Decision-making Process

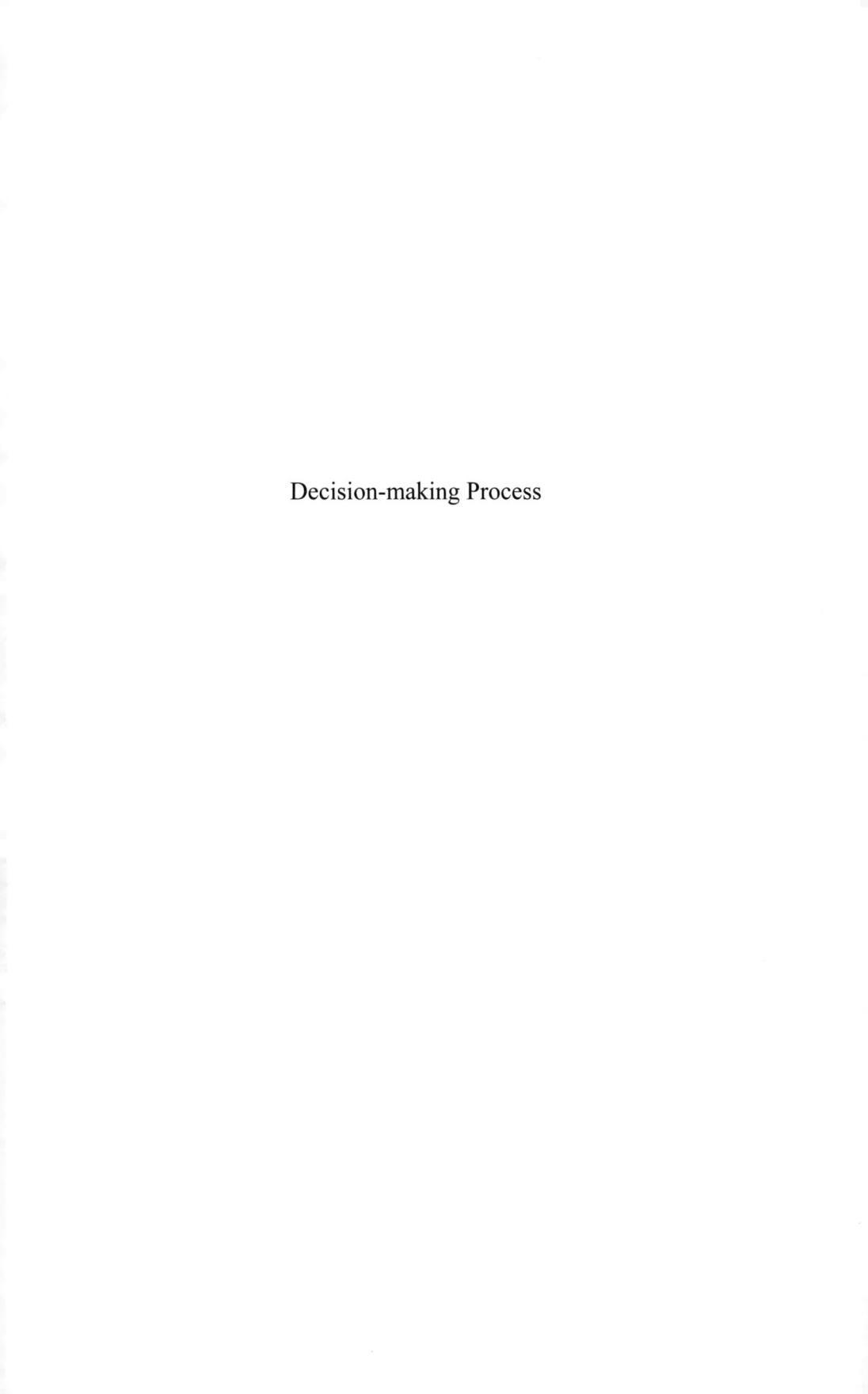

Dedication

Some days after the completion of this book, Jean-Yves Jaffray, who actively contributed to it, passed away, struck down by cancer. He was a pioneer of new approaches to decision theory. He was among the first to bridge the gap between expected utility and the maximin rule, thus enlarging the notion of subjective probability to encompass belief functions. He was a founding father of a group of international scientists (RUD) which actively pursues this line of investigation. The decision theory community at large will forever miss his outstanding creativity and vision, as well as his generosity, his integrity, his modesty, his sense of humor, his faithfulness and, in the end, his amazing courage. Several generations of researchers are indebted to him for their scientific vocation. His seminal works will certainly remain a major source of inspiration for future generations of scientists in decision theory. This book is dedicated to his memory.

Alain Chateauneuf,
Michèle Cohen,
Christophe Gonzales,
Patrice Perny,
and the Editors

Decision-making Process

Concepts and Methods

Edited by
Denis Bouyssou
Didier Dubois
Marc Pirlot
Henri Prade

First published in France in 2006 by Hermes Science/Lavoisier in 3 volumes entitled *Concepts et méthodes pour l'aide à la décision* © LAVOISIER, 2006
First published in Great Britain and the United States in 2009 by ISTE Ltd and John Wiley & Sons, Inc.

Apart from any fair dealing for the purposes of research or private study, or criticism or review, as permitted under the Copyright, Designs and Patents Act 1988, this publication may only be reproduced, stored or transmitted, in any form or by any means, with the prior permission in writing of the publishers, or in the case of reprographic reproduction in accordance with the terms and licenses issued by the CLA. Enquiries concerning reproduction outside these terms should be sent to the publishers at the undermentioned address:

ISTE Ltd
27-37 St George's Road
London SW19 4EU
UK

www.iste.co.uk

John Wiley & Sons, Inc.
111 River Street
Hoboken, NJ 07030
USA

www.wiley.com

© ISTE Ltd, 2009

The rights of Denis Bouyssou, Didier Dubois, Marc Pirlot and Henri Prade to be identified as the authors of this work have been asserted by them in accordance with the Copyright, Designs and Patents Act 1988.

Library of Congress Cataloging-in-Publication Data

Concepts et méthodes pour l'aide à la décision. English
 Decision-making process / edited by Denis Bouyssou ... [et al.].
  p. cm.
 Includes bibliographical references and index.
 ISBN 978-1-84821-116-2
 1. Decision support systems. 2. Decision making--Mathematical models. I. Bouyssou, D. (Denis) II. Title.
 T58.62.C76 2009
 658.4'03--dc22

2009002905

British Library Cataloguing-in-Publication Data
A CIP record for this book is available from the British Library
ISBN: 978-1-84821-116-2

Printed and bound in Great Britain by CPI Antony Rowe, Chippenham and Eastbourne.

FSC
Mixed Sources
Product group from well-managed forests and other controlled sources
Cert no. SGS-COC-2953
www.fsc.org
© 1996 Forest Stewardship Council

Contents

Preface xxi

Chapter 1. From Decision Theory to Decision-aiding Methodology 1
Alexis TSOUKIÀS

    1.1. Introduction 1
    1.2. History 4
        1.2.1. Genesis and youth 4
        1.2.2. Maturity 10
    1.3. Different decision-aiding approaches 16
    1.4. The decision-aiding process 20
        1.4.1. The problem situation 21
        1.4.2. The problem formulation 22
        1.4.3. The evaluation model 23
        1.4.4. The final recommendation 24
    1.5. Conclusion 25
    1.6. Acknowledgements 26
    1.7. Bibliography 26

Chapter 2. Binary Relations and Preference Modeling 49
Denis BOUYSSOU, Philippe VINCKE

    2.1. Introduction 49
    2.2. Binary relations 50
        2.2.1. Definitions 50
        2.2.2. Properties of a binary relation 52
        2.2.3. Graphical representation of a binary relation 53
        2.2.4. Matrix representation of a binary relation 53
        2.2.5. Example 53
    2.3. Binary relations and preference structures 54
    2.4. Classical preference structures 57

2.4.1. Total order 57
  2.4.1.1. Definition 57
  2.4.1.2. Numerical representation 59
2.4.2. Weak orders 60
  2.4.2.1. Definition 60
  2.4.2.2. Numerical representation 61
2.4.3. Classical problems 62
  2.4.3.1. Choosing on the basis of binary relation 62
  2.4.3.2. Aggregating preferences 63
  2.4.3.3. Particular structure of the set of objects 63
2.5. Semi-orders and interval orders 66
2.5.1. Semi-order 66
  2.5.1.1. Definition 66
  2.5.1.2. Weak order associated with a semi-order 67
  2.5.1.3. Matrix representation 68
  2.5.1.4. Numerical representation 68
2.5.2. Interval order 69
  2.5.2.1. Definition 69
  2.5.2.2. Weak orders associated with an interval order 70
  2.5.2.3. Matrix representation 71
  2.5.2.4. Numerical representation 71
2.5.3. Remarks 72
2.6. Preference structures with incomparability 73
2.6.1. Partial order 73
2.6.2. Quasi-order 74
2.6.3. Synthesis 76
2.7. Conclusion 76
2.7.1. Other preference structures 76
2.7.2. Other problems 77
2.8. Bibliography 78

Chapter 3. Formal Representations of Uncertainty 85
Didier DUBOIS, Henri PRADE

3.1. Introduction 85
3.2. Information: a typology of defects 88
  3.2.1. Incompleteness and imprecision 89
  3.2.2. Uncertainty 91
  3.2.3. Gradual linguistic information 94
  3.2.4. Granularity 96
3.3. Probability theory 98
  3.3.1. Frequentists and subjectivists 98
  3.3.2. Conditional probability 101
  3.3.3. The unique probability assumption in the subjective setting 104

3.4. Incompleteness-tolerant numerical uncertainty theories 107
    3.4.1. Imprecise probabilities 108
    3.4.2. Random disjunctive sets and belief functions 112
    3.4.3. Quantitative possibility theory 118
        3.4.3.1. Possibility theory and belief functions 119
        3.4.3.2. Possibility theory and imprecise probabilities 119
        3.4.3.3. Clouds and generalized p-boxes 121
        3.4.3.4. Possibility-probability transformations 122
    3.4.4. Possibility theory and non-Bayesian statistics 126
3.5. Qualitative uncertainty representations 127
3.6. Conditioning in non-additive representations 130
    3.6.1. Conditional events and qualitative conditioning 132
    3.6.2. Conditioning for belief functions and imprecise probabilities . . . 134
3.7. Fusion of imprecise and uncertain information 138
    3.7.1. Non-Bayesian probabilistic fusion 140
    3.7.2. Bayesian probabilistic fusion 141
    3.7.3. Fusion in possibility theory 142
    3.7.4. Fusion of belief functions 144
    3.7.5. Merging imprecise probability families 146
3.8. Conclusion 147
3.9. Acknowledgements 147
3.10. Bibliography 147

Chapter 4. Human Decision: Recognition plus Reasoning 157
Jean-Charles POMEROL
4.1. Introduction: the neurobiology of decision, reasoning and/or recognition 157
4.2. Procedural rationality and limited rationality 159
    4.2.1. Savage's expected utility model 159
    4.2.2. Challenging utility expectation 162
    4.2.3. Bounded rationality 164
    4.2.4. Multicriterion decision 169
    4.2.5. Other models 170
4.3. Decision based on recognition 172
    4.3.1. Diagnosis and decision 172
    4.3.2. Case-based decision 173
4.4. Recognition, reasoning and decision support 175
    4.4.1. Interactive decision support systems 175
    4.4.2. Scenarios 176
4.5. Cognitive biases 178
    4.5.1. Biases linked to probabilities 180
    4.5.2. Representations, levels of satisfaction and the anchor effect 182
4.6. Conclusion 185
4.7. Acknowledgements 187
4.8. Bibliography 187

viii   Decision-making Process

Chapter 5. Multiple Objective Linear Programming 199
Jacques TEGHEM

    5.1. Introduction 199
    5.2. Basic concepts and main resolution approaches 201
       5.2.1. The problem 201
       5.2.2. Dominance relation and efficient solutions 203
       5.2.3. Ideal point, payoff matrix and nadir point 205
       5.2.4. Scalarizing functions 206
       5.2.5. Theorems to characterize efficient solutions 208
       5.2.6. The main resolution approaches 209
          5.2.6.1. A priori preferences 210
          5.2.6.2. A posteriori preferences 213
          5.2.6.3. Progressive preferences or interactive approach 213
    5.3. Interactive methods 215
       5.3.1. The step method 215
          5.3.1.1. Initialization $(m = 0)$ 215
          5.3.1.2. General iteration $(m \geq 1)$ 217
       5.3.2. The Steuer and Choo method 219
          5.3.2.1. Initialization $(m = 0)$ 220
          5.3.2.2. General iteration $(m \geq 1)$ 220
       5.3.3. Interactive methods based on a utility function 222
          5.3.3.1. Principle of the Zionts and Wallenius method 222
          5.3.3.2. Principle of the Geoffrion *et al.* method 223
    5.4. The multiple objective integer programming 224
       5.4.1. Methods of generating $E(P)$ 226
          5.4.1.1. The Klein and Hannan method 226
          5.4.1.2. The Sylva and Crema method 226
          5.4.1.3. The Kiziltan and Yucaoglu method 227
       5.4.2. Interactive methods 228
          5.4.2.1. Gonzales *et al.* method 228
          5.4.2.2. The MOMIX method 229
    5.5. The multiple objective combinatorial optimization 231
       5.5.1. Exact methods 233
          5.5.1.1. Direct methods 235
          5.5.1.2. The two phases method 237
          5.5.1.3. Comments 240
       5.5.2. Metaheuristics 241
          5.5.2.1. Simulated annealing 241
          5.5.2.2. Tabu search 243
          5.5.2.3. Genetic algorithms 243
    5.6. The multiple objective stochastic linear programming 245
       5.6.1. The equivalent deterministic problem 247
       5.6.2. Determination of the first compromise 248

                5.6.2.1. Payoff matrix 248
                5.6.2.2. Weights associated with the objectives 249
                5.6.2.3. First compromise 249
            5.6.3. Interactive phases 249
                5.6.3.1. Information given to the decision maker 249
                5.6.3.2. First interaction with the decision maker 250
                5.6.3.3. Computational phase 250
        5.7. The multiple objective fuzzy linear programming 253
            5.7.1. Comparison of two fuzzy numbers 253
                5.7.1.1. Area compensation 254
                5.7.1.2. Determination of $I(\widetilde{a} \geq \widetilde{b})$ 256
                5.7.1.3. Equivalent crisp constraint 257
            5.7.2. Treatment of a fuzzy objective function 257
            5.7.3. The crisp (deterministic) equivalent problem 258
        5.8. Conclusion 258
        5.9. Bibliography 258

Chapter 6. Constraint Satisfaction Problems 265
Gérard VERFAILLIE, Thomas SCHIEX

        6.1. Introduction 265
        6.2. The CSP framework 266
            6.2.1. Syntactical part 267
            6.2.2. Semantical part 268
            6.2.3. Assignments 269
            6.2.4. Queries 269
        6.3. Complexity 271
        6.4. Related problems 272
        6.5. Reasoning on a CSP 274
            6.5.1. Local consistency 275
            6.5.2. Arc-consistency 275
            6.5.3. Path-consistency 278
            6.5.4. Other local consistency properties 280
            6.5.5. General constraint propagation mechanisms 282
        6.6. Looking for a CSP solution 283
            6.6.1. Tree search 283
            6.6.2. Variable elimination 288
            6.6.3. Greedy search 291
            6.6.4. Local search 292
        6.7. Experimental evaluations and lessons learned 294
            6.7.1. Pure constraint satisfaction problems 294
            6.7.2. Constraint optimization problems 294
        6.8. Polynomial classes 295
            6.8.1. Acyclic constraint networks 296

6.8.2. Simple temporal constraint networks 297
6.9. Existing tools 297
6.10. Extensions of the basic framework 298
    6.10.1. Continuous domains 298
    6.10.2. Conditional problems 300
    6.10.3. Dynamic problems 301
    6.10.4. Constraints and preferences 301
6.11. Open problems 308
    6.11.1. Constraints and uncertainties 308
    6.11.2. Deciding or reasoning under time constraints 309
    6.11.3. Interactive decision 310
    6.11.4. Distributed decision 310
6.12. Books, journals, websites and conferences 311
6.13. Bibliography 311

Chapter 7. Logical Representation of Preferences 321
Jérôme LANG

7.1. Introduction 321
7.2. Basics of propositional logic 324
7.3. Principles and elementary languages 326
7.4. Weights, priorities and distances 329
    7.4.1. Weights 329
        7.4.1.1. Bibliographical notes 332
    7.4.2. Priorities 332
        7.4.2.1. Best-out 333
        7.4.2.2. Discrimin 333
        7.4.2.3. Leximin 334
        7.4.2.4. Bibliographical notes 334
    7.4.3. Distances 335
        7.4.3.1. Bibliographical notes 337
7.5. Preference logics: conditionals and *ceteris paribus* preferences 338
    7.5.1. *Ceteris paribus* preferences 338
        7.5.1.1. Preferences between non-contradictory formulae 339
        7.5.1.2. *Ceteris paribus* comparisons and their generalizations . . . 340
        7.5.1.3. Preference relation induced by *ceteris paribus* preferences . 342
        7.5.1.4. CP-nets 343
        7.5.1.5. Comments and bibliographical notes 345
    7.5.2. Defeasible preferences and conditional preference logics 345
        7.5.2.1. Bibliographical notes 351
    7.5.3. Logical modeling of incomplete and/or contradictory preferences 352
7.6. Discussion 353
    7.6.1. Cognitive and linguistic relevance, elicitation 353
    7.6.2. Expressivity 353

7.6.3. Complexity and algorithms	354
7.6.4. Spatial efficiency	354
7.7. Acknowledgements	355
7.8. Bibliography	355

Chapter 8. Decision under Risk: The Classical Expected Utility Model .. 365
Alain CHATEAUNEUF, Michèle COHEN, Jean-Marc TALLON

8.1. Introduction	365
8.1.1. Decision under uncertainty	366
8.1.2. Risk versus uncertainty	366
8.2. Risk and increasing risk: comparison and measures	367
8.2.1. Notation and definitions	367
8.2.1.1. First-order stochastic dominance	368
8.2.1.2. Second-order stochastic dominance	369
8.2.2. Behavior under risk	370
8.2.2.1. Model-free behavioral definitions	370
8.2.2.2. Certainty equivalent, risk premium and behavior comparison	371
8.3. Expected utility (EU) model	372
8.3.1. Mixing probability distributions	372
8.3.2. Generalized mixture	373
8.3.3. Axiomatic foundation of the EU model	373
8.3.3.1. Linear utility theorem	374
8.3.3.2. Von Neumann–Morgenstern theorem for distributions with finite support in $(\mathcal{C}, \mathcal{G})$	375
8.3.3.3. Von Neumann–Morgenstern theorem for distributions with bounded suport in $(\mathcal{C}, \mathcal{G})$	376
8.3.3.4. Von Neumann–Morgenstern theorem for distributions with bounded support in $(\mathbb{R}, \mathcal{B})$	376
8.3.4. Characterization of risk aversion in the EU model	377
8.3.4.1. Characterization of first- and second-order dominance in the EU model	377
8.3.5. Coefficient of absolute risk aversion, local value of the risk premium	378
8.3.5.1. Coefficient of absolute risk aversion	378
8.3.5.2. Local value of the risk premium	378
8.3.5.3. Variance and EU model	379
8.4. Problems raised by the EU model	379
8.4.1. Allais paradox	379
8.4.2. Interpreting the utility function	380
8.4.3. Weak and strong risk aversion under expected utility	380
8.4.4. Notion of SSD as a risk indicator in the EU model	381
8.5. Some alternative models	381
8.5.1. Machina's model	381
8.5.2. Models with security and potential levels	382

8.6. Acknowledgements 382
8.7. Bibliography 382

Chapter 9. Decision under Uncertainty: The Classical Models 385
Alain CHATEAUNEUF, Michèle COHEN, Jean-Yves JAFFRAY

9.1. Introduction 385
9.2. Subjective expected utility (SEU) 386
   9.2.1. Definitions and notation 386
   9.2.2. The SEU criterion 386
9.3. Savage's theory 387
   9.3.1. Savage's axioms and their interpretation and implications 387
      9.3.1.1. Preferences on the acts 387
   9.3.2. Construction of Savage's theory 391
      9.3.2.1. From qualitative to subjective probabilities 391
      9.3.2.2. Subjective lotteries and linear utility 392
      9.3.2.3. Extension of SEU to all acts 394
   9.3.3. The Ellsberg paradox 394
9.4. Anscombe and Aumann theory 396
   9.4.1. The Anscombe–Aumann axiom system 396
   9.4.2. Comments and discussion 397
   9.4.3. The Anscombe-Aumann representation theorem 397
   9.4.4. Return to the Ellsberg paradox 398
9.5. Conclusion 399
9.6. Bibliography 399

Chapter 10. Cardinal Extensions of the EU Model Based on the Choquet Integral 401
Alain CHATEAUNEUF, Michèle COHEN

10.1. Introduction 401
10.2. Notation and definitions 402
   10.2.1. The notion of comonotony 403
   10.2.2. The Choquet integral 404
   10.2.3. Characterization of the Choquet integral 405
10.3. Decision under uncertainty 405
   10.3.1. Ellsberg's paradox 405
      10.3.1.1. Interpretation of Ellsberg's paradox in the framework of Savage 406
      10.3.1.2. Interpretation of Ellsberg's paradox in the framework of Anscombe and Aumann 406
   10.3.2. Schmeidler's model in Anscombe–Aumann framework 407
      10.3.2.1. Comonotonic independence 408
      10.3.2.2. Representation of preferences by a Choquet integral in Anscombe–Aumann's framework 408

        10.3.3. Choquet expected utility (CEU) models in Savage's framework . 409
            10.3.3.1. Simplified version of Schmeidler's model in Savage's
                framework 409
            10.3.3.2. Choquet expected utility model in Savage's framework . . 411
            10.3.3.3. Example of computation of such a Choquet integral 412
            10.3.3.4. The comonotonic sure-thing principle 412
        10.3.4. Uncertainty aversion 413
        10.3.5. The multiprior model 415
            10.3.5.1. The axiomatic of the model 415
            10.3.5.2. Comparing multiprior model with Choquet utility model . 416
            10.3.5.3. CEU model and lower and upper envelopes of a probability
                distributions family 417
    10.4. Decision under risk 418
        10.4.1. EU model and Allais paradox 419
        10.4.2. The rank-dependent expected utility model 420
            10.4.2.1. Definition of the rank-dependent expected utility model . . 420
            10.4.2.2. Key axiom of RDU's axiomatization: comonotonic sure-
                thing principle 422
        10.4.3. From the CEU to the RDU model using first-order stochastic
            dominance 424
            10.4.3.1. RDU representation is a Choquet integral 424
            10.4.3.2. From the CEU to the RDU 424
        10.4.4. Risk aversion notions and characterization in the RDU model . . 425
            10.4.4.1. Strong risk aversion 426
            10.4.4.2. Monotone risk aversion 426
            10.4.4.3. Left monotone risk aversion 427
            10.4.4.4. Characterization of risk aversion notions in the RDU model 428
    10.5. Bibliography 429

Chapter 11. A Survey of Qualitative Decision Rules under Uncertainty . . 435
Didier DUBOIS, Hélène FARGIER, Henri PRADE, Régis SABBADIN

    11.1. Introduction 435
    11.2. Quantitative versus qualitative decision rules 437
    11.3. Ordinal decision rule without commensurateness 441
    11.4. Axiomatics of qualitative decision theory 445
        11.4.1. Savage's theory: a refresher 445
        11.4.2. The relational approach to decision theory 449
        11.4.3. Qualitative decision rules under commensurateness 452
    11.5. Toward more efficient qualitative decision rules 457
        11.5.1. Refining qualitative criteria 458
        11.5.2. A bridge between generalized maxmin criteria and expected utility 460
        11.5.3. Weighted Leximax/Leximin criteria 463

11.5.4. The representation of uncertainty underlying Leximax(Leximin)
and Leximin(Leximax) criteria 465
11.6. Conclusion 466
11.7. Bibliography 467

Chapter 12. A Cognitive Approach to Human Decision Making 475
Éric RAUFASTE, Denis J. HILTON

12.1. Introduction 475
12.2. Humans do not match current rational models 476
   12.2.1. Overconfidence and calibration of judgement 476
   12.2.2. Preference reversals and framing effects 477
   12.2.3. Subjectivation of expected utility: prospect theory 478
   12.2.4. Questions raised by the standard model 480
12.3. A global descriptive approach to decision making 481
   12.3.1. The concept of multicriteria decision making 482
   12.3.2. The notion of dominance structure 483
      12.3.2.1. The dominance rule 483
      12.3.2.2. The search for dominance 483
      12.3.2.3. Dominance structures 483
   12.3.3. Steps in the decision making process 484
      12.3.3.1. Pre-edition 484
      12.3.3.2. Search for a focal alternative 485
      12.3.3.3. The test of dominance 485
      12.3.3.4. Dominance structuring 486
12.4. Attentional focusing 487
12.5. Evaluation heuristics and ecological rationality 489
   12.5.1. Logical rationality and ecological rationality 489
   12.5.2. The representativeness heuristic 491
   12.5.3. The availability heuristic 492
   12.5.4. The anchoring-adjustment heuristic 493
   12.5.5. Conclusion on heuristics 494
12.6. The role of affect in decision making 495
   12.6.1. The positive role of emotions 495
   12.6.2. Affect and expected utility 496
12.7. Conclusion 498
12.8. Bibliography 499

Chapter 13. Bayesian Networks 505
Jean-Yves JAFFRAY

13.1. Introduction 505
13.2. Definitions and notation 507
   13.2.1. Joint and marginal probabilities 507
   13.2.2. Independence 508

13.2.3. Conditional probabilities	509
13.2.4. Conditional independence	510
13.2.5. Bayesian network	511
13.2.6. Graphical conditional independence criterion in BNs: d-separation	513
13.2.6.1. d-separation	515
13.3. Evidential data processing in a BN	516
13.3.1. Pearl's method	517
13.3.2. The junction tree method	523
13.3.2.1. Construction of the junction tree	523
13.3.2.2. Evidential data processing in a junction tree	525
13.4. Constructing a BN	528
13.4.1. Score-based methods	528
13.4.2. Conditional independence based methods	529
13.4.3. Search among Markov equivalence classes	529
13.4.4. Causality	530
13.4.5. Conditioning by intervention in causal graphs	531
13.5. BNs and influence diagrams	532
13.5.1. Dynamic decision making under uncertainty	532
13.5.1.1. An example of dynamic decision problem under risk	533
13.5.1.2. Decision tree of the problem	533
13.5.1.3. Optimization by dynamic programming	534
13.5.1.4. Limits of the classical method	535
13.5.2. Influence diagrams	535
13.5.2.1. Origin of the influence diagrams	535
13.5.2.2. Semantics of IDs	536
13.5.2.3. The methods of Shachter and Shenoy	536
13.5.2.4. The junction tree method	537
13.6. Conclusion	537
13.7. Software	538
13.8. Bibliography	538

Chapter 14. Planning under Uncertainty with Markov Decision Processes   541
Régis SABBADIN

14.1. Introduction	541
14.2. Markov decision processes	542
14.2.1. Problem formulation	542
14.2.1.1. States, actions, transitions and policies	542
14.2.1.2. Reward, criterion, value function, optimal policy	543
14.2.2. Classical solution algorithms for MDP	544
14.2.2.1. Finite horizon: backwards induction	544
14.2.2.2. Infinite horizon: value iteration and policy iteration	544
14.2.3. Example: car race	546
14.2.4. Recent advances in Markov decision processes	548

14.3. Partially observed MDPs 549
  14.3.1. POMDP model, continuous-MDP transformation 549
  14.3.2. Computing optimal policies in a POMDP 550
    14.3.2.1. t-policy tree 551
    14.3.2.2. Value iteration algorithm for POMDP 553
  14.3.3. POMDP example 553
  14.3.4. Concluding remarks 554
14.4. Real-time dynamic programming and reinforcement learning 555
  14.4.1. Introduction 555
  14.4.2. Real-time dynamic programming 555
    14.4.2.1. Gauss–Seidel algorithm 555
    14.4.2.2. Asynchronous dynamic programming 556
    14.4.2.3. Real-time dynamic programming 557
  14.4.3. Reinforcement learning 558
    14.4.3.1. Indirect reinforcement learning 558
    14.4.3.2. Direct reinforcement learning 559
  14.4.4. Concluding remarks 560
14.5. Factored Markov decision processes 561
  14.5.1. State space factorization, stationary homogenous Bayesian networks 561
  14.5.2. Factored representation of actions 563
  14.5.3. Factored representation of rewards 563
  14.5.4. Factored representation of value functions and policies and computation of optimal policies 564
  14.5.5. Concluding remarks 564
14.6. Possibilistic Markov decision processes 565
  14.6.1. Background on qualitative possibility theory 565
  14.6.2. Possibilistic counterparts of expected utility 566
  14.6.3. Possibilistic Markov decision processes 568
    14.6.3.1. Finite horizon 568
    14.6.3.2. Possibilistic value iteration 570
    14.6.3.3. Policy iteration algorithm 572
  14.6.4. Concluding remarks 573
14.7. Conclusion 573
14.8. Bibliography 574

Chapter 15. Multiattribute Utility Theory 579
Mohammed ABDELLAOUI, Christophe GONZALES

15.1. Introduction 579
15.2. Introduction to utility theory 580
  15.2.1. Utility functions 580
  15.2.2. Decision under certainty, uncertainty and risk 581
  15.2.3. Multiattribute utility functions 583

15.2.4. Decompositions of utility functions 584
15.3. Decomposition under certainty 586
    15.3.1. Additive decomposition in two-dimensional spaces 586
    15.3.2. Extension to more general outcome sets 594
15.4. Decompositions under uncertainty 597
    15.4.1. Decomposition in two-dimensional spaces 599
    15.4.2. Extension of the two-dimensional decomposition 603
15.5. Elicitation of utility functions 605
    15.5.1. Elicitation under certainty 606
    15.5.2. Elicitation under uncertainty 609
15.6. Conclusion 613
15.7. Bibliography 614

Chapter 16. Conjoint Measurement Models for Preference Relations . . . 617
Denis BOUYSSOU, Marc PIRLOT

16.1. Introduction 617
    16.1.1. Brief overview of conjoint measurement models 618
    16.1.2. Chapter contents 620
16.2. Fundamental relations and trivial models 623
    16.2.1. Binary relations on a product set 623
    16.2.2. Independence and marginal preferences 624
    16.2.3. Marginal traces on levels 625
    16.2.4. Marginal traces on differences 626
    16.2.5. Three models for general relations on a Cartesian product 628
16.3. Models using marginal traces on levels 629
    16.3.1. Definition of the models 629
    16.3.2. Completeness of marginal traces and monotonicity of F 631
    16.3.3. Model ($L8$) and strict monotonicity w.r.t. traces 634
    16.3.4. Complete characterization of the models on levels 636
        16.3.4.1. Uniqueness and regular representations 637
    16.3.5. Relations compatible with dominance 637
    16.3.6. Strict compatibility with dominance 640
    16.3.7. The case of weak orders 641
    16.3.8. Examples 642
16.4. Models using marginal traces on differences 644
    16.4.1. Models definition 644
    16.4.2. Completeness of marginal traces on differences and
            monotonicity of G 646
    16.4.3. Characterization of model ($D11$) 650
    16.4.4. Remarks 651
        16.4.4.1. Goldstein's model 651
        16.4.4.2. Marginal preferences 651
        16.4.4.3. Uniqueness of the representation 652

xviii   Decision-making Process

    16.4.5. Examples 653
  16.5. Models using both marginal traces on levels and on differences 655
    16.5.1. Relationships between traces on differences and on levels 657
    16.5.2. Study of models $(L1D0)$ to $(L1D11)$ and $(L2D0)$ to $(L2D11)$. 661
    16.5.3. Examples 664
  16.6. Conclusion 665
  16.7. Bibliography 667

Chapter 17. Aggregation Functions for Decision Making 673
Jean-Luc MARICHAL

  17.1. Introduction 673
  17.2. Aggregation properties 676
    17.2.1. Elementary mathematical properties 677
    17.2.2. Stability properties related to scale types 678
    17.2.3. Algebraic properties 680
  17.3. Means 682
    17.3.1. Quasi-arithmetic means 685
    17.3.2. Lagrangian and Cauchy means 687
  17.4. Associative aggregation functions 688
    17.4.1. Strictly increasing functions 689
    17.4.2. Archimedean semigroups 690
    17.4.3. A class of non-decreasing and associative functions 693
    17.4.4. Internal associative functions 695
    17.4.5. t-norms, t-conorms, and uninorms 697
  17.5. Non-additive integrals 698
    17.5.1. Motivations 698
    17.5.2. The Choquet integral 700
    17.5.3. The Sugeno integral 704
  17.6. Aggregation on ratio and interval scales 709
  17.7. Aggregation on ordinal scales 711
  17.8. Conclusion 714
  17.9. Bibliography 714

Chapter 18. Subjective Evaluation 723
Michel GRABISCH

  18.1. Introduction 723
  18.2. What is subjective evaluation? 725
    18.2.1. General definition and related domains 725
    18.2.2. Definition of our scope 726
  18.3. A multicriteria approach to subjective evaluation 727
    18.3.1. The importance of affect in evaluation 728
    18.3.2. Measurement theory, notion of scale 729
    18.3.3. Unipolar and bipolar scales 733

        18.3.4. The MACBETH approach 735
        18.3.5. Construction of the model of subjective evaluation 738
    18.4. Construction of the aggregation function 740
        18.4.1. Case of cardinal unipolar scales 740
        18.4.2. Case of cardinal bipolar scales 743
    18.5. The case of ordinal scales 747
        18.5.1. Introduction 747
        18.5.2. The Sugeno integral 749
        18.5.3. The symmetric Sugeno integral and bipolar models 750
    18.6. Identification of the parameters of the aggregation function 752
        18.6.1. Cardinal case 753
        18.6.2. Ordinal case 755
    18.7. Interpretation of the aggregation function 758
        18.7.1. Index of importance of a criterion 759
        18.7.2. Index of interaction 760
        18.7.3. Maximum improving index 764
        18.7.4. Conjunction and disjunction indices 765
        18.7.5. Veto and index of veto 765
    18.8. Particular families of capacities and bicapacities 766
    18.9. Applications 768
    18.10. Conclusion 771
    18.11. Bibliography 771

Chapter 19. Social Choice Theory and Multicriteria Decision Aiding . . . 779
Denis BOUYSSOU, Thierry MARCHANT, Patrice PERNY

    19.1. Introduction 779
    19.2. Introductory examples 780
        19.2.1. Uninominal systems 781
        19.2.2. Systems based on rankings 786
    19.3. Some theoretical results 789
        19.3.1. Arrow's theorem 789
            19.3.1.1. Arrow's theorem and fuzzy preferences 794
        19.3.2. Some other results 795
            19.3.2.1. Impossibility results 796
            19.3.2.2. Characterizations 796
            19.3.2.3. Generalizations of the Borda method 799
            19.3.2.4. A characterization of simple majority 799
            19.3.2.5. Analysis 801
    19.4. Multicriteria decision aiding and social choice theory 801
        19.4.1. Relevance and limits of social choice results 801
        19.4.2. Some results in close relation with multicriteria analysis 803
            19.4.2.1. TACTIC 803
            19.4.2.2. Multi-attribute value theory (MAVT) 804

xx   Decision-making Process

        19.4.2.3. Weighted sum 804
        19.4.2.4. ELECTRE and PROMETHEE 804
   19.5. Bibliography 805

Chapter 20. Metric and Latticial Medians 811
Olivier HUDRY, Bruno LECLERC, Bernard MONJARDET,
Jean-Pierre BARTHÉLEMY

   20.1. Introduction 811
        20.1.1. Medians in general 811
        20.1.2. Medians of binary relations 812
        20.1.3. Medians in lattices 813
   20.2. Median relations 814
        20.2.1. The model 814
        20.2.2. The median procedure 815
        20.2.3. The $\mathcal{R}$-medians of a profile of relations 816
        20.2.4. The $\mathcal{M}$-medians of a profile of relations 820
        20.2.5. The $\mathcal{T}$-medians of a profile of tournaments 820
   20.3. The median linear orders ($\mathcal{L}$-medians) of a profile of linear orders . . 822
        20.3.1. Binary linear programming formulation 822
        20.3.2. Formulation using weighted directed graphs 824
        20.3.3. Equivalent formulations for the search of a median order of a
            profile of linear orders 825
        20.3.4. Complexity of the search of a median order of a profile of linear
            orders 829
        20.3.5. Exact and approximate methods 830
        20.3.6. Properties of median orders 833
   20.4. Medians in lattices and semilattices 836
        20.4.1. Ordered structures 837
        20.4.2. Symmetric difference distance in semilattices and remoteness . . 840
        20.4.3. Medians in median semilattices 841
        20.4.4. Other semilattices 844
        20.4.5. Applications 845
   20.5. Conclusion 846
   20.6. Acknowledgements 849
   20.7. Bibliography 849

List of Authors 857

Index 861

Preface

The idea of publishing a treatise presenting the state of the art on concepts and methods for decision-support stems from the fact that decision is a multidisciplinary topic of investigation. Indeed, it lies at the heart of various areas of science such as economics, psychology, political science, management, operational research and artificial intelligence. A recurrent temptation is, for any specific research community, to protect its identity against influences from other areas. It therefore seemed to us quite important to stand against such an attitude, and try to put across the contributions of the various communities which have become involved in this topic in a unified perspective. In order to grasp all dimensions of decision-support, we have to think in terms of empirical studies, mathematical models and algorithms as well as logic-based and other types of computerized representation tools. Psychologists, economists, sociologists, mathematicians, computer scientists – and decision makers – have every interest to get together and speak with one another, in order to implement decision-support tools that are at the same time useful and cogent.

The classical approach

In order to be convinced of the relevance of such a multidisciplinary standpoint, it is useful to briefly revisit the history of decision sciences. Right after the end of World War II, the landscape of this area looked empty. Operational research had inherited from the neo-classic economics tradition the idea of 'rational decision', and promoted an approach based on the optimization of a single objective function under constraints. The development of linear programming by George Dantzig (and later on, of non-linear programming and dynamic programming) provided efficient tools for implementing this approach on real-sized problems (encountered in military logistics, in production research and delivery management for industrial firms). In the same years, John von Neumann and Oscar Morgenstern, followed by Leonard Savage, broadened the scope of the constraint-based optimization paradigm to situations where consequences of decisions are risky or uncertain. Very soon the so-called 'Decision

Analysis School' (led by scholars such as Howard Raiffa and Ward Edwards) demonstrated the usefulness of such theoretical results on practical case studies in decision analysis. The extension of these approaches to the construction of objective functions accounting for several criteria was proposed by Gérard Debreu, Duncan Luce and later on by Ralph Keeney and Howard Raiffa in situations of certainty, uncertainty or risk. All in all, the mid-1970s witnessed a well-established, blossoming field which can be dubbed *classical decision theory*.

Questioning the classical theory

Considering such achievements, why bother advancing research in decision sciences? The point is that concurrently to contributions to the validation of the classical theory, radical criticisms of this theory appeared. Noticeably, the works of Herbert Simon cast doubts on the optimization-based approach to decision as being the unique admissible paradigm of rationality. In addition, classical methods of operational research could not tackle all large-sized optimization problems. The emergence of complexity theory, proposed by Jack Edmonds and Richard Karp, suggested that the perspective of more and more powerful computers was not sufficient to overcome this difficulty in the near future.

On the side of decision under risk and uncertainty, the Bayesian approach, stemming from the work of Savage, appeared like the prototype of a rigorous and elegant approach to rational decision. However, it was undermined due to empirical studies run by economists (Maurice Allais and Daniel Ellsberg) and psychologists (Daniel Kahneman, Amos Tversky and Paul Slovic). Results of such studies demonstrated that, in some cases, human behavior consistently violated the principles of expected utility theory when selecting best decisions. Probability measures seemed to lose their status of a unique rational tool for modeling uncertainty when information about decision consequences is missing. The fact that expected utility theory could not always account for the behavior of decision makers triggered the search for new formal models relying on non-probabilistic representations of uncertainty. Following the pioneering works of David Schmeidler and John Quiggin new, more flexible and realistic mathematical models were proposed. Expected utility was replaced by another more general integral, proposed by Gustave Choquet in the 1950s.

New trends in operational research

In the area of operational research, scholars became more and more aware of the practical limitations of the optimization-based approach to all decision problems. It was not always crystal-clear that a theoretically optimal solution turned out to be an operationally good one from the viewpoint of the user. One of the reasons for such a discrepancy lies in the presence of more than one criterion to be taken into account in order to class a solution to a decision problem as sufficient. From this point of view, multiattribute utility theory was not entirely satisfying. It assumed the preferences of the decision maker to be well structured. However, it was prone to neglect the practical difficulty of comparing two alternatives with respect to several dimensions. Following Bernard Roy, new decision analysis methods dedicated to the case of multiple criteria emerged in the 1970s and 1980s. They acknowledged the ordinal and ill-defined nature of information available in real-world problems, paving the way for more realistic methodologies for multicriteria decision-support. The idea that an optimization algorithm could force a decision maker to use a computed solution was given up. It was acknowledged that the role of a formal method was to help the decision maker build a satisfactory solution. Moreover, the need to consider several criteria presupposed a study of the dependencies between these criteria and the extent to which they can compensate each other, laying bare the possibility of incomparability between solutions. Finally, the analogy between voting theory (where information from voters is essentially ordinal) and multiple criteria decision-making triggered the development of new approaches designed to handle the latter problem.

The emergence of artificial intelligence

Some time passed before the field of artificial intelligence (AI) became concerned with decision problems. This occurred in the 1990s in connection with planning problems under uncertainty and partial observability found in robotics, and the design of user-centered computerized recommender systems and web services. Traditionally, since the late 1950s, artificial intelligence used to focus on declarative knowledge representation and automated reasoning methods, as well as general solving techniques that may apply to a large class of problems. A systematic use of propositional and first-order logics as knowledge representation or programming tools was promoted by scholars such as John McCarthy and Alain Colmerauer. It prompted the emergence of qualitative approaches, even if probability theory and the expected utility approach was also finally accepted, in more recent years. Qualitative approaches especially make sense when it is very time-consuming or costly to build fully fledged utility functions in some application at hand and a coarse representation of preference and uncertainty is good enough to come up with a reasonable decision. In recent years, AI tried to exploit the formal setting of the classical decision theory. The foundations of some ordinal representations were studied. Some of these works come very close to formal results in voting theory, albeit adapting them to specific representation frameworks. In such an ordinal setting, possibility theory is the natural counterpart to probability theory in the classical decision theory. Formal similarities between voting theory, decision under uncertainty and multiple criteria decision-making can therefore be laid bare where voters, states of nature and criteria play the same role in each respective problem.

The emphasis of artificial intelligence on representation issues for decision problems makes sense particularly in problems where the set of states of the world is huge, so that the explicit description of a probability or possibility distribution on the state space becomes too burdensome a task. The recent years have therefore witnessed the emergence of powerful tools for the compact representation of uncertainty or preference, especially graphical representations such as Bayesian networks, influence diagrams and conditional preference networks (often called CP-nets). As well as computer languages for logic programming or constraint-based programming, generic problem-solvers for Boolean or combinatorial decision problems are provided: in such approaches, the user is simply requested to express the problem under concern in the appropriate declarative language. This elementary approach (from the standpoint of expressiveness) was enriched by the introduction of soft constraints, bridging the gap with more traditional quantified frameworks for decision analysis.

This treatise

By and large, the progressive questioning of the claims deriving from the classical theory led to a very wide and active research area devoted to decision analysis and decision science. Many new concepts and topics emerged from this critical assessment of the foundations of decision theory: non-additive frameworks for uncertainty representation, Choquet integral, possibility theory, bounded rationality models, non-transitive preference representations, incomparability, interactions and dependencies between criteria, processing of ordinal information and avoiding threshold effects in quantitative representations (among others). Recent developments are too scattered and numerous to be extensively described in these pages, let alone to be able to predict their evolution. Nevertheless, one specific feature of current trends deserves to be emphasized; these works now involve various disciplines. Economists and operational researchers were joined by psychologists, organizational sociologists and scholars in artificial intelligence and theoretical computer sciences. Interestingly, and as a hint to why this state is unsurprising *ex post*, let us highlight the key role played by John von Neumann, a mathematician who is a pioneer in decision theory and operational research as much as in computer science.

The goal of this treatise is to survey the main results and methods in decision theory and decision-support, in order to enable the reader to enter this area and grasp its extent beyond the specifics of the various areas that contributed to this problem. Each chapter provides a state-of-the-art overview of a particular approach to decision, in terms of modeling, representation or problem-solving tool. The book is composed of three parts. The first part is devoted to mathematical concepts useful for the modeling of decision problems, as well as compact representation techniques and combinatorial problem-solving methods. The second part focuses on decision under uncertainty and the third part reviews the various approaches to multiple criteria decision-making. The fact that all chapters of this book are written by French-speaking authors should not be surprising; research in France and French-speaking countries dealing with decision problems has been very active in the last 50 years, following a long tradition initiated by Borda and Condorcet more than two centuries ago. In the following, we provide a more extensive description of the contents of this book.

Chapters 1–7: modeling tools

The first chapter, written by Alexis Tsoukias, places the current trends of decision theory in a historical perspective, stressing the interaction between this field and others such as cognitive sciences, organization theory, psychology and artificial intelligence, etc. It brings forward a clear distinction between the practice and the process of decision-making from the theory and the techniques used to 'solve' decision problems. The latter are simply tools that are instrumental within a general methodology for decision-support, whose basic features are discussed by the author. A general decision-support process is described that can serve as a guideline to practitioners independently of the specific tool to be employed.

A basic notion in decision theory, whether under uncertainty or multiple criteria, is that of a preference relation. This kind of construction naturally appears for pairwise comparison of alternatives that account for the decision maker opinion. In Chapter 2, Denis Bouyssou and Philippe Vincke present the main mathematical structures instrumental in modeling preference (total order, weak order, interval order and semi-order) and discuss various ways of representing them (by graphs, matrices and numerical functions). A brief account of the problem of preference aggregation is provided, a crucial issue in several chapters of this treatise. This chapter in no way considers the issue of eliciting preferences from the decision maker. This issue is dealt with in the third part of this treatise.

Uncertain information is pervasive in decision problems (as well as in many others). There is a recurrent confusion between two kinds of uncertainty, which is not always easy to resolve in the purely probabilistic setting and is at the origin of many difficulties and debates. In Chapter 3, Didier Dubois and Henri Prade make a careful distinction between these two forms of uncertainty: aleatory uncertainty (which results from the intrinsic variability of natural phenomena) and epistemic uncertainty (mainly due to a lack of information about the reality under concern). Of course, both types of uncertainty may be simultaneously present in a given problem. The authors show that specific representation frameworks are suitable for each kind of uncertainty: probability measures for aleatory uncertainty, sets (e.g. logic and intervals) for incomplete information and new uncertainty theories combining the two ingredients. Basic concepts useful for reasoning and decision are surveyed, especially conditioning and information fusion methods.

Decision-making is a human activity and, as such, influenced by psycho-physiological effects and subject to cognitive limitations of the human mind. In Chapter 4,

Jean-Charles Pomerol interprets decision-making activity as driven by reasoning and emotion according to recent discoveries in neurobiology. Several basic concepts such as bounded rationality are introduced. Decision can be triggered by the recognition of patterns in the state of the world. As a consequence, the author presents the basic principles of case-based decision-making. He discusses cognitive biases related to the perception of probabilities.

Multiple criteria analysis is often distinguished from multiple criteria optimization. The main difference relates to the techniques for describing solutions. Multiple criteria analysis is characterized by a small number of well-defined options that can be explicitly enumerated. Multiple criteria optimization deals with intentionally described (possibly infinite) sets of options defined by means of constraints. In Chapter 5, Jacques Teghem provides an introduction to multiple criteria optimization, a field where technical difficulties relevant to optimization combine two conceptual difficulties inherent to reasoning with multiple criteria. The scope of the chapter is limited to multiple criteria linear programming, where both constraints and objective functions can be represented by linear expressions in terms of decision variables. After a refresher on basic notions, including efficient solutions, Teghem reviews the main techniques used in various multiple criteria linear programming problems according to whether variables are continuous, discrete or Boolean. Building on exact and interactive methods, the author also considers approximate methods with special focus on the use of meta-heuristics. The last two sections of this chapter are devoted to the case of imperfect information: aleatory data (subject to probabilistic randomness) and imprecise data (fuzzy multiple criteria linear programming).

Mathematical programming, whether linear or not, is no longer the only tool capable of solving decision problems where the set of solutions is implicitly described and may involve a large (possibly infinite) number of solutions. Constraint-based programming is a tool stemming from artificial intelligence, which strengthens and enriches the gamut of available decision optimization techniques. Many real-world problems such as scheduling, resource management, pattern recognition and diagnosis can be modeled as constraint satisfaction problems (CSPs). Chapter 6 provides an outline of current tools that address such problems. Gérard Verfaillie and Thomas Schiex also deal with extensions of CSPs where the satisfaction of constraints can be a matter of degree.

Traditionally, preferences are defined over sets of alternatives described by vectors of local evaluations along various attributes. Global preference is analytically determined by means of a formal preference aggregation model merging preferences according to each criterion. This process is more precisely described in the third part.

In Chapter 7, Jérôme Lang takes a more general point of view relying on logical representations of preference. He presents compact preference representation languages allowing a simpler expression of preferences between complex entities, expressed by the decision maker in natural languages. These languages are supplemented with efficient algorithms that can compute whether one alternative is preferred to another and find optimal solutions. Such languages are the topic of extensive research in AI. The author shows how propositional logic-based formalisms can be instrumental for the representation of preference. Various logics of preference are surveyed, starting from so-called *ceteris paribus* preferences, ending with conditional preference logics and graphical representations such as CP nets. The chapter concludes with a brief insight into the potential of multiple-valued and paraconsistent logics.

Chapters 8–14: decision under uncertainty

This part is a compendium of various mathematical or empirical models for decision under uncertainty. First, the various existing criteria for decision-making under uncertainty are reviewed (in the historical order of their appearance): expected utility, subjective expected utility, non-additive extensions thereof and qualitative criteria. One chapter is devoted to the empirical validity of such criteria from the viewpoint of cognitive psychology. The final two chapters of this part focus on mastering the combinatorial complexity of multistage decision-making problems under uncertainty: Bayesian networks, influence diagrams and Markov decision processes for planning under uncertainty.

Chapter 8, written by Alain Chateauneuf, Michèle Cohen and Jean-Marc Tallon, outlines the theory of decision under risk after von Neumann and Morgenstern. Assumption of decision under risk is that a probability distribution over the states of the world is available. In such a situation, any decision is a matter of choosing between lotteries. von Neumann and Morgenstern proposed necessary and sufficient conditions for the justification of:

1) the existence and uniqueness (up to a linear transformation) of a utility function quantifying the attractiveness of the various consequences of the tentative decisions, according to the decision maker;

2) the criterion of expected utility as *the* rational evaluation basis for ranking decisions.

This chapter puts some emphasis on the issue of representing the attitude of the decision maker in the face of risk. Several approaches to model risk aversion, even if intuitively distinct, turn out to be equivalent in this setting which shows some limitation in expressiveness. Another limitation is highlighted by means of the Allais paradox whereby decision makers, when faced with both sure and uncertain gains, may consistently violate the independence axiom. Modern approaches to decision under risk that weaken the independence axiom are surveyed.

Chapter 9, written by Alain Chateauneuf, Michèle Cohen and Jean-Yves Jaffray is a refresher on the classical theory of decision under uncertainty according to Savage, who axiomatically justified subjective expected utility as a criterion for ranking decisions. Contrary to the case of decision under risk, the decision maker does not know the probabilities of the states of nature. Decisions are construed as functions (also called *acts*) from the state space to a set of consequences. Savage proposed a set of postulates on the preference between acts implying that this preference can be represented by an expected utility with respect to a subjective probability distribution. These postulates imply that the set of states is infinite. In other words, in this approach, even if the decision maker is ignorant about the current situation, they behave as if they knew of a probability distribution on states and ranked decisions using the criterion proposed by von Neumann and Morgenstern. The chapter presents other settings where the same result was proved, especially the elegant proposal of Anscombe and Aumann where the state space is finite but decisions have random consequences modeled by lotteries on a finite set of possible results. The authors then recall the history of empirical criticisms of this approach, which also suffers from the Allais paradox and also from the Ellsberg paradox. The latter shows that many decision makers are likely to violate the sure-thing principle (the key axiom of Savage theory) in the face of incomplete information, which is incompatible with a probabilistic representation of uncertainty.

Chapter 10, written by Alain Chateauneuf and Michèle Cohen, surveys the numerous decision models and criteria that were proposed as a consequence of the various critiques of the classical theory. These models were proposed to accommodate the Allais and Ellsberg paradoxes, and to offer refined views of risk and uncertainty aversion. This chapter considers both extensions of the classical theories under risk and under uncertainty. In the case of uncertainty, the main step was taken by David Schmeidler within the Anscombe–Aumann setting. He suggested that the independence axiom only applies to comonotonic decisions, no mixture of which can help hedging against the variability of consequences. Under this restriction, the criterion takes the form of a Choquet integral with respect to a monotonic set function representing uncertainty. Other extensions were later proposed to accommodate the Choquet integral, for instance in the Savage setting, and are surveyed in this chapter. Let us mention the multiprior model of Gilboa and Schmeidler, in which decisions are ranked according to their minimal expected utility with respect to a family of probabilities (coinciding with a Choquet integral w.r.t a lower envelope), and the generalization to belief functions of Hurwicz criterion taking a weighted average between the best and the worst consequences. These approaches use representations of uncertainty presented in Chapter 3. The last section of this chapter considers the generalization of the von Neuman-Morgenstern model proposed by Quiggin (the so-called 'rank-dependent' model). The basic idea is that the decision maker has a subjective perception of objective probabilities. This is encoded by means of a function that models the subjective perception of objective probabilities, and the criterion is again Choquet integral with respect to this distorted probability measure. This model addresses the Allais paradox, distinguishing attitude towards risk (the probability distortion function) and towards sure consequences (the utility function). More recent variants of this approach are discussed.

Chapter 11, written by D. Dubois, H. Fargier, H. Prade and R. Sabbadin, studies what remains of the classical theory when utility and uncertainty functions are no longer numerical and are expressed by preference relations studied in Chapter 2. In the pure relational framework, rational decision rules are qualitative or possibility theory-based counterparts to Condorcet pairwise majority rule, and impossibility results similar to those in the voting framework are found. When a common qualitative value scale is used, criteria for decision under uncertainty extend the maximin and maximax criteria introduced by Shackle and Wald in the early 1950s in the case of total uncertainty. The most general one is the Sugeno integral, a qualitative counterpart to the Choquet integral. This chapter discusses in detail prioritized pessimistic and optimistic extensions of maximin and maximax criteria respectively, the underlying uncertainty theory being possibility theory. In this approach, the attitude of the decision maker is only expressed by the choice of a set function representing uncertainty. In order to cope with the lack of discrimination of qualitative decision criteria, techniques to refine the obtained ranking of decisions are surveyed. In particular, it is shown that the prioritized pessimistic and optimistic extensions of maximin and maximax criteria can be refined by expected utility criteria with respect to a so-called big-stepped probability function, the utility functions being respectively concave or convex.

Chapter 12, written by Eric Raufaste and Dennis Hilton, considers decision under uncertainty from the viewpoint of cognitive psychology. They report on studies evaluating the extent to which normative decision theories faithfully account for the actual behavior of decision makers. This chapter echoes Chapter 4, which discusses this issue in a broader context. The works of Daniel Kahneman and Amos Tversky demonstrated at length, in a series of experiments, that human beings may fail to comply with normative assumptions. The authors present the so-called Prospect Theory, somewhat akin, through the use of distortion functions, to the Quiggin decision model while using a bipolar value scale. Indeed, the bipolar behavior of human decision makers can be examined, since a decision maker does not have the same attitude in the face of gains and in the face of losses. The authors then broaden the scope of the chapter towards a global descriptive approach to human decision, including the case of several dimensions and the search for Pareto-dominance. An important cause of deviation between theoretical models and human behavior is the so-called attentional focusing, namely the fact that a decision maker concerned with one aspect of the decision process tends to neglect other aspects. It makes the choice process prone to manipulation through the way possible choices are described to the user (framing effect). This chapter also highlights the systematic use of heuristics by decision makers as shortcuts to speed up the choice process. The study of such heuristics, as carried out by Gigerenzer, enable some human errors to be predicted. This chapter also discusses the role of emotions in the decision process.

The next two chapters consider computational issues for large decision-making problems, especially within the classical expected utility approach. In Chapter 13, Jean-Yves Jaffray surveys the theoretical background of Bayesian networks and influence diagrams. A Bayesian network is a concise representation of a large joint probability distribution on a Cartesian product of finite universes. Its merit is to highlight the local conditional independence properties between groups of variables via the so-called *d-separation* property. A Bayesian net enables the determination of posterior probabilities to be carried out via local computations for the purpose of belief revision when some variables are instantiated. This technique is especially efficient when paths relating variables in the graph are unique. Bayesian nets are extended to the handling of decision trees. These are structures involving decision nodes and chance nodes; the decision maker tries to find the best decision sequences (policies) in order to maximize the overall expected utility. The computation of optimal policies is made easier by folding the decision tree in order to do away with redundancies. Local computation techniques similar to those in Bayesian nets mentioned in this chapter are possible due to the additive separability of expected utility. The extension of such methods to more general decision rules such as the Choquet integral is problematic because this separability property no longer holds.

Chapter 14, written by Régis Sabbadin, also studies combinatorial aspects of decision under uncertainty for tree-like structures, such as those found in planning problems. Here a temporal dimension is added. The basic idea is that each decision causes the system state to evolve to another state, the aim being to reach a prescribed final state of interest to the user. Uncertainty lies first in the non-determinism of actions whose result is poorly known. These problems are formalized by means of so-called *Markov decision processes* (MDPs) where the result of actions only depends on the previous, supposedly known, state. The optimized criterion is again expected utility along trajectories, and the computation methods are based on dynamic programming which is again possible due to the additive separability of expected utility. This chapter surveys several methods for solving MDP problems, and also considers the more difficult case of *partially observed* MDPs (POMDPs) where the actual result of past actions cannot be completely known. An account is given of decision processes whose transition probabilities are only known via learning. The determination of an optimal policy is carried out simultaneously with the probability learning process. MDPs often contain redundant parts that can be factorized, in order to speed up computations. Concise representations of MDPs exist that are similar to those for decision trees presented in the previous chapter.

The last part of Chapter 14 is devoted to the qualitative counterpart of MDPs where the representation of non-deterministic actions and of the information about the current state is based on possibility theory. Optimistic and pessimistic qualitative criteria presented in Chapter 11 are taken advantage of. From a computational point of view, such criteria preserve a form of separability that makes them amenable to dynamic programming techniques such as the expected utility techniques. This conforms with the fact pointed out in Chapter 11 that possibilistic criteria can be refined by expected utility. Moreover, the increase in complexity when moving from MDPs to POMDPs is significantly smaller than in the probabilistic setting. Without denying the expressive power of probabilistic POMDPs, the qualitative approach to planning under uncertainty is therefore equally attractive.

Chapters 15–20: multiple criteria decision

The third part of this treatise is devoted to multiple criteria decision analysis and, more generally, to aggregation methods for multiple and potentially conflicting judgements or pieces of advice. There are three groups of chapters.

The first group deals with decision-support methods based on conjoint measurement theory. This theory aims at determining conditions under which a binary relation, modeling preferences and defined product set can be represented numerically. The conditions that allow such a numerical representation lead generally to results having a constructive proof, and therefore provide guidelines for the elicitation and the structuring of preferences expressed by a decision maker.

Chapter 15, written by Mohammed Abdellaoui and Christophe Gonzales, presents the classical theory of conjoint measurement which deals with the numerical representation of structures that are complete and transitive. An original aspect of this chapter is its unified presentation framework including (1) the case of sure information that mainly leads to additive value functions and (2) the situations under risk and uncertainty that lead to various decompositions (additive, multiplicative or multilinear) of utility functions according to von Neumann and Morgenstern. Particular attention is paid in this chapter to encoding methods, i.e. to procedures for the elicitation of preferences from a decision maker. The extension of these methods to new decision models under uncertainty (as in rank-dependent expected utility) is also considered for situations under risk and uncertainty.

Chapter 16, written by Denis Bouyssou and Marc Pirlot, is devoted to the study of conjoint measurement models where transitivity or completeness are no longer assumed. It is shown that the use of different forms of the one-dimensional 'traces' of a binary relation on a Cartesian product is instrumental in the derivation of a numerical representation for non-necessarily transitive relations. Models thus obtained can be viewed as offering a general framework that encompasses different aggregation methods proposed in the literature. In particular, it is shown how these general models enable an axiomatic analysis of multicriteria methods based on outranking relations to be performed (as in the ELECTRE method and related approaches).

In the above two chapters, the different components of the Cartesian product of the evaluation domains were not assumed to be expressed on a common scale. The second group of chapters in this part deals with methods where it makes sense to evaluate objects according to different points of view on a common scale. Such a hypothesis may appear to be quite bold. However, it is frequently made when grading student's work, or more generally when different experts on a panel use the same evaluation scale.

Chapter 17, written by Jean-Luc Marichal, presents an overview of the various existing models for aggregating scores belonging to a common scale. In particular, it includes a survey of different types of averages, associative aggregation functions and aggregations based on the use of non-additive measures (in particular, Choquet and Sugeno integrals). Particular attention is paid to the question of the meaningfulness of such aggregation schemes, i.e. to the question of knowing whether the algebraic manipulations performed by the aggregation may lead to opposite conclusions if the evaluation unit on the common scale is changed.

The second chapter of this group (Chapter 18), authored by Michel Grabisch, is devoted to the practical use and interpretation of the aggregation schemes presented in the Chapter 17. It is shown, using the MACBETH approach, how it is possible in practice to evaluate objects on a common scale. Particular emphasis is put on the distinction between unipolar and bipolar scales. For bipolar scales, there exists a neutral point expressing indifference inside the scale, and the aggregation of ratings above the neutral level can be made according to a different logic from that used for ratings below this level. It leads to considering aggregation schemes that are more general than those considered in the previous chapter (e.g. based on an integral with respect to a bi-capacity). The interpretation of parameters involved in such representations (especially in terms of interaction between criteria) and their practical elicitation are discussed in detail.

The third and last group of chapters is devoted to the links between multiple criteria analysis and social choice theory. It should indeed be clear that the aggregation of evaluations according to different criteria is not unrelated to the aggregation of individual opinions regarding various candidates to an election.

Chapter 19, written by Denis Bouyssou, Thierry Marchant and Patrice Perny, offers a simple introduction to social choice theory. It is shown, by means of various examples, why the aggregation methods proposed in social choice theory do not satisfy all the expectations that we might have. These problems are related to more general results (such as the famous Arrow theorem) that examine the difficulty of designing a purely ordinal aggregation of various points of view. This chapter provides a brief survey of the literature, and stresses the relevance of many classical results in social choice theory for the design or the use of a multiple criteria method for decision analysis.

Chapter 20, authored by Olivier Hudry, Bruno Leclerc, Bernard Monjardet and Jean-Pierre Barthélémy, concludes this book. It deals with the analysis of aggregation methods based on the search for medians of a collection of binary relations, i.e. relations that minimize a distance to preference relations in such a collection. This type of method is very old in social choice theory (and dates back at least to Condorcet). These techniques are analyzed in great detail according to the type of relations to be aggregated and the nature of the result under concern. Different algorithmic formulations of these medians are proposed and their complexity studied. The problem of determining a median of a collection of relations is an example of a more general one: that of finding medians in a lattice or in a semi-lattice. The results that are thus obtained at the more general level shed a powerful light on the former problem of aggregation of preference relations.

Hopefully, the collection of survey articles gathered in this book offers a broad overview on the representation and the computational aspects of decision problems and the foundations of decision under uncertainty and multiple points of view. It will guide the reader trough the abundant literature that exists on the topic. The authors of surveys proposed here are renowned contributors to the study of the questions covered in this volume. This volume also demonstrates that research on the use of formal methods for the study of decision problems is active in French-speaking countries.

Denis Bouyssou, Didier Dubois, Marc Pirlot and Henri Prade

Chapter 1

From Decision Theory to Decision-aiding Methodology

1.1. Introduction

Quite often I get asked what my job is. When I reply that I work in decision aiding, people remain perplexed and quite often ask 'aiding what decisions?'.

Indeed, decision making is an activity that every person does every day. We all make decisions constantly, from the simplest 'should I take my umbrella?' [POO 92] to the more complex 'how should the international disarmament treaty be applied?' [JPV 98]. We also make decisions at all levels e.g. individual: 'should I get a divorce?' [WAT 83], organizational: 'how do we schedule the crew shifts?' [CAP 98] and inter-organizational: 'which trace for the highway?' [OST 93].

During such decision processes we often ask for help, advice or support from friends, experts or consulting companies. Several questions arise. Is it conceivable that a decision-aiding methodology could exist independently from any specific domain, one which could be used in all such situations? Can an expert in decision aiding exist who is not an expert in any particular domain? What would the difference be between such an expert and a psychotherapist, a physician, a lawyer, an expert in logistics or your best friend?

What characterizes decision aiding, both from a scientific and a professional point of view, is the fact that it is both formal and abstract. By 'formal' the use of formal

---

Chapter written by Alexis TSOUKIÀS.

languages is meant, ones which reduce the ambiguity of human communication. By 'abstract' the use of languages that are independent from a specific domain of discourse is meant. The basic idea is that the use of such languages implies the adoption of a model of 'rationality': a key concept in decision aiding. Does it make sense to use such a language always and in any context? Obviously not. Being abstract and formal presents several disadvantages:

– it is much less effective with respect to human communication;
– it has a cost (not necessarily monetary);
– reducing ambiguity might not be desirable; and
– it imposes a limiting framework on people's intuition and creativity.

Nevertheless, there are also several advantages which, in some circumstances, can be interesting [BOUY 00]:

– It allows the participants in a decision process to talk the same language, a fact that improves transparency of the process and possibly increases participation (for an example see [BAN 01]).

– It allows the identification of the underlying structure of a decision problem (if there is any) and therefore allows the re-use of procedures and models (see any textbook on Operational Research, e.g. [WIL 90]).

– It is not affected by the biases of human reasoning that are due to education or tradition [RIV 94].

– It may help to avoid the common errors that are due to an informal use of formal methods. A typical case is the use of averages as a universal grading procedure [BOUY 00].

In general terms, a formal and abstract language allows us to better analyze, understand, explain and justify a problem or a solution. It should be noted that organizations, companies, institutions, entreprises and ourselves ask for and use formal methods of decision aiding. Students are promoted using the average of their grades. Traffic restrictions are applied based on a pollution index. Credit demands are rejected because of the client's credit rating. Production is scheduled, highways are designed and networks are administrated using formal methods of decision support. In reality, decision aiding is present in many aspects of our everyday life. People do not necessarily use this term, but there is always a formal and abstract language which is used in all the above examples. Therefore, when the expression 'decision aiding' is used, the use of a formal and abstract language in order to handle problem situations faced by individuals and/or organizations is meant.

In this chapter we first examine a brief history of the evolution of this domain from a scientific and a professional point of view (section 1.2). Such a historical reconstruction pretends neither to be complete nor rigorously organized. Several readers might feel disappointed that some very important scientific achievements are not recognized. Indeed, this is an essay which reflects my very personal point of view and is biased by at least three factors.

– Scientific: I am not an expert in all areas of decision theory and operations research and I tend to emphasize in my presentation what I know better.

– Professional: the real world experiences of decision aiding that I had the opportunity to conduct do not cover all different aspects of practicing decision aiding, so that I have a partial vision of this complex reality.

– Geographical: being a (western) European I have not been exposed to the bulk of the contributions produced in decision theory and operations research just behind the corner [e.g. KEN 83, KWA 62] and this is a severe limitation.

In section 1.3, I will present and discuss different decision-aiding approaches that have been introduced during the 60 years of existence of this discipline: normative, descriptive, prescriptive and constructive approaches. I will try to explain the differences among these approaches by examining the origin of their particular 'models of rationality'. In section 1.4, I will place myself within a constructive decision-aiding approach and I will discuss how a decision-aiding process is structured. In order to do that I will examine the 'artifacts' produced by such a process: the representation of a problem situation, the definition of a problem formulation, the construction of an evaluation model and the formulation of a final recommendation. Such a presentation will allow me to differentiate decision aiding from other areas of scientific investigation such as automatic decision making.

The ultimate message I wish to deliver with this chapter is that decision aiding is a human activity that can be (and actually has been) the subject of scientific investigation. Different decision theories have been developed with specific characteristics. At the same time, different decision-aiding practices have been developed either as a result of testing theoretical conjectures or as a result of aiding real decision makers (individuals, organization or collective entities) in their work.

There is no one-to-one correspondence between theories and practices. Nevertheless, I consider that all such theories and practices define a whole which I will call 'decision-aiding methodology'. The reader should note that in the text I use the term methodology in a very precise way: *reasoning about methods*. I claim that we have several methods, but we should establish a common methodology for decision-aiding purposes. Such reflections are discussed in the conclusions section. At the end of the chapter a long but definitely partial list of references is provided (an exhaustive presentation of the literature being impossible).

1.2. History

1.2.1. *Genesis and youth*

We can fix the origin of decision aiding as sometime just before the second world war, in the studies conducted by the British army on their new radar system installation and their efforts to break the German secret communication code (1936–37). The reader can get a flavor of this period in [BOW 04, KIR 02]. It is the first time the term 'operational research' ('operations research' in the USA) appears.

The problem of how decisions are or ought to be taken by individuals, organizations and institutions was previously discussed by Aristotle [ARI 90] and, more recently, during the 18th century (see [BERN 38] on probability, [EUL 36] on combinatorial problems and [BOR 81, CON 85] on voting and social choice procedures) and also at the beginning of the 20th century ([PAR 06] on economic problems under multiple dimensions, [FAY 49, TAYL 11] on the scientific management of enterprises, [DEF 36, DEF 37, KOL 33, RAM 31] on probability theory and [TUR 37] on decidability).

In all these contributions, the concept of decision is central. It should be mentioned that, in order to argue for their thesis that probability only exists in terms of subjective belief, both Ramsey and de Finetti have used what is known today as comparison of lotteries and the associated preferences of a decision maker. "If the option of α for certain is indifferent with that of β if p is true and γ if p is false, we can define the subject's degree of belief in p as the ratio of the difference between α and γ to that between β and γ. This amounts roughly to defining the degree of belief in p by the odds at which the subject could bet on p, the bet being conducted in terms of differences of values as defined" [RAM 31, p. 179–180].

In any case, it was the undeniable success of operations research in supporting military and intelligence activities of the allies that grounded the idea that decision making (and decision aiding) can be studied using a scientific approach and that general models of decision support were possible. Towards the end of the 1940s, several fundamental contributions appeared in linear programming [DAN 48, KAN 39], decision and game theory [NAS 50, NAS 51, VON 44] and in algorithmics and the definition of machines able to solve any problem [TUR 50].

It was during that period that the first scientific societies of operations research (in the UK in 1948, in the USA in 1950) and the first scientific journals appeared [BLA 50]. The first real-world applications of this new discipline (in non-military applications) appeared [DAN 51] as well as the first companies specializing in decision aiding (but this term was not used at that time). The best-known example is the Rand corporation. Within Rand, operations research was developed into a science to be applied to the multiple problems of the new post-war industrialization.

Such first contributions and experiences were characterized by the search for formal structures underlying precise decision problems and the use of mathematics and logic as a modeling language. For an interesting presentation of the origins of these contributions as have been perceived by their authors themselves, see [LEN 91]. The first steps in this direction strengthened the idea that complex decision problems can be modeled through the use of a simple rationality model (maximize a utility function of the decision maker's decision variables, a function which is expected to faithfully represent the decision maker's preferences). Von Neumann's, Morgenstern's and Nash's contributions [NAS 50, VON 44] showed under what conditions such functions exist. Further on, the linear programming algorithm developed by Dantzig [DAN 48] (the famous Simplex algorithm) introduced the first tools by which such problems could be effectively solved (even for large dimensions). Turing and also Wiener [WIE 48] and Ashby [ASH 56] went further to consider the possibility of formulating a general theory of computation and conceived 'general problem solver' machines.

At that time, some critical contributions to this paradigm started to appear (although they were not always conceived as criticism). In 1951, Arrow [ARR 51] published his famous impossibility theorem, showing that aggregating the preferences of rational individuals, under conditions considered natural (universality, independence, respect of unanimity and non-dictatorship) is impossible. (If the result has to be rational, that is a complete order). Arrow's result closed the discussion opened by Borda and Condorcet in the sense that we know there is no universal preference aggregation procedure [BOUY 92, VIN 82a, VIN 82b]. At the same time, it paved the way for the huge literature on social choice theory [KEL 78, KEL 91, NUR 87, NUR 99, SEN 70, SEN 86, TAY 95].

Allais [ALL 53] published his famous paradox in 1953 where he showed that the axioms, introduced by von Neumann and Morgenstern as necessary and sufficient conditions for the existence of an utility function (and implicitly assumed necessary in order to exhibit a rational behavior), are systematically violated in the behavior of real decision makers when they are confronted by very simple choices [COO 58, MAY 54]. Such an empirical falsification of the expected utility theory opened another research direction on integrating the findings of cognitive science into decision theory [e.g. ALL 79].

In 1947, Simon [SIM 47] observed decision processes occurring within real organizations and concluded that the behavior of real decision makers is far from the postulates of decision theory, at least as this theory was formulated at that time. During the 1950s, Simon [SIM 54, SIM 56, SIM 57] developed his 'bounded rationality' theory. This states that a decision maker facing a choice behaves on the basis of a local satisfaction criterion, in the sense that they will choose the first solution which they subjectively consider as satisfactory without trying to attain an unrealistic (and useless) optimal solution. Actually, Simon considers decision theory to be based on three implicit hypotheses (see the discussion in [MOS 84]):

– decision makers always know their problems well;

– such problems can always be formulated as an effectiveness (or efficiency) problem; and

– the information and the resources necessary to find a solution are always available.

None of these hypotheses is true as, in reality (following Simon):

– decision makers never have a very precise idea of their problem;

– often their problems can be formulated as the search for a 'satisfying compromise'; and

– solving a problem is always constrained by the available resources and time.

The innovation introduced by Simon is radical. Decision theory at that moment always considered the rationality model to exist independently from the decision maker and their decision process. Simon put at the center of his reflection the decision process (the mental activities of a decision maker) and postulated that a rationality model has to be found within such a process and not outside of it. The problem with this hypothesis is that, while an 'exogenous rationality model' is compatible with an optimization model (indeed the classic rationality model is based on optimization), this is not always the case with a subjectively established model (at least not automatically or necessarily). Simon's work opened several research directions, both towards the creation of new decision-aiding approaches [e.g. LEM 77] and towards what today is known as 'artificial intelligence' [SIM 69]. It should be noted that the idea of looking for a satisfying solution has an immediate application to the problem of finding an acceptable compromise when the decision is subject to the presence of multiple criteria [VIN 92].

At the end of the 1950s, several 'classic' books appeared. These books were used to train generations of researchers and practitioners [BER 58, CHA 61, CHU 57, CONW 67, DAN 63, FAU 68, FOR 62, GAS 58, HIL 67, LUC 57, VAJ 56].

The 1950s and 1960s saw significant increases in research, university classes and applications in different domains. Typical big clients of such studies were the companies' managing networks (water distribution, telecommunications, electricity suppliers, railways and airlines). In addition, several consulting companies specializing in operations research and decision support appeared. It should be remembered that these years were when the world was trying to reconstruct itself after the war and tremendous resources were invested in finding viable and efficient solutions to important industrial and economic problems. Unsurprisingly, there were both successes and failures. Such experiences allowed the first critical approaches to the now well-established classic decision theory to become stronger (for early discussions, see [ACK 62, ADE 69, CHU 67, CRO 69, KOO 56]).

At the beginning of the 1960s, Zadeh published his famous paper [ZAD 65] about fuzzy sets. The paper introduced a new perspective on the treatment of uncertainty, ambiguity and linguistic variables. Zadeh's innovation had a major impact on the future of the discipline, since it concerns a fundamental aspect of formal languages: set theory. The extension of set theory through the introduction of a membership function, a 'measure' of an element's membership to a given set, allowed the increase of both the expressivity and the flexibility of formal languages and therefore of the decision-aiding models using them.

Another domain which introduced major contributions to the development of alternative approaches to decision theory is cognitive science and psychology [EDW 54, FES 64, LIC 69, LIC 71, SHE 64, SLO 68]. Allais' intuition to experimentally validate the axioms of decision theory was followed by several researchers [e.g. TVE 67, TVE 69, TVE 77a]. Tversky showed that the properties, intuitively considered as rational for preference relations, are more a theoretical imposition and not necessarily corresponding to the behavior of real decision makers. Tversky showed that preference can well be intransitive [TVE 69] and that similarity can be non-symmetric [TVE 77a].

Such results emphasized the necessity of pursuing a more thorough study of the fundamental structures on which decision-aiding models rely, namely the structure of preference relations [DUS 41, LUC 56, SCO 58] and of the functions which represent them (value or utility functions [FIS 70, KRA 71]). For further work on this subject, see [FIS 85, PIR 97, ROB 79, ROU 85] (see also the recent survey [OZT 05]).

Remaining within the influence of the psychological studies, during the 1960s a psychotherapy movement known as 'relational psychotherapy' appeared, based on an approach claimed by the authors to be 'constructive' [BAT 72, GOF 68, WAT 67]. Within such an approach, the importance of how a problem is formulated was emphasized as well as the importance of the relationship between the one who asks for help and the one who provides such help (the patient and the therapist in their terminology). This approach also emphasized the fact that a problem is not something given within a decision process: the process of defining and solving a problem is the same. From such a perspective, the solution of a problem is a construction and not the result of a search in a space of solutions nor a classic inference from a set of sentences (see the classical dichotomy in artificial intelligence literature [SIM 83]).

The first organizational studies concerning the behavior of decision makers and the structuring of decision processes within real complex organizations were carried out in the 1960s. It was again Simon who provided significant direction in this research [CYE 63, EME 62, MAR 58]. In these works, it was shown that the behavior of an organization (supposed to be composed by rational decision makers) does not correspond to the rational behavior as described by decision theory. (The reader can study an extreme model in [COH 72], the famous model where organizations are seen as garbage cans.) The problem, already observed by Weber [WEBE 22] in his studies during the 190s on the bureaucracies, is that within an organization different forms of rationality may co-exist [SIM 76]. Later on, related research was condensed in Mintzberg's work [MEL 78, MINT 76, MINT 83].

During the 1960s, the concept of 'decision' and 'value' was the focus of interesting research in philosophy which posed the question: is it possible to define the concept of 'good' in a formal way? Von Wright [VONWR 63] (see also [HAL 57]) published his 'Logic of Preference' within which the sentence 'x is preferred to y' is considered true if all the worlds where x is true are preferred to the worlds where y is true. This research direction was followed by [CHI 66a, CHI 66b, HAN 66a, HAN 66b, JEF 65] and by the work done in [RES 67, RES 69]. Von Wright continued the development of his theory in [VONWR 72] (see also [HUB 74]). From this research direction, what is known today as deontic logic [HILP 71] was further developed. See also the more recent [AQV 86, NUT 97] and [MUL 79] for a criticism.

Returning to more formal aspects of operations research and decision aiding, it should be noted that the first works concerning algorithmic complexity appeared during the 1960s. Hartmanis and Stearns [HART 65] were the first to pose the problem in the form we know today. On this basis, Karp [KAR 75] proposed the classification currently in use. This gave the formal basis used by Garey and Johnson [GARE 79] in order to compile their famous 'encyclopedia' (see also [PAP 82]). This research opened a big issue in optimization. Several algorithms used to solve classic operations research problems (and others) appeared to be less useful in practice since, in the presence of large instances of the problem, the resources required to reach an optimal solution are immense and independent of the computer used.

We also mention the problem of satisfying a logical clause and the famous 'traveling salesman problem' [FLO 56, MOR 42]. Little *et al.* [LIT 63] introduced one of the most widely-used algorithms in combinatorial optimization: Branch and Bound. For a survey see [LAW 85]. Looking for an optimal solution, besides its cognitive, theoretical and epistemological problems, also became a practical problem.

The research program of artificial intelligence [e.g. NIL 71] oriented towards the creation of 'thinking machines' and the establishment of general problem solving procedures was boosted by the work of Newell and Simon [NEW 63, NEW 72]. The idea of looking for a satisfying solution (instead of an optimal one) was a partial reply to the problem of the resources required to arrive at a conclusion for any decision process. The question was re-formulated under a more logical approach by McCarthy and Hayes [MCC 69], who opened the way to what is known today as non-monotonic reasoning, and by Minsky [MIN 75] who suggested the use of new techniques to represent 'knowledge', the latter being seen as the source of efficient problem solving.

The first work on the problem of evaluating alternative decisions using multiple criteria, where the criteria could be conflicting, appeared during the 1960s. In reality this is the case in most decision situations. It was the choice (and sometimes the necessity) of researchers and of practitioners that pushed them to simplify problems using a single decision criterion. In 1955 Charnes *et al.* proposed the idea of Goal Programming [CHA 55]. This work was further developed in [CHA 61] opening the way to what is known today as multi-objective programming [BEN 71, GEO 68, GEO 73, SHE 64, ZEL 73]. Bernard Roy presented his ideas on this issue for the first time in 1966 and then in 1968 [BEN 66, ROY 68] opening the way to an approach known as outranking-based methods. Raiffa produced his famous RAND report on these types of problems in 1969 [RAI 69]. The first international conference in this domain [COC 73] took place in 1972. Keeney and Raiffa published their reference book [KEE 76] extending utility theory [FIS 70] in the presence of multiple criteria in 1976.

The presence of multiple criteria poses a fundamental question. The concept of 'vector optimum' makes little sense from a mathematical point of view (at least in the natural terms of minimizing the value of a function). The only objective definition that can be introduced is the one of efficient solution [PAR 06]. A solution is considered efficient if there are no other solutions at least as good as the current one and strictly better under at least one criterion (dominance). The problem is that the set of efficient solutions can be extremely large and therefore useless from a practical point of view. Technically, the different approaches can be distinguished by the procedure used to explore the set of efficient solutions in order to find the 'best compromise' (again a concept with no precise mathematical definition).

On the one hand, we have approaches based on the establishment of a function that aggregates the different criteria in a single criterion (a multi-attribute utility function), the problem thus becoming once more that of optimization. On the other hand, we have approaches based on the idea that the criteria can be seen as individuals having preferences. We then use methods originating in social theory (for instance voting procedures) in order to obtain a global preference relation representing the whole set of criteria. Graph theory is used to obtain a final solution (since such comprehensive preference relations can be easily seen as a graph).

Details of differences between these two approaches are provided later. However, it should be noted that it quickly appeared that there were deeper differences than just the technical ones. These differences were concerned with how decision aiding is conceived and implemented rather than the technical procedures and the use of a specific method (for an interesting discussion on this issue see [ROY 93a]). See section 1.3 for a discussion of such issues.

This first part of the history is concluded by noting that, at the end of the 1960s, operations research and decision theory were enjoying a period of strong development both in theory and in practice. This development, together with the establishment of a dominant paradigm, allowed the appearance of critical approaches which occupied the scene during the period referred to as the 'maturity period'. It is interesting to note the following:

– The discussion about alternative decision theories has been rooted in practical problems; it is the quest to help real decision makers involved in real decision processes that pushed the research to explore 'innovative' or 'alternative' approaches within the discipline.

– The development of operations research (OR) and decision theory created branches (such as game theory, mathematical programming, decision analysis, etc.) which began their own independent evolution.

1.2.2. *Maturity*

In this partial reconstruction of the evolution of decision theory, the following focuses on some research directions briefly introduced in the previous section. As emphasized previously, the passing of decision aiding into 'maturity' [BOUY 93] implied the establishment of different branches or specializations:

– the structuring and formulation of decision problems;
– the contribution of cognitive sciences;
– the intersection of artificial intelligence and decision theory;
– the treatment of uncertainty; and
– the development of multiple criteria decision analysis.

Such directions have been followed either within the OR and decision theory communities or by researchers coming from other fields sharing an interest towards the concept of decision support. These directions do not diverge, but rather have several common points and potential areas of convergence.

As in other empirical sciences, OR and decision theory entered their first official crisis for a practical reason. Towards the end of the 1960s, the British OR society wanted to create a kind of chartered directory of OR professionals. The reason was simple: provide the practitioners of the domain a quality label allowing the discipline and its practice to be better promoted. Not surprisingly, ORSA (in the USA) published almost at the same time its suggestion about the guidelines of OR practice [ORS 71].

The initiative was followed by several questions: what are the boundaries of the discipline and how are they fixed? should existing methods be used? who decides whether a decision support method belongs to the discipline? and, given a new method, how will it be legitimated to enter these boundaries? The difficulty in finding convincing answers to these questions highlighted the differences between diverse decision theories and their critics. This debate reached a conclusion only very recently; the British society finally modified its statutes in order to create the above mentioned directory in 2001.

The reader can get an idea of this discussion in the famous articles of Ackoff [ACK 79a, ACK 79b]. A reconstruction of this discussion is also available in the introduction of [ROS 89] and more recently in [KIR 06]. An interesting perspective on the discussion about the operations research crisis is also in [BOUY 03].

During the 1970s (mainly in the UK) there appeared new approaches to decision aiding, based on work done within the Tavistock Institute [EMER 59, FRI 69, STI 67, TRI 93] and by Stafford Beer [BEE 59, BEE 66]. The reader can see a presentation of such approaches in [ROS 89]. The better-known approaches include: soft systems methodology [CHE 81]; strategic choice [FRI 69, FRI 87]; cognitive mapping [EDE 83, EDE 88]; robustness analysis [ROS 78, ROS 96].

Recall that, in classic decision theory, a decision problem is formulated in a unique way. It is always a problem of maximizing a function on the outcomes of all potential actions. There is no alternative to this formulation; the decision maker has to adapt the information available and the perception of the problem to the axioms of the theory. In contrast, the new approaches claimed that the most important part within a decision-aiding process is that concerning the structuring and formulation of the decision problem. This practice was already being followed in certain psychotherapy methodologies [WAT 74]. Within such new approaches the attention is focused on the interactions between the client(s) and the analyst(s).

Several techniques were proposed in order to arrive at a definition of a representation of the problem situation on which all the participants could agree (see also the work done in [BANV 98, LAN 87, LAN 95, MOS 84]). What these approaches suggest is that, once the decision makers have understood their problem, solving it is a secondary issue and in most cases a simple one. Little attention is indeed paid to how the problem can be formulated in logical/mathematical terms (this aspect has been criticized on several occasions). However, it cannot be denied that structuring and formulating a problem remains one of the most critical parts within a decision-aiding process, as several real-world experiences have shown [BAN 99, BELT 97, CHE 90, ROS 89, STA 03]. This is discussed further in section 1.4.

As previously mentioned, decision theory has also been criticized on a cognitive basis. Several experiences (conducted mainly in the laboratory) have shown that decision makers do not behave as decision theory axioms pretend. Such experiences have also shown that the frame within which, and the precise way, a decision problem is formulated have a great influence on the behavior of the decision maker. For instance, asking for preferences between two alternatives presented in terms of gains or losses gives totally different answers. More generally, the cognitive context of the decision process is fundamental for the final result. For the first experiments conducted in this direction, see [KAH 79, TVE 80, TVE 93].

A first tentative reply to these theoretical and practical problems was the extension of utility theory through the introduction of 'belief coefficients' which were expected to take the cognitive context into account. The theory is now known as 'prospect theory' [KAH 79]. Although the complete axiomatization of this theory is still to be done [e.g. WAK 93], it has been the subject of a large research area that is still extremely active today [BLE 01, CHAT 99, GIL 01, KAH 02, KAH 03, KAS 03, LUC 94, LUC 96, SLO 02, VONW 86, WAK 02].

Another tentative answer developed at the same time (not necessarily in opposition to the previous one) had the identification of 'decision strategies', the procedures used by decision makers when facing a problem situation, as an objective. One of the first to observe such behaviors was Tversky [TVE 72]. Similar types of studies can also be found in [BART 92, GIG 99, MONT 76, MONT 83]. The common pattern of this research is always the same: the identification of regularities in the behavior of the decision makers, such as the progressive elimination of alternatives or the research for dominance structures. The reader can see reviews of this approach in [BART 02, SVE 96]. What such approaches basically contributed was the centering of decision aiding on the decision maker, their cognitive effort and the decision context. For the first time, decision aiding was focused on the decision process and not on the decision theory.

The reader will recognize some of Simon's cognitive criticism in the approach presented above. Simon's contribution found a fertile area of expansion in artificial intelligence (AI). One of the principal points of view of Simon was that decision theory payed (at that time) little attention to the process of problem solving and the necessary resources. In Simon's mind, AI could fill this gap. Indeed, a large part of the research conducted in this area concerned (and concerns) well-known decision problems. It is therefore interesting to observe how these two research areas evolved.

One common area of interest between artificial intelligence and operations research concerned optimization and planning algorithms with mutual benefits for both research areas. Indeed, the problem of establishing a plan in order to solve a problem has been often viewed in AI as the exploration of a tree structure where the nodes represent 'states of the world' and the arcs represent transitions from one state to another [FIK 71, NIL 80, RUS 95].

The goal of such exploration is to establish a path from a state of the world which represents the present situation to a state of the world which represents the solution. Such an exploration is mostly based on the estimation of the length of the path remaining in order to reach the desired state of the world (the solution), as can be seen in the famous A* algorithm ([HAR 68]). Indeed the state space tree has a structure similar to that generated by a Branch and Bound algorithm and it is explored using similar principles. In doing that, AI researchers used (and use) concepts derived from integer and dynamic programming methods developed in OR [e.g. BON 96, BOU 99b].

At the same time, AI researchers developed the so-called 'constraint satisfaction' based methods [TSA 93, VAN 89]. Such methods have been largely applied in typical operations research problems [APT 99, BAR 98, BOC 98, BRAI 99, DUB 96]. Practically, the two communities were sharing (and still share) a common concern: how to efficiently solve problems which are or can be considered decision problems. From this point of view, the development of heuristics for the solution of hard optimization problems common to both communities should be noted [AAR 97, GLO 86, GLO 97, GOL 89, PIR 96]. A partial bibliography on the above issues can be found in [JAU 88].

Another interesting interaction was developed around what is known today as 'qualitative decision theory'. The issue here is to extend decision theory through the use of symbolic approaches not requiring the imposition of further hypotheses in order to quantify information [BOU 94, BOU 99a, BOU 00, BRA 96, BRA 97, BRA 00, DOY 91, DOY 94, DOY 99, DUB 95, LEH 96, LEH 01b, TAN 94, WEL 91]. The problem is how to formulate a theory where the preferences are simply order relations and uncertainty is purely qualitative. The reader can see an exhaustive presentation and discussion of this issue in [DUB 02]. The result is that, if we want to remain within the frame of Savage's axioms, such a theory is too weak. Indeed, as pointed out in [DUB 02], the decision rules obtained within such an approach are either not decisive or overconfident, thus not interesting from an operational point of view. The reasons for such a negative result are related to the impossibility results present in social choice theory (the resulting decision rule is likely dominance).

Last, but not least, a field of interesting research has been established in 'preferential entailment'. Doyle [DOY 85] and Shoham [SHO 87] have observed that a reasoning system with only simple inferencing capabilities was not able to take into account preferences which are considered a fundamental element of human capability to solve problems. Their suggestion was to enhance inference systems, namely those able to perform non-monotonic reasoning, with an ordering relation among the possible interpretations of a logical clause in order to obtain preferred consequences instead of only true ones.

Such an idea has been followed by several other researchers [ALC 85, BRA 01, DOY 89, DOY 90, DOY 94, GÄR 88, GÄR 94, KRAU 90, LEH 01a] from different perspectives. Nevertheless, the problem of aggregating such orders remains once more within the frame of Arrow's impossibility theorem, as Doyle and Wellman have shown [DOY 91] (see also [DUB 02]).

Such results may appear negative. However, they also open interesting research perspectives, such as relaxing the axiomatic frame within which to look for a solution [e.g. WEY 84] or exploring the so-called 'non-rationalizable' choice functions [SEN 71, SEN 93].

Another major innovation within the frame of decision theory has been the introduction of fuzzy sets and, more particularly, of possibility theory [DUB 88, ZAD 78]. In order to obtain a general view of how these formalisms contributed to decision theory, see two other reference books on this subject [FOD 94, SLOW 98].

The focus here is two specific contributions:

– The consideration of preference relations as fuzzy subsets [FOD 94, KAC 88]: this allows us to relate such concepts to the already existing literature on valued binary relations and graphs [e.g DOI 86]. The use of fuzzy sets theory has therefore been extended to other decision-aiding concepts such as choice sets, kernels, etc. [BIS 00, KIT 93]. See [SLOW 98, Chapters 1 and 2] and, for a recent review, [OZT 05].

– The development of new aggregation procedures: aggregating 'uncertainty measures' or 'fuzzy measures' are similar to aggregating preferences [PER 92, BOUY 00, Chapter 7]. Consequently, a literature has been developed on the use of new aggregation operators, mainly based on the use of fuzzy integrals [GRA 00, GRA 95].

More generally speaking, possibility theory introduced the use of formalisms for representing uncertainty different from probability. The motivation for that was the consideration that the additive property of probability was problematic and the consequent conceptual discussion when subjective estimation of uncertainty is considered [e.g. NAU 01]. The ordinal nature of possibility distributions allowed their use in a more flexible way for several different domains of decision aiding [e.g. SAB 98, SAB 01, SLOW 90] although it did not solve all conceptual problems related to uncertainty modeling. That said, the reader should remember that since the late 1980s there has been a large discussion on innovating the whole field of decision under uncertainty and risk [COH 80, FAR 05, GIL 89, GIL 93, GIL 02a, GIL 02b, JAF 88, JAF 89, JAF 93, MAC 82, MAC 92, MAC 95, NAU 95, QUI 93, SCHM 89].

The discussion on handling uncertainty is concluded by recalling the contributions based on the use of other logic formalisms that allow the inevitable uncertainties, ambiguities and inconsistencies which characterize a decision-aiding process to be taken into account [FORT 02, PER 98, TSO 95, TSO 02a, TSO 02b].

In the first part of this historical reconstruction, it was argued that the formulation of a decision problem as an optimization one is a simplification of reality. Decision problems are almost always situations where we find several different dimensions, several points of view and several participating actors and stakeholders, each of them carrying within the decision process their values, preferences and criteria. The optimization simplification does not always allow the consideration of the complexity of the decision process.

Remember that, from a technical point of view, multiple criteria decision-aiding methods can be grouped into two categories based on how the set of the potential alternatives is explored (for a recent survey see [FIG 05]):

1) the establishment of an utility function synthesizing the different criteria; and

2) the use of pairwise comparison procedures and majority principles for establishing a final recommendation.

Within the first category, we find methods based on the construction of a multi-attribute utility function [KEE 76] and the methods which interactively explore the set of efficient solutions of a multi-objective program [GAR 97, VAND 89]. Specific heuristics possibly apply to these types of problems (particularly in the case of difficult ones such as in combinatorial optimization, see [ULU 94]). For an excellent reference survey, see [EHR 02]. The construction of the utility function can be obtained either directly [e.g. VONW 86] or indirectly (through, for instance, the AHP method [SAA 80], the UTA method [JAC 82] or the MACBETH method, [BAN 94]).

We find the methods known as 'outranking methods' within the second category. This name was given by Bernard Roy [ROY 85] to the preference relation representing the concept 'at least as good as'. Such methods are based on the principle: when we compare x to y under multiple criteria, x will be at least as good as y if it is the case for a weighted majority of criteria and there are no strong 'blocking minorities' [TSO 02b]. The reader can obtain more details on these methods in [ROY 91, ROY 96, SCHÄ 85, SCHÄ 96, VIN 92]. Recently, the possibility of constructing such a relation from holistic evaluations of the alternatives provided by the decision maker was shown in [GRE 99, PAW 94]. More generally, the extension of the theory of rough sets through the use of dominance-based decision rules [GRE 01, SLOW 05] allows us to take into account purely ordinal evaluations. For an axiomatic characterization of this approach in terms of conjoint measurement and on the equivalence between 'outranking based' and 'decision rules' based models, see [GRE 04, SLOW 02].

Such different methods each present advantages and disadvantages. The construction of an utility function is more restrictive (in the sense of the conditions to be fulfilled) and requires a considerable cognitive effort on the part of the decision maker (not necessarily intuitive). On the other hand, it allows us to obtain a rich result and is axiomatically well founded. The outranking methods are much more flexible (since there are less conditions to respect), but there is a risk of a very poor result and they are sometimes difficult to justify from an axiomatic point of view. For an interesting discussion on this issue, see [BELTS 02], [BOUY 00, Chapter 6] and [BOUY 06, Chapters 4–6].

However, the separation of the above methods into categories can be misleading. Adopting a conjoint measurement point of view, Bouyssou and Pirlot [BOUY 02, BOUY 04a, BOUY 04b, BOUY 05a, BOUY 05b] have shown that it is possible to give a common axiomatization to all such methods. Moreover, authors from different backgrounds [BELTS 02, DAL 94, FRE 88, GOO 98, KEE 92, KEE 99, ROY 90, ROY 92, ROY 93a, ROY 94, STE 03] have often claimed that, if any differences exist among the methods, these depend in reality more on how the decision-aiding process is implemented and less on the specific method adopted.

This historical reconstruction is summarized as follows:

– Despite the specialization of the last years, OR and decision theory can still be viewed as a unique discipline (as its founders did more than 60 years ago).

– OR and decision theory are deeply rooted in practising decision support, aiding real decision makers in real problem situations and involved in real decision processes. Even the more abstract theoretical results have originated from precise practical problems and the research for models fitting real demands. Theoretical soundness has always been accompanied by empirical validation.

– The evolution of the discipline has certainly been influenced by the vitality of the research conducted within it, but it has greatly benefit from cultural contamination from other disciplines such as philosophy, psychology, organization theory, political science, logic, mathematics and computer science.

– There is an increasing interest in issues such as how to structure and formulate a problem, conduct and implement a decision-aiding process, handle the relations with the client of the decision support requested, and train young people in the profession of OR and/or decision analyst. The issue here is to take the development of decision theories (which are in excellent shape) one step further towards a decision-aiding methodology: *a body of knowledge and a coherent structure of reasoning about theories and practices concerning deciding and aiding to decide*. Within such a methodology, it is possible to distinguish different approaches. Their principal differences are sketched in section 1.3.

1.3. Different decision-aiding approaches

In order to be able to assist someone in decision making, we must be able to elaborate on preferences. Indeed, what we know are their problems and desires (the problem situation). This is an elaboration based on the use of a formal language. To move from the problem situation to a decision-aiding model, and the actions such a model might imply, requires the use of a 'model of rationality'. This is a tool enabling the translation of 'informal' information (which is also naturally ambiguous) to a formal representation (where even ambiguity is represented in an unambiguous way). The question is where this model of rationality comes from.

In the following example the term 'client' is used to represent the person or collective entity that asks for decision support. The client is potentially, but not necessarily, a decision maker. Consider a client with a health problem who has a number of diagnoses and a certain number of proposed treatments. Assume that there is some uncertainty associated with the diagnoses and therefore with the outcomes of the treatments. What do we suggest to this client to do?

The classic approach in decision theory is straightforward. With each diagnosis (the states of the nature) is associated a probability and with each treatment (the potential actions) the respective outcomes. Using any of the standard protocols for constructing the client's value function on the set of the outcomes, we are able to define an utility function (including uncertainty) which, when maximized, identifies the solution which should be adopted (since by definition, it is the one which maximizes the client's expected utility).

The existence of such a function is guaranteed by a certain umber of axioms that represent what, following the theory, should be the principles of a rational decision maker's behavior [SAV 54]. Preferences are supposed to be transitive (and complete). The presence of cycles implies that the decision maker will be ready to infinitely increase what they are ready to pay for any of the solutions, and this is considered inconsistent with the idea of rationality. Similarly preferences about uncertain outcomes ought to be independent from probabilities [FIS 70, p. 107]

$$P \succ Q, \ 0 < \alpha < 1 \ \Rightarrow \ \alpha P + (1-\alpha)R \succ \alpha Q + (1-\alpha)R,$$

thus allowing the construction of a mathematical expectation. It should be noted that there has been no observation of the client behavior and the question of what other decision makers do in similar situations has not been posed. It is the decision maker who has to adapt themselves and their behavior to the axioms. Otherwise, they are not rational and the information and their preferences ought to be modified. This type of approach is usually called *normative*.

It should be noted that although the model handles uncertainty, there is no uncertainty at all associated with the model itself: the diagnoses are all the possible diagnoses and so are the treatments. The only issue is to find the best choice for the client. As with laws or ethical norms, the legitimation of the model of rationality is external to the problem situation. The model of rationality is a law of behavior imported into the decision process. Several classics on this approach include [FIS 70, FIS 82, LUC 57, SAV 54, WAK 89]. For a discussion on how rational such an approach is, see [MON 00].

However, it might be the case that the client's behavior does not respect the axioms of the classic decision theory. As an alternative, one could look for a model of rationality based on empirical legitimation instead of a theoretical model. If other decision makers followed a certain strategy in order to make a decision under similar circumstances, why not apply the same to the present one? This is the basic idea of the approach usually call *descriptive*: define models and decision strategies based on the observation of real decision makers [HUM 83, KAH 81, POU 94, VONW 86].

Once again it should be noted that we impose a model of rationality which is independent of the problem situation. Nevertheless, there are more degrees of freedom. The client's personality is considered as a source of information. The problem is not necessarily formulated as an optimization one (several alternatives are possible). On the other hand, as for the normative approach, we are sure about the problem and the model: we are looking for the best treatment for the client given the diagnoses, the treatments and the uncertainties of the outcomes. Some of these ideas can be found at the origin of the research on expert systems [HAT 92].

The problem is that we can find ourselves in a situation where the client cannot be associated with any model of rationality more or less ready made. They might exhibit intransitive and/or incomplete preferences. Their perception of the uncertainty might escape any effort to quantify or to measure it. Moreover, the client might be aware that they have to improve the structure of their preferences; however, perhaps there is no time, will or resources available to do that. Nevertheless, we have to suggest a recommendation and we have to do it *here and now*. An approach could be to look for a contingent rationality model without searching for it outside the decision process, but within it. Obviously the validity of such a model is strictly local, but its legitimation is clear: the client themself. Such an approach is referred to as *prescriptive*.

Identifying such a model of rationality has to obey the constraints of the formal language we are using and take into account what the procedures can and cannot do with the available information [BOUY 00]. See [BEL 88, BELTS 02, KEE 92, LAR 95, TVE 77b, VAND 02, VIN 92, WEB 90] for a discussion of such an approach. The fact that we do not impose a model of rationality but that we look for it within the problem situation allows us to be more pragmatic and not to force the client to accept a model of rationality imposed from outside. However, we have to recognize two hypotheses within such an approach. The first is that the client's problem is what has been presented to us and the second is that the client has a model of rationality (possibly a very personal one). The issue is to identify it.

The reality of decision aiding is that quite often the client does not have a very clear idea of the problem, at least not clear enough to allow the identification of a model of rationality. Are we sure these are all the possible diagnoses? Did we really consider all the possible treatments? Is it certain that the problem is to find a treatment for the client? What if at the end we discover that the best thing for the client is to take a long vacation (possibly together with the analyst)? In other terms, finding the solution of a well-formulated problem is always possible. The risk is to find a solution to a problem the client does not have. The problem is that nobody really knows what the problem is. In such situations we might adopt an approach referred to as *constructive*: we have to construct the problem and its solution at the same time.

Within such an approach we do not have to look just for the method that best adapts to the client's problem. Together with the client we have to establish a representation of the problem situation, formulate a formal problem with the consensus of the client and then establish an evaluation model which will help to formulate the final recommendation. There is a fundamental learning dimension in such a process. The models we are going to formulate are the result of a mutual learning process: the client learns to reason about their problem in an abstract and formal way (the point of view of the analyst) and the analyst learns to reason about the client's problem following the client's point of view. Nothing can be considered as given or fixed and everything has to be constructed. See [BELTS 02, BOUY 00, CHE 81, GEN 02, HAB 90, LAN 83a, LAN 83b, LAN 96, ROS 89, ROY 96, SCH 88, WAT 67] for more references to such an approach.

In Table 1.1 [DIA 04] the principal differences of the different approaches are presented.

Approach	Characteristics	Process to obtain the model
Normative	Exogenous rationality, ideal economic behavior	To postulate
Descriptive	Exogenous rationality, empirical behavior models	To observe
Prescriptive	Endogenous rationality, coherence with the decision situation	To unveil
Constructive	Learning process, coherence with the decision process	To reach a consensus

Table 1.1. *Differences between approaches*

Some remarks to conclude this section are as follows:

1) It is clear that the differences among the approaches do not concern the methods used to solve a decision problem. It is possible to use a constructive approach and a combinatorial optimization procedure if this fits the situation. On the other hand, imposing the use of a method (as flexible as possible) on the client corresponds to using a normative or a descriptive approach since the legitimation of this choice is external to the client.

2) There is no unique model of rationality and rational behavior. A client exhibiting cyclic preferences is not less rational than another client perfectly consistent with decision theory's axioms. Transitivity of preferences is necessary only if we interpret the sentence 'x is preferred to y' as 'I am ready to pay more for x than for y'. If we interpret the same sentence as 'there are more reasons in favor of x than in favor of y' [SCH 88, TSO 02b] then it is possible to understand that cyclic preferences (in this case) are due to the existence of a cyclic structure of arguments. This is exactly the case with Condorcet's paradox [CON 85].

3) The presence of inconsistency in the client's arguments is not necessarily a problem; it can be seen as a source of information for conducting the decision-aiding process.

4) Conducting a decision-aiding process is decision aiding itself. Asking the question: 'where do you want to go this evening?' implies that the set of alternatives is constrained to only external locations, the possibility of remaining at home not being considered. Asking 'do you prefer to hear classical music or jazz?' implies that the subject wants to hear music, silence not being considered. This type of implicit hypotheses enters the decision model just by the way in which the decision-aiding process is conducted and should be an important source of reflection in our profession.

In the following section, we focus on this last concept (the decision-aiding process) in order to see how its structuring allows decision theory to operate in practice.

1.4. The decision-aiding process

As already noted, Simon has suggested that a decision is not an act, but a process. Following such a suggestion, rationality cannot be conceived with respect to an objective (substantial rationality), but with respect to the process itself (procedural rationality). Rationality becomes a local coherence (with respect to a certain temporal instance of the process) and is therefore bounded [SIM 57, SIM 79]. In the following, a descriptive model of the decision process presented in [OST 93] is described.

It is assumed that the client is involved within one or more decision processes and that their demand for decision support refers to one of these decision processes. The activities associated with such a support are grouped under the name of *decision-aiding process*. The following elements are identified:

– at least two participants, the client and the analyst;

– at least two objects of the process: the client's concerns and the analyst's motivations;

– a set of resources including the client's knowledge of their concern's domain, the analyst's methodological knowledge and the time; and

– a converging object (a meta-object) consisting of a shared (among the participants) representation of the client's concerns (one or more artifacts [EAS 91, SIM 69]).

The decision-aiding process is considered as a distributed cognition process. Nevertheless, the author's point of view will be operational and not cognitive. The hypothesis that the participants actively try to create a shared representation is made. We attempt to analyze the artifacts which such a process generates (for an expanded discussion see [PAS 00, STA 03, TSO 07]):
– a representation of the problem situation;
– a problem formulation;
– an evaluation model; and
– a final recommendation.

1.4.1. *The problem situation*

A representation of the problem situation is the result of an effort aimed at replying to questions of the following type:
– Who has a problem?
– Why is this a problem?
– Who decides on this problem?
– What is the commitment of the client on this problem?
– Who is going to pay for the consequences of a decision?

The construction of such an artifact allows, on the one hand, the client to better understand their position within the decision process for which they asked for decision support and, on the other hand, the analyst to better understand their role within this decision process.

From a formal point of view, a representation of the problem situation is a triple:

$$\mathcal{P} = \langle \mathcal{A}, \mathcal{O}, \mathcal{S} \rangle$$

where $\mathcal{A}$ is the set of participants in the decision process; $\mathcal{O}$ is the set of stakes each participant brings within the decision process; and $\mathcal{S}$ is the set of resources the participants commit on their stakes and the other participants' stakes.

Such a representation is not fixed within the decision-aiding process, but will usually evolve. Actually, one reason that such a representation is constructed is to help to understand the misunderstandings during the client–analyst interaction.

1.4.2. *The problem formulation*

For a given representation of the problem situation, the analyst might propose to the client one or more problem formulations. This is a crucial point of the decision-aiding process. The representation of the problem situation has a descriptive or explicative scope. The construction of the problem formulation introduces what is reffered to as a model of rationality. A problem formulation reduces the reality of the decision process within which the client is involved to a formal and abstract problem. The result is that one or more of the client's concerns are transformed into formal problems on which we can apply a method (already existing, adapted from an existing one or created ad hoc) of the type studied in decision theory.

Example 1.1. Consider the case of a client having the problem of buying new buses in order to improve the service offered to the customers. Different problem formulations are possible:

– choose one among the potential suppliers;

– choose one among the offers received (a supplier may have made more than one); or

– choose combinations of offers.

The choice of one among the above formulations is not neutral. The first is focused on the suppliers rather than the offers and enables us to think about the will to establish a more strategic relationship with one of them. The second one is a more contingent formulation and introduces the implicit hypothesis that all buses will be bought from the same supplier. The third is also a contingent problem formulation, but also considers the possibility of buying from different suppliers. Obviously choosing one of the above formulations will strongly influence the outcome of the decision-aiding process and the final decision.

From a formal point of view, a problem formulation is a triple:

$$\Gamma = \langle \mathbb{A}, \mathbb{V}, \Pi \rangle$$

where $\mathbb{A}$ is the set of potential actions the client may undertake within the problem situation as represented in $\mathcal{P}$; $\mathbb{V}$ is the set of points of view under which the potential actions are expected to be observed, analyzed, evaluated and compared, including different scenarios for the future; Π is the problem statement, the type of application to perform on the set $\mathbb{A}$ and an anticipation of what the client expects [BAN 96, OST 90, ROY 93b]; for a detailed example see [STA 03].

Obtaining the client's consensus on a problem formulation can lend insight, since instead of having an ambiguous description of the problem we have an abstract and formal problem. Several decision-aiding approaches will stop here, considering that formulating (and understanding) a problem is equivalent to solving it; this limits decision aiding to helping to formulate problems, the solution being a personal issue of the client. Other approaches will instead consider the problem formulation as given. Within a constructive approach, the problem formulation is one among the products of the decision-aiding process. It is expected to be used in order to construct the evaluation model.

1.4.3. *The evaluation model*

By evaluation model, the traditional decision-aiding models conceived through any operations research, decision theory or AI method is meant. Classic decision-aiding textbooks focus their attention on the construction of this model. In a normative approach there is no freedom, the structure of the model being predefined. Within other approaches more degrees of freedom are possible, at least as far as some of the model's parameters are concerned.

An evaluation model is an n-tuple:

$$\mathcal{M} = \langle A, D, E, H, \mathcal{U}, \mathcal{R} \rangle$$

where A is a set of alternatives to which the model will apply; D is a set of dimensions (attributes) under which the elements of A are observed, measured, described, etc. (such a set can be structured, for instance through the definition of an hierarchy); E is a set of scales associated with each element of D; H is a set of criteria (if any) under which each element of A is evaluated in order to take into account the client's preferences (recall that a criterion is a preference model); $\mathcal{U}$ is a set of uncertainty measures associated with D and/or H; $\mathcal{R}$ is a set of operators enabling synthetic information about the elements of A or of $A \times A$ to be obtained, namely aggregation operators (acting on preferences, measures, uncertainties, etc.).

The reader can observe that a large part of the existing decision-aiding models and methods can be represented through the above description. Additionally, such a description allows us to focus our attention on a number of important remarks:

1) It is easy to understand why the differences among the decision-aiding approaches do not depend on the adopted decision-aiding method. The fact that we work with only one evaluation dimension or a single criterion can be the result of applying a constructive approach. We can conduct a decision-aiding process constructively and end by using a combinatorial optimization algorithm. What is important is to show that such tools are a consequence of the decision-aiding process and not to choose them before the problem has been formulated or the evaluation model constructed.

2) The technical choices (typology of the measurement scales, different preference, difference models or different aggregation operators) are not neutral.

24   Decision-making Process

Even when the client can formulate their problem clearly and is convinced about its formulation (possibly using one of the techniques aiding in formulating problems), the choice of a certain technique, procedure or operator can have important consequences that are not discussed at the moment of problem formulation (for a critical discussion see [BOUY 00]). Characterizing such techniques, procedures and operators is therefore crucial, since it allows a control of their applicability to the problem as has been formulated during the decision-aiding process.

3) The evaluation models are subject to validation processes, namely [LAN 83a]:
    - conceptual validation (verify the suitability of the concepts used);
    - logical validation (verify the logical consistency of the model);
    - experimental validation (verify the results using experimental data); and
    - operational validation (verify the implementation and use of the model in everyday life).

1.4.4. *The final recommendation*

The final recommendation represents the return to reality for the decision-aiding process. Usually the evaluation model will produce a result, say Φ. The final recommendation should translate such a result from the abstract and formal language in which Φ is formulated to the current language of the client and the decision process in which they are involved. Some elements are very important in constructing this artifact:

– the analyst has to be sure that the model is formally correct;

– the client has to be sure that the model represents them, that they understand it and that they should be able to use its conclusions (the client should feel they are the 'owner' of the results as well as be satisfied by them); and

– the recommendation should be 'legitimated' with respect to the decision process for which the decision aiding has been asked.

We should pay some attention to this last observation. The decision-aiding process is an activity that introduces a certain distance between the participants and the reality of the decision process and its organizational dimension. Returning to reality requires a check of whether the results are legitimated. We should check whether such results are accepted or not by the participants in the decision process and understand the reasons for their position (such reasons can be completely independent from the decision process itself). Being able to put into practice the final recommendation definitely depends on such legitimation: no legitimation, no implementation [CHU 67].

The presentation of the decision-aiding process through its artifacts is concluded with the following two remarks:

– Not all such artifacts are necessarily created in all decision-aiding processes. There might be cases where the evaluation model is not constructed, the client being satisfied by being enabled to correctly formulate the problem. A final recommendation might not always be formulated. This presentation tries to give an account of the possible outcomes of a decision-aiding process.

– The identification of artifacts within the decision-aiding process in the form of checklists is of course a simplification of the complexity of real decision-aiding situations. The scope of such a presentation is mainly conceived for training purposes, i.e. what a novice analyst should check when involved in a decision-aiding process. Experienced analysts may conduct a decision-aiding process in a more holistic way, but the analysis of such an approach goes beyond the scope of this chapter.

1.5. Conclusion

In this chapter a personal perspective on the evolution of decision theory has been outlined. The focus was mainly on the appearance and growth of several alternative approaches to the so-called classic decision theory. This was done in relation both to empirical validation and to the evolution of related scientific domains such as cognitive sciences, organization theory and artificial intelligence.

The first hypothesis developed in the chapter is that such alternative approaches are ultimately related to the classic decision theory. This is because they all share the fundamental idea that decision making and decision aiding are human activities that can be scientifically investigated. It is also possible to use an abstract and formal language in aiding decision makers to handle the issues arising within the decision processes. The plural 'decision theories' is more appropriate for emphasizing the existence of several different theoretical approaches and methods studying and implementing the above idea [WHI 75].

The second hypothesis developed is that decision aiding is a broader concept than the one of decision theory. This is true as the former includes not only the theoretical aspects of this activity, but also the practices and the behaviors that can be observed along the decision-aiding process. One of the characteristics of the decision theories' evolution is the appearance of approaches aiming to include large parts of the decision-aiding process in their field of investigation.

Decision aiding is practiced every day by individuals and organizations and, in a proportion of cases larger than the number of relevant scientific publications would suggest, decision theories are correctly used. It should be noted that the level of analysis of such decision-aiding practices is far less important if compared to the extremely fine theoretical achievements which the decision theories can show. Under such a perspective our scientific area, despite its maturity, is still lacking the establishment of 'best practices analysis', as is the case for similar professions such as lawyers, physicians and psychotherapists.

A third hypothesis developed concerns what decision theory and operations research owes to other scientific fields such as mathematics, cognitive science, organization theory, artificial intelligence and more general computer science. Several critical advances in our field have been possible thanks to the integration of findings obtained in such areas. At the same time, the focus of our research on concepts such as decision, preference, optimal and compromise solution provided invaluable contributions to these areas (and not only these, OR and decision theory are applied in fields such as molecular biology, archaeology, engineering, sociology and political science). The ultimate interdisciplinary nature of decision theory and decision aiding can be best observed through its practice.

Last, but not least, a personal classification of the decision-aiding approaches was presented. The differences between such approaches, on the basis of the origin of the model of rationality used in order to construct the artifacts of the decision-aiding process, were discussed. Under such a perspective a model of the decision-aiding process, sufficiently large to include most of the existing methods and techniques, was outlined. This chapter therefore contributes to the establishment of a decision-aiding methodology (from the Greek $\mu\epsilon\theta o\delta o\lambda o\gamma\iota\alpha$: $\lambda\acute{o}\gamma o\zeta\mu\epsilon\acute{o}\delta\omega\nu$, reasoning about methods).

1.6. Acknowledgements

This chapter was initiated while visiting DIMACS, Rutgers University, under a NSF CCR 00-87022 grant. It was finished while visiting the SMG, Université Libre de Bruxelles under a FNRS grant. Both supports are gratefully acknowledged. In order to compile the historical part of this essay I have used the 50 year history compiled by S. Gass for INFORMS [GAS 05] extensively. Ofer Melnik at DIMACS helped with the English. I am indebted to Ken Bowen, Luis Dias, Marc Pirlot and Bernard Roy for some very interesting discussions on earlier versions of this chapter. Three anonymous referees provided helpful comments.

This chapter was originally published in the *European Journal of Operational Research* [TSO 08] and appears here with permission from Elsevier.

1.7. Bibliography

[AAR 97] E. Aarts and J.K. Lenstra. *Local Search in Combinatorial Optimization*. John Wiley, New York, 1997.

[ACK 62] R.L. Ackoff. Some unsolved problems in problem solving. *Operational Research Quarterly*, 13:1–11, 1962.

[ACK 79a] R.L Ackoff. The future of operational research is past. *Journal of Operational Research Society*, 30:93–104, 1979.

[ACK 79b] R.L. Ackoff. Resurrecting the future of operational research. *Journal of the Operational Research Society*, 30:189–199, 1979.

[ADE 69] R.M. Adelson and J.M. Norman. Operational research and decision making. *Operational Research Quarterly*, 20:399–413, 1969.

[ALC 85] C. Alchourron, P. Gärdenfors, and D. Makinson. On the logic of theory change: Partial meet contraction and revision functions. *Journal of Symbolic Logic*, 50:510–530, 1985.

[ALL 53] M. Allais. Le comportement de l'homme rationnel devant le risque : Critique des postulats et axiomes de l'école américaine. *Econometrica*, 21:503–46, 1953.

[ALL 79] M. Allais and O. Hagen, editors. *Expected Utility Hypotheses and the Allais Paradox*. D. Reidel, Dordrecht, 1979.

[APT 99] Kr. Apt. The essence of constraint propagation. *Theoretical Computer Science*, 221:179–210, 1999.

[AQV 86] L. Aqvist. Deontic logic. In D. Gabbay and F. Guenther, editors, *Handbook of Philosophical Logic, vol II*, pages 605–714. D. Reidel, Dordrecht, 1986.

[ARI 90] Aristotle. *Ethica Nicomachea*. Oxford University Press, Oxford, 1990. Originally published in 350 BC, English edition by I. Bywater.

[ARR 51] K.J. Arrow. *Social Choice and Individual Values*. John Wiley, New York, 1951. 2nd edition, 1963.

[ASH 56] W.R. Ashby. *An Introduction to Cybernetics*. Chapman & Hall, London, 1956.

[BAN 96] C.A. Bana e Costa. Les problématiques de l'aide à la décision: vers l'enrichissement de la trilogie choix-tri-rangement. *RAIRO/ Recherche Opérationnelle*, 30(2):191–216, 1996.

[BAN 94] C.A. Bana e Costa and J.C. Vansnick. MACBETH: An interactive path towards the construction of cardinal value functions. *International Transactions in Operational Research*, 1(4):387–500, 1994.

[BAN 99] C.A. Bana e Costa, L. Ensslin, E.C. Correa, and J.-C. Vansnick. Decision support systems in action: Integrated application in a multicriteria decision aid process. *European Journal of Operational Research*, 113:315–335, 1999.

[BAN 01] C.A. Bana e Costa, F.N. da Silva, and J.-C. Vansnick. Conflict dissolution in the public sector: A case-study. *European Journal of Operational Research*, 130:388–401, 2001.

[BANV 98] C. Banville, M. Landry, J.-M. Martel, and C. Boulaire. A stakeholder approach to MCDA. *Systems Research and Behavioral Science*, 15:15–32, 1998.

[BAR 98] P. Barth and A. Bockmayr. Modelling discrete optimization problems in constraint logic programming. *Annals of Operations Research*, 81:467–495, 1998.

[BART 92] J.-P. Barthélemy and E. Mullet. A model of selection by aspects. *Acta Psychologica*, 79:1–19, 1992.

[BART 02] J.-P. Barthélemy, R. Bisdorff, and G. Coppin. Human centered processes and decision support systems. *European Journal of Operational Research*, 136:233–252, 2002.

[BAT 72] G. Bateson. *Steps to an Ecology of Mind*. Chandler Publ. Group, S. Francisco, 1972.

[BEE 59] S. Beer. What has cybernetics to do with operational research? *Operational Research Quarterly*, 10:1–21, 1959.

[BEE 66] S. Beer. *Decision and Control; The Meaning of Operational Research and Management Cybernetics*. John Wiley, New York, 1966.

[BEL 88] D. Bell, H. Raiffa, and A. Tversky, editors. *Decision Making: Descriptive, Normative, and Prescriptive Interactions*. Cambridge University Press, Cambridge, 1988.

[BELT 97] V. Belton, F. Ackermann, and I. Shepherd. Integrated support from problem structuring through alternative evaluation using COPE and V-I-S-A. *Journal of Multi-Criteria Decision Analysis*, 6:115–130, 1997.

[BELTS 02] V. Belton and T. Stewart. *Muliple Criteria Decision Analysis: An Integrated Approach*. Kluwer Academic, Dordrecht, 2002.

[BEN 66] R. Benayoun, B. Roy, and B. Sussman. ELECTRE: une méthode pour guider le choix en présence des points de vue multiples. Technical report, SEMA-METRA International, Direction Scientifique, 1966. Note de travail 49.

[BEN 71] R. Benayoun, J. de Montgolfier, J. Tergny, and O.I. Larichev. Linear programming with multiple objective functions: Step method (STEM). *Mathematical Programming*, 1(3):366–375, 1971.

[BER 58] C. Berge. *Théorie des graphes et ses applications*. Collection Univesitaire des Mathématiques, Dunod, Paris, 1958.

[BERN 38] D. Bernoulli. Specimen theoriae novae de mensura sortis, Commentarii Academiae Scientiarum Imperialis Petropolitanae (5, 175–192, 1738). *Econometrica*, 22:23–36, 1954. Translated by L. Sommer.

[BIS 00] R. Bisdorff. Logical foundation of fuzzy preferential systems with application to the ELECTRE decision aid methods. *Computers & Operations Research*, 27(7–8):673–687, June 2000.

[BLA 50] P.M.S. Blackett. Operational research. *Operational Research Quarterly*, 1:3–6, 1950. Now Journal of the Operational Research Society.

[BLE 01] H. Bleichrodt, J.L. Pinto, and P.P. Wakker. Making descriptive use of prospect theory to improve the prescriptive use of expected utility. *Management Science*, 47:1498–1514, 2001.

[BOC 98] A. Bockmayr and T. Kasper. Branch and infer: a unifying framework for integer and finite domain constraint programming. *Informs Journal on Computing*, 10:287–300, 1998.

[BON 96] B. Bonet and H. Geffner. Arguing for decisions: A qualitative model of decision making. In *Uncertainty in Artificial Intelligence: Proceedings of the 12th Conference (UAI-1996)*, pages 98–105. Morgan Kaufmann, San Francisco, 1996.

[BOR 81] J.C. Borda. Mémoire sur les élections au scrutin. *Comptes rendus de l'Académie des sciences, translated by Alfred de Grazia as Mathematical Derivation of a Election System, Isis, vol 44, pp 42–51*, 1781.

[BOU 94] C. Boutilier. Toward a logic for qualitative decision theory. In *Proceedings of the 4th International Conference on Knowledge Representation and Reasoning, KR'94*, pages 75–86. Morgan Kaufmann, San Francisco, 1994.

[BOU 00] C. Boutilier. Decision making under uncertainty: operations research meets AI (again). In *Proceedings of the 17th National Conference on Artificial Intelligence, AAAI-2000*, pages 1145–1150. AAAI Press, Menlo Park, 2000.

[BOU 99a] C. Boutilier. Knowledge representation for stochastic decision processes. In M.J Wooldridge and M. Veloso, editors, *Artificial Intelligence Today. Recent Trends and Developments*, pages 111–152. Springer Verlag, Berlin, 1999.

[BOU 99b] C. Boutilier, T. Dean, and S. Hanks. Decision-theoretic planning: Structural assumptions and computational leverage. *Journal of Artificial Intelligence Research*, 11:1–94, 1999.

[BOUY 92] D. Bouyssou. Democracy and efficiency - a note on 'arrow's theorem is not a surprising result'. *European Journal of Operational Research*, 58:427–430, 1992.

[BOUY 03] D. Bouyssou. La crise de la recherche opérationnelle: 25 ans après. *Mathématiques et Sciences Humaines*, 161:7–27, 2003.

[BOUY 02] D. Bouyssou and M. Pirlot. Non transitive decomposable conjoint measurement. *Journal of Mathematical Psychology*, 46:677–703, 2002.

[BOUY 04a] D. Bouyssou and M. Pirlot. 'Additive difference' models without additivity and subtractivity. *Journal of Mathematical Psychology*, 48(3):263–291, 2004.

[BOUY 04b] D. Bouyssou and M. Pirlot. Preferences for multiattributed alternatives: Traces, dominance, and numerical representations. *Journal of Mathematical Psychology*, 48(3):167–185, 2004.

[BOUY 05a] D. Bouyssou and M. Pirlot. A characterization of concordance relations. *European Journal of Operational Research*, 167:427–443, 2005.

[BOUY 05b] D. Bouyssou and M. Pirlot. Following the traces: An introduction to conjoint measurement without transitivity and additivity. *European Journal of Operational Research*, 163:287–337, 2005.

[BOUY 93] D. Bouyssou, P. Perny, M. Pirlot, A. Tsoukiàs, and Ph. Vincke. A manifesto for the new MCDM era. *Journal of Multi-Criteria Decision Analysis*, 2:125–127, 1993.

[BOUY 00] D. Bouyssou, T. Marchant, M. Pirlot, P. Perny, A. Tsoukiàs, and Ph. Vincke. *Evaluation and Decision Models: A Critical Perspective*. Kluwer Academic, Dordrecht, 2000.

[BOUY 06] Denis Bouyssou, Thierry Marchant, Marc Pirlot, Alexis Tsoukiàs, and Philippe Vincke. *Evaluation and Decision Models with Multiple Criteria: Stepping Stones for the Analyst*. International Series in Operations Research and Management Science, Volume 86. Springer, Boston, 1st edition, 2006.

[BOW 04] K. Bowen. Sixty years of operational research. *European Journal of Operational Research*, 153:618–623, 2004.

[BRA 96] R.I. Brafman and M. Tennenholtz. On the foundations of qualitative decision theory. In *Proceedings of the 13th National Conference on Artificial Intelligence, AAAI96*, pages 1291–1296. MIT Press, Cambridge, 1996.

[BRA 97] R.I. Brafman and M. Tennenholtz. Modeling agents as qualitative decision makers. *Artificial Intelligence*, 94:217–268, 1997.

[BRA 00] R.I. Brafman and M. Tennenholtz. An axiomatic treatment of three qualitative decision criteria. *Journal of the ACM*, 47:452–482, 2000.

[BRA 01] R.I. Brafman and N. Friedman. On decision-theoretic foundations for defaults. *Artificial Intelligence*, 133:1–33, 2001.

[BRAI 99] S.C. Brailsford, C.N. Potts, and B.M. Smith. Constraint satisfaction problems: algorithms and applications. *European Journal of Operational Research*, 119:557–581, 1999.

[CAP 98] A. Caprara, P. Toth, D. Vigo, and M. Fischetti. Modeling and solving the crew rostering problem. *Operations Research*, 46:820–830, 1998.

[CHA 55] A. Charnes, W.W. Cooper, and R. Ferguson. Optimal estimation of executive compensation by linear programming. *Management Science*, 1:138–151, 1955.

[CHA 61] A. Charnes and W.W. Cooper. *Management Models and Industrial Applications of Linear Programming*. John Wiley, New York, 1961.

[CHAT 99] A. Chateauneuf and P.P. Wakker. An axiomatization of cumulative prospect theory for decision under risk. *Journal of Risk and Uncertainty*, 18:137–145, 1999.

[CHE 81] P. Checkland. *Systems Thinking, Systems Practice*. John Wiley, New York, 1981.

[CHE 90] P. Checkland and J. Scholes. *Soft Systems Methodology in Action*. John Wiley, New York, 1990.

[CHI 66a] R.M. Chisholm and E. Sosa. On the logic of intrinsically better. *American Philosophical Quarterly*, 3:244–249, 1966.

[CHI 66b] R.M. Chisholm and E. Sosa. Intrinsic preferability and the problem of supererogation. *Synthese*, 16:321–331, 1966.

[CHU 67] C.W. Churchman. Wicked problems. *Management Science*, 14:B141–B142, 1967.

[CHU 57] C.W. Churchman, R.L. Ackoff and E.L. Arnoff. *Introduction to Operations Research*. John Wiley, New-York, 1957.

[COC 73] J.L. Cochrane and M. Zeleny. *Multiple Criteria Decision Making*. University of South Carolina Press, Columbia, 1973.

[COH 80] M. Cohen and J.-Y Jaffray. Rational behavior under complete ignorance. *Econometrica*, 48:1281–1299, 1980.

[COH 72] M.D. Cohen, J.G. March, and J.P. Olson. A garbage can model of organizational choice. *Administrative Science Quarterly*, 17:1–25, 1972.

[CON 85] Marquis de Condorcet. *Essai sur l'application de l'analyse à la probabilité des décisions rendues à la pluralité des voix*. Imprimerie Royale, Paris, 1785.

[CONW 67] R.W. Conway, W.L. Maxwell, and L.W. Miller. *Production Scheduling*. Addison Wesley, Reading, 1967.

[COO 58] C.H. Coombs. On the use of inconsistency in preferences in psychological measurement. *Journal of Experimental Psychology*, 55:1–7, 1958.

[CRO 69] J.D. Croston and G. Gregory. A critique of operational research and decision making by Adelson and Norman. *Operational Research Quarterly*, 20:215–220, 1969.

[CYE 63] R.M. Cyert and J.G. March. *A Behavioral Theory of the Firm*. Prentice Hall, Englewood Cliffs, 1963.

[DAL 94] H.G. Daellenbach. *Systems and Decision Making. A Management Science Approach*. John Wiley, New York, 1994.

[DAN 48] G.B. Dantzig. *Programming in a Linear Structure*. USAF, Washington D.C., 1948.

[DAN 51] G.B. Dantzig. Application of the simplex method to a transportation problem. In T.C. Koopmans, editor, *Activity Analysis of Production and Allocation*, pages 359–373. John Wiley, New York, 1951.

[DAN 63] G.B. Dantzig. *Linear Programming and Extensions*. Princeton University Press, Princeton, 1963.

[DEF 36] B. de Finetti. La logique de la probabilité. In *Actes du Congres International de Philosophie Scientifique a Paris 1935, Tome IV*, pages 1–9. Hermann et Cie, Paris, 1936.

[DEF 37] B. de Finetti. La prévision: Ses lois logiques, ses sources subjectives. In *Annales de l'Institut Henri Poincaré 7*, pages 1–68. Paris, 1937. Translated into English by Henry E. Kyburg Jr., Foresight: Its Logical Laws, its Subjective Sources. In Henry E. Kyburg Jr. and Howard E. Smokler (1964, Eds.), Studies in Subjective Probability, 53-118, Wiley, New York.

[DIA 04] L.C. Dias and A. Tsoukiàs. On the constructive and other approaches in decision aiding. In C.A Hengeller Antunes, J. Figueira, and J. Clímaco, editors, *Proceedings of the 56th Meeting of the EURO MCDA Working Group*, pages 13–28. CCDRC, Coimbra, 2004.

[DOI 86] J.P Doignon, B. Monjardet, M. Roubens, and Ph. Vincke. Biorder families, valued relations and preference modelling. *Journal of Mathematical Psychology*, 30:435–480, 1986.

[DOY 85] J. Doyle. Reasoned assumptions and pareto optimality. In *Proceedings of the 9th International Joint Conference on Artificial Intellignce, IJCAI85*, pages 87–90. Morgan Kaufmann, San Francisco, 1985.

[DOY 89] J. Doyle. Constructive belief and rational representation. *Computational Intelligence*, 5:1–11, 1989.

[DOY 90] J. Doyle. Rationality and its roles in reasoning. In *Proceedings of the 8th National Conference on Artificial Intelligence (AAAI'90)*, pages 1093–1100. MIT Press, Cambridge, 1990.

[DOY 94] J. Doyle. Reasoned assumptions and rational psychology. *Fundamenta Informaticae*, 20:35–73, 1994.

[DOY 91] J. Doyle and M.P. Wellman. Impediments to universal preference-based default theories. *Artificial Intelligence*, 49:97–128, 1991.

[DOY 94] J. Doyle and M.P. Wellman. Representing preferences as ceteris paribus comparatives. In *Decision-Theoretic Planning: Papers from the 1994 Spring AAAI Symposium*, pages 69–75. AAAI Press, Menlo Park, California, 1994.

[DOY 99] J. Doyle and R.H Thomason. Background to qualitative decision theory. *AI Magazine*, 20:55–68, 1999.

[DOY 91] J. Doyle, Y. Shoham, and M.P. Wellman. A logic of relative desire. In *Methodologies for Intelligent Systems, 6th International Symposium, ISMIS 91*, pages 16–31. Springer-Verlag, Berlin, 1991.

[DUB 88] D. Dubois and H. Prade. *Possibility Theory*. Plenum Press, New York, 1988.

[DUB 95] D. Dubois and H. Prade. Possibility theory as a basis for qualitative decision theory. In *Proceedings of the 14th International Joint Conference on Artificial Intelligence, IJCAI95*, pages 1924–1930. Morgan Kaufmann, San Francisco, 1995.

[DUB 96] D. Dubois, H. Fargier, and H. Prade. Possibility theory in constraint satisfaction problems: handling priority, preference and uncertainty. *Applied Intelligence*, 6:287–309, 1996.

[DUB 02] D. Dubois, H. Fargier, P. Perny, and H. Prade. Qualitative decision theory: from Savage's axioms to non-monotonic reasoning. *Journal of the ACM*, 49:455–495, 2002.

[DUS 41] B. Dushnik and E.W. Miller. Partially ordered sets. *American Journal of Mathematics*, 63:600–610, 1941.

[EAS 91] S. Easterbrook. Handling conflict between domain descriptions with computer-supported negotiation. *Knowledge Acquisition*, 3:255–289, 1991.

[EDE 88] C. Eden. Cognitive mapping. *European Journal of Operational Research*, 36:1–13, 1988.

[EDE 83] C. Eden, S. Jones, and D. Sims. *Messing About in Problems*. Pergamon Press, Oxford, 1983.

[EDW 54] W. Edwards. The theory of decision making. *Psychological Bulletin*, 41:380–417, 1954.

[EHR 02] M. Ehrgott and X. Gandibleux. *Multiple Criteria Optimization. State of the art annotated bibliographic surveys*. Kluwer Academic, Dordrecht, 2002.

[EME 62] R. Emerson. Power dependence relations. *American Sociological Review*, 27:31–41, 1962.

[EMER 59] F. Emery. Characteristics of socio-technical systems. Technical report, Tavistock Institute, Document 527, London, 1959.

[EUL 36] L. Euler. Solutio problematis ad geometriam situs pertinentis. *Opera Omnia*, 7:128–140, 1736.

[FAR 05] H. Fargier and R. Sabadin. Qualitative decision under uncertainty: back to expected utility. *Artificial Intelligence*, 164:245–280, 2005.

[FAU 68] R. Faure. *Éléments de la recherche opérationnelle*. Gauthier-Villars, Paris, 1968.

[FAY 49] H. Fayol. *General and Industrial Management*. Pitman and Sons, New York, 1949. First edition in 1916.

[FES 64] L. Festinger. *Conflict, Decision and Dissonance*. Stanford University Press, Stanford, 1964.

[FIG 05] J. Figueira, S. Greco, and M. Ehrgott. *Multiple Criteria Decision Analysis: State of the Art Surveys*. Springer Verlag, Boston, Dordrecht, London, 2005.

[FIK 71] R. Fikes and N. Nilsson. Strips: A new approach to the application of theorem proving to problem solving. *Artificial Intelligence*, 2:189–208, 1971.

[FIS 70] P.C. Fishburn. *Utility Theory for Decision Making*. Wiley, New York, 1970.

[FIS 82] P.C. Fishburn. Nontransitive measurable utility. *Journal of Mathematical Psychology*, 26:31–67, 1982.

[FIS 85] P.C. Fishburn. *Interval Orders and Interval Graphs*. John Wiley, New York, 1985.

[FLO 56] M.M. Flood. The travelling-salesman problem. *Operations Research*, 6:61–75, 1956.

[FOD 94] J. Fodor and M. Roubens. *Fuzzy Preference Modelling and Multicriteria Decision Support*. Kluwer Academic Publishers, 1994.

[FOR 62] L.R. Ford and D.R. Fulkerson. *Flows in Networks*. Princeton University Press, Princeton, 1962.

[FORT 02] Ph.. Fortemps and R. Słowiński. A graded quadrivalent logic for ordinal preference modelling: Loyola-like approach. *Fuzzy Optimization and Decision Making*, 1:93–111, 2002.

[FRE 88] S. French. *Decision Theory - An Introduction to the Mathematics of Rationality*. Ellis Horwood, Chichester, 1988.

[FRI 69] J.K. Friend and W.N. Jessop. *Local Government and Strategic Choice*. Tavistock Publications, London, 1969.

[FRI 87] J.K. Friend and A. Hickling. *Planning under Pressure: The Strategic Choice Approach*. Pergamon Press, New York, 1987.

[GAR 97] L.R. Gardiner and D. Vanderpooten. Interactive multiple criteria procedures: Some reflections. In J.N. Clíimaco, editor, *Multicriteria Analysis*, pages 290–301. Springer Verlag, Berlin, 1997.

[GARE 79] M. Garey and D. Johnson. *Computers and Intractability*. Freeman and Co., New York, 1979.

[GÄR 88] P. Gärdenfors. *Knowledge in Flux*. MIT Press, Cambridge, 1988.

[GÄR 94] P. Gärdenfors and D. Makinson. Nonmonotonic inference based on expectations. *Artificial Intelligence*, 65:197–245, 1994.

[GAS 58] S.I Gass. *Linear Programming: Methods and Applications*. McGraw-Hill, New York, 1958.

[GAS 05] S.I. Gass and A.A. Assad. *An Annotated Timeline of Operations Research: An Informal History*. Springer Verlag, Berlin, 2005.

[GEN 02] J.-L. Genard and M. Pirlot. Multiple criteria decision aid in a philosophical perspective. In D. Boyssou, E. Jacquet-Lagrèze, P. Perny, R. Słowiński, D. Vanderpooten, and Ph. Vincke, editors, *Aiding Decisions with Multiple Criteria: Essays in Honour of Bernard Roy*, pages 89–117. Kluwer Academic, Dordrecht, 2002.

[GEO 68] A.M. Geoffrion. Proper efficiency and the theory of vector optimization. *Journal of Mathematical Analysis and Application*, 22:618–630, 1968.

[GEO 73] A.M. Geoffrion, J.S. Dyer, and A. Feinberg. An interactive approach for multicriteria optimization with an application to the operation of an accademic department. *Management Science*, 19:357–369, 1973.

[GIG 99] G. Gigerenzer and P.M. Todd. *Simple Heuristics That Make Us Smart*. Oxford University Press, New York, 1999.

[GIL 89] I. Gilboa and D. Schmeidler. Maxmin expected utility with a non-unique prior. *Journal of Mathematical Economics*, 18:141–153, 1989.

[GIL 93] I. Gilboa and D. Schmeidler. Updating ambigous beliefs. *Journal of Economic Theory*, 59:33–49, 1993.

[GIL 01] I. Gilboa and D. Schmeidler. A cognitive model of individual well-being. *Social Choice and Welfare*, 12:269–288, 2001.

[GIL 02a] I. Gilboa and D. Schmeidler. A cognitive foundation of probability. *Mathematics of Operations Research*, 27:68–81, 2002.

[GIL 02b] I. Gilboa, D. Schmeidler and P.P. Wakker. Utility in case-based decision theory. *Journal of Economic Theory*, 105:483–502, 2002.

[GLO 86] F. Glover. Future paths for integer programming and links to artificial intelligence. *Computers and Operations Research*, 13:533–549, 1986.

[GLO 97] F. Glover and M. Laguna. *Tabu Search*. Kluwer Academic, Dordrecht, 1997.

[GOF 68] E. Goffman. *Asylums; Essays on the Social Situation of Mental Patients and Other Inmates*. Alding Publishing Co., Chicago, 1968.

[GOL 89] D.E. Goldberg. *Genetic Algorithms in Search, Optimization and Machine Learning*. Addison Wesley, Reading, 1989.

[GOO 98] P. Goodwin and G. Wright. *Decision Analysis for Management Judgment*. John Wiley, New York, 1998. Second Edition.

[GRA 95] M. Grabisch, H.T Nguyen, and E.A Walker. *Fundamentals of Uncertainty Calculi, with Applications to Fuzzy Inference*. Kluwer Academic, Dordrecht, 1995.

[GRA 00] M. Grabisch, T. Murofushi, M. Sugeno, and J. Kacprzyk. *Fuzzy Measures and Integrals. Theory and Applications*. Physica Verlag, Berlin, 2000.

[GRE 99] S. Greco, B. Matarazzo, and R. Słowiński. The use of rough sets and fuzzy sets in MCDM. In T. Gal, T. Stewart, and T. Hanne, editors, *Advances in MCDM Models, Algorithms, Theory, and Applications*, pages 14.1–14.59. Kluwer Academic, Dordrecht, 1999.

[GRE 01] S. Greco, B. Matarazzo, and R. Słowiński. Rough sets theory for multicriteria decision analysis. *European Journal of Operational Research*, 129:1–47, 2001.

[GRE 04] S. Greco, B. Matarazzo, and R. Słowiński. Axiomatic characterization of a general utility function and its particular cases in terms of conjoint measurement and rough-set decision rules. *European Journal of Operational Research*, 158:271–292, 2004.

[HAB 90] J. Habermas. *Logic of the Social Sciences*. MIT Press, Boston, 1990.

[HAL 57] S. Halldén. *On the Logic of Better*. Library of Theoria, Lund, 1957.

[HAN 66a] B. Hansson. Foundamental axioms for preference relations. *Synthese*, 18:423–442, 1966.

[HAN 66b] B. Hansson. Choice structures and preference relations. *Synthese*, 18:443–458, 1966.

[HAR 68] P.E. Hart, N.J. Nilsson, and B. Raphael. A formal basis for the heuristic determination of minimum cost paths. *IEEE Transactions on Systems Science and Cybernetics*, 4:100–107, 1968.

[HART 65] J. Hartmanis and R.E Stearns. On the computational complexity of algorithms. *Transactions of the American Mathematical Society*, 117:285–305, 1965.

[HAT 92] A. Hatchuel and B. Weil. *L'expert et le système*. Economica, Paris, 1992.

[HIL 67] F.S. Hillier and G.J. Lieberman. *Introduction to Operations Research*. Holden Day, Oakland, 1967.

[HILP 71] R. Hilpinen. *Deontic Logic: Introductory and Systematic Readings*. Reidel, Dordrecht, 1971.

[HUB 74] O. Huber. An axiomatic system for multidimensional preferences. *Theory and Decision*, 5:161–184, 1974.

[HUM 83] P.C. Humphreys, O. Svenson, and A. Vári. *Analysis and Aiding Decision Processes*. North-Holland, Amsterdam, 1983.

[JAC 82] E. Jacquet-Lagrèze and Y. Siskos. Assessing a set of additive utility functions for multicriteria decision making: the UTA method. *European Journal of Operational Research*, 10:151–164, 1982.

[JAF 88] J.Y. Jaffray. Choice under risk and the security factor: an axiomatic model. *Theory and Decision*, 24:169–200, 1988.

[JAF 89] J.Y. Jaffray. Utility theory for belief functions. *Operations Research Letters*, 8:107–112, 1989.

[JAF 93] J.-Y. Jaffray and P.P. Wakker. Decision making with belief functions: compatibility and incompatibility with the sure-thing principle. *Journal of Risk and Uncertainty*, 7:255–271, 1993.

[JAU 88] B. Jaumard, S.O. Peng, and B. Simeone. A selected artificial intelligence bibliography for operations researchers. *Annals of Operations Research*, 12:1–50, 1988.

[JEF 65] R.C. Jeffrey. *The Logic of Decision*. McGraw-Hill, New York, 1965.

[JPV 98] P. Journée, P. Perny, and D. Vanderpooten. A multicriteria methodology for the verification of arms control agreements in Europe. *Foundations of Computing and Decision Sciences*, 23(2):64–85, 1998.

[KAC 88] J. Kacprzyk and M. Roubens. *Non-conventional Preference Relations in Decision Making*. Springer Verlag, LNMES n. 301, Berlin, 1988.

[KAH 03] D. Kahneman. A perspective on judgment and choice: mapping bounded rationality. *American Psychologist*, 58:697–720, 2003.

[KAH 79] D. Kahneman and A. Tversky. Prospect theory: an analysis of decision under risk. *Econometrica*, 47:263–291, 1979.

[KAH 02] D. Kahneman and S. Frederick. Representativeness revisited: attribute substitution in intuitive judgment. In T. Gilovich, D. Griffin, and D. Kahneman, editors, *Heuristics and Biases: The Psychology of Intuitive Judgment*, pages 49–81. Cambridge University Press, Cambridge, 2002.

[KAH 81] D. Kahneman, P. Slovic, and A. Tversky. *Judgement Under Uncertainty - Heuristics and Biases*. Cambridge University Press, Cambridge, 1981.

[KAN 39] L.V. Kantorovich. *Mathematical Methods in the Organization and Planning of Production*. Publication House of the Leningrad State University, Leningrad, 1939. Translated into English in: Management Science, vol. 6, 1960, 366–422.

[KAR 75] R.H. Karp. On the complexity of combinatorial problems. *Networks*, 5:44–68, 1975.

[KAS 03] J.X. Kasperson, R.E. Kasperson, N. Pidgeon, and P. Slovic. The social amplification of risk: Assessing fifteen years of research and theory. In N. Pidgeon, R.E. Kasperson, and P. Slovic, editors, *The Social Amplification of Risk*, pages 13–46. Cambridge University Press, Cambridge, 2003.

[KEE 92] R.L. Keeney. *Value-Focused Thinking. A Path to Creative Decision Making*. Harvard University Press, Cambridge, 1992.

[KEE 76] R.L. Keeney and H. Raiffa. *Decisions with Multiple Objectives: Preferences and Value Tradeoffs*. John Wiley, New York, 1976.

[KEE 99] R.L. Keeney, J.S. Hammond, and H. Raiffa. *Smart Choices: A Guide to Making Better Decisions*. Harvard University Press, Boston, 1999.

[KEL 78] J.S. Kelly. *Arrow Impossibility Theorems*. Academic Press, New York, 1978.

[KEL 91] J.S. Kelly. Social choice bibliography. *Social Choice and Welfare*, 8:97–169, 1991.

[KEN 83] Hua-Lo Keng. *Selected Papers*. Springer Verlag, Berlin, 1983. edited by H. Halberstam.

[KIR 02] M.W. Kirby. *A History of Operational Research in Britain*. World Scientific, London, 2002.

[KIR 06] M.W. Kirby. A festering sore: the issue of professionalism in the history of the operational research society. *Journal of the Operational Research Society*, 57:161 – 172, 2006.

[KIT 93] J. Kitainik. *Fuzzy Decision Procedures with Binary Relations*. Kluwer Academic, Dordrecht, 1993.

[KOL 33] A.N. Kolmogorov. *Grundbegriffe der Warscheinlichkeitsrechnung*. Springer, Berlin, 1933. Translated into English by Nathan Morrison (1950), Foundations of the Theory of Probability, Chelsea, New York. Second English edition 1956.

[KOO 56] B.O. Koopman. Fallacies in operations research. *Operations Research*, 3:422–426, 1956.

[KRA 71] D.H. Krantz, R.D. Luce, P. Suppes, and A. Tversky. *Foundations of Measurement*, volume 1: Additive and polynomial representations. Academic Press, New York, 1971.

[KRAU 90] S. Kraus, D. Lehmann, and M. Magidor. Non-monotonic reasoning, preferential models and cumulative logics. *Artificial Intelligence*, 44:167–207, 1990.

[KWA 62] Mei-Ko Kwan. Graphic programming using odd or even points. *Chinese Mathematics*, 1:273–277, 1962.

[LAN 83a] M. Landry, J.L. Malouin, and M. Oral. Model validation in operations research. *European Journal of Operational Research*, 14:207–220, 1983.

[LAN 83b] M. Landry, D. Pascot, and D. Briolat. Can DSS evolve without changing our view of the concept of problem? *Decision Support Systems*, 1:25–36, 1983.

[LAN 87] M. Landry. Les rapports entre la complexité et la dimension cognitive de la formulation des problèmes. In *L'aide à la décision dans l'organisation, AFCET, Paris*, pages 3–31, 1987.

[LAN 95] M. Landry. A note on the concept of problem. *Organization Studies*, 16:315–343, 1995.

[LAN 96] M. Landry, C. Banville, and M. Oral. Model legitimisation in operational research. *European Journal of Operational Research*, 92:443–457, 1996.

[LAR 95] O.I. Larichev and H.M. Moskovich. Unstructured problems and developmennt of prescriptive decision making methods. In P. Pardalos, Y. Siskos, and C. Zopounidis, editors, *Advances in Multicriteria Analysis*, pages 47–80. Kluwer Academic, Dordrecht, 1995.

[LAW 85] E. Lawler and A. Rinnooy Kan. *The Traveling Salesman Problem: A Guided Tour of Combinatorial Optimization*. John Wiley, New York, 1985.

[LEH 96] D. Lehmann. Generalized qualitative probability: Savage revisited. In *Proceedings of the 12th Conference on Uncertainty in Artificial Intelligence, UAI96*, pages 381–388. Morgan Kaufmann, San Francisco, 1996.

[LEH 01a] D. Lehmann. Nonmonotonic logics and semantics. *Journal of Logic and Computation*, 11:229–256, 2001.

[LEH 01b] D. Lehmann. Expected qualitative utility maximization. *Games and Economic Behavior*, 35:54–79, 2001.

[LEM 77] J.-L. Le Moigne. *La Théorie du système général: Théorie de la modélisation*. Presses Universitaires de France, Paris, 1977.

[LEN 91] J.K Lenstra, A.H.G Rinnooy Kan, and A. Schrijver, editors. *History of Mathematical Programming: A Collection of Personal Reminiscences*. North-Holland, Amsterdam, 1991.

[LIC 69] W. Lichtenstein, P. Slovic, and D. Zink. Effect of instruction in expected value on optimality of gambling decisions. *Journal of Experimental Psychology*, 79:236–240, 1969.

[LIC 71] W. Lichtenstein and P. Slovic. Reversals of preferences between bids and choices gambling decisions. *Journal of Experimental Psychology*, 89:46–55, 1971.

[LIT 63] J.D.C. Little, K.G. Murty, D.W. Sweeney, and C. Karel. An algorithm for the travelling salesman problem. *Operations Research*, 11:972–989, 1963.

[LUC 56] R.D. Luce. Semiorders and a theory of utility discrimination. *Econometrica*, 24:178–191, 1956.

[LUC 57] R.D. Luce and H. Raiffa. *Games and Decisions*. John Wiley, New York, 1957.

[LUC 94] R.D. Luce and D. von Winterfeldt. What common ground exists for descriptive, prescriptive, and normative utility theories? *Management Science*, 40:263–279, 1994.

[LUC 96] R.D. Luce. The ongiong dialog between empirical science and measurement theory. *Journal of Mathematical Psychology*, 40:78–98, 1996.

[MAC 82] M.J Machina. Expected utility without the independence axiom. *Econometrica*, 50:277–323, 1982.

[MAC 92] M.J Machina and D. Schmeidler. A more robust definition of subjective probability. *Econometrica*, 60:745–780, 1992.

[MAC 95] M.J Machina and D. Schmeidler. Bayes without Bernoulli: Simple conditions for probabilistically sophisticated choice. *Journal of Economic Theory*, 67:106–128, 1995.

[MAR 58] J.G. March and H.A. Simon. *Organizations*. John Wiley, New York, 1958.

[MAY 54] K. O. May. Intransitivity, utility and the aggregation of preference patterns. *Econometrica*, 22:1–13, 1954.

[MCC 69] J. McCarthy and P.J. Hayes. Some philosophical problems from the standpoint of artificial intelligence. In D. Michie, editor, *Machine Intelligence, vol. 4*, pages 463–502. Edinburgh University Press, Edinburgh, 1969.

[MEL 78] J. Mélèse. *Approche systèmique des organisations*. Ed. Hommes et Techniques, Paris, 1978.

[MIN 75] M. Minsky. A framework for representing knowledge. In P.M. Winston, editor, *The Psychology of Computer Vision*, pages 211–277. McGraw-Hill, New York, 1975.

[MINT 83] H. Mintzberg. *Power In and Around Organizations*. Prentice Hall, Englewood Cliffs, 1983.

[MINT 76] H. Mintzberg, D. Raisinghani, and A. Théoret. The structure of unstructured decision processes. *Administrative Science Quarterly*, 21:246–272, 1976.

[MON 00] Ph. Mongin. Does optimization implies rationality? *Synthese*, 124:73–111, 2000.

[MONT 76] H. Montgomery and O. Svenson. On decision rules and information processing strategies for choices among multiattribute alternatives. *Scandinavian Journal of Psychology*, 17:283–291, 1976.

[MONT 83] H. Montgomery. Decision rules and the search for a dominance structure: towards a process models of decision making. In P.C. Humphreys, O. Svenson, and A. Vári, editors, *Analysing and Aiding Decision Processes*, pages 343–369. North-Holland, Amsterdam, 1983.

[MOR 42] G. Morton and A.H. Land. A contribution to the travelling-salesman problem. *Journal of the Royal Statistical Society, Series B*, 17:185–194, 1942.

[MOS 84] J. Moscarola. Organizational decision processes and ORASA intervention. In R. Tomlinson and I. Kiss, editors, *Rethinking the Process of Operational Research and Systems Analysis*, pages 169–186. Pergamon Press, Oxford, 1984.

[MUL 79] J.D. Mullen. Does the logic of preference rest on a mistake? *Metaphilosophy*, 10:247–255, 1979.

[NAS 50] J.F. Nash. The bargaining problem. *Econometrica*, 18:155–162, 1950.

[NAS 51] J.F. Nash. Non-cooperative games. *Annals of Mathematics*, 54:286–295, 1951.

[NAU 95] R.F Nau. Coherent decision analysis with inseparable probabilities and utilities. *Journal of Risk and Uncertainty*, 10:71–91, 1995.

[NAU 01] R.F. Nau. De Finetti was right: probability does not exist. *Theory and Decision*, 51:89–124, 2001.

[NEW 63] A. Newell and H.A. Simon. GPS, a program that simulates human thought. In E.A Feigenbaum and J. Feldman, editors, *Computers and Thought*, pages 279–293. McGraw-Hill, New York, 1963.

[NEW 72] A. Newell and H.A. Simon. *Human Problem Solving*. Prentice Hall, Englewood Cliffs, 1972.

[NIL 71] N.J. Nillson. *Problem Solving Methods in Artificial Intelligence*. McGraw-Hill, New York, 1971.

[NIL 80] N. Nilsson. *Principles of Artificial Intelligence*. Tioga, Palo Alto, 1980.

[NUR 87] H. Nurmi. *Comparing Voting Systems*. D. Reidel, Dordrecht, 1987.

[NUR 99] H. Nurmi. *Voting Paradoxes and How to Deal with Them?* Springer Verlag, Berlin, 1999.

[NUT 97]   D. Nute. *Defeasible Deontic Logic*. Kluwer Academic, Dordrecht, 1997.

[ORS 71]   ORSA. Guidelines for the practice of operations research. *Operations Research*, 19:1123–1148, 1971.

[OST 90]   A. Ostanello. Action evaluation and action structuring: different decision aid situations reviewed through two actual cases. In C.A. Bana e Costa, editor, *Readings in Multiple Criteria Decision Aid*, pages 36–57. Springer Verlag, Berlin, 1990.

[OST 93]   A. Ostanello and A. Tsoukiàs. An explicative model of 'public' interorganizational interactions. *European Journal of Operational Research*, 70:67–82, 1993.

[OZT 05]   M. Öztürk, A. Tsoukiàs, and Ph Vincke. Preference modelling. In M. Ehrgott, S. Greco, and J. Figueira, editors, *State of the Art in Multiple Criteria Decision Analysis*, pages 27 – 72. Springer Verlag, Berlin, 2005.

[PAP 82]   C.H. Papadimitriou and K. Steiglitz. *Combinatorial Optimisation, Algorithms and Complexity*. Prentice Hall, Englewood Cliffs, 1982.

[PAR 06]   V. Pareto. *Manuale di Economia Politica*. Piccola Biblioteca Scientifica, Milan, 1906. Translated into English by Ann S. Schwier (1971), Manual of Political Economy, MacMillan, London.

[PAS 00]   E. Paschetta and A. Tsoukiàs. A real world MCDA application: evaluating software. *Journal of Multi-Criteria Decision Analysis*, 9:205–226, 2000.

[PAW 94]   Z. Pawlak and R. Słowiński. Decision analysis using rough sets. *International Transactions on Operational Research*, 1:107–114, 1994.

[PER 92]   P. Perny and B. Roy. The use of fuzzy outranking relations in preference modelling. *Fuzzy Sets and Systems*, 49:33–53, 1992.

[PER 98]   P. Perny and A. Tsoukiàs. On the continuous extension of a four valued logic for preference modelling. In *Proceedings of the IPMU 1998 conference, Paris*, pages 302–309, 1998.

[PIR 96]   M. Pirlot. General local search methods. *European Journal of Operational Research*, 92:493–511, 1996.

[PIR 97]   M. Pirlot and Ph. Vincke. *Semi Orders*. Kluwer Academic, Dordrecht, 1997.

[POO 92]   D. Poole. Decision-theoretic defaults. In *Proceedings of the Ninth Biennial Conference of the Canadian Society for Computational Studies of Intelligence*, pages 190–197. Morgan Kaufmann, San Francisco, 1992.

[POU 94]   E.C. Poulton. *Behavioral Decision Theory: A New Approach*. Cambridge University Press, Cambridge, 1994.

[QUI 93]   J. Quiggin. *Generalized Expected Utility Theory: The Rank-dependent Model*. Kluwer Academic, Dordrecht, 1993.

[RAI 69] H. Raiffa. Preferences for multi-attributed consequences. Technical report, RM-5868-DOT, The RAND Corporation, Santa Monica, California, 1969.

[RAM 31] F.P. Ramsey. *Foundations of Mathematics and other Logical Essays*. Routledge & P. Kegan, London, 1931. Collection of papers publishded posthumously, edited by R.B Braithwaite.

[RES 67] N. Rescher. Semantic foundations for the logic of preference. In N. Rescher, editor, *The Logic of Decision and Action*, pages 37–62. University of Pittsburgh, Pittsburgh, 1967.

[RES 69] N. Rescher. *Introduction to Value Theory*. Prentice Hall, Englewood Cliffs, 1969.

[RIV 94] P. Rivett. *The Craft of Decision Modelling*. John Wiley, New York, 1994.

[ROB 79] F.S. Roberts. *Measurement Theory, with Applications to Decision Making, Utility and the Social Sciences*. Addison-Wesley, Boston, 1979.

[ROS 78] J. Rosenhead. An education in robustness. *Journal of the Operational Research Society*, 29:105–111, 1978.

[ROS 89] J. Rosenhead. *Rational Analysis of a Problematic World*. John Wiley, New York, 1989. 2nd revised edition in 2001.

[ROS 96] J. Rosenhead. What's the problem? an introduction to problem structuring methods. *Interfaces*, 26:117–131, 1996.

[ROU 85] M. Roubens and Ph. Vincke. *Preference Modeling*. LNEMS 250, Springer Verlag, Berlin, 1985.

[ROY 68] B. Roy. Classement et choix en présence de points de vue multiples: La méthode ELECTRE. *Revue Francaise d'Informatique et de Recherche Opérationnelle*, 8:57–75, 1968.

[ROY 85] B. Roy. *Méthodologie multicritère d'aide à la décision*. Economica, Paris, 1985.

[ROY 90] B. Roy. Decision-aid and decision-making. *European Journal of Operational Research*, 45:324–331, 1990.

[ROY 91] B. Roy. The outranking approach and the foundations of ELECTRE methods. *Theory and Decision*, 31:49–73, 1991.

[ROY 92] B. Roy. Science de la décision ou science de l'aide à la décision ? *Revue Internationale de Systémique*, 6:497–529, 1992.

[ROY 93a] B. Roy. Decision science or decision-aid science? *European Journal of Operational Research*, 66:184–203, 1993.

[ROY 94] B. Roy. On operational research and decision aid. *European Journal of Operational Research*, 73:23–26, 1994.

[ROY 96] B. Roy. *Multicriteria Methodology for Decision Aiding*. Kluwer Academic, Dordrecht, 1996.

[ROY 93b] B. Roy and D. Bouyssou. *Aide Multicritère à la Décision: Méthodes et Cas.* Economica, Paris, 1993.

[RUS 95] S. Russel and P. Norvig. *Artificial Intelligence: A Modern Approach.* Prentice Hall, New York, 1995.

[SAA 80] T.L. Saaty. *The Analytic Hierarchy Process, Planning, Piority Setting, Resource Allocation.* McGraw-Hill, New York, 1980.

[SAB 98] R. Sabbadin, H. Fargier, and J. Lang. Towards qualitative approaches to multi-stage decision making. *International Journal of Approximate Reasoning*, 19:441–471, 1998.

[SAB 01] R. Sabbadin. Possibilistic Markov decision processes. *Engineering Applications of Artificial Intelligence*, 14:287–300, 2001.

[SAV 54] L.J. Savage. *The Foundations of Statistics.* John Wiley, New York, 1954. Second revised edition, 1972.

[SCH 88] G. Schaffer. Savage revisited. In D. Bell, H. Raiffa, and A. Tversky, editors, *Decision Making: Descriptive, Normative and Prescriptive Interactions*, pages 193–235. Cambridge University Press, Cambridge, 1988.

[SCHÄ 85] A. Schärlig. *Décider sur plusieurs critères, panorama de l'aide à la décision multicritère.* Presses Polytechniques Romandes, Lausanne, 1985.

[SCHÄ 96] A. Schärlig. *Pratiquer Electre et Prométhée.* Presses Polytechniques et Universitaires Romandes, Lausanne, 1996.

[SCHM 89] D. Schmeidler. Subjective probability and expected utility without additivity. *Econometrica*, 57:571–587, 1989.

[SCO 58] D. Scott and P. Suppes. Foundational aspects of theories of measurement. *Journal of Symbolic Logic*, 23:113–128, 1958.

[SEN 70] A.K. Sen. *Collective Choice and Social Welfare.* North-Holland, Amsterdam, 1970.

[SEN 71] A.K. Sen. Choice functions and revealed preferences. *Review of Economic Studies*, 38:307–317, 1971.

[SEN 86] A.K. Sen. Social choice theory. In K.J. Arrow and M.D. Intriligator, editors, *Handbook of Mathematical Economics*, volume 3, pages 1073–1181. North-Holland, Amsterdam, 1986.

[SEN 93] A.K. Sen. Internal consistency of choice. *Econometrica*, 61:495–521, 1993.

[SHE 64] R.N. Shepard. On subjectively optimum selection among multiattribute alternatives. In M.W Shelly and G.L Bryan, editors, *Human Judgement and Optimality*, pages 257–281. John Wiley, New York, 1964.

[SHO 87] Y. Shoham. Non-monotonic logic: meaning and utility. In *Proceedings of the 10th International Joint Conference in Artificial Intelligence, IJCAI87*, pages 388–393. Morgan Kaufmann, San Francisco, 1987.

[SIM 47] H.A. Simon. *Administrative Behavior: A Study of Decision Making Processes in Administrative Organizations*. MacMillan, New York, 1947.

[SIM 54] H.A. Simon. A behavioral model of rational choice. *Quarterly Journal of Economics*, 69:99–118, 1954.

[SIM 56] H.A. Simon. Rational choice and the structure of the environment. *Psychological Review*, 63:129–138, 1956.

[SIM 57] H.A. Simon. A behavioral model of rational choice. In H.A. Simon, editor, *Models of Man: Social and Rational; Mathematical Essays on Rational Human Behavior in a Social Setting*, pages 241–260. John Wiley, New York, 1957.

[SIM 69] H.A. Simon. *The Science of the Artificial*. MIT Press, Camridge, 1969.

[SIM 76] H.A. Simon. From substantial to procedural rationality. In S.J. Latsis, editor, *Method and Appraisal in Economics*, pages 129–148. Cambridge University Press, Cambridge, 1976.

[SIM 79] H.A. Simon. Rational decision making in business organizations. *American Economic Review*, 69:493–513, 1979.

[SIM 83] H.A. Simon. Search and reasoning in problem solving. *Artificial Intelligence*, 21:7–29, 1983.

[SLO 68] P. Slovic and S. Lichtentstein. The relative importance of probabilities and payoffs in risk taking. *Journal of Experimental Psychology Monographs*, 78:1–18, 1968.

[SLO 02] P. Slovic, M. Finucane, E. Peters, and D.G. MacGregor. Rational actors or rational fools? implications of the affect heuristic for behavioral economics. *The Journal of Socio-Economics*, 31:329–342, 2002.

[SLOW 90] R. Słowiński and J. Teghem, editors. *Stochastic versus Fuzzy Approaches to Multiobjective Mathematical Programming under uncertainty*. Kluwer Academic, Dordrecht, 1990.

[SLOW 98] R. Słowiński, editor. *Fuzzy Sets in Decision Analysis, Operations Research and Statistics*. Kluwer Academic, Dordrecht, 1998.

[SLOW 02] R. Słowiński, S.Greco, and B.Matarazzo. Axiomatization of utility, outranking and decision-rule preference models for multiple-criteria classification problems under partial inconsistency with the dominance principle. *Control and Cybernetics*, 31:1005–1035, 2002.

[SLOW 05] R. Słowiński, S. Greco, and B. Matarazzo. Rough set based decision support. In E.K. Burke and G.Kendall, editors, *Search Methodologies: Introductory Tutorials in Optimization and Decision Support Techniques*, pages 475–527. Springer Verlag, Berlin, 2005.

[STA 03] I. Stamelos and A. Tsoukiàs. Software evaluation problem situations. *European Journal of Operational Research*, 145:273–286, 2003.

[STE 03] Th.J. Stewart and F.B. Losa. Towards reconciling outranking and value measurement practice. *European Journal of Operational Research*, 145:645–659, 2003.

[STI 67] J. Stringer. Operational research for multi-organizations. *Operational Research Quarterly*, 8:5–20, 1967.

[SVE 96] O. Svenson. Decision making and the search for fundamental psychological regularities: what can we learn from a process perspective? *Organisational Behaviour and Human Decision Processes*, 65:252–267, 1996.

[TAN 94] S.W. Tan and J. Pearl. Qualitative decision theory. In *Proceeding of the 12th National Conference on Artificial Intelligence, AAAI94*, pages 928–933. MIT Press, Cambridge, 1994.

[TAY 95] A. Taylor. *Mathematics and Politics: Strategy, Voting, Power, and Proof*. Springer Verlag, Berlin, 1995.

[TAYL 11] F.W. Taylor. *The Principles of Scientific Management*. Harper and Row, New York, 1911.

[TRI 93] E. Trist and H. Murray. *The Social Engagement of Social Science: A Tavistock Anthology, vol. 2*. University of Pennsylvania Press, Philadelphia, 1993.

[TSA 93] C. Tsang. *Foundations of Constraint Satisfaction*. Academic Press, New York, 1993.

[TSO 95] A. Tsoukiàs and Ph. Vincke. A new axiomatic foundation of partial comparability. *Theory and Decision*, 39:79–114, 1995.

[TSO 02a] A. Tsoukiàs. A first-order, four valued, weakly paraconsistent logic and its relation to rough sets semantics. *Foundations of Computing and Decision Sciences*, 12:85–108, 2002.

[TSO 02b] A. Tsoukiàs, P. Perny, and Ph. Vincke. From concordance/discordance to the modelling of positive and negative reasons in decision aiding. In D. Bouyssou, E. Jacquet-Lagrèze, P. Perny, R. Słowiński, D. Vanderpooten, and Ph. Vincke, editors, *Aiding Decisions with Multiple Criteria: Essays in Honour of Bernard Roy*, pages 147–174. Kluwer Academic, Dordrecht, 2002.

[TSO 07] A. Tsoukiàs. On the concept of decision aiding process. *Annals of Operations Research*, 154:3–27, 2007.

[TSO 08] A. Tsoukiàs. From decision theory to decision aiding methodology. *European Journal of Operations Research*, 187:138–161, 2008.

[TUR 37] A. Turing. On computable numbers, with an application to the entscheidungsproblem. *Proceedings of the London Mathematical Society*, 42:230–265, 1937.

[TUR 50] A. Turing. Computing machinery and intelligence. *Mind*, 49:433–460, 1950.

[TVE 67] A. Tversky. Additivity, utility and subjective probability. *Journal of Mathematical Psychology*, 4:175–201, 1967.

[TVE 69] A. Tversky. Intransitivity of preferences. *Psychological Review*, 76:31–48, 1969.

[TVE 72] A. Tversky. Elimination by aspects: A theory of choice. *Psychological Review*, 79:281–299, 1972.

[TVE 77a] A. Tversky. Features of similarity. *Psychological Review*, 84:327–352, 1977.

[TVE 77b] A. Tversky. On the elicitation of preferences: Descriptive and prescriptive considerations. In D. Bell, R.L. Keeney, and H. Raiffa, editors, *Conflicting Objectives in Decisions*, pages 209–222. John Wiley, New York, 1977.

[TVE 80] A. Tversky and D. Kahneman. The framing of decisions and the psychology of choice. *Science*, 211:453–458, 1981.

[TVE 93] A. Tversky and I. Simonson. Context-dependent preferences. *Management Science*, 39:1179–1189, 1993.

[ULU 94] E.L. Ulungu and J. Teghem. Multi-objective combinatorial optimization: a survey. *Journal of Multi-Criteria Decision Analysis*, 3:83–104, 1994.

[VAJ 56] S. Vajda. *The Theory of Games and Linear Programming*. John Wiley, New York, 1956.

[VAN 89] P. Van Hentenryck. *Constraint Satisfaction in Logic Programing*. MIT Press, Cambridge, 1989.

[VAND 89] D. Vanderpooten and Ph. Vincke. Description and analysis of some representative interactive multicriteria procedures. *Mathematical and Computer Modelling*, 12:1221–1238, 1989.

[VAND 02] D. Vanderpooten. Modelling in decision aiding. In D. Bouyssou, E. Jacquet-Lagrèze, P. Perny, R. Słowiński, D. Vanderpooten, and Ph. Vincke, editors, *Aiding Decisions with Multiple Criteria: Essays in Honour of Bernard Roy*, pages 195–210. Kluwer Academic, Dordrecht, 2002.

[VIN 82a] Ph. Vincke. Aggregation of preferences: a review. *European Journal of Operational Research*, 9:17–22, 1982.

[VIN 82b] Ph. Vincke. Arrow's theorem is not a surprising result. *European Journal of Operational Research*, 10:22–25, 1982.

[VIN 92] Ph. Vincke. *Multicriteria Decision-Aid*. John Wiley, New York, 1992.

[VON 44] J. von Neumann and O. Morgenstern. *Theory of Games and Economic Behavior*. Princeton University Press, Princeton, 1944. Second edition in 1947, third in 1954.

[VONW 86] D. von Winterfeldt and W. Edwards. *Decision Analysis and Behavioral Research*. Cambridge University Press, Cambridge, 1986.

[VONWR 63] G.H von Wright. *The Logic of Preference*. Edinburgh University Press, Edinburgh, 1963.

[VONWR 72] G.H von Wright. The logic of preference reconsidered. *Theory and Decision*, 3:140–169, 1972.

[WAK 89] P.P. Wakker. *Additive Representations of Preferences. A New Foundation of Decision Analysis*. Kluwer Academic, Dordrecht, 1989.

[WAK 93] P.P. Wakker and A. Tversky. An axiomatization of cumulative prospect theory. *Journal of Risk and Uncertainty*, 7:147–176, 1993.

[WAK 02] P.P. Wakker and H. Zank. A simple preference-foundation of cumulative prospect theory with power utility. *European Economic Review*, 46:1253–1271, 2002.

[WAT 67] P. Watzlawick, J.H. Beavin, and D.D. Jackson. *Pragmatics of Human Communication*. W.W. Norton, New York, 1967.

[WAT 74] P. Watzlawick, J.H. Weakland, and R. Fisch. *Change: Principles of Problem Formation and Problem Resolution*. Norton, New York, 1974.

[WAT 83] P. Watzlawick. *The Situation is Hopeless, But Not Serious: (The Pursuit of Unhappiness)*. Norton, New York, 1983.

[WEB 90] E.U. Weber and O. Cockunoglu. Descriptive and prescriptive models of decision making: implications for the development of decision aid. *IEEE Transactions on Systems, Mans and Cybernetics*, 20:310–317, 1990.

[WEBE 22] M. Weber. *Wirtschaft und Gesellschaft*. Mohr, Tubingen, 1922.

[WEL 91] M.P. Wellman and J. Doyle. Preferential semantics for goals. In *Proceedings of the 9th National Conference on Artificial Intelligence, AAAI91*, pages 698–703. AAAI Press, Menlo Park, 1991.

[WEY 84] J.A Weymark. Arrow's theorem with social quasi-orderings. *Public Choice*, 42:235–246, 1984.

[WHI 75] D.J. White and K. Bowen. *The Role and Effectiveness of Theories of Decision in Practice*. Hodder and Stoughton, London, 1975.

[WIE 48] N. Wiener. *Cybernetics*. MIT Press, Cambridge, 1948.

[WIL 90] H.P. Williams. *Model Building in Mathematical Programming*. John Wiley, New York, 1990. Third edition.

[ZAD 65] L.A. Zadeh. Fuzzy sets. *Information Control*, 8:338–353, 1965.

[ZAD 78] L.A. Zadeh. Fuzzy sets as a basis for theory of possibility. *Fuzzy Sets and Systems*, 1:3–28, 1978.

[ZEL 73] M. Zeleny. Compromise programming. In J. L. Cochrane and M. Zeleny, editors, *Multiple Criteria Decision Making*, pages 262–301. University of South Carolina Press, Columbia, SC, 1973.

Chapter 2

Binary Relations and Preference Modeling

2.1. Introduction

This book is dedicated to concepts, results, procedures and software aiming at helping people make a decision. It is then natural to investigate how the various courses of action that are involved in this decision compare in terms of preference. The aim of this chapter is to propose a brief survey of the main tools and results that can be useful to do so.

The literature on preference modeling is vast. This can first be explained by the fact that the question of modeling preferences occurs in several disciplines, such as the following:

– in Economics, where we try to model the preferences of a 'rational consumer' [e.g. DEB 59];

– in Psychology, in which the study of preference judgments collected in experiments is quite common [KAH 79, KAH 81];

– in Political Sciences, in which the question of defining a collective preference on the basis of the opinion of several voters is central [SEN 86];

– in Operations Research, in which optimizing an objective function implies the definition of a direction of preference [ROY 85]; and

– in Artificial Intelligence, in which the creation of autonomous agents able to take decisions implies the modeling of their vision of what is desirable and what is less so [DOY 92].

Chapter written by Denis BOUYSSOU and Philippe VINCKE.

Moreover, the question of preference modeling can be studied from a variety of perspectives [BEL 88], including:

– a *normative* perspective, where one investigates preference models that are likely to lead to a 'rational behavior';

– a *descriptive* perspective, in which adequate models to capture judgements obtained in experiments are sought; or

– a *prescriptive* perspective, in which one tries to build a preference model that is able to lead to an adequate recommendation.

Finally, the preferences that are to be modeled can be expressed on a variety of objects depending on the underlying decision problem. For instance, we may compare:

– vectors in $\mathbb{R}^p$ indicating the consumption of p perfectly divisible goods;

– candidates in an election;

– probability distributions modeling the possible financial results of various investment prospects;

– alternatives evaluated on several criteria expressed in incommensurable units when comparing sites for a new factory;

– projects evaluated on a monetary scale conditionally on the occurrence of various events or on the actions of other players.

It would be impossible within the scope of this chapter to exhaustively summarize the immense literature on the subject. More realistically, we will try here to present in a simple way the main concepts used in building models of preference. This will give the reader the necessary background to tackle the remaining chapters in this book. The reader willing to deepen their understanding of the subject is referred to [ALE 06, FIS 70, FIS 85, KRA 71, PIR 97, ROB 79, ROU 85].

This chapter is organized as follows. Section 2.2 is devoted to the concept of the *binary relation* since this is the central tool in most models of preference. Section 2.3 defines a 'preference structure'. Section 2.4 introduces two classical preference structures: complete orders and weak orders. Sections 2.5 and 2.6 introduce several more general preference structures. Section 2.7 concludes with the mention of several important questions that we cannot tackle here.

2.2. Binary relations

2.2.1. *Definitions*

A binary relation T on a set A is a subset of the Cartesian product $A \times A$, i.e. a set of ordered pairs (a, b) of elements of A. If the ordered pair (a, b) belongs to the set T, we will often write $a \, T \, b$ instead of $(a, b) \in T$. In the opposite case, we write

$(a, b) \notin T$ or $a \neg T b$. Except when explicitly mentioned otherwise, we will suppose in all what follows that the set A is *finite*.

Remark 2.1. Since binary relations are sets, we can apply the classical operations of set theory to them. For instance, given any two binary relations T_1 and T_2 on A, we will write:

$$T_1 \subset T_2 \Leftrightarrow [a\ T_1\ b \Rightarrow a\ T_2\ b, \forall a, b \in A],$$

$$a\ (T_1 \cup T_2)\ b \Leftrightarrow a\ T_1\ b \text{ or } a\ T_2\ b,$$

$$a\ (T_1 \cap T_2)\ b \Leftrightarrow a\ T_1\ b \text{ and } a\ T_2\ b.$$

Moreover, the *product* $T_1 \cdot T_2$ will be defined by:

$$a\ T_1 \cdot T_2\ b \Leftrightarrow \exists c \in A : a\ T_1\ c \text{ and } c\ T_2\ b.$$

We denote by T^2 the relation $T \cdot T$, i.e. the product of the relation T with itself.

Given a binary relation T on A, we define:

– its inverse relation T^- such that:

$$a\ T^-\ b \Leftrightarrow b\ T\ a;$$

– its complement, i.e. the binary relation T^c such that:

$$a\ T^c\ b \Leftrightarrow a \neg T\ b;$$

– its dual relation T^d such that:

$$a\ T^d\ b \Leftrightarrow b \neg T\ a;$$

– its symmetric part I_T such that:

$$a\ I_T\ b \Leftrightarrow [a\ T\ b \text{ and } b\ T\ a];$$

– its asymmetric part P_T such that:

$$a\ P_T\ b \Leftrightarrow [a\ T\ b \text{ and } b \neg T\ a];$$

– its associated equivalence relation E_T such that:

$$a\ E_T\ b \Leftrightarrow \left\{ \begin{array}{c} a\ T\ c \Leftrightarrow b\ T\ c, \\ c\ T\ a \Leftrightarrow c\ T\ b, \end{array} \right\}, \forall c \in A.$$

Remark 2.2. It is easy to check that we have:

$$T^d = T^{-c} = T^{c-},$$

$$I_T = T \cap T^-,$$

$$P_T = T \cap T^d.$$

2.2.2. Properties of a binary relation

A binary relation T on A is said to be:
- *reflexive* if $a\ T\ a$;
- *irreflexive* if $a\ \neg T\ a$;
- *symmetric* if $a\ T\ b \Rightarrow b\ T\ a$;
- *antisymmetric* if $a\ T\ b$ and $b\ T\ a \Rightarrow a = b$;
- *asymmetric* if $a\ T\ b \Rightarrow b\ \neg T\ a$;
- *weakly complete* if $a \neq b \Rightarrow a\ T\ b$ or $b\ T\ a$;
- *complete* if $a\ T\ b$ or $b\ T\ a$;
- *transitive* if $a\ T\ b$ and $b\ T\ c \Rightarrow a\ T\ c$;
- *negatively transitive* if $a\ \neg T\ b$ and $b\ \neg T\ c \Rightarrow a\ \neg T\ c$;
- *Ferrers* if $[a\ T\ b$ and $c\ T\ d] \Rightarrow [a\ T\ d$ or $c\ T\ d]$; and
- *semi-transitive* if $[a\ T\ b$ and $b\ T\ c] \Rightarrow [a\ T\ d$ or $d\ T\ c]$

for all $a, b, c, d \in A$.

Remark 2.3. The above properties are not independent. For instance, it is easy to check that
- a relation is asymmetric $\Leftrightarrow$ it is irreflexive and antisymmetric;
- a relation is complete $\Leftrightarrow$ it is weakly complete and reflexive;
- an asymmetric and negatively transitive relation is transitive; and
- a complete and transitive relation is negatively transitive.

Whatever the properties of T, it is clear that
- P_T is always asymmetric;
- I_T is always symmetric; and
- E_T is always reflexive, symmetric and transitive.

Remark 2.4. It is possible to reformulate the above properties in a variety of ways. For instance, observe that:
- T is complete $\Leftrightarrow T \cup T^- = A \times A$;
- T is asymmetric $\Leftrightarrow T \cap T^- = \varnothing$;
- T is transitive $\Leftrightarrow T^2 \subset T$;
- T is Ferrers $\Leftrightarrow T \cdot T^d \cdot T \subset T$; and
- T is semi-transitive $\Leftrightarrow T \cdot T \cdot T^d \subset T$.

An *equivalence* is a reflexive, symmetric and transitive binary relation (hence, the binary relation E_T defined earlier is an equivalence whatever the properties of T). Let

E be an equivalence on A. Given an element $a \in A$, the equivalence class associated with a, denoted by $[a]_E$, is the set $\{b \in A : a \, E \, b\}$. It is always true that $a \in [a]_E$. It is easy to show that $\forall a, b \in A$, either $[a]_E = [b]_E$ or $[a]_E \cap [b]_E = \emptyset$. An equivalence therefore partitions A into *equivalence classes*. The set of all these equivalence classes is called the quotient of A for E and is denoted A/E.

2.2.3. *Graphical representation of a binary relation*

A binary relation T on A can be represented as a directed graph (A, T) where A is the set of vertices of the graph and T is the set of the arcs of the graph (i.e. ordered pair of vertices). The particular properties of a binary relation can easily be interpreted using the sagittal representation of the graph (A, T). The reflexivity of T implies the presence of a loop on each vertex. The symmetry of T means that when there is an arc going from a to b, there is also an arc going from b to a. The transitivity of T means that as soon as there is a path of length 2 going from a to b, there is an arc from a to b. Taking the inverse relation is tantamount to inverting the orientation of all arcs in the graph. Taking the complement consists of adding all missing arcs and deleting all existing ones.

Observe that a symmetric relation can be more conveniently represented using a non-oriented graph, in which the ordered pairs (a, b) and (b, a) of the relation are represented using a single edge between the vertices a and b.

2.2.4. *Matrix representation of a binary relation*

Another way to represent a binary relation T on A is to associate with each element of A a row and a column of a square matrix M^T of dimension $|A|$. The element M^T_{ab} of this matrix, being at the intersection of the row associated with a and at the intersection of the column associated with b, is 1 if $a \, T \, b$ and 0 otherwise.

With such a representation, the reflexivity of T implies the presence of 1 on the diagonal of the matrix, provided that the elements of A have been associated in the order of the row and columns of the matrix. Under this hypothesis, the symmetry of T is equivalent to the fact that M^T is equal to its transpose. Taking the inverse relation consists of transposing the matrix M^T. The matrix associated with the product of two binary relations is the boolean product of the two corresponding matrices.

2.2.5. *Example*

Let $A = \{a, b, c, d, e\}$. Consider the binary relation

$$T = \{(a, b), (b, a), (b, c), (d, b), (d, d)\}.$$

A matrix representation of T is the following:

	a	b	c	d	e
a	0	1	0	0	0
b	1	0	1	0	0
c	0	0	0	0	0
d	0	1	0	1	0
e	0	0	0	0	0

A sagittal representation of the graph (A, T) is depicted in Figure 2.1.

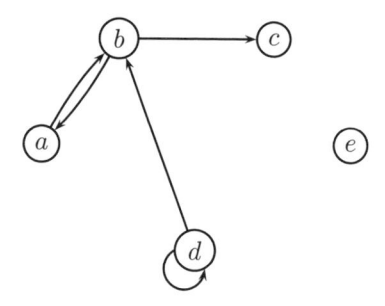

Figure 2.1. *Sagittal representation of the graph (A, T)*

2.3. Binary relations and preference structures

Consider an ordered pair (a, b) of objects. It is classically assumed that there can only be two answers to the question 'is object a at least as good as object b?': yes or no, these two answers being exclusive. Asking such a question for all ordered pais of objects leads to the definition of a *binary relation* S on the set A of all objects letting $a\ S\ b$ if and only if the answer to the question 'is a at least as good as b?' is yes. In view of its definition, it is natural to consider that S is reflexive; we will do so in all that follows.

Definition 2.1. A preference structure on A is a reflexive binary relation S on A.

Remark 2.5. The preceding definition raises a question of *observability*. If the idea of preference is to be based on observable behavior, the primitive may be taken to be choices made on various subsets of objects. This change of primitive is at the heart of 'revealed preference' theory in which the relation S is inferred from choices that are observable. Such an inference requires that choices are essentially 'binary', i.e. that choices made on pairs of objects are sufficient to infer choice made on larger sets of objects. The conditions allowing such a rationalization of a choice function through a binary relation are classical [e.g. SEN 70, SEN 77]. They have recently been severely questioned [MAL 93, SEN 93, SUG 85].

Remark 2.6. In some cases, we may envisage answers other than yes or no to the question 'is a at least as good as b?', such as the following:

– answers such as 'I do not know';

– answers including information on the *intensity* of the preference, e.g. 'a is strongly/weakly/moderately preferred to b';

– answers including information on the *credibility* of the proposition 'a is at least as good as b', e.g. 'the credibility of the 'a is at least as good as b' is greater than the credibility of the proposition 'c is at least as good as d' or even 'the credibility of the proposition 'a is at least as good as b' is $\alpha \in [0;1]$'.

Admitting such answers implies using a language that is richer than that of binary relations, e.g.:

– the language of *fuzzy relations* [DOI 86, FOD 94, PER 92], each assertion of the type $a \ S \ b$ having a *degree of credibility*;

– languages tolerating hesitation [e.g. ROY 87];

– languages using the idea of *intensity of preference* [COS 94, DOI 87], an assertion such that $a \ S \ b$ and $b \ \neg S \ a$ being further qualified (weak, strong or extreme preference, for instance); or

– languages making use of *non-classical logics* [TSO 92, TSO 95, TSO 97] allowing the capture of the absence of information or, on the contrary, the existence of contradictory information (with such languages, the truth value of the assertion $a \ S \ b$ can take values different from just 'true' or 'false' and include 'unknown' and 'contradictory').

We do not consider such extensions in this chapter.

Let us consider a preference S on a set A. For all pairs of objects $\{a, b\}$, we are in one of the following four situations (see Figure 2.2):

1) $[a \ S \ b$ and $b \ S \ a]$, denoted by $a \ I_S \ b$, interpreted as 'a is *indifferent* to b';

2) $[a \ \neg S \ b$ and $b \ \neg S \ a]$, denoted by $a \ J_S \ b$, interpreted as 'a is *incomparable* to b';

3) $[a \ S \ b$ and $b \ \neg S \ a]$, denoted by $a \ P_S \ b$, interpreted as 'a is *strictly preferred* to b'; and

4) $[a \ \neg S \ b$ and $b \ S \ a]$, denoted by $b \ P_S \ a$, interpreted as 'b is *strictly preferred* to a'.

	$b\,S\,a$	$b\,\neg S\,a$
$a\,S\,b$	$a\,I\,b$	$a\,P\,b$
$a\,\neg S\,b$	$b\,P\,a$	$a\,J\,b$

Figure 2.2. *Four exhaustive and mutually exclusive situations*

When there is no risk of ambiguity, we use I, J and P instead of I_S, J_S and P_S.

By construction, I and J are symmetric and P is asymmetric. Since S is reflexive, I is reflexive and J is irreflexive. The three relations P, I and J are:

– mutually exclusive, i.e. $P \cap I = P \cap J = I \cap J = \emptyset$ and
– exhaustive, i.e. $P \cup P^- \cup I \cup J = A^2$.

Remark 2.7. Many works use $\succsim$ instead of S, $\succ$ instead of P and $\sim$ instead of I.

Remark 2.8. Given a preference structure of S on A, it may be useful to consider the relation induced by S on the quotient set A/E_S, where E_S denotes the equivalence associated with S. This allows the simplification of many results.

Remark 2.9. Since a preference structure is a reflexive binary relation, we can use the graphical and matrix representations introduced earlier to represent it. In order to simplify graphical representations, we will systematically omit reflexivity loops and will use the conventions introduced in Figure 2.3.

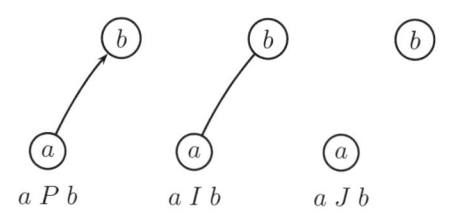

Figure 2.3. *Graphical conventions*

Example 2.1. Let $A = \{a, b, c, d, e\}$ and the preference structure $S = \{\,(a,a), (a,b), (a,c), (a,e), (b,a), (b,b), (b,c), (c,b), (c,c), (d,a), (d,b), (d,c), (d,d), (e,a), (e,c), (e,e)\,\}$. We have:

$$P = \{(a,c), (d,a), (d,b), (d,c), (e,c)\},$$
$$I = \{(a,a), (a,b), (a,e), (b,a), (b,b), (b,c), (c,b), (c,c), (d,d), (e,a), (e,e)\},$$
$$J = \{(b,e), (d,e), (e,b), (e,d)\}.$$

Using the above conventions, we obtain the matrix representation (Figure 2.4) and the graphical representation (Figure 2.5) of T.

$\circlearrowright$	a	b	c	d	e
a	1	1	1	0	1
b	1	1	1	0	0
c	0	1	1	0	0
d	1	1	1	1	0
e	1	0	1	0	1

Figure 2.4. *Matrix representation*

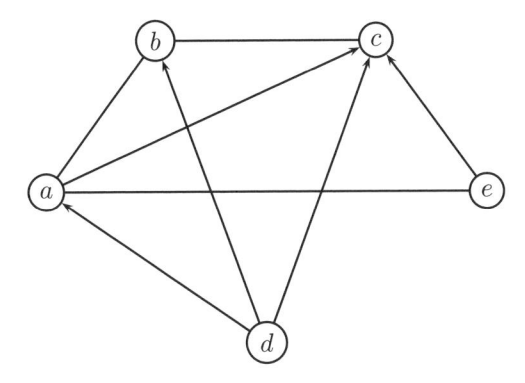

Figure 2.5. *Graphical representation*

2.4. Classical preference structures

2.4.1. *Total order*

2.4.1.1. *Definition*

A preference structure S is a total order if:
- S is complete;
- S is transitive; and
- S is antisymmetric.

In a total order, the incomparability relation is empty ($J = \emptyset$) and the indifference relation I is limited to pairs of identical objects ($I = \{(a,a) : a \in A\}$). The strict

58   Decision-making Process

preference is that P is weakly complete and transitive. A total order therefore consists of a ranking of the objects from A from best to worst (using the relation P) without the possibility of *ex aequo*.

Remark 2.10. It is easy to check that an equivalent definition of a total order consists of saying that S is complete and the only circuits in this relation are loops.

It is clear that, if S is a total order,
– P is weakly complete and transitive;
– I is transitive;
– $I \cdot P \subset P$; and
– $P \cdot I \subset P$.

Remark 2.11. Checking if a preference structure is a total order is quite simple using the matric representation of S. Indeed, labeling rows and columns of the matrix according to P, we obtain a matrix that has only 0 below the diagonal and 1 elsewhere. The relation P corresponds to off-diagonal 1's. In the graphical representation, if vertices are ranked according to P, all arcs are going from left to right.

Example 2.2. Let $A = \{a, b, c, d, e\}$. Consider the preference structure $S = \{(a, a), (a, b), (a, c), (a, d), (a, e), (b, b), (b, c), (b, d), (b, e), (c, c), (c, d), (c, e), (d, d), (d, e), (e, e)\}$.

It is easy to check that it is a total order using the matrix representation shown in Figure 2.6 or its graphical representation shown in Figure 2.7.

↻	a	b	c	d	e
a	1	1	1	1	1
b	0	1	1	1	1
c	0	0	1	1	1
d	0	0	0	1	1
e	0	0	0	0	1

Figure 2.6. *Matrix representation of a total order*

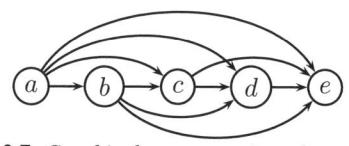

Figure 2.7. *Graphical representation of a total order*

2.4.1.2. *Numerical representation*

Let S be a total order on A. We may associate a number with each object in such a way that this number reflects the position of the object in the relation S. We leave the easy proof of the following result to the reader.

Theorem 2.1. *A preference structure S on a finite set A is a total order if and only if there is a function $g : A \to \mathbb{R}$ such that $\forall a, b \in A$:*

$$\begin{cases} a\ S\ b \Leftrightarrow g(a) \geq g(b), \\ g(a) = g(b) \Rightarrow a = b. \end{cases}$$

Remark 2.12. The numerical representation of a total order is not unique. It is easy to show that given a numerical representation g satisfying the conditions of Theorem 2.1, any increasing transformation applied to g leads to another admissible representation. Conversely, if g and h are two numerical representations of the same total order in the sense of Theorem 2.1, there is an increasing function ϕ such that $g = \phi \circ h$. The scale g is said to be an *ordinal scale*.

Let g be a function satisfying the condition of the above theorem. It is possible to compare differences such as $g(a) - g(b)$ and $g(c) - g(d)$. These comparisons are nevertheless clearly dependent upon the choice of the particular function g: another legitimate choice can lead to other comparisons of differences. Hence, in general, it is impossible to give a particular meaning to these comparisons.

Remark 2.13. Theorem 2.1 remains true if A is countably infinite (g is defined by an easy induction argument). It is clear that the result is no more true in the general case. Let us illustrate this fact by two examples:

1) It is well known that the cardinality of $\mathcal{P}(\mathbb{R})$ (i.e. the set of subsets of $\mathbb{R}$) is strictly greater than that of $\mathbb{R}$. Any total order on $\mathcal{P}(\mathbb{R})$ cannot have a numerical representation in the sense of Theorem 2.1. A natural question arises: is Theorem 2.1 true when attention is restricted to sets A, having at most the cardinality of $\mathbb{R}$? This is not so, as shown by the following famous example.

2) Let $A = \mathbb{R} \times \{0, 1\}$. It is easy to show that A has the same cardinality as $\mathbb{R}$. Consider the lexicographic order defined, letting:

$$(x, y)\ P\ (z, w) \Leftrightarrow \begin{cases} x > z \text{ or} \\ x = z \text{ and } y > w, \end{cases}$$

and

$$(x, y)\ I\ (z, w) \Leftrightarrow x = z \text{ and } y = w.$$

It is easy to show that the structure $S = P \cup I$ is a total order. It does not have a numerical representation in the sense of Theorem 2.1. Indeed, suppose that g is such a representation. We would have $\forall x \in \mathbb{R}$, $(x,1)\,P\,(x,0)$ so that $g(x,1) > g(x,0)$. There exists a rational number $\mu(x)$ such that $g(x,1) > \mu(x) > g(x,0)$. We have $(y,1)\,P\,(y,0)\,P\,(x,1)\,P\,(x,0) \Leftrightarrow y > x$. Hence, $y > x$ implies $\mu(y) > \mu(x)$. The function μ built above is therefore a bijection between $\mathbb{R}$ and $\mathbb{Q}$, a contradiction.

Beardon *et al.* [BEA 02] propose a detailed analysis of the various situations in which a total order does not have a numerical representation. The necessary and sufficient conditions ensuring that a total order has a numerical representation are known [BRI 95, DEB 54, FIS 70, KRA 71]. They amount to supposing that S on A has a behavior that is 'close' to that of $\geq$ in $\mathbb{R}$.

2.4.2. *Weak orders*

2.4.2.1. *Definition*

A preference structure S is a weak order if:
– S is complete; and
– S is transitive.

Weak orders generalize total orders since they do not have to be antisymmetric. Hence, indifference between distinct elements is allowed in weak orders.

Remark 2.14. An equivalent definition of a weak order is that S is complete and any circuit of S has no P arc.

It is clear that, if S is a weak order,
– P is transitive;
– P is negatively transitive;
– I is transitive (I is therefore an equivalence);
– $I \cdot P \subset P$;
– $P \cdot I \subset P$; and
– the relation S induces a total order on the quotient set A/I.

Remark 2.15. Let T be an asymmetric and negatively transitive binary relation on A. Let $S = T \cup (T^- \cap T^d)$. It is easy to show that S is a weak order.

Remark 2.16. If the rows and columns of the matrix representation of a weak order are ordered according to a relation that is compatible with P (the ordering of the rows and columns for indifferent elements being unimportant), we obtain a matrix in which the 1's are separated from the 0's by a stepped frontier that is below the diagonal and touches the diagonal. In a similar way, the graphical representation of a weak order generalizes that of a total order.

Example 2.3. Let $A = \{a, b, c, d, e\}$. Consider the preference structure $S = (a, a), (a, b), (a, c), (a, d), (a, e), (b, a), (b, b), (b, c), (b, d), (b, e), (c, c), (c, d), (c, e), (d, c), (d, d), (d, e), (e, e)\}$. It is easy to check that this is a weak order, considering the matrix representation depicted in Figure 2.8 or the graphical representation depicted in Figure 2.9.

$\circlearrowright$	a	b	c	d	e
a	1	1	1	1	1
b	1	1	1	1	1
c	0	0	1	1	1
d	0	0	1	1	1
e	0	0	0	0	1

Figure 2.8. *Matrix representation of a weak order*

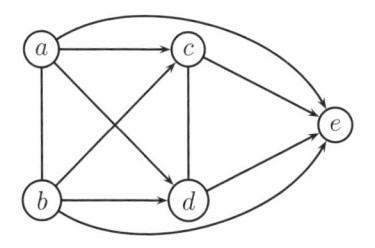

Figure 2.9. *Graphical representation of a weak order*

2.4.2.2. Numerical representation

Remembering that weak order induces a total order on the quotient set A/I, it is easy to prove the following result.

Theorem 2.2. *A preference structure S on a finite set A is a weak order if and only if (iff) there is a function* $g : A \to \mathbb{R}$ *such that* $\forall a, b \in A$

$$a \, S \, b \Leftrightarrow g(a) \geq g(b).$$

Remark 2.17. As above, the numerical representation of a weak order is defined up to an increasing transformation. The function g is an ordinal scale and most of the assertions that can be obtained using arithmetic operations on the values of g have a truth value that depends on the function g that was chosen: they are not meaningful in the sense of [ROB 79].

Remark 2.18. It is clear that the above result remain true when A is countably infinite (since in this case a total order structure always has a numerical representation). As was the case with total orders, extending this result to arbitrary sets implies the introduction of additional conditions.

2.4.3. *Classical problems*

In most studies involving preferences, the weak order model is used: the function g representing the weak order is the function that should be maximized. Depending on the context, it is referred to as the value function, objective function, criterion or value function. It is striking that decision problems have been dealt with so often in this way without much investigation on the adequateness of g as a model of preference.

We discuss here a few classical questions that have been dealt with using the weak order model.

2.4.3.1. *Choosing on the basis of binary relation*

Suppose that we have a weak order S on a set A and consider the situation (common in Economics) in which a choice must be made in a subset $B \subseteq A$. How should the information contained in S be used to guide such a choice? A natural way to define the set $C(B, S)$ of chosen objects (note that since we do not require $C(B, S)$ to be a singleton, it would be more adequate to speak of objects that are susceptible to be chosen) in B on the basis of S is to let

$$C(B, S) = \{b \in B : Not[\, a \; P \; b\,] \text{ for all } a \in B\}.$$

An object a belongs to the choice set as soon as there is no other object that is strictly preferred to a. It is not difficult to show that $C(B, S)$ is always non-empty as soon as B is finite (the general case raises difficult questions, see [BER 75]) and S is a weak order. Let us observe that, when B is finite, imposing that S is a weak order is only a sufficient condition for the non-emptyness of $C(B, S)$.

A classic result [SEN 70] states that, when B is finite, $C(B, S)$ is non-empty as soon as P is acyclic in B (it is never true that, for all $a_1, a_2, \ldots, a_k$ in B, $a_1 \; P \; a_2, a_2 \; P \; a_3, \ldots, a_{k-1} \; P \; a_k$ and $a_k \; P \; a_1$). The use of structures that are more general than the weak order also allows a simple answer to the problem to be derived.

We note that there are situations (e.g. a competitive exam) in which it is desirable to rank order all elements in a subset $B \subseteq A$ and also to define the choice set $C(B, S)$. The weak order model allows a trivial answer to this problem to be derived since the restriction of a weak order on A to a subset $B \subseteq A$ is a weak order on B.

2.4.3.2. *Aggregating preferences*

Suppose that you have collected $n \geq 2$ preference structures on A, for example because the objects are evaluated according to various points of view (voters, criteria or experts). In such a situation, it is natural to try to build a 'collective' preference structure S that aggregates the information contained in $(S_1, S_2, \ldots, S_n)$.

In general, one looks for a mechanism (e.g. an electoral system or an aggregation method) that is able to aggregate *any* n-tuple of preference structures on A into a collective preference structure. When the weak order model is used, defining such a mechanism amounts to defining an aggregation function F from $\mathcal{WO}(A)^n$ in $\mathcal{WO}(A)$, where $\mathcal{WO}(A)$ is the set of all weak orders on A.

The work of Arrow [ARR 63] has clearly shown the difficulty of such a problem. Imposing a small number of apparently reasonable conditions on F (unanimity, independence with respect to irrelevant alternatives and absence of dictator) leads to a logical impossibility: it is impossible to simultaneously satisfy all these principles (for a rich synthesis of such results, see [CAM 02, SEN 86]). The simple majority method can be used to illustrate the problem uncovered by Arrow's result. This method consists of declaring that 'a is collectively at least as good as b' if there are more weak orders in which 'a is at least as good as b' than weak orders for which 'b is at least as good as a'. Such a method seems highly reasonable and in line with our intuitive conception of democracy.

It does not always lead to a collective weak order; it may even lead to a collective relation having a cycle in its asymmetric part. This is the famous Condorcet paradox: $A = \{a, b, c\}$, $n = 3$, $a\ P_1\ b\ P_1\ c, c\ P_2\ a\ P_2\ b$ and $b\ P_3\ c\ P_3\ a$ gives the simplest example of such a situation. Using a collective preference structure in which strict preference may be cyclic in order to choose and/or to rank order is far from being an easy task. Many works have investigated the question [e.g. LAS 97, MOU 86, SCH 86].

2.4.3.3. *Particular structure of the set of objects*

In many situations, it is natural to suppose that the set of objects A has a particular structure. This will be the case in the following situations:

– decision with multiple criteria in which the elements of A are vectors of evaluations on several dimensions, attributes or criteria ($A \subseteq A_1 \times A_2 \times \cdots \times A_n$ where A_i is the set of possible evaluations of the objects on the ith dimension);

– decision under risk in which the elements on A are viewed as probability distribution on a set of consequences ($A \subseteq \mathcal{P}(C)$ where $\mathcal{P}(C)$ is a set of probability distributions on a set of consequences C); or

– decision under uncertainty in which the elements of A are characterized by consequences occurring contingently upon the occurrence of 'several states of nature'

($A \subseteq C^n$ where C is a set of consequences, supposing that n distinct states of nature are distinguished).

In all these cases it is tempting to add to the weak order model additional conditions that will allow us to take advantage of the particular structure of the set A. Among these condition, let us mention the following:

1) *Preference independence* [KEE 76, KRA 71, WAK 89]: in the case of decision-making with multiple criteria, this implies that the comparison of two objects differing only on a subset of criteria is independent from their common evaluations:

$$(a_I, c_{-I}) \ S \ (b_I, c_{-I}) \Leftrightarrow (a_I, d_{-I}) \ S \ (b_I, d_{-I})$$

where I is a subset of criteria $\{1, 2, \ldots, n\}$ and where (a_I, c_{-I}) denotes the object $e \in A$ such that $e_i = a_i$ if $i \in I$ and $e_i = c_i$ otherwise.

2) *Independence with respect to probabilistic mixing* [FIS 70, FIS 88]: in the case of decision-making under risk, this implies that the preference relation between two probability distributions is not altered when they are both mixed with a common probability distribution:

$$a \ S \ b \Leftrightarrow (a\alpha c) \ S \ (b\alpha c)$$

where $(a\alpha b)$ denotes the convex combination of the probability distributions a and b with the coefficient $\alpha \in (0; 1)$.

3) *The sure-thing principle* [FIS 70, SAV 54, WAK 89]: in the case of decision-making under uncertainty, this implies that the preference between two acts does not depend on common consequences obtained in some states of nature, i.e.

$$(a_I, c_{-I}) \ S \ (b_I, c_{-I}) \Leftrightarrow (a_I, d_{-I}) \ S \ (b_I, d_{-I})$$

where I is a subset of states of nature and (a_I, c_{-I}) denotes the act $e \in A$ such that $e_i = a_i$ if $i \in I$ and $e_i = c_i$ otherwise.

When these conditions are applied to sets of objects that are sufficiently 'rich' (and when it is required that S behaves coherently with this richness [FIS 70, WAK 89]), we obtain some famous models based on that of the classical theory:

– The model of *additive value functions* in the case of decision with multiple criteria:

$$a \ S \ b \Leftrightarrow \sum_{i=1}^{n} u_i(a_i) \geq \sum_{i=1}^{n} u_i(b_i)$$

where u_i is a real-valued function on A_i and the evaluation of object a on the ith criterion is denoted by a_i.

– The *expected utility* model in the case of decision making under risk:

$$a \ S \ b \Leftrightarrow \sum_{c \in C} p_a(c) u(c) \geq \sum_{c \in C} p_b(c) u(c)$$

where u is a real-valued function on C and $p_a(c)$ is the probability to obtain consequence $c \in C$ with object a.

– The *subjective expected utility* model in the case of decision-making under uncertainty:

$$a \ S \ b \Leftrightarrow \sum_{i=1}^{n} p_i u(a_i) \geq \sum_{i=1}^{n} p_i u(b_i)$$

where u is a real-valued function on C and the p_is are non-negative numbers summing to 1 that can be interpreted as the subjective probabilities of the various states of nature.

One of the major aims of these models is to allow a numerical representation g of S that is much more specific than that given by Theorem 2.2. The additional conditions mentioned above imply that, when A is adequately rich (e.g. that $A = A_1 \times A_2 \times \cdots \times A_n$ in the case of decision making with multiple criteria, and that each A_i has a rich structure [WAK 89]), g can be additively decomposed. The numerical representation obtained is an interval scale (unique up to the choice of origin and unit). It is then possible to use sophisticated elicitation techniques to assess g and, therefore, structure a preference model [KEE 76, KRA 71, WAK 89].

These additional conditions were subjected to many empirical tests. In the fields of decision making under risk and uncertainty, it was shown that the conditions at the heart of the expected utility model (independence axiom and sure-thing principle) were falsified in a predictable and reproducible way [ALL 53, ELL 61, KAH 79, MCC 79]. This has generated numerous studies investigating models using only weakening of these additional conditions (see [FIS 88, MAC 82, QUI 82, QUI 93, YAA 87] for decision under risk and [DUB 01, GIL 87, GIL 89, SCH 89, WAK 89] for decision under uncertainty).

Dutch book-like arguments (adhering to these generalized models may transform an individual into a 'money pump') have often been used to criticize these models [RAI 70]. The validity of such arguments nevertheless raises difficult questions (see [MAC 89, MCC 90] for a criticism of such arguments for decision making under risk).

Finally, let us mention that other structures for A can be usefully studied. For instance, when A is endowed with a topological structure, it is natural to investigate numerical representation having continuity properties [BOS 02a, BRI 95, JAF 75]. Similarly, if A is endowed with a binary operation allowing the combination of its elements (this is the case in decision under risk using 'probabilistic mixing' of two objects), a numerical representation is sought that is somehow compatible (most often through addition) with this operation [KRA 71].

2.5. Semi-orders and interval orders

In weak orders, the indifference relation I is transitive. This hypothesis is sometimes inadequate since it amounts to supposing a perfect discrimination between close but distinct objects. Luce [LUC 56] was the first to suggest a preference structure in which indifference may be intransitive [PIR 97]. He suggested the following example.

Example 2.4. Consider a set A consisting of 101 cups of coffee numbered from 0–100 and identical except that there are i grains of sugar in the ith cup. It is likely that an individual comparing these cups will not be able to detect a difference between two consecutive cups. Hence, it is likely that we obtain:

$$a_0 \ I \ a_1, a_1 \ I \ a_2, \ldots, a_{99} \ I \ a_{100}.$$

If the relation I is assumed to be transitive, we should have $a_0 \ I \ a_{100}$, which seems unlikely as the individual is supposed to prefer sugared coffee.

The two preference structures introduced in this section aim to model situations in which indifference is not transitive, while maintaining our other hypotheses (transitivity of P, no incomparability) made so far.

2.5.1. *Semi-order*

2.5.1.1. *Definition*

A preference structure S is a semi-order if:
– S is complete;
– S is Ferrers; and
– S is semi-transitive.

Remark 2.19. It is easy to check that an equivalent definition of a semi-order is to suppose that S is complete and all circuits of S have more I arcs than P arcs.

Moreover, it is easy to prove that if S is a semi-order:
– P is transitive;
– P is Ferrers;
– P is semi-transitive;
– $P \cdot I \cdot P \subset P$;
– $P \cdot P \cdot I \subset P$;
– $I \cdot P \cdot P \subset P$; and

– $P^2 \cap I^2 = \emptyset$.

As will become apparent later, semi-orders arise when an indifference threshold is introduced when comparing objects evaluated on a numerical scale. As an easy exercise, the reader may wish to check that any weak order is a semi-order.

Remark 2.20. The graphical representation of a semi-order is characterized by the fact that the four configurations depicted in Figure 2.10 are forbidden (whatever appears on the diagonal and with the possibility that two indifferent elements may be identical).

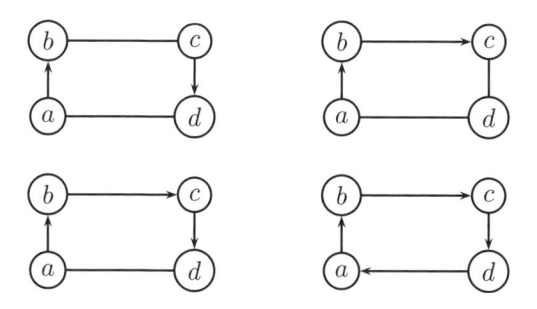

Figure 2.10. *Forbidden configurations in a semi-order*

2.5.1.2. *Weak order associated with a semi-order*

Let S is be a binary relation on A. The binary relation $S^{\pm}$ on A defined by

$$a \, S^{\pm} \, b \Leftrightarrow \left\{ \begin{array}{l} b \, S \, c \Rightarrow a \, S \, c, \\ c \, S \, a \Rightarrow c \, S \, b, \end{array} \right\} \forall c \in A$$

is called the trace of S. It is clear that the trace of a relation is always reflexive and transitive. We leave the easy proof of the following result to the reader.

Theorem 2.3. *Let S be a reflexive binary relation on A. S is a semi-order if and only if its trace $S^{\pm}$ is complete.*

Remark 2.21. When S is a semi-order, the weak order $S^{\pm}$ is obtained by ranking the elements of A according to their degree in S (i.e. number of arcs leaving a vertex minus the number of arcs entering it). One can check that a weak order is always identical to its trace.

2.5.1.3. *Matrix representation [JAC 78]*

By ordering the row and columns of the matrix representation of a semi-order, by using an order that is compatible with the trace of the relation, we obtain a matrix in which the 1s are separated from the 0s by frontiers that are stepped and located below the diagonal. This follows immediately from the definition of the trace. In contrast with what happens with weak orders, the frontier separating the 1s and the 0s does not necessarily touch the diagonal.

Example 2.5. Let $A = \{a, b, c, d, e, f\}$. Consider the preference structure $S = \{(a,a), (a,b), (a,c), (a,d), (a,e), (a,f)\ (b,a), (b,b), (b,c), (b,d), (b,e), (b,f), (c,b), (c,c), (c,d), (c,e), (c,f), (d,c), (d,d), (d,e), (d,f), (e,c), (e,d), (e,e), (e,f), (f,e), (f,f)\}$. We obtain the matric representation shown in Figure 2.11. This relation is not a weak order: we have e.g. $e\ S\ c$ and $c\ S\ b$ but $e\ \neg S\ b$.

S	a	b	c	d	e	f
a	1	1	1	1	1	1
b	1	1	1	1	1	1
c	0	1	1	1	1	1
d	0	0	1	1	1	1
e	0	0	1	1	1	1
f	0	0	0	0	1	1

Figure 2.11. *Matrix representation of a semi-order*

2.5.1.4. *Numerical representation*

Theorem 2.4. *Let A be a finite set. The following propositions are equivalent.*

1) S is a semi-order on A.

2) There is a function $g : A \to \mathbb{R}$ and a constant $q \geq 0$ such that $\forall a, b \in A$:

$$a\ S\ b \Leftrightarrow g(a) \geq g(b) - q.$$

3) There is function $g : A \to \mathbb{R}$ and a function $q : \mathbb{R} \to \mathbb{R}^+$ such that $\forall a, b \in A$:

$$g(a) > g(b) \Rightarrow g(a) + q(g(a)) \geq g(b) + q(g(b))$$

and

$$a\ S\ b \Leftrightarrow g(a) \geq g(b) - q(g(b)).$$

Proof: see [FIS 85], [PIR 97, theorem 3.1], [SCO 58] or [SUP 89, Chapter 16].

This result shows that semi-orders naturally arise when objects evaluated on a numerical scale are compared on the basis of the scale, however, differences that are less than a constant threshold are not perceived or are not considered to be significant. The threshold is not necessarily constant provided that we never have $g(a) > g(b)$ and $g(b) + q(g(b)) > g(a) + q(g(a))$. Let us observe that the generalization of this result to arbitrary sets raises delicate problems [BEJ 92, CAN 02, FIS 73, FIS 85].

Remark 2.22. Let us build the numerical representation of the semi-order for which we gave the matrix representation earlier. Having chosen an arbitrary positive value for q, e.g. $q = 1$, the function g is built associating increasing values to the elements f, e, d, c, b, a (i.e. considering the lower elements in the weak order $S^{\pm}$ first), while satisfying the desired numerical representation. In such a way, we obtain: $g(f) = 0$, $g(e) = 0.5$, $g(d) = 1.1$, $g(c) = 1.2$, $g(b) = 2.15$ and $g(a) = 3$.

Remark 2.23. The numerical representation of a semi-order is not unique. All increasing transformation applied to g gives another acceptable representation provided that the same transformation is applied to q. However, all representations of a semi-order cannot be obtained in this way as shown by the following example. The scale that is built is more complex than an ordinal scale.

Example 2.6. Let $A = \{a, b, c, d\}$. Consider the preference structure $S = \{(a, d), (a, a), (b, b), (c, c), (d, d), (a, b), (b, a), (b, c), (c, b), (b, d), (d, b), (c, d), (d, c)\}$. It is easy to check, e.g. using a matrix representation, that this structure is a semi-order. Table 2.1 gives two numerical representations of S that cannot be obtained from one another by an increasing transformation.

	a	b	c	d	threshold
g	2	1.1	1	0	1.5
g'	2	1	1	0	1.5

Table 2.1. *Two numerical representations of a semi-order*

2.5.2. Interval order

2.5.2.1. Definition

A preference structure S is an interval order if:
- S is complete; and
- S is Ferrers.

This structure generalized all structures introduced so far. As we will see later, it arises naturally when one wishes to compare intervals on an ordinal scale.

70 Decision-making Process

Remark 2.24. It is easy to check that an equivalent definition of an interval order consists of saying that S is complete and that all circuits in S have at least two consecutive I arcs.

It is easily checked that, if S is an interval order,
- P is transitive;
- P is Ferrers; and
- $P \cdot I \cdot P \subset P$.

Remark 2.25. The graphical representation of an interval order is characterized by the fact that the three configurations depicted on Figure 2.12 are forbidden (anything can appear on the diagonal).

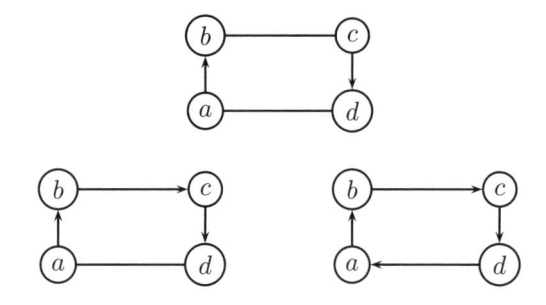

Figure 2.12. *Forbidden configurations in an interval order*

2.5.2.2. *Weak orders associated with an interval order*

Let S be a binary relation on A. Let us define a relation S^+ on A, setting

$$a\ S^+\ b \Leftrightarrow [b\ S\ c \Rightarrow a\ S\ c, \forall c \in A].$$

Similarly, we define the relation S^- setting

$$a\ S^-\ b \Leftrightarrow [c\ S\ a \Rightarrow c\ S\ b, \forall c \in A].$$

The relation S^+ (respectively S^-) is called the right trace (respectively left trace) of S. It is clear that S^+ and S^- are always reflexives and transitives.

The proof of the following result is easy and left to the reader.

Theorem 2.5. *Let S be a reflexive binary relation on A. The following three propositions are equivalent:*

1) S is an interval order;
2) S^+ is complete; and
3) S^- is complete.

Remark 2.26. When S is an interval order, the weak order S^+ (respectively S^-) can be obtained ranking the elements of A according to their out-degree (respectively in-degree) in S.

2.5.2.3. *Matrix representation*

Let us rank the rows of the matrix representation in a way that is compatible with S^+ taking care to rank indifferent elements according to S^+ using an order that is compatible with S^-. Let us perform a similar operation on the columns of the matrix, permuting the roles of S^+ and S^-. We obtain a matrix in which the 1s are separated from the 0s by a stepped frontier that is below the diagonal.

Example 2.7. Let $A = \{a, b, c, d, e, f\}$. Consider the following structure: $S = \{$ (a, a), (a, b), (a, c), (a, d), (a, e), (a, f), (b, a), (b, b), (b, c), (b, d), (b, e), (b, f), (c, b), (c, c), (c, d), (c, e), (c, f), (d, c), (d, d), (d, e), (d, f), (e, c), (e, d), (e, e), (e, f), (f, e), (f, f) $\}$.

We obtain the following matrix representation:

S	a	b	d	c	e	f
a	1	1	1	1	1	1
b	1	1	1	1	1	1
c	0	1	1	1	1	1
d	0	0	1	1	1	1
e	0	0	1	1	1	1
f	0	0	0	1	1	1

This structure is an interval order. It is not a semi-order since $f \ S \ c$ and $c \ S \ b$ but $f \ \neg S \ d$ and $d \ \neg S \ b$. It is therefore impossible to represent this structure using a stepped matrix with a similar order on rows and columns.

2.5.2.4. *Numerical representation*

The proof of the following result can be found in [PIR 97, theorem 3.11] or [FIS 85].

Theorem 2.6. *Let A be a finite set. The following propositions are equivalent:*
1) S *is an interval order on* A; *and*

2) there are two functions $g : A \to \mathbb{R}$ and $q : \mathbb{R} \to \mathbb{R}^+$ such that $\forall a, b \in A$:

$$a \, S \, b \Leftrightarrow g(a) + q(g(a)) \geq g(b).$$

We refer to [BRI 95, CHA 87, FIS 73, FIS 85, NAK 02, OLO 98] for the problems involved in generalizing this result to arbitrary sets.

Remark 2.27. For instance, it is possible to build the numerical representation of the interval order presented earlier as follows. The values of g are arbitrarily chosen provided they increase from the first to the last row of the matrix. The values of $g + q$ are then defined in such a way that they increase from the first to the last column of the matrix and they satisfy the desired representation. For instance, we successively obtain:

$$g(f) = 0, g(e) = 5, g(c) = 10, g(d) = 15, g(b) = 20, g(a) = 25,$$
$$(g+q)(f) = 12, (g+q)(e) = 17, (g+q)(d) = 19,$$
$$(g+q)(c) = 23, (g+q)(b) = 28, (g+q)(a) = 30.$$

Letting $\underline{g} = g$ and $\overline{g} = (g+q)$, it is clear that the numerical representation of an interval order amounts to associating an interval $[\underline{g}, \overline{g}]$ with each $a \in A$ such that:

$$\begin{cases} a \, P \, b \Leftrightarrow \underline{g}(a) > \overline{g}(b), \\ a \, I \, b \Leftrightarrow \begin{cases} \underline{g}(a) \leq \overline{g}(b), \\ \underline{g}(b) \leq \overline{g}(a), \end{cases} \end{cases}$$

which leads to the representation depicted in Figure 2.13.

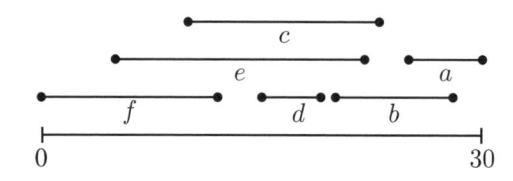

Figure 2.13. *Interval representation of an interval order*

2.5.3. *Remarks*

Remark 2.28. Interval orders may be generalized using a threshold depending on both objects compared. One then obtains a threshold representation of all relations for which the asymmetric part is acyclic [ABB 93, ABB 95, AGA 93, ALE 06, DIA 99, SUB 94]. We do not tackle such models here.

Remark 2.29. In an interval order, the relation P is transitive and hence is acyclic. For all non-empty finite subsets $B \subset A$, $C(B, S)$ is therefore always non-empty. Using one of the structures introduced in this section does not raise major problems when it comes to linking preferences and choices.

Remark 2.30. We saw that when A has a particular structure and S is a weak order, it is interesting to use such a structure to try to arrive at a numerical representation that is more constrained than an ordinal scale. These extensions make central use of the transitivity of indifference in order to build these numerical representations. It is therefore not simple to do similar things on the basis of a semi-order or an interval order [DOM 71, KRA 67, LUC 73, SUP 89].

Remark 2.31. Building a collective preference that is a semi-order or an interval order does not significantly contribute to the solution of the aggregation problem of weak orders uncovered by Arrow's theorem [SEN 86]. As soon as $|A| \geq 4$, the theorem still holds if the collective preference is required to be complete and Ferrers (or complete and semi-transitive).

2.6. Preference structures with incomparability

In all the structures envisaged so far, we assumed that S was complete. This hypothesis may seem innocuous, in particular when preferences are inferred from observed choices. It is not without problems however. Indeed, it may well happen that:

– information is poor concerning one or several of the elements of A;

– comparing elements of A implies synthesizing on several conflicting points of view; and

– the objects are not familiar to the individual.

In such cases, it may prove useful for preference modeling to use structures that explicitly include incomparability [FLA 83, ROY 85].

2.6.1. *Partial order*

A preference structure S is a partial if:
– S is reflexive;
– S is antisymmetric; and
– S is transitive.

Intuitively, a partial order is a structure in which, given two distinct objects, either object is strictly preferred to the other or the two objects are incomparable, with strict preference being transitive.

74 Decision-making Process

Remark 2.32. It is easy to check that, if S is a partial order,
- P is transitive; and
- I is limited to loops.

A fundamental result [DUS 41, FIS 85] shows that all partial orders on a finite set can be obtained intersecting a finite number of total orders on this set. The minimal number of total orders that are needed for this is called the *dimension* of the partial order. This easily implies the following result.

Theorem 2.7. *Let A be a finite set. The following propositions are equivalent:*
1) *S is a partial order on A; and*
2) *there is a function $g : A \to \mathbb{R}$ such that $\forall a, b \in A$:*

$$\begin{cases} a \, S \, b \Rightarrow g(a) \geq g(b), \\ g(a) = g(b) \Rightarrow a = b. \end{cases}$$

Example 2.8. Let $A = \{a, b, c, d, e\}$. Consider the preference structure: $S = \{ (a,a), (a,b), (a,c), (a,d), (b,b), (b,d), (b,e), (c,c), (c,e), (d,d), (d,e), (e,e) \}$. A graphical representation of this structure is depicted in Figure 2.14.

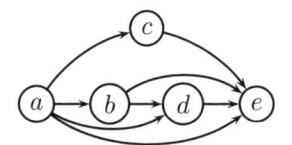

Figure 2.14. *Graphical representation of a partial order*

It is easy to check that the structure is partial order with dimension 2, obtained by intersecting the two total orders (using obvious notation):

$a > b > d > c > e$ and

$a > c > b > d > e$.

Let us note that the detection of a partial order of dimension 2 can be done in polynomial time. On the contrary, the determination of the dimension of a partial order is NP-difficult [DOI 84, FIS 85].

2.6.2. *Quasi-order*

A preference structure S is a quasi-order if:

– S is reflexive; and
– S is transitive.

Quasi-orders generalize partial orders by allowing indifference between distinct elements, the indifference relation being transitive.

Remark 2.33. It is easy to check that, if S is a quasi-order,
– P is transitive;
– I is transitive;
– $P \cdot I \subset P$; and
– $I \cdot P \subset P$.

As with partial orders, it is easy to show that any quasi-order on a finite set can be obtained intersecting a finite number of weak orders [BOS 02b, DON 98]. This implies the following result.

Theorem 2.8. *Let A be a finite set. The following propositions are equivalent:*

1) S is a quasi-order on A; and

2) there is a function $g : A \to \mathbb{R}$ such that $\forall a, b \in A$:

$$a\ S\ b \Rightarrow g(a) \geq g(b).$$

Remark 2.34. Alternatively, we can build a numerical representation of a quasi-order considering a set of numerical representations of weak orders [OK 02].

Example 2.9. Let $A = \{a, b, c, d, e, f\}$. Consider the preference structure $S=\{(a,a), (a,b), (a,c), (a,d), (a,e), (a,f)\ (b,b), (b,d), (b,e), (b,f), (c,c), (c,e), (c,f), (d,b), (d,d), (d,e), (d,f), (e,e), (e,f), (f,e), (f,f)\}$. It is easy to check that this is a quasi-order. Its graphical representation is depicted in Figure 2.15.

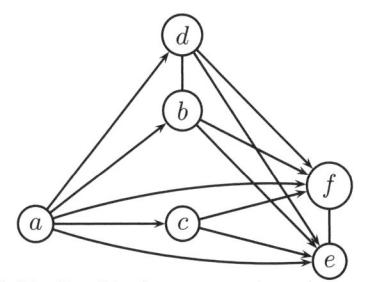

Figure 2.15. *Graphical representation of a quasi-order*

Remark 2.35. It is possible to extend classical models of decision under risk to deal with quasi-orders [AUM 62, FIS 70]. The multi-attribute case was only studied in the finite case [FIS 70, SCO 64]. Let us also mention that allowing for incomparability in the collective preference does not significantly contribute to the solution of the problem uncovered by Arrow's theorem [WEY 84].

Remark 2.36. Roubens and Vincke [ROU 85] proposed definitions of partial semi-orders and interval orders. They allow an intransitive indifference relation at the same time as incomparability situations. We do not detail this point here.

2.6.3. *Synthesis*

We summarize in Table 2.2 the properties of preference structures that have been introduced so far.

Structures	Definition
Total order	S complete S antisymmetric S transitive
Weak order	S complete S transitive
Semi-order	S complete S Ferrers S semi-transitive
Interval order	S complete S Ferrers
Partial order	S reflexive S antisymmetric S transitive
Quasi-order	S reflexive S transitive

Table 2.2. *Common preference structures*

2.7. Conclusion

2.7.1. *Other preference structures*

In all the structures introduced so far, the relation P was transitive and, hence, was acyclic. This seems a natural hypothesis. Abandoning it implies reconsidering the links existing between 'preference' and 'choice' as we already saw. Nevertheless, it is possible to obtain such preferences in experiments [MAY 54, TVE 69] when subjects are asked to compare objects evaluated on several dimensions. They are also common in social choice due to Condorcet's paradox. Indeed, a famous result [MCG 53] shows that with a simple majority, any complete preference structure can be be obtained as the result of the aggregation of individual weak orders. With other aggregation methods, all preference structures may occur [BOU 96].

The literature on Social Choice abounds with studies of adequate choice procedure on the basis of such preferences. The particular case of *tournaments* (complete and antisymmetric relations) have been explored in depth [LAS 97, MOU 86].

More recently, it was shown that it is possible to build numerical representations of such relations [BOU 86, BOU 99, BOU 02, FIS 82, FIS 88, FIS 91b, FIS 91a, FIS 92, TVE 69, VIN 91]. In the models proposed in [BOU 02], we have sets A being Cartesian products (as in decision under uncertainty or in decision with multiple attributes):

$$a \; S \; b \Leftrightarrow F(p_1(a_1, b_1), p_2(a_2, b_2), \ldots, p_n(a_n, b_n)) \geq 0$$

where p_i are functions from A_i^2 to $\mathbb{R}$, F is a function from $\prod_{i=1}^n p_i(A_i^2)$ to $\mathbb{R}$ and where, for example, F can be increasing in all its arguments. This model generalizes the classical additive difference model proposed in [TVE 69] in which:

$$a \; S \; b \Leftrightarrow \sum_{i=1}^n \varphi_i(u_i(a_i) - u_i(b_i)) \geq 0$$

where u_i are functions from A_i to $\mathbb{R}$ and φ_i are odd increasing functions on $\mathbb{R}$.

Similarly, in the models studied in [FIS 82, FIS 88] for the case of decision-making under risk, the numerical representation is such that:

$$a \; S \; b \Leftrightarrow \sum_{c \in C} \sum_{c' \in C} p_a(c) p_b(c') \phi(c, c') \geq 0$$

where ϕ is a function from C^2 to $\mathbb{R}$ and $p_a(c)$ is the probability to obtain the consequence $c \in C$ with object a.

A common criticism of such models is that cycles leave the door open to apparently 'irrational' behavior and make an individual vulnerable to Dutch books [RAI 70]. As in the case of decision under risk mentioned earlier, it is not clear that the arguments are actually convincing [FIS 91a].

2.7.2. *Other problems*

This brief survey of classical preference structures used in preference modeling will hopefully give the reader enough clues to tackle a vast and complex literature. This chapter has neglected many important questions, including:

– the question of the approximation of preference structure by another one, e.g. the search for a total order at minimal distance of a tournament [BAR 89, BAR 81, BER 72, CHA 92, HUD 96, MON 79, SLA 61];

– the way to collect and validate preference information in a given context [WIN 86];

– the links between preference modeling and the question of meaningfulness in measurement theory [ROB 79];

– the statistical analysis of preference data [COO 64, GRE 88]; and

– deeper questions on the links between value systems and preferences [BRO 91, COW 88, TSO 92, WRI 63].

2.8. Bibliography

[ABB 93] ABBAS M., VINCKE PH., "Preference structures and threshold models", *Journal of Multicriteria Decision Analysis*, vol. 2, p. 171–178, 1993.

[ABB 95] ABBAS M., "Any complete preference structure without circuit admits an interval representation", *Theory and Decision*, vol. 39, p. 115–126, 1995.

[AGA 93] AGAEV R., ALESKEROV F., "Interval choice: classic and general cases", *Mathematical Social Sciences*, vol. 26, p. 249–272, 1993.

[ALE 06] ALESKEROV F., BOUYSSOU D., MONJARDET B., *Utility Maximization, Choice and Preference*, Springer-Verlag, Heidelberg, 2nd edition, 2006.

[ALL 53] ALLAIS M., "Le comportement de l'homme rationnel devant le risque: critique des postulats et axiomes de l'école américaine", *Econometrica*, vol. 21, p. 503–46, 1953.

[ARR 63] ARROW K. J., *Social Choice and Individual Values*, Wiley, New York, 2nd edition, 1963.

[AUM 62] AUMANN R. J., "Utility theory without the completeness axiom", *Econometrica*, vol. 30, p. 445–462, 1962, Correction: Econometrica, 1964, vol. 32, 1–2.

[BAR 81] BARTHÉLÉMY J.-P., MONJARDET B., "The median procedure in cluster analysis and social choice theory", *Mathematical Social Sciences*, p. 235–267, 1981.

[BAR 89] BARTHÉLÉMY J.-P., GUÉNOCHE A., HUDRY O., "Median linear orders: heuristics and a branch and bound algorithm", *European Journal of Operational Research*, p. 313–325, 1989.

[BEA 02] BEARDON A. F., CANDEAL J. C., HERDEN G., INDURÁIN E., MEHTA G. B., "The non-existence of a utility function and the structure of non-representable preference relations", *Journal of Mathematical Economics*, vol. 37, p. 17–38, 2002.

[BEJ 92] BEJA A., GILBOA I., "Numerical representations of imperfectly ordered preferences (A unified geometric exposition)", *Journal of Mathematical Psychology*, vol. 36, p. 426–449, 1992.

[BEL 88] BELL D. E., RAIFFA H., TVERSKY A., "Descriptive, normative, and prescriptive interactions in decision making", BELL D. E., RAIFFA H., TVERSKY A., Eds., *Decision Making: Descriptive, Normative, and Prescriptive Interactions in Decision Making*, Cambridge University Press, p. 9–32, 1988.

[BER 72] BERMOND J.-C., "Ordres à distance minimum d'un tournoi et graphes partiels sans circuits maximaux", *Mathématiques et Sciences Humaines*, vol. 37, p. 5–25, 1972.

[BER 75] BERGSTROM T. X., "Maximal elements of acyclic relations on compact sets", *Journal of Economic Theory*, vol. 10, p. 403–404, 1975.

[BOS 02a] BOSI G., MEHTA G. B., "Existence of a semicontinuous or continuous utility function: a unified approach and an elementary proof", *Journal of Mathematical Economics*, vol. 38, p. 311–328, 2002.

[BOS 02b] BOSSERT W., SPRUMONT Y., SUZUMURA K., "Upper semicontinuous extensions of binary relations", *Journal of Mathematical Economics*, vol. 37, p. 231–246, 2002.

[BOU 86] BOUYSSOU D., "Some remarks on the notion of compensation in MCDM", *European Journal of Operational Research*, vol. 26, p. 150–160, 1986.

[BOU 96] BOUYSSOU D., "Outranking relations: do they have special properties?", *Journal of Multiple Criteria Decision Analysis*, vol. 5, p. 99–111, 1996.

[BOU 99] BOUYSSOU D., PIRLOT M., "Conjoint measurement without additivity and transitivity", MESKENS N., ROUBENS M., Eds., *Advances in Decision Analysis*, Dordrecht, Kluwer, p. 13–29, 1999.

[BOU 02] BOUYSSOU D., PIRLOT M., "Non-transitive decomposable conjoint measurement", *Journal of Mathematical Psychology*, vol. 46, p. 677–703, 2002.

[BRI 95] BRIDGES D. S., MEHTA G. B., *Representations of Preference Orderings*, Springer-Verlag, Berlin, 1995.

[BRO 91] BROOME J., *Weighting Goods*, Basil Blackwell, London, 1991.

[CAM 02] CAMPBELL D. E., KELLY J. S., "Impossibility theorems in the Arrovian framework", ARROW K. J., SEN A. K., SUZUMURA K., Eds., *Handbook of Social Choice and Welfare*, vol. 1, p. 35–94, North-Holland, Amsterdam, 2002.

[CAN 02] CANDEAL J. C., INDURÁIN E., ZUDAIRE M., "Numerical representability of semiorders", *Mathematical Social Sciences*, vol. 43, p. 61–77, 2002.

[CHA 87] CHATEAUNEUF A., "Continuous representation of a preference relation on a connected topological space", *Journal Mathematical Economics*, vol. 16, p. 139–146, 1987.

[CHA 92] CHARON-FOURNIER I., GERMA A., HUDRY O., "Utilisation des scores dans des méthodes exactes déterminant les ordres médians des tournois", *Mathématiques, Informatique et Sciences Humaines*, vol. 119, p. 53–74, 1992.

[COO 64] COOMBS C. H., *A Theory of Data*, Wiley, New York, 1964.

[COS 94] BANA E COSTA C. A., VANSNICK J.-C., "MACBETH: An interactive path towards the construction of cardinal value functions", *International Transactions in Operational Research*, vol. 1, num. 4, p. 489–500, 1994.

[COW 88] COWAN T. A., FISHBURN P. C., "Foundations of preference", EBERLEIN G., BERGHEL H., Eds., *Essays in Honor of Werner Leinfellner*, Dordrecht, D. Reidel, p. 261–271, 1988.

[DEB 54] DEBREU G., "Representation of a preference ordering by a numerical function", THRALL R., COOMBS C., DAVIES R., Eds., *Decision Processes*, New York, Wiley, p. 159–175, 1954.

[DEB 59] DEBREU G., *Theory of Value: An Axiomatic Analysis of Economic Equilibrium*, John Wiley & Sons Inc., New York, 1959.

[DIA 99] DIAYE M.-A., "Variable interval models", *Mathematical Social Sciences*, vol. 38, p. 21–33, 1999.

[DOI 84] DOIGNON J.-P., DUCAMP A., FALMAGNE J.-C., "On realizable biorders and the biorder dimension of a relation", *Journal of Mathematical Psychology*, vol. 28, p. 73–109, 1984.

[DOI 86] DOIGNON J.-P., MONJARDET B., ROUBENS M., VINCKE PH., "Biorder families, valued relations and preference modelling", *Journal of Mathematical Psychology*, vol. 30, num. 4, p. 435–480, 1986.

[DOI 87] DOIGNON J.-P., "Threshold representation of multiple semiorders", *SIAM Journal on Algebraic and Discrete Methods*, vol. 8, p. 77–84, 1987.

[DOM 71] DOMOTOR Z., STELZER J., "Representation of finitely additive semi-ordered qualitative probability structures", *Journal of Mathematical Psychology*, vol. 8, p. 145–168, 1971.

[DON 98] DONALDSON D., WEYMARK J. A., "A quasiordering is the intersection of orderings", *Journal of Economic Theory*, vol. 78, p. 382–387, 1998.

[DOY 92] DOYLE J., WELLMAN M., "Modular utility representation for decision-theoretic planning", *Proceedings of the First International Conference on Artificial Intelligence Planning Systems*, p. 236–242, 1992.

[DUB 01] DUBOIS D., PRADE H., SABBADIN R., "Decision-theoretic foundations of qualitative possibility theory", *European Journal of Operational Research*, vol. 128, p. 459–78, 2001.

[DUS 41] DUSHNIK B., MILLER E., "Partially ordered sets", *American Journal of Mathematics*, vol. 63, p. 600–610, 1941.

[ELL 61] ELLSBERG D., "Risk, ambiguity and the Savage axioms", *Quarterly Journal of Economics*, vol. 75, p. 643–669, 1961.

[FIS 70] FISHBURN P. C., *Utility Theory for Decision-making*, Wiley, New York, 1970.

[FIS 73] FISHBURN P. C., "Interval representations for interval orders and semiorders", *Journal of Mathematical Psychology*, vol. 10, p. 91–105, 1973.

[FIS 82] FISHBURN P. C., "Nontransitive measurable utility", *Journal of Mathematical Psychology*, vol. 26, p. 31–67, 1982.

[FIS 85] FISHBURN P. C., *Interval Orders and Intervals Graphs*, Wiley, New York, 1985.

[FIS 88] FISHBURN P. C., *Nonlinear Preference and Utility Theory*, Johns Hopkins University Press, Baltimore, 1988.

[FIS 91a] FISHBURN P. C., "Non-transitive preferences in decision theory", *Journal of Risk and Uncertainty*, vol. 4, p. 113–134, 1991.

[FIS 91b] FISHBURN P. C., "Nontransitive additive conjoint measurement", *Journal of Mathematical Psychology*, vol. 35, p. 1–40, 1991.

[FIS 92] FISHBURN P. C., "Additive differences and simple preference comparisons", *Journal of Mathematical Psychology*, vol. 36, p. 21–31, 1992.

[FLA 83] FLAMENT C., "On incomplete preference structures", *Mathematical Social Sciences*, vol. 5, p. 61–72, 1983.

[FOD 94] FODOR J., ROUBENS M., *Fuzzy Preference Modelling and Multiple Criteria Decision Support*, Kluwer, Dordrecht, 1994.

[GIL 87] GILBOA I., "Expected utility with purely subjective non-additive probabilities", *Journal of Mathematical Economics*, vol. 16, p. 65–68, 1987.

[GIL 89] GILBOA I., SCHMEIDLER D., "Maxmin expected utility with a non-unique prior", *Journal of Mathematical Economics*, vol. 18, p. 141–153, 1989.

[GRE 88] GREEN P. E., TULL D. S., ALBAUM G., *Research for Marketing Decisions*, Prentice Hall, Englewood Cliffs, NJ, 1988.

[HUD 96] HUDRY O., WOIRGARD F., "Ordres médians et ordres de Slater des tournois", *Mathématiques, Informatique et Sciences Humaines*, vol. 133, p. 23–56, 1996.

[JAC 78] JACQUET-LAGRÈZE É., "Représentation de quasi-ordres et de relations probabilistes transitives sous forme standard et méthodes d'approximation", *Mathématiques et Sciences Humaines*, vol. 63, p. 5–25, 1978.

[JAF 75] JAFFRAY J.-Y., "Existence of a continuous utility function: an elementary proof", *Econometrica*, vol. 43, p. 981–983, 1975.

[KAH 79] KAHNEMAN D., TVERSKY A., "Prospect theory: an analysis of decision under risk", *Econometrica*, vol. 47, p. 263–291, 1979.

[KAH 81] KAHNEMAN D., SLOVIC P., TVERSKY A., *Judgement Under Uncertainty: Heuristics and Biases*, Cambridge University Press, Cambridge, 1981.

[KEE 76] KEENEY R. L., RAIFFA H., *Decisions with Multiple Objectives: Preferences and Value Tradeoffs*, Wiley, New York, 1976.

[KRA 67] KRANTZ D. H., "Extensive measurement in semiorders", *Philosophy of Science*, vol. 34, p. 348–362, 1967.

[KRA 71] KRANTZ D. H., LUCE R. D., SUPPES P., TVERSKY A., *Foundations of Measurement*, vol. 1: Additive and polynomial representations, Academic Press, New York, 1971.

[LAS 97] LASLIER J.-F., *Tournament Solutions and Majority Voting*, Springer-Verlag, Berlin, 1997.

[LUC 56] LUCE R. D., "Semi-orders and a theory of utility discrimination", *Econometrica*, vol. 24, p. 178–191, 1956.

[LUC 73] LUCE R. D., "Three axiom systems for additive semiordered structures", *SIAM Journal of Applied Mathematics*, vol. 25, p. 41–53, 1973.

[MAC 82] MACHINA M. J., "Expected utility without the independence axiom", *Econometrica*, vol. 50, p. 277–323, 1982.

[MAC 89] MACHINA M. J., "Dynamic consistency and non-expected utility models of choice under uncertainty", *Journal of Economic Literature*, vol. 27, p. 1622–1688, 1989.

[MAL 93] MALISHEVSKI A. V., "Criteria for judging the rationality of decisions in the presence of vague alternatives", *Mathematical Social Sciences*, vol. 26, p. 205–247, 1993.

[MAY 54] MAY K. O., "Intransitivity, utility and the aggregation of preference patterns", *Econometrica*, vol. 22, p. 1–13, 1954.

[MCC 79] MCCRIMMON K. R., LARSSON S., "Utility theory: Axioms versus paradoxes", ALLAIS M., HAGEN O., Eds., *Expected Utility Hypotheses and the Allais Paradox*, Dordrecht, D. Reidel, p. 27–145, 1979.

[MCC 90] MCCLENNEN E. L., *Rationality and Dynamic Choice: Foundational Explorations*, Cambridge University Press, 1990.

[MCG 53] MCGARVEY D. C., "A theorem on the construction of voting paradoxes", *Econometrica*, vol. 21, p. 608–610, 1953.

[MON 79] MONJARDET B., "Relations à éloignement minimum de relations binaires: note bibliographique", *Mathématiques, Informatique et Sciences Humaines*, vol. 67, p. 115–122, 1979.

[MOU 86] MOULIN H., "Choosing from a tournament", *Social Choice and Welfare*, vol. 3, p. 271–291, 1986.

[NAK 02] NAKAMURA Y., "Real interval representations", *Journal of Mathematical Psychology*, vol. 46, p. 140–177, 2002.

[OK 02] OK E. A., "Utility representation of an incomplete preference relation", *Journal of Economic Theory*, vol. 104, p. 429–449, 2002.

[OLO 98] OLORIZ E., CANDEAL J. C., INDURÁIN E., "Representability of interval orders", *Journal of Economic Theory*, vol. 78, p. 219–227, 1998.

[PER 92] PERNY P., ROY B., "The use of fuzzy outranking relations in preference modelling", *Fuzzy Sets and Systems*, vol. 49, p. 33–53, 1992.

[PIR 97] PIRLOT M., VINCKE PH., *Semiorders. Properties, Representations, Applications*, Kluwer, Dordrecht, 1997.

[QUI 82] QUIGGIN J., "A theory of anticipated utility", *Journal of Economic Behaviour and Organization*, vol. 3, p. 323–343, 1982.

[QUI 93] QUIGGIN J., *Generalized Expected Utility Theory: The Rank-dependent Model*, Kluwer, Dordrecht, 1993.

[RAI 70] RAIFFA H., *Decision Analysis: Introductory Lectures on Choices under Uncertainty*, Addison-Wesley, Reading, 1970.

[ROB 79] ROBERTS F. S., *Measurement Theory with Applications to Decision Making, Utility and the Social Sciences*, Addison-Wesley, Reading, 1979.

[ROU 85] ROUBENS M., VINCKE PH., *Preference Modelling*, Springer Verlag, Berlin, 1985.

[ROY 85] ROY B., *Méthodologie Multicritère d'aide à la Décision*, Economica, Paris, 1985.

[ROY 87] ROY B., VINCKE PH., "Pseudo-orders: Definition, properties and numerical representation", *Mathematical Social Sciences*, vol. 14, p. 263–274, 1987.

[SAV 54] SAVAGE L. J., *The Foundations of Statistics*, Wiley, New York, 1972, 2nd revised edition, 1954.

[SCH 86] SCHWARTZ T., *The Logic of Collectice Choice*, Columbia University Press, 1986.

[SCH 89] SCHMEIDLER D., "Subjective probability and expected utility without additivity", *Econometrica*, vol. 57, p. 571–587, 1989.

[SCO 58] SCOTT D., SUPPES P., "Foundational aspects of theories of measurement", *Journal of Symbolic Logic*, vol. 23, p. 113–128, 1958.

[SCO 64] SCOTT D., "Measurement structures and linear inequalities", *Journal of Mathematical Psychology*, vol. 1, p. 233–247, 1964.

[SEN 70] SEN A. K., *Collective Choice and Social Welfare*, Holden Day, San Francisco, 1970.

[SEN 77] SEN A. K., "Social choice theory: a re-examination", *Econometrica*, vol. 45, p. 53–89, 1977.

[SEN 86] SEN A. K., "Social choice theory", ARROW K. J., INTRILIGATOR M. D., Eds., *Handbook of Mathematical Economics*, vol. 3, p. 1073–1181, North-Holland, Amsterdam, 1986.

[SEN 93] SEN A. K., "Internal consistency of choice", *Econometrica*, vol. 61, p. 495–521, 1993.

[SLA 61] SLATER P., "Inconsistencies in a schedule of paired comparisons", *Biometrika*, vol. 48, p. 303–312, 1961.

[SUB 94] SUBIZA B., "Numerical representation of acyclic preferences", *Journal of Mathematical Psychology*, vol. 38, p. 467–476, 1994.

[SUG 85] SUGDEN R., "Why be consistent? A critical analysis of consistency requirements in choice theory", *Economica*, vol. 52, p. 167–183, 1985.

[SUP 89] SUPPES P., KRANTZ D. H., LUCE R. D., TVERSKY A., *Foundations of Measurement*, vol. 2: Geometrical, threshold, and probabilistic representations, Academic Press, New York, 1989.

[TSO 92] TSOUKIÀS A., VINCKE PH., "A survey on nonconventional preference modelling", *Ricerca Operativa*, vol. 61, p. 5–49, 1992.

[TSO 95] TSOUKIÀS A., VINCKE PH., "A new axiomatic foundation of partial comparability", *Theory and Decision*, vol. 39, p. 79–114, 1995.

[TSO 97] TSOUKIÀS A., VINCKE PH., "Extended preference structures in MCDA", CLÍMACO J., Ed., *Multicriteria Analysis*, p. 37–50, Springer-Verlag, Berlin, 1997.

[TVE 69] TVERSKY A., "Intransitivity of preferences", *Psychological Review*, vol. 76, p. 31–48, 1969.

[VIN 91] VIND K., "Independent preferences", *Journal of Mathematical Economics*, vol. 20, p. 119–135, 1991.

[WAK 89] WAKKER P. P., *Additive Representations of Preferences: A New Foundation of Decision Analysis*, Kluwer, Dordrecht, 1989.

[WEY 84] WEYMARK J. A., "Arrow's theorem with quasi-orderings", *Public Choice*, vol. 42, p. 235–246, 1984.

[WIN 86] VON WINTERFELDT D., EDWARDS W., *Decision Analysis and Behavioral Research*, Cambridge University Press, Cambridge, 1986.

[WRI 63] VON WRIGHT G. H., *The Logic of Preference*, Edinburgh University Press, Edinburgh, 1963.

[YAA 87] YAARI M. E., "The dual theory of choice under risk", *Econometrica*, vol. 55, p. 95–115, 1987.

Chapter 3

Formal Representations of Uncertainty

3.1. Introduction

The recent development of uncertainty theories that account for the notion of belief is linked to the emergence, in the 20th century, of decision theory and artificial intelligence (AI). Nevertheless, this topic was dealt with very differently by each area. Decision theory insisted on the necessity to found representations on the empirical observation of individuals choosing between courses of action, regardless of any other type of information. Any axiom in the theory should be liable to empirical validation. Probabilistic representations of uncertainty can then be justified with a subjectivist point of view, without necessary reference to frequency. Degrees of probability then evaluate to what extent an agent believes in the occurrence of an event or in the truth of a proposition. In contrast, AI adopted a more introspective approach aiming at formalizing intuitions and reasoning processes through the statement of reasonable axioms, often without reference to probability. Until the 1990s, AI essentially focused on purely qualitative and ordinal (in fact, logical) representations.

Historically, the interest in formalizing uncertainty began in the middle of the 17th century, involving scholars such as Pascal, Fermat, Huyghens, the chevalier de Méré and Jacob Bernoulli. Two distinct notions were laid bare and studied: the objective notion of chance, related to the analysis of games, and the subjective notion of probability in connection with the issue of the reliability of witnesses in legal matters. In pioneering works such as those of Bernoulli, chances were quickly related to the evaluation of frequency and were therefore naturally additive. However, probabilities were not considered so in the first stand.

Chapter written by Didier DUBOIS and Henri PRADE.

However, with the fast developments of hard sciences in the 18th century, the interest in the subjective side of probability waned and the additive side of probability became prominent; so much so that some late works on non-additive probabilities (for instance, those of Lambert) became unpalatable to other contemporaneous scholars [SHA 78]. From then on, under the influence of Laplace and for a long times, probabilities would be additive whether frequentist or not. It was therefore very natural that in the 20th century, pioneering proposals formalizing probability independently from frequency [DEF 37, RAM 80] tried to justify the additivity axiom, especially in the framework of a theory of gambles for economic decision problems.

The rise of computer and information sciences in the last part of the 20th century renewed the interest for human knowledge representation and reasoning. The latter is often tainted with imprecision, uncertainty and contradiction. These new fields were developed independently of progress made in probability and decision theories. They focused on qualitative logical formalisms (especially in AI), as well as the representation of the gradual nature of linguistic information (especially fuzzy set theory). This trend has also triggered the revival of non-additive probabilities for modeling uncertainty, a revival already pioneered by the works of Good [GOO 62], Smith [SMI 61], Shackle [SHA 61], Dempster [DEM 67], Kyburg [KYB 74] and Shafer [SHA 76].

In addition, the logic school rediscovered ancient modal concepts of possibility and necessity, quite relevant for epistemic issues, introduced by Aristotle and exploited by medieval religious philosophy. At the heart of the logical approach, the idea of incomplete knowledge is basic and comes close to issues in imprecise probability (as opposed to the use of a unique probability distribution advocated by the Bayesian school). In the imprecise probability view, possibility and necessity respectively formalize subjective plausibility and certainty by means of upper and lower probability bounds. Such non-classical incertainty functions appeared independently within decision theory itself. This was due to the questioning of the empirical validity of Savage's postulates underlying expected utility theory [SCH 89], after observing systematic violations of some of these postulates.

The gap created in the early 20th century between logicians (mainly interested by the foundation of mathematics) and statisticians is now reducing. To date, logic in its classical and non-classical versions (modal, non-monotonic, probabilistic and possibilistic) is again considered as a formal tool for the representation of human knowledge and the mechanization of reasoning processes; it is no longer confined to metamathematics.

It therefore sounds more natural to propose that, when statistical data is missing, the probabilistic knowledge possessed by an individual be represented by a set of logical propositions each having its probability, rather than by a probability distribution over an exhaustive set of mutually exclusive elements. However, the former representation generally characterizes a family of probability functions and not a unique distribution. This logical view of probability is present in the 19th century in the works of Boole [BOO 58] whose magnum opus *The Laws of Thought* laid the formal foundations of probabilistic logic at least as much as those of classical logic. In addition, AI and cognitive psychology share the concern of studying the laws of thought (even if with totally different goals).

The aim of this chapter is to propose a unified overview of various approaches to representations of uncertainty which have come to light during the last 50 years or so in the areas of AI and decision theory. The focus is on ideas and intuitions rather than on mathematical details. It is pointed out that apart from the central issue of belief representation, other aspects of the imperfection of information are currently studied for their own sake, such as the non-Boolean nature of linguistic predicates and the concept of granularity.

This chapter is organized as follows. Section 3.2 considers the notion of information in its semantic side and proposes a typology of defects of information items possessed by a cognitive entity (a human agent or a computer). Section 3.3 recalls some basics of probability theory, which in any case stands as a landmark. Injecting incomplete information into probability theory leads to a hierarchy of representations involving convex sets of probabilities, including Shafer's theory of evidence [SHA 76] and the numerical variant of possibility theory [DUB 88a, DUB 00].

These approaches are reviewed in section 3.4, which also discusses bridges between possibility and probability. It is shown that some results and methods in non-Bayesian statistics can be reinterpreted and systematized in possibility theory, such as the maximum likelihood principle and confidence intervals. Moreover, the insufficient reason principle of Laplace can be extended to derive a probability measure from a possibility measure, or conversely in order to justify possibility distributions as cautious substitutes of subjective probability distributions.

Section 3.5 presents ordinal and logical representations of uncertainty. Qualitative possibility theory [DUB 98b] is tailored to handle incomplete information and is shown to stand as the simplest among ordinal approaches to uncertainty.

Section 3.6 discusses the important notion of conditioning in uncertainty theories, using the key concept of conditional events as a guideline. The bottom line is that, in probability theory, Bayesian conditioning is a unique tool instrumental for several distinct problems, but each problem requires a specific conditioning tool in the non-additive frameworks.

Finally, section 3.7 deals with uncertain fusion information and shows that the framework of uncertainty theories leaving room to incompleteness leads to a reconciliation of probabilistic fusion modes (based on averaging) and logical modes (based on conjunction and disjunction).

3.2. Information: a typology of defects

The term *information* refers to any collection of symbols or signs, produced either through the observation of natural or artificial phenomena or by cognitive human activity, with a view to helping an agent understand the world or the current situation, make decisions or communicate with other human or artificial agents. In this section we focus on the mathematical representation of information items. We draw several important distinctions in order to charter this area.

A first distinction separates on the one hand so-called *objective* information, stemming from sensor measurements and the direct perception of events, and on the other hand *subjective* information typically uttered by individuals (e.g. testimonies) or conceived without resorting to direct observations.

Another distinction is between *quantitative* information modeled in terms of numbers, typically objective information (sensor measurements, from the direct perception of events or from subjective information) and *qualitative* or symbolic information (typically subjective information, e.g. expressed in natural language). Nevertheless, this partition is not as strict as it looks: subjective information can be numerical and objective information can be qualitative (e.g. a color identified by means of a symbolic sensor). Quantitative information can assume various formats: numbers, intervals and functions. Structured symbolic information is often encoded in logical or graphical representations. There are hybrid representations such as weighted logics or probabilistic networks.

Yet another very important distinction must be drawn between singular and generic information. *Singular* information refers to a particular situation or a response to a question on the current state of affairs: e.g. an observation (a patient has fever at a given time point) or a testimony (the crazy driver's car was blue). *Generic* information refers to a collection or a population of situations; it could be a physical law, a statistical model built from a representative sample of observations or a piece of commonsense knowledge such as 'birds fly'. This distinction is important when considering problems of inference or revision of uncertain information. Moreover, topics such as induction or learning processes deal with the construction of generic knowledge from several items of singular information. Conversely, statistical prediction can be viewed as the use of some piece of generic knowledge on the frequency of an event to derive a degree of belief in the singular occurrence of this event in a specific situation [HAC 75].

An agent is assumed to have some information about the current world. The *epistemic state* of the agent is assumed to be made of three components: generic knowledge, singular observations and beliefs [DUB 04a]. Beliefs are understood as pertaining to the current situation. They are singular and derived from the two former kinds of information. They are instrumental in making decisions. Decision making involves another kind of information possessed by an agent which this chapter does not deal with: preferences.

In order to represent the epistemic state of an agent, a representation of the state of the world is needed in agreement with the point of view of this agent, i.e. highlighting the relevant aspects by means of suitable attributes. Let v be the vector of attributes relevant to the agent and S the domain of v. S is called a *frame*; it is the set of (descriptions of) all states of the world. A subset A of S, viewed as a disjunction of possible worlds, is called an *event* and is seen as a proposition that asserts $v \in A$. It is not assumed that the set S be explicitly known as a primitive object. It can also be reconstructed, at least partially, from pieces of information supplied by the agent in the form of asserted propositions.

Four kinds of qualification of the imperfection of pieces of information expressible on the frame S can be considered: incomplete (or yet imprecise), uncertain, gradual and granular information.

3.2.1. *Incompleteness and imprecision*

A piece of information is said to be *incomplete* in a given context if it is not sufficient to allow the agent to answer a relevant question in this context. We interpret imprecision as a form of incompleteness, in the sense that an imprecise response provides only incomplete information. The kind of question which the agent tries to answer is of the form 'what is the current value of some quantity v?' or, more generally, 'does v satisfy some property of interest?' The notion of imprecision is not an absolute one. For instance, if the quantity of concern is the age of a person, the term *minor* is precise if the proper frame is $S = \{minor, major\}$ and the question of interest is 'can the person vote?' On the contrary, if $S = \{0, 1, \ldots, 150\}$ (in years), the term *minor* is imprecise; it provides incomplete information if the question of interest is the date of birth of the person.

The typical form of a piece of incomplete information is $v \in A$ where A is a subset of S containing more than one element. An important remark is that elements in A seen as possible values of v are mutually exclusive (since the quantity takes on a single value). Hence, a piece of imprecise information takes the form of a disjunction of mutually exclusive values. For instance, to say that 'Pierre is between 20 and 25 years old' i.e. $v = $ age(Pierre) $\in \{20, 21, 22, 23, 24, 25\}$ is to suppose $v = 20$ or $v = 21$ or $v = 22$ or $v = 23$ or $v = 24$ or $v = 25$. In classical logic, incompleteness explicitly appears as a disjunction. Asserting the truth of $p \vee q$ means that one of the following propositions $p \wedge q$, $p \wedge \neg q$ or $\neg p \wedge q$ is true. More generally, one of the models of $p \vee q$ is true.

A set used for representing a piece of incomplete information is called a *disjunctive set*. It contrasts with the conjunctive view of a set considered as a collection of elements. A conjunctive set represents a precise piece of information. For instance, consider the quantity $v = sisters(Pierre)$ whose range is the set of subsets of possible names for Pierre's sisters. The piece of information $v = \{Marie, Sylvie\}$ is precise and means that Pierre's sisters are Marie *and* Sylvie. Indeed, the frame is then $S = 2^{NAMES}$, where $NAMES$ is the set of all female first names. In this setting, a piece of incomplete information would be encoded as a disjunction of conjunctive subsets of $NAMES$.

A piece of incomplete information defines a so-called *possibility distribution* on S. If the available information is of the form $v \in A$, it means that any value of v not in A is considered impossible, but any value of v in the set A is possible. The possibility distribution encoding the piece of information $v \in A$, denoted by π_v, is the characteristic function of A. It is a mapping from S to $\{0, 1\}$ such that $\pi_v(s) = 1$ if $s \in A$, and 0 otherwise. Conventions for $\pi_v(s)$ are therefore 1 for *possible* and 0 for *impossible*.

In the possibilistic framework, extreme forms of partial knowledge can be captured:
– complete knowledge: for some state $s_0, \pi_v(s_0) = 1$ and $\pi_v(s) = 0$ for other states s (only s_0 is possible); and
– complete ignorance: $\pi_v(s) = 1, \forall s \in S$ (all states are totally possible).

Two pieces of incomplete information can be compared in terms of information content: a piece of information $v \in A_1$ is said to be *more specific* than a piece of information $v \in A_2$ if and only if A_1 is a proper subset of A_2. In terms of respective possibility distributions, say π_1 for $v \in A_1$ and π_2 for $v \in A_2$, it corresponds to the inequality $\pi_1 < \pi_2$. Note that a possibility distribution always contains some subjectivity in the sense that it represents information possessed by an agent at a given time point, i.e. it reflects an epistemic state. This information is likely to evolve upon the arrival of new pieces of information; in particular, it often becomes more specific. The acquisition of a new piece of information comes down to deleting possible values of v. If $v \in A_1$ is more specific than $v \in A_2$, the first epistemic state is accessible from the second one by the acquisition of new information of the same type.

Given a collection of pieces of incomplete information of the form $\{v \in A_i : i = 1, \ldots, n\}$, the least arbitrary possibility distribution that represents this collection is the least specific disjunctive set among those that are compatible with each piece of information $v \in A_i$, i.e. $v \in \cap_{i=1,\ldots,n} A_i$. It corresponds to computing the possibility distribution $\pi_v = \min_{i=1,\ldots,n} \pi_i$. These notions lie at the roots of possibility theory [DUB 88a, ZAD 78] in its Boolean version.

This type of representation of incomplete information can be found in two areas: classical logic and interval analysis. In both settings, either logic or interval analysis, the kind of information represented is the same. What differs is the type of variable used to describe the state space S: Boolean in the first case and numerical in the second case.

In propositional logic, a collection of information items is a set K, often called belief base, of Boolean propositions p_i expressed by well-formed formulae by means of literals and connectives. Given n Boolean variables with domain $\{true, false\}$, then $S = \{true, false\}^n$ is made of 2^n elements called *interpretations*. They are maximal conjunctions of literals, which is equivalent to assigning a value in $\{true, false\}$ to each variable. Models of K form a disjunctive subset of S containing all interpretations that make all propositions in K true. K is then understood as the conjunction of propositions p_i. If models of p_i form the set A_i, the set of models of K form the set $\cap_{i=1,\ldots,n} A_i$ which corresponds to a *possibilistic* handling of incomplete information.

In interval analysis [MOO 66], numerical information items take the form of closed real intervals $v_i \in [a_i, b_i]$ describing incomplete knowledge of parameters or inputs of a mathematical model described by a real function f. A typical problem is to compute the set of values of $f(v_1, \ldots, v_n)$ when the v_i lie in the sets $[a_i, b_i]$, that is, $A = \{f(s_1, \ldots, s_n) : s_i \in [a_i, b_i], i = 1, \ldots, n\}$.

3.2.2. *Uncertainty*

A piece of information is said to be *uncertain* for an agent when the latter does not know whether this piece of information is true or false. If a primitive item of information is a proposition, i.e. a statement that an event occurred or will occur or a proposition is modeled by a subset of possible values of the form $v \in A$, we may assign a token of uncertainty to it. This token, or uncertainty qualifier, is located at the metalevel with respect to the pieces of information. It can be numerical or symbolic (e.g. linguistic). For instance, consider the statements:

– the probability that the activity takes more than one hour is 0.7;
– it is very possible that it will snow tomorrow; and
– it is not absolutely certain that Jean will come to the meeting tomorrow.

In these examples, uncertainty qualifiers are a number (a probability) and symbolic modalities (possible, certain). The most usual representation of uncertainty consists of assigning to each proposition or event A, viewed as a subset of S, a number $g(A)$ in the unit interval. $g(A)$ evaluates the likelihood of A, the confidence of the agent in the truth of proposition asserting $v \in A$. This proposition can only be true or false by convention, even if the agent may ignore this truth value. The requirements

$$g(\emptyset) = 0; \quad g(S) = 1 \tag{3.1}$$

sound natural, as do the monotonicity with respect to inclusion:

$$\text{if } A \subseteq B \text{ then } g(A) \leq g(B). \tag{3.2}$$

Indeed, the contradictory proposition $\emptyset$ is impossible, and the tautology S is certain. Moreover, if A is more specific than B in the wide sense (hence implies it), the agent cannot be more confident in A than in B. All things being equal, the more imprecise a proposition the more certain it is. In an infinite setting, continuity properties with respect to converging monotonic sequences of sets must be added. Under these properties, the function g is sometimes called a *capacity* [CHO 53] (with explicit reference to electricity) and sometimes a *fuzzy measure* [SUG 77]. In order to stick to the uncertainty framework, it is referred to as a *confidence function* here. Easy but important consequences of postulates (3.1) and (3.2) are:

$$g(A \cap B) \leq \min(g(A), g(B)); \quad g(A \cup B) \geq \max(g(A), g(B)). \tag{3.3}$$

An important particular case of confidence function is the probability measure $g = P$ which satisfies the additivity property

$$\text{if } A \cap B = \emptyset, \text{ then } P(A \cup B) = P(A) + P(B). \tag{3.4}$$

Given an elementary piece of incomplete information of the form $v \in E$, held as certain, other types of confidence functions taking on values in $\{0, 1\}$ can be defined:
- a *possibility measure* Π such that $\Pi(A) = 1$ if $A \cap E \neq \emptyset$ and 0 otherwise; and
- a *necessity measure* N such that $N(A) = 1$ if $E \subseteq A$ and 0 otherwise.

It is easy to see that $\Pi(A) = 1$ if and only if proposition $v \in A$ is not inconsistent with information item $v \in E$, and that $N(A) = 1$ if and only if proposition $v \in A$ is entailed by information item $v \in E$. This is the Boolean version of possibility theory [DUB 88b].

$\Pi(A) = 0$ means that A is impossible if $v \in E$ is true. $N(A) = 1$ expresses that A is certain if $v \in E$ is true. Moreover, to say that A is impossible ($A \cap E = \emptyset$) is to say that the opposite event is $\overline{A}$ is certain. So, functions N and Π are totally related to each other by the conjugateness property

$$N(A) = 1 - \Pi(\overline{A}). \tag{3.5}$$

This conjugateness relation is the main difference between necessity and possibility measures on the one hand and probability measures on the other, which are self-conjugate in the sense that $P(A) = 1 - P(\overline{A})$.

Uncertainty of the possibilistic type is clearly at work in classical logic. If K is a propositional belief base with a set of models E and p is the syntactic form of proposition $v \in A$, then $N(A) = 1$ if and only if K implies p and $\Pi(A) = 0$ if and only if $K \cup \{p\}$ is logically inconsistent. Note that the presence of p in K means that $N(A) = 1$, while its negation $\neg p$ in K is used to mean $\Pi(A) = 0$. However, in propositional logic, it cannot be stated that $N(A) = 0$ or $\Pi(A) = 1$. To do so, a modal logic is needed [CHE 78] that prefixes propositions with modalities such as possible ($\Diamond$) and necessary ($\Box$). In a modal belief base K^{mod}, $\Diamond p \in K^{mod}$ encodes $\Pi(A) = 1$, and $\Box p \in K^{mod}$ encodes $N(A) = 1$ (which is encoded by $p \in K$ in classical logic). Conjugateness relation (3.5) is well known in modal logic, where it reads: $\Diamond p = \neg \Box \neg p$.

It is easy to check that each of possibility and necessity measures saturates one of inequalities (3.3):

$$\Pi(A \cup B) = \max(\Pi(A), \Pi(B)). \tag{3.6}$$

$$N(A \cap B) = \min(N(A), N(B)). \tag{3.7}$$

Possibility measures are said to be *maxitive* and characterized (in the finite setting) by maxitivity property (3.6). Similarly, necessity measures are said to be *minitive* and are characterized (in the finite setting) by minitivity property (3.7). These properties are taken as postulates even when possibility and necessity values lie in $[0, 1]$. In the Boolean setting, they read $\Diamond(p \vee q) = \Diamond p \vee \Diamond q$ and $\Box(p \wedge q) = \Box p \wedge \Box q$ and are well known in modal logics. In fact, it also holds that $N(A) > 0$ implies $\Pi(A) = 1$, and the Boolean possibilistic setting is therefore captured by the modal logic KD45, which is typical of Hintikka's epistemic logic [HIN 62].

In general, possibility measures are distinct from necessity measures. Maxitivity and minitivity properties cannot simultaneously hold for all events, except if $N = \Pi$ corresponds to precise information ($E = \{s_0\}$). It then also coincides with a Dirac probability measure, since then $g(A) = 1$ if and only if $g(\overline{A}) = 0$. However, note that it may occur that $N(A \cup B) > \max(N(A), N(B))$ and $\Pi(A \cap B) < \min(\Pi(A), \Pi(B))$. Namely, it is easy to check that if it is not known whether A is true or false (because $A \cap E \neq \emptyset$ and $\overline{A} \cap E \neq \emptyset$), then $\Pi(A) = \Pi(\overline{A}) = 1$ and $N(A) = N(\overline{A}) = 0$. However, by definition $\Pi(A \cap \overline{A}) = \Pi(\emptyset) = 0$ and $N(A \cup \overline{A}) = N(S) = 1$. The possibilistic approach therefore distinguishes between three extreme epistemic states:

- the certainty that $v \in A$ is true: $N(A) = 1$ which implies $\Pi(A) = 1$;
- the certainty that $v \in A$ is false: $\Pi(A) = 0$ which implies $N(A) = 0$; and
- the ignorance as to whether $v \in A$: $\Pi(A) = 1$ and $N(A) = 0$.

The item of Boolean information $v \in E$ may also lead to the definition of a probability measure. Whenever this is the only available information, the Insufficient

Reason principle of Laplace proposes assigning (in the finite setting) the same probability weight to each element in E (by symmetry, i.e. lack of reason not to act so), which implies letting

$$P(A) = \frac{Card(A \cap E)}{Card(E)}.$$

The idea is that E should be defined in such a way that all its elements have equal probability. This probability measure is such that $P(A) = 1$ if and only if $E \subseteq A$ and $P(A) = 0$ if and only if $E \cap A = \emptyset$. It plays the same role as the pair (Π, N) and it refines it since it measures to what extent A overlaps E. Nevertheless, probabilities thus computed depend on the number of elements inside E. In the case of total ignorance ($E = S$) some contingent events (different from S and $\emptyset$) will be more probable than others, which sounds paradoxical. The possibilistic framework proposes a less committal representation of ignorance: all contingent events and only them are equally possible and certain (they have possibility 1 and necessity 0). The situation of total ignorance is not faithfully rendered by a single probability distribution.

3.2.3. *Gradual linguistic information*

The representation of a proposition as an entity liable to being true or false (or, of an event that may occur or not) is a convention. This convention is not always reasonable. Some kinds of information which an agent can assert or understand do not lend themselves easily to this convention. For instance, the proposition 'Pierre is young' could be neither totally true, nor totally false: it sounds more true if Pierre is 20 years old than if he is 30 (in the latter case, it nevertheless makes little sense to say that Pierre is not young). Moreover, the meaning of 'young' will be altered by linguistic hedges expressing intensity: it makes sense to say 'very young', 'not too young', etc. In other words, the proposition 'Pierre is young' is clearly not Boolean. It underlies a ranking, in terms of relevance, of attribute values to which it refers. This kind of information is taken into account by the concept of *fuzzy set* [ZAD 65]. A fuzzy set F is an application from S to a (usually) totally ordered scale L often chosen as the interval $[0, 1]$. $F(s)$ is the membership degree of element s to F. It is a measure of the adequacy between situation s and proposition F.

It is natural to use fuzzy sets when dealing with a piece of information expressed in natural language and referring to a numerical attribute. Zadeh [ZAD 75a, ZAD 75b, ZAD 75c] introduced the notion of *linguistic variable* ranging in a finite ordered set of linguistic terms. Each term represents a subset of a numerical scale associated with the attribute and these subsets forms a partition of this scale. For instance, the set of terms $F \in \{young, adult, old\}$ forms the domain of the linguistic variable $age(Pierre)$. It partitions the scale of this attribute. Nevertheless, it seems that transitions between age zones corresponding to terms are gradual rather than abrupt. In the case of the predicate *young*, it sounds somewhat arbitrary to define a precise threshold $s_\star$ on a continuous scale such that $F(s) = 0$ if $s > s_\star$ and 1 otherwise. Such linguistic terms are referred to as *gradual predicates*. You can spot them by the possibility of altering their meaning by intensity adverbs such as the linguistic hedge 'very'. The membership scale [0, 1] is but the mirror image of the continuous scale of the attribute (here, the age). Not all predicates are gradual. For instance, it is clear that 'single' is Boolean.

It is important to tell degrees of adequacy (often called *degrees of truth*) from degrees of confidence or belief. Already, within natural language, the sentences 'Pierre is very young' and 'Pierre is probably young' convey different meanings. According to the former sentence, the membership degree of *age(Pierre)* to $F = young$ is clearly high; according to the latter, it is not totally excluded that Pierre is old. A membership degree is interpreted as a degree of adequacy if the value $age(Pierre) = s$ is known and the issue under concern is to provide a linguistic qualifier to describe Pierre. The term 'young' is adequate to degree $F(s)$.

The standpoint of fuzzy set theory is to consider any evaluation function as a set. For instance, a utility function can be viewed as a fuzzy set of *good* decisions. This theory defines gradual, non-Boolean extensions of classical logic and its connectives (disjunction, conjunction, negation and implication). Of course, natural questions may be raised such as the measurement of membership functions and the commensurability between membership functions pertaining to different attributes. These are the same questions raised in multifactorial evaluation. The membership degree $F(s)$ can actually be seen as a degree of similarity between the value s and the closest prototype of F, namely some s_0 such that $F(s_0) = 1$. $F(s)$ is inversely proportional to the distance between this prototype s_0 and the value s. The membership degree often has such a metric interpretation, which relies on the existence of a distance in S.

When the only available information is of the form $v \in F$, where F is a fuzzy set (for instance 'Pierre is very young') then, as in the Boolean case, the membership function is interpreted as a possibility distribution attached to v: $\pi_v = F$ [ZAD 78]. Now, however, it is a gradual possibility distribution on the scale L, here [0, 1]. Values s such that $\pi_v(s) = 1$ are the most plausible values for v. The plausibility of a value s for v is then all the greater as s is close to a totally plausible value.

Possibility theory is driven by the principle of minimal specificity. It states that any hypothesis not known to be impossible cannot be ruled out. A possibility distribution is said to be at least as specific as another one if and only if each state is at least as possible according to the latter as to the former [YAG 83]. In the absence of sufficient information, each state is allocated the maximal degree of possibility: this is the minimal specificity principle. Then, the least specific distribution is the least restrictive and informative, or the least committal.

Plausibility and certainty evaluations induced by the information item $v \in F$ concerning a proposition $v \in A$ can be computed in terms of possibility and necessity degrees of event A:

$$\Pi(A) = \max_{s \in A} \pi_v(s); \quad N(A) = 1 - \Pi(\overline{A}) = \min_{s \notin A} 1 - \pi_v(s) \tag{3.8}$$

It is clear that a gradual information item is often more informative than Boolean information: $v \in F$, where F is gradual, is more specific than $v \in A$ when $A = \text{support}(F) = \{s, F(s) > 0\}$ because the former suggests a plausibility ranking between possible values of v in A. This representation of uncertainty through the use of gradual linguistic terms leads to quantifying plausibility in terms of distance to an ideally plausible situation, not in terms of frequency of occurrence, for instance.

3.2.4. *Granularity*

In the previous sections, assumptions that underlie the definition of the set S of states of affairs were not laid bare. Nevertheless, the choice of S has a clear impact on the possibility or not to represent relevant information. In decision theory, for instance, it is often assumed that S is infinite or detailed enough to completely describe the problem under concern. Nevertheless, this assumption is sometimes hard to sustain. On the real line, for instance, only so-called measurable sets can be assigned a probability even if, intuitively, it should be possible to do so to any event that makes sense in a situation [GOO 62]. In fact, using real numbers is often due to the continuous approximation of information that is intrinsically discrete, or perceived as such.

For instance, probability distributions derived from statistical data can be viewed as idealizations of histograms (which are finite entities) not only because they represent a finite number of observations but also from our inability to perceive the difference between very close values. This indistinguishability can also be encountered when representing preferences of an agent accounting for indifference thresholds on the utility function.

Moreover, the set S is seldom taken for granted. In the approach by De Finetti [DEF 74], as in the logical approach to AI, the primitive information consists of a collection of propositions expressed in some prescribed language to which an agent assigns degrees of confidence. The state space S is then generated from these propositions (mathematically, its subsets form the smallest Boolean algebra containing the subsets of models of these propositions). This way of proceeding has non-trivial consequences for representing and revising information.

For instance if a new proposition is added, it may result in a modification or a refinement of the set S. This is called a *granularity change* for the representation. A set S_2 is a refinement of S_1 [SHA 76] if there is an onto mapping ρ from S_2 to S_1 such that the reciprocal images of elements in S_1 via ρ, namely the sets $\{\rho^{-1}(s) : s \in S_1\}$, form a partition of S_2 (Zadeh [ZAD 97] speaks of S_1 being a 'granulation' of S_2).

It is clear that the probabilistic representation of incomplete information by means of the Insufficient Reason principle does not resist a change of granularity: the image on S_1 of a uniform probability on S_2 via ρ is not generally a uniform probability. This principle applied to S_1 inside equivalence classes of S_2 may not produce a uniform probability on S_2 either. The probabilistic representation of ignorance therefore sounds paradoxical as it seems to produce information out of the blue while changing the frame. This anomaly does not appear with the possibilistic representation: the image of a uniform possibility distribution on S_2 via ρ is a uniform possibility distribution indeed. Conversely, applying the minimal specificity (or symmetry) principle in two steps (to S_2 then S_1) produces a uniform possibility distribution on S_1.

The simplest case of granularity change is the following: let Ω be a set of entities described by means of attributes $V_1, V_2, \ldots, V_k$ with respective domains $D_1, D_2, \ldots, D_k$. Then S is the Cartesian product $D_1 \times D_2 \times \cdots \times D_k$. Each element in S can be refined into several elements if a $(k+1)$th attribute is added. Suppose a collection of individuals Ω exists, described by such attributes. Nothing forbids different individuals from sharing the same description in terms of these attributes. Then let Ξ be a subset of Ω. It is not generally possible to describe it by means of S. Indeed, let R be the equivalence relation on Ω defined by the identity of descriptions of elements w of Ω: $w_1 R w_2$ if and only if $V_i(w_1) = V_i(w_2), \forall i = 1, \ldots, k$. Let $[w]_R$ be the equivalence class of w. Each element in S corresponds to an equivalence class in Ω. Then, the the set Ξ can only be approximated by the language of S but not exactly described by it. Let Ξ^* and Ξ_* be the upper and lower approximations of Ξ, defined

$$\Xi^* = \{w \in \Omega : [w]_R \cap \Xi \neq \emptyset\}; \quad \Xi_* = \{w \in \Omega : [w]_R \subseteq \Xi\}. \tag{3.9}$$

The pair (Ξ^*, Ξ_*) is called a *rough set* by Pawlak [PAW 91]. Only sets Ξ^* and Ξ_* of individuals can be perfectly described by combinations of attribute values $V_1, V_2, \ldots, V_k$ corresponding to the subsets of S. Note that histograms and numerical images correspond to this very notion of indistinguishability and granularity, equivalence classes corresponding to boxes of the histogram and to pixels.

When changing granularity by adding a new attribute that is logically independent from others, each element in S_1 is refined into as many elements in S_2 and a uniform probability on one set is compatible with a uniform probability on the other. In the case of adding a proposition that is not logically independent from others, the induced refinement is not always that homogenous.

3.3. Probability theory

Probability theory is the oldest of uncertainty theories, the most mathematically developed as well as the most widely acknowledged. Probability theory can be envisaged from a purely mathematical side, which is often the case since the emergence of Kolmogorov axioms in the 1930s (and typically in France where statistics is a branch of applied mathematics). Under this view, the starting point is a sample space Ω, an algebra of measurable subsets $\mathcal{B}$ and a measure of probability P i.e. a mapping from $\mathcal{B}$ in $[0, 1]$ such that

$$P(\emptyset) = 0; \; P(\Omega) = 1; \tag{3.10}$$

$$\text{if } A \cap B = \emptyset \text{ then } P(A \cup B) = P(A) + P(B). \tag{3.11}$$

The triple $(\Omega, \mathcal{B}, \mathcal{P})$ is called a probability space. A random variable is construed as a mapping V from Ω in some representation space S (often the real line). In the simplest case, S is assumed to be a finite set, which prescribes a finite partitioning of Ω according to the procedure described in section 3.2.4. The family of measurable sets $\mathcal{B}$ can be defined as the Boolean algebra induced by this partition. The probability distribution associated with the random variable V is then characterized by an assignment of weights $p_1, p_2, \ldots, p_{card(S)}$ to elements of S i.e. $p_i = P(V^{-1}(s_i))$, such that

$$\sum_{i=1}^{card(S)} p_i = 1.$$

Beyond a basically consensual mathematical framework (up to discussions on the meaning of zero probabilities and the issue of infinite additivity), significantly diverging views of what a probability degree may mean can be found in the literature [FIN 83]. This section reviews some of these controversies, emphasizing the limitations of uncertainty representations relying on the use of a unique probability distribution.

3.3.1. *Frequentists and subjectivists*

We consider probability theory as a tool for representing information. For this purpose, probabilities must be given a concrete meaning. Traditionally, there is at least three interpretations of probability degrees. The oldest and simplest is in terms of counting equally possible cases, due to Laplace at the turn of the 19th century. For instance, Ω is assumed finite and p_i is proportional to the number of elements in

$V^{-1}(s_i)$. The probability of an event is the number of favorable cases, where this event occurs, divided by the total number of possible cases. The validity of this approach relies on (i) Laplace's Insufficient Reason principle stating that equally possible states are equally probable and (ii) the capability of constructing S in such a way that its elements are indeed equipossible. This can be helped by appealing to symmetry considerations, justifying assumptions of purely random phenomena (as in games with unbiased coins, dice, etc.).

To date, the most usual interpretation of probability is frequentist. Observations (that form a relevant sampling of the set Ω) are collected (say a finite subset $\Omega(n) \subset \Omega$ with n elements). These observations are supposedly independent and made in the same conditions. Frequencies of observing $V = s_i$ can be calculated as:

$$f_i = \frac{card(V^{-1}(s_i) \cap \Omega(n))}{n}$$

or, if S is infinite, a histogram associated with the random variable V can be set up considering frequencies of members of a finite partition of S.

It is assumed that, as the number of observations increases, $\Omega(n)$ becomes fully representative of Ω and that frequencies f_i converge to 'true' probability values $p_i = \lim_{n \to \infty} f_i$. The connection between frequency and probability dates to Bernoulli's law of large numbers and proves that when tossing a fair coin a great number of times, the proportion of heads tends to become equal to the proportion of tails.

This definition of probabilities requires a sufficient number of observations (ideally infinite) of the phenomenon under concern. Then, assigning a probability to an event requires a population of situations and reveals a trend in this population. A probability distribution is then viewed as generic knowledge. This framework also forbids assigning probabilities to non-repeatable events. Only statistical prediction is allowed, that is, a degree of confidence in obtaining 'head' at the next toss of the coin reflects the proportion of heads observed so far in a long sequence of experiments. However, the idea that statistical experiments are rigorously repeatable is debatable. The frequentist assumption of independent observations collected in identical conditions is often only approximately verified. One might suspect some contradiction between the identity of experimental conditions and the independence of the observations, as when measuring the same quantity several times with the same sensor.

In general, even when they are independent, experimental conditions under which observations are collected may only be similar to one another. A frequentist approach can then still be developed [GIL 00]. In the case of non-repeatability (e.g. testimonies or elections), one is led to a subjectivist view of probabilities which then directly represents degrees of belief of agent about the occurrence of singular events or the truth of relevant propositions for the problem at hand. This point of view meets a caveat: how do we justify the additivity law of probabilities seen as degrees of belief?

In the case of repeatable phenomena, considered random, the use of frequencies is in agreement with additivity axiom (3.11). The role of frequencies for non-repeatable events is played by amounts of money bet on the occurrence or the non-occurrence of singular events [DEF 37, RAM 80].

The degree of confidence of an agent in the occurrence of event A is the price $P(A)$ this agent (referred to as a player) would accept to pay in order to buy a lottery ticket that brings back 1 Euro if event A occurs (and 0 Euro if not). The more the player believes in the occurrence of A, the less risk is involved in buying a lottery ticket for a price close to 1 Euro. In order to force the latter to propose a fair price, it is moreover assumed that the person that sells lottery tickets (the banker) will not accept the transaction if prices proposed by the player are too low. In particular, if the proposed price is too low, the banker is allowed to exchange roles with the player. In this case, the latter is obliged to sell the lottery ticket at price $P(A)$ and to pay 1 Euro to the banker if event A occurs.

This approach relies on a principle of coherence that presupposes a rational agent, i.e. a player that tries to avoid sure loss. Suppose that the player buys two lottery tickets pertaining to two opposite propositions A and $\overline{A}$. The principle of coherence then enforces $P(A) + P(\overline{A}) = 1$. Indeed, only one of the two events A or $\overline{A}$ occurs in this one-shot setting. Prices must therefore be such that $P(A) + P(\overline{A}) \leq 1$, lest the player surely loses $P(A) + P(\overline{A}) - 1$ Euros. However, if the player proposes prices such that $P(A) + P(\overline{A}) < 1$ then the banker would also turn into a player in order to avoid sure loss. Similarly, with three mutually exclusive propositions A, B and $\overline{A \cup B}$, it can be shown that only $P(A) + P(B) + P(\overline{A \cup B}) = 1$ is rational. Since $P(\overline{A \cup B}) = 1 - P(A \cup B)$, it follows that $P(A \cup B) = P(A) + P(B)$.

This framework can be used on problems having a true answer, e.g. 'what is the date of birth of the current Brazilian president?' Clearly no statistical data can be accurately useful for an agent to answer this question if this agent does not know the answer beforehand. The above procedure might result in a subjective probability distribution on possible birth dates, and the resulting outcome can be checked. Note that here uncertainty is due to incomplete information, while in a coin-tossing experiment it is due to the variability of the outcomes.

The subjectivist approach sounds like a simple reinterpretation of the frequentist probability framework. Actually, as pointed out by De Finetti and his followers [COL 02, DEF 74], this is not so straightforward. In the subjectivist approach, there is no sample space. The starting point is a set of Boolean propositions $\{A_j : j = 1, n\}$ to which an agent assigns coherent degrees of confidence c_i and a set of logical constraints between these propositions. The state space S is then constructed on the basis of these propositions and constraints. By virtue of the principle of coherence, the agent is assumed to choose degrees of confidence c_j according to some probability measure P in such a way that $c_j = P(A_j), \forall j = 1, \ldots, n$. While the frequentist approach is to start from a unique probability measure (obtained by estimation from statistical data) that models the repeatable phenomenon under study, there is no equivalent in the subjective setting. There may even be several probability measures such that $c_j = P(A_j), \forall j = 1, \ldots, n$. Each of them is rational, but the available information may not allow their isolation. There may also be no probability measure satisfying these constraints if the agent is not coherent. Computing the probability $P(A)$ of any event A based on the knowledge of pairs $\{(A_j, c_j) : i = 1, n\}$ requires the solution of a linear programming problem whose variables are probability weights p_i attached to elementary events [DEF 37], namely:

maximize (or minimize) $\sum_{s_i \in A} p_i$ under the constraints

$$c_j = \sum_{s_k \in A_j} p_k, \forall j = 1, \ldots, n.$$

In this sense, the subjectivist approach to probability is an extension of the logical approach to knowledge representation and of classical deduction [ADA 75]. Moreover, the subjectivist approach does not require the σ-additivity of P (i.e. axiom (3.11) for an infinite denumerable set of mutually exclusive events), contrary to the frequentist Kolmogorovean approach. More differences between subjective and frequentist probabilities can be laid bare when the notion of conditioning comes into play.

3.3.2. *Conditional probability*

It is obvious that assigning a probability to an event is not carried out in the absolute. It is done inside a certain context embodied by the frame S. In practice, S never contains *all* possible states of the world, but only those that our current knowledge or working assumptions do not rule out. For instance, in the dice-tossing problem, S contains the six facets of the dice, not the possibility for the dice to break into pieces. It is suggested to write the probability $P(A)$ in the form $P(A \mid S)$ to highlight this aspect. If the agent later obtains new information that leads to the further restriction of the set of states of the world, the context of these probabilities will change. Let $C \subset S$ be the current relevant context and $P(A \mid C)$ be the probability of A in such a context. The transformation from $P(A)$ to $P(A \mid C)$ essentially consists of renormalizing probabilities assigned to states where C is true i.e.

$$P(A \mid C) = \frac{P(A \cap C)}{P(C)}. \tag{3.12}$$

This definition retrieves $P(A)$ under the form $P(A \mid S)$. It is easy to justify in the frequentist case since $P(A \mid C)$ is the limit of a relative frequency.

Two known results can then be derived.
– *The total probability theorem*: if $\{C_1, \ldots, C_k\}$ forms a partition of S, then

$$P(A) = \sum_{i=1}^{k} P(A \mid C_i) P(C_i).$$

– *Bayes theorem*:

$$P(C_j \mid A) = \frac{P(A \mid C_j) P(C_j)}{\sum_{i=1}^{k} P(A \mid C_i) P(C_i)}.$$

The first result enables the probability of an event to be computed for a general context S given known probabilities of this event in more specific contexts, provided that these contexts form a partition of possible states and that probabilities of each of these contexts are known. It is instrumental for backward calculations in causal event trees.

Bayes theorem can deal with the following classification problem: Consider k classes C_j of objects forming a partition of S. If the probability $P(A \mid C_j)$ of property A for objects of each class C_j is known, as well as the prior probabilities $P(C_j), j = 1\ldots, k$ that an object is of class C_j, then for any new object which is known to possess property A, it is possible to derive the probability $P(C_j \mid A)$ that this object belongs to class C_j. In diagnosis problems, replace class by fault type and property by symptom.

Bayes' theorem is also instrumental in model inference, or learning from statistical data. Then:
– the set of classes is replaced by the range of values $\theta \in \Theta$ of the model parameter;
– $P(A \mid \theta)$ is the likelihood function known when the type of statistical model is known and θ is fixed;
– the set A represents a series of observed outcomes;
– a prior probability distribution is given on the parameter space Θ (in case of ignorance, a non-informative prior according to the objective Bayesian school is used); and
– the posterior probability $P(\theta \mid A)$ is viewed as the new knowledge of the parameter model after observing A, which leads to a possible update of this model.

In a subjectivist framework, the situation of conditioning is different. The probability $P(A \mid C)$ is now assigned by the agent to the hypothetical occurrence of the conditional event $A \mid C$. Conditional probability is now considered as a primitive notion (no longer derived from a probability measure). Namely, $A \mid C$ represents the occurrence of event A in the hypothetical context where C is true. The quantity $P(A \mid C)$ is then still interpreted as an amount of money bet on A, but now this amount is given back to the player if event C does not occur and the bet is then called off [DEF 74]. In this operational framework, it can be shown that coherence requires that the equality $P(A \cap C) = P(A \mid C) \cdot P(C)$ be satisfied.

The definition of conditional probability under the form of a quotient presupposes that $P(C) \neq 0$, which may turn out to be too restrictive. Indeed, in the framework proposed by De Finetti where elicited probabilities may be assigned to any conditional event, the available set of beliefs to be reasoned from takes the form of a collection of conditional probabilities $\{P(A_i \mid C_j), i = 1, \ldots, m; j = 1, \ldots, n\}$ corresponding to various potential contexts (some of which have zero probability of occurring in the current world). However, by defining conditional probability as any solution to equation $P(A \cap C) = P(A \mid C) \cdot P(C)$, it still makes sense as a non-negative number when $P(C) = 0$ [COL 02]. Besides, in the tradition of probability theory, an event of zero probability is understood as practically impossible, not intrinsically impossible. In other words, it is an exceptional event only (such as the dice breaking into pieces). The general reasoning problem in the conditional setting is to compute probability $P(A \mid C)$ from a set of known conditional probabilities $\{P(A_i \mid C_j), i = 1, \ldots, m; j = 1, \ldots, n\}$ [PAR 94], a problem much more general than that underlying the theorem of total probability.

Under this view, probabilistic knowledge consists of all values $P(A_i \mid C_j)$ known in all contexts. An agent only selects the appropriate conditional probability based on the available knowledge on the current situation, a view completely contrasting with that of revising a probability measure based on the arrival of new knowledge. Indeed, some scholars justify conditional probability as the result of a revision process. The quantity $P(A \mid C)$ is then viewed as the *new* probability of A when the agent hears that event C occurred [GÄR 88].

Basic to belief revision is the principle of minimal change: agents minimally revise their beliefs in order to absorb the new information item interpreted by the constraint $P(C) = 1$. A simple encoding of the principle of minimal change is to suppose that probabilities of states that remain possible do not change in relative value, which enforces the usual definition of conditioning [TEL 84].

Another, more general, approach is to look for the new probability measure P_+ that minimizes an informational distance to the prior probability P under the constraint $P_+(C) = 1$ [DOM 85]. If relative entropy is chosen as a measure of distance, it can be shown that P_+ is indeed the conditional probability relative to C.

Note that interpreting the context C as the constraint $P_+(C) = 1$ is questionable in the frequentist setting as, in this case, a probability measure refers to a class of situations (a population) while the information item C often refers to a unique situation (one of the specific problems which the agent tries to solve). Indeed, the constraint $P(C) = 1$ might misleadingly suggest that C is true for the whole population while C occurred only in the specific situation the agent is interested in. In the subjectivist scope, conditioning is but hypothetical and the known occurrence of C only helps in selecting the correct reference class.

3.3.3. *The unique probability assumption in the subjective setting*

The so-called *Bayesian* approach to subjective probability postulates the unicity of the probability measure that represents beliefs of an agent, as a prerequisite to any further consideration [e.g. LIN 82]. Indeed, if the agent decides to directly assign subjective probabilities to elements of S, the principle of coherence leads to the specification of a unique probability distribution by fear of a sure loss of money (this is also called the Dutch book argument).

If the available knowledge is insufficient to uniquely characterize a probability distribution, the Bayesian approach may appeal to selection principles such as that of Insufficient Reason that exploits the symmetries of a problem, or the maximum entropy principle [JAY 79, PAR 94]. Resorting to the latter in the subjectivist framework is questionable because it only selects the uniform distribution whenever possible, as in the following example.

Example 3.1. Suppose the agents describe their knowledge of a biased coin by providing rough estimates of the probability p of getting a tail. If they consider the bias is towards tail and, if cautious, they just provide an estimate p in the form of an interval such as $[0.5, 0.8]$. Applying the maximum entropy principle enforces the choice of the uniform distribution, while selecting $p = 0.65$ (the mid-point of the interval) sounds more sensible and faithful to the trend expressed by the incomplete information supplied by the agent.

In any case (and in the above example), the Bayesian credo states that any epistemic state of an agent is representable by a unique prior probability distribution. An additional argument in favor of this claim is Savage Decision Theory (see Chapter 9). It demonstrates that in an infinite setting, if the agent makes decisions in an uncertain environment while respecting suitable rationality axioms (in particular the fact that the preference between two acts does not depend on states in which they have the same consequences), the decision process can be explained as if the agent's knowledge were encoded as a unique probability distribution and decisions were rank-ordered according to their expected utility. In addition, the subjectivist approach is somewhat convergent with the frequentist approach because it is agreed that if the agent possesses reliable statistical information in the form of frequencies, they should be used to quantify belief in the next event.

The systematic use of a unique probability as the universal tool for representing uncertainty nevertheless raises some serious difficulties:

– There is no difference between uncertainty due to incomplete information and uncertainty due to variability in past results observed by the agent. In the dice game, how can a uniform distribution provided by an agent that describes the epistemic state of the dice be interpreted in a non-ambiguous way? Namely, it may be the case that the agent knows the dice is unbiased and that the limit frequency distribution should be uniform (pure randomness). However, if the agents ignore everything about that particular dice, because they were not given a chance to try it, then the uniform distribution is but the result of the symmetry principle (the agent has no reason to bet more money on one facet rather than another), expressing ignorance. What this means is that there is no bijection between the possible epistemic states of the agent (which are clearly different in the above two situations) and probability distributions, even if it is correct to consider that the proposed prices for buying the lottery tickets by the player do result from their epistemic state. It does not make perfect sense to *identify* betting rates to degrees of confidence or belief. This limitation in expressivity is somewhat problematic in a dynamical framework where the amount of available information evolves, as shown later. When a new piece of information is obtained, should agents modify their bets by means of a revision rule, or revise their epistemic state and propose new betting rates accordingly?

– It was pointed out earlier that the choice of frame S depends on the language used, hence on the source of information. One agent may perceive distinct situations another agent will not discern. If several points of view or several languages are simultaneously used in a problem, there will be several frames $S_1, S_2, \ldots, S_p$ (rightly called 'frames of discernment' [SHA 76]) involved to describe the same quantity V and compatibility relations between these frames. Each subset of S_i may only be represented by a rough subset of S_j (in the sense of section 3.2.4). It may become impossible to represent mutually consistent epistemic states on the various frames of discernment by means of a unique probability distribution on each set S_i. Indeed, a uniform distribution on one set may fail to correspond with a uniform distribution on another. For instance, consider the example of the possibility of extra-terrestrial life [SHA 76].

Example 3.2. Generally, people ignore whether there is life or not. Hence $P_1(Life) = P_1(Nolife) = \frac{1}{2}$ on $S_1 = \{Life, Nolife\}$. However, if the agent discerns between animal life ($Alife$) and vegetable life only ($Vlife$), with frame $S_2 = \{Alife, Vlife, Nolife\}$, the ignorant agent is bound to propose $P_2(Alife) = P_2(Vlife) = P_2(Nolife) = \frac{1}{3}$. Since $Life$ is the disjunction of $Vlife$ and $Alife$, distributions P_1 and P_2 are incompatible while they are assumed to stem from the same epistemic state.

The same phenomenon occurs on the continuous real line when a piece of incomplete information of the form $x \in [a, b]$ is represented by a uniform probability density on $[a, b]$. The latter representation is not scale-invariant. Indeed, consider a continuous increasing function f. Stating $x \in [a, b]$ is then equivalent to stating $f(x) \in [f(a), f(b)]$. However, if x has a probability distribution with uniform density, the density of $f(x)$ is generally not uniform. It looks as if ignorance on $[a, b]$ can create information on $[f(a), f(b)]$.

– The usual debate between normative and descriptive representations of information is relevant when dealing with uncertainty. If the Bayesian approach is normatively attractive, it may prove to be a poor model to account for the way agents handle confidence degrees [KAH 79]. More recent experimental studies seem to suggest that a human agent may, in some situations, follow the rules of possibility theory instead [RAU 03].

– Finally, there is a practical measurement difficulty in the case of subjective probabilities. The agent is not capable of supplying, even via price assessments, infinitely precise probability values. What can be expressed consists of fuzzy probabilities (as surprisingly acknowledged even by Luce and Raiffa [LUC 81]). Such probabilities would be more faithfully represented by intervals, if not fuzzy intervals. In some situations, they are only linguistic terms (*very probable, quite improbable*, etc.). One may therefore argue that subjective probabilities should be represented in a purely symbolic way or, on the contrary, by fuzzy subsets (as in section 3.2.3) of $[0, 1]$ [BUD 95, COO 05, ZAD 84]. Some authors even propose higher-order probabilities [e.g. MAR 75] which sounds like recursively solving a problem by creating the same problem one step higher.

Note that these defects essentially affect the Bayesian representation of subjective belief in the case of poor information. They are partially irrelevant in the case of frequentist probabilities based on sufficient experimental data. For instance, the lack of scale-invariance of probability densities is no paradox in the frequentist view. If the collected information in terms of values for $x \in [a, b]$ justifies a uniform distribution, it is unsurprising that the encoding of the same information in terms of values for $f(x)$ may not lead to a uniform distribution. However, the frequentist framework does not pretend to express subjective ignorance.

These caveats motivated the development of alternative representations of subjective uncertainty. In some of them, the numerical framework is replaced by ordinal structures that underlie subjectivist numerical representations. In other representations, incompleteness is acknowledged as such and injected into probability theory yielding various approaches, some being more general than others. In all approaches, possibility theory (qualitative or quantitative, [DUB 98b]) is retrieved as the simplest non-trivial non-probabilistic representation of uncertainty.

3.4. Incompleteness-tolerant numerical uncertainty theories

It is now clear that representations of belief using subjective probabilities, under the Bayesian approach, tend to confuse uncertainty due to variability and uncertainty due to incompleteness of information, because of the principle of symmetry or indifference. This choice of representation is often motivated by the stress put on the subsequent decision step supposed to justify any attempt at representing uncertainty. However, it is legitimate to look for representations of uncertainty that maintain a difference between variability and incompleteness [FER 96]. For instance in risk analysis, an ambiguous response due to a lack of information does not lead to the same kind of decision as when it is due to uncontrollable but precisely measured variability. In section 3.2.1, it was pointed out that incompleteness can be conveniently modeled by means of disjunctive sets, in agreement with interval analysis and classical logic.

Allowing for incompleteness in uncertainty representations comes down to combining disjunctive sets and probabilities. There are two options:

1) consider disjunctive sets of probabilities, assuming the agent is not in a position to single out a probability distribution; or

2) randomize the disjunctive set based representation of incompleteness of section 3.2.1.

Representing incompleteness is coupled with modal notions of possibility and necessity. The generalized probability frameworks will be based on numerical extensions of such modalities. The first line was studied at length by Walley [WAL 91], who relies on the use of upper and lower expectations characterizing closed and convex sets of probabilities. The second option, due to Dempster [DEM 67] and Shafer [SHA 76] was further developed by Smets [SME 94, SME 98]. It is equivalent to randomizing the modal logic of incompleteness, assigning to each event degrees of belief and plausibility. The resulting theory turns out to be a special case of the former mathematically, but is philosophically different.

In the first theory, the agent represents subjective knowledge by means of maximal buying prices of gambles. The imprecise probability approach can also be interpreted as performing sensitivity analysis on a probabilistic model, i.e. there exists a true probability distribution but it is unknown and lies in some subjectively assessed probability family. In the Shafer–Smets approach, the agent uses degrees of belief and plausibility without any reference to some unknown probability.

Numerical possibility theory [DUB 88a, DUB 98b, DUB 00, ZAD 78] whose axioms were laid bare in section 3.2.2 and used in the representation of linguistic information in section 3.2.3 turns out to be a special case of the two above approaches, now interpreted in terms of imprecise probability. Section 3.2.3 is dedicated to this special case.

All numerical representations of incompleteness-tolerant uncertainty have the following common feature: the uncertainty of each event A, a subset of S, is characterized by two (upper and lower) evaluations referred to as degrees of *epistemic possibility* and *certainty*, denoted Ep and Cer respectively (adopting a subjectively biased language). Epistemic possibility refers to a lack of surprise. These two degrees define confidence functions on the frame S (in the sense of section 3.2.2) such that

$$\forall A \subseteq S, Cer(A) \leq Ep(A). \tag{3.13}$$

They are supposedly self-conjugate, i.e.

$$\forall A \subseteq S, Cer(A) = 1 - Ep(\overline{A}). \tag{3.14}$$

The first condition (3.13) postulates that an event must be epistemically possible prior to being certain. The second condition (3.14) states that an event becomes more certain as its opposite becomes less epistemically possible. These functions formally generalize possibility measures ($Ep(A) = \Pi(A)$) and necessity measures ($Cer(A) = N(A)$) of sections 3.2.2 and 3.2.3 respectively and also probability measures ($P(A) = Ep(A) = Cer(A)$). This framework has the merit of unambiguously encoding three epistemic states pertaining to event A as follows:

1) The case when A is certainly true: $Cer(A) = 1$ (hence $Ep(A) = 1, Ep(\overline{A}) = 0, Cer(\overline{A}) = 0$).

2) The case when A is certainly false: $Ep(A) = 0$ (hence $Cer(A) = 0$).

3) The case when the agent does not know if A is true or false: $Cer(A) = 0$ and $Ep(A) = 1$ (then $Ep(\overline{A}) = 1; Cer(\overline{A}) = 0$).

The amount of incompleteness of the information pertaining to A is the difference $Ep(A) - Cer(A)$. When information on A is totally missing, there is a maximal gap between certainty and epistemic possibility. The non-certainty of A ($Cer(A) = 0$) is carefully distinguished from the certainty of its negation $\overline{A}$. The distinction between ignorance and what could be understood as a random variability of A (or totally conficting information about it) is also made (the latter occurs when $Cer(A) = Ep(A) = \frac{1}{2} = P(A)$). The two approaches to the representation of uncertainty presented here, namely imprecise probabilities and belief functions, use pairs of set-functions of the (Cer, Ep) kind.

3.4.1. *Imprecise probabilities*

Suppose that the information possessed by an agent is represented by a family of probability measures on S. This situation may sometimes correspond to the idea of an imprecise probabilistic model. This imprecision may have various origins as follows:

– In the frequentist framework, the assumptions that frequencies converge may no longer be made. At the limit, it is only known that the frequency of each elementary event belongs to an interval [WAL 82].

– There may be incomplete information about which is the right stochastic model of a repeatable phenomenon. For instance, the nature of a parametric model is known but the value of some parameter such as the mean or the variance is incompletely known. Bayesians then choose a prior probability distribution on possible values of parameters. This is precisely what is not assumed by imprecise probabilists [BER 05].

– Pieces of incomplete information are supplied by an agent about a probability distribution (support, mean value, mode, median and some quantiles) in a non-parametric framework [BAU 06].

– In the subjectivist framework, conditional propositions along with (bounds of) probabilities incompletely characterize a subjective probability after De Finetti [DEF 37] and his followers [COL 02].

– Walley [WAL 91] gives up the idea of exchangeable bets and allows the agent to propose maximal buying prices and minimal selling prices for gambles that may differ from each other. Gambles are functions from S to the real line, where $f(s)$ is the relative gain in state s, generalizing events. The maximal buying (respectively minimal selling) price of a gamble is interpreted as a lower (respectively upper) expectation, thus defining closed convex sets of probabilities called *credal sets* that can be interpreted as epistemic states [LEV 80].

– Gilboa and Schmeidler [GIL 89] provide a decision-theoretic justification of the assumption that an agent uses a family of prior probabilities for making choices among acts by relaxing the Savage axiom in a suitable way. In order to hedge against uncertainty, when evaluating the potential worth of each act the agent selects the probability measure ensuring the least expected utility value (see also Chapter 10).

In this section, the certainty function $Cer(A)$ and epistemic possibility function $Ep(A)$ are interpreted as lower and upper bounds, respectively, of a probability $P(A)$ for each event A. The additivity of P forces the following inequalities to be respected by these bounds [GOO 62]: $\forall A, B \subseteq S$, such that $A \cap B = \emptyset$,

$$\begin{aligned} Cer(A) + Cer(B) &\leq Cer(A \cup B) \leq Cer(A) + Ep(B) \\ &\leq Ep(A \cup B) \leq Ep(A) + Ep(B). \end{aligned} \quad (3.15)$$

Then Cer and Ep are clearly monotonic under inclusion and self-conjugate (since $Cer(\overline{A})$ must be a lower of bound $1 - P(A)$, it follows that $P(A) \geq Cer(A), \forall A$ is equivalent to $P(A) \leq Ep(A), \forall A$). Nevertheless, this approach is not satisfactory as it may be the case that the set of probabilities that function Cer is assumed to bound from below (or, for function Ep, from above), namely the set $\{P : \forall A \subseteq S, P(A) \geq Cer(A)\}$, is empty.

Conversely, we may start from a family $\mathcal{P}$ of probability measures and compute the bounds [SMI 61]:

$$P_*(A) = \inf_{P \in \mathcal{P}} P(A); \quad P^*(A) = \sup_{P \in \mathcal{P}} P(A). \tag{3.16}$$

Letting $Cer(A) = P_*(A)$ and $Ep(A) = P^*(A)$, functions P_* and P^* duly verify properties (3.13–3.15). P_* and P^* are referred to as *lower and upper envelopes* respectively [WAL 91]. The width of interval $[P_*(A), P^*(A)]$ represents in some way the degree of ignorance of the agent relative to proposition A. When this interval coincides with the whole unit interval, the agent has no information about A. When this interval narrows down to a point, probabilistic information is maximal.

Generally, the only knowledge of upper and lower envelopes of events is not enough to recover $\mathcal{P}$. This is typically the case if $\mathcal{P}$ is not convex. Indeed, the set of probability measures $\mathcal{P}(P_*) = \{P : \forall A \subseteq S, P(A) \geq P_*(A)\}$ called the *core* of P_*, and derived from the lower envelope, is convex and contains the convex closure of the original set $\mathcal{P}$ (if $P_1 \in \mathcal{P}(P_*)$ and $P_2 \in \mathcal{P}(P_*)$ then $\forall \lambda \in [0,1], \lambda \cdot P_1 + (1-\lambda) \cdot P_2 \in \mathcal{P}(P_*)$). $\mathcal{P}$ and $\mathcal{P}(P_*)$ induce the same lower and upper envelopes. In fact, the strict inclusion $\mathcal{P} \subset \mathcal{P}(P_*)$ may hold even if $\mathcal{P}$ is convex, because upper and lower probability bounds on events cannot characterize the sets of closed convex sets of probability functions. To achieve this characterization, we need all lower expectations of all gambles associated with a convex set $\mathcal{P}$ and the notion of coherence ensuring estimates of these lower expectations are maximal. This is why Walley [WAL 91] uses gambles as generalizations of events for developing his theory; the logic of gambles is the proper language for describing (convex) credal sets.

Coherent lower probabilities $\underline{P}$ are lower probabilities that coincide with the lower envelopes of their core, i.e. for all events A of X, $\underline{P}(A) = \min_{P \in \mathcal{P}(\underline{P})} P(A)$. It also means for every event A, the bounds are reachable i.e. there is a probability distribution P in $\mathcal{P}(\underline{P})$ such that $P(A) = \underline{P}(A)$. A characteristic property of a coherent upper probability (hence generated by a non-empty set of probabilities) was found by Giles [GIL 82]. Let us use the same notation for A and its characteristic function (a gamble with values in $\{0,1\}$: $A(s) = 1$ if $s \in A$ and 0 otherwise). A set-function Ep is a coherent lower probability if and only if for any family $A_0, A_1, \ldots, A_k$ of subsets of S, and any pair of integers (r,s) such that $\sum_{i=1}^{k} A_i(\cdot) \geq r + s \cdot A_0(\cdot)$, the expression

$$\sum_{i=1}^{k} Ep(A_i) \geq r + s \cdot Ep(A_0)$$

holds. This condition makes sense in terms of gambles and involves optimal minimal selling prices of an agent who sells $k+1$ lottery tickets corresponding to events $A_0, A_1, \ldots, A_k$ and is protected against a sure loss of money. It also provides a tool to compute least upper probability bounds (in case assigned bounds are not optimal) and, in this sense, restoring coherence is like achieving a deductive closure in the logical sense. Since all representations considered in this paper correspond to particular instances of coherent lower probabilities, we will restrict ourselves to such lower probabilities on events.

An important particular case of coherence is obtained by weakening probabilistic additivity, requiring a condition stronger than equation (3.15), called *2-monotonicity* [CHO 53]:

$$Cer(A) + Cer(B) \leq Cer(A \cup B) + Cer(A \cap B), \forall A \subseteq S. \qquad (3.17)$$

A 2-monotonic function is also called a *convex capacity*. Its adjoint function Ep is said to be 2-alternating, which corresponds to property (3.17) where the inequality is reversed. Due to equation (3.17), it is ensured that the core $\mathcal{P}(Cer) = \{P : \forall A \subseteq S, P(A) \geq Cer(A)\}$ is not empty and that Cer is a coherent lower probability. However, a coherent lower probability is not always 2-monotone. The property of 2-monotonicity can be extended to k-monotonicity for $k = 3, 4, \ldots$, changing the equality (appearing in the probabilistic additivitity property written with k events) into inequality. However, while probabilistic 2-additivity implies k-additivity $\forall k > 2$, this is no longer true for k-monotonicity: the latter does not imply $k+1$-monotonicity (even if $k+1$-monotonicity implies k-monotonicity). There is therefore a countable hierarchy of types of coherent upper and lower probabilities [CHA 89].

An important example of credal set is generated by so-called *probability intervals*. They are defined over a finite space S as lower and upper probability bounds restricted to singletons s_i [CAM 94]. They can be seen as a set of intervals $L = \{[l_i, u_i], i = 1, \ldots, n\}$ defining the family

$$\mathcal{P}_L = \{P | l_i \leq p(s_i) \leq u_i, \forall s_i \in S\}.$$

It is easy to see that $\mathcal{P}_L$ is totally determined by only $2|S|$ values. $\mathcal{P}_L$ is non-empty provided that $\sum_{i=1}^{n} l_i \leq 1 \leq \sum_{i=1}^{n} u_i$. A set of probability intervals L will be called reachable if, for each s_i, each bound u_i and l_i can be reached by at least one distribution of the family $\mathcal{P}_L$. Reachability is equivalent to the condition

$$\sum_{j \neq i} l_j + u_i \leq 1 \text{ and } \sum_{j \neq i} u_j + l_i \geq 1.$$

Lower and upper probabilities $P_*(A), P^*(A)$ are calculated by

$$P_*(A) = \max(\sum_{s_i \in A} l_i, 1 - \sum_{s_i \notin A} u_i),$$

$$P^*(A) = \min(\sum_{s_i \in A} u_i, 1 - \sum_{s_i \notin A} l_i).$$

De Campos *et al.* [CAM 94] have shown that these bounds are coherent and the lower bounds are 2-monotonic.

Another practical example of credal set is a *p-box* [FER 03]. It is defined by a pair of cumulative distributions $(\underline{F}, \overline{F})$ on the real line such that $\underline{F} \leq \overline{F}$, bounding the cumulative distribution of an imprecisely known probability function P. It is a form of generalized interval. The probability family $\mathcal{P}_{p-box} = \{P, \overline{F}(x) \geq P((-\infty, x]) \geq \underline{F}(x), \forall x \in \mathbb{R}\}$ is a credal set. A *p*-box is a covering approximation of a parameterized probability model whose parameters (such as mean and variance) are only known to belong to an interval.

3.4.2. *Random disjunctive sets and belief functions*

The approach adopted in the theory of evidence [SHA 76] is somewhat reversed with respect to that of the imprecise probability schools. Instead of augmenting the probabilistic approach with higher order uncertainty due to incompleteness described by sets of probabilities, the idea is to inject higher order probabilistic information to the disjunctive set approach to incompleteness.

Instead of a representation of the form $x \in A$ where A is a set of possible values of x, a (generally) discrete probability distribution is defined over the various possible assertions of the form $x \in A$ (assuming a finite frame S). Let m be a probability distribution over the power set 2^S of S. The function m is referred to as *mass assignment*, $m(A)$ the *belief mass* allocated to the set A and *focal set* any subset A of S such that $m(A) > 0$. Let $\mathcal{F}$ be the collection of focal sets. Usually, no positive mass is assigned to the empty set ($m(\varnothing) = 0$ is assumed). However, the Transferable Belief Model (TBM) after Smets [SME 94] does not make this assumption. $m(\varnothing)$ therefore represents the degree of internal contradiction of the mass assignment. The condition $m(\varnothing) = 0$ is a form of normalization. As m is a probability distribution, the condition $\sum_{A \subseteq S} m(A) = 1$ must hold anyway.

In this hybrid representation of uncertainty, it is important to understand the meaning of the mass function. It is also essential not to confuse $m(A)$ with the probability of occurrence of event A. Shafer [SHA 76] stated that $m(A)$ is the belief mass assigned to A only and to none of its subsets. One may also see $m(A)$ as the amount of probability pending over elements of A without yet being assigned, by lack of knowledge. An explanation in the subjective line consists of saying that $m(A)$ is the probability that only the agent knows that $x \in A$. There is therefore an epistemic modality implicitly present in $m(A)$, but absent from $P(A)$. It explains why function m is not required to be inclusion-monotonic. $m(A) > m(B) > 0$ is allowable even if $A \subset B$, when the agent is sure that what is known is of the form $x \in A$. In the language of modal logic, one should write $m(A) = P(\Box A)$ where $\Box$ represents a modality such as 'only the agent knows that...'. In particular, $m(S)$ is the probability that the agent is completely ignorant.

In practice, a mass assignment results from a situation where the available pieces of information only partially determine the quantity of interest. This is typically the case when there is only a compatibility relation (instead of a mapping) between a probability space and the frame S of interest to the agent. Let Ω be a set of possible observations and P a probability measure on Ω supposedly available. Suppose there is a multimapping Γ that defines for each value $\omega \in \Omega$ of the quantity v the set $\Gamma(\omega)$ of possible values of the unknown quantity x in S. If the agent knows $v = \omega$, they only know that $x \in \Gamma(\omega)$ and nothing else. From the knowledge of a probability function on Ω, only a mass assignment on S is derived, namely:

$$\forall A \subseteq S, m(A) = P(\{\omega : \Gamma(\omega) = A\}) \text{ if } \exists \omega \in \Omega, A = \Gamma(\omega),$$

and 0 otherwise. This technique for generating a mass assignment from a multiple-valued function was proposed by Dempster [DEM 67].

Example 3.3. Consider an unreliable watch. The failure probability ϵ is known. The set Ω describes the possible states of the watch $U = \{KO, OK\}$. The agent wishes to know what time it is. S is therefore the set of possible time-points. Suppose the watch indicates time t. Then the multimapping Γ is such that $\Gamma(OK) = \{t\}$ (if the watch is in order, it provides the right time) and $\Gamma(KO) = S$ (if the watch does not work properly, the time is unknown). The induced mass assignment on S is therefore $m(\{t\}) = 1 - \epsilon$ and $m(S) = \epsilon$, which is indeed the probability of not knowing what time it is.

The mass assignment obtained in this example is called a *simple support* because the mass is shared between a single subset A of S and S itself. It is a good model of an unreliable source asserting $x \in A$ that an agent believes is irrelevant with probability ϵ. This value is assigned to S so that $m(A) = 1 - \epsilon$.

The probability space Ω can be considered as a sample space as in the framework of frequentist probabilities. However, it is then assumed that observations are imprecise.

Example 3.4. Consider an opinion poll pertaining to a French presidential election. The set of candidates is $S = \{a, b, c, d, e\}$. There is a population Ω of n individuals that supply their preferences. However, since the opinion poll takes place well before the election, individuals may not have made a final choice even if they do have an opinion. The opinion of individual i is modeled by the subset $\Gamma(i) \subseteq S$. For instance, a left-wing vote is modeled by $\Gamma(i) = \{a, b\}$; for an individual having no opinion, $\Gamma(i) = S$, etc. In this framework, if individual responses of this form are collected, $m(A)$ is the proportion of opinions of the form $\Gamma(i) = A$.

Another method for constructing Γ can be devised when the frame S is multidimensional $S_1 \times S_2 \times \ldots \times S_k$, a probability distribution P is available on part of the frame such as $S_1 \times S_2 \times \ldots \times S_i$, and there is a set of constraints relating the various parameters $x_1, x_2, \ldots, x_k$, thus forming a relation R on S. R represents all admissible tuples in S. Let $U = S_1 \times S_2 \times \ldots \times S_i$. Then if $u = (s_1, s_2, \ldots, s_i)$, denote the set of tuples in S starting with u as $[u]$; then $\Gamma(\omega) = R \cap [u]$. The above watch example is of this kind.

A mass assignment m induces two set-functions: a belief function Bel and a plausibility function Pl, defined:

$$Bel(A) = \sum_{E \subseteq A, E \neq \varnothing} m(E) \qquad (3.18)$$

$$Pl(A) = \sum_{E \cap A \neq \varnothing} m(E). \qquad (3.19)$$

When $m(\varnothing) = 0$, it is clear that $Bel(S) = Pl(S) = 1, Pl(\varnothing) = Bel(\varnothing) = 0$ and $Bel(A) = 1 - Pl(\overline{A})$ i.e. these functions are another example of certainty ($Cer = Bel$) and epistemic possibility ($Ep = Pl$). Belief functions Bel are k-monotonic for any positive integer k, i.e.

$$Bel(\cup_{i=1,\ldots,k} A_i) \geq \sum_{i=1}^{k} (-1)^{i+1} \sum_{I:|I|=i} Bel(\cap_{j \in I} A_j). \qquad (3.20)$$

Plausibility functions satisfy a similar property, reversing the direction of the above inequality.

Conversely, knowing function Bel, a unique mass assignment m can be calculated from the equations that define $Bel(A)$ for all subsets of S, considering values $m(E)$ as unknowns. This is the Moebius transform. This transform, say $M(g)$, actually applies to any set-function g and in particular to the lower envelope P_* of a probability family. Solving these equations is always possible and yields a unique solution in the form of a set-function $m = M(P_*)$ such that $\sum_{A \subseteq S} m(A) = 1$ which, however, may not be everywhere positive.

Links between the cardinality of subsets with positive mass and the order of the k-monotonicity of a confidence function were studied by Chateauneuf and Jaffray [CHA 89]. The positivity of the Moebius transform of a confidence function is characteristic of belief functions. This property shows that belief functions are a special case of coherent lower envelopes, i.e. that $Bel(A) = \inf\{P(A) : P \in \{P : P \geq Bel\}\}$. Nevertheless, this property is generally not exploited in the setting of belief functions. For instance, the TBM [SME 94] considers $Bel(A)$ as the degree of belief in A for an agent, not as a lower bound of some unknown objective or subjective probability. This non-probabilistic point of view affects calculation rules (for conditioning or combination) that must then be devised independently, instead of being induced by probability theory. Smets [SME 97] tried to justify $Bel(A)$ as a genuine non-probabilistic degree of belief through an axiomatic derivation.

Two important particular cases of belief functions must be pointed out:

1) Probability functions are retrieved by assuming focal sets are singletons. It is clear that if $m(A) > 0$ implies $\exists s \in S, A = \{s\}$, then $Bel(A) = Pl(A) = P(A)$ for the probability function such that $P(\{s\}) = m(\{s\}), \forall s \in S$. Conversely, Bel is a probability function if and only if $Bel(A) = Pl(A) \forall A \subseteq S$.

2) Plausibility functions are possibility measures (or via adjunction, belief functions are necessity measures) if and only if focal sets are nested, i.e. $\forall A \neq B \in \mathcal{F}, A \subset B$ or $B \subset A$. Then, $Pl(A \cup B) = \max(Pl(A), Pl(B))$ and $Bel(A \cap B) = \min(Bel(A), Bel(B))$.

Belief functions were first defined on finite frames. Their extension to infinite sets poses tricky mathematical problems in the general case [SHA 79]. Nevertheless, it is possible to define a belief function on the real numbers, based on a continuous mass density bearing on closed intervals [STR 84]. For any pair of real numbers $x \leq y$, the mass density $m([x, y])$ is defined by the bi-dimensional probability density $p(x, y)$ taking value 0 if $x > y$. Then, belief and plausibility degrees of intervals of the form $[-\infty, s]$ (which are actually a lower cumulative distribution $F_*(s) = Bel([-\infty, s])$ and an upper distribution $F^*(s) = Pl([-\infty, s])$) can be obtained as integrals of $p(x, y)$ on the domains $\{(x, y), y \leq s\}$ and $\{(x, y), x \leq s\}$, respectively [SME 05].

Contrary to the case of probabilities, these cumulative functions are not sufficient to reconstruct the mass density function (except when focal intervals are nested), nor to compute belief and plausibility or other events. Clearly the pairs (F_*, F^*) are p-boxes that provide a useful summary of the information contained in a belief function, when the question of interest is one of violating a threshold. The lack of information is all the greater as F_* and F^* stand far away from each other. The credal set $\mathcal{P}(\underline{F}, \overline{F})$ induced by any p-box is in fact representable by a belief function whose focal elements are of the form $\{x, \overline{F}(x) \geq \alpha\} \setminus \{x, \underline{F}(x) \geq \alpha\}$ [KRI 05]. However, the belief function equivalent to the probability box induced by a belief function is less informative than the original.

Smets [SME 90] tried to reconcile the theory of exchangeable bets (justifying subjective probabilities) and the postulate that beliefs of an agent are represented by belief functions. A major objection to subjective probability theory is its lack of distinction between situations of known variability (unbiased dice) and ignorance (unknown dice), as emphasized in section 3.2. The theory of belief functions enables this distinction to be captured: the case of total ignorance is expressed by the mass assignment $m^?(S) = 1$, encoding a situation where $Bel(A) = 0, Pl(A) = 1, \forall A \neq S, \emptyset$ (corresponding to the uninformative possibility distribution $\pi^?$ in section 2.1). In contrast, a uniform probability distribution correctly states that all realizations of a variable v are known to be equiprobable.

If agents ignore all information about variable v, they are therefore led to propose a uniform probability distribution on S following the Insufficient Reason principle of Laplace. If the agent has some knowledge in the form of a belief function with mass assignment m, Smets [SME 90] suggests that the agent should bet with a probability distribution defined by replacing each focal set E by a uniform probability distribution with support E, then computing the convex mixing of these probabilities weighted by masses $m(E)$. This is the so-called *pignistic* probability defined by the distribution $BetP$:

$$BetP(s) = \sum_{E: s \in E} \frac{m(E)}{Card(E)}. \tag{3.21}$$

This transformation of a belief function into a probability function was originally proposed by Dubois and Prade [DUB 82] with a view to generalizing the Laplace principle. Smets [SME 90] provided an axiomatic justification, finding the probability function satisfying a linearity property (the pignistic probability of a convex sum of belief functions is the convex sum of their pignistic probabilities) and a property of anonymity (the pignistic probability of an event should not change when realizations of this event are exchanged). In fact, the pignistic probability has been known in cooperative game theory since the 1950's under the name *Shapley value*. Smets axioms are mathematically the same as those proposed by Shapley [SHA 53] in a quite different context.

Belief functions can be compared in terms of their informative content. Note that belief functions model imprecise and uncertain information at the same time;

we may wish to evaluate their imprecision and their uncertainty separately. A natural imprecision index of a belief function is the expected cardinality of its mass assignment:

$$Imp(m) = \sum_{E \subseteq S} m(E) \cdot Card(E). \quad (3.22)$$

It is clear that $Imp(m^?) = Card(S)$ and $Imp(m) = 1$ if the mass assignment is a probability. It can be checked that $Imp(m) = \sum_{s \in S} Pl(\{s\})$, i.e. it only depends on the plausibility of the singletons. This numerical index is in agreement with relations comparing belief functions in terms of their imprecision:

– A mass assignment m_1 is said to be at least as specific as a mass assignment m_2 if $\forall s \in S, Pl_1(\{s\}) \leq Pl_2(\{s\})$. This is a natural requirement due to the property of the cardinality-based imprecision index, viewing the function $Pl(\{s\}) \forall s \in S$ (referred to as the *contour function* by Shafer [SHA 76]) as a possibility distribution.

– A mass assignment m_1 is said to be more precise than a mass assignment m_2 if and only if for all events A, the interval $[Bel_1(A), Pl_1(A)]$ is included in the interval $[Bel_2(A), Pl_2(A)]$. Due to the adjunction property between Pl and Bl, it is enough that inequality $\forall A, Pl_1(A) \leq Pl_2(A)$, holds. In other words, the narrower the interval $[Bel(A), Pl(A)]$, the closer it is to a single probability. If $\mathcal{P}(m) = \{P, P(A) \leq Pl(A), \forall A\}$, m_1 being more precise than m_2 means that the credal set $\mathcal{P}(m_1)$ is a subset of $\mathcal{P}(m_2)$. The function m is therefore maximally precise when it coincides with a unique probability, and minimally precise if $m = m^?$.

– A mass function m_1 is a *specialization* of a mass assignment m_2 if and only if the following three conditions are verified:

1) Any focal set of m_2 contains at least one focal set of m_1.
2) Any focal set of m_1 is included in at least one focal set of m_2.
3) There is a stochastic matrix W whose term w_{ij} is the fraction of the mass $m_1(E_i)$ of the focal set E_i of m_1 that can be reallocated to the focal set F_j of m_2 in order to retrieve the mass $m_2(F_j)$, namely, $m_2(F_j) = \sum_i w_{ij} \cdot m_1(E_i)$, with constraint $w_{ij} > 0$ only if $E_i \subseteq F_j$.

The latter relation is more demanding than the former: if m_1 is a specialization of m_2, then m_1 is also more precise and more specific than m_2. It is also obvious that if m_1 is a specialization of m_2, then $Imp(m_1) \leq Imp(m_2)$. The converse properties do not hold. Comparing contour functions is less demanding than comparing plausibilities, and $Pl_1 < Pl_2$ does not imply that m_1 is a specialization of m_2 [DUB 86b].

Example 3.5. $S = \{s_1, s_2, s_3\}$. Suppose $m_1(\{s_1, s_2\}) = \frac{1}{2}$, $m_1(\{s_1, s_3\}) = \frac{1}{2}$, $m_2(\{s_1\}) = \frac{1}{2}$ and $m_2(S) = \frac{1}{2}$. It is easy to see that none of these mass assignments is a specialization of another (the inclusion requirements between focal sets are violated). However, m_1 is less precise than m_2 (because $Pl_1(A) = Pl_2(A)$ except if $A = \{s_2, s_3\}$, for which $Pl_1(\{s_2, s_3\}) = 1 > Pl_2(\{s_2, s_3\}) = 0.5$). However, the two contour functions are the same.

The uncertainty of a belief function can be evaluated by a generalization of entropy $H(P) = -\sum_{i=1}^{card(S)} p_i \cdot ln p_i$. Several extensions were proposed [DUB 87]:

– A measure of dissonance: $D(m) = -\sum_{E \subseteq S} m(E) \cdot ln Pl(E)$, maximal for uniform probability distributions, minimal ($= 0$) as soon as $Pl(E) = 1$ for all focal sets E (i.e. they intersect: $\cap \{E : m(E) > 0\} \neq \emptyset$).

– A measure of confusion: $D(m) = -\sum_{E \subseteq S} m(E) \cdot ln Bel(E)$, high (in fact, maximal for index obtained by deleting the logarithm and the minus sign from this expression; [DUB 93b]) for uniform mass assignments over all sets with cardinality $\frac{card(S)}{2}$ and minimal ($= 0$) as soon as $m(E) = 1$ for a focal set (incomplete and crisp information).

– Klir and Parviz [KLI 92] proposed measuring the uncertainty of a mass assignment m by means of the entropy of its pignistic probability, which evaluates the amount of indecision of an agent faced with a betting situation under uncertainty. More recently, other suggestions include maximizing and minimizing $H(P)$ when P ranges in the credal set associated with the belief function.

3.4.3. *Quantitative possibility theory*

Like imprecise probability and evidence theories, possibility theory represents uncertainty by means of two adjoint set-functions: a necessity measure N that is 'minitive' and a possibility measure Π that is 'maxitive'. They have already been introduced in sections 3.2.2 and 3.2.3.

In this section, one sees these set-functions as lower and upper probabilities since they can be generated from mass functions associated with nested focal sets. While Zadeh [ZAD 78] defines possibility distributions from linguistic pieces of information, the idea of considering possibility measures as counterparts to probability measures is due to the economist Shackle [SHA 61], who named the degree of potential surprise of event A the quantity $N(\overline{A}) = 1 - \Pi(A)$.

Possibility theory, in its numerical variant, proposes a very simple model of uncertainty tailored for imprecise information and it can encode particular families of probabilities in a very concise way. This model not only enables us to represent linguistic information (according to Zadeh), but it also generalizes the set-based representation of information (propositional logic and interval analysis). It can, in an approximate way, represent imprecise statistical information [DUB 00].

3.4.3.1. *Possibility theory and belief functions*

More precisely, let m be a mass function on a finite set S. One defines the possibility distribution π induced by m, also called its contour function, by letting $\pi(s) = \text{Pl}(\{s\})$ (plausibility of singletons), i.e.

$$\forall s \in S, \pi(s) = \sum_{s \in E} m(E). \tag{3.23}$$

It is easy to see that π takes its values on [0, 1] and is normalized ($\pi(s) = 1$ for some state $s \in S$) as soon as the focal sets have a common non-empty intersection (in particular, this is the case when they are nested). Recovering m from π is possible only when the focal sets are nested or disjoint. Assume that the focal sets are nested. Then they can be rank ordered in an increasing sequence $E_1 \subset E_2 \subset \ldots \subset E_n$ where $E_i = \{s_1, \ldots, s_i\}$, then

$$\pi(s_i) = \sum_{j=i}^{n} m(E_j).$$

The possibility and necessity measures Π and N, defined by equation (3.8) from π, coincide with the plausibility and belief functions induced by m. The mass function can then be recalculated from π as follows (letting $\pi(s_{n+1}) = 0$):

$$m_\pi(E_i) = \pi(s_i) - \pi(s_{i-1}), i = 1, \ldots, n. \tag{3.24}$$

We can therefore see that, in the finite consonant case, m_π and π contain the same information and that $Pl = \Pi$ and $Bel = N$. However, in the infinite case, the relation between consonant random sets and possibility measures is more complex in the general case [MIR 02, MIR 04].

For possibility measures, the precision and specialization orderings coincide with the specificity ordering of possibility distributions on the singletons. m_{π_1} is a specialization of m_{π_2} if and only if $\Pi_1(A) \leq \Pi_2(A), \forall A \subseteq S$ if and only if $\pi_1(s) \leq \pi_2(s), \forall s \in S$ [DUB 86b].

In the general case, π is only an approximation of m and it can be checked that π is the least specific possibility distribution such that $Pl \geq \Pi$ and $Bel \leq N$ [DUB 90b]. It is worth noticing that if the focal sets are imprecise observations coming from a random experiment, equation (3.23) represents the possibilistic counterpart of a histogram.

3.4.3.2. *Possibility theory and imprecise probabilities*

As belief functions mathematically correspond to a particular case of family of probability measures, this is especially true for possibility distributions. Let us again consider the case of an increasing sequence of nested sets $E_1 \subset E_2 \subset, \ldots, \subset E_k$. Let $\nu_1 \leq \nu_2 \leq \ldots \leq \nu_k$ be lower bounds of probability and let $\mathcal{P} = \{P, P(E_i) \geq \nu_i, \forall i = 1, \ldots, k\}$. This is typically the kind of information provided by an expert who expresses himself in an imprecise way about the value of a parameter. He suggests that $x \in E_i$ with a confidence degree at least equal to ν_i. Then $P_*(A) = \inf_{P \in \mathcal{P}} P(A)$ is a necessity measure and $P^*(A) = \sup_{P \in \mathcal{P}} P(A)$ is a possibility measure, based on the possibility distribution [DUB 92a]:

$$\forall s \in S, \pi(s) = \min_{i=1,\ldots,k} \max(E_i(s), 1 - \nu_i) \tag{3.25}$$

with $E_i(s) = 1$ if $s \in E_i$ and 0 otherwise. See De Cooman and Aeyels [DEC 99] for an extension of this result to the infinite case.

In this framework, each E_i is a kind of confidence set (an interval in the case where $S = \mathbb{R}$) and the probability of belonging to this set is at least ν_i. The probability of not belonging to E_i is therefore at most $1 - \nu_i$. This confidence set weighted by a certainty degree corresponds to the possibility distribution $\max(E_i(s), 1 - \nu_i)$. The above equation is nothing but the conjunction of these local distributions. It is clear that distribution π encodes in a very compact way the family of probabilities $\mathcal{P}$. Conversely, a possibility distribution π encodes the credal set defined by $\mathcal{P}(\pi) = \{P, P(A) \leq \Pi(A), \forall A \text{ measurable}\} = \{P, P(A) \geq N(A), \forall A \text{ measurable}\}$.

In the case where $S = \mathbb{R}$, an important particular case of possibility distribution is a *fuzzy interval*. Distribution π is assumed to be upper semi-continuous and quasi-concave ($\forall a, b, c \in \mathbb{R}, \pi(c) \geq \min(\pi(a), \pi(b))$); its level cuts $\{s, \pi(s) \geq \alpha\}, \alpha \in (0, 1]$ are then nested closed intervals $[a_\alpha^-, a_\alpha^+]$. We can associate with π a mass density m_π uniformly distributed over its level cuts. The lower and upper cumulative functions $F_*(s) = N([-\infty, s])$ and $F^*(s) = \Pi([-\infty, s])$ are of the form

$$F^*(s) = \pi(s), s \in (-\infty, a_1^-], \text{ and } 1 \text{ if } s \geq a_1^- \tag{3.26}$$

and

$$F_*(s) = 1 - \pi(s), s \in [a_1^+, +\infty) \text{ and } 0 \text{ if } s \leq a_1^+, \tag{3.27}$$

respectively.

Let us consider an interval $A = [x, y]$ including the core of π. The inequality $P(A) \leq \Pi(A)$ implies $F(x) + 1 - F(y) \leq \max(\pi(x), \pi(y))$ where F is the cumulative function of P. One can check that the credal set $\mathcal{P}(\pi)$ is precisely equal to $\{P, \forall x \leq a_1^-, \forall y \geq a_1^+, F(x) + 1 - F(y) \leq \max(\pi(x), \pi(y))\}$. It is generally strictly included in the credal set $\{P, F^* \geq F \geq F_*\}$ [DUB 91] of the corresponding p-box. The *mean interval* $[e^-(\pi), e^+(\pi)]$ of π is the set of mean values of the probability distributions in $\mathcal{P}(\pi)$. Its bounds are nevertheless the mean values induced by F^* and F_*, respectively.

3.4.3.3. *Clouds and generalized p-boxes*

Interestingly, the notion of cumulative distribution is based on the existence of the natural ordering of numbers. On a finite set, no obvious notion of cumulative distribution exists. In order to make sense of this notion over X, we must equip it with a complete preordering. It is reduced to a family of nested confidence sets $\emptyset \subseteq A_1 \subseteq A_2 \subseteq \ldots \subseteq A_n \subset S$, with $A_i = \{s_1, \ldots, s_i\}$. Consider two cumulative distributions according to this ordering, which form a *p*-box. The credal set $\mathcal{P}$ can then be represented by the following restrictions on probability measures

$$\alpha_i \leq P(A_i) \leq \beta_i \qquad i = 1, \ldots, n \tag{3.28}$$

with $\alpha_1 \leq \alpha_2 \leq \ldots \leq \alpha_n \leq 1$ and $\beta_1 \leq \beta_2 \leq \ldots \leq \beta_n \leq 1$. If we take $S = \mathbb{R}$ and $A_i = (-\infty, s_i]$, it is easy to see that we retrieve the usual definition of a *p*-box.

The credal set $\mathcal{P}$ described by such a generalized *p*-box can be encoded by a pair of possibility distributions π_1, π_2 s.t. $\mathcal{P} = \mathcal{P}(\pi_1) \cap \mathcal{P}(\pi_2)$ where π_1 comes from constraints $\alpha_i \leq P(A_i)$ and π_2 from constraints $P(A_i) \leq \beta_i$. Again, it is representable by a belief function [DES 07c].

A *cloud* [NEU 04] can be seen as an interval-valued fuzzy set F such that $(0,1) \subseteq \cup_{x \in S} F(s) \subseteq [0,1]$, where $F(s)$ is an interval $[\delta(s), \pi(s)]$. It implies that $\pi(s) = 1$ for some s (π is a possibility distribution) and $\delta(s') = 0$ for some s' ($1 - \delta$ is also a possibility distribution). A probability measure P on S is said to belong to a cloud F if and only if $\forall \alpha \in [0,1]$:

$$P(\delta(s) \geq \alpha) \leq 1 - \alpha \leq P(\pi(s) > \alpha) \tag{3.29}$$

under all suitable measurability assumptions. From this definition, a cloud (δ, π) is equivalent to the cloud $(1 - \pi, 1 - \delta)$. If S is a finite space of cardinality n, let $A_i = \{s_i, \pi(s_i) > \alpha_{i+1}\}$ and $B_i = \{s_i, \delta(s_i) \geq \alpha_{i+1}\}$. A cloud can therefore be defined by the following restrictions [DES 07c]:

$$P(B_i) \leq 1 - \alpha_i \leq P(A_i) \text{ and } B_i \subseteq A_i \quad i = 1, \ldots, n \tag{3.30}$$

where $1 = \alpha_0 > \alpha_1 > \alpha_2 > \ldots > \alpha_n > \alpha_{n+1} = 0$, $\emptyset = A_0 \subset A_1 \subseteq A_2 \subseteq \ldots \subseteq A_n \subseteq A_{n+1} = S$ and $\emptyset = B_0 \subseteq B_1 \subseteq B_2 \subseteq \ldots \subseteq B_n \subseteq B_{n+1} = S$.

Let $\mathcal{P}(\delta, \pi)$ be the credal set described by the cloud (δ, π) on a frame S. Clouds are closely related to possibility distributions and *p*-boxes as follows [DES 07c]:

– $\mathcal{P}(\delta, \pi) = \mathcal{P}(\pi) \cap \mathcal{P}(1 - \delta)$ using the credal sets induced by the two possibility distributions π and $1 - \delta$.

– A cloud is a generalized *p*-box with $\pi_1 = \pi$ and $\pi_2(s_{i+1}) = 1 - \delta(s_i)$ if and only if the sets $\{A_i, B_i, i = 1, \ldots, n\}$ form a nested sequence (i.e. there is a complete order with respect to inclusion). In other words, it means that π and δ are comonotonic. A comonotonic cloud is a generalized *p*-box and generates upper and lower probabilities that are plausibility and belief functions.

– When the cloud is not comonotonic, $\mathcal{P}(\delta, \pi)$ generates lower probabilities that are not even 2-monotone [DES 07c]. It is anyway possible to approximate upper and lower probabilities of events from the outside by possibility and necessity measures based on π and $1 - \delta$:

$$\max(N_\pi(A), N_{1-\delta}(A)) \leq P(A) \leq \min(\Pi_\pi(A), \Pi_{1-\delta}(A)).$$

The belief and plausibility functions of the random set $m(A_i \setminus B_{i-1}) = \alpha_{i-1} - \alpha_i$ are inner approximations of $\mathcal{P}(\delta, \pi)$, which become exact when the cloud is monotonic.

When $\pi = \delta$, the cloud is said to be thin. In the finite case, $\mathcal{P}(\pi, \pi) = \emptyset$. To ensure it is not empty, we need a one-step index shift such that (assuming the $\pi(s_i)$ are decreasingly ordered) $\delta(s_i) = \pi(s_{i+1})$ (with $\pi(s_{n+1}) = 0$). $\mathcal{P}(\delta, \pi)$ then contains a single probability distribution p such that $p(s_i) = \pi(s_i) - \pi(s_{i+1})$. In the continuous case, $\mathcal{P}(\pi, \pi)$ contains an infinity of probability measures and corresponds to a random set whose realizations are doubletons (the end-points of the cuts of π).

The strong complementarity between possibilistic and probabilistic representations of uncertainty is noticeable. While a probability distribution naturally represents precise pieces of information with their variability (what is called statistical data), a possibility distribution encodes imprecise, but consonant, pieces of information (expressed by the nestedness of focal sets).

One may consider that the possibilistic representation is more natural for uncertain subjective information, in the sense that from a human agent one rather expects consonant pieces of information with some imprecision, rather than artificially precise but scattered pieces of information. The fact that a probability measure is lower bounded by a necessity measure and upper bounded by a possibility measure ($N(A) \leq P(A) \leq \Pi(A), \forall A$) expresses a compatibility principle between possibility and probability: for any event, being probable is more demanding than being possible, and being somewhat certain is more demanding than being probable [ZAD 78]. A probability measure P and a possibility measure Π are said to be *compatible* if and only if $P \in \mathcal{P}(\pi)$.

3.4.3.4. *Possibility-probability transformations*

It is legitimate to look for transformations between probabilistic and possibilistic representations of information. There are several reasons for that. On the one hand, with a view of fusing heterogenous pieces of information (linguistic pieces of information, measurements issued from sensors), we may wish to have a unique representation framework at our disposal. Besides, the useful information extracted from probability distributions is often much less informative than the original distribution (a prediction interval, a mean value, etc.).

Conversely, the subjectivist interpretation of probabilities by the betting theory can be regarded as a probabilistic formalization of the often incomplete pieces of information provided by an agent. Lastly, possibility theory allows us to systematize notions that already exist in the practice of statisticians under an incompletely developed form. The transformation between a probability measure P and a possibility measure Π should obey natural requirements as follows:

– *Possibility-probability consistency*: P and Π should be compatible.

– *Ordinal faithfulness*: we cannot require the equivalence between $P(A) \geq P(B)$ and $\Pi(A) \geq \Pi(B), \forall A, B \subseteq S$, since the ordering induced on the events by P will always be more refined than that induced by Π. Then one should only ensure an ordinal equivalence between the distributions p and π, i.e. $p(s_i) \geq p(s_j)$ if and only if $\pi(s_i) \geq \pi(s_j), \forall s_i, s_j \in S$. We may also only require a weaker ordinal equivalence, for instance considering that $p(s_i) > p(s_j)$ implies $\pi(s_i) > \pi(s_j)$ but $p(s_i) = p(s_j)$ does not entail $\pi(s_i) = \pi(s_j)$.

– *Informativity*: probabilistic representation is more precise, thus richer than possibilistic representation. Information is lost when going from the first to the second; information is gained in the converse way. From possibility to probability, one should try to preserve the symmetries existing in the possibilistic representation. From probability to possibility, we should try to lose as little information as possible if the probability measure is statistically meaningful. The case of a subjective probability is different since it often corresponds to poorer knowledge artificially increased by the probabilistic representation, so that a least commitment principle might prevail.

3.4.3.4.1. From possibility to probability

To change a possibility distribution into a probability distribution, it is natural to use the pignistic transformation [SME 90]. If $card(S) = n$, let us denote $\pi_i = \pi(s_i), i = 1, \ldots, n$, assuming that $\pi_1 \geq \pi_2 \geq \ldots \geq \pi_n$. The pignistic transform is a probability distribution p ordinally equivalent to π, such that $p_1 \geq p_2 \geq \ldots \geq p_n$, with $p_i = p(s_i), i = 1, \ldots, n$:

$$p_i = \sum_{j=i}^{n} \frac{\pi_j - \pi_{j+1}}{j}, \forall i = 1, \ldots, n. \qquad (3.31)$$

In the case of a fuzzy interval, the mass density associated with $[a_\alpha^-, a_\alpha^+]$ is changed into a uniform probability over this interval, and one considers the uniform probabilistic mixture obtained by integrating over $\alpha \in [0, 1]$. This amounts to building the probability measure of the process obtained by picking a number $\alpha \in [0, 1]$ at random and then an element $s \in [a_\alpha^-, a_\alpha^+]$ at random [CHA 88]. The mean value of the pignistic probability is the middle of the mean interval of π introduced in section 3.4.3.2. This transformation generalizes the Laplace Insufficient Reason principle, since it yields the corresponding uniform probability when applied to a uniform possibility distribution over an interval.

3.4.3.4.2. From subjective probability to possibility

For the converse change, from probability to possibility, one should distinguish the case where one starts with a subjective probability from the situation where there exist statistics justifying the probability distribution. In the subjectivist framework, and in agreement with the debatable nature of the unique probability provided by an expert, one assumes that the knowledge of the agent is a belief function with mass m over a finite frame S. The elicitation process forces them to provide a probability distribution p that is considered to be the pignistic transform of m. By default, one considers that the least biased belief function is the least informative one, if it exists, among those whose pignistic transform is p [SME 00]. If we look for the mass assignment that maximizes the imprecision index $Imp(m) = \sum_{j=i}^{n} \pi_j$ (equation (3.22)), it can be proved that this mass assignment is unique, that it is consonant and that it is also minimally specific (w.r.t. the plausibility of singletons) [DUB 03]. By noticing that the pignistic transformation is a one-to-one mapping between probability and possibility, the least biased representation of the agent's knowledge leading to the subjective probability distribution p is obtained by reversing equation (3.31):

$$\pi_i = \sum_{j=1}^{n} \min(p_i, p_j), \forall i = 1, \ldots, n. \qquad (3.32)$$

This transformation has been independently introduced by Dubois and Prade; see [DUB 83].

3.4.3.4.3. From objective probability to possibility

In the case of an objective probability distribution, when changing representation one should try to lose as little information as possible. This leads to the search for a possibility distribution π among the most specific ones such that $P \in \mathcal{P}(\pi)$ and which is ordinally equivalent to p.

Let us first consider the discrete case. If $p_1 > p_2 > \ldots > p_n$ and $E_i = \{s_1, \ldots, s_i\}$, it is enough to let $\Pi(E_i) \geq P(E_i) \forall i = 1, \ldots, n$ in order to make p and π compatible. By forcing equalities, we obtain a unique possibility distribution, maximally specific and ordinally equivalent to p [DUB 82]:

$$\pi_i = \sum_{j=i}^{n} p_j, \forall i = 1, \ldots, n. \qquad (3.33)$$

Unicity is preserved when the inequalities between the p_i are no longer strict but the transformation is written $\pi_i = \sum_{j:p_j \leq p_i} p_j, \forall i = 1, \ldots, n$ which maintains ordinal faithfulness. If we relax this constraint, we may obtain possibility distributions compatible with p that are more specific than the former. In particular, equation (3.33) always yields a possibility distribution that is maximally specific and consistent with p. For instance, if p is a uniform distribution, there are $n!$ ways of ordering S and equation (3.33) gives $n!$ non-uniform possibility distributions, maximally specific and consistent with p.

In the case of a unimodal continuous density p over $\mathbb{R}$, this possibility-probability transformation can be extended by considering the level cuts of p, i.e. the subsets $E_\lambda = \{s, p(s) \geq \lambda\}, \lambda \in (0, \sup p]$. If we denote $E_\lambda = [x(\lambda), y(\lambda)]$, then the possibility distributions that are maximally specific and ordinally equivalent to p are defined by

$$\pi(x(\lambda)) = \pi(y(\lambda)) = 1 - P(E_\lambda). \tag{3.34}$$

Indeed, it can be proved more generally that, if $P(E_\lambda) = q$, the measurable set A having the smallest measure such that $P(A) = q$ is E_λ [DUB 93a, DUB 04b]. If p is unimodal, E_λ is the interval with length $L = y(\lambda) - s(\lambda)$ that is the most legitimate representative of the probability density p, in the sense where E_λ is the interval with length L having maximal probability $P(E_\lambda) \geq P([a, b]), \forall a, b$ such that $b - a = L$.

Transformation equation (3.34) can therefore be related to a view of a prediction interval as an imprecise substitute of a probability density, with a given confidence level (often 0.95). Most of the time, this type of interval is defined for symmetrical densities and the considered intervals are centered around the mean. The interval with confidence 0.95 is often defined by the 0.025 and 0.975 percentiles. Characterizing the prediction interval with confidence 0.95 by these percentiles when the distributions are non-symmetrical is not very convincing since this may eliminate values with higher density than those of the values in this interval. It is much more natural to look for λ such that $P(E_\lambda) = 0.95$.

More generally, the α level cut of the possibility distribution π obtained by equation (3.34) from p is the smallest interval with confidence $1 - \alpha$ deducible from p. We can find in the statistical literature a proposal for comparing probability densities according to their 'peakedness' [BIR 48]. This is a comparison of their possibilistic transforms in terms of their relative specificity. Moreover, the information ordering of probability measures by means of the entropy index refines the partial specificity of their possibilistic transforms [DUB 07].

Transformation equation (3.34) builds a family of nested sets around the mode of p. One may systematically build a possibility measure consistent with p by considering any characteristic value s^* in the support of p and a family of subsets A_λ nested around s^*, indexed by $\lambda \in [0, \omega]$ such that $A_\omega = \{s^*\}$ and $A_0 = support(p)$.

For instance, if s^* is the mean mea of p with standard deviation σ, and if one sets $A_\lambda = [mea - \lambda \cdot \sigma, mea + \lambda \cdot \sigma]$, the Chebychev inequality gives us $P(\overline{A_\lambda}) \leq$

$\min(1, \frac{1}{\lambda^2})$. The possibility distribution obtained by letting $\pi(mea-\lambda\cdot\sigma) = \pi(mea+\lambda\cdot\sigma) = \min(1, \frac{1}{\lambda^2})$ is therefore consistent with any probability measure with mean mea and standard deviation σ.

The probability-possibility transforms can yield other probabilistic inequalities. It has been shown that a symmetrical triangular possibility distribution with bounded support $[a, b]$ is consistent with any unimodal symmetrical probability function having the same support, and contains the prediction intervals of all these probability measures [DUB 04b]. Moreover, it is the most specific one having these properties (it is consistent with the uniform density over $[a, b]$). This provides, for this distribution family, a probabilistic inequality that is much stronger than that of Chebychev, and justifies the use of triangular fuzzy intervals for representing incomplete probabilistic information. See Baudrit and Dubois [BAU 06] for possibilistic representations of probability families induced by partial knowledge of distribution characteristics.

3.4.4. *Possibility theory and non-Bayesian statistics*

Another interpretation of numerical possibility distributions is the likelihood function in non-Bayesian statistics [DUB 97, SME 82]. In the framework of an estimation problem, one is interested in the determination of the value of some parameter $\theta \in \Theta$ that defines a probability distribution $P(\cdot \mid \theta)$ over S. Suppose that we observed event A. The function $P(A \mid \theta), \theta \in \Theta$ is not a probability distribution, but a likelihood function $\mathcal{L}(\theta)$. A value a of θ is considered as being all the more plausible if $P(A \mid a)$ is higher and the hypothesis $\theta = a$ will be rejected if $P(A \mid a) = 0$ (or is below some relevance threshold). Often, this function is renormalized so that its maximum is equal to 1. We are allowed to let $\pi(a) = P(A \mid a)$ (thanks to this renormalization) and to interpret this likelihood function in terms of possibility degrees. In particular, it can be checked that $\forall B \subseteq \Theta$ bounds for the value of $P(A \mid B)$ can be computed as:

$$\min_{\theta \in B} P(A \mid \theta) \leq P(A \mid B) \leq \max_{\theta \in B} P(A \mid \theta)$$

which shows that the maxitivity axiom corresponds to an optimistic computation of $P(A \mid B) = \Pi(B)$. It is easy to check that letting $P(A \mid B) = \max_{\theta \in B} P(A \mid \theta)$ is the only way for building a confidence function about θ from $P(A \mid \theta), \theta \in \Theta$. Indeed, the monotonicity w.r.t. inclusion of the likelihood function $\mathcal{L}$ forces $P(A \mid B) \geq \max_{\theta \in B} P(A \mid \theta)$ to hold [COL 03].

The maximum likelihood principle originally due to Fisher consists of choosing the value of the parameter $\theta = \theta^*$, induced by the observation A, that maximizes $P(A \mid \theta)$. It is clear that this selection principle for the estimation of a parameter is in total agreement with possibility theory.

Another element of non-Bayesian statistical analysis is the extraction of a confidence interval for θ on the basis of repeated observations. Let us suppose that the observations $s_1, s_2, \ldots, s_k$ result in an estimation $\hat{\theta}$ of the actual value θ^*. Let I_θ be a confidence interval for θ such that $P(I_\theta \mid s_1, s_2, \ldots, s_k) \geq 1 - \epsilon$. One can choose the tightest interval E_ϵ of values of θ with probability $1 - \epsilon$, by taking a cut of the density $p(I_\theta \mid s_1, s_2, \ldots, s_k)$ (as suggested by the probability-possibility transformations). It is the smallest confidence interval containing the value of θ^* with a confidence level $1 - \epsilon$. One often takes $\epsilon = 0,05$, which is arbitrary. It is clear that by letting ϵ vary between 0 and 1, one obtains a family of nested sets E_ϵ providing information about θ^*. Statistical analysis by means of confidence intervals can thus be understood as the construction of a possibility distribution that provides an imprecise estimate of the value of parameter θ. It can be viewed as a possibility distribution (of order 2) over probability measures $P(\cdot|\theta)$.

3.5. Qualitative uncertainty representations

It seems more natural in an ordinal framework to represent the relative confidence that an agent has between various propositions expressing their knowledge rather than trying to force them to deliver numerical evaluations. It is indeed easier to assert that a proposition is more credible than another, rather than assessing a belief degree (whose meaning is not always simple to grasp), or even to guess a frequency for each of them. The idea of representing uncertainty by means of relations over a set of events dates back to De Finetti [DEF 37], Koopman [KOO 40] and Ramsey [RAM 80], who tried to find an ordinal counterpart to subjective probabilities. Later, philosophers of logic such as Lewis [LEW 86] have considered other types of relations, including comparative possibilities in the framework of modal logic. This section offers an overview of ordinal representations of uncertainty, in relation to their numerical counterparts.

The ordinal approaches represent uncertainty by means of a relative confidence relation between propositions (or events) interpreted as subsets of the set S of the states of the world. Such a relation expresses the more or less high confidence of an agent in some propositions rather than in others. Let us denote by $\geq_\kappa$ the confidence relation defined on the set of propositions (subsets of S). $A \geq_\kappa B$ means that the agent is at least as confident in the truth of A as in the truth of B. This relation is in general a partial preorder, since the agent may not know the relative confidence between all the propositions. $>_\kappa$ denotes the strict part of $\geq_\kappa$ (i.e. $A >_\kappa B$ if and only if $A \geq_\kappa B$ but not $B \geq_\kappa A$). It states that the agent is strictly more confident in A than in B. The agent has equal confidence in A and in B when both $A \geq_\kappa B$ and $B \geq_\kappa A$ hold, which is denoted $A =_\kappa B$. These relations are supposed to satisfy the following properties:

– *reflexivity* of $\geq_\kappa$: $A \geq_\kappa A$, $\forall A$;

– *non-triviality* $S >_\kappa \emptyset$;
– *coherence with logical deduction*, expressed by two properties:
   1) $A \subseteq B$ entails $B \geq_\kappa A$ (monotony w.r.t. inclusion of $\geq_\kappa$); and
   2) if $A \subseteq B, C \subseteq D$ and $A >_\kappa D$, then $B >_\kappa C$ (well-ordered relation);
– *transitivity* of $>_\kappa$: if $A >_\kappa B$ and $B >_\kappa C$ then $A >_\kappa C$.

These four hypotheses are difficult to challenge. The two coherence conditions w.r.t. deduction are independent except if the relation $\geq_\kappa$ is complete (i.e. we have $A \geq_\kappa B$ or $B \geq_\kappa A$, $\forall A, B$) or transitive. Transitivity and completeness of $\geq_\kappa$ become natural if the confidence relation can be represented by a confidence function g with values in $[0, 1]$. In this case, the confidence relation $\geq_\kappa$ is a complete preorder. A confidence function g represents a confidence relation as soon as

$$A \geq_\kappa B \text{ if and only if } g(A) \leq g(B), \forall A, B.$$

All the set-functions used for modeling uncertainty (probability measures, possibility measures and belief functions) correspond to complete preorders between propositions, satisfying particular properties. (This is except for the set-functions studied by Friedman and Halpern [FRI 96] under the name of *plausibility measures*, which induce partial preorders of relative confidence. This name *plausibility measures* is misleading as they have no relationship to Shafer's plausibility functions.)

Comparative probability relations are the first relations of uncertainty that were introduced [DEF 37, KOO 40]. They have been studied in detail by Savage [SAV 72] in the framework of decision theory. A comparative probability relation $\geq_{prob}$ is a complete and transitive confidence relation on the propositions, which satisfies the *preadditivity* property if A, B, C are three subsets such that $A \cap (B \cup C) = \emptyset$,

$$B \geq_{prob} C \text{ if and only if } A \cup B \geq_{prob} A \cup C.$$

It is clear that any relation between events induced by a probability measure is preadditive. The converse is false as shown by Kraft *et al.* [KRA 59] by means of the following counter-example on a set S with five elements. Let a comparative probability relation satisfy the following properties:

$$s_4 >_{prob} \{s_1, s_3\};$$

$$\{s_2, s_3\} >_{prob} \{s_1, s_4\};$$

$$\{s_1, s_5\} >_{prob} \{s_3, s_4\};$$

$$\{s_1, s_3, s_4\} >_{prob} \{s_2, s_5\}.$$

The reader can easily check that a comparative probability relation satisfying the above conditions exists, but that there does not exist a probability measure satisfying them. A comparative probability relation is therefore an object that is partially non-probabilistic and less easy to handle than a probability function. In particular, a probability measure on a finite set is completely defined by the probabilities of the elements, but a comparative probability relation is not fully characterized by its restriction on singletons.

Confidence relations that have this simplicity are possibility and necessity relations. Comparative possibility relations were independently introduced in the 1970s [LEW 76] in the framework of modal logics of counterfactuals as well as from a decision theory perspective [DUB 86a]. Comparative possibility relations $\geq_\Pi$ are complete and transitive confidence relations satisfying the following characteristic property of *disjunctive stability*:

$$\forall C, B \geq_\Pi A \text{ entails } C \cup B \geq_\Pi C \cup A.$$

Their numerical counterparts in the finite setting are (and are only) the possibility functions Π with values in a totally ordered set L with bottom element 0 and top element 1. Each possibility relation can be entirely specified by means of a unique complete preorder $\geq_\pi$ on the states of the world. $s_1 \geq_\pi s_2$ means that the state s_1 is in general at least as plausible (i.e. normal, unsurprising) as state s_2. The possibility relation on events is then defined as follows:

$$B \geq_\Pi A \text{ if and only if } \exists s_1 \in B, \forall s_2 \in A, s_1 \geq_\pi s_2.$$

The degree of possibility of event A therefore reflects the plausibility of the state of the world which is the most normal where A is true. The case where the preorder on the events is induced by a partial order on S was studied by Halpern [HAL 97]. Possibility relations are not invariant by negation. Comparative necessity relations are defined by duality: $B \geq_N A$ if and only if $\overline{A} \geq_\Pi \overline{B}$. The relation $B \geq_N A$ means that A is at least as certain as B. These necessity relations satisfy a characteristic property called *conjunctive stability*:

$$\forall C, B \geq_N A \text{ entails } C \cap B \geq_N C \cap A.$$

The corresponding set-functions are necessity measures such that $N(A \cap B) = \min(N(A), N(B))$. Any possibility distribution π from S to a totally ordered set L representing $\geq_\pi$ (i.e. $\pi(s_1) \geq \pi(s_2)$ if and only if $s_1 \geq_\pi s_2$) is defined up to a monotonic transformation. The complete preorder $\geq_\pi$ encodes under a very simple form the generic knowledge of an agent about the relative plausibility of the states of the world. One often assumes then that for each state s, $\pi(s) > 0$, expressing that no state of the world is totally excluded.

Possibility and necessity relations enjoy a remarkable property. By 'belief' we mean any event A such that $A >_\Pi \overline{A}$. Then the set of beliefs induced by a possibility relation $\geq_\Pi$ is deductively closed. In particular, if A and B are beliefs, the conjunction $A \cap B$ is also a belief. A belief is said to be accepted if an agent accepts it as true (and therefore applies the inference rules of classical logic to it). It follows that possibility relations account for the notion of accepted belief [DUB 04a].

This property remains when the possibility relation is restricted to a context $C \subseteq S$. By 'belief in context C', one implies any event A such that $A \cap C >_\Pi \overline{A} \cap C$. The set of beliefs induced by a possibility relation $\geq_\Pi$ in a context C is also deductively closed. This result relies on the following property of possibility relations (referred to as 'negligibility'): if A, B, C are three disjoint sets, then

$$A \cup C >_\Pi B \text{ and } A \cup B >_\Pi C \text{ entails } A >_\Pi B \cup C.$$

This property clearly indicates that $A >_\Pi B$ means that the plausibility of B is negligible w.r.t. that of A, since in cumulating with B events that are less plausible than A, the plausibility of A cannot be attained. This feature is typical of possibility theory.

There are two main ways of generalizing comparative probability and possibility relations in weakening their characteristic axioms. A first method consists of adopting a restricted form of disjunctive stability, replacing equivalence by implication in the preadditivity axiom: if A, B, C are three subsets such that $A \cap (B \cup C) = \varnothing$:

$$B \geq_\kappa C \text{ entails } A \cup B \geq_\kappa A \cup C. \tag{3.35}$$

The results proved in Dubois [DUB 86a] and Chateauneuf [CHA 96] show that the class of set-functions captured by the weak preadditivity axiom (3.35) exactly contains the pseudo-additive (or decomposable) confidence functions g, i.e. such that there exists an operation $\oplus$ on the codomain of g such that for each pair of disjoint subsets $A, B, g(A \cup B) = g(A) \oplus g(B)$. The cases where $\oplus = \max$ and $\oplus = +$ cover possibility and probability measures, respectively.

The other extension consists of restricting the scope of the weak preadditivity axiom to subsets A, B, C such as $A \cap (B \cup C) = \varnothing$ and $C \subseteq B$. Any relative confidence relation $\geq_\kappa$ obeying this restriction of the preadditivity axiom is representable by a plausibility function in the sense of Shafer [WON 93].

3.6. Conditioning in non-additive representations

The generalization of the notion of probabilistic conditioning to other theories of uncertainty is not straightforward for two reasons.

– As pointed out in section 3.3.2, probabilistic conditioning is often directly defined as a ratio of two quantities and not as the probability of a genuine conditional event. However, splitting the conditional event from the probability measure, one may better understand how to generalize the notion of conditioning.

– Probabilistic conditioning has been used for several types of very different tasks: learning from observations, prediction from a statistical model and the revision of uncertain information. Moreover, there are several ways of formally generalizing the probabilistic conditioning. It is not obvious that the various tasks can be modeled by the same form of conditioning.

First, a clarification is required. The quantity $P(A \mid C)$ is often presented as the probability of event A when C is true. The example below, due to Romano Scozzafava, shows that it is a misconception.

Example 3.6. Let us consider balls drawn from a bag S containing five balls numbered from 1 to 5. It is clear that $P(even \mid \{1,2,3\}) = P(even \mid \{3,4,5\}) = \frac{1}{3}$. If one understands these results as: *if the ball is in $\{1,2,3\}$, then the probability that it is even is $\frac{1}{3}$* and *if the ball is in $\{3,4,5\}$, then the probability that it is even is $\frac{1}{3}$*, one is logically led to conclude that the probability of the ball being even is $\frac{1}{3}$ *in any case* since $S = \{1,2,3\} \cup \{3,4,5\}$. However, $P(Pair \mid S) = \frac{2}{5}$.

The reason for this paradox is a misinterpretation of the conditional probability $P(A \mid C)$. In fact, this is the probability of A when one does not know anything else than the truth of C (e.g. if it is only known that the number of the ball is in the set $\{1,2,3\}$ in the example above). Note that 'knowing only that the ball is in $\{1,2,3\}$ or that the ball is in $\{3,4,5\}$' is not equivalent to knowing nothing. Thus, one should understand $P(A \mid C)$ as the probability of an event $A \mid C$ which involves a non-classical implication. The conditional event $A \mid C$ is different from the material implication $\overline{C} \cup A$ since it is generally false that $P(A \mid C) = P(\overline{C} \cup A)$. Moreover, it is not true that $P(A \mid C) \leq P(A \mid C \cap B)$ (lack of monotonicity) while, of course, $P(\overline{C} \cup A) \leq P(\overline{C \cap B} \cup A)$.

It is important to distinguish the prediction problem from the revision problem. When dealing with prediction, we have at our disposal a model of the world under the form of probability distribution P issued e.g. from a representative set of statistical data. This is what we call 'generic information' or 'generic knowledge' (e.g. medical knowledge synthesized by causal relations between diseases and symptoms). Assume we have some observations on the current state of the world, i.e. a particular situation referred to as singular information, under the form of a proposition C (e.g. some medical test results for a patient). One then tries to formulate some statements A about the current world with their associated degrees of belief (e.g. predict the disease of the patient). The conditional probability $P(A \mid C)$ (e.g. the frequency of observation of

A in context C) is then used for estimating a degree of belief that the current world satisfies A.

The revision scenario is different: given a probability distribution P (which may or may not represent generic information), one learns that the probability of an event C is 1 (and not $P(C) < 1$ as it was supposed before). Then the problem is to determine the new probability measure P' such that $P(C) = 1$, which is the closest to P in some sense, in order to comply with a minimal change principle. It can then be shown that if we use an appropriate relative information measure, it follows that $P'(A) = P(A \mid C)$, $\forall A$ [WIL 80]. Note that, in the prediction problem, generic knowledge remains unaffected by singular evidence which is handled separately.

Finally, learning can be viewed as bridging the gap between generic and singular information. Bayes' theorem is instrumental for letting prior knowledge be altered by singular evidence when the validity of predictions have been checked. An important problem is to see what remains of Bayesian learning when prior knowledge is incomplete. While the answer to this question is not yet well understood, the imprecise Dirichlet model [BER 05] provides some insight into this problem for imprecise probabilities. For belief functions, little has been done as it is a theory of handling singular uncertain evidence and not so much an extension of Bayesian probabilistic modeling. In the following, we focus on prediction, revision and fusion of evidence.

3.6.1. *Conditional events and qualitative conditioning*

De Finetti [DEF 36] was the first to regard the conditional probability $P(A \mid C)$ as the probability of a *tri-event* $A \mid C$ that should be read 'if what is known is described by C then conclude A', where A and C represent classical propositions (interpreted as subsets of S). A tri-event $A \mid C$ partitions the set of states $s \in S$ into three subsets: either

– $s \in A \cap C$, then s is said to be an *example* of the rule 'if C then A'; the tri-event is then true (value 1) at s; or

– $s \in \overline{A} \cap C$, then s is said to be a *counter-example* of the rule 'if C then A'; the tri-event is then false (value 0) at s; or

– $s \in \overline{C}$, then s is said to be *irrelevant* to the rule 'if C then A', i.e. the rule does not apply to s; the tri-event then takes a third truth value (I) at s.

The third truth value can be interpreted in various ways. According to Goodman *et al.* [GOO 91], it corresponds to an hesitation between true and false, i.e. $I = \{0, 1\}$. This is philosophically debatable but suggests the equivalence between a tri-event and a family of subsets of S, lower bounded by $A \cap C$ (this is the case when we choose $I = 0$) and upper bounded by $\overline{C} \cup A$ representing material implication (this is the case when we choose $I = 1$). It is easy to check that any subset B such as

$A \cap C \subseteq B \subseteq \overline{C} \cup A$ satisfies the identity $A \cap C = B \cap C$. One therefore has an Bayesian-like equality of the form:

$$A \cap C = (A \mid C) \cap C \qquad (3.36)$$

as this identity is valid for any representative of the family $\{B : A \cap C \subseteq B \subseteq \overline{C} \cup A\}$. This family is an interval in the algebra of subsets of S, fully characterized by the nested pair $(A \cap C, \overline{C} \cup A)$.

The third truth value I may be also seen as expressing 'inapplicable' [CAL 87]. This underlies the definition of a conjunction of conditional events, by means of a truth table with three values, in a non-monotonic three-valued extension of propositional logic [DUB 94a]. Lastly, for De Finetti and his followers [COL 02], the truth value I should be changed into the probability $P(A \mid C)$. Indeed, the probability $P(A \mid C)$ is then seen as the price of a lottery ticket in a conditional bet that yields (if condition C is satisfied) 1 Euro when A takes place and 0 when A does not take place. If condition C (which is the precondition for the game to take place) turns to be false, the price paid is reimbursed (the bet is called off).

Relation (3.36) is the Boolean variant of Bayes equation $P(A \cap C) = P(A \mid C) \cdot P(C)$. Moreover, $P(A \mid C)$ is indeed a function of $P(A \cap C)$ and $P(\overline{C} \cup A)$ only, since (if $P(C) > 0$):

$$P(A \mid C) = \frac{P(A \cap C)}{P(A \cap C) + 1 - P(\overline{C} \cup A)}. \qquad (3.37)$$

It is therefore possible to separate the tri-event from the conditional probability. There are therefore two ways of generalizing the probabilistic conditioning of confidence functions g that differ from probabilities:

1) Either one states that $g(A \cap C)$ only depends on $g(A \mid C)$ and $g(C)$ via a function ϕ. This is the approach followed by Cox [PAR 94]. The constraints induced by the Boolean algebra of events, together with some natural technical conditions such as the strict increasing of ϕ, enforce $g(A \cap C) = g(A \mid C) \cdot g(C)$ in practice.

2) Alternatively, the conditional measure $g(A \mid C)$ is directly defined by replacing P by g in equation (3.37).

The equivalence between the two approaches, which holds for probabilities, is no longer true for more general set-functions.

In the case of non-numerical possibility theory, with possibility values on a finite scale L, only the first option generalizing equation (3.36) is possible. We then state, for lack of product operation:

$$\Pi(A \cap C) = \min(\Pi(A \mid C), \Pi(C)). \qquad (3.38)$$

This equation has no unique solution. Nevertheless, in the spirit of possibility theory, one is led to select the least informative solution, i.e. for $C \neq \emptyset$ and $A \neq \emptyset$:

$$\Pi(A \mid C) = 1 \text{ if } \Pi(A \cap C) = \Pi(C), \text{ and } \Pi(A \cap C) \text{ otherwise.} \quad (3.39)$$

This is similar to conditional probability, but there is no longer any division by $\Pi(C)$. If $\Pi(C) = 0$, then $\Pi(A \mid C) = 1$ provided that $A \neq \emptyset$. Conditioning by an impossible event destroys information.

The conditional necessity measure is then defined by $N(A \mid C) = 1 - \Pi(\overline{A} \mid C)$. It coincides with the necessity of the material implication except if $\Pi(A \cap C) = \Pi(C)$. Note that the dual equation $N(A \cap C) = \min(N(A \mid C), N(C))$ is not very interesting, since its minimal solution is $N(A \mid C) = N(A \cap C) = \min(N(A), N(C))$ which is the same as stating $\Pi(A \mid C) = \Pi(\overline{C} \cup A)$. On the other hand, the solution of equation (3.38) captures ordinal conditioning of the previous section, since it can be checked that $N(A \mid C) > 0 \iff \Pi(A \cap C) > \Pi(\overline{A} \cap C)$ when $\Pi(C) > 0$. This means that a proposition A is accepted as true in context C if it is more plausible than its negation in this context. The non-monotonic nature of this type of conditional possibility can be seen by noticing that we may have both $N(A \mid C) > 0$ and $N(\overline{A} \mid B \cap C) > 0$, i.e. the arrival of information B may lead to the rejection of proposition A which was previously accepted in context C. See Benferhat et al. [BEN 97] for a more detailed study of non-monotonicity in this framework.

3.6.2. *Conditioning for belief functions and imprecise probabilities*

Most of the time, the information encoded by a probability distribution refers to a population (the set of situations that correspond to the results of the statistical tests). This is a form of generic information, typically frequentist. This information can be used for inferring beliefs about a particular situation for which we have incomplete but clear-cut observations. This is called prediction. If $P(A \mid C)$ is the (frequentist) probability of having A in context C, the confidence of the agent in proposition A when they know information C is estimated by quantity $P(A \mid C)$, assuming that the current situation is typical of environment C. The belief of the agent in proposition A in the current situation changes from $P(A)$ to $P(A \mid C)$ when it has been observed that C is true in the current situation and nothing else. Conditioning is used here for updating the beliefs of the agent about the current situation by exploiting generic information.

In the example of section 3.6, the probability measure P represents the medical knowledge (often compiled under the form of a Bayesian network). The singular information C represents the results of tests for a patient. $P(A \mid C)$ is the probability of having disease A for patients for whom C has been observed; this value also estimates the singular probability (belief) that this patient has this disease. Note that in this type of inference, the probability measure P does not change; only singular beliefs change. One only applies the available generic knowledge to a reference class C. This is referred to as *focusing* [DUB 98a].

When probability P is subjective, it may also have a singular nature (when betting on the occurrence of a non-repeatable event). In this case, conditioning can be interpreted as updating a singular probability *by a piece of information of the same nature*. In this case, information C is interpreted as $P(C) = 1$, which represents a constraint that has to be taken into account when revising P.

An example of this is the case when some investigator suspects Peter, Paul and Mary of being involved in a criminal affair with probabilistic confidence degrees $\frac{1}{4}$, $\frac{1}{4}$ and $\frac{1}{2}$ respectively, and then learns that Peter has an alibi i.e. $P(\{\text{Mary, Paul}\}) = 1$ [DUB 96]. We then have to revise these singular probabilities. The use of conditional probability for handling this revision of the probabilities is often proposed (and justified by the minimal change principle) which yields probabilities $\frac{1}{3}$ and $\frac{2}{3}$ for Paul and Mary, respectively. However, the problem of revising P is different from that of updating singular beliefs on the basis of generic information.

Lastly, one may also want to justify the revision of a frequentist probability after the occurrence of major events. In the example of the opinion poll about a future election, let us suppose that the frequentist probability of being elected has been obtained for each candidate (i.e. everyone supplied a precise favorite candidate). Suppose now that a candidate withdraws. What becomes of the probabilities? Applying Bayesian conditioning in this situation is questionable, since it assumes that the votes of the electors that previously supported the withdrawn candidate are transferred to the other candidates in proportion to the number of potential votes previously estimated. It would be more convincing to make the assumption that the transfer will be done towards the nearest neighbors of the withdrawn candidate in terms of political affinity (which corresponds to the 'imaging' rule proposed by Lewis [LEW 76]). This case questions the alleged universality of Bayesian conditioning, even for probabilities. In such a situation, it would be better to run the opinion poll again.

In the case where the generic knowledge of the agent is represented by imprecise probabilities, Bayesian plausible inference is generalized by performing a sensitivity analysis on the conditional probability. Let $\mathcal{P}$ be a family of probability measures on S. For each proposition A, a lower bound $P_*(A)$ and an upper bound $P^*(A)$ of the probability degree of A are known. In the presence of singular observations summarized under the form of a context C, the belief of an agent in a proposition A is represented by the interval $[P_*(A \mid C), P^*(A \mid C)]$ defined by

$$P_*(A \mid C) = \inf\{P(A \mid C), P(C) > 0, P \in \mathcal{P}\}$$

$$P^*(A \mid C) = \sup\{P(A \mid C), P(C) > 0, P \in \mathcal{P}\}.$$

It may happen that the interval $[P_*(A \mid C), P^*(A \mid C)]$ is larger than $[P_*(A), P^*(A)]$, which corresponds to a loss of information in specific contexts. This property reflects the idea that the more singular information is available about a situation, the less informative is the application of generic information to it (since the number of statistical data that fit this situation may become very small). We see that this form of conditioning does not correspond at all to the idea of enriching generic information; it is only a matter of querying it.

Belief and plausibility functions in the sense of Shafer [SHA 76] are, mathematically speaking, important particular cases of lower and upper probabilities although these functions were independently introduced without any reference to the idea of imprecise probability. Information is supposed to be represented by the assignment of non-negative weights $m(E)$ to subsets E of S. In a generic knowledge representation perspective, $m(E)$ is e.g. the proportion of imprecise results of the form $x \in E$ in a statistical test on a random variable x. In this framework, plausible inference in context C consists of evaluating the weight function $m(\cdot \mid C)$ induced by the mass function m on the set of states C, taken as the new frame. Three cases should be considered:

1) $E \subseteq C$: In this case, $m(E)$ remains assigned to E.

2) $E \cap C = \emptyset$: In this case, $m(E)$ no longer matters and is eliminated.

3) $E \cap C \neq \emptyset$ and $\overline{E} \cap C \neq \emptyset$: In this case, some fraction $\alpha_E \cdot m(E)$ of $m(E)$ remains assigned to $E \cap C$ and the rest, i.e. $(1 - \alpha_E) \cdot m(E)$, is allocated to $\overline{E} \cap C$. Note that this sharing process is unknown.

The third case corresponds to incomplete observations E that neither confirm nor disconfirm C. We do not have enough information in order to know if, in each of the situations corresponding to these observations, C is true or not, since only E is known. Suppose that the values $\{\alpha_E, E \subseteq S\}$ were known. It is always known that $\alpha_E = 1$ and $\alpha_E = 0$ in the first and second cases, respectively. Then, we can build a mass function $m_\alpha^C(\cdot)$. Note that a renormalization of this mass function is generally necessary as soon as $Pl(C) < 1$ (letting $m_\alpha(\cdot \mid C) = \frac{m_\alpha^C(\cdot)}{Pl(C)}$). If we denote the belief and plausibility functions obtained by focusing on C by $Bel_\alpha(A \mid C)$ and $Pl_\alpha(A \mid C)$, based on the allocation vector α, the conditional belief and plausibility degrees on C are defined by

$$Bel(A \mid C) = \inf_\alpha Bel_\alpha(A \mid C)$$

and

$$Pl(A \mid C) = \sup_\alpha Pl_\alpha(A \mid C).$$

One still obtains belief and plausibility functions [JAF 92] and necessity and possibility measures if we start with such measures [DUB 92a]. The following results show that what is obtained is a generalization of Bayesian inference:

$$Bel(A \mid C) = \inf\{P(A \mid C) : P(C) > 0, P \geq Bel\} = \frac{Bel(A \cap C)}{Bel(A \cap C) + Pl(\overline{A} \cap C)},$$

$$Pl(A \mid C) = \sup\{P(A \mid C) : P(C) > 0, P \geq Bel\} = \frac{Pl(A \cap C)}{Pl(A \cap C) + Bel(\overline{A} \cap C)}.$$

It is easy to see that $Pl(A \mid C) = 1 - Bel(\overline{A} \mid C)$, and that these formulae generalize probabilistic conditioning under equation (3.37). $Bel(A \mid C)$ is indeed a function of $Bel(A \cap C)$ and of $Bel(\overline{C} \cup A)$ (and similarly for $Pl(A \mid C)$). Note that if $Bel(C) = 0$ and $Pl(C) = 1$ (complete ignorance regarding C), then all the focal sets of m overlap C without being contained in C. In this case, $Bel(A \mid C) = 0$ and $Pl(A \mid C) = 1, \forall A \neq S, \emptyset$; one cannot infer anything in context C.

The other conditioning, referred to as 'Dempster conditioning' and proposed by Shafer [SHA 76] and Smets [SME 94], systematically assumes $\alpha_E = 1$ as soon as $E \cap C \neq \emptyset$. It supposes a transfer of the full mass of each focal set E to $E \cap C \neq \emptyset$ (followed by a renormalization). This means that we interpret the new information C as modifying the initial belief function in such a way that $Pl(\overline{C}) = 0$; situations where C is false are considered as impossible. If we denote the plausibility function after revision as $Pl(A \parallel C)$, we have:

$$Pl(A \parallel C) = \frac{Pl(A \cap C)}{Pl(C)}.$$

This constitutes another generalization of probabilistic conditioning in the sense of equation (3.36). The conditional belief is then obtained by duality $Bel(A \parallel C) = 1 - Pl(\overline{A} \parallel C)$. Note that with this conditioning the size of focal sets diminishes, thus information becomes more precise, and the intervals $[Bel, Pl]$ become tighter (they are always tighter than those obtained by focusing). Dempster conditioning therefore corresponds to a process where information is enriched, which contrasts with focusing. If $Bel(C) = 0$ and $Pl(C) = 1$ (complete ignorance about C), conditioning on C in the sense of Dempster rule significantly increases the precision of resulting beliefs.

In the more general framework of imprecise probabilities, a blind application of revision by a piece of information C consists of adding the supplementary constraint $P(C) = 1$ to the family $\mathcal{P}$, i.e.

$$P_*(A \parallel C) = \inf\{P(A \mid C), P(C) = 1, P \in \mathcal{P}\}.$$

$$P^*(A \parallel C) = \sup\{P(A \mid C), P(C) = 1, P \in \mathcal{P}\}.$$

However, it may happen that the set $\{P \in \mathcal{P}, P(C) = 1\}$ is empty (it is always the case in the classical Bayesian framework since $\mathcal{P}$ is a singleton). One then applies the maximal likelihood principle [GIL 92] and we replace the condition $P(C) = 1$ by $P(C) = P^*(C)$ in the above equation. In this way, we generalize Dempster conditioning (which is recovered if P^* is a plausibility function).

This type of conditioning has nothing to do with the previously described focusing problem since, in the view of Shafer and Smets, the mass function m does not represent generic knowledge but rather uncertain singular information (non-reliable testimonies, more or less valuable clues) collected about a particular situation. These authors consider a form of reasoning under uncertainty where generic knowledge is not taken into account, but where all the pieces of information are singular.

In the crime example, suppose that the organizer of the crime tossed a coin for deciding whether a man or a woman is recruited to be the killer. This piece of uncertain singular information is represented by the mass function $m(\{\text{Peter, Paul}\}) = \frac{1}{2}$ (there is no information available about Peter alone and Paul alone), and $m(\{\text{Mary}\}) = \frac{1}{2}$. Now, if we learn that Peter has an alibi, the focal set {Peter, Paul} reduces to {Paul} and we deduce, after revision, that $P(\{\text{Mary}\}) = P(\{\text{Paul}\}) = \frac{1}{2}$. Note that the Bayesian approach would split the mass $m(\{\text{Peter, Paul}\})$ equally between Peter and Paul. Bayesian conditioning then yields $P(\{\text{Mary}\}) = 2 \cdot P(\{\text{Paul}\}) = \frac{2}{3}$, which may sound debatable when dealing with uncertain singular pieces of information (let alone at a court of law).

3.7. Fusion of imprecise and uncertain information

The problem of fusing distinct pieces of information from different sources has become increasingly important in several areas such as robotics (multisensor fusion), image processing (merging of several images), risk analysis (expert opinions fusion) or databases (fusion of knowledge bases). However, fusion has received little attention in the probabilistic tradition. In the frequentist view, one works with a unique probability distribution issued from a set of observations. In the subjectivist tradition, one often considers that uncertainty is expressed by a unique agent. In the last thirty years, the problem of fusing pieces of information has emerged as a fundamental issue when representing information from several sources.

The fusion of pieces of information differs from the fusion of multiple criteria or multiple agent preferences. In the latter case, one usually looks for a compromise between points of view or agents. Each agent may be led to accept options that they had not proposed at the beginning. In contrast, the aim of information fusion is to lay bare what is true among a collection of data that are often imprecise and inconsistent. Consequently, the operations that are natural for fusing different pieces of information are not necessarily those needed for fusing preferences.

The fusion problem can be stated in similar terms independently from the representation of uncertainty that is used: in each uncertainty theory, one can find the same fusion modes even if they are expressed by different operations. In addition, the fusion problem differs from the revision of information upon the arrival of a new piece of information (which is based on the notion of conditioning). The fusion problem is by nature symmetric; sources play similar roles even if they may be (and are often) heterogenous. This contrasts with revision, where prior information is minimally changed on the basis of new information. When fusing pieces of information, there may be no prior knowledge available. If there is any, it is modified by the pieces of information coming from several sources in parallel.

In its simplest form a fusion problem, when the sources provide incomplete pieces of information, can be stated as follows. Assume there are two sources 1 and 2 that inform us about the value of a variable x taking its value in S. According to the first source $x \in A_1$, while according to the second source $x \in A_2$. The fusion problem consists of deducing the most useful plausible information contained in what the sources delivered. It is obvious that the result should depend on the quality of the sources. There are three kinds of assumptions as follows:

1) *The two sources are reliable.* One concludes that $x \in A_1 \cap A_2$. This reasoning presupposes that the pieces of information that we start with are coherent. If $A_1 \cap A_2 = \emptyset$, then the hypothesis that the two sources are reliable no longer holds.

2) *At least one of the two sources is reliable.* One concludes that $x \in A_1 \cup A_2$. This reasoning no longer presupposes that the pieces of information that we start with are coherent. Thus if $A_1 \cap A_2 = \emptyset$, one can still deduce a non-trivial piece of information (except if x is an all-or-nothing variable). However, there is an important loss in precision.

3) *The two sources are identical and provide independent information.* In this case, one can consider that $A_1 \cap A_2$ is the set of values that are the most plausible (since both sources declare them as feasible). The values in $(A_1 \cap \overline{A_2}) \cup (\overline{A_1} \cap A_2)$ are less plausible but not excluded (since at least one of the two sources declare them as possible).

These three kinds of combination can be found in all formalisms. The first one is called *conjunctive fusion*, since it performs the intersection of the sets of values that are possible for x according to each source. This is the usual fusion mode in classical logic. If several propositions of the form $x \in A_i$ are asserted as true, the values resulting from the combination are those for which all the propositions are true.

The second is called *disjunctive fusion*. It corresponds to a classical mode for dealing with inconsistency in logic [RES 70]. If the propositions of the form $x \in A_i$ are contradictory, then one looks for maximal consistent subsets of propositions, assuming that reality corresponds to one of these subsets (here reduced to $\{A_1\}$ and $\{A_2\}$).

The third mode is of another nature: the hypothesis of independence of the sources allows for a counting process. For each value of x, one counts the number of sources that do not exclude it. This number reflects the plausibility of each of these values. This is typically what is done in statistics, but in the latter case each observation is assumed to be precise ($x = a_i$) and comes from the same unique aleatory source in an independent way. Moreover, it is also assumed that many more than two observations are reported. Collecting statistical data agrees with the third fusion mode, which may be termed *cumulative fusion*. In the above elementary case, it can be expressed by the arithmetic mean of the characteristic functions of A_1 and A_2, or in the form of a mass distribution such that $m(A_1) = m(A_2) = \frac{1}{2}$.

In the following, we explain how these three modes of fusion can be expressed in the different uncertainty formalisms studied in this chapter: probabilities, possibilities, belief functions and imprecise probabilities. The closure condition supposes that when one fuses pieces of information that are expressed in a given formalism then the combination result should be also expressible in this formalism. We shall see that this assumption may be problematic. Requiring this condition may forbid some fusion modes. For instance, it is clear that cumulative fusion does not preserve the all-or-nothing nature of the pieces of information in the above elementary case, contrary to the situations for conjunctive or disjunctive fusions. In order to define all fusion modes in all formalisms, we shall see that the result of the fusion brings us from a particular setting to a more general one (for example from possibilities or probabilities to belief functions).

3.7.1. *Non-Bayesian probabilistic fusion*

It is assumed that source i provides a probability measure P_i on S. One looks for a function f which is non-decreasing, monotonic, from $[0,1]^n$ to $[0,1]$ such that the set-function $P = f(P_1, \ldots, P_n)$ is still a probability measure. Existing results show that, especially under mild conditions, $f(0, \ldots, 0) = 0$ and $f(1, \ldots, 1) = 1$, the only possible fusion function is the weighted average [LEH 81], i.e.

$$\forall A \subseteq S, f(P_1(A), \ldots, P_n(A)) = \sum_{i=1}^{n} \alpha_i \cdot P_i(A),$$

where $\sum_{i=1}^{n} \alpha_i = 1$ with $\alpha_i \geq 0, \forall i$. This amounts to requiring that aggregation commutes with marginalization.

This is a cumulative fusion mode. It considers the sources as independent aleatory generators of precise values and the weight α_i reflects the number of observations produced by source i. In the framework of expert opinion fusion, it is assumed that each expert produces a probability measure expressing what they know about the value of a parameter x. The weight α_i reflects the reliability of expert i, understood as the probability that expert i is correct. These weights are estimated by testing the expert on questions, the answer to which is supposedly known [COO 91].

This is the only fusion mode allowed by this approach. One may also fuse probability densities by means of other operations such as the geometric mean, provided that the result is renormalized, which broadens the spectrum of possible fusion operations [FRE 85]. However, the commutation with marginalization operation is then lost.

3.7.2. *Bayesian probabilistic fusion*

Another approach to the fusion problem presupposes that sources provide precise evaluations $x_1, \ldots, x_n$ of the value of x, but that these evaluations are inexact. The probability $P(x_1, \ldots, x_n \mid x = s_j)$ that sources jointly provide the n-tuple of values $x_1, \ldots, x_n$ when the real value of x is equal to s_j is assumed to be known. This information models the joint behavior of the sources. Moreover, prior probabilities p_j that $x = s_j, \forall j$ are also assumed to be available. Under these hypotheses one can compute, by means of Bayes' theorem, the probability $P(x = s_j \mid x_1, \ldots, x_n)$ that the real value of x is equal to s_j when each source i provides a value x_i:

$$P(x = s_j \mid x_1, \ldots, x_n) = \frac{P(x_1, \ldots, x_n \mid s_j) \cdot p_j}{\sum_{k=1}^{n} P(x_1, \ldots, x_n \mid s_k) \cdot p_k}. \tag{3.40}$$

Despite its appeal, this approach is very demanding in pieces of information. The probability $P(x_1, \ldots, x_n \mid x = s_j)$ reflects the dependency between sources. It is seldom available, since it requires a great number of values to be specified. In practice, it is easier to obtain the marginal probabilities $P(x_i \mid x = s_j)$ that each source i provides the value x_i when the real value of x is equal to s_j. By default, sources are assumed to be conditionally independent of the true value of x, which gives:

$$P(x = s_j \mid x_1, \ldots, x_n) = \frac{P(x_1 \mid s_j) \cdot \ldots \cdot P(x_n \mid s_j) \cdot p_j}{\sum_{k=1}^{n} P(x_1, \ldots, x_n \mid s_k) \cdot p_k}. \tag{3.41}$$

We need a prior probability about the value sources are assumed to provide information on. Such prior information is often missing since, if it were available, one might not even need the pieces of information provided by sources. In practice, one is obliged to provide a subjective estimate of the prior probability (taken as uniform by default), which may influence the result. Nevertheless, let us note that this fusion mode is conjunctive (since the product of the likelihood functions is performed). One might think of defining a disjunctive fusion mode by computing $P(x = s_j \mid x_1$ or $\ldots$ or $x_n)$, the probability that the real value for x is equal to s given at least one of the values provided by the sources.

3.7.3. *Fusion in possibility theory*

In this framework, each source i is assumed to provide a possibility distribution π_i defined on S. For fusing such pieces of information, the whole panoply of fuzzy set aggregation operations is available [DUB 88a, Chapter 2], [CAL 02, FOD 00]. In particular, the three basic information fusion modes can be expressed and a resulting possibility distribution π on S obtained under the form $\pi(s) = f(\pi_1(s), \ldots, \pi_n(s)), \forall s \in S$ for an appropriate operation f.

For conjunctive fusion, one can use triangular norms [KLE 00] which are semigroup operations of the unit interval (hence associative), monotonically increasing and with neutral element 1. The main operations of this kind are the minimum operation, the product and the linear conjunction $\max(0, a + b - 1)$. The advantage of choosing

$$\pi(s) = \min(\pi_1(s), \ldots, \pi_n(s)), \forall s \in S$$

is the idempotency of this operation. If all sources provide the same distribution π, it is this distribution that is taken as the result. This property enables us to cope with the case where the sources are redundant (e.g. when experts have the same background knowledge), without requiring any assumption about the independence of the sources. However, if one is sure that the information sources are independent, it may be desirable to have a reinforcement effect (if all the sources are considered to have a low plausibility, there will be a very low global plausibility). This effect is captured by the product: $\pi(s) = \pi_1(s) \cdot \pi_2(s) \cdot \ldots \cdot \pi_n(s), \forall s \in S$.

The reinforcement effect obtained with the linear conjunction $\max(0, a + b - 1)$ is much stronger, since values that are not considered as being plausible but are not impossible are eliminated after the fusion. In fact, this operation applies when it is known that a certain number k of sources lie [MUN 92]. Then an information item of the form $x \in A$ proposed by a source is modeled as $\pi_i(s) = 1$ if $s \in A$ and $1 - \frac{1}{k+1}$ otherwise, which is greater as k is large. The linear conjunction enables us to confidently eliminate values which at least $k+1$ sources declare impossible.

All these operations clearly generalize the conjunctive fusion of two all-or-nothing pieces of information and presuppose that the possibility distributions provided by the sources are not contradictory. Nevertheless, the resulting possibility distribution will often be sub-normalized ($\pi(s) < 1, \forall s \in S$). The quantity $Cons = \max_{s \in S} \pi(s)$ measures the degree of consistency between the sources. The fusion result may be renormalized if it is certain that the sources are reliable (since the true value of x is among the values that are not eliminated by any source, even if its possibility is very low). When sources are independent, we obtain

$$\pi(s) = \frac{\pi_1(s) \cdot \ldots \cdot \pi_n(s)}{\max_{s \in S} \pi_1(s) \cdot \ldots \cdot \pi_n(s)}, \forall s \in S. \qquad (3.42)$$

Renormalization preserves associativity if the combination operation is the product. However, when renormalization is applied to a minimum operation, associativity is lost [DUB 88b]. Let us note the striking similarity between Bayesian fusion equation (3.41) and possibilistic fusion equation (3.42), especially when letting $\pi_i(s) = P(x_i \mid x = s)$, justified above. The difference between the two fusion operations lies in the presence of the prior probability in equation (3.41) and in the type of renormalization (probabilistic or possibilistic). The two resulting distributions are even proportional if a uniform prior probability is chosen in equation (3.41). This coincidence between Bayesian and possibilistic approaches indicates their mutual coherence, and confirms the conjunctive nature of Bayesian fusion. However, the similarity of numerical results should not hide a serious difference at the interpretation level. In the probabilistic framework, it is assumed that the posterior probability of each possible value of x can be computed in a precise way. In the possibilistic framework, and in agreement with the non-Bayesian probabilistic tradition, fusion only provides a likelihood degree for the possible values of x. This information is poorer than a probability degree; probabilistic information is too rich in the case of partial ignorance.

When the value of the consistency index is too low, renormalization makes the conjunctive fusion numerically unstable [DUB 88b]. Inconsistency is all the more likely as the number of sources is high. In this case, disjunctive fusion becomes more appropriate and relevant. For the latter fusion mode, triangular co-norms [KLE 00] can be used. They are semi-groups of the unit interval, monotonically increasing and with neutral element 0. Co-norms u are obtained by the De Morgan duality from triangular norms t under the form $u(a, b) = 1 - t(1 - a, 1 - b)$. The main operations of this kind for disjunctive fusion are the maximum operation, the probabilistic sum $a + b - ab$ and the bounded sum $\min(1, a + b)$.

This type of fusion operation does not require any renormalization step. However, since it supposes only that one source is reliable, the obtained result may be very imprecise (particularly if the number of sources is high) due to the higher risk of scattered pieces of information. It is then possible to use milder fusion modes.

For example, a quantified fusion may be used. It is assumed that there are k reliable sources among n. A conjunctive fusion is first performed inside each group of k sources, and these partial results are then combined disjunctively. One may optimize the value of k by trying to maximize the informativeness of the result (in order to choose k not too small), while minimizing inconsistencies (choosing k not too large) [DUB 94b]. One may also look for maximal sub-groups of sources that are together consistent, then perform conjunctive fusion inside these groups and finally combine these partial results disjunctively [DUB 01a]. This can be done for cuts of each possibility distribution, which no longer leads to a possibility distribution for the result but a belief function [DES 07b].

Finally, one may also apply a cumulative fusion mode to possibilistic pieces of information, under the form of a weighted arithmetic mean $\sum_{i=1}^{n} \alpha_i \cdot \pi_i$ when the sources are numerous and independent. Nevertheless, the convex combination of possibility measures is not a possibility measure but again a belief function, since the consonance of focal sets is not preserved by convex sum. Only the disjunctive fusion of possibility measures based on the maximum operation provides a possibility measure [DUB 90a].

3.7.4. *Fusion of belief functions*

It is now assumed that the two sources provide two mass functions m_1 and m_2 defined on frame S. Shafer [SHA 76] has proposed a conjunctive combination rule that may be related to the Bayesian fusion method and generalizes set intersection. It amounts to performing the intersection of each focal set A_1 of m_1 with each focal subset A_2 of m_2 and to allocate mass $m_1(A_1) \cdot m_2(A_2)$ to the subset $A_1 \cap A_2$ (which may be empty). In order to obtain a normal mass function, the result is renormalized by dividing by the sum of masses allocated to non-empty subsets. It therefore leads to an associative combination rule:

$$\forall A \subseteq S, m(A) = \frac{\sum_{A_1, A_2 : A = A_1 \cap A_2} m_1(A_1) \cdot m_2(A_2)}{\sum_{A_1, A_2 : A_1 \cap A_2 \neq \emptyset} m_1(A_1) \cdot m_2(A_2)}. \quad (3.43)$$

It is easy to check that this fusion rule is also commutative, but non-idempotent. This rule supposes that the information *sources* (not the underlying variables) are independent. The normalization factor is an evaluation of the consistency between the sources. One may also notice that the plausibility function Pl induced by m, restricted to the singletons in S, satisfies the property: $\forall s, Pl(\{s\})$ is proportional to the product $Pl_1(\{s\}) \cdot Pl_2(\{s\})$ (equality holds if the sources are consistent, i.e. $\forall A_1, A_2 : A_1 \cap A_2 \neq \emptyset$).

Applying this combination rule to two possibility measures Π_1 and Π_2, it can be seen that the resulting mass function is not necessarily consonant (if the focal sets A_1 of m_1 and A_2 of m_2 are nested, it may not be the case for the subsets of the form $A_1 \cap A_2$). Nevertheless, possibilistic fusion rule equation (3.42) is an approximation of Dempster rule in this case, since it provides a possibility distribution that is proportional to $Pl(\{s\})$.

This fusion rule may also be applied to probability distributions p_1 and p_2. It amounts to performing products $p_1(s) \cdot p_2(s), \forall s \in S$ and renormalizing the distribution thus obtained. If one combines a mass function m_1 with a probability function p, what is obtained is a probability distribution proportional to $p(s) \cdot Pl_1(s)$. Combining three mass functions m_1, m_2 and m_3 by Dempster rule, where the last one is a probability ($m_3 = p$), is equivalent to applying the Bayesian fusion rule to sources 1 and 2 while viewing $Pl_1(\{s\})$ and $Pl_2(\{s\})$ as likelihood functions and m_3 as a prior probability.

Dempster rule is also numerically unstable when the sources are not very consistent, i.e. when the renormalization factor in equation (3.43) is small [DUB 88b]. In this case, one may use the disjunctive counterpart to the Dempster rule, which amounts to replacing intersection by union in equation (3.43), i.e. [DUB 86b]:

$$m(A) = \sum_{A_1, A_2 : A = A_1 \cup A_2} m_1(A_1) \cdot m_2(A_2).$$

Renormalization is then of no use, since this disjunctive fusion is a union of random sets, but the result is more imprecise. The resulting belief function Bel is the product of Bel_1 and Bel_2: $Bel(A) = Bel_1(A) \cdot Bel_2(A), \forall A \subseteq S$. Applied to probability distributions p_1 and p_2, the result of the disjunctive fusion is no longer a probability measure but a belief function whose focal sets are singletons or 2-element subsets (the closure property is violated).

Rather than adopting a disjunctive combination uniformly, alternative options have been proposed for handling the mass of conflict $CONF = \sum_{A_1, A_2 : A_1 \cap A_2 = \emptyset} m_1(A_1) \cdot m_2(A_2)$ when it is too large:

– Smets [SME 98] suggested abstaining from renormalizing, thus laying bare the conflict. Then the un-normalized Dempster rule is equivalent to multiplying commonality functions $Q_i(A) = \sum_{A \subseteq E} m_i(E)$.

– Yager [YAG 87] proposed to assign the mass of conflict to the whole frame S, turning inconsistency into ignorance.

– Dubois and Prade [DUB 88b] allocate the mass $m_1(A_1) \cdot m_2(A_2)$ to the set $A_1 \cap A_2$ if it is not empty, and to the disjunction $A_1 \cup A_2$ otherwise.

– Other authors share the mass $m_1(A_1) \cdot m_2(A_2)$ between A_1 and A_2 when they are disjoint [SMA 06], and more generally between $A_1 \cap A_2$, $A_2 \setminus A_1$, and $A_1 \setminus A_2$ regardless of whether A_1 and A_2 are disjoint or not [YAM 08].

Under such schemes, associativity is generally lost. An extensive comparative discussion of fusion rules in the theory of evidence is provided by Smets [SME 07].

Belief functions are also compatible with a combination mode based on weighted average. Indeed, the weighted arithmetic mean of mass functions is a mass function. The belief function $Bel = \sum_{i=1}^{n} \alpha_i \cdot Bel_i$ has a mass function $\sum_{i=1}^{n} \alpha_i \cdot m_i$. This is a generalization of non-Bayesian probabilistic fusion, which also applies to the fusion of possibility measures without preserving the nestedness of focal sets. The weighted arithmetic mean of products of belief functions is therefore a belief function.

The arithmetic mean is instrumental for the discounting of a belief function provided by a source with low reliability as pointed out by Shafer [SHA 76]. Let α be the probability that the source providing the belief function Bel_1 is reliable. It means that with a probability $1 - \alpha$ nothing is known, which corresponds to a second source providing the non-informative mass function $m_2(S) = 1$. The weighted arithmetic mean of these mass functions is $m = \alpha \cdot m_1 + (1 - \alpha) \cdot m_2$. The mass allocated to the informative subset $A \subset S$ decreases since $m(A) = \alpha \cdot m_1(A)$, while the mass allocated to the whole frame, i.e. the tautology $(m(S) = \alpha \cdot m_1(S) + (1-\alpha))$ increases.

It is not very easy to find natural idempotent *conjunctive* fusion rules for belief functions using mass functions. Dubois and Yager [DUB 92b] propose a methodology for building such fusion rules by duplicating focal sets and sharing masses in order to make the two mass functions commensurate. However, there is no unique combination scheme resulting from this process, even if this approach enables the minimum rule to be retrieved if the two belief functions are consonant [DES 07a].

Dubois *et al.* [DUB 01b] show that the minimum rule of possibility theory can be interpreted as a minimal commitment fusion of consonant belief functions, in the sense of the commonality-based information ordering. Recently, Denoeux [DEN 08] proposed using the decomposition of a non-dogmatic belief function $(m(S) > 0)$ as a Dempster combination of simple support functions:

$$m = \oplus_{A \subset S} A^{w(A)}$$

where $A^{w(A)}$ denotes the simple support belief function with mass function m_A such that $m_A(A) = 1 - w(A)$ and $m(S) = w(A)$. In fact, not all belief functions can be expressed this way, unless we admit that some terms in the above equation are fictitious simple support belief functions for which $w(A) > 1$. The decomposition then exists and is unique for non-dogmatic belief functions [SME 98].

The idea of the idempotent rule is then to combine weight functions w event-wise using the minimum. However, when applied to consonant belief functions, it does not retrieve the minimum rule of possibility theory. The question of finding a canonical idempotent fusion rule in the theory of evidence consistent with that of possibility theory is still an unresolved problem.

3.7.5. *Merging imprecise probability families*

The fusion of imprecise probabilities is not really in agreement with the fusion of belief functions. Given two familles $\mathcal{P}_1$ and $\mathcal{P}_2$ of probabilities provided by two reliable sources, it is natural to consider that the result of a fusion is the intersection $\mathcal{P} = \mathcal{P}_1 \cap \mathcal{P}_2$, when non-empty. In contrast with Dempster rule, this fusion mode is idempotent. But, while it sounds hard to justify Dempster fusion rule in terms of imprecise probabilities, in the same way it is not easy to express the mass function induced by $\mathcal{P}_1 \cap \mathcal{P}_2$ in terms of the mass functions induced by $\mathcal{P}_1$ and $\mathcal{P}_2$. One may apply the idempotent fusion of imprecise probabilities to belief functions, by performing the intersection of sets $\mathcal{P}_i = \{P : P(A) \geq Bel_i(A), \forall A \subseteq S\}$ for $i = 1, 2$. However, the lower bounds of the induced probabilities are not generally belief functions. Chateauneuf [CHA 94] explores these issues in some detail, although many questions remain unanswered.

3.8. Conclusion

This chapter offers an overview of uncertainty representation frameworks where the problems of collecting observations tainted with variability and of representing incomplete information are carefully distinguished. The former naturally leads to a probabilistic approach. The latter situation is more naturally described in terms of sets of mutually exclusive elements and belongs to the realm of logic (if the variables describing a problem are Boolean), or of interval analysis (for numerical variables). The existing new uncertainty theories are hybrids of these basic approaches, some variants being purely ordinal. It includes the case of linguistic information dealing with numerical variables (fuzzy set theory).

This synergy between uncertainty representation frameworks is fruitful since it provides very expressive formal tools for the faithful representation of pieces of information along with their imperfections. It contrasts with the Bayesian theory of subjective probabilities, which appears to be incapable of ensuring a clear distinction between uncertainty due to variability and uncertainty due to ignorance.

The unified view offered here also enables formal notions from set theory or probability theory to be generalized to other settings. For example, one can introduce conditioning independent of the notion of probability even in symbolic representations of the logical type, or use logical connectives for combining probabilities, fuzzy sets or random sets. Finally, injecting interval analysis into the notion of mathematical expectation leads to non-additive Choquet integrals studied in Chapters 10 and 17.

3.9. Acknowledgements

The authors thank Claudette Cayrol for her useful comments on the original French version of this text. This version is augmented and updated.

3.10. Bibliography

[ADA 75] ADAMS E., LEVINE H., "On the uncertainties transmitted from premises to conclusions in deductive inferences", *Synthese*, vol. 30, p. 429–460, 1975.

[BAU 06] BAUDRIT C., DUBOIS D., "Practical representations of incomplete probabilistic knowledge", *Computational Statistics and Data Analysis*, vol. 51, num. 1, p. 86–108, 2006.

[BEN 97] BENFERHAT S., DUBOIS D., PRADE H., "Non-monotonic reasoning, conditional objects and possibility theory", *Artificial Intelligence*, vol. 92, p. 259–276, 1997.

[BER 05] BERNARD J.-M., "An introduction to the imprecise Dirichlet model for multinomial data", *International Journal of Approximate Reasoning*, vol. 39, num. 2-3, p. 123-150, 2005.

[BIR 48] BIRNBAUM Z. W., "On random variables with comparable peakedness", *Annals of Mathematical Statistics*, vol. 19, p. 76–81, 1948.

[BOO 58] BOOLE G., *An Investigation of the Laws of Thought on which are Founded the Mathematical Theory of Logic and Probabilities*, MacMillan, reprinted by Dover, New York, 1958.

[BUD 95] BUDESCU D., WALLSTEIN T., "Processing linguistic probabilities: general principles and empirical evidence", BUSEMEYER J., HASTIE R., MEDIN D., Eds., *The Psychology of Learning and Motivation: Decision-Making from the Perspective of Cognitive Psychology*, p. 275–318, Academic Press, 1995.

[CAL 87] CALABRESE P., "An algebraic synthesis of the foundations of logic and probability", *Information Sciences*, vol. 42, p. 187–237, 1987.

[CAL 02] CALVO T., MAYOR G., MESIAR R., Eds., *Aggregation Operators: New Trends and Applications*, vol. 97 of *Studies in Fuzziness and Soft Computing*, Physica-Verlag, Heidelberg, 2002.

[CAM 94] DE CAMPOS L. M., HUETE J., MORAL S., "Probability intervals: a tool for uncertain reasoning", *International Journal of Uncertainty, Fuzziness and Knowledge-Based Systems*, vol. 2, p. 167–196, 1994.

[CHA 88] CHANAS S., NOWAKOWSKI M., "Single value simulation of fuzzy variable", *Fuzzy Sets and Systems*, vol. 25, p. 43–57, 1988.

[CHA 89] CHATEAUNEUF A., JAFFRAY J., "Some characterizations of lower probabilities and other monotone capacities through the use of Moebius inversion", *Mathematical Social Sciences*, vol. 17, p. 263–283, 1989.

[CHA 94] CHATEAUNEUF A., "Combination of compatible belief functions and relation of specificity", FEDRIZZI M., KACPRZYK J., YAGER R., Eds., *Advances in the Dempster-Shafer Theory of Evidence*, p. 98–114, Wiley, New York, 1994.

[CHA 96] CHATEAUNEUF A., "Decomposable capacities, distorted probabilities and concave capacities", *Mathematical Social Sciences*, vol. 31, p. 19–37, 1996.

[CHE 78] CHELLAS B., *Modal Logic*, Cambridge University Press, Cambridge, UK, 1978.

[CHO 53] CHOQUET G., "Theory of capacities", *Annales de l'Institut Fourier*, vol. 5, num. 4, p. 131–295, 1953.

[COL 02] COLETTI G., SCOZZAFAVA R., *Probabilistic Logic in a Coherent Setting*, Kluwer Academic Pub, 2002.

[COL 03] COLETTI G., SCOZZAFAVA R., "Coherent conditional probability as a measure of uncertainty of the relevant conditioning events", *Proceedings of ECSQARU03*, LNAI 2711, Aalborg, Springer Verlag, p. 407–418, 2003.

[COO 91] COOKE R. M., *Experts in Uncertainty*, Oxford University Press, Oxford, UK, 1991.

[COO 05] DE COOMAN G., "A behavioural model for vague probability assessments", *Fuzzy Sets and Systems*, vol. 154, num. 3, p. 305–358, 2005.

[DEC 99] DE COOMAN G., AEYELS D., "Supremum-preserving upper probabilities", *Information Sciences*, vol. 118, p. 173–212, 1999.

[DEF 36] DE FINETTI B., "La logique de la probabilité", *Actes du Congrès Inter. de Philosophie Scientifique (1935)*, Paris, France, Hermann et Cie Editions, p. IV1–IV9, 1936.

[DEF 37] DE FINETTI B., "La prévision: ses lois logiques, ses sources subjectives", *Annales de l'Institut Poincaré*, vol. 7, p. 1–68, 1937.

[DEF 74] DE FINETTI B., *Theory of Probability*, Wiley, New York, 1974.

[DEM 67] DEMPSTER A. P., "Upper and lower probabilities induced by a multivalued mapping", *Annals of Mathematical Statistics*, vol. 38, p. 325–339, 1967.

[DEN 08] DENOEUX T., "Conjunctive and disjunctive combination of belief functions induced by nondistinct bodies of evidence", *Artifical Intelligence*, vol. 172, num. 2-3, p. 234-264, 2008.

[DES 07a] DESTERCKE S., DUBOIS D., CHOJNACKI E., "Cautious conjunctive merging of belief functions", MELLOULI K., Ed., *Symbolic and Quantitative Approaches to Reasoning with Uncertainty (ECSQARU)*, vol. 4724 of *Lecture Notes in Artificial Intelligence, LNAI*, http://www.springerlink.com, Springer, p. 332–343, 2007.

[DES 07b] DESTERCKE S., DUBOIS D., CHOJNACKI E., "Possibilistic information fusion using maximal coherent subsets", *IEEE International Conference on Fuzzy Systems*, London, UK, http://www.ieee.org/, IEEE, p. 445–450, 2007.

[DES 07c] DESTERCKE S., DUBOIS D., CHOJNACKI E., "Relating practical representations of imprecise probabilities", DE COOMAN G., VEJNAROVA J., ZAFFALON M., Eds., *International Symposium on Imprecise Probability: Theories and Applications (ISIPTA)*, Prague (Czech Republic), http://www.sipta.org, SIPTA, p. 155–164, 2007.

[DOM 85] DOMOTOR Z., "Probability kinematics: conditional and entropy principles", *Synthese*, vol. 63, p. 74–115, 1985.

[DUB 82] DUBOIS D., PRADE H., "On several representations of an uncertain body of evidence", GUPTA M., SANCHEZ E., Eds., *Fuzzy Information and Decision Processes*, p. 167–181, North-Holland, Amsterdam, 1982.

[DUB 83] DUBOIS D., PRADE H., "Unfair coins and necessity measures: a possibilistic interpretation of histograms", *Fuzzy Sets and Systems*, vol. 10, num. 1, p. 15–20, 1983.

[DUB 86a] DUBOIS D., "Belief structures, possibility theory and decomposable confidence measures on finite sets", *Computers and Artificial Intelligence (Bratislava)*, vol. 5, p. 403–416, 1986.

[DUB 86b] DUBOIS D., PRADE H., "A set-theoretic view of belief functions: logical operations and approximations by fuzzy sets", *International Journal of General Systems*, vol. 12, p. 193–226, 1986.

[DUB 87] DUBOIS D., PRADE H., "Properties of information measures in evidence and possibility theories", *Fuzzy Sets and Systems*, vol. 24, p. 161–182, 1987.

[DUB 88a] DUBOIS D., PRADE H., *Possibility Theory*, Plenum Press, New York, 1988.

[DUB 88b] DUBOIS D., PRADE H., "Representation and combination of uncertainty with belief functions and possibility measures", *Computational Intelligence*, vol. 4, num. 4, p. 244–264, 1988.

[DUB 90a] DUBOIS D., PRADE H., "Aggregation of possibility measures", KACPRZYK J., FEDRIZZI M., Eds., *Multiperson Decision Making using Fuzzy Sets and Possibility Theory*, p. 55–63, Kluwer, Dordrecht, 1990.

[DUB 90b] DUBOIS D., PRADE H., "Consonant approximations of belief functions", *International Journal of Approximate Reasoning*, vol. 4, num. 5/6, p. 419–449, 1990.

[DUB 91] DUBOIS D., PRADE H., "Random sets and fuzzy interval analysis", *Fuzzy Sets and Systems*, vol. 42, p. 87–101, 1991.

[DUB 92a] DUBOIS D., PRADE H., "When upper probabilities are possibility measures", *Fuzzy Sets and Systems*, vol. 49, p. 65–74, 1992.

[DUB 92b] DUBOIS D., YAGER R., "Fuzzy set connectives as combinations of belief structures", *Information Sciences*, vol. 66, p. 245–275, 1992.

[DUB 93a] DUBOIS D., PRADE H., SANDRI S., "On possibility/probability transformations", LOWEN R., ROUBENS M., Eds., *Fuzzy Logic. State of the Art*, p. 103–112, Kluwer Academic Publishing, Dordrecht, 1993.

[DUB 93b] DUBOIS D., RAMER A., "Extremal properties of belief measures in the theory of evidence", *International Journal of Uncertainty, Fuzziness and Knowledge-Based Systems*, vol. 1, num. 1, p. 57–68, 1993.

[DUB 94a] DUBOIS D., PRADE H., "Conditional objects as non-monotonic consequence relationships", *Special issue on Conditional Event Algebra, IEEE Transactions on Systems, Man and Cybernetics*, vol. 24, num. 12, p. 1724–1740, 1994.

[DUB 94b] DUBOIS D., PRADE H., "Possibility theory and data fusion in poorly informed environments", *Control Engineering Practice*, vol. 2, num. 5, p. 811–823, 1994.

[DUB 96] DUBOIS D., PRADE H., SMETS P., "Representing partial ignorance", *IEEE Transactions on Systems, Man and Cybernetics*, vol. 26, num. 3, p. 361–377, 1996.

[DUB 97] DUBOIS D., MORAL S., PRADE H., "A semantics for possibility theory based on likelihoods", *Journal of Mathematical Analysis and Applications*, vol. 205, p. 359–380, 1997.

[DUB 98a] DUBOIS D., MORAL S., PRADE H., "Belief change rules in ordinal and numerical uncertainty theories", DUBOIS D., PRADE H., Eds., *Belief Change*, p. 311–392, Kluwer Academic Publishing, 1998.

[DUB 98b] DUBOIS D., PRADE H., "Possibility theory: qualitative and quantitative aspects", SMETS P., Ed., *Handbook on Defeasible Reasoning and Uncertainty Management Systems. Volume 1: Quantified Representation of Uncertainty and Imprecision*, p. 169–226, Kluwer Academic Publ., Dordrecht, The Netherlands, 1998.

[DUB 00] DUBOIS D., NGUYEN H. T., PRADE H., "Possibility theory, probability and fuzzy sets: misunderstandings, bridges and gaps", DUBOIS D., PRADE H., Eds., *Fundamentals of Fuzzy Sets*, The Handbooks of Fuzzy Sets Series, p. 343–438, Kluwer, Boston, Mass., 2000.

[DUB 01a] DUBOIS D., PRADE H., "Possibility theory in information fusion", DELLA RICCIA G., LENZ H., KRUSE R., Eds., *Data Fusion and Perception*, Vol. 431 in the CISM Courses and Lectures, p. 53–76, Springer-Verlag, Berlin, 2001.

[DUB 01b] DUBOIS D., PRADE H., SMETS P., "New semantics for quantitative possibility theory", *ISIPTA '01, Proceedings of the Second International Symposium on Imprecise Probabilities and their Applications, Ithaca, NY, USA*, Shaker, p. 152-161, 2001.

[DUB 03] DUBOIS D., PRADE H., SMETS P., "A definition of subjective possibility", *Badania Pperacyjne i Decyzje (Operation Research and Decisions)*, vol. 4, p. 7–22, 2003, Revised version in *International Journal of Approximate Reasoning*, vol. 48(2), p. 352–364, 2008.

[DUB 04a] DUBOIS D., FARGIER H., PRADE H., "Ordinal and probabilistic representations of acceptance", *Journal of Artificial Intelligence Research (JAIR)*, vol. 22, p. 23–56, 2004.

[DUB 04b] DUBOIS D., FOULLOY L., MAURIS G., PRADE H., "Possibility/probability transformations, triangular fuzzy sets, and probabilistic inequalities", *Reliable Computing*, vol. 10, p. 273–297, 2004.

[DUB 07] DUBOIS D., HUELLERMEIER E., "Comparing probability measures using possibility theory: a notion of relative peakedness", *International Journal of Approximate Reasoning*, vol. 45, p. 364–385, 2007.

[FER 96] FERSON S., GINZBURG L. R., "Different methods are needed to propagate ignorance and variability", *Reliability Engineering and System Safety*, vol. 54, p. 133–144, 1996.

[FER 03] FERSON S., GINZBURG L., KREINOVICH V., MYERS D., SENTZ K., Construction probability boxes and Dempster-Shafer structures, Report num. SANDD2002-4015, Sandia National Laboratories, 2003.

[FIN 83] FINE T., *Theories of Probability*, Academic Press, New York, 1983.

[FOD 00] FODOR J., YAGER R., "Fuzzy set-theoretic operators and quantifiers", DUBOIS D., PRADE H., Eds., *Fundamentals of Fuzzy Sets*, The Handbook of Fuzzy Sets Series, p. 125–193, Kluwer Academic Publ., Dordrecht, 2000.

[FRE 85] FRENCH S., "Group consensus probability disributions: a critical survey", *Bayesian Statistics 2*, p. 183–202, Elsevier Science, 1985.

[FRI 96] FRIEDMAN N., HALPERN J., "Plausibility measures and default reasoning", *Proceedings of the 13th National Conference on Artificial Intelligence*, Portland, OR, p. 1297–1304, 1996.

[GÄR 88] GÄRDENFORS P., *Knowledge in Flux: Modeling the Dynamics of Epistemic States*, MIT Press, Cambridge, Mass, 1988.

[GIL 82] GILES R., "Foundations for a theory of possibility", GUPTA M., SANCHEZ E., Eds., *Fuzzy Information and Decision Processes*, p. 1836–195, North-Holland, 1982.

[GIL 89] GILBOA I., SCHMEIDLER D., "Maxmin expected utility with a non-unique prior", *Journal of Mathematical Economics*, vol. 18, p. 141–153, 1989.

[GIL 92] GILBOA I., SCHMEIDLER D., "Updating ambiguous beliefs", MOSES Y., Ed., *Theoretical Aspects of Reasoning About Knowledge (Proceedings of the 4th Conference TARK'92)*, p. 143–162, 1992.

[GIL 00] GILBOA I., SCHMEIDLER D., "Case-based knowledge and induction", *IEEE Transactions on Systems, Man, and Cybernetics, Part A*, vol. 30, num. 2, p. 85–95, 2000.

[GOO 62] GOOD I., "Subjective Probability as the measure of a non-measurable set", NAGEL E., ET AL., Eds., *Logic, Probability and Philosophy of Science*, Stanford University Press, Stanford, 1962.

[GOO 91] GOODMAN I., NGUYEN H., WALKER E., *Conditional Inference and Logic for Intelligent Systems: A Theory of Measure-Free Conditioning*, North-Holland, Amsterdam, 1991.

[HAC 75] HACKING I., *The Emergence of Probability*, Cambridge University Press, Cambridge, UK, 1975.

[HAL 97] HALPERN J., "Defining relative likelihood in partially-ordered preferential structures", *Journal of Artifical Intelligence Research*, vol. 7, p. 1–24, 1997.

[HIN 62] HINTIKKA J., *Knowledge and Belief*, Cornell University Press, Ithaca, NY, 1962.

[JAF 92] JAFFRAY J., "Bayesian updating and belief functions", *IEEE Transactions on Systems, Man and Cybernetics*, vol. 22, p. 1144–1152, 1992.

[JAY 79] JAYNES E., "Where do we stand on maximum entropy", LEVINE I., TRIBUS M., Eds., *The Maximum Entropy Formalism*, MIT Press, Cambridge USA, 1979.

[KAH 79] KAHNEMANN D., SLOVIC P., TVERSKY A., Eds., *Judgment Under Uncertainty: Heuristics and Biases*, Cambridge University Press, Cambridge, UK, 1979.

[KLE 00] KLEMENT E., MESIAR R., PAP E., *Triangular Norms*, Kluwer Academic Pub., Boston, 2000.

[KLI 92] KLIR G., PARVIZ B., "Probability-possibility transformation: a comparison", *International Journal of General Systems*, vol. 21, p. 291–310, 1992.

[KOO 40] KOOPMAN B., "The bases of probability", *Bulletin of American Mathematical Society*, vol. 46, p. 763–774, 1940.

[KRA 59] KRAFT C., PRATT J., SEIDENBERG A., "Intuitive probability on finite sets", *Annals of Mathematical Statistics*, vol. 30, p. 408–419, 1959.

[KRI 05] KRIEGLER E., HELD H., "Utilizing belief functions for the estimation of future climate change", *International Journal of Approximate Reasoning*, vol. 39, p. 185-209, 2005.

[KYB 74] KYBURG H., *The Logical Foundations of Statistical Inference*, Reidel, Dordrecht, The Netherlands, 1974.

[LEH 81] LEHRER K., WAGNER C., *Rational Consensus in Science and Society*, Reidel, Dordrecht, 1981.

[LEV 80] LEVI I., *The Enterprise of Knowledge*, The MIT Press, Cambridge, Mass., 1980.

[LEW 76] LEWIS D., "Probabilities of conditionals and conditional probabilities", *The Philosophical Review*, vol. 85, p. 297–315, 1976.

[LEW 86] LEWIS D., *Counterfactuals*, Basil Blackwell (1973), 2nd edition, Billing and Sons Ltd., Worcester, UK, 1986.

[LIN 82] LINDLEY D., "Scoring rules and the inevitability of probability", *International Statistical Review*, vol. 50, p. 1–26, 1982.

[LUC 81] LUCE R., RAIFFA H., *Games and Decisions*, Wiley, New York, 1981.

[MAR 75] MARSCHAK J., "Personal probabilities of probabilities", *Theory and Decision*, vol. 6, p. 121–125, 1975.

[MIR 02] MIRANDA E., COUSO I., GIL P., "Relationships between possibility measures and nested random sets", *International Journal of Uncertainty, Fuzziness and Knowledge-Based Systems*, vol. 10, num. 1, p. 1–15, 2002.

[MIR 04] MIRANDA E., COUSO I., GIL P., "A random set characterization of possibility measures", *Information Science*, vol. 168, num. 1–4, p. 51–75, 2004.

[MOO 66] MOORE R. E., *Interval Analysis*, Prentice Hall, Englewood Cliffs, NJ, 1966.

[MUN 92] MUNDICI D., "The logic of Ulam games with lies", BICCHIERI C., DALLA CHIARA M., Eds., *Knowledge: Belief and Strategic Interaction*, p. 275–284, Cambridge Univ. Press, 1992.

[NEU 04] NEUMAIER A., "Clouds, fuzzy sets and probability intervals", *Reliable Computing*, vol. 10, p. 249-272, 2004.

[PAR 94] PARIS J., *The Uncertain Reasoner's Companion*, Cambridge University Press, 1994.

[PAW 91] PAWLAK Z., *Rough Sets: Theoretical Aspects of Reasoning about Data*, Kluwer Academic Publ., Dordrecht, 1991.

[RAM 80] RAMSEY F. P., "Truth and probability", KYBURG J., SMOKLER H., Eds., *Studies in Subjective Probability*, p. 23–52, Krieger Pub. Co, Huntington, NY, 1980.

[RAU 03] RAUFASTE E., DA SILVA NEVES R., MARINÉ C., "Testing the descriptive validity of possibility theory in human judgments of uncertainty", *Artificial Intelligence*, vol. 149, p. 197–218, 2003.

[RES 70] RESCHER N., MANOR R., "On inference from inconsistent premises", *Theory and Decision*, vol. 1, p. 179–219, 1970.

[SAV 72] SAVAGE L., *The Foundations of Statistics*, Wiley (1954); 2nd edition, Dover Publications Inc., New York, 1972.

[SCH 89] SCHMEIDLER D., "Subjective probability and expected utility without additivity", *Econometrica*, vol. 57, p. 571–587, 1989.

[SHA 53] SHAPLEY L. S., "A value for n-person games", KUHN, TUCKER, Eds., *Contributions to the Theory of Games, II*, p. 307–317, Princeton University Press, 1953.

[SHA 61] SHACKLE G. L., *Decision, Order and Time in Human Affairs*, (2nd edition), Cambridge University Press, UK, 1961.

[SHA 76] SHAFER G., *A Mathematical Theory of Evidence*, Princeton University Press, 1976.

[SHA 78] SHAFER G., "Non-additive probabilities in the work of Bernoulli and Lambert", *Archive for History of Exact Sciences*, vol. 19, p. 309–370, 1978.

[SHA 79] SHAFER G., "Allocations of probability", *Annals of Probability*, vol. 7, p. 827–839, 1979.

[SMA 06] SMARANDACHE F., DEZERT J., "Proportional conflict redistribution rules for information fusion", SMARANDACHE F. D. J., Ed., *Applications and Advances of DSmT for Information Fusion. Vol. 2.*, p. 3–68, American Research Press, Rehoboth, N.M., 2006.

[SME 82] SMETS P., "Possibilistic inference from statistical data", *Proceedings of the 2nd World Conference on Mathematics at the Service of Man*, Las Palmas (Canary Islands), Spain, p. 611–613, Jun-Jul 1982.

[SME 90] SMETS P., "Constructing the pignistic probability function in a context of uncertainty", HENRION M., *et al.*, Eds., *Uncertainty in Artificial Intelligence*, p. 29–39, North-Holland, Amsterdam, 1990.

[SME 94] SMETS P., KENNES R., "The transferable belief model", *Artificial Intelligence*, vol. 66, p. 191–234, 1994.

[SME 97] SMETS P., "The normative representation of quantified beliefs by belief functions", *Artificial Intelligence*, vol. 92, p. 229–242, 1997.

[SME 98] SMETS P., "The transferable belief model for quantified belief representation", *Handbook of Defeasible Reasoning and Uncertainty Management Systems*, vol. 1, p. 267–301, Kluwer Academic, Dordrecht, The Netherlands, 1998.

[SME 00] SMETS P., "Quantified possibility theory seen as an hypercautious transferable belief model", *Rencontres Francophones sur les Logiques Floues et ses Applications (LFA 2000)*, La Rochelle, France, Cepadues-Editions, p. 343–353, Oct 2000.

[SME 05] SMETS P., "Belief functions on real numbers", *International Journal of Approximate Reasoning*, vol. 40, p. 181–223, 2005.

[SME 07] SMETS P., "Analyzing the combination of conflicting belief functions", *Information Fusion*, vol. 8, num. 4, p. 387–412, 2007.

[SMI 61] SMITH C., "Consistency in statistical inference and decision", *Journal of the Royal Statistical Society*, vol. B-23, p. 1–37, 1961.

[STR 84] STRAT T., "Continuous belief functions for evidential reasoning", *National Conference on Artificial Intelligence (AAAI-84)*, Los Altos, CA, W. Kaufmann, p. 308–313, 1984.

[SUG 77] SUGENO M., "Fuzzy measures and fuzzy integral: a survey", GUPTA M., SARIDIS G., GAINES B., Eds., *Fuzzy Automata and Decision Processes*, p. 89–102, North-Holland, Amsterdam, 1977.

[TEL 84] TELLER P., "Conditionalization, observation and change of preference", HARPER W., HOOKER C., Eds., *Foundations of Probability Theory, Statistical Inference, and Statistical Theories of Science*, vol. 1, p. 205–259, D. Reide, Los Altos, CA, 1984.

[WAL 82] WALLEY P., FINE T., "Towards a frequentist theory of upper and lower probability", *The Annals of Statistics*, vol. 10, p. 741–761, 1982.

[WAL 91] WALLEY P., *Statistical Reasoning with Imprecise Probabilities*, Chapman and Hall, 1991.

[WIL 80] WILLIAMS P., "Bayesian conditionalization and the principle of minimum information", *British Journal for the Philosophy of Sciences*, vol. 31, p. 131-144, 1980.

[WON 93] WONG S., YAO Y., BOLLMAN P., BURGER H., "Axiomatization of qualitative belief structure", *IEEE Transactions on Systems Man and Cybern*, vol. 21, p. 726–734, 1993.

[YAG 83] YAGER R., "An introduction to applications of possibility theory", *Human Systems Management*, vol. 3, p. 246–269, 1983.

[YAG 87] YAGER R. R., "On the Dempster-Shafer framework and new combination rules", *Information Sciences*, vol. 41, num. 2, p. 93–137, 1987.

[YAM 08] YAMADA K., "A new combination of evidence based on compromise", *Fuzzy Sets and Systems*, vol. 159, num. 13, p. 1689–1708, 2008.

[ZAD 65] ZADEH L., "Fuzzy sets", *Information and Control*, vol. 8, p. 338–353, 1965.

[ZAD 75a] ZADEH L., "The concept of a linguistic variable and its application to approximate reasoning, Part I", *Information Sciences*, vol. 8, p. 199–249, 1975.

[ZAD 75b] ZADEH L., "The concept of a linguistic variable and its application to approximate reasoning, Part II", *Information Sciences*, vol. 8, p. 301–357, 1975.

[ZAD 75c] ZADEH L., "The concept of a linguistic variable and its application to approximate reasoning, Part III", *Information Sciences*, vol. 9, p. 43–80, 1975.

[ZAD 78] ZADEH L., "Fuzzy sets as a basis for a theory of possibility", *Fuzzy Sets and Systems*, vol. 1, p. 3–28, 1978.

[ZAD 84] ZADEH L. A., "Fuzzy probabilities", *Information Processing and Management*, vol. 20, num. 3, p. 363–372, 1984.

[ZAD 97] ZADEH L., "Toward a theory of fuzzy information granulation and its centrality in human reasoning and fuzzy logic", *Fuzzy Sets and Systems*, vol. 90, p. 111–127, 1997.

Chapter 4

Human Decision: Recognition plus Reasoning

4.1. Introduction: the neurobiology of decision, reasoning and/or recognition

Language is a human activity – "Decision making is, in fact, as defining a human trait as language" [DAM 96] – and its neurobiological aspect has been the subject of many investigations. Also, decision making is no less a human activity than language, yet it was not until the later years of the 20th century that any investigations into its neurobiological component were made [DAM 94, DAM 96].

Broadly summarized, the work of these researchers led to two important results. The first, due to Damasio and some others, was the finding that there is an integrating center for rational decision making situated in the ventro-medial part of the pre-frontal cortex of the brain [BER 03, DAM 94, FUR 96]. Deterioration of this zone causes irrational behavior in hitherto rational subjects (see for example the case of Phineas Gage, [DAM 94]). One of the ways in which subjects with damage in this part of the brain are affected is an indifference to, or inaccurate estimation of, risk [ADO 96, DAM 94]. According to Adolphs *et al.* [ADO 96, p. 162],

> "Subjects with VM (ventromedial) frontal lesions, however, do not show this switch in strategy. They invariably lose money on the task as a result of continuously choosing cards from the risky decks, even after they have had substantial experience with the decks, and have lost money on them. Interestingly, the VM frontal patients are quite aware that they are losing money, and some even figure out the fact that the decks from which they are choosing are likely to be more risky. None of this knowledge, however, appears

Chapter written by Jean-Charles POMEROL.

to influence their abnormal behavior, and they continue to choose from risky decks despite continued losses."

Another interpretation, by the author of this chapter [POM 97b], has not been the subject of experiment before now. It appears as though the subjects become unable to arbitrate between the short and the long term, preferring more or less immediate satisfaction to future gains (or losses), giving the impression that risk has not been taken into account. This lack of ability to anticipate is clearly the case in fronto-temporal dementia [BER 03, SCH 98].

The second result, on which Damasio has placed much emphasis, is the role of the emotions in decision making [DAM 03, KOE 07]. It is this that has led him to play down the part of reasoning in decision. We shall return to this role of the affective side in section 4.5, which is devoted to biases and in particular to the 'frame effect'. It is difficult to deny that the emotions play a role in decision making, and emotions can actually be modeled as shown by [SIM 95]. Various models can be proposed at the cognitive level, including reinforcement and short-circuiting effects. In the literature, the process of 'intuitive' decision making is always that of immediate decision making triggered by an affective, visual or other stimulus. This opposition or complementarity between recognition of a pattern and reasoning has already been recognized as intuition versus analysis [e.g. ARK 86, HAM 87, ROU 83]. Klein [KLE 93] used the expression 'recognition-primed decision making', the recognition being that of matching to some pattern in making the decision. According to Berthoz [BER 96, p. 89], "The brain is a matching machine and a simulator of alternative, not a 'representational' machine".

The two drivers of decision making, reasoning and/or recognition, are both intimately involved in human decision making. But is it in fact specifically human? Or does the reasoning component grow during the course of evolution, thus indirectly confirming its place in the frontal lobe, the most recent part of the brain? Between an earthworm taking the decision to retreat from a drop of acid and a sheep fleeing from the shadow of a glider that it has mistaken for a predator, nature offers a wide range of decisions based on the recognition of more or less complex stimuli. First of all, between earthworm and sheep, it is the complexity of the stimulus that grows. According to Berthoz [BER 96, p. 84],

"But we have also proposed the idea that,..., higher central loops that have increasingly gained complexity during evolution operate on another mode that we have called a projective process. In this mode, signals are processed in internal loops having no direct link with sensors."

Afterwards comes a capacity for Pavlovian learning in birds and mammals. Is it therefore not the beginnings of reasoning when the dog fetches its leash when its master puts on his coat? These capacities culminate in man where, at a much higher level, they enable learning and reasoning.

A final point to mention is that one must have a memory in order to reason. As Newell and Simon pointed out [NEW 72], 'intelligent' information processing systems all have the form of a stimulus detector/interpreter, one or more memories and the capacity for symbolic reasoning. The brain is no exception to this. Therefore, in human development, memory, reasoning and decision making have grown in concert. We may include language in this list since language has features in common with decision making. In both cases, there is an ability to form a chain involved, placing end-to-end sounds, words (for language), images and memories of events and alternatives (for decision making) [CAL 91, CAL 94]. Reasoning through scenarios strongly resembles a language adapted to decision making.

In this chapter we shall review the two aspects of decision making. First of all we shall state the standard and indispensable framework of decision models, then we shall examine the point of view of its detractors. Next we shall consider decision by recognition, then decision by reasoning and finally decision biases, which will take us back to the brain.

4.2. Procedural rationality and limited rationality

4.2.1. *Savage's expected utility model*

Savage's model (see Chapter 9 and [DUB 03]) is well known and has been much discussed; however, it will be useful here to recall the model and to see what it really means in terms of alternative.

The first purpose of Savage's model [SAV 54] is to provide a formalized, coherent framework in which to consider decision making. First of all, Savage rightly emphasizes the difference between what the decision maker does not control (the events E) and what he controls (the alternatives A). Taking the simple example of whether or not to take one's umbrella the following day, we have two possible alternatives (TU) and (NTU). We may assume that there are only two events the following day: either it rains (R) or stays fine (NR). We define the function of the set $A \times E$ in the set of outcomes or consequences C (in general $C = \mathbb{R}$) by the matrix shown in Table 4.1.

	R	NR
TU	1	0
NTU	–2	2

Table 4.1. *A decision matrix*

Here the set of outcomes is $\{-2, 1, 0, 2\}$. Savage states that if the decision maker satisfies a certain number of coherence axioms on the choice of alternatives (in the case where the alternatives A are isomorphous with $\mathbb{R}$) then there exist probabilities on E and a utility function U (i.e. a mapping of $C \in \mathbb{R}$) such that the alternative chosen by the decision maker gives the maximum utility expectation for the probabilities in question. Savage's theorem is often used inversely in supposing that if we have a coherent set of probabilities on E (future events), then the decision maker will be wise (rational?) to choose the alternative that maximizes the utility expectation.

Savage's model formalizes extremely important notions before it is even necessary to consider the theorem itself. The first notion is that of the strict separation between the alternatives, the outcomes and the events. This is a fundamental point since most people unschooled in decision making are incapable of seeing the difference. They consequently attribute to their alternatives – in general to their intelligence – what is merely luck. A large dose of modesty is needed to admit that you were just lucky rather than intelligent when the outcome of a decision is good. Thus, if the probability of rain is 75% and you don't take your umbrella, you can have the same outcome, 2, if it doesn't rain. It is luck, because you have been a poor decision maker. The inverse is also true: you can take an excellent decision, and if a low-probability event occurs, the outcome is catastrophic (in this case we don't hesitate to blame bad luck). This separation between event and alternative, leading to the distinction between alternative and outcome, is, as Howard [HOW 88] humorously puts it, perhaps the most important contribution of decision theory. To be convinced, just watch how people play the stock exchanges.

We may nevertheless wonder if it is realistic to separate the world into alternatives and events. There are alternatives that can modify events. For example, if the alternative of a company director is to fix a price, and if the events are the re-alternatives of his competitors, it is clear that the two cannot be separated (especially in an oligopoly). To deal with this we need other models, in this case from game theory. The separation between the decision maker and the environment, including the social environment, is in general merely a simplifying assumption (see [BOL 79] for a reasoned criticism of this type of modeling), but is a necessary assumption if any analytical light is to be shed on decision and rationality.

In a more limited context, Gilboa and Schmeidler [GIL 95] give two examples of decision where the separation between alternative and event does not lead to the kind of thinking that will actually solve the problem. The first case is of a company director wishing to recruit a salesman. The possible alternatives are the candidates. In this particular case, the events do not arise naturally. The states of the environment represent the qualities of the candidates, e.g. honesty, performance and mobility. Describing the states of the environment is equivalent to knowing all the qualities of all the candidates according to each criterion. The uncertainty is of not knowing whether or not the candidates have the qualities they are supposed to have, and it is this uncertainty that decision makers try to reduce to a minimum by getting information.

In this type of situation, multicriterion decision [e.g. POM 00] is a much more realistic way of handling the problem.

A second example of Gilboa and Schmeidler is strategic decisions. Here the reasoning horizon is quite long, so that each event is actually a series of events occurring successively over a long period. As each sub-event can take on numerous guises, there ensues a combinatory explosion in the number of events. To illustrate the difficulty, put yourself in the place of George W. Bush before the Iraq war. Once again the alternatives are clear: 'to go or not to go'. The events are more obvious than in the previous example: the strength of the adversary, the attitude of his allies and public opinion are all events that could affect the outcome. But the long-term events are just as important, if not more so, as the short-term ones: what will be the impact on Arab countries? It is absolutely impossible to cover all possible events. In fact, only a few more or less likely scenarios can be assessed. In the latter case, Savage's model provides a reasonably well-adapted framework, but the complexity of the events, and above all their dispersion in time, reduces any hope of utility expectation that would involve a prior assessment of these events. In fact, we are merely able to evaluate a few scenarios that form a tiny sub-set of the set of possible scenarios (and this itself is no mean achievement).

The most suitable model is therefore the decision tree which explicitly takes into account the succession of events [RAI 68] but which does not solve the intrinsic difficulty of giving credible conditional probabilities to the various non-independent chained events. Utility expectation cannot be of any help in any of these cases, which is why Gilboa and Schmeidler [GIL 95, GIL 00] plead for case-by-case reasoning in this type of situation.

It is perhaps important at this point to give an idea of the paradoxes that arise if the model is not correctly posed. Consider the following example where the decision consists of choosing between two horses, 'Stagger Home' and 'Knacker's Delight'. Which of the following two models described in Tables 4.2 and 4.3 is the correct one [cf. POU 90]?

Bet on	My horse wins	My horse loses
Stagger Home	50	–5
Knacker's Delight	45	–6

Table 4.2. *Model 1*

In the first model you must always bet on Stagger Home because he dominates the game (even with a leg in plaster?). In the second model, it depends on the probability: you must bet on Knacker's Delight once the probability of Stagger Home winning is lower than 50/106. As can be seen, the model works well provided you choose the

Bet on	p Stagger Home wins	$(p-1)$ Knacker's Delight wins
Stagger Home	50	−5
Knacker's Delight	−6	45

Table 4.3. *Model 2*

correct one. In the first model, the alternatives and events are interlinked; the second correct model excludes this.

In the light of this misleading model it is easier to understand why the formalized framework of Savage represents an important step forward in thinking about decision making, before even considering utility expectation.

4.2.2. *Challenging utility expectation*

The other important discussion stemming from Savage's framework actually goes back further than the publication of the book in 1954; it concerns the question of the existence of accuracy probabilities, or any other measurement that can be applied to events.

The same question arises, for example, with possibility measures or fuzzy measures [BOU 96, BOU 03, DUB 85]. In any case, we need to be able to distinguish between events on the basis of the greater or smaller chance they have of occurring. This is an extremely difficult problem. For repeated events, it is possible to record the frequency and from this deduce the probability. For example, if you take the same train every day, after a few months you can predict that your chance of arriving at work on time is, say, 80%. This is an example of frequentist probability.

In certain fields such as medicine, such frequency-based data is available. By contrast, if we want to know what the price of a barrel of oil will be in six months (higher than today's price or not?) we have changed context and it is now extremely risky and presumptuous to give probabilities. Frequentist probability is of no help here. What Savage's model says is that even if there is no probability, if you respect the coherence of your decisions, it is as if you were measuring the importance of events with a probability. In other words, a coherent choice of alternatives reveals what you believe to be the probability of the events.

Two criticisms of the model are possible. The first criticism is of the axioms and in particular the axiom of independence (Savage's sure-thing principle [SAV 54]), which requires the utility function to be linear with respect to the probabilities [ALL 53]. This independence condition is of the same type as the independence in probability or in coordinates in multicriterion decision that entails the existence of a function of additive choice [KEEN 76, WAK 89]. This correspondence is not surprising given that if each event is assimilated to a criterion, Table 4.1 is none other than a multicriterion decision matrix and the choice of a valid alternative for all the events comes down to aggregating the set of criteria. In Cohen and Tallon [COH 00] there is a complete review of those decision models in risk and uncertainty that weaken the axiom of independence.

The second criticism of the axioms concerns overall coherence in the choice of alternatives by the decision maker. Some of these are highly theoretical and do not correspond to experience, especially constant alternatives whose outcome does not depend on events.

If we set aside the criticisms of the axioms, we may state that Savage probabilities doubtless exist in theory but do not actually correspond to anything for real-life decision makers. This criticism is especially important if we intend to apply the Savage model inversely. That is, we now assume that the decision maker is capable of expressing probabilities about future events and we then deduce that if they want to remain perfectly rational, they must maximize their utility expectation. Those probabilities that the decision maker gives are called *a priori* probabilities because they are given before any observations are made in order to be updated in a Bayesian manner afterwards. They are also called 'subjective' because they obviously depend on the subject (i.e. they are based on nothing in particular). Here, the most radical criticism is to say that such probabilities are also 'subjective' in the other meaning of the term, i.e. they have no objective basis [DEF 37, NAU 01]. This leads to models of non-probabilized uncertainty, e.g. taking maximin as a decision criterion (i.e. the decision that is the argument of $\text{Max}_A \text{Min}_E U(a,e)$). More sophisticated risk models blend expectancy with the influence of the worst existing outcomes [ESS 97, JAF 88].

Even if it is reasonable to think that subjective probabilities do not actually exist, we do have to concede from a purely pragmatic point of view that this does not prevent people from making decisions. We must therefore come back to observing the decision makers. Two types of behavior emerge: on the one hand, we can put our faith in experts who are assumed to be capable of giving probabilities that are not too absurd, and on the other hand we can settle for sub-rational behavior. This brings us to the framework defined by Simon and to bounded rationality.

The criticisms leveled at probabilities can also be applied to the utility function since we know that it is not unique in representing the preorder. As soon as we use cardinality, either in multicriterion decisions [POM 00] or when we use the utility expectancy criterion, the final decision is dependent on the chosen utility. This throws serious doubts on the validity of the model. This issue of cardinality is linked to the commensurability of uncertainty and utility [DUB 03].

4.2.3. *Bounded rationality*

From observing the way municipal decision makers in his home town of Milwaukee made their decisions, Simon quickly became aware of the gap between actual practise and the expected utility model. From then on he spent a large part of his life trying to understand the mechanisms of human decision [SIM 91]. Many issues in Simon's work in the field of decision can be found in [POM 02].

While utility expectation does not offer good guidance, the 'Taylorian' vision of Dewey [SIM 77] is no more relevant:

– what is the problem?
– what are the possible alternatives?
– which one is best?

This simplistic vision, still in vogue with many engineers, is hardly operational:

– "Unfortunately, problems do not come to the administrators carefully wrapped in bundles with the value elements and the factual elements neatly sorted" [SIM 97]. The decision environment is essentially ambiguous and depends on the individual interpretation of the decision maker [BOL 79, MAR 76].

– "The alternatives are not given, they have to be constructed" [KEEN 92, ROY 00].

– The best for which criterion? This brings us back to Savage or multicriteria analysis.

It was in view of these observations that Simon was to emphasize the diachronic aspect of the decision process and introduce his well-known three stages that were to become four [SIM 77]. According to Simon, the process begins with three stages:

1) gathering all the possible alternatives;

2) determining the set of consequences of the possible alternatives;

3) evaluating all the possible consequences.

The novelty when compared with Dewey is clear: Simon is interested in the process, he does not say 'what are the possible alternatives?' but 'we have to gather them'. Note also that the vain question of the best alternative is avoided in this approach.

Simon next adds several other aspects to the various phases of decision, in particular concerning the way the problem is posed and the quest for information. This was to culminate in the famous four phases:

1) intelligence;

2) design;

3) choice; and

4) review.

The role of the information is fundamental in the first two phases; we only choose between those alternatives that we know and that we are able to document. As Simon puts it: "the information drives the decision".

In contradiction to the reproaches that are sometimes leveled at this approach, Simon himself is perfectly well aware of the way the various phases are entangled and he gives examples of about-turns. He even suggests that each phase can be considered recursively as a decision [SIM 77, p. 43]. However, what is undoubtedly most important in this phase scheme is that, according to Simon, it would be difficult to pin the decision to the moment of choice: "All the images falsify decision by focusing on the final moment" [SIM 77, p. 40]. This change of attitude was to bring decision out of the realms of mythology or epic (such as Caesar crossing the Rubicon or de Gaulle launching Concorde) and to tie it to management and to information processing. Finally, note that Simon knew perfectly well that, the decision having been made, it still has to be applied:

> "In the foregoing discussion I have ignored the fourth phase of decision making: the task of carrying out decisions. I shall merely observe by the way that seeing that decisions are executed is again decision-making activity."

(Note that "fourth" should read "fifth"; the review phase was not mentioned in the first edition of [SIM 77, p. 43] which was published in 1960.)

Simon then adds [SIM 77, p. 44]: "Executing policy, then, is indistinguishable from making more detailed policy." Basically, for Simon alternative and decision are inseparable, and execution merely means focusing on the details of smaller and smaller decisions that are closer and closer to the ground. This idea, which to the author of this chapter is fundamental, has not yet been sufficiently exploited in management.

In the framework defined by Simon, decision and information can be related, but it contains little about choice and the role of the future. This is where we come up against the cognitive limits of humans and their inability to know events in the indefinite future, yet which is necessary if one is to apply Savage's model. In other words, the combinatory explosion in the number of scenarios is too much for the brain to cope with [POM 01]. This leads to some awkward questions such as: how can a decision maker evaluate all the consequences of an alternative and compare them? Simon actually gives an interesting definition of the knowledge of a decision maker as his ability to evaluate the consequences [SIM 97, p. 85]. This problem of evaluating the consequences is central to any decision process. In the context of Savage, evaluating the consequences assumes a knowledge of all future events and their probabilities.

The evaluation of the consequences, the constraints and the aims all form a complex whole in which it is not always easy to identify where reasoning has its place. In theory, we know what to do: we just have to maximize a utility function on a set of choices. The difficulty comes in determining what actually is the role of reason when there is neither a clear set of choices nor a utility function, and we have but a sketchy knowledge of the future. This is the framework for Simon's thoughts on rationality.

In fact, when it comes to 'Administrative Behavior', Simon knows that the questions listed at the beginning of this section and, in particular, the one about the evaluation of the consequences in uncertainty, cannot be solved by a human brain within a utility expectancy model. Absolute rationality, where according to Dewey we are meant to choose the best possible alternative after evaluating all the possible consequences into the indefinite future, was afterwards named by Simon as substantive rationality. Thus, according to Simon [SIM 97, p. 93–94], substantive rationality is a failure because of the following:

– Rationality requires complete knowledge and total anticipation of the consequences of choices. In practice, knowledge about consequences is always fragmentary especially in risk or uncertainty. In the American tradition, one speaks of risk when the decision maker possesses a degree of probability measure on the events and of uncertainty in the other cases. Here, the term 'uncertainty' is used to cover both cases. This exhaustiveness issue is also central in Janis and Mann [JAN 77], see also [KLE 02, p. 109].

– Consequences belong in the future and the imagination has to make up for the lack of any experience to attribute values to them, but these values can only be imperfectly predicted.

– Rationality requires the choice among all possible known alternatives (intangible data) [MAR 93, p. 159]. In actual practice, only a small number of alternatives come to mind.

– The decision maker does not have a total preorder on the consequences, i.e. they have no utility function [MAR 93, p. 159], no total preorder that presupposes that the alternatives are comparable [JAN 77]. Moreover, the preferences are not exogenous and independent of the choice and alternatives [MAR 78, MAR 93, MAR 94].

As we can see, Simon's criticism is based on the difficulty (except in very simple cases) to correctly use the model of maximum expected utility (subjective expected utility (SEU)). Each of the criticisms stated above corresponds to an implicit assumption in the model of expected utility. To quote Simon [SIM 83, p. 14]:

> "When these assumptions are stated explicitly, it becomes obvious that SEU theory has never been applied and never can be applied – with or without the largest computers – in the real world."

The amount of knowledge necessary to apply the model certainly justifies Simon's use of the adjective 'Olympian' [SIM 83, p. 19]. Simon therefore strives to replace these Olympian assumptions by realistic assumptions. These assumptions were to become the foundation of what in 1955 (reprinted in [SIM 79, Chapter 11]) would become limited rationality. They can be summarized as follows:

– The impossibility of ascribing probabilities to all events and even of merely enumerating all the possible events with their combinations.

– The fact that the decision maker's preferences are not rational in the sense that they maximize a utility function; they are actually multicriterion and also changeable, which leads to the impossibility of having an overall utility function for the choice.

– The decisions are spread out over time and, in organizations, form a time process within which the sub-decisions are not mutually independent, but may be taken at different moments and levels with non-identical criteria. Furthermore, preferences, alternatives and aims cannot be separated ("Closely related to the idea that alternatives generate their goals is the fact that alternative is itself an important goal in the lives of many people" [MAR 93, p. 15]). The fact that the sub-decisions are taken locally on partial criteria is clearly, and mathematically, opposed to any overall optimization [SIM 83, p. 18].

– Information is fundamental and very strongly conditions decision making. This becomes particularly clear when one sees the (small) number of alternatives that an individual is actually capable of studying. Attention also plays a considerable role in framing the problem and conditioning the subsequent decision making. Attention is a rare resource; a person can only fix their attention on a small number of problems at once, or even just one if they are very preoccupied.

In other words, since we do not have the wisdom of the gods, we must be satisfied with sub-optimal or 'satisficing' decisions. In practice, given the limitations just pointed out, the decision process stops once the decision maker has found a solution that gives them satisfaction within the assumptions that appear as the most likely or that seem to dominate the other decisions while never being catastrophic.

Simon [SIM 84, p. 594] specifically refers to the maximin aspect of 'satisficing'; he also states that an alternative is satisfactory once it reaches or exceeds a certain level of expectancy for the set of criteria considered by the decision maker [MAR 93, p. 161]. The notion of level of expectancy is linked to the form of the utility. Note also that the level of expectancy varies during the search and is adapted locally according to the difficulty of reaching it [SEL 02]. This notion of 'satisficing' tends to become more and more preponderant in the work of Simon after 1960 [e.g. SIM 83].

The limited rationality of 1955 gives way progressively to 'bounded rationality' [SIM 72]. More often, this bounded rationality takes the form of an algorithm already underlying in 1955 in the form of a 'satisficing rule'. The algorithmic aspect underlines the sequential and heuristic aspect of decision processes. According to Gigerenzer and Selten [GIG 02a], limited rationality can be summed up as the use of fast, rough-cut and robust rules (1) for searching, (2) for stopping the search and (3) for choosing [GIG 02].

This vision justified the use of the term procedural rationality [SIM 76] which Simon from then on opposes to substantive rationality. The above evolution was accompanied by a growing interest by Simon in artificial intelligence ("Alternatives of action and consequences of action are discovered sequentially through search processes" [MAR 93, p. 191]). The heuristic process is characteristic of procedural rationality, for the rationality is in the searching, whereas at the next higher level (meta [PIT 02]) reflection on 'problem solving' becomes substantive [MAR 93, p. 200]. The searching is rational, and we therefore have a form of procedural rationality obeying a program just like heuristic searching. The criterion for stopping the search is the satisfaction of the decision maker when they have reached a 'satisficing' level in terms of expectancy.

Emphasis should be placed on the fourth level of rationality for it has a double aspect. There is firstly the information aspect, i.e. the quantity of information that an individual can process is limited. In the 'information society' in which we are immersed, we can see that the gap is widening dramatically between potentially available information and what a person can grasp (this is still truer with the Internet). Simon [SIM 55] is explicit:

> "Broadly stated, the task is to replace the global rationality of Economic Man with a kind of rational behavior that is compatible with the access to information and the computational capacities that are actually possessed by organisms, including man, in the kinds of environments in which such organisms exist."

This first aspect leads to the second idea that cognitive resources are limited, which gives rise to some interesting developments [BEL 88]. In fact, with 'Administrative Behavior', we find in the chapters devoted to psychology the first reflections on the role in decision of attention, information and stress, reflections that were to lead on to the problem of cognitive load related to decision. Given the limited cognitive capacity of humans, attention is a rare resource. It also plays an important role in decision and this theme is expanded ("... the ways in which attention is allocated is critical to understanding decision") [MAR 93, p. 4] and is finally one of the key factors for understanding the garbage can model [COH 72].

During the development of Simon's thinking, where the brain was treated as a symbol processing system, cognitive limitation became a central element in limited rationality:

> "In its simplest form, the theory of limited rationality is a theory of 'how to live' in an infinite world while only disposing of very modest computing means;

means that are not dependent on the size of the real world, but only on the local environment and what you can do there" [SIM 84, p. 595].

Simon often emphasized that man has to get by with what he has, and that does not include an exhaustive study of the whole of the alternatives and their consequences. Simon was subsequently often to set procedural rationality, which is the rationality of examining the consequences in view of information limitations, cognitive capacity and the attention of the decision maker against substantive rationality. The latter is the rationality of the gods and is optimizing, while the former simply aims for satisfactory (satisficing) solutions:

> "The idea of limited, consequential rationality found in the book has become more or less standard in modern theories of decision-making, at least outside the hard core of orthodox neoclassical economic theory" [MAR 93, p. 9].

The model of bounded rationality is, for Simon, a centrist model [SIM 97, p. 331]. It stands between the point of view of those economists who only accept non-limited rationality, in the Olympian sense, and who are only beginning to examine models other than those of expected utility maximization and the point of view of those who flee from the word rationality and who defend intuition and purely reactive behavior in management (i.e. of the 'case-based reasoning' type). This is not sufficient to explain why the notion of limited rationality had such an immense following for over half a century. A more convincing explanation is that it was the first time that anybody had tried to set up a scientific framework based on the fact that the real decisions of real decision makers in real organizations could be a subject for investigation, with real measurements of efficiency (efficiency criterion). This framework also took into account cognitive limitations and limitations of information and individuals' reasoning.

4.2.4. *Multicriterion decision*

We have seen that Simon was one of the first to state with some scientific authority the existence of more or less contradictory criteria in decision since it is one of the components of limited rationality. The phenomenon has of course been known for much longer by flesh and blood decision makers, and we even know of Benjamin Franklin's procedure for tackling the question. This consists of listing the arguments 'pro' and 'con' and then simplifying the table, the 'pros' and 'cons' of similar weights cancelling, until one of the columns is empty (letter to Joseph Priestley, see [ZIO 92]). It is not the purpose of this section to deliver a lesson on multicriterion decision; diverse and varied monographs exist on the subject and its applications [BOUY 00, POM 00, ROY 85, ROY 93].

Multicriterion decision is part and parcel of the human condition. Everyone wants to have their cake and eat it, and a similar proverb surely exists in many languages.

This problem has no solution yet people always end up making decisions [KEE 77] unless they are disciples of French politician Henri Queuille (*petit père Queuille* (1901–1993) was a president of the radical council of the *Quatrième République* who claimed that there existed no problem to which a non-decision did not eventually provide a solution). As already mentioned, arbitrating between the short and the long term is the first inevitable and painful multicriterion choice. How can we reach a compromise [SIM 97]? From a neurobiological point of view we know now that the integrating center for the various impulsions is the ventro-medial part of the pre-frontal cortex and that certain abnormal behaviors are caused by an integration failure, the irrational side being interpreted either as short-term dictatorship or as an uncontrolled emotional receptivity.

As in the first example of Gilboa and Schmeilder, multicriterion decision is more focused on the description of the characteristics of the possible alternatives than on the events to come. In this regard, it is more worthwhile to be able to evaluate such and such a characteristic than to look at the uncertainty of this characteristic across all possible events. This is why most followers of multicriteria analysis appear to ignore uncertainty: "Information versus uncertainty" always gives the same alternative. Similarly, rapid decision making is worth more than long investigations on events in the future, provided of course that the decision is not irreversible [POM 97a]. This is evident in games such as the 'beer' game [STE 89] and studies in the field of decision with delayed feedback [KLEI 85, KLEI 93]. "The ability to select relevant variables seems to be more important than procedural sophistication in the processing of that information", according to Kleinmuntz [KLEI 85, p. 696]. In addition, "When viewed from this continuous perspective, decision making success critically depends upon two major factors: (1) the availability of the feedback and (2) the opportunity for taking corrective alternatives based upon that feedback", [KLEI 85, p. 682].

However, people do not like the tension generated by multicriterion choice [see BER 03, KOT 91]. They often seek to rationalize their choice either by searching for dominance [MONT 83, MONT 87] (this choice of dominance actually being confirmed by neurobiologists [BER 03, p. 306]), or by using analogy-based reasoning and not aggregation, which is seen as a scientist's attempt at rationalization. Often the decision maker will, following the paths of heuristic search and of limited rationality, prefer to proceed by trial and error via interactive methods [POM 00] and local adaptations according to levels of expectancy [LÉV 86, SEL 02].

4.2.5. *Other models*

We have seen the problems posed by the use of probabilities and utility expectation within the model of Savage. We have also mentioned that it is possible to get rid of probabilities by considering other models such as MaxMin. In decision practice, sensitivity to the worst outcome is a well-attested phenomenon [MAR 87, TVE 95]. We even find the expression "extremeness aversion" in [TVE 93].

We can try to construct models that take into account the probabilities and the aversion to large losses (ruin) [e.g. COH 88, JAF 88, LEL 94, RUB 88]. A more complete approach consists of taking into account the difference in value between the outcomes versus the difference between the probability of their occurring [SHAF 93]. These models try to 'flavor' the choice criteria by introducing aversion to large losses or large differences in gains. We shall turn to the problem of low-probability events in section 4.5, which are one of the main sources of error in human decision [MAR 87, MORE 02]. The use of belief functions by Dempster [DEM 67] and Shafer [SHA 76] enable mixing of beliefs about the probability of future events with partial ignorance. In the model of Smets [SME 90], a so-called pignistic transformation is used to transform belief functions into probabilities at the moment of decision making [DUB 96].

In quite another way, it is perfectly legitimate to consider that probabilities provide illusory information and to replace them by possibilities [DUB 85] which are sub-additive measures (i.e. the measure of two disjoint events can be less than the sum of the measures of each event). A distribution of event possibilities merely lists them from the most to the least probable, and only the order counts. It is then possible, using a Choquet integral, to integrate over the whole set of outcomes in order to obtain a possibilistic expected utility together with other decision criteria within a possibilistic framework of axioms [DUB 95, DUB 01]. We then speak of qualitative decisions since only the relative plausibility of events is taken into account; no absolute measure of their probability of occurring is involved. In Dubois *et al.* [DUB 03], there is a review of the various models and criteria that are based on weaker measures than probabilities.

Recent and abundant investigations have shown that a model can be constructed within this framework as coherent as that of Savage [DUB 02]. A Savage-type model can also be obtained by weakening the assumption of a total order on the alternatives. In this case, instead of probabilities we obtain a preorder on events refered to as qualitative probabilities [GIL 03, LEH 96].

Finally, we can simply have a preorder on the events and a preorder on the outcomes to obtain an entirely qualitative decision model [DUB 03]. Decision a is then preferred to decision b if the set of events in which the outcome of a is better than that of b is 'greater' than the set of events in which b outclasses a. It is remarkable that a Savage-type axiomatic model can be reconstructed within such a framework [DUB 03]. However, the decision rule so obtained is not very satisfactory because we get outcomes of the Arrow theorem type, which amounts to only considering the most plausible event to dictate the decision (the dictator phenomenon of Arrow [DUB 02, DUB 03]). Note too that this model is free of a strong but hidden constraint in the Savage model, namely the commensurability of utilities and probabilities. In Savage's model, there is a relation between the degree of uncertainty and the scale used to measure the outcomes. Since we know the value of a certain equivalent of a lottery, we can establish a direct relation between outcomes (the value of the certain equivalent) and probability in the lottery.

4.3. Decision based on recognition

4.3.1. *Diagnosis and decision*

As we have seen, it is not possible to deal with human decision without at least having thought of the future. On the other hand, as we have already mentioned, a peacefully grazing herbivore's decision to flee obeys a simple reaction triggered by a stimulus. This reaction is encoded in the genes of the animal who probably has no representation of the future, and is the result of evolutionary learning.

Such behavior exists in humans too in the form of reflexes, so that you do not need to think before ducking to avoid a snowball in your face. When we enter the domain of reasoning where, at the very least, the decision maker has the time to envisage representations of the future, it is useful to distinguish the two phases of diagnosis and look-ahead. In this way we arrive at the following simplified decision process scheme (Figure 4.1).

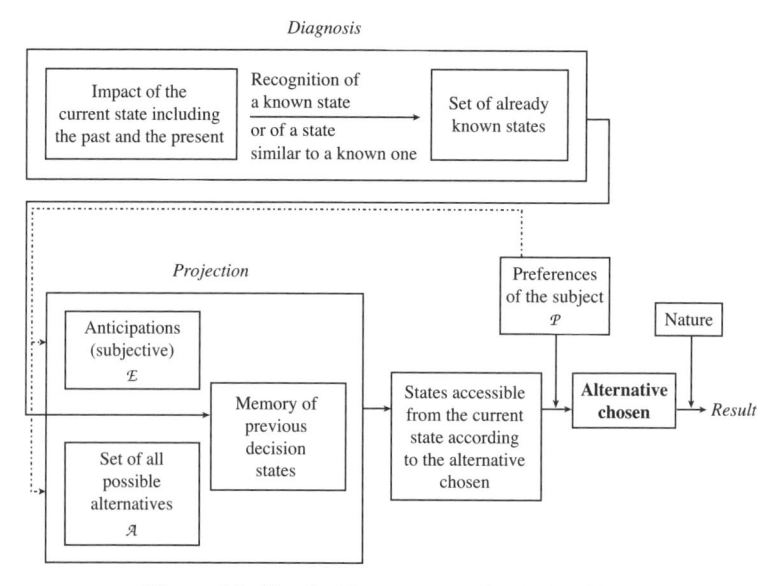

Figure 4.1. *The decision process (after [POM 97a])*

The diagnosis phase consists of recognizing what is the current state of the world, i.e. the past and the present. Next, we try to anticipate the consequences of the decision in question in the light of our vision of the future; this is the projection phase. This is the step which establishes the essential distinction between human decision and animal decision. The incorporation of a larger and larger projection component happened progressively in the course of evolution, but only became a species characteristic in man (homo sapiens or his ancestors?). This also explains why there remains in human behavior a large area of decision that is either reflex or based on decision patterns. Rouse [ROU 83, p. 620] states that "humans, if given a choice, would prefer to act as context-specific pattern recognizers rather than attempting to calculate or optimize".

We have argued that the decision directly triggered by a recognition of the state of the world, i.e. when the diagnosis calls a standard reaction, is an important, perhaps frequent and even rational process within industrial processes [POM 97a]. Expert systems worked on this basis: a good diagnosis brings with it the decision whether we represent the states of the world in the form of rules as in expert systems or in the form of cases [KOL 93, RIE 89]. The diagnosis phase consists of recognizing a state of the world. If we have an exhaustive list of 'diagnosable states' associated with a list of decisions and a one-to-one mapping between the two, we obtain the principle of decision tables [POM 97a].

The situation is often more complicated, especially when the diagnosis does not allow us to identify a case already recorded in the memory. We shall examine the model of Gilboa and Schmeidler which tackles this question of recognition when the 'recognizable' states are not recorded in the memory.

4.3.2. *Case-based decision*

The principle of case-based decision is simple. We assume there exists a decisional case base in the memory, these cases representing the whole experience of the system. Confronted with a new situation, the decision maker recognizes a case already met and triggers the decision that best fits this case (a decision that has also been recorded in the memory). If we stay within the simple case of the decision table, the problems that arise are purely representational, i.e. we need to have a quite highly evolved language or representation to capture the richness of each case and enable easy pattern matching. These are questions of artificial intelligence which we shall not explore further here; see the literature [e.g. KOL 93].

In reality, case-based reasoning cannot be reduced to matching since these systems also (and above all) require learning ability. The case base must be able to expand with new, unrecorded cases and must also facilitate the decision if the system meets hitherto unrecorded cases. The question that then arises is how close the cases are to one another. When can we say, to a given degree, that one case is close to another and that the latter is a reasonable model for the decision being made? What we have to do is to define distance between cases.

Gilboa and Schmeidler [GIL 95, GIL 00] proposed a framework to formally bring together case-based decision and reasoning. Their idea is that each case is a triplet (p, a, r) where $p \in P$ (the set of problems), $a \in A$ (the set of possible alternatives) and $r \in R$ (the set of outcomes). Case-based reasoning applies to problems. Gilboa and Schmedler therefore define a function for similarity between problems:

$$S : P^2 \to [0, 1]. \tag{4.1}$$

This function gives the 'distance' between the two problems. The decision maker also has a utility function on the results:

$$U = R \to \mathbb{R}. \tag{4.2}$$

The set of cases in the memory is denoted M. With this notation, it is possible to measure the relevance or utility of the alternative a to a problem p given by:

$$U_p(a) = \sum_{(q,a,r \in M)} s(p, q)\, u(r). \tag{4.3}$$

In other words, for fixed a and p we take all the problems q in memory such that $(q, a, r) \in M$ are weighted by their similarity distance to p (i.e. $s(p, q)$), which is higher the closer q is to p. It is then natural to choose the alternative a that maximizes $Up(a)$.

Gilboa and Schmeidler [GIL 95] provide axioms that ensure consistency in their model. In the manner of Savage, if the choice of alternatives obeys the axioms of consistency whatever the memories, a theorem guarantees the existence of a similarity function such that the choice is that of maximizing $Up(a)$. The reasoning is the same as in Savage's model, a coherent choice of the alternatives involving the existence of a similarity distance between the problems (instead of the probabilities about events in Savage). This similarity shows – and this is a major weakness of this type of model – that the reasoning about the future (i.e. uncertainty) is contained in the similarity function.

In Gilboa and Schmeidler [GIL 00], the model is extended to the similarity between pairs (problem, alternative) and triplets (problem, alternative, outcome). When comparing Savage's model with case-based reasoning as we have just set out, the main advantage is that instead of knowing all states of the world and their outcomes in front of various alternatives, it is sufficient to have a memory of past cases. Note also that one of the useful points of the model is that it is enriched little by little by the introduction of new cases, as well as by the refinement of the similarity function, as the model is used (learning).

In recent work, Gilboa and Schmeidler [GIL 03] propose an axiomatic model to derive probabilities from a memory of a case. The main factor is the number of occurrences of the case, and the higher the number the higher the associated subjective probability. This is basically another way of modeling the phenomenon of availability (see section 4.5) or reinforcement already seen in [AND 83, AND 95], or of representation [TVE 82b, TVE 82c].

4.4. Recognition, reasoning and decision support

The processes at work in human decisions are complex, as evidenced by the work of neurobiologists [BER 03, DAM 94, DAM 96, DAM 03]. Conscious, deliberate reasoning is not all that is involved. We have seen that the other main direction in decision is recognition. Even in animals such as the toad, recognition is tempered by context and learning [BER 03]. Researchers wondered whether the best way of taking account of this complexity was actually to 'leave man in the loop' and to design interactive decision support systems (DSS).

4.4.1. *Interactive decision support systems*

DSSs tend to complement man in his reasoning by providing rational models and, for recognition, extracting the relevant information features (stimuli) that are too numerous for human processing. There exists a vast literature on these systems [e.g. ADA 02, ADA 03, BON 81, BUR 01, HUM 01, KEE 78, LÉV 89, MOR 02, SPR 82].

In fact, when there is enough time to deliberatein decision making, the process always comes back to the ability to construct representations of the future world and to project oneself there. Consequently, decision support is first of all an aid to the construction of scenarios and seeks to amplify this specifically human aptitude to consciously project into the future.

As emphasized by Berthoz [BER 03] and as confirmed by the analysis of accidents concerning bad decisions [BOY 91, MORE 02, PER 84], decision begins with the perception and above all interpretation of stimuli in situation (or in context). Thus a DSS, like any information processing system, is made up of a perception-interpretation module, of a model base with which to make computations and projection (for example through statistical regression) and a database to serve as a memory (Figure 4.2).

```
┌─────────────────────────────────────┐
│  ┌──────────┐        ┌──────────┐   │
│  │ Database │◄──────►│Model base│   │
│  └──────────┘        └──────────┘   │
│       ↘              ↙              │
│         ┌──────────┐                │
│         │  Dialog  │                │
│         └──────────┘                │
└──────────────┬──────────────────────┘
               ↓
              User
```

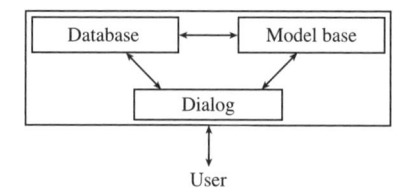

Figure 4.2. *Structure of DSS (after [SPR 87])*

Without going into details [see BON 81, LÉV 89, MOR 02, TUR 88], suffice it to say that DSS designers have a tendency to attach more importance to the projection part of the model than perception and diagnosis [POM 93, section 2]. This is how DSS acquired the image of 'what if' analyzers or 'look ahead machines' [POM 97a]. This is not a false image, but it is simplistic in that it entirely neglects decision pattern recognition with no projection taking place, either through lack of time or because it is unnecessary, evolutionary learning or simply learning having provided suitable responses.

To conclude, we can say that the field of interactive DSS is a very active one and that these systems perform a frequent and invaluable service in many companies. However, it remains very difficult to treat them with a general theory, each system having a very precise purpose tending to lend it an ad hoc nature. The only reasonably fertile general idea consists of analyzing them as heuristic search systems [BON 81, LÉV 89, LÉV 95]. What happens is that the decision maker remains in the loop and engages in a heuristic search guided and facilitated by the system. This heuristic search essentially allows them to explore the future ('what if' analysis) and to explore it at two levels: the level of data and the level of models [POM 03a]. It is this twofold degree of freedom that makes systems such as spreadsheets so popular and effective [POM 02a, POM 03a]. Obviously, the heuristic search ceases once a 'satisficing' solution has been found. This takes us directly into bounded rationality.

4.4.2. *Scenarios*

Since the world of possibilities is very large if not infinite, human decision aided by machine was to be endowed with scenarios (a small number compared with all possible ones). These scenarios were projected up to a time horizon that was dependent on the context but that could be very distant, especially with strategic decisions, hence the need for DSS. Even for a small number of scenarios, the combinatorics rapidly become impossible for a human brain to handle.

The use of scenarios turned out to be the most common and reliable way of exploring the future. In its most formalized version, it takes the form of a decision tree

[RAI 68, SHA 96, VON 86] or other graphic forms. When conditional probabilities can be attached to various successive events, a backward folding type of reasoning is obtained that rigorously allows the scenario with the best utility expectation to be found. May we remind the non-specialist that the best eventual scenario is not, except in restricted cases, simply the continuation of the best intermediate scenarios; there is always opposition between the short and the long term!

Numerous other graphic methods have been derived from decision trees, in particular by reducing the requirement for probability independence between all the events e.g. influence networks, Bayesian networks [OLI 90, SHE 94], various qualitative methods [OLI 90], and even methods without probabilities for representing the decision context [BRÉ 02, POM 02b].

One of the important aspects of decision practice that is corroborated by our observations [BRÉ 02, POM 95] is linked to the simplification of scenarios in human reasoning. This is the use of alternatives considered as robust *vis-à-vis* the set of events belonging to an 'event' node, which allows the node in question to be eliminated [POM 01] and to obtain sequences of 'relatively good alternatives' that are often used in practice.

Another way of mitigating the combinatory explosion consists of pushing as many alternatives as possible to the end of the scenario ('alternative postponement'; [see POM 01]). This can be interpreted as a search for information (when this is possible) before the action or as an illustration of the old decision method consisting of always having two irons in the fire, i.e. we push back the choices when the real states of the world are revealed. In dynamic programming this ability to keep as many possibilities open for as long as possible is studied under the name of flexibility [ROS 01]. These pragmatic ways of reasoning, although not issuing from substantive rationality, are perfectly rational and fit well into reasoning by scenarios.

The DSS is then confronted with the question of the choice of scenarios: multicriterion choice, naturally, and conscious multicriterion choice, in that experience rapidly shows people that you cannot win on every front. The way humans make choices has not been well elucidated. According to neurobiologists, the brain works more through inhibition of potential solutions than by choice. In other words, after a complicated physiological process involving numerous parts of the brain, a dominant solution eventually inhibits all the other possible solutions. (Note here that we meet the 'search for dominance' phenomenon described by Montgomery [MONT 83, MONT 87]. We can all see this behavior when, after his purchase, an individual persuades themself that they have chosen the best car or washing machine within their constraints.)

In the discharging of neurons there would appear to be threshold effects that result in 'winner takes all'. This type of phenomenon can certainly be modeled in multicriterion decision by giving at one point a weight or a relative importance to the criteria, a phenomenon that cannot be identified in the brain and that remains hidden in the neurons. As pointed out by Keen [KEE 77], what is astonishing in decision is that theoretically there is no solution but in practice one is nevertheless chosen (except in the case of Buridan's ass, which of course is academic!).

In the choice of scenarios, robustness is an important factor. Here we mean robustness relative to events; we will not enter into the questions of robustness relative to data and to the parameters of the models [ROY 98, ROY 02, VIN 99]. In the case of robustness related to events and the probability of their happening (or any other measure), we find ourselves in the Savage framework. It is an extremely complex problem to escape from the maximin criterion which is obviously robust against all events, and to know what constitutes a negligible event or not [LEH 96, MON 98]. It is also all the more difficult when we realize that a bad appraisal of small probabilities is a great weakness of the human brain.

We find this negligence in many accidents. For example, the one or two days of cold weather per century in Florida, assumed by the designers of the space shuttle booster rocket joints, was wrong by a factor of ten. Very cold spells actually occur at least once every ten years. This unfortunately led to the explosion of the shuttle [MORE 02]. Note that in analyzing the accident befalling the shuttle Challenger, although the engineers correctly considered that the failure rate for launching such shuttles is around 1%, the management put the figure at 1 in 100,000. This difference by a factor of a thousand brings with it different behavior patterns: at 1% the matters are taken seriously but at 1 in 100,000 one is negligent. According to Schelling [SCH 62, p. vii]:

> "There is a tendency in our planning to confuse the unfamiliar with the improbable. The contingency we have not considered looks strange; what looks strange is thought improbable; what is improbable need not to be considered seriously."

This relative inability of the brain to process and appreciate probabilities, even when they exist in a realistic way, will be discussed in the next section together with other examples of cognitive bias.

4.5. Cognitive biases

There are some unavoidable obstacles in the way of attempts at rationality in decision. The first is that of low probabilities: should we choose an alternative that can lead to catastrophic outcomes such as the death of the decision maker in the event of very low probability occurrences? For example, should we drive, or go out, in extremely windy weather? Either we take an extremely pessimistic decision criterion such as maximin and stay in bed all the time, or we treat exceptions as exceptions, coming up against logical incoherence [DUB 03].

The principle of independence, or sure-thing principle, is another obstacle because it imposes a rationality that no one accepts: if you are in the higher price range, there are good reasons for choosing the fastest car but which has the highest fuel consumption. In the lower price range, however, you will attach more importance to consumption and will choose the model with the lowest even if it is less fast. This assumption of linearity of preferences in relation to probabilities (or to multicriterion weightings) is very strong. (See section 4.2.2; it is purely mathematical and is in no way rational since it is not stupid to change one's choice according to level of satisfaction.) The non-respecting of other axioms that we have not discussed here also brings about severe incoherence. Such is the case with the axiom of 'irrelevant alternatives' [POM 00] since, when one is not satisfied, one obtains paradoxes such as the so-called Talleyrand method to force the choice [WOL 91]. To push decision makers towards the median choice, all that is needed is the introduction of very bad or very expensive choices.

These facts are evident from experience, just like the violation of the principle of independence. Since the founding criticism of Allais [ALL 53], numerous decision experiments have been carried out in particular by Kahneman and Tversky [TVE 67, TVE 69, TVE 82a, TVE 83]. It is these results that we would like to outline briefly [KAH 82, KAH 00], relating them particularly to the problems discussed in this chapter.

We shall not dwell much on aspects relating to the emotions and the affective nature of certain decisions, as in the 'frame effect' or the way the context of a decision is presented [SLO 88, TVE 88]. Numerous experiments have demonstrated the reality of this effect, identified a long time ago by Tversky and Kahmeman. Zickar and Highhouse [ZIC 98], however, showed that the size of this effect depends on individual character traits. In Slovic *et al.* [SLO 02] there is argument for, and numerous examples of, the involvement of feelings and emotion in decisions: an effect that is obviously sensitive to the way the facts are presented. If we present the same risk situation in terms of possible deaths or in terms of possible survivors, the judgement of most people is reversed. This is clearly pure irrationality, and it is the same whether the public is being manipulated on small probabilities with the so-called principle of precaution. We are not a long way from techniques of manipulation which naturally take advantage of these biases, especially those of a sympathetic nature [CIA 01, JOU 87].

Among the effects that are directly linked to the theory, two categories are quoted here: questions relating to probabilities and those connected with the anchor effect and expectancy level. A complete review of these biases can be found in Bell *et al.* [BEL 88], Kahneman *et al.* [KAH 82], Kahneman and Tversky [KAH 00], von Winterfeldt and Edwards [VON 86] and Chapter 12 of this book.

4.5.1. *Biases linked to probabilities*

We have already noted that low probabilities are not correctly perceived by humans, being either ignored [MAR 87] or overestimated [TVE 95]. Actually, with probability in the range $10^{-3} - 10^{-6}$, it is difficult to realize the difference accurately and dispassionately as the brain has no appropriate yardstick. However, catastrophic flooding that happens every three years or every three thousand years makes a big difference to the inhabitants. It is in fact around the level of probability of 10^{-3} that there appears to occur this modification in the perception of risk. People tend to dismiss the risk under 10^{-4}, which corresponds to the probability of twelve or thirteen heads in a row in a session of heads or tails. Under 10^{-3}, risk is accepted within certain limits provided it is accompanied by the idea (or the illusion) of control. That is, the person thinks that they must be careful and is persuaded that they are capable of doing so [MCK 93, PER 84].

For a driver in France covering 20,000 km in a year, the risk of injury in an accident was 1/300 and the risk of death 1/4,300 (1997 figures). The risk of death accepted by climbers making at least one ascent per year in France is between 1/500 and 1/1,000. For an air passenger doing 20,000 km a year, the risk of dying is 10^{-5}, which is negligible. The automobile risk gives an idea of the maximum limit acceptable to an individual who is in control and free from any drug or alcohol influence or constraints, of the order $10^{-2} - 10^{-3}$. Another example of this psychological limit is in the 18th century, 3% of the ships that were built eventually sunk in the sea. The activities of ship owners and of sailors were considered risky and generated substantial income (at least for the ship owner) if successful. Today the risk of shipwreck is around 3/1,000 for all ships, and maritime transport has become just another activity (according to naval historian Christian Buchet on TV Europe No.1, 2005).

At the other end of the probability scale, the effect of certainty is well authenticated. The choice leading to a certain gain is always preferred to the hope of a lottery win, which brings more money with a probability $1 - \epsilon$ and nothing with a probability ϵ. In this case however, the rationality is obvious and proverbial: a bird in the hand is worth two in the bush. However, we come back to the previous discussion, for while the behavior appears rational for $\epsilon = 10^{-3}$, it is more difficult to justify it for $\epsilon = 10^{-6}$. However, human nature is such that it is averse to risk for gain [KAH 00, part 3].

Man doesn't like to lose! From the work of Kahmeman and Tversky [KAH 79], it is abundantly clear and has been confirmed many times by experiment that human attitude to risk is not the same if it is a question of winning or losing. We have already noted the role played by large losses (the probability of ruin) and the aversion engendered in the choices [COH 87, MAR 87, TVE 93, TVE 95] but, more generally, all losses are the subject of risk taking (man is a risk taker with losses) whereas man is prudent with gains (i.e. he is risk-averse for gain).

Human Decision: Recognition plus Reasoning   181

In other words, to avoid a certain loss of −10 man chooses lotteries of the style depicted in Figure 4.3.

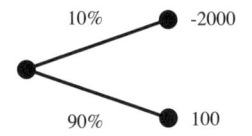

Figure 4.3. *A losing lottery*

That is, he prefers a lottery with a utility expectancy of −110 to a certain loss of −10, man in general being a bad loser! This touches on game addiction and the idea that you can make up for your losses by making riskier choices. On the other hand, for gains, a certain gain of 10 will be preferred to the lottery depicted in Figure 4.4 with an expectancy of 18.

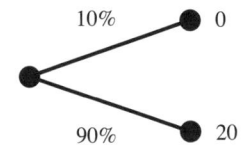

Figure 4.4. *A winning lottery*

It occurs as if e.g. the 'real utilities' measured in monetary terms were modified by the subject (see Chapters 8 and 9), and we obtain the well-known concave/convex utility curve depicted in Figure 4.5.

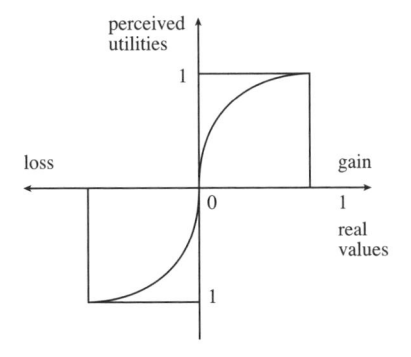

Figure 4.5. *Subjective utilities*

This gain/loss dissymmetry discovered by Kahneman and Tversky [KAH 79] is a fundamental notion for the understanding of human behavior.

We will not dwell on the effects relating to Bayes' rule or the inability to take into account conditional probabilities. It is patently obvious that the brain is not a spontaneous calculator, so when it becomes a question of handling probabilities or making calculations on conditional probabilities, the brain is a non-starter. The cognitive load is very large by the time there are four or five events and all possible processings. It is here that science and decision support tools are unbeatable. Medical decision [GRE 90] which cannot be seriously treated without Bayes and processing has made spectacular progress in the last 50 years. This question of conditional probabilities and coupling with events also plays a big role in reliability. Accident risk can be greatly minimized if we wrongly consider that events are independent when they are not. Perrow [PER 84] emphasizes these problems of coupling and sequencing in serious accidents.

One last effect related to probabilities that deserves attention is the illusion of control of risk [BAR 94, KAH 82, KAH 93, MAR 87, MCK 93, SLO 82]. This so-called risk control is purely irrational and is a pre-Savage regression that mixes what the decision maker controls and what they do not. If we do not accept the separation between alternatives and events, we can only arrive at paradoxes of the type described in section 4.2.1 with horse betting. In risk control, the only reasonable idea is the search for information, hence the role of forecasts such as in weather which, in certain countries, is given in terms of probabilities. The search for information also leads to the idea of the postponed alternative (section 4.4.2), i.e. we let nature take its course while seeking to know more about the true state of the world before deciding.

With the illusion that we are controlling uncertainty, we open the door to irrationality which returns in force with the principle of precaution and the manipulation of public opinion that follows. During the winter of 2003, several local authorities started preparing for the Seine to burst its banks on the centennial of the last occurrence (1906). This is a well-known effect of bad use of the law of large numbers [KAH 72]. We can make many complaints regarding the notion of probability and decision theory, but certainly not about being over-taught to future decision makers!

4.5.2. *Representations, levels of satisfaction and the anchor effect*

We have seen that the attitude to risk is inverted around a point that we arbitrarily set to zero in Figure 4.5. In fact, everything happens as if each of us has a neutral point or level of expectancy and that we measure our preferences from there: desire above, dislike below. This notion of expectancy level has been known for a long time [LEW 44, SIE 57] and was taken up again by Tversky and Kahneman [TVE 74]. It is clearly an important notion in practice when lose or gain one dollar does not have the same significance for a Rockefeller as for a tramp. We have previously seen that there exist gain difference models in decision [SHAF 93] and in multicritia [BOUY 86, FIS 91, FIS 92].

The notion of level of expectancy is semantically close to that of reference level, which leads us to the concept of the anchor effect. The anchor point is the point where, led by emotions and experience, the individual evaluates their choices. For example, a happy holiday spent on a sunny island will serve as a reference point for choosing future holidays. This phenomenon of the anchor effect can have an interesting range of dimensions: cognitive and memory-based, representational and eventually narrative.

With cognitive and memory-based anchor effect, certain events are marked in the memory and will orientate the choices through the emotions as soon as they are recognized. We are not a long way from the 'frame effect' as this point. An individual who has had a disagreeable experience, even after a good decision, (section 4.2) will hesitate to make the same decision. The reference level can be manipulated through the emotions exactly as in the 'frame effect'. It even appears that this manipulation is more effective than context [KÜH 98].

Less obvious, although well documented in cognitive science and artificial intelligence, is the recuperation effect. Recent or memorized events have a greater weight than older events. These recent events will tend to govern choice in problem solving; Anderson [AND 83] and Newell [NEW 90] actually modeled the effect to make their systems humanly plausible. Even worse, the brain creates false correlations between completely independent events [CHA 69]. If certain numbers are imposed on the brain and subjects are then asked how many nations are in the UNO, the result is therefore influenced by those previously given numbers [PIA 95]. This can also be interpreted as an anchor effect [TVE 74].

One should be extremely wary of this effect of recuperation. The phenomenon is particularly sensitive when estimating probabilities, especially when they are experimentally not very sensitive to the decision maker (less than a few tenths). Between a probability of 10^{-2} and 10^{-4}, there is every reason to fear that an unenlightened decision maker may be extremely sensitive to anchor effects, recuperation or representation (see following section) that stem from previous experience having nothing at all to do with the current phenomenon. However, we have seen that between these two levels is found a psychological limit and a difference in behavior that is completely rational on a human scale.

The second component of the anchor effect is the 'representativeness effect'. This means events that are easy to depict will be given a higher probability than those that are less easy to imagine [MAR 94, SLO 82, SLO 88, TVE 82c]. Thus an airplane pilot may well anchor on the non-deployment of his undercarriage if the indicator light does not come on (a common situation well known to pilots in training), and meanwhile forget that he is about to run out of fuel (accident at Portland [MORE 02]). This representativeness effect is also a threat in diagnosis, the current state in that field being that it is highly dependent on our representations. This can lead to many accidents due to errors in diagnosis, such as Three Mile Island and many others in aviation [BOY 91, MORE 02, PER 84].

The third component of the anchor effect, and doubtless the least well known, is the narrative aspect. Here we come back to scenarios: a scenario is a sort of story. As we have seen, making a decision consists of inhibiting all possible scenarios except one which will dominate, and that this domination will occur before the action ("rationale construction for alternative" [POM 03]) or after the alternative (post-decision rationalization). In any case, this rationalization effect always exists and is preferentially related to the context [BRÉ 02]. The more credible (attractive?) the story, the greater the chance that the decision will be made. The narrative mode is in general a fundamental cognitive mode [BOL 95, BRU 86, BRU 90].

It has been said that making a decision in an organization that people will stick to is like telling them a story that they believe [WEI 01]. This idea of telling a story – to oneself or to others – is leading us rather a long way from rationality. It brings us closer to language however, with which decision has many points in common at least from a phylogenetic point of view. Even without invoking Vico [VIC 44], we would be wrong to ignore this aspect because historically before reasoning there were mythology and lyrical poetry which, in the form of stories, were the first ways in which man structured his world and accumulated knowledge. More scientifically, Tversky and Kahneman [TVE 82b] showed that the easier a story is to construct, the greater the chance the decision will be made. See also Kahneman and Lovallo [KAH 93] and Boland [BOL 79], who stated

> "…the decision maker will build convincing explanations of what happened using the data made focally available and will tend to discount the importance of factors on which data is not presented."

All these aspects that bring together decision and artificial intelligence belong to the domain of representation by case, or more generally of AI-type modeling [AND 83, NEW 90, SIM 95]. The latter references demonstrate that the subject attracted the attention of the pioneers of artificial intelligence. The questions of whether we should lean toward 'human reasoning' at the expense of rationality and the role of evolution in these biases remain open. It is not easy to give an straightforward answer to the question of whether these biases and/or these decisional heuristics are advantages or disadvantages for the species.

Evaluation can only be multicriterion. There are, first of all, heuristic decisions which have the advantage of rapidity and robustness, even though they may not have Olympian qualities [GIG 02, section 2.3]. There is no need to point out that speed is of the essence for the survival of the individual. A famous general, when asked what was the main factor in his victories, replied: "I don't know, but I know the reason for the defeats: too late!" The same can obviously be said for 'recognition-primed decision'.

Cognitive psychology (Chapter 12) is tending to reassess the usefulness of other biases in a positive light, but we must be guarded. Note too, as pointed out by one author to whom I am grateful, that the rationality of the species is not necessarily that of a given individual (think of the elimination of the least adapted reproducers, for example).

Taking a few examples of biases, it appears difficult to justify the frame effect or the anchor effects that allow minds to be manipulated. On the other hand, aversion to risk in gain is certainly a useful behavior trait (look before you leap), but what is the point of risk taking in loss? You do not recover by gambling or on the stock exchange; instead you are occasionally lucky. Perhaps this bias facilitates progress in the cultural and technical domains, since it can be argued that we need big risk takers to make big discoveries. It is surely wiser for the species to neglect small probabilities (of the order 10^{-4} and less) and to accept the certainty effect.

The most ambivalent bias is that of risk control, for it leads to extremely dangerous behavior in many human activities (e.g. finance, gambling and controlling machines). On the other hand however, without this bias, no one would feel tempted to leave their territory to explore the big wide world.

4.6. Conclusion

In this chapter we have made the link between decision theory and human decision. In contrast to what some researchers in biology and psychology believe, these links are deep and useful.

They are deep, for if we fail to bear in mind Savage's model, its limits and now the results on qualitative decision, it is quite simply impossible to think rationally about decision in risk. It is Savage's model that enables us to understand the difference between good and bad luck and rational decisions. We can discuss whether the assumptions in the model are realistic or rational, but we cannot deny that outside the games of chance studied since the 18th century, the quantitative or qualitative Savage framework is the only one that allows a distinction to be made between a lucky bad decision maker and an unlucky good decision maker. It is, for example, by referring to this model and also thanks to the psychologists Tversky and Kahneman that we have understood the inversion of attitude to risk, according to whether the individual thinks in terms of losses or gains.

If we are interested in the biological aspect of decision, we must take an evolutionary point of view and conclude that even if common mortals consider that language and decision are specifically human traits, and even knowing that evolution proceeds by mutations, there exists a continuum between the neurons of the cockroach that make it 'decide' to flee or to feign death, and human neurons. This evolution over 400 million years explains the great complexity of the circuits involved in decision in the brain and the different areas concerned, from the primitive part of the brain to the most recent part, the pre-frontal cortex [BER 03].

What we can say is that the part that is most closely involved in the body and the emotions, relying on the oldest parts of the brain, interferes with the 'reasoning' part and that the integration of the information happens in the pre-frontal cortex. The reasoning part is above all our ability to project ourselves into the future and, by complex and poorly identified phenomena, to make one alternative dominate the others in the Pareto sense (for this is indeed multicriterion decision). This domination can, moreover, very well result from a 'search for dominance' subsequent to the decision. The part played by emotion and intuition (Sacha Guitry, lampooning popular wisdom, said "beware of your first impression, it's always the right one") has never been denied by decision specialists, and the phenomena of diagnosis by quasi-instantaneous recognition of stimuli or more complex decisional patterns followed by the decision are (fortunately) well known. We even know how to model them by using case-based reasoning.

It is therefore rather saddening to see neurobiologists such as Berthoz caricaturing utility expectation, which remains the most rational means to make a decision provided that we have probabilities and a utility that aggregates. These are assumptions that are obviously not confirmed in daily life, just as there is no such thing as a perfect market. It is moreover amusing to note that it is often the same people who, for ideological reasons, are the detractors of Savage and Debreu.

The limits of utility expectancy have been denounced since Simon introduced his counter-model of bounded rationality which offers a frame for reasoning – if not a model in the classical sense of the term – allowing the experimentation and design of numerous reasoning and problem-solving systems, starting from decision models [e.g. AND 83, AND 95, NEW 72, NEW 90]. This also gave people the right to speak of heuristic exploration and 'what if' bounded rationality. Although obviously as old as homo sapiens, this provides a frame for and a rational way of treating the subject which explains its popularity.

In this conclusion we shall not return to bias in human decision which, for the most part linked to poor processing of probabilities by the untrained brain (such as mental arithmetic, a skill that new generations are completely lacking), are now well known and should systematically be brought in for all high-stake decisions. As for the other more psychological biases, we urge the reader to take care when making a decision and to remember that in the normative model, it would not be possible to see this bias. Then, even when Savage is no great help, if there are no probabilities or clear utility functions, one can at least try to see through decision pitfalls such as the representation effect, irrelevant alternatives (see Talleyrand method in [WOL 91]) and other traps [JOU 87].

We end by reminding those who must make decisions that once they have striven to control all their biases, "a decision is only good if it is rooted in friendly words and convincingly argued" [SFE 80]. This citation from an author highly critical of decision (but without good arguments) reminds us of the narrative and social sides of decision, uniting decision and language and making homo sapiens unique.

4.7. Acknowledgements

Thank you to Jean-Yves Jaffray for his careful re-reading of this work.

4.8. Bibliography

[ADA 02]   Adam F., Brézillon P., Humphreys P., Pomerol J.-Ch. (Eds.), 2002, Decision making and decision support in the Internet sge, *Proceedings of the IFIP W.G. 8.3 Conference*, Oak Free Press, Cork, Ireland.

[ADA 03]   Adam F., Brézillon P., Courbon J.-Cl. (Eds), 2003, Decision support systems in the Internet age, *Journal of Decision Systems*, vol. 12(2).

[ADO 96]   Adolphs R., Tranel D., Bechara A., Damasio H., Damasio A.R., 1996, Neuropsychologigal approaches to reasoning and decision making, in *Neurobiology of decision-making*, Damasio A.R., Damasio H. and Christen Y. (Eds), Springer, Berlin, 157–179.

[ALL 53]   Allais M., 1953, Le comportement de l'homme rationnel devant le risque: criticism des postulats and axiomes de l'école américaine, *Econometrica*, vol. 21, 503–546.

[AND 83]   Anderson J.R., 1983, *The Architecture of Cognition*, Harvard University Press, Cambridge, MA.

[AND 95]   Anderson J.R., 1995, *Cognitive Psychology and its Implications*, Freeman, New York.

[ARK 86]   Arkes H.R., Hammond K.R., 1986, *Judgment and Decision Making: an Interdisciplinary Reader*, Cambridge University Press, Cambridge USA.

[BAR 94]   Barki H., Rivard S., Talbot J., 1994, Risk management by information systems project leaders, *Journal of Management Information Systems*, vol. 10, 254–265.

[BEL 88]   Bell E.D., Raiffa H., Tversky A. (Eds.), 1988, *Decision Making*, Cambridge University Press, Cambridge, USA.

[BER 96] Berthoz A., 1996, Neural basis of decision in perception and in the control of movement, in *Neurobiology of Decision-making*, Damasio A.R., Damasio H. and Christen Y. (Eds), Springer, Berlin, 83–100.

[BER 03] Berthoz A., 2003, *La Décision*, Odile Jacob, Paris.

[BOL 79] Boland Jr. R.J., 1979, Control, causality and information system requirements, *Accounting, Organizations and Society*, vol. 4, 259–272.

[BOL 95] Boland Jr. R.J., R.V. Tenkasi, 1995, Perspective making and perspective taking in communities of knowing, *Organization Science*, vol. 6, 350–372.

[BON 81] Bonczek R.H., Holsapple C.W., Whinston A.B., 1981, *Foundations of Decision Support Systems*, Academic Press, NY.

[BOU 96] Bouchon-Meunier B., Nguyen H.T., 1996, Les incertitudes dans les systèmes intelligents, *Que Sais-Je?*, vol. 3110, PUF, Paris.

[BOU 03] Bouchon-Meunier B., Marsala C. (Eds.), 2003, Logique floue, principes, aide à la décision, Vol. 1 *Traitement des données complexes and commande en logique floue*, Vol. 2 *du traité Information-Commande-Communication*, Hermès-Lavoisier, Paris.

[BOUY 86] Bouyssou D., 1986, Some remarks on the notion of compensation in MCDM, *European Journal of Operational Research*, vol. 26, 150–160.

[BOUY 00] Bouyssou D., Marchant T., Pirlot M., Perny P., Tsoukias A., Vincke Ph., 2000, *Evaluation and Decision Models, A Critical Perspective*, Kluwer, NY.

[BOY 91] Boy G., 1991, *Intelligent Assistant Systems*, Academic Press, NY.

[BRÉ 02] Brézillon P., Pasquier L., Pomerol J-Ch., 2002, Reasoning with contextual graphs, *European Journal of Operational Research*, vol. 136, 290–298.

[BRU 86] Bruner J.S., 1986, *Actual Minds, Possible Works*, Harvard University Press, Cambridge MA.

[BRU 90] Bruner J.S., 1990, *Acts of Meaning*, Harvard University Press, Cambridge MA.

[BUR 01] Burstein F. (Ed.), 2001, Decision support in the new millennium, *Journal of Decision Systems*, vol. 10(3).

[CAL 91] Calvin W.-H, 1991, *The Ascent of Mind: Ice Age, Climate and the Evolution of Intelligence*, Bantam Books, New York.

[CAL 94] Calvin W.-H, 1994, La naissance de l'intelligence, *Pour la Science*, vol. 206, 110–117.

[CHA 69] Chapman L.J., Chapman J.P., 1969, Illusory correlation as an obstacle to the use of valid psychodiagnostic signs, *Journal of Abnormal Psychology*, vol. 74, 271–280.

[CIA 01] Cialdini R.B., 2001, Harnessing the science of persuasion, *Harvard Business Review*, October 2001, 72–79.

[COH 87] Cohen M., Jaffray J.-Y., Said T., 1987, Experimental comparison of individual behavior under risk and uncertainty for gains and losses, *Organizational Behavior and Human decision Processes*, vol. 39, 1–22.

[COH 88] Cohen M., Jaffray J.-Y., 1988, Is Savage's independence axiom a universal rationality principle?, *Behavioral Science*, vol. 33, 38–47.

[COH 00] Cohen M., Tallon J.-M., 2000, Décision dans le risque and l'incertain: l'apport des modèles non additifs, copy from University of Paris I.

[COH 72] Cohen D.M., March J.G., Olsen J.P., 1972, A garbage can model of organizational choice, *Administrative Science Quarterly*, vol. 17, 1–25.

[DAM 94] Damasio A.R., 1994, *Descartes' Error*, Putnam's Sons, NY.

[DAM 03] Damasio A.R., 2003, *Looking for Spinoza: Joy, Sorrow and the Feeling Brain*, Harcourt, New-York.

[DAM 96] Damasio A.R., Damasio H., Christen Y. (Eds), 1996, *Neurobiology of Decision-making*, Springer, Berlin.

[DEF 37] De Finetti B., 1937, La prévision: ses lois logiques, ses sources subjectives, *Annales de l'Institut Henri Poincaré*, vol. 7, 1–68.

[DEM 67] Dempster, A.-P., 1967, Upper and lower probabilities induced by a multivalued mapping, *Annals of Mathematical Statistics*, vol. 38, 325–339.

[DUB 85] Dubois D., Prade H., 1985, *Théorie des Possibilités*, Masson, Paris. *Possibility Theory, An Approach to Computerized Processing of Uncertainty* (translation), Plenum Press (1988).

[DUB 95] Dubois D., Prade H., 1995, Possibility theory as a basis for qualitative decision theory, *Proc. IJCAI-95*, Montréal, 1924–1930.

[DUB 96] Dubois D., Prade H., Smets Ph., 1996, Representing partial ignorance, *IEEE Transalternatives on Systems, Man, and Cybernetics*, vol. 26, 361–377.

[DUB 01] Dubois D., Prade H., Sabbadin R., 2001, Decision-theoretic foundations of qualitative possibility theory, *European Journal of Operational Research*, vol. 128, 459–478.

[DUB 02] Dubois D., Fargier H., Prade H., Perny P., 2002, Qualitative decision theory: from Savage's axioms to non-monotonic reasoning, *Journal of the ACM*, vol. 49(4), 455–495.

[DUB 03] Dubois D, Fargier H., Perny P., 2003, Qualitative decision theory with preference relations and comparative uncertainty: an axiomatic approach, *Artificial Intelligence*, vol. 148, 219–260.

[ESS 97] Essid S., 1997, Choice under risk with certainty and potential effects: a general axiomatic model, *Mathematical Social Science*, vol. 34, 223–247.

[FIS 91] Fishburn P.C., 1991, Non-transitive preferences in decision theory, *Journal of Risk and Uncertainty*, vol. 4, 113–134.

[FIS 92] Fishburn P.C., 1992, Additive differences and simple preference comparisons, *Journal of Mathematical Psychology*, vol. 36, 21–31.

[FUR 96] Furster J.M. 1996, Frontal lobe and the cognitive foundation of behavioral alternative, in *Neurobiology of Decision-making* Damasio A.R., Damasio H. and Christen Y. (Eds), Springer, Berlin, 115–123.

[GIG 02] Gigerenzer G., 2002, The adaptive toolbox, in *Bounded Rationality: The Adaptive Toolbox*, Gigerenzer G. and Selten R. (Eds.), MIT Press, MA, 37–50.

[GIG 02a] Gigerenzer G., Selten R. (Eds.), 2002a, *Bounded Rationality: The Adaptive Toolbox*, MIT Press, MA.

[GIG 02b] Gigerenzer G., Selten R., 2002b, Rethinking rationality, in *Bounded Rationality: The Adaptive Toolbox*, Gigerenzer G. and Selten R. (Eds.), MIT Press, MA, 1–12.

[GIL 95] Gilboa I., Schmeidler D., 1995, Case-based decision theory, *Quarterly Journal of Economics*, vol. 110, 605–639.

[GIL 00] Gilboa I., Schmeidler D., 2000a, Case-based knowledge and induction, *IEEE Transalternatives on Systems, Man and Cybernetics*, vol. 30, 85–95.

[GIL 03] Gilboa I., Schmeidler D., 2003, Inductive inference: an axiomatic approach, *Econometrica*, vol. 71(1), 1–26.

[GRE 90] Grenier B., 1990, *Evaluation de la décision médicale*, Masson, Paris.

[HAM 87] Hammond K.R. Hamm R.M., Gassia J., Pearson T., 1987, Direct comparison of the efficacy of intuitive and analytical cognition expert judgment, *IEEE Transactions on Systems, Man, and Cybernetics*, vol. 17(5), 753–770.

[HOW 88] Howard R.A., 1988, Decision analysis: practice and promise, *Management Science*, vol. 34, 679–695.

[HUM 01] Humphreys P., Brézillon P. (Eds.), 2001, Decision systems in alternative, *Journal of Decision Systems*, vol. 10(2).

[JAF 88] Jaffray, J.-Y., 1988, Choice under risk and security factor. An axiomatic model, *Theory and Decision*, vol. 24, 169–200.

[JAN 77] Janis I.L., Mann L., 1977, *Decision Making: A Psychological Analysis of Conflict, Choice and Commitment*, Free Press, NY.

[JOU 87] Joule R.V., Beauvois J.L., 1987, *Petit traité de manipulation à l'usage des honnêtes gens*, Presses Universitaires de Grenoble, Grenoble.

[KAH 72] Kahneman D., Tversky A., 1972, Subjective probability: a judgment of representativeness, *Cognitive Psychology*, vol. 3, 430–454.

[KAH 79] Kahneman D., Tversky A., 1979, Prospect theory, an analysis of decision under risk, *Econometrica*, vol. 47, 263–291.

[KAH 93] Kahneman D., Lovallo D., 1993, Timid choices and bold forecast: a cognitive perspective on risk taking, *Management Science*, vol. 39, 17–31.

[KAH 00] Kahneman D., Tversky A. (Eds.), 2000, *Choices, Values and Frames*, Cambridge University Press, Cambridge UK.

[KAH 82] Kahneman D., Slovic P., Tversky A. (Eds.), 1982, *Judgment Under Uncertainty: Heuristics and Biases*, Cambridge University Press, Cambridge, UK.

[KEE 77] Keen P.G.W., 1977, The evolving concept of optimality, in *Multiple Criteria Decision Making*, M.K. Starr and M. Zeleny (Eds.), TIMS study in management science 6, North Holland, 31–57.

[KEE 78] Keen P.G.W., Scott-Morton M.S., 1978, *Decision Support Systems*, Addison-Wesley, Reading.

[KEEN 92] Keeney R.L., 1992, *Value-Focused Thinking*, Harvard University Press, MA.

[KEEN 76] Keeney R.L., Raiffa H., 1976, *Decisions with Multiple Objectives*, Wiley & Sons, NY.

[KLE 93] Klein G.A., 1993, A recognition-primed decision (RPD) model of rapid decision making, in *Decision Making in Alternative, Models and Methods*, G.A. Klein, J. Orasanu, R. Calderwood, C.E. Zsambok (Eds.), Ablex, Nordwood N.J., 138–147.

[KLE 02] Klein G.A., 2002, The fiction of optimization, in *Bounded Rationality: The Adaptive Toolbox*, Gigerenzer G. and Selten R. (Eds.), MIT Press, MA, 103–121.

[KLEI 85] Kleinmuntz D.N., 1985, Cognitive heuristics and feedback in a dynamic decision environment, *Management Science*, vol. 31, 680–702

[KLEI 93] Kleinmuntz D.N., 1993, Information processing and misperceptions of the implications of feedback in dynamic decision making, *System Dynamics Review*, vol. 9, 223–237

[KOE 07] Koenigs M., Young L., Adolphs R., Tranel D., Cushman F., Hauser M., Damasio A., 2007, Damage to the prefrontal cortex increases utilitarian moral judgements, *Nature*, vol. 446, 908–911.

[KOL 93] Kolodner J., 1993, *Case-based Reasoning*, Morgan Kaufmann, San Francisco.

[KOT 91] Kottemann J.E., Davis D.R., 1991, Decisional conflict and user acceptance of multicriteria decision-making aids, *Decision Sciences*, vol. 22, 918–926.

[KÜH 98] Kühberger A., 1998, The influence of framing on risky decisions: a meta-analysis, *Organizational Behavior and Human decision Processes*, vol. 75, 23–55.

[LEH 96] Lehmann D., 1996, Generalized qualitative probability: Savage revisited, in the *Proceedings of the Conference on Uncertainty in AI*, Portland, Oregan; Morgan Kaufmann Publishing, San Francisco, 381–388.

[LEL 94] Leland J.W., 1994, Generalized similarity judgments: an alternative explanation for choices anomalies, *Journal of Risk and Uncertainty*, vol. 9, 151–172.

[LÉV 86] Lévine P., Pomerol J-Ch., 1986, PRIAM an interactive method for choosing among multiple attribute alternatives, *European Journal of Operational Research*, vol. 25, 272–280.

[LÉV 89] Lévine P., Pomerol J.-Ch., 1989, *Systèmes Interactifs d'aide à la décision and systèmes experts*, Hermes, Paris.

[LÉV 95] Lévine P., Pomerol J.-Ch., 1995, The role of the decision maker in DSSs and representation levels, *Proceedings of 26th Hawaii International Conference On System Sciences*, J.F. Nunamaker Jr. and R.H. Sprague (Eds.), vol. 3, IEEE, 42–51.

[LEW 44] Lewin K., Dembo T., Festinger L., Sears P., 1944, Level of aspiration, in *Personality and the Behavior Disorders*, J.M. Hunts (Ed.), Ronald Press, NY, 333–378.

[MAR 78] March J.G., 1978, Bounded rationality, ambiguity and the engineering of choice, in *Decision Making*, D.E. Bell, H. Raiffa and A. Tversky (Eds.), Cambridge University Press, 1988.

[MAR 94] March J.G., 1994, *A Primer on Decision Making*, The Free Press, New York.

[MAR 76] March J.G., Olsen J.P. (Eds.), 1976, *Ambiguity and Choice in Organizations*, Universitetsforlaget, Bergen.

[MAR 87] March J.G., Shapira Z., 1987, Managerial perspectives on risk and risk taking, *Management Science*, vol. 33, 1404–1418.

[MAR 93] March J.G., Simon H.A., 1993, *Organizations*, 2nd edition, Basil Backwell, Oxford, UK.

[MCK 93] McKenna F.P., 1993, It won't happen to me: unrealistic optimism or illusion of control, *British Journal of Psychology*, vol. 84, 39–50.

[MON 98] Monnet J.-M., Lagrange J.-Ph., Pomerol J.-Ch., Teulier R., 1998, A formal framework for decision-making in case-based reasoning. *Proceedings IPMU*, Paris, vol. 2, 1274–1281.

[MONT 83] Montgomery H., 1983, Decision rules and the search for a dominance structure: towards a process model of decision making, in *Analysing and Aiding Decision Processes*, P.C. Humphreys, O. Svenson and A. Vari (Eds), North-Holland, 343-369.

[MONT 87] Montgomery H., 1987, Image theory and dominance search theory: How is decision making actually done?, *Acta Psychologica*, vol. 66, 221–224.

[MOR 02] Mora M., Forgionne G., Gupta J. (Eds.), 2002, *Decision Making Support Systems*, Idea Group Publishing, Hershey PA.

[MORE 02] Morel C., 2002, *Les décisions absurdes*, Galimard, Paris.

[NAU 01] Nau R.F., 2001, De Finetti was right: probability does not exist, *Theory and Decision*, vol. 51, 89–124.

[NEW 90] Newell A., 1990, *Unified Theories of Cognition*, Harvard University Press, MA.

[NEW 72] Newell A., Simon H.A., 1972, *Human Problem Solving*, Prentice Hall, Englewood Cliffs.

[OLI 90] Oliver R.M., Smith J.Q. (Eds.), 1990, *Influence Diagrams, Belief Nets and Decision Analysis*, John Wiley & Sons, Chichester.

[PER 84] Perrow C., 1984, *Normal Accidents*, Basic Books, NY.

[PIA 95] Piattelli-Palmarini M., 1995, *La réforme du jugement ou comment ne plus se tromper*, Odile Jacob, Paris.

[PIT 02] Pitrat J., 2002, Herbert Simon et le méta, *Revue d'Intelligence Artificielle*, vol. 16, 87–99.

[POM 93] Pomerol J-Ch., 1993, Multicriteria DSSs: State of the art and problem, *Central European Journal for Operations Research and Economics*, vol. 2/3, 197–212.

[POM 97a] Pomerol J-Ch., 1997a, Artificial intelligence and human decision making, *European Journal of Operational Research*, vol. 99, 3–25.

[POM 97b] Pomerol J-Ch., 1997b, Cognition and Decision: about some recent results in neurobiology, in *ISDSS97 Proceedings*, Lausanne, 115–125.

[POM 01] Pomerol J-Ch., 2001, Scenario development and practical decision making under uncertainty, *Decision Support Systems*, vol. 31, 197–204.

[POM 02] Pomerol J-Ch., 2002, L'apport de Herbert Simon dans le management et la décision, *Revue d'Intelligence Artificielle*, vol. 16, 221–249.

[POM 03] Pomerol J-Ch., 2003, Decision making biases and context, in DSS from theory to practice, *Journal of Decision Systems*, vol. 12(3–4), 235–252.

[POM 00] Pomerol J-Ch., S. Barba-Romero, 2000, *Multicriterion Decision Making in Business*, Kluwer, New York.

[POM 02a] Pomerol J-Ch., Adam F., 2002, From human decision making to DMSS architecture, in *Decision Making Support Systems*, M. Mora, G. Forgionne and J. Gupta (Eds.), 40–70.

[POM 03a] Pomerol J-Ch., Adam F., 2003, Multi-level and Multi-model DSSs, in *DSS in the Uncertainty of the Internet Age*, T. Bui, H. Sroka, S. Stanek and J. Goluchowski (Eds.), Karol Adamiecki University of Economics Press, Katowice, Poland, 333–346.

[POM 95] Pomerol J-Ch., Roy B., Rosenthal-Sabroux S.C., Saad A., 1995, An intelligent DSS for the multicriteria evaluation of railway timetables, *Foundations of Computer and Decision Science*, vol. 20(3), 219–238.

[POM 02b] Pomerol J-Ch., Brézillon P., Pasquier L, 2002, Operational representation for practical decision making, *Journal of Management Information Systems*, vol. 18(4), 101–116.

[POU 90] Poundstone W., 1990, *Les labyrinthes de la raison*, Belfond, Paris.

[RAI 68] Raiffa H.A., 1968, *Decision Analysis*, McGraw-Hill, New-York.

[RIE 89] Riesbeck C.K., Schank R.C., 1989, *Inside Case-based Reasoning*, Laurence Erlbaum, Hillsdale N.J.

[ROS 01] Rosenhead J., 2001, Robustness analysis: keeping your options open, in Rosenhead J. and Mingers J. (Eds.), *Rational Analysis for a Problematic World Revisited: Problem Structuring Methods for Complexity Uncertainty and Conflict*, Wiley, Chichester, 181–207.

[ROU 83] Rouse, W.B., 1983, Models of human solving: Detection Diagnosis and Compensation for system failures, *Automatica*, vol. 19(6), 613–625.

[ROY 85] Roy B., 1985, *Méthodologie multicritère d'aide à la décision*, Economica, Paris.

[ROY 98] Roy B., 1998, A missing link in operational research decision aiding: robustness analysis, *Foundations of Computer and Decision Science*, vol. 23, 141–160.

[ROY 00] Roy B., 2000, Réflexions sur le thème, quête de l'optimum and aide à la décision, in *Decision, Prospective and Auto-Organisation*, Mélanges en l'honneur de Jacques Lesourne, J. Thépot, M. Godet, F. Roubelat and A.E. Saad (Eds.), Dunod, Paris, 61–83.

[ROY 02] Roy B., 2002, Robustesse de quoi and vis-à-vis de quoi, mais aussi robustesse pourquoi en aide à la décision? *Proceedings of the 56th Meeting of the European Working Group on Multiple Criteria Decision Aiding*, Coimbra, October 2002.

[ROY 93] Roy B., Bouyssou D., 1993, *Aide Multicritère à la Décision: Méthodes and cas*, Economica, Paris.

[RUB 88] Rubinstein A., 1988, Similarity and decision-making under risk (is there a utility theory resolution to the Allais paradox?), *Journal of Economic Theory*, vol. 46, 145–153.

[SAV 54] Savage L.J., 1954, *The Foundations of Statistics*, 2nd edition, Dover Publications, 1972, New York.

[SCH 62] Schelling T. C., 1962, Preface in R. Wohlstetter: *Pearl Harbour: Warning and Decision*, Stanford University Press, Stanford. French translation: Pearl Harbour n'était pas possible, Stock, 1964.

[SCH 98] Schoenbaum G., Chiba A., Gallagher M., 1998, Orbito-frontal cortex and basolateal amygdala encode expected outcomes during learning, *Nature Neurosciences*, vol. 1, 155–159.

[SEL 02] Selten R., 2002, What is bounded rationality, in *Bounded Rationality: The Adaptive Toolbox*, Gigerenzer G. and Selten R. (Eds.), MIT Press, MA, 13–36.

[SFE 80] Sfez L., 1980, *Je reviendrai des terres nouvelles*, Hachette Littérature, Paris.

[SHA 76] Shafer G., 1976, *A Mathematical Theory of Evidence*, Princeton University Press, NJ.

[SHA 96] Shafer G., 1996, *The Art of Causal Conjecture*, MIT Press, Cambridge, MA.

[SHAF 93] Shafir E.B., Osherson D.N., Smith E.E., 1993, The advantage model: a comparative theory of evaluation and choice under risk, *Organisational Behavior and Human Decision Processes*, vol. 55, 325–378.

[SHE 94] Shenoy P., 1994, A comparison of graphical techniques for decision analysis, *European Journal of Operational Research*, vol. 78, 1–21.

[SIE 57] Siegel S., 1957, Level of aspiration and decision making, *Psychological Review*, vol. 64, 253–262.

[SIM 55] Simon H.A., 1955, A behavioral model of rational choice, *Quarterly Journal of Economics*, 69, 99–118.

[SIM 72] Simon H.A., 1972, Theories of bounded rationality, in *Decision and Organization*, C.B. McGuire and R. Radner (Eds.), North Holland, Amsterdam, 161–176.

[SIM 76] Simon H.A., 1976, From substantive to procedural rationality, in *Methods and Appraisal in Economics*, S.J. Latsis (Ed.), Cambridge University Press, NY, 129–148.

[SIM 77] Simon, H.A., 1977, *The New Science of Management Decision*, Prentice Hall, Englewood Cliffs, NJ.

[SIM 79] Simon H.A., 1979, *Models of Thought*, Yale University Press, New Haven.

[SIM 83] Simon, H.A., 1983, *Reason in Human Affairs*, Basil Blackwell, Oxford, UK.

[SIM 84] Simon, H.A., 1984, Commentaires dans le cadre du Colloque de la Grande Motte, in *Sciences de l'Intelligence, Sciences de l'Artificiel*, Demailly A. and Le Moigne J.L. (Eds), Presses Universitaires de Lyon, 1986, 577-619.

[SIM 91] Simon, H.A., 1991, *Models of my Life*, Basic Books, New York.

[SIM 95] Simon H.A., 1995, Explaining the Ineffable: AI on the Topics of Intuition, Insight and Inspiration, *Proceedings of IJCAI-95*, 939–948.

[SIM 97] Simon H.A., 1997, *Administrative Behavior*, 4th edition, The Free Press, NY.

[SLO 82] Slovic P., Fischhoff B., Lichtenstein S., 1982, Facts versus fears: understanding perceived risk, in *Judgment under Uncertainty: Heuristics and Biases*, Kahneman D., Slovic P. and Tversky A. (Eds.), Cambridge University Press, Cambridge, UK, 463–489.

[SLO 88] Slovic P., Fischhoff B., Lichtenstein S., 1988, Response mode, framing and information-processing effects in risk assessment, in *Decision Making*, Bell D.E., Raiffa H. and Tversky A. (Eds.), Cambridge University Press, Cambridge, MA, 152–166.

[SLO 02] Slovic P., Finucane M., Peters E., MacGregor D.G., 2002, The affect heuristic, in *Heuristics and Biases: The Psychology of Intuitive Judgment*, Gilovich T., Griffin D. and Kahneman D. (Eds.), Cambridge University Press, Cambridege, MA, 397–420.

[SME 90] Smets Ph., 1990, Constructing the pignistic probability function in a context of uncertainty, in *Uncertainty in Artificial Intelligence*, M. Heurion, D. Schachter, N. Kanal and J. Leurmer (Eds.), Vol 5, North Holland, 29–40.

[SPR 87] Sprague R.H., 1987, DSS in context, *Decision Support Systems*, vol. 3, 197–202.

[SPR 82] Sprague R.H., Carlsson E.D., 1982, *Building Effective Decision Support Systems*, Prentice Hall, NJ.

[STE 89] Sterman J.-D., 1989, Modelling managerial behavior: Misperceptions of feedback in a dynamics decision-making experiment, *Management Science*, vol. 35, 321–339.

[TUR 88] Turban E., 1988, *Decision Support and Expert Systems*, MacMillan, NY.

[TVE 67] Tversky A., 1967, Additivity, utility and subjective probability, *Journal of Mathematical psychology*, vol. 4, 175–202.

[TVE 69] Tversky A., 1969, Intransitivity of preferences, *Psychological Review*, vol. 76, 31–48.

[TVE 74] Tversky A., Kahneman D., 1974, Judgment under uncertainty: heuristics and biases, *Science*, vol. 185, 1124–1131.

[TVE 82a] Tversky A., Kahneman D., 1982a, Judgment under uncertainty: Heuristics and biases, in *Judgment under Uncertainty: Heuristics and Biases*, Kahneman D., Slovic P. and Tversky A. (Eds.), Cambridge University Press, Cambridge, UK, 3–20.

[TVE 82b] Tversky A., Kahneman D., 1982b, Subjective probability: A judgment of representativeness, in *Judgment under Uncertainty: Heuristics and Biases*, Kahneman D., Slovic P. and Tversky A. (Eds.), Cambridge University Press, Cambridge, UK, 32–47.

[TVE 82c] Tversky A., Kahneman D., 1982c, Availability: A heuristic for judging frequency and probability, in *Judgment under Uncertainty: Heuristics and Biases*, Kahneman D., Slovic P. and Tversky A. (Eds.), Cambridge University Press, Cambridge, UK, 163–178.

[TVE 83] Tversky A., Kahneman D., 1983, Extensional versus Intuitive Reasoning: the Conjunction Fallacy in Probability Judgment, *Psychological Review*, vol. 90, 293–315.

[TVE 88] Tversky A., Kahneman D., 1988, Rational Choice and the Framing of Decisions, in *Decision Making*, Bell D.E., Raiffa H. and Tversky A. (Eds.), Cambridge University Press, Cambridge, MA, 167–192.

[TVE 93] Tversky A. and Simonson I., 1993, Context-Dependent Preferences, *Management Science*, 39, 1179-1189.

[TVE 95] Tversky A., Wakker P., 1995, Risk attitudes and Decision Weights, *Econometrica*, vol. 63, 1255–1280.

[VIC 44] Vico G., 1744, *Principes d'une science nouvelle relative à la nature commune des nations* (traduction 1986), Nagel, Paris.

[VIN 99] Vincke Ph., 1999, Robust solutions and methods in decision aid, *Journal of Multicriteria Decision Analysis*, vol. 8, 181–187.

[VON 86] von Winterfeldt D., Edwards W., 1986, *Decision Analysis and Behavioral Research*, Cambridge University Press, Mass, 1986.

[WEI 01] Weinberger D., 2001, Garbage in, Great Staff Out, *Harvard Business Review*, vol. 79(8), 30–32.

[WAK 89] Wakker P.P., 1989, *Additive Representations of Preferences*, Kluwer, Dordrecht.

[WOL 91] Woolsey R. 1991, The fifth column: La Méthode de Charles Maurice de Talleyrand or Maximized acceptance with Optimized Agendas, *Interfaces*, vol. 21, 103–105.

[ZIC 98] Zickar M.J., Highhouse S., 1998, Looking closer on the effects of the framing on Risky Choice: An Item Response Theory Analysis, *Organizational Behavior and Human Decision Processes*, vol. 75, 75–91.

[ZIO 92] Zionts S., 1992, The State of multiple criteria decision making: past, present and future, in *Multiple Criteria Decision Making*, A. Goicoechea, L. Duckstein and S. Zionts (Eds.), Springer, Berlin, 33–43.

Chapter 5

Multiple Objective Linear Programming

5.1. Introduction

Decision problems are often modeled using constrained optimization models; for this reason, mathematical programming is a basic and unavoidable tool of Operations Research. Since the beginning in the 1940s with Dantzig's simplex algorithm for linear programming, many developments of mathematical programming have been proposed, either to extend the models (nonlinear or integer programming, combinatorial optimization, etc.) or to improve the efficiency of algorithms (gradient or penalty methods, Lagrangian relaxation, cutting methods, Branch and Bound, polyhedral theory, interior point methods, etc.).

The mainstream of research in this field concerns mainly exclusively single objective optimization models i.e. well-defined mathematical models governed by the classical paradigm of existence, characterization of optimal solutions and then convergent algorithms.

Even if these single-objective models are justified and really efficient in many situations, in many applications it appears that a single objective can in no way at all represent the reality of the application.

At the end of the 1970s, the necessity of a *multicriteria decision aid* therefore appeared. It was due to highly renowned scientists – Roy and Geoffrion for the so-called French and American schools, respectively – that the way to this field was opened, despite the scepticism of a large majority of operational researchers at that

---

Chapter written by Jacques TEGHEM.

time. An extraordinary lucidity was required to dare to turn off the beaten track. Now, multicriteria decision is a full part of operations research and decision theory.

Effectively, the consideration of the new *multicriteria paradigm*, i.e. accepting several conflicting criteria in a same model, gave rise to a collapse of all basic notions of single-objective algorithms:

– There are no more optimal solutions because there generally does not exist any feasible solution simultaneously optimizing all the criteria of the model: the improvement of one criterion is made to the detriment of another.

– Consequently, there are no more convergent methods which can only be a tool to first analyze and obtain knowledge of a problem, then to help the *decision maker* to find satisfying solutions which are good compromises between the conflicting criteria.

– Consequently, the methods do not appear as black boxes providing THE ideal (optimal) solution to the decision maker any longer. Multicriteria methods support the decision – proposed by the *analyst* – and interact with the decision maker. They are required to progressively express their preferences, based on their knowledge of the problem, to derive the proposed solutions.

Many multicriteria methods, in particular for multiple-objective programming, are *interactive methods*. They require the decision maker to generate a good compromise according to their preferences during the procedure. The final solution will therefore depend not only on the chosen method but also on the personality of the decision maker.

We can easily understand the reticence of many scientists at this time regarding such an innovation. Despite the development and increasing success of multicriteria methods, there is still a lack of understanding. Many reputable scientists are still opposed to any multicriteria approaches that they do not perceive to be appropriately rigourous.

It is true that, as for any new discipline, axiomatic progress of multicriteria methodology must still be carried out. Many researchers in this field are themselves convinced of this, and are working in this direction.

In any case, it is important to strongly underline that the multicriteria paradigm does not eliminate the single-criterion paradigm, which continues to be essential and allows the development of exceptionally powerful tools for optimization and decision. The paradigms must coexist; it is the details of the considered application which dictates the choice of paradigm.

In this chapter we will only consider multiple-objective programming: the set of all feasible solutions is defined *a priori* (the set is stable) in an implicit way by the satisfaction of the constraints (the set is implicitly defined) and each feasible solution is exclusive of any other (the set is globalized) [VIN 92]. The criteria are defined by objectives, i.e. by real functions of the variables (they are real criteria) [VIN 92]. Another class of problems – often called multicriteria analysis – is not considered in this chapter [ROY 85, ROY 93, VIN 92]. See Chapters 4 and 12 for details of multicriteria analysis.

The chapter is structured as follows. In section 5.2 we present basic concepts and principles of the main resolution approaches. Section 5.3 is devoted to the description of some typical methods of multiple-objective mathematical programming with continuous variables, essentially of linear programming. Multiple-objective linear programming with integer programming will be studied in section 5.4. The particular case of multiple-objective combinatorial optimization will be presented in section 5.5, in which we will emphasize the adaption of metaheuristics to multiple objective problems. Sections 5.6 and 5.7 will treat multiple-objective linear programming in a framework of uncertainty (the data are random) and in a framework of imprecision (the data are fuzzy), respectively.

5.2. Basic concepts and main resolution approaches

5.2.1. *The problem*

We consider a multiple-objective optimization problem (MOP):

$$\left. \begin{array}{l} \text{'min'} \ z_k(x) \quad k = 1, \ldots, K \\ x \in \mathcal{D} \end{array} \right\} \tag{5.1}$$

where $\mathcal{D} \subset \mathbb{R}^n$ is the set of feasible solutions and the kth objective function $z_k(x)$ represents the kth partial preference function of the decision maker. The notation '' implies that the problem is not well-defined mathematically, except in very particular cases which free the problem of its multiple-objective substance. A feasible solution minimizing the K objective functions i.e. the notion of optimal solution does not exist. The notation 'min' only means that the direction of preference for each objective is of a decreasing $z_k(x)$.

The resolution of such a problem consists of determining one of several good compromises i.e. solutions $x \in \mathcal{D}$ corresponding to the global preference of the decision maker. In addition to the decision space R^n, it is useful to also consider the objective space R^K which allows us to represent the evaluation of a solution x by a point $z(x) = (z_1(x), \ldots, z_K(x))$.

We will denote the set of points of R^K corresponding to the image of feasible solutions of $\mathcal{D}$ (Figure 5.1) by $Z_\mathcal{D}$:

$$Z_\mathcal{D} = \{z(x) \in R^K | x \in \mathcal{D}\}. \tag{5.2}$$

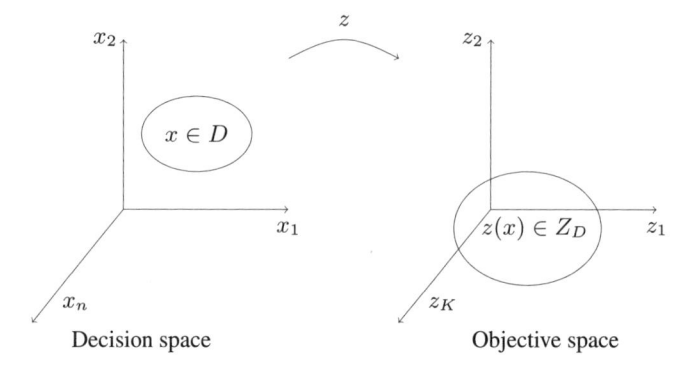

Figure 5.1. *Decision and objective spaces*

Equivalently, the problem of MOP can be written

$$\left. \begin{array}{ll} \text{`min'} z_k & k = 1, \ldots, K \\ z = (z_1, \ldots, z_K) \in Z_\mathcal{D} & \end{array} \right\} \quad (5.3)$$

The particular case of multiple-objective linear programming problem (MOLP) is written

$$\left. \begin{array}{ll} \text{`min'} z_k(x) = c_k \cdot x & k = 1, \ldots, K \\ x \in \mathcal{D} = \{x \in R^n \mid Tx \leq d, x \geq 0\} & \end{array} \right\} \quad (5.4)$$

where $c_k : (1 \times n) \;\forall\, k$, $T : (m \times n)$, $x : (n \times 1)$ and $d : (m \times 1)$.

The set $\mathcal{D}$ is then a convex polyhedron of R^n and the linear form of the objectives allows us to establish that $Z_\mathcal{D}$ is also a convex polyhedron of R^K, of which the vertices are the image of the vertices of $\mathcal{D}$ (Figure 5.2).

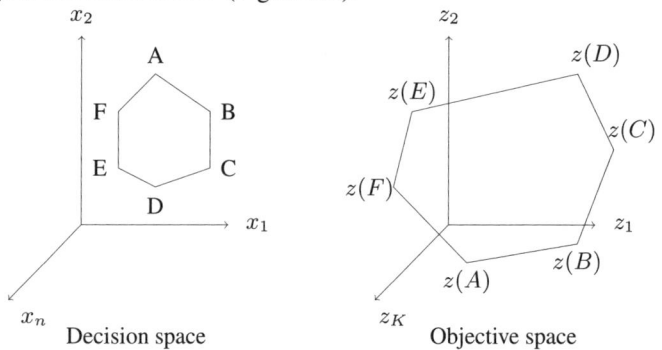

Figure 5.2. *The case of a linear problem*

5.2.2. *Dominance relation and efficient solutions*

In order for a solution $x \in \mathcal{D}$ to be a satisfying compromise, it appears logical to request that no other feasible solution $y \in \mathcal{D}$ gives values of each objective at least as good as those corresponding to x and even better for at least one objective. Such a minimal condition justifies the following definitions.

Definition 5.1. Dominance relation: a point $z \in Z_\mathcal{D}$ *dominates* a point $z' \in Z_\mathcal{D}$ if and only if (iff)

$$z_k \leq z'_k \qquad k = 1, \ldots, K \tag{5.5}$$

and at least one of these K inequalities is strict (i.e. $z \neq z'$). A point $z \in Z_\mathcal{D}$ is *not dominated* if there does not exist any point $z' \in Z_\mathcal{D}$ which dominates it.

Definition 5.2. Efficient solution: a solution $x \in \mathcal{D}$ is *efficient* – or Pareto optimal – if the point $z(x)$ is not dominated. A point $z \in Z_\mathcal{D}$ is *not dominated* in the objective space if the cone, having this point as vertex and formed by the axes z_k, does not contain any other point of $Z_\mathcal{D}$. In other words, if $C^\leq$ is the cone $\{z \in R^K | z \leq 0\}$, $\bar{z}$ is not dominated if

$$\{C^\leq + \bar{z}\} \cap Z_\mathcal{D} = \{\bar{z}\}. \tag{5.6}$$

The set of efficient solutions is the set of interesting solutions from the point of view of multiple objectives. Generally, this set has a large cardinality and even for a problem in continuous variables, a non-countable infinite cardinality. This definition is illustrated by Figures 5.3–5.5 for the three situations of a MOP, MOLP and multiple-objective integer linear programming (MOILP, i.e. a MOLP with integer variables) problem, respectively.

Remark 5.1. 1) The set of efficient solutions of a MOLP problem never contains any isolated point. In particular, two efficient vertices of $\mathcal{D}$ are always linked by a set of edges whose points are all efficient solutions. On the other hand, a facet of polyhedron $\mathcal{D}$ may contain an edge of efficient solutions without every point being efficient solutions (see [STE 86] for a detailed analysis of the structure of the set of efficient solutions).

2) The dominance relation can be defined differently by

$$z \in Z_\mathcal{D} \text{ dominates } z' \in Z_\mathcal{D} \text{ iff } z_k < z'_k \qquad \forall k. \tag{5.7}$$

A point is said to be *weakly non-dominated* if there does not exist any $z' \in Z_\mathcal{D}$ verifying $z'_k < z_k \; \forall k$.

A solution $x \in \mathcal{D}$ is said to be *weakly efficient* if the point $z(x)$ is weakly dominated. An efficient solution is always weakly efficient but the inverse is not true.

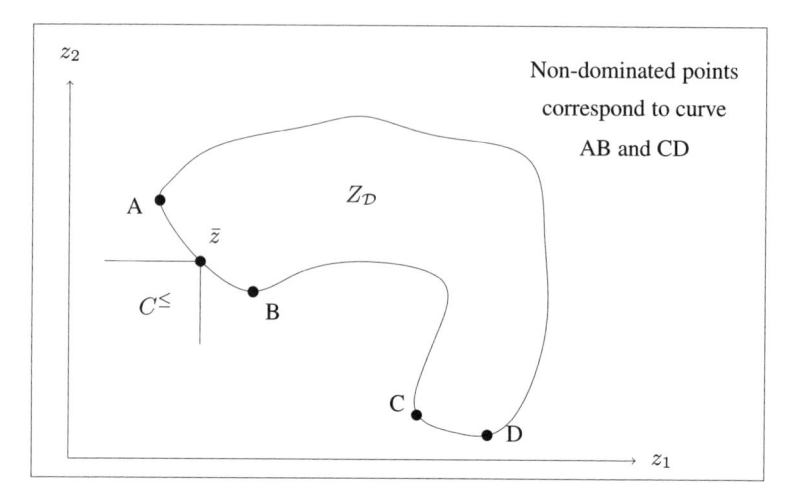

Figure 5.3. *Objective space of a MOP problem*

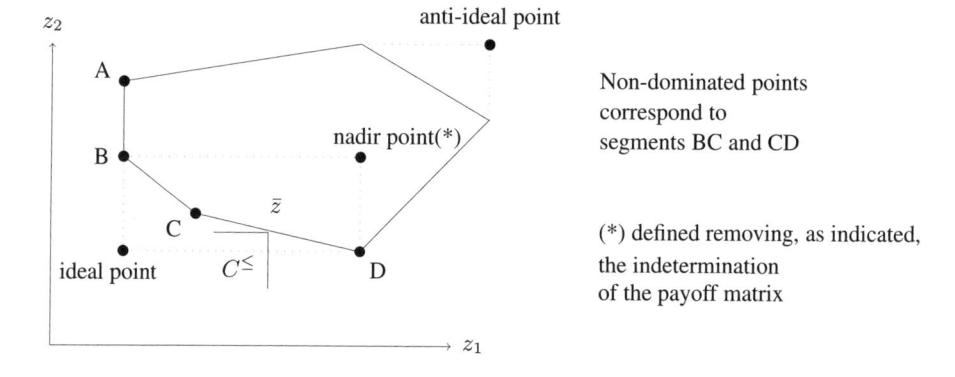

Figure 5.4. *Objective space of a MOLP problem*

In Figure 5.4, all the points of the edge (AB) give the optimal value of objective z_1 and are therefore weakly non-dominated. Nevertheless, among them, only the point B corresponds to an efficient solution. The notion of weakly efficient solution is not very useful from a practical point of view, but sometimes necessary from a technical point of view.

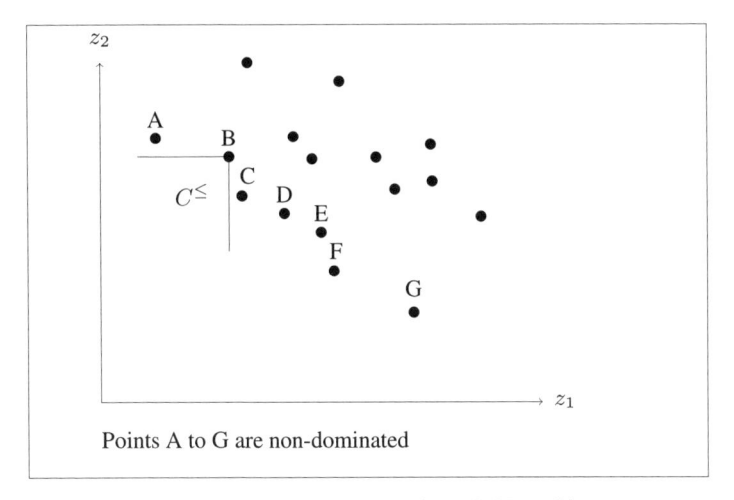

Figure 5.5. *Objective space of a MOILP problem*

5.2.3. *Ideal point, payoff matrix and nadir point*

The *ideal point* is the point of R^K with coordinates

$$M_k = \min_{x \in \mathcal{D}} z_k(x) \qquad k = 1, \ldots, K. \tag{5.8}$$

Let $\widetilde{x}^{(l)}$ be an optimal solution – not necessarily unique – of objective z_l. We note

$$z_{kl} = z_k(\widetilde{x}^{(l)}). \tag{5.9}$$

The matrix $(K \times K)$ defined by the elements z_{kl} is called the *payoff matrix*:

$$\begin{array}{c} \\ z_1 \\ \vdots \\ z_k \\ \vdots \\ z_K \end{array} \begin{pmatrix} \widetilde{x}^{(1)} & \ldots & \widetilde{x}^{(l)} & \ldots & \widetilde{x}^{(K)} \\ M_1 & \ldots & z_{1l} & \ldots & z_{1K} \\ \vdots & & \vdots & & \vdots \\ z_{k1} & \ldots & z_{kl} & \ldots & z_{kK} \\ \vdots & & \vdots & & \vdots \\ z_{K1} & \ldots & z_{Kl} & \ldots & M_K \end{pmatrix}.$$

The coordinates of the ideal point $M_k = z_{kk}$ appear on the diagonal of this matrix. The payoff matrix is unequivocally determined only if, for each objective l, the solution $\widetilde{x}^{(l)}$ is unique. On the other hand, if an objective l has several optimal solutions (and therefore, in case of equation (5.4) (MOLP), an infinity) the column

l of the payoff matrix will depend on the chosen solution $\widetilde{x}^{(l)}$. To remove this indetermination, we can define for example:

$$z_{kl} = \min z_k(x)$$

$$\begin{cases} x \in \mathcal{D} \\ z_l(x) = M_l \end{cases}$$

i.e. to evaluate each objective k on the solution $\widetilde{x}_l$ giving the best value. We note

$$m_k = \max_{l=1,\ldots,K} z_{kl} \quad k = 1,\ldots,K. \tag{5.10}$$

The point m with coordinates $(m_1, \ldots, m_k)$ is called the *nadir point* (if the payoff matrix is not univocally determined, it depends on the matrix chosen). It must not be confused with the *anti-ideal point*, defined by the coordinates $\max_{x \in \mathcal{D}} z_k(x)$. See Figure 5.4 for illustrations of ideal, nadir and anti-ideal points.

Remark 5.2. In multiple objective methods (section 5.3), the interval $[M_k, m_k]$ is often used to measure the variation of the values of objective z_k on the set of efficient solutions. Nevertheless, it is only an estimation of the interval of variation because it is possible that m_k is lower than or greater than the maximal value of z_k on the set of efficient solutions [STE 86].

5.2.4. *Scalarizing functions*

It appears logical to take only the efficient solutions into consideration as potential satisfying compromises. However, this does not resolve the decision problem which requires the selection of a unique 'good compromise'. For this selection, it is necessary to have additional information about the structure of the decision maker preferences. Such information is generally obtained through a dialogue with the decision maker and can be defined in terms of *preference parameters*. The most common are:

– *the weights* λ_k $(k = 1, \ldots, K)$ which measure the relative importance of each objective (they are often normalized: $\sum_{k=1}^{K} \lambda_k = 1$, $\lambda_k \geq 0$);

– *the substitution rates or tradeoffs* which reflect the idea of compensation between a loss on one objective and a gain on another;

– *the reference points* which represent points of R^K whose coordinates are desirable values (to try to reach) or non-desirable values (to try to move away) of the different objectives; and

– *the reservation levels* which correspond to the minimal requirement imposed for the values of certain objectives.

The multiple objective methods often use one of these preference parameters. Reservation levels allow us to limit an interesting area inside $Z_\mathcal{D}$. The weights, the substitution rates or the reference points are generally used to aggregate the different objectives into a single function. These aggregation functions are called *scalarizing functions*.

Very often, these functions have a technical role internal to the method; their optimization allows us to generate a feasible solution. They must not be confused with utility functions (see section 5.2.6.1.1).

Ideally, a scalarizing function must be defined so that:

– its optimization always gives rise to an efficient solution; and

– each efficient solution corresponds to its optimization for some value of the preference parameters.

From a practical point of view, its optimization must be relatively easy.

The three most common scalarizing functions, s_1, s_2 and s_3, are as follows. All three use weights λ_k as preference parameters and s_2, s_3 also use a reference point $\bar{z}$ defined by the coordinates $\bar{z}_k = M_k - \epsilon_k$, $k = 1, \ldots, K$ where ϵ_k is an arbitrary small positive value:

– The weighted sum:

$$s_1(z, \lambda) = \sum_{k=1}^{K} \lambda_k z_k. \tag{5.11}$$

– The weighted Tchebytchev distance:

$$s_2(z, \lambda, \bar{z}) = \max_{k=1,\ldots,K} (\lambda_k \mid z_k - \bar{z}_k \mid). \tag{5.12}$$

– The augmented weighted Tchebytchev distance:

$$s_3(z, \lambda, \bar{z}) = \max_{k=1,\ldots,K} (\lambda_k \mid z_k - \bar{z}_k \mid) + \rho(\sum_{k=1}^{K} \mid z_k - \bar{z}_k \mid) \qquad \rho > 0. \tag{5.13}$$

We note that the minimization of a Tchebytchev distance generates a 'min max' problem:

$$\min_{x \in \mathcal{D}} \max_{k=1,\ldots,K} \left(\lambda_k \mid z_k - \bar{z}_k \mid + \rho \left(\sum_{k=1}^{K} \mid z_k - \bar{z}_k \mid \right) \right). \tag{5.14}$$

Nevertheless, if an additional variable δ is introduced, such a problem is equivalent to

$$\min \delta - \rho \sum_{k=1}^{K} \mid z_k(x) - \bar{z}_k \mid \lambda_k(z_k(x) - \bar{z}_k) \leq \delta \qquad k = 1, \ldots, K \text{ and } x \in \mathcal{D} \tag{5.15}$$

i.e. linear programming if the multiple-objective problem is of this type.

5.2.5. *Theorems to characterize efficient solutions*

The above scalarizing functions allow us to characterize, completely or partially, the set of efficient solutions. The interest of these theorems is essentially theoretical because their implementation corresponds to the resolution of multiparametric problems. This is not easy to tackle if the number of parameters (equal to the number of objectives) is large.

We note

$$\Lambda = \{\lambda_k \mid \sum_{k=1}^{K} \lambda_k = 1 \text{ and } \lambda_k > 0, \quad k = 1, \ldots, K.\} \tag{5.16}$$

Theorem 5.1. *(Often called the Geoffrion Theorem.) Consider the parametric problem*

$$\min_{x \in \mathcal{D}} s_1(z(x), \lambda) \tag{5.17}$$

with $\lambda \in \Lambda$.

1) *If x is an optimal solution of problem (5.17), x is an efficient solution.*

2) *If x is an efficient solution and $Z_\mathcal{D}$ is a convex set, then there exists $\lambda \in \Lambda$ such that x is an optimal solution of problem (5.17).*

Remark 5.3. 1) If the weights λ_k are not all strictly positive, the condition (1) will only provide the weak efficiency of x in the case where x is not the unique optimal situation.

2) For equation (5.4), the set $Z_\mathcal{D}$ is convex. The resolution of the parametric problem (5.17) allows us to determine the set of all efficient solutions.

We note that $Z_\mathcal{D}$ is no longer convex if there are discrete variables in the problem. In such a case, the resolution of the parametric problem (5.17) only allows us to generate a subset of efficient solutions which are called supported efficient solutions (see section 5.4).

In Figure 5.5, the points A, C, F and G correspond to the supported efficient solutions and points B, D and E to *non-supported efficient solutions*.

Let $\bar{z}$ be a reference point verifying $\bar{z}_k \leq M_k \ \forall \ k$ and $\bar{z} \neq M$.

Theorem 5.2. *(Often called the Bowman Theorem.) Consider the parametric problem*

$$\min_{x \in \mathcal{D}} s_2(z(x), \lambda, \bar{z}) \tag{5.18}$$

A solution x is an efficient solution iff x is an unique optimal solution of problem (5.18).

If we consider the augmented weighted Tchebytchev distance, we can cancel the unicity character of the optimal solution.

Theorem 5.3.

$$\min_{x \in \mathcal{D}} s_3(z(x), \lambda, \overline{z}) \qquad (5.19)$$

1) If x is an optimal solution of problem (5.19), x is an efficient solution.

2) If x is an efficient solution, there exist $\lambda \in \Lambda$ and ρ, a small enough positive value, such that x is an optimal solution of problem (5.19).

Let us note that Theorems 5.2 and 5.3 are valid even if $\mathcal{D}$ is not a convex set.

Theorem 5.4. *(Often called the Soland theorem.) Consider the parametric problem*

$$\min z_l(x) \qquad z_k(x) \leq \alpha_k k \neq l x \in \mathcal{D} \qquad (5.20)$$

with $\alpha_k \in \mathbb{R}$. A solution x is efficient iff x is an optimal solution of problem (5.20).

5.2.6. *The main resolution approaches*

Faced with a multiple objective problem, the aim of the decision maker is to determine an efficient solution that they estimate to be satisfactory. We can distinguish three classes of approaches, depending on the moment at which the decision maker is involved in the process of selection of best compromise:

– If the decision maker's preferences are known (or built) previously to the model, we speak of an *a priori articulation* of preferences.

– On the other hand, if the decision maker expresses their preference after the determination of the set of efficient solutions by the model, we talk of an *a posteriori articulation* of preferences.

– For the case where the preferences are expressed progressively according to the progress of the method and the better knowledge of the interactions between the objectives, we use the term progressive *articulation of preferences*.

We briefly present these three approaches and the general principle of the different corresponding techniques.

5.2.6.1. *A priori preferences*

The main advantage of this approach is its computational simplicity because the initial knowledge of the preferences of the decision maker (however expressed) allows us to transform the multiple-objective problem into a single-objective optimization problem. An optimal solution of the latter will then be considered as a best compromise.

There exist many methods by which scalarizing functions are introduced, aggregating the different objectives into a single objective and then optimizing it. Obviously, this is a naive and indirected way of tackling a multiple-objective problem. The reader will find a description of these methods in different books, in particular those of [STE 86] for the MOLP problem and of [COL 02] for the general MOP.

We will only present here three often-used, different techniques related to this approach, corresponding to some theoretical or practical justification.

5.2.6.1.1. Multiattribute utility

This approach, often termed multiattribute utility approach (MAUT), was developed by US researchers. Researchers based in France have often been critical of its applicability [ROY 85, ROY 93, VIN 92]. The aim is to determine, to estimate or to build a *utility function*:

$$U(x) = U(z_1(x), \ldots, z_K(x)) \tag{5.21}$$

aggregating the objectives in an unique function which represents the mecanism of global preference of the decision maker. The assumption is made that they always react, consciously or not, by comparing various solutions according to the function $U(x)$ i.e.

$$xPx' \quad \text{if} \quad U(x) > U(x') \tag{5.22}$$

where P represents the global preference relation of the decision maker.

If such a function is available, the multiple objective problem

$$\text{'}\min_{x \in \mathcal{D}}\text{'} z_k(x) \quad k = 1, \ldots, K \tag{5.23}$$

is reduced to the single objective problem

$$\max_{x \in \mathcal{D}} U(x). \tag{5.24}$$

The most-used utility model is the *additive model* in which U is a separable function for the K objectives:

$$U(x) = \sum_{k=1}^{K} U_k(z_k(x)), \tag{5.25}$$

where the functions U_k are (strictly) decreasing and generally concave.

The main criticism of the utility theory is precisely that the assumption of the existence of such a function allowing us to compare, in the absolute two solutions, is not realistic in many (almost all) multiple-objective problems. Moreover, even with the assumption of the existence of such a utility function, there exist theoretical and practical difficulties concerning the MAUT approach. The criticisms of the French school are also related to the fact that these difficulties are often quite insurmountable. We will not present this important technique in this chapter; see Chapter 15.

5.2.6.1.2. *Hierarchical optimization*

It is assumed here that the decision maker gives the different objectives an order of importance. First of all, they want to optimize one of the objectives (e.g. z_1). Then, according to results, they would like to discriminate the optimal solutions of z_1, optimizing z_2 first (second objective in the order of importance), then z_3, etc.

This technique induces a sequence of single-objective optimization. First

$$\tilde{z}_1 = \min_{x \in \mathcal{D}} z_1(x), \tag{5.26}$$

then

$$\tilde{z}_2 = \min_{x \in \mathcal{D} \cap \{x | z_1(x) = \tilde{z}_1\}} z_2(x) \tag{5.27}$$

and, successively for $k = 3, \ldots, K$

$$\tilde{z}_k = \min_{x \in \mathcal{D} \cap \{x | z_l(x) = \tilde{z}_l,\ l=1,\ldots,k-1\}} z_k(x). \tag{5.28}$$

Clearly, such treatment of a multiple objective problem is only realistic in very particular situations and only makes sense if the set of optimal solutions is not quickly reduced to an unique solution.

5.2.6.1.3. *Goal programming*

We present here the technique of goal programming in its simplest form. The application of goal programming first requires from the decision maker the definition of the following:

– Reference levels α_k for each objective $k = 1, \ldots, K$. Depending the situation and the concerned objective, these goals α_k can be:

    1) an aspiration level α_k that the value of objective k is expected to satisfy;

    2) a level α_k that the value of objective k must be as close to as possible.

(For other situations related to levels α_k, see [STE 86, p. 282]). Let $K^{(i)}$ and $K^{(ii)}$, with $K^{(i)} \cup K^{(ii)} = \{1, \ldots, K\}$, be the sets of indexes of objectives for which the goals are respectively of type (1) and (2).

– Importance weights λ_k associated with objectives $k = 1, \ldots, K$.

Each objective is then formulated by a constraint defined with new variables representing the deviations in terms of the reference levels α_k:

– for type (1):

$$z_k(x) - y_k = \alpha_k, \ y_k \geq 0 \qquad k \in K^{(i)} \qquad (5.29)$$

– for type (2):

$$z_k(x) - y_k^+ + y_k^- = \alpha_k, \ y_k^+ \geq 0, \ y_k^- \geq 0 \qquad k \in K^{(ii)} \qquad (5.30)$$

(y_k^+ and y_k^- not simultaneously strictly positive).

These deviation variables are nothing else but slack variables, by excess or by default, relative to the levels α_k. A compromise is then determined by minimization of the weighted sum of these deviations:

$$\min \sum_{k \in K^{(1)}} \lambda_k y_k + \sum_{k \in K^{(2)}} \lambda_k (y_k^+ + y_k^-)$$

$$z_k(x) - y_k = \alpha_k \qquad k \in K^{(1)}$$
$$z_k(x) - y_k^+ + y_k^- = \alpha_k \qquad k \in K^{(2)}$$
$$x \in \mathcal{D}$$
$$y_k \geq 0, \ k \in K^{(1)}; \ y_k^+ \geq 0, \ y_k^- \geq 0; \ k \in K^{(2)}.$$

In such a manner, the obtained compromise will closely depend on the reference levels α_k and on the weights λ_k, defined *a priori*. It is therefore necessary to at least realize a sensibility analysis of the compromise regarding these parameters. It would be better, however, to allow the decision maker to modify and fit the values of the parameters α_k and/or λ_k in an interactive form (see section 5.2.6.3 below) of goal programming. A sequence of compromises is therefore determined that the decision maker may converge to a satisfying solution. The goal programming is often used in the form of a hierarchical optimization, by the definition of very different weights of values.

For instance, if

$$\lambda_1 \gg \lambda_2 \gg \cdots \gg \lambda_K,$$

the optimization consists of:

– first giving the *priority* to the only constraint related to objective z_1;

– deciding between obtained solutions taking into account the constraint related to objective z_2, and so on.

See the chapter devoted to the recent developments of goal programming by Jones and Tamiz in [EHR 02].

5.2.6.2. *A posteriori preferences*

This approach consists of determining the set E of efficient solutions of the problem described by equation (5.1), to furnish this set to the decision maker who will choose from its *best compromise*.

The major drawback of this approach is of course the difficulty of implementation because it requires the resolution of a multiparametric problem of type (5.17–5.19) or (5.20); this is generally a difficult task and costly in computational time. It is specially true when the variables are continuous and/or Z_D is not convex. However, in the case of problem (5.4), we can use the simplex algorithm to solve the parametric problem (5.17) [STE 86].

Nevertheless, the interest of this approach is not only theoretical. We will see in sections 5.4 and 5.5, devoted to discrete variables, that this approach can be useful if the set E does not have too large a cardinality. On the other hand, with the use of metaheuristics, it is possible to determine an approximation $\widehat{E}$ of E formed by a sample of representative (potential) efficient solutions.

The *a posteriori* approach can also be adapted in an interactive version (see section 5.2.6.3 below). At iteration k, a sample $\widehat{E}_k$ is provided to the decision maker. On base of their preferences, a new sample $\widehat{E}_{k+1}$ more in accordance to these preferences is then determined.

5.2.6.3. *Progressive preferences or interactive approach*

The idea on which the interactive approach is based is that the structure of global preference of the decision maker is not established *a priori*, or even that such a structure exists permanently in a constant manner. The global preference can move as the information is obtained about the interactions between the objectives for the different possible solutions.

It can only be generated progressively during *a learning process*. Through the analysis of the problem and the information obtained by the decision maker regarding the proposed solutions, it will allow little by little the interactions between the objectives to be discovered and simultaneously the global preference of the decision maker to be determined. Clearly, such an approach is quite different from the *a priori* approach. The aim of an interactive approach is therefore to give the decision maker a tool to help them progressively delimit a *best compromise*.

The use of this tool requires the participation of the decision maker: the link between them and the analyst (or the model) will take place inside a *dialog* formed of a sequence of interactions, each one containing a *computational phase* (managed by the analyst) and an *information phase* (managed by the decision maker) (Figure 5.6).

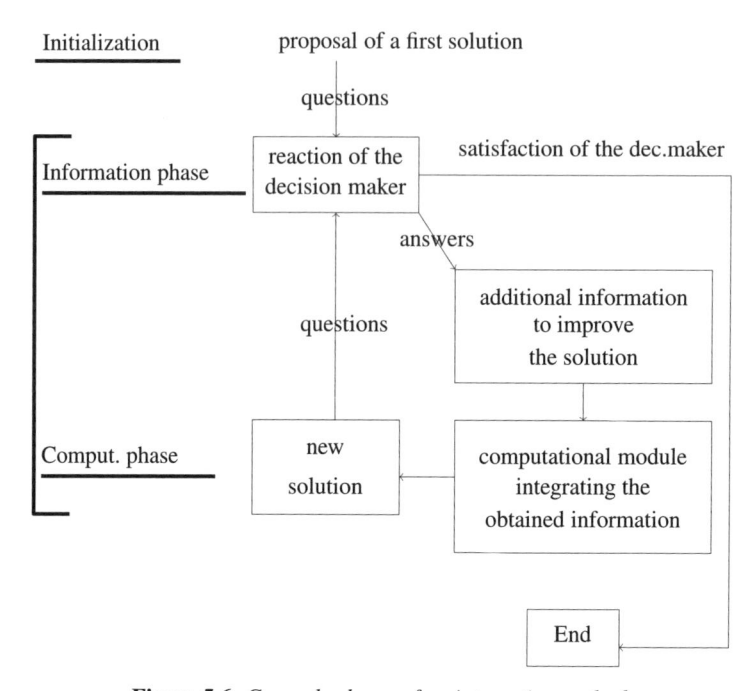

Figure 5.6. *General scheme of an interactive method*

5.2.6.3.1. Computational phase

The computational phase integrates all the information given by the decision maker to provide them with a new (or several) solution(s). The computational module must be such that:

– the proposed solution(s) is (are) always efficient; and
– any efficient solution can be proposed during the process.

5.2.6.3.2. Information phase

The information phase allows, through an exchange of questions and answers about the proposed solution, its qualities and its drawbacks regarding the preceding proposed solutions, the generation of useful information to help determine a more satisfying solution for the decision maker. The quality of an interactive method essentially depends on the simplicity and the flexibility of this information phase as follows:

– It is important to have few and identical questions at each phase which are easy to understand. These questions must not require any technical knowledge of the computational module. The decision maker must accept the notion of what an efficient solution is, such that the decision maker understands that it is impossible to simultaneously improve all the objectives. The answers must be easy to formulate and quick to obtain. For this reason, it is preferable to collect qualitative instead of quantitative information because the latter are always more difficult to collect and also often needlessly precise.

– It is important to allow the decision maker, as they work through the problem, to return to previous judgements they have made during some preceding phases. Effectively, their preferences may have been modified, taking into account the additional information obtained. There is therefore a process of trial and error.

Ideally, we must not speak of convergence (in the mathematical sense) of an interactive method. The only possible convergence which will stop the method is of a 'psychological' nature, which will see the decision maker satisfied by the final compromise because they are positive there does not exist a way of obtaining a more satisfying one. Due to the importance of this interactive approach, we will devote the next section (section 5.3) to it, describing some typical methods in detail.

5.3. Interactive methods

There are many interactive methods, sometimes only differing by a small amount. We will only present four here (the most typical) and we refer the reader interested in a more exhaustive presentation to specialized publications such as [ROY 93, VIN 92].

We present these methods only in the framework of a multiple objective linear programming problem of type (5.4), even if some of them are able to be applied either to nonlinear problems or even to some multicriteria analysis problems.

For some interactive methods designed for nonlinear problems, see [COL 02] and the chapter written by Miettinen in [EHR 02].

5.3.1. *The step method [BENA 71]*

The step method (STEM) was one of the first multiple objective mathematical programming methods proposed in 1971 for equation (5.4). We present it not in its initial version [BENA 71], but with some improvements which were proposed afterwards.

5.3.1.1. *Initialization* $(m = 0)$

The objectives are optimized individually to obtain (section 5.2.3):
– the ideal point $(M_1, \ldots, M_K)$;
– the payoff table z_{kl} $\quad k, l = 1, \ldots, K$;

- the nadir point $(m_1, \ldots, m_k)$; and
- the estimation of the variation interval of z_k on the set of efficient solutions $[M_k, m_k]$.

Normalized variation coefficients (or technical weights) are calculated as

$$\pi_k = \frac{\alpha_k}{\sum\limits_{k=1}^{K} \alpha_k} \tag{5.31}$$

with

$$\alpha_k = \frac{m_k - M_k}{|m_k|} \frac{1}{\|c_k\|} \tag{5.32}$$

where $\|c_k\|$ is the Euclidean norm of vector c_k.

Remark 5.4. It is important not to mistake coefficients π_k for the weights λ_k which express (e.g. in an utility function) the importance given to the objective z_k by the decision maker. The coefficients π_k have only a secondary technical role in the scalarizing function which takes place temporarily at each iteration in the computational module. In this function, these coefficients are used to attract more attention to an objective with a larger relative variation interval.

There exists a great amount of literature on these technical weights and many authors proposed simply defining

$$\alpha_k = \frac{m_k - M_k}{|m_k|}$$

and not taking into account the norm of the coefficients c_k which depend on the unit scale used to define it. Sometimes neglecting such weights is suggested.

The *first compromise* $\widehat{x}^{(1)}$ is obtained by minimization of the augmented weighted Tchebytchev norm to the ideal point, so that the efficient character of $\widehat{x}^{(1)}$ is assured (see Theorem 5.3):

$$\min_{x \in \mathcal{D}} (\max_{k=1,\ldots,K} (\pi_k(c_k x - \bar{z}_k)) + \rho \sum_{k=1}^{K} \pi_k(c_k x - \bar{z}_k)))$$

where $\bar{z}_k = M_k - \epsilon_k$, ϵ_k an arbitrary small positive value.

The augmented character of the weighted Tchebytchev distance is only required in the case of non-unicity of the optimal solution minimizing this distance (Theorem 5.2).

The technique of M is therefore useful to transform the problem into the following equivalent linear problem

$$(P_0) \begin{cases} \min & M\delta - \sum_{k=1}^{K} \xi_k \\ & \pi_k(c_k x - \bar{z}_k) \leq \delta - \xi_k, \quad k \in K^{(0)} = \{1, \ldots, K\} \\ & x \in \mathcal{D}^{(0)} \equiv \mathcal{D} \\ & \delta \geq 0, \xi_k \geq 0 \quad k = 1, \ldots, K \end{cases}$$

The optimal solution of this problem is the first compromise $\widehat{x}^{(1)}$ provided to the decision maker, who does not bring in this initial phase.

Remark 5.5. In practice $\bar{z}_k = M_k$. In problem (5.17), the (classic) notation ($M_k, k = 1, \ldots, K$) represents a number arbitrarily large; this has nothing to do with the other (classic) notation M representing the ideal point.

5.3.1.2. *General iteration* $(m \geq 1)$

Let $\widehat{x}^{(m)}$ be the compromise obtained at the end of iteration $m - 1$.

5.3.1.2.1. Information phase

This compromise is provided to the decision maker through:

$$z_k^{(m)} = z_k(\widehat{x}^{(m)}); \quad [M_k, m_k] \quad k = 1, \ldots, K$$

i.e. the values taken by the objectives regarding the variation intervals given by the payoff table:

– If the decision maker is satisfied with these values, taking into account the preceding iterations, the procedure stops and $\widehat{x}^{(m)}$ is the accepted compromise.

– On the other hand, two questions are asked of the decision maker.

1) Knowing that to determine another compromise, at least one objective must be deteriorated, which objective do you accept to relax (to deteriorate)?

2) For this objective, what is the maximal level of deterioration you can accept?

Let us say that the first question is elementary, of qualitative nature and that it is easy to answer. It is more delicate to answer the second question, due to its quantitative nature and the difficulty of fixing this acceptable loss without knowledge of the corresponding gain (or variation) of the other objectives in compensation.

Remark 5.6. If the decision maker hesitates to fix this deterioration level, it is still possible to examine several increasing values of this loss and after the resolution of the corresponding problems P_m (see below), by selecting $\widehat{x}^{(m+1)}$ among the proposed solutions. Another way is analyze parametrically the deteriorated value of the indicated objective; this is done using the STRANGE (STRAtegy for Nuclear Generation of Electricity) method (see section 5.6).

Let k_m be the objective indicated by the decision maker to be relaxed (see below $k_m \in K^{(m-1)}$) in the answer to question (1) and let Δ_{k_m} be the maximal level of relaxation of objective z_{k_m}, obtained in the answer to question (2).

5.3.1.2.2. Computational phase

We present two options for this computational phase. The first is that presented in the initial version of the method. It was the subject of criticism given the fact that the decision maker has no flexibility to modify any advice given previously and which therefore always has an irrevocable character. The second is an adaptation we have proposed in the framework of the STRANGE method (see section 5.6) to overcome this drawback.

Answer to question (1) with restrictive constraints. The next compromise $\widehat{x}^{(m+1)}$ is determined by the optimal solution of problem

$$(P_m) \begin{cases} \min & M\delta - \sum_{k=1}^{K} \xi_k \\ \pi_k(c_k x - \overline{z}_k) & \leq \delta - \xi_k & k \in K^{(m)} \\ c_{k_m} x & \leq z_{k_m}^{(m)} + \Delta_{k_m} \\ x & \in \mathcal{D}^{(m)} \\ \delta & \geq 0 \\ \xi_k & \geq 0 & k \in K^{(m)} \end{cases}$$

where $K^{(m)}$ and $\mathcal{D}^{(m)}$ are defined

$$K^{(m)} = K^{(m-1)} \setminus \{k_m\}$$

and

$$\mathcal{D}^{(m)} = \mathcal{D}^{(m-1)} \cap \{x \mid c_{k_{m-1}} x \leq z_{k_{m-1}}^{(m)}\}.$$

The meaning of this modelization is therefore that each objective can be relaxed only once. When it is chosen, it no longer takes place in the following iterations. It is not taken into account in the calculation of the Tchebytchev distance (or equivalently, its coefficient π_k is set to zero). In addition, when an objective is relaxed, its value will no longer be deteriorated in the next iterations. The value corresponding to the accepted compromise

$$z_{k_{m-1}}^{(m)} = z_{k_{m-1}}(\widehat{x}^{(m)})$$

is considered by the decision maker as the worst acceptable value, whatever the variations of the other objectives.

The consequences of such a procedure are that a convergence of the method is imposed (artificially) with at most K iterations and that the decision maker is prevented from changing their advice. This is all the more embarrassing as the compromise $\widehat{x}^{(m+1)}$ is strongly related to the deterioration level Δ_{k_m} provided by the decision maker, which is really difficult to fix.

Answer to question (2) without restrictive constraints. The next compromise $\widehat{x}^{(m+1)}$ is determined by the optimal solution of problem P_m in which the sets $K^{(m)}$ and $\mathcal{D}^{(m)}$ are defined

$$K^{(m)} = K \backslash \{k_m\}$$

and

$$\mathcal{D}^{(m)} = \mathcal{D}.$$

With this version of the computational phase, an objective is withdrawn from the computation of the distance to the ideal point during the iteration of its relaxation. It is then considered again during the next iterations. The number of iterations is therefore no longer bounded and the convergence can then be fixed only by the decision maker. At no iterations, the set of feasible (and therefore efficient) solutions is limited. An accepted value for the relaxed objective can possibly still be deteriorated at a next iteration. This allows a large flexibility of assessment for the decision maker.

Remark 5.7.   1) We present and comment on this method with more details that the others described in this section because it is the one for which we find the principle more satisfying, and has been adapted in the method STRANGE (section 5.6). Its main drawback is to propose at each iteration to the decision maker only one new compromise. Moreover, this compromise is strongly related to the maximal level of relaxation Δ_{k_m} which is often reached:

$$z_{k_m}^{(m+1)} = z_{k_m}^{(m)} + \Delta_{k_m}.$$

A way to remedy this is to take into account the suggestions made in Remark 5.6 above.

2) Many variants of the STEM method have been proposed, each introducing one or another improvement. Among the more important are the methods of Roy [ROY 76] (referred to as the 'target point' method) and of Vincke and Vanderpooten [VAN 89]. There are also the methods of reference point of Wierzbicki [WIE 82] and that of Korhonen and Laakso [KOR 86] (a little different from the STEM method but nevertheless in the same spirit). The latter has the advantage of proposing, at each iteration, a large number of possible compromises in a direction proposed by the decision maker. For more details on these methods, see [ROY 93, STE 86, VIN 92].

5.3.2. *The Steuer and Choo method [STE 86]*

This method has the great advantage of being very general (its principle can be applied to nonlinear problems). In addition, it proposes to the decision maker (at each iteration) choosing the new compromise from a set of efficient solutions obtained in the direction they proposed.

5.3.2.1. *Initialization* ($m = 0$)

We consider equation (5.4) as described before. The objectives are optimized individually to obtain the ideal point $(M_1, \ldots, M_K)$. As before, we note

$$\bar{z}_k = M_k - \epsilon_k \qquad k = 1, \ldots, K$$

where ϵ_k is an arbitrary small positive value.

Let

$$\Pi = \{\pi_k \ (k = 1, \ldots, K) \mid \pi_k \geq 0, \sum_{k=1}^{K} \pi_k = 1\}$$

be the initial set of possible weight vectors. Two parameters must be initially fixed with the agreement of the decision maker (and in function of their available time):

– p the number of compromises calculated at each iteration; and

– r ($0 < r < 1$) a reduction factor which will speed up the convergence process (accordingly it will be small).

5.3.2.2. *General iteration* ($m \geq 1$)

5.3.2.2.1. Computational phase

Let $\Pi^{(m)}$ be the set of weight vectors at iteration m.

If $m = 1$, $\Pi^{(m)} = \Pi$. If $m > 1$, let $(\bar{\pi}_k^{(m-1)}, k = 1, \ldots, K)$ be the weight vector which has allowed us to determine the compromise $\hat{x}^{(m-1)}$ chosen by the decision maker at the preceding iteration. The set $\Pi^{(m)}$ is then reduced regarding $\Pi^{(m-1)}$ and defined by

$$\Pi^{(m)} = \{\pi_k, \ k = 1, \ldots, K \mid l_k^{(m)} \leq \pi_k \leq u_k^{(m)}, \sum_{k=1}^{K} \pi_k = 1\}.$$

The interval $[l_k^{(m)}, u_k^{(m)}]$ is defined by

$$\begin{aligned}[l_k^{(m)}, u_k^{(m)}] &= [0, r^{m-1}] && \text{if } \bar{\pi}_k^{(m-1)} \leq \frac{r^{m-1}}{2} \\ &= [1 - r^{m-1}, 1] && \text{if } \bar{\pi}_k^{(m-1)} \geq 1 - r^{m-1}{2} \\ &= [\bar{\pi}_k^{(m-1)} - \tfrac{r^{m-1}}{2}, \bar{\pi}_k^{(m-1)} + \tfrac{r^{m-1}}{2}] && \text{else.} \end{aligned}$$

The range of the interval of possible values for π_k at this mth iteration is therefore equal to r^{m-1}; it converges to zero as one progresses through the method.

The aim is to choose p weight vectors $\{\pi_k,\ k = 1,\ldots,K\} \in \Pi^{(m)}$ as representative as possible (see remark below). For each of them, solve the linear problem

$$
\begin{aligned}
\min \quad & M\delta - \sum_{k=1}^{K} \xi_k \\
& \pi_k(c_k x - \overline{z}_k) \leq \delta - \xi_k \quad k = 1,\ldots,K \\
& x \in \mathcal{D} \\
& \delta \geq 0 \\
& \xi_k \geq 0 \quad k = 1,\ldots,K.
\end{aligned}
$$

There are therefore p resolutions. At each one, the problem differs only by the coefficients π_k. We obtain p efficient solutions.

5.3.2.2.2. Information phase

The values of the K objectives corresponding to these p solutions are presented to the decision maker so that they can compare them. The decision maker is asked to select from these p solutions the one they prefer; this corresponds to compromise $\widehat{x}^{(m)}$. The corresponding weight vector is noted $\overline{\pi}_k^{(m)}$ (see section 5.3.2.2.1).

If the decision maker is satisfied by the compromise, the procedure stops; otherwise a new iteration begins. This method has the advantage of submitting to the decision maker at each iteration a representative sample of possible compromises. At the beginning, the sample covers the set of efficient solutions. Then, as long as the decision maker specifies their preferences, the search for best compromise focuses progressively on the more interesting region, building a finer sample of possible compromises there. Despite a mathematical convergence of the method (induced by the factor r^m converging to zero) the decision maker can however modify their advice to orientate the search to a different region of the efficient frontier, according to the learning accumulated during the preceding iterations.

The main drawbacks include

– the *a priori* definition of the parameter r; nevertheless we can reduce the intervals $[l_k^{(m)}, u_k^{(m)}]$ in a more systematic manner (but no as fine) without the definition of this parameter;

– the large number p of solutions required to provide a representative sample in case of large-scale problems, which increases the computational time.

Remark 5.8. The representative character of the p weight vectors inside $\Pi^{(m)}$ does not necessarily induce the representative character of the p corresponding solutions among the set of efficient solutions. For this reason, Steuer and Choo propose to compute (in a particular manner) $2p$ weight vectors and after to 'filter' the $2p$ obtained solutions with the aim of extracting the p most representative ones.

Steuer also suggests specific formulae to fix the parameters p and r. (See [STE 86] for more details).

5.3.3. *Interactive methods based on a utility function*

The American school proposed various interactive methods which assume the existence of an utility function not known explicitly. The aim of the interactions with the decision maker consist of progressively estimating this utility function. In particular, we can quote two of the more well-known methods of this type:

– Zionts and Wallenius [ZIO 83] use an utility function (very restrictive) of type $s_1(z, \lambda)$ and the iterations lead to the determination of the weights λ.

– Geoffrion et al. [GEO 72] consider a general utility function; the interactive aspect essentially concerns the substitution rates.

We will only examine the principle of these two exemplary methods here; we refer the interested reader to [ROY 93, STE 86, VIN 92] for more details and applications of those principles.

5.3.3.1. *Principle of the Zionts and Wallenius method [ZIO 83]*

At each iteration m, an efficient vertex $\widehat{x}^{(m)}$ of the polyhedron $\mathcal{D}$ is determined by optimization of the function $s_1(z, \lambda^{(m)})$, where $\lambda^{(m)}$ is chosen in a set

$$\Lambda^m \subset \Lambda^1 = \{\lambda_k > 0, \sum_{k=1}^{K} \lambda_k = 1\}.$$

Each of the non-basic variables $j \in J$ is examined to test if their introduction in the basis will produce an efficient vertex. Those for which this is the case are called efficient non-basic variables; let $J_e \subset J$ be the set of these variables.

The analysis of the simplex tableau corresponding to $\widehat{x}^{(m)}$ indicates that increasing one unit of x_j, $j \in J_e$ produces a variation $a_{0j}^{(k)}$ of the objective z_k, where $-a_{0j}^{(k)}$ is the coefficient of x_j in the expression of z_k. Let us note that the information produced by these marginal costs is only local.

The decision maker is asked if such a variation $\{a_{0j}^{(k)}, k = 1, \ldots, K\}$ is acceptable. If the answer is positive, it means that the weights λ_k must satisfy the relation:

$$\sum_{k=1}^{K} \lambda_k(z_k(\widehat{x}^{(m)}) - a_{0j}^{(k)}) < \sum_{k=1}^{K} \lambda_k z_k(\widehat{x}^{(m)})$$

i.e.

$$\sum_{k=1}^{K} \lambda_k a_{0j}^{(k)} > 0.$$

In case of a negative answer, the weights λ_k must satisfy the relation:

$$\sum_{k=1}^{K} \lambda_k a_{0j}^{(k)} < 0.$$

These relations are then imposed to reduce the set Λ^m to Λ^{m+1} in accordance with the answer with the decision maker for each $j \in J_e$. A new weight vector $\lambda^{(m+1)}$ is chosen in Λ^{m+1} to build the vertex $\widehat{x}^{(m+1)}$.

The main drawbacks of this method are:

– only (efficient) vertices are generated;

– the decision maker is asked many questions which are difficult to answer due to the local character of the given information (even if the decision maker has the opportunity not to answer the question corresponding to some variables x_j, $j \in J_e$).

5.3.3.2. *Principle of the Geoffrion et al. method [GEO 72]*

At each iteration m, the method questions the decision maker on the marginal substitution rates of the objective z_k regarding a reference objective (let z_1) for the compromise $\widehat{x}^{(m)}$; we obtain

$$\Delta z_{k1}(\widehat{x}^{(m)}).$$

The jth coordinate of the gradient of the utility function $U(\cdot)$

$$\frac{\partial U(\cdot)}{\partial x_j}(\widehat{x}^{(m)}) = \sum_{k=1}^{K} \frac{\partial U(\cdot)}{\partial z_k}(\widehat{x}^{(m)}) \cdot \frac{\partial z_k}{\partial x_j}(\widehat{x}^{(m)})$$

is equal to (within a multiplicative coefficient $\frac{\partial U(\cdot)}{\partial z_1}(\widehat{x}^{(m)})$)

$$\sum_{k=1}^{K} \Delta z_{k1}(\widehat{x}^{(m)}) c_{kj}.$$

The direction search $d^{(m)}$ of a new compromise is chosen as the best direction, i.e. optimizing a linear combination of the coordinates of the gradient vector of $U(\cdot)$. If $y^{(m)}$ is the optimal solution of the problem

$$\min_{y \in D} \sum_{k=1}^{K} \Delta z_{k1}(\widehat{x}^{(m)}) \sum_{j=1}^{n} c_{kj} y_j,$$

this direction corresponds to the vector $d^{(m)} = y^{(m)} - \widehat{x}^{(m)}$.

Several solutions are then proposed to the decision maker in this direction

$$x^{(m+1;t)} = \widehat{x}^{(m)} + \alpha_t \cdot d^{(m)} \qquad t = 1, \ldots, T$$

for different values of the step α_t. The decision maker chooses the new compromise $\widehat{x}^{(m+1)}$ as the preferred solution $x^{(m+1;t)}$.

The principle of this method is very general and can be applied to nonlinear programming. It can appear seductive if we accept:

– that the decision maker always reacts in accordance with the same utility function from a theoretical point of view; and

– that the decision maker can answer the required questions to determine the marginal substitution rates.

5.4. The multiple objective integer programming

Due to the importance of integer variables in the modelization of many real applications, some works have been naturally devoted to multiple objective integer linear programming (MOILP), i.e.

$$\begin{aligned}
\text{`min'} z_k &= c_k x \qquad k = 1, \ldots, K \\
x &\in \mathcal{D} = \{X \in \mathbb{Z}^n | TX \leq d,\ X \geq 0\}
\end{aligned} \qquad (5.33)$$

In the particular case of binary variables, i.e. when $\mathbb{Z}^n$ is replaced by $\{0,1\}^n$, we will speak of multiple objective binary linear programming (MOBLP).

Nevertheless, the introduction of discrete variables into the multiple objective paradigm generates particular difficulties, essentially due to the non-convexity of the set $\mathcal{D}$ of feasible solutions.

On the one hand, the simple combination of an ILP method with a MOLP method does not generally give efficient algorithms to generate the set $E(P)$ of efficient solutions. It is therefore necessary to build specific methods to tackle MOILP problems. On the other hand, as noted previously, the optimization of a weighted sum of the objectives

$$\min_{x \in \mathcal{D}} \sum_{k=1}^{K} \lambda_k c_k x,$$

in addition to the technical difficulty in solving this parametric problem, generates only a subset of efficient solutions referred to as *supported*; we denote this subset $SE(P)$.

As an illustration, we consider the elementary problem (see Figure 5.7):

$$\begin{aligned}\text{'max'} \quad z_1 &= x_1 \\ z_2 &= x_2\end{aligned}$$

$$3x_1 + 4x_2 \leq 12$$

$$x_1,\ x_2 \in \mathbb{Z}^+.$$

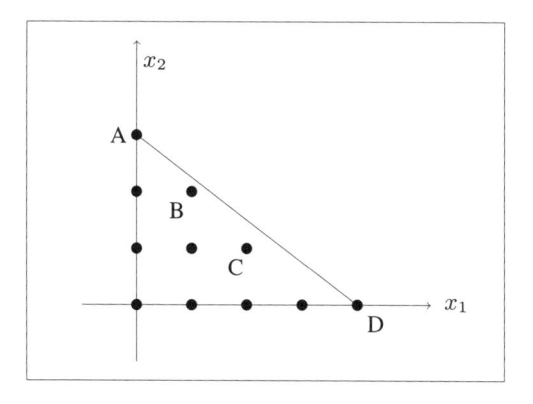

Figure 5.7. *Illustration: $SE(P)$ and $NSE(P)$*

The only optimal solutions generated by the optimization of the function

$$\lambda x_1 + (1-\lambda)x_2 \qquad \lambda \in [0,1]$$

are the solutions

$A(0,3)$ for $\lambda \in [0, \frac{3}{7}]$ and
$D(4,0)$ for $\lambda \in [\frac{3}{7}, 1]$

which are the two supported efficient solutions.

Nevertheless, the solutions $B(1,2)$ and $C(2,1)$ are also efficient, but not supported. We will refer to $NSE(P) = E(P) \setminus SE(P)$ as the set of non-supported efficient solutions. A difficulty of another nature is the cardinality of the discrete set $E(P)$ which can be, in some cases, very large.

In this section, we will analyze a selection of exemplary methods for a problem MOILP (or MOBLP) [CLI 97, TEG 86a, TEG 86b]. We distinguish methods generating $E(P)$ (section 5.4.1) from those interactive methods (section 5.4.2). In section 5.5, we will consider the methods devoted to multiple objective combinatorial optimization (MOCO) problems i.e. problems of type MOBLP but with a particular structure.

5.4.1. *Methods of generating* $E(P)$

5.4.1.1. *The Klein and Hannan method [KLE 82]*

At each iteration, the method solves a single objective ILP problem, becoming more and more constrained.

An objective is arbitrarily chosen (e.g. $z_1(x)$) and the problem

$$\min_{x \in \mathcal{D}} z_1(x) \tag{5.34}$$

is solved at the initial step. $\widehat{E(P)}$ is initialized with the optimal solution if it is unique or with the only non-dominated optimal solutions otherwise.

At the step m, let $\{x^r : r = 1, \ldots, R\}$ be the efficient solutions generated at the preceding iterations. The problem

$$\left[\begin{array}{l} \min z_1 x \\ x \in \mathcal{D} \\ \bigcap_{r=1}^{R}\left(\bigcup_{k=2}^{K} z_k(x) \leq z_k(x^r) - \epsilon^k\right) \quad \text{with} \quad \epsilon^k \geq 1 \end{array}\right. \tag{5.35}$$

is then solved. The constraints require that the feasible solutions of problem (5.35) improve at least one objective $k \neq 1$ for the efficient solutions x^r.

The optimal solution of problem (5.35) is added to $\widehat{E(P)}$ if it is unique or to the non-dominated optimal solutions otherwise. The procedure stops when the problem (5.35) is impossible to solve. If $\varepsilon_k = 1 \ \forall \ k$ at each iteration, then the final set $\widehat{E(P)}$ is $E(P)$ (supposing the data c_k are integers). On the other hand, $\widehat{E(P)}$ is a representative sample of $E(P)$. Obviously, problem (5.35) can be difficult to solve.

5.4.1.2. *The Sylva and Crema method [SYL 04]*

The implementation of the previous method was improved recently [SYL 04]. In the problems described by equations (5.34) and (5.35), the objective $z_1(x)$ is replaced by the objective $\sum_{k=1}^{K} \lambda_k z_k(x)$ where λ is an arbitrary vector (e.g. $\lambda_k = \frac{1}{k}, \ \forall \ k$) with the aim that any optimal solution will be efficient. Morover, in the case $\varepsilon_k > 1$, the sample $\widehat{E(P)}$ is not built from an extreme solution of $E(P)$.

However, problem (5.35) is expressed by adding the additional constraints

$$c_k x \leq (c_k x^r - \varepsilon_k) y_k^r + M_k (1 - y_k^r) \quad k = 1, \ldots, K; \ r = 1, \ldots, R$$
$$\sum_{k=1}^{K} y_k^r \geq 1 \quad r = 1, \ldots, R$$
$$y_k^r \in \{0, 1\} \quad k = 1, \ldots, K; \ r = 1, \ldots, R$$

to $\mathcal{D}$, where M_k is an upper bound of the optimal value of objective z_k.

5.4.1.3. *The Kiziltan and Yucaoglu method [KIZ 83]*

This method is a direct adaptation of the multiple objective framework of the well-known Balas algorithm for a problem with binary variables; it therefore solves an MOBLP problem. The algorithm examines the nodes of a tree to determine if an efficient solution can be found by moving down in the tree. The procedure stops when all the nodes are fathomed.

The rules of the method are to never treat a single objective optimization and to always work with a vector optimization. The main phase of the algorithm is the solution of the problem:

$$\text{'min'} \sum_{j \in F_l} c^j x_j + \sum_{j \in B_l} c^j$$

$$\sum_{j \in F_l} t^j x_j \leq d_l$$

$$x_j \in \{0, 1\} \qquad j \in F_l$$

at node N^l, where F_l represents the set of free variables at node N^l; B_l represents the set of variables fixed to node N^l; c^j is the vector of coordinates $(c_k)_j$, $k = 1, \ldots, K$; t^j is the jth column of T; and $d_l = d - \sum_{j \in B_l} t^j$.

For the different objectives, the vectors

$$\overline{Z}^l = \sum_{j \in B_l} c^j$$

$$\underline{Z}^l = \sum_{j \in B_l} c^j + Y_l \text{ with } y_{lk} = \sum_{j \in F_l} \min(0, (c_k)_j)$$

represent the upper and lower bounds of Z at node N_l, respectively.

Two exclusive cases can appear:

1) $d^l \geq 0$: the node N^l is feasible. In this case, $\overline{Z}^l$ is compared to the list of L of upper bound vectors, already obtained and non-dominated:
  - $\overline{Z}^l$ is added to the list if it is not dominated by any element of L; and
  - the elements of L dominated by $\overline{Z}^l$ are removed from the list L.

2) $d^l \not\geq 0$: the node N^l is unfeasible (let us underline that, contrary to the single objective case, such a node is not always fathomed).

Fathom rules are applied:
- if the node N^l is unfeasible and there exists i such that

$$\sum_{j \in F_i} \min(0, t_{ij}) > d_i^l;$$

– if $\underline{Z}^l$ is dominated by one of the list L; or
– if $\overline{Z}^l = \underline{Z}^l$.

The backtracking rule is the usual rule applied in the single objective case. A non-fathomed node is separated in the following manner:

– if N^l is unfeasible, we select a variable x_j, $j \in F_l$, on basis of a minimal unfeasibility criterion $\min\limits_{j \in F_l} \sum\limits_i \max(0, t_{ij} - d_i^l)$; or

– if N^l is feasible, the variable x_j is arbitrarily selected in the set $\{j \in F_l | c^j \not\geq 0\}$.

At the end of the implicit enumeration, the list L corresponds to $E(P)$. Note, however, that as in the previous methods, it is only possible to generate a subset $\widehat{E(P)}$ of $E(P)$.

5.4.2. Interactive methods

5.4.2.1. *Gonzales et al. method [GON 85]*

This method is the interactive concretization of a principle referred to as *two phases* (see section 5.5): the first phase consists of determining $SE(P)$ and the second phase consists of determining $NSE(P)$. However, this principle is integrated in an interactive approach. During the first phase, a set $\widetilde{S} \subseteq SE(P)$ of cardinality K is selected and formed by the decision maker. During the second phase, possible solutions of $NSE(P)$ preferred by the decision maker are integrated in $\widetilde{S}$ to replace other solutions.

5.4.2.1.1. First phase

At the initial step, the K single objective problems are solved according to:

$$\min_{x \in \mathcal{D}} z_k(x) \ k = 1, \ldots, K$$

and we note $\widetilde{x}_k$ is a non-dominated optimal solution of objective k. The set $\widetilde{S}$ is initialized

$$\widetilde{S} = \{\widetilde{x}_k, \ k = 1, \ldots, K\}$$

and we note

$$\widetilde{Z} = \{z(\widetilde{x}_k), \ k = 1, \ldots, K.\}$$

At the general iteration, a linear search direction $g(x)$ is determined: it is the inverse image, in the decision space $\mathcal{R}^n$, of the hyperplane determined by the K points of $\widetilde{Z}$ in the objective space $\mathcal{R}^K$.

A new solution is generated by solving the problem $\min_{x \in \mathcal{D}} g(x)$. Let x^* be this solution and $z^* = z(x^*)$ be the corresponding point in the objective space.

Three cases can arise:

1) $z^* \notin \widetilde{Z}$ and the decision maker prefers x^* to at least one solution of $\widetilde{S}$. In this case, x^* replaces the least preferred solution in $\widetilde{S}$.

2) $z^* \notin \widetilde{Z}$ but the decision maker prefers all the solutions of $\widetilde{S}$ to x^*; in this case point 2 of the second phase (section 5.4.2.1.2) is started.

3) $z^* \in \widetilde{Z}$; in this case, point 1 of the second phase is started.

5.4.2.1.2. Second phase

1) At the mth iteration, a non-supported solution $\widetilde{x}_m$ is determined by solving the problem

$$\min g(x)$$
$$x \in \mathcal{D}$$
$$g(x) \geq \widetilde{g} - \varepsilon$$

with $\widetilde{g} = g(\widetilde{x}_{m-1})$. If $m = 1$, $\widetilde{g}$ is the value of $g(x)$ at point (3) of the first phase (section 5.4.2.1.1):

(a) If $\widetilde{x}_m$ is preferred to one of the solutions of $\widetilde{S}$, $\widetilde{x}_m$ replaces the least preferred solution in $\widetilde{S}$. $g(x)$ is updated and iteration $m+1$ is started.

(b) Otherwise, the procedure stops and the decision maker chooses the most preferred solution from $\widetilde{S}$.

2) In this case, the decision maker is not interested by solutions different to those of $\widetilde{S}$. However, before stopping the procedure, it is possible to begin a search of non-supported solutions in the neighborhood of the preferred solution of $\widetilde{S}$, by solving the above problem where $g(x)$ is the objective function which generated this point. A similar search can also be made at point 1(b).

Remark 5.9. This method appears general and easy to implement. Nevertheless, the division of the algorithm in two phases makes it relatively heavy for an interactive approach

5.4.2.2. *The MOMIX method [LHO 95]*

This method uses the concept of interactive *branch and bound*, introduced by Marcotte and Soland [MAR 86]. It consists of analyzing a MOILP problem with the help of a branch and bound tree in which we circulate according to the preferences of the decision maker: at each node, they will choose which sub-node to examine. If the basic idea appears interesting, its implementation seems complicated in the Marcotte and Soland method. The main reasons are that:

– the sets of feasible solutions corresponding to each sub-nodes are not disjoined; and

– the order to improve the objectives is fixed once and for all independently of the proposed compromise at each iteration.

For these reasons, the management of the circulation into the tree is very difficult and requires the storage of a large amount of information. The MOMIX method takes up this interesting idea but with a completely different arrangement of the branching and separation processes, allowing an easier management of the *branch and bound*.

We can distinguish two main phases as follows.

5.4.2.2.1. Initial phase

The initial phase consists, as in the STEM method (see section 5.3.1), of determining a first compromise $x^{(0)}$ by minimization of the weighted Tchebytcheff distance (possibly augmented). We therefore solve the problem $P^{(m)}$ (with $m = 0$):

$$\begin{bmatrix} \min \delta \\ \Pi_k^{(m)}(c_k x - M_k^{(m)}) \leq \delta \quad k = 1, \ldots, K. \\ x \in D^{(m)} \end{bmatrix} \quad (5.36)$$

where $D^{(0)} = D$, $M_k^{(m)}$ is the optimal value of objective k on $D^{(m)}$ and

$$\Pi_k^{(m)} = \frac{\alpha_k^{(m)}}{\sum_{i=1}^{K} \alpha_i^{(m)}}$$

is the weight of objective k with e.g.

$$\alpha_k^{(m)} = \frac{m_k^{(m)} - M_k^{(m)}}{\max(|m_k^{(m)}|, |M_k^{(m)}|)} \cdot \frac{1}{\|c_k\|}$$

where $m_k^{(m)}$ is the kth coordinate of the nadir point on $D^{(m)}$ and $\|c_k\|$ is the Euclidean norm of c_k.

5.4.2.2.2. Interactive phases

The interactive phases use an interactive branch and bound with two steps:

1) A *'depth first'* process allows us to quickly obtain a good compromise by iterative improvement of an objective chosen at each iteration by the decision maker. Then, at the mth iteration:

- let $x^{(m-1)}$ be the $(m-1)$th compromise and $z_k^{(m-1)} = c_k x^{(m-1)}$ the corresponding value for objective k;

- the decision maker indicates the objective $l_m(1) \in \{1, \ldots, K\}$ to improve in priority; and

- a new compromise is obtained by solving problem (5.36) with

$$D^{(m)} = D^{(m-1)} \cap \{x : z_{l_m(1)}(x) < z_{l_m(1)}^{(m-1)}\}$$

so that objective $l_m(1)$ is improved.
Some fathoming and stopping tests are defined. In particular:
- $D^{(m)} = \emptyset$;
- $m_k^{(m)} - M_k^{(m)} \leq \epsilon_k \, \forall k \, (\epsilon_k > 0, \text{fixed})$;
- $\hat{z}$, the vector of best values found previously, is preferred to the ideal point $M^{(m)}$ related to $D^{(m)}$;
- during q iterations (q fixed by the decision maker), no improvement of $\hat{z}$ has been fixed; and
- a number of Q iterations have been made.

2) The *backtracking process* then checks if there exists a better compromise for $\hat{z}$ in $D^{(m-1)} \setminus D^{(m)}$ of the feasible region neglected at each iteration during the depth first process. It proceeds in the following way:
- the node corresponding to the compromise $x^{(m-1)}$ is separated in K branches;
- let $l_m(k), k = 1, \ldots, K$ be the priority order in which the decision maker wants to improve the K objectives regarding the compromise; and
- the K sub-nodes are defined by the addition of the constraints:

$$\begin{bmatrix} z_{l_m(1)}(x) < z_{l_m(1)}^{(m-1)} & \text{(examined during the depth first phase)} & (\star) \\ z_{l_m(2)}(x) < z_{l_m(2)}^{(m-1)} \text{ and } & z_{l_m(1)}(x) \geq z_{l_m(1)}^{(m-1)} & (\star\star) \\ \vdots & \vdots & \\ z_{l_m(\bar{k})}(x) < z_{l_m(\bar{k})}^{(m-1)} \text{ and } & z_{l_m(k)}(x) \geq z_{l_m(k)}^{(m-1)} \, k = 1, \ldots, \bar{k} & \\ \vdots & \vdots & \\ z_{l_m(K)}(x) < z_{l_m(K)}^{(m-1)} \text{ and } & z_{l_m(k)}(x) \geq z_{l_m(k)}^{(m-1)} \, k = 1, \ldots, K & (\star\star\star) \end{bmatrix}.$$

We therefore obtain a partition of the set of feasible solutions of the preceding node. For each sub-node, we can amend equation (5.36) to search for a possible better compromise. Figure 5.8 illustrates the procedure.

The same fathoming and stopping tests can be introduced. More importantly, it appears unusual (at least for a consistent decision maker) to examine the kth sub-nodes for $k > 2$ or 3. Effectively, they correspond to a simultaneous deterioration of the objectives that the decision maker wants to improve.

5.5. The multiple objective combinatorial optimization

Combinatorial optimization concerns the study of optimization problems with binary variables which present a particular structure, more often at the level of the

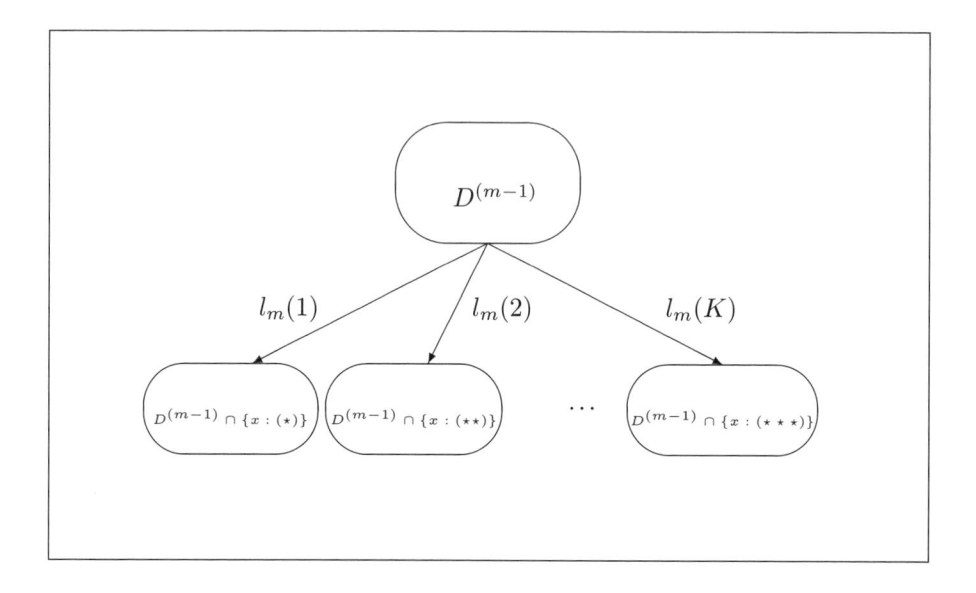

Figure 5.8. *'Branching' procedure*

constraints. There are many problems of this type: assignment, knapsack, traveling salesman, vehicle routing, location, covering or partitioning, and production scheduling. Combinatorial optimization is certainly one of the more powerful and frequently used tools of operations research, allowing us to treat a large class of applications [WOL 98].

A stream of recent research publications appear to analyze combinatorial optimization in a multiple objective framework i.e. multiple objective combinatorial optimization (MOCO). This stream was strengthened by the success of metaheuristics [PIR 03, TEG 02], which have been adapted by several researchers to multiple objective problems i.e. multiple objective metaheuristics (MOMH).

We can only present the main areas of this research field here, which is undergoing huge development. We will essentially focus on the methodological aspect. Section 5.5.1 is devoted to exact methods which determine the set $E(P)$ of efficient solutions of a problem (P). The adaptation of metaheuristics, with the aim of determining a good approximation $\widehat{E(P)}$ of $E(P)$, will be analyzed in section 5.5.2.

For the reader interested in the literature, see:

– two papers related to MOCO: [ULU 94a] opens the road to this field and [EHR 02, Chapter 8] is more recent;

– three surveys devoted to MOMH: [PIR 03, Chapter 7], [JAS 02] and [EHR 02, Chapter 6] (the latter exclusively analyzes evolutionary algorithms);

– several studies related to particular problems: shortest paths [SKI 00, ULU 91], transportation [CUR 93], location [CUR 90] and production scheduling [LOU 03, TKI 02].

5.5.1. *Exact methods*

A MOCO problem,

$$\begin{array}{ll}\text{'min'} z_k = c_k x & k = 1, \ldots, K \\ x \in D = \{x \in \{0,1\}^n | Tx \le d\} & \end{array} \quad (5.37)$$

of type MOBLP, is characterized by a particular structure of the constraints $Tx \le d$ (and more rarely of the objectives z_k). In addition to those described in section 5.4, we can note the following additional difficulties.

Difficulty 1. The previously established fact of existence of non-supported efficient solutions remains valid even if the set D verifies the *total unimodularity property*. If the matrix T is totally unimodular (matrix for which every square sub-matrix has a determinant equal to –1, 0 or +1) and if the vector d has integer coordinates, the vertices of the polyhedron D have integer coordinates so that the resolution of the single objective problem with binary variables, defined

$$\left[\min_{x \in D} cx \right],$$

is equivalent to the resolution of the relaxed problem in continuous variables

$$\left[\min_{x \in \{x \in \mathcal{R}^n | Tx \le d\}} cx \right].$$

A classical problem verifying this property is the single objective assignment problem (AP), i.e. the following problem with $K = 1$

$$\begin{bmatrix} \text{"min"} \sum_{i=1}^{n} \sum_{j=1}^{n} c_{ij}^{(k)} x_{ij} & k = 1, \ldots, K \\ \sum_{i=1}^{n} x_{ij} = 1 & j = 1, \ldots, n \\ \sum_{j=1}^{n} x_{ij} = 1 & i = 1, \ldots, n \\ x_{ij} \in \{0,1\} & \end{bmatrix}.$$

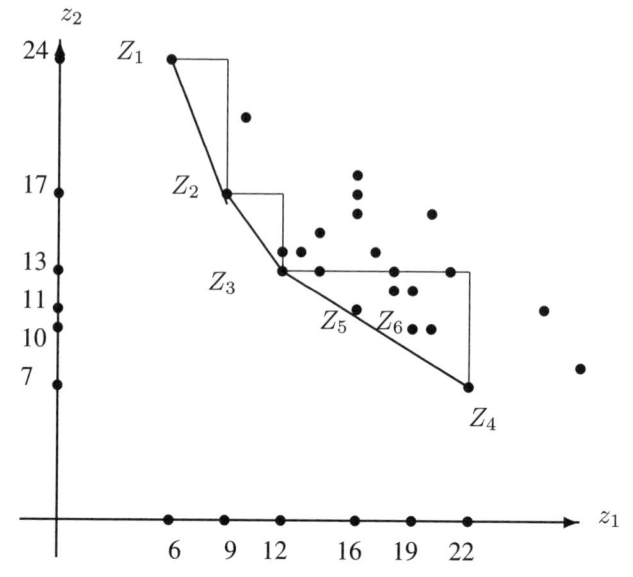

Figure 5.9. *The feasible values of the illustration in the objective space*

Nevertheless, despite this property, the multiple objective assignment problem (MOAP) has non-supported efficient solutions, as illustrated by the following didactic example with two objectives:

$$C^{(1)} = \begin{bmatrix} 5 & 1 & 4 & 7 \\ 6 & 2 & 2 & 6 \\ 2 & 8 & 4 & 4 \\ 3 & 5 & 7 & 1 \end{bmatrix} \text{ and } C^{(2)} = \begin{bmatrix} 3 & 6 & 4 & 2 \\ 1 & 3 & 8 & 3 \\ 5 & 2 & 2 & 3 \\ 4 & 2 & 3 & 5 \end{bmatrix}$$

which define the two matrices of costs $c_{ij}^{(k)}$ $i, j = 1, \ldots, 4$; $k = 1, 2$. Figure 5.9 represents the corresponding values of the 24 feasible solutions in the bi-objective space.

It appears there exist four supported efficient solutions (corresponding to points 1, 2, 3 and 4) and two non-supported efficient solutions (corresponding to points 5 and 6); the 18 other solutions are not efficient. Note that in the space (z_1, z_2), the points corresponding to the non-supported efficient solutions must necessarily be located in the rectangular triangles defined by the points corresponding to two adjacent supported solutions (in the space (z_1, z_2)).

Difficulty 2. This is of a different type to that described above. On the one hand, the different types of combinatorial optimization problems are each characterized by a specific structure of the polyhedron D. These specificities are used to build efficient algorithms to determine an optimal solution of the single objective problems.

On the other hand, the more classic approach to generating a set of efficient solutions for a MOILP problem consists of adding an additional constraint at each iteration (see section 5.4). Such an approach is difficult to apply to a MOCO problem because it implies the loss of the specific form of D and therefore the impossibility of using existing single-objective methods for this type of problem.

The difficulty is therefore to try to elaborate methods to build $E(P)$ without the introduction of additional constraints. It is a major reason why there exists relatively few exact methods of generating $E(P)$.

Difficulty 3. Finally, for some structures of problems, the number of efficient solutions can be very large. For instance, for a bi-objective knapsack problem (MOKP, see below), Visée *et al.* [VIS 98] counts 1708 efficient solutions (among them only 101 supported) for a problem of 500 objects. However, let us note that for other problems, e.g. a production scheduling problem, this number can be small [LOU 03]; the MOAP problem corresponds to an intermediate situation [TUY 00].

5.5.1.1. *Direct methods*

We refer to an extension of an existing method for the corresponding single-objective problem as a direct method. Each time a new feasible solution is obtained, the vector of objective function values is calculated and compared with those of the solutions of the list $\widehat{E(P)}$, containing the feasible solutions already obtained and non-dominated by any other already generated solution. We call $\widehat{E(P)}$ the set of potential efficient solutions; $\widehat{E(P)}$ plays the role of *incumbent solution* in a method for a single objective.

At each iteration, the list $\widehat{E(P)}$ is actualized. In an exact method, $E(P) = \widehat{E(P)}$ at the end of the procedure.

Such a principle can be applied, for instance, to the methodology of dynamic programming [CAR 90]. It can also be applied in an effective manner for branch and bound methods, as for the Kiziltan and Yucaoglu method described in section 5.4.

However, the amount of calculation is obviously greater than in the single objective case. In particular, in a branch and bound method, less nodes of the tree will be fathomed. We will give an example of a direct method [ULU 97] for a multiple objective knapsack problem (MOKP) of the type

$$\left[\begin{array}{l} \text{"max"} z_k(x) = \sum_{j=1}^{n} c_j^{(k)} x_j \quad k = 1, \ldots, K \\ \sum_{j=1}^{n} w_j x_j \leq W \\ x_j \in \{0, 1\} \quad j = 1, \ldots, n. \end{array}\right. \quad (5.38)$$

to a multiple objective method.

We assume the variables to be sorted in the order Θ which is defined in the following manner:

- Θ_k is the list of variables ranked by decreasing efficiencies for objective k

$$\frac{c_j^{(k)}}{w_j} \quad (k = 1, \ldots, n);$$

- $r_j^{(k)}$ is the rank of the variable x_j in the order Θ_k; and
- Θ is the order of the variables ranked by increasing values

$$\sum_{k=1}^{K} r_j^{(k)}.$$

At each node of the tree, we define:

- B_1 (B_0) is the set of indices of variables fixed to 1 (0) (initially $B_1 = B_0 = \emptyset$).
- F is the set of free variables which always follows in the order Θ for those already fixed. If $i-1$ is the largest index of a fixed variable, $B_1 \cup B_0 = \{1, \ldots, i-1\}$ and $F = \{i, \ldots, n\}$. Initially, $i = 1$.

We note:

- $\overline{W} = W - \sum_{j \in B_1} w_j$ is the remaining capacity.

- $\underline{Z}$ is the vector of coordinates $\underline{z}_k = \sum_{j \in B_1} c_j^{(k)}$, corresponding to the values of the objectives for the partial solution $B_1 \cup B_0$. $\widehat{E(P)}$ contains all the solutions corresponding to the non-dominated vector $\underline{Z}$ and is actualized at each iteration. Initially, $\underline{z}_k = 0 \ \forall k$ and $\widehat{E(P)} = \emptyset$.

- $\overline{Z}$ is the vector of coordinates $\overline{z}_k$ corresponding to the upper bound of objective z_k at the current node. This upper bound can be calculated separately for each objective, e.g. by the manner proposed by Martello and Toth [MAR 90]. Initially, $\overline{z}_k = \infty \ \forall k$.

The node will be fathomed if one of the two following conditions is satisfied:
1) $\{j \in F | w_j < \overline{W}\} = \emptyset$; or
2) $\overline{Z}$ is dominated by one vector $z(x)$, $x \in \widehat{E(P)}$.

When a node is fathomed, we backtrack in a classical manner: if t is the last index of B_1, the new node corresponds to

$$\begin{aligned} B_1 &\longleftarrow B_1 \setminus \{t\} \\ B_0 &\longleftarrow B_0 \cap \{1, \ldots, t-1\} \cup \{t\} \\ F &\longleftarrow \{t+1, \ldots, n\} \end{aligned}$$

When a node is not fathomed, a new node is considered. It is generated in the following manner, where s is the index of the variable defined by

$$\begin{aligned} s &= \max\{l \in F | \sum_{j=i}^{l} w_j \leq \overline{W}\} & \text{if } w_i \leq \overline{W} \\ s &= i - 1 & \text{if } w_i > \overline{W} \end{aligned}$$

– If $s \geq i$:
$$\begin{aligned} B_1 &\longleftarrow B_1 \cup \{i, \ldots, s\} \\ B_0 &\longleftarrow B_0 \\ F &\longleftarrow \{s+1, \ldots, n\} \end{aligned}.$$

– If $s = i - 1$:
$$\begin{aligned} B_1 &\longleftarrow B_1 \cup \{r\} \text{ with } r = \min\{j \in F | w_j \leq \overline{W}\} \\ B_0 &\longleftarrow B_0 \cup \{i, \ldots, r-1\} \\ F &\longleftarrow \{r+1, \ldots, n\} \end{aligned}.$$

The algorithm stops when the initial node is fathomed, then $E(P) = \widehat{E(P)}$.

5.5.1.2. *The two phases method*

This approach is well adapted to a bi-objective (MOCO) problem [ULU 94b].

5.5.1.2.1. *The first phase to generate $SE(P)$*

Let $S \cup S'$ be the list of supported efficient solutions already generated, with S the extreme solutions and S' the non-extreme solutions. S is initialized with the non-dominated optimal solutions for the two objectives. The solutions of S are ordered in the increasing order of the values z_1. Let us consider two successive solutions x^r and x^s: we therefore have

$$z_{1r} < z_{1s} \quad \text{and} \quad z_{2r} > z_{2s} \quad \text{with} \quad z_{kl} = z_k(x^l) \ k = 1, 2; \ l = r, s.$$

The single objective problem

$$\min z_\lambda(x) = \lambda_1 z_1(x) + \lambda_2 z_2(x)$$
$$x \in D$$
with $\lambda_1 = z_{2r} - z_{2s}$ and $\lambda_2 = z_{1s} - z_{1r}$

is considered and solved by an algorithm corresponding to the single objective optimization problem. The objective function $z_\lambda(x)$ corresponds, in the objective space, to the line determined by the points $z(x^r)$ and $z(x^s)$.

We note that $\{x^t, t = 1, \ldots, T\}$ is the optimal solution of this problem and $\{Z^t, t = 1, \ldots, T\}$ is the corresponding image in the objective space. Two cases can occur:

1) $\{z(x^r), z(x^s)\} \cap \{Z^t,\ t = 1, \ldots, T\} = \emptyset$

In this case, the solutions x^t are supported efficient solutions and the sets S and S' are actualized in the following manner:

$$\begin{array}{rll} S & \longleftarrow\ S \cup \{x^1\} \cup \{x^T\} & (\text{if } T \geq 1) \\ S' & \longleftarrow\ S' \cup \{x^2, \ldots, x^{T-1}\} & (\text{if } T > 2) \end{array}.$$

At the next iterations, the pairs (x^r, x^1) and (x^T, x^s) must be considered.

2) $\{z(x^r), z(x^s)\} \subset \{Z^t,\ t = 1, \ldots, T\}$

In this case, the solutions x^t are also supported efficient solutions but the points Z^t are located on the line segment $[z(x^r), z(x^s)]$, i.e. $x^1 \equiv x^r$ and $x^T \equiv x^s$ so that:

$$S' \longleftarrow S' \cup \{x^2, \ldots, x^{T-1}\}.$$

This first phase stops when all the pairs (x^r, x^s) of S are examined without any extension of S. We then have

$$SE(P) = S \cup S'$$

as in Figure 5.10.

5.5.1.2.2. *The second phase: generation of* $NSE(P)$

The image in the objective space of the non-supported efficient solutions is necessarily located in the rectangular triangles $\triangle_{rs}$ determined by $z(x^r)$ and $z(x^s)$ with x^r, x^s being two successive solutions of $SE(P)$ (see Figure 5.11). It is therefore necessary to analyze $|SE(P)| - 1$ triangles.

This second phase is certainly more technical and more difficult to implement, and strongly depends on the considered problem and on the single objective method used. The interested reader could refer to [TUY 00] for the implementation of this second

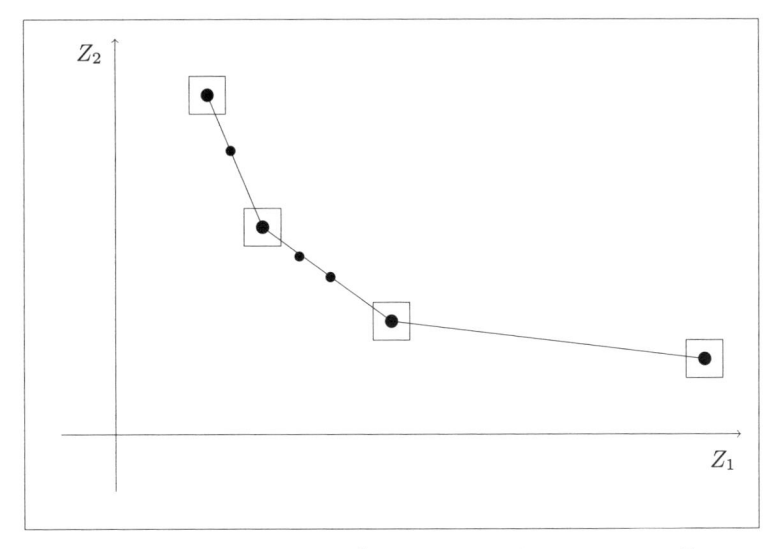

Figure 5.10. $SEP = S \cup S'$: ◼ solutions of S; • solutions of S'

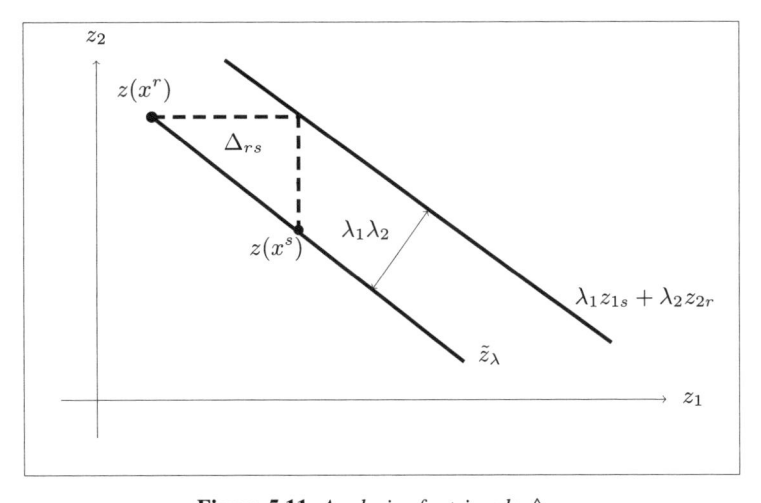

Figure 5.11. *Analysis of a triangle* $\triangle_{rs}$

phase in the case of a bi-objective MOAP problem, and to [VIS 98] in the case of a bi-objective MOKP problem.

We will only emphasize here that a triangle $\triangle_{rs}$ is generally analyzed with the objective function $z_\lambda(x)$, for which the optimal value determined at phase 1 is equal to

$$\widetilde{z}_\lambda = \lambda_1 z_{1s} + \lambda_2 z_{2s} = \lambda_1 z_{1r} + \lambda_2 z_{2r}$$

(see Figure 5.11).

To have a solution x inside the triangle $\triangle_{rs}$, the conditions $z_1(x) \leq z_{1r}$ and $z_2(x) \leq z_{2s}$ apply. In addition, it is necessary that the increase $L(x)$ of the value $\widetilde{z}_\lambda$ verifies the inequality

$$\widetilde{z}_\lambda + L(x) \leq \lambda_1 z_{1s} + \lambda_2 z_{2r}$$

i.e.

$$L(x) \leq \lambda_1 \lambda_2.$$

This allows us to eliminate all the solutions x which do not satisfy the upper bounds for $z_1(x)$, $z_2(x)$ and $L(x)$.

We also note that each time a non-supported efficient solution is determined in the triangle $\triangle_{rs}$, the upper bound of $L(x)$ can be decreased, reducing the set of solutions x to examine.

5.5.1.3. *Comments*

Clearly, due to a large computational time, these two exact methods can only solve small or medium dimension problems, e.g.

– the direct method described in section 5.5.1.1 allows us to solve bi-objective MOKP problems with 500 objects [VIS 98];

– the two phases method described in section 5.5.1.2 allows us to solve bi-objective MOAP problems with $n = 50$ [TUY 00].

These two exact methods can easily be transformed in interactive procedures:

– For the direct method, the decision maker must periodically express satisfaction levels on the objectives required to effectively introduce a solution in the set $\widehat{E(P)}$; these satisfaction levels can be strengthened during the procedure. At the end of the algorithm, $\widehat{E(P)}$ will contain the efficient solutions corresponding to the preferences of the decision maker.

– In the two phases method, the decision maker can choose the two solutions x^r and x^s preferred from $SE(P)$ at the end of the first phase. The second phase will then analyze only one triangle $\triangle_{rs}$.

5.5.2. *Metaheuristics*

Due to the difficulty of the exact methods in determining the set $E(P)$ for a MOCO problem, and taking into account the performances of the metaheuristics [PIR 03, TEG 02] for single objective combinatorial optimization problems, it appears natural to adapt metaheuristics to MOCO problems. The aim is to determine a good approximation $\widehat{E(P)}$ of $E(P)$.

Important research has been developed during the last 10 years on this MOMH approach. Two recent surveys have been written on this field: [EHR 02] and [JAS 08].

In this section, we assume that the reader is familiar with the general mechanism of these metaheuristics. We present only some principles of MOMH and some representative methods for the adaptation of simulated annealing, tabu search or genetic algorithms.

5.5.2.1. *Simulated annealing*

Two main difficulties must be overcome for the adaptation of a local search to a multiple objective framework.

Difficulty 1. First of all, it is necessary to define an acceptance rule of a neighboring solution y randomly chosen at each iteration in the neighborhood $N(x)$ of the current solution x.

Effectively, in the single objective case, only two situations can appear for the comparison of y and x:

1) either y is at least as good as x ($z(y) \leq z(x)$) and in this case, y is taken as the new current solution; or

2) either y makes the value of the objective function ($z(y) > z(x)$) worse and, nevertheless, y will be accepted as the new current solution but with a probability p less than 1, classically defined by

$$p = e^{\frac{-\triangle z}{T}}$$

where $\triangle z = z(y) - z(x)$ and T is the value of the temperature parameter.

In the multiple objective case, three situations may be considered for comparison of y and x:

1) y dominates x: $\triangle z_k = z_k(y) - z_k(x) \leq 0 \, \forall \, k$;
2) y is dominated by x: $\triangle z_k \geq 0 \, \forall \, k$; and
3) y and x are mutually non-dominated: $\exists k$ and $k' \mid \triangle z_k < 0$ and $\triangle z_{k'} > 0$.

Obviously, y will be accepted with a probability of 1 in situation (1); but what should be done in the two other situations?

In any case, it appears difficult to avoid the use of a scalarizing function $s(z, \lambda)$ (see section 5.2.4) to aggregate the different objectives and so to be able to define the acceptance probability p. This probability is generally defined by

$$p = \begin{cases} 1 & \text{if } \triangle s \leq 0 \\ e^{\frac{-\triangle s}{T}} & \text{if } \triangle s > 0 \end{cases}$$

with $\triangle s = s(z(y), \lambda) - s(z(x), \lambda)$.

The way to project the space $\mathcal{R}^K$ on the straight line $\triangle s$ and the acceptance rule depend on the scalarizing function used (generally s_1 or s_3).

Difficulty 2. Another difficulty is to completely cover $E(P)$. Effectively, the use of a weight vector λ inside the scalarizing function induces a preferential search direction in the objective space $\mathcal{R}^K$. Without enough diversity in the vector λ, good values for $z(x)$ will only be obtained in this direction.

In the two most typical methods, this diversity is introduced differently:

– In the multiple objective simulated annealing (MOSA) method of Ulungu *et al.* [ULU 95, ULU 99], a set of diversified weight vectors $\lambda^l; l = 1, \ldots, L$ is initially introduced. These L vectors are uniformly generated so that functions $s(z, \lambda^l)$ are used in enough directions to cover all of the efficient frontier. The simulated annealing is applied L times generating L sets $\widehat{E_l(P)}, l = 1, \ldots, L$. They are then filtered by pairwise comparisons of the solutions so that only non-dominated solutions are kept to form the final approximation $\widehat{E(P)}$.

– In the Pareto simulated annealing (PSA) method [CZY 98], a population of L solutions is considered, each having an independent development initially with a different vector λ^l. During the procedure, an exchange of information is organized between the current solutions so that a modification of the weight vectors is made to enforce a good dispersion of the solutions. Only the neighbor solutions y non-dominated by the solution x are considered, and the weights of the objectives are increased or decreased by a value δ to move the point $z(y)$ away from $z(x)$ in the objective space.

The parameter L is an important one in both methods, depending essentially on the dimension of the treated problem. δ is an additional parameter of the PSA method.

The MOSA method has been applied to assignment problems [TUY 00], to knapsack problems [ULU 99] and to production scheduling problems [LOU 02]. An interactive version has been proposed and applied to a case study [TEG 00, ULU 98].

The PSA method has also been used for several applications [CZY 96, CZY 98, JAS 97, VIA 00] and also in an interactive way [HAP 98].

5.5.2.2. *Tabu search*

The same two difficulties as described in section 5.5.2.1 exist for the multiple objective adaptation of another local search, referred to as a Tabu search.

To determine the best non-Tabu solution inside a (sub)neighborhood of the current solution, a scalarizing function $s(z, \lambda)$ is used. However, a Tabu solution can be chosen if it satisfies an aspiration criterion.

In the method of Gandibleux *et al.* [GAN 97], a dynamic modification of weights can be introduced to keep a diversification of the search direction to the Pareto front. The weight λ_k of the objective z_k is decreased by a quantity $\underline{\delta}_k$ ($\overline{\delta}_k$) if the new current solution corresponds to a small (large) deterioration of the objective z_k. However, in this case, the modification of this objective z_k becomes Tabu during a certain number of iterations.

The Hansen method [HAN 00] uses a population of solutions, similar to the PSA method. At each iteration, a distance between the images of these solutions in the objective space is measured. The weight of an objective is modified proportionally to this distance so that the solutions are more diversified.

Let us also mention the quite different method of Ben Abdelaziz *et al.* [BEN 99], which avoids the use of a scalarizing function due to the random choice of the new current solution in the neighborhood. However, the current solution is redefined periodically by optimization of a weighted sum of the two objectives with the worst values.

These three methods have been applied to knapsack problems [BEN 99, GAN 00] and to the traveling salesman problem [HAN 00].

5.5.2.3. *Genetic algorithms*

The genetic algorithms, or the more general evolutionary algorithms, are those which have been the most adapted to multiple objective frameworks. The Internet site [COE 08] recently cited more than 900 references. Several recent books have been devoted to this field, in particular [COE 02, DEB 00] and [EHR 02, Chapter 6].

Nevertheless, this research initially treated only multiple objectives nonlinear programming (MONLP) problems, which we do not cover in this chapter [see COL 02]. It was only in a second phase that research with MOCO streams occured. We can only highlight a few important aspects and recent methods among the more effective. Of course, these multiple objective algorithms incorporate the classical notions of genetic algorithms: population of solutions, selection and crossover and mutation operators [TEG 02].

There exist two difficulties to overcome for the adaption of a genetic algorithm for a multiple objective problem.

Difficulty 1. The first concerns the fitness function of the solutions, which must take into account the multiple objective character of the problem.

Even if some algorithms use a scalarizing function, as in sections 5.5.2.1 and 5.5.2.2, most of them introduce an evaluation mechanism based on the dominance relation. The basic idea involves ranking the solutions of the population using the following relation. Non-dominated solutions have rank 1, then after they are provisionally withdrawn, rank 2 is given to the non-dominated solutions regarding the remaining population, and so on to define solutions with rank 3, 4, etc.

The selection is then made on the basis of this ranking: the solutions with small rank have a larger probability to be selected. Many variants exist, in particular, an elite form which allows the potential efficient solutions of the current list $\widehat{E(P)}$ to participate at this ranking and therefore at this selection. For instance, this is the case in the non-sorting genetic algorithm (NSGA) method of [SRI 94].

Difficulty 2. Nevertheless, as with the use of a scalarizing function, this evaluation mecanism has a tendency to produce a convergence of the population to a particular region of the Pareto frontier (this aspect is called 'genetic drift'). It is therefore necessary to introduce enough diversity to cover all these frontiers.

Several mechanisms are possible:

1) The 'fitness sharing' consists of penalizing the evaluation of very close solutions in the decision or in the objective space (NSGA method [SRI 94]).

2) The 'crowding distance' used by [DEB 01] first selects the solutions with a small rank (for instance with rank 1 or 2), but then completes the selection with the solutions of superior rank which are the furthest ones from the preceding solutions.

3) The evaluation of a solution can also be based on the number of solutions dominated by this solution. For example in the strength pareto evolutionary algorithm (SPEA) of Zitzler and Thiele [ZIT 98], if P_0 is the current population, the fitness function $F(x)$ of a solution $x \in \widehat{E(P)} \cup P_0$ is calculated by:

$$\begin{aligned} x \in \widehat{E(P)} &: F(x) = \frac{|\{y \in P_0 | z(x) \leq z(y)\}|}{|P_0| + 1} \\ y \in P_0 &: F(y) = 1 + \sum_{\{x \in \widehat{E(P)} | z(x) \leq z(y)\}} F(x) \end{aligned}$$

Many other variants exist. Clearly, we have only touched upon this very rich research field: the interested reader should refer to the specialized literature cited above.

To conclude this section, let us say that recent development of metaheuristics (for single or multiple objective optimization) is oriented to hybrid methods combining genetic algorithms with local searches, the latter applied after the crossover of solutions (sometimes referred to as mutation of the solutions). Ishibuchi and Murata [ISH 98] are the first to propose such hybridization for a multiple objective context: their multiple objective genetic local algorithm (MOGLS) (extended by [MUR 00]) uses a scalarizing function with a randomly generated weight vector to evaluate the solutions. Each iteration combines a crossover operator and a local search applied to the resulting solutions. Moreover, a part of the solutions of $\widehat{E(P)}$ is added to the new population. Among many hybrid methods [JAS 08], we want to cite the Jaszkiewicz method [JAS 02] which appears as one of the more efficient. Finally, other metaheuristics have been adapted to a multiple objective context. For instance, in [GOM 04, GOM 05] a 'scatter search' method is applied to knapsack problems.

Remark 5.10. It is not easy to analyze the respective performances of the different MOMH methods, i.e. to compare the sets $\widehat{E(P)}$ generated by the different methods and to measure their proximity to $E(P)$. Effectively, no quality measure allows us to easily measure if each individual solution of $\widehat{E(P)}$ is close to a solution of $E(P)$ (generally unknown) and if the global solutions of $\widehat{E(P)}$ are dispersed enough to completely approximate the set $E(P)$.

Many quality measures are described in the specialized literature, each one having advantages and drawbacks. It is therefore necessary to use several of these measures to be able to analyze the performance of a MOMH method.

5.6. The multiple objective stochastic linear programming

Little research has been devoted to multiple objective stochastic linear programming (MOSLP) problems i.e. MOLP problems in which some of the coefficients are random variables. The problem of stochastic linear programming is, as for a multiple objective problem, badly defined from the mathematical point of view. It is necessary to give a sense of the optimization of a random variable as well as of the inequalities between two random variables. It is therefore necessary to associate it with a deterministic equivalent problem.

Two main approaches have been proposed to define this equivalent problem: the *recourse* and the *chance constraint* approaches. See [TEG 03] for some elements of stochastic linear programming and [BIR 97] for a more detailed presentation.

When the coefficients are continuous random variables, the equivalent problems are generally nonlinear programming problems which often require important mathematical developments. The case of discrete random variables (considering their realizations as different scenarios) seems better adapted to many applications, in particular investment planning on a time horizon. This is the case for the two applications [KUN 87, TEG 85] for which the method described below has been developed.

The MOSLP problem can be written

$$\left[\begin{array}{ll} \text{'min'} & z_k = c_k(w)x \\ & x \in D = \{x | T(w)x \leq d(w),\ x \geq 0\} \end{array}\right. \tag{5.39}$$

where $c_k(w), T(w)$ and $d(w)$ are random variables defined on a probability space $(\Omega, \mathbf{a}, \mathbb{P})$.

One of the first methods devoted to this problem was PROTADE (PRObabilistic TRAde of DEvelopment) proposed by Goicoechea [GOI 82], where only the vectors c_k are random but with deterministic constraints. The method STRANGE [TEG 86c] considers that all the coefficients are discrete random variables.

Each objective k depends on a set of scenarios $\{s_k \mid s_k = 1, \ldots, s_K\}$. To each of these scenarios a plausibility level p_{ks_k} is assigned. We denote the realization of vector c_k under the scenario s_k as c_{ks_k}, so that

$$P(c_k = c_{ks_k}) = p_{ks_k};\ \sum_{s_k=1}^{S_k} p_{ks_k} = 1.$$

It is important to note that p_{ks_k} is a subjective probability.

Similarly, various realizations are considered for the coefficients (T, d) of the constraints. We denote these realizations by (T_r, d_r) $r = 1, .., R$ and the corresponding subjective probability by q_r. We then have

$$P(T = T_r,\ d = d_r) = q_r;\ \sum_{r=1}^{R} q_r = 1.$$

Remark 5.11. 1) In many applications, the scenarios are the same for each objective so that

$$P(c_k = c_{ks}) = p_{ks} \qquad s = 1, .., S.$$

The method can be applied without any difficulty in the case where they are different.

Multiple Objective Linear Programming   247

2) The reason for different scenarios, i.e. for the objectives $(s_k;\ s_k = 1,\ldots,S_k)$ and for the constraints $(r = 1,\ldots,R)$, is due to the applications which have motivated the model. In the objectives, it is the costs (raw materials and investments) which are uncertain; in the constraints, it is the available resources or the demands which are uncertain. In such cases, there is no relation between these uncertainties related to the objectives and the constraints.

5.6.1. *The equivalent deterministic problem*

As explained before, the random character of the data requires the definition of an associated deterministic problem accepted as equivalent. One advantage of STRANGE is the ease with which this equivalent problem can be formulated keeping the data as defined in the initial problem.

Each objective is considered separately with each scenario to obtain $\sum_{k=1}^{K} S_k$ new objectives, i.e.

$$z_{ks_k} = c_{ks_k}\, x \qquad k = 1,\ldots,K;\ s_k = 1,\ldots,S_k.$$

The uncertainty existing for the constraints is globally measured with the help of a new additional objective, denoted z_{K+1}. The idea of the stochastic programming with recourse is used to define this new objective. The vectors $(m \times 1)$ of slack variables $y^{(r)+}$ and $y^{(r)-}$, by excess and by default, respectively, between $T_r\, x$ and d_r in case of scenario r, are introduced in the constraint

$$T_r\, x + y^{(r)+} - y^{(r)-} = d_r \qquad r = 1,\ldots,R.$$

The new objective to minimize is then

$$z_{K+1} = \sum_{r=1}^{R} q_r (\beta^{(r)}\, y^{(r)-}),$$

where $\beta^{(r)}$ is a vector $(1 \times m)$ of possible penalties allowing different treatment of the non-satisfaction of the constraints in each scenario r.

This objective is therefore a global measure of the non-satisfaction of the constraints and, in the real case studies treated with STRANGE, it has a precise meaning similar to supply risk. The objective z_{K+1} does not depend on any scenario. To unify the notations, we note

$$z_{K+1} = z_{K+1,\, s_{K+1}}$$

where $S_{K+1} = 1$.

The (multiple objective) associated deterministic problem is therefore:

$$(P') \begin{bmatrix} \text{"min"} \ z_{ks_k}(x) = c_{ks_k} x & k = 1, \ldots, K+1; \ s_k = 1, \ldots, S_k \\ (x, \ y^{(r)+}, \ y^{(r)-}) \in \mathcal{D}^{(0)} \end{bmatrix}$$

where $\mathcal{D}^{(0)}$ is defined by

$$\mathcal{D}^{(0)} = \{(x, \ y^{(r)+}, \ y^{(r)-}) \ r = 1, \ldots, R \mid T_r \ x + y^{(r)+} - y^{(r)-} = d_r;$$

$$x \geq 0; \ y^{(r)+} \geq 0; \ y^{(r)-} \geq 0\}.$$

5.6.2. *Determination of the first compromise*

The principle used is similar to the STEM method (see section 5.3.1) with the exception that it is adapted to the particular context. This is particularly true for the definition of the payoff matrix and for the consideration of 'expected' distance of the initial random objectives from their ideal values in the definition of the augmented weighted Tchebytchef distance.

5.6.2.1. *Payoff matrix*

For each objective $(k, s_k) \ k = 1, \ldots, K+1$, $s_k = 1, \ldots, S_k$ and for each scenario $r, r = 1, \ldots, R$, the following single objective problem is solved

$$\begin{cases} \min z_{ks_k}(x) \\ T_r x + y^{(r)+} - y^{(r)-} = d_r \\ x \geq 0, \ y^{(r)+} \geq 0, \ y^{(r)-} \geq 0 \end{cases}$$

and an optimal solution $x_{ks_k}^{(r)}$ is obtained.

We define $\widetilde{x}_{ks_k}$ as the best solution $x_{ks_k}^{(r)}$ for the objective (k, s_k), i.e.

$$z_{ks_k}(\widetilde{x}_{ks_k}) = \min_{r \in \{1, \ldots, R\}} z_{ks_k}(x_{ks_k}^{(r)}).$$

This determines the coordinates of the ideal point in the objective space

$$M_{ks_k} = z_{ks_k}(\widetilde{x}_{ks_k})$$

which is the best possible value for the objective (k, s_k).

Remark 5.12. If $\widetilde{x}_{ks_k}$ is not an unique solution, the particular procedure described in section 5.2.3 is applied to remove the indetermination of a column of the payoff matrix. This happens frequently for the objective $(K+1, S_{K+1})$; effectively, there generally exists an infinity of feasible solutions for which the uncertain constraints are all satisfied $(y^{(r)-} = 0 \ \forall r)$, giving the optimal value zero for the objective z_{K+1}.

5.6.2.2. *Weights associated with the objectives*

Similarly to the STEM method (section 5.3.1), and with

$$m_{ks_k} = \max_{(lt_l)} z_{(ks_k)(lt_l)}$$

a variation coefficient (or technical weight) is associated with each objective

$$\pi_{ks_k} = \frac{\alpha_{ks_k}}{\sum_{k=1}^{K+1}\sum_{s_k=1}^{S_k} \alpha_{ks_k}}$$

with

$$\alpha_{ks_k} = \frac{m_{ks_k} - M_{ks_k}}{m_{ks_k}} \frac{1}{\| c_{ks_k} \|}.$$

5.6.2.3. *First compromise*

The first compromise is obtained by resolving the single objective problem

$$(P_0') \begin{bmatrix} \min M\delta - \sum_{k=1}^{K+1} \xi_k \\ \sum_{s_k=1}^{S_k} p_{ks_k}(c_{ks_k} x - M_{ks_k})\pi_{ks_k} \leq \delta - \xi_k \quad k = 1, \ldots, K+1 \\ (x, y^{(r)+}, y^{(r)-}) \in \mathcal{D}^{(0)}; \; \xi_k \geq 0 \quad k = 1, \ldots, K+1. \end{bmatrix}$$

Let $\tilde{x}^{(1)}$ be the optimal solution which is the first compromise.

5.6.3. *Interactive phases*

5.6.3.1. *Information given to the decision maker*

For each compromise $\tilde{x}^{(m)}$, two pieces of information are given to the decision maker:

1) The most important is the value obtained with this compromise by each objective (ks_k), i.e. the value of each initial objective k if the scenario s_k will be realized:

$$z_{ks_k}^{(m)} = z_{ks_k}(\tilde{x}^{(m)}) \quad k = 1, \ldots, K+1; \; s_k = 1, \ldots, S_k.$$

This information is given to the decision maker regarding the variation interval $[M_{ks_k}, m_{ks_k}]$ of this objective. They therefore obtain a complete view of the consequences of the compromise $\tilde{x}^{(m)}$.

2) In addition, the 'expected' value of each objective k can be provided:

$$\bar{z}_k^{(m)} = \sum_{s_k=1}^{S_k} p_{ks_k} z_{ks_k}^{(m)}.$$

250 Decision-making Process

Moreover, to facilitate the comparison of these values for the different objectives, it is useful for the decision maker to obtain (1) and (2) in relative values, i.e.

$$z'^{(m)}_{ks_k} = \frac{z^{(m)}_{ks_k} - M_{ks_k}}{m_{ks_k} - M_{ks_k}},$$

$$\bar{z}'^{(m)}_k = \frac{\bar{z}^{(m)}_k - \overline{M}_k}{\overline{m}_k - \overline{M}_k},$$

where

$$\overline{M}_k = \sum_{s_k=1}^{S_k} p_{ks_k} M_{ks_k},$$

$$\overline{m}_k = \sum_{s_k=1}^{S_k} p_{ks_k} m_{ks_k}.$$

The relative values 0 and 1 correspond to the ideal value and the worse value (in the payoff table), respectively.

5.6.3.2. *First interaction with the decision maker*

With this information, the decision maker must decide if the compromise is satisfying or if they want to determine a better compromise. For the latter case, they must indicate an objective $(ks_k)^*$ for which a relaxation will be accepted, i.e. a rise in the value $z^{(m)}_{(ks_k)^*}$. As far as possible, the decision maker is also asked to fix an upper bound $\Delta_{(ks_k)^*}$ of the value $z^{(m+1)}_{(ks_k)^*}$, so that this value will be in the interval

$$[z^{(m)}_{(ks_k)^*},\ \Delta_{(ks_k)^*}].$$

5.6.3.3. *Computational phase*

A parametric analysis is carried out to completely explore the road indicated by the decision maker, i.e. the consequences of each possible level of relaxation of the objective $(ks_k)^*$. With the notation

$$M_{(ks_k)^*} + \underline{\lambda}(m_{(ks_k)^*} - M_{(ks_k)^*}) = z^{(m)}_{(ks_k)^*},$$

$$M_{(ks_k)^*} + \overline{\lambda}(m_{(ks_k)^*} - M_{(ks_k)^*}) = \Delta_{(ks_k)^*},$$

the possible values for $z^{(m+1)}_{(ks_k)^*}$ correspond to the values $\lambda \in [\underline{\lambda}, \overline{\lambda}]$ of the parameter λ. The single objective parametric linear programming problem

$$(P'_m)\ \begin{bmatrix} \min M\delta - \sum_{k=1}^{K+1} \xi_k \\ \sum_{s_k=1}^{S_k} p_{ks_k}(c_{ks_k}\,x - M_{ks_k})\pi_{ks_k} \leq \delta - \xi_k \quad k=1,\ldots,K+1 \\ c_{(ks_k)^*}\,x = M_{(ks_k)^*} + \lambda(m_{(ks_k)^*} - M_{(ks_k)^*}) \quad \underline{\lambda} \leq \lambda \leq \overline{\lambda} \\ (x, y^{(r)+}, y^{(r)-}) \in \mathcal{D}^{(m)};\ \xi_k \geq 0 \quad k=1,\ldots,K+1 \end{bmatrix}$$

is considered.

For the definition of $\mathcal{D}^{(m)}$, two options are proposed to the decision maker corresponding to the introduction, or not, of restrictive constraints (see section 5.3.1).

5.6.3.3.1. *Option (a): with restrictive constraints.*

$\mathcal{D}^{(m)}$ is defined by

$$\mathcal{D}^{(m)} = \mathcal{D}^{(m-1)} \cap \{x \mid z_{(ks_k)^*}(x) \leq z_{(ks_k)^*}(\widetilde{x^{(m)}})\}$$

and, simultaneously, the weight $\pi_{(ks_k)^*}$ is set definitively to zero for all of the remaining procedure. The number of interactive phases is therefore limited to a maximal number of

$$\sum_{k=1}^{K+1} S_k$$

iterations.

5.6.3.3.2. *Option (b): without restrictive constraints.*

In this case,

$$\mathcal{D}^{(m)} = \mathcal{D}^{(0)} \quad \forall m$$

and the weight $\pi_{(ks_k)^*}$ is set to zero, but only during the mth iteration corresponding to the relaxation of the objective $(ks_k)^*$. After this, its value is re-established, here the number of iterations is no longer limited.

The parametric problem (P'_m) is solved by the dual simplex algorithm: the optimal solution $x^{(m+1)}(\lambda)$ is determined by the sequence of stability intervals of the optimal basis corresponding to the bounds

$$\underline{\lambda} = \lambda_0 < \lambda_1 < \cdots < \lambda_p = \overline{\lambda}.$$

For each objective (ks_k) $k = 1, \ldots, K+1$; $s_k = 1, \ldots, S_k$, we therefore obtain the values

$$z_{(ks_k)}(x^{(m+1)}(\lambda)) \quad \underline{\lambda} \leq \lambda \leq \overline{\lambda}.$$

These values are presented numerically and graphically to the decision maker: they are piecewise linear with constant slope on each interval:

$$[\lambda_{i-1}, \lambda_i] \quad i = 1, \ldots, p.$$

To make the task of the decision maker easier (see section 5.6.3.3.3), the relative values of each objective are presented simultaneously with the same scale on a unique figure. The decision maker therefore obtains a complete, precise and easy view of the possible consequences of the choice they must make (see Figure 5.12, a numerical illustration described in [TEG 03]).

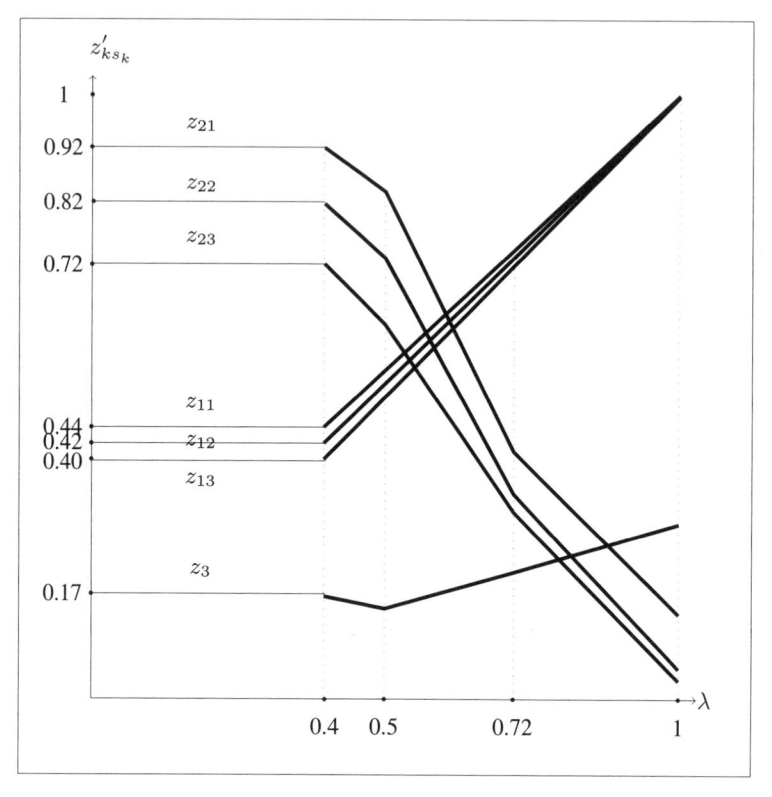

Figure 5.12. *Parametric analysis of an interactive phase for a numerical example* ($K = 2, S_k = 3, k = 1, 2$; *relaxation of* z_{13})

5.6.3.3.3. Option (c): second interaction with the decision maker.

With such complete information, the decision maker must fix the level $\tilde{\lambda} \in [\underline{\lambda}, \overline{\lambda}]$ of relaxation preferred so that the new compromise is more satisfying:

$$\widetilde{x^{(m+1)}} = x^{(m+1)}(\tilde{\lambda}).$$

Remark 5.13. To close this section, we indicate some research concerning MOSLP:

– A monograph [SLO 90] has been devoted to these models and also to those where the data are fuzzy numbers (see section 5.7). In particular, the reader can find a more theoretical review of MOSLP problems [SLO 90, Chapter II.1], an extension of the STRANGE method to problems with integer variables [SLO 90, Chapter II.2] and the treatment of models in which the information on the random variables is not complete in [SLO 90, Chapter II.4] (see also [NAD 94, URL 90]).

– In many applications, it appears difficult to estimate the realizations of the scenarios. In this case, the only available information is the variation intervals of the coefficients; such a situation is analyzed in [CHA 96, TEG 94, URL 92].

– Teghem [TEG 94] also proposes an approach for the case where the scenarios (corresponding to possible states of the nature) are globally defined for all the coefficients in the objectives as well as in the constraints.

5.7. The multiple objective fuzzy linear programming

The fuzzy modelization craze in many scientific fields during the past two decades was remarkable; decision aiding is just one example. This approach allows us to model uncertainty when it is more related to an imprecision of definition or understanding of the data than to a random nature. Its success is due to a pragmatic ease of modelization and treatment, as well as to the results obtained.

There are several books concerning fuzzy modelization (in particular those of [DUB 80, SLO 98]). Some of the literature treat, more specifically, multiple objective fuzzy linear programming (MOFLP) problems of the type

$$\begin{array}{l} \text{`min'} \quad z_k(x) = \widetilde{c}_k x \quad k = 1, \ldots, K \\ x \in D = \{x | \widetilde{T} x \leq \widetilde{d}, \ x \geq 0\} \end{array} \quad (5.40)$$

where elements of $\widetilde{c}$, $\widetilde{T}$ and $\widetilde{d}$ are fuzzy numbers [SLO 90, Chapters 1, 3], [LAI 92], [EHR 02, Chapter 4] and [TEG 03, Chapters 10, 11].

It is not possible to present a survey of these numerous references. As in the previous section, we simply discuss one recent method which appears attractive and easy to implement. For similar reasons as explained in the previous section, an MOFLP problem is badly defined and it is necessary to define a crisp (or deterministic) equivalent problem. The different methods essentially differ by the following:

– in comparing two fuzzy numbers to determine the constraints of the equivalent problem; and

– in treating the optimization of a fuzzy number to determine the objective function(s) of the equivalent problem.

We describe the answers to these questions regarding the multi-objective fuzzy area compensation (MOFAC) method [FOR 01] in the following section.

5.7.1. *Comparison of two fuzzy numbers*

It is therefore necessary to analyze the relations $\widetilde{a} \leq \widetilde{b}$, $\widetilde{a} = \widetilde{b}$, $\widetilde{a} \geq \widetilde{b}$ where $\widetilde{a}$ and $\widetilde{b}$ are two fuzzy numbers, supposed normalized and convex, which in equation (5.40)

(MOFLP) correspond to the left hand side ($\sum_{j=1}^{n} \tilde{t}_{ij} x_j$) and to the right hand side ($\tilde{d}_i$) of a fuzzy constraint, respectively.

5.7.1.1. *Area compensation*

The idea proposed by Fortemps and Roubens [FOR 96] consists of analyzing the global area defined by the membership functions of $\tilde{a}$ and $\tilde{b}$. If $[\underline{a}_\alpha, \overline{a}_\alpha]$ and $[\underline{b}_\alpha, \overline{b}_\alpha]$ are the α-cuts of $\tilde{a}$ and $\tilde{b}$, this area, denoted $S(\tilde{a}, \tilde{b})$, is defined by

$$S(\tilde{a}, \tilde{b}) = \int_0^1 \left(\max(\overline{a}_\alpha, \overline{b}_\alpha) - \min(\underline{a}_\alpha, \underline{b}_\alpha) \right) d\alpha$$

corresponding to the sum of the areas numbered 1–6 in Figure 5.13.

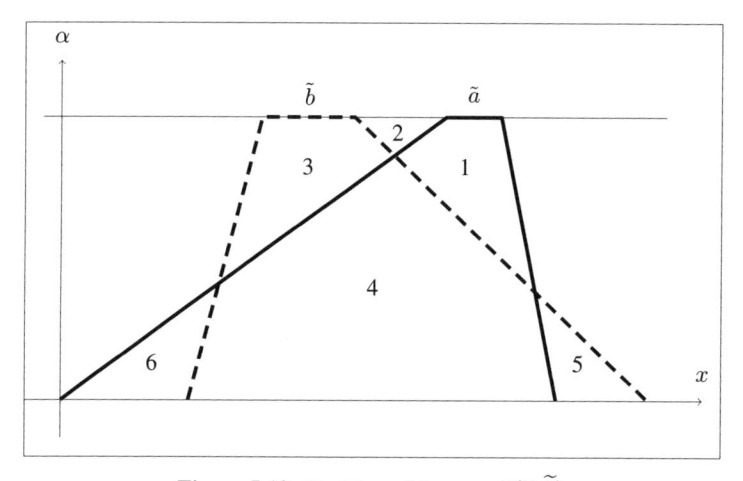

Figure 5.13. *Partition of the area* $S(\tilde{a}, \tilde{b})$

This global area is separated into three parts: $S(\tilde{a} > \tilde{b})$, $S(\tilde{a} = \tilde{b})$, $S(\tilde{a} < \tilde{b})$, favorable to the relations $\tilde{a} > \tilde{b}, \tilde{a} = \tilde{b}, \tilde{a} < \tilde{b}$ respectively, such that

$$S(\tilde{a}, \tilde{b}) = S(\tilde{a} > \tilde{b}) + S(\tilde{a} = \tilde{b}) + S(\tilde{a} < \tilde{b})$$

where

$$S(\tilde{a} > \tilde{b}) = \int_0^1 \left(\overline{a}_\alpha - \min(\overline{a}_\alpha, \overline{b}_\alpha) + \underline{a}_\alpha - \min(\underline{a}_\alpha, \underline{b}_\alpha) \right) d\alpha$$

$$S(\tilde{a} = \tilde{b}) = \int_0^1 \left(\min(\overline{a}_\alpha, \overline{b}_\alpha) - \max(\underline{a}_\alpha, \underline{b}_\alpha) \right) d\alpha.$$

Geometrically, these three numbers correspond to the areas of Figure 5.13 as follows:

$$\begin{aligned} S(\tilde{a} > \tilde{b}) &= \text{area}(1) + \text{area}(3) + 2 \times \text{area}(2) \\ S(\tilde{a} = \tilde{b}) &= \text{area}(4) - \text{area}(2) \\ S(\tilde{a} < \tilde{b}) &= \text{area}(5) + \text{area}(6). \end{aligned}$$

To obtain three normalized indices measuring the intensity of these three relations, the following definitions are introduced:

$$\begin{aligned} I(\tilde{a} > \tilde{b}) &= \frac{S(\tilde{a} > \tilde{b})}{S(\tilde{a}, \tilde{b}) + S(\tilde{a} = \tilde{b})} \\ I(\tilde{a} = \tilde{b}) &= \frac{2S(\tilde{a} = \tilde{b})}{S(\tilde{a}, \tilde{b}) + S(\tilde{a} = \tilde{b})} \\ I(\tilde{a} < \tilde{b}) &= \frac{S(\tilde{a} < \tilde{b})}{S(\tilde{a}, \tilde{b}) + S(\tilde{a} = \tilde{b})} \end{aligned}$$

so that

$$I(\tilde{a} > \tilde{b}) + I(\tilde{a} = \tilde{b}) + I(\tilde{a} < \tilde{b}) = 1.$$

It must be noted that these three indices are not necessarily included in the interval $[0, 1]$ and that they can either be strictly greater than 1 or negative. We also introduce

$$I(\tilde{a} \neq \tilde{b}) = 1 - I(\tilde{a} = \tilde{b}) = I(\tilde{a} > \tilde{b}) + I(\tilde{a} < \tilde{b}).$$

Although these indices appear difficult to calculate (due to the minimum and maximum operators used in their definition formula), this is not the case (see section 5.7.1.2 below) for the indices

$$I(\tilde{a} \geq \tilde{b}) = I(\tilde{a} > \tilde{b}) + \frac{1}{2}I(\tilde{a} = \tilde{b})$$

where

$$I(\tilde{a} \geq \tilde{b}) + I(\tilde{a} \leq \tilde{b}) = 1.$$

These definitions give coherent values for the comparison of a fuzzy number $\tilde{a}$ with itself as

$$I(\tilde{a} > \tilde{a}) = I(\tilde{a} \neq \tilde{a}) = 0;\ I(\tilde{a} = \tilde{a}) = 1;\ I(\tilde{a} \geq \tilde{a}) = \frac{1}{2}.$$

5.7.1.2. *Determination of $I(\tilde{a} \geq \tilde{b})$*

The reason to not state in the definitions above that the values of the indices belong to the interval $[0, 1]$ is that we can derive an easy formula to calculate these values. If we set

$$E_*(\tilde{a}) = \int_0^1 \underline{a}_\alpha \, d\alpha$$
$$E^*(\tilde{a}) = \int_0^1 \overline{a}_\alpha \, d\alpha$$
$$\text{and} \quad \mathcal{F}(\tilde{a}) = \tfrac{1}{2}(E_*(\tilde{a}) + E^*(\tilde{a})),$$

taking into account $\min(x, y) + \max(x, y) = x + y$, then

$$I(\tilde{a} \geq \tilde{b}) = \frac{E^*(\tilde{a}) - E_*(\tilde{b})}{(E^*(\tilde{a}) - E_*(\tilde{a})) + (E^*(\tilde{b}) - E_*(\tilde{b}))}$$

or

$$I(\tilde{a} \geq \tilde{b}) = \frac{1}{2} + \frac{\mathcal{F}(\tilde{a}) - \mathcal{F}(\tilde{b})}{(E^*(\tilde{a}) - E_*(\tilde{a})) + (E^*(\tilde{b}) - E_*(\tilde{b}))}.$$

Finally, we derive

$$I(\tilde{a} \geq \tilde{b}) \geq \frac{1}{2} \iff \mathcal{F}(\tilde{a}) \geq \mathcal{F}(\tilde{b}).$$

$E_*(\tilde{a})$ and $E^*(\tilde{a})$ correspond to the hatched areas of Figure 5.14a and b, respectively.

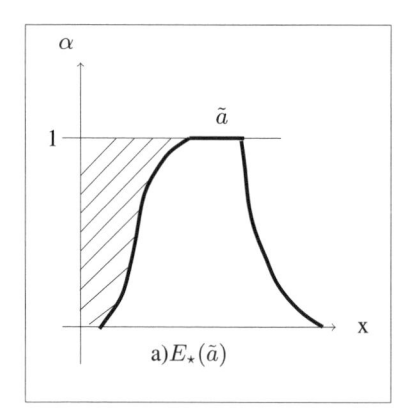

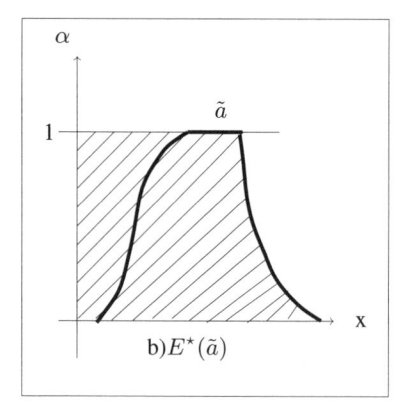

Figure 5.14. *The areas $E_*(\tilde{a})$ and $E^*(\tilde{a})$*

If we interpret a fuzzy number as a feasible set of probability distributions, the interval $[E_*(\tilde{a}), E^*(\tilde{a})]$ can be viewed as the interval of the expected values of these distributions [DUB 87]. The function $\mathcal{F}$, defining the middle of this interval, then appears as a 'defuzzyfication' function which gives a natural order on the set of fuzzy numbers. Moreover [FOR 96], this function is linear, verifying

$$\mathcal{F}(c\tilde{a}) = c\mathcal{F}(\tilde{a})$$
$$\mathcal{F}(\tilde{a}+\tilde{b}) = \mathcal{F}(\tilde{a}) + \mathcal{F}(\tilde{b})$$

5.7.1.3. *Equivalent crisp constraint*

The principle described above allows the transformation of a fuzzy constraint

$$\sum_{j=1}^{n} \tilde{t}_{ij} x_j \leq \tilde{d}_i$$

into a crisp constraint, if a satisfaction level σ_i is fixed. It is only necessary to impose

$$I\left(\sum_{j=1}^{n} \tilde{t}_{ij} x_j \geq \tilde{d}_i\right) \geq \sigma_i$$

and, due to the linearity of the operators E_* and E^* and the non-negativity of the variables x_j, this corresponds to

$$\frac{E^*(\tilde{d}_i) - \sum_{j=1}^{n} E_*(\tilde{t}_{ij}) x_j}{E^*(\tilde{d}_i) - E_*(\tilde{d}_i) + \sum_{j=1}^{n} \left(E^*(\tilde{t}_{ij}) - E_*(\tilde{t}_{ij})\right) x_j} \geq \sigma_i$$

or

$$\sum_{j=1}^{n} \left(\sigma_i E^*(\tilde{t}_{ij}) + (1-\sigma_i) E_*(\tilde{t}_{ij})\right) x_j \leq \sigma_i E_*(\tilde{d}_i) + (1-\sigma_i) E^*(\tilde{d}_i).$$

Note that the particular value $\sigma_i = 1/2$ which appears quite logical, simply corresponds to

$$\sum_{j=1}^{n} \mathcal{F}(\tilde{t}_{ij}) x_j \leq \mathcal{F}(\tilde{d}_i)$$

i.e. to the application of the 'defuzzyfication' function $\mathcal{F}$ to the initial fuzzy constraint.

5.7.2. *Treatment of a fuzzy objective function*

In the spirit of the area compensation described in section 5.7.1, a fuzzy objective function

$$\tilde{z}_k(x) = \sum_{j=1}^{n} \tilde{c}_{kj} x_j$$

can be transformed into a crisp objective function by application of the 'defuzzyfication' function $\mathcal{F}$, i.e.

$$z_k(x) = \sum_{j=1}^{n} \mathcal{F}\left(\widetilde{c}_{kj}\right) x_j.$$

5.7.3. *The crisp (deterministic) equivalent problem*

Combining sections 5.7.1 and 5.7.2, we obtain a MOLP problem of the same dimension. It is especially easy to formulate if all the satisfaction levels are fixed to $1/2$. This problem can then be treated by any method for a MOLP problem.

To highlight the simplicity of this approach, note that other methods proposed to tackle MOFLP problems either require the introduction of many parameters, produce a nonlinear crisp equivalent problem or, if the crisp problem is linear, increase its dimension compared to the dimension of the initial problem.

Among the numerous methods discussed, we can also mention the fuzzy linear programming (FLIP) method of Slowinski [SLO 86], [SLO 90, Chapter 2.3] and the fuzzy linear programming based on aspiration levels (FULPAL) method of Rommelfanger [SLO 90, Chapter 3.5].

5.8. Conclusion

Unbelievably, it is quite impossible to treat all multiple objective programming and its various extensions in a single chapter. Nevertheless, we hope to have introduced the reader to this field and its many parts (except for nonlinear programming). Each section provides a good introduction to the existing literature, but to obtain a deeper knowledge, the specialist books and survey papers cited in each section must be read also. Attention has been focused on the methodologies and their main principles, without mention of the several possible applications. The reader can refer to [WHI 90] for a sample of these applications.

5.9. Bibliography

[BEN 99] BEN ABDELAZIZ F., CHOACHI J., KRICHEN S. A hybrid heuristic for multiobjective knapsack problems. In S. Voss, S. Martello, I. Osman, C. Roucairol (eds), *Meta-Heuristics: Advances and Trends in Local Search Paradigms for Optimization*, Kluwer Academic Publisher, Dordrecht, pp. 205–212 (1999).

[BENA 71] BENAYOUN R., DE MONTGOLFIER J., TERGNY J., LARICHEV O. Linear programming with multiple objective functions: Step method (STEM). *Mathematical Programming* 1(2), 366–373 (1971).

[BIR 97] BIRGE J.R., LOUVEAUX F. *Introduction to Stochastic Programming,* Springer-Verlag, Berlin (1997).

[CAR 90] CARRAWAY R.L., MORIN T.L., MOSKOVITZ H. Generalized dynamic programming for multicriteria optimization. *European Journal of Operational Research,* 44, 95–104 (1990).

[CHA 96] CHANAS S., KUTCHA D. Multiobjective programming in optimization of interval objective function: A generalized approach. *European Journal of Operational Research* 94, 594–598 (1996).

[CLI 97] CLÍMACO J., FERREIRA C., CAPTIVO M.E. Multicriteria integer programming: An overview of the different algorithmic approaches. In J. Climaco (ed), *Multicriteria Analysis,* Springer Verlag, Berlin, pp. 248–258 (1997).

[COE 02] COELLO COELLO C.A., VAN VELDHUIZEN D.A., LAMON G.B. *Evolutionary Algorithms for Solving Multi-objective Problems.* Kluwer Academic Publishers, New York (2002).

[COE 08] COELLO COELLO C.A.
http://www.lania.mx/~coello/EMOO/EMOObib.html (2008).

[COL 02] COLLETTE Y., SIARRY P. *Optimisation Multiobjectif,* Editions Eyrolles, Paris (2002).

[CUR 90] CURRENT J., MIN H., SCHILLING D. Multiobjective analysis of facility location decisions. *European Journal of Operational Research,* 49, 295–307 (1990).

[CUR 93] CURRENT J., MARSH M. Multiobjective transportation network design: taxonomy and annotation. *European Journal of Operational Research,* 65, 4–19 (1993).

[CZY 96] CZYZAK P., JASZKIEWICZ A. A multiobjective metaheuristic approach to the localisation of a chain of petrol stations by the capital budgeting model. *Control and Cybernetics,* 25, 177–187 (1996).

[CZY 98] CZYZAK P., JASZKIEWICZ A. Pareto simulated annealing: a metaheuristic technique for multiple objective combinatorial optimization. *Journal of Multi-Criteria Decision Analysis,* 7, 34–47 (1998).

[DEB 00] DEB K. *Multi-objective Optimization using Evolutionary Algorithms.* John Wiley & Sons, Chichester, UK (2000).

[DEB 01] DEB K., AGRAWAL S., PRATAB A., MEYARIVAN T. A Fast Elitist Non-Dominated Sorting Genetic Algorithm for Multi-objective optimization: NSGA-II. In *Proceedings of the Parallel Problem Solving from Nature VI Conference,* Springer, Berlin, pp. 849–858 (2001).

[DUB 80] DUBOIS D., PRADE H. *Fuzzy Sets and Systems Theory: Theory and Applications.* Academic Press, London (1980).

[DUB 87] DUBOIS D., PRADE H. The mean value of a fuzzy number. *Fuzzy Sets and Systems,* 24, 279–300 (1987).

[EHR 02] EHRGOTT M., GANDIBLEUX X. *Multiple Criteria Optimization: State of the Art and Annotated Bibliographic Surveys.* Kluwer Academic Publisher, Dordrecht (2002).

[FOR 96] FORTEMPS PH., ROUBENS M. Ranking and defuzzification methods based on area compensation. *Fuzzy Sets and Systems*, 82, 319–330 (1996).

[FOR 01] FORTEMPS PH., TEGHEM J. *Multi-objective Fuzzy Linear Programming: The MOFAC Method in Preferences and Decisions under Incomplete Knowledge,* J. Fodor, B. de Baets and P. Perny (Eds), Physica-Verlag, New York pp. 11–32 (2001).

[GAN 97] GANDIBLEUX X., MEZDAOUI N., FRÉVILLE A. A tabu search procedure to solve multiobjective combinatorial optimization propblems. In R. Caballero, F. Ruiz and R. Steuer (eds), *Advances in Multiple Objective and Goal Programming*, vol. 455, Lectures Notes in Economics and Mathematical Systems, Springer-Verlag, Berlin, 291–300 (1997).

[GAN 00] GANDIBLEUX X., FRÉVILLE A. Tabu search based procedure for solving the 0/1 multiobjective knapsack problem: the two objective case. *Journal of Heuristics*, 6(3), 361–383 (2000).

[GEO 72] GEOFFRION A.M., DYER J.S., FEINBERG A. An interactive approach for multicriterion optimization. *Management Science*, 19(4), 357–368 (1972).

[GOI 82] GOICOECHA A., HANSEN D.R., DUCKSTEIN L. *Multiobjective Decision Analysis with Engineering and Business Application,* John Wiley, New York (1982).

[GOM 04] GOMEZ DA SILVA C., CLÍMACO J., FIGUEIRA J. A scatter search method for bi-criteria multidimensional $\{0, 1\}$-knapsack problem using surrogate relaxation. *Journal of Mathematical Modelling and Algorithms*, 3(3), 183–208 (2004).

[GOM 05] GOMEZ DA SILVA C., CLÍMACO J., FIGUEIRA J. A scatter search method for bi-criteria knapsack problems. *European Journal of Operational Research*, 169(2), 373–391 (2005).

[GON 85] GONZALES J.J., REEVES G.R., FRANZ L.S. An Interactive Procedure for Solving Multiple Objective Integer Linear Programming Problems. In Haimes Y. and Chankong (eds), *Decision Making with Multiple Objectives*, Springer-Verlag, Berlin, pp. 250–260 (1985).

[HAN 00] HANSEN M.P. Tabu search for multiobjective combinatorial optimization: TAMOCO. *Control and Cybernetics*, 29(3), 799–818 (2000).

[HAP 98] HAPKE M., JASZKIEWICZ A., SLOWINSKI R. Interactive analysis of multiple-criteria project scheduling problems. *European Journal of Operational Research*, 107(2), 315–324 (1998).

[ISH 98] ISHIBUCHI H., MURATA T. Multi-Objective Genetic Local Search Algorithm and Its Application to Flowshop Scheduling. *IEEE Transactions on Systems, Man and Cybernetics Part C: Applications and Reviews*, 28(3), 392–403 (1998).

[JAS 97] JASZKIEWICZ A. A metaheuristic approach to multiple objective nurse scheduling. *Foundation of Computing and Decision Sciences Journal*, 22(3), 169–184 (1997).

[JAS 02] JASZKIEWICZ A. Genetic local search for multiple objective combinatorial optimization. *European Journal of Operational Research*, 137(1), 50–71 (2002).

[JAS 08] JASZKIEZWICZ A. http://www.idss.cs.put.poznan.pl/jaszkiewicz/MOMHLib/ (2008).

[KIZ 83] KIZILTAN G., YUCAOĞLU E. An Algorithm for Multiobjective Zero: One Linear Programming. *Management Science*, 29(12), 1444–1453 (1983).

[KOR 86] KORHONEN, P. LAASKO, J. A visual interactive method for solving the multiple criteria problems. *European Journal of Operational Research*, 14, 277–287 (1986).

[KLE 82] KLEIN D., HANNAN E. An Algorithm for Multiple Objective Integer Linear Programming Problem. *European Journal of Operational Research*, 9, 378-385 (1982).

[KUN 87] KUNSCH P.L., TEGHEM J. Nuclear fuel cycle optimization using multiobjective linear programming. *European Journal of Operational Research*, 31, 240-249 (1987).

[LAI 92] LAI Y.J., HWANG C.L. Fuzzy Mathematical Programming: methods and applications. *Lecture Notes in Economics and Mathematical Systems*, no. 394, Springer-Verlag, Berlin (1992).

[LHO 95] L'HOIR H., TEGHEM J. Portfolio selection by MOLP using an interactive Branch and Bound. *Foundations of Computing and Decision Sciences*, 20(3), 175–185, (1995).

[LOU 02] LOUKIL T., TEGHEM J., TUYTTENS D. Solving multi-objective production scheduling problems using metaheuristics. *European Journal of Operational Research*, 161, 42–61 (2005).

[LOU 03] LOUKIL T., TEGHEM J. Multiple criteria production scheduling problems. A literature survey and classified bibliography. Technical Report Polytechnique Faculty of Mons (2003).

[MAR 86] MARCOTTE O., SOLAND R.M. An Interactive Branch-and-Bound Algorithm for Multiple Criteria Optimization. *Management Science*, 32, 1, 61–75 (1986).

[MAR 90] MARTELLO S., TOTH P. *Knapsack Problems: Algorithms and Computer implementations*. John Wiley & Sons, New York (1990).

[MUR 00] MURATA T., ISHIBUCHI H. Cellulary genetic local search for multi-objective optimization. *Proceedings of the Genetic Evolutionary Computation Conference* 2000, 307–314 (2000).

[NAD 94] NADEAU R., URLI B., KISS LASZLO N. Promise: a DSS for multiple objective stochastic linear programming problems. *Annals of Operations Research*, 51, 45–59 (1994).

[PIR 03] PIRLOT M., TEGHEM J. *Résolution de problèmes de recherche opérationnelle par les métaheuristiques*. Traité IC2, Hermes (2003).

[ROY 76] ROY B. From optimization to multicriteria decision aid: three main operational attitudes. In Thiriez, H. and Zionts, S. (eds). *Multiple Criteria Decision Making Lecture Notes in Economics and Mathematical Systems*, 130, Springer-Verlag, Berlin, 1–30 (1976).

[ROY 85] ROY B. *Méthodologie multicritère d'aide à la décision*. Economica, Paris, 1985.

[ROY 93] ROY B., BOUYSSOU D. *Aide multicritère à la décision: méthodes et cas*. Economica, Paris (1993).

[SKI 00] SKRIVER A.J.V. A classification of bicriteria shortest path (BSP) algorithms. *Asia-Pacific Journal of Operational Research*, 17(2), 199–212 (2000).

[SLO 86] SLOWINSKI R. A multicriteria fuzzy linear programming method for water supply system development planning. *Fuzzy Sets and Systems*, 19, 217-237 (1986).

[SLO 90] SLOWINSKI R., TEGHEM J. *Stochastic versus Fuzzy Approaches to Multiobjective Mathematical Programming under Uncertainty.* Kluwer Academic Publisher, Dordrecht (1990).

[SLO 98] SLOWINSKI R. Fuzzy sets in decision analysis, operations research and statistics. In *Operations Research and Statistics*. Kluwer Academic Publisher, Dordrecht (1998).

[SRI 94] SRINIVAS N., DEB K. Multiple objective optimization using nondominated sorting in genetic algorithms. *Evolutionary Computation*, 2(2), 239–254 (1994).

[STE 86] STEUER R. *Multiple Criteria Optimization: Theory, Computation and Application*. Wiley (1986).

[SYL 04] SYLVA J., CREMA A. A method for finding the set of non dominated solutions for multiple objective integer linear programs. *European Journal of Operational Research*, 158, 46–55 (2004).

[TEG 85] TEGHEM J., KUNSCH P.L. Multi-objective decision making under uncertainty: an example for power systems. In Haimes Y.Y. and Chankong V. (Eds), *Decision Making with Multiple Objective*, pp. 443–456, Springer-Verlag, Berlin (1985).

[TEG 86a] TEGHEM J., KUNSCH P. Interactive methods for multi-objective integer linear programming. In G.Fandel *et al.*, *Lecture Notes in Economics and Mathematical Systems*, vol. 273, pages 75–86. Springer-Verlag, Berlin (1986).

[TEG 86b] TEGHEM J., KUNSCH P. Survey of techniques to determine the efficient solutions for multi-objective integer linear programming. *Asia-Pacific Journal of Operation Research*, 3, 95–108, 1986.

[TEG 86c] TEGHEM J., DUFRANE D., THAUVOYE M., KUNSCH P.L. 'STRANGE': an interactive method for multi-objective linear programming under uncertainty. *European Journal of Operational Research*, 26, 65–82 (1986).

[TEG 94] TEGHEM J. New developments in multiobjective stochastic linear programming. In Skiadas C. and Jansen J. (Eds), *Applied Stochastic Models and Data Analysis*, pp. 938–948 (1994).

[TEG 00] TEGHEM J., ULUNGU E.L., TUYTTENS D. An interactive heuristic method for multi-objective combinatorial optimization. *Computers & Operations Research*, 27, 621–634 (2000).

[TEG 02] TEGHEM J., PIRLOT M. *Optimisation Approchée en Recherche Opérationnelle.* Traité IC2. Hermes (2002).

[TEG 03] TEGHEM J. *Programmation linéaire (2nd edition).* Collection Statistique et Mathématiques Appliquées. Editions de l'Université de Bruxelles et Ellipses (2003).

[TKI 02] T'KINDT V., BILLAUT J. CH. *Multicriteria Scheduling.* Springer-Verlag, Berlin (2002).

[TUY 00] TUYTTENS D., TEGHEM J., FORTEMPS PH. , VAN NIEUWENHUYZE P. Performance of the mosa method for the bicriteria assignment problem. *Journal of Heuristics*, 6, 295–310, 2000.

[ULU 91] ULUNGU E.L., TEGHEM J. Multi-objective shortest path problems: a survey. In D. Glückaufova *et al.* (Eds). *Proceedings of the International Workshop on MCDM*, pp.176–178, Institute of Economics, Czechoslovak Academy of Sciences, Prague, 1991.

[ULU 94a] ULUNGU E.L., TEGHEM J. Multi-objective combinatorial optimization problems: A survey. *Journal of Multi-Criteria Decision Analysis*, 3, 83–104, 1994.

[ULU 94b] ULUNGU E.L., TEGHEM J. The two-phases method: an efficient procedure to solve bi-objective combinatorial optimization problem. *Foundations of Computing and Decision Sciences*, 20(2), 149–165, 1994.

[ULU 95] ULUNGU E.L., TEGHEM J., FORTEMPS PH. Heuristics for multiobjective combinatorial optimization problems by simulated annealing. In Wei Q. *et al.* (Eds) *MCDM: Theory and Applications*, pp. 218–238, Sci-Tech. Information Services, Windsor, UK, 1995.

[ULU 97] ULUNGU E.L., TEGHEM J. Solving multi-objective knapsack problem by a branch-and-bound procedure. In J.N. Clímaco, *Multicriteria Analysis*, pages 269–278. Springer-Verlag, Berlin 1997.

[ULU 98] ULUNGU E.L., TEGHEM J., OST CH. Efficiency of interactive multi-objective simulated annealing through a case study. *Journal of the Operational Research Society*, 49, 1044–1050 (1998).

[ULU 99] ULUNGU E.L., TEGHEM J., FORTEMPS PH. , TUYTTENS D. Mosa method: a tool for solving multiobjective combinatorial optimization problems. *Journal of Multi-Criteria Decision Analysis*, 8, 221–236, 1999.

[URL 90] URLI B., NADEAU R. Stochastic MOLP with incomplete information: an interactive approach with recourse. *Journal of Operational Research Society*, 41(12), 1143–1152 (1990).

[URL 92] URLI B. An interactive method to multiobjective linear programming problems with interval coefficients. *INFOR*, 30(2), 127–137 (1992).

[VAN 89] VANDERPOOTEN, D., VINCKE, PH. Description and analysis of some representative interactive multicriteria procedures. *Mathematical and Computer Modelling*, 12(10–11), 1221–1238 (1989).

[VIA 00] VIANA A., PINHO DE SOUSA J. Using metaheuristics in multiobjective ressource constrained project scheduling. *European Journal of Operational Research*, 120(2), 359–374 (2000).

[VIN 92] VINCKE PH. *Multicriteria Decision Aid*. John Wiley & Sons, New York (1992).

[VIS 98] VISÉE M., TEGHEM J., PIRLOT M., ULUNGU E.L. Two-phases method and branch and bound to solve bi-objective knapsack problem. *Journal of Global Optimization*, 12, 139–155 (1998).

[WHI 90] WHITE D.J. A bibliography on the application of mathematical programming multiple objective methods. *Journal of the Operational Research Society*, 41(8), 669–691 (1990).

[WIE 82] Wierczbicki, A.P. A mathematical basis for satisficing decision making. *Mathematical Modelling*, 3, 391–405 (1982).

[WOL 98] WOLSEY L.A. *Integer Programming*. Series in Discrete Mathematics and Optimization. Wiley, Chichester (1998).

[ZIO 83] ZIONTS S., WALLENIUS J. An interactive multiple objective linear programming method for a class of underlying nonlinear utility functions. *Management Science*, 29(5), 519–529 (1983).

[ZIT 98] ZITZLER E., THIELE L. Multi objective Evolutionary Algorithms: A comparative case study and strength Pareto approach. *IEEE Transactions on Evolutionary Computation*, 3(4), 257–271 (1998).

Chapter 6

Constraint Satisfaction Problems

6.1. Introduction

Around 60 years ago, American scientists working at the frontier of mathematics and computer science had an idea. They decided that most of their logistics problems, such as the deployment of the American army raised just after the second world war, shared a common mathematical structure which justified their study globally to look for common algorithmic answers. Some years later, *linear programming* and the so-called *simplex* algorithm were born [DAN 63]. They paved the way for years of research and improvement and enabled the development of software tools which are now capable of exactly solving optimization problems, involving hundreds of thousands of real variables linked by linear constraints and a linear criterion.

30 years later, other scientists working in the area of artificial intelligence (AI) and, more specifically, in computer vision, had another idea. They concluded that another generic framework could be designed to represent arbitrary constraint satisfaction problems involving variables with finite domains. The *Constraint Satisfaction Problem* (CSP) was born [MAC 77a, MON 74, WAL 75]. Similarly to what happened with linear programming, the research which has organized itself around this problem has led to the development of efficient solving tools. These tools are now used in various domains such as planning, scheduling, resource management, design, configuration, computer vision, diagnosis, natural language processing, structure recognition, etc.

The CSP framework actually follows from two essential observations:

Chapter written by Gérard VERFAILLIE and Thomas SCHIEX.

– Many real problems involve nonlinear constraints which are not always conveniently represented or approximated by linear constraints. This is especially true if this transformation leads to an extreme increase in the problem size or to a unbearable distortion of the original problem. Despite its computational power, linear programing is inherently limited by its definition: all the constraints, as well as the optimization criterion, must be linear.

– In most real problems, constraints do not usually involve all the variables of the problem but only a small fraction of them. A global constraint satisfaction problem results from the conjunction of a large number of local constraints which are intimately interdependent in that they share one or more variables. In such a situation, local processing (even if relatively naive and simply enumerative because of the arbitrary form of the constraints) can exhibit good performances as long as the result of each processing is propagated in the network comprising variables and constraints.

The CSP framework allows either *decision* problems (deciding on the value of some variables according to a set of constraints and an optimization criterion) or *inference* problems (proving, from a set of constraints, that other constraints hold on some variables) to be both represented. In a decision problem, such as a configuration problem (configuration of a car or a kitchen, for example), the variables allow the possible choices (usable components together with their characteristics) to be represented. The constraints allow technological constraints (component incompatibilities, characteristics limitations) as well as user requirements to be captured. In an inference problem, such as a diagnosis problem, the variables allow observable parameters (alarms, test results) and non-observable parameters (component states) to be represented. The constraints can capture the existing knowledge of the system, i.e. relations between components and, for each component, relations between observable and non-observable parameters in normal and abnormal modes.

6.2. The CSP framework

There are four essential components in the CSP framework: the *variables*, their *domains*, the *constraints*, and their *relations*. A CSP instance can be defined by a 4-tuple (V, D, C, R) where:

– V is a sequence of n *variables*.

– D is a sequence of n *domains*. For every variable $v_i \in V$, $1 \leq i \leq n$, there is one associated domain $D_i \in D$ which represents all the possible values for v_i. These domains are finite but of an arbitrary nature, numerical or not (see section 6.10.1 for an extension to continuous domains).

– C is a sequence of e *constraints*. For every constraint $c_j \in C$, $1 \leq j \leq e$, there is one associated sub-sequence V_j of V which represents the variables that are involved in c_j.

– R is a sequence of e *relations*. For every constraint $c_j \in C$, $1 \leq j \leq e$, there is one associated relation $R_j \in R$ on the domains of the variables in V_j. This relation defines a subset of the Cartesian product of the domains of the variables in V_j, which itself represents all the combinations of values for the variables in V_j that are allowed by c_j. These relations are absolutely arbitrary. They can be defined in *extension* by the explicit list of all the allowed (or forbidden) combinations of values, or in *intension* by an equation involving the variables in V_j. More generally, they can also be defined by a Boolean function (or *characteristic function*) f_j. This may have the form of a computer code which takes as an input a combination of values of the variables in V_j. It outputs *true* or *false* according to the satisfaction of constraint c_j by the input combination of values.

6.2.1. *Syntactical part*

V and C represent the so-called *syntactical* part or, more adequately, the *structural* part of a CSP instance. It can be represented as an undirected (hyper)graph whose vertices are the variables in V and (hyper)edges are the constraints in C. This (hyper)graph is often called the *constraint graph* or the instance *macrostructure*. Figure 6.1 shows the macrostucture associated with a CSP instance involving 4 variables and 4 constraints: 3 binary constraints (c_1 involving variables v_1 and v_2, c_2 involving v_2 and v_4 and c_3 involving v_3 and v_4) and one ternary constraint (c_4 involving variables v_1, v_2, and v_3). We define the *arity* a_j of a constraint c_j as the number of variables it involves: $a_j = |V_j|$. We define the *degree* d_i of a variable v_i as the number of constraints that involve it: $d_i = \sum_{c_j \in C}(v_i \in V_j)$. In the example of Figure 6.1, constraint c_4 has arity 3 and variable v_1 has degree 2.

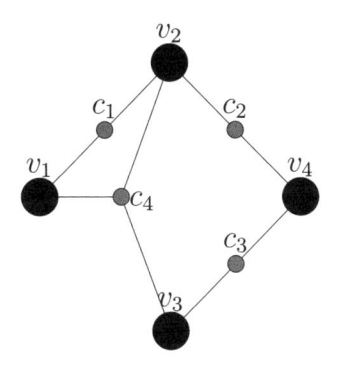

Figure 6.1. *An example of macrostructure*

6.2.2. *Semantical part*

D and R represent the so-called *semantical* part of a CSP instance. Similarly to the syntactical part, it can be represented as a n-partite undirected (hyper)graph. (An undirected (hyper)graph is said to be n-partite if and only if there exists a partition of its vertices such that every (hyper)edge connects only vertices from different elements of the partition.) This hypergraph has vertices which are the possible values in the domains of D, the elements of the partition are the domains themselves and the (hyper)edges are the allowed combinations of values in the relations of R.

This (hyper)graph is often called the *consistency graph* or the *microstructure*. Figure 6.2 shows the microstructure associated with a CSP instance whose macrostructure is that of Figure 6.1. For the sake of readability, the (hyper)edges that represent combinations of values that are allowed because of the absence of constraint are omitted. Because there is no constraint between v_1 and v_3, all the possible combinations of values of both variables are implicitly allowed but they are not explicitly represented. As an example, the domain associated with variable v_4 is $\{1, 2, 3\}$. The relation associated with constraint c_2 between variables v_2 and v_4 is defined by the inequation $v_2 < v_4$, which allows the pairs of values $(1, 2)$, $(1, 3)$ and $(2, 3)$. The relation associated with constraint c_4 between variables v_1, v_2 and v_3 is defined by the inequality $v_1 + v_2 + v_3 \leq 3$, which allows only the 3-tuple $(1, 1, 1)$.

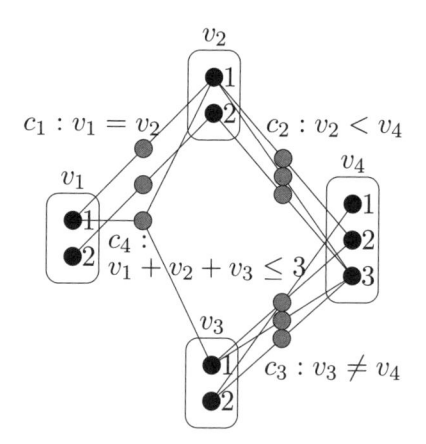

Figure 6.2. *An example of microstructure*

We must emphasize the fact that domains must be finite, but may be of an arbitrary nature. A domain can be defined in extension by a list of values as in the example of Figure 6.2. It can be also defined in intension by a type of values and a unary constraint as far as type and constraint together define a finite domain. Examples of values include the set of integers between 3 and 9, the set of integers between 2 and 5 or between 7 and 12, or the set of integers that are a multiple of 3 and between 1 and 20. It is also possible to define domains having symbols, vectors, structures, objects or sets as values.

Analogously, constraints may be of arbitrary nature. We have seen in the example of Figure 6.2 linear numerical constraints ($v_1 + v_2 + v_3 \leq 3$) and nonlinear constraints ($v_3 \neq v_4$). However, many other types of not necessarily linear constraints can be used. Examples include $c_1 \vee c_2$ where c_1 and c_2 are two linear constraints, $x \cdot y = z$ or $x^y \geq z$. On domains of arbitrary nature, numerical or not, we can imagine many other types of constraints. For example, the *all-different* constraint involves a set of variables V' and ensures that all the variables in V' take different values. For example, the *element* constraint involves an ordered set of variables V', an integer variable i and another variable v, and enforces the ith variable of V' to be equal to v.

6.2.3. Assignments

A variable is said to be assigned if a value in its domain has been associated with it. Let A be the assignment of a set $V(A) \subseteq V$ of variables. Assignment A is said to be *complete* if all the variables are assigned by it ($V(A) = V$). It is said to be *partial* otherwise. Let $c_j \in C$ be a constraint such that all its variables are assigned by A ($V_j \subseteq V(A)$). Constraint c_j is said to be *satisfied* by A if the restriction of A to the variables in V_j belongs to relation R_j ($A[V_j] \in R_j$). (Note that if A is an assignment and V' a set of variables such that $V' \subseteq V(A)$, $A[V']$ denotes the projection of A on V'.) Assignment A is said to be *consistent* if all the constraints whose variables are all assigned by A are also satisfied by A ($\forall c_j \in C | V_j \subseteq V(A), A[V_j] \in R_j$). It is said to be *inconsistent* otherwise. A *solution* is a complete and consistent assignment ($[V(A) = V] \wedge [\forall c_j \in C, A[V_j] \in R_j]$) or, more explicitly, an assignment of all the variables that satisfy all the constraints. A CSP instance is said to be consistent if it has a solution. It is said to be inconsistent otherwise.

In the example of Figure 6.2, the partial assignment $\{(v_1 = 1), (v_2 = 1), (v_4 = 1)\}$ is inconsistent because it does not satisfy constraint c_2 whose variables are all assigned. The partial assignment $\{(v_1 = 1), (v_2 = 1), (v_4 = 2)\}$ is consistent because c_1 and c_2, the two constraints whose variables are all assigned, are both satisfied. The complete assignment $\{(v_1 = 1), (v_2 = 1), (v_3 = 1), (v_4 = 2)\}$ is consistent and is one of the two solutions of this CSP instance which is itself consistent.

6.2.4. Queries

Many *queries* can be expressed on a CSP instance. We can consider for example:

1) to decide whether or not it is consistent;
2) to produce a solution when it is consistent;

3) to produce all the solutions;

4) to compute the number of solutions;

5) to decide whether or not a given value of a given variable belongs to a solution;

6) to decide whether or not a given combination of values of a given set of variables belongs to a solution;

7) to remove from every domain all the values that do not belong to a solution;

8) to remove from every relation all the combination of values that do not belong to a solution.

The second query is, by far, the most frequently addressed. It directly answers the decision problem: to find a decision (a plan in planning, a system schema in design, etc.) that satisfies all the constraints, whether they follow from the the laws of physics or from user requirements. The first query appears in many reasoning tasks: in diagnosis, it captures the problem of deciding whether or not a set of assumptions is consistent with the observations and the system behavior model, including normal and abnormal modes. In the example of Figure 6.2, the answers to the different queries considered are the following:

1) *yes*, this instance is consistent;

2) $\{(v_1 = 1), (v_2 = 1), (v_3 = 1), (v_4 = 2)\}$ is a solution;

3) $\{\{(v_1 = 1), (v_2 = 1), (v_3 = 1), (v_4 = 2)\}, \{(v_1 = 1), (v_2 = 1), (v_3 = 1), (v_4 = 3)\}\}$ is the set of solutions;

4) this instance has 2 solutions;

5) *yes*, for example, $(v_1 = 1)$ belongs to a solution; on the contrary, *no*, $(v_1 = 2)$ belongs to no solution;

6) *yes*, for example, $\{(v_1 = 1), (v_3 = 1)\}$ belongs to a solution; on the contrary, *no*, $\{(v_1 = 1), (v_3 = 2)\}$ belongs to no solution;

7) removal of value 2 from the domains of v_1, v_2 and v_3 and of value 1 from the domain of v_4;

8) removal of the combination $\{(v_1 = 2), (v_2 = 2)\}$ from the relation associated with constraint c_1, of the combination $\{(v_2 = 2), (v_4 = 3)\}$ from the relation associated with constraint c_2 and of the combinations $\{(v_3 = 2), (v_4 = 1)\}$ and $\{(v_3 = 2), (v_4 = 3)\}$ from the relation associated with constraint c_3.

Figure 6.3 shows the microstructure of the CSP instance of Figure 6.2 after having answered queries (7) and (8).

In its basic version, the CSP is not an optimization problem but a pure satisfaction problem. However, if an optimization criterion exists and is a function of a given subset $V_c \subseteq V$ of the variables, the problem of finding a solution such that the optimization criterion takes a value above a given threshold k becomes a constraint

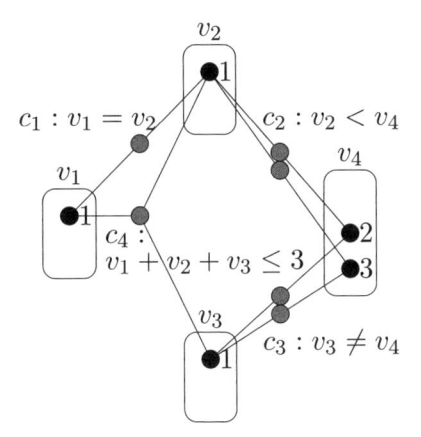

Figure 6.3. *The microstructure obtained after the removal of the values and combination of values that belong to no solution*

satisfaction problem. A variable v_c is added to V, representing the value taken by the optimization criterion together with two constraints. One constraint connects v_c to the variables of V_c and specifies the optimization criterion. The other unary constraint on v_c states $v_c \succ k$ (i.e. $x \succ y$ indicates that value x of the criterion is better than value y).

In the rest of this chapter, we will denote the number of variables in an instance by n, the number of constraints by e and the maximum domain cardinality by d.

6.3. Complexity

From the theoretical complexity point of view [GAR 79, PAP 94], deciding the consistency of an arbitrary CSP instance belongs to the class of the *non-deterministic polynomial (NP) complete* problems. It belongs to the class of the NP problems because a certificate of consistency is given by a solution which has a polynomial size (of $O(n)$) and can be verified in polynomial time (of $O(e)$, if we consider that checking the satisfaction of a constraint by a given assignment is an elementary operation achieved in constant time). A problem p is said to be complete for a class C if any instance of any problem $p' \in C$ can be transformed in polynomial time into an equivalent instance of p. It is complete for this class because it is a generalization of the the *Boolean expression satisfiability problem* (SAT) [GU 97] problem which has itself been shown to be complete for this class [COO 71]. The SAT problem is actually a restriction of the CSP where all variables are Boolean and all constraints are clauses. (Note that a clause is a disjunction of literals, a literal being a Boolean variable or its negation e.g. $a \vee \neg b \vee c$.)

The main practical consequence of this property is that it is very unreasonable (except if we assume that NP problems are also polynomial) to try to design an algorithm that solves the general CSP, which is complete and correct and whose worst case complexity is polynomial. An algorithm that aims to answer a decision problem is said to be complete if it always gives an answer (positive or negative). It is said to be correct if this answer is always correct (positive for consistent instances and negative otherwise.) Generality, at least one of completeness or polynomial complexity must be relaxed; relaxing the requirement of a correct answer does not seem to be sensible.

If we abandon the requirement of polynomial complexity, we can consider complete generic algorithms such as *tree search* or *variable elimination* (see sections 6.6.1 and 6.6.2). If instead we relax the requirement of completeness, we can use generic incomplete algorithms such as *greedy search* or *local search* (see sections 6.6.3 and 6.6.4). Finally, if we relax the requirement of generality, we can study complete polynomial time algorithms dedicated to specific *sub-problems* of the CSP itself (see section 6.8).

Given that the complexity theory only considers worst case complexity, we may also be interested in the mean complexity or in the complexity empirically observed on a given set of reference instances. Section 6.7 provides the main lessons that have been learnt from the numerous experiments performed.

6.4. Related problems

Considering the SAT problem [GU 97], we have already seen that this problem is a sub-problem of the CSP defined by the restriction to Boolean variables and to clauses. Conversely, it is easy to show that any CSP instance can be transformed into an equivalent SAT instance. The essential idea of this transformation consists of associating a SAT Boolean variable with every variable-value pair in the CSP instance. It is then possible to associate: a SAT clause with every CSP variable stating that this variable must take at least one value in its domain; a SAT clause with every pair of values in the domain of every CSP variable which forbids the simultaneous use of both values; and a SAT clause with every combination of values forbidden by a CSP constraint which forbids the simultaneous use of the values appearing in the combination.

We can also consider the related *integer linear programming* (ILP) [GAR 72, NEM 88] problem which is a variant of the *linear programming* (LP) [DAN 63] problem where some of the variables are required to take integer values. Without any optimization criterion and with bounded domains, the ILP problem is a sub-problem of the CSP using integer variables and linear constraints. Conversely, the previous idea used to transform a CSP instance into an equivalent SAT instance can be directly reused for ILP. (Any clause has a linear formulation obtained by transforming Boolean values into 0/1 variables and by replacing disjunction in the clause by addition, $\neg x$ by $(1 - x)$ and by stating that the transformed expression must be greater than or equal to 1. For example, The clause $a \vee \neg b \vee c$ is equivalent to the linear inequality $x_a + (1 - x_b) + x_c \geq 1$.)

It must be stressed that the CSP, SAT and ILP problems are all NP-complete.

If we look to *graph theory* [GON 84], we can observe that various classical problems on graphs can be naturally stated as CSP. The most famous one is probably the graph coloring problem which consists of associating a color with every vertex of a graph in such a way that all adjacent vertices take different colors. The CSP formulation associates a variable with every vertex whose domain is made of all available colors, and a difference constraint with every edge in the graph. Conversely, for binary CSP (CSP instances where all constraints involve at most two variables), it is easy to show that finding a solution of the CSP is equivalent to finding a clique (a complete sub-graph) of size n in the consistency graph (microstructure) of the CSP, as far as all the edges representing the absence of constraints are explicitly represented (see section 6.2).

As for *operations research*, several classical OR problems can easily be expressed as CSP. The *job-shop scheduling* problem, which consists of ordering a set of tasks taking into account task durations, earliest starting times, latest ending times, non-preemption, temporal precedence constraints and temporal non-overlapping constaints, is a classical example [BAP 01]. The CSP formulation associates with every task a variable representing its starting time, with every precedence constraint a linear constraint and with every non-overlapping constraint a nonlinear constraint which is the disjunction of two linear constraints.

A strong relation, often ignored, also exists between CSP and *relational databases* [MAI 83]. Each relation r of a relational database can indeed be interpreted as a constraint which applies to the attributes of r. Every attribute can be interpreted as a variable. The complete relational database can then be seen as a CSP instance. The join of all the relations of the database is the set of all the solutions of the CSP.

Let us consider a database with 3 relations r_1, r_2 and r_3, r_1 applying to attributes a_1 and a_2, r_2 applying to attributes a_1, a_2 and a_3 and r_3 applying to attributes a_2 and a_3. An example of a conjunctive query is: find all combinations of values for attributes a_1 and a_3 such that $\exists a_2, r_1(a_1, a_2) \wedge r_2(a_1, a_2, a_3)$. Answering a conjunctive query R to the database is equivalent to projecting the set of the solutions of the CSP defined by the contents of R onto the free variables of R.

The main differences that justify the use of significantly different methods include the fact that relations in databases are often very large tables that can be handled and accessed only at a significant cost. However, another difference is the fact that databases queries often require the production of all solutions and not just one. Nevertheless, approaches trying to bring together methods which have been developed in each area have been considered (e.g. [KAN 94]).

6.5. Reasoning on a CSP

We have seen that a CSP instance follows from the conjunction of a large number of constraints which are both local and interdependent because of shared variables. The intuition behind the reasoning mechanisms that will be considered is that reasoning directly on the global instance is far too complex, but that reasoning on local sub-instances can at least produce information that will be useful for the global level reasoning.

More precisely, let us consider a CSP instance P involving a set of variables V, a set of constraints C and a sub-instance P' defined by a subset C' of C and the set of variables $V' \subset V$ involved in those constraints. Let us consider a subset $V'' \subseteq V'$ and imagine that we can prove that a given assignment A of the variables in V'' never participates in a solution of P' (see Figure 6.4).

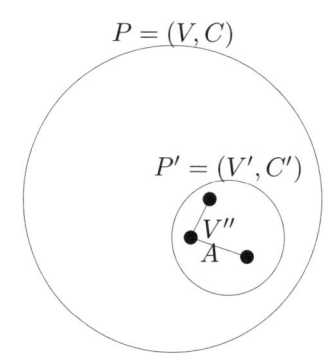

$$P = (V, C)$$

$$P' = (V', C')$$

Figure 6.4. *Reasoning on a local sub-instance*

We can conclude that A will not participate in a solution of P and therefore add explicitly to the definition of P the fact that A is forbidden. This is the basic operation used in the most frequently used reasoning mechanisms in CSP processing. These mechanisms can be considered as *deduction* mechanisms which allow constraints that were only implicit in the CSP instance definition to be made explicit. Because they remove combinations of values from existing relations or values from existing domains, they can be also considered as *simplification* or *filtering* mechanisms. The most extreme case of simplification arises when a relation or a domain becomes empty after several removals. In this case, no solution can exist and the inconsistency of P is proved. These mechanisms can therefore be seen as *inconsistency detection* mechanisms.

Let us add that the removal of a combination of values A can lead to the removal of another combination of values A' that had no explicit reason to be eliminated up until now, but that can now be proved to never appear in any solution of a sub-instance P' following the removal of A: a form of propagation of information inside the constraint network. This is why these mechanisms are often denoted as *constraint propagation* mechanisms.

6.5.1. *Local consistency*

In order to achieve a well-defined level of deduction, we usually rely on a so-called *local consistency* property, denoted as π. Let P be a CSP instance. This property applies to combinations of values of variables in P or, equivalently, on partial assignments. It should be checkable locally by considering only limited sets of variables and constraints in P. The fact that an assignment A fails to satisfy it should imply that A does not participate in any solution of P. Removing A from P (forbidding A in P) does not change the set of solutions of P. The instance obtained is therefore said to be equivalent to P. In these conditions, starting from an instance P, we iteratively eliminate all the combinations of values that do not satisfy π, with two possible results:

1) a relation or a domain becomes empty and the inconsistency of P is proved; or

2) the instance obtained satisfies π; this instance, denoted as $\pi(P)$, is a simplified instance equivalent to P.

It is important to note that, because π is a local consistency property that never considers the instance from a global point of view, nothing guarantees that $\pi(P)$ is consistent in the second situation. Concisely, we can say that local inconsistency implies inconsistency (situation 1), but that local consistency does not imply consistency (situation 2). We can also say that local consistency enforcing mechanisms are incomplete: they cannot always detect inconsistency.

6.5.2. *Arc-consistency*

As an illustration, let us consider one of the most simple and most frequently used levels of local consistency, known as *arc-consistency* [MAC 77a] in the case of binary CSP instances.

A value val of a variable v is said to be arc-consistent for a constraint c, that links v to another variable v', if there exists at least one value val' in the domain of v' that is consistent with val, or such that the assignment $\{(v = val), (v' = val')\}$ satisfies the constraint c (see Figure 6.5). A value is said to be arc-consistent if it is arc-consistent for all the constraints that involve its variable. Ultimately, a CSP instance is said to be arc-consistent if all the values of all its variables are arc-consistent.

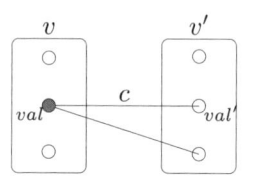

Figure 6.5. *Sub-instance considered by arc-consistency*

The most naive algorithm which can filter an instance by arc-consistency simply scans all the values and removes those that do not satisfy the arc-consistency property. This process must be repeated as long as the current one has deleted at least one value. Indeed, a value val of a variable v that was previously arc-consistent for a constraint c that connects v to v', due to the existence in the domain of v' of a value val' consistent with val, can become arc-inconsistent if val' is the only value consistent with val in the domain of v' and if it was deleted in the last run (propagation of removals in the constraint network).

Figure 6.6 shows the effect of this filtering on a CSP instance involving 3 variables v_1, v_2 and v_3 each having two possible values 1 and 2. Each variable is connected by two constraints c_1 and c_2, c_1 specifying that $v_1 = v_2$ and c_2 enforcing that $v_2 > v_3$. The eliminated values are indicated in black. If v_1, v_2 and v_3 are processed in this order, a first scan allows value 1 of v_2 to be removed because there is no value in the domain of v_3 that is compatible with it. Value 2 of v_3 can also be removed because there is no value in the domain of v_2 that is compatible with it. Because values have been removed, a second scan is needed. It removes value 1 of v_1 because no value compatible with it now remains in the domain of v_2. A third scan is needed, but it produces no value removal. The instance obtained is arc-consistent and equivalent to the original instance.

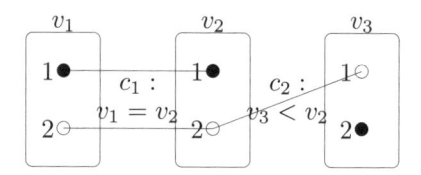

Figure 6.6. *Arc-consistency: example of simplification*

Figure 6.7 shows the result of this filtering on another instance, similar to the previous instance, except that constraint c_2 is now defined as $v_2 \neq v_3$. No value is removed here because the original instance is already arc-consistent.

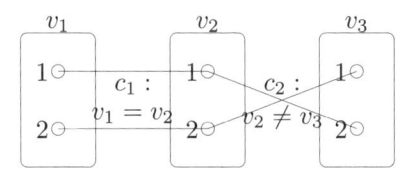

Figure 6.7. *Arc-consistency: example of lack of simplification*

Figure 6.8 shows the result of this filtering on another instance, similar to the previous two, where constraint c_1 allows just the pair $(1,1)$ and constraint c_2 just the pair $(2,2)$. The first scan removes value 2 of v_1 and values 1 and 2 of v_2. The domain of v_2 is then empty. No further scan is needed because it is now proved that this instance is inconsistent.

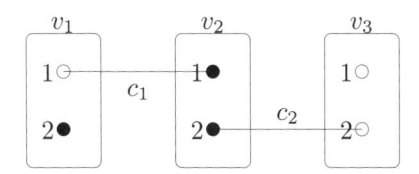

Figure 6.8. *Arc-consistency: example of inconsistency detection*

Figure 6.9 shows the effect of this filtering on another instance where the three constraints c_1, c_2 and c_3 are all defined to be difference constraints. As in Figure 6.7, no value is removed because the original instance is already arc-consistent. However, it is clearly inconsistent which shows that local consistency does not necessarily implies consistency.

Many algorithms, more sophisticated than the algorithm described above, have been proposed to filter an instance by arc-consistency. One of the most famous is called AC3 [MAC 77a]. It relies on a set Q of variable-constraint pairs that must be checked. Initially, Q is set to contain all possible pairs (v, c) such that v is a variable and c a constraint involving it. Every time a pair $(v, c) \in Q$ is considered, it is removed from Q and the domain of v is reduced by eliminating all the values that are arc-inconsistent for c. If the domain of v is effectively reduced, then all pairs (v', c') such that $v' \neq v$ and c' involves v are added to Q (propagation). The algorithm stops when a domain becomes empty (situation 1) or when Q becomes empty (situation 2).

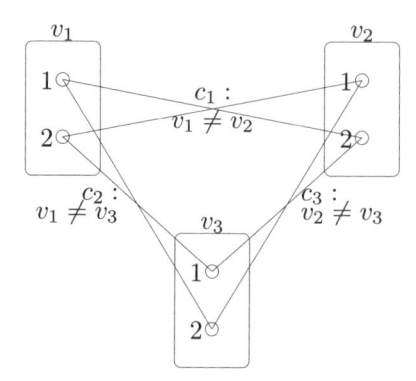

Figure 6.9. *Arc-consistency: example of lack of inconsistency detection*

Its temporal complexity is of $O(e \cdot d^3)$, where e is the number of constraints and d is the maximum domain size. Other algorithms, with an improved optimal temporal complexity of $O(e \cdot d^2)$, have been proposed (specifically AC4 [MOH 86] and AC6 [BES 94]). However, since its ease of implementation and its possible adaptation to specific conditions (numerical continuous domains or constraints relying on dedicated filtering methods) often lead to it being chosen as the default arc-consistency enforcing algorithm. Recent improvements of AC3 [BES 01, ZHA 01] allow most of its good properties in terms of ease of implementation and of adaptation capabilities to be kept, while offering the optimal temporal complexity of $O(e \cdot d^2)$ of AC4 and AC6.

Arc-consistency has been generalized to non-binary constraints [MAC 77b], leading to an unavoidable increase in temporal complexity with the arity of the constraints handled. Conversely, it has been specialized to more efficiently handle constraint types such as *functional* or *monotonic* constraints (for example, inequality constraints) [HEN 92].

6.5.3. *Path-consistency*

Filtering by arc-consistency therefore considers only sub-instances defined by one constraint and the two variables it connects. We may consider that such sub-instances are too local to lead to sufficient simplifications or to detect inconsistency. This is why fewer local properties have been proposed. Among these, the most famous (but not necessarily the most used) is called *path-consistency* [MAC 77a].

If we limit ourselves to binary CSP instances, let us consider three variables v, v' and v'' and the constraints that connect them: c between v and v', c' between v and v'' and c'' between v' and v''. If there is no constraint between two variables, a universal constraint allowing all pairs is considered. A pair (val, val'), comprising a value val

of v and a value val' of v' which satisfies c, is said to be path-consistent according to v'' if there is at least one value val'' in the domain of v'' such that the assignment $\{(v = val), (v' = val'), (v'' = val'')\}$ also satisfies c' and c'' (see Figure 6.10). It is said to be path-consistent if it is path-consistent with respect to all other variables. A CSP instance is said to be path-consistent if all possible allowed pairs of values are path-consistent.

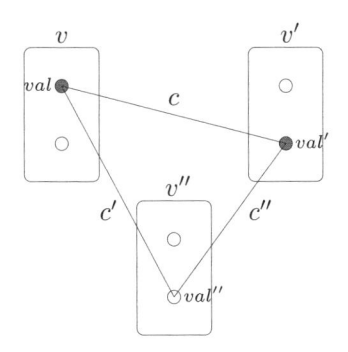

Figure 6.10. *Sub-instance considered by path-consistency*

As for arc-consistency, the most naive algorithm which can filter by path-consistency consists of scanning all possible pairs of values that are not forbidden by constraints (including pairs of values from variables that are not connected by constraints) and in removing every pair that does not satisfy the path-consistency property. This process must be repeated until no pairs of values are removed.

Figure 6.11 shows the result of this filtering on a CSP instance involving 3 variables v_1, v_2 and v_3 each having two possible values 1 and 2 and connected by two constraints c_1 and c_2, c_1 specifying that $v_1 \neq v_3$ and c_2 that $v_2 \neq v_3$. As no constraint links v_1 and v_2, all the pairs of values between these two variables are implicitly allowed. The eliminated pairs of values are shown in bold. For example, the pair $\{(v_1 = 1), (v_2 = 2)\}$ is eliminated because there is no value in the domain of v_3 that is simultaneously compatible with $(v_1 = 1)$ and $(v_2 = 2)$. The final instance obtained is path-consistent and equivalent to the original one.

Figure 6.12 shows the result of this filtering on the instance of Figure 6.9. Here, the pairs of values $\{(v_1 = 1), (v_2 = 2)\}$ and $\{(v_1 = 2), (v_2 = 1)\}$ are eliminated, resulting in an empty relation. Path-consistency filtering has therefore proved the inconsistency of the instance, which was not previously achieved by arc-consistency filtering. This, however, still does not imply that path-consistency filtering is complete: on some instances, it may also be unable to detect inconsistency.

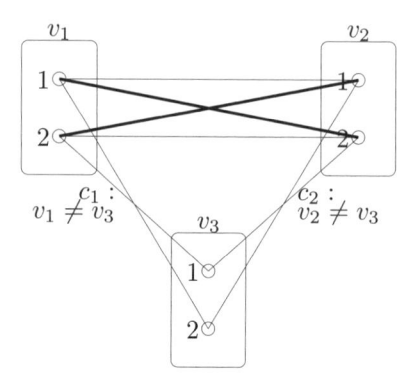

Figure 6.11. *Path-consistency: example of simplification*

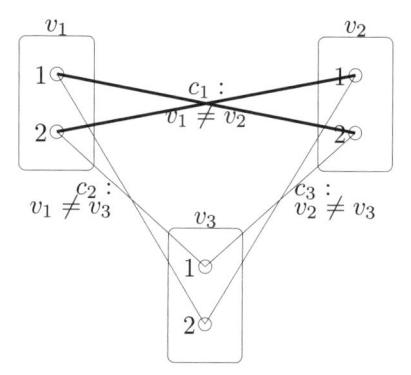

Figure 6.12. *Path-consistency: example of inconsistency detection*

We can observe that the elimination of pairs of values by path-consistency filtering may turn a previously arc-consistent value into a non-arc-consistent one. It is therefore possible that arc-consistency filtering activates path-consistency filtering and conversely. Whereas arc-consistency filtering has time complexity of $O(e \cdot d^2)$, with $e < n^2$, the time complexity of path-consistency is of $O(n^3 \cdot d^3)$.

6.5.4. *Other local consistency properties*

The notion of (i, j)-*consistency* [FRE 78] allows arc and path-consistency notions to be generalized. Informally, a CSP instance is said to be (i, j)-consistent if every consistent assignment of i variables can be extended in a consistent way on any set of j new variables. In the case of binary CSP, arc-consistency is equivalent to $(1,1)$-consistency and path-consistency is equivalent to the combination of $(1,1)$ and $(2,1)$-consistency.

We must however emphasize an important difference between, on one hand, arc-consistency filtering (and more generally $(1,j)$ consistency filtering) and, on the other hand, path-consistency filtering (and more generally (i,j) consistency for $i > 1$). Whereas the former only reduces variable domains by deleting values, the latter may reduce the relations associated with constraints by eliminating combinations of values and even by creating new constraints where none existed before. The constraint graph may be modified and may become in the worst case complete. The memory space needed to store in extension all the eliminated combinations of values may become intractable. This is why most of the contributions in the area are essentially dealing with local consistencies that may be stronger than arc-consistency, but still remove values and not combinations of values.

The simplest of these properties in this direction, called *path inverse consistency*, is simply $(1,2)$-consistency and can easily be generalized to $(1,j)$-consistency. In another direction, the *neighborhood inverse consistency* [FRE 96] considers for every variable v the sub-instance $P(v)$ defined by v, all the variables directly linked to v by a constraint and all the constraints that link these variables together (see Figure 6.13). A value val of a variable v is said to be neighborhood inverse consistent if it participates in at least one solution of $P(v)$. One can find in [VER 99] a generalization of neighborhood inverse consistency, taking into account arbitrary sub-instances. [DEB 01] also provides an overview of most of the local consistencies that have been proposed beyond arc-consistency.

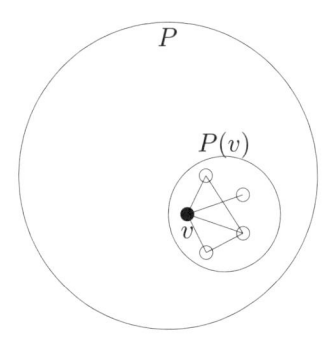

Figure 6.13. *The sub-instance considered by neighborhood inverse consistency*

6.5.5. *General constraint propagation mechanisms*

Even if local consistency properties allows the nature of the results obtained by filtering on every instance to be characterized and those obtained by two different properties to be compared, the notion of local consistency property is not necessary to define constraint propagation mechanisms.

The only compulsory element is a filtering mechanism that can, based on reasoning on a sub-instance P', reduce the domain of any variable of P' by removing values that are known to participate in no solution of P' and therefore in no solution of P. This mechanism may not necessarily remove all the values that do not participate in a solution of P', but only some of them, even if the maximum number is desirable. In fact, the best compromise between the reduction in the instance size and the computational cost of the reasoning must be sought. This mechanism must however be *correct* in the sense that it should not eliminate values that do participate in solutions. The precise mechanism used may depend on the very nature of the constraints in P'.

This paves the way to the use of various existing algorithms, for example: linear programming algorithms such as the *simplex* one if P' is only made of linear constraints [DAN 63]; or maximum matching algorithms if P' is made of a single *all-different* constraint [RÉG 96]. The term of global constraint is used to describe these constraints, often of very large arity but with a specific nature that allows dedicated efficient filtering algorithms to be exploited.

Figure 6.14 depicts a schema of a general constraint propagation mechanism where each constraint is associated with a specific filtering mechanism of the domains of the variables it involves. The filtering mechanism associated with a constraint c can then be managed as a *daemon* which reacts to the modification of the domain of any variable of c and filters the domains of the other variables of c accordingly.

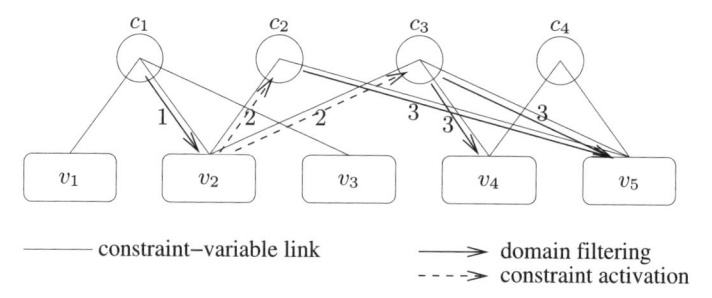

Figure 6.14. *Schema of a general constraint propagation mechanism*

The plain bold arrows show the domain filterings that are tried and the dotted bold arrows indicate the constraint activations that follow an effective filtering. The numbers associated with these arrows represent the temporal sequence of the domain filterings and constraint activations. In a first step, the domain of v_2 is filtered according to c_1 and the current domains of v_1 and v_3. In a second step, this filtering activates constraints c_2 and c_3 which both involve v_2. In a third step, these activations lead to domain filterings of the domain of v_5 according to c_2 and the current domain of v_2 and of the domains of v_4 and v_5 according to c_3 and the current domain of v_2.

The propagation is performed each time a domain filtering yields an effective domain reduction. For the sake of efficiency, the daemon associated with every constraint is usually tuned to the type of underlying constraint. For example, the daemon associated with a constraint $x \leq y$ will only react to domain reductions that increase the lower bound of the domain of x or decrease the upper bound of the domain of y, resulting in an increase in the lower bound of the domain of y (or a decrease in the upper bound of the domain of x, respectively) [e.g. HEN 92].

6.6. Looking for a CSP solution

6.6.1. *Tree search*

Many approaches for finding one or more solutions of a CSP instance have been proposed. Among them, tree search defines in some sense a reference which serves as a source of comparison for other approaches. The essential idea of tree search is to deal with the huge search space associated with a CSP instance by partitioning it and exploring all the elements of the partition successively, possibly by recursively partitioning them when needed, resulting in a partitioning tree.

Three essential parameters define a tree search procedure: the partitioning mechanism, the order of exploration of the sub-spaces defined by the partitioning and the stopping criterion of the recursive partitioning.

For the partitioning mechanism itself, different approaches exist. Let P be an instance to be partitioned. The most frequently used mechanism consists of choosing a variable v of P and in associating with every value val in its domain the sub-instance that follows from adding constraint $v = val$ to P. Each instance is therefore split into as many sub-instances as there are values in the domain of v. For very large domains (or continuous domains, see section 6.10.1), the mechanism used consists of choosing a variable v of P, in splitting its domain in two sub-domains (or more generally in k sub-domains) and in associating with every sub-domain D' the sub-instance that follows from adding constraint $v \in D'$ to P. Each instance is therefore split into as many instances as there are sub-domains.

Another more general approach consists of considering a constraint c that is not a constraint of P and in generating two sub-instances: the first follows from adding constraint c to P and the other from adding the negation $\neg c$ of c to P. Such a mechanism is especially convenient for problems where some of the constraints in P are disjunctions of elementary constraints.

Considering the *exploration order*, different approaches also exist. A *breadth-first* strategy gives the priority to the oldest non-partitioned sub-instance (or node). A *depth-first* strategy gives the priority to the newest one. A *best-first* strategy evaluates every non-partitioned sub-instance and gives the priority to the most promising one. In most cases, a depth-first strategy is used for CSP solving, leading to the so-called *backtrack* algorithm [BIT 75]. It is named the backtrack algorithm mainly because it can be easily implemented, does not require all the as yet unpartitioned sub-instances to be stored and therefore requires only a polynomial space. However, the main weakness of this strategy is that it is less heuristically guided than a best-first one and is very dependent on the first choices performed at the top of the partitioning tree.

When a variable-value partitioning and a depth-first strategy are used, the complete definition of the exploration performed includes the order in which variables are assigned (variable ordering heuristics) and the order in which possible values are explored (value ordering heuristics).

For *variable ordering*, two general principles are used: (1) to reduce as far as possible the width of the tree by giving priority to variables with small domains and (2) to reduce as far as possible its depth by giving priority to the most constrained variables [DEC 87]. The heuristics that order variables according to increasing values of the ratio between domain size and degree in the constraint graph is a good compromise between these two points of view [BES 96].

For *value ordering*, the only general principle is to give priority to values that most likely lead to a solution, which is usually highly problem-dependent. For both types of heuristics (on variables and on values), we distinguish *static* heuristics (order decided for the whole search before it starts) from *dynamic* heuristics (each choice made during the search according to the current accumulated knowledge).

Other more complex exploration strategies have been proposed. Among the most remarkable, we can cite the *limited discrepancy search* algorithm [HAR 95] which uses a sequence of searches at increasing Hamming distance from an initial assignment heuristically generated. (The Hamming distance between two assignments is the number of variables with different assigned values.) There are also algorithms based on *randomization and restart* [GOM 98], which use a sequence of truncated tree searches using possibly heuristically biased randomized heuristics for value and variable orderings.

For the *stopping criterion* of the recursive partitioning, two cases must be considered: stop on a consistency proof or on an inconsistency proof.

Usually, stopping on a *consistency proof* occurs when all the variables have been assigned and no inconsistency has been detected, resulting in a solution. It may, however, occur earlier: for example when arc-consistency filtering is performed on every sub-instance and reduces the domains of non-assigned variables to singletons. This proves consistency and directly produces a solution.

In order to stop on an *inconsistency proof*, an inconsistency detection mechanism is required. The most simple one is known as *backward-checking*. After every new assignment of a variable v, it simply checks the satisfaction of all the constraints that connect v to previously assigned variables and stops as soon as one of these constraints is unsatisfied.

Figure 6.15 shows the search tree associated with the proof of inconsistency of the 3-queens instance. (The n-queens problem consists of positioning n queens on a $n \times n$ chessboard in such a way that no two queens attack each other if on the same line, same column or same diagonal. The 3-queens instance is inconsistent, but the 4-queens one, which will be considered later, is consistent.) Because exactly one queen will appear on each row, a CSP variable is associated with each row and represents the column on which the queen will be positioned on this row. The variables are assigned in the row order from top to bottom. For every variable, the values are chosen in the column order from left to right. The assignments are indicated by crosses in the corresponding position on the chessboard. The inconsistency detections are indicated by a bold cross just below the corresponding node. The numbers on the right of each node represent the order in which these nodes are generated and explored. The third branch of the tree is not represented because it is symmetric with respect to the first.

A slightly more sophisticated mechanism for inconsistency detection is called *forward-checking* [HAR 80, NAD 89]. Every time a new variable v is assigned, it considers all the non-assigned variables that are connected to v by a constraint and removes from their domains all the values that are incompatible with the value currently assigned to v. The search stops as soon as one domain becomes empty. This can be seen as a limited form of arc-consistency filtering where the domains of non-assigned variables are filtered from assigned variables only. Figure 6.16 shows the tree associated with the proof of inconsistency of the same 3-queens instance. The values removed by forward-checking are indicated in gray.

An even more sophisticated mechanism consists of using a complete arc-consistency filtering after each variable assignment, including the filtering of non-assigned variables from assigned and non-assigned variables [HAR 80, NAD 89, SAB 94]. As previously, the search stops as soon as one domain becomes empty.

Figure 6.17 shows the tree associated with the proof of inconsistency of the same 3-queens instance. The values filtered by arc-consistency that would not have been removed by forward-checking are indicated in dark gray. This tree is, in this specific

286   Decision-making Process

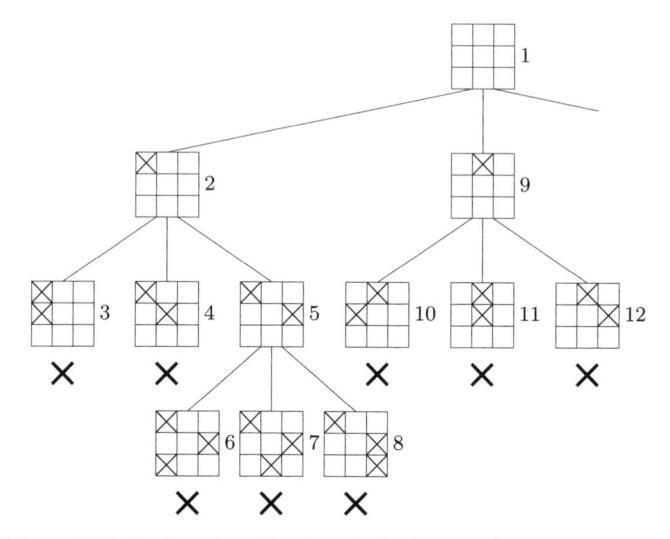

Figure 6.15. *Backtrack and backward-checking on the 3-queens instance*

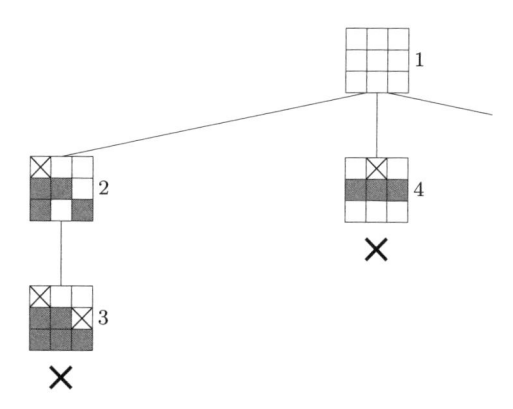

Figure 6.16. *Backtrack and forward-checking on the 3-queens instance*

case, reduced to the root node because arc-consistency filtering suffices to detect inconsistency.

Figure 6.18 shows the tree associated with the proof of consistency of the 4-queens instance. The inconsistency detections (respectively consistency) are indicated by a a cross (respectively a circle) in bold below the corresponding node. In this case, arc-consistency filtering does not simplify the original instance which is already arc-consistent. However, as soon as the first queen is placed on the first column,

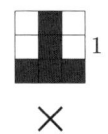

Figure 6.17. *Backtrack, forward-checking and arc-consistency on the 3-queens instance*

inconsistency is detected (third queen's domain becomes empty). As soon as it is placed on the second column, consistency is established (the domains of the non-assigned variables are all reduced to singletons). The two remaining branches of the tree are not shown because they are symmetrical with respect to the first two.

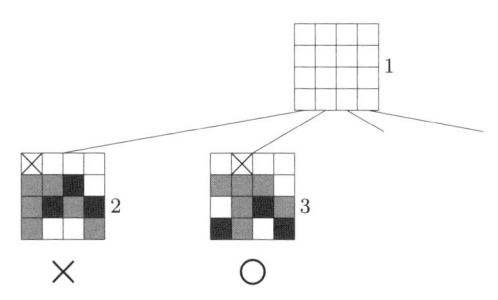

Figure 6.18. *Backtrack, forward-checking and arc-consistency on the 4-queens instance*

In the general case, an arbitrary local consistency filtering mechanism (as presented in section 6.5) can be used to detect inconsistency at each node of the search tree. The more powerful the mechanism is, the earlier the inconsistencies can be detected and the shallower is the tree (see Figures 6.15–6.17), but the computation performed at each node is more expensive. A compromise must be found. The current wisdom, built on practical experience, is that arc-consistency filtering (or in some cases stronger local consistencies between arc and path-consistency) are reasonable compromises [DEB 97].

We must stress the influence of the filtering mechanism used at each node on the dynamic variable and value-ordering heuristics. For example, variable-ordering heuristics relying on domain sizes (see above) become really efficient only when they can exploit the updated size of the filtered domains.

Another parameter of a depth-first search is the backtracking mechanism used when a variable could not be assigned successfully (failure of all the possible values). The usual *chronological* mechanism consists of reconsidering the choice made for the previous variable in the assignment order. Other mechanisms, often called *intelligent backtracking*, have been considered. They are all inspired by the observation that the choice made for the previous variable may not be related to the failure observed. If it is not responsible, changing it will not avoid the failure and will lead to repeated useless work. To avoid this useless work as much as possible, the idea consists of isolating a set V' of assigned variables whose values may be related to the failure, and to directly reconsider the choice made for the most recently assigned variable in V' (*backjumping*). To identify a set of variables whose assignment could be related to the failure, different mechanisms based either on the constraint graph [DEC 90] or on information collected during search and filtering [PRO 93] have been proposed.

Another parameter is the ability to use a constraint *learning* mechanism during a search [FRO 94, SCH 94]. As for backjumping, the idea is to isolate a set V' of assigned variables, whose current assignment A' may be responsible for the failure, and to record the inconsistency of A' inside a constraint involving V' and forbidding A' in order to increase the ability of detecting inconsistency during the rest of the search.

Whatever the sophistication used, the worst case *temporal complexity* of the tree search is of $O(d^n)$. In the worst case, the partitioning is carried out until complete assignments are considered and neither consistency or inconsistency stop it. A plain enumeration of all complete assignments would then have been just as efficient.

When optimization problems are considered (defined by a set of constraints and a criterion v_c to be optimized as introduced in section 6.2.4), the usual approach is to perform the search ignoring the criterion. As soon as a solution is found, it is evaluated. Let k be its value. The constraint $v_c \succ k$ is then added to the set of constraints and the search either proceeds or starts again. Each time a new improved solution is found, the same mechanism is used until inconsistency is proved. In this case, the last solution found is proved to be optimal. The optimization problem is therefore solved as a sequence of increasingly constrained satisfaction problems.

6.6.2. *Variable elimination*

The iterated elimination of the variables of a CSP instance is another way of resolving a large size instance by solving a sequence of smaller size instances. The so-called *bucket elimination* [DEC 99] algorithm is directly inspired by the *non-serial dynamic programming* method, introduced in [BER 72, SEI 81, SHE 90].

The main idea is to eliminate each variable from the instance, one after the other, following an arbitrary order. Let us consider a variable v, $C' \subseteq C$ the set of all the constraints involving v and $V' \subseteq V$ the set of all the variables involved in at least one of the constraints in C' (excluding v itself). Eliminating v consists of computing the set of the combinations of values for the variables in V' that can be consistently extended to v (by satisfying all the constraints in C') and in recording them in a constraint c on the variables in V'. Once c is computed and added to the instance, we can eliminate variable v and constraints in C' from the instance, because we know that the combinations of values that can be chosen for variables in V' can always be consistently extended to v. This process can be repeated until all the variables have been eliminated or until inconsistency has been detected: no combination of values for V' can be consistently extended to v.

Figure 6.19 shows a graph coloring instance using two colors: red and green. The associated CSP instance has 5 variables, each one associated with one vertex $(a, b, c, d$ and $e)$ and having two possible values (r and g), and 5 difference constraints, each one associated with one edge. This instance is inconsistent.

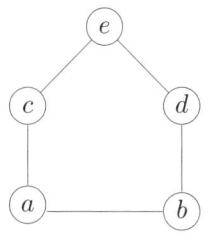

Figure 6.19. *Example 1: a graph to color using only two colors*

Let us assume that we eliminate variables in the order (e, d, c, b, a). Table 6.1 shows, for each variable v, the constraints that are taken into account and the constraint that is created and added when variable v is eliminated. Let us consider the elimination of variable e. We have $C' = \{c \neq e, d \neq e\}$ and $V' = \{c, d\}$. The only combinations of values for the variables in V' that can be extended to e, in such a way that all the constraints in C' are satisfied, are (r, r) and (g, g). We therefore add the equality constraint $c = d$ to the instance and remove e and the constraints in C' from it.

Variables	Constraints considered	Constraint added
e	$\{c \neq e, d \neq e\}$	$c = d$
d	$\{b \neq d, c = d\}$	$b \neq c$
c	$\{a \neq c, b \neq c\}$	$a = b$
b	$\{a \neq b, a = b\}$	$\emptyset$
a		

Table 6.1. *Example 1: variable elimination using the order (e, d, c, b, a)*

Let us now consider the elimination of variable d. We have $C' = \{b \neq d, c = d\}$ and $V' = \{b, c\}$ because of the new constraint between c and d created by the elimination of variable e. The only combinations of values of the variables in V' that can be extended to d while satisfying the constraints in C' are (r,g) and (g,r). We therefore add the difference constraint $b \neq c$ and remove d and the constraints in C'. Finally, when we eliminate b, we obtain $C' = \{a \neq b, a = b\}$ and $V' = \{a\}$. There is no value for a that can be extended to b while satisfying the constraints in C' (C' defines an inconsistent sub-instance), which proves the inconsistency of the original instance.

In the case of a consistent instance (see Figure 6.20 and Table 6.2), the elimination of all the variables without encountering inconsistency proves the consistency of the original instance. A solution can then be built without any backtrack by assigning variables in the inverse order of their elimination and by choosing for every variable v a value that is consistent with the previous choices and with the constraints in C' associated with v. The work performed during the elimination itself guarantees that such a value exists. Table 6.3 shows one of the solutions that can be built in this way.

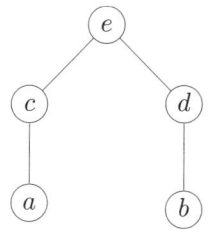

Figure 6.20. *Example 2: another graph to color using only two colors*

Variables	Constraints considered	Constraint added
e	$\{c \neq e, d \neq e\}$	$c = d$
d	$\{b \neq d, c = d\}$	$b \neq c$
c	$\{a \neq c, b \neq c\}$	$a = b$
b	$\{a = b\}$	
a		

Table 6.2. *Example 2: variable elimination using the order (e, d, c, b, a)*

The *time complexity* of this algorithm is of $O(d^{w+1})$ where w is the maximum arity of the constraints created by the elimination process. Its *space complexity* is of $O(d^w)$. Maximum arity w is always strictly smaller than n, but depends on the order chosen for variable elimination. Finding an order that minimizes w is an *NP-hard* problem. The minimum value of w (called the *induced width* and denoted by w^*) depends on the constraint graph. If this graph is a tree $w^* = 1$, which guarantees an efficient

Variables	Constraints considered	Constraint added	Assignment
e	$\{c \neq e, d \neq e\}$	$c = d$	r
d	$\{b \neq d, c = d\}$	$b \neq c$	v
c	$\{a \neq c, b \neq c\}$	$a = b$	v
b	$\{a = b\}$		r
a			r

Table 6.3. *Example 2: variable assignment using the order (a, b, c, d, e)*

algorithm. If the graph is complete $w^* = n - 1$, which guarantees exponential space and time behavior. This is similar to the worst case time complexity of backtrack, but with a far higher space complexity. This is in fact even worse because backtrack practical time complexity is often far better than its worst case complexity, whereas practical variable elimination time and space complexity tends to be close to its worst case complexity.

Whereas a backtrack algorithm processes variables by assigning them, a bucket elimination algorithm processes them by computing and recording the impact they have on the rest of the instance. Both approaches can cooperate and combinations have been proposed [LAR 03a], based on the idea that eliminating a variable should be preferred to assigning it when the elimination creates only a small arity constraint.

Relations between assignment and variable elimination become even clearer using (hyper)tree decompositions of a constraint network [DEC 89, GOT 00] where nodes represent sub-instances. A backtrack algorithm equipped with constraint recording capabilities [JÉG 03] appears to be very similar to a variable elimination algorithm [SHE 90].

6.6.3. *Greedy search*

Greedy search is the first method that comes to the mind of a newcomer to constraint satisfaction problems. It relies on two heuristics: one for ordering variables and one for choosing values. It simply assigns variables in the order indicated by the first heuristics, using the value indicated by the second one, without ever reconsidering previous choices. It can be seen as a depth-first search limited to its first branch.

Obviously, nothing guarantees that the final assignment is a solution. This method is therefore not really adapted to CSP solving. It is better adapted to optimization problems with a limited impact of constraints (for example, problems where producing consistent assignments is not really difficult). In such a case, both heuristics simply aim to produce a good quality solution. Using repeated random samplings biased by these heuristics [BRE 96] is a simple method to improve the solution quality even further.

6.6.4. *Local search*

Local search can be seen as an extension of greedy search. If the assignment generated by greedy search is not a solution, we can modify it using local changes focused on its flaws i.e. unsatisfied constraints, in order to produce a solution.

At first sight, we may think that there is a contradiction between CSP which is a satisfaction problem and local search which is designed for optimization problems. This contradiction disappears if we consider that CSP can also be seen as a pure optimization problem where the goal is to minimize the number of unsatisfied constraints.

The *min-conflicts* algorithm [MIN 92] is an example of a local search algorithm applied to CSP. It consists of performing repeated trials until either one is successful or a maximum fixed number of trials has been reached. Each trial starts with a random generation of a complete assignment. It consists of modifying this assignment until either a solution is reached (successful trial) or a maximum fixed number of modifications has been reached (unsuccessful trial). A modification consists of randomly choosing a variable among those that are involved in unsatisfied constraints, and then randomly choosing a value for this variable among those that minimize the number of unsatisfied constraints given the assignment of the other variables.

Four essential parameters specify a local search: the initial assignment generation, the neighborhood function, the neighbor choice function and the stopping criterion.

The *initial assignment generation* is equivalent to a greedy search. If several trials are performed, using different initial assignments, it should include a random component (see previous section).

The *neighborhood function* associates with every complete assignment A the set of all its neighbor complete assignments, obtained from A by performing a single modification. It can be defined by the set of all possible modifications that can be applied to a complete assignment. For CSP solving, the most frequently used neighborhood function associates with every complete assignment A the set of all the assignments that can be obtained by changing the value of only one variable in A. It can be generalized by allowing the value of k variables to be changed in A.

Different options exist for the neighbor choice function. This choice can be random. We may also choose the assignment that improves or strictly improves over the current assignment, or the best assignment in the neighborhood considering the number of unsatisfied constraints. To avoid being stuck in local optima, we may be forced to choose a neighbor that is worse than the current assignment, sometimes bounding the loss in quality. Note that an assignment is a local optimum if there is no better assignment in its neighborhood. A local optimum is not necessarily a global optimum. See Figure 6.21, where the nodes represent assignments and where two nodes are connected by an edge when the two corresponding assignments are neighbors. The number on the right of each node represents the cost of the assignment and the goal is to find an assignment of minimum cost. Assignment A_3 is a local optimum, but not a global one because A_4 is strictly better.

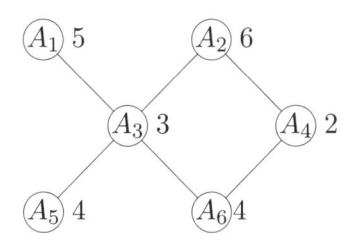

Figure 6.21. *Example of a local optimum:* A_3

The *stopping criterion* may depend on the CPU time or on the number of trials or modifications from the beginning of the search or from the last improving modification.

Considered as an optimization problem, CSP can be handled using classical local search algorithms [AAR 97] such as *simulated annealing* [KIR 83], *taboo search* [GLO 93], *genetic algorithms* [GOL 89] or *ant colony optimization* [DOR 96]. On problems combining constraints and optimization, the combination of constraint satisfaction and optimization criterion value in the function to be optimized remains nevertheless a non-trivial issue.

Contrary to tree search and variable elimination, local search is incomplete: it may be unable to prove the consistency of a consistent instance and it cannot prove the inconsistency of an inconsistent instance. It usually does not exploit constraint propagation mechanisms just before search, on the initial instance, in order to simplify it or to detect inconsistency. During search, constraints are only passively checked.

Various combinations or tree search, constraint propagation, and local search have been considered. An example of such a combination consists of applying local search to partial assignments, i.e. not only to complete assignments [JUS 02, PRA 05]. This can be considered as a mixture between tree search and local search allowing local search and constraint propagation to be combined and, in some cases, inconsistency to be proved.

6.7. Experimental evaluations and lessons learned

The conclusions that can be drawn from the numerous experimental evaluations, performed either on real problems and instances or on randomly generated problems, are quite different. They depend upon the nature of the problem: pure constraint satisfaction or constraint optimization problems.

6.7.1. *Pure constraint satisfaction problems*

The main lessons that can be derived are as follows:

– The solving time observed using e.g. backtrack algorithms are often far smaller than the time expected via a worst-case analysis, without being negligible. Reaching the worst-case is extremely rare except for well-designed pathological instances.

– *Under-constrained* instances (few constraints or weak constraints) are usually easily solved because they are consistent and a solution can rapidly be found.

– *Over-constrained* instances (many constraints or strong constraints) are also often easy to solve because they are inconsistent and the proof of inconsistency is easy to build.

– Really difficult instances appear at the frontier between consistency and inconsistency. For such instances, proving consistency or inconsistency is a difficult task. Experimentally, on randomly generated instances we can observe a sudden *complexity peak* when this frontier is crossed (peak of the median or mean solving time of one instance, see Figure 6.22). The height of this peak increases exponentially with the size of the instances considered. Moreover, at a given distance from the peak, it is simpler to solve an under-constrained instance than an over-constrained one. Similarly to what has been observed in physical systems that change phase (liquid to solid), this is referred as a *phase transition* phenomenon [HOG 96]. On randomly generated instances, the position of this peak can be easily estimated with a reasonable precision. This therefore allows us to predict beforehand whether an instance is consistent or difficult to solve, given general statistics such as the number of variables, the domain sizes, the number and the tightness of constraints. However, this prediction ability does not extend from the very simple models used for random instance generation to real instances with complex features. For these, it seems unrealistic to reliably predict their consistency or their solving time using only a few global indicators.

6.7.2. *Constraint optimization problems*

In this case, the main lessons learned are as follows:

– Solving *optimization* problems is usually harder than solving pure *satisfaction* problems. This can be explained by the fact that solving an optimization problem using tree search reduces to a sequence of satisfaction problems. Among these, the two

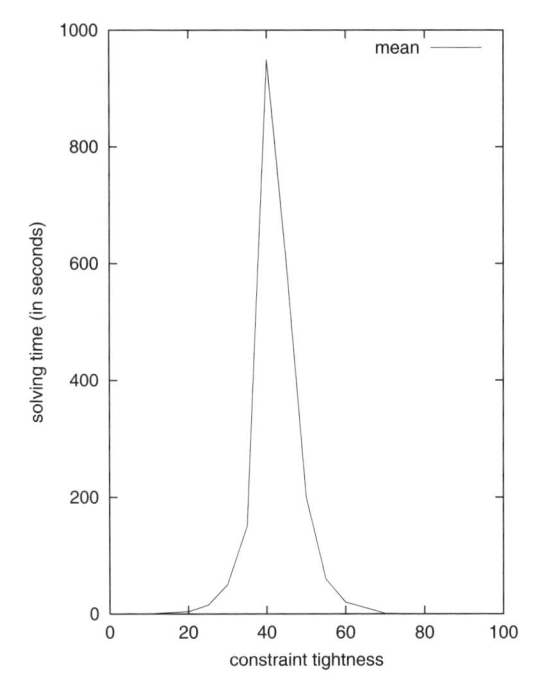

Figure 6.22. *Mean CPU time for solving a set of randomly generated instances having the same global characteristics: phase transition phenomenon at the consistency/inconsistency frontier*

final problems (finding an optimal solution and proving its optimality, which requires proving that there is no better solution) are both close to the frontier between consistent and inconsistent instances, which is the region where the complexity peak occurs.

– If we consider the quality of the solutions found as a function of CPU time, we often observe that *local search* behaves far better than *tree search* and is generally able to quickly produce good quality solutions (see Figure 6.23). This can be explained by the disordered and opportunistic behavior of local search opposed to the ordered and systematic behavior of tree search. The latter can take a lot of time to reconsider its first (possibly bad) choices.

6.8. Polynomial classes

Even if the general CSP is *NP-complete* (see section 6.3), there may be sub-classes of the general problem for which polynomial time algorithms exist. A lot of effort has been dedicated to try to identify such *polynomial* classes. We present two such classes that, despite the restriction they bring to the general case, still allow some

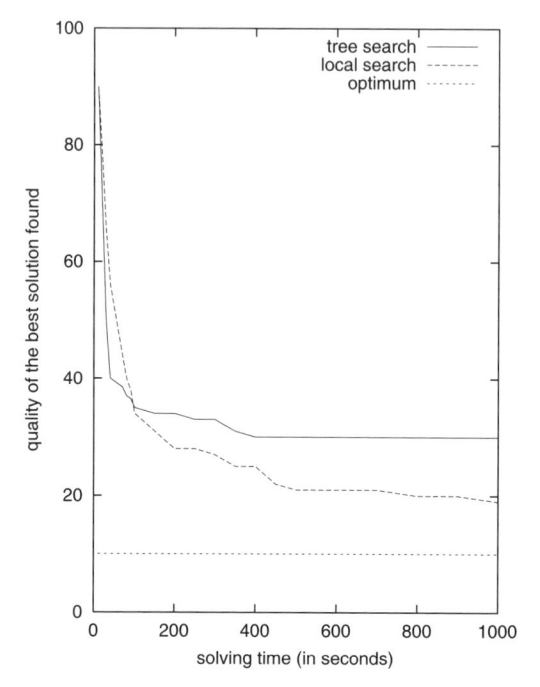

Figure 6.23. *Evolution of the quality of the best solution found on a given instance as a function of time*

real problems to be represented. In the first class of *acyclic constraint networks*, the restriction lies in the so-called syntactical or structural part of the problem: the constraint graph. In the second class of *simple temporal constraint networks*, the restriction lies on the semantical part of the problem: the nature of the constraints. An algebraic characterization of polynomial classes based on the semantics of the constraints (so-called polynomial languages) is given in [JEA 95].

6.8.1. *Acyclic constraint networks*

Let us consider a constraint network with binary constraints such that its constraint graph is *acyclic* or equivalently is a *tree* or a *forest*. (A forest is an acyclic graph and a tree is an acyclic connected graph. A forest is therefore a set of disconnected trees. If the constraint graph is a forest, each tree can be processed separately.) It can be solved in two ways:

– The first method consists of filtering the network by *arc-consistency* (see section 6.5.2). If filtering leads to an empty domain, then the problem is proven to be inconsistent. Otherwise, it is possible to show that it is consistent and that a solution can be produced without backtrack by assigning any variable with any value in its domain (remaining after filtering), and then recursively assigning each of its neighbor variables with any value in its domain that is compatible with the previously chosen values. Such a value always exists by arc-consistency itself. In fact, this is a case where local consistency filtering, despite its polynomial time complexity, is complete.

– The second method consists of choosing an arbitrary variable v and in building the rooted tree defined by the constraint graph and the choice of v as its root. (The rooted tree defined by a tree and one of its vertex s is obtained by taking s as the root and by recursively considering neighbor vertices as sons of s.) Then, we can simply apply a *bucket elimination* algorithm (see section 6.6.2) which eliminates variables from the leaves to the root of the tree. The constraints added are unary constraints similar to filtered domains because the induced width is equal to 1. As before, if an empty domain appears, the network is inconsistent. Otherwise it is consistent and a solution can be produced without backtrack by assigning variables in the inverse order, from the root to the leaves.

If both methods have the same asymptotic temporal complexity of $O(n \cdot d^2)$, the latter is less expensive in practice because it is actually equivalent to performing arc-consistency filtering in one direction only for each constraint. This is also called *directional arc-consistency* [DEC 87] and we are in a situation where directional arc-consistency is complete.

6.8.2. *Simple temporal constraint networks*

A simple temporal constraint network is a binary constraint network involving integer or real variables (where discrete or continuous domains behave similarly and can be treated the same). The variables represent temporal events with the restriction that any constraint connecting a variable t_i and a variable t_j can be written as $l_{ij} \leq t_i - t_j \leq u_{ij}$ [DEC 91]. Despite its simplicity, such a framework allows many real-time management problems to be represented. The so-called PERT (project evaluation and review technique) [KEL 61] graphs which are largely used in project management are a specific case of such problems.

The problem defined here is a linear programming problem (linear constraints only, no criterion). However, the specific nature of the linear constraints involved implies that the problem can be solved either by *path-consistency* filtering (see section 6.5.3), or equivalently by an *all-pairs shortest path* algorithm such as the Floyd-Warshall algorithm [GON 84]. Both algorithms have the same complexity of $O(n^3)$.

6.9. Existing tools

Historically, the first software tools for constraint programming were developed on the foundations of *logic programming*. This followed the work of [JAF 87] who showed that *unification between terms*, a fundamental mechanism of logic programming, can be interpreted as a specific constraint solving problem. It could also, under some simple assumptions, be extended to handle various constraint systems such as linear constraints over real variables [COL 90, JAF 92] or arbitrary constraints over finite domains [COD 96, DIN 88]. However, during the 1990s, constraint programming tended to drift slowly away from the limiting framework of logic programming.

These research projects have given birth to commercial tools such as *CP Optimizer* [ILO 08], *Chip* [COS 08], or *SICStus Prolog* [SIC 08], but also to free academic tools such as *Choco* [LAB 08], *ECLiPSe* [ECL 08], *Comet* [HEN 08], *GNU Prolog* [DIA 08], *Gecode* [SCH 08] and *FaCiLe* [BRI 08].

6.10. Extensions of the basic framework

Several extensions of the basic CSP framework have been proposed in several directions. We only present four of them: the handling of *continuous domains*, the so-called *conditional* and *dynamic* problems and the simultaneous handling of *constraints* and *preferences*.

6.10.1. *Continuous domains*

Before any consideration about continuous domains, we remind ourselves that real numbers cannot be directly represented in a computer which is fundamentally a discrete and finite machine. Real numbers are usually approximated by floating point numbers or by intervals whose bounds are floating point numbers. As the number of different floating point numbers that can be represented in a computer is finite we are again handling finite domains, but with two important differences compared to the previous case: (1) the size of the domains is such that it is generally not reasonable to enumerate them, and (2) the real numbers between two successive floating point numbers cannot be explicitly represented and processed.

Two types of methods of the original CSP framework on finite domains have been extended to continuous domains: *filtering* methods and *tree search* methods.

A first type of filtering method relies on the results of *interval analysis* [MOO 66] which extends the usual operations on real numbers to intervals. In interval arithmetic, addition is simply defined as $\forall a, b, c, d / (a \leq b) \wedge (c \leq d), [a,b] + [c,d] = [a+c, b+d]$, because the set of real numbers z such that $z = x + y$, $x \in [a,b]$, and $y \in [c,d]$ is indeed the interval $[a+c, b+d]$. More generally, an operation $\otimes_f$ on reals is extended to an operation $\otimes_i$ on intervals of real numbers, such that $\forall x \in [a,b], \forall y \in [c,d], x \otimes_f y \in [a,b] \otimes_i [c,d]$.

Table 6.4 depicts an example of filtering using interval analysis on an instance involving 3 variables x, y and z. The variables have $[0, 10]$, $[1, 3]$ and $[0, 2]$ as their respective domains (all reals) and two constraints $x = 4y$ and $y \leq z$. Every row represents the state of the domains of the variables at a given step of the algorithm. A dash means that the domain is not changed compared to the previous step. The first row represents the initial domains. The second row represents the domain of x after its filtering with respect to the constraint $x = 4y$ and the domain of y, since $y \in [1, 3]$ and $x = 4y$, $x \in 4 \cdot [1, 3] = [4, 12]$ and $x \in [0, 10]$, $x \in [4, 12] \cap [0, 10] = [4, 10]$. The domains after the complete filtering appear on the last row. The constraints of this tiny example are linear but this method also applies to nonlinear constraints such as $x \cdot y = z$ or $x^y geqz$.

		Domains		
Constraint	Filtered variable	x	y	z
		$[0, 10]$	$[1, 3]$	$[0, 2]$
$x = 4y$	x	$[4, 10]$	–	–
$x = 4y$	y	–	$[1, 2.5]$	–
$y \leq z$	y	–	$[1, 2]$	–
$y \leq z$	z	–	–	$[1, 2]$
$x = 4y$	x	$[4, 8]$	–	–
		$[4, 8]$	$[1, 2]$	$[1, 2]$

Table 6.4. *Example of filtering based on interval analysis*

Figure 6.24 represents the filtering on continuous domains as the *projection* of a constraint on a domain. $d(x)$ and $d(y)$ are the initial domains of x and of y. The constraint c considered here is $|x - x_c|^2 + |y - y_c|^2 \leq r^2$. $P(c, x, y)$ is the projection on y of the combination of the constraint c and of the domain $d(x)$ of x. The new domain $d'(y)$ of y is the intersection of $P(c, x, y)$ and of its previous domain $d(y)$. Note that it is possible to use any super-set of $P(c, x, y)$ instead of $P(c, x, y)$. The main problem underlying filtering consists of designing mechanisms which allow the domains of the variables to be as much as possible reduced without enumerating values and without eliminating any value that participates in a solution. Interval analysis is one way of achieving this goal. Other ways have been proposed, such as filtering by *2B consistency* [LHO 93] or *box consistency* [BEN 94], which are approximations of arc-consistency filtering based on interval bound reasoning. See [COL 99] for a synthetic overview.

Considering tree search, the *partitioning* mechanism which is the most often used consists of splitting the domain of a chosen variable into two sub-domains of the same size. However, more complex splitting mechanisms in several sub-domains of different sizes can also be considered.

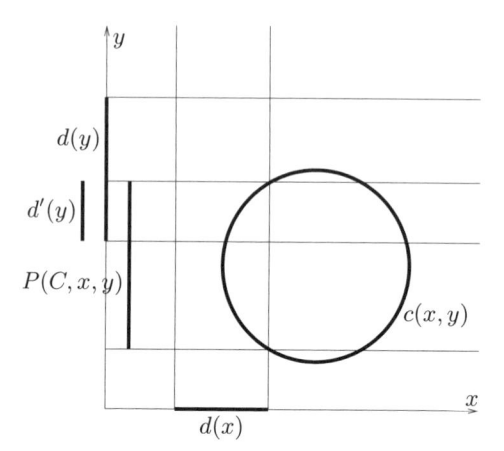

Figure 6.24. *Example of constraint projection*

Numerica [HEN 97] is an example of a tool dedicated to modeling and solving CSP on continuous variables.

6.10.2. *Conditional problems*

The *conditional* CSP framework has been introduced in order to represent problems whose solutions do not all have the same structure and involve different sets of variables and constraints: the existence of some variables and constraints in the problem may depend on the assignment of other variables. Such a situation may appear in various problems such as configuration ones. In a car configuration problem, the choice of a motor type (gas oil or not) may define two different sets of variables and associated constraints which describe the specific choices and the constraints to be satisfied in each case.

The so-called *dynamic* CSP framework [MIT 90] has been proposed to model such situations, although the term *conditional* would probably have been better suited. This framework associates an *activation state* with every variable and introduced two types of variables (variables that are always active and those that can become active or not) and two types of constraints (compatibility constraints which are similar to usual ones and activation constraints which define, often as rules, the activation conditions of the potentially active variables). For example, an activation constraint may be 'if $v = val$, then v' is active'.

It must be stressed that the conditional CSP framework can be considered simply as syntactic sugar. It is easy to transform any conditional CSP into a classical one where every potentially active variable includes, in its domain, a special *null* value representing the fact that it is not active. This is done by modifying the compatibility constraints in order to capture the fact that the *null* value is compatible with all other values and by reformulating, using the *null* values, all the activation constraints as classical constraints.

6.10.3. *Dynamic problems*

The *dynamic* CSP framework [DEC 88] has been introduced to capture situations where local modifications are introduced in the problem to be solved because of changes in the problem environment or objectives, for example in planning and scheduling problems.

In the CSP framework, any problem modification can be expressed by the addition or the removal of constraints (unary, binary or n-ary). The difficulty lies in the fact that adding a constraint may invalidate the result of a previous search (a previous solution may violate some of the new constraints), whereas removing a constraint may invalidate a previous reasoning (a previous filtering may no longer be valid).

Specific dynamic reasoning and search methods have been proposed to deal with these issues, which can cope with constraint additions or removals without requiring a complete restart from scratch in case of invalidation [VER 05]. Another more recent direction of research consists of developing methods that can anticipate potential changes. Examples include computing *robust* solutions (which are more likely to resist predictable changes [HÉB 04]) or *flexible* solutions (which can be simply adapted to the changes that occurred). Such methods are related to the problems considered in section 6.11.1.

6.10.4. *Constraints and preferences*

We have seen that the basic CSP framework only allows pure satisfaction problems to be expressed: a constraint can either be satisfied or not. If it is not satisfied, then it completely invalidates the current assignment. This framework does not allow partial or gradual satisfaction or dissatisfaction to be expressed. It cannot deal with inconsistent problems or compare different assignments which each violate some constraints (although not necessarily the same ones and are therefore not equivalent). It cannot deal with consistent problems where solutions are not all equivalent from the user point of view. To deal with these issues, several extensions of the CSP framework have been proposed:

– *Additive* CSP is where a positive number, which represents a violation cost, is associated with each constraint and where the cost of a complete assignment is defined as the sum of all violated constraint costs. The specific case where all constraints have the same cost of 1 defines the Max-CSP problem where we seek an assignment that maximizes the number of satisfied constraints (or minimizes the number of violated ones) [FRE 92, SHA 81].

– *Possibilistic* CSP is where a number between 0 and 1, which represents a priority, is associated with each constraint. The level of a complete assignment is defined as the maximum priority among all violated constraints [ROS 76, SCH 92].

– *Fuzzy* CSP is where a number between 0 and 1 is associated with each combination of values A_c of the variables of a constraint c. This number can be interpreted as the membership degree of A_c to the fuzzy relation c (interpreted using fuzzy set theory [ZAD 78]) or as the satisfaction degree of c by A_c. The level of a complete assignment A is then defined as the minimum of all the constraints of their satisfaction degrees by A [DUB 96]. (Note that it is possible to transform a possibilistic CSP into a fuzzy CSP. This is done by associating a membership degree $1 - p$ with every combination of values forbidden by a constraint whose priority is p, whereas allowed combinations receive a degree of 1.)

– *Probabilistic* CSP is where a number between 0 and 1 is associated with each constraint c, which represents the probability that c exists in the real problem. The level of an assignment is then defined as the probability of being a solution of the real problem given the probability of existence of the constraints it violates [FAR 93a].

These extensions all share similar characteristics:

– A *level* (we could equivalently speak of priority, importance, degree, weight, cost, etc.), numerical or not, is associated with either (1) every constraint, or (2) for every constraint, with every combination of values of its variables. Case 1 can be seen as a specific sub-case of case 2, where the level associated with a combination of values A_c of the variables of a constraint c is equal to an identity level when A_c satisfies c, and to the level of c otherwise. Only two different levels are used for all combinations of values of the variables of c.

– The level associated with a complete assignment A is the result of combining the levels associated with either (1) the constraints violated by A or (2) the projections of A on the variables of each constraint. Each constraint is therefore a function which maps assignments to levels and provides a local evaluation of the assignment. The different local evaluations are then combined to define a global evaluation.

– Assignments with a preferred global evaluation are sought. The problem can therefore be seen as an optimization problem where the criterion to be optimized is a function of the constraint satisfaction.

This observation has lead to the definition of generic frameworks such as *Semiring CSP* (SCSP) [BIS 95, BIS 97] or *Valued CSP* (VCSP) [SCH 95]. These frameworks are presented and compared in [BIS 99]. They rely on similar algebraic structures and cover classical, additive, possibilistic, fuzzy and probabilistic CSP, as well as many other extensions. The main difference between SCSP and VCSP lies in the ability of the SCSP to represent partially ordered sets of levels, whereas the VCSP framework assumes totally ordered levels. Adding this assumption to SCSP makes them equivalent to VCSP.

If we consider the example of VCSP, a VCSP is defined as a 5-tuple (V, D, C, S, F). The first three elements are the same as in classical CSP: a sequence V of variables, a sequence D of domains and a sequence C of constraints. The fourth element S is a so-called valuation structure, defined by a valuation set E and equipped with a total order $\prec$, a binary combination operator $\otimes$, a minimum element $\bot$ and a maximum element $\top$. The fifth element F is a valuation function which associates an element of E with either (1) every constraint, or (2) for every constraint with each combination of values of its variables.

E is used to associate a level with the constraints or with the combinations of values of variables of each constraint, and also with complete assignments. $\prec$ is used to compare different elements of E and $\otimes$ to combine them. (Note that in the VCSP framework, elements of E represent levels of dissatisfaction. Smaller elements are therefore preferred.) $\bot$ is used to express a complete satisfaction and $\top$ to express a complete dissatisfaction. Some reasonable properties are expected such as commutativity, associativity and monotonicity of $\otimes$, as well as the existence of an identity element and of an absorbing element for $\otimes$ (which must be $\bot$ and $\top$, respectively). The standard query, which is equivalent to the usual CSP query in the classical case (see section 6.2.4), is to produce an optimal assignment (minimum according to $\prec$).

For example:
– For *classical* CSP, E contains two elements t (*true*) and f (*false*) with $t = \bot$, $f = \top$, and $t \prec f$. $\otimes$ is the logical *and* and the level f is associated with every constraint.

– For *possibilistic* CSP, E is the set of reals between 0 and 1, with $0 = \bot$ and $1 = \top$. $\prec$ is the usual order on reals and $\otimes = max$. A strictly positive level is associated with every constraint, indicating its priority.

– For *additive* CSP, E is the set of non-negative integers completed with a special $+\infty$ level, with $0 = \bot$ and $+\infty = \top$. $\prec$ is the usual order on integers and $\otimes = +$. A strictly positive level is associated with every constraint, indicating its violation cost.

It is worth considering these problems from the point of view of relaxations. A *relaxation* of a problem is a classical CSP defined by a subset C' of the constraints in the problem. A relaxation is associated with a level equal to the combination of the levels of all the relaxed constraints (those in $C - C'$). It is easy to show that every optimal assignment A is associated with an optimal consistent relaxation of the same level (the relaxation that relaxes all the constraints violated by A). Conversely, it is easy to show that every optimal consistent relaxation C' is associated with a set of optimal assignments of the same level (the set of solutions of C'). Looking for an optimal assignment is therefore equivalent to looking for an optimal consistent relaxation.

Let us consider the CSP instance whose microstructure appears in Figure 6.25. (This instance has been obtained from the instance of Figure 6.2 by eliminating value 1 of v_3 and value 3 of v_4, and by modifying constraint c_4 (≤ 4 instead of ≤ 3).) This instance is inconsistent: no complete assignment can simultaneously satisfy the four constraints. Table 6.5 shows the unsatisfied constraints for every possible assignment. The problem of choosing an assignment can be considered as a multiple criteria optimization problem.

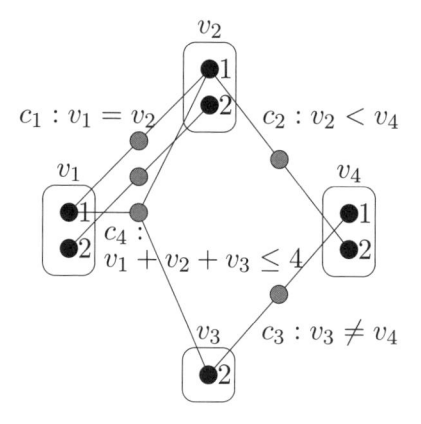

Figure 6.25. *An inconsistent CSP instance*

	Variables				Constraints			
	v_1	v_2	v_3	v_4	c_1	c_2	c_3	c_4
A_1	1	1	2	1		×		
A_2	1	1	2	2			×	
A_3	1	2	2	1	×	×		×
A_4	1	2	2	2	×	×	×	×
A_5	2	1	2	1	×	×		×
A_6	2	1	2	2	×		×	×
A_7	2	2	2	1		×		×
A_8	2	2	2	2			×	× × ×

Table 6.5. *Unsatisfied constraints for each of the 8 possible complete assignments. Each row is associated with a complete assignment. The unsatisfied constraints are marked with a cross*

Optimal solutions depend on the valuation structure and function considered:
– In *classical* CSP, all the assignments have the same level f and are equivalent.

– In *Max-CSP* (additive CSP with a cost of 1 associated with every constraint), A_1 and A_2 are the two optimal assignments i.e. those that violate the smallest number of constraints.

– In *additive* CSP and if the constraint violation costs are 1, 5, 2 and 1, respectively, A_2 becomes the only optimal assignment with a cost of 2.

– If instead, we use *possibilistic* CSP and if the priorities are 0.1, 0.5, 0.2 and 0.1, respectively, A_2 and A_6 are the two optimal assignments both with a level of 0.2, even though A_2 violates less constraints than A_6. This is called the *drowning* effect, induced by the idempotent combination operator used. To avoid this effect, a usual approach consists of shifting from possibilistic CSP to *lexicographic* CSP [FAR 93b], where two assignments are compared using a *leximin* approach [MOU 88]. In such a framework, A_2 would become the only optimal assignment.

Figure 6.26 shows the lattice of relaxations based on the inclusion relation, as well as the frontier between consistency and inconsistency. We can see that:

– In the *Max-CSP* case, the two consistent optimal relaxations are $\{c_1, c_2, c_4\}$ and $\{c_1, c_3, c_4\}$, which both relax one constraint.

– In the *additive* CSP case and if the constraints costs are 1, 5, 2 and 1, respectively, $\{c_1, c_2, c_4\}$ becomes the only consistent optimal relaxation.

– In the *possibilistic* CSP case, if the constraint priorities are 0.1, 0.5, 0.2 and 0.1, respectively, the four optimal consistent relaxations are $\{c_1, c_2, c_4\}$, $\{c_1, c_2\}$, $\{c_2, c_4\}$ and $\{c_2\}$. However, the latter three are only subsets of the first and are not maximal for inclusion. It is possible to add constraints to each of them without loosing consistency. In the *lexicographic* CSP case, $\{c_1, c_2, c_4\}$ becomes the only optimal consistent relaxation.

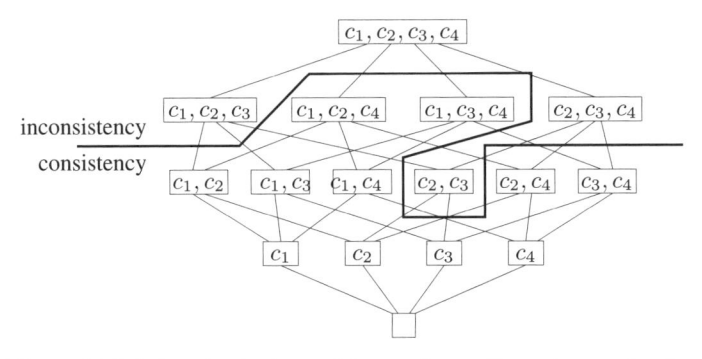

Figure 6.26. *Relaxation lattice and the consistency/inconsistency frontier*

If we consider additional properties of the combination operator $\otimes$, we can distinguish *idempotent* VCSP (which use an idempotent operator) from *strictly monotonic* VCSP (which use a strictly monotonic operator). (An operator $\otimes$ is idempotent if and only if $\forall a,\ a \otimes a = a$. This is the case for max and for the logical *and* which is actually equivalent to max on a set of two elements.) Among the first, we find classical, possibilistic and fuzzy CSP. Among the second, we find classical, additive, probabilistic and lexicographic CSP. It must be stressed that the only idempotent operator in the VCSP framework is max (which captures classical, fuzzy and possibilistic CSP). The the only VCSP structure that is both idempotent and strictly monotonic corresponds to classical CSP. There are structures that are neither idempotent, nor strictly monotonic (see Figure 6.27).

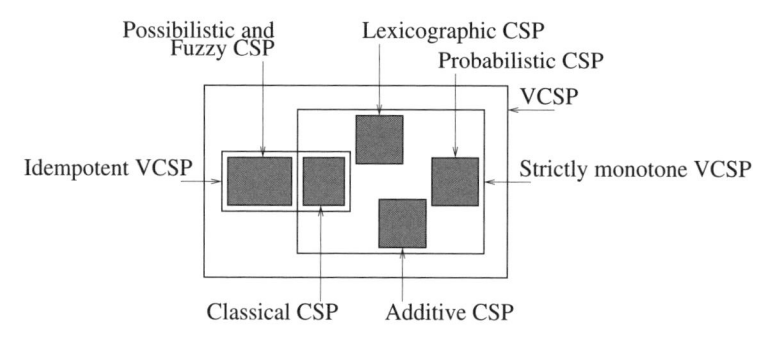

Figure 6.27. *Different VCSP classes*

Although this classification may initially appear to be purely theoretical, its practical impact is strong. From the semantical point of view, we have seen in the example of Figure 6.25 that non-strictly monotonic VCSP such as possibilistic or fuzzy CSP are suffering from the so-called drowning effect: more unsatisfied constraints may lead to no change in the level of an assignment. Conversely, from a computational point of view, we shall see that the non-idempotent VCSP, such as lexicographic, probabilistic or additive CSP, are usually much more difficult to solve.

Considering the reasoning methods presented in section 6.5 such as arc-consistency filtering, they can be simply extended to idempotent VCSP (possibilistic and fuzzy CSP [DUB 96, ROS 76, SCH 92]), but this extension is not so obvious for non-idempotent VCSP (additive, lexicographic and probabilistic CSP). The reason for this difficulty lies in the fact that filtering algorithms work by adding deduced constraints to the filtered instance in order to ensure propagation in the constraint network. If the operator used for combining violation levels is idempotent, adding a deduced constraint to the instance produces an equivalent instance. However, if it is not idempotent, equivalence is no longer guaranteed. This is why dedicated filtering methods have been developed which work on non-idempotent VCSP:

– methods based on *inconsistency counts* (arc-consistency or directed arc-consistency counts [FRE 92, LAR 96, LAR 99, WAL 94]), which add no deduced constraint and therefore perform no propagation in the constraint network; and

– real *propagation*-based methods (soft arc-consistency [COO 04, LAR 02, LAR 03b, SCH 00]), which actually add deduced constraints, but compensate for these additions, defining so-called equivalence preserving transformations.

Considering the *search* methods presented in section 6.6:

– Tree search methods such as the *backtrack* algorithm (see section 6.6.1) can be easily extended to the *depth-first branch and bound* algorithm. Among the different parameters that define this algorithm, the one that has the strongest influence on efficiency is clearly the mechanism that computes at each node n of the tree a *lower bound* on the optimum of the sub-instance associated with n. This mechanism is equivalent to the inconsistency detection mechanism used in classical CSP. Indeed, this lower bound allows us to backtrack each time it is greater than or equal to the level of the best solution found so far (this guarantees that no optimal solution is lost because in such a case all the assignments below the current node cannot have a level better than the best one found so far). To compute such a lower bound, mechanisms such as the backward and forward-checking can be easily extended. However, similarly to what occurs with classical CSP, more sophisticated mechanisms such as directed arc-consistency counts or soft arc-consistency presented previously produce stronger lower bounds with a better global efficiency.

– Variable elimination methods such as *bucket elimination* (see section 6.6.2) can be directly extended to the VCSP framework. They were actually initially designed to solve optimization problems such as VCSP [BER 72]. Let us consider a variable v, $C' \subseteq C$ the set of all the constraints involving v and $V' \subseteq V$ the set of all the variables involved in at least one of the constraints in C', excluding v itself. Eliminating v consists of computing, for every combination of values for the variables in V', the optimum level of its extension to v, taking into account constraints in C' and in recording these levels in a constraint c on the variables in V'.

– Regarding greedy and local search methods (see sections 6.6.3 and 6.6.4), they are explicit optimization methods and their adaptation to the VCSP framework is obvious.

Overall, we should remember that although the VCSP search space is exactly the same as the classical CSP search space, solving VCSP is usually much harder than solving CSP.

The first reason has already been presented in section 6.7.2 for tree search methods. To solve an optimization problem, we must solve a sequence of satisfaction problems among which the latter two are located close to the consistency/inconsistency frontier where the hardest problems are.

The second reason lies in the weakened pruning power of the lower bounds used in VCSP solving, such as directed arc-consistency counts or soft arc-consistency, compared to the pruning power or inconsistency detection mechanisms used in CSP solving such as hard arc-consistency. Experiments on randomly generated instances confirm this phenomenon: contrary to the classical CSP case where complexity decreases suddenly after the consistency/inconsistency frontier, complexity actually starts to increase tremendously after this frontier in the VCSP case.

Once again, the idempotent possibilistic and fuzzy CSP have a specific behavior because they can always be resolved by solving a sequence of classical CSP called α-*cuts*. The α-cut of a possibilistic CSP is the classical CSP that contains only constraints whose priority is greater than or equal to α. It is, for example, possible to start by solving the α-cut defined by α set to the maximum priority over all the constraints. Every time an α-cut is consistent, it is known for sure that the optimum of the possibilistic CSP is strictly lower than α and it is possible to take the priority immediately below as a new value for α. As soon as an α-cut is inconsistent, then it is known that the optimum of the possibilistic CSP is α. If k is the number of different levels of priority used in the possibilistic CSP, its solution requires at most k classical CSP solvings. Using dichotomic search on priority levels, it is even possible to reduce to only $O(\log(k))$ classical CSP solvings.

Considering *polynomial classes*, it is worth noting that the complexity of acyclic constraint networks (see section 6.8.1) remains unchanged when shifting from classical CSP to VCSP. More generally, and quite logically, all the computational complexity arguments that are based purely on the graph structure remain valid when the VCSP framework is considered.

6.11. Open problems

There are still a number of topics that can be qualified as open problems, considering that ongoing research has not yet reached the level of maturity observed on the previously described topics. We only consider four of them, chosen because we consider that they are fundamental for dealing with real problems. They include simultaneous handling of *constraints* and *uncertainty*, solving under hard or soft *real time constraints* and *interactive* and *distributed* solving.

6.11.1. *Constraints and uncertainties*

When CSP is used to represent constrained decision problems, the CSP variables are used to represent either decisions made by the agent or deterministic consequences of these decisions. An example is the cost of an action or the system state following its execution. They cannot represent decisions made by the environment or by other agents that would not be under the control of the agent itself such as, for example, the system state following the execution of a non-deterministic action.

Using a uniform representation for decisions coming from the agent, the environment or from other agents would lead to an incorrect modeling as showed by the following example where the problem is to decide whether an umbrella should be carried or not. Let us assume that three Boolean variables are used: um (representing the decision to carry or not an umbrella), ra (representing the fact that it rains or not) and we (representing the fact that the agent will be wet or not). Four constraints allow the problem itself to be modeled: $(\neg um \wedge ra) \rightarrow we$, $(um \wedge ra) \rightarrow \neg we$, $(\neg ra) \rightarrow \neg we$, $\neg we$. The first three constraints represent laws of physics. The latter represents the requirement of the agent who does not want to be wet. One of the solutions of this CSP is $\neg um$, $\neg ra$, $\neg we$, which would mean that the agent has the ability to decide whether it rains or not.

This example brings to light the necessity of splitting variables into *controllable* and *uncontrollable* variables from the agent point of view, as it has been proposed in [FAR 96]. This allows queries to be expressed: e.g. finding an assignment of the controllable variables that is consistent whatever the values of the uncontrollable variables (as long as they satisfy the constraints that involve them). If additional knowledge is available on uncontrollable variables such as a probability distribution on every uncontrollable variable, the problem becomes a *stochastic CSP* [FAR 95, WAL 02]. This allows queries such as finding an assignment of the controllable variables whose probability of being a solution is maximum, given the possible values for the uncontrollable variables.

Replacing probabilities by possibilities, possibilistic variants of these queries can also be defined [DUB 95]. We can observe the proximity between works on stochastic CSP and those on *stochastic satisfiability* [LIT 01]. We can also observe that *probabilistic CSP* (see section 6.10.4) offers yet another way of capturing uncertainty. In this case, uncertainty is associated with the existence of some constraints rather than the possible values of some uncontrollable variables.

6.11.2. *Deciding or reasoning under time constraints*

In practice, very few real decision making or reasoning problems exist with absolutely no constraints on the time needed to produce an output. This time constraint is specifically strong when the process is interacting with the environment (online situation analysis or planning for autonomous systems) or with a user (see the following section): decision and reasoning must follow the timing imposed by the environment or the user.

The development of increasingly efficient methods only offers a partial answer to this problem because even the most efficient available tools cannot always solve arbitrary instances to optimality in the available time. A natural question that arises is the level of compromise between the solving time and the quality of the result obtained. The *utility* of the result is an increasing function of its quality, but also a decreasing function of its delivery time.

This is why people have considered the use of concepts such as *bounded* reasoning from a resource or time point of view, or *anytime* reasoning which is able to provide a result at any time with a increasing quality as a function of the running time [BOD 94, DEA 88, RUS 91, ZIL 96].

In the CSP framework, or rather in the VCSP framework, most results have been dedicated either to the adaptation of the algorithms to the instance to solve and to the time available for solving it [LOB 98], or to the development of methods that produce good quality profiles (evolution of the quality, or more generally of lower and upper bounds on the optimum, as a function of time) [GIV 97].

6.11.3. *Interactive decision*

All the methods developed in the CSP framework assume an automatic solving of decision making problems. However, in many situations, such as the management of large systems including human supervision, if users require the support of software tools for decision making, they do not necessarily want the decisions to be automatically made by the software. Typically, some decisions may be too important to be left to the software or the software does not have at its disposal all the information needed to compare decisions and to select the best one (either because information is too complex to be formalized, or because people do not want all the information to be formalized and therefore explicit).

The problem of the interaction between a user and a decision making software follows from such situations. The main approaches that have been considered up to now in this direction using the CSP framework include interleaving of user and software choices, visualization by the software of the consequences of user choices, production of explanations in the case of inconsistency and interactive restoration of consistency [e.g. AMI 02].

6.11.4. *Distributed decision*

Another restriction of the existing CSP methods is that they assume that all the data required to model and solve the problem are collected and processed by a single computing agent. However, an increasing number of real decision making problems occur in a distributed context where data are distributed between different agents and processed locally by these agents. Even when a centralization of all data and processing is technically possible, it is not necessarily accepted for confidentiality reasons or to preserve the locality of the decisions.

The *distributed CSP* framework tries to answer these requirements. In a distributed CSP, the set of variables of the network is divided between different agents (one variable belongs to precisely one agent). The set of constraints is divided between internal constraints that involve variables belonging to only one agent (these constraints are assigned to this agent) and external constraints that involve variables from more than one agent (these constraints are often duplicated inside each corresponding agent). A distributed CSP can be seen as a set of CSP, one per agent, interconnected by external constraints. The intra-agent connectivity is *a priori* stronger than the inter-agent connectivity. Otherwise, we should probably reconsider the choice of a distributed approach or the current organization of the distribution.

The methods developed to solve such CSP try to preserve the autonomy and the asynchronism of local decisions while guaranteeing the consistency of the global decision using a minimum number and size of messages [MOD 05, YOK 00]. Recent works also focus on the preservation of confidentiality of local data during solving [WAL 05].

6.12. Books, journals, websites and conferences

There are a number of good references on this research area. Some of them are more oriented towards the pure CSP framework (definitions, properties, algorithms, etc.), such as [DEC 03, TSA 93]. Others are more oriented towards constraint programming, logic or not (software, solvers, etc.), such as [APT 03, MAR 98, HEN 89]. The recent extensive *Handbook of Constraint Programming* [ROS 06] covers both aspects and much more.

At the international level, the *Association for Constraint Programming* [ACP 08] maintains a web site [CPO 08] and uses a mailing list [CSP 08]. Beyond general artificial intelligence conferences and journals, publications on the topic appear in the international *Constraints* journal [CON 08] and in annual conferences such as CP (International Conference on Principles and Practice of Constraint Programming) and CPAIOR (International Conference on Integration of Artificial Intelligence and Operations Research Techniques in Constraint Programming for Combinatorial Optimization Problems).

6.13. Bibliography

[AAR 97] AARTS E., LENSTRA J., Eds., *Local Search in Combinatorial Optimization*, John Wiley & Sons, 1997.

[ACP 08] ACP, "Association for Constraint Programming", 2008, http://slash.math.unipd.it/acp/.

[AMI 02] AMILHASTRE J., FARGIER H., MARQUIS P., "Consistency Restoration and Explanations in Dynamic CSP: Application to Configuration", *Artificial Intelligence*, vol. 135, num. 1, p. 199–234, 2002.

[APT 03] APT K., *Principles of Constraint Programming*, Cambridge University Press, 2003.

[BAP 01] BAPTISTE P., PAPE C. L., NUIJTEN W., *Constraint-based Scheduling: Applying Constraint Programming to Scheduling Problems*, Kluwer Academic Publishers, 2001.

[BEN 94] BENHAMOU F., MCALLESTER D., HENTENRYCK P. V., "CLP(Intervals) Revisited", *Proceedings of the International Symposium on Logic Programming (ILPS-94)*, Ithaca, NY, USA, p. 124–138, 1994.

[BER 72] BERTELÉ U., BRIOSCHI F., *Nonserial Dynamic Programming*, Academic Press, 1972.

[BES 94] BESSIÈRE C., "Arc-consistency and arc-consistency again", *Artificial Intelligence*, vol. 65, num. 1, p. 179–190, 1994.

[BES 96] BESSIÈRE C., RÉGIN J., "MAC and Combined Heuristics: Two Reasons to Forsake FC (and CBJ?)", *Proceedings of the 2nd International Conference on Principles and Practice of Constraint Programming (CP-96, LNCS 1118)*, Cambridge, MA, USA, p. 61–75, 1996.

[BES 01] BESSIÈRE C., RÉGIN J., "Refining the Basic Constraint Propagation Algorithm", *Proceedings of the 17th International Joint Conference on Artificial Intelligence (IJCAI-01)*, Seattle, WA, USA, p. 309–315, 2001.

[BIS 95] BISTARELLI S., MONTANARI U., ROSSI F., "Constraint Solving over Semirings", *Proceedings of the 14th International Joint Conference on Artificial Intelligence (IJCAI-95)*, Montreal, Canada, p. 624–630, 1995.

[BIS 97] BISTARELLI S., MONTANARI U., ROSSI F., "Semiring-based Constraint Solving and Optimization", *Journal of ACM*, vol. 44, num. 2, p. 201–236, 1997.

[BIS 99] BISTARELLI S., MONTANARI U., ROSSI F., SCHIEX T., VERFAILLIE G., FARGIER H., "Semiring-Based CSPs and Valued CSPs: Frameworks, Properties and Comparison ftp://ftp.cert.fr/pub/verfaillie/vcsp-constraints.ps", *Constraints*, vol. 4, num. 3, p. 199–240, 1999.

[BIT 75] BITNER J., REINGOLD E., "Backtraking Programming Techniques", *Communications of the ACM*, vol. 18, num. 11, p. 651–656, 1975.

[BOD 94] BODDY M., DEAN T., "Deliberation Scheduling for Problem Solving in Time-Constrained Environments", *Artificial Intelligence*, vol. 67, num. 2, p. 245–285, 1994.

[BRE 96] BRESINA J., "Heuristic-Biased Stochastic Sampling", *Proceedings of the 13th National Conference on Artificial Intelligence (AAAI-96)*, Portland, OR, USA, p. 271–278, 1996.

[BRI 08] BRISSET P., "FaCiLe", 2008, http://www.recherche.enac.fr/opti/facile/.

[COD 96] CODOGNET P., DIAZ D., "Compiling Constraints in CLP(FD)", *Journal of Logic Programming*, vol. 27, num. 3, p. 185–226, 1996.

[COL 90] COLMERAUER A., "An Introduction to Prolog III", *Communications of the ACM*, vol. 33, num. 7, p. 69–90, 1990.

[COL 99] COLLAVIZZA H., DELOBEL F., RUEHER M., "Comparing Partial Consistencies", *Reliable Computing*, vol. 5, p. 1–16, 1999.

[CON 08] CONSTRAINTS, "Constraints: An International Journal", 2008, http://ai.uwaterloo.ca/ vanbeek/Constraints/constraints.html.

[COO 71] COOK S., "The Complexity of Theorem Proving Procedures", *Proceedings of the 3rd Annual ACM Symposium on Theory of Computing*, p. 151–158, 1971.

[COO 04] COOPER M., SCHIEX T., "Arc Consistency for Soft Constraints", *Artificial Intelligence*, vol. 154, num. 1-2, p. 199–227, 2004.

[COS 08] COSYTEC, "CHIP", 2008, http://www.cosytec.com/.

[CPO 08] CPO, "Constraint Programming Online", 2008, http://slash.math.unipd.it/cp/.

[CSP 08] CSPLIST, "CSP mailing list", 2008, csp@carlit.toulouse.inra.fr.

[DAN 63] DANTZIG G., *Linear Programming and Extensions*, Princeton University Press, 1963.

[DEA 88] DEAN T., BODDY M., "An Analysis of Time-Dependent Planning", *Proceedings of the 7th National Conference on Artificial Intelligence (AAAI-88)*, St. Paul, MN, USA, p. 49–54, 1988.

[DEB 97] DEBRUYNE R., BESSIÈRE C., "Some Practical Filtering Techniques for the Constraint Satisfaction Problem", *Proceedings of the 15th International Joint Conference on Artificial Intelligence (IJCAI-97)*, Nagoya, Japan, p. 412–417, 1997.

[DEB 01] DEBRUYNE R., BESSIÈRE C., "Domain Filtering Consistencies", *Journal of Artificial Intelligence Research*, vol. 14, p. 205–230, 2001.

[DEC 87] DECHTER R., PEARL J., "Network-based Heuristics for Constraint Satisfaction Problems", *Artificial Intelligence*, vol. 34, num. 1, p. 1–38, 1987.

[DEC 88] DECHTER R., DECHTER A., "Belief Maintenance in Dynamic Constraint Networks", *Proceedings of the 7th National Conference on Artificial Intelligence (AAAI-88)*, St. Paul, MN, USA, p. 37–42, 1988.

[DEC 89] DECHTER R., PEARL J., "Tree Clustering for Constraint Networks", *Artificial Intelligence*, vol. 38, num. 3, p. 353–366, 1989.

[DEC 90] DECHTER R., "Enhancement Schemes for Constraint Processing : Backjumping, Learning and Cutset Decomposition", *Artificial Intelligence*, vol. 41, num. 3, p. 273–312, 1990.

[DEC 91] DECHTER R., MEIRY I., PEARL J., "Temporal Constraint Networks", *Artificial Intelligence*, vol. 49, p. 61–95, 1991.

[DEC 99] DECHTER R., "Bucket Elimination: a Unifying Framework for Reasoning", *Artificial Intelligence*, vol. 113, p. 41–85, 1999.

[DEC 03] DECHTER R., *Constraint Processing*, Morgan Kaufmann, 2003.

[DIA 08] DIAZ D., "GNU Prolog", 2008, http://gnu-prolog.inria.fr/.

[DIN 88] DINCBAS M., HENTENRYCK P. V., SIMONIS H., AGGOUN A., GRAF T., BERTHIER F., "The Constraint Logic Programming Language CHIP", *Proceedings of the International Conference on Fifth Generation Computer Systems*, Tokyo, Japan, p. 249–264, 1988.

[DOR 96] DORIGO M., MANIEZZO V., COLORNI A., "The Ant System: Optimization by a Colony of Cooperating Agents", *IEEE Transactions on Systems, Man, and Cybernetics*, vol. 26, num. 1, p. 29–41, 1996.

[DUB 95] DUBOIS D., PRADE H., "Possibility Theory as a Basis for Qualitative Decision Theory", *Proceedings of the 14th International Joint Conference on Artificial Intelligence (IJCAI-95)*, Montreal, Canada, p. 1925–1930, 1995.

[DUB 96] DUBOIS D., FARGIER H., PRADE H., "Possibility Theory in Constraint Satisfaction Problems: Handling Priority, Preference and Uncertainty", *Applied Intelligence*, vol. 6, num. 4, p. 287–309, 1996.

[ECL 08] ECLIPSE, "ECLiPSe", 2008, http://eclipse.crosscoreop.com/.

[FAR 93a] FARGIER H., LANG J., "Uncertainty in Constraint Satisfaction Problems: A Probabilistic Approach", *Proceedings of the European Conference on Symbolic and Quantitavive Approaches of Reasoning under Uncertainty (ECSQARU-93)*, Grenada, Spain, p. 97–104, 1993.

[FAR 93b] FARGIER H., LANG J., SCHIEX T., "Selecting Preferred Solutions in Fuzzy Constraint Satisfaction Problems", *Proceedings of the 1st European Congress on Fuzzy and Intelligent Technologies (EUFIT-93)*, Germany, 1993.

[FAR 95] FARGIER H., LANG J., MARTIN-CLOUAIRE R., SCHIEX T., "A Constraint Satisfaction Framework for Decision under Uncertainty", *Proceedings of the 11th International Conference on Uncertainty in Artificial Intelligence (UAI-95)*, Montreal, Canada, p. 167–174, 1995.

[FAR 96] FARGIER H., LANG J., SCHIEX T., "Mixed Constraint Satisfaction: a Framework for Decision Problems under Incomplete Knowledge", *Proceedings of the 13th National Conference on Artificial Intelligence (AAAI-96)*, Portland, OR, USA, p. 175–180, 1996.

[FRE 78] FREUDER E., "Synthesizing Constraint Expressions", *Communications of the ACM*, vol. 21, num. 11, p. 958–966, 1978.

[FRE 92] FREUDER E., WALLACE R., "Partial Constraint Satisfaction", *Artificial Intelligence*, vol. 58, p. 21–70, 1992.

[FRE 96] FREUDER E., ELFE C., "Neighborhood Inverse Consistency Preprocessing", *Proceedings of the 13th National Conference on Artificial Intelligence (AAAI-96)*, Portland, OR, USA, p. 202–208, 1996.

[FRO 94] FROST D., DECHTER R., "Dead-end Driven Learning", *Proceedings of the 12th National Conference on Artificial Intelligence (AAAI-94)*, Seattle, WA, USA, p. 294–300, 1994.

[GAR 72] GARSINKEL R., NEMHAUSER G., *Integer Programming*, John Wiley & Sons, 1972.

[GAR 79] GAREY M., JOHNSON D., *Computers and Intractability : A Guide to the Theory of NP-completeness*, W.H. Freeman and Company, 1979.

[GIV 97] DE GIVRY S., VERFAILLIE G., SCHIEX T., "Bounding the Optimum of Constraint Optimization Problems ftp://ftp.cert.fr/pub/verfaillie/cp97.ps", *Proceedings of the 3rd International Conference on Principles and Practice of Constraint Programming (CP-97)*, Schloss Hagenberg, Austria, 1997.

[GLO 93] GLOVER F., LAGUNA M., "Tabu Search", *Modern Heuristic Techniques for Combinatorial Problems*, p. 70–141, Blackwell Scientific Publishing, 1993.

[GOL 89] GOLDBERG D., *Genetic Algorithms in Search, Optimization, and Machine Learning*, Addison-Wesley Publishing Company, 1989.

[GOM 98] GOMES C., SELMAN B., KAUTZ H., "Boosting Combinatorial Search Through Randomization", *Proceedings of the 15th National Conference on Artificial Intelligence (AAAI-98)*, Madison, WI, USA, p. 431–437, 1998.

[GON 84] GONDRAN M., MINOUX M., VAJDA S., *Graphs and Algorithms*, John Wiley & Sons, 1984.

[GOT 00] GOTTLOB G., LEONE N., SCARCELLO F., "A Comparison of Structural CSP Decomposition Methods", *Artificial Intelligence*, vol. 124, num. 2, p. 243–282, 2000.

[GU 97] GU J., PURDOM P., FRANCO J., WAH B., "Algorithms for the Satisfiability (SAT) Problem: A Survey", *DIMACS Series in Discrete Mathematics and Theoretical Computer Science*, vol. 35, p. 19–152, 1997.

[HAR 80] HARALICK R., ELLIOT G., "Increasing Tree Search Efficiency for Constraint Satisfaction Problems", *Artificial Intelligence*, vol. 14, num. 3, p. 263–313, 1980.

[HAR 95] HARVEY W., GINSBERG M., "Limited Discrepancy Search", *Proceedings of the 14th International Joint Conference on Artificial Intelligence (IJCAI-95)*, Montreal, Canada, p. 607–613, 1995.

[HÉB 04] HÉBRARD E., HNICH B., WALSH T., "Super Solutions in Constraint Programming", *Proceedings of the International Conference on Integration of Artificial Intelligence and Operations Research Techniques in Constraint Programming for Combinatorial Optimisation Problems (CP-AI-OR-04)*, Nice, France, p. 157–172, 2004.

[HEN 89] HENTENRYCK P. V., *Constraint Satisfaction in Logic Programming*, MIT Press, 1989.

[HEN 92] HENTENRYCK P. V., DEVILLE Y., TENG C., "A Generic Arc-consistency Algorithm and its Specializations", *Artificial Intelligence*, vol. 57, num. 2-3, p. 291–321, 1992.

[HEN 97] HENTENRYCK P. V., MICHEL L., DEVILLE Y., *Numerica*, MIT Press, 1997.

[HEN 08] HENTENRYCK P. V., MICHEL L., "COMET", 2008, http://www.comet-online.org/.

[HOG 96] HOGG T., HUBERMAN B., WILLIAMS C., "Phase Transitions and the Search Problem", *Artificial Intelligence: Special Issue on Frontiers in Problem Solving: Phase Transitions and Complexity*, vol. 81, num. 1-2, 1996.

[ILO 08] ILOG, "CP Optimizer", 2008, http://www.ilog.com/products/cpoptimizer/.

[JAF 87] JAFFAR J., LASSEZ J., "Constraint Logic Programming", *Proceedings of the 14th ACM Symposium on Principles of Programming Languages*, Munich, Germany, p. 111–119, 1987.

[JAF 92] JAFFAR J., MICHAYLOV S., STUCKEY P., YAP R., "The CLP(R) Language and System", *ACM Transactions on Programming Languages and Systems*, vol. 14, num. 3, p. 339–395, 1992.

[JEA 95] JEAVONS P., COHEN D., GYSSENS M., "A Unifying Framework for Tractable Constraints", *Proceedings of the 1st International Conference on Principles and Practice of Constraint Programming (CP-95, LNCS 976)*, Cassis, France, p. 276–291, 1995.

[JÉG 03] JÉGOU P., TERRIOUX C., "Hybrid Backtracking bounded by Tree-decomposition of Constraint Networks", *Artificial Intelligence*, vol. 146, num. 1, p. 43–75, 2003.

[JUS 02] JUSSIEN N., LHOMME O., "Local Search with Constraint Propagation and Conflict-based Heuristics", *Artificial Intelligence*, vol. 139, p. 21–45, 2002.

[KAN 94] KANELLAKIS P., GOLDIN D., "Constraint Programming and Database Query Languages", *Proceedings of the International Conference on Theoretical Aspects of Computer Software (TACS-04)*, Sendai, Japan, p. 96–120, 1994.

[KEL 61] KELLEY J., "Critical Path Planning and Scheduling: Mathematical Basis", *Operations Research*, vol. 9, p. 296–320, 1961.

[KIR 83] KIRKPATRICK S., GELATT C., VECCHI M., "Optimization by Simulated Annealing", *Science*, vol. 220, num. 4598, p. 671–680, 1983.

[LAB 08] LABURTHE F., "CHOCO", 2008, http://choco-solver.net/.

[LAR 96] LARROSA J., MESEGUER P., "Exploiting the Use of DAC in MAX-CSP", *Proceedings of the 2nd International Conference on Principles and Practice of Constraint Programming (CP-96, LNCS 1118)*, Cambridge, MA, USA, p. 308–322, 1996.

[LAR 99] LARROSA J., MESEGUER P., SCHIEX T., "Maintening Reversible DAC for Max-CSP", *Artificial Intelligence*, vol. 107, p. 149–163, 1999.

[LAR 02] LARROSA J., "Node and Arc Consistency in Weighted CSP", *Proceedings of the 18th National Conference on Artificial Intelligence (AAAI-02)*, Edmonton, Alberta, Canada, p. 48–53, 2002.

[LAR 03a] LARROSA J., DECHTER R., "Boosting Search with Variable Elimination in Constraint Optimization and Constraint Satisfaction Problems", *Constraints*, vol. 8, num. 3, p. 303–326, 2003.

[LAR 03b] LARROSA J., SCHIEX T., "In the Quest of the Best Form of Local Consistency for Weighted CSP", *Proceedings of the 18th International Joint Conference on Artificial Intelligence (IJCAI-03)*, Acapulco, Mexico, p. 239–244, 2003.

[LHO 93] LHOMME O., "Consistency Techniques for Numerical Constraint Satisfaction Problems", *Proceedings of the 13th International Joint Conference on Artificial Intelligence (IJCAI-93)*, Chambéry, France, p. 232–238, 1993.

[LIT 01] LITTMAN M., MAJERCIK S., PITASSI T., "Stochastic Boolean Satisfiability", *Journal of Automated Reasoning*, vol. 27, num. 3, p. 251–296, 2001.

[LOB 98] LOBJOIS L., LEMAÎTRE M., "Branch and Bound Algorithm Selection by Performance Prediction ftp://ftp.cert.fr/pub/verfaillie/estim-aaai98.ps", *Proceedings of the 15th National Conference on Artificial Intelligence (AAAI-98)*, Madison, WI, USA, p. 353–358, 1998.

[MAC 77a] MACKWORTH A., "Consistency in Networks of Relations", *Artificial Intelligence*, vol. 8, num. 1, p. 99–118, 1977.

[MAC 77b] MACKWORTH A., "On Reading Sketch Maps", *Proceedings of the 5th International Joint Conference on Artificial Intelligence (IJCAI-77)*, Cambridge, MA, USA, p. 598–606, 1977.

[MAI 83] MAIER D., *The Theory of Relational Databases*, Computer Science Press, 1983.

[MAR 98] MARRIOTT K., STUCKEY P., *Programming with Constraints: An Introduction*, MIT Press, 1998.

[MIN 92] MINTON S., JOHNSTON M., PHILIPS A., LAIRD P., "Minimizing Conflicts: a Heuristic Repair Method for Constraint Satisfaction and Scheduling Problems", *Artificial Intelligence*, vol. 58, p. 160–205, 1992.

[MIT 90] MITTAL S., FALKENHAINER B., "Dynamic Constraint Satisfaction Problems", *Proceedings of the 8th National Conference on Artificial Intelligence (AAAI-90)*, Boston, MA, USA, p. 25–32, 1990.

[MOD 05] MODI P., SHEN W., TAMBE M., YOKOO M., "Adopt: Asynchronous Distributed Constraint Optimization with Quality Guarantees", *Artificial Intelligence*, vol. 161, p. 149–180, 2005.

[MOH 86] MOHR R., HENDERSON T., "Arc and Path Consistency Revisited", *Artificial Intelligence*, vol. 28, num. 2, p. 225–233, 1986.

[MON 74] MONTANARI U., "Networks of Constraints: Fundamental Properties and Applications to Picture Processing", *Information Sciences*, vol. 7, num. 2, p. 95–132, 1974.

[MOO 66] MOORE R., *Interval Analysis*, Prentice Hall, 1966.

[MOU 88] MOULIN H., *Axioms of Cooperative Decision Making*, Cambridge University Press, 1988.

[NAD 89] NADEL B., "Constraint Satisfaction Algorithms", *Computational Intelligence*, vol. 5, p. 188–299, 1989.

[NEM 88] NEMHAUSER G., WOLSEY L., *Integer and Combinatorial Optimization*, John Wiley & Sons, 1988.

[PAP 94] PAPADIMITRIOU C., *Computational Complexity*, Addison-Wesley Publishing Company, 1994.

[PRA 05] PRALET C., VERFAILLIE G., "About the Choice of the Variable to Unassign in a Decision Repair Algorithm", *RAIRO Operations Research*, vol. 39, p. 55–74, 2005.

[PRO 93] PROSSER P., "Hybrid Algorithms for the Constraint Satisfaction Problems", *Computational Intelligence*, vol. 9, num. 3, p. 268–299, 1993.

[RÉG 96] RÉGIN J., "Generalized Arc Consistency for Global Cardinality Constraint", *Proceedings of the 13th National Conference on Artificial Intelligence (AAAI-96)*, Portland, OR, USA, p. 209–215, 1996.

[ROS 76] ROSENFELD A., HUMMEL R., ZUCKER S., "Scene Labeling by Relaxation Operations", *IEEE Transactions on Systems, Man, and Cybernetics*, vol. 6, num. 6, p. 173–184, 1976.

[ROS 06] ROSSI R., BEEK P. V., WALSH T., Eds., *Handbook of Constraint Programming*, Elsevier, 2006.

[RUS 91] RUSSEL S., WEFALD E., *Do the Right Thing*, MIT Press, 1991.

[SAB 94] SABIN D., FREUDER E., "Contradicting Conventional Wisdom in Constraint Satisfaction", *Proceedings of the 11th European Conference on Artificial Intelligence (ECAI-94)*, Amsterdam, The Netherlands, p. 125–129, 1994.

[SCH 92] SCHIEX T., "Possibilistic Constraint Satisfaction Problems or "How to handle soft constraints ?" ftp://ftp.cert.fr/pub/verfaillie/icuai92.ps", *Proceedings of the 8th International Conference on Uncertainty in Artificial Intelligence (UAI-92)*, Stanford, CA, USA, p. 269–275, 1992.

[SCH 94] SCHIEX T., VERFAILLIE G., "Nogood Recording for Static and Dynamic Constraint Satisfaction Problems ftp://ftp.cert.fr/pub/verfaillie/ijait.ps", *International Journal of Artificial Intelligence Tools*, vol. 3, num. 2, p. 187–207, 1994.

[SCH 95] SCHIEX T., FARGIER H., VERFAILLIE G., "Valued Constraint Satisfaction Problems : Hard and Easy Problems ftp://ftp.cert.fr/pub/verfaillie/ijcai95.ps", *Proceedings of the 14th International Joint Conference on Artificial Intelligence (IJCAI-95)*, Montreal, Canada, p. 631–637, 1995.

[SCH 00] SCHIEX T., "Arc Consistency for Soft Constraints", *Proceedings of the 6th International Conference on Principles and Practice of Constraint Programming (CP-00)*, Singapore, p. 411–424, 2000.

[SCH 08] SCHULTE C., STUCKEY P., "GECODE", 2008, http://www.gecode.org/.

[SEI 81] SEIDEL P., "A New Method for Solving Constraint Satisfaction Problems", *Proceedings of the 7th International Joint Conference on Artificial Intelligence (IJCAI-81)*, Vancouver, Canada, p. 338–342, 1981.

[SHA 81] SHAPIRO L., HARALICK R., "Structural Descriptions and Inexact Matching", *IEEE Transactions on Pattern Analysis and Machine Intelligence*, vol. 3, p. 504–519, 1981.

[SHE 90] SHENOY P., "Valuation-based Systems for Discrete Optimization", *Proceedings of the 6th International Conference on Uncertainty in Artificial Intelligence (UAI-90)*, Cambridge, MA, USA, p. 385–400, 1990.

[SIC 08] SICSTUS, "SICStus Prolog", 2008, http://www.sics.se/isl/sicstuswww/site/.

[TSA 93] TSANG E., *Foundations of Constraint Satisfaction*, Academic Press Ltd., 1993.

[VER 99] VERFAILLIE G., MARTINEZ D., BESSIÈRE C., "A Generic Customizable Framework for Inverse Local Consistency ftp://ftp.cert.fr/pub/verfaillie/aaai99.ps", *Proceedings of the 16th National Conference on Artificial Intelligence (AAAI-99)*, Orlando, FL, USA, p. 169–174, 1999.

[VER 05] VERFAILLIE G., JUSSIEN N., "Constraint Solving in Uncertain and Dynamic Environments: A Survey", *Constraints*, vol. 10, num. 3, p. 253–281, 2005.

[WAL 75] WALTZ D., "Generating Semantic Descriptions from Drawings of Scenes with Shadows", WINSTON P., Ed., *The Psychology of Computer Vision*, p. 19–91, McGraw-Hill, 1975.

[WAL 94] WALLACE R., "Directed Arc Consistency Preprocessing", *Proceedings of the ECAI-94 Workshop on Constraint Processing (LNCS 923)*, p. 121–137, Springer, 1994.

[WAL 02] WALSH T., "Stochastic Constraint Programming", *Proceedings of the 15th European Conference on Artificial Intelligence (ECAI-02)*, Lyon, France, p. 111–115, 2002.

[WAL 05] WALLACE R., FREUDER E., "Constraint-based Reasoning and Privacy/Efficiency Tradeoffs in Multi-agent Problem Solving", *Artificial Intelligence*, vol. 161, p. 209–227, 2005.

[YOK 00] YOKOO M., HIRAYAMA K., "Algorithms for Distributed Constraint Satisfaction: A Review", *Autonomous Agents and Multi-Agent Systems*, vol. 3, p. 185–207, 2000.

[ZAD 78] ZADEH L., "Fuzzy Sets as a Basis for a Theory of Possibility", *Fuzzy Sets and Systems*, vol. 1, p. 3–28, 1978.

[ZHA 01] ZHANG Y., YAP R., "Making AC-3 an Optimal Algorithm", *Proceedings of the 17th International Joint Conference on Artificial Intelligence (IJCAI-01)*, Seattle, WA, USA, p. 316–321, 2001.

[ZIL 96] ZILBERSTEIN S., "Using Anytime Algorithms in Intelligent Systems", *AI Magazine*, vol. 17, num. 3, p. 73–83, 1996.

Chapter 7

Logical Representation of Preferences

7.1. Introduction

The specification of a decision making problem includes the agent's preferences on the available alternatives. We have to distinguish between *preference modeling*, which consists of choosing a mathematical model for preferences and studying its properties, from *preference representation* (or *specification*), which consists of choosing a language for expressing, storing and processing an agent's preferences efficiently. A third important problem is *preference elicitation*, which consists of interacting with the agent in order to acquire enough information about their preferences.

Preference representation languages aim to represent preferences in a modular and local way. This is carried out by means of preference statements describing basic elements of preference, e.g. 'in context γ I prefer φ to ψ' where γ, φ and ψ express properties that each alternative may or may not satisfy. Such languages have been studied in two different communities. The artificial intelligence community has produced a considerable amount of work on languages for *compact preference representation*, whereas *preference logics* has been studied in the philosophical logic community. These two streams of work have very different motivations.

Compact preference representation is clearly driven by computational issues, and consists of expressing and processing preferences over large domains (having generally a combinatorial structure) using as few computational resources (space and time) as possible. Preference logics are driven by more philosophical considerations, such as understanding and reasoning with preferences.

Chapter written by Jérôme LANG.

However, the links between the work in these two communities are surprisingly strong, as they have developed (sometimes) very related languages. In this chapter we choose to speak about these two streams of works in a more or less unified manner.

Because these two areas have given rise to an important number of works, we cannot speak about every approach in detail. When discussing compact preference representation we will therefore focus on logical representation languages. *Graphical languages* for compact representation will be presented in a logical manner, but with somewhat less space than they deserve. Likewise, when talking about preference logics we will focus on works that are related (or useful), at least to some extent, to compact representation.

A naive idea would consist of expressing preferences *explicitly*, simply by enumerating all possible alternatives together with their utility (in the case of cardinal preferences), or the list of all pairs of alternatives contained in the relation (in the case of ordinal, or more generally relational, preferences). Obviously, the explicit representation is practical only when the number of alternatives is small enough with respect to the available computational resources. This assumption is often unrealistic, in particular when the set of alternatives has a combinatorial (or multiattribute) structure, i.e. when each alternative consists of a tuple of values, one for each of a given set of decision variables (or attributes). In this case, the set of alternatives is the Cartesian product of the value domains and, of course, its cardinality grows exponentially with the number n of variables. Let us examine two motivating examples.

Example 7.1. An agent has to express their preferences about a meal composed of a first course, a main course, a dessert and a wine, with a choice of six possibilities for each; this makes 6^4 alternatives. This would not be a problem if the preferences of the four variables were separable. In this case, it would be sufficient to represent them independently. The joint preference on the set of meals would, for instance, be determined by an aggregation function. Here, the preference structure on the 6^4 alternatives would come down to four preference structures, each on 6 alternatives. However, this becomes much more complicated when the agent wishes to express *dependencies* between variables, as in 'I prefer white wine if one of the dishes is fish and none is meat, red wine if at least one of the dishes is meat and none is fish, and in all other cases I have no preference between red and white wine'.

Example 7.2. Consider the following problem of a committee selecting applicants for a job: a committee has to select not a single applicant but k applicants among n. The set of all possible alternatives can no longer be identified with the set of applicants, but has a combinatorial structure (it is the set of all the subsets of k applicants among n). A member of the committee can express their preferences in an explicit way only if the dependencies between applicants can be ignored. This means that the members cannot express *correlations* between applicants, such as e.g. 'My preferred applicant is A, the next is B then C; but since A and B work on similar subjects and C works on another, I prefer to hire A and C, or even B and C, than A and B.'

For such problems, the size of the set of alternatives and the impossibility of decomposing the preference structure into smaller structures (each bearing on one of the variables) make it impossible in practice to ask the agents to give a utility function or a preference relation on the set of all the alternatives in an *explicit* way (under the form of a table or a list). Therefore, expressing a utility function or a preference relation on such sets of alternatives requires a language allowing the preference structure to be expressed as *succinctly* or *compactly* as possible. These languages, called *compact representation languages*, should also be as expressive as possible and close enough to human intuition, i.e. cognitively relevant. (Ideally, the specification of the preference structure in the representation language should be easily translated from the agent's preferences expressed in natural language, and should allow for efficient elicitation techniques.) Finally, these languages should be equipped with efficient algorithms for automating inference or searching for an optimal decision.

Such preference representation languages have been particularly studied in artificial intelligence. Some of these languages are based on propositional (and sometimes first-order) logic; some others, often called 'graphical', are not far from these logic-based languages however. They consist of expressing elementary preferences locally (on subsets of variables) by 'preference statements' that correspond to logical formulae with a specific syntax. Of course, the issue of compact representation is also very relevant for representing *beliefs* on the state of the world. For instance, *Bayesian networks* (see Chapter 13) are the most familiar compact representation languages of joint probability distributions on combinatorial sets of states.

For the sake of concision, we will focus in this chapter on formalisms directly based on propositional logic, and will briefly present (some) graphical languages under an equivalent logical form. Section 7.2 gives the basics of propositional logic required to understand the rest of the chapter. Section 7.3 gives the basic principles of logical preference representation. In section 7.4, we show how classical propositional logic can be used as a tool for logical preference representation by associating propositional formulae expressing preferences with weights, priorities or a distance between interpretations. In section 7.5 we focus on 'preference logics', whose first aim is to interpret statements of the form 'I desire φ' or 'I prefer φ to ψ' with respect to the underlying preference relation between elementary alternatives. We will first consider *ceteris paribus* preferences, then preferences expressed in conditional logics. This section will be completed by some brief considerations on the role of non-classical logics (such as paraconsistent or multivalued logics) for preference modeling in the presence of poor or inconsistent information. To conclude, we provide an informal discussion about the arguments regarding the choice of a language for a given problem.

For pedagogical reasons, given that this book is dedicated to a large readership who does not necessarily have a strong knowledge of propositional logic, the different languages will be presented rather informally and in a very progressive way. More importance is given to examples than to technical results or algorithms. A non-beginner may therefore skip the first parts of this chapter.

7.2. Basics of propositional logic

$\mathcal{L}_{PS}$ is a propositional language built from a finite set of propositional symbols PS, the usual connectives $\wedge$ (conjunction), $\vee$ (disjunction), $\neg$ (negation), $\rightarrow$ (implication) and $\leftrightarrow$ (equivalence) and the two propositional constants $\top$ (tautology) and $\bot$ (contradiction). The elements of $\mathcal{L}_{PS}$ are called *formulae*. Formally, the set of formulae $\mathcal{L}_{PS}$ is defined inductively by:

- for every $v \in PS$, v is a formula;
- the symbols $\top$ and $\bot$ are formulae;
- for all formulae $\varphi, \psi \in \mathcal{L}_{PS}$, $\neg\varphi, \varphi\wedge\psi, \varphi\vee\psi, \varphi \rightarrow \psi$ and $\varphi \leftrightarrow \psi$ are formulae.

If $\varphi \in \mathcal{L}_{PS}$, $Var(\varphi)$ is the set of propositional symbols appearing in φ. A *literal* l is a propositional symbol or the negation of a propositional symbol. A *clause* δ is a disjunction of literals. A *cube* γ is a conjunction of literals. A cube γ' (respectively, a clause δ') is a *subcube* (respectively, a *subclause*) of γ (δ) if the literals of γ' (δ') form a subset of the literals of γ (δ). A formula is under conjunctive normal form (CNF) if it is a conjunction of clauses, and under disjunctive normal form (DNF) if it is a disjunction of cubes.

Example 7.3. Let $PS = \{a, b, c, d\}$; $a, \neg a$ are literals, $\delta = \neg a \vee c \vee \neg d$ is a clause and $\gamma = \neg a \wedge \neg b \wedge d$ a cube. We have $Var(\delta) = \{a, c, d\}$ and $Var(\gamma) = \{a, b, d\}$. $\gamma' = \neg a \wedge d$ is a subcube of γ. $(\neg a \vee c \vee \neg d) \wedge (a \vee b) \wedge \neg b$ is a CNF formula and $(b \wedge \neg c) \vee (\neg a \wedge \neg b \wedge d) \vee c$ is a DNF formula.

An *interpretation* w for $\mathcal{L}_{PS}$ is a function from PS to $\{\top, \bot\}$ assigning a truth value to every propositional symbol. The set of interpretations for $\mathcal{L}_{PS}$ is denoted by Ω_{PS} – it is isomorphic to 2^{PS}. The satisfaction relation $\models \subseteq \Omega_{PS} \times \mathcal{L}_{PS}$ is defined inductively as follows (where $w \not\models \varphi$ is an abbreviation for not $(w \models \varphi)$):

- if $\varphi = v$ where $v \in PS$, then $w \models \varphi$ if and only if $w(v) = \top$;
- $w \models \top$;
- $w \not\models \bot$;
- $w \models \neg\varphi$ if not $(w \models \varphi)$;
- $w \models \varphi \wedge \psi$ if $w \models \varphi$ and $w \models \psi$;
- $w \models \varphi \vee \psi$ if $w \models \varphi$ or $w \models \psi$;

- $w \models \varphi \rightarrow \psi$ if $w \models \neg\varphi \vee \psi$;
- $w \models \varphi \leftrightarrow \psi$ if $w \models (\varphi \rightarrow \psi) \wedge (\psi \rightarrow \varphi)$.

An interpretation w on PS is written by listing the literals it satisfies: for example, if $PS = \{a, b, c, d\}$ then the interpretation w in which a and c are false and b and d are true is written $(\neg a, b, \neg c, d)$ or more simply $\bar{a}b\bar{c}d$. The formula $(\neg a \vee c \vee \neg d) \wedge (a \vee b) \wedge \neg b$ is not satisfied by w, while it is satisfied by $w' = (a, \neg b, c, d)$. If $X \subseteq PS$, $w^{\downarrow X}$ is the restriction of w to X. For example, if $w = \bar{a}b\bar{c}d$ then $w^{\downarrow \{b,c\}} = b\bar{c}$.

For every formula $\varphi \in \mathcal{L}_{PS}$, $Mod(\varphi) = \{w \in \Omega_{PS} \mid w \models \varphi\}$. $Mod(\varphi)$ is the set of the *models of* φ. If $Mod(\varphi) \neq \emptyset$ then φ is *satisfiable*. if $Mod(\varphi) = \Omega_{PS}$ then φ is *valid*. if $Mod(\varphi) \subseteq Mod(\psi)$ then ψ is a *logical consequence* of φ, denoted by $\varphi \models \psi$. If $Mod(\varphi) = Mod(\psi)$ then φ and ψ are *logically equivalent*, denoted by $\varphi \equiv \psi$. Every formula can be written as an equivalent CNF formula and as an equivalent DNF formula.

$Diff(w, w')$ represents the set of all propositional symbols which are not assigned the same truth value by w and w'. For example, if $w = (\neg a, b, \neg c, d)$ and $w' = (\neg a, \neg b, c, d)$, then $Diff(w, w') = \{b, c\}$.

Propositional logic allows us to express *cardinality constraints* such as 'at least/at most/exactly k formulae among p must be satisfied', which we denote $[\geq k] : \varphi_1, \ldots, \varphi_p$, $[\leq k] : \varphi_1, \ldots, \varphi_p$ and $[= k] : \varphi_1, \ldots, \varphi_p$, respectively. Such expressions, called *cardinality formulae* [BEN 94, HEN 91], are strictly speaking not formulae of $\mathcal{L}_{PS}$. We can consider them as such, however, since they can be expressed by formulae of $\mathcal{L}_{PS}$. For example, $[\geq 2] : \varphi_1, \varphi_2, \varphi_3$ is short for $(\varphi_1 \wedge \varphi_2) \vee (\varphi_1 \wedge \varphi_3) \vee (\varphi_2 \wedge \varphi_3)$. It is important to note that these cardinality formulae can be expressed by polynomially long plain formulae (i.e. without suprapolynomial increase of size), modulo the addition of new propositional symbols to the language. Their use for syntactic convenience does not therefore lead to a complexity gap.

Often, the description of existing alternatives makes use of non-binary variables. However, the assumption that all variables are binary does not lead to a loss of generality compared to the more general case where all variables take their values on *finite* domains. On the one hand, most models we will expose can be easily adapted to this more general case but on the other hand, propositional logic easily allows for representing preferences on variables whose domains are finite.

The simplest way of doing this (but not the most economical from the point of view of the number of variables) is the following. Let $VAR = \{x_1, \ldots, x_n\}$ be a finite set of variables and for each i, $D_i = \{v_i^1, \ldots, v_i^{|D_i|}\}$ the (finite) domain of x_i. For every subset $U \subseteq VAR$, we note $D_U = \times \{D_i \mid x_i \in U\}$. We note $D = D_{VAR}$, the set of all alternatives. Let $PS_D = \{(x_i = v_i^j) \mid x_i \in VAR, v_i^j \in D_i\}$ and

$$K_D = \bigwedge_{x_i \in VAR} [=1] : (x_i = v_i^1), \ldots, (x_i = v_i^{|D_i|}),$$

expressing that each variable takes a unique value. K_D can be completed into $K = K_D \wedge K'$ by domain-specific constraints, defining the set of feasible alternatives as previously.

7.3. Principles and elementary languages

In this section, we make the important assumption that the set of alternatives is $W = Mod(K) \subseteq \Omega_{PS}$, where K is a propositional formula expressing constraints defining the set of feasible alternatives. For example, in the recruiting committee example, if at most two candidates among $\{a, b, c, d, e\}$ can be hired then $K = [\leq 2] : a, b, c, d, e$. The preference structure is therefore defined on $Mod(K)$. Thus, alternatives are identified with propositional interpretations. By default, we take $K = \top$ i.e. $W = Mod(\top) = \Omega_{PS}$.

A *utility function* on W is a function $u : W \to \mathbb{R}$. A *preference relation* $\succeq$ on W is a preorder, i.e. a reflexive and transitive relation (not necessarily complete). The *strict preference* induced by $\succeq$ is the strict order $\succ$ defined by $w \succ w'$ if and only if $w \succeq w'$ and not $(w' \succeq w)$. The *indifference relation* induced by $\succeq$ is the equivalence relation $\sim$ defined by $w \sim w'$ if and only if $w \succeq w'$ and $w' \succeq w$. If u is a utility function then the preference relation $\succeq_u$ induced by u is defined by $w \succeq_u w'$ if and only if $u(w) \succeq u(w')$.

A common way for an agent to express their preferences consists of enumerating a set of goals, each of which can be represented by a propositional formula, possibly with additional information such as weights, priorities, contexts or distances. In the rest of the chapter, GB is a called a 'goal base' (analogous to 'knowledge base') and u_{GB} (respectively, R_{GB}) denotes the utility function (respectively, the preference relation) induced by GB.

We illustrate the various representation languages on an example, in which an agent has to express their preferences on airplane tickets. The relevant criteria are the following:

1) The destination: we consider 7 possible destinations, namely Amsterdam (A), Cairo (C), Hong Kong (HK), Istanbul (I), Naples (N), New York (NY) and Rome (R). Each of them is represented by a propositional symbol.

2) The price of the ticket: cheap, medium-priced or expensive, each possibility being represented by a propositional symbol.

3) The duration of stay: short, medium or long, each possibility being represented by a propositional symbol.

4) The decision to buy a ticket or not, represented by the propositional symbol ticket.

The set of possible alternatives is described by the set of formulae K (interpreted conjunctively), containing:

– exclusion constraints for the variables corresponding to destination, price and duration:
¬ (A ∧ C), ¬ (A ∧ HK), ¬ (A ∧ I) etc.
¬ (cheap ∧ medium-priced), ¬ (cheap ∧ expensive), ¬ (medium-priced ∧ expensive);
¬ (short ∧ medium), ¬ (short ∧ long), ¬ (medium ∧ long);

– a constraint expressing that buying a ticket is equivalent to buying a ticket for one of these 7 destinations, with a given price and a given duration:
ticket ↔ (A ∨ C ∨ HK ∨ I ∨ N ∨ NY ∨ R) ∧ (cheap ∨ medium-priced ∨ expensive) ∧ (short ∨ medium ∨ long);

– lastly, a constraint expressing that it is not possible to find a cheap ticket to Hong Kong:
HK → ¬ cheap.

A *preference representation language* is a pair $\mathcal{R} = \langle L_\mathcal{R}, Ind_\mathcal{R} \rangle$ where

– $L_\mathcal{R}$ is a language formed from a logical language $\mathcal{L}_{PS}$ and other constructs that we will detail later.

– $Ind_\mathcal{R}$ is a function from $L_\mathcal{R}$ to $\mathcal{P}$, where $\mathcal{P}$ is the set of all preference relations on 2^{PS} mapping each element of $L_\mathcal{R}$ to the induced preference relation. In the case of *cardinal* preference representation languages, the preference relation is obtained by the intermediary of a utility function. In this case we denote the function mapping each element of $L_\mathcal{R}$ to the induced utility function by $Ind_\mathcal{R}^U$. We then have $Ind_\mathcal{R}(\Phi) = \succeq_{Ind_\mathcal{R}^U(\Phi)}$.

We denote the set of all preference relations representable in $L_\mathcal{R}$ by $S_\mathcal{R} \subseteq \mathcal{P}$ i.e. $S_\mathcal{R} = Ind_\mathcal{R}(L_\mathcal{R})$. In the case of cardinal preference representation languages, we note $S_\mathcal{R}^U = Ind_\mathcal{R}^U(L_\mathcal{R})$. We then have $S_\mathcal{R} = Ind_\mathcal{R}(L_\mathcal{R}) = \{\succeq_u, u \in Ind_\mathcal{R}(L_\mathcal{R})\}$.

The most basic way of representing preferences in propositional logic consists of specifying a goal under the form of a propositional formula G and then defining $u_G(w) = 1$ if $w \models G$ and $u_G(w) = 0$ if $w \models \neg G$. The preference relation induced by G is *dichotomous*. It is therefore very rough, since it only allows us to distinguish 'good' alternatives (those of utility 1) from 'bad' alternatives (those of utility 0). For example, $G = $ (HK ∨ I ∨ R) ∧ (¬ HK → cheap) ∧ (¬expensive) expresses that the agent wants to go to Hong Kong, Istanbul or Rome, that they do not want to pay for an expensive ticket and that they accept paying for a non-cheap ticket only if they go to Hong Kong. Let us call this language $\mathcal{R}_{dicho}$; we have $Ind_{dicho}(G) = u_G$, and it is clear that S_{dicho} is the set of all dichotomous preference relations on Ω_{PS}.

This very rough representation technique can be refined by specifying a finite set GB of propositional formulae and by *counting* the formulae satisfied by a given alternative. Let $GB = \{G_1, \ldots, G_n\}$ be a set of propositional formulae and let us note:

- $sat(w, GB) = \{i | w \models G_i\}$; and
- $nonsat(w, GB) = \{1, \ldots, n\} \setminus sat(w, GB_i)$.

Then $u_{GB}(w) = |sat(w, GB)|$. We will denote the language defined this way by $\mathcal{R}_{card}$. We can check that S_{card}^U is the set of all integer-valued utility functions and S_{card} is the set of all complete preorders.

Example 7.4. Let $GB = \{G_1, G_2, G_3, G_4, G_5, G_6\}$ with G_1 = ticket, G_2 = HK ∨ I ∨ R, G_3 = HK ∨ I, G_4 = HK, G_5 = (¬ HK → cheap) ∧ (HK → medium-priced) and G_6 = ¬ expensive. This goal base deliberately contains apparent redundancies. For example, G_2, G_3 and G_4 together express that the agent ideally wants to go to Hong Kong, that their second choice is Istanbul and their third choice is Rome, since an interpretation containing HK (respectively I, R) satisfies all three formulae (respectively two formulae, one formula) of $\{G_2, G_3, G_4\}$. Let $w_1, \ldots, w_6$ be six interpretations such that
$w_1 \models$ I ∧ medium-priced, $w_2 \models$ HK ∧ expensive, $w_3 \models$ A ∧ cheap,
$w_4 \models$ I ∧ cheap, $w_5 \models$ HK ∧ medium-priced, $w_6 \models$ ¬ ticket.
We have
$u_{GB}(w_1) = 4$, $u_{GB}(w_2) = 4$, $u_{GB}(w_3) = 3$,
$u_{GB}(w_4) = 5$, $u_{GB}(w_5) = 6$, $u_{GB}(w_6) = 2$.

Instead of defining the preference according to the *number* of goals satisfied, one may consider the *subset* of goals satisfied. Again, let $GB = \{G_1, \ldots, G_n\}$, then $w \succeq_{GB} w'$ if and only if $sat(w, GB) \supseteq sat(w', GB)$. This partial preorder is the Pareto preorder induced by GB. w is strictly preferred to w' if $sat_{GB}(w)$ strictly contains $sat_{GB}(w')$, i.e. if w satisfies all the goals satisfied by w' and at least another goal. We will denote the language defined this way by $\mathcal{R}_{Pareto}$. $\mathcal{R}_{Pareto}$ allows us to express all preorders on Ω.

Example 7.5. Let us take the same set of goals GB as in example 7.4. We have $sat(w_1, GB) = \{1, 2, 3, 6\}$, $sat(w_2, GB) = \{1, 2, 3, 4\}$, $sat(w_3, GB) = \{1, 5, 6\}$, $sat(w_4, GB) = \{1, 2, 3, 5, 6\}$, $sat(w_5, GB) = \{1, 2, 3, 4, 5, 6\}$ and $sat(w_6, GB) = \{5, 6\}$. We therefore have $w_5 \succ_{GB} w_4$, $w_4 \succ_{GB} w_1$, $w_4 \succ_{GB} w_2$, $w_4 \succ_{GB} w_3$ and $w_3 \succ_{GB} w_6$. Note that w_1, w_2 and w_3 are pairwise incomparable, as well as w_1 and w_6 and w_2 and w_6.

In the rest of this chapter we will define more sophisticated languages, of which the previous three elementary languages will constitute degenerate cases.

7.4. Weights, priorities and distances

7.4.1. Weights

An immediate generalization of R_{card} consists of associating a numerical weight with each formula of GB, representing its importance. The utility function u_{GB} can typically be defined by aggregating the weights of the formulae that are not satisfied:

$$R_F^- : \begin{array}{|l} GB = \{\langle G_1, \alpha_1\rangle, \ldots, \langle G_n, \alpha_n\rangle\}; \\ u_{GB}(w) = -F(\{\alpha_i | w \models \neg G_i\}) \end{array}$$

where F is a function from $\mathbb{R}^+ \times \mathbb{R}^+$ to $\mathbb{R}^+$, non-decreasing, commutative and associative (which explains *a posteriori* why we write $F(\{\alpha_i | w \models \neg G_i\})$) (see [LAF 00] for justification, in particular for associativity).

In this case, since $u_{GB}(w) \leq 0$, it is more intuitive to speak of a *disutility function* (where $disu_{GB}(w) = -u_{GB}(w)$). The goals G_i are called *negative goals*, or *constraints*. Some usual choices for F are, for example, the sum (weights are then called *penalties* and the language is denoted by R_{pen}) or the maximum. Symmetrically, one can induce a (positive) utility function by aggregating the weights of the goals that are *satisfied*:

$$u_{GB}(w) = F(\{\alpha_i | w \models G_i\}).$$

The goals G_i are then *positive goals* and the weights are rewards.

In many practical situations, it is sufficient to consider negative goals only or positive goals only. This implies that the utility function always has the same sign, which is acceptable if the utility is considered as a relative rather than an absolute notion (i.e. only differences of utility matter). However, in the general case, one may need both kinds of goals. In this case, positive preferences (goals) have to be formally distinguished from negative preferences (constraints); this principle is known as *bipolarity*, i.e.

$$R_{F_1, F_2, F_3}^{+-} : \begin{array}{|l} GB = GB = \langle GB^+, GB^-\rangle, \text{ with} \\ GB^+ = \{\langle \alpha_1, G_1^+\rangle, \ldots, \langle \alpha_n, G_n^+\rangle\}; \\ GB^- = \{\langle \beta_1, G_1^-\rangle, \ldots, \langle \beta_p, G_p^-\rangle\} \\ u_{GB}(w) = F_1(F_2\{\alpha_i | w \models G_i^+\}), F_3(\{\beta_j | w \models \neg G_j^-\}) \end{array}$$

where F_2 and F_3 are non-decreasing, commutative and associative and F_1 is non-decreasing in its first argument and non-increasing in its second argument. $u_{GB}(w)$ is therefore a function of the weights of the goals satisfied by w and the weights of the constraints violated by w.

We will not pursue here the discussion on the choice of satisfactory aggregation functions (see discussions on bipolarity in [BEN 02a, LAN 02b]). In the following example we will stick to the choice: $F_1(x,y) = x - y$, $F_2 = F_3 = +$, i.e. $u_{GB}(w) = \sum\{\alpha_i | w \models G_i^+\} - \sum\{\beta_j | w \models \neg G_j^-\}$. Note, however, that the framework defined in this way is not *truly* bipolar, since positive and negative goals are handled in an homogenous way.

Example 7.6. Let $GB = \langle GB^+, GB^- \rangle$, where

$$GB^+ = \{\, \langle 8, \text{A}\rangle, \langle 8, \text{C}\rangle, \langle 15, \text{HK}\rangle, \langle 12, \text{I}\rangle, \langle 9, \text{N}\rangle, \langle 10, \text{NY}\rangle, \langle 10, \text{R}\rangle \,\} \text{ and}$$

$$\begin{aligned}
GB^- = \{\ &\langle 5, \text{cheap}\rangle, &&\langle 5, \text{cheap} \vee \text{medium-priced}\rangle, \\
&\langle 3, \text{short} \rightarrow \text{cheap}\rangle, &&\langle 3, \neg\,\text{long} \rightarrow (\text{cheap} \vee \text{medium-priced})\rangle, \\
&\langle 4, \text{A} \vee \text{N} \vee \text{R} \rightarrow \text{short}\rangle, &&\langle 4, \text{A} \vee \text{N} \vee \text{R} \rightarrow \text{short} \vee \text{medium}\rangle, \\
&\langle 4, \text{I} \vee \text{C} \rightarrow \text{medium}\rangle, &&\langle 10, \text{NY} \rightarrow \text{medium}\rangle, \\
&\langle 10, \text{HK} \rightarrow \text{medium} \vee \text{long}\rangle, &&\langle 5, \text{HK} \rightarrow \text{long}.\rangle \ \}
\end{aligned}$$

Let $PS = PV \cup DV \cup LV \cup \{\text{ticket}\}$, with $PV = \{$ cheap, medium-priced, expensive$\}$, $DV = \{$ short, medium, long$\}$ and $LV = \{$ A, C, HK, I, N, NY, R$\}$. The exclusion constraints imply that every interpretation satisfying ticket can be rewritten in a simpler way as a triple (d, p, l) where $d \in DV$, $p \in PV$ and $l \in LV$. The utility function induced by GB is defined in Table 7.1 for the alternatives satisfying ticket. As to the unique interpretation of w^* not satisfying $\neg$ ticket, we have $u_{GB}(w^*) = 0$.

	ch, short	ch, medium	ch, long	mp, short	mp, medium	mp, long	exp, short	exp, medium	exp, long
A	8	4	0	0	−1	−5	−8	−9	−10
C	4	8	4	−4	3	−1	−12	−5	−6
HK	imp.	imp.	imp.	−8	5	10	−16	−3	5
I	8	12	8	0	7	3	−8	−1	−6
N	9	5	1	1	0	−4	−7	−8	−9
NY	0	10	0	−8	5	−5	−16	−3	−10
R	10	6	2	2	1	−3	−6	−7	−8

Table 7.1. *Utility function indexed by GB (ch and mp: cheap and medium-priced)*

This requires a few comments. The two negative goals $\{\langle 5, \text{cheap}\rangle, \langle 5, \text{cheap} \vee \text{medium-priced}\rangle\}$ together express that a penalty of 5 applies when the ticket bought is not cheap, and that (in addition to this), another penalty of 5 applies if the ticket is expensive. This means that, independently of the rest, buying an expensive (respectively, medium-priced) ticket results in a penalty of 10 (respectively, 5). The two negative goals ⟨3, short → cheap⟩ and ⟨3, ¬ long → (cheap ∨ medium-priced))} imply that in addition to the previous penalties, a penalty applies if the duration of the stay is not long enough with respect to the price of the ticket, i.e. a penalty of 3 for a medium-priced ticket if the stay is short or for a expensive ticket if the stay is of medium length, and a penalty of 6 for an expensive ticket if the duration of stay is short.

We end this section by mentioning two representation languages very close to the previous ones: GAI-nets (generalized additive independence) and valued constraints. These *graphical* languages are more general and more specific than the language consisting of weighted formulae. They are more general because the variables are not necessarily binary but have more general domains with a finite number of values. They are more specific because they impose specific syntactical restrictions on the weighted formulae allowed.

Let $V = \{x_1, \ldots, x_n\}$ the set of variables, and let D_i be the domain of x_i; for $Z \subseteq X$, let $D_Z = \times_{x_i \in Z} D_i$. The starting point of GAI-nets is the notion of generalized additive independence [BAC 95, FIS 70]. Let $Z_1, \ldots, Z_k$ be subsets of V (not necessarily disjoints) such that $V = \bigcup_i Z_i$. Let $u : D_V \to \mathbb{R}$ be a utility function. $Z_1, \ldots, Z_k$ satisfies the property of generalized additive independence (for u), which we will denote by $GAI_u(Z_1, \ldots, Z_k)$, if and only if there exist k local utility functions $u_i : D_{Z_i} \to \mathbb{R}$ such that

$$u(w) = \sum_{i=1}^{k} u_i(w^{\downarrow Z_i})$$

(see Chapter 15). The interest of such a decomposition is clear: a utility function u for which $GAI_u(Z_1, \ldots, Z_k)$ holds can be represented by k local utility functions; the size of the representation of u is therefore only $\sum_{i=1}^{k} \Pi_{j, x_j \in Z_k} |D_{x_j}|$ instead of $\Pi_{j=1}^{n} |D_{x_j}|$.

It has to be noted that such a representation under the form of local utilites can be seen as a valued constraint satisfaction problem (Chapter 6) which immediately gives optimization algorithms allowing us to find an alternative of maximal utility. Lastly, when variables are binary, the representation of a utility function under the form of k local utility functions can be seen as a representation by weighted formulae, where the formulae must be Z_k-cubes. Therefore, GAI-nets on binary variables can be obtained as a sub-language of weighted goals by the latter syntactical restriction.

7.4.1.1. *Bibliographical notes*

Associating numerical weights with propositional formulae is natural and appears in many places in the literature. We mention here a few works concerning the representation of utility functions in logical languages with weights.

The principle of associating additive penalties with propositional formulae appears in [DUP 94, HAD 92, PIN 91]. See [CHE 06, UCK 07, UCK 08] for further developments on the expressivity, succinctness and complexity of weighted goals. Using weighted goals with the *minimum* or *maximum* aggregation function has been considered in a few papers on possibilistic logic for preference representation [BEN 01, DUB 94, LAN 91, SAB 98]. In particular, Benferhat *et al.* [BEN 01] argue that there are three ways of representing preferences in possibilistic logic, depending on whether the weighted formulae correspond to (i) 'level cuts' of a goal expressed by a fuzzy set (for example 'I would like to arrive rather early'), (ii) non-fuzzy goals with different piriority levels and (iii) sets of solutions more or less acceptable (for example 'if x satisfies $\varphi \wedge \psi$ then x is totally satisfactory, and if φ is not satisfied, x is nevertheless rather satisfactory if it satisfies ξ').

The notion of bipolar preference has been developed in many recent works [GRA 00, GRE 02, LAB 03, TSO 02b]; see also [BEN 02a, BEN 02b, LAN 02b, TOR 01] for bipolar preference representation languages based on propositional logic.

GAI-nets were introduced by Bacchus and Grove [BAC 95]; preference elicitation in GAI-nets is addressed in [BRA 05, BRA 07, GON 04]. UCP-nets [BOU 01] combine some aspects of GAI-nets and CP-nets (section 7.5.1.4): a UCP-net can be seen as a GAI-net whose independence structure verifies some specific properties that we will not mention here. Expected utility networks [MUR 99] allow for a joint modular representation of utility functions (like GAI-nets) and probabilities of states of the world (like Bayesian networks). GAI-nets are technically close both to valued constraints [BIS 99] (see also Chapter 6) and to valuation networks [SHE 89]. A logic of soft constraints is constructed in [WIL 06].

7.4.2. *Priorities*

The ordinal counterpart of logical languages with weights is the family of *logical languages with priorities*. A *stratified*, or *prioritized preference base* GB is a tuple $\langle GB_1, ..., GB_n \rangle$, where GB_i is the set of goals of GB of priority i. (Strictly speaking, GB_i should be defined as a *multiset* rather than a set; the same formula may appear several times in one of the GB_i.) By convention, we consider that GB_1 and GB_n contain the formulae of greatest and least priority, respectively. We then have to define a preorder relation on Ω_{PS} from GB, i.e. induce a preorder on alternatives from a preorder on formulae. We now give a summary of the most usual choices.

7.4.2.1. Best-out

This criterion consists of comparing the alternatives according to the priority of the most important non-satisfied goals. Let $\rho(w, GB) = \min\{i, nonsat(w, GB_i) \neq \varnothing\}$.

$R_{best-out}$:
$$w \geq_{GB}^{best-out} w' \text{ if } \rho(w, GB_i) \geq \rho(w', GB_i).$$

Note that $S_{best-out}$ is the set of all complete preference relations. For a simple transformation of priorities into weights, this representation language suffers from a so-called 'drowning effect': the presence of a non-satisfied formula of priority i inhibits the effect of all formulae of priority $j \geq i$. The following two refinements of the best-out criterion avoid this drowning effect.

7.4.2.2. Discrimin

This criterion consists of comparing two alternatives according to the more important goals satisfied by one alternative and not the other.

$R_{discrimin}$:

- $w >_{GB}^{discrimin} w'$ if $\exists i \leq n$ such that

$$\left(\begin{array}{l} sat(w, GB_i) \supset sat(w', GB_i) \\ \forall j \leq i, sat(w, GB_j) = sat(w', GB_j) \end{array} \right);$$

- $w \sim_{GB}^{discrimin} w'$ if $\forall i \leq n, sat(w, GB_i) = sat(w', GB_i)$;
- $w \geq_{GB}^{discrimin} w'$ if $w >_{GB}^{discrimin} w'$ or $w \sim_{GB}^{discrimin} w'$.

This preference relation is, in general, not complete. Note that if GB contains a single priority level, i.e. $GB = GB_1$, then $\geq_{GB}^{discrimin}$ coincides with $\geq_{GB}^{Pareto}$, therefore $S_{discrimin}$ is the set of all preference relations.

Example 7.7. Take the set of goals of example 7.4 with the following stratification: $GB = \{GB_1, GB_2, GB_3\}$ with $GB_1 = \{\varphi_1 = \text{ticket}, \varphi_2 = \neg \text{expensive}\}; GB_2 = \{(\varphi_3 = \neg \text{HK} \rightarrow \text{cheap}) \land (\text{HK} \rightarrow \text{medium-priced})\}$ and $GB_3 = \{\varphi_4 = \text{HK} \lor \text{I} \lor \text{R}, \varphi_5 = \text{HK} \lor \text{I}, \varphi_6 = \text{HK}\}$. Let us neglect the duration of stay, and let the alternatives $w_1 = (\text{I, medium-priced}); w_2 = (\text{HK, expensive}); w_3 = (\text{A, cheap}); w_4 = (\text{I, cheap}); w_5 = (\text{HK, medium-priced})$ and $w_6 = \neg \text{ticket}$. Table 7.2 shows the formulae of GB satisfied by each of these six alternatives.

We have $w_5 >_{GB}^{discrimin} w_4 >_{GB}^{discrimin} w_3 >_{GB}^{discrimin} w_1, w_1 >_{GB}^{discrimin} w_2$ and $w_1 >_{GB}^{discrimin} w_6$; w_2 and w_6 are incomparable for $>_{GB}^{discrimin}$.

	w_1	w_2	w_3	w_4	w_5	w_6
$sat(.,GB_1)$	1,2	1	1,2	1,2	1,2	2
$sat(.,GB_2)$	∅	3	3	3	3	3
$sat(.,GB_3)$	4,5	4,5,6	∅	4,5	4,5,6	∅

Table 7.2. *Formulae satisfied by alternatives*

7.4.2.3. *Leximin*

$R_{leximin}$ consists of comparing two alternatives by identifying first the most important priority level for which the two alternatives do not satisfy the same number of goals, and then to prefer the one that satisfies more goals at this level. We denote the cardinality of $sat(w, GB_i)$ by $\#sat(w, GB_i)$, that is, the number of goals of level i satisfied by w.

$R_{leximin}$:

- $w >_{GB}^{leximin} w'$ if $\exists i \leq n$ such that

$$\left(\begin{array}{l} \#sat(w, GB_i) > \#sat(w', GB_i) \\ \forall j < i, \ \#sat(w, GB_j) = \#sat(w', GB_j) \end{array} \right);$$

- $w \sim_{GB}^{leximin} w'$ if $\forall i \leq n, \#sat(w, GB_i) = \#sat(w', GB_i)$;
- $w \geq_{GB}^{leximin} w'$ if $w >_{GB}^{leximin} w'$ or $w \sim_{GB}^{leximin} w'$.

An equivalent expression of this criterion consists of defining the vector $\vec{s}_{GB}(w) = \langle \#sat_{GB}^q(w), \ldots, \#sat_{GB}^1(w) \rangle$ and comparing $\vec{s}_{GB}(w)$ and $\vec{s}_{GB}(w')$ according to the lexicographical order. $\geq_{GB}^{leximin}$ is a complete preorder. The following implications hold:

- $w >_{GB}^{bestout} w' \Rightarrow w >_{GB}^{discrimin} w' \Rightarrow w >_{GB}^{leximin} w'$;
- $w \geq_{GB}^{discrimin} w' \Rightarrow w \geq_{GB}^{leximin} w' \Rightarrow w \geq_{GB}^{bestout} w'$.

Consider example 7.7 once more: now we have $w_2 \sim_{GB}^{leximin} w_6$ (the rest being unchanged).

Note that if GB contains a single priority level then $\geq_{GB}^{leximin}$ coincides with $\geq_{GB}^{card}$; $S_{leximin}$ is therefore the set of all complete preference relations.

7.4.2.4. *Bibliographical notes*

The *discrimin* criterion was initially proposed by [BEH 77] and reused in different contexts in many works [BEN 93, BRE 89, CAY 92, DUB 92, FAR 93, GEF 92,

JON 08, LIU 08, NEB 91]. The *leximin* criterion has been studied for many years in the literature of social choice and decision theory [e.g. MOU 88]. Its use with the aim of ranking interpretations given a priority order on formulae appears in [BEN 93, DUB 92, FAR 93, LEH 95]. See also [DUB 97, DUB 01].

[BRE 02] proposes a new logical connective (the no-commutative disjunction $\otimes$, where $\varphi \otimes \psi$ reads 'I desire that φ be satisfied and, if it is not, then I desire that ψ be satisfied'). This allows us to specify priorities between formulae in a more implicit way; this representation language is independent of the criterion chosen for generating the preference relation on alternatives. [BRE 04] gives a more expressive representation language allowing for the coexistence in a same preference base of several criteria for interpreting priorities. While the previous criteria do not allow for compensations between different strata, [BEN 98] allow for including commensurability constraints between combinaisons of goals (e.g. 'I am indifferent between the simultaneous satisfaction of goals 2, 3 and 5, and the simultaneous satisfaction 1 and 7').

[DEL 03] generalize prioritized goals by introducing temporal preferences. [BIE 05] use prioritized goals in in the context of planning.

7.4.3. *Distances*

A *pseudo-distance* on propositional interpretations is a function $d : \Omega_{PS} \times \Omega_{PS} \to \mathbb{N}$ satisfying

Sep $\forall w, w', d(w, w') = 0 \Leftrightarrow w = w'$ and
Sym $\forall w, w', d(w, w') = d(w', w)$.

If φ is a formula of L_{PS} and $w, w' \in \Omega_{PS}$ then $d(w, \varphi) = \min_{w' \models \varphi} d(w, w')$ and $d(\varphi, \psi) = \min_{w \models \varphi, w' \models \psi} d(w, w')$.

A well-known example is the *Hamming distance* d_H, defined as the number of propositional symbols taking a different value in w and w', i.e.

$$d_H(w, w') = |Diff(w, w')|.$$

For instance, if $w = (\neg a, b, \neg c, d)$ and $w' = (\neg a, \neg b, c, d)$, then $d(w, w') = 2$. The *binary distance* d_δ is defined by

$$d_\delta(w, w') = \begin{cases} 0 & \text{if } w = w' \\ 1 & \text{if } w \neq w'. \end{cases}$$

Representing preferences using a pseudo-distance is based on the intuitive idea that when an agent expresses a goal G then, ideally, w must satisfy G. If this is not the case, then the 'further' the interpretation w from G, the less satisfactory is the solution. Formally, a pair $\langle\{G\}, d\rangle$, where G is a propositional formula and d a pseudo-distance, induces the utility function

$$u_{GB}(w) = -d(w, G) = -\min_{w' \models G} d(w, w').$$

This principle is then generalized by considering a set of goals. The pseudo-distances to each of these goals is aggregated by an aggregation function F, non-decreasing in each of its arguments (as in section 7.4.1):

$$R_{d,F} \left| \begin{array}{l} GB = \langle\{G_1, ..., G_n\}, d\rangle; \\ u_{GB}(w) = F(d(w, G_1), ..., d(w, G_n)). \end{array} \right.$$

Example 7.8. Consider the following partition of the set of variables: $PS = P \cup DV \cup LV \cup \{\text{ticket}\}$ with $PV = \{\text{cheap, medium-priced, expensive}\}$, $DV = \{\text{short, medium, long}\}$ and $LV = \{\text{A, C, HK, I, N, NY, R}\}$. Now we define the distance d by

$$\begin{aligned} d(w, w') &= d_P(w^{\downarrow PV}, w'^{\downarrow PV}) + d_D(w^{\downarrow DV}, w'^{\downarrow DV}) + d_L(w^{\downarrow LV}, w'^{\downarrow LV}) \\ &+ d_b(w^{\downarrow\{\text{ticket}\}}, w'^{\downarrow\{\text{ticket}\}}) \end{aligned}$$

where d_P (respectively, d_D, d_L, d_b) is a 'local' distance on Ω_{PV} (respectively, on Ω_{DV}, Ω_{LV} and $\Omega_{\{\text{ticket}\}}$), defined as in Tables 7.3–7.6.

d_{PV}	cheap	mp	exp
cheap	0		
mp	10	0	
exp	10	5	0

Table 7.3. *Definition of d_{PV}*

d_{LV}	short	medium	long
short	0		
medium	6	0	
long	6	3	0

Table 7.4. *Definition of d_{LV}*

Let $GB = \{G_1, \ldots, G_8\}$ with $G_1 = \text{ticket} \to \text{cheap}$, $G_2 = \text{ticket} \to (\text{HK} \vee \text{NY} \vee \text{I} \vee \text{R})$, $G_3 = \text{short} \to \text{cheap}$, $G_4 = \neg\text{long} \to \text{cheap} \vee \text{medium-priced}$, G_5

d_b	ticket	¬ticket
ticket	0	
¬ticket	12	0

Table 7.5. *Definition of d_b*

d_{DV}	A	C	HK	I	N	NY	R
A	0						
C	10	0					
HK	10	10	0				
I	10	5	10	0			
N	5	10	10	6	0		
NY	6	10	6	10	10	0	
R	4	10	10	6	1	10	0

Table 7.6. *Definition of d_{DV}*

= A ∨ N ∨ R → short, G_6 = I ∨ C ∨ NY → medium, G_7 = HK → long, G_8 = ticket. Consider the three alternatives w_1 = (R, medium, medium-priced); w_2 = (N, short, cheap); w_3 = (¬ticket). Table 7.7 lists the distances of w_1, w_2, w_3 to the G_i's.

For example, $d(w_1, \text{cheap}) = d(w_1, (\text{R, medium, cheap})) = 5$, i.e. the closest interpretation to w_1 among those satisfying cheap is (R, medium, cheap).

7.4.3.1. *Bibliographical notes*

The idea of using distances between propositional interpretations in knowledge representation appears in belief revision and update, notably in [KAT 91, KAT 92] and in belief merging, notably in [KON 98, KON 02, REV 97]. The idea also appears in later work, more specifially dedicated to preferences [BEN 02b, LAF 00, LAF 01]. Two closely related notions are (1) 'supermodels' [GIN 98], defined as interpretations that not only satisfy a given formula but that still satisfy it when they are subject to small perturbations; and (2) similarity-based reasoning as in [DUB 95a].

	G_1	G_2	G_3	G_4	G_5	G_6	G_7	G_8	u
w_1	5	0	0	0	3	0	0	0	−5
w_2	0	1	0	0	0	0	0	0	−1
w_3	0	0	0	0	0	0	0	12	−12

Table 7.7. *Utility function induced by GB*

7.5. Preference logics: conditionals and *ceteris paribus* preferences

Section 7.4 dealt with compact representation of ordinal, qualitative or numerical preferences. The formalisms presented, even if they made use of logic, were not *preference logics* in the meaning we give in this section. A preference logic consists of a semantic and/or a formal system meant to interpret dyadic preferences between propositional formulae, or monadic 'absolute' preferences.

The starting point of this section is that individuals often express relative or absolute preferences that refer not to isolated alternatives, but to logical formulae representing *sets of alternatives* which are generally not singletons, nor even disjoints subsets. Of course, the preferences thus expressed between formulae must be linked in some way to the preference structure of the agent on the set Ω_{PS} of alternatives.

The central issue in preference logics is the choice of a *lifting* operator inducing preferences over formulae (or sets of alternatives) from preferences over interpretations (or alternatives). This lifting problem has been considered formally in several places, especially [BAR 04, HAL 97]. It is, to some extent, the reverse process of the induction of a preference relation on interpretations from a priority relation on formulae discussed in section 7.4.2. Hansson [HAN 01b, Chapter 5] discusses these two opposed approaches: the *holistic* approach considers preferences between alternatives as primary and preferences between formulae as derived from them, whereas the *aggregative* approach considers preferences between formulae as primary.

In section 7.5.1, we present a family of preference logics built on the *ceteris paribus* principle for interpreting preferences expressed by an individual between logical formulae. This section owes a lot to Hansson's book [HAN 01b]. In section 7.5.2 we present another family of preference logics, also based on *conditional logics*. Lastly, in section 7.5.3 we briefly discuss the interest of some non-classical (multivalued or paraconsistent) logics, not for compact representation of preferences, but for modeling incomplete and/or contradictory preferences.

7.5.1. Ceteris paribus *preferences*

When an agent expresses in natural language a preference such as 'I prefer a flat on the sixth floor to a flat on the ground floor', they surely do not want to say that they prefer *any* flat on the sixth floor to *any* flat on the ground floor, independently of their other properties. This preference statement does not exclude that the agent prefers a vast and luxurious flat on the ground floor to a studio on the sixth floor. The principle at work in the interpretation of a such a preference statement is that the alternatives must be compared *all other things being equal* (*ceteris paribus*) or, more generally, all irrelevant properties being equal.

We now proceed in three steps: first, we will see which meaning to give to comparisons between logical formulae that are not contradictory; we will then state the principle of *ceteris paribus* comparisons and its generalization based on 'maximally similar' pairs of alternatives; lastly, we will briefly evoke a few languages that are less expressive but more efficient from a computational point of view, especially CP-nets.

7.5.1.1. *Preferences between non-contradictory formulae*

Interpreting the statement 'φ is preferred to ψ', written formally $\varphi \triangleright \psi$, is unproblematic when φ and ψ are complete formulae (corresponding each to a unique alternative). Such a statement corresponds directly to its semantical counterpart $w \succ w'$, where $Mod(\varphi) = \{w\}$ and $Mod(\psi) = \{w'\}$. In a similar way, the indifference between φ and ψ, written formally as $\varphi \bowtie \psi$, corresponds to $w \sim w'$. Defining a logic of preferences where preference and indifference do not bear on complete formulae comes down to translating in logical terms the desirable properties of preference relations (transitivity, acyclicity of strict preference, etc.). We do not go deeper into the details of these constructions; see [HAN 01a, section 2].

Now, when expressing relative or absolute preferences, individuals often refer not only to isolated alternatives, but also to logical formulae representant *sets of alternatives* that are generally not singletons, nor even disjoint subsets. There is nothing exceptional in expressing a statement such as 'I prefer icecream to cake', whereas it might be inconceivable (in this context) to eat both an icecream and a piece of cake. This statement actually refers to a comparison between icecream-and-no-cake and cake-and-no-icecream. This convention, observed by Hallden [HAL 57] and von Wright [WRI 63], is written formally: $\varphi \triangleright \psi$ is translated by $\varphi \wedge \neg\psi > \neg\varphi \wedge \psi$, where $>$ has to be defined (the subject of section 7.5.1.2).

However, this principle fails whenever one of these propositions is a logical consequence of the other (since it would then consist of comparing a formula to a logical contradiction). Some natural statements fall into this limit case: consider $\varphi = $ 'I work hard and earn a lot of money' and $\psi = $ 'I work hard' [HAN 01b]. In order to take this limit case into account, Hansson [HAN 89] proposes a generalization of the latter principle: define $\varphi \backslash \psi$ ('φ and if possible not ψ') as being equal to φ if $\varphi \wedge \neg\psi$ is inconsistent, and to $\varphi \wedge \neg\psi$ otherwise. The informal statement 'φ is preferred to ψ' is then traslated into $\varphi \backslash \psi > \psi \backslash \varphi$.

Hansson [HAN 01b] proposes an even more general translation obtained from the previous one by replacing $\varphi \backslash \psi$ by $\varphi \backslash_\Sigma \psi$, where Σ is a logical theory defined as being equal to φ if $\varphi \wedge \neg\psi \wedge \Sigma$ is inconsistent, and to $\varphi \wedge \neg\psi$ otherwise.

In a similar way, the indifference between φ and ψ is translated by $\varphi \backslash \psi \approx \psi \backslash \varphi$, where $\approx$ remains to be defined. We will say that the preferences of the form $\varphi \triangleright \psi$ and $\varphi \bowtie \psi$ expressed between formulae that are non-necessarily exclusive are under *general* form, and that their translations into preferences of the form $\alpha > \beta$ or $\alpha \approx \beta$ (between exclusive formulae) are under *exclusive* form.

We can moreover introduce *contexts* into conditional preferences: intuitively, if γ is a propositional formula, $\gamma : \varphi \triangleright \psi$ (respectively, $\gamma : \varphi \bowtie \psi$) means that the preference of φ to ψ (respectively, the indifference between φ and ψ) applies only when γ is true. This introduction of contexts is rather unproblematic, since it suffices to rewrite $\gamma : \varphi \triangleright \psi$ into $\gamma \wedge \varphi \triangleright \gamma \wedge \psi$ and $\gamma : \varphi \bowtie \psi$ into $\gamma \wedge \varphi \bowtie \gamma \wedge \psi$.

7.5.1.2. Ceteris paribus *comparisons and their generalizations*

The previous translations do not say how the preferences of the form $\varphi > \psi$ and $\varphi \approx \psi$ are related to the preference relation between alternatives. A particularly intuitive principle is the *ceteris paribus* interpretation of preference statements. This consists of interpreting preferences between two logical formulae φ and ψ such as 'everything else being equal, I prefer an interpretation satisfying $\varphi \wedge \neg\psi$ to an interpretation satisfying $\psi \wedge \neg\varphi$' (and similarly for indifference).

These principles are based on the works of von Wright [WRI 63]. Hansson suggests rewriting them by taking the previous limit case into account, i.e. by replacing $\varphi \wedge \neg\psi$ by $\varphi \backslash \psi$. A preference relation $\succeq$ therefore satisfies $\varphi \triangleright \psi$ if and only if $w \succ w'$ holds for every pair (w, w') of alternatives such that

1) $w \models \varphi \backslash \psi$;
2) $w' \models \psi \backslash \varphi$; and
3) w and w' coincide on all other issues (everything else being equal)

and similarly for $\bowtie$, replacing $\succ$ by $\sim$.

The problem that arises is then how to interpret formally 'everything else being equal' (i.e. *ceteris paribus*). When φ and ψ are opposed literals, i.e. $\varphi = p$ and $\psi = \neg p$ or *vice versa*, this is unproblematic: w and w' are identical *ceteris paribus* if they give the same truth value to all propositional symbols other than p. When φ and ψ are complex formulae, the interpretation of $\varphi > \psi$ and $\varphi \approx \psi$ is much more involved.

Hansson proposes a very general interpretation of $\varphi > \psi$ that goes much beyond the *ceteris paribus* principle and is based on the notion of *representation function*. Let φ and ψ be two consistent propositional formulae, then $f(\varphi, \psi)$ is a non-empty subset of $Mod(\varphi) \times Mod(\psi)$. Intuitively, $f(\varphi, \psi)$ is the set of pairs of alternatives that will be compared when interpreting the formula $\varphi > \psi$ or the formula $\varphi \approx \psi$. Formally, let $\succeq$ be a preference relation between alternatives and f a representation function. Then $\succeq$ satisfies $\varphi >_f \psi$ if, for every pair of alternatives $\langle w, w' \rangle \in f(\varphi, \psi)$, $w \succ w'$ holds.

A few concrete propositions for representation functions are as follows. Let us first introduce the notion of equivalence of models modulo a subset of variables: for $X \subseteq PS$, w and w' are said to be X-equivalent, denoted by $w =_X w'$, if w and w' give the same truth value to all the propositional symbols that are not in X.

We can choose $f_\forall(\varphi, \psi) = Mod(\varphi) \times Mod(\psi)$, which leads to the interpretation of $\varphi > \psi$ as 'every model of φ is preferred to every model of ψ'. This is much too weak a definition to be practically interesting [WRI 63].

Von Wright [WRI 72] proposes a first extension of the *ceteris paribus* principle to formulae that are not opposed literals, making the following choice. Let $Var(\varphi)$ be the set of propositional symbols appearing in φ, and define f_V by $\langle w, w' \rangle \in f_V(\varphi, \psi)$ if and only if $w \models \varphi$, $w' \models \psi$ and w coincides with w' on all the symbols outside $Var(\varphi) \cup Var(\psi)$.

[DOY 91a, TAN 94a, TAN 94b] propose similar definitions but consider, instead of $Var(\varphi)$, the support $S(\varphi)$ defined as the set of propositional symbols on which φ depends. Formally, φ depends on $x \in PS$ if there exists no formula φ' logically equivalent to φ in which the symbol x does not appear [LAN 98]. Of course, we have $S(\varphi) \subseteq Var(\varphi)$.

Then let (1) $\langle w, w' \rangle \in f_S(\varphi, \psi)$ if and only if $w \models \varphi$, $w' \models \psi$ and $w =_{\overline{S(\varphi) \cup S(\psi)}} w'$ (cf. [TAN 94b], which considers only the case where $\psi = \neg \varphi$), and (2) $\langle w, w' \rangle \in f_{DSW}(\varphi, \psi)$ if $w \models \varphi$, $w' \models \psi$ and there exists an alternative w^* such that $w^* =_{S(\varphi)} w'$ and $w^* =_{S(\psi)} w'$ [DOY 91a]. When $\psi = \neg \varphi$, the two definitions are equivalent (since $S(\varphi) = S(\psi)$) and, informally, reduce to: w and w' give the same truth value to all propositional symbols that are irrelevant to φ.

In presence of a context γ, an issue is whether the previously defined functions can allow the variables associated with the context to vary. For instance, when expressing $a \vee b : p > \neg p$ in the CP-net formalism (see following section), one compares alternatives giving the same value to all variables except p; abp and $\bar{a}b\bar{p}$ remain incomparable. In order to give more expressivity to the representation language, some approaches [COS 04, LAN 02a, WIL 04b] suggest adding a set of variables $X \subseteq PS$ which are allowed to vary to a contextual preference $\gamma : \varphi > \psi$. Thus, $\gamma : \varphi > \psi[X]$ induces $w \succ w'$ if and only if $w \models \varphi$, $w' \models \psi$ and $w =_{\bar{X}} w'$. Of course, it is natural to require that $S(\varphi) \cup S(\psi) \subseteq X$.

Hansson [HAN 01b] proposes using a representation function induced by a comparative similarity relation $\leq_T$, where $\langle w_1, w_2 \rangle >_T \langle w_3, w_4 \rangle$ means that w_1 is closer to w_2 than w_3 is to w_4. Given such a relation (defined outside the logical language), the representation function f_T is defined by $f_T(\varphi, \psi) = \min(\leq_T, Mod(\varphi) \times Mod(\psi))$. Therefore $\succ_{f_T}$ consists of comparing an alternative satisfying φ and an alternative satisfying ψ, as soon as these two alternatives are as similar as possible among the pairs of alternatives such that one satisfies φ and the other ψ. The comparison principle induced by this representation function goes much beyond the basic *ceteris paribus* principle.

7.5.1.3. *Preference relation induced by* ceteris paribus *preferences*

It now remains to make explicit the preference relation $\succeq_{GB}$ induced by a set of preference statements and a representation function f.

Let $GB = \{\varphi_1 > \psi_1, \ldots, \varphi_p > \psi_p, \varphi_{p+1} \sim \psi_{p+1}, \ldots, \varphi_q \sim \psi_q\}$ be a set of preference statements under exclusive form, and f a representation function. Define the satisfaction of a preference statement under exclusive form by a preference relation $\succeq$ as follows:

1) $\succeq$ satisfies $\varphi_i > \psi_i$ if we have $w \succ w'$ for every $\langle w, w' \rangle \in f(\varphi, \psi)$; and
2) $\succeq$ satisfies $\varphi_i \approx \psi_i$ if we have $w \sim w'$ for every $\langle w, w' \rangle \in f(\varphi, \psi)$.

Lastly, $\succeq$ satisfies GB if and only if $\succeq$ satisfies each of the preference statements of GB. GB is said to be *consistent* if there exists a preference relation $\succeq$ satisfying GB. The inconsistency of a set of preference items under exclusive form is caused by the presence of a preference cycle containing at least a strict preference such as $\{a > \neg a, \neg a > a\}$ or $\{a > \neg a, \neg a \approx a\}$.

Finally, when GB is consistent, the preference relation $\succeq_{GB}$ induced by GB is the intersection of all the preference relations satisfying GB.

We can show (see [BOU 04a] in the particular case of CP-nets) that $\succeq_{GB}$ can be characterized equivalently in the following constructive way. Define first the local preference relation $\succeq_i$ associated with the preference statement G_i by:

– if G_i is of the form $\varphi_i > \psi_i$, then $w \succeq_i w'$ if and only if $\langle w, w' \rangle \in f(\varphi, \psi)$; and
– if G_i is of the form $\varphi_i \approx \psi_i$, then $w \succeq_i w'$ if and only if $\langle w, w' \rangle \in f(\varphi, \psi)$ or $\langle w', w \rangle \in f(\varphi, \psi)$.

We then have the following result: if GB is consistent, then $\succ_{GB}$ is the reflexive and transitive closure of $\cup\{\succ_i, i = 1 \ldots, q\}$. This characterization allows us to determine if $w \succeq w'$ by searching for a finite sequence $w_0 = w, w_1, \ldots, w_{r-1}, w_r = w'$ of alternatives such that for every $j \in \{0, \ldots, r-1\}$ there exists an $i \in \{1, \ldots, q\}$ such that $w_j \succeq_i w_{j+1}$. The previous result allows us to say that $w \succeq w'$ if and only if such a sequence exists, and that w is a non-dominated alternative for $\succeq_G$ if and only if there exists no alternative w' nor any $i \in \{1, \ldots, q\}$ such that $w' \succ_i w$.

Example 7.9. Let GB be the following set of contextual preference statements:

$$\text{expensive} \lor \text{HK} : \text{long} \triangleright \text{medium} \triangleright \text{short}$$
$$\text{cheap} \land \neg \text{HK} : \text{short} \triangleright \text{medium} \triangleright \text{long}$$
$$\text{medium-priced} \land \neg \text{HK} : \text{short} \bowtie \text{medium} \bowtie \text{long}$$
$$\top : \text{cheap} \triangleright \text{medium-priced} \triangleright \text{expensive}$$
$$\top : \text{HK} \land \text{medium-priced} \triangleright \neg \text{HK} \land \text{cheap}$$
$$\top : \text{HK} \land \text{expensive} \triangleright \neg \text{HK} \land \text{medium-priced}$$

We can check that the induced preference relation (HK, medium-priced, long) is preferred to (¬ HK, expensive, short). Indeed, we have the following chain of strict preferences:

(HK,medium-priced,long)
$\succ$ (HK,medium-priced,medium) (application of expensive ∨ HK: long ▷ medium)
$\succ$ (HK,expensive,medium) (application of ⊤: medium-priced ▷ expensive)
$\succ$ (¬ HK,medium-priced,medium) (application of ⊤: HK ∧ expensive ▷ ¬ HK ∧ medium-priced)
$\succ$ (¬ HK,expensive,medium) (application of ⊤: medium-priced ▷ expensive)
$\succ$ (¬ HK,expensive,short) (application of expensive ∨ HK: medium ▷ short)

We also have (HK, medium-priced, medium) $\succ$ (¬ HK, cheap,long) (by application of ⊤: HK ∧ medium-priced ▷ ¬ HK ∧ cheap and of cheap ∧ ¬ HK: medium ▷ long). On the other hand, it is not possible to derive a preference (nor an indifference) between the alternatives (HK, medium-priced, medium) and (¬ HK, cheap, short), which are therefore incomparable.

7.5.1.4. *CP-nets*

An important and recent stream of work in artificial intelligence focuses on a graphical preference representation language which is also based on *ceteris paribus* comparisons: *CP-nets*. This language is both more general and less general than the language of *ceteris paribus* preferences, for similar reasons to those evoked for GAI-nets in section 7.4.1. It is more general because variables are not necessarily binary, and less general because the preference statements that can be expressed must comply with a fixed restricted syntax. For the sake of brevity, assume that all variables are binary. If X and Y are two disjoint subsets of PS, and $x \in \Omega_X, y \in \Omega_Y$ are two 'partial alternatives' giving a value to the variables of X and Y respectively, then the partial alternative (x, y) is the concatenation of x and y, giving to each variable of X (respectively, Y) the value given by x (respectively, y).

We now introduce the notion of *preferential independence*. Let $\{X, Y, Z\}$ be a partition of the set of variables PS and $\succeq$ a preference relation. X is *preferentially independent of Y given Z* (for the preference relation $\succeq$) if and only if for all $x_1, x_2 \in 2^X, y_1, y_2 \in 2^Y$ and $z \in D_Z$,

$$(x_1, y_1, z) \succeq (x_2, y_1, z) \text{ iff } (x_1, y_2, z) \succeq (x_2, y_2, z).$$

Unlike probabilistic independence, preferential independence is an oriented notion: it may be the case that X is independent of Y given Z without Y being independent of X given Z. (If X is preferentially independent of $\bar{X}$ and $\bar{X}$ preferentially independent of X, then X is said to be *separable*.)

A CP-net [BOU 04a, BOU 99] on PS is a pair $\langle \mathcal{G}, \mathcal{C} \rangle$ where $\mathcal{G}$ is an oriented graph whose vertices are PS, and $\mathcal{C} = \{C(x) | x \in PS\}$ is a set of *conditional preference tables*. Let U be the set of parents of x in $\mathcal{G}$. $C(x)$ associates with each $u \in \Omega_U$ a strict preference on x, i.e. $x \succ \bar{x}$ or $\bar{x} \succ x$.

The edges of $\mathcal{G}$ express preferential independencies: if $Par(x)$ denotes the set of parents of x in $\mathcal{G}$, then each variable x is independent of $\overline{\{x\} \cup Par(x)}$ given $Par(x)$. The conditional preferences tables contain elementary contextual preferences interpreted with the *ceteris paribus* principle.

Example 7.10. $PS = \{x, y, z\}; \mathcal{G} = \begin{array}{c} \nearrow y \downarrow \\ x \rightarrow z \end{array}$.

The conditional preference tables are:

| $x \succ \bar{x}$ |

| $x : y \succ \bar{y}$ |
| $\bar{x} : \bar{y} \succ y$ |

| $x \vee y : z \succ \bar{z}$ |
| $\neg(x \vee y) : \bar{z} \succ z$ |

The preference relation induced by this CP-net is

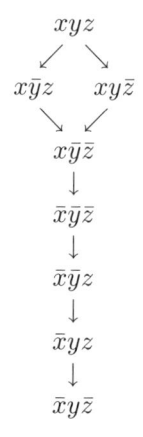

$$\begin{array}{c}
xyz \\
\swarrow \quad \searrow \\
x\bar{y}z \qquad xy\bar{z} \\
\searrow \quad \swarrow \\
x\bar{y}\bar{z} \\
\downarrow \\
\bar{x}\bar{y}\bar{z} \\
\downarrow \\
\bar{x}\bar{y}z \\
\downarrow \\
\bar{x}yz \\
\downarrow \\
\bar{x}y\bar{z}
\end{array}$$

Many works on CP-nets make the additional assumption that the graph $\mathcal{G}$ is *acyclic*. Under this assumption, the set of *ceteris paribus* preference statements expressed by the tables of the CP-net is consistent. The associated requests, consisting of comparing two alternatives or of searching for a non-dominated alternative, are computationally reasonable [BOU 04b].

When variables are binary, the language R_{cpnets} of CP-nets can therefore be seen as a restriction of the language of contextual *ceteris paribus* preferences, where the preference statements $\gamma : \varphi > \psi$ are such that (a) φ and ψ are complementary literals and (b) for every variable x, $\bigvee\{\gamma_i \mid GB \text{ contains } \gamma : x > \neg x \text{ or } \gamma : \neg x > x\}$ is a tautology.

Note that CP-nets cannot represent all preference relations: the computational gain comes with a loss of expressivity. Several extensions of CP-nets have been proposed in order to enhance their expressivity: [DOM 02c, WIL 04b, WIL 04a] allow for expressing relative importance relations between variables.

7.5.1.5. *Comments and bibliographical notes*

The principle consisting of interpreting preferences along with the *ceteris paribus* principle is due to von Wright [WRI 63] and has been considerably revisited by Hansson [HAN 89, HAN 01b] who, noticeably, has proposed the generalization based on representation functions and who has studied in detail the logical properties. [ROY 09] give an axiomatization of von Wright's *ceteris paribus* preference logic. The *ceteris paribus* principle was independently rediscovered by researchers from the AI community [DOY 91a, DOY 91b].

[TAN 94a, TAN 94b] add to these *ceteris paribus* preferences some *normality* considerations between worlds. [MCG 02] show how to compute utility functions that are compatible with the (partial) order induced by a set of *ceteris paribus* preference statements.

The work on CP-nets is concerned with more practical issues such as preference elicitation and computation of optimal outcomes. For an extensive presentation of CP-nets see [BOU 04a, BOU 04b] as well as [DOM 02a]. See also [BRA 04, DOM 02b] for the problem of the consistency checking in CP-nets and [GOL 05] for the complexity of dominance and of consistency in CP-nets. [DUB 05] explore the links between CP-nets and possibilistic logic, and [DOM 03] the link between CP-nets and valued constraint satisfaction problems.

7.5.2. *Defeasible preferences and conditional preference logics*

We now give a summary of another stream of logical formalism logics for representing conditional and *defeasible* preferences, based on *conditional logics*. Consider the following statements:

1) John desires to go to Brittany this weekend.

2) If there is a storm warning on Brittany next weekend, then John desires to stay in Paris.

Statement (1) corresponds to a *defeasible* or a *default* preference; (1) applies not only if we know that there is no risk of storm but more generally if there is no specific information about the weather forecast. This makes the assumption that the state of the world is *normal* (no storm warning), given that a later announcement of a storm warning would invalidate statement (1) and give priority to statement (2), which is more specific. There is therefore no real inconsistency between (1) and (2), which should be read the following way: 'normally, John desires to go to Brittany, except in the exceptional states where there is a storm notification'.

Reasoning on such preferences is *non-monotonic*, in the sense that the application of a preference statement sometimes has to be revised (or invalidated) after a more specific piece of information is learned. (This kind of reasoning has been studied a lot in AI under the name 'non-monotonic reasoning'. However, it is more concerned with factual beliefs and generic rules with exceptions than with preferences in the decision-theoretic sense.)

What is the interest in this principle consisting of implicitly assuming that the state of the world is normal, allowing us to draw defeasible conclusions about the agent's preferences? First, it fits the intuition and the expression of preferences in natural language, where normality assumptions about the state of the world are often made implicitly. Then, it allows for a succinct and modular description of preferences: succinct because avoiding specifying explicitly all the exceptional conditions in which a preference statement does not apply leads to an economy of representation; modular because a set of such preference statements can be completed at any time, without generating an inconsistency. Returning the statements above, to the preference statements (1) and (2) we add the following statement.

3) If, on the platform at Montparnasse station, John instantly falls in love with someone who is leaving for Brittany, then he desires to go to Brittany whatever the meteorological conditions.

This statement will then have priority over statement (2) in the 'doubly exceptional circumstance' `storm_notification` $\land$ `in_love`, statement (2) having priority over statement (1) in the simply exceptional circumstance `storm_warning` $\land$ $\neg$ `in_love`.

A neat way of formalizing these contextual preferences consists of using *conditional logics*. The idea of using conditionals for representing defeasible preferences comes back to [BOU 94]. The language of propositional conditional logics contains, in addition to the language of classical propositional logic, a *dyadic modality* $I(.|.)$. If

φ and ψ are formulae of the language, so is $I(\psi|\varphi)$. (More common notation in the literature on conditional logics is $\varphi \Rightarrow \psi$ instead of $I(\psi|\varphi)$.) This inductive definition allows us to express nested conditionals such as $I(a|I(b|c))$. However, as long as we are interested only in preference representation we do not need these formulae with nested modalities, therefore we will consider only formulae of depth no more than 1. A formula of depth 0 is a classical propositional formula; if φ and ψ are of depth 0 then $I(\psi|\varphi)$ is of depth 1. Finally, if φ and ψ are of depth 1 then $\neg\phi$, $\varphi \wedge \psi$ and $\varphi \vee \psi$ are of depth 1. Let us call LC^1_{PS} the set of all formulae of depth lower than or equal to 1 built on the set of propositional symbols PS. $I(\psi)$ is short for $I(\psi|\top)$.

The semantics of the conditional logic CO [BOU 94] interprets formulae of LC^1_{PS} in terms of complete preference relations: a model of CO is a pair $M = \langle W, \geq \rangle$ where $W \subseteq 2^{PS}$ is a set of possible worlds and $\geq$ is a *complete preorder* on W. This identification of a world with its valuation is possible because of the restriction to formulae of depth lower than or equal to 1.

A model $M = \langle W, \geq \rangle$ of CO satisfies a conditional desire $I(\varphi|\psi)$ if and only if

$$Max(\geq, Mod(\psi)) \subseteq Mod(\varphi).$$

Thus, $I(\varphi|\psi)$ ('ideally φ if ψ') holds if, in the preferred worlds where ψ is true, φ is true.

At first glance, it may appear paradoxical to favor an optimistic interpretation of conditional desires; most approaches in qualitative decision making argue towards using a pessimistic criterion for the choice of an action (see Chapter 11). However, the paradox is easily resolved. When an agent specifies $I(\psi|\top)$, for example, they express that they have a preference for ψ, which is not the same thing as saying they have the intention to choose an action making ψ true, which can be seen in the following example.

Example 7.11. Let $GB = \{D(\neg i), D(i|p)\}$, where i and p mean 'take a umbrella' and 'it is raining', respectively. $D(\neg i)$ expresses that ideally, the agent prefers not to carry an umbrella; this does not mean that if they have the choice between taking their umbrella or leaving it at home, they will choose to leave it at home.

This example illustrates that interpreting conditional desires and interpreting preferences on acts are, to some extent, independent problems. It is perfectly possible to interpret conditional desires in terms of ideality while having at the same time a pessimistic criterion for preferences between acts [LAN 03]. That being said, it is possible to replace the max-max criterion of the ideality semantics by other criteria such as min-min, max-min or min-max. See [LAN 02b] for a discussion.

It now remains to make explicit the way a unique preference relation over alternatives can be induced from a set of preference statements expressed by conditional desires. Since a model of CO is isomorphic to a complete preference relation over alternatives, an intuitive answer would consist of mapping a set of conditional desires to the set of complete preference relations corresponding to its models.

Since the question reduces to: draw *one* preference relation $\geq_{GB}$ from GB and K (therefore to see conditional logic as a language for describing preference relations in an implicit and compact way), the most straightforward choice (called standard) would then consist of defining $\geq_{GB}$ as the intersection of preference relations corresponding to the models of GB. Let $GB = \{D(\varphi_1|\psi_1), \ldots, D(\varphi_p|\psi_p)\}$ be a set of conditional desires and K a formula expressing, as before, feasibility constraints. $\geq_{GB}^{cond,S}$ is defined: for all $w, w' \in Mod(K)$, $w \geq_{GB}^{cond,S} w'$ if and only if for every $M \models GB$ we have $w \geq_M w'$. $\geq_{GB}^{cond,S}$ thus built is a preference relation (i.e. a preorder).

GB generally has too many models, which implies that $\geq_{GB}^{cond,S}$ is much too weak. Consider the example: $GB = \{D(a|\top)\}$. For all $w, w' \in \{(a,b), (a, \neg b), (\neg a, b), (\neg a, \neg b)\}$, we have $w \geq_{GB}^{cond,S} w'$ if and only if $w = w'$ and therefore $w >_{GB}^{cond,S} w'$ is never verified: all alternatives are non-dominated.

A way of remedying the latter problem consists of selecting *one* model satisfying GB: the one maximizing preference 'interpretation wise' or, equivalently, the preference relation obtained by Z-completion of GB [BOU 94, p. 79]. This principle [ADA 75, PEA 90] was initially used in for reasoning with rules tolerating exceptions: it consists of interpreting each default rule $\varphi \Rightarrow \psi$ by the constraint $Prob(\psi|\varphi) \geq 1 - \varepsilon$ where ε is infinitely smal, and then in ranking interpretations according to their probability.

In the context of preferences with exceptions, this principle can be described in the following way. Let $GB = \{I(\psi_i|\varphi_i), i = 1, \ldots, n\}$ be a set of conditional desires (for the sake of simplicity, and without loss of generality we let $K = \top$). Define the satisfaction of a set of conditional desires by an integer-valued utility function and the *canonical* non-positive integer-valued utility function $u_{GB}^* : \Omega_{PS} \to Z^-$ associated with GB as follows:

– for each conditional desire $I(\psi|\varphi)$, $u \models I(\psi|\varphi)$ if and only if $\max_{w \models \varphi \wedge \psi} u(w) > \max_{w \models \varphi \wedge \neg \psi} u(w)$;

– let $u : \Omega_{PS} \to Z^-$ be a non-positive integer-valued utility function, then $u \models \mathcal{D}$ if and only if $u \models I(\psi_i|\varphi_i)$ for every $I(\psi_i|\varphi_i)$ in $\mathcal{D}$; and

– for every $w \in \Omega_{PS}$, $u_\mathcal{D}^*(w) = \max_{u \models \mathcal{D}} u(w)$.

We can check that $u_{GB}^* \models GB$. Lastly, define $\succeq_{GB}^Z = \succeq_{u_{GB}^*}$, that is, $w \succeq_{GB}^Z w'$ if and only if $u_{GB}^*(w) \geq u_{GB}^*(w')$. Intuitively, $\succeq_{GB}^Z$ makes alternatives "gravitate towards preference" [BOU 94]. We can compute u_{GB}^* more simply than its definition suggests, using the following algorithm [PEA 90]. Let Δ be a set of conditional desires and $\delta = I(\psi \mid \varphi) \in \Delta$; we say that Δ *tolerates* δ if and only if $\varphi \wedge \psi \wedge \bigwedge \{\varphi' \rightarrow \psi' \mid I(\psi' \mid \varphi') \in \Delta\}$ is satisfiable. Consider the following algorithm:

$\Delta := GB; k := 0;$
repeat
$\quad \Delta_k = \{\delta \in \Delta \mid \delta \text{ tolerated by } \Delta\};$
$\quad \Delta := \Delta \setminus \Delta_k;$
$\quad k := k + 1$
until $\Delta = \varnothing$

We can show that $u^*_{GB}(w) = -\max\{k \mid I(\psi \mid \varphi) \in \Delta_k \text{ and } w \models \varphi \wedge \neg \psi\}$.

This construction process can also be seen as transforming a set of conditional desires into a set of classical propositional formulae obtained by replacing each conditional desire $I(\psi|\varphi)$ by the material implication $\varphi \rightarrow \psi$, these formulae being ranked by a priority relation. Intuitively, this priority relation is such that if a rule r is more specific than a rule r', then the material implication associated with r has priority over the material implication associated with r', as it can be seen in the following example.

Example 7.12.
$$GB = \{I(\neg b), I(b \mid a), I(\neg b | a \wedge c)\}$$

We find out that only $I(\neg b)$ is tolerated by GB, hence $\Delta_1 = \{I(\neg b)\}$. Then $\Delta_2 = \{I(b \mid a)\}$ and $\Delta_3 = \{I(\neg b | a \wedge c)\}$, hence $u^*_{GB}(abc) = -3$, $u^*_{GB}(a\bar{b}c) = u^*_{GB}(a\bar{b}\bar{c}) = -2$, $u^*_{GB}(\bar{a}\bar{b}\bar{c}) = u^*_{GB}(\bar{a}bc) = u^*_{GB}(ab\bar{c}) = -1$ and $u^*_{GB}(\bar{a}\bar{b}c) = u^*_{GB}(\bar{a}\bar{b}\bar{c}) = 0$.

Once this priority relation has been obtained, we can use the criteria defined in section 7.4.2. The criterion that allows us to recover the original definition is the *best-out* criterion. This criterion has one major drawback: it is subject to the drowning effect [BEN 93] as can be seen in the following example.

Example 7.13. Let $GB = \{\text{I(cheap)}, \text{I(medium-priced}| \neg \text{ cheap)}, \text{I(long|HK)}, \text{I(} \neg \text{ short|cheap)}, \text{I(short|cheap)}, \text{I(HK|} \neg \text{ cheap)}, \text{I(lh)}\}$, where each propositional symbol is defined as in example 7.6 and lh in the desire I(lh) means that the agent prefers to fly with Lufthansa. The Z-completion process creates three levels of priorities. The formula with the greatest priority is the material implication associated with I($\neg$ short|cheap), i.e. cheap $\rightarrow \neg$ short. The formulae of intermediate priority are $\neg$ cheap $\rightarrow$ medium-priced, $\neg$ cheap $\rightarrow$ HK and HK $\rightarrow$ long (recall that there exists no interpretation where HK and cheap are simultaneously true). Lastly, the formulae of weakest priority are lh, cheap and cheap → short. Thus, (¬ HK, medium-priced, medium, lh) is not preferred to (¬ HK, expensive, medium, lh). On the other hand, the preference for Lufthansa is abandoned as soon as the ticket is not cheap or the stay is not short.

The advantage of this characterization by means of a stratified preference base defined from GB is that the drowning effect can be avoided by interpreting GB according to criteria other than *best-out*, especially *discrimin* and *leximin* as seen in section 7.4.2. This resolves the previous problems but leaves the formulae cheap and lh at the same priority level, which is not justified. An alternative approach to interpreting these conditional rules that does not use a completion step (even if it deals with specificity) is proposed by [LAN 96] and extended (with weights expressing rule strength, as well as polarities) in [LAN 02b].

Finally, conditional logics of preferences allow for expressing relative *plausibility* (or *normality*) of worlds, and then allow for a logical formalization of *qualitative decision theory* (Chapter 11). A model of the logic QDT (qualitative decision theory) [BOU 94] is a triple $M = \langle W, \succeq_P, \succeq_N \rangle$ where W is a set of worlds (that we assume to be finite for the sake of simplicity) identified with propositional interpretations as before. $\succeq_P$ is a complete preorder expressing preference and $\succeq_P$ is a complete preorder expressing *normality*. $I(.|.)$ is defined as before, whereas $N(B|A)$ ('normally B if A') is defined by $M \models N(B|A)$ if and only if the most normal worlds among those satisfying A also satisfy B. [BOU 94] then defines the notion of *ideal goal*, that combines normality and preference as follows. $M \models IG(B|A)$ if and only if $Max(\succeq_P, Max(\succeq_N, Mod(A))) \subseteq Mod(B)$, i.e. $IG(B|A)$ is true if the most preferred A-worlds among the most normal worlds satisfy B.

This interpretation of ideal goals only allows a weak interaction between preference and normality, since only the most plausible worlds are taken into consideration. Moreover, undesirable properties appear: for example, *normally* p implies that p is an ideal goal. The definition of conditional desires in [LAN 03] avoids these pitfalls. A model M (defined as before) satisfies $I(B|A)$ if and only if the most preferred among the most normal $A \wedge B$-worlds are preferred to the most preferred among the most normal $A \wedge \neg B$-worlds. In other words, $\forall w' \in Max(\succeq_N, Mod(A \wedge \neg B))$ $\exists w \in Max(\succeq_N, Mod(A \wedge B))$ such that $w \succ_P w'$.

Example 7.14. This is adapted from a classical example from the deontic logics literature:

1) John does not wish to have a fence around his cottage ($I(f)$).
2) If John has a dog, then he wishes to have a fence ($I(f|d)$).
3) John wishes to have a dog ($I(d)$).

That is, $GB = \{I(\neg f), I(f|d), I(d)\}$. Whereas GB is unsatisfiable with the semantics of [BOU 94] (and remains so if I is replaced by IG), it becomes satisfiable with the semantics of [LAN 03]; it suffices to consider a model where having a dog is exceptional:
$\succeq_N$: $\bar{d}f, \bar{d}\bar{f} \succ_N df, d\bar{f}$
$\succeq_P$: every complete preorder satisfying $df \succ_P d\bar{f} \succ_P \bar{d}f$.
Note that GB possesses several other models [LAN 03].

We wonder about how normality should be interpreted in an example such as the above where all variables are controllable. The interpretation of $\succ_N$ in terms of *plausibility* is not relevant here; 'normality' here can be interpreted as the distance to the actual matter of facts [LAN 03].

Whereas conditional logics call for *dyadic* modalities, a few works call for *monadic* modalities or predicates for representing preferences. In particular, [HAN 01b, Chapter 8] studies logics for expressing monadic preferences (φ is good/bad).

We end this section by mentioning a few approaches to reasoning about preferences that are based on Reiter's default logic (we discuss them here because of the existence of strong links between default logic and conditional logics).

The system of [THO 00] considers both defaults of the 'preference' type and defaults of the 'belief' type, with a procedural strategy that differs totally from the semantical definitions of the previous approaches. The goals are derived in two steps: first an application of 'belief' defaults, allowing us to determine the plausible properties of the actual state of the world, then an application of 'preference' defaults. This strict separation into two separate steps allows us to avoid the 'wishful thinking' paradox (when using inference rules in an uncontrolled way without formally distinguishing between beliefs and preferences) [THO 00].

'Decision-theoretic defaults' [BRA 95, POO 92] are also interpreted in terms of both normality and preference, this time using the classical criterion of expected utility. The interpretation of a default $A : B$ in [POO 92] is that if A is true, then the action *accept* B is better (in terms of expected utility) than the actions *accept* $\neg B$ and *accept neither B nor $\neg B$*.

7.5.2.1. *Bibliographical notes*

Conditional logics have existed since the works of Lewis [LEW 73] and have been the subject of many research papers, both in philosophical logic and in AI. They were initially developed for reasoning with counterfactuals. (A conditional $A \Rightarrow B$ is translated into the statement 'if A were true, then B would be true', interpreted: the closest A-worlds satisfy B.) The specificity of the dyadic conditional modality (and also of conditional objects [DUB 95b]) is that a conditional rule has three possible truth values. $D(\varphi|\psi)$ is satisfied in w if $w \models \psi \wedge \varphi$, violated if $w \models \psi \wedge \neg\varphi$ and unapplicable if $w \models \neg\psi$. Since their semantics are often defined in terms of preorder relations between worlds, it is not surprising that they have played a role in preference representation.

Finally, representing preferences by conditional desires is close, to some extent, to the representation of obligations and permissions (and especially confluctual obligations such as 'contrary-to-duty' obligations). Table 7.8 lists three different interpretations of conditionals (see [MAK 93, TOR 97] for a deeper discussion on the various interpretations of rankings on sets of alternatives).

	$\geq$	$I(\varphi|\psi)$
epistemic interpretation	normality	normally φ if ψ
preferential interpretation	preference	ideally φ if ψ
deontic interpretation	permission	φ obligatory if ψ

Table 7.8. *Three interpretations of rankings*

7.5.3. *Logical modeling of incomplete and/or contradictory preferences*

We only mention briefly a stream of works very different to that considered in the rest of the chapter: the use of non-classical logics for modeling certain classes of preferences. Here the goal is neither compact representation nor the interpretation of preference statements between logical formulae, but using logic for axiomatizing a given mathematical model of preferences structures.

The first works on the subject, notably [HAN 68, RES 67], axiomatize ordinal preferences in first-order logic. For example, transitivity is expressed by $\forall xyz R(x,y) \wedge R(y,z) \rightarrow R(x,z)$. More recent extensions of these approaches make use of non-classical logics for modeling complex preferences that cannot simply be modeled by orderings (see [ÖZT 05, TSO 92] for a synthesis):

– *Paraconsistent logics* allow for the presence of 'local' and 'non-explosive' contradictions, i.e. they allow a formula which is inconsistent in classical logic (such $A \wedge \neg A$) to become consistent and not entail any other formula of the language. These logics are therefore of interest for the axiomatization of conflictual preferences. [TSO 02a] makes use of Belnap's four-valued logic [BEL 77] (whose so-called 'truth values' are true, false, indefinite and inconsistent). The distinction between the lack of information concerning the preference between two alternatives A and B, and the excess of information resulting from the presence of elements in favor of the (strict) preference of A over B and elements in favor of the (strict) preference of B over A, is expressed. A continuous extension of these approaches, allowing us to express intensities of preference and conflict, is developed in [PER 98].

– *Multivalued logics* and particularly *fuzzy logics* are multivalued logics with a continuum of truth values. They allow the introduction of a notion of intensity in ordinal preferences. Fuzzy/multivalued logics make the concept of truth gradual, and thus introduce intermediate truth degrees such as 'completely true' and 'rather true' which apply to statements referring to vague propositions or predicates. They are naturally relevant for the axiomatization of *fuzzy preferences*. A fuzzy preference relation specifies, for each pair (x, y) of alternatives, the degree to which x is preferred to y (or the degree to which y is preferred to x). There exist two possible interpretations of a fuzzy preference relation R: $\mu_R(x, y)$ represents either a degree of intensity of preference (the degree to which x is preferred to y) or a degree of uncertainty concerning the preference of x over y [FOD 98, ORL 78, ROY 77].

7.6. Discussion

In this chapter, we have discussed several families of logical formalisms allowing the expression of preferences in a structured and/or succinct way. This variety does not make the choice of a suitable language easy. We provide a few hints allowing the evaluation of the different formalisms. The choice between them must, of course, be guided by the characteristics of the problem at hand.

7.6.1. *Cognitive and linguistic relevance, elicitation*

A language for preference representation has to be as close as possible to the way individuals know their preferences and express them in natural language (in other terms, the preferences expressed in a given language should be intuitively understandable by an individual). If philosophers and computer scientists have focused on the links between logic and preferences, these logics for preference representation have not yet been evaluated by cognitive psychologists and linguists.

Preference elicitation consists of building interactive algorithms allowing the minimization of the number of questions asked of an agent, while maximizing the informational usefulness of the preferences obtained. A preference representation language should be, if possible, coupled to efficient elicitation algorithms, whose output consists of preferences expressed in the target language.

7.6.2. *Expressivity*

Evaluating the expressivity of a language L consists of determining the set preference (preference relations or utility functions) expressible in L. To make it short, we will only consider here the expressivity of languages for ordinal preferences, using S_L as defined in section 7.3. Table 7.9 lists a quick survey of the expressivity of the languages evoked in this chapter. Most results are straightforward; those which are not generally come from [COS 04].

L	Section	Syntax	S_L
R_{dicho}	7.3	G	all dichotomous preorders
R_{card}	7.3	$\{G_1,\ldots,G_n\}$	all complete preorders
R_{Pareto}	7.3	$\{G_1,\ldots,G_n\}$	all preorders
R_{pond}	7.4.1	$\{\langle G_1,\alpha_1\rangle,\ldots,\langle G_p,\alpha_p\rangle\}$	all complete preorders
$R_{GAI-nets}$	7.4.1	local utility functions	all complete preorders
$R_{best-out}$	7.4.2	$\{G_1,\ldots,G_n\}$ + stratification	all complete preorders
$R_{discrimin}$	7.4.2	$\{G_1,\ldots,G_n\}$ + stratification	all preorders
$R_{leximin}$	7.4.2	$\{G_1,\ldots,G_n\}$ + stratification	all complete preorders
R_{dist}	7.4.3	$\{G_1,\ldots,G_p\} + d$	all complete preorders
R_{CP}	7.5.1.3	$\{C_i : G_i \sharp G'_i, i=1\ldots p\}, \sharp \in \{\triangleright,\bowtie\}$	all preorders
$R_{CP-nets}$	7.5.1.4	$\langle \mathcal{G},\mathcal{C}\rangle$	some preorders
R^S_{cond}	7.5.2	$\{D(G_1|C_1),\ldots,D(G_p|C_p)\}$	some preorders
R^Z_{cond}	7.5.2	$\{D(G_1|C_1),\ldots,D(G_p|C_p)\}$	all complete preorders

Table 7.9. *'Ordinal' expressivity of languages*

7.6.3. *Complexity and algorithms*

Once a preference structure has been represented in a given language L, a key question is to identify the computational difficulty of the following decision problems (we do not give any technical results here. For some of the languages considered in this chapter, see [LAN 04] for corresponding complexity results):

– *Comparison*: given two alternatives w and w', determine if $w \succeq w'$.

– *Optimality*: given an alternative w, determine if w is non-dominated, i.e. if there does not exist an alternative w' such that $w' \succ w$.

– *Optimization*: find one (or all) non-dominated alternative(s).

– *Inference*: given a property represented by a logical formula φ, determine if there exists a non-dominated alternative satisfying φ.

In addition to assessing the complexity of the latter decision problems, it is crucial to construct algorithms for finding a non-dominated alternative given a preference specification in a particular language.

7.6.4. *Spatial efficiency*

The spatial efficiency (or succinctness power) of a language is a relative notion. A language L is said to be at least as succinct as a language L' if, informally, any preference structure that can be expressed in L' can also be expressed in L without any superpolynomial increase of size or, formally, if there exists (a) a function $f : L' \to L$

such that $Ind_{L'} = Ind_L \circ f$ or (b) a polynomial p such that for every $\Phi \in L'$, $|f(\Phi)| \leq p(|\Phi|)$ where $|.|$ represents the size of the input. Clearly, if L is at least as succinct as L' then L is at least as expressive as L', i.e. $S_L \subseteq S_{L'}$ [COS 04].

7.7. Acknowledgements

Many thanks to Didier Dubois and Alexis Tsoukiàs for proofreading the French version of this chapter and for the many helpful comments.

7.8. Bibliography

[ADA 75] ADAMS E., *The Logic of Conditionals*, D. Reidel, Dordrecht, 1975.

[BAC 95] BACCHUS F., GROVE A., "Graphical models for preference and utility", *Proceedings of the 11th International Conference on Uncertainty in Artificial Intelligence (UAI-95)*, p. 3–10, 1995.

[BAR 04] BARBERA S., BOSSERT W., PATTANAIK P., "Ranking sets of objects", *Handbook of Utility Theory*, p. 895–978, Kluwer Academic Publishers, Dordrecht, 2004.

[BEH 77] BEHRINGER F., "On optimal decisions under complete ignorance: A new criterion stronger than both Pareto and Maxmin", *European Journal of Operational Research*, vol. 1, num. 5, p. 295–306, 1977.

[BEL 77] BELNAP N., "A useful four-valued logic", *Modern Uses of Multiple Valued Logic*, D. Reidel, Dordrecht, 1977.

[BEN 93] BENFERHAT S., CAYROL C., DUBOIS D., LANG J., PRADE H., "Inconsistency management and prioritized syntax-based entailment", *Proceedings of the 13th International Joint Conference on Artificial Intelligence (IJCAI'93)*, p. 640–645, 1993.

[BEN 94] BENHAMOU B., SAIS L., "Two proof procedures for cardinality based language in propositional calculus", *11th International Symposium on Theoretical Aspects of Computer Science (STACS'94)*, LNCS 775, Springer Verlag, p. 71–82, 1994.

[BEN 98] BENFERHAT S., DUBOIS D., LANG J., PRADE H., SAFFIOTTI A., SMETS P., "A general approach for inconsistency handling and merging information in prioritized knowledge bases", *Proceedings of the 6th International Conference on Knowledge Representation and Reasoning (KR'98)*, 1998.

[BEN 01] BENFERHAT S., DUBOIS D., PRADE H., "Towards a possibilistic logic handling of preferences", *Applied Intelligence*, vol. 14, num. 3, p. 403–417, 2001.

[BEN 02a] BENFERHAT S., DUBOIS D., KACI S., PRADE H., "Bipolar possibilistic representations", *Proceedings of the 18th International Conference on Uncertainty in Artificial Intelligence (UAI-02)*, p. 45–52, 2002.

[BEN 02b] BENFERHAT S., DUBOIS D., KACI S., PRADE H., "Possibilistic representation of preference: relating prioritized goals and satisfaction levels expressions", *Proceedings of KR2002*, 2002.

[BIE 05] BIENVENU M., MCILRAITH S., "Qualitative dynamical preferences for planning", *Proceedings of the IJCAI-05 Workshop on Advances in Preference Handling*, p. 13–18, 2005.

[BIS 99] BISTARELLI S., FARGIER H., MONTANARI U., ROSSI F., SCHIEX T., VERFAILLIE G., "Semiring-Based CSPs and Valued CSPs: Frameworks, Properties, and Comparison", *CONSTRAINTS: An International Journal*, vol. 4, num. 3, p. 199–240, 1999.

[BOU 94] BOUTILIER C., "Toward a logic for qualitative decision theory", *Proceedings of the 4th International Conference on Principles of Knowledge Representation and Reasoning (KR'94)*, p. 75–86, 1994.

[BOU 99] BOUTILIER C., BRAFMAN R., HOOS H., POOLE D., "Reasoning with conditional *ceteris paribus* preference statements", *Proceedings of the 15th International Conference on Uncertainty in Artificial Intelligence (UAI-99)*, p. 71–80, 1999.

[BOU 01] BOUTILIER C., BACCHUS F., BRAFMAN R., "UCP-networks: a directed graphical representation of conditional utilities", *Proceedings of the 17th Conference on Uncertainty in Artificial Intelligence (UAI-2001)*, p. 56–64, 2001.

[BOU 04a] BOUTILIER C., BRAFMAN R., DOMSHLAK C., HOOS H., POOLE D., "CP-nets: a tool for representing and reasoning with conditional ceteris paribus statements", *Journal of Artificial Intelligence Research*, vol. 21, p. 135–191, 2004.

[BOU 04b] BOUTILIER C., BRAFMAN R. I., DOMSHLAK C., HOOS H., POOLE D., "Preference-Based Constrained Optimization with CP-nets", *Computational Intelligence*, vol. 20, num. 2, p. 137–157, 2004.

[BRA 95] BRAFMAN R., FRIEDMAN N., "On decision-theoretic foundations for defaults", *Proceedings of International Joint Conference on Artificial Intelligence (IJCAI-95)*, p. 1458–1465, 1995.

[BRA 04] BRAFMAN R., DIMOPOULOS Y., "Extended Semantics and Optimization Algorithms for CP-Networks", *Computational Intelligence*, vol. 20, num. 2, p. 218–245, 2004.

[BRA 05] BRAZIUNAS D., BOUTILIER C., "Local Utility Elicitation in GAI Models", *Proceedings of the 21st Conference on Uncertainty in Artificial Intelligence*, p. 42–49, 2005.

[BRA 07] BRAZIUNAS D., BOUTILIER C., "Minimax regret based elicitation of generalized additive utilities", *Proceedings of the 23rd Conference on Uncertainty in Artificial Intelligence (UAI-07)*, p. 25–32, 2007.

[BRE 89] BREWKA G., "Preferred subtheories: an extended logical framework for default reasoning", *Proceedings of the 11th International Joint Conference on Artificial Intelligence (IJCAI'89)*, p. 1043–1048, 1989.

[BRE 02] BREWKA G., "Logic programming with ordered disjunction", *Proceedings of the 18th National Conference on Artificial Intelligence (AAAI-02)*, p. 100–105, 2002.

[BRE 04] BREWKA G., "A rank-based Description Language for Qualitative Preferences", *Proceedings of 16th European Conference on Artificial Intelligence (ECAI04)*, p. 303–307, 2004.

[CAY 92] CAYROL C., "Un modèle logique pour le raisonnement révisable", *Revue d'Intelligence Artificielle*, vol. 6, p. 255–284, 1992.

[CHE 06] CHEVALEYRE Y., ENDRISS U., LANG J., "Expressive Power of Weighted Propositional Formulas for Cardinal Preference Modelling", *Proceedings of the 10th International Conference on Principles of Knowledge Representation and Reasoning (KR-2006)*, AAAI Press, p. 145–152, 2006.

[COS 04] COSTE-MARQUIS S., LANG J., LIBERATORE P., MARQUIS P., "Expressive power and succinctness of propositional languages for preference representation", *Proceedings of the 9th International Conference on the Principles of Knowledge Representation and Reasoning (KR-2004)*, p. 203–212, 2004.

[DEL 03] DELGRANDE J., SCHAUB T., TOMPITS H., "A Framework for Compiling Preferences in Logic Programs", *Theory and Practice of Logic Programming*, vol. 3, num. 2, p. 129–187, March 2003.

[DOM 02a] DOMSHLAK C., Modelling and reasoning about preferences with CP-nets, PhD thesis, Ben-Gurion University, 2002.

[DOM 02b] DOMSHLAK C., BRAFMAN R. I., "CP-nets: Reasoning and Consistency Testing", *Proceedings of the 8th International Conference on the Principles of Knowledge Representation and Reasoning (KR-2002)*, p. 121–132, 2002.

[DOM 02c] DOMSHLAK C., BRAFMAN R. I., "Introducing Variable Importance Tradeoffs in CP-nets", *Proceedings of the 18th International Conference on Uncertainty in Artificial Intelligence (UAI-02)*, 2002.

[DOM 03] DOMSHLAK C., ROSSI F., VENABLE K. B., WALSH T., "Reasoning about soft constraints and conditional preferences: complexity results and approximation techniques", *Proceedings of the 18th International Joint Conference on Artificial Intelligence (IJCAI-03)*, p. 215–220, 2003.

[DOY 91a] DOYLE J., SHOHAM Y., WELLMAN M. P., "A logic of relative desire", *Proceedings of the 6th International Symposium on Methodologies for Intelligent Systems (ISMIS-91)*, p. 16–31, 1991.

[DOY 91b] DOYLE J., WELLMAN M. P., "Preferential semantics for goals", *Proceedings of the 9th National (American) Conference on Artificial Intelligence (AAAI-91)*, p. 698–703, 1991.

[DUB 92] DUBOIS D., LANG J., PRADE H., "Inconsistency in possibilistic knowledge bases: to live or not live with it", ZADEH L., KACPRZYK J., Eds., *Fuzzy Logic for the Management of Uncertainty*, p. 335–351, Wiley, Oxford, 1992.

[DUB 94] DUBOIS D., LANG J., PRADE H., "Possibilistic logic", GABBAY D., HOGGER C., ROBINSON J., Eds., *Handbook of Logic in Artificial Intelligence and Logic Programming*, vol. 3, p. 439–513, Clarendon Press, Oxford, 1994.

[DUB 95a] DUBOIS D., ESTEVA F., GARCIA P., GODO L., PRADE H., "Similarity-based consequence relation", *Proceedings of the 3rd European Conference on Symbolic Quantitative Approaches to Reasoning and Uncertainty (ECSQARU-95)*, Lecture Notes in Computer Science 946, Springer Verlag, p. 171–179, 1995.

[DUB 95b] DUBOIS D., PRADE H., "Conditionals: from Philosophy to Computer Science", Chapter Conditional objects, possibility theory and default rules, p. 301–336, Oxford University Press, Oxford, 1995.

[DUB 97] DUBOIS D., FARGIER H., PRADE H., "Beyond min aggregation in multicriteria decision: (Ordered) weighted min, discri-min, leximin", YAGER R., KACPRZYK J., Eds., *The Ordered Weighted Averaging Operators – Theory and Applications*, p. 181–192, Kluwer Academic Publishing, Norwell, 1997.

[DUB 01] DUBOIS D., FORTEMPS P., "Leximin Optimality and Fuzzy Set Theoretic Operations", *European Journal of Operational Research*, vol. 130, p. 20–28, 2001.

[DUB 05] DUBOIS D., KACI S., PRADE H., "CP-nets and possibilistic logic: two approaches to preference handling. Steps towards a comparison", *Proceedings of the IJCAI-05 Workshop on Advances on Preferences Handling*, p. 79–84, 2005.

[DUP 94] DUPIN DE SAINT CYR F., LANG J., SCHIEX T., "Penalty logic and its link with Dempster-Shafer theory", *Proceedings of UAI'94*, Morgan Kaufmann, p. 204–211, 1994.

[FAR 93] FARGIER H., LANG J., SCHIEX T., "Selecting preferred solutions in fuzzy constraint satisfaction problems", *Proceedings of the 1st European Conference on Fuzzy Information Technologies*, p. 1128–1134, 1993.

[FIS 70] FISHBURN P., *Utility Theory for Decision Making*, Wiley, Oxford, 1970.

[FOD 98] FODOR J., ORLOVSKI S., PERNY P., ROUBENS M., "The use of fuzzy preference models in multiple criteria: choice, ranking and sorting", *Handbook of Fuzzy Sets*, Kluwer Academic Publishers, Dordrecht, 1998.

[GEF 92] GEFFNER H., *Default Reasoning: Causal and Conditional Theories*, MIT Press, Cambridge, 1992.

[GIN 98] GINSBERG M. L., PARKES A. J., ROY A., "Supermodels and Robustness", *Proceedings of the 15th National (American) Conference on Artificial Intelligence (AAAI-98)*, p. 334–339, 1998.

[GOL 05] GOLDSMITH J., LANG J., TRUSZCZINSKI M., WILSON N., "The computational complexity of dominance and consistency in CP-nets", *Proceedings of IJCAI-05*, p. 144–149, 2005.

[GON 04] GONZALES C., PERNY P., "GAI networks for utility elicitation", *Proceedings of the 9th International Conference on the Principles of Knowledge Representation and Reasoning (KR-2004)*, p. 224–233, 2004.

[GRA 00] GRABISCH M., LABREUCHE C., "The Sipos integral for the aggregation of interacting bipolar criteria", *Proceedings of the 8th International Conference on Information Processing and Management of Uncertainty in Knowledge-based Systems (IPMU)*, p. 395–401, 2000.

[GRE 02] GRECO S., MATARAZZO B., SLOWINSKI R., "Bipolar Sugeno and Choquet integrals", *Proceedings of EUROFUSE02 Workshop on Information Systems*, p. 191–196, 2002.

[HAD 92] HADDAWY P., HANKS S., "Representations for decision theoretic planning: utility functions for deadline goals", *Proceedings of the 3th International Conference on the Principles of Knowledge Representation and Reasoning (KR-92)*, p. 71–82, 1992.

[HAL 57] HALLDÉN S., *On the Logic of 'Better'*, Library of Theoria, Lund, 1957.

[HAL 97] HALPERN J., "Defining relative likelihood in partially-ordered preferential structures", *Journal of Artificial Intelligence Research*, vol. 7, p. 1–24, 1997.

[HAN 68] HANSSON B., "Fundamental axioms for preference relations", *Synthese*, vol. 18, p. 423–442, 1968.

[HAN 89] HANSSON S. O., "A new semantical approach to the logic of preferences", *Erkenntnis*, vol. 31, p. 1–42, 1989.

[HAN 01a] HANSSON S. O., "Preference Logic", GABBAY D., GUENTHNER F., Eds., *Handbook of Philosophical Logic*, p. 319–393, Kluwer, Dordrecht, 2001.

[HAN 01b] HANSSON S. O., *The Structure of Values and Norms*, Cambridge University Press, 2001.

[HEN 91] HENTENRYCK P. V., DEVILLE Y., "The cardinality operator: a new logical connective for constraint logic programming", *Proceedings of the 8th International Conference on Logic Programming (ICLP-91)*, p. 745–759, 1991.

[JON 08] DE JONGH D., LIU F., "Preference, Priorities and Belief", 2008, Report, ILLC, University of Amsterdam.

[KAT 91] KATSUNO H., MENDELZON A., "On the difference between updating a knowledge base and revising it", *Proceedings of the 2nd International Conference on the Principles of Knowledge Representation and Reasoning (KR-91)*, p. 387–394, 1991.

[KAT 92] KATSUNO H., MENDELZON A., "Propositional Knowledge Base Revision and Minimal Change", *Artificial Intelligence*, vol. 52, num. 3, p. 263–294, 1992.

[KON 98] KONIECZNY S., PINO-PÉREZ R., "On the logic of merging", *Proceedings of the 6th International Conference on the Principles of Knowledge Representation and Reasoning (KR-98)*, p. 488–498, 1998.

[KON 02] KONIECZNY S., LANG J., MARQUIS P., "Distance-based merging: a general framework and some complexity results", *Proceedings of the 8th International Conference on the Principles of Knowledge Representation and Reasoning (KR 2002)*, p. 97–108, 2002.

[LAB 03] LABREUCHE C., GRABISCH M., "Modeling Positive and Negative Pieces of Evidence in Uncertainty.", *Proceedings of the 7th European Conference on Symbolic Quantitative Approaches to Reasoning and Uncertainty (ECSQARU-03)*, p. 279–290, 2003.

[LAF 00] LAFAGE C., LANG J., "Logical representation of preferences for group decision making", *Proceedings of the 7th International Conference on the Principles of Knowledge Representation and Reasoning (KR 2000)*, p. 457–468, 2000.

[LAF 01] LAFAGE C., LANG J., "Propositional distances and preference representation", *Proceedings of the 6th European Conference on Symbolic Quantitative Approaches to Reasoning and Uncertainty (ECSQARU-01)*, p. 48–59, 2001.

[LAN 91] LANG J., "Possibilistic logic as a logical framework for min-max discrete optimization and prioritized constraints", *Proceedings of the International Workshop on Fundamentals of Artificial Intelligence Research*, vol. 535 of *Lecture Notes in Computer Science*, Springer, p. 113–125, 1991.

[LAN 96] LANG J., "Conditional desires and utilities: an alternative logical approach to qualitative decision theory", *Proceedings of the 12th European Conference on Artificial Intelligence (ECAI-96)*, p. 318–322, 1996.

[LAN 98] LANG J., MARQUIS P., "Complexity results for independence and definability in propositional logic", *Proceedings of the 6th International Conference on Knowledge Representation and Reasoning (KR'98)*, Trento, 1998, 356–367.

[LAN 02a] LANG J., "From preference representation to combinatorial vote", *Proceedings of the 8th International Conference on the Principles of Knowledge Representation and Reasoning (KR 2002)*, p. 277–288, 2002.

[LAN 02b] LANG J., VAN DER TORRE L., WEYDERT E., "Utilitarian desires", *International Journal on Autonomous Agents and Multi-Agent Systems*, vol. 5, p. 329–363, 2002.

[LAN 03] LANG J., VAN DER TORRE L., WEYDERT E., "Hidden uncertainty in the logical representation of desires", *Proceedings of the Eighteenth International Joint Conference on Artificial Intelligence (IJCAI'03)*, p. 685–690, 2003.

[LAN 04] LANG J., "Logical preference representation and combinatorial vote", *Annals of Mathematics and Artificial Intelligence*, vol. 42, num. 1, p. 37–71, 2004.

[LEH 95] LEHMANN D., "Another Perspective on Default Reasoning", *Annals of Mathematics and Artificial Intelligence*, vol. 15, num. 1, p. 61–82, 1995.

[LEW 73] LEWIS D., *Counterfactuals*, Blackwell, 1973.

[LIU 08] LIU F., Changing for the better: preference dynamics and agent diversity, PhD thesis, 2008.

[MAK 93] MAKINSON D., "Five faces of minimality", *Studia Logica*, vol. 52, p. 339–379, 1993.

[MCG 02] MCGEACHIE M., DOYLE J., "Efficient Utility Functions for Ceteris Paribus Preferences", *Proceedings of the 18th National (American) Conference on Artificial Intelligence (AAAI-02)*, p. 279–284, 2002.

[MOU 88] MOULIN H., *Axioms of Cooperative Decision Making*, Cambridge University Press, Cambridge, 1988.

[MUR 99] MURA P. L., SHOHAM Y., "Expected utility networks", *Proceedings of the 15th International Conference on Uncertainty in Artificial Intelligence (UAI-99)*, p. 366–373, 1999.

[NEB 91] NEBEL B., "Belief Revision and Default Reasoning: Syntax-Based approaches", *Proceedings of the 2nd International Conference on Knowledge Representation and Reasoning (KR'91)*, p. 417–428, 1991.

[ORL 78] ORLOVSKY S., "Decision making with a fuzzy preference relation", *Fuzzy Sets and Systems*, vol. 1, p. 155–167, 1978.

[ÖZT 05] ÖZTÜRK M., TSOUKIÀS A., VINCKE P., "Preference modelling", EHRGOTT M., GRECO S., FIGUEIRA J., Eds., *State of the Art in Multiple Criteria Decision Analysis*, p. 27–72, Springer Verlag, 2005.

[PEA 90] PEARL J., "System Z: a natural ordering of defaults with tractable applications for default reasoning.", *'Proceedings of the 3rd Conference on Theoretical Aspects of Reasoning about Knowledge (TARK-90)*, p. 121–135, 1990.

[PER 98] PERNY P., TSOUKIAS A., "On the continuous extension of a four valued logic for preference modelling", *Proceedings of the 6th International Conference on Information Processing and Management of Uncertainty in Knowledge-Based Systems (IPMU-98)*, p. 302–309, 1998.

[PIN 91] PINKAS G., "Propositional nonmonotonic reasoning and inconsistency in symmetric neural networks", *Proceedings of the 12th International Joint Conference on Artificial Intelligence (IJCAI91)*, Morgan-Kaufmann, p. 525–530, 1991.

[POO 92] POOLE D., "Decision-theoretic defaults.", *Proceedings of the Canadian Conference on Artificial Intelligence*, p. 190–197, 1992.

[RES 67] RESCHER N., *Semantic Foundations for the Logic of Preference*, University of Pittsburgh Press, Pittsburgh, 1967.

[REV 97] REVESZ P., "On the semantics of arbitration", *International Journal of Algebra and Computation*, p. 133–160, 1997.

[ROY 77] ROY B., "Partial preference analysis and decision aid: the fuzzy outranking relation concept", *Conflicting Objectives in Decision*, p. 40–75, Wiley, 1977.

[ROY 09] ROY O., VAN BENTHEM J., GIRARD P., "Everything else being equal: A modal logic approach to ceteris paribus preferences", *Journal of Philosophical Logic*, 2009, To appear.

[SAB 98] SABBADIN R., "Decision as abduction", *Proceedings of the 13th European Conference on Artificial Intelligence (ECAI-98)*, p. 600–604, 1998.

[SHE 89] SHENOY P., "A valuation-based language for expert systems.", *International Journal of Approximate Reasoning*, vol. 3, num. 5, p. 383–411, 1989.

[TAN 94a] TAN S., PEARL J., "Qualitative decision theory", *Proceedings of the 11th National (American) Conference on Artificial Intelligence (AAAI-94)*, p. 928–933, 1994.

[TAN 94b] TAN S., PEARL J., "Specification and evaluation of preferences for planning under uncertainty", *Proceedings of the 4th International Conference on Principles of Knowledge Representation and Reasoning (KR'94)*, p. 530–539, 1994.

[THO 00] THOMASON R., "Desires and defaults: a framework for planning with inferred goals", *Proceedings of the 7th International Conference on the Principles of Knowledge Representation and Reasoning (KR 2000)*, p. 702–713, 2000.

[TOR 97] VAN DER TORRE L., Reasoning about obligations, PhD thesis, Erasmus University Rotterdam, 1997.

[TOR 01] VAN DER TORRE L., WEYDERT E., "Parameters for utilitarian desires in a qualitative decision theory", *Applied Intelligence*, vol. 14, num. 3, p. 285–302, 2001.

[TSO 92] TSOUKIÀS A., VINCKE P., "A survey on non conventional preference modelling", *Ricerca Operativa*, vol. 61, p. 5–49, 1992.

[TSO 02a] TSOUKIÀS A., "A first-order, four valued, weakly paraconsistent logic and its relation to rough sets semantics", *Foundations of Computing and Decision Sciences*, vol. 27, p. 77–96, 2002.

[TSO 02b] TSOUKIÀS A., PERNY P., VINCKE P., "From concordance/discordance to the modelling of positive and negative reasons in decision aiding", JACQUET-LAGRÈZE E., PERNY P., SLOWINSKI R., VANDERPOOTEN D., VINCKE P., Eds., *Aiding Decisions with Multiple Criteria: Essays in Honour of Bernard Roy*, p. 147–174, Kluwer Academic, Dordrecht, 2002.

[UCK 07] UCKELMAN J., ENDRISS U., "Preference Representation with Weighted Goals: Expressivity, Succinctness, Complexity", *Proceedings of the AAAI Workshop on Preference Handling for Artificial Intelligence (AiPref-2007)*, p. 85–92, 2007.

[UCK 08] UCKELMAN J., ENDRISS U., "Preference Modeling by Weighted Goals with Max Aggregation", *Proceedings of the 11th International Conference on Principles of Knowledge Representation and Reasoning (KR-2008)*, p. 579–588, September 2008.

[WIL 04a] WILSON N., "Consistency and Constrained Optimisation for Conditional Preferences", *Proceedings of the 16th European Conference on Artificial Intelligence (ECAI-04)*, p. 888–892, 2004.

[WIL 04b] WILSON N., "Extending CP-nets with stronger conditional preference statements", *Proceedings of AAAI-04*, p. 735–741, 2004.

[WIL 06] WILSON N., "A logic of soft constraints based on partially ordered preferences", *Journal of Heuristics*, vol. 12, num. 4-5, p. 241–262, 2006.

[WRI 63] VON WRIGHT G. H., *The Logic of Preference*, Edinburgh University Press, Edinburgh, 1963.

[WRI 72] VON WRIGHT G. H., "The Logic of Preference Reconsidered", *Theory and Decision*, vol. 3, p. 140–169, 1972.

Chapter 8

Decision under Risk: The Classical Expected Utility Model

8.1. Introduction

We make most of our decisions without definitely knowing their consequences: the outcome of each decision depends on the realization of some uncertain event.

To help an individual facing a decision problem under uncertainty, the axiomatic approach that we adopt in this chapter takes the following steps:

1) Assume that the decision maker has well-defined preferences.

2) Propose a set of 'rationality' axioms that are sufficiently intuitive.

3) Derive from these axioms a representation of the decision maker's preferences.

4) Evaluate all possible decisions with this representation and take the one that scores best.

Importantly, if the decision maker agrees with the set of axioms, they will also agrees with the model derived from these axioms. This model will then help them to take the right decisions.

We deal with a specific uncertain environment in this chapter, known as *risk*, in which the probability of each event is known. In this setting, we define the main properties of decision under risk, the different possible behavior under risk and their comparison. We then study the standard model of behavior under risk: the expected

Chapter written by Alain CHATEAUNEUF, Michèle COHEN and Jean-Marc TALLON.

utility model. We provide axiomatic foundation, study the properties of the model and its behavioral implications. We then discuss the problems raised by this expected utility model, which cannot account for some observed behavior. We then expose a few alternative models, although the main generalization of the expected utility model, in which decisions are evaluated by Choquet integrals, is presented in Chapter 10.

8.1.1. *Decision under uncertainty*

A decision problem under uncertainty is usually described through a set S called the set of states of nature (or states of the world), identifying events with subsets of S. We will only need to use the sub-family of 'relevant' events for the problem at hand and will then use the smallest σ-algebra $\mathcal{A}$ including this sub-family.

We denote a set of possible outcomes or consequences by $\mathcal{C}$, and an algebra containing the singletons of $\mathcal{C}$ by $\mathcal{G}$. A *decision* or *act* is defined as a measurable mapping from $(S, \mathcal{A})$ to $(\mathcal{C}, \mathcal{G})$. We denote the set of all such mappings from S to consequences $\mathcal{C}$ by $\mathfrak{X}$.

We assume that a decision maker has a well-defined preference relation $\succsim$ on $\mathfrak{X}$. Strict preference is denoted $\succ$ and indifference is denoted $\sim$. The preference relation on $\mathfrak{X}$ *induces* (through constant acts) a preference relation on the set $\mathcal{C}$ of consequences. Abusing notation, we also denote this preference relation as $\succsim$ on $\mathcal{C}$.

We aim to represent the decision maker's preferences $(\mathfrak{X}, \succsim)$ by a real valued utility function, that is, a mapping V from $\mathfrak{X}$ to $\mathbb{R}$ such that: $X \succsim Y$ if and only if $V(X) \geq V(Y)$. This function will take different forms depending on the set of axioms imposed.

8.1.2. *Risk versus uncertainty*

We can distinguish different forms of uncertainty according to the information the decision maker has on the states of nature. The two extreme situations are:

1) *risk*, in which there exists a *unique probability distribution* P on $(S, \mathcal{A})$, and this distribution is objectively known; and

2) *complete ignorance*, in which no information whatsoever is available about the events.

The distinction between risk and uncertainty is due to [KNI 21]. In between these two extreme cases, we can distinguish between different situations depending on how much information we have on the probability of the various events.

In this chapter, we assume that the decision maker is in a situation of risk. The probability distribution P is known, which is exogenous on the set of states of natures.

The set $(S, \mathcal{A})$ endowed with this probability measure is therefore a probability space $(S, \mathcal{A}, P)$.

Since each decision X induces a probability distribution P_X on $(\mathcal{C}, \mathcal{G})$, and under the rather natural assumption that two decisions with the same probability distribution are equivalent, the preference relation defined on the set of probability distributions with support in $\mathcal{C}$. This relation is denoted $\succsim$ with a slight abuse of notation.

Furthermore, we identify the consequence c of $\mathcal{C}$ with the Dirac measure δ_c in $\mathcal{L}$, and will indifferently use the notation $\delta_c \succsim P_X, c \succsim P_X$ or $c \succsim X$. We therefore work on the set $\mathcal{L}$ of probability distributions on $(\mathcal{C}, \mathcal{G})$ endowed with the relation $\succsim$. The decision maker must therefore compare probability distributions.

Let $\mathcal{L}_0 \subset \mathcal{L}$ be the set of probability distributions with *finite support* in $\mathcal{C}$; in this case, the probability distribution of decision X is denoted $P_X = (x_1, p_1, \ldots, x_n, p_n)$ where $x_1 \precsim, \ldots, \precsim x_n, p_i \geq 0$ and $\sum_i p_i = 1$. Such distributions with finite supports are called lotteries.

In the following section, we provide intrinsic definitions (i.e. independent of representation models) of measures of risk and risk aversion.

8.2. Risk and increasing risk: comparison and measures

In this section, we take $\mathcal{X}$ to be the set of $\mathcal{A}$– measurable functions that are real-valued and bounded from $(S, \mathcal{A}, P)$ to $(\mathbb{R}, \mathcal{B})$, that is, the set of *real, bounded, random variables*. A mapping $X : (S, \mathcal{A}) \to (\mathbb{R}, \mathcal{B})$ is measurable if, for all $B \in \mathcal{B}$, $X^{-1}(B) \in \mathcal{A}$ where $X^{-1}(B) = \{s \in S : X(s) \in B\}$ and $\mathcal{B}$ is the algebra of Borel sets.

8.2.1. *Notation and definitions*

A decision in $\mathcal{X}$ is a random variable X whose probability distribution P_X is defined for all $B \subset \mathbb{R}$, $P_X(B) = P\{s \in S \mid X(s) \in B\}$. We will restrict our attention to bounded random variables. P_X has a cumulative distribution function $F_X(x) = P(\{s \in S : X(s) \leq x\})$. Its expected value or mean is denoted $E(X)$. We define the function $G_X(x) = P(\{s \in S : X(s) > x\}) = 1 - F_X(x)$ to be the survival function.

We now provide definitions for the comparison of various probability distributions. The preference relations so defined will be partial, and are sometimes called stochastic orders.

8.2.1.1. *First-order stochastic dominance*

Definition 8.1. Let X and Y be elements of $\mathcal{X}$. Then X first-order stochastically dominates (FSD) Y if, for all $x \in \mathbb{R}$, $F_X(x) \leq F_Y(x)$.

Remark 8.1. – If X FSD Y, the graph of Y is above the graph of X.
– This condition can be expressed through survival functions: $Pr\{X > x\} \geq Pr\{Y > x\}$: for all x the probability of having more than x is always larger for X than for Y.
– This notion implies that $E(X) \geq E(Y)$.
– The relation FSD only partially ranks the elements of $\mathcal{L}$.

Let X and Y be two acts whose consequences are described in each state of nature $s \in S$ in Table 8.1.

	s_1	s_2	s_3	s_4
$Pr(\{s\})$	0.1	0.2	0.3	0.4
X	1	2	3	4
Y	2	1	2	3

Table 8.1. *Example of FSD*

The cumulative distribution functions of X and Y are:

$$F_X(x) = \begin{cases} 0 \text{ if } x < 1 \\ 0.1 \text{ if } 1 \leq x < 2 \\ 0.3 \text{ if } 2 \leq x < 3 \\ 0.6 \text{ if } 3 \leq x < 4 \\ 1 \text{ if } 4 < x \end{cases} \quad F_Y(x) = \begin{cases} 0 \text{ if } x < 1 \\ 0.2 \text{ if } 1 \leq x < 2 \\ 0.6 \text{ if } 2 \leq x < 3 \\ 1 \text{ if } 3 \leq x < 4 \\ 1 \text{ if } 4 < x, \end{cases}$$

respectively. It is easily seen that for all x in $\mathbb{R}$, $F_X(x) \leq F_Y(x)$ and hence X FSD Y. We now provide a characterization of this notion.

Proposition 8.1. *X first-order stochastically dominates (FSD) Y if and only if for all increasing functions u from $\mathbb{R}$ to $\mathbb{R}$, $\int u(x)dF_X(x) \geq \int u(x)dF_Y(x)$.*

8.2.1.2. Second-order stochastic dominance

We can also compare probability distributions according to their risks: there exist several possible definitions of what it means for a distribution to be more risky than another. For each of these notions, there is an associated notion of risk aversion and these different definitions are independent of the decision model that is retained.

The usual notion of increasing risk is the one associated with second-order stochastic dominance (SSD), introduced in economics by Rothschild and Stiglitz [ROT 70].

Definition 8.2. Let X and Y be in $\mathfrak{X}$, X second-order stochastically dominates (SSD) Y if for all $T \in \mathbb{R}$,

$$\int_{-\infty}^{T} F_Y(x)dx \geq \int_{-\infty}^{T} F_X(x)dx.$$

We have the following implication: $[X \text{ FSD } Y] \Rightarrow [X \text{ SSD } Y]$. The converse is false. The relation SSD also only partially ranks the elements of $\mathcal{L}$. When X and Y have the same mean, we have the following definition.

Definition 8.3. For X and Y in $\mathfrak{X}$, Y is a mean preserving spread (MPS) of X if (i) $E(X) = E(Y)$ and (ii) X SSD Y.

We also say that Y is more risky than X with the same mean.

Example 8.1. Let X and Z be two acts whose decisions in each state of nature $s \in S$ are reported in Table 8.2.

	s_1	s_2	s_3	s_4
$\Pr(\{s\})$	0.1	0.2	0.3	0.4
X	1	2	3	4
Z	4	1	4	3

Table 8.2. *Example of SSD*

Computing the cumulative distribution functions of X and Z, we obtain

$$F_X(x) = \begin{cases} 0 \text{ if } x < 1 \\ 0.1 \text{ if } 1 \leq x < 2 \\ 0.3 \text{ if } 2 \leq x < 3 \\ 0.6 \text{ if } 3 \leq x < 4 \\ 1 \text{ if } 4 < x \end{cases} \quad F_Z(x) = \begin{cases} 0 \text{ if } x < 1 \\ 0.2 \text{ if } 1 \leq x < 2 \\ 0.2 \text{ if } 2 \leq x < 3 \\ 0.6 \text{ if } 3 \leq x < 4 \\ 1 \text{ if } 4 < x, \end{cases}$$

respectively. We can check that $E(X) = E(Y)$ and that the surface between 0 and T of the difference between $F_Z(x)$ and $F_X(x)$ is always positive, which implies that X SSD Z and hence Z MPS X. The following proposition makes the definition of MPS more intuitive.

Proposition 8.2. *Let X and Y be two random variables with the same mean. The following three assertions are equivalent [ROT 70]:*

1) Y is a mean preserving spread of X, that is Y MPS X.

2) Y has the same distribution as $(X + \theta)$ where θ is a random variable such that $E(\theta|X) = 0$ almost everywhere.

3) For all increasing and concave u from $\mathbb{R} \to \mathbb{R}$, $\int u(x)dF_X(x) \geq \int u(x)dF_Y(x)$.

Characterization (2) reveals the intuition behind the definition since it expresses the fact that Y is a mean preserving spread of X when Y can be obtained by adding some *noise* to X. After we define an expected utility decision maker (section 8.3), we will interpret condition (3) behaviorally.

Remark 8.2. Several other notions of increasing risk can be defined, which we will not develop here, although they are sometimes more suited for particular comparative static problems. (See [CHA 97, CHA 04] for some of these definitions and their properties, as well as applications.) Some of these notions will be developed in Chapter 10.

Remark 8.3. If Y MPS X, then the variance of Y is greater than or equal to that of X. The converse is not always true (see section 8.3.5.3). The variance could be intuitively used as a measure of increases in risk but, as we shall see, it might lead to inconsistencies.

8.2.2. *Behavior under risk*

8.2.2.1. *Model-free behavioral definitions*

For a decision maker with a preference relation $\succsim$ on $\mathfrak{X}$, we define some typical behavior under risk. Let us first recall that comparing $E(X)$ and X amounts to comparing $\delta_{E(X)}$ and X.

We can define various notions of risk aversion. We will focus on two of them in this chapter.

Definition 8.4. *An agent is weakly risk averse if, for any random variable X in $\mathfrak{X}$, the expected value is preferred to the random variable itself [ARR 65, PRA 64]:*

$$\forall X \in \mathfrak{X}, \ E(X) \succsim X.$$

Decision under Risk 371

They are *weakly risk seeking* if

$$\forall X \in \mathfrak{X}, \ X \succsim E(X).$$

They are *risk neutral* if

$$\forall X \in \mathfrak{X}, \ X \sim E(X).$$

This definition is usually not strong enough to rank two distributions with the same mean. One can also use another definition as follows.

Definition 8.5. A decision maker is *strongly risk averse* if for any two random variables X, Y in $\mathfrak{X}$ with the same expected value, such that Y is more risky than X according to second-order stochastic dominance, the less risky variable X is preferred to Y:

$$\forall X, Y \in \mathfrak{X}, \quad Y \operatorname{MPS} X \implies X \succsim Y.$$

They are *strongly risk seeking* if

$$\forall X, Y \in \mathfrak{X}, \quad Y \operatorname{MPS} X \implies Y \succsim X.$$

They are *risk neutral* if

$$\forall X, Y \in \mathfrak{X}, \quad Y \operatorname{MPS} X \implies Y \sim X.$$

If a decision maker does not always rank a couple of random variables (Y MPS X) in the same way, they will not fit into any of these categories.

Remark 8.4. It is easy to see that for all X, X MPS $E(X)$. Hence, a strongly risk averse decision maker will necessarily be weakly risk averse. The converse does not hold in general.

8.2.2.2. *Certainty equivalent, risk premium and behavior comparison*

8.2.2.2.1. *Certainty equivalent*

For each random variable X in $\mathfrak{X}$, its *certainty equivalent*, if it exists, is the certain outcome c_X in $\mathcal{C}$ that is indifferent to X: $c_X \sim X$. In this chapter, any random variable in $\mathfrak{X}$ has a unique certainty equivalent.

8.2.2.2.2. Risk premium

The *risk premium* attached to X is denoted ρ_X. It is the difference between the expected value of X and its certainty equivalent: $\rho_X = E(X) - c_X$.

This premium can be interpreted as the maximum amount the decision maker is willing to pay to exchange the variable X with its mean. This premium is negative whenever the decision maker is weakly risk seeking.

The risk premium captures the intensity of (weak) aversion to risk. It is possible to use it to compare, in a partial manner, different behaviors.

Definition 8.6. Decision maker 1 is *more weakly risk averse* than decision maker 2 if, for all $X \in \mathfrak{X}$, the risk premium ρ_X^1 of decision maker 1 is greater than or equal to the risk premium ρ_X^2 of decision maker 2.

8.3. Expected utility (EU) model [VON 47]

We now return to the decision problem faced by a decision maker endowed with a preference relation $\succsim$ on $\mathfrak{X}$ and the associated relation on $\mathcal{L}$. We now expose the axiomatic foundation of the classical model of decision under risk: the *expected utility* (EU) model due to von Neumann–Morgenstern [VON 47]. We study how notions of risk aversion defined above translate in this model.

We consider here the set $\mathcal{L}$ of probability distributions on $(\mathcal{C}, \mathcal{G})$ where $\mathcal{C}$ is a set endowed with an algebra $\mathcal{G}$ which contains, by assumption, all the *singletons*.

Before giving the axioms, we first need to define a mixture operation on the set of probability distributions.

8.3.1. *Mixing probability distributions*

For all $P, Q \in \mathcal{L}$ and $\alpha \in [0, 1]$, we refer to the α-mixture of P and Q as the distribution $R = \alpha P + (1 - \alpha) Q$ such that, for all A in $\mathcal{A}$, $R(A) = \alpha P(A) + (1 - \alpha) Q(A)$. The mixture of two distributions can be interpreted, when P and Q are discrete, as a two-stage lottery. In the first stage, the distributions P and Q are drawn with probability α and $(1 - \alpha)$, respectively. In the second stage, a consequence is chosen according to the distribution drawn at the first stage. $\mathcal{L}$ is then a convex subset of a vector space.

8.3.2. *Generalized mixture*

For any $\alpha_1, \ldots, \alpha_n \in [0,1]$ such that $\sum \alpha_i = 1$ and for all $P_1, \ldots, P_n \in \mathcal{L}$, one can define in a similar way the mixture of these n distributions P_i as the distribution $R = \sum \alpha_i P_i$ such that for all $A \in \mathcal{G}$, $R(A) = \sum \alpha_i P_i(A)$.

Any distribution with finite support can therefore be written as a mixture of Dirac distributions: $P = \sum_{i=1}^{i=n} p_i \delta_{x_i}$. This can also be referred to as a 'convex combination of consequences'.

8.3.3. *Axiomatic foundation of the EU model*

The model is based on three fundamental axioms: a weak order axiom, a continuity axiom and an independence axiom, to which an extra axiom is added in certain cases. Intuitive presentations of the axioms as well as elegant proofs of the von Neumann–Morgenstern [VON 47] theorem (both in the finite and infinite case) can be found in [FIS 70, FIS 82, HER 53, JAF 78, JEN 67, KRE 88] for example. We follow here the presentation of Jaffray [JAF 78].

Axiom 8.1. *Weak order: the preference relation $\succsim$ on $\mathcal{L}$ is a complete weak order that is non-trivial.*

The relation $\succsim$ is thus reflexive, transitive and complete. Furthermore, there exists at least one couple P, Q in $\mathcal{L}$ such that $P \succ Q$.

The completeness assumption, i.e. the fact that the decision maker is assumed to be able to rank all alternatives, is rather strong in some contexts. It is nevertheless widely accepted in standard economic models.

Adding the continuity axiom to this weak order axiom allows the relation $\succsim$ to be represented by a function often called the *utility function* $V : \mathfrak{X} \to \mathbb{R}$, such that:

$$X \succsim Y \iff V(X) \geq V(Y).$$

The precise formulation of the continuity axiom depends on the topological structure of $\mathfrak{X}$ on which preferences are defined [DEB 54, GRA 72]. When this set is a set of probability distributions, as is the case here, the continuity axiom can be expressed as follows.

Axiom 8.2. *Continuity: the preference relation $\succsim$ on $\mathcal{L}$ is continuous (in the sense of [JEN 67]): for all P, Q, R in $\mathcal{L}$ such that $P \succ Q \succ R$, $\exists \alpha, \beta \in \,]0,1[$ such that $\alpha P + (1-\alpha) R \succ Q$ and $Q \succ \beta P + (1-\beta) R$.*

This axiom requires that there does not exist a consequence c_M that is so desirable (actually infinitely desirable) that if a distribution P_0 was offered this consequence with the smallest (positive) probability, this distribution would be preferred to any other distribution that would not have c_M as a possible consequence. Axiom 8.2 also prevents the existence of an infinitely undesirable consequence c_m (think of c_M as being paradise and c_m as being hell, as in Pascal's bet).

The independence axiom that we now give is central to the construction of the expected utility model.

Axiom 8.3. *Independence: for all P, Q, R in $\mathcal{L}$ and all $\alpha \in]0, 1]$,*

$$P \succsim Q \iff \alpha P + (1-\alpha)R \succsim \alpha Q + (1-\alpha)R.$$

This axiom can be interpreted as follows (building on the interpretation of the mixture we gave above). A decision maker that prefers P to Q and who has to choose between the two mixtures $\alpha P + (1-\alpha)R$ and $\alpha Q + (1-\alpha)R$ would reason in the following manner. If an event of probability $(1-\alpha)$ occurs, they get the distribution R independently of their choice. However, if the complement event occurs, they face the choice between P and Q. Since P is preferred, the mixture $\alpha P + (1-\alpha)R$ is preferred. The logic behind this axiom is therefore intuitive. For an interesting discussion around the independence axiom see [FIS 82].

However, axiom 8.3 has attracted a lot of criticism: numerous experimental studies (such as the Allais paradox) have shown that most decision makers make decisions that contradict this axiom. We will return on this issue in section 8.4.1. The representation theorem can be decomposed into two important results as follows.

8.3.3.1. *Linear utility theorem*

Theorem 8.1. *Let $(\mathcal{L}, \succsim)$ be a convex subset of a vector space on $\mathbb{R}$ endowed with a preference relation $\succsim$. The following two conditions are equivalent:*

1) $(\mathcal{L}, \succsim)$ satisfy weak order, continuity and independence.

2) There exists a linear function U from $\mathcal{L}$ to $\mathbb{R}$ that represents the weak order i.e. such that (a) for all X, Y from $\mathcal{L}$, $X \succsim Y \iff U(X) \geq U(Y)$ and (b) for all α in $[0, 1]$, $U(\alpha X + (1-\alpha)Y) = \alpha U(X) + (1-\alpha)U(Y)$.

Proof. We only give a sketch of the proof. It consists of proving the following points:

1) For all P, Q in $\mathcal{L}$ and μ in $]0, 1]$, $P \succ Q \implies P \succ \mu Q + (1-\mu)P$.

2) For all P, Q in $\mathcal{L}$ and λ, μ in $[0, 1]$, $[P \succ, Q, \lambda > \mu] \implies \lambda P + (1-\lambda)Q \succ \mu P + (1-\mu)Q$.

3) For all P, Q, R in $\mathcal{L}$ such that $P \succ Q \succ R$, there exists α in $]0,1[$ such that $Q \sim \alpha P + (1-\alpha)R$.

4) For all P_1, P_2 in $\mathcal{L}$ such that $P_1 \succ P_2$, there exists a linear utility function on the set $\mathcal{L}_{12}$ defined by: $\mathcal{L}_{12} = \{P \in \mathcal{L}, P_1 \succsim P \succsim P_2\}$.

5) This linear utility on $\mathcal{L}_{12}$ is unique up to a positive affine transformation.

6) Extrapolating, there exists a linear utility function on $(\mathcal{L}, \succsim)$ which is unique up to a positive affine transformation.

This theorem is true as soon as $\mathcal{L}$ is a convex subset of a vector space. In order to be able to express the function U as an expected utility, it is necessary to explore several cases according to the structure of $\mathcal{C}$:

– When the distributions do not have finite support, the algebra $\mathcal{G}$ must be rich enough and, furthermore, one needs to add a dominance axiom.

– When $\mathcal{C}$ is already ordered by a complete weak order (in particular when $\mathcal{C}$ is a subset of $\mathbb{R}$), it is necessary to impose a stronger axiom (sometimes labeled monotonicity axiom) that ensures the compatibility of the preference relation on $\mathcal{X}$ and the preference relation on $\mathcal{C}$.

8.3.3.2. *Von Neumann–Morgenstern theorem for distributions with finite support in* $(\mathcal{C}, \mathcal{G})$

We restrict our attention to the set $\mathcal{L}_0$ of distributions with finite support over $\mathcal{C}$. Any distribution P can then be written $P = (x_1, p_1, \ldots, x_n, p_n)$ (i.e. P yields consequence x_i with probability p_i and $\sum p_i = 1$). $(\mathcal{L}_0, \succsim)$ is a convex set and the previous axioms are sufficient for the representation theorem of $\succsim$ as an expected utility.

Theorem 8.2. *Let $\mathcal{L}_0$ be the set of distributions with finite support in $\mathcal{C}$ endowed with the preference relation $\succsim$. The following two statements are equivalent:*

1) $(\mathcal{L}_0, \succsim)$ satisfies weak order, continuity and independence.

2) There exists a utility function U representing the relation $\succsim$ such that

$$U(P) = Eu(P) = \sum_{i=1}^{n} p_i u(x_i),$$

where u is a strictly increasing function from $\mathcal{C}$ to $\mathbb{R}$ defined by $u(x) = U(\delta_x)$ and unique up to a positive affine transformation (that is, any function $v = au + b$ with $a > 0$ is also admissible).

We easily understand in this formulation why the expected utility model is said to be linear: it deals with probabilities in a linear way since $U(\alpha P + (1-\alpha)Q) = \alpha U(P) + (1-\alpha)U(Q)$.

8.3.3.3. Von Neumann–Morgenstern theorem for distributions with bounded suport in $(\mathcal{C},\mathcal{G})$

This theorem can be generalized to the set $\mathcal{L}$ of probability distributions on $(\mathcal{C},\mathcal{G})$. We first assume that $\forall c \in \mathcal{C}$, the sets $\{c' \in \mathcal{C}, c' \precsim c\}$ and $\{c' \in \mathcal{C}, c' \succsim c\}$ belong to the algebra $\mathcal{G}$. We furthermore impose the following dominance axiom, which will guarantee that the utility function u is bounded and therefore that $\int_\mathcal{C} u \, dP$ is well defined.

Axiom 8.4. *Dominance: for all P in $\mathcal{L}$ and c_0 in $\mathcal{C}$,*

1) $P\{c \in \mathcal{C}/c \succsim c_0\} = 1$ *implies* $P \succsim \delta_{c_0}$; *and*
2) $P\{c \in \mathcal{C}/c \precsim c_0\} = 1$ *implies* $P \precsim \delta_{c_0}$.

Axiom 8.4 expresses the fact that if all the outcomes of the distribution P are preferred to the outcome c_0, then P is preferred to the degenerate distribution on c_0.

For a distribution P with bounded support in $(\mathcal{C},\mathcal{G})$, define its cumulative distribution function F as follows. F is a mapping from $\mathcal{C}$ to $[0,1]$ defined by $F(x) = P\{X \precsim x\}$. We can then state the von Neumann–Morgenstern theorem in this setting as follows.

Theorem 8.3. *Let $\mathcal{L}$ be the set of probability distributions with bounded support in $(\mathcal{C},\mathcal{G})$ endowed with the preference relation $\succsim$. The following two statements are equivalent:*

1) $(\mathcal{L},\succsim)$ *satisfies weak order, continuity, independence and dominance.*
2) *There exists a utility function U representing the relation $\succsim$ with*

$$U(P) = Eu(P) = \int_\mathcal{C} u(x) dF(x),$$

where u is a strictly increasing, bounded mapping from $\mathcal{C}$ to $\mathbb{R}$ defined by $u(x) = U(\delta_x)$, unique up to a positive affine transformation.

Remark 8.5. In the remainder, a decision maker who obeys the axioms of the von Neumann–Morgenstern model will be referred to as an EU decision maker.

Remark 8.6. The behavior of an EU decision maker is entirely characterized by the function u.

8.3.3.4. Von Neumann–Morgenstern theorem for distributions with bounded support in $(\mathbb{R},\mathcal{B})$

When $\mathcal{C}$ is a subset of $\mathbb{R}$, axioms 8.1–8.3 combined with axiom 8.4 are not sufficient to obtain the representation. We need to express the compatibility between the preference relation $\succsim$ and the order relation $\geq$ that exists on $\mathbb{R}$; we then need to replace axiom 8.4 by a stronger axiom as follows.

Axiom 8.5. *Monotonicity: for all x, y in $\mathbb{R}$, $x \geq y \iff x \succsim y$.*

We can then state the theorem in this setting as follows.

Theorem 8.4. *Let $\mathcal{L}$ be the set of probability distributions with bounded support in $\mathbb{R}$ endowed with the preference relation $\succsim$. The following two statements are equivalent:*

1) $(\mathcal{L}, \succsim)$ satisfies weak order, continuity, independence and monotonicity.

2) There exists a utility function U representing the relation $\succsim$ such that

$$U(P) = Eu(P) = \int_{\mathbb{R}} u(x) dF(x),$$

where u is a strictly increasing function from $\mathbb{R}$ to $\mathbb{R}$ defined by $u(x) = U(\delta_x)$, which is unique up to a positive affine transformation.

8.3.4. Characterization of risk aversion in the EU model

In the remainder of section 8.3, we consider the set $\mathcal{X}$ of random variables with bounded support in $(\mathbb{R}, \mathcal{B})$ and the associated set of distributions with bounded support in $(\mathbb{R}, \mathcal{B})$.

How are the two notions of risk aversion, previously introduced, characterized in the EU model? The following proposition shows that they cannot be distinguished in this model.

Proposition 8.3. *The following three assertions are equivalent for an expected utility decision maker [ROT 70]:*

1) The decision maker is weakly risk averse.

2) The decision maker is strongly risk averse.

3) The decision maker utility function u is concave.

The equivalence (1)–(3) is straightforward. The equivalence (2)–(3) was proved by Rothschild and Stiglitz [ROT 70].

Remark 8.7. Proposition 8.3 therefore reveals that an EU decision maker cannot make a distinction between weak and strong risk aversion. In the EU model, one can simply speak of *risk aversion* without ambiguity.

8.3.4.1. Characterization of first- and second-order dominance in the EU model

We can now interpret propositions 8.2 and 8.3(3) in the EU model as follows:

– Proposition 8.2: X first-order stochastically dominates Y if and only if any EU decision maker preferes X to Y.

– Proposition 8.3(3): a random Y is a mean preserving spread of X if and only if $E(X) = E(Y)$ and any weakly risk averse EU decision maker prefers X to Y.

8.3.5. Coefficient of absolute risk aversion, local value of the risk premium

In the EU model, it is possible to define the intensity of risk aversion for a decision maker through properties of u.

8.3.5.1. Coefficient of absolute risk aversion

Definition 8.7. When the function u which characterizes the behavior of an EU decision maker is strictly increasing and twice continuously differentiable with strictly positive derivative, we call the coefficient of absolute risk aversion the function R_A from $\mathbb{R}$ to $\mathbb{R}$ defined by

$$R_A(x) = -\frac{u''(x)}{u'(x)}.$$

Note that this coefficient is independent of the choice of the function u representing the preferences. Any other function $v = au + b, a > 0$ will have the same coefficient.

8.3.5.2. Local value of the risk premium

When the distribution X with an expected value x and a variance σ^2 takes its values in an interval $[x - h, x + h]$ where h is *small* with respect to x, one can show [ARR 65, PRA 64] that the risk premium is proportional to the coefficient of absolute risk aversion:

$$\rho_X(x) \approx -\frac{\sigma^2}{2}\frac{u''(x)}{u'(x)} = \frac{\sigma^2}{2}R_A(x).$$

This approximation is useful as, in the expression for the risk premium, it serves to distinguish an objective part which depends solely on the variance of the distribution from a subjective part that is linked to the decision maker's preferences, $R_A(x)$. This result can be used to derive the following theorem that compares the behavior of two EU decision makers.

Theorem 8.5. Let 1 and 2 be two EU decision makers, with utility functions u_1 and u_2 respectively, that are assumed to be strictly increasing and twice continuously differentiable. The following assertions are equivalent [ARR 65, PRA 64]:

1) 1 is more risk averse than 2: $\rho_X^1 \geq \rho_X^2$.

2) There exists an increasing and concave function φ from $\mathbb{R}$ to $\mathbb{R}$ such that $u_1 = \varphi(u_2)$.

3) The coefficient of absolute risk aversion for u_1 is greater than or equal to the coefficient of absolute risk aversion for u_2 for all $x \in \mathbb{R}$: $R_A^1(x) \geq R_A^2(x)$.

Remark 8.8. The notions of risk premium and coefficient of absolute risk aversion can also be defined for decision makers that are not necessarily risk averse. The theorem can be applied to compare such decision makers.

Remark 8.9. The equivalence between (1) and (2) remains true even when u_1 and u_2 are not twice continuously differentiable.

8.3.5.3. *Variance and EU model*

We saw in remark 8.7 that the notion of an increase in risk in the sense of second-order stochastic dominance was justified in the EU model. The variance is not a good indicator of riskiness as the following example shows [ING 87].

Example 8.2. Consider two lotteries $P = (0, 1/2; 4, 1/2)$ and $Q = (1, 7/8; 9, 1/8)$. We have $E(P) = E(Q)$ and $Var(Q) > Var(P)$. Take a decision maker that satisfies the axioms of the EU model, who exhibits weak aversion with a concave utility function given by $u(x) = \sqrt{x}$. One can check that for this decision maker $Q \succ P$, i.e. the expected utility of the lottery P, which has the smallest variance, is lower than the expected utility of Q. In the EU model, a risk averse decision maker might therefore prefer a random variable with higher variance (holding means constant).

Note, however, that when $u(x)$ is a second-order polynomial (as in the capital asset pricing model, CAPM), a risk averse decision maker will always prefer the variable with the lowest variance of two random variables with the same mean. One can actually show that with such a utility function, the expected utility of a distribution depends only on its mean and variance.

The EU model is widely used in economics. It has useful properties that make it very tractable. In particular, in a dynamic setting, it is compatible with dynamic programming and backward induction. However, it has been criticized on a number of different grounds.

8.4. Problems raised by the EU model

We analyze here a few problems raised by the EU model [see MAC 87].

8.4.1. *Allais paradox*

As early as 1953, Allais [ALL 53] built a couple of alternatives for which a majority of subjects, confronted with these choices, selected in contradiction with the independence axiom. We present here the original Allais experiment. Subjects were confronted with a choice between the following lotteries (e.g. in Euros):
 – L_1: win 1M with certainty; or
 – L_2: win 1M with probability 0.89, 5M with probability 0.10 and nothing with probability 0.01,

and also with a choice between:
 – L'_1: win 1M with probability 0.11 and nothing with probability 0.89; or

– L'_2: win 5M with probability 0.10 and nothing with probability 0.90.

Most subjects chose L_1 over L_2 and L'_2 over L'_1. This choice violates the independence axiom (axiom 8.3). Indeed, let P be the lottery yielding 1M with probability 1 and Q the lottery yielding nothing with probability $1/11$ and 5M with probability $10/11$. One can check that:

$$L_1 = 0.11\,P + 0.89\,\delta_1$$
$$L_2 = 0.11\,Q + 0.89\,\delta_1$$
$$L'_1 = 0.11\,P + 0,89\,\delta_0$$
$$L'_2 = 0.11\,Q + 0,89\,\delta_0$$

where δ_0 is the lottery win of nothing with probability 1 and δ_1 is the lottery win of 1M with probability 1. The observed choices are therefore in contradiction with the independence axiom.

This experiment has been run many times on various subjects with similar results: about 66% of the choices are in contradiction with the independence axiom. These results have led researchers to acknowledge some descriptive deficiencies of the EU model. However, most remain convinced that the normative aspect of the model should be given more weight.

8.4.2. *Interpreting the utility function*

On top of experimental violations of the independence axiom, the expected utility model raises a theoretical issue concerning the interpretation of the utility function u. This function captures two distinct behavioral features at the same time: (1) it captures the decision maker's risk attitude (concavity of u implies that the decision maker is risk averse) and (2) it captures the decision maker's attitude towards certain outcomes (concavity of u implies a decreasing marginal utility of wealth, say). It is therefore impossible to represent in this model a decision maker that would be risk seeking and would have a decreasing marginal utility.

Since the EU model is so parsimonious, it cannot separate risk attitudes from attitudes towards wealth under certainty. This distinction is possible in more flexible but less parsimonious models, which will be presented in Chapter 10.

8.4.3. *Weak and strong risk aversion under expected utility*

As stated in remark 8.7, weak and strong risk aversions cannot be distinguished in the expected utility model. We can indeed interpret proposition 8.3 as a limit of the expected utility model: any agent who is weakly risk averse but not strongly risk averse cannot satisfy the model's axioms. We can show [CHA 97, CHA 04] that several notions of risk aversion, corresponding to different stochastic orders on random variables, are confounded in the expected utility model. It is therefore not surprising that this model lacks flexibility to account for a wide range of different behavior in the face of increases in risk in different problems. The more general rank-dependent expected utility model that will be presented in Chapter 10 does not face this problem.

8.4.4. *Notion of SSD as a risk indicator in the EU model*

Despite the fact that second-order stochastic dominance is well-characterized in the EU model, this notion can lead to some counter-intuitive results. We will focus on two of them.

First, in the classical portfolio choice problem when the decision maker has the choice between any mixture of a risky asset and a riskless asset, a natural prediction would be that if the risky asset becomes riskier in the sense of MPS, then any risk averse investor should reduce his position in this asset. Rothschild and Stiglitz [ROT 71] have shown that this is not always the case in the expected utility model.

The second issue deals with insurance choices. A decision maker that is more risk averse than another is not necessarily ready to pay at least as much as the other to get the same risk reduction (in the sense of MPS) [e.g. ROS 81].

8.5. Some alternative models

There exist several decision models under risk that, to fit the observed behavior better, weaken one or several of the von Neumann–Morgenstern axioms. We briefly expose a few of them. A review of these models and the experimental evidence can be found in Harless and Camerer [HAR 94].

8.5.1. *Machina's model*

In the model in Machina [MAC 82], the independence axiom is dropped while weak order and continuity are retained. Still, the function used to represent preferences is smooth (i.e. Fréchet differentiable). As a consequence, this model is locally very similar to the EU model since the function can be approximated by a linear function.

8.5.2. *Models with security and potential levels*

Several experiments have shown that violations of the EU model disappear when the compared distributions have the same maximum and minimum. Cohen [COH 92], Essid [ESS 97], Gilboa [GIL 88] and Jaffray [JAF 88] axiomatized a model in which the independence axiom is satisfied only for distributions with the same minimum [GIL 88, JAF 88] or same minimum and maximum [COH 92, ESS 97]. This is a rather weak condition. One therefore needs to add some other axioms in addition to weak order and continuity. The representation takes the form of the combination of three criteria: the minimum, maximum and expected utility. This model is compatible with many experiments that have shown that the iso-utility curves are parallel (as in the EU model) when the distributions have the same extremal points, while they move away from parallel lines when extrema are different.

Other models exist in the literature [e.g. HAR 94]. Probably the most well-known model compatible with Allais' experiment is the rank-dependent expected utility model [QUI 82], based on the Choquet integral which will be presented in some detail in Chapter 10.

8.6. Acknowledgements

Thank you to two referees for their useful suggestions, which improved the exposition of the chapter.

8.7. Bibliography

[ALL 53] Allais M. "Le comportement de l'homme rationnel devant le risque: critique des postulats et axiomes de l'école américaine". *Econometrica*, vol. 21, 503–546, 1953.

[ARR 65] Arrow K.J. *The Theory of Risk Aversion, in Aspects of the Theory of Risk Bearing.* Helsinki: Ynjo Jahnsonin Saatio, 1965.

[CHA 97] Chateauneuf A., Cohen M.D. and Meilijson I. "New tools to better model behavior under risk and uncertainty: An overview". *Finance*, vol. 18, 25–46, 1997.

[CHA 04] Chateauneuf A., Cohen M.D. and Meilijson I. "Four notions of mean-preserving increase in risk, risk attitudes and applications to the rank-dependent expected utility model". *Journal of Mathematical Economics*, vol. 40(6), 547–571, 2004.

[COH 92] Cohen M.D. "Security level, potential level, expected utility: a three-criteria decision model under risk". *Theory and Decision*, vol. 33(2), 1–34, 1992.

[DEB 54] Debreu G. "Representation of a preference ordering by a numerical function". In *Decision Processes*, Thrall, Coombs and Davies (eds), Wiley, New York, 159–165, 1954.

[ESS 97] Essid S. "Choice under risk with certainty and potential effects: A general axiomatic model". *Mathematical Social Sciences*, vol. 34(3), 223–247, 1997.

[FIS 70] Fishburn P. *Utility Theory for Decision Making*. Wiley, New York, 1970.

[FIS 82] Fishburn P. *The Foundations of Expected Utility*. Reidel, Dordrecht, 1982.

[GIL 88] Gilboa I. "A Combination of Expected Utility and Maxmin Decision Criteria". *Journal of Mathematical Psychology*, vol. 32, 405–420, 1988.

[GRA 72] Grandmont J.M. "Continuity Properties of von Neumann-Morgenstern Utility". *Journal of Economic Theory*, vol. 4(1), 45–57, 1972.

[HAR 94] Harless D.W. and Camerer C.F. "The predictive utility of generalized expected utility theories". *Econometrica*, vol. 62(6), 1251–1289, 1994.

[HER 53] Herstein I. and Milnor J. "An axiomatic approach to measurable utility". *Econometrica*, vol. 21, 291–297, 1953.

[ING 87] Ingersoll J. *Theory of Financial Decision Making*. Rowman and Littlefield, Totowa, NJ., 1987.

[JAF 78] Jaffray J.Y. Duplicate from the University of Paris VI, 1978.

[JAF 88] Jaffray J.Y. "Choice under risk and the security factor. An axiomatic model". *Theory and Decision*, vol. 24(2), 169–200, 1988.

[JEN 67] Jensen, N "An introduction to Bernoullian utility theory: (1) Utility functions". *Swedish Journal of Economics*, vol. 69, 163–183, 1967.

[KNI 21] Knight F. *Risk, Uncertainty and Profit*. Houghton Miffin, Boston, 1921.

[KRE 88] Kreps D. *Notes on the Theory of Choice*. Underground classics in economics, Westview Press, 1988.

[MAC 82] Machina M. "Expected utility analysis without the independence axiom". *Econometrica*, vol. 50, 277–323, 1982.

[MAC 87] Machina M. "Choice under uncertainty: Problems solved and unsolved". *Journal of Economic Perspectives*, vol. 1, 121–154, 1987.

[PRA 64] Pratt J. "Risk aversion in the small and in the large". *Econometrica*, vol. 32, 122–136, 1964.

[QUI 82] Quiggin J. "A theory of anticipated utility". *Journal of Economic Behavior and Organisation*, vol. 3, 323–343, 1982.

[ROS 81] Ross S. "Some stronger measures of risk aversion in the small and in the large with applications". *Econometrica*, vol. 49, 621–638, 1981.

[ROT 70] Rothschild M. and Stiglitz J. "Increasing Risk: I. A definition". *Journal of Economic Theory*, vol. 2, 225–243, 1970.

[ROT 71] Rothschild M. and Stiglitz J. "Increasing Risk: II. Its economic consequences". *Journal of Economic Theory*, vol. 3, 66–84, 1971.

[VON 47] Von Neumann J. and Morgenstern O. *Theory of Games and Economic Behavior*. Princeton University Press, Princeton, N.J., 1947.

Chapter 9

Decision under Uncertainty: The Classical Models

9.1. Introduction

This chapter is dedicated to classical decision models under uncertainty. Following Knight [KNI 21], the term *risk* is reserved to situations in which events have 'objective' probabilities with which the decision maker agrees. This is typically the case in games of chance such as card games and roulette; risk also encompasses all situations in which reliable statistical data are available. In addition to situations of risk, there seems to be a great variety of other situations of uncertainty that the decision maker can encounter: upper/lower probability intervals, possibilities/necessities, complete ignorance and small samples. Rather surprisingly, the classical models of decision making under uncertainty enforce the universal use of a probabilistic representation: every situation of uncertainty is identifiable to a situation of *subjective* risk. This means that every decision maker behaves as if they had probabilistic beliefs on all the events; on the other hand, these beliefs can vary from one decision maker to another.

The justification of this representation is based on axioms of 'rational behavior'. The most famous model giving an axiomatic justification of the subjective expected utility (SEU) criterion is due to Savage [SAV 54]: uncertainty reduces to subjective risk and decisions are ranked according to the expected utilities (EU) of their consequences. Anscombe and Aumann [ANS 63] also justify the SEU criterion, with a different model and in a different framework.

Chapter written by Alain CHATEAUNEUF, Michèle COHEN and Jean-Yves JAFFRAY.

9.2. Subjective expected utility (SEU)

9.2.1. *Definitions and notation*

S is the set of *states of nature*, $\mathcal{E} \subset 2^S$ is a set of parts of S, $A \in \mathcal{E}$ is an *event* and $\mathcal{C}$ is the set of *consequences*.

Decisions are identified to *acts*, which are applications from S into $\mathcal{C}$. Axiom P8 will add a 'measurability' requirement. An act f is a *simple step act* (respectively, *step act*) when there exists a finite (respectively, denumerable) partition $\{E_i, i \in I\}$ of S, with $E_i \in \mathcal{E}$ for every $i \in I$ such that $f(E_i) = \{c_i\}$ i.e. a singleton. In particular, a *constant* act δ_c is characterized by $\delta_c(S) = \{c\}$.

A *grafting* is an operation which associates with two acts f, g and an event E, a third act, their graft h defined by $h(s) = f(s)$ for $s \in E$, $h(s) = g(s)$ for $s \in E^c$; such an act is denoted by $h = fEg$.

Preferences are represented by binary relation $\succsim$ on the set of acts $\mathbb{V}$.

9.2.2. *The SEU criterion*

Preferences $\succsim$ comply with SEU theory when they can be explained by the expected utility criterion, i.e. when there exist a (subjective) probability measure P on the events and a utility function u on the consequences such that, for all acts f, g:

$$f \succsim g \iff \int_S u(f(.))dP \geq \int_S u(g(.))dP.$$

Savage [SAV 54] (and later Anscombe and Aumann [ANS 63]) proposed axiomatic justifications of this criterion. Anscombe and Aumann [ANS 63] require a special structure for the consequence set, which is the set of all lotteries (finite support distributions) on the outcome set. Moreover, they assume the validity of the EU criterion for comparing these lotteries. Savage's framework is more general and may seem more natural since it does not require any particular structure of the consequence set. On the other hand, his approach is rather complex. Anscombe and Aumann have a simpler task, since they can take advantage of the properties of linear utility on the lotteries. We begin with the presentation of Savage's theory.

9.3. Savage's theory [SAV 54]

9.3.1. *Savage's axioms and their interpretation and implications*

Note that the axiom system presented here is somewhat different from that of Savage. The theory presented here leads to a representation of the beliefs on the events by a σ-additive probability measure (as opposed to a simply additive probability in Savage's).

9.3.1.1. *Preferences on the acts*

The first axiom postulates the existence of a rich structure on both the set of the events and the set of the acts and requires that the preference relation be a weak order (reflexivity, transitivity and completeness).

Axiom 9.1. **P1**: *weak ordering of the acts*

1) The set of the events $\mathcal{E}$ is a σ-algebra.

2) The set of the acts $\mathbb{V}$ contains all step acts and is closed with respect to the grafting operation.

3) $\succsim$ is a weak order on $\mathbb{V}$.

Conditions (1) and (2) are technical; the structures imposed on $\mathcal{E}$ and $\mathbb{V}$ could not be dispensed with, even though they imply the existence of unrealistic acts (e.g. acts giving good consequences conditionally on unfavorable events). Condition (3) is standard in decision theory. Note, however, that standard rationality arguments such as the avoidance of money pumps forbid preference cycles but cannot justify completeness.

The next axiom is the key axiom of Savage's theory. It states that a common modification of the common part of two acts cannot modify the preference order between them.

Axiom 9.2. **P2**: *sure-thing principle*
For all acts f, g, h, h' and for every event E,

$$fEh \succsim gEh \iff fEh' \succsim gEh'.$$

Remark 9.1. Here again money pump arguments can only justify the following weakened version of axiom 9.2, referred to below as **P′2**:

$$fEh \succ gEh \implies fEh' \succsim gEh'.$$

This is an important remark because *backward induction* is an efficient method for solving dynamic decision problems. However, its validity does not rely on **P2** but only on **P′2**; this opens the gate to alternative theories which, despite the fact they use different representations of uncertainty, remain operational.

Let us finally note that actual behavior often violates the sure-thing principle **P2** and also **P′2**; see the Ellsberg paradox [ELL 61] below (section 9.3.3). The Allais paradox [ALL 53] can be presented as a violation of these axioms.

9.3.1.1.1. Induced preferences

The axiom system will make it possible to derive several other binary relations from a single primitive preference relation $\succsim$ on the acts. These will be interpreted as conditional preferences, preferences under certainty or preferences on the events.

9.3.1.1.2. Conditional preferences given events

For any event $E \in \mathcal{E}$, **P2** allows us to define on the set of acts $\mathbb{V}$ a binary relation, *preference given E*, by:

$$f \succsim_E g \iff \text{for every } h, fEh \succsim gEh.$$

Relation $\succsim_E$ can be *trivial*, i.e. such that $f \succsim_E g$ for all $f, g \in \mathbb{V}$, in which case event E is called a *null* event; in particular, $\varnothing$ is a null event.

Let us note that $\succsim_E$ only depends on the restrictions of f and g to E. This relation is generally interpreted when E is not null as the expression of the decision maker's preferences conditionally to E. Note, however, this is only an interpretation [GHI 02].

It is clear that for every event $E \in \mathcal{E}$, $\succsim_E$ (preference given E) is a weak order.

9.3.1.1.3. Preferences under certainty

Preferences on acts $\succsim$ also induce *preferences under certainty*, $\succsim_\mathcal{C}$, by

$$c' \succsim_\mathcal{C} c'' \iff \delta_{c'} \succsim \delta_{c''} \text{ for all } c', c'' \in \mathcal{C}.$$

Relation $\succsim_\mathcal{C}$ is also a weak order.

The introduction of $\succsim_\mathcal{C}$ is not interesting unless there exists *intrinsic* preferences under certainty, i.e. which do not depend on the information in the following axiom.

Axiom 9.3. P3: *existence of intrinsic preferences under certainty*
For all consequences $c', c'' \in \mathcal{C}$, for every non-null event $E \in \mathcal{E}$,

$$c' \succsim_\mathcal{C} c'' \iff \delta_{c'} \succsim_E \delta_{c''}.$$

This axiom is more restrictive than it seems. For example, it does not leave the possibility of expressing the influence on the ordering of consequences of an emotional trauma. Certain theories allow *state-dependent* preferences and do not require this axiom [KAR 93].

9.3.1.1.4. Preferences on the events

We next define a preference relation on the events. For this, we shall use a particular class of step acts: the one-step acts.

Given $c', c'' \in \mathcal{C}$ such that $c' \succ_C c''$, act f_A offers prize (c'/c'') on A when

$$f_A(s) = c' \text{ if } s \in A, \quad f_A(s) = c'' \text{ if } s \in A^c.$$

A preference relation $\succsim_\mathcal{E}$ on the set of events $\mathcal{E}$ can then be defined as follows.

Definition 9.1. For all $A, B \in \mathcal{E}$, $A \succsim_\mathcal{E} B \iff$ there exists a prize (c'/c'') such that acts f_A, f_B offering that prize on A and B, respectively, satisfy $f_A \succsim f_B$.

Axiom 9.4 states that the value of the prize does not matter at all, which will make relation $\succsim_\mathcal{E}$ a weak order. Its interpretation is: if, for a given prize, we prefer f_A to f_B, it is because we believe A to be more likely to obtain than B.

Axiom 9.4. **P4**: *non-influence of the prize*
For all consequences $c', c'', k', k'' \in \mathcal{C}$ such that $c' \succ_C c''$ and $k' \succ_C k''$, for every act f_A (respectively, f_B) offering prize (c'/c'') on event A (respectively, $B) \in \mathcal{E}$ and every act g_A (respectively, g_B) offering prize (k'/k'') on event A (respectively, B):

$$f_A \succsim f_B \iff g_A \succsim g_B.$$

To prevent $\succsim_\mathcal{E}$ being trivial, there must exist at least one feasible prize.

Axiom 9.5. **P5**: *non-triviality of preferences under certainty*
There exists consequences $c', c'' \in \mathcal{C}$ such that $c' \succ_C c''$. Note that E is null if and only if $E \sim_\mathcal{E} \emptyset$.

Together, the preceding assumptions (axioms P1–P5) are sufficient to endow relation $\succsim_\mathcal{E}$ with properties **Q1** and **Q2** of a *qualitative probability* (see section 9.3.2.1 below). We shall need the following definition.

Definition 9.2. An event $A \succ_\mathcal{E} \emptyset$ is an *atom* (for $\succsim_\mathcal{E}$) when there is no event $B \subset A$ such that: $A \succ_\mathcal{E} B \succ_\mathcal{E} \emptyset$.

Axiom 9.6 implies that set S is *atomless* for $\succsim_\mathcal{E}$, a property which will prove to be crucial for the existence of a unique subjective probability. This axiom also implies continuity properties, related to those of the continuity axiom of linear utility theory.

Axiom 9.6. P6: *continuity*
For every pair of acts $f, g \in \mathbb{V}$ such that $f \succ g$, for every consequence $c \in \mathcal{C}$, there exists a finite partition $\{E_i, i \in I\}$ of S such that, for all $i \in I$:
   1) $f_i \succ g$ where $f_i(s) = f(s)$ for $s \notin E_i$ and $f_i(s) = c$ for $s \in E_i$;
   2) $f \succ g_i$ where $g_i(s) = g(s)$ for $s \notin E_i$ and $g_i(s) = c$ for $s \in E_i$.

Axiom 9.6 can be interpreted as follows. If the modification of f on E_i cannot reverse preferences, then each E_i must be judged sufficiently unlikely. One therefore assumes:

1) the existence of partitions composed of arbitrarily unlikely events, which will imply the absence of atoms;

2) that every f_i which is sufficiently close to f (for the distance of weak convergence) must be ranked in the same way as f with respect to g, which is a continuity property.

The last axiom in the original Savage system is a dominance (or monotony) axiom, as follows.

Axiom 9.7. P7: *dominance*
For every event $E \in \mathcal{E}$:
   1) $f \succ_E \delta_c$ for every $c \in g(E)$ implies $f \succ_E g$;
   2) $f \prec_E \delta_c$ for all $c \in g(E)$ implies $f \prec_E g$.

Axiom 9.7 states that if we prefer f to any consequence which can result from g, then we should prefer f to g. Axioms 9.8 and 9.9 are not part of the original system of Savage; they will ensure that the subjective probability constructed is always σ-additive.

Axiom 9.8. P8: *measurability*
For every act $f \in \mathbb{V}$ and for every consequence $c \in \mathcal{C}$, sets $\{s \in S : f(s) \succsim_\mathcal{C} c\}$ and $\{s \in S : f(s) \precsim_\mathcal{C} c\}$ belong to $\mathcal{E}$.

Axiom 9.9. P9: *event-wise continuity*
For all events $A, B \in \mathcal{E}$ and for every sequence of events $(A_n)_{n \in \mathcal{N}}$, if $A_n \downarrow A$, $A_n \succsim_\mathcal{E} B$ for every n then $A \succsim_\mathcal{E} B$.

9.3.2. *Construction of Savage's theory*

This section is based on Jaffray's notes [JAF 78]. Savage proves that:

1) There exist, on the event set, qualitative probabilities and subjective (quantitative) probabilities which are compatible with them. Every act generates then a (subjective) probability measure on the consequence set.

2) Preferences on the acts generate preferences on these probability measures, and these preferences satisfy the von Neumann–Morgenstern [VON 47] axioms for decision making under risk.

9.3.2.1. *From qualitative to subjective probabilities*

9.3.2.1.1. Existence of qualitative probabilities

By definition, relation $\succsim_\mathcal{E}$ is a *qualitative probability* on $\mathcal{E}$ when it satisfies the following three properties:

1) **Q1**: $\succsim_\mathcal{E}$ is a weak order $S \succ_\mathcal{E} \emptyset$ and, for all $A \in \mathcal{E}$, $S \succsim_\mathcal{E} A \succsim_\mathcal{E} \emptyset$.
2) **Q2**: For all $A_1, A_2, B_1, B_2, \in \mathcal{E}$,
   a) $[A_1 \cap A_2 = \emptyset, A_1 \succsim_\mathcal{E} B_1, A_2 \succsim_\mathcal{E} B_2] \Longrightarrow A_1 \cup A_2 \succsim_\mathcal{E} B_1 \cup B_2$;
   b) $[A_1 \cap A_2 = \emptyset, A_1 \succ_\mathcal{E} B_1, A_2 \succsim_\mathcal{E} B_2] \Longrightarrow A_1 \cup A_2 \succ_\mathcal{E} B_1 \cup B_2$.
3) **Q3**: For all $A, B \in \mathcal{E}$ and $(A_n)_{n \in \mathcal{N}}$, $[A_n \downarrow A, A_n \succsim_\mathcal{E} B$ for all $n] \Longrightarrow A \succsim_\mathcal{E} B$.

The validity of properties **Q1** and **Q2** is a direct consequence of axioms 9.1–9.5 (**P1** – **P5**). To establish the validity of **Q2**, the following intermediate property is useful:

$$A_1 \succsim_\mathcal{E} B_1 \Longleftrightarrow A_1 \cup E \succsim_\mathcal{E} B_1 \cup E \text{ for every } E \text{ such that } E \cap [A_1 \cup B_1] = \emptyset$$

which is a straightforward consequence of axiom 9.2. Finally, property **Q3** is simply axiom 9.9 (**P9**). Therefore relation $\succsim_\mathcal{E}$ is a qualitative probability of $\mathcal{E}$.

Remark 9.2. Conditions **Q1** and **Q2** are due to De Finetti [DEF 37]. Villegas [VIL 64] added axiom **Q3** in order to obtain a σ-additive version of subjective probability theory.

9.3.2.1.2. Existence of a compatible subjective probability

A probability P on $\mathcal{E}$ is *compatible* with $\succsim_\mathcal{E}$ if $P(A) \geq P(B) \Longleftrightarrow A \succsim_\mathcal{E} B$.

It can easily be seen that conditions **Q1** and **Q2** are necessary for the existence of a probability P on $\mathcal{E}$ which is compatible with $\succsim_\mathcal{E}$. A counter-example due to Kraft *et al.* [KRA 59] shows that these conditions are not sufficient to insure the existence of a compatible probability. However, by adding the assumption that set $\mathcal{E}$ is atomless, Villegas [VIL 64] obtained the following result.

Theorem 9.1. *When $\mathcal{E}$ is atomless, **Q1**, **Q2** and **Q3** are sufficient conditions for the existence of a unique subjective probability P on $(S, \mathcal{E})$ compatible with qualitative probability $\succsim_{\mathcal{E}}$. Moreover:*

1) $E \in \mathcal{E}$ is null if and only if $P(E) = 0$; and

2) for every $E \in \mathcal{E}$ and every $\rho \in (0, 1)$, there exists $A \subset E$ such that $P(A) = \rho P(E)$.

Sketch of proof. Every event A can be divided into two sub-events A_1 and A_2 satisfying $A_1 \sim_{\mathcal{E}} A_2$; this implies, by an inductive argument, that there exists a 2^n-partition $\{E_i\}$ of the sure event S with $E_i \sim_{\mathcal{E}} E_j$ for all i, j. Necessarily, a compatible probability P is such that $P(E_i) = 1/2^n$ for all i. Moreover, probability $P(A)$ of an event A of $\mathcal{E}$ such that

$$\bigcup_{1 \leq i \leq k+1} E_i \succ_{\mathcal{E}} A \succsim_{\mathcal{E}} \bigcup_{1 \leq i \leq k} E_i,$$

shall satisfy

$$P(A) \in \left[\frac{k}{2^n}, \frac{k+1}{2^n} \right[.$$

By taking the limit $(n \mapsto \infty)$, $P(A)$ will be uniquely determined. Finally, one proves the additivity and the σ-additivity of P.

The preceding result can be interpreted roughly as follows: $\mathcal{E}$ contains all events linked to the outcomes of an arbitrary sequence of coin throws, where the coin used is believed to be unbiased by the decision maker. To evaluate the probability of any given event, they only need to compare it with events linked to the throwing sequence, to which probabilities of the form $k/2^n$ are already attributed.

The absence of atoms in Savage's axiom system is essentially due to axiom 9.6 (**P6**): for every non-null event A, one can find a partition $\{E_i\}$ such that $A \succ_{\mathcal{E}} E_i \succ_{\mathcal{E}} \emptyset$ for every i and, in particular, E_{i_0} such that $B = E_{i_0} \cap A$ satisfies $A \succ_{\mathcal{E}} B \succ_{\mathcal{E}} \emptyset$.

Together, Savage's axioms imply both the absence of atoms and the validity of conditions **Q1**, **Q2** and **Q3**. They therefore imply the existence of a unique subjective probability on the events. We are therefore now facing a problem of decision making under risk (subjective risk). However, as we shall see, the decision maker's behavior will not differ from their behavior under objective risk.

9.3.2.2. *Subjective lotteries and linear utility*

Now that a (unique) subjective probability P has been constructed on the events, we can associate with every act f the probability measure P_f which it generates on consequence set $\mathcal{C}$ (P_f is the image of P by f). We denote the set of these probability measures by $\mathcal{L}_0$. In particular, a simple step act generates a (subjective) *lottery* on $\mathcal{C}$, i.e. a probability measure with finite support. If the only feasible consequences of f are the set $\{x_i, i = 1, \ldots, n\}$, this set is the support of P_f and $P_f(x_i) = P(f^{-1}(x_i))$, $i = 1, \ldots, n$.

We then need to show that two acts generating the same lottery are necessarily indifferent for relation $\succsim$. This is a crucial step in the construction of Savage, and also one of the most delicate ones. It basically exploits two properties: (i) the sure-thing principle (**P2**); and (ii) the existence, for every event A and every $\rho \in [0, 1]$, of an event $B \subset A$ such that $P(B) = \rho P(A)$.

It results from **P1** that $\mathcal{L}_0$ is the set of all lotteries on $\mathcal{C}$. There then exists a preference relation on lottery set $\mathcal{L}_0$, induced by the preferences existing on the acts, which we also denote by $\succsim$ i.e.

$$P \succsim Q \iff \text{there exist simple step acts } f \text{ and } g \text{ such that}$$

$$P_f = P, P_g = Q \text{ and } f \succsim g.$$

Relation $\succsim$ on $\mathcal{L}_0$ is clearly a weak order, thus satisfying axiom 9.1 of linear utility theory. The next step consists of proving that it moreover satisfies axioms 9.2 (independence) and 9.3 (continuity).

The proof of these results confirms that axiom 9.6 is indeed a continuity axiom (and not only a non-atomicity axiom); it also stresses the narrow links between **P2** and Anscombe-Aumann's axiom **AA2** (see section 9.4.1). Indeed, the Allais paradox [ALL 53] constitutes a violation of both.

The theorem of von Neumann–Morgenstern therefore applies to $\mathcal{L}_0$: there exists on $\mathcal{L}_0$ a linear utility function U and an associated von Neumann–Morgenstern utility u. Returning to acts, we can therefore state:

– The restriction to simple step acts of preference relation $\succsim$ can be explained by an expected utility criterion with respect to subjective probability measure P on the events and utility function u on the consequences. For two such acts f and g:

$$f \succsim g \iff Eu(P_f) \geqslant Eu(P_g) \iff \sum_{i=1}^{n} P_f(\{x_i\})u(x_i) \geqslant \sum_{j=1}^{n'} P_g(\{y_j\})u(y_j).$$

The extension of the validity of the expected utility criterion from simple step acts to general acts remains to be demonstrated.

9.3.2.3. *Extension of SEU to all acts*

Savage's axiom 9.7 (**P7**) which concerns acts implies the validity of dominance axiom Anscombe-Aumann's dominance axiom **AA4** for the probability measures these acts generate on $\mathcal{C}$. It therefore follows that utility function u is bounded.

Moreover, by using axiom 9.8 (**P8**), one can show that u is also measurable so that the integral

$$\int_S u(f(.))dP = \int_C u(.)dP_f$$

exists and has a finite value. Its value can then be associated with act f. It still remains to show that the expected utility criterion is valid for preferences on the whole set of acts. First the extension from simple step acts (for which this criterion is valid) to generalized step acts is made by a similar reasoning to that used in EU theory. The extension to general acts follows; it uses the fact that every act is indifferent to a generalized step act.

Theorem 9.2. *Under axioms* **P1** − **P9**, *preference relation* $\succsim$ *on* $\mathbb{V}$ *is representable by a utility function* $U(.)$ *of the form:*

$$U(.): f \mapsto \int_S u(f(.))dP = \int_C u(.)dP_f$$

where $P(.)$ is a σ-additive probability on the events of E and $u(.)$ is the von Neumann–Morgenstern utility on the probability set formed by the images of P generated by the acts. Moreover, P is unique, whereas $U(.)$ and $u(.)$ are unique up to a strictly increasing affine transformation.

The empirical validity of theorem 9.2 (Savage's model) has serious limitations. The Allais paradox not only exhibits a pattern of behavior which is incompatible with EU under risk, but a pattern which is also incompatible with SEU under uncertainty.

There are other experiments, specific to uncertainty situations, where subjects display behavioral patterns which are incompatible with the existence of subjective probabilities (and *a fortiori* with SEU), such as the famous Ellsberg paradox.

9.3.3. *The Ellsberg paradox*

Ellsberg [ELL 61] describes the following situation. An urn contains 90 balls: 30 are red and 60 are blue or yellow in unknown proportions. There are therefore k blue balls and $(60 - k)$ yellow balls, with k of value $0 - 60$. A random drawing of a ball from the urn will lead to the realization of one of the events R, B and Y, according to the color of the ball drawn. Ellsberg asks the subjects to choose between the following options: a bet on R (decision X_1) or a bet on B (decision X_2) and a bet on $R \cup Y$ (decision X_3) or a bet on $B \cup Y$ (decision X_4).

Table 9.1 gives the payments (in €) associated with each decision for each possible event.

	R	B	Y
X_1	100	0	0
X_2	0	100	0
X_3	100	0	100
X_4	0	100	100

Table 9.1. *Ellsberg's acts: Savage's framework*

Typically, a majority of subjects choose X_1 and X_4, thus revealing preferences: $X_1 \succ X_2$ and $X_4 \succ X_3$. This constitutes a violation of the sure-thing principle **P2**. A modification of event y of the common consequence €0 of X_1 and X_2, consisting of replacing it by a different common consequence €100 which transforms X_1 into X_3 and X_2 into X_4, should leave preferences unchanged, i.e. lead to $X_3 \succ X_4$ whenever $X_1 \succ X_2$.

Since they do not respect **P2**, these subjects cannot abide by the SEU criterion. As a matter of fact, their behavior is incompatible with the very existence of subjective probabilities p_R, p_B, p_Y for elementary events R, B, Y. $X_1 \succ X_2$ would imply $p_R > p_B$ whereas $X_4 \succ X_3$ would imply $p_B + p_Y > p_R + p_Y$: a contradiction.

To represent the situation described by Ellsberg, we have taken $S' = \{R, B, Y\}$ as a set of states of nature and identified the bets with applications (acts) $X : S' \to \mathbb{R}$.

We might have adopted another approach and taken a set of states of nature composed of 61 states, $S = \{s_0, s_1, \ldots, s_k, \ldots, s_{60}\}$, where a state s_k corresponds to the composition of the urn '30 red balls, k blue balls and $(60 - k)$ yellow balls'. The decisions are then identifiable with applications from S into $\mathcal{Y}$, the set of lotteries on $\mathcal{C} = \{0, 100\}$ (i.e. the set of all probability measures on $\mathcal{C}$ which have a finite support).

The uncertain prospect offered by the decision giving a gain of €100 if the ball drawn is blue and of €0 otherwise (X_2) is therefore characterized by application g_2, associating with every state of nature s_k of S the corresponding lottery

$$(0, \frac{90-k}{90}\ 100, \frac{k}{90}).$$

This is equivalent to the lottery giving a null gain with probability $(90-k)/90$ and a gain of €100 with probability $k/90$.

9.4. Anscombe and Aumann theory [ANS 63]

The set of states of nature S is *finite*. The algebra of events is $\mathcal{A} = 2^S$. We denote by $\mathcal{Y}$ the set of lotteries on an outcome set $\mathcal{C}$ (i.e. the set of all probability measures with finite support in $\mathcal{C}$). The set of acts $\mathbb{F}_0$ is then defined as the set of all applications from S into $\mathcal{Y}$.

An act of this kind is called a 'horse lottery' by reference to the sweepstake tickets, which offer different random gains (lottery tickets) depending on which horse wins the race.

In this model, consequences are not outcomes (elements of $\mathcal{C}$) but lotteries on $\mathcal{C}$, which are elements of $\mathcal{Y}$. The set $\mathcal{Y}$ is a mixture set (see section 8.3.1). By using this structure we can define, for all f and h in $\mathbb{F}_0$ and every α in $[0, 1]$, act $\alpha f + (1 - \alpha)h$ by

$$(\alpha f + (1 - \alpha)h)(s) = \alpha f(s) + (1 - \alpha)h(s)$$

for every s in S. For this operation, $\mathbb{F}_0$ is itself a mixture set.

Preferences are defined by a weak order on set of acts $\mathbb{F}_0$, denoted by $\succsim$. Relation $\succsim$ induces a preference relation (also denoted by $\succsim$) on the set of lotteries, by identifying a lottery y of $\mathcal{Y}$ with the *constant act* δ_y in $\mathbb{F}_0$ (the act taking the same value, consequence y, for every s in S):

$$\text{for all } y, z \text{ in } \mathcal{Y}, y \succsim z \Leftrightarrow \delta_y \succsim \delta_z.$$

9.4.1. *The Anscombe–Aumann axiom system*

The Anscombe–Aumann axiom system consists of the following five axioms.

Axiom 9.10. AA1: *ordering*
Preference relation $\succsim$ is a weak order on $\mathbb{F}_0$.

Axiom 9.11. AA2: *continuity*
For all X, Y, Z in X_0 satisfying $X \succ Y \succ Z$, there exist $\alpha, \beta \in]0, 1[$ such that:

$$\alpha X + (1 - \alpha)Z \succ Y \succ \beta X + (1 - \beta)Z.$$

Axiom 9.12. AA3: *independence*
For all X, Y, Z in $\mathbb{F}_0$ and for every $\alpha \in]0, 1]$,

$$X \succsim Y \iff \alpha X + (1 - \alpha)Z \succsim \alpha Y + (1 - \alpha)Z.$$

Axiom 9.13. AA4: *monotony*
For all X, Y in $\mathbb{F}_0$,

$$[X(s) \succsim Y(s) \text{ for every } s \in S] \Rightarrow X \succsim Y.$$

Axiom 9.14. AA5: *non-triviality of preferences*
There exists at least one pair of acts X, Y such that

$$X \succ Y.$$

9.4.2. Comments and discussion

The introduction of a set of lotteries $\mathcal{Y}$ among the primitive concepts presupposes the existence of 'exogeneous' probabilities, i.e. which have no relation to the beliefs of the decision maker. This was not the case with the model of Savage, in which the existence of a probability is always a result and never an assumption.

In the model of Anscombe and Aumann [ANS 63], the outcome of an act is determined in two steps. During the first step, the uncertainty about the states of nature is resolved and the true state identified. During the second step, the lottery associated with this state is resolved and the final outcome determined. One of the important points of the proof of the representation theorem consists of showing that the order of resolution of the two kinds of uncertainty is irrelevant to the decision maker.

The mixture set structure of $\mathbb{F}_0$ suggests the formal use of the axioms of von Neumann and Morgenstern [VON 47]. However, since the acts of $\mathbb{F}_0$ are more complex than probability measures, these axioms acquire a wider significance. In particular, in this framework, the independence axiom (in the presence of the other axioms) implies the validity of Savage's sure-thing principle (axiom **P2**).

9.4.3. *The Anscombe-Aumann representation theorem*

Theorem 9.3. *Under axioms* **AA1** − **AA5**, *preference relation $\succsim$ on $\mathbb{F}_0$ is representable by a utility function:*

$$V(.) : X \mapsto \sum_{s \in S} U(X(s)) P(\{s\})$$

where $P(.)$ is an additive probability measure on $(S, \mathcal{E})$ and $U(.)$ is the linear utility function on $(\mathcal{L}, \succsim_\mathcal{L})$. P is unique and $V(.)$, as for $U(.)$, is unique up to a strictly increasing linear transformation.

In theorem 9.3, every type of uncertainty is reducible to subjective risk, and the criterion under risk (under objective risk (lotteries) as under subjective risk) is the EU criterion. The proof has several steps.

First, by restricting axioms **AA1–AA3** to the constant acts δ_y, identified with lotteries y, we note that the von Neumann–Morgenstern theory applies to these constant acts. It is then easily seen that the following representation is valid for general acts:

$$X \succsim Y \iff U(X) \geqslant U(Y) \text{ where } U(X) = \sum_{s \in S} U_s(X(s))$$

where each U_s is a linear utility, i.e. where $U_s(X(s))$ is the expectation of a utility function u_s with respect to lottery $X(s)$. The preceding linear utilities U_s depend on state s.

Secondly, by taking into account axioms **AA4–AA5**, one can show that the U_s are in fact proportional and that there therefore exists a unique probability measure P such that ratio $U_s/P(\{s\})$ is independent of s. It then suffices to set $U_s/P(\{s\}) = U$ to obtain $U(X) = \sum_{s \in S} U(X(s))P(\{s\})$.

Remark 9.3. In the Anscombe–Aumann framework, since S is finite, the question of the σ-additivity of probability P is pointless.

Remark 9.4. Fishburn [FIS 70] has extended the Anscombe–Aumann theory to an infinite set of states of nature. In his extension, subjective probability P is only finitely additive.

9.4.4. *Return to the Ellsberg paradox*

Let us now show that the Ellsberg paradox can be interpreted in the Anscombe–Aumann theory framework as a violation of the independence axiom 9.12 (**AA3**). Let us use the formalization $S = \{s_0, s_1, \ldots, s_k, \ldots, s_{60}\}$, where state s_k corresponds to urn content '30 red balls, k blue balls and $60 - k$ yellow balls'.

The uncertain prospect described by act X_i in Savage's framework is now characterized in the framework of Anscombe and Aumann [ANS 63]. This is carried out by mapping g_i, associating with each state of nature s_k in S, a lottery as indicated in Table 9.2. Rows 1–4 of the table indicate what becomes of acts X_1, X_2, X_3, X_4 in this new framework. Note that acts g_1, g_4, δ_0 are now constant acts.

Axiom 9.12 (**AA3**) and the equalities of mixtures of acts in rows 7 and 8 of Table 9.2 imply that:

$$g_1 \succ g_2 \iff \frac{1}{2}g_1 + \frac{1}{2}f \succ \frac{1}{2}g_2 + \frac{1}{2}f \iff \frac{1}{2}g_3 + \frac{1}{2}\delta_0 \succ \frac{1}{2}g_4 + \frac{1}{2}\delta_0 \iff g_3 \succ g_4.$$

Choices g_1 and g_4 in the experiment are therefore a violation of axiom 9.12 (**AA3**).

Act	Consequence on $s_k, k = 0, \ldots, 60$
$g_1(\approx X_1)$	$(0, 60/90;\ 100, 30/90)$
$g_2(\approx X_2)$	$(0, (90-k)/90\ \ 100, k/90)$
$g_3(\approx X_3)$	$(0, k/90\ \ 100, (90-k)/90)$
$g_4(\approx X_4)$	$(0, 30/90\ \ 100, 60/90)$
δ_0	$(0, 90/90)$
f	$(0, (30+k)/90;\ 100, (60-k)/90)$
$g_1/2 + f/2 = g_3/2 + \delta_0/2$	$(0, (90+k)/180;\ 100, (90-k)/180)$
$g_2/2 + f/2 = g_4/2 + \delta_0/2$	$(0, 120/180;\ 100, 60/180)$

Table 9.2. *Ellsberg acts: Anscombe–Aumann's framework*

9.5. Conclusion

The possibility of justifying the most crucial axioms of the theories of Savage [SAV 54] and Anscombe and Aumann [ANS 63] by rationality arguments, has secured the rank of dominant normative model to the SEU model. Moreover, its use being simple, SEU has become a major tool in economic theory as well as in domains of application as diverse as insurance, finance, management, health care and the environment.

On the other hand, the limitations of SEU as a descriptive model (i.e. its inability to take into account fairly common behavior (Ellsberg's paradox)) may create difficulties in applications, e.g. when assessing subjective probabilities or constructing the utility function.

There exist other models in the literature which are more flexible than SEU. However, the two axiom systems which we have presented in this chapter have invariably been the source of inspiration of the alternative 'new' theories.

9.6. Bibliography

[ALL 53] Allais, M. "Le comportement de l'homme rationnel devant le risque: critique des postulats and axiomes de l'école américaine". *Econometrica*, vol. 21, 503–546, 1953.

[ANS 63] Anscombe, F. and Aumann, R. "A definition of subjective probability". *Annals of Mathematical Statistics*, vol. 34, 199–205, 1963.

[DEF 37] deFinetti, B. "La prévision: ses lois logiques, ses sources subjectives". *Annales de l'Institut Henri Poincaré*, vol. 7(1), 1–68, 1937.

[ELL 61] Ellsberg, D. "Risk, ambiguity, and the Savage axioms". *The Quarterly Journal of Economics*, vol. 75(4), 643–669, 1961.

[FIS 70] Fishburn, P. *Utility Theory for Decision Making*. Wiley, New York, 1970.

[GHI 02] Ghirardato, P. "Revisiting Savage in a conditional world". *Economic Theory*, vol. 20(1), 83–92, 2002.

[JAF 78] Jaffray, J.Y. *Théorie de la Decision*. Polycopie, Paris University VI, 1978.

[KAR 93] Karni, E. and D. Schmeidler. "On the uniqueness of subjective probabilities". *Economic Theory*, vol. 3(2), 267–77, 1993.

[KNI 21] Knight, F. *Risk, Uncertainty and Profit*. Houghton Miffin, Boston and New York., 1921.

[KRA 59] Kraft, C.H., Pratt, JW. and Seidenberg, A. "Intuitive probability on finite sets". *Annals of Mathematical Statistics*, vol. 30, 408–419, 1959.

[SAV 54] Savage, L. *The Foundations of Statistics*, John Wiley, New York, 1954.

[VIL 64] Villegas, C. "On qualitative probability σ-algebras". *Annals of Mathematical Statistics*, vol. 35, 1787–1796, 1964.

[VON 47] von Neumann, J. and Morgenstern, O. *Theory of Games and Economic Behavior*, Princeton University Press, Princeton, NJ, 1947.

Chapter 10

Cardinal Extensions of the EU Model Based on the Choquet Integral

10.1. Introduction

It has been proven that the classical models of decision under risk (the expected utility (EU) model [VON 47]) and under uncertainty (the subjective expected utility (SEU) model [SAV 54]) are often violated by observed behaviors. The most famous evidence is the Allais paradox [ALL 53] under risk and the Ellsberg paradox [ELL 61] under uncertainty. Among others, these two paradoxes have called into question these classical models.

To take into account these behaviors, Schmeidler [SCH 89] (under uncertainty) and Quiggin [QUI 82] and Yaari [YAA 87] (under risk) have built new axiomatizations of behavior for which the EU (or SEU) model is a particular case.

The comonotonic (terminology is from common monotony) independence axiom is an appealing and intuitive axiom which requires that the usual independence axiom holds only when hedging effects are absent. Under this axiom, Schmeidler, Quiggin and Yaari have independently characterized the preferences by means of a functional (a Choquet integral), under uncertainty as well as under risk. The Choquet integral has therefore proven to be an important tool for decision making under risk and uncertainty.

These models – referred to as Choquet expected utility (CEU) models – explain most of the observed paradoxes. They also offer simple but flexible representations,

---

Chapter written by Alain CHATEAUNEUF and Michèle COHEN.

allow for more diversified patterns of behavior under uncertainty as well as under risk and allow the separate perception of uncertainty or of risk from the valuation of outcomes.

The aim of this chapter is mainly to emphasize the role of the models of behavior based on the Choquet integral.

10.2. Notation and definitions

Let us recall some notation from the previous chapters. S is the set of *states of nature*, $\mathcal{E} \subset 2^S$ is a σ-algebra of subsets of S, $A \in \mathcal{E}$ is an *event* and $\mathcal{C}$ is the set of *consequences*. A decision is identified with an *act*, which is a mapping from S to $\mathcal{C}$. The set of acts will be denoted $\mathbb{V}$ and the set of consequences $\mathcal{C}$.

The *preferences* between acts are represented by a binary relation denoted $\succsim$ on the set of acts $\mathbb{V}$. Strict preference will be denoted $\succ$ and indifference $\sim$. The preference relation on $\mathbb{V}$ *induces* (thanks to constant acts) a preference relation on the set $\mathcal{C}$ of consequences. Abusing notation, we denote this preference relation on $\mathcal{C}$ as $\succsim$.

An act f is a *simple step act* if there exists a finite partition $\{A_i, i \in I\}$ of S, with $A_i \in \mathcal{E}$ for all $i \in I$, such that $f(A_i) = \{c_i\}$ i.e. a singleton. When f is a simple step act, we will denote $f = (c_1, A_1, \ldots, c_n, A_n)$ where $c_1 \precsim \ldots \precsim c_n$. In particular, a *constant* act δ_c is characterized by $\delta_c(S) = c, c \in \mathcal{C}$.

In this chapter, we differentiate the following two particular cases:

1) When the set of consequences is a subset of $\mathbb{R}$ and consequently *already ordered*, the set of acts will be denoted $\mathbb{X}$. Furthermore, a simple step act will be denoted $X = (x_1, A_1, \ldots, x_n, A_n)$ where $x_1 \leq \ldots \leq x_n$.

We define the characteristic function of A_i. 1_{A_i} is defined by $1_{A_i}(s) = 1$ if $s \in A_i$, $1_{A_i}(s) = 0$. Otherwise, we have

$$X = \sum_{i=1}^{i=n} x_i 1_{A_i}.$$

2) When the set of consequences $\mathcal{Y}$ is *a set of lotteries* (or equally, distributions of probability with finite support) on a given set $\mathcal{C}$ of outcomes and when the set S of states of nature is *finite*, the set of acts (equally the set of mappings from S to $\mathcal{Y}$) will be denoted $\mathbb{F}_0$. In this case acts are called 'horse lotteries'. Since the set of consequences $\mathcal{Y}$ is a mixture set (see Chapter 8), one can use this structure in order to define, for all f and h in $\mathbb{F}_0$ and all α in $[0, 1]$, the act $\alpha f + (1 - \alpha)h$ by:

$$(\alpha f + (1 - \alpha)h)(s) = \alpha f(s) + (1 - \alpha)h(s) \text{ for all } s \in S.$$

For this operation, $\mathbb{F}_0$ is also a mixture space.

10.2.1. *The notion of comonotony*

The notion of comonotony is crucial for the axiomatic of models that we will develop in this chapter.

Definition 10.1. Two acts f and g of $\mathbb{V}$ are said to be comonotonic if there exists no pair $s, s' \in S$ such that $f(s) \succ f(s')$ and $g(s) \prec g(s')$.

When the set of consequences is a subset of $\mathbb{R}$ ordered with the usual order $\geq$, the definition is as follows.

Definition 10.2. Two acts X and Y of $\mathbb{X}$ are said to be comonotonic if for all $s, s' \in S$,

$$(X(s) - X(s'))(Y(s) - Y(s')) \geq 0$$

If two acts X and Y are comonotonic, they both vary in the same direction from one state s to another state $s\prime$. Thus, it is impossible to ensure against the 'variability' of the payments of a financial asset X by purchasing an other asset Y which would be comonotonic with it. In other words, *two comonotonic acts with value in $\mathbb{R}$ cannot be used for hedging purposes*.

Let us illustrate this notion with the following example.

Example 10.1. Consider the five mappings defined on the space $S = \{s_1, s_2, s_3\}$ by:

	s_1	s_2	s_3
X_1	1	2	3
X_2	-5	0	9
X_3	10	5	0
X_4	7	3	5
X_5	2	2	2

Since every mapping is comonotonic with a constant mapping, X_5 is comonotonic with all other decisions. The decisions X_1 and X_2 are comonotonic. X_1 and $-X_3$ are comonotonic (we also say that X_1 and X_3 are anti-comonotonic). X_4 presents no comonotonic relation with X_1, X_2 or X_3. Note that comononotonicity is not transitive: X_4 is comonotonic with X_5, X_5 is comonotonic with X_1 and nevertheless X_4 and X_1 are not comonotonic.

For more information on comonotony, see [CHA 97, DEN 94].

10.2.2. *The Choquet integral*

In order to understand the models of decision under uncertainty that we will develop in the following section, let us define the Choquet integral [CHO 53] by first giving the definition of a capacity.

Definition 10.3. A (normalized) capacity v on $(S, \mathcal{E})$ is a set-function from $\mathcal{E}$ to $[0, 1]$ satisfying $v(\phi) = 0, v(S) = 1$ and monotone i.e.

$$\forall A, B \in \mathcal{E}, A \subset B \Rightarrow v(A) \leq v(B).$$

A capacity is said to be *convex* if:

$$\forall A, B \in \mathcal{E}, \ v(A \cup B) + v(A \cap B) \geq v(A) + v(B).$$

Another usual denomination is supermodular or monotone of order 2.

When S is finite, one considers $\mathcal{E} = 2^S$.

Definition 10.4. For any measurable mapping X from $(S, \mathcal{E})$ to $\mathbb{R}$, the Choquet integral $\int_{Ch} X dv$ is defined by:

$$\int_{Ch} X dv = \int_{-\infty}^{0} [v(X > t) - 1] dt + \int_{0}^{\infty} v(X > t) dt \qquad (10.1)$$

– First note that the Choquet formula remains unchanged if strict inequalities are replaced by weak ones.

– Note also that if v is a probability measure P, $\int_{Ch} X dv$ reduces to $\int X dP = E_P(X)$, the mathematical expectation of X with respect to P.

– When X takes only a finite number of values, one can write:

$$X = (x_1, A_1, \ldots, x_i, A_i, \ldots, x_n, A_n)$$

where $x_i \in \mathbb{R}, x_1 \leq \ldots \leq x_i \leq \ldots \leq x_n$ and where $A_i \in \mathcal{E}, (A_i)$ is a partition of S. The Choquet integral of X is then given by:

$$\int_{Ch} X dv = x_1 + (x_2 - x_1) v [X \geq x_2] + \ldots + (x_n - x_{n-1}) v [X \geq x_n].$$

– Let $\mathcal{C}$ be a set of consequences, f a mapping from S in $\mathcal{C}$ and u a non-decreasing mapping from $\mathcal{C}$ in $\mathbb{R}$. By setting $X = u \circ f$, X is a mapping from S to $\mathbb{R}$. Then we can therefore define for a given u and v:

$$\int_{Ch} u(f) dv = \int_{-\infty}^{0} [v(u(f) > t) - 1] dt + \int_{0}^{\infty} v(u(f) > t) dt \qquad (10.2)$$

We will refer to equation (10.2) as the Choquet expected utility (CEU) of the act f i.e. $CEU(f)$.

10.2.3. Characterization of the Choquet integral

Schmeidler [SCH 86] gave a characterization of functionals which are Choquet integrals. This characterization will be a crucial tool for the decision model initiated by Schmeidler and more generally for all Choquet expected utility models (CEU).

Theorem 10.1. *Characterization of the Choquet integral [SCH 86]*
Let us consider the functional $I : \mathbb{X} \to \mathbb{R}$ satisfying $I(1_S) = 1$ and the following two conditions:

1) Comonotonic additivity: if X and Y in $\mathbb{X}$ are comonotonic, this implies $I(X + Y) = I(X) + I(Y)$ (hence $I(0) = 0$).

2) Monotonicity: $X \geq Y$ on S implies $I(X) \geq I(Y)$.

Then defining v by $v(A) = I(1_A)$ on $\mathcal{E}$, we obtain for all X in $\mathbb{X}$:

$$I(X) = \int_{Ch} X\,dv, \text{ or equally, } I(X) = \int_{-\infty}^{0} [v(X > t) - 1]\,dt + \int_{0}^{\infty} [v(X > t)]\,dt.$$

Conversely, any Choquet integral

$$I : X \in \mathbb{X} \to I(X) = \int_{Ch} X\,dv \in \mathbb{R}$$

satisfies $I(1_S) = 1$ and conditions (1) and (2).

This theorem is at the root of decision models under uncertainty based on the Choquet integral.

10.3. Decision under uncertainty

Let us recall that by decision under uncertainty we mean, in contrast to decision under risk, situations when a given objective probability distribution on the set S of states of the world is not available to the decision maker. We saw in Chapter 9 that the classical SEU model of decision under uncertainty imposes the use of a *probabilistic* representation, dictating that any situation of uncertainty should become a situation of *subjective* risk. This model contradicts the observed behaviors as shown by Ellsberg's paradox.

10.3.1. Ellsberg's paradox

Ellsberg's paradox is important in constructing extensions of the classical model. Described in detail in Chapter 9, we simply recall it here. Ellsberg [ELL 61] proposes the following situation: an urn contains 90 balls of which 30 are red (R) and 60 are blue (B) or yellow (Y) in some unknown proportion. The number of blue balls may be 0 – 60 and the complement consists of yellow balls. We draw (at random) one ball from the urn and ask the subjects to make the two following decisions: bet on R (decision X_1) or bet on B (decision X_2), then bet on $(R \cup Y)$ (decision X_3) or bet on $(B \cup Y)$ (decision X_4).

10.3.1.1. *Interpretation of Ellsberg's paradox in the framework of Savage*

Table 10.1 lists the value of consequences for each decision (expressed in €) according to the event.

| | 30/90 | 60/90 | |
| | Red | Blue | Yellow |
	R	B	Y
X_1	100	0	0
X_2	0	100	0
X_3	100	0	100
X_4	0	100	100

Table 10.1. *Ellsberg's acts: Savage's framework*

Typically, the majority of subjects make the choices: $X_1 \succ X_2$ and $X_4 \succ X_3$. As demonstrated in Chapter 9, such behavior is incompatible with Savage's sure-thing principle, one of the major axioms of theory.

Moreover, as noticed by Machina and Schmeidler [MACH 92], such subjects are not even probabilistically sophisticated. This means that they do not ascribe subjective probabilities p_R, p_B, p_Y to states of nature (i.e. elementary events R, B, Y) and then use the first-order stochastic dominance axiom. (Let us recall that, if X and Y are real random variables, the first-order stochastic dominance rule stipulates that if $\forall t \in \mathbb{R}, P\{X \geq t\} \geq P\{Y \geq t\}$, then X should be weakly preferred to Y. The preference becomes strict if $P\{X \geq t\} > P\{Y \geq t\}$ for some $t_0 \in \mathbb{R}$.) The first-order stochastic dominance axiom is a widely accepted rule for partially ordered random variables. Otherwise, $X_1 \succ X_2$ would imply $p_R > p_B$ and $X_4 \succ X_3$ would imply $p_B + p_Y > p_R + p_Y$: a contradiction.

10.3.1.2. *Interpretation of Ellsberg's paradox in the framework of Anscombe and Aumann*

In the previous presentation of the Ellsberg paradox, uncertainty is modeled through the set of the states of the world $S' = \{R, B, Y\}$ and bets are interpreted as mappings $X : S' \to \mathbb{R}$.

We have seen in Chapter 9 that Ellsberg's paradox is robust. However, if we consider Ellsberg's experiment in the context of Anscombe and Aumann [ANS 63], the independence axiom 9.12 (**AA3**) is violated.

The composition of the urn is now uncertain. The set S of states of nature is composed of 61 states: $S = \{s_0, s_1, \ldots, s_k, \ldots, s_{60}\}$ where a state s_k represents a given composition of the urn: '30 red balls, k blue balls and $60 - k$ yellow balls'.

Let us refer to the set of all lotteries on $\mathcal{C} = \{0, 100\}$, or equally of all probability distributions on $\mathcal{C}$, as $\mathcal{Y}$ with finite support. The uncertain prospect described by the act X_i in Savage's framework is now characterized in the framework of Anscombe and Aumann [ANS 63] by the mapping g_i from S to $\mathcal{Y}$, $g_i \colon S \to \mathcal{Y}$ in the following way.

To each state of nature s_k of S, the consequence $g_i(s_k)$ is the lottery:

$$(X_i(R), 30/90; X_i(B), k/90; X_i(J), (60-k)/90)$$

or equally the lottery offering $X_i(R)$ with probability $30/90$, $X_i(B)$ with probability $k/90$ and $X_i(J)$ with probability $(60-k)/90$ (see Table 9.2).

Assume, as implicitly assumed by Schmeidler [SCH 89] and Anscombe–Aumann [ANS 63], that under risk the decison maker maximizes an expected utility (see Chapter 8) with a von Neumann utility function u. This utility function can be assumed without loss of generality such that $u(0) = 0, u(100) = 1$. We can therefore establish through a direct computation that, in the Anscombe–Aumann framework, the expected utility model under uncertainty cannot explain preferences described above. We can actually imagine that the decision maker ascribes probabilities to the events s_k, and that they behave in accordance with the Anscombe–Aumann expected utility model, i.e. prefers h to g if and only if $\sum p_k u(h(s_k)) \geq \sum p_k u(g(s_k))$. Then, a simple computation shows that $g_1 \succ g_2$ would give $30 > \sum k p_k$ while $g_4 \succ g_3$ would give $30 < \sum k p_k$: a contradiction.

10.3.2. *Schmeidler's model in Anscombe–Aumann framework*

In order to explain such paradoxes and to separate the perception of uncertainty from the valuation of outcomes, Schmeidler [SCH 89] has proposed a model which relaxes the usual independence condition while offering a flexible but simple formula. As previously discussed, Schmeidler [SCH 89] has developed his model in the framework of Anscombe–Aumann [ANS 63]. In this section, the set S of sets of nature is therefore finite and the events are the elements of $\mathcal{E} = 2^S$. The set of consequences Y is the set of lotteries on a given set of outcomes $\mathcal{C}$ (i.e. $\mathcal{Y}$ is the set of probability distributions on $\mathcal{C}$ with finite support). The set of acts is the set of mappings $\mathbb{F}_0$ from S to $\mathcal{Y}$, also called 'horse lotteries'. Let $\succsim$ be the preference relation of the decision maker on the set $\mathbb{F}_0$.

10.3.2.1. *Comonotonic independence*

Let us recall that, in the Anscombe–Aumann framework, the subjective expected utility model (SEU) (see Chapter 9) is obtained mainly through the following axiom.

Axiom 10.1. *Independence axiom [ANS 63]*
For all f, g, h in $\mathbb{F}_0$ and for all α in $]0, 1[$, $f \succ g$ implies

$$\alpha f + (1 - \alpha)h \succ \alpha g + (1 - \alpha)h.$$

We have seen that most behavior contradicts axiom 10.1 (interpretation of Ellsberg's paradox in Anscombe and Aumann framework). In order to weaken this axiom, Schmeidler introduced the definition of comonotonic acts which led to the following weakened axiom.

Axiom 10.2. *Axiom of comonotonic independence [SCH 89]*
For all pairwise comonotonic acts f, g and h in $\mathbb{F}_0$ and for all α in $]0, 1[$, $f \succ g$ implies

$$\alpha f + (1 - \alpha)h \succ \alpha g + (1 - \alpha)h.$$

Roughly speaking, comonotonic independence requires the direction of preferences to be retained, as long as hedging effects are not involved. This intuition (crucial in Schmeidler's model) will appear more transparent in Schmeidler's representation theorem [SCH 89].

By adding weak order and continuity conditions to this key axiom, Schmeidler [SCH 89] derived the characterization of his model where typical preferences observed in section 10.3.1 become admissible.

10.3.2.2. *Representation of preferences by a Choquet integral in Anscombe–Aumann's framework*

Schmeidler shows that the preference relation $\succsim$ on $\mathbb{F}_0$ (the acts in Anscombe–Aumann's framework) satisfying the axioms previously described is represented by a Choquet integral with respect to a unique capacity v. More precisely, for all f and g in $\mathbb{F}_0$:

$$f \succsim g \text{ if and only if } \int_{Ch} u(f(.))dv \geq \int_{Ch} u(g(.))dv$$

where u is the von Neumann utility function on the set $\mathcal{Y}$ of lotteries on $\mathcal{C}$. Notice that capacity v is substituted to probability P in Anscombe–Aumann's theorem.

The strategy of Schmeidler's proof consists of first noting that axiom 10.2 entails axiom 10.1 on the set of constant acts $\mathbb{F}_0^c$. The existence of a von Neumann–Morgenstern utility function u on the set $\mathcal{Y}$ of lotteries is therefore established, as is the ability of linking any act

$$f = (y_1, A_1, \ldots, y_n, A_n) = \sum_{i=1}^{i=n} y_i 1_{A_i}$$

in a natural way where $y_i \in \mathcal{Y}$ with the real random variable

$$u(f) = \sum_{i=1}^{i=n} x_i 1_{A_i}$$

where $x_i = u(y_i), i = 1, \ldots, n$.

By denoting the set of such variables by $\mathcal{X}_0$, Schmeidler shows in a second step that the preorder induced on $\mathcal{X}_0$ (denoted $\succsim_0$) is representable by a Choquet integral. Equally, there exists a capacity v on S such that:

$$\forall (X, Y) \in \mathcal{X}_0^2, \ X \succsim_0 Y \text{ if and only if } \int_{Ch} X \, dv \geq \int_{Ch} Y \, dv.$$

10.3.3. *Choquet expected utility (CEU) models in Savage's framework*

By Choquet expected utility (CEU) models, we mean those non-additive models directly connected to the Choquet integral which, following the pioneering work of Schmeidler [SCH 89] in Anscombe–Aumann's framework, have been derived in Savage's framework [e.g. GIL 87, WAK 90].

Savage's framework seems more natural than that of Anscombe–Aumann, where consequences are lotteries but the axiomatization becomes more sophisticated.

Although Savage's framework allows for more general consequence sets $\mathcal{C}$, we will confine $\mathcal{C} = \mathbb{R}$ within section 10.3.3 *only*, permitting a simple exposure of the main properties of CEU models.

We therefore consider a decision maker making their choices within the set $\mathbb{X}$ of acts consisting of all ε-measurable and bounded functions $X : (S, \mathcal{E}) \to \mathbb{R}$, where S is a set of states of nature and $\mathcal{E}$ a σ-algebra of subsets of S. This decision maker is in a situation of uncertainty, and $\succsim$ is a preference relation on $\mathbb{X}$.

10.3.3.1. *Simplified version of Schmeidler's model in Savage's framework*

In Savage's framework, which fits the first and simple presentation of Ellsberg's paradox, a *simplified* translation of the comonotonic independence axiom of Schmeidler is as follows.

Axiom 10.3. *Axiom of comonotonic independence [CHA 94a]*
If $X, Y, Z \in \mathbb{V}$ and Z are comonotonic with X and Y, then

$$X \sim Y \Rightarrow X + Z \sim Y + Z.$$

For $\mathcal{C} = \mathbb{R}$, the definition of comonotonic acts is that of definition 10.2.

This axiom of comonotonic independence requires us to maintain the direction of preferences when adding the same act, as long as no asymmetric reduction of uncertainty is involved through hedging effects. On the contrary, in the case of asymmetric reduction of uncertainty (through hedging effects), this axiom allows us to modify the direction of preferences.

Example 10.2 below demonstrates how such a behavior under uncertainty can be taken into account in a case where the acts give results dependent upon the realization of the event A or of the complementary event $\bar{A}$.

Example 10.2. Assume at the beginning indifference between X and Y ($X \sim Y$). Z is comonotonic with Y but not with X. Z may be used as a hedge against X but not against Y, and consequently an uncertain averse decision maker may express (after addition of the variable Z) the strict preference $X + Z \succ Y + Z$.

	A	$\bar{A}$
X	25,000	15,000
Y	12,000	30,000
Z	15,000	25,000
$X + Z$	40,000	40,000
$Y + Z$	27,000	55,000

Under the key comonotonic independence axiom and other classical axioms such as weak order and continuity, it is then possible to derive a simplified version of Schmeidler's model where preferences can be represented by a Choquet integral with respect to a capacity v [CHA 94a], i.e.

$$\text{for all } X, Y \in X, \ X \succsim Y \text{ if and only if } \int_{Ch} X \, dv \geq \int_{Ch} Y \, dv.$$

Note that this model is simplified in the sense that utility of outcomes is linear, a consequence of the independence axiom of Chateauneuf [CHA 94a]. Such a result is deduced from the fundamental theorem of Schmeidler [SCH 86], which characterizes the Choquet integral [CHO 53] and appears as a crucial tool for Schmeidler's model and more generally for Choquet expected utility (CEU) models.

10.3.3.2. *Choquet expected utility model in Savage's framework*

When utility of results is no longer necessarily linear, we obtain the following classical definition of the Choquet expected utility model.

Definition 10.5. A decision maker satisfies the Choquet expected utility (CEU) model if the decision maker's preferences on the set of acts $\mathbb{V}$ can be represented with the help of a utility function under certainty $u \colon \mathbb{R} \to \mathbb{R}$, increasing and defined up to an increasing affine transformation and with the help of a personal evaluation of the likelihood of events through a capacity v. Preference representation is given by

$$I(u(X)) = \int_{Ch} u(X) dv,$$

the Choquet integral of $u(X)$ with respect to capacity v, defined for $X \in \mathbb{X}$ by

$$\int_{Ch} u(X) dv = \int_{-\infty}^{0} [v(u(X) > t) - 1] \, dt + \int_{0}^{\infty} [v(u(X) > t)] \, dt \quad (10.3)$$

Note that this CEU model generalizes equation (10.1) with a function u which is not necessarily linear. For a simple *step* act

$$X = (x_1, A_1, \ldots, x_n, A_n) = \sum_{i=1}^{i=n} x_i 1_{A_i}$$

where $x_i \in \mathbb{R}$, $A_i \in \mathcal{E}$ and (A_i) is a partition of S, we obtain:

$$\begin{aligned}\int_{Ch} u(X) dv &= u(x_1) + (u(x_2) - u(x_1)) v\left[X \geq x_2\right] \\ &\quad + \ldots + (u(x_n) - u(x_{n-1})) v\left[X \geq x_n\right].\end{aligned}$$

Remark 10.1. One can interpret the behavior of a decision maker using the model

$$\int_{Ch} u(X) dv$$

as follows. The decision maker values X by first evaluating the utility of the minimum result x_1 obtained with certainty, and then adding the additional increases of utility $u(x_{i+1}) - u(x_i)$, $1 \leq i \leq n-1$ weighted by personal belief $v\left[X \geq x_{i+1}\right]$ of occurence.

	ϕ	$\{s_1\}$	$\{s_2\}$	$\{s_3\}$	$\{s_1,s_2\}$	$\{s_1,s_3\}$	$\{s_2,s_3\}$	S
v	0	1/3	0	0	1/3	1/3	2/3	1
$u(X)$		a	b	c				

Table 10.2. *Computation of CEU*

10.3.3.3. *Example of computation of such a Choquet integral*

Let $S = \{s_1, s_2, s_3\}$. Let v be a capacity on S as below and X an act such that the values of $u(X)$ are given in Table 10.2.

The evaluation of the Choquet integral $I = \int_{Ch} u(X) dv$ depends upon the ranking of a, b, c:

- If $a < b < c$,

$$\int_{Ch} u(X) dv = a + (b-a)v(\{s_2, s_3\}) + (c-b)v(\{s_3\})$$
$$= 1/3 a + 2/3 b$$

- If $c < a < b$,

$$\int_{Ch} u(X) dv = 2/3 c + 1/3 a.$$

- If $b < c < a$,

$$\int_{Ch} u(X) dv = 2/3 b + 1/3 a.$$

- etc.

A classical integral, with an additive measure, would naturally take the same value whatever the ranking of consequences. We will now provide the key axiom of CEU theory.

10.3.3.4. *The comonotonic sure-thing principle*

The main feature of the CEU model is to take into account possible hedging effects. For this purpose, the crucial axiom in the axiomatization of CEU is the comonotonic sure-thing principle [e.g. CHE 96, GIL 87], a weakening of Savage's sure-thing principle which can be stated in the following way.

Axiom 10.4. *The comonotonic sure-thing principle*
Let

$$X = \sum_{i=1}^{n} x_i 1_{A_i}$$

and

$$Y = \sum_{i=1}^{n} y_i 1_{A_i},$$

where $\{A_i\}$ is a partition of S and $x_1 \leq \ldots \leq x_i \leq \ldots \leq x_n$ and $y_1 \leq \ldots \leq y_i \leq \ldots \leq y_n$ are such that $x_{i_0} = y_{i_0}$ for some $1 \leq i_0 \leq n$. Then $X \succsim Y$ implies $X' \succsim Y'$ for the acts X' and Y' obtained from acts X and Y by merely replacing the i_0th common result by any other common result which preserves the ranking i_0 for both acts X and Y.

Axiom 10.4 states that, as long as acts remain *comonotonic* (i.e. no hedging effect), there is no reason to change the direction of preferences when a common outcome is modified. Note, however, that even when combined with standard axioms of weak order, continuity and monotonicity, the comonotonic sure-thing principle fails to fully characterize CEU. For instance, Wakker [WAK 89] completes the axiomatization of the CEU model by strengthening axiom 10.4 to an axiom of *comonotonic trade-off consistency*.

We now turn to the ability of Schmeidler's model to handle uncertainty aversion and, symmetrically, uncertainty appeal.

10.3.4. *Uncertainty aversion*

In his seminal papers, Schmeidler [SCH 89] has demonstrated the great ability of his model to capture the concept of uncertainty aversion. He defined uncertainty aversion through convexity of preferences i.e.

$$\forall f, g \in \mathbb{F}_0, \forall \alpha \in [0,1], \ f \sim g \Rightarrow \alpha f + (1-\alpha)g \succsim f,$$

interpreting this axiom as 'smoothing' or averaging potential outcomes makes the decision maker better off. This definition is particularly meaningful since, as proved by Schmeidler [SCH 86, SCH 89], uncertainty aversion is equivalent to the capacity v being *convex*.

Proposition 10.1. *Schmeidler [SCH 86]*
Let $I : \mathbb{X} \to \mathbb{R}$ be a Choquet integral with respect to a capacity v, i.e.

$$\forall X \in \mathbb{X}, \ I(X) = \int_{Ch} X \, dv,$$

the following conditions (1) and (2) are equivalent:
  1) v is convex;
  2) $core(v) \neq \phi$ where

$$core(v) = \left\{ \begin{array}{l} \text{simply additive probabilities } P \text{ on } \mathcal{E} \\ \text{such that } P(A) \geq v(A), \forall A \in \mathcal{E} \end{array} \right\}$$

and for all X in $\mathbb{X}$:

$$I(X) = Min\left\{\int XdP, P \in core(v)\right\}.$$

Proposition 10.1 offers an attractive interpretation of uncertainty aversion in terms of *pessimism*. In Schmeidler's model, an uncertainty averse decision maker behaves as follows. They consider for every act, among all probability distributions P in *core* of v, the one giving the minimum expected utility $E_P u(f)$ of this act, and then choose the act which maximizes this minimum i.e.

$$\forall f, g \in \mathbb{F}_0, f \succsim g \text{ if and only if } \min_{P \in core(v)} \int_S u(f) dP \geq \min_{P \in core(v)} \int_S u(g) dP.$$

Such an interpretation remains true for the CEU model (i.e. in Savage's framework) since for such a model, convexity of preferences is equivalent to v convex (and u concave) [see CHA 02]. Moreover, in the simple case of the CEU model with constant marginal utility ($u(x) = x, \forall x \in \mathbb{R}$), we can give a direct interpretation in terms of hedging effects since convexity of preferences is equivalent to the following uncertainty aversion axiom [CHA 94a].

Axiom 10.5. *Uncertainty aversion*
For $X, Y, Z \in \mathbb{X}$, Y *and* Z *comonotonic,*

$$X \sim Y \Rightarrow X + Z \succsim Y + Z.$$

Note that this uncertainty aversion axiom implies the comonotonic independence axiom and therefore characterizes the simplified Schmeidler's model where, moreover, v is convex.

Axiom 10.5 allows us to take hedging effects into account since Z is not a hedge against Y but may be a hedge against X. $X + Z$ may therefore display a reduction of uncertainty with respect to $Y + Z$, and therefore $X + Z$ may be preferred to $Y + Z$ by an uncertainty averse decision maker.

Such an interpretation is particularly suitable for interpreting behavior in Ellsberg's example. Let us describe uncertainty in Ellsberg's example (section 10.3.1) by:

$$S = \{R, B, Y\}, \mathcal{E} = 2^S.$$

Let $\mathcal{P}$ be the set of all probability distributions on $(S, 2^S)$ compatible with the information i.e.

$$\mathcal{P} = \{\text{ probability distributions on } (S, 2^S) \text{ such that } P(R) = 1/3\}$$

	φ	R	B	Y	R∪B	R∪Y	B∪Y	S
v	0	1/3	0	0	1/3	1/3	2/3	1

Table 10.3. *Capacity in Ellsberg's example*

where v is defined by $v(A) = \underset{\mathcal{P}}{Inf} P(A), \forall A \in \mathcal{E}$; we obtain Table 10.3.

It is straightforward to show that v is a convex capacity and that $\mathcal{P} = core(v)$. (Note that v is actually an infinite monotone capacity or else a belief function.) Let us compute

$$I(X) = \int_{Ch} X \, dv$$

for all considered acts:

$$I(X_1) = 1/3 \times 100 > I(X_2) = 0 \times 100 \text{ thus } X_1 \succ X_2$$
$$I(X_4) = 2/3 \times 100 > I(X_3) = 1/3 \times 100 \text{ thus } X_4 \succ X_3.$$

Consequently, one can explain the behavior in Ellsberg's paradox by uncertainty aversion.

10.3.5. *The multiprior model*

We now consider the max-min model of Gilboa and Schmeidler [GIL 89]. In this model, the agents have a set of *a priori* probability laws (not a single one as in the Bayesian paradigm) and use the maximin criterion for evaluating decisions through this set of initial beliefs (*multiple prior*).

10.3.5.1. *The axiomatic of the model*

Gilboa and Schmeidler [GIL 89] consider Anscombe–Aumann's framework [ANS 63] where the set of consequences is a set $\mathcal{Y}$ of laws with finite support over a set $\mathcal{C}$. This axiomatic is very simple and is mainly derived from the following two axioms. The first is the axiom of certainty independence.

Axiom 10.6. *Certainty independence*
For all f, g of $\mathbb{F}_0$ and h constant decision of $\mathbb{F}_0$, then for all $\alpha \in]0, 1[$:

$$f \succ g \Longrightarrow \alpha f + (1 - \alpha)h \succ \alpha g + (1 - \alpha)h.$$

Axiom 10.6 is weaker than the usual independence axiom, since it applies only when adding a 'common consequence' which is constant. This axiom is implied by the comonotonic independence axiom (axiom 10.3). The second axiom is one of uncertainty aversion previously defined in Schmeidler's model [SCH 89].

Axiom 10.7. *Uncertainty aversion*
For all f, g in $\mathbb{F}_0$ and $\alpha \in]0, 1[$,

$$f \sim g \Longrightarrow \alpha f + (1 - \alpha)g \succsim f.$$

Proposition 10.2. *Gilboa and Schmeidler [GIL 89]*
 Under the axiom of weak order, an axiom of monotony, an axiom of continuity and axioms 10.6 and 10.7, there exists a set of probability measures $\mathcal{P}$, closed and convex, and a von Neumann utility function $u : \mathcal{Y} \to \mathbb{R}$ such that:

$$f \succsim g \Longleftrightarrow \min_{P \in \mathcal{P}} \int u(f)dP \geq \min_{P \in \mathcal{P}} \int u(g)dP.$$

The function u is unique up to a positive affine transformation, while the set $\mathcal{P}$ is unique if closed in the weak-star topology.

The interpretation of this representation is fairly simple. The decision maker behaves as if they had a set of *a priori* beliefs (instead of a unique one as in the expected utility model). In order to evaluate an act, they compute the expected utility of this act with respect to all probability distributions considered in $\mathcal{P}$, and then take the minimum. This last operation represents an attitude of pessimism or uncertainty aversion. Note that by reversing the last preference in axiom 10.7, this model takes into account uncertainty loving and therefore optimistic behavior.

10.3.5.2. *Comparing multiprior model with Choquet utility model*

The multiprior model is closely linked with the Choquet utility model. With this model, it is possible to interpret the Choquet capacity in terms of beliefs. From proposition 10.1:

$$v \text{ is convex} \iff \begin{cases} core(v) \neq \emptyset \text{ and} \\ \int_{Ch} u(X)dv = \min_{P \in core(v)} \int u(X)dP \text{ for all } X \in \mathbb{X}. \end{cases}$$

When the decision maker's capacity is convex, the decision maker behaves as in a multiprior model whose set of probability measures is given by the core of a convex capacity. Nevertheless, one should note that every closed and convex family of probability measures is not necessarily the core of a convex capacity and, therefore, that the multiprior model is a more general model than the Choquet utility case with a convex capacity. Moreover, the behavior described by a Choquet integral with respect to a non-convex capacity cannot be described by the multiprior model.

Remark 10.2. The behavior of a decision maker of the multiprior type may be considered as excessively pessimistic. In fact, in the next section we present the models of Jaffray [JAF 89a, JAF 89b] and Jaffray–Philippe [JAF 97], which represent less extreme behavior.

10.3.5.3. *CEU model and lower and upper envelopes of a probability distributions family*

Jaffray [JAF 89a, JAF 89b] and Jaffray and Philippe [JAF 97] have proven that, under some conditions, it was possible to write a Choquet integral with respect to any capacity v as a convex combination of two terms. These terms are the minimum and the maximum of expected utilities with respect to a family of probability distributions, the weight between the two representing an index of pessimism.

As shown previously in the Ellsberg experiment, the uncertainty can be summarized by the lower envelope

$$v(.) = \underset{P \in \mathcal{P}}{Inf} P(.).$$

In this case the capacity v is convex, therefore allowing the simpler formula as in proposition 10.1. Indeed, if v is a convex capacity on $(S, \mathcal{E})$, then

$$\forall X \in \mathbb{X}, \min \left\{ \int X dP, P \in core(v) \right\} = \int_{Ch} X dv.$$

Such situations of uncertainty summarized by a lower envelope (i.e. a convex capacity) have been defined by Jaffray [JAF 89a, JAF 89b] as being 'regular uncertainty'.

Definition 10.6. We have a situation of *regular uncertainty* when the situation of uncertainty, defined by a family of probability distributions $\mathcal{P}$ on $(S, \mathcal{E})$, is completely characterized by its lower envelope c where

$$c(A) = \underset{P \in \mathcal{P}}{Inf} P(A)$$

and c is convex, meaning that $\mathcal{P} = \{P \text{ on } (S, 2^S), P \geq c\}$. We will denote the upper envelope of $\mathcal{P}: C = \underset{P \in \mathcal{P}}{Sup} P(.)$ by C, where $C(A) = 1 - c(\bar{A})$, $\forall A \in \mathcal{E}$.

This 'regular uncertainty' can be encountered in natural situations as shown by Dempster [DEM 67]. Let us assume (as in [DEM 67]) that $(\Omega, 2^\Omega, \pi)$ is a finite probability space and that Γ is a correspondence from Ω to $\mathcal{E}^* = \mathcal{E} - \{\phi\}$, where $\mathcal{E} = 2^S$ and S is a finite state space. Let us interpret Γ as implying that if $\varpi \in \Omega$ occurs, then the true state s belongs to $\Gamma(\varpi)$ (such a state space $(\Omega, 2^\Omega, \pi)$ is called a message space). We can then state that each event $A \in \mathcal{E}$ occurs with a probability at least equal to $c(A)$ where

$$c(A) = \sum_{B \subset A} m(B),$$

and

$$m(B) = \sum_{\{\varpi \in \Omega, \Gamma(\varpi) = B\}} \pi(\{\varpi\}).$$

It can be shown that c is a belief function (i.e. a particular case of a convex capacity) [e.g. JAF 89b, SHA 76].

In such situations of regular uncertainty, it can be the case that a CEU decision maker does not necessarily exhibit uncertainty aversion, i.e. does not necessarily have a subjective assessment of events represented by a capacity $v = c$, but by a subjective assessment of events represented by a capacity $v = \alpha c + (1 - \alpha)C$ with $\alpha \in [0, 1]$, c being convex.

Such a behavior, where the value of α can be interpreted as the pessimism index due to Hurwicz, has been studied and axiomatized by Jaffray and Philippe [JAF 97] who have shown that this behavior was compatible both with the CEU model and with the Jaffray models [JAF 89a, JAF 89b].

10.4. Decision under risk

From this point onwards, we assume that there is an 'objective' probability distribution P on $(S, \mathcal{E})$ and that the decision maker knows it. We then say that the decision maker is facing a *problem of decision under risk*.

Moreover, to make the exposition simpler, we suppose that the probability distribution P is σ-additive and non-atomic i.e. $\forall A \in \mathcal{E}$, such that $P(A) > 0$, $\forall \alpha \in (0, 1]$, $\exists B \in \mathcal{E}, B \subset A$ such that $P(B) = \alpha P(A)$. Due to these assumptions, the set $\mathbb{X}$ of acts generates any real bounded random variable.

Any element X of $\mathbb{X}$ is then a random variable whose probability distribution is P_X. Let us denote the cumulative distribution function of X as F_X i.e. $\forall x \in \mathbb{R}, F_X(x) = P\{s \in S/X(s) \leq x\} = P_S\{X \leq x\}$, its expected value as $E(X)$ and the set of all probability distributions of elements of $\mathbb{X}$ as $\mathcal{L}$.

Since every X of $\mathbb{X}$ induces a probability distribution $L(X)$ on $\mathbb{R}$, the preference relation $\succsim$ on $\mathbb{X}$ also induces a preference relation on $\mathcal{L}$ that (by abuse of notation) we also denote $\succsim$ under the following condition H_0.

– Condition H_0 Neutrality: two random variables with the same probability distribution are always indifferent.

Hence, under this condition, any axiomatization on $(\mathbb{X}, \succsim)$ can be replaced by an axiomatization on $(\mathcal{L}, \succsim)$.

Remark 10.3. Any discrete act X of $\mathbb{X}$ can be written:

$$X = (x_1, A_1, \ldots, x_k, A_k, \ldots \mathcal{X}_n, A_n),$$

where $A_i (i = 1, \ldots, n)$ is a partition of S and x_i the consequence of X on each A_i. Under risk, the probability distribution of this random variable is denoted:

$$L(X) = (x_1, p_1, \ldots, x_k, p_k, \ldots, x_n, p_n)$$

with

$$x_1 \leq x_2 \leq \ldots \leq x_n, p_i = P(A_i) \geq 0 \text{ and } \sum p_i = 1.$$

In the following, it can be useful to use the notation:

$$L(X) = (x_1, 1 - q_1; x_2, q_1 - q_2; \ldots; x_{n-1}, q_{n-2} - q_{n-1}; x_n, q_{n-1}) \quad (10.4)$$

where, for $i = 1, \ldots, n-1$,

$$q_i = \sum_{j=i+1}^{j=n} p_j.$$

In this section, we identify any consequence c with its Dirac probability distribution $\delta_{\{c\}}$.

10.4.1. *EU model and Allais paradox*

In Chapter 8 we studied the classical model of decision under risk in detail: the expected utility (EU) model. From as early as 1953, Allais [ALL 53] built a couple of alternatives for which a majority of subjects, confronted with those choices, choose in contradiction with the independence axiom and therefore in violation of the EU model (see section 8.4.1).

As this experiment (known as the Allais 'paradox') has been fundamental in the questioning of the EU model, let us first recall the original Allais paradox [ALL 53]. Subjects were asked to choose between the lotteries (say in thousand Euros) L_1 (win 1M with certainty) or L_2 (win 1M with probability 0.89, 5M with probability 0.10 and 0 with probability 0.01), and then (independently) to choose between the lotteries L'_1 (win 1M with probability 0.11 and 0 with probability 0.89) or L'_2 (win 5M with probability 0.10 and 0 with probability 0.90).

Most subjects choose L_1 over L_2 and L'_2 over L'_1. These simultaneous choices violate the independence axiom. Indeed, defining P as the lottery yielding 1M with probability 1 and Q as the lottery yielding 0 with probability 1/11 and 5M with probability 10/11, we can check that:

$$L_1 = 0.11P + 0.89\delta_1$$
$$L_2 = 0.11Q + 0.89\delta_1$$
$$L'_1 = 0.11P + 0.89\delta_0$$
$$L'_2 = 0.11Q + 0.89\delta_0$$

where δ_0 is the lottery 'win 0 with probability 1' and δ_1 is the lottery 'win 1M with probability 1'. The observed choices are therefore in contradiction with the independence axiom. Note that under the independence axiom:

$$L_1 \succeq L_2 \implies P \succeq Q \implies L'_1 \succeq L'_2.$$

This experiment has been run many times on various populations of subjects with similar results: about 66% of the choices are in contradiction with the independence axiom.

Not only are observed behaviors in contradiction with EU theory, but the EU model also raised a theoretical difficulty: the interpretation of the function u (called von Neumann's utility) characterizing the decision maker's behavior. As pointed out by Allais himself, the function u has in fact the double role of expressing the decision maker's attitude with respect to risk (concavity of u implying risk aversion) and the decision maker's valuation of differences of preferences under certainty (concavity of u implying diminishing marginal utility of wealth). This evidence has led researchers to build more flexible models, a pioneering famous work in this stream being [KAH 79]. We will focus in what follows on the rank-dependent expected utility (RDU), more directly related with Choquet integral. The RDU model presented in the next section will not only disentangle attitude towards risk and satisfaction of outcomes, but will also be compatible with observed behaviors in Allais experiment.

10.4.2. *The rank-dependent expected utility model*

10.4.2.1. *Definition of the rank-dependent expected utility model*

The rank-dependent expected utility (RDU) model is due to Quiggin [QUI 82] under the description of 'anticipated utility'. Variants of this model are due to Yaari [YAA 87], Segal [SEG 87, SEG 93] and Allais [ALL 88]. More general axiomatizations can be found in Wakker [WAK 94] and Chateauneuf [CHA 99].

Definition 10.7. A decision maker behaves in accordance with the RDU model if the decision maker's preferences on $(\mathcal{L}, \succeq)$ are characterized by two functions u and f. A continuous, increasing, cardinal (if defined up to an affine increasing transformation) utility function $u: \mathbb{R} \to \mathbb{R}$ plays the role of *utility on certainty*. An increasing *probability-transformation* function $f: [0,1] \to [0,1]$ satisfies $f(0) = 0, f(1) = 1$. Such a decision maker prefers the random variable X to the random variable Y if and only if $V(X) \geq V(Y)$, where the functional V is given by:

$$V(Z) = V_{u,f}(Z) = \int_{-\infty}^{0} [f(P(u(Z) > t)) - 1] \, dt + \int_{0}^{\infty} f(P(u(Z) > t)) \, dt.$$

We can note the following:

– If the transformation function f is the identity function $f(p) \equiv p$, then $V(Z) = V_{u,I}(Z)$ is the expected utility $E[u(Z)]$ of the random variable Z.
– If the utility u is the identity function $u(x) \equiv x$, then $V(Z) = V_{I,f}(Z)$ is the Yaari functional [YAA 87]. In fact, Yaari independently axiomatized his model, referred to as 'Dual Theory'. This model is as parcimonious as the EU model since it only uses one function f. However, this model allows us to distinguish strong risk aversion from weak risk aversion, which is not possible in EU model.
– If both transformation and utility are identity functions, then $V(Z) = V_{I,I}(Z)$ is simply the expected value $E[Z]$ of the random variable Z.

When Z is discrete, $V(Z)$ can be written as

$$\begin{aligned} V(Z) &= u(x_1) + f(q_1)[u(x_2) - u(x_1)] + \ldots \\ &+ f(q_2)[u(x_3) - u(x_2)] + \ldots + f(q_{n-1})[u(x_n) - u(x_{n-1})]. \end{aligned}$$

We can then interpret the evaluation of an RDU decision maker. They certainly evaluate first the utility of the worst outcome $u(x_1)$, and then weight the additional possible increases of utility $u(x_i) - u(x_{i-1})$ by their personal transformation $f(q_i)$ of the probability v_i of having *at least* x_i.

According to this interpretation, if the decision maker behaves in such a way that $f(p) \leq p$, it means that they underestimate all the additional utilities of gains. In this sense, we will call them *pessimistic under risk*. In the same way, u now reflects their satisfaction for wealth and the concavity of u reveals diminishing marginal utility.

Remark 10.4. Let us note that various attempts to generalize EU model by a functional:

$$(x_1, p_1; \ldots; x_k, p_k; \ldots; x_n, p_n) \longmapsto \sum f(p_i) u(x_i)$$

with $f : [0,1] \longrightarrow [0,1]$ and $f(0) = 0, f(1) = 1$ failed because the only functionals compatible with the first-order stochastic dominance is obtained for $f(p) = p$, meaning that this functional is reduced to EU.

10.4.2.1.1. Allais paradox is compatible with RDU model

As an exercise, we can evaluate the different lotteries of the Allais example in an RDU model. Setting $u(0) = 0$ (without loss of generality) we have

$$V(L_1) = u(1); V(L_2) = u(1)(f(0.99) - f(.0.10)) + u(5)f(0.10)$$

$$V(L_1') = u(1)f(0.11)$$

and

$$V(L_2') = u(5)f(0.10).$$

$L_1 \succ L_2$ implies $u(5)f(0.10) < u(1)[1-f(0.99)+f(0.10)]$ and $L_2' \succ L_1'$ implies $u(5)f(0.10) > u(1)f(0.11)$. The simultaneous choices $L_1 \succ L_2$ and $L_2' \succ L_1'$ are therefore explained by RDU theory for any f satisfying $1 - f(099) > f(0.11) - f(0.10)$, revealing that the same probability difference 0.01 is considered as more important in the neighborhood of certainty.

10.4.2.2. Key axiom of RDU's axiomatization: comonotonic sure-thing principle

Axiom 10.8. *Comonotonic sure-thing principle under risk*
The justification of the description of this axiom results from a natural interpretation of P, Q, P', Q' as probability distributions of pairwise comonotonic random variables.

Let P and Q be two lotteries of $\mathcal{L}$ and $P = (x_1, p_1; \ldots; x_k, p_k; \ldots; x_n, p_n)$ and $Q = (y_1, p_1; \ldots; y_k, p_k; \ldots; y_n, p_n)$ be such that $x_{k_0} = y_{k_0}$. Then $P \succeq Q$ implies $P' \succeq Q'$ for lotteries obtained from lotteries P and Q simply by replacing the common outcome x_{i_0} by a common k_0th outcome x_{i_0}' in both P' and Q'.

Axiom 10.8 [CHA 99] is very similar to the ordinal independence axiom of Green and Julien [GRE 88], to the irrelevance axiom of Segal [SEG 87] and to the comonotonic independence of Chew and Wakker [CHE 96]; see also [CHE 89, QUI 82] and [WAK 94]. It is clearly much weaker than Savage's sure-thing principle, which requires no restriction on x_{i_0}'.

Remark 10.5. In the statement of axiom 10.8, the common modification of the two lotteries does not change the order of the common outcomes in their respective distributions. The corresponding random variables canonically associated with the distributions X and Y, taking values x_k and y_k respectively on sets E_k with probability p_k ($k = 1, \ldots, n$) stay comonotonic.

	Probabilities		
	0.01	0.89	0.1
L_1	1M	1M	1M
L_2	0	1M	5M
L'_1	1M	0	1M
L'_2	0	0	5M

Table 10.4. *Allais' lotteries*

To capture the real meaning of axiom 10.8, let us return to Allais' experiment where subjects have to choose first between L_1 and L_2 then (independently) between L'_1 and L'_2. The four different lotteries are described in Table 10.4.

The common modification from L_1 to L'_1 and from L_2 to L'_2 does not preserve the rank of the common outcome in both modified lotteries. More precisely, the common value 1M (with probability 0.89) in L_1 and L_2 corresponds to an intermediate value. The common value 0M (with the same probability) corresponds to the smallest value. Thus, the two choices L_1 and L'_2 do not contradict the previous comonotonic sure-thing principle.

This attractive axiom is central in the characterization of RDU. However, as in the case of CEU, this axiom fails to fully characterize RDU even when considered jointly with the standard axioms of weak order, continuity and monotony.

A complete characterization of RDU model can be obtained e.g. with the help of *non-contradictory comonotonic trade-offs* [WAK 94] or else with a *comonotonic mixture independence axiom*. The latter is an adaptation of mixture independence, which underlines the role played not only by comonotony but also by the extrema outcomes [CHA 99].

More precisely, Chateauneuf [CHA 99] adds axiom 10.9 to the usual axioms of weak order, monotony, continuity and the comonotonic sure-thing principle under risk in order to characterize the RDU model.

Axiom 10.9. *Comonotonic mixture independence*
For every p in $[0, 1]$,
  1) $P_1 = (1-p)\delta_{x_1} + p\delta_a \sim Q_1 = (1-p)\delta_{y_1} + p\delta_b$ *and*
  2) $P_2 = (1-p)\delta_{x_1} + p\delta_c \sim Q_2 = (1-p)\delta_{y_1} + p\delta_d$ *imply*
  3) $\alpha P_1 + (1-\alpha)P_2 \sim \alpha Q_1 + (1-\alpha)Q_2$ *for every α in $[0, 1]$.*
For every p in $[0, 1]$,
  4) $R_1 = (1-p)\delta_a + p\delta_{z_1} \sim S_1 = (1-p)\delta_b + p\delta_{t_1}$ *and*
  5) $R_2 = (1-p)\delta_c + p\delta_{z_1} \sim S_2 = (1-p)\delta_d + p\delta_{t_1}$ *imply*

6) $\alpha R_1 + (1-\alpha)R_2 \sim \alpha S_1 + (1-\alpha)S_2$ for every α in $[0,1]$.

Axiom 10.9 underlines the role played not only by comonotonicity but also by the security factors x_1 and y_1 in (1) and (2) and potential factors z_1 and t_1 in (4) and (5) [see COH 92, JAF 88].

10.4.3. From the CEU to the RDU model using first-order stochastic dominance [WAK 90]

Let us first show that the RDU representation can be viewed as a Choquet integral.

10.4.3.1. *RDU representation is a Choquet integral*

In the RDU model, the function f from $[0,1]$ to $[0,1]$ is increasing and satisfies $f(0) = 0$ and $f(1) = 1$. The corresponding 'transformed' probability foP is therefore a capacity and the RDU functional is a Choquet integral with respect to this capacity $v = foP$. More precisely,

$$V(Z) = \int_{Ch} u(Z) d(foP) = -\int_{-\infty}^{\infty} u(x) df(P(Z > x)) = -\int_{-\infty}^{\infty} u(x) df(1-F(x)).$$

Remark 10.6. Let us note that if f is a convex function, then $v = foP$ is a convex capacity [e.g. CHA 91, DEN 94]. Moreover, if f is below the diagonal (i.e. satisfies $f(p) \leq p$, $\forall p \in [0,1]$), then it can be easily seen that $core(v) \neq \phi$.

10.4.3.2. *From the CEU to the RDU*

It has been recognized by several authors [e.g. CHA 91, WAK 90] that the RDU model under risk can be derived from the CEU model under uncertainty simply by postulating the respect of first-order stochastic dominance. We will use this approach first to obtain Yaari's model from the simplified version of Schmeidler's model (section 10.2.3.1), then to obtain the RDU model from the Choquet expected utility model.

Being under risk, we suppose that the objective probability P is compatible with the preference relation on $(\mathbb{V}, \succeq)$. More precisely, we suppose the following axiom.

Axiom 10.10. *First-order stochastic dominance*

$$[A, B \in \mathcal{A}, P(A) \geq P(B)] \Rightarrow A \succeq B.$$

Let us note that axiom 10.10 is actually weaker than the first-order stochastic dominance axiom but proves to be equivalent in this framework.

10.4.3.2.1. From the simplified Schmeidler model to the Yaari model

Let us suppose that the preference relation on $(\mathbb{V}, \succeq)$ satisfies the comonotonic independence axiom 10.3 as well as the usual axioms of non-trivial weak-order, continuity and monotonicity. The preference relation is then represented by a Choquet integral with respect to a capacity v such that $A \succeq B$ implies $v(A) \geq v(B)$. The axioms then state that $P(A) \geq P(B)$ implies $v(A) \geq v(B)$.

This gives us an intuition of the result. There exists a unique transformed increasing function $f : [0,1] \to [0,1]$ satisfying $f(0) = 0, f(1) = 1$ such that $v = f \circ P$.

It can then be seen that the simplified Schmeidler model reduces to the Yaari model under the assumption of first-order stochastic dominance [CHA 94a, WAK 90].

10.4.3.2.2. From the general CEU model to the RDU model

Let us suppose that the preference relation on $(\mathbb{V}, \succeq)$ satisfies all the axioms to obtain the general CEU model characterized by v and u (see definition 10.5), then $A \succeq B$ implies $v(A) \geq v(B)$. Moreover, if the objective measure P on S satisfies first-order stochastic dominance then, since $P(A) \geq P(B)$ implies $v(A) \geq v(B)$, there exists a unique transformation function f such that $v = f \circ P$. We obtain the following result [WAK 90].

Let the preference relation on $(\mathbb{V}, \succeq)$ satisfy all the axioms to obtain general CEU, and let P be a probability distribution on S satisfying first-order stochastic dominance. Then the preference relation on $(\mathbb{V}, \succeq)$ can be represented by the RDU model.

10.4.4. Risk aversion notions and characterization in the RDU model

We defined two notions of risk aversion (RA) in Chapter 8: strong RA and weak RA. In the EU model, both notions have the same characterization: concavity of u. Let us recall these two notions here. The most natural way to define risk aversion is the following.

Definition 10.8. A decision maker is *weakly risk averse* if they always prefer to any random variable X the certainty of its expected value $E(X)$. They are *weakly risk seeking* if they always prefer any random variable X to the certainty of its expected value $E(X)$ and *risk neutral* if they are always indifferent between X and $E(X)$.

Another possible way to define some type of risk aversion is to define it as aversion to some type of (mean preserving) increase in risk. All kinds of stochastic orders can then generate many different kinds of risk aversion. There therefore exist many different definitions of risk aversion. However, their different meanings have been hidden by the fact that, under expected utility theory, all are equivalent. They all reduce to the concavity of the utility function (see section 8.4.3).

We now provide usual definitions of (mean preserving) increase in risk with corresponding definitions of risk aversion.

10.4.4.1. *Strong risk aversion*

Y is a general mean preserving increase in risk (MPIR) of X if

$$\int_{-\infty}^{t} F_Y(x)dx \geq \int_{-\infty}^{t} F_X(x)dx$$

for all $t \in \mathbb{R}$ and

$$\int_{-\infty}^{+\infty} F_Y(x)dx = \int_{-\infty}^{+\infty} F_X(x)dx.$$

This usual concept of (mean preserving) increasing risk is classically used in economics [ROT 70] and we define the corresponding notion of strong risk aversion as follows.

Definition 10.9. A decision maker is *strongly risk averse* if they are averse to any general (mean preserving) increase in risk, i.e. for any X and Y in $\mathbb{V}$ such that Y is a MPIR of X, X is preferred to Y. They are strongly risk seeking if Y is preferred to X and risk neutral if indifferent.

10.4.4.2. *Monotone risk aversion*

Quiggin [QUI 92] first noted that strong risk aversion may be too strong a concept and introduced a new notion, *monotone (mean-preserving) increase in risk*, defined in terms of comonotonic random variables instead of a general mean-preserving increase in risk.

Y is a (mean preserving) monotone increase in risk (MPMIR) of X if and only if $Y \stackrel{d}{=} X + Z$, where Z is such that $E(Z) = 0$ and X and Z are *comonotonic*. (Note that notation $\stackrel{}{\underset{d}{=}}$ represents equality of probability distributions.)

Before giving an important property of this notion, let us recall that $F^{-1}(p) = \inf\{z \in \mathbb{R} | F(z) \geq p\}$. We can then interpret $F^{-1}(p)$ as the highest gain among the least favorable $p\%$ of the outcomes.

Landsberger and Meilijson [LAN 94b] proved that for two random variables with equal mean this notion is equivalent to the statistical notion of 'dispersion' introduced by Bickel and Lehmann [BIC 76]: Y is *more dispersed than X* if

$$F_Y^{-1}(q) - F_Y^{-1}(p) \geq F_X^{-1}(q) - F_X^{-1}(p),$$

where F^{-1} is defined from $(0, 1]$ into $\mathbb{R}$ by

$$F^{-1}(p) = \inf\{z \in \mathbb{R} | F(z) \geq p\},$$

for all $0 < p < q < 1$. Thus, if Y is MPMIR of X, all the interquantile intervals are shorter for X than for Y. Let us then define the corresponding notion of monotone risk aversion.

Definition 10.10. A decision maker is *monotone risk averse* if averse to any monotone increase in risk i.e. for every pair (X, Y) where Y is MPMIR of X, they always prefer X to Y. They are monotone risk seeking if Y is always preferred to X and risk neutral if always indifferent between X and Y.

This notion of *monotone risk aversion* [e.g. COH 95] is particularly fitted to RDU theory where comonotony plays a fundamental part at the axiomatic level.

10.4.4.3. *Left monotone risk aversion*

The order induced by monotone increasing risk is a very partial order since it can order very few pairs of random variables. The following notion compares more pairs. This notion of increasing risk is asymmetric in the sense that it treats downside and upside risks differently. This notion will prove to be particularly suitable for deductible insurance [VER 97].

The following definition, due to Jewitt [JEW 89], was referred to as location-independent risk (see also Landsberger and Meilijson [LAN 94a]). (However, note that in the original definition the notion is given for X and Y with possibly different meanings.) The motivation of Jewitt was to find a notion of increase in risk that models coherent behavior in a context of partial insurance.

Y is said to be a *left monotone mean preserving increase in risk* (LIR) of X if

$$\int_{-\infty}^{F_Y^{-1}(p)} F_Y(x)dx \geq \int_{-\infty}^{F_X^{-1}(p)} F_X(x)dx$$

for all $p \in (0, 1)$. We define the corresponding notion of left monotone risk aversion as follows.

Definition 10.11. A decision maker is *left monotone risk averse* (respectively, left monotone risk seeking) if they are averse to any left monotone increase in risk, i.e. for any X and Y in $\mathbb{V}$ such that Y is a left monotone MPIR of X, X is preferred to Y (respectively, Y to X).

Remark 10.7. It can readily be seen that strong risk aversion $\Rightarrow$ left motone risk aversion $\Rightarrow$ monotone risk aversion $\Rightarrow$ weak risk aversion. The reverse implications are generally not true. However, in the EU model, all these notions are equivalent and are reduced to the concavity of u.

10.4.4.4. *Characterization of risk aversion notions in the RDU model*

Contrary to the EU model, each of the different notions of aversion to risk has a specific characterization in the RDU model. Machina [MACH 82a, MACH 82b] was the first to notice that the equivalence between different notions of risk aversion in the EU model does not carry over to generalized models. Gathering several results from different papers, we obtain the following results. Let an RDU decision maker be characterized by two differentiable functions u and f.

1) An RDU decision maker is *strongly risk averse* (respectively strongly risk seeking) if and only if the utility function u is concave and the transformation function f is convex (respectively u convex and f concave) [CHE 87]. Note that f convex implies that the capacity $f o P$ is convex.

2) An RDU decision maker is *left monotone risk averse* if and only if their transformation function f is star-shaped at 1 from above (i.e. if for any x of $\mathbb{R}_+$, $x < 1$, $(1 - f(x))/(1 - x)$ is increasing) and their utility function u is concave [CHA 04].

3) An RDU decision maker is *left monotone risk seeking* if and only if the transformation function f is star-shaped at 1 from below (i.e. if for any x of $\mathbb{R}_+$, $x < 1$, $(1 - f(x))/(1 - x)$ is decreasing) and the utility function u is convex [CHA 04].

4) The characterization of monotone risk aversion is based on two indices:

a)
$$P_f = \inf_{0<v<1} \left[\frac{1 - f(v)}{f(v)} \Big/ \frac{1 - v}{v} \right]$$

referred to as the index of *pessimism*, which is ≥ 1 as soon as $f(p) \leq p$ and

b)
$$G_u = \sup_{y \leq x} \frac{u'(x)}{u'(y)}$$

referred to as the index of *non-concavity* if u is not differentiable [CHA 97]. In this case G_u becomes more complex:

$$G_u = \sup_{x_1 < x_2 \leq x_3 < x_4} \left[\frac{u(x_4) - u(x_3)}{x_4 - x_3} \Big/ \frac{u(x_2) - u(x_1)}{x_2 - x_1} \right]$$

and is referred to as the index of *greediness*. $G_u \geq 1$ is always satisfied and the value 1 corresponds exclusively to concavity.

An RDU decision maker with probability transformation function f and differentiable utility u is *monotone risk averse* if and only if their index of pessimism is greater than their index of non-concavity, i.e. $P_f \geq G_u$ [CHA 05]. The most significant feature of this result is that a decision maker does not need to have a concave utility function u to be monotone risk averse.

5) The characterization of monotone risk seeking is based on two indices:

a)
$$O_f = \inf_{0<v<1} \left[\frac{f(v)}{1 - f(v)} \Big/ \frac{v}{1 - v} \right]$$

referred to as the index of *optimism*, which is ≥ 1 as soon as $f(p) > p$, and
b)
$$T_u = \sup_{x<y} \frac{u'(x)}{u'(y)}$$
referred to as the index of *non-convexity*, which always satisfies $T_u \geq 1$ and the value 1 corresponds exclusively to convexity.

A RDEU decision maker with probability perception function f and utility function u is *monotone risk seeking* if and only if the decision maker's index of optimism exceeds the index of non-convexity: i.e. $O_f \geq T_u$.

6) For a weakly risk-averse RDU decision maker, there is no known characterization but sufficient conditions, not implying concavity of u [CHA 94b].

An interesting point can be made from all these results. RDU models not only allow the separation of transformation of probability from valuation of outcomes but also explain diversified behaviors e.g. weakly risk seeking with a diminishing marginal utility of wealth or a dislike of risk (to be weakly risk averse) while accepting a (mean preserving) increase in risk i.e. without being a strongly risk-averse decision maker.

All the cardinal extensions of the EU model proposed in this chapter allow a better representation of real behavior under uncertainty.

Recent years have shown an increase in interest in new cardinal generalizations of the subjective EU model, building upon the Choquet models initiated by Schmeidler, Quiggin and Yaari. The interested reader should see [CHA 07, GAJ 08, GHI 04, GHI 05, GIL 04, KLI 05, MAC 06]. In the following chapter, we shall investigate 'ordinal' extensions of the EU model.

10.5. Bibliography

[ALL 53] Allais M. "Le comportement de l'homme rationnel devant le risque: critique des postulats et axiomes de l'école américaine". *Econometrica*, vol. 21, 503–546, 1953.

[ALL 88] Allais M. "The general theory of random choices in relation to the invariant cardinal utility function and the specific probability function" In *Risk, Decision and Rationality*, B. R. Munier (Ed.), Reidel: Dordrecht, 233–289, 1988.

[ANS 63] Anscombe F.J. and Aumann R.J. "A definition of subjective probability". *Annals of Mathematical Statistics*, vol. 34, 199–205, 1963.

[BIC 76] Bickel P.J. and Lehmann E.L. "Descriptive statistics for non-parametric models, III. Dispersion". *Annals of Statistics*, vol. 4, 1139–1158, 1976.

[CHA 91] Chateauneuf A. "On the use of capacities in modeling uncertainty aversion and risk aversion". *Journal of Mathematical Economics*, vol. 20, 343–369, 1991.

[CHA 94a] Chateauneuf A. "Modeling attitudes towards uncertainty and risk through the use of Choquet integral". *Annals of Operations Research*, vol. 52, 3–20, 1994.

[CHA 94b] Chateauneuf A. and Cohen M.D. "Risk-seeking with diminishing marginal utility in a non-expected utility model". *Journal of Risk and Uncertainty*, vol. 9, 77–91, 1994.

[CHA 97] Chateauneuf A., Cohen M.D. and Kast R. "A review of some results related to comonotony". *Cahiers d'Ecomath*, vol. 97(32), 1–29, 1997.

[CHA 99] Chateauneuf A. "Comonotonicity axioms and RDU theory for arbitrary consequences". *Journal of Mathematical Economics*, vol. 32, 21–45, 1999.

[CHA 02] Chateauneuf A. and Tallon J.M. "Diversification, convex preferences and non-empty core in the Choquet expected utility model". *Economic Theory*, vol. 19, 509–523, 2002.

[CHA 04] Chateauneuf A., Cohen M.D. and Meilijson I. "Four notions of mean-preserving increase in risk, risk attitudes and applications to the Rank-Dependent Expected Utility Model". *Journal of Mathematical Economics*, vol. 40, 547–571, 2004.

[CHA 05] Chateauneuf A., Cohen M.D. and Meilijson I. "More pessimism than greediness: A characterization of monotone risk aversion in the Rank Dependent Expected Utility model". *Economic Theory*, vol. 25(3), 649–668, 2005.

[CHA 07] Chateauneuf A., Eichberger J. and Grant S. "Choice Under uncertainty with the best and worst in mind: Neo-additive capacities". *Journal of Economic Theory*, vol. 137, 538–567, 2007.

[CHE 89] Chew S. and Epstein L. "A unifying approach to axiomatic non-expected utility theory". *Journal of Economic Theory,* vol. 49, 207–240, 1989.

[CHE 96] Chew S. and Wakker P. "The comonotonic sure-thing principle". *Journal of Risk and Uncertainty*, vol. 12, 5–27, 1996.

[CHE 87] Chew S., Karni E. and Safra. Z. "Risk aversion in the theory of expected utility with Rank Dependent preferences". *Journal of Economic Theory*, vol. 42, 370–381, 1987.

[CHE 93] Chew S., Epstein L. and Wakker P. "A unifying approach to axiomatic non-expected utility theory: correction and comment". *Journal of Economic Theory*, vol. 59, 183–188, 1993.

[CHO 53] Choquet G. "Théorie des capacités". *Annals of Fourier Institute* (Grenoble), vol. V, 131–295, 1953.

[COH 92] Cohen M.D. "Security level, potential level, expected utility : a three-criteria decision model under risk". *Theory and Decision*, vol. 33(2), 1–34, 1992.

[COH 95] Cohen M. D. "Risk aversion concepts in expected and non-expected utility models". *The Geneva Papers on Risk and Insurance Theory*, vol. 20, 73–91, 1995.

[DEM 67] Dempster A.P. "Upper and lower probabilities induced by a multivalued mapping". *Annals of Mathematical Statistics*, vol. 38, 325–339, 1967.

[DEN 94] Denneberg D. *Non-additive Measure and Integral*. Kluwer Academic Publishers, Dordrecht, 1994.

[ELL 61] Ellsberg D. "Risk, ambiguity and the Savage axioms". *Quarterly Journal of Economics*, vol. 75, 643–669, 1961.

[GAJ 08] Gajdos T., Hayashi T., Tallon J.-M. and Vergnaud J.-C. "Attitude toward imprecise information". *Journal of Economic Theory*, vol. 140, 27–65, 2008.

[GHI 04] Ghirardato P., Macceroni F. and Marinacci M. "Differentiating ambiguity and ambiguity attitude". *Journal of Economic Theory*, vol. 118, 133–173, 2004.

[GHI 05] Ghirardato P., Macceroni F. and Marinacci M. "Certainty independence and the separation of utility and beliefs". *Journal of Economic Theory*, vol. 120, 129–136, 2005.

[GIL 87] Gilboa I. "Expected utility with purely subjective non-additive probabilities". *Journal of Mathematical Economics*, vol. 16, 65–88, 1987.

[GIL 04] Gilboa I. (Ed). *Uncertainty in Economic Theory, Essays in Honor of David Schmeidler's 65th Birthday*. Routledge, 2004.

[GIL 89] Gilboa I. and Schmeidler D. "Maxmin expected utility with a non-unique prior". *Journal of Mathematical Economics*, vol. 18, 141–153, 1989.

[GRE 88] Green J. and Jullien B. "Ordinal independence in non-linear utility theory". *Journal of Risk and Uncertainty*, vol. 1, 355–387, 1988.

[JAF 88] Jaffray J.Y. "Choice under risk and the security factor. An axiomatic model". *Theory and Decision*, vol. 24(2), 169–200, 1988.

[JAF 89a] Jaffray J.Y. "Généralisation du critère de l'utilité espérée aux choix dans l'incertain régulier". *Recherche Opérationnelle*, vol. 23, 237–267, 1989a.

[JAF 89b] Jaffray J.Y. "Linear utility for belief functions". *Operations Research Letters*, vol. 8, 107–112, 1989b.

[JAF 97] Jaffray J.Y. and Philippe F. "On the existence of subjective upper and lower probabilities". *Mathematics of Operations Research*, vol. 22, 165–185, 1997.

[JEW 89] Jewitt I. "Choosing between risky prospects: the characterization of comparative statics results, and location independent risk". *Management Science*, vol. 35, 60–70, 1989.

[KAH 79] Kahneman D. and Tversky A. "Prospect theory: an analysis of decision under risk". *Econometrica*, vol. 47, 263–291, 1979.

[KLI 05] Klibanoff P., Marinacci M. and Mukerji S. "A Smooth Model of Decision Making under Ambiguity". *Econometrica*, vol. 73(6), 1849–1892, 2005.

[LAN 94a] Landsberger M. and Meilijson. I. "The generating process and an extension of Jewitt's location independent risk concept", *Management Science*, vol. 40, p. 662–669, 1994a.

[LAN 94b] Landsberger M. and Meilijson I. "Comonotone allocations, Bickel-Lehmann dispersion and the Arrow-Pratt measure of risk aversion". *Annals of Operations Research*, vol. 52, 97–106, 1994b.

[MAC 06] Macceroni F., Marinacci M. and Rustichini A. "Ambiguity aversion, robustness, and the variational representation of preferences". *Econometrica*, vol. 74(6), 1447–1498, 2006.

[MACH 82a] Machina M. "Expected utility analysis without the independence axiom". *Econometrica*, vol. 50, 277–323, 1982a.

[MACH 82b] Machina M. "A stronger characterization of declining risk aversion". *Econometrica*, vol. 50(4), 1069–1079, 1982b.

[MACH 92] Machina M. and Schmeidler D. "A more robust definition of subjective probability". *Econometrica*, vol. 60, 745–780, 1992.

[QUI 82] Quiggin J. "A theory of anticipated utility". *Journal of Economic Behavior and Organisation*, vol. 3, 323–343, 1982.

[QUI 92] Quiggin J. "Increasing risk: another definition". In *Progress in Decision, Utility and Risk Theory*, A. Chikan (Ed.), Dordrecht: Kluwer, 1992.

[ROT 70] Rothschild M. and Stiglitz J. "Increasing Risk: I. A definition". *Journal of Economic Theory*, vol. 2, 225–243, 1970.

[SAV 54] Savage L. *The Foundations of Statistics*. New York. Wiley, (Second edition 1972, Dover), 1954.

[SCH 86] Schmeidler D. "Integral representation without additivity". *Proceedings of the American Mathematical Society*, vol. 97, 255–261, 1986.

[SCH 89] Schmeidler D. "Subjective probability and expected utility without additivity". *Econometrica*, vol. 57, 517–587, 1989.

[SEG 87] Segal U. "Anticipated utility: a measure representation approach". *Annals of Operations Research*, vol. 19, 359–374, 1987.

[SEG 93] Segal U. "The measure representation: A correction". *Journal of Risk and Uncertainty*, vol. 6, 99–107, 1993.

[SHA 76] Shafer G. *A Mathematical Theory of Evidence*. Princeton University Press, Princeton, NJ, 1976.

[VER 97] Vergnaud J.C. "Analysis of risk in a non-expected utility framework and applications to the optimality of the deductible". *Revue Finance*, vol. 18(1), 155–167, 1997.

[VON 47] Von Neumann J. and Morgenstern O. *Theory of Games and Economic Behavior*. Princeton University Press, Princeton, NJ, 1947.

[WAK 89] Wakker P. "Continuous subjective expected utility with non-additive probabilities". *Journal of Mathematical Economics*, vol. 18(1), 1–27, 1989.

[WAK 90] Wakker P. "Under Stochastic Dominance Choquet Expected Utility and Anticipated Utility are identical". *Theory and Decision*, vol. 29, 119–132, 1990.

[WAK 94] Wakker P. "Separating marginal utility and risk aversion". *Theory and Decision*, vol. 36, 1–44, 1994.

[YAA 87] Yaari M. "The dual theory of choice under risk". *Econometrica*, vol. 55, 95–115, 1987.

Chapter 11

A Survey of Qualitative Decision Rules under Uncertainty

11.1. Introduction

Traditionally, decision making under uncertainty (DMU) relies on a probabilistic framework. When modeling a decision maker's rational choice between acts, it is assumed that the uncertainty about the state of the world is described by a probability distribution, and that the ranking of acts is carried out according to the expected utility of the consequences of these acts. This proposal was made by economists in the 1950s, and justified on an axiomatic basis by Savage [SAV 54] and his school (see Chapter 9). More recently, in artificial intelligence, this setting has been applied to problems of planning under uncertainty, and is at the root of the influence diagram methodology for multiple stage decision problems (see Chapters 13 and 14).

However, in parallel to these developments, artificial intelligence has witnessed the emergence of a new decision paradigm called *qualitative decision theory* [DOY 99], where the rationale for choosing among decisions no longer relies on probability theory nor on numerical utility functions. Motivations for this new proposal are twofold. There exists a tradition of symbolic processing of information in artificial intelligence, and it is not surprising this tradition should try and stick to symbolic approaches when dealing with decision problems. Formulating decision problems in a symbolic way may be more compatible with a declarative expression of uncertainty and preferences in the setting of some logic-based language [BOU 94, THO 00].

Chapter written by Didier DUBOIS, Hélène FARGIER, Henri PRADE and Régis SABBADIN.

In addition, the emergence of new information technologies such as information systems or autonomous robots has generated many new decision problems involving intelligent agents [BRA 97]. An information system is supposed to help an end user retrieve information and choose between courses of action, based on a limited knowledge of the user needs. It is not clear that numerical approaches to DMU, developed in the framework of economics, are fully adapted to these new problems. Expected utility theory might sound too sophisticated a tool for handling queries of end users. Numerical utility functions and subjective probabilities presuppose a rather elaborate elicitation process that is worth launching for making complex decisions that need to be carefully analyzed [see BOU 00].

Users of information systems are not necessarily capable of describing their state of uncertainty by means of a probability distribution, nor may they be willing to quantify their preferences [BOU 94]. This is typical of electronic commerce, or recommender systems (that provide advice or suggestions) for example.

In many cases, it sounds more satisfactory to implement a choice method that is fast and based on rough information about the user preferences and knowledge. Moreover, the expected utility criterion makes full sense for repeated decisions whose successive results accumulate (for instance money in gambling decisions). In contrast, some decisions made by end users are rather one-shot, in the sense that obtaining wrong advice one day cannot always be compensated by good advice the next. Note that this kind of application often needs multiple-criteria decision making rather than DMU. However, there is a strong similarity between the two problems [DUB 00b], and some notions and results in this chapter can be expressed in the setting of multiple-criteria decision making.

In the case of autonomous robots, conditional plans are often used to monitor the robot behavior and the environment of the robots is sometimes only partially observable. The theory of partially observable Markov decision processes leads to highly complex methods due to handling infinite state spaces. A qualitative, finitistic, description of the goals of the robot and of its knowledge of the environment might lead to more tractable methods [e.g. SAB 01]. Besides, the expected utility criterion is often adopted because of its mathematical properties (it enables dynamic programming principles to be used). However, it is not clear that this criterion is always the most cogent one e.g. cautious policies should be followed in risky environments. Dynamic programming techniques are also compatible with qualitative settings such as possibility theory (see [DUB 05, FAR 98] and Chapter 14).

There is a need for qualitative decision rules. However, there is no real agreement on what 'qualitative' means. Some authors assume incomplete knowledge about classical additive utility models, whereby the utility function is specified via symbolic constraints [e.g. BAC 96, LAN 96]. Others use sets of integers and the like to describe rough probabilities or utilities [GIA 00, TAN 94]. Lehmann [LEH 01] injects some qualitative concepts of negligibility in the classical expected utility framework. However, some approaches are genuinely qualitative in the sense that they do not involve any form of quantification. We take it for granted that a qualitative decision theory is one that does not resort to the full expressive power of numbers for the modeling of uncertainty, nor for the representation of utility.

This chapter proposes an overview of qualitative decision theory, focused on discussing the rationale of the various possible decision rules and their properties. It is stressed that two kinds of approach exist, according to whether degrees of uncertainty and degrees of utility are commensurate (i.e. belong to a unique measurement scale) or not. Savage-like axiomatics are proposed for each of these two approaches. In this setting, acts are modeled as functions from the set of states to the set of consequences, and decision rules stem from properties which the preference relation over acts is requested to satisfy.

The natural uncertainty theory at work in qualitative frameworks is generally possibility theory rather than probability theory. However, qualitative decision rules are often either indecisive (due to incomparability incurred or ties) or too adventurous (concentrating on most plausible states of nature and neglecting other ones). Some rules lack discrimination simply because the measurement scale is too coarse. Recent results show how to refine some criteria, using a specific form of standard expected utility encoding lexicographic refinements.

The chapter is organized as follows. A survey of qualitative decision rules is proposed, including those that assume commensurability between utility and uncertainty (section 11.2). Section 11.3 then motivates a decision rule that does not presuppose it, and shows its potential limitations. Section 11.4 presents Savage-like representation results for such qualitative decision rules, on the basis of axioms expressing properties of the preference relation between acts. Finally, section 11.5 explains how to refine them in order to tackle this weakness, acknowledging the lack of discrimination power of qualitative decision rules.

11.2. Quantitative versus qualitative decision rules

A decision problem can be cast in the following framework: consider a set S of states (of the world) and a set X of potential consequences of decisions. States encode possible situations, states of affairs, etc. An act is viewed as a mapping f from the state space to the consequence set, namely, in each state $s \in S$, an act f produces a well-defined result $f(s) \in X$. The decision maker must rank acts without knowing what is the current state of the world in a precise way. The consequences of an act can often be ranked in terms of their relative appeal: some consequences are judged better than others. This is often modeled by means of a numerical utility function u which assigns a utility value $u(x) \in \mathbb{R}$ to each consequence $x \in X$.

Classically, there are two approaches when modeling the lack of knowledge of the decision maker about the state of affairs. The most widely-found assumption is that there is a probability distribution p on S. It is either obtained from statistics (this is called decision under risk, Von Neumann and Morgenstern [NEU 47]; see Chapter 8) or it is a subjective probability [SAV 54] supplied by the agent via suitable elicitation methods. Then the most usual decision rule is based on the expected utility criterion:

$$EU_{p,u}(f) = \sum_{s \in S} p(s)u(f(s)). \tag{11.1}$$

An act f is strictly preferred to act g if and only if $EU_{p,u}(f) > EU_{p,u}(g)$. The expected utility criterion is by far the most commonly used. This criterion makes sense especially for repeated decisions whose results accumulate. It also clearly presupposes subjective notions like belief and preference to be precisely quantified. In particular, in the expected utility model, the way in which the preference on consequences is numerically encoded will affect the induced preference relation on acts. The model exploits some extra information not contained solely in preference relations on X, namely, the absolute order of magnitude of utility grades. Moreover, the same numerical scale is used for utilities and degrees of probability. This is based on the notion *certainty equivalent*, i.e. the idea that a lottery (involving uncertainty) can be compared to a sure gain or a sure loss (involving utility only) in terms of preference.

Another proposal is the maximin criterion often credited to Wald [WAL 50]. It applies when no information about the current state is available, and it ranks acts according to its worst consequence:

$$W_u^-(f) = \min_{s \in S} u(f(s)). \tag{11.2}$$

It is a (very) pessimistic criterion. An optimistic counterpart $W_u^+(f)$ to W_u^- is obtained by turning minimum into maximum in equation (11.2). Clearly, the maximin and maximax criteria do not need numerical utility values. Only a total ordering on consequences is needed. No knowledge about the state of the world is necessary. However, these criterion have the major defect of being extremely pessimistic and over-optimistic, respectively. In practice, they are never used for this reason. Hurwicz has proposed to use a weighted average of $W_u^-(f)$ and its optimistic counterpart, where the weight bearing on $W_u^+(f)$ is viewed as a degree of optimism of the decision maker. Other decision rules have been proposed, especially some that generalize both $EU_{p,u}(f)$ and W_u^- (see [JAF 89, SCH 89] and Chapter 10). However, all these extensions again require the quantification of preferences and/or uncertainty.

Qualitative extensions of the maximin criterion, which account for some knowledge about the state of affairs, nevertheless exist. Boutilier [BOU 94] is inspired by preferential inference of non-monotonic reasoning, whereby a proposition A entails another one B by default if B is true in the most normal situations where A is true. He assumes that states of nature are ordered in terms of their relative plausibility using a weak order relation $\trianglerighteq$ on S. He proposes to make decisions on the basis of the most plausible states of nature in accordance with the available information, neglecting other states. If the available information is that $s \in A$, a subset of states, and if A^* is the set of maximal elements in A according to the plausibility ordering $\trianglerighteq$, then the criterion is defined by

$$W^-_{\trianglerighteq,u}(f) = \min_{s \in A^*} u(f(s)). \tag{11.3}$$

Another refinement of the Wald criterion is the possibilistic qualitative criterion. It is based on a utility function u on X and a possibility distribution π on S [DUB 88a, DUB 98b], both mapping on the same totally ordered value scale V, with top 1 and bottom 0. The ordinal value $\pi(s)$ represents the relative plausibility of state $s \in S$. A pessimistic criterion $W^-_{\pi,u}(f)$ is proposed of the form [DUB 95b]:

$$W^-_{\pi,u}(f) = \min_{s \in S} \max(\nu(\pi(s)), u(f(s))). \tag{11.4}$$

Here, V is equipped with its involutive order-reversing map ν; in particular $\nu(1) = 0$, $\nu(0) = 1$. $\nu(\pi(s))$ therefore represents the degree of potential surprise [SHA 61] caused if the state of the world were s. In particular, $\nu(\pi(s)) = 1$ for impossible states. The value of $W^-_{\pi,u}(f)$ is small as soon as there exists a highly plausible state ($\nu(\pi(s)) = 0$) with low utility value. This criterion is actually a prioritized extension of the Wald maximin criterion $W^-_u(f)$. The latter is recovered if $\pi(s) = 1$ for all $s \in S$. The decisions are again made according to the merits of acts in their worst consequences, now restricted to the most plausible states, such as equation (11.3). However, the set of most plausible states $S^* = \{s, \pi(s) \geq \nu(W^-_{\pi,u}(f))\}$ now depends on the act itself. It is defined by the compromise between belief and utility expressed in the min-max expression. However, contrary to the other qualitative criteria, the possibilistic qualitative criterion presupposes that degrees of utility $u(f(s))$ and possibility $\pi(s)$ share the same scale and can be compared.

The optimistic counterpart to this criterion [DUB 95b] is:

$$W^+_{\pi,u}(f) = \max_{s \in S} \min(\pi(s), u(f(s))). \tag{11.5}$$

This expression is due to Zadeh [ZAD 78] but its interpretation as a decison criterion was first proposed by Yager [YAG 79]. The pessimistic criterion was first proposed as such by Whalen [WHA 84]. Similar ideas have actually appeared in the works of Shackle [SHA 49], a forerunner of possibility theory.

These two criteria have been used for a long time in fuzzy information processing for the purpose of triggering fuzzy rules in expert systems [CAY 82] and flexible querying of an incomplete information database [DUB 88b]. They were used in scheduling under flexible constraints and uncertain task durations, when minimizing the risk of delayed jobs [DUB 95a].

These optimistic and pessimistic possibilistic criteria are actually particular cases of a more general criterion based on the Sugeno integral [SUG 74], a qualitative counterpart to the Choquet integral used in extensions of expected utility approaches; see [GRA 00a] and Chapter 17. One expression of this criterion can be written as follows:

$$S_{\gamma,u}(f) = \max_{\lambda \in V} \min(\lambda, \gamma(F_\lambda)) \tag{11.6}$$

where $F_\lambda = \{s \in S, u(f(s)) \geq \lambda\}$ is a set of preferred states for act f and $\gamma(A)$ is the degree of likelihood of event A. The set-function γ reflects the decision maker attitude in uncertainty. This expression achieves a trade-off between the degrees of likelihood of preferred events and the figures of merit of the worst consequences when they occur. If the set of states is rearranged in decreasing order of merit via f in such a way that $u(f(s_1)) \geq \ldots \geq u(f(s_n))$, then denoting $A_i = \{s_1, \ldots, s_i\}$, it turns out that $S_{\gamma,u}(f)$ is the median of the set

$$\{u(f(s_1)), \ldots, u(f(s_n))\} \cup \{\gamma(A_1), \ldots, \gamma(A_{n-1})\}.$$

For instance, consider act f resulting in a good consequence x if event A occurs and a bad consequence y (with $u(x) > u(y)$) otherwise. It is easily seen that $S_{\gamma,u}(f)$ is the median of $\{u(x), u(y), \gamma(A)\}$. In other words:

– if A is likely enough, $\gamma(A) \geq u(x)$ and $S_{\gamma,u}(f) = u(x)$, then the decision maker thinks they can get x;

– if A is unlikely to a sufficient degree, $\gamma(A) \leq u(y)$ and $S_{\gamma,u}(f) = u(y)$, then the decision maker thinks they can get only y;

– otherwise ($u(x) > \gamma(A) > u(y)$), the value of act f exactly reflects the likelihood of the successful event ($S_{\gamma,u}(f) = \gamma(A)$).

In this approach, the attitude of the decision maker in uncertainty is encoded by the choice of a likelihood function γ. If optimistic, they select a possibility measure $\gamma = \Pi$, i.e. a function $\Pi(A) = \max_{s \in A} \pi(s)$, where $\pi(s) \in V$ is the grade of plausibility of event A. $\Pi(A) = 1$ as soon as the decision maker thinks the opposite event A^c of A has no certainty of occurring. They then bet on the occurrence of A, hence $S_{\gamma,u}(f) = u(x)$ (more generally $S_{\Pi,u} = W^+_{\pi,u}$). If pessimistic, they select a necessity measure $\gamma = N$, adjoint to a possibility measure: $N(A) = 1 - \Pi(A^c)$, which evaluates the grade of certainty of A. $N(A) = 0$ as soon as the decision maker is uncertain about A. They then bet on the non-occurrence of A. Then $S_{\gamma,u}(f) = u(y)$ (more generally $S_{N,u} = W^-_{\pi,u}$).

11.3. Ordinal decision rule without commensurateness

Several of the above decision rules presuppose that utility functions and uncertainty functions share the same range, so it makes sense to write $\min(\pi(s), u(f(s)))$ for instance. In contrast, one may look for a natural decision rule that computes a preference relation on acts from a purely symbolic perspective, no longer assuming that utility and partial belief are commensurate, that is, share the same totally ordered scale [DUB 97]. The decision maker then only supplies a likelihood relation $\succeq_L$ between events and a preference relation $\succeq_P$ on consequences. The strict part $\succ_L$ of the likelihood relation $\succeq_L$ is defined by $A \succ_L B$ if and only if $A \succeq_L B$, but not $B \succeq_L A$, and the indifference relation $\sim_L$ induced by $\succeq_L$ is defined in the usual way: $A \sim_L B$ if and only if $A \succeq_L B$ and $B \succeq_L A$. $A \succeq_L B$ means that event A is at least as likely as B.

In the most realistic model, the strict part $\succ_L$ of a likelihood relation on the set of events is irreflexive, transitive and non-trivial ($S \succ_L \emptyset$). Moreover, it should be faithful to deductive inference, which means for the strict part of the likelihood relation:

$$\forall A, B, C, D, A \succ_L B \text{ implies } A \cup C \succ_L B \cap D.$$

Finally, if $A \subseteq B$ then it should hold that $B \succeq_L A$ (inclusion-monotony). The inclusion-monotony property states that if A implies B, then A cannot be more likely than B. Let $s_i \trianglerighteq s_j$ denote the plausibility relation between states induced by $\succeq_L$ on elements of S.

The preference relation on the set of consequences X is assumed to be a weak order (a complete preordering, e.g. see Chapter 2). Namely, $\succeq_P$ is a reflexive and transitive relation, and completeness means $x \succeq_P y$ or $y \succeq_P x$. $x \succeq_P y$ therefore means that consequence x is not worse than y. The induced strict preference relation is derived as usual: $x \succ_P y$ if and only if $x \succeq_P y$ and not $y \succeq_P x$. It is assumed that X has at least two elements x and y such that $x \succ_P y$. The assumptions pertaining to $\succeq_P$ are natural in the scope of numerical representations of utility, however, we do not require that the likelihood relation is also a weak order.

If the likelihood relation on events and the preference relation on consequences are not comparable, a natural way of lifting the pair $(\succ_L, \succeq_P)$ to X^S is as follows: an act f is more promising than an act g if and only if the event formed by the disjunction of states in which f gives better results than g is more likely than the event formed by the disjunction of states in which g gives results better than f. A state s is more promising for act f than for act g if and only if $f(s) \succ_P g(s)$. Let $[f \succ_P g]$ be an event made of all states where f outperforms g, that is $[f \succ_P g] = \{s \in S, f(s) \succ_P g(s)\}$. Accordingly, we define the preference between acts $\succeq$, the corresponding indifference $\sim$ and strict preference $\succ$ relations as follows:

- $f \succ g$ if and only if $[f \succ_P g] \succ_L [g \succ_P f]$;

– $f \succeq g$ if and only if $\neg(g \succ f)$, i.e. if and only if $[f \succ_P g] \succeq_L [g \succ_P f]$; and
– $f \sim g$ if and only if $f \succeq g$ and $g \succeq f$.

This is the Likely Dominance rule [DUB 97]. It is the first one that comes to mind when information is only available under the form of an ordering of events and an ordering of consequences and when the preference and uncertainty scales are not comparable. Events are only compared to events, and consequences to consequences. The properties of the relations $\succeq, \sim$ and $\succ$ on X^S will depend on the properties of $\succeq_L$ with respect to Boolean connectives. An interesting remark is that if $\succeq_L$ is a comparative probability ordering then the strict preference relation $\succ$ in X^S is not necessarily transitive, nor acyclic.

Example 11.1. A very classical and simple example of undesirable lack of transitivity is when $S = \{s_1, s_2, s_3\}$ and $X = \{x_1, x_2, x_3\}$ with $x_1 \succ_P x_2 \succ_P x_3$, and the comparative probability ordering is generated by a uniform probability on S. Suppose three acts f, g, h are such that

– $f(s_1) = x_1 \succ_P f(s_2) = x_2 \succ_P f(s_3) = x_3$,
– $g(s_3) = x_1 \succ_P g(s_1) = x_2 \succ_P g(s_2) = x_3$,
– $h(s_2) = x_1 \succ_P h(s_3) = x_2 \succ_P h(s_1) = x_3$.

Then $[f \succ_P g] = \{s_1, s_2\}$; $[g \succ_P f] = \{s_3\}$; $[g \succ_P h] = \{s_1, s_3\}$; $[h \succ_P g] = \{s_2\}$ and $[f \succ_P h] = [h \succ_P f] = \{s_2, s_3\}$. The likely dominance rule yields $f \succ g, g \succ h, h \succ f$ (while, of course, $f \succ f$ does not hold). Note that the presence of this cycle does not depend on figures of utility that could be attached to consequences to the extent that the ordering of utility values is respected for each state. Moreover, the undesirable cycle remains as long as probabilities $p(s_1) > p(s_2) > p(s_3)$ of states remain close to each other, so that $p(s_i) + p(s_j) > p(s_k), \forall i, j, k$ distinct. In contrast, the ranking of acts induced by expected utility completely depends on the choice of utility values, even if we keep the constraint $u(x_1) > u(x_2) > u(x_3)$. The reader can check that, by symmetry, any of the three linear orders $f \succ g \succ h, g \succ h \succ f, h \succ f \succ g$ can be obtained by the expected utility criterion, by suitably quantifying the utility values of states without changing their preference ranking.

This situation can be viewed as a counterpart to the Condorcet paradox in social choice. Indeed, the problem of ranking acts can be cast in the setting of a voting problem (see [MOU 88] and Chapter 19). Let $\mathcal{V}$ be a set of voters, C be a set of candidates and let $\succeq_i$ be a relation on C that represents the preference of voter i on the set of candidates. $\succeq_i$ is a weak order, by assumption. The decision method consists of constructing a relation R on C that aggregates the relations $\{\succeq_i, i \in V\}$ as follows.

Let $\mathcal{V}(c_1, c_2) = \{i \in \mathcal{V}, c_1 \succ_i c_2\}$ be the set of voters who find c_1 more valuable than c_2, and $|\mathcal{V}(c_1, c_2)|$ the cardinality of that set. Then the social preference relation

Qualitative Decision Rules under Uncertainty   443

R on C is defined as follows by Condorcet: $c_1 R c_2$ if and only if $|\mathcal{V}(c_1, c_2)| > |\mathcal{V}(c_2, c_1)|$.

This is the so-called pairwise majority rule. It is well known that such a relation is often not transitive and may contain cycles. More generally, Arrow [ARR 51] proved that the transitivity of R is impossible under natural requirements on the voting procedure such as independence of irrelevant alternatives, unanimity, and non-dictatorship (i.e. there should be no voter i enforcing their preference relation: $R \neq \succeq_i, \forall i \in \mathcal{V}$).

Condorcet procedure is therefore a special case of the likely dominance rule based on a uniform probability distribution, letting $\mathcal{V} = S, C = X^S$, and considering for each $s \in S$ the relation R on acts such that $\forall f, g \in X^S : f \succeq_s g$ if and only if $f(s) \succ_P g(s)$. Computing the probability $Prob([f \succ_P g])$ is a weighted version of $|V(c_1, c_2)|$ with $\mathcal{V} = S, c_1 = f, c_2 = g$, which explains the intransitivity phenomenon. Such weighted extensions of Condorcet procedure are commonly found in multicriteria decision making [VIN 92]. However, the likely dominance rule makes sense for any inclusion-monotonic likelihood relation between events and is then much more general than the Condorcet pairwise majority rule even in its weighted version.

Assume now that a decision maker supplies a weak order of states $\triangleright$ and a weak order of consequences $\succeq_P$ on X. Let $\succeq_\Pi$ be the induced possibilistic ordering of events [DUB 86, LEW 73]. Namely, denote any (most plausible) state $s \in A$ by $\max(A)$ such that $s \triangleright s', \forall s \in A$. Then define $A \succeq_\Pi B$ if and only if $\max(A) \trianglerighteq \max(B)$. The preference acts in accordance with the likely dominance rule, for any two acts f and g, is: $f \succ g$ if and only if $[f \succ_P g] \succ_\Pi [g \succ_P f]$; $f \succeq g$ if and only if $\neg(g \succ f)$. Then, the undesirable intransitivity of the strict preference vanishes.

Example 11.1. (continued)
Consider again the 3-state + 3-consequence example. If a uniform probability is changed into a uniform possibility distribution, then it is easy to check that the likely dominance rule yields $f \sim g \sim h$. However, if $s_1 \triangleright s_2 \triangleright s_3$ then

- $[f \succ_P g] = \{s_1, s_2\} \succ_\Pi [g \succ_P f] = \{s_3\}$;
- $[g \succ_P h] = \{s_1, s_3\} \succ_\Pi [h \succ_P g] = \{s_2\}$;
- $[f \succ_P h] = \{s_1\} \succ_\Pi [h \succ_P f] = \{s_2, s_3\}$.

So $f \succ g \succ h$ follows. It contrasts with the cycles obtained with a probabilistic approach. However the indifference relation between acts is generally not transitive.

Let us study the likely dominance rule induced by a single possibility distribution (and the possibilistic likelihood relation it induces):

1) If the decision maker is ignorant about the state of the world, all states and all events are equipossible except for $\emptyset$. If f and g are such that $[g \succ_P f] \neq \emptyset$ and $[f \succ_P g] \neq \emptyset$, then neither $f \succ g$ nor $g \succ f$ holds, following the likely dominance rule. The case when $[f \succ_P g] \neq \emptyset$ and $[g \succ_P f] = \emptyset$ corresponds to when f Pareto-dominates g, i.e. $f \succeq_P g$ and $\exists s \in S, f(s) \succ_P g(s)$. The preference relation induced on acts by the likely dominance rule then reduces to Pareto-dominance. This method, although natural, is not at all decisive (it corresponds to a unanimity rule in voting theories).

2) Conversely, if there is a total ordering $s_1 \triangleright s_2 \triangleright \ldots \triangleright s_n$ of S, then for any A, B such that $A \cap B = \emptyset$, it holds that $A >_\Pi B$ or $B >_\Pi A$, then $\forall f \neq g$, either $f \succ g$ or $g \succ f$. Moreover, this is a lexicographic ranking:

$f \succ g$ if and only if $\exists k$ such that $f(s_k) \succ_P g(s_k)$ and $f(s_i) \sim_P g(s_i), \forall i < k$.

This corresponds to the following procedure. Check if f is better than g in the most normal state: if yes prefer f, if f and g give equally preferred results in s_1 do the same test in the second most normal state, and so on. This comes down to a lexicographic ranking of vectors $(f(s_1), \ldots, f(s_n))$ and $(g(s_1), \ldots, g(s_n))$. It is a form of dictatorship by most plausible states, in voting theory terms. It also coincides with Boutilier's criterion, except that ties can be broken by less normal states.

3) More generally any weak order splits S into a well-ordered partition $E_1 \cup E_2 \cup \ldots \cup E_n = S, E_i \cap E_j = \emptyset (\forall i \neq j)$ such that states in each E_i are equally plausible and any state in E_i is more plausible than all states in $E_j, \forall j > i$. Then, the ordering of events is defined as follows:

- $f \succ g$ if and only if $\exists k \geq 1$ such that: $\forall s \in E_1 \cup E_2 \cup \ldots \cup E_{k-1}, f(s) \sim_P g(s)$, and $\forall s \in E_k, f(s) \succeq_P g(s)$ and $\exists s \in E_k, f(s) \succ_P g(s)$

- $f \sim g$ if and only if either $\forall s \in S, f(s) \sim_P g(s)$, or $\exists k \geq 1$ such that: $\forall s \in E_1 \cup E_2 \cup \ldots \cup E_{k-1}, f(s) \sim_P g(s)$, and $\exists s \neq s' \in E_k, f(s) \succ_P g(s)$ and $g(s') \succ_P f(s')$.

This decision criterion is a blending of lexicographic priority and unanimity among states. Informally, the decision maker proceeds as follows. f and g are compared on the set of most normal states E_1: if f Pareto-dominates g in E_1, then f is preferred to g. If there is a disagreement in E_1 about the relative performance of f and g then f and g are not comparable. If f and g have equally preferred consequences in each most normal state then the decision maker considers the set of second-most normal states E_2, etc.

This is basically a prioritized Pareto-dominance relation. Preferred acts are selected by restricting choices to the most plausible states of the world, and a unanimity rule is used on these maximally plausible states. Ties are broken by lower level oligarchies. This procedure is therefore similar to Boutilier's decision rule in that it focuses on the most plausible states, but Pareto-dominance is required instead of the maximin rule on them and ties can be broken by subsets of lower plausibility. This decision rule is cognitively appealing, but it has a limited expressive and decisive power.

One may also apply the maximin rule in a prioritized way: the maximin decision rule can be substituted to unanimity within the likely dominance rule inside the oligarchies of states. It is also easy to imagine a counterpart to the likely dominance rule where expected utility applies inside the oligarchies of states [LEH 96]. However reasonable these refined decision rules may look, they need to be formally justified.

11.4. Axiomatics of qualitative decision theory

A natural question is whether it is possible to found rational decision making in a purely qualitative setting, under an act-driven Savage framework. The idea of the approach is to extract the decision maker's likelihood relation and the decision maker's preference on consequences from the decision maker's preference pattern on acts, as only the latter is observable from human behavior. Enforcing 'rationality' conditions on the way the decision maker should rank acts then determines the kind of uncertainty theory implicitly 'used' by the decision maker for representing the available knowledge on states. It also prescribes a decision rule. Moreover, this framework is operationally testable, since choices made by individuals can be observed and the uncertainty theory at work is determined by these choices. However, it is right away assumed that states of nature are imperfectly perceived: it comes down to considering a finite set S representing states in a granular way, each element in S clustering indiscernible states of nature according to the decision maker's language and perception.

As seen in sections 11.2 and 11.3, two research lines can be followed in agreement with this definition: the relational approach and the absolute approach. Following the relational approach [DUB 02, DUB 03a], the decision maker uncertainty is represented by a partial ordering relation among events (expressing relative likelihood), and the utility function is simply encoded as another ordering relation between potential consequences of decisions. The advantage is that it is faithful to the kind of elementary information users can directly provide. The other approach, which can be dubbed the absolute approach [DUB 00c, DUB 01b], presupposes the existence of a totally ordered scale (typically a finite one) for grading both likelihood and utility. Both approaches lead to an act-driven axiomatization of the qualitative variant of possibility theory [DUB 98b, ZAD 78].

11.4.1. *Savage's theory: a refresher*

The Savage framework (already described in Chapter 9) is adapted to our purpose of devising a purely ordinal approach because its starting point is indeed based on relations even if its representation is eventually made on an interval scale. Suppose a decision maker supplies a preference relation $\succeq$ over acts $f : S \to X$. X^S usually denotes the set of all such mappings. In Savage's approach, any mapping in the set X^S is considered to be a possible act (even if it is an imaginary one rather than a feasible one). The first requirement stated by Savage is:

Axiom 11.1. P1: $(X^S, \succeq)$ *is a weak order.*

Axiom 11.1 is unavoidable in the scope of expected utility theory. If acts are ranked according to expected utility, then the preference over acts will be transitive, reflexive and complete ($f \succeq g$ or $g \succeq f$ for any f, g). What this axiom also implies (if X and S are finite) is that there exists a totally ordered scale, say V, that can serve to evaluate the worth of acts. Indeed the indifference relation ($f \sim g$ if and only if $f \succeq g$ and $g \succeq f$) is an equivalence relation, and the set of equivalence classes, denoted $X^S/\sim$ is totally ordered via the strict preference $\succ$. If $[f]$ and $[g]$ denote the equivalence classes of f and g, $[f] \succ [g]$ holds if and only if $f \succ g$ holds for any pair of representatives of each class. It is therefore possible to rate acts on $V = X^S/\sim$ and $[f]$ is interpreted as the qualitative utility level of f.

An event is modeled by a subset of states and understood as a disjunction thereof. The set of acts is closed under the following combination involving acts and events. Let $A \subseteq S$ be an event, f and g two acts, and denote by fAg the act such that:

$$fAg(s) = f(s) \text{ if } s \in A, \text{ and } g(s) \text{ if } s \notin A.$$

For instance, f may mean 'bypass the city', g 'cross the city' and A represents the presence of a traffic jam in the city. Then S represents descriptions of the state of the road network, and X represents a timescale for the time spent by an agent who drives to their working place. Act fAg then means: bypass the city if there is a traffic jam, and cross the city otherwise. More generally the notation $f_1 A_1 f_2 A_2, \ldots, A_{n-1} f_n A_n$, where $A_1, \ldots, A_{n-1}, A_n$ is a partition of S, denotes the act whose result is $f_i(s)$ if $s \in A_i, \forall i = 1, \ldots, n$. fAg is actually short for $fAgA^c$ where A^c is the complement of A.

Savage proposed an axiom that he called the *sure-thing principle*. It requires that the relative preference between two acts does not depend on states where the acts have the same consequences. In other words, the preference between act fAh and act gAh does not depend on the choice of act h.

Axiom 11.2. P2: $\forall A, f, g, h, h', fAh \succeq gAh$ *if and only if* $fAh' \succeq gAh'$.

For instance, if you bypass the city (f) rather than cross it (g) in case of a traffic jam (A), this preference does not depend on what you would do in case of fluid traffic

(A^c), say, cross the city ($h = g$), bypass it anyway ($h = f$) or make a strange decision such as staying at home. Grant et al. [GRA 00b] pointed out that the name 'sure-thing principle' for this postulate was not fully justified since it is hard to grasp where the sure-thing is. Grant et al. propose several expressions of a genuine sure-thing principle, one version they called the weak sure-thing principle being as follows.

Axiom 11.3. **WSTP**: $fAg \succeq g$ and $gAf \succeq g$ implies $f \succeq g$.

Axiom 11.3 really means that the weak preference of act f over act g does not depend on whether A occurs or not. It is obvious that axiom 11.3 is implied by axioms 11.1 and 11.2, since from $fAg \succeq g = gAg$ and axiom 11.2 we derive $f = fAf \succeq gAf$ and using transitivity of $\succeq$ due to axiom 11.1, $f \succeq g$ follows.

The sure-thing principle enables two notions to be simply defined, namely conditional preference and null events. An act f is said to be weakly preferred to another act g, *conditioned* on event A if and only if $\forall h, fAh \succeq gAh$. This is denoted by $(f \succeq g)_A$. Conditional preference $(f \succeq g)_A$ means that f is weakly preferred to g when the state space is restricted to A, regardless of the decision made when A does not occur. Note that $f \succeq g$ is short for $(f \succeq g)_S$. Moreover $(f \succeq g)_\emptyset$ always holds for any f and g, since it is equivalent to the reflexivity of $\succeq$ (i.e. $h \succeq h$). Clearly, the sure-thing principle enables $(f \succeq g)_A$ to hold as soon as $fAh \succeq gAh$ for *some* act h.

An event A is said to be *null* if and only if $\forall f, \forall g, (f \succeq g)_A$ holds. Any non-empty set of states A on which no act makes a difference then behaves like the empty set in the perspective of choosing a best decision.

Conditional preference enables the weak sure-thing principle to be expressed like a unanimity principle in the terminology of voting theory, provided that the sure-thing principle holds.

Axiom 11.4. **U**: $(f \succeq g)_A$ and $(f \succeq g)_{A^c}$ implies $f \succeq g$ (unanimity).

Note that in the absence of axiom 11.2, axiom 11.4 implies axiom 11.3 but not the converse. The unanimity postulate has been formulated by Lehmann [LEH 96].

Among acts in X^S are *constant acts* such that: $\exists x \in X, \forall s \in S, f(s) = x$. They are denoted f_x. It seems reasonable to identify the set of constant acts $\{f_x, x \in X\}$ and X. The preference $\succeq_P$ on X can be induced from $(X^S, \succeq)$ as follows:

$$\forall x, y \in X, x \succeq_P y \text{ if and only if } f_x \succeq f_y.$$

This definition is self-consistent provided that the preference between constant acts is not altered by conditioning. The third Savage postulate is as follows.

Axiom 11.5. P3: $\forall A \subseteq S$, A not null, $(f_x \succeq f_y)_A$ if and only if $x \succeq_P y$.

Clearly, Pareto-dominance should imply weak preference for acts. And indeed under **P1**, **P2**, and **P3**, $f \succeq_P g$ (that is, $\forall s \in S, f(s) \succeq_P g(s)$) implies $f \succeq g$.

The preference on acts also induces a likelihood relation among events. For this purpose, it is enough to consider the set of *binary acts* of the form $f_x A f_y$, which due to **P3** can be denoted xAy, where $x \in X, y \in X$ and $x \succ_P y$. Clearly for fixed $x \succ_P y$, the set of binary acts $\{x,y\}^S$ is isomorphic to the set of events 2^S. However the restriction of $(X^S, \succeq)$ to $\{x,y\}^S$ may be inconsistent with the restriction to $\{x',y'\}^S$ for other choices of consequences $x' \succ_P y'$. A relative likelihood $\succeq_L$ among events can however be recovered, as suggested by Lehmann [LEH 96]:

$\forall A, B \subseteq S, A \succeq_L B$ if and only if $xAy \succeq xBy, \forall x, y \in X$ such that $x \succ_P y$.

In order to obtain a weak order of events, Savage introduced yet another postulate as follows.

Axiom 11.6. P4: $\forall x, y, x', y' \in X$ such that $x \succ_P y, x' \succ_P y'$, it holds that $xAy \succeq xBy$ if and only if $x'Ay' \succeq x'By'$.

Under axiom 11.6, the choice of $x \in X, y \in X$ with $x \succ_P y$ does not affect the ordering between events in terms of binary acts, namely: $A \succeq_L B$ is short for $\exists x \succ_P y, xAy \succeq xBy$.

Lastly, Savage assumed that the ordering $\succ$ is not trivial.

Axiom 11.7. P5: X contains at least two elements x, y such that $f_x \succ f_y$ (or $x \succ_P y$).

Under **P1–P5**, the likelihood relation on events is a comparative probability ordering [see FIS 86], i.e. satisfies the preadditivity property

If $A \cap (B \cup C) = \emptyset$, then $B \succeq_L C$ if and only if $A \cup B \succeq_L A \cup C$.

Such relations are induced by probability measures, but the converse is not true [KRA 58].

Savage introduces yet another postulate that enables him to derive the existence (and uniqueness) of a numerical probability measure on S that can represent the likelihood relation $\succeq_L$.

Axiom 11.8. P6: *for any f, g with $f \succ g$ in X^S and any $x \in X$, there is a partition $\{E_1, \ldots, E_n\}$ of S such that $\forall i = 1, \ldots n, xE_i f \succ g$ and $f \succ xE_i g$.*

Under the postulates **P1–P6**, not only can $\succeq_L$ be represented by a unique numerical probability function but $(X^S, \succeq)$ can be represented by the expected utility of acts:

$$u(f) = \int_{s \in S} u(f(s))\, dP(s),$$

where the numerical utility function u represents the relation $\succeq_P$ on X uniquely, up to an affine transformation. According to postulate **P6**, the probability of subset E_i can be made arbitrary small, without altering the relation $f \succ g$ when x is very bad (so that $xE_i f \succ g$) or very good (so that $f \succ xE_i g$). Clearly, such a postulate makes sense only if the state space S is infinite, which goes against our assumptions. In contrast, we assume that both S and X are finite in this chapter, and **P6** is trivially violated in such a finite setting. There is, to our knowledge, no joint representation of subjective probability and expected utility that would assume a purely finite setting for both states and consequences.

11.4.2. *The relational approach to decision theory*

The relational approach introduced in [DUB 97] (further developed in [DUB 02, DUB 03a]) tries to lay bare the formal consequences of adopting a purely ordinal point of view on DMU, while retaining as much as possible from Savage's axioms (especially the sure-thing principle which is the cornerstone of theory). To this end, an axiom of ordinal invariance, originally due to [FIS 75] in another context, is then added [FAR 99]. This axiom says that what matters for determining the preference between two acts is the relative merit of consequences of acts for each state, not the figures of merit of these consequences or the relative positions of these acts relative to other acts. More rigorously, two pairs of acts (f, g) and (f', g') such that

$$\forall s \in S, f(s) \succeq_P g(s) \quad \text{if and only if } f'(s) \succeq_P g'(s)$$
$$\text{and } g(s) \succeq_P f(s) \quad \text{if and only if } g'(s) \succeq_P f'(s)$$

are called statewise order-equivalent. (As pointed out in [DUB 07b], only one of these two equivalence conditions is explicitly stated in [DUB 02] and [DUB 03a], even though the intent was clearly to have both of them, and the proofs of subsequent results presuppose it. However, stating only one of these equivalence conditions is not sufficient for proving the representation theorem.) This is denoted $(f, g) \equiv (f', g')$. It means that, in each state, consequences of f, g and of f', g' are rank-ordered likewise. The ordinal invariance axiom is as follows.

Axiom 11.9. OI: $\forall f, f'g, g' \in X^S$, if $(f, g) \equiv (f', g')$ then ($f \succeq g$ if and only if $f' \succeq g'$).

Axiom 11.9 expresses the purely ordinal nature of the decision criterion. It is easy to check that the likely dominance rule obeys this. This is obvious noticing that if $(f, g) \equiv (f', g')$ then, by definition, $[f \succ_P g] = \{s, f(s) \succ_P g(s)\} = [f' \succ_P g']$. More specifically, under axiom 11.9, if the weak preference on acts is reflexive and the induced weak preference on consequences is complete, the only possible decision rule is likely dominance. **OI** implies the validity of Savage **P2** and **P4** axioms. Adopting axiom 11.9 and sticking to a transitive weak preference on acts leads to problems exemplified in the previous section by the probabilistic variant of the likely dominance rule. Indeed, the following result was proved in [DUB 02].

Theorem 11.1. *If $(X^S, \succeq)$ is a weak order on acts satisfying axiom 11.9, and S and X have at least three elements, let $\succeq_L$ be the likelihood relation induced by axiom* **P4** *(implied by* **OI***). Then there is a permutation of the non-null elements of S, such that*

$$\{s_1\} \succ_L \{s_2\} \succ_L \ldots \succ_L \{s_{n-1}\} \succ_L \{s_n\} \ldots \succ_L \emptyset$$

and $\forall i = 1, \ldots, n-2, \{s_i\} \succ_v \{s_{i+1}, \ldots, s_n\}$.

In the general case where X has more than two elements, the ordinal invariance axiom forbids a Savagean decision maker to believe that there are two equally likely states of the world, each of which is more likely than a third state. This is clearly not acceptable in practice. Nevertheless, if X only has two consequences of distinct values, then such a trivialization is avoided.

If we analyze the reason why this phenomenon occurs, it is found that axiom 11.1 (**P1**) plays the crucial role. **P1** assumes the full transitivity of the likelihood relation $\succeq_L$. Giving up the transitivity of $\succeq_L$ suppresses the unnatural restriction of an almost total plausibility ordering of states, to the extent that we wish to keep the sure-thing principle. We are led to formulate a weak form of **P1** [DUB 02] as follows.

Axiom 11.10. WP1: $(X^S, \succ)$ *is a transitive, irreflexive, partially ordered set.*

Dropping the transitivity of $\succeq$ cancels some useful consequences of the sure-thing principle under axiom 11.1 (**P1**), which are nevertheless consistent with the likely dominance rule. For instance, axiom 11.3 (**WSTP**) (or equivalently, the unanimity axiom **U**) will not follow from the relaxed framework. We must add it to get it. As a consequence, if one insists on sticking to a purely ordinal view of DMU, we come up to the framework defined by axioms **WP1, WSTP** (or **U**), **P3, P5** and **OI**. The likelihood relation induced by **P4** is in agreement with the classical deduction:

$$\text{if } B \succ_L A \text{ then } B \cup C \succ_L A \text{ and } B \succ_L A \cap C. \tag{11.7}$$

The null events are then all subsets of a subset N of null states. Moreover, if X has more than two elements, the likelihood relation satisfies the following strongly non-probabilistic property [DUB 95c]: for any three pairwise disjoint non-null events A, B, C,

$$B \cup C \succ_L A \text{ and } A \cup C \succ_L B \text{ imply } C \succ_L A \cup B. \tag{11.8}$$

The statement $B \succ_L A$ really means that event B is *much* more likely than A, because B will never be more likely than any disjunction of events nor more likely than A. This likelihood relation can always be represented by a family of *possibility relations*. Namely, there is a family $\mathcal{F}$ of possibility relations $\succeq_\Pi$ on S and a weak order relation $\succeq_P$ on X such that the preference relation on acts is defined by the likely dominance rule restricted to possibility relations [DUB 04b]:

$$f \succ g \text{ if and only if } \forall \succeq_P \in \mathcal{F}, [f \succ_P g] \succ_\Pi [g \succ_P f].$$

In [DUB 04b], it is shown that this ordinal Savagean framework actually leads to a representation of uncertainty at work in the non-monotonic logic system of Kraus *et al.* [KRA 90] (see Friedman and Halpern [FRI 96] who also study property (11.8)).

A more general setting starting from a reflexive weak preference relation on acts is used in Dubois *et al.* [DUB 03a]. In this framework **P3** is replaced by a monotonicity axiom on both sides, implied by Savage's framework, namely for any event A:

Axiom 11.11. Monotonicity: *If* $h \succ_P f$ *and* $f \succeq g$ *then* $fAh \succeq g$; *if* $g \succ_P h$ *and* $f \succeq g$ *then* $f \succeq gAh$.

Two additional axioms (also valid in Savage's framework) enable a unique possibility relation to be enforced as the resulting likelihood relation between disjoint events [DUB 03a]:

Axiom 11.12. EUN: $\forall A, B \subseteq S, (f \succeq g)_A$ *and* $(f \succeq g)_B$ *jointly imply* $(f \succeq g)_{A \cup B}$.

Axiom 11.13. ANO *If* $s_1 \sim_L s_2$ *then:*

$$\forall f, g, f \succeq g \text{ if and only if } f(s_1)\{s_2\}f(s_2)\{s_1\}f \succeq g(s_1)\{s_2\}g(s_2)\{s_1\}g.$$

Axiom 11.12 (EUN) extends unanimity U to any disjunction of events. Axiom 11.13 is an anonymity property ensuring that exchanging consequences of two equally plausible states does not alter the preferences between acts. Note that $f(s_1)\{s_2\}f(s_2)\{s_1\}f$ represents act f where states s_1 and s_2 have been exchanged. The following result is obtained.

Theorem 11.2. *The two following properties are equivalent:*

– Relation $\succeq$ on X^S is reflexive and complete, has a transitive strict part with at least two non-null states and it satisfies axioms **OI, A1, A5, LM, RM, EUN, ANO**.

– There exists a complete preorder $\succeq_P$ on X and a unique non-trivial possibility relation $\succeq_\Pi$ on events, such that $\forall f, g \in X^S$, $f \succeq g$ if and only if $[f \succ g] \succ_\Pi [g \succ f]$.

While these results do characterize the possibilistic approach to uncertainty in qualitiative decision theory, the family of 'rational' decision rules in the purely relational approach to decision under uncertainty is very restrictive. This restricted family only reflects the situation faced in voting theories where natural axioms lead to impossibility theorems [e.g. ARR 51, SEN 86]. This kind of impediment was already pointed out by Doyle and Wellman [DOY 91] for preference-based default theories. These results question the very possibility of a purely ordinal solution to this problem, in the framework of transitive and complete preference relations on acts.

The likely dominance rule lacks discrimination, not because of indifference between acts, but because of incomparability. Actually, it may be possible to weaken axiom **OI** while avoiding the notion of certainty equivalent of an uncertain act. It must be stressed that **OI** requires more than the simple ordinal nature of preference and uncertainty (i.e. more than separate ordinal scales for each of them). Condition **OI** also involves a condition of independence with respect to irrelevant alternatives (in the sense of [ARR 51]). It states that the preference $f \succ g$ only depends on f and g. This unnecessary part of the condition could be cancelled within the proposed framework, thus leaving room for a new family of rules not considered in this chapter, for instance involving a third act or some prescribed consequence considered as an aspiration level [PER 06].

11.4.3. *Qualitative decision rules under commensurateness*

Let us now consider the axiomatization of absolute qualitative criteria (11.4–11.6), based on the Sugeno integral in the scope of Savage theory. Note that the maximin and maximax criteria, to which possibilistic decision rules reduce when total ignorance prevails ($\forall s \in S, \pi(s) = 1$), were axiomatized very early by Chernoff [CHE 54]. Arrow and Hurwicz [ARR 72] characterized the pair of criteria $(W_u^-(f), W_u^+(f))$ for decision making under total ignorance. Interestingly, they carefully distinguish it from equiprobable states, and credit Shackle [SHA 49] for the invention of these criteria. More recently, Brafman and Tennenholtz [BRA 00] axiomatically characterize the refinement $W_{\trianglerighteq,u}^-$ of the maximin rule to unequally plausible states, due to Boutilier, in terms of conditional policies (rather than acts). Finally the first axiomatization of possibilistic decision rules was proposed by Dubois and Prade [DUB 95b] in the style of decision under risk, assuming a possibility distribution is known, and adapting Von Neumann and Morgenstern axioms [NEU 47] (see [DUB 99b] for the complete study).

Clearly, pessimistic, optimistic possibilistic criteria and the Sugeno integral satisfy axiom 11.1 (**P1**). However, the sure-thing principle can be severely violated by the Sugeno integral. It is easy to show that there may exist $f, g, h, h\prime$ such that $fAh \succ gAh$ while $gAh\prime \succ fAh\prime$. It is enough to consider binary acts (events) and notice that, if A is disjoint from $B \cup C$, generally nothing prevents a fuzzy measure γ from satisfying $\gamma(B) > \gamma(C)$ along with $\gamma(A \cup C) > \gamma(A \cup B)$ (for instance, Shafer's belief functions). The possibilistic criteria equations (11.4) and (11.5) violate the sure-thing principle to a lesser extent, since

$$\forall A \subseteq S, \forall f, g, h, h', W_{\pi,u}^-(fAh) > W_{\pi,u}^-(gAh) \Rightarrow W_{\pi,u}^-(fAh') \geq W_{\pi,u}^-(gAh')$$

and likewise for $W_{\pi,u}^+$. Moreover, only one part of **P3** holds for Sugeno integrals. The obtained ranking of acts satisfies the following axiom.

Axiom 11.14. WP3: $\forall A \subseteq S, \forall x, y \in X, \forall f, x \succeq_P y \Rightarrow xAf \succeq yAf$.

Besides, axiom **P4** is violated by Sugeno integrals, but only to some extent. Namely, the preference relation between binary acts satisfies a weak form of it as follows.

Axiom 11.15. WP4: $\forall x \succ_P y, x' \succ_P y' \in X : xAy \succ xBy \Rightarrow x'Ay' \succeq x'By'$

Axiom 11.15 forbids preference reversals when changing the pair of consequences used to model events A and B. Moreover, the strict preference is maintained if the pair of consequences is changed into more extreme ones:

$$\text{if } u(x') > u(x) > u(y) > u(y')$$
$$\text{then } S_{\gamma,u}(xAy) > S_{\gamma,u}(xBy) \Rightarrow S_{\gamma,u}(x'Ay') > S_{\gamma,u}(x'By'). \quad (11.9)$$

The Sugeno integral and its possibilistic specializations are weakly Pareto-monotonic since $f \succeq_P g$ implies $S_{\gamma,u}(f) \geq S_{\gamma,u}(g)$. However, we may have $f(s) \succ_P g(s)$ for some state s, while $S_{\gamma,u}(f) = S_{\gamma,u}(g)$. This is the so-called drowning effect, which also appears in the violations of **P4**. This is because some states are neglected when comparing acts.

The basic properties of the Sugeno integrals exploit disjunctive and conjunctive combinations of acts. Namely, given a preference relation $(X^S, \succeq)$, and two acts f and g, define $f \wedge g$ and $f \vee g$ as

$$f \wedge g(s) = f(s) \text{ if } g(s) \succeq_P f(s) \text{ and } g(s) \text{ otherwise}$$
$$f \vee g(s) = f(s) \text{ if } f(s) \succeq_P g(s) \text{ and } g(s) \text{ otherwise.}$$

Act $f \wedge g$ always produces the worst consequences of f and g in each state, while $f \vee g$ always makes the best of them. They are the union and intersection of fuzzy sets viewed as acts. Obviously

$$S_{\gamma,u}(f \wedge g) \leq \min(S_{\gamma,u}(f), S_{\gamma,u}(g)) \text{ and } S_{\gamma,u}(f \vee g) \geq \max(S_{\gamma,u}(f), S_{\gamma,u}(g))$$

from weak Pareto monotonicity. These properties hold with equality whenever f or g is a constant act. The latter equality is in fact characteristic of Sugeno integrals for monotonic aggregation operators [MAR 00]. This characterization can actually be expressed by means of axioms 11.16 and 11.17, called restricted conjunctive and disjunctive dominance (**RCD** and **RDD**) on the preference structure $(X^S, \succeq)$ [DUB 00c].

Axiom 11.16. RCD: *If f is a constant act, $f \succ h$ and $g \succ h$ jointly imply $f \wedge g \succ h$.*

Axiom 11.17. RDD: *If f is a constant act, $h \succ f$ and $h \succ g$ jointly imply $h \succ f \vee g$.*

The area of significance of qualitative decision theory and, more precisely, that of axioms 11.16 and 11.17, is restricted to the case where X and S are finite and where the value scale is coarse. For instance, **RCD** means that limiting from above the potential utility values of an act g that is better than another one h, to a constant value that is better than the utility of act h, still yields an act better than h.

This is in contradiction with expected utility theory and debatable in that setting. Indeed, suppose g is a lottery where you win 1000 Euros against nothing with equal chances. Suppose the certainty equivalent of this lottery is 400 Euros received for sure, and h is the fact of receiving 390 Euros for sure. It is likely that if f represents the certainty-equivalent of g, $f \wedge g$ will be felt strictly less attractive than h, as the former means you win 400 Euros against nothing with equal chances. Axiom 11.16 implies that such a lottery should never be preferred to receiving $400\,\epsilon$ Euros for sure, for arbitrary small values of ϵ. This axiom is thus strongly counter-intuitive in the context of economic theory, with a continuous consequence set X. However, the area of significance of qualitative decision theory is precisely when both X and S are finite.

Two presuppositions actually underlie axiom 11.16 (and similarly for axiom 11.17):

1) There is no compensation effect in the decision process: in case of equal chances, winning 1000 Euros cannot compensate for the possibility of not earning anything. It fits with the case of one-shot decisions where the notion of certainty equivalent can never materialize: you can only get 1000 Euros or get nothing if you just play once. You cannot get 400 Euros. The latter can only be obtained in the average, by playing several times.

2) There is a big step between one level $\lambda_i \in V$ in the qualitative value scale and the next one λ_{i+1} with $V = \{1 = \lambda_1 > \ldots > \lambda_m = 0\}$. The preference pattern $f \succ h$ always means that f is significantly preferred to h so that the preference level of $f \wedge g$ can never get very close to that of h when $g \succ h$. The counter-example above is obtained by precisely bringing these two preference levels very close to each other so that $f \wedge g$ can become less attractive than the sure gain h. Level λ_{i+1} is in some sense considered negligible compared to λ_i.

The Sugeno integral can be axiomatized in the style of Savage [DUB 00c].

Theorem 11.3. *If the preference structure $(X^S, \succeq)$ satisfies **P1**, **WP3**, **P5**, **RCD** and **RDD**, then there a finite chain V of preference levels, a V-valued capacity function γ, and a V-valued utility function u on the set of consequences X, such that the preference relation on acts is defined by $f \succeq g$ if and only if $S_{\gamma,u}(f) \geq S_{\gamma,u}(g)$.*

Proof. Clearly, **P1**, **WP3** and **P5** jointly imply Pareto-monotonicity between acts. In the representation method, V is the quotient set $X^S/\sim$ and the utility value $u(x)$ is the equivalence class of the constant act f_x. Because the sure-thing principle is lacking, the degree of likelihood $\gamma(A)$ is the equivalence class of the binary act $1A0$, having extreme consequences. It yields the most refined likelihood relation between events due to equation (11.9). The equality $u(xA0) = \min(u(x), u(1A0))$ can then be proved using **RCD**. Finally, due to **RDD**, $u(xA0 \vee yB0) = \max(u(xA0), u(yB0))$ can be obtained. The result is easy to obtain by expressing any act f in a canonical form $\vee_{x \in X} x F_x 0$, with $F_x = \{s, u(f(s)) \geq u(x)\}$.

Axioms **RDD** and **RCD** can be replaced in Theorem 11.3 by non-compensation assumptions.

Axiom 11.18. NC:

$$\begin{cases} 1_L Ay \sim y & \text{or} \quad 1_L Ay \sim 1_L A0 \\ \text{and} \\ xA0_L \sim x & \text{or} \quad xA0_L \sim 1_L A0_L \end{cases}$$

Axiom 11.18 formalizes the following intuition: in order to evaluate act $1_L Ay$, there is no middle term between values $u(y)$ and $\gamma(1_L A0)$.

Theorem 11.3 still holds if, in the expression of **RCD** and **RDD**, we consider any two comonotonic acts f and g (i.e. $f(s) >_P f(s') \Rightarrow g(s) \succeq_P g(s'), \forall s, s' \in S$). Indeed, the Sugeno integrals are 'linear' for operations maximum and minimum with respect to disjunctions and conjunctions of comonotonic acts f, g: $S_{\gamma,u}(f \wedge g) = \min(S_{\gamma,u}(f), S_{\gamma,u}(g))$ and $S_{\gamma,u}(f \vee g) = \max(S_{\gamma,u}(f), S_{\gamma,u}(g))$. In this sense, the Sugeno integral is a qualitative counterpart to the Choquet integral.

It is easy to check that these equalities hold with any two acts f and g for the pessimistic and the optimistic possibilistic preference functionals, $W^-_{\pi,u}(f \wedge g) = \min(W^-_{\pi,u}(f), W^-_{\pi,u}(g))$ and $W^+_{\pi,u}(f \vee g) = \max(W^+_{\pi,u}(f), W^+_{\pi,u}(g))$, respectively. The criterion $W^-_{\pi,u}(f)$ can therefore be axiomatized by strengthening axiom **RCD** as follows.

Axiom 11.19. CD: $\forall f, g, h, f \succ h$ and $g \succ h$, $f \wedge g \succ h$ *(conjunctive dominance)*.

Axiom 11.19 means that if two acts f, g are individually better than a third act, the act $f \wedge g$ which yields the worse result of both acts still remains better than the third. It makes sense in the scope of a one-shot decision. Together with **P1, WP3, RDD** and **P5, CD** implies that the set-function γ is a necessity measure and therefore $S_{\gamma,u}(f) = W^-_{\pi,u}(f)$, for some possibility distribution π.

In order to determine why axiom 11.19 leads to a pessimistic criterion, Dubois et al. [DUB 01b] have noticed that it can be equivalently replaced by the following property.

Axiom 11.20. PESS: $\forall A \subseteq S, \forall f, g, fAg \succ g$ implies $g \succeq gAf$ *(pessimism)*.

Axiom 11.20 can be explained as follows. If changing g into f when A occurs results in a better act, the decision maker has enough confidence in event A to consider that improving the results on A is worthwhile. However, in this case, there is less confidence on the complement A^c than in A, and any possible improvement of g when A^c occurs is neglected. Alternatively, the reason why $fAg \succ g$ holds may be that the consequences of g when A occurs are very bad and the occurrence of A is not unlikely enough to neglect them, while the consequences of g when A^c occurs are acceptable. Suppose then that consequences of f when A occurs are also acceptable; then $fAg \succ g$. However, act gAf remains undesirable because, regardless of whether the consequences of f when A^c occurs are acceptable or not, act gAf still possesses plausibly bad consequences when A occurs; hence $g \succeq gAf$.

For instance, g means losing ($= A$) or winning ($= A^c$) 10,000 Euros with equal chances according to whether A occurs or not and f means winning either nothing ($= A$) or 20,000 Euros ($= A^c$) conditioned on the same event. Then fAg is clearly safer than g as there is no risk of losing money. However, if axiom 11.20 holds, then the chance of winning much more money (20,000 Euros) by choosing act gAf is neglected because there is still a good chance to lose 10,000 Euros with this lottery. Such behavior is clearly cautious.

Similarly, the optimistic criterion $W^+_{\pi,u}(f)$ can be axiomatized by strengthening axiom 11.17 as follows.

Axiom 11.21. DD: $\forall f, g, h, h \succ f$ and $h \succ g$, $h \succ f \vee g$ (disjunctive dominance.)

Together with **P1, WP3, RCD, P5**, axiom 11.21 implies that the set-function γ is a possibility measure and so $S_{\gamma,u}(f) = W^+_{\pi,u}(f)$ for some possibility distribution π. The optimistic counterpart to property axiom PESS that can serve as a substitute to axiom 11.21 for the representation of criterion $W^+_{\pi,u}$ is as follows.

Axiom 11.22. OPT: $\forall A \subseteq S, \forall f, g, g \succ fAg$ implies $gAf \succeq g$ (optimism).

11.5. Toward more efficient qualitative decision rules

The absolute approach to qualitative decision criteria is simple (especially in the case of possibility theory). Naturally, a complete preorder on acts is obtained. The restriction of the pessimistic approach to the most plausible states, at work in possibilistic criteria, makes them more realistic than the maximin criterion, and more flexible than purely ordinal approaches based on the likely dominance rule.

However, approaches based on an absolute qualitative value scale have their own shortcomings. First, one has to accept the commensurability assumption between utility and degrees of likelihood. It assumes the existence of a common scale for grading uncertainty and preference. It can be questioned, although it is already taken for granted in classical decision theory (via the notion of certainty equivalent of an uncertain event). It is already implicit in the Savage approach, and looks acceptable for decision under uncertainty (but more debatable in social choice). As a consequence, the acts are then totally preordered. This is not actually a drawback from a normative point of view.

More importantly, absolute qualitative criteria lack discrimination due to many indifferent acts. The obtained ranking of decisions is bound to be coarse since there cannot be more classes of preference-equivalent decisions than levels in the finite scale used. The above possibilistic decision rule and the maximin rule are consistent with Pareto dominance only in the wide sense: they can consider two acts as indifferent even if one Pareto-dominates the other. The sure-thing principle may be violated (even if not drastically for possibilistic criteria). This section describes approaches that attempt to remedy this problem.

11.5.1. *Refining qualitative criteria*

The main reason for the lack of discrimination power of absolute qualitative criteria is the fact that they do not use all the available information for discriminating among acts. An act f can be considered indifferent to another act g, even if f is at least as good as g in all states and strictly in some states (including some of the most plausible ones). This defect is absent from the expected utility model.

We may consider refining the optimistic possibilistic criterion by the pessimistic one or vice versa [DUB 00a]. Along this line, Giang and Shenoi [GIA 00, GIA 05] have tried to obviate the need for making assumptions on the pessimistic or optimistic attitude of the decision maker and therefore improve the discrimination power in the absolute qualitative setting. They use a totally ordered set of possibility measures on a two-element set $\{0, 1\}$ containing the values of the best and the worst consequences, as a utility scale. Each such possibility distribution represents a qualitative lottery. Let $V_\Pi = \{(a, b), \max(a, b) = 1, a, b \in V\}$. Coefficient a represents the degree of possibility of obtaining the worst consequence, and coefficient b the degree of possibility of obtaining the best. This set can be viewed as a bipolar value scale ordered by the complete preordering relation:

$$(a, b) \geq_V (c, d) \text{ if and only if } (a \leq c \text{ and } b \geq d).$$

The fact this relation is complete is due to the fact that pairs (a, b) and (c, d) such that $(a, b) >_V (c, d)$ and $(c, d) >_V (a, b)$ cannot both lie in V_Π, since then either $\max(a, b) < 1$ or $\max(c, d) < 1$. The bottom of this utility scale is $(1, 0)$, its top is $(0, 1)$ and its neutral point $(1, 1)$ means 'indifferent'. The canonical example of such a scale is the set of pairs $(\Pi(A^c), \Pi(A))$ of degrees of possibility for event $A = $ 'getting the best consequence', and its complement. The inequality $(\Pi(A^c), \Pi(A)) >_V (\Pi(B^c), \Pi(B))$ means that A is more likely (certain or plausible) than B (because it is equivalent to $\Pi(A) > \Pi(B)$ or $N(A) > N(B)$). In fact, the induced likelihood ordering between events

$$A \succeq_{L\Pi} B \text{ if and only if } (\Pi(A^c), \Pi(A)) \geq_V (\Pi(B^c), \Pi(B))$$

is self-conjugate i.e. $A \succeq_{L\Pi} B$ is equivalent to $B^c \succeq_{L\Pi} A^c$.

Each consequence x is assumed to have a utility value (α, β) in V_Π. The proposed preference functional map acts, viewed as n–tuples $f = ((\alpha_1, \beta_1), \ldots, (\alpha_n, \beta_n))$ of values in V_Π, to V_Π itself. The uncertainty is described by possibility weights $(\pi_1, \ldots, \pi_n)$ with $\max_{i=1,\ldots,n} \pi_i = 1$. The utility of an act f, called *binary possibilistic utility*, is computed as the pair

$$W_{GS}(f) = (\max_{i=1,\ldots,n} \min(\pi_i, \alpha_i), \max_{i=1,\ldots,n} \min(\pi_i, \beta_i)) \in V_\Pi.$$

This form results from simple and very natural axioms on possibilistic lotteries, which are counterparts to the Von Neumann and Morgenstern axioms [NEU 47]: a complete preorder of acts, increasing in the wide sense according to the ordering in V_Π, substitutability of indifferent lotteries and the assumption that any consequence of an act is valued on V_Π. More recently, Weng [WEN 06a] proposed a Savage-style axiomatization of binary possibilistic utility. It puts together the axiomatizations of the optimistic and the pessimistic possibilistic criteria by Dubois et al. [DUB 01b], adding to the axioms justifying the Sugeno integral two additional conditions: (i) the self-conjugateness of the preference relation on binary acts, and (ii) a postulate enforcing axiom 11.22 on the subset of acts $\{f : f \succeq h, f \in X^S\}$ weakly preferred to an act h that plays the role of a neutral point separating favorable from unfavorable acts in X^S.

Pessimistic and optimistic possibilistic criteria turn out to be special cases of this bipolar criterion. They correspond respectively to either using the negative part of V_Π only (not being able to separate $(1,1)$ from $(0,1)$ in case of pessimism) or using the positive part of V_Π only (not being able to separate $(1,0)$ from $(1,1)$ in case of optimism). The decision rule of Giang and Shenoy can capture the lexicographic use of possibilistic criteria $W^-_{\pi,n(u)}$ and $W^+_{\pi,u}$, where the optimist one is used when the pessimistic one cannot discriminate (or vice versa) [GOD 05, WEN 05]. However, this criterion has a major drawback. Whenever two states s_i and s_j are such that $\alpha_i = 1$ and $\beta_j = 1$ (a bad or neutral, and a good or neutral state, respectively) and these states have maximal possibility $\pi_i = \pi_j = 1$, then $W_{GS}(f) = (1,1)$ results, expressing indifference. This limited expressiveness seems to be unavoidable when using finite bipolar scales [GRA 04].

Lehmann [LEH 01] axiomatizes a refinement of the maximin criterion whereby ties between equivalent worst states are broken by considering their respective likelihoods. This decision rule takes the form of an expected utility criterion with qualitative (infinitesimal) utility levels. An axiomatization is carried out in the Von Neumann–Morgenstern style [NEU 47].

The lack of discrimination of the maximin rule itself was actually addressed a long time ago by Cohen and Jaffray [COH 80] who improve it by comparing acts on the basis of their worst consequences of *distinct* merits, i.e. one considers only the set $D(f,g) = \{s, u(f(s)) \neq u(g(s))\}$ when performing a minimization. Denoting the strict preference between acts by $f \succ_D g$,

$$f \succ_D g \text{ if and only if } \min_{s \in D(f,g)} f(s) > \min_{s \in D(f,g)} g(s) \qquad (11.10)$$

and the weak preference is $f \succeq_D g$ if and only if $\neg(g \succ_D f)$. This refined rule always rates an act f better than another act g whenever f is at least as good as g in all states and better in some states (strict compatibility with Pareto-dominance). However, only a partial ordering of acts is then obtained. This last decision rule is actually no longer based on a preference functional (i.e. it cannot be encoded by a numerical function, such as expected utility). This decision rule has been independently proposed by Fargier and Schiex [FAR 93] and used in fuzzy constraint satisfaction problems [DUB 99a] under the name *discrimin ordering*.

This criterion can be further refined by the so-called *Leximin* ordering [MOU 88]. The idea is to reorder utility vectors $\vec{f} = (u(f(s_1)), \ldots u(f(s_n)))$ by non-decreasing values as $(f_{(1)}, \ldots, f_{(n)})$, where $f_{(k)}$ is the kth smallest component of $\vec{f}$ (i.e. $f_{(1)} \leq \ldots \leq f_{(n)}$). Similarly, a *Leximax* preorder can be envisaged as a refinement of the one induced by the maximum. Let $\vec{f}, \vec{g} \in L^N$. Define the Leximin ($\succeq_{lmin}$) and Leximax ($\succeq_{lmax}$) rules as:

- $\vec{f} \succeq_{lmin} \vec{g} \Leftrightarrow$ either $\forall j, f_{(j)} = g_{(j)}$ or $\exists i, \forall j < i, f_{(j)} = g_{(j)}$ and $f_{(i)} > g_{(i)}$
- $\vec{f} \succeq_{lmax} \vec{g} \Leftrightarrow$ either $\forall j, f_{(j)} = g_{(j)}$ or $\exists i, \forall j > i, f_{(j)} = g_{(j)}$ and $f_{(i)} > g_{(i)}$.

The two possible decisions f and g are indifferent if and only if the corresponding reordered vectors are the same. The Leximin-ordering is a refinement of the discrimin ordering, hence of both the Pareto-ordering and the maximin-ordering [DUB 96]: $f \succ_D g$ implies $f \succ_{lmin} g$. Leximin optimal decisions are always discrimin maximal decisions, and thus indeed min-optimal and Pareto-maximal: $\succ_{lmin}$ is the most selective among these preference relations. The Leximin ordering can discriminate more than any symmetric aggregation function; e.g. in the numerical setting when the sum of the $u(f(s_i))$s equals the sum of the $u(\mathbf{f}(s_i))$s, this does not mean that the reordered vectors are the same.

11.5.2. *A bridge between generalized maxmin criteria and expected utility*

Criteria of the discrimin and Leximin type unfortunately never take into account the available information on the state of affairs, contrary to possibilistic criteria. One idea is to refine the latter by changing minimum into Leximin and maximum into Leximax in each of them in order to integrate the plausibility of states within the lexicographic approach. It turns out that this can be encoded by means of an extreme form of expected utility [FAR 05].

First note that, in a finite setting, the qualitative Leximin and Leximax rules can be simulated by means of a sum of utilities provided that the levels in the qualitative (finite) utility scale V are mapped to values sufficiently far away from one another on a numerical scale. Consider an increasing mapping ϕ from V to the reals. It is possible to define this mapping in such a way as to refine the maximax ordering:

$$\max_{i=1,\ldots n} f_i > \max_{i=1,\ldots n} g_i \text{ implies } \sum_{i=1,\ldots n} \phi(f_i) > \sum_{i=1,\ldots n} \phi(g_i). \quad (11.11)$$

For instance, the transformation $\phi(\lambda_i) = N^i$ with $N > n$ achieves this goal. It is a super-increasing mapping in the sense that $\phi(\lambda_i) > \sum_{j<i} \phi(\lambda_i), \forall i = 1, \ldots, m$. In order to map V to [0, 1] so that $\phi(\lambda_0) = 0$ and $\phi(\lambda_m) = 1$, just take

$$\phi(\lambda_i) = \frac{N^i - 1}{N^m - 1}.$$

It can actually be checked that the Leximax ordering is equivalent to applying the Bernoulli criterion with respect to such a convex utility function $\phi(.)$:

$$f >_{Leximax} g \text{ if and only if } \sum_{i=1,\ldots n} \phi(f_i) > \sum_{i=1,\ldots n} \phi(g_i). \tag{11.12}$$

A similar encoding of the Leximin procedure by a sum can be achieved using another super-increasing mapping (for instance, the transformation $\psi(\lambda_i) = (1 - N^{-i})/(1 - N^{-m})$):

$$\min_{i=1,\ldots n} f_i > \min_{i=1,\ldots n} g_i \text{ implies } \sum_{i=1,\ldots n} \psi(f_i) > \sum_{i=1,\ldots n} \psi(g_i). \tag{11.13}$$

The Leximin ordering comes down to applying the Bernoulli criterion with respect to such a concave utility function $\psi(.)$. Notice that these transformations are not possible when V is not finite [MOU 88] although the Leximin and Leximax procedures still make mathematical sense even in this case. The qualitative pessimistic and optimistic criteria under total ignorance are therefore refined by means of a classical criterion with respect to a risk-averse and risk-prone utility function respectively, as can be seen by plotting V against numerical values in $\phi(V)$ and $\psi(V)$.

These refinement principles have been extended to possibilistic criteria [FAR 05] using weighted averages. Consider first the optimistic possibilistic criterion $W^+_{\pi,\mu}$ under a given possibility distribution π. We can again define an increasing mapping χ from V to the reals such that $\chi(\lambda_0) = 0$ and especially:

$$\max_i \min(\pi(s_i), u(f(s_i))) > \max_i \min(\pi(s_i), u(g(s_i)))$$

implies (11.14)

$$\sum_{i=1,\ldots n} \chi(\pi(s_i)) \cdot \chi(u(f(s_i))) > \sum_{i=1,\ldots n} \chi(\pi(s_i)) \cdot \chi(u(g(s_i))). \tag{11.15}$$

A sufficient condition is that:

$$\forall i \in \{1, \ldots, m\}, \chi(\lambda_i)^2 \geq N\chi(\lambda_{i-1}) \cdot \chi(\top) \tag{11.16}$$

for $N > n$. The increasing mapping $\chi(\lambda_i) = N/(N^{2^{m-i}}), i = 1,\ldots, m$ and $\chi(\lambda_0) = 0$ with $N = n + 1$ can be chosen with $n = |S|; m = |V|$. The mapping is such that $\chi(\lambda_m) = 1$.

Moreover, let $\{E_0, \ldots, E_k\}$ be the well-ordered partition of S induced by π, E_k containing the most plausible states and E_0 the null states. Let

$$K = \frac{1}{\sum_{i=1,k} |E_i| \cdot \chi(\pi(s_i))}.$$

Define $\chi^*(\lambda_i) = K\chi(\lambda_i)$; the following holds:

– $p = \chi^*(\pi(\cdot))$ is a probability assignment respectful of the possibilistic ordering of states. In particular, p is uniform on equipossible states (the sets E_i). Moreover, if $s \in E_i$ then $p(s)$ is greater than the sum of the probabilities of all less probable states i.e. $p(s) > P(E_{i-1} \cup \ldots \cup E_0)$. Such probabilities, here said to be *big-stepped*, generalize the linear big-stepped probabilities that form a super-increasing sequence of numbers assigned to singletons. They are introduced by Snow [SNO 99] and also studied in Benferhat *et al.* [BEN 99] in connection with non-monotonic reasoning. Linear big-stepped probabilities are recovered when the E_i's are singletons.

– $\chi(u(\cdot))$ is a big-stepped numerical utility function (a super-increasing sequence of reals $u_l > \ldots > u_1$ such that $\forall l \geq i > 1, u_i > n \cdot u_{i-1}$) that can be encoded by a convex real mapping.

– The preference functional

$$EU_+(f) = \sum_{i=1,\ldots n} \chi^*(\pi(s_i)) \cdot \chi(u(f(s_i)))$$

is an expected (big-stepped) utility criterion for a risk-seeking decision maker, and $W^+_{\pi,u}(f) > W^+_{\pi,u}(g)$ implies $EU_+(f) > EU_+(g)$. Namely this is precisely equation (11.15) up to the multiplicative constant K i.e. the expected utility criterion so-obtained refines the possibilistic optimistic criterion. As a refinement, it is perfectly compatible with but more decisive than the optimistic utility. Since it is based on expected utility, it obviously satisfies the sure-thing principle as well as the strict Pareto-dominance, actually recovering Savage's five first axioms. Moreover, it does not use any other information but the original ordinal one. It can be shown that it is not the only criterion in this family of sound 'unbiased' refinements, but it is the most efficient among them (up to an equivalence relation), since it refines any unbiased refinement of the possibilistic optimistic criterion (see [FAR 05] for more details).

The pessimistic criterion can be similarly refined. Note that, using the order-reversing map ν of V, $W^-_{\pi,u}(f) = \nu(W^+_{\pi,\nu(u)}(f))$. Then, choosing the same mapping

χ^* as above, we may have

$$\min_i \max(\pi(s_i), u(f(s_i))) > \min_i \max(\pi(s_i), u(g(s_i)))$$

implies

$$\sum_{i=1,\ldots n} \chi^*(\pi(s_i)) \cdot \phi(u(f(s_i))) > \sum_{i=1,\ldots n} \chi^*(\pi(s_i)) \cdot \phi(u(g(s_i))) \quad (11.17)$$

where $\phi(\lambda_i) = 1 - \chi(\nu(\lambda_i))$ (equal to $1 - (n+1)/((n+1)^{2^i})$ here). Function $\phi(u(\cdot))$ is a super-increasing numerical utility function that can be encoded by a concave real mapping. The expected utility criterion

$$EU_-(f) = \sum_{i=1,\ldots n} \chi^*(\pi((s_i))) \cdot \phi(u(f(s_i)))$$

is a risk-averse one, refining $W_{\pi,\mu}$ in the sense that $W^-_{\pi,\mu}(f) > W^-_{\pi,\mu}(g)$ implies $EU_-(f) > EU_-(g)$.

These results highlight the deep agreement between qualitative possibilistic criteria and expected utility. The former is simply coarser than the latter, and as such cannot account for compensative effects. Actually, both types of criteria are subsumed within a more abstract algebraic approach using operations on a semi-ring by Chu and Halpern [CHU 04] and Weng [WEN 06b].

11.5.3. *Weighted Leximax/Leximin criteria*

The orderings induced by $EU_+(f)$ and $EU_-(f)$ actually correspond to generalizations of Leximin and Leximax to prioritized minimum and maximum aggregations, thus bridging the gap between possibilistic criteria and classical decision theory. To make this generalization clear, let us simply consider that Leximin and Leximax orderings are defined on sets of tuples whose components belong to a totally ordered set $(\Omega, \unrhd)$, say $Leximin(\unrhd)$ and $Leximax(\unrhd)$. Now, suppose $(\Omega, \unrhd) = (V^l, Leximin)$ or $(\Omega, \unrhd) = (V^l, Leximax)$, with any $l \in \mathbb{N}$. Lexicographic ordering relations can be recursively defined by nesting procedures such as $Leximin(Leximin(\geq))$, $Leximax(Leximin(\geq))$, $Leximin(Leximax(\geq))$ and $Leximax(Leximax(\geq))$, in order to compare V-valued matrices.

Consider for instance the procedure $Leximax(Leximin(\geq))$ which defines the relation $\succeq_{lmax(\succeq lmin)}$. It applies to matrices $[a]$ of dimension $p \times q$ with coefficients a_{ij} in $(V, \geq)$. These matrices can be totally ordered in a very refined way by this relation. Denote row i of $[a]$ by $a_{i.}$. Let $[a^\star]$ and $[b^\star]$ be rearranged matrices $[a]$ and

$[b]$ such that terms in each row are reordered increasingly and rows are arranged lexicographically top-down in decreasing order. $[a] \succ_{lmax(\succeq lmin)} [b]$ is defined as follows:
$$\exists k \leq p \text{ such that } \forall i < k, a^\star_{i\cdot} =_{lmin} b^\star_{i\cdot} \text{ and } a^\star_{k\cdot} >_{lmin} b^\star_{k\cdot}.$$

Relation $\succeq_{lmax(\succeq lmin)}$ is a complete preorder. $[a] \simeq_{lmax(\succeq lmin)} [b]$ if and only if both matrices have the same coefficients up to the above described rearrangement. Moreover, relation $\succeq_{lmax(\succeq lmin)}$ refines the ranking obtained by the optimistic criterion:
$$\max_i \min_j a_{ij} > \max_i \min_j b_{ij} \text{ implies } [a] \succ_{lmax(\succeq lmin)} [b]$$

In particular, if $[a]$ Pareto-dominates $[b]$ in the strict sense ($\forall i, j, a_{ij} \geq b_{ij}$ and $\exists i^\star, j^\star$ such that $a_{i^\star j^\star} > b_{i^\star j^\star}$), then $[a] \succ_{lmax(\succeq lmin)} [b]$.

Comparing acts f and g in the context of a possibility distribution π can be done using relations $\succeq_{lmax(\succeq lmin)}$ applied to $n \times 2$ matrices on $(V, \leq)$. n is the number of states in S, namely on the matrix $[f]_{\pi,u}$ and $[g]_{\pi,u}$ with coefficients $f_{i1} = \pi(s_i)$ and $f_{i2} = u(f(s_i))$, $g_{i1} = \pi(s_i)$ and $g_{i2} \mu(g(s_i))$).

The big-stepped expected utility $EU_+(f)$ defined in the previous section precisely encodes the relation $\succeq_{lmax(\succeq lmin)}$ as follows.

Theorem 11.4. *[FAR 05]:* $EU_+(f) \geq EU_+(f)$ *if and only if* $[f]_{\pi,u} \succeq_{lmax(\succeq lmin)} [g]_{\pi,u}$.

In other terms, EU_+ applies a Leximax procedure to utility degrees weighted by possibility degrees. Similarly, EU_- applies a Leximin procedure to utility degrees weighted by 'impossibility degrees'.

Theorem 11.5. *[FAR 05]:* $EU_-(f) \geq EU_-(g)$ *if and only if* $[f]_{n(\pi),u} \succeq_{lmin(\succeq lmax)} [g]_{n(\pi),u}$.

In other words, $EU_-(f)$ just encodes the application of a procedure Leximin(Leximax) not directly on $[f]_{\pi,u}$ and $[g]_{\pi,u}$ but on the corresponding π-reverse matrix $[f]_{n(\pi),u}$ and $[g]_{n(\pi),u}$ with coefficients $f_{i1} = \nu(\pi(s_i))$ and $f_{i2} = u(f(s_i))$, $g_{i1} = \nu(\pi(s_i))$ and $g_{i2} = u(g(s_i))$.

As a consequence, the additive preference functionals $EU_+(f)$ and $EU_-(f)$ refining the possibilistic criteria are qualitative despite their numerical encoding. Moreover, the two orderings $\succeq_{lmax(\succeq lmin)}$ and $\succeq_{lmin(\succeq lmax)}$ of acts are defined even on coarse ordinal scales V while *obeying Savage's five first axioms of rational decision*. Weng [WEN 05] has extended this approach to the binary possibilistic utility of Giang and Shenoy, recalled in section 11.5.1.

11.5.4. *The representation of uncertainty underlying Leximax(Leximin) and Leximin(Leximax) criteria*

The two relations $\succeq_{lmax(\succeq lmin)}$ and $\succeq_{lmin(\succeq lmax)}$ coincide if the utility functions are Boolean, and then compare events by their likelihood. The corresponding uncertainty representation is precisely the lexi-refinement of possibility orderings

$$\succeq_\Pi \ (A \succeq_\Pi B \text{ if and only if } \Pi(A) \geq \Pi(B))$$

already identified by [DUB 98a]:

$$A \succeq_{l\Pi} B \text{ if and only if } \vec{\pi}_A \succeq_{lmax} \vec{\pi}_B \tag{11.18}$$

where $\vec{\pi}_A$ is the vector $(a_1, \ldots, a_n)$ such that $a_i = \pi(s_i)$ if $s_i \in A$ and $a_i = 0$ otherwise. This relation among events is called the Leximax likelihood [DUB 98a, DUB 04a]. It is a complete preordering whose strict part refines the possibilistic ordering of events together with its adjoint necessity ordering ($A \succeq_N B$ if and only if $\Pi(B^c) \geq \Pi(A^c)$).

This is not surprising since $\succeq_{lmin}$ and $\succeq_{lmax}$ are conjugate: $\vec{u} \succeq_{lmin} \vec{v}$ if and only if $(\nu(v_1), \ldots, \nu(v_k)) \succeq_{lmax} (\nu(u_1), \ldots, \nu(u_k))$. If $\vec{u}$ and $\vec{v}$ are Boolean and encode events A and B, it comes down to $A \succeq_{l\Pi} B$ if and only if $B^c \succeq_{l\Pi} A^c$. Relation $\succeq_{l\Pi}$ is therefore self-conjugate.

Another natural way of refining a possibility relation is to delete, in the spirit of Cohen–Jaffray's decision rule $\succ_D$, states common to two events A and B [DUB 98a]:

$$A >_{D\Pi} B \text{ if and only if } \Pi(A \setminus B) > \Pi(B \setminus A).$$

This partial ordering relation, called *possibilistic likelihood* also refines the weak order induced by the necessity measure. It is preadditive as in probability relations, and also self-adjoint.

The relation $\succeq_{l\Pi}$ refines the above possibilistic likelihood relation and coincides with it for linear plausibility rankings of states (by which S is totally ordered). In the case of a uniform distribution, the Leximax likelihood relation coincides with a qualitative probability relation induced by a uniform probability distribution (comparing the cardinality of sets, $A \succ_{l\Pi} B$ if and only if $|B| > |A|$).

The uncertainty representation underlying the $\succeq_{lmax(\succeq lmin)}$ and $\succeq_{lmin(\succeq lmax)}$ decision rules is therefore probabilistic, although qualitative. The Leximax likelihood relation is a special qualitative probability relation representable by means of the big-stepped probability P, involved in functionals $EU_+(f)$ and $EU_-(f)$, i.e. $A \succeq_{l\Pi} B$ if and only if $P(A) \geq P(B)$. Another formulation of the reason why the Leximax likelihood relation is self-conjugate therefore consists of noticing that $EU_+(f)$ and $EU_-(f)$ share the same big-stepped probability function P.

11.6. Conclusion

This chapter is an overview of qualitative criteria for decision under uncertainty. These results also apply, to some extent, to multicriteria decisions, where the various objectives play the role of states and the likelihood relation is used to compare the relative importance of groups of objectives [DUB 01a, DUB 03b]. Indeed, the commensurability assumptions of the absolute possibilistic approach are often more difficult to advocate between objectives having different natures in multicriteria evaluation than for states of the world in decision under uncertainty. To reconcile the two frameworks, evaluation methods in this chapter should be articulated with conjoint measurement methods described by Bouyssou and Pirlot (see Chapters 16 and 19).

Qualitative criteria can be instrumental in solving discrete decision problems involving finite state spaces, or problems where it is not natural or very difficult to elicit numerical utility functions or probabilities including:

– when the problem is located in a dynamic environment involving a large state space, a non-quantifiable goal to be reached, and a partial information on the current state (this case can be found in robotic planification problems [SAB 01]);

– when only a very high level description of a decision problem is available, where states and consequences of decisions are coarsely defined (e.g. in some kinds of strategic decision making);

– or when there is no time to quantify utilities and probabilities because advice is requested quickly (as in recommender systems).

Possibilistic criteria were also used in scheduling problems, in order to produce robust sequencings of tasks, ensuring moderate and balanced violations of due-dates in case of unexpected events [DUB 95a]. These criteria are compatible with dynamic programing in multistep decision problems [FAR 98].

A number of natural properties any realistic decision theory should satisfy in information system applications are as follows:

1) Faithfulness to available information supplied by decision makers, as poor as it be: an ordinal declarative approach sounds closer to human capabilities.

2) Cognitive relevance: the number of levels in the value scale must be small enough (according to well-known psychological studies, people cannot understand the meaning of more than seven value levels).

3) Good discrimination: especially respecting the strict Pareto-dominance.

4) Decisive power: avoiding incomparability and favor linear rankings.

5) Taking into account the decision maker's attitude in the face of risk and uncertainty.

6) Taking into account the available information on the current state of affairs.

These requirements are often conflicting. Expected utility is information demanding, and hardly compatible with the limited perception capabilities of human decision makers. The maximin criterion of Wald and its refinements neglects available information on the state of affairs. In the present overview, two kinds of qualitative decision rules, compatible with the two first requirements, have been laid bare. Approaches based on ordinal preference relations, including the likely dominance rule, are in full agreement with Pareto-dominance. They satisfy the sure-thing principle, but either leave room to incomparability to a large extent, or focus too much on the most plausible states.

Approaches based on an absolute value scale improve the expressivity of maximin and maximax criteria by injecting the respective plausibility of states. They provide rankings of decisions but lack discrimination power. There is some inconsistency between the requirement of a fine-grained discrimination (respecting Pareto-dominance) and the requirement of a total (especially transitive) ranking of acts in the qualitative framework. Enforcing both conditions seems to bring us back to a special case of expected utility as explained in section 11.5.2. In a purely qualitative setting, nested lexicographic criteria seem to maximize the number of satisfied natural requirements listed above.

Many problems remain open in this area:

– How do we refine the coarse ranking induced by the Sugeno integral? Recent results [DUB 07a] suggest it can be refined by means of the Choquet integral.

– The likely dominance rule compares two acts independently of others. More expressive decision rules involving the comparison with a third reference act can be envisaged by weakening the ordinal invariance axiom [PER 06].

– How do qualitative criteria behave in a dynamic environment where new information is acquired, in the absence of the sure-thing principle to ensure dynamic consistency? It requires the study of conditional acts and qualitative conditional preference functionals. See [DUB 07c] for a preliminary study in the case of possibilistic criteria.

11.7. Bibliography

[ARR 51] ARROW K. J., *Social Choice and Individual Values*, Cowles Foundations and Wiley, New York, 1951.

[ARR 72] ARROW K., HURWICZ L., "An optimality criterion for decision-making under ignorance", CARTER C., FORD J., Eds., *Uncertainty and Expectations in Economics*, Oxford, Basil Blackwell and Mott Ltd, p. 1–12, 1972.

[BAC 96] BACCHUS F., GROVE A. J., "Utility independence in a qualitative decision theory", *Proceedings of the Fifth International Conference on Principles of Knowledge Representation and Reasoning (KR'96)*, Cambridge, Mass., USA, p. 542–552, 1996.

[BEN 99] BENFERHAT S., DUBOIS D., PRADE H., "Possibilistic and standard probabilistic semantics of conditional knowledge bases", *Journal of Logic and Computation*, vol. 9, p. 873–895, 1999.

[BOU 94] BOUTILIER C., "Toward a logic for qualitative decision theory", *Proceedings of the 4th International Conference on Principles of Knowledge Representation and Reasoning (KR'94)*, Bonn, Germany, USA, p. 75–86, 1994.

[BOU 00] BOUYSSOU D., MARCHANT T., PIRLOT M., PERNY P., TSOUKIÀS A., VINCKE P., *Evaluation and Decision Models: A Critical Perspective*, Kluwer Academic Publishers, Dordrecht, 2000.

[BRA 97] BRAFMAN R., TENNENHOLTZ M., "Modeling agents as qualitative decision makers", *Artificial Intelligence*, vol. 94, p. 217–268, 1997.

[BRA 00] BRAFMAN R., TENNENHOLTZ M., "On the axiomatization of qualitative decision criteria", *Journal of the ACM*, vol. 47, p. 452–482, 2000.

[CAY 82] CAYROL M., FARRENY H., PRADE H., "Fuzzy pattern matching", *Kybernetes*, vol. 11, p. 103–116, 1982.

[CHE 54] CHERNOFF H., "Rational selection of decision functions", *Econometrica*, vol. 22, p. 422–444, 1954.

[CHU 04] CHU F. C., HALPERN J. Y., "Great expectations. Part II: generalized expected utility as a universal decision rule", *Artificial Intelligence*, vol. 159, num. 1-2, p. 207–229, 2004.

[COH 80] COHEN M., JAFFRAY J., "Rational behavior under complete ignorance", *Econometrica*, vol. 48, num. 5, p. 1281–99, 1980.

[DOY 91] DOYLE J., WELLMAN M. P., "Impediments to universal preference-based default theories", *Artificial Intelligence*, vol. 49, p. 97–128, 1991.

[DOY 99] DOYLE J., THOMASON R. H., "Background to qualitative decision theory", *AI Magazine*, vol. 20, num. 2, p. 55–68, 1999.

[DUB 86] DUBOIS D., "Belief Structures, Possibility Theory and Decomposable Confidence Measures on Finite Sets", *Computers and Artificial Intelligence*, vol. 5, num. 5, p. 403–416, 1986.

[DUB 88a] DUBOIS D., PRADE H., *Possibility Theory*, Plenum Press, New York (NY), 1988.

[DUB 88b] DUBOIS D., PRADE H., TESTEMALE C., "Weighted fuzzy pattern matching", *Fuzzy Sets and Systems*, vol. 28, p. 313–331, 1988.

[DUB 95a] DUBOIS D., FARGIER H., PRADE H., "Fuzzy constraints in job-shop scheduling", *Journal of Intelligent Manufacturing*, vol. 6, p. 215–234, 1995.

[DUB 95b] DUBOIS D., PRADE H., "Possibility theory as a basis for qualitative decision theory", *Proceedings of the International Joint Conference on Artificial Intelligence (IJCAI'95)*, p. 1925–1930, 1995.

[DUB 95c] DUBOIS D., PRADE H., "Numerical representations of acceptance", *Proceedings of International Conference on Uncertainty in Artificial Intelligence (UAI'95)*, p. 149–156, 1995.

[DUB 96] DUBOIS D., FARGIER H., PRADE H., "Refinements of the maximin approach to decision-making in a fuzzy environment", *Fuzzy Sets Systems*, vol. 81, num. 1, p. 103–122, 1996.

[DUB 97] DUBOIS D., FARGIER H., PRADE H., "Decision making under ordinal preferences and comparative uncertainty", *Proceedings of International Conference on Uncertainty in Artificial Intelligence (UAI'97)*, p. 157–164, 1997.

[DUB 98a] DUBOIS D., FARGIER H., PRADE H., "Possibilistic likelihood relations", *Proceedings of the International Conference on Information Processing and Management of Uncertainty (IPMU'98)*, Paris, France, EDK, p. 1196–1203, 1998.

[DUB 98b] DUBOIS D., PRADE H., "Possibility theory: qualitative and quantitative aspects", SMETS P., Ed., *Handbook on Defeasible Reasoning and Uncertainty Management Systems Volume 1: Quantified Representation of Uncertainty and Imprecision*, Dordrecht, Kluwer Academic, p. 169–226, 1998.

[DUB 99a] DUBOIS D., FORTEMPS P., "Computing improved optimal solutions to max-min flexible constraint satisfaction problems", *European Journal of Operational Research*, vol. 118, p. 95–126, 1999.

[DUB 99b] DUBOIS D., GODO L., PRADE H., ZAPICO A., "On the possibilistic decision model: from decision under uncertainty to case-based decision", *International Journal of Uncertainty, Fuzziness and Knowledge-Based Systems*, vol. 7, p. 631–670, 1999.

[DUB 00a] DUBOIS D., GODO L., PRADE H., ZAPICO A., "Advances in qualitative decision theory: refined rankings", *7th Ibero-American Conference on AI and 15th Brazilian Symposium on AI, IBERAMIA-SBIA'2000, LNAI 1952*, Berlin, Springer, p. 427–436, 2000.

[DUB 00b] DUBOIS D., GRABISCH M., MODAVE F., PRADE H., "Relating decision under uncertainty and multicriteria decision making models", *International Journal of Intelligent Systems*, vol. 15, num. 10, p. 967–979, 2000.

[DUB 00c] DUBOIS D., PRADE H., SABBADIN R., "Qualitative decision theory with Sugeno integrals", GRABISCH M., MUROFUSHI T., SUGENO M., Eds., *Fuzzy Measures and Integrals: Theory and Applications*, Heidelberg, Physica Verlag, p. 314–322, 2000.

[DUB 01a] DUBOIS D., MARICHAL J.-L., PRADE H., ROUBENS M., SABBADIN R., "The use of the discrete Sugeno integral in decision-making: a survey", *International Journal of Uncertainty, Fuzziness and Knowledge-Based Systems*, vol. 9, p. 539–561, 2001.

[DUB 01b] DUBOIS D., PRADE H., SABBADIN R., "Decision-theoretic foundation of qualitative possibility theory", *European Journal of Operational Research*, vol. 128, p. 478–495, 2001.

[DUB 02] DUBOIS D., FARGIER H., PERNY P., PRADE H., "Qualitative decision theory: from Savage's axioms to non-monotonic reasoning", *Journal of the ACM*, vol. 49, p. 455–495, 2002.

[DUB 03a] DUBOIS D., FARGIER H., PERNY P., "Qualitative models for decision under uncertainty: an axiomatic approach", *Artificial Intelligence*, vol. 148, p. 219–260, 2003.

[DUB 03b] DUBOIS D., FARGIER H., PERNY P., PRADE H., "A characterization of generalized concordance rules in multicriteria decision making", *International Journal of Intelligent Systems*, vol. 18, p. 751–774, 2003.

[DUB 04a] DUBOIS D., FARGIER H., "An axiomatic framework for order of magnitude confidence relations", *Proceedings of UAI'04*, Banff, CA, 2004.

[DUB 04b] DUBOIS D., FARGIER H., PRADE H., "Ordinal and probabilistic representations of acceptance", *Journal of Artificial Intelligence Research*, vol. 22, p. 23–55, 2004.

[DUB 05] DUBOIS D., FORTEMPS P., "Selecting preferred solutions in the minimax approach to dynamic programming problems under flexible constraints", *European Journal of Operational Research*, vol. 19, p. 441–471, 2005.

[DUB 07a] DUBOIS D., FARGIER H., "Lexicographic refiniments of Sugeno integrals", MELLOULI K., Ed., *European Conference on Symbolic and Quantitative Approaches to Reasoning with Uncertainty (ECSQARU)*, Lecture Notes in Artificial Intelligence, LNAI, Hammamet, Tunisia, http://www.springerlink.com, Springer, p. 611–622, 2007.

[DUB 07b] DUBOIS D., FARGIER H., PERNY P., "Corrigendum to qualitative decision theory with preference relations and comparative uncertainty: an axiomatic approach", *Artificial Intelligence*, vol. 171, p. 361–362, 2007.

[DUB 07c] DUBOIS D., FARGIER H., VANTAGGI B., "An axiomatization of conditional possibilistic preference functionals", MELLOULI K., Ed., *European Conference on Symbolic and Quantitative Approaches to Reasoning with Uncertainty (ECSQARU)*, vol. 4724 of *Lecture Notes in Artificial Intelligence, LNAI*, Hammamet, Tunisia, http://www.springerlink.com, Springer, p. 803–815, 2007.

[FAR 93] FARGIER H., LANG J., SCHIEX T., "Selecting preferred solutions in fuzzy constraint satisfaction problems", *Proceedings of 1st European Congress on Fuzzy and Intelligent Technologies (EUFIT'93)*, Aachen, Germany, p. 1128–1134, 1993.

[FAR 98] FARGIER H., LANG J., SABBADIN R., "Towards qualitative approaches to multi-stage decision making", *International Journal of Approximate Reasoning*, vol. 19, p. 441–471, 1998.

[FAR 99] FARGIER H., PERNY P., "Qualitative models for decision under uncertainty without the commensurability assumption", LASKEY K., PRADE H., Eds., *Proceedings of the 15th Conference on Uncertainty in Artificial Intelligence*, Stockholm, Sweden, p. 157–164, 1999.

[FAR 05] FARGIER H., SABBADIN R., "Qualitative decision under uncertainty: Back to expected utility", *Artificial Intelligence*, vol. 164, p. 245–280, 2005.

[FIS 75] FISHBURN P. C., "Axioms for lexicographic preferences", *Review of Economic Studies*, vol. 42, p. 415–419, 1975.

[FIS 86] FISHBURN P. C., "The axioms of subjective probabilities.", *Statistical Science*, vol. 1, p. 335–358, 1986.

[FRI 96] FRIEDMAN N., HALPERN J. Y., "Plausibility measures and default reasoning", *Proceedings of AAAI'96*, p. 1297–1304, 1996.

[GIA 00] GIANG P. H., SHENOY P. P., "A qualitative utility theory for Spohn's theory of epistemic beliefs", *Proceedings of the 16th Conference on Uncertainty in Artificial Intelligence*, p. 220–227, 2000.

[GIA 05] GIANG P. H., SHENOY P. P., "Two axiomatic approaches to decision-making using possibility theory", *European Journal of Operational Research*, vol. 162, p. 450–467, 2005.

[GOD 05] GODO L., ZAPICO A., "Lexicographic refinements in the context of possibilistic decision theory", *Proceedings of International Conference in Fuzzy Logic and Technology (EUSFLATÕ05)*, Barcelona, Universitat Politecnica, p. 569–575, 2005.

[GRA 00a] GRABISCH M., MUROFUSHI T., (EDS.) M. S., *Fuzzy Measures and Integrals: Theory and Applications*, Physica Verlag, Heidelberg, 2000.

[GRA 00b] GRANT S., KAJI A., POLAK B., "Decomposable choice under uncertainty", *Journal of Economic Theory*, vol. 92, p. 169–197, 2000.

[GRA 04] GRABISCH M., "The Moebius transform on symmetric ordered structures and its application to capacities on finite sets", *Discrete Mathematics*, vol. 287, p. 17–34, 2004.

[JAF 89] JAFFRAY J.-Y., "Linear utility theory for belief functions", *Operations Research Letters*, vol. 8, p. 107–112, 1989.

[KRA 58] KRAFT C. H., PRATT J. W., SEIDENBERG A., "Intuitive probability on finite sets", *Annals of Mathematical Statistics*, vol. 30, p. 408–419, 1958.

[KRA 90] KRAUS S., LEHMANN D., MAGIDOR M., "Nonmonotonic reasoning, preferential models and cumulative logics", *Artificial Intelligence*, vol. 44, num. 1-2, p. 167–207, 1990.

[LAN 96] LANG J., "Conditional desires and utilities: an alternative logical approach to qualitative decision theory", *Proceedings of the 12th European Conference on Artificial Intelligence (ECAI'96)*, Budapest, p. 318–322, 1996.

[LEH 96] LEHMANN D., "Generalized qualitative probability: Savage revisited", *Proceedings of International Conference on Uncertainty in Artificial Intelligence (UAI'96)*, p. 381-388, 1996.

[LEH 01] LEHMANN D., "Expected qualitative utility maximization", *Games and Economic Behavior*, vol. 35, num. 1–2, p. 54–79, 2001.

[LEW 73] LEWIS D., *Counterfactuals*, Basil Blackwell, London, 1973.

[MAR 00] MARICHAL J.-L., "On Sugeno integrals as an aggregation function", *Fuzzy Sets and Systems*, vol. 114, num. 3, p. 347–365, 2000.

[MOU 88] MOULIN H., *Axioms of Cooperative Decision Making*, John Wiley, New York, 1988.

[NEU 47] NEUMANN J. V., MORGENSTERN O., *Theory of Games and Economic Behavior*, Princeton University Press, 1947.

[PER 06] PERNY P., ROLLAND A., "Reference-dependent qualitative models for decision making under uncertainty", BREWKA G., CORADESCHI S., PERINI A., TRAVERSO P., Eds., *ECAI*, IOS Press, p. 422–426, 2006.

[SAB 01] SABBADIN R., "Possibilistic Markov decision processes", *Engineering Applications of Artificial Intelligence*, vol. 14, p. 287–300, 2001.

[SAV 54] SAVAGE L., *The Foundations of Statistics*, John Wiley, New York, 1954.

[SCH 89] SCHMEIDLER D., "Subjective probability and expected utility without additivity", *Econometrica*, vol. 57, p. 571–587, 1989.

[SEN 86] SEN A. K., "Social choice theory", ARROW K., INTRILLIGATOR M., Eds., *Handbook of Mathematical Economics*, Chapter 22, p. 1073–1181, Elsevier Sciences Publishers, North Holland, 1986.

[SHA 49] SHACKLE G., *Expectation in Economics*, Cambridge University Press, U.K, 1949.

[SHA 61] SHACKLE G., *Decision Order and Time In Human Affairs*, Cambridge University Press, U.K, 1961.

[SNO 99] SNOW P., "Diverse Confidence Levels in a Probabilistic Semantics for Conditional Logics", *Artificial Intelligence*, vol. 113, num. 1–2, p. 269–279, 1999.

[SUG 74] SUGENO M., Theory of fuzzy integral and its applications, PhD thesis, Tokyo Institute of Technology, Tokyo, 1974.

[TAN 94] TAN S., PEARL J., "Specification and Evaluation of Preferences Under Uncertainty", JON DOYLE, ERIK SANDEWALL P. T., Ed., *Proceedings of the 4th International Conference on Principles of Knowledge Representation and Reasoning (KR'94), Bonn, Germany, USA*, Bonn, FRG, Morgan Kaufmann, p. 530–539, May 1994.

[THO 00] THOMASON R., "Desires and Defaults: A Framework for Planning with Inferred Goals", *Proceedings of KR'2000*, p. 702–713, 2000.

[VIN 92] VINCKE P., *Multicriteria Decision Aid*, John Wiley, New York, 1992.

[WAL 50] WALD A., *Statistical Decision Functions*, John Wiley, New York, 1950.

[WEN 05] WENG P., "Qualitative decision making under possibilistic uncertainty: Towards more discriminating criteria", *Proceedings of the 21st Conference in Uncertainty in Artificial Intelligence (UAI'05)*, Edinburgh, UK, p. 615–622, 2005.

[WEN 06a] WENG P., "An axiomatic approach in qualitative decision theory with binary possibilistic utility", *Proceedings of the 17th European Conference on Artificial Intelligence (ECAI 2006)*, Riva del Garda, Italy, IOS Press, p. 467–471, 2006.

[WEN 06b] WENG P., "Axiomatic Foundations for a Class of Generalized Expected Utility: Algebraic Expected Utility", *Proceedings of the 22nd Conference in Uncertainty in Artificial Intelligence*, Cambridge, MA, USA, p. 520–527, 2006.

[WHA 84] WHALEN T., "Decision making under uncertainty with various assumptions about available information.", *IEEE Transactions on Systems, Man and Cybernetics*, vol. 14, p. 888–900, 1984.

[YAG 79] YAGER R., "Possibilistic decision making", *IEEE Transactions on Systems, Man and Cybernetics*, vol. 9, p. 388–392, 1979.

[ZAD 78] ZADEH L., "Fuzzy sets as a basis for a theory of possibility", *Fuzzy Sets and Systems*, vol. 1, p. 3–28, 1978.

Chapter 12

A Cognitive Approach to Human Decision Making

12.1. Introduction

The initial studies in the psychology of decision making under uncertainty were based on expected utility theory. However, this theory rapidly appeared to be incompatible with subjects' actual behavior, which followed another kind of rationality rooted in millions of years of evolution under the pressure of natural selection. For instance, a double tendency exists in every individual: risk aversion, a drive to avoid risky situations, and the drive to realize one's potential, which incites us towards risk-taking behaviors. Since these conflicting motivations can be found in other mammals, they were probably acquired long before invention of money, number systems, spoken language and more generally, of any symbolic system. Evolution also equipped us with a cognitive architecture capable of processing information through two very different functioning modes. The first makes use of a lower level of automatic, fast, subconscious processes essentially based on the detection or activation of associations. The second 'symbolic' mode is slower. It is cognitively more costly as it requires attentional resources for inhibiting and guiding automatic processes. However, it alone enables formal reasoning and mathematical models such as expected utility theory. Due to its high 'cognitive cost', formal reasoning is unlikely to be used in everyday life. Mundane reasoning is therefore largely determined by automatic processes, that is, by a processing mode that sometimes differs markedly from classical norms of rationality.

Chapter written by Éric RAUFASTE and Denis J. HILTON.

12.2. Humans do not match current rational models

The fact that humans do not match rational models can be demonstrated by two complementary approaches. These show that there are systematic deviations between the statistical structure of reality and the representation people have of it. In particular, we discuss the bias of overconfidence and the lack of internal coherence of mental representations.

12.2.1. *Overconfidence and calibration of judgement*

Formal models of reasoning generally use the language of probability to represent uncertainty. The birth of the modern theory of probability is often dated to the 17th century, when French mathematicians set themselves the task of calculating the chances of winning at games of cards or tennis [BER 96, HAC 75]. Can one suppose, however, that ordinary people use objective probabilities (even when available) to express or calculate their chances of winning? Or do they systematically mis-estimate the chances of their judgements and predictions of being correct compared to an objective standard?

One way of addressing these questions is to examine the quality of the calibration of human judgements [ALP 82]. Imagine that 100 people are asked the question: 'What was the age of Martin Luther King at his death?', and then asked to state an upper and lower bound such that they are 90% sure that the correct response falls in this interval. If this group of respondents is well calibrated, 90 of them should give responses that fall in the interval and only 10 responses should fall outside the interval. One can also establish whether an individual is well calibrated by asking them 100 general knowledge questions of this type. If this individual is well calibrated, 90 of the correct responses should fall inside the intervals that they gives and only 10 outside.

In a recent study [HIL 09] that used 10 such questions about general knowledge with various samples of French students (university students in economics, management and psychology and *Grande Ecole* business students), we obtained overall surprise rates of between 71–80%. As the expected surprise was only 10% for well-calibrated participants, we are led to conclude that these students are overconfident in the quality of their judgements. These results correspond to those found by other researchers [e.g. LIC 82]. For example, Russo and Schoemaker [RUS 92] found that managers only gave the correct response during 42–62% of cases, even though their supposed domains of expertise were tapped by the questions posed. In the studies conducted by Klayman *et al.* [KLA 99], the correct response fell within participants' confidence interval in only 43% of cases. In addition, this bias seems to be difficult to eradicate: thus Fischhoff *et al.* [FIS 77] found that financial incentives had little or no effect on performance on this task.

(Indeed, the most spectacular demonstration of the resistance of miscalibration to financial incentives that we know of was made by Denis Bouyssou while he was a professor in a Paris business school. As part of his course on decision analysis, he invited his students to bet on the accuracy of their judgements using similar techniques to those described in this chapter. His average win from classes of 30 or so students was 4,000 francs (about €600), which he always graciously reimbursed to the students at the end of the course in the form of champagne.)

Experts are not immune from overconfidence in their judgements, which could prove costly. Stephan [STE 98] found high levels of miscalibration in German traders who were asked questions about future currency exchange rates and market indicators. Physicians prescribe and dose painkillers based on their estimates of their patients' pain level but Marquié et al. [MAR 03] found systematic error in physicians' estimates of patients' pain. The finding that overconfidence is observed in experts answering questions in their domain of everyday expertise suggests that overconfidence is not necessarily an artefact created by an over-sampling of trick questions in the set posed to participants, as suggested by Gigerenzer et al. [GIG 91] and Juslin [JUS 94].

What is more, overconfidence in judgement can have negative effects on performance. Biais et al. [BIA 05] therefore used a calibration questionnaire composed of general knowledge questions to measure overconfidence in finance students. They then showed that overconfident students were likely to lose in an experimental market game, and above all to make poor deals in times where there was high ambiguity about the relation between stated price and actual value. It is in such situations that overconfidence about the diagnosticity of market signals (stated prices) as indicators of true value of assets can prove most costly.

While people are better calibrated when the judgement task is easy [FIS 77], and miscalibration is less extreme when measured by other methods than confidence intervals [KLA 99], the robustness of this phenomenon indicates that people often, indeed systematically, underestimate what they do not know. In a later part of this chapter, we will discuss processes capable of explaining why overconfidence in judgement occurs, such as judgemental heuristics. In the following section, we continue our examination of whether human judgement follows normative standards, by demonstrating that they often show considerable internal inconsistency (for example, in the domain of preference formation).

12.2.2. *Preference reversals and framing effects*

Imagine that a new disease spreads throughout your town. Two vaccines are available. One is certain to save 200 lives, but no more, whereas the other has one chance out of three to save 600 lives and two chances out of 3 of saving none. You are responsible for the choice of the vaccine that will be applied. Which one do you choose?

Now, imagine a new disease arrives. Two other vaccines are available. With the first, it is certain that 400 persons will die. With the second, there is one chance out of three that no one dies and two chances out of three that 600 die. Which one do you choose?

Experimental results [TVE 81] show that the majority of subjects significantly prefer the more certain option in the first choice (certainty of saving 200 lives). Participants prefer the more uncertain option in the second choice (possibility of saving 600 lives). The problems are logically equivalent, however.

This is a demonstration of what psychologists call 'framing effects'. Slovic and Lichtenstein [LIC 71, SLO 68] have shown that superficial characteristics of problems, irrelevant from a rational standpoint, have a qualitative and quantitative impact on the final choice to the point that such preference reversals can appear. Thus, bets having a high probability of winning a little amount are chosen more often than equivalent bets with a low probability of winning a large amount. Moreover, when subjects are asked to provide a value for the bets, highly valued bets are those associated with a large-but-unlikely gain, despite the same participants having preferred bets having a high probability of making a small gain.

Numerous studies have since confirmed the possibility of inducing preference reversals between rationally equivalent options [SLO 95]. Indeed, preferences generally do not preexist in individuals' minds but rather are constructed during the decision making process, which is influenced by that construction. We first present a psychological theory of expected utility, which is aimed at explaining framing effects. However, we will see that a finer analysis of the cognitive mechanisms underlying the construction of preferences is necessary.

12.2.3. *Subjectivation of expected utility: prospect theory*

Prospect theory, proposed by the cognitive psychologists Kahneman and Tversky in 1979 [KAH 79], constitutes a first formalization of the acknowledged effect framing has on decision making. Kahneman received the Nobel Prize in Economics for his work on the psychology of decision making under uncertainty. Let α be an action prospect (vaccines A or B in the example above) with potential outcomes r_i having some utilities $u(r_i)$ (e.g. patient's survival, cost of treatment, etc.), and having some probabilities of occurrence $p(r_i)$ (success rate). Classical decision theory computes the expected utility of a possible action $U(\alpha)$ by summing the utility multiplied by the probability products of all the potential consequences of the action, i.e.

$$U(\alpha) = \sum u(r_i).p(r_i).$$

Prospect theory 'subjectivizes' this approach by substituting a subjective function (value) for the objective utility (amount), and a subjective function (weighting) for the objective probabilities. Let $v(.)$ be the subjective value felt in response to the objective price of the outcome of the action under consideration, and $\pi(.)$ the weighting felt with regard to the objective probability of the outcome realization. The resulting subjective value will be:

$$V(\alpha) = \sum v(u(r_i)).\pi(p(r_i)).$$

The question is to determine properties of the subjective functions $v(.)$ and $\pi(.)$ as a function of the objective utilities and probabilities. Prospect theory postulates two fundamental properties for the shape of the value function (empirically verified). It is convex in the domain of losses and concave in the region of gains. It is not symmetric as a loss produces a negative reaction of higher intensity than the positive reaction produced by the corresponding gain (Figure 12.1).

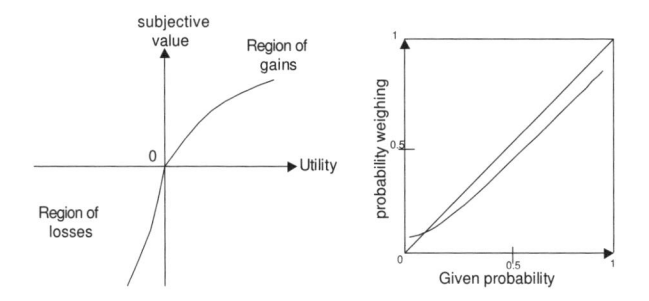

Figure 12.1. *Subjectivization functions in prospect theory*

The S-shape of the value function represents an aversion to risky choices in the region of gains and a tendency towards risky choices in the region of losses. As an example, let us compare the prospect of a €1000 gain that is 75% probable and the certainty of a €750 gain. The classical theory computes a €750 expected utility in both cases (indifference). However, because the subjective value function is concave in the region of gains, the subjective value of €750 will be greater than three-quarters of the subjective value of €1000. The cautious prospect will therefore be chosen.

The weighting function $\pi(.)$ also has particular properties (a curve satisfying those properties is presented in Figure 12.1(b)). Only one is of interest here: low objective probabilities are weighted too much and high objective probabilities are not weighted enough. Then a reduction in uncertainty from 5% to 0% will generally have more effect than a reduction from 10% to 5%. Individuals will therefore generally be more ready to pay an insurance policy that totally eliminates a risk than a policy that reduces the risk in the same proportion but without removing the randomness attached to the final outcome.

In a more recent version, Tversky and Kahneman [TVE 92] refined their approach by taking into account the interaction between the uncertainty and utility conditions. In the original version the weighting was therefore the same whether utility was in the region of gains or in the regions of losses. In the later version, weighting functions change with the utility region under consideration. Risk seeking and risk aversion are no longer determined by the utility function but by the conjunction of utility *and* the level of uncertainty. A more specific pattern of attitudes towards risks is given in Table 12.1.

	Low probabilities	High probabilities
Region of gains	Risk seeking	Risk aversion
Region of losses	Risk aversion	Risk seeking

Table 12.1. *Attitudes towards risk depending on the type of outcomes and the degree of uncertainty*

12.2.4. *Questions raised by the standard model*

Despite being a descriptive but not a normative approach, prospect theory has a number of postulates that make it somewhat similar to the standard expected utility theory. Those postulates leave room for discussion, and other phenomena described in the literature cannot be captured by prospect theory.

One of the more questionable postulates states that utilities can be measured on a numerical scale. Baron and Spranca [BAR 97] introduced the notion of 'protected values' defined as values that cannot be negotiated, particularly not against money. Such values stem from deontological rules about actions, that is, about the way in which outcomes are produced. For example, even if some behavior enables money to be made, say by killing somebody, a decision maker may not want to do it because this way of making money is morally unacceptable to them.

Protected values have several properties, one of which is of particular interest here. Protected values are not sensitive to differences in quantity. This property induces people to refuse to attach numerical values to human lives, thus producing results that are incoherent according to formal models. (Note that this phenomenon should not be confused with the 'psychophysical numbing' sometimes evoked to account for the tendency of undervaluing individual human lives as the number of endangered lives increases.) Protected values exist in every culture, even though their nature varies from one culture to another. The very existence of those values calls into question the idea that utilities can be measured by means of a simple numerical scale.

As regards processing of uncertainty, classical approaches to expected utility use uncertainty functions of a probabilistic (or Bayesian) nature. If numerical scales are not always compatible with the way humans evaluate utility, as when protected values are involved, it is also possible that numerical scales are no more suitable for evaluating uncertainty. As a matter of fact, in a series of experiments (some of which were conducted with psychology undergraduates and some expert radiologists [RAU 98a, RAU 03]) we showed that a possibilistic (qualitative) approach to uncertainty judgements was more in agreement with human judgement than a probabilistic (quantitative) approach. Specifically, conjunctions and disjunctions of elementary judgements appeared to be combined through min, max and order-reversing algorithms rather than through additive and multiplicative processes. These results entail a qualitative approach to uncertainty, which is fundamentally different to the probabilistic approach. In the remainder of this chapter, we cover other phenomena that prospect theory does not capture.

Perhaps more embarrassing than the previous two points is the fact that prospect theory summarizes a number of empirical phenomena but does not enable understanding of their origin. Where do the properties of the subjective value and weighting functions described above come from? In addition, some studies have shown that public reactions are determined by various factors as diverse as the perception of social inequalities in the distribution of risks and benefits, or aversion to situations that induce a feeling of not being in control. Some persons therefore prefer taking their car because of a fear of aircraft accidents, while the objective risk is notoriously higher in personal vehicles. Explaining such effects requires study of the very origin of the subjective value function. It was shown, for example, that the nature of the task proposed to the subject had a decisive effect on the final decision. Tasks where subjects have to choose between various options lead to results different from tasks where subjects have to put a price on the same options. It is then necessary to study the cognitive mechanisms leading to decisions, and first of all the construction of a mental representation of the decision making situation.

12.3. A global descriptive approach to decision making

Some researchers study cognitive processes underlying judgement and decision making under risk in domains far more complex and less structured than classical laboratory settings. Participants in these studies are senior managers, aircraft pilots, doctors, insurance brokers and traders. While the traditional approach to decision making emphasizes choice among possible options and the rational way of making the choice, investigation of human cognitive processes in naturalistic settings shows that professionals acting in their own domain of expertise seem to devote the bulk of their attention to building and updating a reliable representation of the problem situation [KLE 93, ZSA 97].

Exploring the set of possible choices seems to be a secondary preoccupation for those experts. From the first studies on chess players [e.g. CHAS 73], numerous works in domains such as military decision making [see ZSA 97] or medicine [e.g. ELS 78, RAU 98b] showed that experts rarely evoke more than one or two options even though a long reflection time is then devoted to analyzing these options. Our own results on expertise in radiology, a specialty where physicians are used to reason based on sets of differential diagnoses rather than on individual hypotheses, show that the maximal diversity can be observed in novices, and minimal diversity in some of the experts [RAU 98b]. Diversity in novices comes from the incapacity to eliminate some irrelevant hypotheses whereas diversity in experts comes from the activation, while reasoning, of knowledge about relevant particular cases. Relevance of the initial selection set of options is therefore a key element. Indeed, what is the point of perfectly ranking the retained options if none of them contains the correct solution? Other work about decision making in the workplace led to a general descriptive model that we now present: 'the search for dominance' [MON 83]. To understand this model, we first need to remind ourselves of some basic notions of multicriteria decision making.

12.3.1. *The concept of multicriteria decision making*

One of the major concerns for researchers in the psychology of decision making was to study the construction of preferences in the case where the options differ on several attributes [EDW 00]. For example, imagine that you would like to buy a video recorder. Numerous parameters can guide your choice. Some parameters can be evaluated on numerical dimensions (price, resolution, etc.). Other parameters refer to a qualitative dimension (for instance, the presence or absence of options such as a video screen or the type of recording devices, flash memory or magnetic tape). Several questions arise. What process can combine the various attributes? How is the relative weight of each attribute determined? The issue of decision making as a whole appears as a particular case of these questions. A classical approach consists of determining the weight of an option from a linear combination of the various attributes:

$$W = a_1 X_1 + a_2 X_2 + a_3 X_3 + \ldots + a_n X_n,$$

where each coefficient a_i represents the weight associated with the attribute i and where each X_i represents the value of this attribute. More sophisticated models exist, such as stochastic models that also include a random component enabling an explanation of why the same individual with the same pattern of attribute weightings may change his choice between morning and afternoon. Here, we will not present normative models of multicriteria decision making but simply consider the general process of choice.

From a purely descriptive standpoint, the decision making processes actually used by subjects do not always take into account the whole set of available attributes.

For example, in the so-called 'lexicographic' procedures, decision makers ground their decisions on the most important attributes [e.g. TVE 72]. If this attribute does not enable differentiation among the options, the second attribute in the order of importance is taken into account, and so on. It can be seen that such a process is non-compensatory in nature: if the first criterion is sufficient for the decision to be taken, other attributes are not even examined. Therefore, they have no chance to balance or compensate for the influence of the most important factor. For the moment we will simply note that multicriteria decision making is not necessarily the result of computing some more or less complex function, but rather that it may be understood as a process.

12.3.2. *The notion of dominance structure*

12.3.2.1. *The dominance rule*

The dominance rule is a normative rule. It states that one should always choose an alternative that is dominated on no attribute by the other alternatives and that is better than all other alternatives on at least one attribute. Although being a crucial element of the theory of rational choice, the dominance rule suffers from a serious drawback: it is not always possible to find an alternative that, strictly speaking, dominates the others.

12.3.2.2. *The search for dominance*

When the mental representation of the problem does not allow detection of a dominant alternative, decision makers must transform their representations in order to make a dominant alternative appear. Reasoning in decision making settings can therefore be construed as a particular case of representation transformation, the purpose of which is to make dominance appear. In this model, the transformation of the problem representation is guided by reasoning rules (logical rules, pragmatic rules, etc.). The search for dominance can pass through the search of new information in the environment, but, it can also directly operate by means of a direct transformation of some of the attributes in the problem. The subject may try to neutralize or counterbalance some attributes in the representation, or else try to introduce new attributes. Hence, it is possible to define the descriptive counterpart of the dominance rule.

12.3.2.3. *Dominance structures*

Montgomery [MON 83, p. 344] defined a dominance structure as 'equivalent to a representation where one alternative has at least one advantage compared to other alternatives, and where all disadvantages associated with that alternative are neutralized or counterbalanced in one way or another'.

To create such a structure, the decision maker can modify their evaluations of attributes, or can modify the attributes under consideration. The dominance structure is more or less distant from the dominance rule: the more the chosen alternative presents disadvantages that must be neutralized or counterbalanced, the greater the distance to pure dominance. An essential feature of the dominance structure resides in its construction. It consists of a construction process that taps various reasoning rules. The rule of dominance can be one of these rules but, in the general case, rules for building a dominance structure ought to be construed as operators enabling local transformations of the representation so that the dominance rule can be applied to the resulting representation. For instance, a rule may consist of excluding the alternatives unlikely to become dominant. Another rule can be used to neutralize a disadvantage of a promising alternative.

In other terms, the decision making process as a whole is construed as the search for a dominance structure by means of the successive application of rules, the scope of which is generally local (with the exception of the rule of dominance). Let us now examine the steps of the decision making process.

12.3.3. *Steps in the decision making process*

According to Montgomery, the decision making process can be decomposed into four main phases: pre-edition, the selection of a focal alternative, the test of dominance and the structuring of dominance (see Figure 12.2). The first two phases are particularly sensitive to affect-driven phenomena, such as social values that determine what is important and what is not.

12.3.3.1. *Pre-edition*

The goal of the pre-edition phase is to separate relevant from less relevant information. The latter can be neglected by subsequent steps of the information processing. For example, in medicine, a small number of diagnostic hypotheses is selected in a few seconds, and hypotheses that do not belong to this initial set are very unlikely to be taken into account later [ELS 78].

The pre-edition phase involves two operations: selecting the relevant facts (attributes) and selecting the choice possibilities (alternatives) to consider. In the case of diagnosis, for example, this step consists of selecting the symptoms that ought to be accounted for and the diagnostic hypotheses in competition. The hypotheses retained are those having a fair probability of constituting a dominance structure while the hypotheses having a low probability of generating a dominance structure are eliminated.

It is noteworthy that this phase is sensitive to factors completely unaccounted for by classical normative theories. For instance, construction of the mental representation depends on socio-cultural factors [SLO 97]. Thus, in the US whatever the nature of the risks under consideration (infectious diseases, pollution, accidents or X-rays)

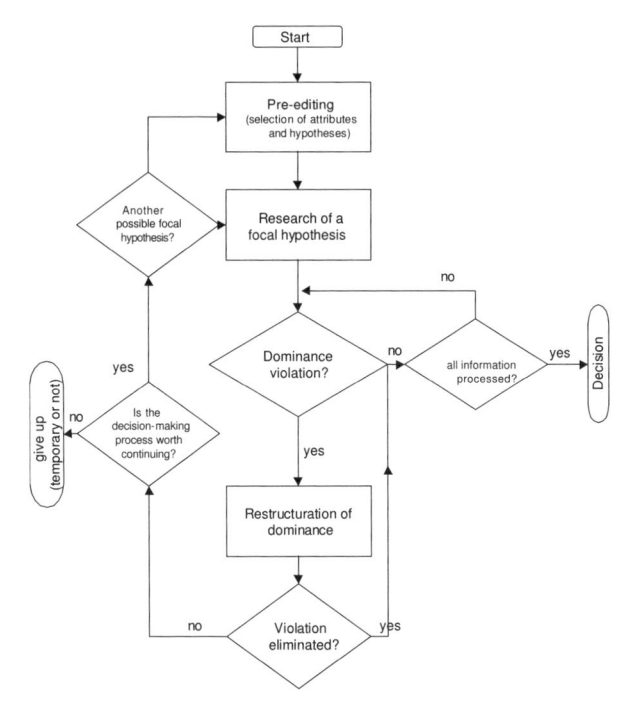

Figure 12.2. *The model of search for dominance (after Montgomery [MON 83])*

white males provide lower risk judgements than white females and black males and females [FLY 94]. More generally, since 1971 many studies showed that males are less sensitive to risks than females (for a review, see [SLO 97]). For almost every danger source, they judge the risks to be lower and the consequences less problematic. Even when studies involve experts in the domain (medicine toxicity, nuclear power, etc.), female scientists deem risks to be higher than their male colleagues.

12.3.3.2. *Search for a focal alternative*

This phase aims to find, among the alternatives selected in the previous phase, the one having the best chance of acquiring the status of a dominance structure.

12.3.3.3. *The test of dominance*

This phase aims to evaluate whether the focal alternative selected in the previous phase can actually be considered as dominant. In particular, the decision maker checks whether the focal hypothesis presents some disadvantages compared to its competitors.

12.3.3.4. *Dominance structuring*

Operations of this phase take place when the focal hypothesis violates a condition for access to the status of a dominance structure. This phase then aims to neutralize this violation. In the case of success, the decision making process returns to the phase of dominance testing until all available information has been processed. In the case of failure, decision makers come back to one of the first two phases, in order to select a new and promising hypothesis or new facts and hypotheses. They can also delay the decision.

At least four structuring methods can be distinguished:

1) 'De-emphasizing' refers to when decision makers reduce the importance (the weight) of an attribute or minimize the differences between alternatives relative to this attribute. For example, decision makers change their criteria as regards what is important or not. They may also decide that the dominated attribute has a low probability of occurrence.

2) 'Bolstering' consists of augmenting the support received by the focal hypothesis. Decision makers can increase the weight of attributes where the focal hypothesis dominates, for example by rehearsing positive arguments in order to make the elements that support the focal hypothesis more vivid in their imagination (see the availability heuristic below). They can also seek new arguments favouring the focal hypothesis.

3) 'Cancellation' is a type of tradeoff where two specific attributes are nullified, one on which the focal hypothesis is dominated, in exchange of the nullification of another specific attribute on which the focal hypothesis dominates. Obviously, using cancellation requires an attribute on which the focal hypothesis dominates.

4) 'Collapsing' is an operation by which two or more attributes are merged into a newer, more comprehensive, attribute. For example, imagine that you want to buy a car. You hesitate between A and B with a preference for B. But B consumes more petrol than A and is therefore dominated on this attribute. You convert the consumption difference into money (e.g. overconsumption by B represents €100 a year) and you integrate the initial cost of buying (e.g. B is initially cheaper than A by €1,000) with the cost overrun caused by overconsumption. You obtain a global cost on which, say, B dominates. Assuming the car will be kept 5 years, the total overconsumption by B represents €500, but as it initially costs €1,000 less, the global balance is €500 in favor of option B. Since the global cost includes consumption, consumption can be eliminated and then a dominance structure has been obtained.

From this global approach to decision making, it is necessary to deepen the details of each specific mechanism. Some of those mechanisms have a cognitive cost (i.e. mental effort is necessary to execute them). The process of setting a particular mental mechanism to work is also subjected to a decision-making process [e.g. PAY 93].

The remainder of this chapter will be limited to some transversal determinants, that is, psychological phenomena that affect various steps in the model of Montgomery. We will principally evoke attentional focusing and heuristic utilization, and will conclude with the issue of emotional determinants.

12.4. Attentional focusing

An often observed phenomenon is the effect of attentional focusing stemming from the fact that individuals essentially base their reasoning and decision making on what is explicitly present in their representation of the problem. Information, knowledge and ideas under the focus of attention are therefore weighted more in reasoning and decision making [LEG 93].

On the contrary, hypotheses excluded from the attentional field have a weak influence on decision making [CHE 03, FIS 78]. In agreement with this principle, Tversky and Koehler [TVE 94] presented and tested a model enabling a better understanding of the origins of subjective probability judgements, namely support theory. According to this theory, confidence judgements about a hypothesis depend on the strength of evidence that support this hypothesis. In turn, this strength depends on the vividness of the representation in the decision maker's mind at the moment where the judgement is made. In other words, the more the representation of a hypothesis – as a happy or unhappy consequence of a choice – is vivid, the more this hypothesis will receive strength. Indeed, focusing one's attention on a prospect allows better perception of its details.

Due to general mechanisms that favor the perception of elements that are coherent with the focal hypothesis, if subjects successively focus their attention on several variants of a hypothesis, the overall quantity of elements supporting that hypothesis will generally be higher compared to subjects who do not clearly represent all the details. The subjective probability associated with that hypothesis will then be reinforced.

Hence, a presentation that inclines subjects to represent the consequences of a risk with a lot of details will generally increase the subjective probability associated with that risk (however, other mechanisms exposed later can oppose this tendency). Reciprocally, the subjective probability felt about a risk can be lowered by describing this risk in abstract terms that do not facilitate concrete representation. One can easily imagine the implications this approach has for the design of risk prevention strategies.

The effect of attentional focusing is all the more important when simultaneously representing the whole set of costs and benefits is difficult. This is the case in 'intertemporal choice', which consists of deciding between action possibilities whose expected costs and benefits are not simultaneous. For example, when investing in technical equipment, cost is immediate whereas expected benefits only occur after some delay. Various studies [e.g. AHL 97, HAU 79] show that an important proportion of subjects underestimate the temporal dimension in their global assessment of benefits. Modeling of such phenomena can be traced back to Samuelson [SAM 37] (for a more recent review, see [LOE 92]).

For example, subjects chose options that offer the fastest payback, even though they are less advantageous in the long run. People may therefore tend to avoid investing in a machine that is costly in the short term despite the fact that it should bring them a greater revenue in later periods such that the final profit will be higher. Such temporal myopia may affect the decision to buy protection such as insurance policies; buying an insurance policy is a typical case of trade-offs combining a short-term certain cost with a long-term potential benefit. This effect is also a consequence of attentional focusing.

In anti-seismic protection of houses, Kunreuther *et al.* [KUN 98] were able to observe an increase in the likelihood of buying protection measures that were onerous in the short term. This increase was linked to the explicit mention of the temporal horizon, of the probabilities of associated damages and of the magnitude of damage reduction brought by the protective measure. In other words, helping subjects to comprehend decision parameters also helps them to include those parameters in the decision making process. However, it does not mean that an explicit description systematically increases buying behaviors.

For example, in a study about the purchase of a warranty at the moment of buying an electronic device [HOG 95], the probability of purchase was higher in subjects who received no information on costs and probabilities of potential repairs than in subjects who received such information. Without this information, subjects simultaneously took into account the respective prices of the product and of the guarantee. However, bringing concrete information about risks induced a direct comparison of the cost of repair and the price of the warranty. In this situation, information reduced the likelihood of purchase by as much as a 5% increase in the price of the warranty.

Other attentional effects have more complex causes than the presence or absence of some aspects of the problem in the representation. Interactions with the task also matter. For example, significantly different preferences seem to be elicited when different methods are used to elicit preferences. Choice therefore operates by direct comparison (both options are simultaneously present in consciousness), which favors the most important dimension. In evaluation, on the other hand, options are processed independently of each other. In lottery experiments, where options that differ on two dimensions are compared, namely financial utility and the uncertainty attached to the outcome, reversals often occur. This depends on whether preferences are measured by asking subjects to provide a direct choice (between options) or by estimating the value of each option ('pricing').

This finding is a violation of the invariance principle according to which, for the same problem, two rational decision procedures should produce the same result. According to the 'compatibility principle' [TVE 88], the relative weight of a given piece of information in a judgement or decision making situation is increased if this piece of information is compatible with the scale used for providing the response. Thus, estimating the price of a bet tends to increase the weight of the value dimension compared to the probability dimension because both the value dimension and the price of a bet are expressed using monetary units. In other words, the question makes the monetary dimension 'salient'. Compatibility effects constitute an important cause of preference reversals [SLO 02].

All pieces of information in the decision making situation do not contribute equally to the various processes. In addition to the compatibility principle proposed below, Tversky *et al.* [TVE 88] proposed a 'prominence principle', describing when individuals choose according to the subjectively most important dimension (then at least partially neglecting other dimensions) but give more balanced weights to the various dimensions when pricing the options. Consequently, the most prominent attribute will weigh more in choice than in appraisal.

Consider the request 'you must decide whether you country should invest 55 million dollars in a road safety program that will save 570 lives, or 12 million dollars in a program that will save only 500 lives'. 68% of subjects choose the more expensive program that saves more lives [TVE 88]. A preference reversal appears when – instead of being asked to choose the program they prefer – subjects are asked to evaluate the price of a program allowing 570 lives to be saved so that it would be as attractive as an existing 12 million dollar program that allows 500 lives to be saved. The percentage of subjects, the appraisal of which would lead a rational decision maker to choose the more expensive program, falls to 4%. Money is usually deemed less important than the lives it might save. This is why in this experiment, according to the prominence principle, money weighs lower in choice than in appraisal.

As well as effects of an attentional origin, specific evaluation mechanisms play a key role in judgement and decision making: heuristics.

12.5. Evaluation heuristics and ecological rationality

12.5.1. *Logical rationality and ecological rationality*

Imagine that a lion is pursuing you. You are 25 sec ahead. You arrive in front of a lake. You have two escape routes, one on the left and one on the right. One leads you to a safe (solid) shelter but you will need 24 sec to reach the shelter. The other is less safe but you can reach the shelter in 20 sec. Which way will you chose?

The point here is that after 5 sec of reflection with no action, you are dead whatever the option you take! From an evolutionist standpoint, it is therefore better to have an imperfect decision system that reacts swiftly, even by providing suboptimal responses, than to have a decision system that provides the perfect response too late. Then a second form of rationality exists, different from logical rationality: so-called 'ecological rationality'. (We use this phrase with its usual meaning in psychology, which refers to the rationality of an organism having to adapt its environment.) One can therefore expect the existence of a difference between actual behaviors of subjects (descriptive models of decision making) and the 'ideal' behavior (normative models). If the ideal cannot be reached, is it still possible to produce behaviors that (at least statistically) provide an advantage in the struggle for life?

Ecological rationality suggests decision-making processes employ what Simon [SIM 56] calls 'bounded rationality', that is, with algorithms (heuristics) that provide a 'satisficing' rather than ideal response, but in a reasonable time. By satisficing, one must understand responses that in a majority of cases will allow the desired goal to be reached. Although it is not possible to compute the whole set of possible consequences of an action, Simon [SIM 56, p. 27] showed that very simple decision-making processes may provide satisficing solutions in reasonable time. He concludes that "...we should be skeptical in postulating for humans, or other organisms, elaborate mechanisms for choosing among diverse needs".

De facto, the ability to produce satisficing responses in a limited time represents a clear adaptive advantage. The theory of evolution by natural selection then suggests that the progressive adaptation of the cognitive system to environmental constraints should endow us with mechanisms allowing decision making at speeds compatible with the requirement of the species' survival. If the adaptive advantage provided by a heuristic persists for the species (by using it rather than by not using it, more individuals survive long enough to reproduce), and if the selection pressure is strong enough, the proportion of individuals using the heuristic will tend to grow in the population. The other side of the coin is that this adaptation is only partial: if heuristics provide satisficing responses in a majority of cases, they nevertheless produce erroneous responses in a minority of cases.

Researchers in the psychology of human decision making have based their study of human heuristics on the existence of such failures. Indeed, while the classical normative theory can only predict the correct response, heuristics can also predict error patterns. If one knows the context and the heuristic that is used, it is generally possible to anticipate the direction of errors. Work by Kahneman *et al.* [KAH 79] thus initiated a research stream known under the name of 'heuristics and biases'. As well as preference reversal cited above, this research program uncovered several heuristic reasoning rules, some examples of which will now be presented.

12.5.2. *The representativeness heuristic*

Let us consider the following problem. Linda is 31 years old, single, outspoken and very bright. She majored in philosophy. As a student, she was deeply concerned with issues of discrimination and social justice and also participated in anti-nuclear demonstrations. Please check the most probable alternative:
– Linda is a bank teller.
– Linda is a bank teller and is active in the feminist movement.

A large majority of participants (over 80%) answer that Linda is more probably a bank teller than bank teller and active in the feminist movement. However, formally it is impossible to have $p(A \cap B) > p(A)$ because every element in $A \cap B$ is also an element of A. Thus, the problem demonstrates a very robust bias. This bias is the other side of the coin of a powerful heuristic: the representativeness heuristic.

The representativeness heuristic consists of judging the probability of a class depending on the perceived similarity between the properties of the target class and the properties of a stimulus that can be viewed as an instance of this class. In other words, we estimate that I is probably an instance of the category C if the properties of I resemble typical properties of the C category. This heuristic is powerful because it allows generalizing of prior knowledge in order to predict the behavior of reality. For example, if I see an unknown animal that resembles a lion, it is not unreasonable to behave as if it were a lion, that is, to preventively protect oneself against the potential danger that a big feline represents.

Applying this heuristic to the Linda problem, one sees that Linda is described in a way very similar to the prototype of exemplars of the category 'feminist': Linda is representative of the class of feminists. In contrast, Linda is not very representative of the class of bank tellers. Then we are prone – due to the representativeness heuristic – to give a high probability to 'bank teller and feminist' because the representative element ('feminist') is only present in this second option. But this choice violates a basic principle of normative theories, 'extensionality': the probability of a subset can never be greater than the probability of a set within which it is included. Every single woman who is feminist and bank teller is a bank teller. The reverse is not true and then the probability to be bank teller AND feminist can never be greater than the probability to be bank teller alone. (Note that the extensionality argument can only hold if 'Linda is a bank teller' is not pragmatically interpreted to mean 'Linda is a bank teller, and not a feminist' [DUL 91, KAH 02].)

12.5.3. *The availability heuristic*

Let us consider a new problem. For each of the following pairs of causes of death, indicate which is the most frequent:
1. Lung cancer or Road accident
2. Emphysema or Homicide
3. Diabetes or Fire and flames

The availability heuristic consists of judging the probability of a class depending on how easily instances of the class come to mind. This heuristic validity stems from the very properties of human memory. Indeed, for reasons bound to human brain functioning, we recall frequent rather than non-frequent events better and more easily. Hence, ease of retrieval of information from memory often constitutes a valid cue to the frequency of the represented element.

However, the coin still has another side. In the three questions above, the majority of subjects answer with the right column elements, whereas the death causes considered in the left column killed many more than those placed in the right column (the statistics are from Slovic *et al.* [SLO 80] from the US in the 1970s, where their experiments were conducted). This bias is linked to the fact that frequency is not the only determinant of the ease with which memories are retrieved.

Information salience, its subjective importance and its associated affective reactions are among the factors that contribute to affect information availability. It is therefore possible to construct situations where an element will be easily retrieved, thereby inducing a high probability judgement despite its relatively low actual frequency. In the preceding examples, the causes of death on the right are easy to represent because they are regularly reported in the media. However, the frequency of mention in the media does not reflect the real frequency of occurrence of these events. Moreover, media shows are often associated with dramatic pictures that, by affectively tagging the event, facilitate later retrieval. On the contrary, in an ordinary population, the presented pathologies do not spontaneously come to mind. They are then judged – erroneously in the present case – to be less probable.

Another example perhaps illustrates the underlying mechanism more clearly. Consider the letter R. Is R more likely to appear in:
1) words that start with R; or
2) words the third letter of which is R.

In this kind of example, two-thirds of individuals choose the answer 'words that start with R'. According to Kahneman and Tversky [KAH 79], it can be explained by the fact that it is easier to mentally generate words that start with a given letter than by words having a given letter in the third position.

It should be remarked that, due to the availability heuristic, bringing subjects to imagine the details of an event (e.g. showing pictures of AIDS patients to induce less risky sexual behaviors) does not necessarily lead to higher probability judgements, as suggested by the focusing effects presented earlier. Indeed, in cases where evoking the details is difficult, as in subjects who are distressed by those pictures and repress them, the estimated probability might be lower [SHE 85]. The event will only be deemed more likely if evoking its details is easy.

12.5.4. *The anchoring-adjustment heuristic*

Let us consider a mental arithmetic exercise to be done in 5 sec, an impossible task for an ordinary non-prodigy subject. Half the participants have to estimate the result of the following operation: $8 \times 7 \times 6 \times 5 \times 4 \times 3 \times 2 \times 1$. The other half must estimate $1 \times 2 \times 3 \times 4 \times 5 \times 6 \times 7 \times 8$. Obviously the results are the same but estimates of the first group are greater than estimates of the second. It can be explained by the fact that subjects mentally compute the first operations during a few seconds then, discovering that there will not be enough time for the whole calculation, extrapolate the effect of the remaining operations starting from the last intermediate result reached.

This situation illustrates the anchoring and adjustment heuristic, more complex than the two previous heuristics because it is a two-step process. In the first step (anchoring), the subject has a value that can serve as a starting point for the extrapolation. In the example, it is the last intermediate result that was calculated. In a second step (adjustment), the subject updates their initial estimate towards the most plausible direction. This heuristic is valid when the anchor is chosen validly and the adjustment sufficient. For example, a private individual willing to buy a second-hand car can start from a global estimate of the mean sale price for vehicles of the same type, age and mileage. This first estimate constitutes the anchor. The buyer may then adjust this price depending on more subjective parameters such as aesthetic quality and state of the paintwork.

This heuristic generates strong biases when the anchor is invalid. The following experiment illustrates such biases. Subjects are presented with a wheel of fortune providing a number between 10 and 200. Depending on the result r, the experimenter asks 'is the percentage of African countries in the UN below or above r?' As a matter of fact, the wheel is under the control of the experimenter who can produce either 10 or 65. In the 65% case, participants are sure that the answer is 'below'. In the 10% case, participants are sure that the answer is 'above'. For the moment, no surprise. The interesting point is that, without being aware of it, subjects just anchored a value in their minds, 10% in a case, 65% in the other case. In a second phase, the experimenter asks 'what is the exact percentage of African countries in the UN?' The effect of an insufficient adjustment then appears: estimates from subjects anchored to 65% are biased in excess whereas estimates anchored to 10% are biased down.

Various explanations of such effects have been proposed [e.g. EPL 06, STR 97] and anchoring-and-adjustment effects are now viewed as a multi-determined phenomenon [e.g. EPL 04].

The anchoring-and-adjustment heuristic is a powerful means to manipulate people, widely used in daily life. When politicians provide a biased statistics, they provide anchors from which people will adjust insufficiently. This is why, in France, demonstrations always give rise to two estimates, most often outrageously divergent, that of the police and that of the demonstrators. In a striking demonstration of the seemingly irresistible nature of anchoring effects, Englich *et al.* [ENG 06] show that high versus low anchors influenced sentence recommendations by experienced legal professionals, even when it was made clear that the anchor was irrelevant (because it came from a question posed by a journalist), or randomly determined (by a dice throw made by the judge him/herself). This anchoring effect still persisted despite the fact that judges corrected for the fact that the demand was made by the prosecutor. According to the traditional explanation, the biases associated with this heuristic stem from insufficient adjustment. However, if anchoring effects are robust, the issue of their explanation is still open [CHA 02, EPL 01].

12.5.5. *Conclusion on heuristics*

The heuristics presented here are far from being an exhaustive sample of all heuristics known in human decision making. An influential research program conducted by Gigerenzer *et al.* [e.g. GIG 99] explores what they call fast and frugal heuristics, because these heuristics consume few cognitive resources. In addition to the human algorithmic 'cognitive toolbox', this approach advocates the need for better comprehension of the functional aspect of heuristics than the bias and heuristics approach, which essentially applied itself to show their dysfunctional side. De facto, the challenge for current psychology of decision making is no longer to demonstrate the existence of deviations between human behavior and the ideal norm of expected utility theory. Such deviations are now accepted. Above all, we now have to understand 'how it works when it works'.

After a period of time focused on the irrationality of human decision making, we observe the return to a conception where humans can reason, if not logically, at least ecologically. After all, humans exhibit a stunning capacity to easily handle very complex operations such as those required by language processing. If one is ready to believe that evolution may also have affected decision making, it is not surprising that humans would be well adapted in matters of decision making. Concomitantly with this resurgence of a more optimistic conception of human rationality, the old antagonism between reason and emotion is also undergoing resorption.

12.6. The role of affect in decision making

For centuries, the prevailing conception was that reason – pure, providing much good – could only be disturbed by emotions that, in contrast, were largely considered as irrational. The drastic change brought by modern cognitive sciences is the conception that emotions can be necessary to the correct functioning of reason. We now know that, without emotions, it becomes very hard or even impossible to make decisions adapted to the complexity of social life.

12.6.1. *The positive role of emotions*

In the introduction of this chapter, we saw that positive and negative presentations of an event induce different choices. Choices presented in terms of gains make us prefer safe options whereas choices presented in terms of losses make us prefer risky options. Other findings, issuing from the study of cognitive deficits induced by cerebral lesions, show that affect also determines attentional focusing, whose effect on the weighting function was presented above.

Damasio *et al.* [DAM 91] showed that, when confronted with a complex decision making situation, subjects do not consciously consider all hypotheses. As we are told, this has long been known in the psychology of decision making in natural situations and corresponds to phenomena described in the 'pre-edition' phase of Montgomery's model. What is new in Damasio's work is the realization that a major determinant of the process selecting the hypotheses to be considered is affect. Subjects consider only a small number of hypotheses, selected on the basis of an emotional sensation. Individuals in whom this capacity is damaged become unable to make acceptable decisions in a reasonable time, even if their IQ remains high. Damasio reports the case of EVR, a patient who had become emotionally deficient after brain surgery but with an intact IQ, still over 130 (i.e. an individual who still belonged to the 2% most intellectually gifted subjects). At the same time, this individual had become unable to make correct decisions in daily life. For an enlightening discussion of the dissociation between intelligence and rationality, see [STA 09].

The previous results question the interaction between affect and conscious processes in decision making. In a subsequent series of experiments by the Damasio team [BEC 97], subjects received four decks of cards (A, B, C and D) and $2000 in fake money. The task was to decide, for each deck, if the next hidden card had to be uncovered. Uncovering a card immediately yielded $100 (for decks A or B) or $50 (for decks C or D). However, the card could also unpredictably yield a punishment. The player knew that the punishment was large in decks A and B and small in decks C and D (which the player ignored). Players did not know when the game would stop (actually, after 100 cards had been picked). Instructions were to play in order to maximize gains and minimize losses, but subjects had no means of precisely computing the net gains or losses associated with each particular deck.

Initially, all players were ignorant. Subjects with functional emotional systems eventually succeeded in finding a profitable strategy, while emotionally deficient subjects did not. Results showed that explicit reasoning (e.g. when the subject consciously decides not to take any more cards in a deck felt to be 'dangerous') was preceded by an unconscious step. Subjects with spared emotional systems began choosing advantageously before consciously understanding which strategy was the best. However, emotionally deficient patients continued choosing disadvantageously even after determining the good strategy. In addition, emotionally spared patients started generating electrodermal responses (temporary drops in the electrical resistance of the skin surface, resulting from the unconscious release of micro-drops of sweat after an excitation of the sympathetic system e.g. after an emotional excitation) as soon as they were presented with a risky choice, even before explicitly knowing that it was a risky choice. On the contrary, emotionally deficient patients never developed electrodermal responses, even though some of them had consciously realized which choices were risky.

On the whole, without emotional processes, explicit knowledge and conscious reasoning seem to be insufficient to ensure profitable behaviors.

12.6.2. *Affect and expected utility*

Since affect helps in determining the favorable options, we can reasonably expect some overlap between affect and the key elements of expected utility theory, that is, utility calculus on one hand, and uncertainty handling on the other. The relationship between utility and affect is quite intuitive and has never really been questioned by psychologists. However, this relationship has several implications not always taken into account by economists. Indeed, some differences exist between purely financial utilities considered by economists and affective (hedonic) utilities considered by psychologists. Economic utilities are therefore monotonic functions of financial benefits whereas hedonic experiences can be non-monotonic functions of financial benefits because they take into account counterfactual comparisons.

For example, depending on the subject's expectancies, a little gain initially unexpected may bring great pleasure whereas a large gain may bring displeasure if it comes in the context of an even larger expectancy. *Ceteris paribus*, people evaluate the outcome of a bet as worse when a counterfactual result is better. This type of finding led psychologists to develop psychological variants of expected utility theory. For example, the theory of 'expected subjective emotion' by Mellers *et al.* [MEL 97] proposed a model of the computation of feeling as a function of objective financial utilities and the probabilities associated with these utilities and of the computation of expected subjective-emotion by summation of the probability feeling products.

It is often considered in psychology that daily affective experience can be summarized fairly well by two independent dimensions of experience, the most important being 'valence'. Valence is the dimension that represents the positive versus negative character of affect. Thus, it differentiates between the region of gains and the region of losses. Experimental studies found that emotions felt about a stimulus are more ambivalent than 'colder' evaluations. Abelson *et al.* [ABE 82] therefore found that Americans could simultaneously feel positive and negative emotions about presidential candidates (e.g. 'he made me feel happy' and 'he made me feel afraid'), whereas their estimates of the candidates' personality (e.g. he is competent, dishonest, etc.) were much more evaluatively coherent. Due to their greater variability, but also because they seem to be bound more closely to the formation of preferences than estimates of the candidates' personality [ZAJ 80], emotions better predicted participants' intentions of vote. It seems that two distinct motivational systems underlie estimates of the positive and negative meanings of a stimulus [HIG 00, RAU 08]. If the two systems are weakly activated, it is indifference. If the two systems are strongly activated, it is ambiguity.

Therefore, contrary to the classical utility approach, gains and losses do not compensate each other. It is probably this dissociation between the two affective subsystems of appraisal which explains the difference that can be observed, in prospect theory, between the slopes of the subjectivation functions for positive and negative utilities.

Affect also influences the uncertainty function. Thus, Johnson and Tversky [JOH 83] showed that, in normal subjects, reading a text relating a tragic death (e.g. a murder described in detail) induced a negative affect that subsequently increased the frequency estimates related to other causes of death that were unrelated to the initial text (e.g. the probability of having a car accident).

This double influence of affect, on both the utility and uncertainty functions, opens a breach in an important postulate of many normative decision theories: independence of utilities and uncertainties. Imagine that you have to choose between two lottery tickets having a 1% chance of winning. If you win with the first, you earn $50. If you win with the second you have the opportunity to meet and kiss your favorite cinema star. Faced with such a choice under uncertainty, 65% of the participants in Rottenstreich and Hsee [ROT 01] chose the kiss of the star. In another condition (certainty condition) where participants had to imagine between directly choosing the $50 or the opportunity to meet and kiss their favorite cinema star, 70% of the participants chose to have the money.

These results illustrate a striking interaction between the level of certainty and the type of utility. In a second experiment, the authors compared the price that students would be willing to pay for a lottery ticket that would allow them to win a voucher for travel to Europe to the value of $500 or a coupon for a $500 reduction on the price of their university's yearly registration. 88% of the students judged the travel coupon more emotionally exciting. Students of one group were then told the tickets had a 1% chance of winning. Students of another group were told the tickets had a 99% chance of winning. The median value of the price the students were ready to pay for the travel coupon ticket was $20 in the low-probability condition (versus $5 for the reduction coupon ticket). In the high-probability condition, the mean value of the travel coupon ticket was $450 against $475 for the reduction coupon ticket. Thus, these experiments show that purely affective factors may create preference reversals due to the interactions between utilities and uncertainties attached to the prospects of gain.

12.7. Conclusion

Throughout this chapter, we have tried to show why psychologists have been led to abandon expected utility theory as a descriptive framework of human decision making processes. We outlined an approach to the multiple determinants that contribute to make human decision making specific. Certainly, human judgement and decision making appears to be strongly biased in some respects, particularly when their decisions are compared to that of formal models. However, when considering the multiplicity of decision making situations humans have to cope with, in addition the imprecise and incomplete character of information to take the decisions, the weakness of attentional resources in the cognitive system and, finally, considering that humans must rapidly take decisions in a social environment that is not so easy to formalize, we must conclude that global human performance is surprisingly good. Despite being efficient on local and well-defined problems, the best artefacts available today are very far from reaching such a global efficiency, and there are few complex situations (if any) over which we would be ready to delegate the full responsibility to an artificial decision making system.

We can therefore admire the efficiency of the heuristics that support human reasoning, judgement and decision making. The human cognitive system evolved in conditions over which uncertainty and incompleteness of available information ruled supreme. In such conditions, current normative theories have little to say about the optimal behavior. It is not surprising that adaptation of the cognitive system has been achieved by means of processes aimed at optimizing the construction of the representation of the decision making situation. We think that it is mainly from this standpoint that behaviors that appear as biases under the auspices of usual normative theories must be understood.

In the many uncertain situations humans have to cope with, it is often impossible to reach a perfect decision. As argued by Hammond [HAM 96], such situations often entail a social trade-off between 'inevitable error' and 'unavoidable injustice'. Thus, perfect decision making is probably beyond hope. In addition, everyone can recall some example of catastrophic human errors in, say, finance, medicine and jurisprudence. But however dramatic some of those tragic errors may appear, we must not neglect the innumerable decisions that day after day turn out to be correct, and are therefore forgotten. First and foremost, we need to understand what adaptive advantage the behavior provides. Only once this is complete may we wonder about the remedies that can be brought to the remaining weaknesses. This is because the solutions designed to correct the biases must not disturb the positive functions fulfilled by these cognitive mechanisms. Otherwise, the remedy may turn out to be worse than the disease.

12.8. Bibliography

[ABE 82] Abelson R.P., Kinder D.R., Peters M.D. and Fiske S.T. "Affective and semantic components in political person perception". *Journal of Personality and Social Psychology*, vol. 42, 619–630, 1982.

[AHL 97] Ahlbrecht M. and Weber M. "An empirical study of intertemporal decision making under risk". *Management Science*, vol. 43, 813–826, 1997.

[ALP 82] Alpert M. and Raiffa H. "A progress report on training probability assessors". In D.E. Kahneman, P. Slovic, and A. Tversky (Eds.) *Judgment Under Uncertainty: Heuristics and Biases* pp. 294-305. Cambridge: Cambridge University Press, 1982.

[BAR 97] Baron J. and Spranca M. "Protected values". *Organizational Behavior and Human Decision Processes*, vol. 70, 1–16, 1997.

[BEC 97] Bechara A., Damasio H., Tranel D. and Damasio A.R. "Deciding advantageously before knowing the advantageous strategy". *Science*, vol. 275, 1293–1295, 1997.

[BER 96] Bernstein P.L. *Against the Gods: The Remarkable Story of Risk*. New York: John Wiley and Sons, 1997.

[BIA 05] Biais B., Hilton D.J., Pouget S. and Mazurier K. "Judgmental overconfidence, self-monitoring and trading performance in an experimental financial market". *Review of Economic Studies*, vol. 72, 297–312, 2005.

[CHA 02] Chapman G.B. and Johnson E.J. "Incorporating the irrelevant: Anchors in judgments of belief and value". In T. Gilovich, D. Griffin, and D. Kahneman (Eds.) *Heuristics and Biases: The Psychology of Intuitive Judgment*. Cambridge: Cambridge University Press, 2002.

[CHAS 73] Chase W.G. and Simon H.A. "Perception in Chess". *Cognitive Psychology*, vol. 4, 55–81, 1973.

[CHE 03] Cherubini P., Mazzocco K. and Rumiati R. "Rethinking the focusing effect in decision-making". *Acta Psychologica*, vol. 113, 67–81, 2003.

[DAM 91] Damasio A.R., Tranel D. and Damasio H.C. "Somatic markers and the guidance of behavior: Theory and preliminary testing". In H.S. Levin, H.M. Eisenberg, and A.L. Benton (Eds.) *Frontal Lobe Function and Dysfunction* p. 217–229. New York: Oxford University Press, 1991.

[DUL 91] Dulany D.L. and Hilton D.J. "Conversational implicatures, conscious representations, and the conjunction fallacy". *Social Cognition*, vol. 9, 85–110, 1991.

[EDW 00] Edwards W., and Newman J.R. "Multiattribute evaluation". in T. Connoly, H.R. Arkes, and K.R. Hammond (Eds.) *Judgment and Decision-making: An Interdisciplinary Reader*, 2nd Edition, pp. 17–34. Cambridge, Cambridge University Press, 2000.

[ELS 78] Elstein A.S., Shulman L.S. and Sprafka S.A. *Medical Problem Solving: An Analysis of Clinical Reasoning*. Cambridge, Massachusetts: Harvard University Press, 1978.

[ENG 06] Englich B., Mussweiler T. and Strack F. "Playing dice with criminal sentences: The influence of irrelevant anchors on experts' judicial decision-making". *Personality and Social Psychology Bulletin*, vol. 32, 188–200, 2006.

[EPL 01] Epley N. and Gilovich T. "Putting adjustment back in the anchoring and adjustment heuristic: Differential processing of self-generated and experimenter-provided anchors". *Psychological Science*, vol. 12, 391–396, 2001.

[EPL 04] Epley N. "A Tale of Tuned Decks? Anchoring as accessibility and anchoring as adjustment". In D. J. Koehler and N. Harvey (Eds.) *The Blackwell Handbook of Judgment and Decision Making* pp. 240–256. Oxford, UK: Blackwell Publishers, 2004.

[EPL 06] Epley N. and Gilovich T. "The anchoring and adjustment heuristic: Why adjustments are insufficient". *Psychological Science*, vol. 17, 311–318, 2006.

[FIS 77] Fischhoff B., Slovic P. and Lichtenstein S. "Knowing with certainty: The appropriateness of extreme confidence". *Journal of Experimental Psychology*, vol. 3, 552–564, 1977.

[FIS 78] Fischhoff B., Slovic P. and Lichtenstein S. "Fault trees: Sensitivity of estimated failure probabilities to problem representation". *Journal of Experimental Psychology: Human Perception and Performance*, vol. 4, 330–344, 1978.

[FLY 94] Flynn J., Slovic P. and Mertz C.K. "Gender, race, and perception of environmental health risks". *Risk Analysis*, vol. 14(6), 1101–1108, 1994.

[GIG 91] Gigerenzer G., Hoffrage U. and Kleinbolting H. "Probabilistic mental models: A Brunswikian theory of confidence". *Psychological Review*, vol. 98, 506–528, 1991.

[GIG 99] Gigerenzer G., Todd P. and the ABC Group. *Simple Heuristics that Make us Smart*. New York: Oxford University Press, 1999.

[HAC 75] Hacking I. *The Emergence of Probability: A Philosophical Study of Early Ideas about Probability, Induction and Statistical Inference*. Cambridge: Cambridge University Press, 1975.

[HAM 96] Hammond K.R. *Human Judgment and Social Policy: Irreducible Uncertainty, Inevitable Error, Unavoidable Injustice*. New York: Oxford University Press, 1996.

[HAU 79] Hausman J. "Individual discount rates and the purchase of utilization of energy-using durables". *Bell Journal of Economics*, vol. 10, 33–54, 1979.

[HIG 00] Higgins E.T. "Beyond pleasure and pain". In E. T. Higgins and A. W. Kruglanski (Eds.) *Motivational Science: Social and Personality Perspectives*. pp. 231–255. Philadelphia, PA: Psychology Press, 2000.

[HIL 09] Hilton D., Régner I., Cabantous L., Charalambides, L. and Vautier, S. "Judgmental overconfidence: Do positive illusions predict miscalibration?" forthcoming.

[HOG 95] Hogarth R.M. and Kunreuther H. "Decision making under ignorance: Arguing with yourself". *Journal of Risk and Uncertainty*, vol. 10, 15–36, 1995.

[JOH 83] Johnson E.J. and Tversky A. "Affect, generalization, and the perception of risk". *Journal of Personality and Social Psychology*, vol. 45, 20–31, 1983.

[JUS 94] Juslin P. "The overconfidence phenomenon as a consequence of informal experimenter-guided selection of almanac items". *Organizational Behavior and Human Decision Processes*, vol. 57, 226–246, 1994.

[KAH 79] Kahneman D. and Tversky A. "Prospect Theory: An analysis of decision under risk". *Econometrica*, vol. 47, 263–291, 1979.

[KAH 02] Kahneman D. and Frederick S. "Representativeness revisited: Attribute substitution in intuitive judgment". In T. Gilovich, D. Griffin, and D. Kahneman (Eds). *Heuristics and Biases: The Psychology of Intuitive Judgment*, pp. 49–81. New York: Cambridge University Press, 2002.

[KLA 99] Klayman J., Soll J., Gonzales-Vallejo C. and Barlas S. "Overconfidence: it depends on how, what and whom you ask". *Organizational Behavior and Human Decision Processes*, vol. 79, 216–247, 1999.

[KLE 93] Klein G.A., Oranasu J., Calderwood R. and Zsambok C.E. *Decision-making in Action: Models and Methods*. Norwood, NJ: Ablex, 1993.

[KUN 98] Kunreuther H., Onculer A. and Slovic P. "Time insensitivity for protective investments". *Journal of Risk and Uncertainty*, vol. 16, 279–299, 1998.

[LEG 93] Legrenzi P., Girotto V. and Johnson-Laird P.N. "Focussing in reasoning and decision making". *Cognition*, vol. 49, 37–66, 1993.

[LIC 71] Lichtenstein S. and Slovic P. "Reversals of preference between bids and choices in gambling decisions". *Journal of Experimental Psychology*, vol. 89, 46–55, 1971.

[LIC 82] Lichtenstein S., Fischhoff B. and Phillips L. "Calibration of probabilities: The state of the art to 1980". In H. Jungermann and G. deZeew (Eds.) *Decision Making and Change in Human Affairs*, Amsterdam: D. Rede, 1982.

[LOE 92] Loewenstein G. and Prelec D. "Anomalies in intertemporal choice: Evidence and an interpretation". *The Quarterly Journal of Economics*, vol. 107, 573–597, 1992.

[MAR 03] Marquié L., Raufaste E., Lauque D., Mariné C., Ecoiffier M. and Sorum P.C. "Pain ratings by patients and physicians: Evidence of systematic pain miscalibration". *Pain*, vol. 102, 289–296, 2003.

[MEL 97] Mellers B.A., Schwartz A., Ho K. and Ritov I. "Decision affect theory: Emotional reactions to the outcomes of risky options". *Psychological Science*, vol. 8, 423–429, 1997.

[MON 83] Montgomery H. "Decision rules and the search for a dominance structure: towards a process model of decision-making". In P.C. Humphreys, O. Svenson, and A. Vari (Eds.) *Analyzing and Aiding Decision Processes* pp. 343–369. Amsterdam: North-Holland, 1983.

[PAY 93] Payne J.W., Bettman J.R. and Johnson E.J. *The Adaptive Decision Maker*. Cambridge: Cambridge University Press, 1993.

[RAU 98a] Raufaste E. and Da Silva Neves R. "Empirical evaluation of possibility theory in human radiological diagnosis". In H. Prade (Ed.) *Proceedings of the 13th Biennial Conference on Artificial Intelligence*, ECAI'98 pp. 124–128. London: John Wiley & Sons, 1998.

[RAU 98b] Raufaste E., Eyrolle H. and Mariné C. "Pertinence generation in radiological diagnosis: Spreading activation and the nature of expertise". *Cognitive Science*, vol. 22, 517–546, 1998.

[RAU 03] Raufaste E., Da Silva Neves R. and Mariné C. "Testing the descriptive validity of Possibility Theory in human judgments of uncertainty". *Artificial Intelligence*, vol. 148, 197–218, 2003.

[RAU 08] Raufaste E. and Vautier S. "An evolutionist approach to information bipolarity: Representations and affects in human cognition". *International Journal of Intelligent Systems*, vol. 23, 878–897, 2008.

[ROT 01] Rottenstreich Y. and Hsee C.K. "Money, kisses, and electric shocks: An affective interpretation of probability weighting function". *Psychological Science*, vol. 12, 185–190, 2001.

[RUS 92] Russo J.E. and Schoemaker P.J.H. "Managing over-confidence". *Sloan Management Review*, vol. 33, 7–17, 1992.

[SAM 37] Samuelson P. "A note on the measurement of utility". *Review of Economic Studies*, vol. 4, 155–161, 1937.

[SHE 85] Sherman S.J., Cialdini R.B., Schwartzman D.F. and Reynolds K.D. "Imagining can heighten or lower the perceived likelihood of contracting a disease: The mediating effect of ease of imagery". *Personality and Social Psychology Bulletin*, vol. 11, 118–127, 1985.

[SIM 56] Simon H.A. "Rational Choice and the structure of the environment". *Psychological Review*, vol. 63, 129–138, 1956. (Reprinted in H.A. Simon (Ed.), *Models of Thought*, vol. I, pp. 20–28. Yale University Press.)

[SLO 95] Slovic P. "The construction of preference". *American Psychologist*, vol. 50, 364–371, 1995.

[SLO 97] Slovic P. "Trust, emotion, sex, politics, and science: Surveying the risk-assessment battlefield". In M. H. Bazerman, D. M. Messick, A. E. Tenbrunsel, and K. A. Wade-Benzoni (Eds.) *Environment, Ethics, and Behavior*, p. 277–313. San Francisco: New Lexington, 1997.

[SLO 68] Slovic P. and Lichtenstein S. "Relative importance of probabilities and payoffs in risk-taking". *Journal of Experimental Psychology Monographs*, vol. 78, 1–18, 1968.

[SLO 80] Slovic P., Fischhoff B. and Lichtenstein S. "Facts and fears: Understanding perceived risk". In R. Schwing and W. A. Albers, Jr (Eds). *Societal Risk Asssessment: How Safe is Safe Enough?*, pp. 184–214. New York: Plenum Press, 1980.

[SLO 02] Slovic P., Griffin D. and Tversky A. "Compatibility effects in judgment and choice". In T. Gilovich, D. Griffin and D. Kahneman (Eds.), *Heuristics and Biases: The Psychology of Intuitive Judgment*, pp. 217–229. Cambridge, UK: Cambridge University Press, 2002.

[STA 09] Stanovich K.E. *What Intelligence Tests Miss: The Psychology of Rational Thought*. New Haven: Yale University Press, 2009.

[STE 98] Stephan E. "Anchoring and adjustment in economic forecasts: the role of incentives, ability and expertise". *Conference on Judgemental Inputs to the Forecasting Process*, University College London, 1998.

[STR 97] Strack F. and Mussweiler T. "Explaining the enigmatic anchoring effect: Mechanisms of selective accessibility". *Journal of Personality and Social Psychology*, vol. 73, 437–446, 1997.

[TVE 72] Tversky A. "Elimination by aspects: A theory of choice". *Psychological Review*, vol. 79, 281–299, 1972.

[TVE 92] Tversky A. and Kahneman D. "Advances in Prospect Theory: Cumulative representation of uncertainty". *Journal of Risk and Uncertainty*, vol. 5, 297–323, 1992.

[TVE 81] Tversky A. and Kahneman D. "The framing of decisions and the psychology of choice". *Science*, vol. 211, 453–458, 1981.

[TVE 94] Tversky A. and Koehler D.J. "Support theory: A non-extensional representation of subjective probability". *Psychological Review*, vol. 101, 547–567, 1994.

[TVE 88] Tversky A., Sattath S. and Slovic P. "Contingent weighting in judgment and choice". *Psychological Review*, vol. 95, 371–384, 1988.

[ZAJ 80] Zajonc R.B. "Feeling and thinking: preferences need no inferences". *American Psychologist*, vol. 36, 102–103, 1980.

[ZSA 97] Zsambok C.E. and Klein G. *Naturalistic Decision Making*. Mahwah, NJ: LEA, 1997.

Chapter 13

Bayesian Networks

13.1. Introduction

We constantly have to make choices and take actions in a world which we perceive to be full of uncertainty. A doctor knows that some disease can be accompanied by a certain symptom, but that sometimes it is not; he moreover knows that the same symptom can also be present with other diseases. A mechanic knows that a car engine which is improperly maintained is likely to break down, but he also knows that replacing it by a new one is not a guarantee that this will not happen. A manufacturer knows that they cannot expect market research to make them certain that their new products will sell well; they also know that a careful study of the economic situation cannot completely eliminate the uncertainty concerning the amount of sales.

Fortunately, information can be useful even when it is not complete. A symptom, which is often present with some disease and not so often with others, directs the doctor's diagnosis towards the first one. Their trust in their own conclusion will possibly be reinforced by the observation of other symptoms (which are themselves non-conclusive separately) or by the arrival of epidemic information. On the other hand, if evidence can strengthen a diagnosis, it can also do the opposite: the absence of a particular symptom can create a hesitation in the doctor's mind regarding the conclusion towards which the present symptoms would direct them. It may also happen that some evidence may make other evidence lose its importance. For a mechanic who is about to check the oil level in a car engine, the warning light on the dashboard is devoid of interest. The availability of direct information on the variable

---

Chapter written by Jean-Yves JAFFRAY.

we are concerned with – the state of the engine for the mechanic – may therefore make indirect information pointless.

A Bayesian network (BN) provides, by means of a graph, precise information on the existence of direct and indirect dependence relations among a set of variables. This graph is completed by numerical data which inform us about the nature and the intensity of these links. More precisely, a BN is a probabilistic model; its graph expresses the validity of conditional independence relations between random variables. Its data tables bring numerical accuracy, in the form of conditional probability distributions, about the degrees of dependence between variables.

Example 13.1. On a car dashboard, the brake warning LED can be lit or not. If it is lit, it means that either the brake fluid is leaking or the disk is damaged. A leak may or may not create a fluid puddle under the car. Figure 13.1 represents this knowledge through an oriented graph. Each node is associated with a binary variable: $L \in \mathbf{L} = \{\text{leak, no leak}\}$, $D \in \mathbf{D} = \{\text{damage, no damage}\}$, $F \in \mathbf{F} = \{\text{puddle, no puddle}\}$ and $V \in \mathbf{V} = \{\text{lit, not lit}\}$. The presence of an arc joining two nodes and its direction express, in a precise way, permanent knowledge. From the structure of the whole network, important conclusions can then be inferred. For instance, the existence of a chain connecting nodes F and D through arcs directed as indicated is consistent with the following rule: when the brake warning is on, the presence of a puddle should suggest that the brake dysfunction is due to a fluid leak rather than to disk damage. The presence of a puddle therefore makes disk damage less plausible: it 'explains away' that potential cause. However, probabilistic data, which always come with the graph in a BN, are required to validate for definite the preceding statement. They allow us to compute the probability that the disk be damaged, knowing both that the warning is on and that there is a puddle under the car, and to compare it with the probability of disk damage knowing only that the warning is on.

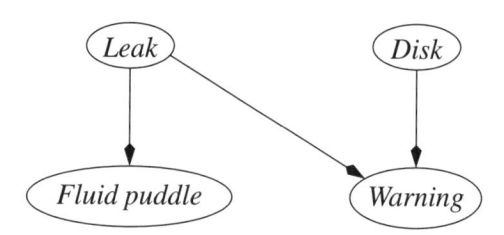

Figure 13.1. *The car example*

The construction of a BN is based on expert knowledge and relevant numerical data. This construction can be partly or completely automated. Efficient algorithms are then available for the propagation of information throughout the network. They provide diagnoses or prognoses in the form of the posterior probability, conditional to the information, that the variable of interest takes a certain value.

Influence diagrams (ID) complement BNs by adding decision nodes and indicating anteriority relations between decisions and data collections. An ID graphically represents a sequential decision problem in a more compact way than a classical decision tree does. With both representations, the determination of an optimal strategy with respect to the expected utility criterion is made by dynamic programming; however IDs inherit from BNs the ability to drastically simplify the probabilistic computations involved.

We present a complete survey, from the theoretical foundations to the practical implementation, of the powerful tools for analysis and decision aiding formed by the BNs and the IDs.

13.2. Definitions and notation

13.2.1. *Joint and marginal probabilities*

A BN is a probabilistic model defined by:

1) a finite algebra of events, with elementary events of the form

$$X_1 = x_1 \ldots \text{ AND } X_k = x_k \ldots \text{ AND } X_n = x_n$$

where $(x_1, \ldots, x_k, \ldots, x_n) \in \mathcal{X}_1 \times \ldots \times \mathcal{X}_k \times \ldots \times \mathcal{X}_n$, is a finite set;

2) a probability distribution P on this algebra, which is determined by the values of the probabilities of the elementary events.

We note

$$p(x_1, \ldots, x_k, \ldots, x_n) =^{def} P(X_1 = x_1 \ldots \text{ AND } X_k = x_k \ldots \text{ AND } X_n = x_n).$$

This implies that each $X_k (k = 1, \ldots, n)$ is a discrete finite random variable (RV) with support $\mathcal{X}_k$ and distribution characterized by probabilities $p(x_k) =^{def} P(X_k = x_k), x_k \in \mathcal{X}_k$. Similarly, the *joint distribution* of pair (X_1, X_2) is fully determined by probabilities $p(x_1, x_2) =^{def} P(X_1 = x_1 \text{ AND } X_2 = x_2), (x_1, x_2) \in \mathcal{X}_1 \times \mathcal{X}_2$. The joint distribution of triple (X_1, X_2, X_3) is fully determined by probabilities $p(x_1, x_2, x_3) =^{def} P(X_1 = x_1 \text{ AND } X_2 = x_2 \text{ AND } X_3 = x_3), (x_1, x_2, x_3) \in \mathcal{X}_1 \times \mathcal{X}_2 \times \mathcal{X}_3$; etc.

Since P is additive, these probabilities are linked by

$$p(x_1, x_2) = \sum_{x_3} p(x_1, x_2, x_3); \; p(x_1) = \sum_{x_2} p(x_1, x_2); \; p(x_2) = \sum_{x_1} p(x_1, x_2).$$

The distribution of (X_1, X_2) is a marginal (distribution) of that of (X_1, X_2, X_3) and the distributions of X_1 and X_2 are marginals of (X_1, X_2) and (X_1, X_2, X_3). These terms refer to their possible representations as *contingency tables*. For example, the contingency table (Table 13.1) with elements $p(x_1, x_2)$ in the main part has elements $p(x_1)$ and $p(x_2)$ in the margins.

$$\begin{array}{ccc|c} \ldots & \ldots & \ldots & \ldots \\ \ldots & p(x_1, x_2) & \ldots & p(x_1) \\ \ldots & \ldots & \ldots & \ldots \\ \hline \ldots & p(x_2) & \ldots & \ldots \end{array}$$

Table 13.1. *Contingency table*

More generally, given a sequence of n random variables, also called an n-dimensional *random vector variable* (RVV.) $(X_1, \ldots, X_k, \ldots, X_n)$, the distribution of part of these variables, $X_J = (X_j, j \in J)$, is a marginal of the distribution of X and its elementary probabilities are obtained by summing the $p(x_1, \ldots, x_k, \ldots, x_n)$ over all the values of the variables which are not in X_J.

Remark 13.1. BNs can also be associated with random variables with an infinite support, in particular with real RVs. This presentation is voluntarily limited to variables with a finite support.

Remark 13.2. From a purely theoretical point of view, properties of vector RV do not differ from those of one-dimensional RV. In fact, any vector RV $(X_1, \ldots, X_k, \ldots, X_n)$ can be considered as a unique RV Z with support

$$Z = \{z = (x_1, \ldots, x_k, \ldots, x_n) \in X_1 \times \ldots \times X_k \times \ldots \times X_n\},$$

the set of all possible configurations of values of these n RVs.

13.2.2. *Independence*

Two RVs X and Y are independent, which is denoted by $X \perp\!\!\!\perp Y$, when

$$p(x, y) = p(x) \times p(y) \forall x, y \in \mathbf{X} \times \mathbf{Y}.$$

The independence relation $\perp\!\!\!\perp$ is symmetric since

$$p(x, y) = p(y, x) \text{ and } p(x) \times p(y) = p(y) \times p(x), \forall x \in X.$$

According to this definition, $X \perp\!\!\!\perp Y$ when the contingency table of pair (X, Y) is the product of its margins; in that case, all the lines of the table are pairwise proportional as are its columns. Each of these properties can be used to provide a simple characterization of independence, which is best expressed as a property of conditional independence. We first recall the definition of this notion.

13.2.3. *Conditional probabilities*

Given two events A and B, with $P(B) > 0$, the conditional probability of A given B is the quantity
$$P(A/B) =^{def} P(A \text{ AND } B)/P(B).$$
Using that definition, given a RV X and an event $Y = y$ such that $p(y) = P(Y = y) > 0$, we can now define the conditional distribution of X given $Y = y$, which is the distribution generated by elementary probabilities

$$\begin{aligned} p(x/y) &= P(X = x/Y = y) =^{def} P(X = x \text{ AND } Y = y)/P(Y = y) \\ &= p(x,y)/p(y), \; \forall y \in Y. \end{aligned}$$

The following two properties are straightforward:

$$X \perp\!\!\!\perp Y \Leftrightarrow p(x/y) = p(x) \forall x \in \mathbf{X}, y \in \mathbf{Y} \text{ such that } p(y) > 0,$$

$$X \perp\!\!\!\perp Y \Leftrightarrow p(y/x) = p(y) \forall y \in \mathbf{Y}, x \in \mathbf{X} \text{ such that } p(x) > 0, \forall x \in \mathbf{X}.$$

The properties on the right-hand side can be interpreted as follows. Observing the value taken by Y does not bring any information about X, in the sense that it will not change our beliefs about X (these are imprecise beliefs, which take the form of a probability distribution). Similarly, observing the value taken by X does not yield any information about Y.

By remark 13.2, the above definition and properties also hold when X and Y are vector random variables. We have already noted that independence relation $\perp\!\!\!\perp$ has property

SYMMETRY: $X \perp\!\!\!\perp Y \Leftrightarrow Y \perp\!\!\!\perp X.$

A simple summation over z in equalities $p(y, z/x) = p(y, z)$ demonstrates that it also satisfies

DECOMPOSITION: $X \perp\!\!\!\perp (Y, Z) \Rightarrow X \perp\!\!\!\perp Y$ and also $X \perp\!\!\!\perp Z.$

This is interpreted as observing that if X does not yield any information about (Y, Z) then it does not yield any information about Y alone. Similarly, if observing (Y, Z) does not yield any information about X, then observing only Y is of no benefit either.

13.2.4. *Conditional independence*

Two RVs X and Y are independent conditionally on a third RV Z, denoted $X \perp\!\!\!\perp Y | Z$, when

$$p(x, y/z) = p(x/z) \times p(y/z), \forall (x, y) \in X \times Y, \forall z \in Z \text{ such that } P(Z = z) > 0$$

This amounts to applying the independence relation $\perp\!\!\!\perp$ to pair (X, Y) for each conditional distribution $P(., ./z)$.

Successive conditionings by $Y = y$ and $Z = z$ lead to the same probabilities, namely $p(x/y, z)$, as a direct conditioning by $(Y, Z) = (y, z)$. The following characterizations are therefore straightforward:

$$X \perp\!\!\!\perp Y | Z \Leftrightarrow p(x/y, z) = p(x/z),$$

$$\forall x \in \mathbf{X}, \forall (y, z) \in \mathbf{Y} \times \mathbf{Z} \text{ such that } p(y, z) > 0$$

and

$$X \perp\!\!\!\perp Y | Z \Leftrightarrow p(y/x, z) = p(y/z),$$

$$\forall y \in \mathbf{Y}, \forall (x, z) \in \mathbf{X} \times \mathbf{Z} \text{ such that } p(x, z) > 0.$$

The properties on the right-hand side can be interpreted as follows. When the value of Z has already been observed, further observation of the value of Y cannot bring any additional information on X, i.e. will not change our present beliefs about X (beliefs which have been updated after the observation of Z). In the same way, observing the value taken by X cannot bring additional information on Y when the value of Z is already known. We say that RV Z contains all the information on X possessed by (Y, Z) and also contains all the information on Y possessed by (X, Z).

Note that for $Z = \varnothing$, conditional independence reduces to independence:

$$X \perp\!\!\!\perp Y | \varnothing \Leftrightarrow X \perp\!\!\!\perp Y.$$

The above definition and properties also hold for vector random variables X, Y and Z, by remark 13.2. It can easily be shown that the following properties hold for conditional independence relation $\perp\!\!\!\perp$:

$$\text{SYMMETRY}: X \perp\!\!\!\perp Y | Z \Leftrightarrow Y \perp\!\!\!\perp X | Z,$$

$$\text{DECOMPOSITION}: X \perp\!\!\!\perp (Y, T) | Z \Rightarrow X \perp\!\!\!\perp T | Z,$$

$$\text{WEAK UNION}: X \perp\!\!\!\perp (Y, T) | Z \Rightarrow X \perp\!\!\!\perp Y | (T, Z),$$

and

CONTRACTION : $X \perp\!\!\!\perp T | Z$ and $X \perp\!\!\!\perp Y | (T, Z) \Rightarrow X \perp\!\!\!\perp (Y, T) | Z$.

These properties identify relation $\perp\!\!\!\perp |$ as a semigraphoïd [PEA 88]. CONTRACTION is a very intuitive property since it basically states that if successive observations do not change beliefs at any moment, beliefs would not have changed if these observations had been simultaneous.

On the other hand, WEAK UNION and DECOMPOSITION, which together form the reciprocal of CONTRACTION, state that there cannot not exist pairs of RVs such that observing one cancels out the effect of observing the other; this property is not so obvious.

13.2.5. *Bayesian network*

The joint distribution of a vector RV $X = (X_1, \ldots, X_k, \ldots, X_n)$ can always be factorized as

$$\begin{aligned} p(x) &= p(x_1, \ldots, x_k, \ldots, x_n) \\ &= p(x_1) \times p(x_2, \ldots, x_k, \ldots, x_n / x_1) \\ &= p(x_1) \times p(x_2/x_1) \times p(x_3, \ldots, x_k, \ldots, x_n / x_1, x_2) \\ &= p(x_1) \times p(x_2/x_1) \times p(x_3/x_1, x_2) \times \ldots \times p(x_k/x_1, x_2, \ldots, x_{k-1}) \times \ldots \\ &\quad \times p(x_n/x_1, \ldots, x_k, \ldots, x_{n-1}) \forall x \in \mathbf{X} \end{aligned}$$

These factors can be simplified by taking advantage of existing conditional probabilities. We can always find a partition of $(X_1, \ldots, X_{k-1})$ into two subsets (X_{PAk}, X_{NPAk}) satisfying $X_k \perp\!\!\!\perp X_{NPAk} | X_{PAk}$ (with perhaps $X_{NPAk} = \emptyset$), hence

$$p(x_k/x_1, x_2, \ldots, x_{k-1}) = p(x_k/x_{PAk})$$

and therefore

$$p(x_1, \ldots, x_k, \ldots, x_n) = \Pi_{k=1,\ldots,n}\, p(x_k/x_{PAk}) \forall x \in X.$$

Smaller sets PA_k make simpler factors; in general, there is no smallest set PA_k such that $X_k \perp\!\!\!\perp X_{NPAk} | X_{PAk}$ but only minimal such sets. Note also that the decomposition depends on the arbitrarily chosen order in which RV $X_1, \ldots, X_k, \ldots, X_n$ are indexed.

To each decomposition of the joint distribution one can associate a directed graph G, in which the n nodes are identified with the n RVs $X_k (k = 1, \ldots, n)$ and where an arc (directed edge) $X_j X_k$ exists if and only if $j \in PAk$; thus X_{PAk} is the set of the parents of X_k in G. We say that P is decomposable according to G. By construction, G is acyclic (has no directed cycle).

A Bayesian network (BN) consists of the pair formed by a directed acyclic graph (DAG) G and a probability distribution P which is minimally decomposable according to G (i.e. is such that P is not decomposable according to a graph resulting from the suppression of any of the arcs of G).

When the n factors $p(x_k/x_{PAk})$ (multi-dimensional tables) are known, the joint distribution $P(.)$ is determined. Note that any enumeration ordering of the variables which is consistent with graph G, i.e. which is a completion of the partial ordering generated by the arcs G, would have resulted in the same decomposition up to a permutation of the factors. There is at least one ordering in which all the non-descendants of X_k in G (except itself), are enumerated before X_k; therefore, for every k, $X_k \perp\!\!\!\perp X_{NPAk}|X_{PAk}$.

More generally, valid conditional independence relations which have not been used for factorizing $P(.)$ and constructing the graph can be found by using the deductive system with relations $X_k \perp\!\!\!\perp X_{NPAk}|X_{PAk}$ as the axiom set and the general properties of semi-graphoids as the inference rules. They can also be detected, as we shall see later, using a purely graphical criterion: d-separation.

Let us first give an example showing the limits of the expressive power of BNs.

Example 13.2. RV $X \in \mathbf{X} = \{0, 1\}$ represents the quality of a certain car part, which can be either defective ($X = 0$) or good ($X = 1$). Values of RV $Z \in \mathbf{Z} = \{0, 1\}$ correspond to two different models for that piece. RV $Y \in \mathbf{Y} = \{1, 2, 3\}$ indicates the factory which the piece comes from. The joint distribution of (X, Y, Z) is given by the $p(x, y, z) \times 216$ table (Table 13.2).

	$Y = 1$		$Y = 2$		$Y = 3$	
	$Z = 0$	$Z = 1$	$Z = 0$	$Z = 1$	$Z = 0$	$Z = 1$
$X = 0$	2	2	2	9	2	1
$X = 1$	6	6	24	108	36	18

Table 13.2. *Probability law for* (X, Y, Z)

Note that $X \perp\!\!\!\perp Z|Y$; moreover, marginal tables $p(x, z) \times 216, p(x, y) \times 216$ and $p(z, y) \times 216$ (Table 13.3) show that $X \perp\!\!\!\perp Z$ but that NOT $X \perp\!\!\!\perp Y$ and NOT $Y \perp\!\!\!\perp Z$.

X, Z		
	Z = 0	Z = 1
X = 0	6	12
X = 1	66	132

X, Y			
	Y = 1	Y = 2	Y = 3
X = 0	4	11	3
X = 1	12	132	54

Z, Y			
	Y = 1	Y = 2	Y = 3
Z = 0	8	26	38
Z = 1	8	117	19

Table 13.3. *Probability laws for* $(X, Z), (X, Y)$ *and* (Z, Y)

By SYMMETRY, $Z \perp\!\!\!\perp X | Y$ and $Z \perp\!\!\!\perp X$. It can be checked that these are the only conditional or unconditional independence properties of (X, Y, Z).

Depending on the variable enumeration ordering chosen, four different graphs can be obtained:

1) $X, Y, Z : X \to Y \to Z$;
2) $Z, Y, X : Z \to Y \to X$;
3) Y, X, Z and $Y, Z, X : Z \leftarrow Y \to X$;
4) X, Z, Y and $Z, X, Y : Z \to Y \leftarrow X$.

The three first graphs express that $Z \perp\!\!\!\perp X | Y$ (or $X \perp\!\!\!\perp Z | Y$) by the absence of arc XZ (or ZX), but not that $X \perp\!\!\!\perp Z$ (nor $Z \perp\!\!\!\perp X$). They allow us to believe, erroneously, that the quality of the piece may depend on its model. On the contrary, the last graph expresses indeed that $X \perp\!\!\!\perp Z$ (or $Z \perp\!\!\!\perp X$), also by the absence of arc XZ (or ZX), but not that $X \perp\!\!\!\perp Z | Y$ (nor $Z \perp\!\!\!\perp X | Y$). It suggests that the quality of the piece may depend on its model, possibly in a different way to depending on the place where it is produced, which does not happen to be the case.

Example 13.2 shows that the graph of a BN cannot in general express all the conditional independence relations satisfied by a set of RVs. On the other hand, as we shall now see, it is possible to identify all the relations which are implicitly expressed by this graph.

13.2.6. *Graphical conditional independence criterion in BNs: d-separation*

The presence/absence of arcs in the graph of a BN is directly linked to the validity of certain conditional independence assertions for the joint distribution of its RV. We can therefore think that there should exist a purely graphic criterion allowing us to recognize the validity of other assertions, in particular those assertions which can be inferred from the initial ones. An example will help us to build such a criterion.

Example 13.3. Returning to the car example (example 13.1), let us add a variable (and node) $S \in \mathbf{S} = \{\text{sand, no sand}\}$ and an arc SD. This is the graph that would be obtained by enumerating the variables as $SDLVF$ and making the following

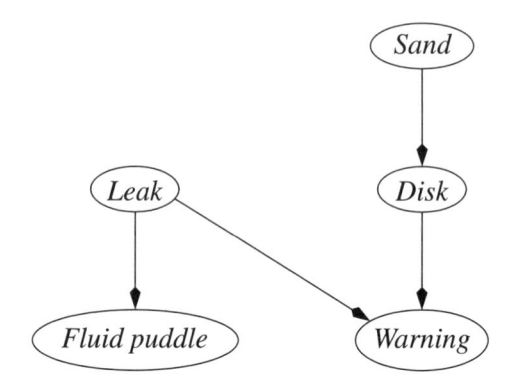

Figure 13.2. *The car example (cont.)*

assumptions: $L \perp\!\!\!\perp (S,D), V \perp\!\!\!\perp S|(L,D)$ and $F \perp\!\!\!\perp (S,D,V)$. From the general properties of relation $\perp\!\!\!\perp$: $L \perp\!\!\!\perp D$ (no link between the two causes of failure); $V \perp\!\!\!\perp S|D$ (the ability of the disk sensor in detecting the existence of damage does not depend on the cause of the damage) and $F \perp\!\!\!\perp V|L$ (the existence of a fluid puddle is closely linked to the importance of the leak, but its detection is not). On the other hand, one can easily construct a probability distribution which is decomposable according to this graph and such that: NOT $L \perp\!\!\!\perp D|V$ (the existence of a reason for the warning being lit makes the other explanation less probable); NOT $V \perp\!\!\!\perp S$ (the presence of sand increases the probability of a disk damage, hence also that of a lit warning); and NOT $F \perp\!\!\!\perp V$ (the presence of a fluid puddle and the warning lighting are both correlated with the existence of a leak).

Let us first see whether or not this criterion can be expressed through a classical separation criterion. Is it true that 'given three disjoint sets of nodes (RV) X, Y and Z, $X \perp\!\!\!\perp Z|Y$ if and only if X and Z are separated by Y?' (i.e. if and only if X and Z belong to different connected components of the subgraph resulting, in the suppression of Y).

It is only necessary to examine the triple of RV L, V, D in the above example to see that this criterion cannot be valid. In structure $L \rightarrow V \leftarrow D$, L and D are not separated, whereas $L \perp\!\!\!\perp D$ and V separates L from D. However, we have NOT $L \perp\!\!\!\perp D|V$.

We can however remark that the separation criterion would provide the correct conclusions for triples V, S, D and F, V, L. In fact, in structure $S \rightarrow D \rightarrow V$, S and V are not separated and indeed NOT $V \perp\!\!\!\perp S$. Similarly, D separates S from V while $V \perp\!\!\!\perp S|D$. We have the same agreement for structure $F \leftarrow L \rightarrow V$, since F and V are not separated and NOT $F \perp\!\!\!\perp S$ and since L separates F and V and $F \perp\!\!\!\perp V|L$.

All this suggests that all we need to do, to obtain a valid criterion, is to amend the separation criterion by taking into account the specificity of triples with two converging arcs, also known as CV-structures. For the particular case of CV-structures where the origins of the arcs are not directly linked by a third arc, we shall use the term V-structures. A CV-structure can indicate the existence of dependence between two variables conditionally to a third variable which has the same effect as L, D and V above, but also conditionally on a variable on which they have a joint effect, as in the following example.

Example 13.4. Two cyclists, Mr X and Mr Y, come face to face on a narrow bike path. They try to avoid bumping into one another by immediately falling back instinctively, randomly and independently, either to their right or to their left. These movements are described by RV X and Y, with values to the left or to the right which satisfy $X \perp\!\!\!\perp Y$. If both move to their right or both to their left, the probability of a collision (event $Z = $ yes) is very small; it is very high otherwise. Thus, Z depends on X and Y, which correspond to a CV-structure and more specifically to a V-structure $X \to Z \leftarrow Y$. If a collision occurs, when Mr X has fallen back on his right (respectively, left), it becomes highly probable that Mr Y has fallen back on his left (respectively, right): i.e. NOT $X \perp\!\!\!\perp Y | Z$. Let us note that, if Z itself is not observed but one of its effects is, for instance RV B (with values {casualties, no casualties}), and B is correlated with Z (link $Z \to U$), the same conclusions can be drawn. Hence, we also have NOT $X \perp\!\!\!\perp Y | B$.

Pearl [PEA 88] introduces the following property.

13.2.6.1. *d-separation*

1) Given three disjoints sets of nodes (RV) X, Y and Z, we say that a chain (non-directed path) C linking X to Y is active relative to Z when, for any pair of arcs of C forming a CV-structure, their common node (or one of its descendants) belongs to Z and, for any pair of consecutive arcs of C forming another structure, the common node does not belong to Z.

2) We say that X and Y are *d-separated* by Z when no chain between X and Y is active relative to Z.

Example 13.5. Let us return to the car example. F is d-separated from S by $\varnothing$ (i.e. in the absence of any information). It is not d-separated from S by V, but by (V, L) as well as by (V, D). Proposition 13.1 below will allow one to conclude that:

$$F \perp\!\!\!\perp S, \text{ NOT } F \perp\!\!\!\perp S | V, F \perp\!\!\!\perp S | (V, L) \text{ AND } F \perp\!\!\!\perp S | (V, D).$$

Proposition 13.1. *Given disjoint sets of nodes (RV) X, Y and Z, the following properties are equivalent:*

– X and Y are d-separated by Z;

– $X \perp\!\!\!\perp Y | Z$ is a logical implication of relations $X_k \perp\!\!\!\perp X_{NPAk} | X_{PAk}$, which have been used for constructing the graph, and of the general properties of conditional independence;

– $X \perp\!\!\!\perp Y | Z$ is true for almost all probability distributions which are decomposable according to the graph.

There is no hope that a graphical criterion would be able to reveal properties which have not been expressed, either directly or indirectly, in the graph. The d-separation criterion therefore cannot be surpassed. Similarly the deductive system, using all the properties of conditional independence as inference rules, is complete in the sense that it can produce all the conditional independence statements which are necessarily valid for every probability distribution which is decomposable according to the graph.

On the other hand, it must be remembered that the strength of these results is somewhat weakened by the fact that the graph of a BN is in general not able to express all the conditional independence relations valid for a given probability distribution.

The major interest of the d-separation criterion is that, while its visual nature makes it easy to use (no computations involved), it can give extremely useful indications. For instance, in the medical domain, it may allow us to identify a minimal exhaustive set of risk factors for a given disease, or to determine which additional examinations are likely to make the diagnosis of another disease more reliable.

13.3. Evidential data processing in a BN

The initial joint distribution (prior distribution) describes in general the relations between various characteristics in a given population (the inhabitants of a region, a fleet of vehicles, etc.). In applications such as medical diagnosis problems, the goal is the determination of the frequencies of some characteristics (diseases) among given subpopulations (an age group, people presenting certain symptoms, etc.). Technically, this amounts to determining the posterior probabilities of certain variables conditional to the available evidence concerning other variables. This is an easy task as long as there are only a few variables, but it may involve computations of prohibitive length with more variables if these computations are performed without care. Computing the marginal distribution of an RV given the joint distribution of 100 RVs may require 99 summations.

Pearl [PEA 88] was the first to realize that it was possible to take advantage of the decomposition of the joint distribution to progressively and efficiently compute a posterior distribution. The idea is that each step of the computation only involves a small part of the permanent and evidential data.

In Pearl's method, every node X_k in graph G:
– is endowed with factor $[p(x_k/x_{PAk})]$ (a $|PA_k| + 1$-dimensional table);
– receives data from the neighboring nodes G in the form of numerical messages;
– makes the computations required for updating the local data; and
– sends itself messages to its neighbors.

Although the validity of this method is limited to the case where G is acyclic, the same principle applies to the general case as we shall see later. This is achieved by replacing G by the corresponding *junction tree*, the nodes of which graph are the cliques of G.

A very simple example is all that is needed for highlighting the main features of Pearl's method.

13.3.1. *Pearl's method*

The joint distribution of triple (X, Y, Z), where $Z \perp\!\!\!\perp X | Y$, can be factorized as

$$p(x, y, z) = p(x) \times p(y/x) \times p(z/y).$$

When these three factors are stored at nodes X, Y and Z, $[p(x)]$, marginal prior distribution of X, can be read directly in X. As soon as a message from X to Y with content $[p(x)]$ has been received by Y, the marginal of Y will itself be computable in Y by the total probability formula: $p(y) = \sum_x p(x) \times p(y/x)$. Y will then itself be able to send a message to Z with content $[p(y)]$, which will allow the computation in Z of its marginal $p(z) = \sum_y p(y) \times p(z/y)$. These messages and computations constitute the initialization phase (Figure 13.3).

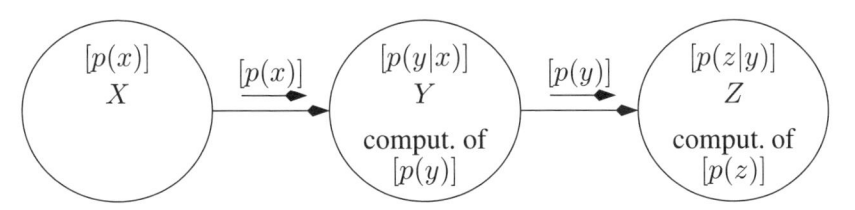

Figure 13.3. *Initialization phase*

Suppose now that it becomes known that $X = x_i$ (Figure 13.4). X will pass this information to Y by sending its marginal posterior distribution, which is the certain distribution $[p(x/x_i)] = [0, \ldots, 1, \ldots, 0]$ (where the 1 is the ith component).

Y will compute its new (posterior) marginal $[p(y/x_i)]$ (which is the ith line of matrix $[p(y/x)]$) and send it in a message to Z, which will then be able to compute its own posterior by $p(z/x_i) = \sum_x p(y/x_i) \times p(z/y)$, a formula that takes into account the fact that

$$Z \perp\!\!\!\perp X | Y \Rightarrow p(z/x_i, y) = p(z/y).$$

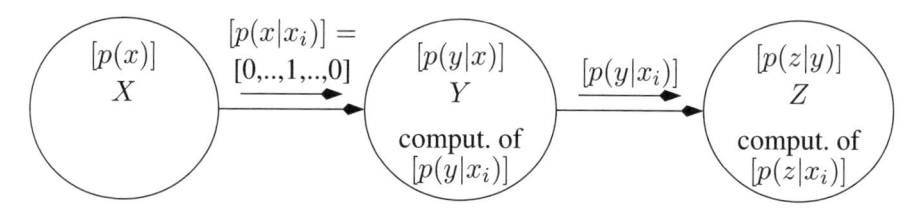

Figure 13.4. *Propagation of information downstream*

Let us now suppose that the evidence concerns Z (Figure 13.5). If it becomes known that $Z = z_k$, the posterior distribution of Z $[p(z/z_k)] = [0, \ldots, 1, \ldots, 0]$ (where the 1 is the kth component) will be certain and Z will have to send to Y the message $[p(z_k/y)]$ (the kth column of matrix $[p(z/y)]$). Y will therefore be able to compute its own posterior distribution $[p(y/z_k)]$ by Bayes' formula $p(y/z_k) \propto p(y) \propto p(z_k/y)$. Proportionality symbol $\propto$ indicates equality modulo a multiplication by a constant (which can always be determined by using the fact that $[p(y/z_k)]$ is a probability vector). Note that $[p(y)]$ is not available in Y unless the initialization phase has been performed previously.

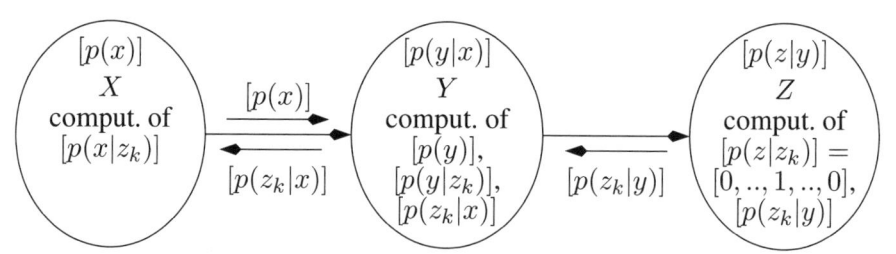

Figure 13.5. *Propagation of information upstream*

It still remains to compute vector $[p(z_k/x)]$ in Y by the formula $p(z_k/x) = \sum_y p(y/x) \times p(z_k/y)$ and to send it to X, the posterior distribution $[p(x/z_k)]$ of which can be computed from formula $p(x/z_k) = \sum_x p(x) \times p(z_k/x)$.

It is not any more difficult to propagate noised evidence e_Y on a variable Y provided the noise is characterized by conditional probabilities $p(e_Y/y)$ ('probability of observing e_Y when $Y = y$'). Everything happens as if e_Y was the observation of the value of a fictitious RV, with a unique parent Y (the same as Z in the graph Figure 13.5) which must therefore receive message $[p(e_Y/y)]$ to compute its updated distribution $[p(y/e_Y)]$ by formula $p(y/e_Y) \propto p(y) \times p(e_Y/y)$ and then, possibly, pass the information to a parent X through message $[p(e_Y/x)]$ computed by formula $p(e_Y/x) = \sum_y p(y/x) \times p(e_Y/y)$, etc.

The possibility of computing the posterior probability of any variable, by propagating the evidence throughout the graph by the means of messages that transmit vectors, exists for any BN with an acyclic graph. In order that every node receives all the information it requires for a correct probability update, all that is needed is:

1) part of the messages transmit all the evidence received by the nodes along the network edges to a center: an arbitrarily selected node (COLLECT phase); and

2) that the center transmits to each node along the network edges all the information it is not aware of yet (DISTRIBUTE phase).

The content of the messages between two adjacent nodes is the following (Figure 13.6). The parent node X transmits to the child node Y all the evidence e_{XY}^+ received on its side (i.e. by nodes which are closer to X than to Y) through a message containing its posterior distribution given that information $[p(x/e_{XY}^+)]$. Correlatively, Y transmits to X the evidence received on its side e_{XY}^- in the form of a likelihood vector $[p(e_{XY}^-/x)]$, which is all that X needs to compute its posterior distribution given all the evidence:

$$p(x/e_{XY}^+, e_{XY}^-) \propto p(x/e_{XY}^+) \times p(e_{XY}^-/x).$$

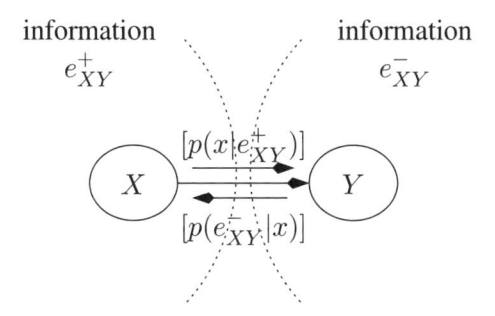

Figure 13.6. *Information exchange between adjacent nodes*

Let us observe the algorithm at work on the car, with the query 'the warning is lit, there is a fluid puddle under the car, what is the probability of a disk damage?'. The evidence (e_F, e_W) consists of two elements: e_F = 'presence of a fluid puddle'

520 Decision-making Process

and e_W = 'the warning is lit'. There may be noise, expressed by a probability of error for each observation, on each of these elements corresponding to a fictitious node in Figure 13.7, which illustrates the COLLECT PHASE with (arbitrary) center L. The content of the messages sent by the various nodes is indicated. The only constraint on the timing of the messages is that a node cannot send an outgoing message before it has received all the incoming messages. In Figure 13.8, which illustrates the DISTRIBUTE phase, only messages which are required to be answered have been represented.

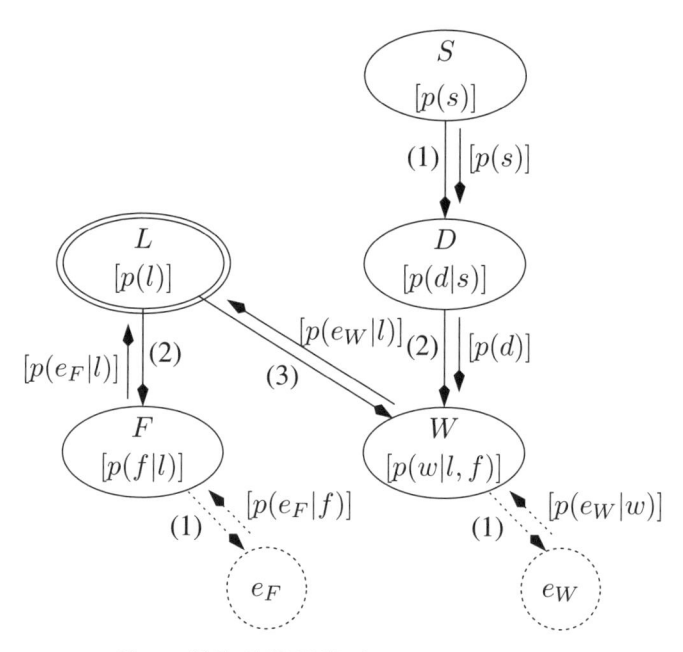

Figure 13.7. *COLLECT phase (car example)*

As soon as there exists cycles in graph G, splitting the evidence in two with respect to arcs XY no longer makes any sense and the principle on which Pearl's method relies does not apply anymore, as illustrated by the following variant of the car example. S and L are now directly linked (a piece of gravel in the sand can make a hole in the fluid circuit) thus creating a cycle (S, L, W, D) (Figure 13.9). The corresponding decomposition of the joint distribution is:

$$p(s, l, d, f, w) = p(s) \times p(l/s) \times p(d/s) \times p(f/l) \times p(v/l, d).$$

If the standard algorithm is applied blindly, identical messages $[p(s)]$ are sent from S to L and D, allowing the computation of $[p(l)]$ in L by $p(l) = \sum_s p(s) \times p(l/s)$

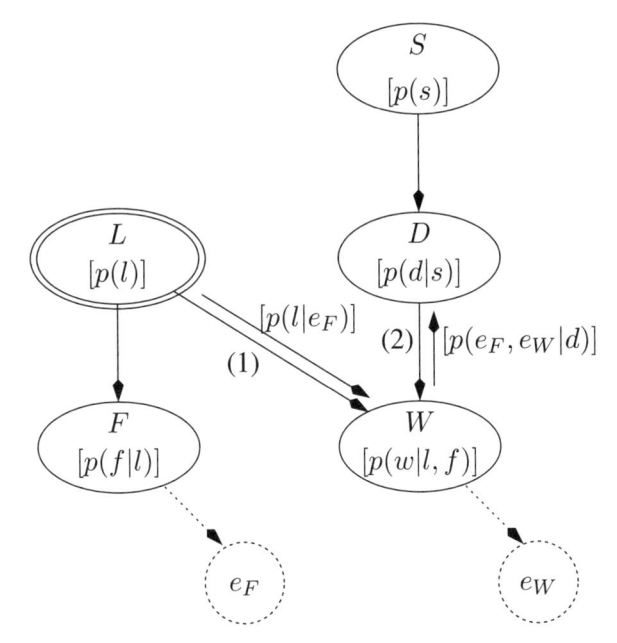

Figure 13.8. *DISTRIBUTE phase (car example)*

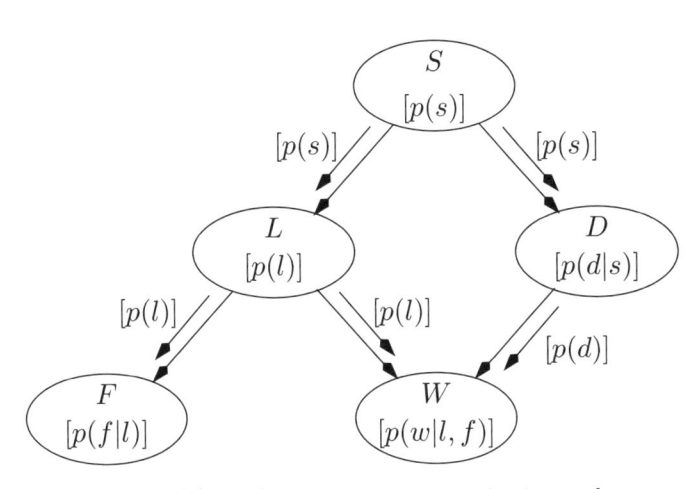

Figure 13.9. *Irrelevant message propagation in a cycle*

and of $[p(d)]$ in D by $p(d) = \sum_s p(s) \times p(d/s)$. Messages $[p(l)]$ and $[p(d)]$ are then sent from L and D, respectively, to W. Unfortunately, the correct expression for the marginal distribution of W is

$$p(w) = \sum_{l,d} p(l,d) \times p(w/l,d) \neq \sum_{l,d} p(l) \times p(d) \times p(w/l,d)$$

since RV L and D are not independent. Pearl's messages are therefore not appropriate for the computation of this distribution.

What can be done to solve this difficulty? A first solution, proposed by Pearl, consists of cutting the cycle by suppressing S then computing (by the standard method) the conditional probabilities of the other variables given $S = s$ for each possible value of $s \in \mathbf{S}$. The prior (unconditional) probabilities are then recovered by the total probability formula. For example, for W, messages $[p(l/s)]$ and $[p(d/s)]$ from L and D to W allow one to compute $[p(w/s)]$ by

$$p(w/s) = \sum_{l,d} p(w/l,d) \times p(l/s) \times p(d/s),$$

a formula justified by the fact that $p(v/s,l,d) = p(v/l,d)$ and that $p(l/s,d) = p(l/s)$. Finally, $[p(w)]$ is calculated by $p(w) = \sum_s p(w/s) \times p(s)$.

Another way to look at this method is to consider that there is only one message propagation process, but that it involves bi-dimensional messages transmitting matrices $[p(l/s)]$ and $[p(d/s)]$.

This 'cut-cycle' principle applies to any BN. However, if n cuts are made, the messages are $(n+1)$-dimensional, which can make computations unfeasible in practice. It is however possible to reduce the amount of computation by limiting the effect of a cut on the dimension of the messages inside the cycle which has been cut i.e. the local cut-cycle method [FAY 00]. In the above example, all that is needed is a one-dimensional message from L to F (which does not depend upon the value of S).

As a matter of fact, it is another solution by Jensen et al. [JEN 90] which has prevailed. A variation of propositions was made by Lauritzen and Spiegelhalter [LAU 88] and Shafer and Shenoy [SHA 90]. Getting rid of the cycles in a network by regrouping some of its nodes is a standard trick. Here, the natural groupings are those appearing in the factorization of the joint distribution. In our example where

$$\begin{aligned} p(s,l,d,f,w) &= p(s) \times p(l/s) \times p(d/s) \times p(f/l) \times p(w/l,d) \\ &= f(s,l) \times g(s,d) \times h(l,f) \times k(l,d,w), \end{aligned}$$

these are SL, SD, LF and LDW.

In order to remain close to Pearl's algorithm, we would like to construct a graph with these groups for its nodes. The graph would be a tree and such that it would only be necessary to enter the evidence concerning a given variable once, at one of the nodes to which it belongs, to be passed by messages later to the others. This requires that a variable belonging to two different groups (nodes) should also belong to all groups (nodes) along the chain which links them; this is known as the *running intersection property* and a tree with this property is a *junction tree*. Such a tree does not exist in our example. The reason is that (1) SL and SD and (2) SD and LDV would have to be linked directly. This would only leave the option of linking LF either to SL or to LDV (and this would not be a junction tree), or to link it to both (ensuring the running intersection property is maintained, but in a graph which is not a tree).

However, there exists a procedure described below which transforms the graph of any BN in such a way that the cliques of the resulting graph can be linked to form a junction tree. In our example, one would obtain the tree of Figures 13.10 and 13.11. The rectangles on the edges in Figure 13.11, which display the variables common to the neighboring cliques, are called *(clique) separators*; it is clear that this tree has the running intersection property. We shall now see how a junction tree can be constructed in the general case and how information is transmitted in it.

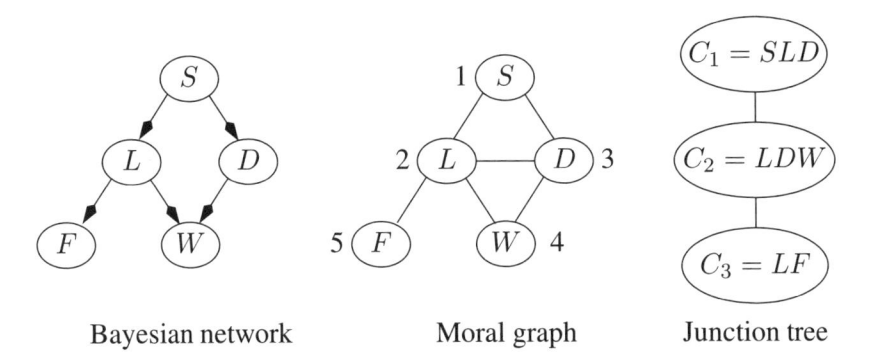

Figure 13.10. *Construction of a junction tree (1st example)*

13.3.2. *The junction tree method*

13.3.2.1. *Construction of the junction tree*

From the factorization of the joint distribution of the RV in the BN

$$p(x_1, \ldots, x_k, \ldots, x_n) = \Pi_{k=1,\ldots,n} p(x_k, x_{PAk}),$$

we only determine that each factor $p(x_k/x_{PAk})$ is a function $f_k(x_k, x_{PAk})$:

$$p(x_1, \ldots, x_k, \ldots, x_n) = \Pi_{k=1,\ldots,n} f_k(x_k, x_{PAk}).$$

524 Decision-making Process

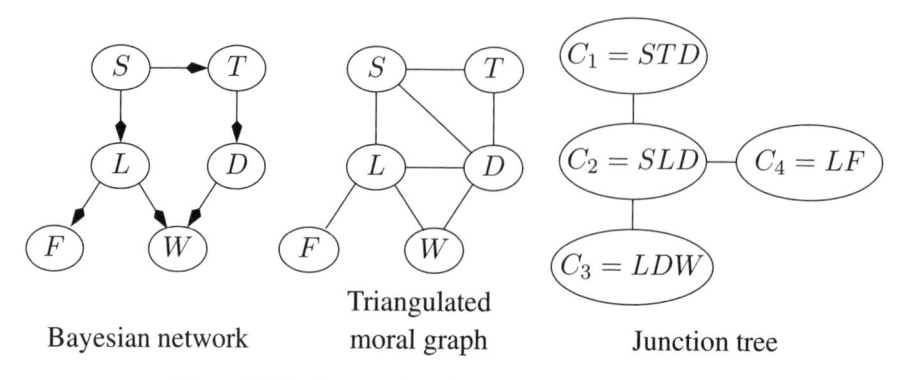

Figure 13.11. *Construction of a junction tree (2nd example)*

Figure 13.12. *Cliques and clique separators (1st example)*

This factorization is graphically represented by the non-directed graph G_M resulting from the graph G of the BN by:
- linking by edges all the parents of a same node of G; and
- deleting the directions of the arcs of G.

G_M is the *moral graph* associated with graph G. Its cliques (maximal complete subgraphs) are sets $X_k \cup X_{PA_k}, k = 1, \ldots, n$.

The existence of a junction tree, the nodes of which are these cliques, is not ascertained unless G_M is *triangulated*, i.e. unless all its cycles of length greater than three have at least one chord.

We therefore proceed to the triangulation of G_M, i.e. we add new edges one by one until we obtain a triangulated graph G_T; the success is certain if we use the following algorithm due to Tarjan and Yannakakis [TAR 84]:

- Label the nodes in increasing order from 1 to n by following the maximal cardinality search rule, which simply requires that the next node labeled should have a maximal number of neighbors among the nodes which have already been labeled.

- For each successive node k in decreasing order from $k = n$ to $k = 1$, link by an edge every pair of neighbors of k which have labels smaller than k and are not adjacent (in the graph containing the edges already added).

A simple procedure then produces a junction tree, in which the nodes are the cliques of G_T:

– Rank the cliques of G_T from 1 to m so that their rank increases with the label of their highest label node: $C_1, \ldots, C_i, \ldots, C_m$.

– Link every clique C_i by an edge with the cliques (or one of them) $C_j, j < i$ with which it has the greatest number of elements in common.

Finding a 'good' triangulation which minimizes the size of the data tables associated with the junction tree is a NP-complete problem. Kjaerulff [KJA 92] compares various graph algorithms (for more results, see [COW 99, NAI 04]).

13.3.2.2. *Evidential data processing in a junction tree*

Let us return to our example. The joint distribution

$$p(s, l, d, f, w) = p(s) \times p(l/s) \times p(d/s) \times p(f/l) \times p(w/l, d)$$

can also be written as

$$p(s, l, d, f, w) = [p(s, l, d)) \times p(l, d, w) \times p(f, l)] / [p(l, d) \times p(l)],$$

hence is of the form

$$p(s, l, d, f, w) = [g(s, l, d) \times h(l, d, w) \times k(f, l] / [r(l, d) \times t(l)]$$

with

$$r(l, d) = \sum_s g(s, l, d) = \sum_v h(l, d, w)$$

and

$$t(l) = \sum_{s,d} g(s, l, d) = \sum_{d,v} h(l, d, w) = \sum_f k(f, l). \tag{13.1}$$

Functions g, h and k are called *clique potentials* (and associated with cliques SLD, LDV and FL), while functions r and t are called *(clique) separator potentials* (and associated with separators LD and L).

We say that *consistency* holds in the junction tree when clique and separator potentials satisfy relations in condition (13.1) up to a multiplicative constant. The marginal probability distributions of the cliques and of the separators are therefore consistent. It can be shown that the converse is also true: if the potentials of the cliques and of the separators are consistent, then they are none other than their probability distributions (up to a multiplicative constant). Furthermore, *local consistency* between the potentials of each separator and those of the two adjacent cliques is sufficient for ensuring full consistency. This means here that relation $t(l) = \sum_{s,d} g(s, l, d)$ is in fact implied by the other relations.

The preceding properties apply to any probability distribution, in particular to a posterior distribution (the conditional of the prior distribution given some evidence). Suppose, for example, the existence of evidence (e_S, e_F) on RVs S and F and that the existing noise only depends on the corresponding variable, i.e.

$$p(s, l, d, f, w/e_S, e_F) \propto p(s, l, d, f, w) \times p(e_S/s) \times p(e_F/f)$$
$$= [G(s, l, d) \times h(l, d, w) \times K(f, l)]/[r(l, d) \times t(l)]$$

with

$$G(s, l, d) = g(s, l, d) \times p(e_S/s) \text{ and } K(f, l) = k(f, l) \times p(e_F/f).$$

Since these new potentials are no longer consistent, they are not equal to the marginal conditional distributions of the cliques and separators. However, we can try to make them consistent by modifying them, while conserving the value of the ratios which should remain equal (up to a constant) to $p(s, l, d, f, w/e_S, e_F)$.

The modifications required can be performed progressively by a procedure of message passing and computations which are similar to those used for the acyclic BN, and also involve the choice of center, COLLECT and DISTRIBUTE phases. Each phase will establish a different part of the consistency relations required (Figures 13.13 and 13.14).

In our example where LDW is chosen as the center, SLD computes and sends matrix $[R(l, d)]$ to LD, where $R(l, d) = \sum_s G(s, l, d)$. This will change potential $[r(l, d)]$, which amounts to multiplying each element $r(l, d)$ by $R'(l, d) = R(l, d)/r(l, d)$. For the quotient of the product of the clique potentials by the product of the separator potentials to remain unchanged, we only need to send matrix $[R'(l, d)]$ to LDV and operate the same transformation on its potential $[h(l, d, v)]$, thus replacing each $h(l, d, v)$ by $h(l, d, v) \times R'(l, d)$. However, since for its part FL computes and sends vector $[T(l)]$ to L where $T(l) = \sum_f K(f, l)$, and since L multiplies the elements of its potential by $T'(l) = T(l)/t(l)$, elements of the potential of LDV will finally be replaced by $H(l, d, v) = h(l, d, v) \times R'(l, d) \times T'(l)$. This ends the COLLECT phase. Potentials are now consistent (1) between SLD and LD and (2) between FL and L.

The DISTRIBUTE phase will secure the other consistency relations without affecting the former. LDV will compute and send matrix $[r''(l, d)]$ to LD, where

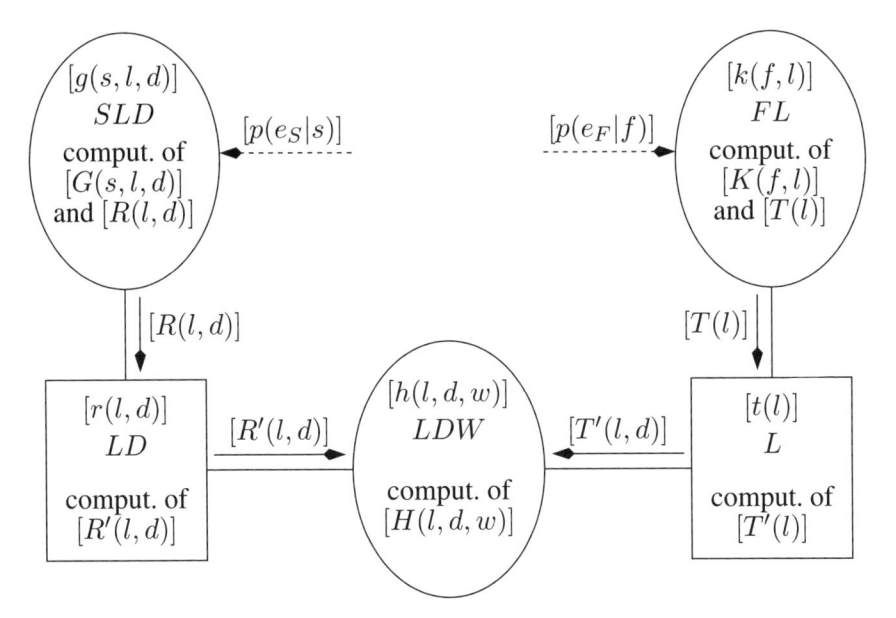

Figure 13.13. COLLECT phase (1st example)

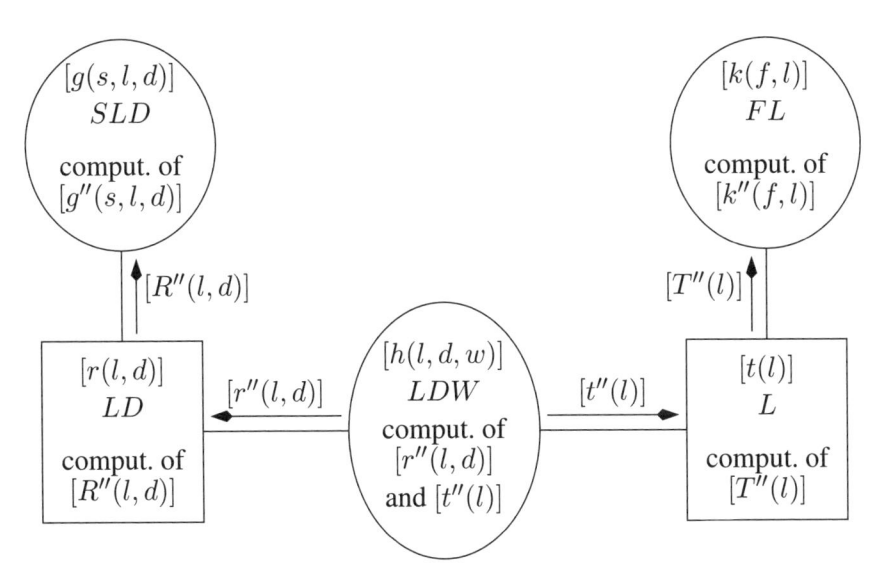

Figure 13.14. DISTRIBUTE phase (1st example)

$r''(l, d) = vH(l, d, v)$. It will substitute it by its present potential $[R(l, d)]$, which amounts to multiplying each element $R(l, d)$ by $R''(l, d) = r''(l, d)/R(l, d)$. Message $[R''(l, d)]$, sent from LD to SLD, allows us to perform the same transformation on potential $[G(s, l, d)]$ which becomes $[G''(s, l, d)]$. Simultaneously, LDV will compute and send vector $[t''(l)]$ to L, where $t''(l) = \sum_{d,v} H(l, d, v)$. It is then substituted by $[T(l)]$ by multiplying each of its elements by $T''(l) = t''(l)/T(l)$. Message $[T''(l)]$ sent from L to FL will perform the same transformation on potential $[K(f, l)]$, which becomes $[K''(f, l)]$.

According to the previously mentioned result, the new potentials (which are consistent) are equal (up to a multiplicative constant) to the marginal distributions of conditional distributions $p(s, l, d, f, v/e_S, e_F)$.

13.4. Constructing a BN

In applications, the construction of a BN is made partly by processing available data and partly on the basis of expert knowledge. This construction presents two distinct aspects:

1) the determination of the structure of the graph; and

2) the estimation of the conditional probability distributions which appear in the factorization of the joint distribution.

It is not clear that these two problems should be solved separately. The most usual methods do however, and treat them in the order above. For phase (2), a mixture of standard statistical techniques applied to the available numerical data and of subjective evaluations performed by experts is generally used. Phase (1), on the other hand, has required the introduction of original methods [JOR 98]. They can be grouped into two main families.

13.4.1. *Score-based methods*

In these methods, an evaluation function or score is used to measure the ability of a BN to represent the joint probability distribution. This is generally known through data in an imprecise, noised and incomplete way. The search space, which may often be the space of all BNs with the same set of nodes, is enormous. There is therefore no attempt to find the maximal score BN, but only to propose a heuristic producing an 'acceptable' solution. Such heuristics use standard search strategies which explore structures which are close to the strategy presently considered, i.e. strategies which can be derived from it by admissible transformations. In order to keep the score computations simple, the evaluation function is generally decomposable into a sum of factors associated with the nodes. The value of a factor remains unchanged unless the set of parents of the corresponding node is modified in the transformation considered.

The best-known evaluation function is the minimum description length (MDL) score which attempts to minimize the length of the message encoding the description of both the graph and the data. The latter takes the compressed form resulting from the decomposition of the distribution according to the graph [FRI 96].

A Bayesian approach, in which the best structure maximizes the posterior distribution, leads (under some assumptions) to the BDe (discrete evaluation) score [HEC 94] which is also decomposable. In that family, the best known algorithms are probably K2 of Cooper and Herskovitz [COO 92] and the Buntine algorithm [BUN 94].

An inefficiency factor in these methods is the existence of multiple BNs satisfying the same set of independence relations, which creates numerous local optima. The methods of section 13.4.3 try to overcome this difficulty.

13.4.2. *Conditional independence based methods*

These methods (inductive causation or IC/IC* [PEA 91], fast causal inference or FCI [SPI 00]) progressively determine the structure of the BN graph depending on the results of conditional independence tests. Some of the algorithms start from a completely undirected graph, suppress edges one by one, and finally give a direction to the remaining ones. Others work the opposite way, and progressively add some arcs or edges. In both cases, the number of tests to be performed increases exponentially with the number of variables, making these algorithms inefficient in large-scale problems.

Moreover, changing the conclusion of some of the tests may result in deep modifications of the structure of the graph built. This is unfortunate, since tests involving many variables will not be significant unless the database is huge. This creates an important limitation to the use of methods of this type.

On the other hand, some of these methods such as IC* have the advantage of being able to detect and express the influence of hidden variables.

13.4.3. *Search among Markov equivalence classes*

All these methods can be considerably improved by taking into account the following. The tests are not able to make a distinction between two structures which are Markov equivalent, i.e. which explicitly or implicitly express the same conditional independence relations. A result of the d-separation criterion is that two BN graphs are Markov-equivalent when they have:

1) the same underlying undirected graph; and

2) the same V-structures.

Each equivalence class can therefore be represented by the corresponding essential graph, i.e. the semi-oriented graph which is obtained by suppressing all the arc directions which are not involved in any V-structure.

In the independence-based methods, it is natural to first construct an essential graph and, when needed, to transform it into a directed graph. Regarding the score methods, we can take the set of the essential graphs as the search space [CHI 96]. It is only required that the score function depend on the equivalence classes. The gain can be substantial. An algorithm based on these ideas is EQ (equivalence classes) [MUN 01].

13.4.4. *Causality*

We have not yet introduced causality and have only mentioned the presence or absence of stochastic correlations between the variables. The dominant position among statisticians is indeed that the direct observation of variables can only reveal correlations and that one must have recourse to experiments, in which some of the variables are controlled, to become able to detect cause and effect relations.

However, when data concerning a triple of RVs X, Y and Z show that $X \perp\!\!\!\perp Y$ but at the same time NOT $X \perp\!\!\!\perp Z$, NOT $Y \perp\!\!\!\perp Z$ and NOT $X \perp\!\!\!\perp Y | Z$, which is expressed graphically by V-structure $X \rightarrow Z \leftarrow Y$, it is tempting to conclude that X and Y are independent causes having a joint effect on Z. Prior to drawing such a conclusion, however, we must eliminate the possibility that X and Z are correlated because they have a common hidden cause (as opposed to one being a cause of the other).

Starting from this remark and extending it to the general case, Pearl [PEA 00] proposes criteria allowing us to recognize if a variable is the potential cause of another i.e. if it is a genuine cause or if there is in fact a spurious association between them. Variable X, when linked with variable Z, is a potential cause of it if there exists a third variable Y such that triple X, Y, Z necessarily forms a V-structure $X \rightarrow Z \leftarrow Y$. It is in fact a genuine cause of Z if the link between X and Z by a common cause can be discarded. It is the nature of the links between X, Y and Z in certain contexts, i.e. conditional to the observation of certain other variables, which may make the discrimination possible. Similarly, we can conclude the presence of a spurious association between X and Y when there exist two contexts which respectively disqualify X as a potential cause of Y, and Y as a potential cause of X.

These are of course just definitions, and we may have doubts about their relevance for capturing causality. We should nonetheless note that the existence of discriminating contexts amounts to the existence of databases which are sufficiently rich to contain all the information that a controlled experience would have provided. Pearl's theory of causality is perhaps not that far from the classical point of view.

In the graphs constructed by algorithms IC and IC* of Pearl and Verma [PEA 91], only the latter allows for the existence of hidden variables. The directions of the arcs are consistent with an interpretation in terms of causality as defined above; for this reason they are called causal graphs.

13.4.5. *Conditioning by intervention in causal graphs*

Consider the following example. The medical observation of a subpopulation has shown that there is a link between the presence/absence of some symptom (variable S) and the development of a certain disease (variable M). The reception of a treatment (variable T) is also linked with the value of S. Finally, the ensuing good or bad health of people (variable E) depends simultaneously on S, M and T. These dependences are expressed by graph G in Figure 13.15. Accordingly, the decomposition of the joint distribution is $p(s,t,m,e) = p(s) \times p(t/s) \times p(m/s) \times p(e/s,t,m)$.

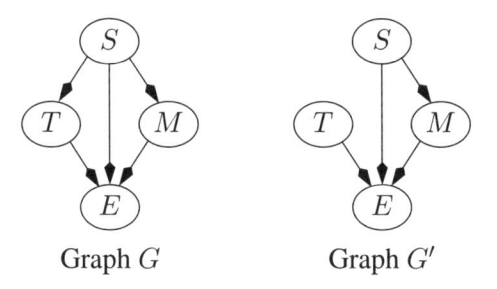

Graph G Graph G'

Figure 13.15. *Conditioning by intervention graph*

The probability that E = good health knowing that M = yes and T = yes in the subpopulation can be computed using Jensen's algorithm. What we really want to know, however, is the efficiency of the treatment i.e. the probability that in the entire population, a person which is ill and treated recovers a good health. This probability is in general different from the preceding one. It may be, for example, that this symptom only appears in the most serious forms of the disease and that only people presenting the symptom have been treated, so that the first probability is smaller than the true probability. This latter probability would be correctly evaluated in the BN of the graph G' of Figure 13.16, which is derived from G by suppressing the parents (here, the unique parent) S of T. It corresponds to the decomposition $p(s,t,m,e/T = \text{yes}) = p(s) \times p(m/s) \times p(e/s,t,m)$ knowing that t = yes and $p(s,t,m,e/T = \text{yes}) = 0$ otherwise. The reason for this modification is clear in a causal graph: if T = yes is enforced, T looses all connections with its causes but its joint influence with other causes on a given variable remains unchanged.

Pearl [PEA 00] asks the following general question: given the data which have been used to construct the BN and no other information, can we correctly predict the effect on certain variables of actions performed on others, when there exists a third group of variables which interact with the first two groups (confounding variables)?

The standard answer of statisticians is negative; they claim that it is necessary to have recourse to additional experiments in which the confounding variables are controlled (i.e. have fixed values).

What Pearl is able to show, by developing a general theory of conditioning by intervention, is that the answer is subtle. If certain graphical conditions are satisfied (back-door and front-door criteria) then the data already contain all the information which a controlled experiment would provided.

The potential practical interest of these results is clear: controlling the experiment is often impossible, and when feasible often extremely costly. Causal graphs therefore constitute a powerful tool, not only for the analysis of situations (diagnostics and prognostics) but also for guiding the action.

13.5. BNs and influence diagrams

We shall now see the contribution of BNs to the representation and resolution of sequential decision making problems under uncertainty.

13.5.1. *Dynamic decision making under uncertainty*

A decision problem is the formal representation of a situation where the decision maker must choose between various alternatives which can have desirable consequences (e.g. financial). Decision making under uncertainty is concerned with problems where, at the time of choice, the decision maker cannot perfectly anticipate the outcomes of their choices. In a dynamical problem, the decision maker does not have a single decision to make but a sequence of decisions. If uncertainty prevails, the decision maker can use the received information to make decisions depend on the information already possessed at the moment of decision. A (decision) strategy (i.e. a sequence of conditional decisions) then has to be selected.

Classically, the progressive arrival of information is presented as the result of successive choices of a fictitious agent, nature (N). Being probabilistic models, BNs can only be useful for modeling decision problems if the assumption that the decison maker's predictions concerning the future actions of N take the form of a probability distribution on the relevant events (for the problem considered) every time. We make that assumption, which places us in the framework of decision making under risk. We moreover assume that the decision maker never forgets what they have learned and that they update their probabilistic beliefs according to Bayes' rule.

In any given problem, the decision maker has to look for the (or a) best strategy according to its decision criterion under risk. We assume here that it is the classical criterion of expected utility maximization (EU criterion). The choice of a strategy by the decision maker determines the results that will be obtained depending on the events. Since events have probabilities, a probability distribution on the space of the consequences can be associated with each strategy. Since the criterion only depends on consequences through their utilities, the criterion value for a strategy that offers consequence c_i with probability p_i is $\sum_i p_i \times u(c_i)$, where $u(.)$ is the decision maker's von Neumann–Morgenstern utility function. The shape of function $u(.)$ depends on the attitude of the decision maker with respect to risk. In the example below, consequences are monetary outcomes and, for the sake of simplicity, the utility function is the identity function $u(.) = Id(.)$ (risk neutrality). The decision maker wants to maximize expected gain or, as in our example, to minimize expected cost.

13.5.1.1. *An example of dynamic decision problem under risk*

Consider the following example. The decision maker, whose car is in bad condition, has to keep it one more year. They can decide immediately whether or not to replace the car engine by a new one (decisions R and $NotR$); they can also (decision G) make their decision based upon the opinion (good or bad) (events B and B^c) given by an expert (a mechanic) after testing the engine. The prior probability that the present engine will cease to function before the end of the year (event A, complementary event A^c) is p, whereas it is only $q(<< p)$ for a new engine. The expert is not fully trustworthy and probabilities $P(B/A)$ and $P(Bc/Ac)$ that his prognostic is wrong are known to the decision maker. The cost of replacing the old engine by a new one c_R, the cost of an engine test c_G and the cost of no longer having a car c_A are all known.

13.5.1.2. *Decision tree of the problem*

Such a problem is traditionally represented through a decision tree, which is in fact a directed tree, since all the arc directions are the same (from the left to the right) they are not indicated. Two kinds of nodes represented by squares and circles alternate: the squares (decision nodes) are associated with times of choice for the decision maker and the circles (chance nodes) correspond to N's choices, i.e. at times where new information is received. The decision maker gains the knowledge (in addition to what is already known) that one of the events of a specific partition of the sure event is true. The tree also contains probabilistic data and, for each of its leaves, the resulting outcome in the case where the strategic choice of the decision maker combined with N's choices lead to that node. In our example, we obtain the tree depicted in Figure 13.16.

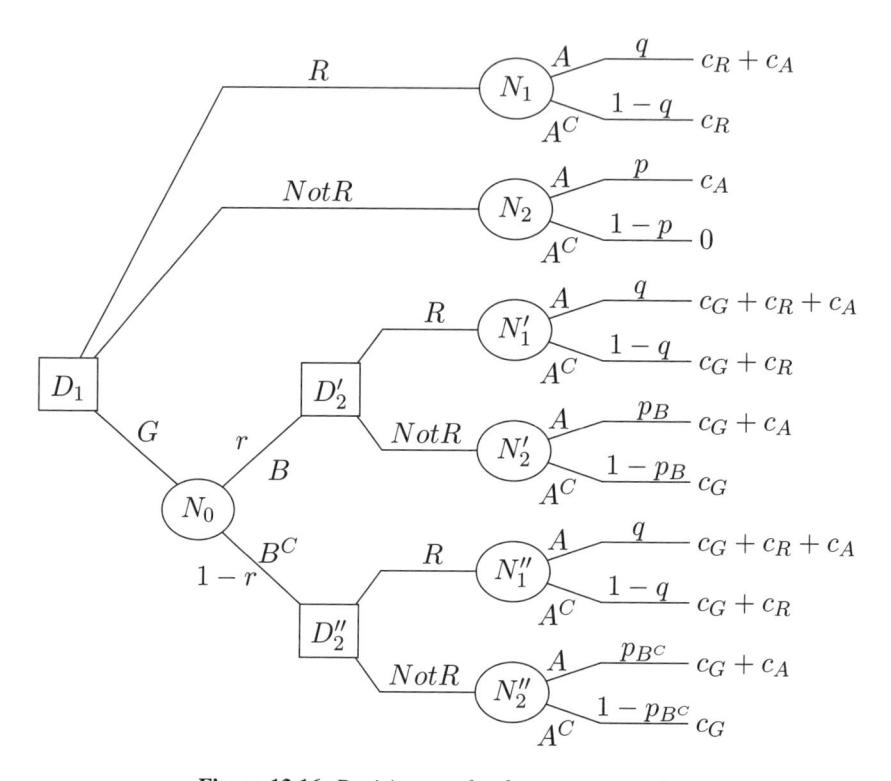

Figure 13.16. *Decision tree for the engine example*

13.5.1.3. *Optimization by dynamic programming*

The form of the EU criterion makes it additively separable. More precisely, an EU like any expectation can be expressed as an expectation of conditional expectations. This property implies the validity of Bellman's principle [BEL 57]. Substrategies of optimal strategies are themselves optimal (except those substrategies which could only be played with zero probability).

An optimal strategy can therefore be found by the dynamic programming algorithm, which operates by rolling back the decision tree and determining, at each decision node met, the best immediate decision. The subsequent decisions are fixed (and already optimized). Since any decision is followed by a choice of N, which randomly picks up a decision subtree, it is necessary to compute the probabilities of N's various feasible choices. This allows us to evaluate the EU criterion at that decision node, which is just the weighted mean (these probabilities being the weights) of the values of the EU criterion at the roots of the subtrees. In other terms, computations only require the alternative use of operators MAX (maximization) and EXP (expectation).

In our example, it is necessary to compute the probability that the expert gives a favorable opinion $r = P(B) = P(B/A) \times P(A) + P(B/A^c) \times P(A^c)$ as well as conditional probabilities $p_B = P(A/B) = P(B/A) \times P(A)/r$ in N_2' and $p_{B^c} = P(A/B^c) = P(B^c/A) \times P(A)/(1-r)$ in N_2''.

An optimal strategy can then be determined as follows. In D_1, the values of the criterion for the first two strategies, which are simple decisions R and $NotR$, are equal to the corresponding expected costs. These values must be compared with the best strategy that begins with the expert's consultation (decision G). If in node D_2' for example, the (conditional) expected cost is smaller than that resulting from decision $NotR$ and, simultaneously, that D_2'' is smaller than that resulting from decision R, the best strategy will be $[G; NotR$ if $B; R$ if $B^c]$; its value is the weighted mean (with weights r and $(1-r)$) of the minimal expected costs in D_2' and D_2''.

13.5.1.4. *Limits of the classical method*

The decision tree technique presents two major drawbacks:

– The representation of most real-life problems requires huge decision trees, which are not easily constructed and are not likely to be displayed at a single instance.

– The evaluations of the substrategies generally require numerous computations of conditional probabilities involving multiple applications of Bayes' rule. Since these computations are performed brutally, without taking advantage of the simplifications allowed by the presence of conditional independences, they are often untractable.

13.5.2. *Influence diagrams*

13.5.2.1. *Origin of the influence diagrams*

Influence diagrams (IDs), also called decision graphs, were initially proposed by Howard and Matheson [HOW 81] as a tool for constructing decision trees more easily. Their basic point was that decision situations are often repetitive – although their contexts may differ – which graphically implies the presence of subtrees with identical structures in the decision tree. This fact can be used to achieve a more compact representation of the problem.

For example, the car engine problem can be represented by the ID of Figure 13.17.

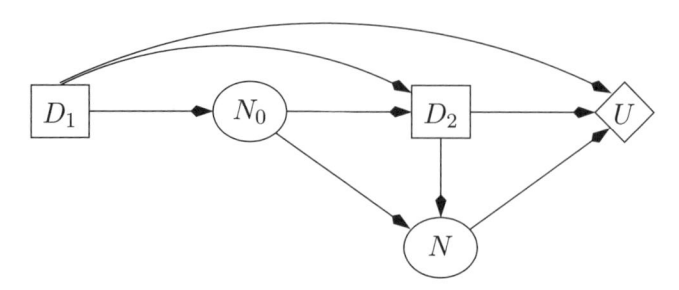

Figure 13.17. *Influence diagram for the car engine example*

13.5.2.2. *Semantics of IDs*

An ID consists of a directed graph and numerical data. A (decision or chance) node of an ID represents a set of nodes of the original decision tree. For a decision node, an incoming arc indicates that the decision may depend on the value of the node at the origin of the arc. The arcs linking chance nodes indicate a probabilistic link. A chance node contains data: its conditional probability distribution given all its parents. The lozenge U is the unique evaluation node. Its incoming arcs indicate which variables influence the result. It also lists the consequences (gains/costs) as functions of these variables (these are the consequences associated with the leaves of the decision tree).

In the example, it is clear that D'_2 and D''_2 can be grouped as node D_2 and that arc $N_0 D_2$ indicates that the decision in D_2 can depend on the event, B or B^c, which is true in N_0. Arcs $N_0 N$ and $D_2 N$ indicate, for their part, that the probabilities of events A and A^c vary from one subtree to the next. As a matter of fact, it has been possible to group branches R and $NotR$ with the others. This is because arc $D_1 D_2$ allows D_2 to be informed by the fact that, if R or $NotR$, D_2 takes the particular value 'no action'. In that case, arc $D_2 N$ informs N that it should not modify the priors of A and A^c.

13.5.2.3. *The methods of Shachter and Shenoy*

Shachter [SHA 86] was the first to determine an optimal decision strategy by working directly on the ID representing the problem studied. The underlying algorithm is still the dynamic programming algorithm. At each step of the computation performed when rolling back, the decision tree corresponds to a transformation of the ID. The suppression of a decision node is related to MAX operations. The suppression of a chance node is related to EXP operations. Reversing the direction of the arc joining two chance nodes corresponds to probability transformations operated by Bayes' rule.

Shenoy [SHE 92] has proposed an elegant variant, the valuation networks method, which relies on the remark that the computations involved in the resolution of a decision problem require only two kinds of operations: COMBINATION and

MARGINALIZATION. A remarkable achievement of Shenoy is his perfectly symmetric treatment of the two kinds of variables (decision and chance variables) and of the various operations (MAX, EXP and probability transformations). Another of his contributions has been to show that we can benefit from a possible decomposition of the utility function u(.) by introducing several evaluation nodes in the ID.

13.5.2.4. *The junction tree method*

Inspired by the model and observations of Shenoy, Jensen *et al.* [JEN 94] have shown that the junction tree method of the BN could be extended to the ID. The fact that information arrivals and decisions are distributed in time creates new constraints in the construction of the junction tree. Starting from the ID (but without its evaluation node(s)), we construct its triangulated moral graph, with the additional rule that the labeling of the nodes which takes place during the triangulation phase respects their temporal ordering. The ordering of the cliques of the junction tree has then the following property. There exists a root R such that, for any pair of adjacent cliques C_1, C_2, where C_1 is closer to R than C_2, all the variables in separator $C_1 \cap C_2$ have ranks smaller than those of the variables in C_2/C_1. This characterizes a strong junction tree (see Figure 13.18). The preceding property is required to make the algorithm of dynamic programming consistent with the standard computations of the junction tree method.

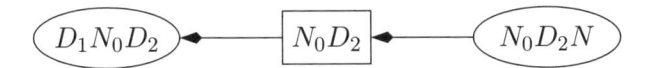

$$\boxed{D_1 N_0 D_2} \longleftarrow \boxed{N_0 D_2} \longleftarrow \boxed{N_0 D_2 N}$$

Figure 13.18. *Strong junction tree for the car engine problem*

This method achieves its main goal: the probabilistic computations are simplified in the same way as in the case of BNs.

13.6. Conclusion

Decision aiding has become considerably richer with Bayesian networks and influence diagrams. These new tools are extremely ambitious and attempt to solve analysis and decision problems of a considerably larger size than those tackled by the classical methods. Forging such tools takes much time. The evidence propagation algorithms and the optimal strategy determination methods already seem to be close to their final form. On the contrary, the construction of a BN that optimally represents the stochastic interactions between the variables of a database is a problem which is still the object of active research. The final place of BNs and IDs in statistics, operations research and artificial intelligence will certainly be important, but cannot yet be perfectly defined.

13.7. Software

Bayesian networks and influence diagrams software is available at the following locations:
- ADA Inc.: http://www.adainc.com/software/
- Bayesian network repository: http://www.cs.huji.ac.il/labs/compbio/Repository/
- Bayesware discoverer: http://www.bayesware.com
- B-Course: http://b-course.hiit.fi/
- BN Power Constructor: http://www.cs.ualberta.ca/ jcheng/bnpc.htm
- IDIS AI resources: http://excalibur.brc.uconn.edu/ baynet/
- Tetrad: http://www.phil.cmu.edu/tetrad/
- HUGIN: http://www.hugin.com/
- NETICA: http://www.norsys.com/

13.8. Bibliography

[BEL 57] Bellman R. *Dynamic Programming*. Princeton University Press, Princeton, NJ, 1957.

[BUN 94] Buntine W. "Operations for learning with graphical models". *Journal of Artificial Intelligence Research*, vol. 2, 159–225, 1994.

[CHI 96] Chickering D.M. "Learning Bayesian networks is NP-complete". In *Learning from Data: Artificial Intelligence and Statistics* V, Springer-Verlag, Berlin/Heidelberg/New York, pp. 121–130, 1996.

[COO 92] Cooper G. and Herskovitz E. "A Bayesian method for the induction of probabilistic networks from data". *Machine Learning*, vol. 9, 309–347, 1992.

[COW 99] Cowell R., Dawid A., Lauritzen S. and Spiegelhalter D. *Probabilistic Networks and Expert Systems*, Springer, Berlin/Heidelberg/New York, 1999.

[FAY 00] Faÿ A. and Jaffray J.Y. "A justification of local conditioning in Bayesian networks". *International Journal of Approximate Reasoning*, vol. 24, 59–81, 2000.

[FRI 96] Friedman N. and Goldszmidt M. "Learning Bayesian networks with local structure". *Proceedings of the 12th Conference on Uncertainty in Artificial Intelligence* (UAI96) vol. 12, 252–262, 1996.

[HEC 94] Heckerman D., Geiger D. and Chickering D. "Learning Bayesian networks: the combination of knowledge and statistical data". *Uncertainty in Artificial Intelligence*, vol. 10, 293–301, 1994.

[HOW 81] Howard R. and Matheson J. "Influence diagrams". In *Principles and Applications of Decision Analysis*, Strategic Decisions Group, Menlo Park CA, 1981.

[JEN 90] Jensen F.V., Lauritzen S. and Olesen K.G. "Bayesian updating in causal probabilistic networks by local computation". *Computational Statistics Quaterly*, vol. 4, 269–282, 1990.

[JEN 94] Jensen F.V, Jensen Fr. and Dittmer S. "From influence diagrams to junction trees". *Uncertainty in Artificial Intelligence*, vol. 10, 367–73, 1994.

[JOR 98] Jordan M. *Learning in Graphical Models*, Kluwer, Dordrecht, 1998.

[KJA 92] Kjaerulff U.B. "Optimal decomposition of probabilistic networks by simulated annealing". *Statistics and Computing*, vol. 2, 7–17, 1992.

[LAU 88] Lauritzen S. and Spiegelhalter D. "Local computations with probabilities on graphical structures and their application to expert systems (with discussion)". *Journal of Royal Statistical Society, Series B*, vol. 50, 157–224, 1988.

[MUN 01] Munteanu P. and Bendou M. "The EQ framework for learning equivalence classes of Bayesian networks". In *Proceedings of 2001 IEEE International Conference on Data Mining*, 417–424, 2001.

[NAI 04] Naim P., Wuillemin P.H., Leray P., Pourret O. and Becker A. *Réseaux Bayésiens*, Eyrolles, Paris, 2004.

[PEA 88] Pearl J. *Probabilistic Reasoning in Intelligent Systems: Networks of Plausible Inference*, Morgan Kaufmann, San Mateo CA, 1998.

[PEA 00] Pearl J. *Causality - Models, Reasoning and Inference*, Cambridge University Press, Cambridge, 2000.

[PEA 91] Pearl J. and Verma T. "A theory of inferred causation". In *Proceedings of 6th International Conference on AI* (AAAI-87, Seattle), 374–379, 1991.

[SHA 86] Shachter R. "Evaluating influence diagrams". *Operations Research*, vol. 34(6), 871–882, 1986.

[SHA 90] Shafer G. and Shenoy P. "Probability propagation". *Annals of Mathematics and Artificial Intelligence*, vol. 2, 327–352, 1990.

[SHE 92] Shenoy P. "Valuation-based systems for Bayesian decision analysis". *Operations Research*, vol. 40(3), 463–484, 1992.

[SPI 00] Spirtes P., Glymour C. and Scheines R. *Causation, Prediction and Search*, MIT Press, Cambridge MA, 2000.

[TAR 84] Tarjan R. and Yannakakis M. "Simple linear-time algorithms to test chordality of graphs, test acyclicity of hypergraphs, and selectively reduce acyclic hypergraphs". *SIAM Journal of Computing*, vol. 13(3), 566–79, 1984.

Chapter 14

Planning under Uncertainty with Markov Decision Processes

14.1. Introduction

The decision-theoretic approach to planning under uncertainty has taken an important place in artificial intelligence (AI) in the past ten years. The main contribution of decision theory to the classic paradigm of planning in AI is linked to its ability to explicitly model uncertainty and preferences over the effects of actions, for example through the use of probabilities and utility functions. This allows for a more flexible search for plans (or decision rules) than in classical planning: a plan which *maximizes* a given criterion is looked for, rather than one that reaches some fixed goal *for sure*. Typically, the criterion to optimize will be the expectation of a random variable representing the accumulation of rewards obtained successively in a problem of sequential decision under uncertainty. In the last part of this chapter we will also see that other criteria, based on non-classical decision theories, have also been considered.

Most recent works in AI on decision-theoretic planning use the framework of *Markov decision processes* (MDP) [PUT 94], initially proposed by the operations research community. These works [e.g. BAR 95, BOU 99, BOU 00, KAE 96, KAE 98] have applied, adapted or extended the MDP framework to various fields of planning in AI: planning under uncertainty in completely or partially observable environments, learning and structured planning problems.

Chapter written by Régis SABBADIN.

In this chapter we will present various approaches to planning under uncertainty in artificial intelligence, based on the Markov decision processes framework. First, we will describe the MDP framework (section 14.2) which grounds the decision-theoretic approach to planning under uncertainty. We will then describe the framework of *partially observed MDP* (POMDP) which extends the MDP framework, allowing us to take into account incomplete information and noisy observations in planning under uncertainty.

The learning community in AI is also linked to the planning under uncertainty community. Reinforcement learning (RL) represents a set of methods, often based on the MDP framework, issued from the cross-fertilization of both communities. Some RL methods will be described in section 14.4. The planning domain is also close to another central domain in AI, concerned with knowledge representation.

It was therefore natural that decision-theoretic approaches to planning under uncertainty would borrow several ideas and approaches from the knowledge representation community, in order to enrich the MDP framework. Indeed, the MDP framework capabilities as a representation language are as poor as its computational capabilities are rich. Several authors have therefore tried to enrich the MDP framework with representational languages such as those traditionally used in AI planning (section 14.5).

In the knowledge representation domain in AI, several non-probabilistic approaches to uncertainty modeling have been explored, some of which have been extended in order to form *non-classical decision theories*. In section 14.6, we will describe a qualitative counterpart to MDP which is based on such a non-classical decision theory: *possibilistic Markov decision processes*.

14.2. Markov decision processes

14.2.1. *Problem formulation*

In its classical formulation [PUT 94], an MDP is described by a four-tuple $<S, A, p, r>$ where S is a set of possible states of the world, A is a set of allowed actions, p is a transition probability function between states and r is an immediate reward function.

14.2.1.1. *States, actions, transitions and policies*

In the case where the set of states is finite (see [PUT 94] for the infinite case), $S = \{s_1, \ldots, s_n\}$ is the set of states that can be reached by the system at any moment in time. Sometimes, the system is only partially observed, in which case the current state of the world is not known precisely but rather is described by a belief state b, which is a probability distribution over S. This case will be described in section 14.3.

$A = \{a_1, \ldots, a_m\}$ is the set of applicable actions at any time, the application of which will cause the state of the world to change (non-deterministically).

The stochastic process describing the evolution in time of the state of the world is also described by the transition probability function which governs it. In an MDP, the state of the world s_t at time-step t will transition to state s_{t+1} at time-step $t+1$ under the effect of action a_t applied at this time-step. This transition is in general stochastic. Furthermore, the process is called Markovian when the transition probability from s_t to s_{t+1} only depends on the action a_t applied and not on the past of the system, described by the trajectory $< s_0, a_0, s_1, \ldots, s_{t-1}, a_{t-1} >$ followed so far. Transition probabilities are denoted $p_t(s_{t+1}|s_t, a_t)$. When the transition probabilities do not depend on the current time-step (in which case the subscript t is omitted), the process is stationary. The set $H \subseteq \mathbb{N}$ of time-steps of the process is called the horizon of the process and can be finite or infinite. When the horizon is infinite, the process is usually stationary.

In the next section we will show that solving an MDP amounts to finding an 'optimal' action for any state of the world encountered, with respect to some optimization criterion. A function $\delta : S \times H \rightarrow A$ assigning an action to any possible state at any time-step is called a decision rule or policy. A policy is stationary when it does not depend on the current time-step.

14.2.1.2. *Reward, criterion, value function, optimal policy*

In an MDP, an immediate reward function $r_t : S \times A \times S \rightarrow \mathbb{R}$ is defined in addition to the transition model. $r_t(s, a, s')$ is the reward obtained when action a has been performed in state s and the state has changed to s'.

The notion of immediate reward function can be extended over trajectories. The reward $V(\tau)$ associated with a trajectory τ is defined as:

$$\tau = < s_0, a_0, s_1, \ldots, s_t, a_t, \ldots >, t \in H : V(\tau) = \sum_{t \in H} r_t(s_t, a_t, s_{t+1}).$$

When H is infinite, the above-defined sum may not converge. The following γ-discounted sum is therefore often used:

$$V(\tau) = \sum_{t \in H} \gamma^t r_t(s_t, a_t, s_{t+1}).$$

The γ-discounted sum surely converges when $0 \leq \gamma < 1$ and when r_t is bounded. When applied to the Markov chain associated with a policy δ in an MDP, this criterion becomes stochastic:

$$V_\delta(s_0) = E\left[\sum_{t \in H} \gamma^t r_t(s_t, \delta(s_t), s_{t+1})|s_0, \delta\right]. \tag{14.1}$$

The expectation is computed over all possible trajectories τ that can be followed, applying policy δ starting from initial state s_0. The problem of finding an optimal policy can be stated as:

$$\text{Find } \delta^*, S \times H \to A, V_{\delta^*}(s) \geq V_\delta(s), \forall s \in S, \forall \delta \in A^{S \times H} \tag{14.2}$$

This problem can be efficiently solved, using classical stochastic dynamic programming methods [BEL 57, BER 87, PUT 94]. The backwards induction algorithm, policy iteration algorithm or value iteration algorithm are the most often used algorithms. We will describe these in the next section.

14.2.2. *Classical solution algorithms for MDP*

14.2.2.1. *Finite horizon: backwards induction*

When $H = \{0, \ldots, N\}$ is finite, the value of a policy δ in any state and at any time-step is described by a time dependent value function $V_{\delta,t}$ which can be computed from the following set of equations:

$$\begin{aligned} V_{\delta,t}(s) &= \sum_{s' \in S} p_t(s'|s, \delta(s)) \cdot \Big(r_t(s, \delta(s), s') + \gamma \cdot V_{\delta,t+1}(s')\Big), t < N, s \in S, \\ V_{\delta,N}(s) &= 0, \forall s \in S. \end{aligned} \tag{14.3}$$

$V_{\delta,t}(s)$ is then computed iteratively, *backwards*, for all s, t. An optimal policy δ^* can also be computed backwards:

$$\begin{aligned} \delta^*(s, t) &= \arg\max_{a \in A} \sum_{s' \in S} p_t(s'|s, a) \cdot \Big(r_t(s, a, s') + \gamma \cdot V^*_{t+1}(s')\Big), \\ V^*_t(s) &= \max_{a \in A} \sum_{s' \in S} p_t(s'|s, a) \cdot \Big(r_t(s, a, s') + \gamma \cdot V^*_{t+1}(s')\Big), \\ V^*_N(s) &= 0, \forall s. \end{aligned} \tag{14.4}$$

14.2.2.2. *Infinite horizon: value iteration and policy iteration*

When the horizon becomes infinite and when the MDP is stationary, it can be shown that the value function V_δ of a stationary policy δ does not depend on time.

Furthermore, it can be computed from the following system of linear equations [HOW 60]:

$$V_\delta(s) = \sum_{s' \in S} p(s'|s, \delta(s)) \cdot \Big(r(s, \delta(s), s') + \gamma \cdot V_\delta(s')\Big), \forall s. \tag{14.5}$$

This system can be solved by a simplex algorithm or by an iterative successive approximations algorithm [PUT 94]:

$$\begin{aligned} V_\delta^0(s) &= 0, \forall s, \\ V_\delta^n(s) &= \sum_{s' \in S} p(s'|s, \delta(s)) \cdot \Big(r(s, \delta(s), s') + \gamma \cdot V_\delta^{n-1}(s')\Big), \forall s. \end{aligned} \tag{14.6}$$

When $n \to \infty$, $V_\delta^n \to V_\delta$ with bounded convergence speed and error [PUT 94].

14.2.2.2.1. Value iteration algorithm

The value iteration algorithm [BEL 57] uses updates which are close to those in equation (14.6) in order to compute an optimal policy. More precisely, it builds a sequence of approximate value functions (V^n):

$$\begin{aligned} V^0(s) &= 0, \forall s, \\ V^n(s) &= \max_{a \in A} \sum_{s' \in S} p(s'|s, a) \cdot \Big(r(s, a, s') + \gamma \cdot V^{n-1}(s')\Big), \forall s. \end{aligned} \tag{14.7}$$

The sequence (V^n) converges (as soon as $0 \leq \gamma < 1$) and its limit function, V^*, is exactly the optimal value function of the MDP, from which the optimal policy δ^* can be computed greedily:

$$\delta^*(s) = \arg\max_{a \in A} \sum_{s' \in S} p(s'|s, a) \cdot \Big(r(s, a, s') + \gamma \cdot V^*(s')\Big), \forall s. \tag{14.8}$$

In practice, there exists a lower value n^* of n, from which the actions maximizing the right-hand side of equation (14.7) form an optimal policy. [PUT 94] gives a set of stopping criteria for the value iteration algorithm.

14.2.2.2.2. Policy iteration algorithm

The policy iteration algorithm [HOW 60] is also based on the updates in equation (14.6). It consists of alternating steps of evaluation and improvement of a current policy. The evaluation step uses equations (14.5) or (14.6) to compute the value of the current policy. The improvement phase transforms the current policy δ into a 'better' policy δ' ($V_{\delta'}(s) \geq V_\delta(s), \forall s$):

$$\delta'(s) = \arg\max_{a \in A} \sum_{s' \in S} p(s'|s, a) \cdot \left(r(s, a, s') + \gamma \cdot V_\delta(s') \right), \forall s. \quad (14.9)$$

The stopping criterion for the policy iteration algorithm is the equality of the value functions of two successive policies δ and δ'. Usually, this algorithm stops after very few improvement steps, but each iteration is costly since it requires a set of linear equations to be solved.

The modified policy iteration algorithm [PUT 94] improves the policy iteration algorithm by applying only a small number of updates in the evaluation step equation (14.6). In practice, the modified policy iteration algorithm is far more efficient, providing that a good choice is made for the upper bound on the number of updates. Note that in the extreme case where only one update is performed at any evaluation step, the modified policy iteration algorithm becomes equivalent to the value iteration algorithm.

14.2.3. *Example: car race*

In order to illustrate the framework of MDP, let us present an example slightly modified from that proposed by [BAR 95]. It is a game of car race simulation, usually played on a sheet of paper where a race track is drawn on a grid. Figure 14.1 shows such a race track.

At any time-step t, the state s_t of a car is described by its position coordinates (x_t, y_t) and its current speed coordinates $(\dot{x}_t, \dot{y}_t)$. The available actions consist of modifying the current speed vector by choosing an acceleration vector $(ax_t, ay_t) \in \{-1, 0, 1\} \times \{-1, 0, 1\}$.

The following equations govern the state dynamics of the car:

$$\begin{aligned}
x_{t+1} &= x_t + \dot{x}_t + ax_t, \\
y_{t+1} &= y_t + \dot{y}_t + ay_t, \\
\dot{x}_{t+1} &= \dot{x}_t + ax_t, \\
\dot{y}_{t+1} &= \dot{y}_t + ay_t.
\end{aligned} \quad (14.10)$$

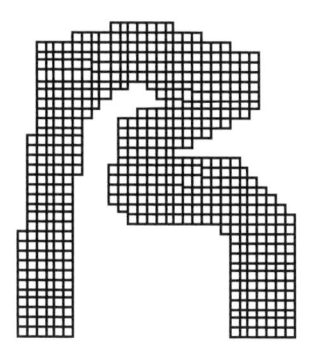

Planning under Uncertainty with Markov Decision Processes   547

Figure 14.1. *Race track example*

In order to introduce some randomness into the problem it is possible that, with probability p, the acceleration is not transmitted to the car in which case $(ax_t, ay_t) = (0,0)$. The state vector of the car comprises a fifth variable n_t, counting the number of 'accidents'. n_t models the number of times the car trajectory has reached a boundary of the circuit. Whenever this happens, n_t is incremented and the car is stopped, i.e.

$$\begin{aligned}
x_{t+1} &= x_t, \\
y_{t+1} &= y_t, \\
\dot{x}_{t+1} &= 0, \\
\dot{y}_{t+1} &= 0, \\
n_{t+1} &= n_t + 1.
\end{aligned}$$

When the car crosses the finish line, or when the number of accidents reaches an upper limit N_{acc}, the system reaches an absorbing state. (Note that an absorbing state in an MDP is simply a state from which the probability of getting out, using any action, is zero and which has a zero-valued reward attached to its self-transition.)

Of course, the goal of this game is to cross the finish line as fast as possible, starting from any position on the start line. This goal is modeled through the reward function $r_t(s_t, a_t, s_{t+1})$, where:

– $r_t(s_t, a_t, s_{t+1}) = \Delta T$ if the current transition does not cross the circuit border or the finish line;

– $r_t(s_t, a_t, s_{t+1}) = T_{acc}$ if the current transition crosses the circuit border;

– $r_t(s_t, a_t, s_{t+1}) = T_\infty$ if the current transition crosses the circuit border and has already done so at least N_{acc} times; and

– $r_t(s_t, a_t, s_{t+1}) = \alpha \cdot \Delta T$ if the current transition crosses the finish line.

α is the proportion of the current move vector that the car has to reach before crossing the finish line.

The criterion to minimize is the total reward criterion $\sum_{t=1}^{\infty} r_t(s_t, a_t, s_{t+1})$, representing the time needed to complete the race. (Note, however, that the problem is easily transformed into a classical maximization MDP problem.) Even though the car race example can be easily modeled as an MDP, the obtained problem has thousands of states. The computational limits of the classical stochastic dynamic programming algorithms are therefore easily reached by such factored problems.

Later in this chapter we will present two kinds of approaches which allow us to overcome such computational limits: *reinforcement learning algorithms* and *factored MDP algorithms*.

14.2.4. *Recent advances in Markov decision processes*

The Markov decision processes framework has been widely used for modeling problems of planning under uncertainty in artificial intelligence in recent years. However, the following limitations of this framework have been acknowledged:

– The assumption of complete observability of the state of the world at any time-step is often unrealistic.

– The assumption of perfect knowledge of the MDP model (transitions, rewards) is also unrealistic. Often, the model is only observed indirectly, using simulations or experiments. Also, only 'qualitative' evaluations of preferences or transition likelihoods are sometimes available.

– Finally, usual MDP algorithms use 'flat' representations of states and actions. However, planning problems in AI often use *factored representations* of states and actions. These factored representations allow us to model very large problems, which cannot be solved using standard algorithms.

In order to overcome these limitations, several approaches have been proposed. We will describe some of them in the remainder of this chapter:

– partially observed MDPs;

– real-time dynamic programming and reinforcement learning;

– factored MDPs; and

– qualitative MDPs.

14.3. Partially observed MDPs

So far, we have made the assumption that we have perfect knowledge of the current state of the system at any time-step. This assumption has allowed us to define policies modeling the behavior of an agent, of the form $\delta : S \to A$. However, it may be that the agent does not precisely observe the current state s of the system, but instead observes the value $\omega \in \Omega$ of some observation variable, indirectly linked to s.

In this case, a possible approach would be to define a policy as a function $\delta : \Omega \to A$, assigning an action to each possible observation, and to solve an MDP over the set of observations. However, such policies do not allow us to distinguish states leading to the same observation. In some cases, this approach allows us to compute useful policies but it can also lead to disastrous policies. For example, [LIT 94] shows some car race example problems in which the computed policies generate endless loops.

If the current observation alone does not allow a good differentiation between possible states of the system, using past observations may lead to a better differentiation. Indeed, POMDP algorithms usually consider *belief states* (probability distributions over S) instead of states themselves, and define policies as functions $\delta : \mathcal{P}(S) \to A$. Observations are used, together with actions, to update the current belief state.

We will see that a POMDP can be transformed into a perfectly observed MDP *over the set of belief states* $\mathcal{P}(S)$. Unfortunately, the new state space is continuous and the obtained problem is far more complex to solve than a usual MDP. Specific solution algorithms for POMDP will be briefly described in this section.

14.3.1. *POMDP model, continuous-MDP transformation*

A partially observed Markov decision process is defined by the tuple

$$< S, A, p, r, \Omega, o >,$$

where $< S, A, p, r >$ defines a classical MDP, Ω is a set of possible observations and $o : S \times A \times \Omega \to [0, 1]$ is an *observation function*. $o(s', a, \omega)$ is the probability of observing ω when action a allows state s' ($\sum_{\omega \in \Omega} o(s', a, \omega) = 1$) to be reached.

The imperfect knowledge of the state of the world is modeled through a *belief state* $b \in \mathcal{P}(S)$. $b(s)$ represents the probability that the current state of the world is s. This belief state is modified by the combined effect of the successive actions and observations:

$$\begin{aligned}
b'(s') &= Pr(s'|b,a,\omega) \\
&= \frac{o(s',a,\omega) \cdot \sum_{s \in S} p(s'|s,a)b(s)}{Pr(\omega|a,b)} \\
&= \frac{o(s',a,\omega) \cdot \sum_{s \in S} p(s'|s,a)b(s)}{\sum_{s,s' \in S} o(s',a,\omega)p(s'|s,a)b(s)}
\end{aligned} \quad (14.11)$$

$b' = \mathcal{T}(b, a, \omega)$ is the resulting belief state when action a has been applied in belief state b and observation ω resulted. $\mathcal{T}$ is called *state estimator function*. Transition probabilities over belief states can be defined from $\mathcal{T}$:

$$\begin{aligned}
Pr(b'|b,a) &= \sum_{\omega \in \Omega} Pr(b'|b,a,\omega) Pr(\omega|a,b) \\
Pr(b'|b,a,\omega) &= 1 \text{ if } b' = \mathcal{T}(b,a,\omega) \text{ and } 0 \text{ else.}
\end{aligned} \quad (14.12)$$

In the same way, the reward function r can be extended to belief states:

$$\begin{aligned}
\rho(b,a,b') &= \sum_{s,s' \in S} b(s) \cdot b'(s') \cdot Pr(b'|b,a) \cdot r(s,a,s') \\
&= \sum_{s \in S} b(s) \cdot Pr(b'|b,a) \cdot \left(\sum_{s' \in S} b'(s') \cdot r(s,a,s') \right).
\end{aligned} \quad (14.13)$$

$< \mathcal{P}(S), A, Pr, \rho >$ is a model of MDP over a continuous state space. A solution to this continuous MDP, coupled with the state estimator $\mathcal{T}$ allows is to optimally control the initial POMDP [AKS 65, SON 78].

14.3.2. *Computing optimal policies in a POMDP*

Even though we have just seen that a POMDP can be translated into an MDP, its continuous state space prevents it from being solved by the usual algorithms presented in section 14.2. However, we will describe in this section a value iteration-like POMDP solution algorithm, exploiting in particular the *piecewise linear and convex* form of the value function $V : \mathcal{P}(S) \to \mathbb{R}$ of an optimal policy. This algorithm uses a tree structure in order to represent a policy and its value function, and defines an iterative method for computing successive approximations of the optimal policy.

14.3.2.1. *t-policy tree*

We have seen that in a POMDP a policy could be defined as a function $\delta : \mathcal{P}(S) \rightarrow A$. However, this 'memoryless' definition cannot be directly exploited by POMDP solution algorithms, since such a function cannot be efficiently stored. In general, it is easier to represent finite-horizon policies as trees of finite depth t, where t is the horizon of the problem.

This *t-policy tree* (Figure 14.2), denoted δ_t, comprises vertices indexed by actions and edges indexed by observations. A branch $\tau =< a_1, \omega_1, ..., a_t, \omega_t >$ represents a sequence of past alternate actions and observations. Of course, several different sequences of MDP states may result in the same actions/observations sequence. However, we can attach a unique belief state to each vertex of the tree, computed from the initial belief state b_0, using equations (14.11).

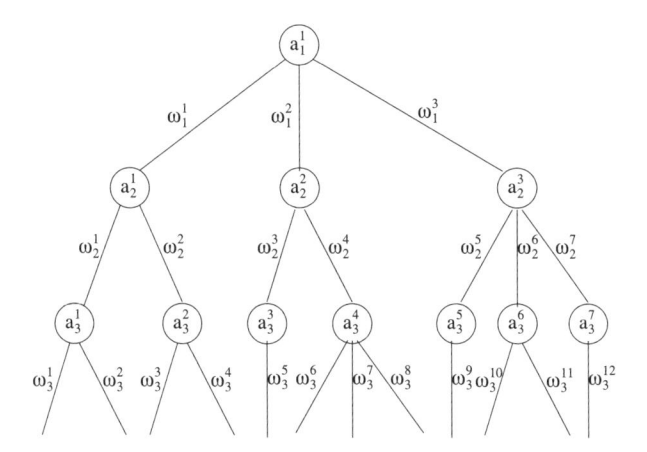

Figure 14.2. *t-policy tree*

Indeed, following a branch transforms the initial belief state b_0 into a sequence of belief states $\tau =< b_0, b_1, ..., b_t >$, where $b_{i+1} = T(b_i, a_i, \omega_i)$. The 'value' of a branch (in terms of MDP) can then be defined as the expected value of all the trajectories compatible with the corresponding actions/observations sequence: $v(\tau) = \sum_{i=1,...,t} \gamma^{i-1} \rho(b_{i-1}, a_i, b_i)$.

We can now compute the value of a policy tree δ_t in b_0 by computing the expectation of the values of all its branches:

$$V_{\delta_t}(b_0) = E_\tau \left[\sum_{i=1,...,t} \gamma^{i-1} \rho(b_{i-1}, a_i, b_i) | b_0, \delta_t \right]. \tag{14.14}$$

This value is exactly the expectation of the sum of the immediate rewards that can be obtained when following the policy defined by δ_t over t time-steps, when the initial state of the world is b_0.

It is now time to describe more precisely the correspondence between the two possible descriptions (stationary and t-tree) of a policy. The stationary policy δ : $\mathcal{P}(S) \to A$ defines the current action for all possible belief states and V_δ is the (infinite horizon) value function of policy δ. As in the classical MDP case, knowing the optimal value function V^* allows us to compute the optimal policy δ^*, using the formula:

$$\delta^*(b) = \arg\max_{a \in A} \sum_{\omega \in \Omega} Pr(b'|b,a) \cdot \left(\rho(b,a,b') + \gamma V^*(b')\right),$$

where $b' = \mathcal{T}(b, a, \omega)$.

The t-policy trees can now be used to build a concise representation of approximations of the optimal value function. To see this, let us start by considering the value of a 1-policy tree δ, in a perfectly observed belief state s:

$$V_\delta(s) = \sum_{s' \in S} p(s'|s, \delta(s)) . r(s, \delta(s), s'),$$

where $\delta(s) = a_1^1 (= \delta(\omega_s)$, in fact, where ω_s is the Dirac probability distribution over S such that $\omega_s(s) = 1$) is the action specified at the root of the policy tree.

More generally, for a t-policy tree and an initial state s,

$$\begin{aligned} V_\delta(s) &= \sum_{s' \in S} p(s'|s, \delta(s)) \cdot \left(r(s, \delta(s), s') + \gamma \sum_{\omega \in \Omega} Pr(\omega|s, \delta(s), s') V_{\delta|\omega}(s') \right) \\ &= \sum_{s' \in S} p(s'|s, \delta(s)) \left(r(s, \delta(s), s') + \gamma \sum_{\omega \in \Omega} o(s', \delta(s), \omega) V_{\delta|\omega}(s') \right) \quad (4.15) \end{aligned}$$

$V_{\delta|\omega}$ denotes the value function of the $(t-1)$-policy tree obtained from δ by taking the subtree which root is the action vertex linked to the root vertex $\delta(s)$ of the t-policy tree by edge ω.

Stated differently, the value of a t-policy tree in a perfectly observed state s can be computed recursively from the values of the $(t-1)$-policy trees attached to the children nodes of the root, resulting from the possible observations. This allows a recursive computation of the value function of a t-policy tree in a given belief state b, since we have:

$$V_\delta(b) = \sum_{s \in S} b(s).V_\delta(s).$$

14.3.2.2. *Value iteration algorithm for POMDP*

In order to compute an optimal policy for a POMDP, the value iteration algorithm has to be adapted. It can use, as for usual MDP, updates similar to those in equations (14.15). However, the value function domain is continuous. In order to overcome this problem, we can observe that the value function can be expressed in a more concise way. Indeed, it can be shown by a recursion proof that the value function V_δ of any t-policy tree can be computed from a finite set of n-dimensions vectors (where $n = |S|$) [SON 71, WHI 91]. This property can be used to design a value iteration algorithm for POMDP, maintaining sets $\mathcal{V}_t$ of n-dimension vectors at each time-step to represent the current value function approximation [CHE 88, KAE 98]. Note, however, that the size of the sets $\mathcal{V}_t$ can grow exponentially with t.

14.3.3. *POMDP example [CAS 94]*

Assume that an agent is in the environment shown in Figure 14.3. There are four possible states here, one of them being a goal state. At any time-step the agent is in one of the four squares and can decide to move either one square left (l) or right (r) (the squares at each end are dead ends). Whenever it moves to the goal square, the agent receives a reward of one unit and is randomly moved to any of the three non-goal squares (with probability $1/3$). The agent never observes its precise position, except when it is on the goal square.

1	2	GOAL	4

Figure 14.3. *Partially observable environment*

This really simple example (three non-goal states, deterministic actions) can be solved exactly. First, note that only five belief states can be encountered, when the agent starts in belief state $b_0 = <1/3, 1/3, 0, 1/3>$. For instance, after a r move in b_0, if the agent does not observe the goal, its belief state is $b_1 = <0, 1/2, 0, 1/2>$. After a new r move, if it still does not observe the goal, its belief state is $b_2 = <0, 0, 0, 1>$: the agent knows it is in the rightmost square. If at any time the agent observes the goal, it receives an immediate reward and goes back to belief state b_0. It is easy to check that only two additional belief states can ever be reached: $b_3 = <1, 0, 0, 0>$ and $b_4 = <0, 1, 0, 0>$.

The belief states transition functions attached to actions r and l are as listed in Table 14.1.

The four first steps of the value iteration algorithm yield the results listed in Table 14.2.

	l					r				
	b_0	b_1	b_2	b_3	b_4	b_0	b_1	b_2	b_3	b_4
b_0	1/3	0	0	2/3	0	1/3	2/3	0	0	0
b_1	1/2	0	0	1/2	0	1/2	1/2	0	0	0
b_2	1	0	0	0	0	0	0	1	0	0
b_3	0	0	0	1	0	0	0	0	0	1
b_4	0	0	0	1	0	1	0	0	0	0

Table 14.1. *Belief states transition probabilities*

$v_t(b_i)$	$t=1$	$t=2$	$t=3$	$t=4$
b_0	$1,\{l,r\}$	$4/3,\{l,r\}$	$16/3,\{r\}$	$23/9,\{r\}$
b_1	$0,\{l,r\}$	$1/2,\{l,r\}$	$7/6,\{r\}$	$10/3,\{r\}$
b_2	$0,\{l,r\}$	$1,\{l\}$	$4/3,\{l\}$	$16/3,\{l\}$
b_3	$0,\{l,r\}$	$0,\{l,r\}$	$1,\{r\}$	$4/3,\{r\}$
b_4	$0,\{l,r\}$	$1,\{r\}$	$4/3,\{r\}$	$16/3,\{r\}$

Table 14.2. *Belief states values*

The optimal infinite horizon policy is represented in Figure 14.4.

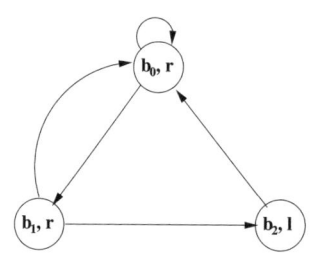

Figure 14.4. *Optimal infinite horizon policy*

14.3.4. *Concluding remarks*

Partially observed MDPs form an extension of MDPs allowing us to take into account imperfect observations in planning under uncertainty. Considering imperfect observations makes the planning problem far more difficult to solve. Much research in AI has therefore been devoted to designing methods for efficiently solving larger and larger problems.

Among the methods proposed for solving large POMDP, some (based on simulations and learning) are also useful for solving completely observed MDP. We will describe succinctly these simulation-based methods in the following section, limiting ourselves to the completely observed case.

14.4. Real-time dynamic programming and reinforcement learning

14.4.1. *Introduction*

The Markov decision processes framework allows us to represent and solve problems of planning under uncertainty. Efficient dynamic programming algorithms allow us to cope with the complexity induced by the sequential aspects of these problems. In the previous section, we have shown that it is possible to extend the MDP framework to the case of partially observed environments. Sometimes, a different kind of partial observability is encountered in the MDP framework, even though the current state of the world is perfectly observed. This is the case where the model of the MDP is unknown. In this case, the functions p and r of the model $< S, A, p, r >$ are *a priori* unknown, and can only be accessed through experiments or simulations.

Reinforcement learning (RL) methods, which we are going to describe, aim to solve such problems. These methods also have the ability to tackle problems of a larger size than usual dynamic programming methods, since they do not require an explicit storage of the size $|S|^2|A|$ transition function. Reinforcement learning methods combine the advantages of learning approaches (*a priori* unknown model) and of the real-time dynamic programming approach, which is a version of the value iteration algorithm which saves time by avoiding updating all states in the state space at each time-step.

14.4.2. *Real-time dynamic programming*

14.4.2.1. *Gauss–Seidel algorithm*

Let us recall the form of the value iteration updates (equations (14.7)):

$$\begin{aligned} V^0(s) &= 0, \forall s, \\ V^t(s) &= \max_{a \in A} \sum_{s' \in S} p(s'|s,a) \cdot \left(r(s,a,s') + \gamma \cdot V^{t-1}(s')\right), \forall s, \forall t \geq \end{aligned} \quad (14.16)$$

Clearly, the value iteration algorithm requires the value function $V^t(s)$ of all states in S to be updated at each time-step. One first remark, leading to the *Gauss–Seidel* variant of the value iteration algorithm [BER 89], is that in these updates, the computation of $V^t(s)$ only uses the values computed at time $t-1$ (based on V^{t-1}). This means that even if some of these values have already been recomputed at time t, they are not used in the present computation. The Gauss–Seidel variant of the value iteration algorithm simply uses the current values when available, in order to compute $V^t(s)$. It has been observed that, in practice, the Gauss–Seidel algorithm converges faster (fewer updates) than the value iteration algorithm.

Furthermore, since the Gauss–Seidel algorithm only takes the most recently computed values of V into account, it is useless to maintain two different value functions V^t and V^{t-1}.

$$V(s) = 0, \forall s,$$
$$V(s) \leftarrow \max_{a \in A} \sum_{s' \in S} p(s'|s, a) \cdot (r(s, a, s') + \gamma \cdot V(s')), \forall s. \qquad (14.17)$$

14.4.2.2. *Asynchronous dynamic programming*

At any time-step of the Gauss–Seidel algorithm, the value of all states in S are updated. This may lead to lots of useless computations, as can be seen in robot navigation problems or in the car race problem, for example. In the latter example, it would be more useful to improve the value function of states in which the car position is close to the finish line, and then progressively update the values of states corresponding to positions closer to the start line.

The asynchronous dynamic programming algorithm generalizes the Gauss–Seidel algorithm by allowing the state values to update to be updated in an asynchronous way. Its principle is to maintain only one value function (as in Gauss–Seidel algorithm) but, unlike it, all state values do not have to be updated in sequence, following the same cycle over S. Instead, the method allows us to focus updates on an area which is likely to provide the most interesting updates of V, temporarily forgetting to update the other states. The asynchronous dynamic programming algorithm will eventually converge to the optimal value function, provided that all states are updated sufficiently often.

The principle (and the efficiency) of the method can be illustrated on the car race example. In this example, the value function represents, for all states, the expectation of the time needed to cross the finish line, applying the best policy. If the value function is uniformly initialized to zero, it is clear that it is initially more interesting to update the values of the states from which it is possible to cross the line. Indeed, for such states, the exact optimal value can be computed by a single application of update equation (14.17). On the other hand, the value of states which are further from the finish line should only be updated when the values of states which are closer have been computed.

The asynchronous dynamic programming algorithm is formally described as:

$$V(s) = 0, \forall s \in S,$$
$$V(s) = \max_{a \in A} \sum_{s' \in S} p(s'|s,a) \cdot (r(s,a,s') + \gamma \cdot V(s')), \forall s \in S_t, \forall t = 1, \ldots$$
(14.18)

In equation (14.18), $S_1, \ldots, S_t, \ldots$ are subsets of S. [BER 89] have shown that, provided that all states are visited infinitely (belong to an infinite number of subsets S_t), equation (14.18) converges toward the optimal value function V^*. Note that, of course, the speed of convergence of equation (14.18) heavily depends on the choice of S_t. It is therefore important to look for good heuristics to choose them. Finally, note that the Gauss–Seidel algorithm is a particular case of the asynchronous dynamic programming algorithm, in which $S_t = \{s_{t \bmod |S|}\}$ is a singleton, for any t.

14.4.2.3. Real-time dynamic programming

The real-time dynamic programming method consists of applying in alternation updates of the value function through asynchronous dynamic programming and process control. The method can be applied on-line (the control being actually applied), but also off-line, as an alternative to the asynchronous dynamic programming method.

More precisely, the main difference with the previous method is that the subsets S_t of states to update are chosen in real time, given the current state s_t of the system and the best *myopic* action a_t. The steps of the algorithm are as follows:

– If the current state of the system is s_t, V is updated over $S_t = f(s_t)$ (f is an arbitrary function assigning a subset of states $S_s = f(s)$ to any state $s \in S$).

– The best myopic action a_t is that which maximizes the expectation of the current value function:

$$a_t = \arg\max_a \sum_{s_{t+1} \in S} p(s_{t+1}|s_t, a) \cdot \left(r(s_t, a_t, s_{t+1}) + \gamma \cdot V(s_{t+1})\right).$$

– The successor state s_{t+1} of (s_t, a_t) is determined either by experiment or by simulation (this is the 'real-time' part of the optimization process).

If the assumptions of asynchronous dynamic programming are verified (in particular the insurance that all states may be visited infinitely often), the real-time dynamic programming method allows us to find an optimal policy. One simple way to enforce the satisfaction of the assumptions is to choose s_{t+1} uniformly at random, from time to time, and to ensure that $\cup f(s_t) = S$.

14.4.3. *Reinforcement learning*

The real-time dynamic programming techniques aim to solve large MDP by avoiding updating the values of all states at each step of the DP algorithm. A further difficulty may occur when solving an MDP. It may be that the model (p, r) of the MDP is not directly available, but accessible only through experiments/simulations. In this case, the objective is not only to solve the MDP, but also to learn its model. Reinforcement learning groups methods which allow this double objective to be reached.

More specifically, there are two families of reinforcement learning methods: *indirect* methods and *direct* methods. Indirect methods first learn the model (p, r) of the MDP, then solve it using classical dynamic programming algorithms. The two phases (learning and optimization) can be interleaved in the real-time dynamic programming way, by focusing the learning on the area of the $S \times A$ space which is the most 'promising' in terms of policy optimization.

Direct methods try to avoid the explicit learning of the model (p, r), by learning directly the value function V (TD_λ algorithm) of a given policy, or a function which allows a direct computation of the optimal policy (Q-learning algorithm).

14.4.3.1. *Indirect reinforcement learning*

14.4.3.1.1. Certainty equivalent

The most simple (and least efficient) indirect reinforcement learning method is the certainty equivalent method [KUM 86]. This method simply consists of randomly exploring the space $S \times A$ (by simulations or experiments) and building estimators $\hat{p}$ and $\hat{r}$ of p and r.

However, this method has several problems:

– It separates arbitrarily the learning and optimization phases, and cannot be really qualified as 'real-time'.

– In the learning phase, the exploration of $S \times A$ is not guided and it is quite likely that lots of useless effort will be spent on exploring 'uninteresting' parts of this space.

These two problems are likely to slow down the search for an optimal policy.

The method can be improved by alternating simulation and optimization and integrating some dynamic programming features, in order to focus learning on really useful parts of $S \times A$.

14.4.3.1.2. Dyna

The Dyna algorithm [SUT 91] progressively builds (as with the certainty equivalent method) a model $(\hat{p}, \hat{r})$ by simulations/experiments. However, Dyna also progressively builds a function $\hat{Q} : S \times A \to \mathbb{R}$, which is an estimator of the function Q:

$$Q(s,a) = \sum_{s' \in S} p(s'|s,a) \cdot (r(s,a,s') + \gamma \cdot V(s')), \tag{14.19}$$

where V is the optimal value function of the MDP (S, A, p, r).

The interest of estimating Q is that both the value function V and the optimal policy δ can be directly computed from Q:

$$V(s) = \max_{a \in A} Q(s,a), \forall s \in S,$$

$$\delta(s) = \arg\max_{a \in A} Q(s,a), \forall s \in S.$$

In the Dyna algorithm, whenever a transition $< s, a, s', r >$ is experienced/simulated the following operations are performed:

1) The model $(\hat{p}, \hat{r})$ is updated.
2) $\hat{Q}$:

$$\hat{Q}(s,a) \leftarrow \sum_{s' \in S} \hat{p}(s'|s,a) \cdot \left(\hat{r}(s,a,s') + \gamma \cdot max_{a' \in A} \hat{Q}(s', a') \right)$$

is updated.

3) Some additional updates of $\hat{Q}$ are performed, by propagating the updated values (through dynamic programming updates).

4) The action to apply in s' is chosen randomly, but the actions which have good $\hat{Q}$-values in s' have a higher probability to be chosen.

Dyna is far more efficient than the certainty equivalent method in practice. However, the 'additional updates' phase has been improved, by guiding the choice of state values to update, to gain more efficiency (leading to the *Queue-Dyna* [PEN 93] and *Prioritized Sweeping* [MOO 93] algorithms).

14.4.3.2. *Direct reinforcement learning*

The indirect reinforcement learning methods we have just described may have a serious drawback for solving really large MDP. They need to store the estimators $\hat{p}$ and $\hat{r}$, which require a storage space in $O(|S|^2|A|)$. The Q-learning algorithm [WAT 92] allows the storage of $\hat{p}$ and $\hat{r}$ to be replaced with the storage of $\hat{Q}$, leading to a factor $|S|$ gain.

The principle of the Q-learning algorithm is to progressively approximate the exact Q-value function, from which an optimal policy can be derived. Note that the exact Q-value function is the solution of the following system of fixed-point equations:

$$Q(s,a) = \sum_{s' \in S} p(s'|s,a) \cdot \left(r(s,a,s') + \gamma \cdot \max_{a' \in A} Q(s',a') \right). \quad (14.20)$$

The solution of this system is progressively obtained by repeating basic updates of the form

$$\hat{Q}(s,a) \leftarrow \hat{Q}(s,a) + \alpha \left(r + \gamma \max_{a' \in A} \hat{Q}(s',a') - \hat{Q}(s,a) \right) \quad (14.21)$$

whenever a transition $< s, a, s', r >$ is observed. α is a 'learning rate' of the algorithm, which decreases to zero when the number of updates increases. The more updates performed, the more confident we are with the current estimator $\hat{Q}$, and the less further experiments should modify it.

Under some simple 'visiting all states/actions' conditions, [WAT 89] has shown that the Q-learning algorithm converges to the exact Q-value function.

14.4.4. *Concluding remarks*

In this section, we have given a very brief and partial glimpse of the real-time dynamic programming methods and the reinforcement learning methods. In particular, we have not described the TD_λ method [SUT 88], the real-time Q-learning methods, or the important methods of parameterized reinforcement learning, which are useful for solving (approximately) even larger problems.

The Q-learning algorithm allows storage space to be saved compared to the Dyna algorithm. On the other hand, since no estimator of the model is maintained, the additional dynamic programming updates of the Dyna family algorithms are no more possible, leading to a need for more simulations/experiments. This means that the choice of a direct or an indirect method should always be guided by the compromise between simulation/experiments time and storage space.

[KAE 96] have compared experimentally Dyna, Prioritized Sweeping and Q-learning, and have shown that Q-learning uses twice as fewer updates as Prioritized Sweeping to converge. However, since Q-learning performs only one update by transition observed, unlike the other methods, it needs twenty times more simulations to converge. This underlines the importance of the compromise between simulations cost and space for the choice between the two types of methods.

14.5. Factored Markov decision processes

Until now, we have assumed a *flat* representation of states and actions in the MDP framework, since the classical MDP solution algorithms are explicitly based on an exhaustive enumeration of the state and action spaces. However, in AI, several languages have been studied for concisely representing states and actions in planning under uncertainty problems.

Generally, these concise representations describe the state of the world by a set of *feature* values rather than by identifying it individually. In the car race example, we have already used such a concise description of the system state, by describing the state s_t of the car through a tuple of values $\vec{X}_t = \{x_t, y_t, \dot{x}_t, \dot{y}_t, nacc_t\}$. in the same way, actions were represented by a vector $\vec{A}_t = \{ax_t, ay_t\}$.

This concise representation has two advantages: (1) it is more natural and easy for a decision maker to model a planning problem in this way and (2) as we will see later, such representations also allow space to be saved in the MDP model description. However, the corresponding drawback is an increased complexity of the obtained optimization problems, which require specific exact or approximate solution methods.

14.5.1. *State space factorization, stationary homogenous Bayesian networks*

Let us first consider the factorization of transition probabilities in a Markovian stochastic process. Let us assume, for example, that the state is described through binary features: $s = \{x_1, \ldots, x_m\}$; then obviously $|S| = 2^m$. For any given action, the explicit representation of transition probabilities by matrices therefore requires space of $O(2^{2m})$, which becomes prohibitive when the number of features is large.

A Bayesian network [PEA 88] (see also Chapter 13) allows such probabilities to be concisely represented in the factored case. A stationary homogenous Bayesian network (SHBN) is a particular BN adapted to the representation of transition probabilities in a Markov chain [DEA 89].

More precisely, a SHBN is made of:

– a graphical model, expressing the dependencies between variables values at two consecutive time-steps; and

– a quantitative model representing explicitly the conditional probabilities between interdependent variables only in a tabular form or, more efficiently, in a tree-structured form.

562   Decision-making Process

The dynamics of the car race example can be modeled graphically by the SHBN of Figure 14.5. The quantitative model associated with the SHBN has to specify the following conditional probabilities: $Pr(x_{t+1}|x_t, y_t, \dot{x}_t)$, $Pr(\dot{x}_{t+1}|x_t, y_t, \dot{x}_t)$, $Pr(y_{t+1}|x_t, y_t, \dot{y}_t)$, $Pr(\dot{y}_{t+1}|x_t, y_t, \dot{y}_t)$ and $Pr(n_{t+1}|n_t, x_t, y_t)$.

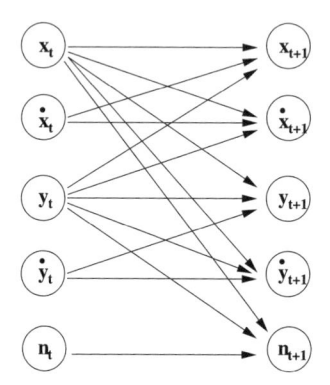

Figure 14.5. *SHBN of the car race example, when the chosen action is* $\vec{A}_t = (0,0)$

Obviously, we have:

$$Pr(\vec{X}_{t+1}|\vec{X}_t) = Pr(x_{t+1}|x_t, y_t, \dot{x}_t) \cdot Pr(\dot{x}_{t+1}|x_t, y_t, \dot{x}_t) \cdot Pr(y_{t+1}|x_t, y_t, \dot{y}_t) \cdot$$

$$Pr(\dot{y}_{t+1}|x_t, y_t, \dot{y}_t) \cdot Pr(n_{t+1}|n_t, x_t, y_t).$$

If, for example, the sizes of the domains of the variables $x_t, \dot{x}_t, y_t, \dot{y}_t$ are all equal to K, and the size of the domain of n_t is equal to N for all t, the factored representation of the conditional probabilities requires a storage size of $4 \times K^4 + N^2 \times K^2$, instead of $K^8 \times N^2$ for a flat representation.

Using a SHBN representation with a tabular representation of the conditional probabilities for interdependent variables allows space to be saved when representing transition probabilities. However, further gains are possible. Let us consider, for example, $Pr(\dot{x}_{t+1}|x_t, y_t, \dot{x}_t)$ and $Pr(\dot{y}_{t+1}|x_t, y_t, \dot{y}_t)$, representing the car speed evolution. When the car crosses the track border, causing an accident, the car stops ($\dot{x}_{t+1} = \dot{y}_{t+1} = 0$). For a large range of (x_t, y_t) values (out of the track), the conditional probabilities $Pr(\dot{x}_{t+1}|\dot{x}_t)$ therefore become unconditional (and can be represented in constant space: $\dot{x}_{t+1} = 0$).

This kind of reasoning motivates a representation of conditional probabilities under the form of a tree, instead of a table. [BOU 00], for example, proposed a tree-structured representation of conditional probabilities, built from an arbitrary order between the variables of a probability table.

14.5.2. *Factored representation of actions*

The above factored representation of transition probabilities requires one SHBN to be built for each possible action. This can be difficult to build, especially when actions themselves are represented by the values of several variables.

However, the above method can be extended by integrating action nodes directly in the SHBN. The extended SHBN in the car race example is shown in Figure 14.6. Note that the edges leaving action nodes allow the dependencies in the conditional probabilities of the factored MDP to be represented.

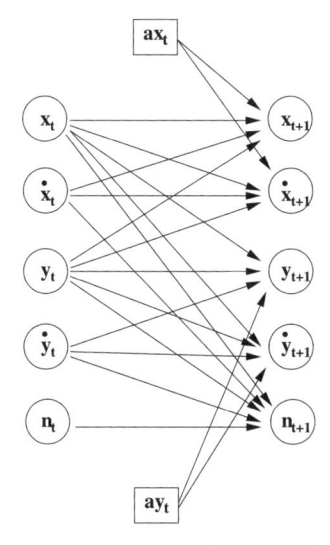

Figure 14.6. *SHBN extended by the addition of action nodes for the car race example*

14.5.3. *Factored representation of rewards*

The rewards of the factored MDP can also be included as nodes in the SHBN. Each reward node represents a local value function, and the incoming edges represent the variables on which the local functions depend. The global reward function of the MDP is then the sum of the local rewards. In the car race example, the 'reward' (which is negative here) is the sum of the time spent on the race track and the time spent in accidents. A SHBN comprising state, action and reward nodes is called stationary homogenous influence diagram (SHID) (see Figure 14.7).

564   Decision-making Process

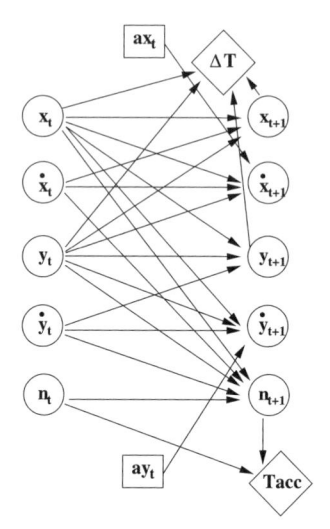

Figure 14.7. *Stationary homogenous influence diagram (SHID) for the car race example*

14.5.4. *Factored representation of value functions and policies and computation of optimal policies*

It would be interesting to compute factored policies and value functions which have the same structure as the factored MDP itself. However, there is no guarantee that the value function associated with any arbitrary policy (be it factored) can be factored as compactly as the MDP itself. Furthermore, there are also no guarantees that an optimal policy for the MDP exists, which has a concise factored expression.

Still, [BOU 00] have proposed *structured* dynamic programming algorithms for computing tree-structured value functions and optimal policies. These algorithms are based on the principle of the value iteration and policy iteration algorithms, but manipulate value functions or policies which are tree-structured.

14.5.5. *Concluding remarks*

Factored MDP have attracted quite a lot of attention in the past years. We have briefly mentioned in this section the structured versions of the classical dynamic programming algorithms. However, several other approaches have also been proposed.

For example, a method based on the *stochastic bisimilarity* principle has been suggested [GIV 03], which solves a factored MDP approximately through an automated reduction of the state space. In this approach, a partition of the state space is generated, such that all transitions from one subset to another have similar probabilities and attached rewards.

Another approach to factored MDP resolution has been proposed by [DIE 95, KEA 99] and [KOL 00]. This approach is based on a parameterized, linear approximation of the value function of a factored MDP. In addition, the two latter papers use simulation-based solution methods for solving the obtained optimization problem.

Along this line of work, [GUE 03] has defined *collaborative multi-agent factored MDP* and dedicated approximation algorithms. Close to that framework, *graph-based MDP* [FOR 06, PEY 06] form a framework which proposes fast approximate solution algorithms for factored MDP which have a specific graph structure.

14.6. Possibilistic Markov decision processes

Transition probabilities for representing the effects of actions in MDP are not always available, especially in AI applications where uncertainty is often ordinal and qualitative. The same remark applies to utilities: it is often more adequate to represent preference over states simply with an ordering relation rather than with additive utilities.

Several authors have advocated a qualitative view of decision making and have proposed qualitative versions of decision theory, together with suitable logical languages for expressing preferences [BOU 94, DUB 95, TAN 94]. A qualitative utility theory based on possibility theory has been proposed [DUB 95], where preferences and uncertainty are both qualitative (see also Chapter 11). This work was extended to sequential decision making [FAR 98, SAB 01a] and possibilistic counterparts of the well-known Bellman's equations were proposed [BEL 57]. This gave rise to the definition of the possibilistic MPDs framework, which was extended to infinite-horizon and partial observability [SAB 99]. Later, this work was extended to structured qualitative decision problems in finite horizon, giving rise to the definition of possibilistic influence diagrams [GAR 08]. In this section we will give a brief overview of these works.

14.6.1. *Background on qualitative possibility theory*

A possibility distribution π on a set of possible worlds or states S is a mapping from S to a bounded, linearly ordered valuation set $(L, >)$. This ordered set is supposed to be equipped with an order-reversing map denoted by n, that is, a bijection of L onto itself such that if $\alpha > \beta \in L$, then $n(\beta) > n(\alpha)$. Let 1_L and 0_L denote the top and bottom elements of L, respectively. Then $n(0_L) = 1_L$ and $n(1_L) = 0_L$. In the numerical setting, $L = [0, 1]$, and function n is generally taken as $1 - \cdot$. Here, it is only assumed that L is a finite chain, and n simply sets L upside down.

A possibility distribution describes knowledge of the unknown value taken by one or several attributes used to describe states of affairs. For instance it may refer to the age of a man, the size of a building, the temperature of a room, etc. Here it will refer to the unknown consequence of a decision. A possibility distribution can represent a state of knowledge (about the state of affairs) distinguishing what is plausible from what is less plausible, what is the normal course of actions from what is not and what is surprising from what is expected.

The function $\pi : S \rightarrow L$ represents a flexible restriction on the actual state of affairs, with the following conventions: $\pi(s) = 0_L$ means that state s is rejected as impossible; $\pi(s) = 1_L$ means that s is totally possible (plausible). Distinct states may simultaneously have a degree of possibility equal to 1_L. Flexibility in this description is modeled by setting $\pi(s)$ between 0_L and 1_L for some states s. The quantity $\pi(s)$ therefore represents the degree of possibility of the state s, some states being more plausible than others. Clearly, if S is the complete range of states, at least one of the elements of S should be fully possible so that $\exists s, \pi(s) = 1_L$ (normalization).

In the above, a possibility distribution encodes imprecise knowledge about a situation; in that case, no choice is at stake, i.e. the actual situation is what it is and π encodes plausible guesses about it. However, there exists a different understanding of a possibility distribution: possibility distributions can also express the states in which an agent *would like to be*, under the form of a flexible constraint on the state space. In this case, possibility is interpreted in terms of graded preference or subjective feasibility and necessity degrees are interpreted as priority levels. Note that when interpreted in terms of preference, possibility distributions need not be normalized: it may be that no state of the world is fully satisfactory. Using the two types of possibility distributions conjointly leads to qualitative possibilistic utility theory.

14.6.2. *Possibilistic counterparts of expected utility*

An ordinal counterpart was proposed [DUB 95], based on possibility theory, of the expected utility theory for one-stage decision making. In this framework, S and X are the (finite) sets of possible states of the world and consequences of actions, respectively. It makes sense, if information is qualitative, to represent not only the incomplete knowledge of the state by a possibility distribution π on S with values in a plausibility scale L but also the decision maker's preference on X by means of another possibility distribution μ with values on a preference scale U. Here, we assume that uncertainty and preferences are commensurate, that is U can be identified to L, which is a finite totally ordered (qualitative) scale. The lowest and greatest elements of this scale are denoted 0_L and 1_L, respectively.

The uncertainty of the agent about the effect of an action a taken in state s is represented by a possibility distribution $\pi(\cdot|s, a) : X \rightarrow L$. $\pi(x|s, a)$ measures to what extent x is a plausible consequence of a in s; $\pi(x|s,a) = 1_L$ means that x is completely plausible, whereas $\pi(x|s,a) = 0_L$ means that it is completely impossible.

In the same way, consequences are ordered in terms of level of satisfaction by a qualitative utility function $\mu : X \to L$. $\mu(x) = 1_L$ means that x is completely satisfactory, whereas if $\mu(x) = 0_L$ it is totally unsatisfactory. Notice that π is normalized (there is at least one completely possible state of the world), but μ may not be (it can be that no consequence is totally satisfactory). The two following qualitative decision criteria were proposed [DUB 95]:

$$u^*(s_0, a) = \max_{x \in X} \min\{\pi(x|s_0, a), \mu(x)\}$$
$$u_*(s_0, a) = \min_{x \in X} \max\{n(\pi(x|s_0, a)), \mu(x)\}$$

where n is the order reversing map of L.

u^* can be seen as an extension of the $maximax$ criterion which assigns the utility of its best possible consequence to an action. On the other hand, u_* is an extension of the $maximin$ criterion which corresponds to the utility of the worst possible consequence. u_* measures to what extent every plausible consequence is satisfactory. u^* corresponds to a very adventurous (optimistic) attitude in the face of uncertainty, whereas u_* is conservative (cautious).

Example 14.1. Consider the omelette example of Savage [SAV 54, p. 13]. The problem is to make a six-egg omelette. Five eggs have already been broken into the pan. The sixth egg may be fresh or rotten. There are three feasible acts: break the egg into the omelette (BIO); break it apart in a cup (BAC) or throw it away (TA). Assume that utilities and degrees of certainty belong to the same totally ordered scale. Here $L = \{0, a, b, c, d, 1\}$ where $0 < a < b < c < d < 1$, equipped with its involutive order-reversing map n. The set of consequences is given in Table 14.3.

Act/State	Fresh egg (F)	Rotten egg (R)
BIO	6-egg omelette (1)	nothing to eat (0)
BAC	6-egg omelette, cup to wash (d)	5-egg omelette, cup to wash (b)
TA	5-egg omelette, a spoiled egg (a)	5-egg omelette (c)

Table 14.3. *States, acts and consequences in Savage's omelette example*

Grades between parentheses indicate a reasonable encoding of the utility ordering of consequences. The reader can easily check that they agree with this ordering. Only two states (fresh F, rotten R) are present. The utilities of the three acts in the egg example are given as functions of $\pi(F)$ and $\pi(R)$:

$$\begin{aligned}
u_*(BIO) &= \min(\max(n(\pi(F)), 1), \max(n(\pi(R)), 0)) = n(\pi(R)), \\
u^*(BIO) &= \max(\min(\pi(F), 1), \min(\pi(R), 0)) = \pi(F), \\
u_*(BAC) &= \min(\max(n(\pi(F)), d), \max(n(\pi(R)), b)) \\
&= \min(d, \max(n(\pi(R)), b)), \\
u^*(BAC) &= \max(\min(\pi(F), d), \min(\pi(R), b)) = \max(b, \min(\pi(F), d)), \\
u_*(TA) &= \min(\max(n(\pi(F)), a), \max(n(\pi(R)), c)) \\
&= \min(c, \max(n(\pi(F)), a)), \\
u^*(TA) &= \max(\min(\pi(F), a), \min(\pi(R), c)) = \max(a, \min(\pi(R), c)).
\end{aligned}$$

The criterion u_* recommends act BAC in case of relative ignorance on the egg state, i.e. when $\min(\pi(F), \pi(R))$ is not low enough (more than c). On the other hand, u^* is more adventurous and recommends BIO as soon as $\pi(F) = 1$. See [DUB 01] or Chapter 11 for a discussion on the foundations of possibilistic decision criteria.

14.6.3. *Possibilistic Markov decision processes*

14.6.3.1. *Finite horizon*

The possibilistic qualitative decision theory was extended to finite-horizon, multi-stage decision making [FAR 98]. In this framework, the qualitative pessimistic utility of a policy $\delta = \{d_0, \ldots, d_N\}$ in state s_0 is defined by the qualitative $minmax$ expectation of the $minimum$ of the degrees of satisfaction of the states of the possible trajectories, and the optimistic utility as the $maxmin$ expectation of the same :

$$\begin{aligned}
u_*(s_0, \delta) &= \min_\tau \max\{\pi(\tau|s_0, \delta), \mu(\tau, \delta)\} \\
u^*(s_0, \delta) &= \max_\tau \min\{\pi(\tau|s_0, \delta), \mu(\tau, \delta)\}
\end{aligned}$$

where, if $\tau = \{s_0, \ldots, s_N\}$,

$$\mu(\tau, \delta) = *_{i \in 0 \ldots N} \mu(s_i, \delta(s_i))$$

and

$$\pi(\tau|s_0, \delta) = \min_{i \in 0 \ldots N-1} \pi(s_{i+1}|s_i, d_i(s_i)).$$

∗ is an operator which aggregates the preference degrees associated with the successive transitions. In practice, we will use either $*_{i \in 0...N} \mu(s_i, d_i(s_i)) = \min_{i \in 0...N} \mu(s_i)$ or $*_{i \in 0...N} \mu(s_i, \delta(s_i)) = \mu(s_N)$ in the finite horizon case.

In order to obtain an intuitive idea of these sequential decision criteria, let us consider the following simple cases:

1) Assume that the transition possibilities only take values 0_L or 1_L. Furthermore, assume that similar binary utilities are attached to goal states only. Then, the best 'pessimistic' policies will be those which can only generate trajectories leading to goal states. The best 'optimistic' policies, on the other hand, will generate at least one such trajectory.

2) Assume now that binary preference degrees are also associated with transitions. Then, the best pessimistic policies will have to generate only trajectories leading to goal states and for which all transitions are satisfying. The best optimistic policies will have to generate at least one such trajectory leading to a goal state and only with satisfying transitions.

3) Assume the same case as before, except that preferences can take any value in L. Then, the pessimistic utility of a policy will be that of the worst possible trajectory (minimum of the end state utility and of the transition possibility degrees). The optimistic utility of a policy, instead, will be that of the best possible trajectory.

The possibilistic counterparts of the Bellman equations in the pessimistic case and optimistic case (for $* \equiv \min$) are the following:

– In the pessimistic case:

$$u_*^t(s) = \max_{a \in A_s} \min_{s' \in S_{t+1}} \min \{\mu(s, a, s'), \max\{n(\pi(s'|s, a)), u_*^{t+1}(s')\}\}$$

$$u_*^N(s) = \mu(s). \qquad (14.22)$$

– In the optimistic case:

$$u^{*t}(s) = \max_{a \in A_s} \max_{s' \in S_{t+1}} \min \{\mu(s, a, s'), \pi(s'|s, a), u^{*t+1}(s')\}$$

$$u^{*N}(s) = \mu(s). \qquad (14.23)$$

It has been shown that any policy computed backwards by successive applications of equation (14.22) (respectively, equation (14.23)) is optimal according to u_* (respectively, u^*) [FAR 98].

Note that because of the idempotency of the $minimum$ operator, there are optimal policies that may not be found by such an algorithm, unlike in the stochastic case. However, every policy returned by the algorithm is optimal and has the property that any subpolicy applied from stage t to N (the horizon) is optimal [FAR 98].

14.6.3.2. *Possibilistic value iteration*

Let us now change slightly the data of the problem, in order to recover one that admits stationary optimal policies in the infinite horizon case. First of all, suppose that the state space, the available actions and the transition functions do not depend on the stage of the problem. Suppose also that a utility function μ on S is given, which expresses the preferences of the agent on the states that the system shall reach and stay in. We finally assume the existence of an action *stay* that keeps the system in the same state (or equivalently, an action *do – nothing* if we assume that the system does not evolve by itself, without any action applied). Under these assumptions, we are able to define a possibilistic counterpart of the *value iteration* algorithm that computes optimal policies from iterated modifications of a possibilistic value function.

First, we have to define the possibilistic counterpart of Q-functions. As in the stochastic case, $\tilde{Q}_*(s,a)$ (respectively, $\tilde{Q}^*(s,a)$) evaluates the 'utility' (either pessimistic or optimistic) of performing a in s. We have a similar property as in the stochastic case, which is that the optimal possibilistic strategy can be obtained from the solution of dynamic programming equations. We can therefore define a possibilistic version of the value iteration algorithm that computes $\tilde{Q}^*$ or $\tilde{Q}_*$: the possibilistic value iteration algorithm [SAB 01a]:

– Pessimistic case:

$$\tilde{Q}_{*t+1}(s,a) = \min_{s' \in S} \min\left\{\mu(s,a,s'), \max\{n(\pi(s'|s,a)), u_{*t}(s')\}\right\}, \quad (14.24)$$

where $u_{*t}(s) = \max_a \tilde{Q}_{*t}(s,a)$ and $\tilde{Q}_{*t}(s, do-nothing) = \mu(s)$.

– Optimistic case:

$$\tilde{Q}^*_{t+1}(s,a) = \max_{s' \in S} \min\left\{\mu(s,a,s'), \pi(s'|s,a), u^*_t(s')\right\}, \quad (14.25)$$

where $u^*_t(s) = \max_a \tilde{Q}^*_t(s,a)$ and $\tilde{Q}^*_t(s, do-nothing) = \mu(s)$.

This algorithm converges to the actual value of $\tilde{Q}_*$ (respectively, $\tilde{Q}^*$) in a finite number of steps. Note that unlike in the stochastic value iteration algorithm, the initialization of u_* (or u^*) is not arbitrary.

Example 14.2. A robot is located somewhere in a room shown in Figure 14.8. The black cells represent obstacles. The point is to define a policy which is able to bring it to the lower-right square of the room. The objective will be partially satisfied if the robot ends in one of the neighbor squares. The state space and the utility function μ on the objective states (taking its values in a finite subset of the interval $[0,1]$) are depicted in Figure 14.8. $\mu(s_{33}) = 1$, $\mu(s_{23}) = \mu(s_{32}) = 0.5$ and $\mu(s) = 0$ for the other states.

The available actions are to move (T)op, (D)own, (L)eft, (R)ight or to (S)tay in place. If the robot chooses to stay, it will *certainly* remain in the same square. If it

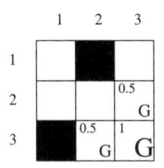

Planning under Uncertainty with Markov Decision Processes 571

Figure 14.8. *State space and utility function*

moves T, D, L or R it will possibly reach the desired square ($\pi = 1$) if it is free but it will be possible that it reaches a neighbor square, as depicted in Figure 14.9 for action R.

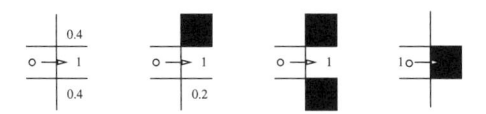

Figure 14.9. *Transition possibilities for moving right*

If the destination cell is an obstacle then the robot will remain in the same cell, as if it had chosen action S. The other transition possibility functions are of course symmetric to these. Let us now compute the optimal (pessimistic) actions after one iteration of the value iteration algorithm.

For any action a and state s, we have

$$\tilde{Q}^1(s,a) = \min_{s' \in S} \max(n(\pi(s'|s,a)), \mu(s'))$$
$$u_*^1(s) = \max_{a \in \{T,D,L,R,S\}} \tilde{Q}^1(s,a). \quad (14.26)$$

Figure 14.10 shows the utility of each state after one iteration, as well as an action that is optimal if the problem is assumed to be solved in one iteration only, for each state with a non-null pessimistic utility. The optimal action is unique, except for state s_{33} for which D and R would be optimal actions as well.

Now we can iterate the process and get an optimal policy. The iterated process is described in Figure 14.11. Note that after 4 iterations, the utility of each state and the associated optimal action no longer change.

Note that the computation of an optimistic optimal policy would lead in this case to the same policy (but with different utilities), as depicted in Figure 14.12.

572   Decision-making Process

Figure 14.10. *Optimal policy, computed at iteration 1*

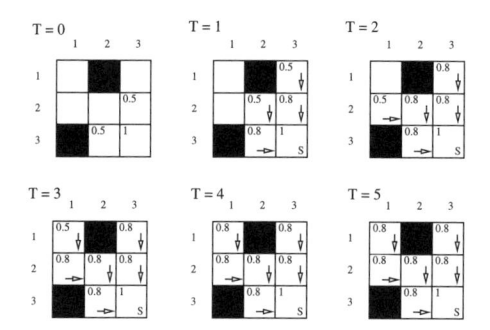

Figure 14.11. *Pessimistic optimal policy computation*

14.6.3.3. *Policy iteration algorithm*

A policy iteration algorithm can also be designed, that alternates the evaluation and improvement phases, as for its stochastic counterpart. In the pessimistic case, it gives:

– Evaluation:
Repeat, until convergence of u_*^δ:

$$\forall s \in S, u_*^\delta(s) = \min_{s' \in S} \max\{n(\pi(s'|s, \delta(s))), u_*^\delta(s')\}. \tag{14.27}$$

– Improvement:

$$\forall s \in S, \delta(s) \leftarrow argmax_{a \in A} \min_{s' \in S} \max\{n(\pi(s'|s, a)), u_*^\delta(s')\}. \tag{14.28}$$

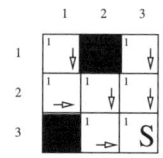

Figure 14.12. *Optimistic optimal policy*

Regarding the value iteration algorithm, initializations of the value function and of the policy cannot be arbitrary. An optimistic counterpart of the algorithm can easily be designed by the use of optimistic utility evaluation, instead of the pessimistic case.

14.6.4. *Concluding remarks*

In this section, we have exemplified non-stochastic approaches to planning under uncertainty, by presenting the possibilistic Markov decision processes framework. For sake of brevity, we have only presented the fully observable 'flat' case, but the possibilistic MDP framework has been extended to handle partially observed environments [SAB 99].

Some results have also been obtained on indirect reinforcement learning methods for possibilistic MDP [SAB 01b]. However, these results are rather preliminary, since possibility theory lacks the statistical ground that would allow possibility distributions to be built from sample observed trajectories in planning under uncertainty problems. Recent results on expected utility refinements of the possibilistic decision criteria [FAR 05] may give new tools for the search for direct reinforcement learning methods.

Finally, structured possibilistic MDPs have also been studied recently, leading to the definition of a *possibilistic influence diagram* framework for the finite horizon case [GAR 08].

14.7. Conclusion

In this chapter, we have proposed a short and non-exhaustive review of recent research in AI on planning under uncertainty based on Markov decision processes. The AI community has adopted the (completely and partially observed) Markov decision processes framework, initially developed in the operations research community, in order to use it as a modeling tool for problems of planning under uncertainty. New, exact or approximate solution algorithms have been proposed in order to tackle the main features of planning under uncertainty problems. In particular, structured representation languages (traditionally developed in AI) have been incorporated to the MDP/POMDP framework, in order to improve its expression power.

The AI community has also proposed some alternative decision criteria for the expected utility criterion. In particular, qualitative criteria are often more adapted to decision problems where a strong interaction with human decision makers is needed. It was therefore natural to extend these criteria in order to provide a framework for planning under uncertainty. We have exemplified this area of work by presenting a qualitative MDP framework based on possibility theory.

The overview proposed in this chapter is obviously too brief, but interested readers are invited to refer to the literature cited on the various subjects that have been briefly described here. The main motivation for writing this chapter was to provide a guide to the literature.

14.8. Bibliography

[AKS 65] AKSTRÖM K. J., "Optimal control of Markov decision processes with incomplete state estimation", *Journal of Mathematical Analysis and Applications*, vol. 10, p. 174–205, 1965.

[BAR 95] BARTO A., BRADTKE S. J., SINGH S. P., "Learning to act using real-time dynamic programming", *Artificial Intelligence*, vol. 72, p. 81–138, 1995.

[BEL 57] BELLMAN R. E., *Dynamic Programming*, Princeton University Press, Princeton, 1957.

[BER 87] BERTSEKAS D. P., *Dynamic Programming: Deterministic and Stochastic Models*, Prentice Hall, Englewood Cliffs, 1987.

[BER 89] BERTSEKAS D. P., TSITSIKLIS J. N., *Parallel and Distributed Computation: Numerical Methods*, Prentice Hall, Englewood Cliffs, 1989.

[BOU 94] BOUTILIER C., "Toward a logic for qualitative decision theory", DOYLE J., SANDEWALL E., TORASSO P., Eds., *Proceedings of 4th International Conference on Principles of Knowledge Representation and Reasoning (KR'94)*, Bonn, Allemagne, p. 75–86, 24-27 mai 1994.

[BOU 99] BOUTILIER C., DEAN T., HANKS S., "Decision-Theoretic Planning: Structural Assumptions and Computational Leverage", *Journal of Artificial Intelligence Research*, vol. 11, p. 1–94, 1999.

[BOU 00] BOUTILIER C., DEARDEN R., GOLDSZMIDT M., "Stochastic Dynamic Programming with Factored Representations", *Artificial Intelligence*, vol. 121, num. 1, p. 49–107, 2000.

[CAS 94] CASSANDRA A. R., KAELBLING L. P., LITTMAN M. L., "Acting Optimally in Partially Observable Stochastic Domains", *Proceedings of 11th National Conference on Artificial Intelligence (AAAI'94)*, Seattle, WA, AAAI Press, p. 1023–1028, 31 July–4 August 1994.

[CHE 88] CHENG H. T., Algorithm for Partially Observable Markov Decision Processes, PhD thesis, University of British Columbia, Canada, 1988.

[DEA 89] DEAN T., KANAZAWA K., "A model for reasoning about persistence and causation", *Computational Intelligence*, vol. 5, num. 3, p. 142–150, 1989.

[DIE 95] DIETTERICH T., FLANN N., "Explanation-based learning and reinforcement learning: A unified view", *Proceedings of 12th International Conference on Machine Learning (ICML'95)*, p. 176–184, 1995.

[DUB 95] DUBOIS D., PRADE H., "Possibility theory as a basis for qualitative decision theory", *Proceedings of 14th International Joint Conference on Artificial Intelligence (IJCAI'95)*, Montreal, Canada, p. 1925–1930, 20–25 August 1995.

[DUB 01] DUBOIS D., PRADE H., SABBADIN R., "Decision-theoretic foundations of qualitative possibility theory", *European Journal of Operations Research*, vol. 128, p. 459–478, 2001.

[FAR 98] FARGIER H., LANG J., SABBADIN R., "Towards qualitative approaches to multi-stage decision making", *International Journal of Approximate Reasoning*, vol. 19, p. 441–471, 1998.

[FAR 05] FARGIER H., SABBADIN R., "Qualitative decision under uncertainty: back to expected utility", *Artificial Intelligence*, vol. 165, p. 245–280, 2005.

[FOR 06] FORSELL N., SABBADIN R., "Approximate linear-programming algorithms for graph-based Markov decision processes", *Proceedings of 17th European Conference on Artificial Intelligence (ECAI'06)*, p. 590–594, 2006.

[GAR 08] GARCIA L., SABBADIN R., "Complexity results and algorithms for possibilistic influence diagrams", *Artificial Intelligence*, vol. 172, p. 1018–1044, 2008.

[GIV 03] GIVAN R., DEAN T., GREIG M., "Equivalence notions and model minimization in Markov decision processes", *Artificial Intelligence*, vol. 147, p. 163–223, 2003.

[GUE 03] GUESTRIN C. E., Planning under uncertainty in complex structured environments, PhD thesis, Stanford University, 2003.

[HOW 60] HOWARD R. A., *Dynamic Programming and Markov Processes*, MIT Press, Cambridge, 1960.

[KAE 96] KAELBLING L. P., LITTMAN M. L., MOORE A. W., "Reinforcement Learning: A Survey", *Journal of Artificial Intelligence Research*, vol. 4, p. 237–285, 1996.

[KAE 98] KAELBLING L. P., LITTMAN M. L., CASSANDRA A. R., "Planning and Acting in Partially Observable Domains", *Artificial Intelligence*, vol. 101, p. 99–134, 1998.

[KEA 99] KEARNS M., MANSOUR Y., NG A., "A sparse sampling algorithm for near-optimal planning in large MDPs", *15th Conference on Uncertainty in Artificial Intelligence (UAI'1999)*, p. 21–30, 1999.

[KOL 00] KOLLER D., PARR R., "Policy iteration for factored MDPs", *16th Conference on Uncertainty in Artificial Intelligence (UAI'2000)*, p. 326–334, 2000.

[KUM 86] KUMAR P. R., VARAIYA P. P., *Stochastic Systems: Estimation, Identification and Adaptive Control*, Prentice Hall, Englewood Cliffs, New Jersey, 1986.

[LIT 94] LITTMAN M. L., "Memoryless policies: Theoretical limitations and practical results", CLIFF L., et al., Eds., *Proceedings of the 3rd International Conference on Simulation of Adaptive Behavior*, Cambridge, MA, MIT Press, 1994.

[MOO 93] MOORE A. W., ATKESON C. G., "Memory-based reinforcement learning: Converging with less data and less real time", *Machine Learning*, vol. 13, p. 103–130, 1993.

[PEA 88] PEARL J., *Probabilistic Reasoning in Intelligent Systems*, San Mateo, CA: Morgan Kaufmann, 1988.

[PEN 93] PENG J., WILLIAMS R. J., "Efficient learning and planning within the Dyna framework", *Adaptive Behavior*, vol. 1, num. 4, p. 437–454, 1993.

[PEY 06] PEYRARD N., SABBADIN R., "Mean field approximation of the policy iteration algorithm for graph-based Markov decision processes", *Proceedings of 17th European Conference on Artificial Intelligence (ECAI'06)*, p. 595–599, 2006.

[PUT 94] PUTERMAN M. L., *Markov Decision Processes*, John Wiley & Sons, New York, 1994.

[SAB 99] SABBADIN R., "A possibilistic model for qualitative sequential decision problems under uncertainty in partially observable environments", LASKEY K., PRADE H., Eds., *Proceedings of 15th Conference Uncertainty in Artificial Intelligence (UAI'99)*, Stockholm, Sweden, Morgan Kaufmann, p. 567–574, July 30–August 1 1999.

[SAB 01a] SABBADIN R., "Possibilistic Markov decision processes", *Engineering Appl. of Artificial Intelligence*, vol. 14, p. 287–300, 2001.

[SAB 01b] SABBADIN R., "Towards Possibilistic Reinforcement Learning Algorithms", *Proceedings of the 10th IEEE International Conference on Fuzzy Systems (FUZZ-IEEE'01)*, vol. 1, Melbourne, p. 404–407, 2–5 December 2001.

[SAV 54] SAVAGE L. J., *The Foundations of Statistics*, John Wiley & Sons, New York, 1954.

[SON 71] SONDIK E. J., The Optimal Control of Partially Observable Markov Processes, PhD thesis, Stanford University, 1971.

[SON 78] SONDIK E. J., "The optimal control of partially observable Markov processes over the infinite horizon: Discounted costs", *Operations Research*, vol. 26, num. 2, p. 282–304, 1978.

[SUT 88] SUTTON R., "Learning to predict by the method of temporal differences", *Machine Learning*, vol. 3, num. 1, p. 9–44, 1988.

[SUT 91] SUTTON R., "Planning by incremental dynamic programming", KAUFMANN M., Ed., *Proceedings of the 8th International Workshop on Machine Learning*, p. 353–357, 1991.

[TAN 94] TAN S. W., PEARL J., "Qualitative decision theory", *Proceedings of 11th National Conference on Artificial Intelligence (AAAI'94)*, Seattle, WA, p. 928–933, 31 July–4 August 1994.

[WAT 89] WATKINS C. J., Learning from Delayed Rewards, PhD thesis, King's College, Cambridge, UK, 1989.

[WAT 92] WATKINS C. J., DAYAN P., "Q-Learning", *Machine Learning*, vol. 3, num. 8, p. 279–292, 1992.

[WHI 91] WHITE C. C., "A survey of solution techniques for the partially observed Markov decision process", *Annals of Operations Research*, vol. 32, p. 215–230, 1991.

Chapter 15

Multiattribute Utility Theory

15.1. Introduction

Important decisions for both individuals and organizations often take into account multiple objectives. From the purchase of a family car to the choice of the most appropriate localization of a nuclear plant, decision makers' choices depend on many different objectives. Most often, the multiobjective nature of important decisions is revealed by assertions such as 'we are willing to pay a little bit more to gain the comfort or prestige of brand A instead of that of brand B' in the case of a car purchase; or 'we agree to increase a little the access time to the airport if, in return, the possibilities of its future extension are also increased, or if this can reduce noise pollution for residents' in the case of the localization of a new airport. These statements involve *tradeoffs* between the different objectives of the decision maker. These tradeoffs result either from an introspective exploration performed by the decision maker themself or from an explicit decision aiding process in which the decision maker expresses their will to make *coherent tradeoffs* in order to make the 'best' possible decision.

The first attempts at multiple objective decision aiding date back to the 1960s with the works by, e.g. Raiffa and Edwards [EDW 71, RAI 69], which gave birth to *Decision Analysis*. In these works, the decision maker's preferences are represented numerically on the set of all possible choices using a numerical function called a *utility function* (or 'utility' for short). The key idea of this approach lies in the fact that, after a utility function has been elicited (i.e. constructed) in a simple decision context, it can be used to assign 'scores' or utilities to all *potential actions* (i.e. the possible choices)

Chapter written by Mohammed ABDELLAOUI and Christophe GONZALES.

that the decision maker faces. These scores can therefore be used to rank the actions from the least desirable to the most desirable one (and conversely).

However, the very fact that such scores can be constructed requires two different kinds of conditions to hold. The first one concerns coherence conditions that must be satisfied by the decision maker's preferences for the latter to be numerically representable by a utility function. The second condition concerns other constraints that must be satisfied in order for the initial multiobjective utility function to be decomposable as a simple combination of mono-objective utility functions (these are also called *multiattribute* and *single-attribute* utility functions, respectively).

The limited cognitive abilities of decision makers make it necessary to use such decompositions for constructing their utility functions. Indeed, as each individual has their own preferences, each decision maker has their own utility function. To elicit utility, the analyst usually asks the decision maker a series of simple choice questions. The presence of more than two attributes is, however, cognitively more demanding (Andersen *et al.* [AND 86] provide an example in which alternatives are represented by 25 attributes). When multiattribute utilities can be decomposed into simple combinations of single-attribute utility functions, the tradeoffs used for their elicitation only need to involve a small set of differing attributes and, therefore, they remain cognitively easy to assess.

The aim of this chapter is to study the most commonly used decompositions. More precisely, we will address in sections 15.3 and 15.4 the additive decomposition of utility functions, the difference between these two sections being in the information available to the decision maker when they actually make their decision. In section 15.3, they know precisely which consequence results from each possible choice. On the other hand, in section 15.4 when the decision maker makes their decisions, they do not yet know with certainty the precise consequence resulting from their choice. Finally, section 15.5 will address the very construction of multiattribute utility functions and the most recent techniques on this matter will be presented.

15.2. Introduction to utility theory

15.2.1. *Utility functions*

From a mathematical point of view, modeling preferences is a trivial task. As an example, assume a decision maker has some preferences over a set of choices $X = \{$eat some lamb, eat some duck, eat an apple pie, eat some carpaccio$\}$. That is, for each pair of elements x, y of X, they can either (i) judge these elements incomparable (for instance, it may be difficult to express a definite preference for duck against the apple pie as one is a main course and the other is a dessert); or (ii) assess a preference for one over the other, or an indifference between both meals x and y. Mathematically, this amounts to representing the decision maker's preferences by a binary relation $\succsim$ defined on $X \times X$. $x \succsim y$ then simply means that 'either the decision maker prefers x to y or they are indifferent between both elements'. Thus, both elements being incomparable translates into Not($x \succsim y$) and Not($y \succsim x$). The decision maker preferring x at least as much as y corresponds to $x \succsim y$, and a strict preference for x over y can be expressed as $x \succsim y$ and Not($y \succsim x$), which is generally denoted by $x \succ y$. Finally, when the decision maker is indifferent between x and y, i.e. when they like x as much as y and conversely, then we have ($x \succsim y$) and ($y \succsim x$), which is usually denoted by $x \sim y$.

However, in practice, directly manipulating relation $\succsim$ for decision aiding tasks is often neither easy nor efficient. For instance, storing in extension the set S of all pairs (x, y) such that $x \succsim y$ may be impossible in complex situations due to the huge number of such pairs. Moreover, searching S, e.g. for determining the most preferred elements, can be very time consuming, unless some structure intrinsic to S is exploited. This explains why in practice instead of using directly $\succsim$ for decision aiding, preferences are often first represented numerically through so-called *utility functions* and the latter are used for decision aiding. The idea underlying utility functions is quite simple: these are functions $u : X \mapsto \mathbb{R}$ attaching a real number to each object of X such that the higher the number the more preferred the object. More formally, this amounts to:

$$\text{for all } x, y \in X, \quad x \succsim y \Leftrightarrow u(x) \geq u(y). \tag{15.1}$$

15.2.2. *Decision under certainty, uncertainty and risk*

In general, it is acknowledged that the decision maker's preferences on the set of possible alternatives is related to their preferences on the possible consequences of their choices. As an illustration, Savage presents the following example [SAV 54, p. 14]: you are cooking an omelette. You have already broken five eggs onto a plate. There remains a sixth egg to be broken and you must decide what you should do with it: (i) break the egg onto the plate already containing the other five eggs; (ii) break this additional egg onto another plate to check it before mixing it with the other eggs; (iii) do not use this egg. How should you decide which of these options is the best one? This can be resolved simply by analyzing the consequences of each decision. Thus, if the egg is safe to eat, option (i) will result in a bigger omelette, but if it is unfit for consumption, the other five eggs will be wasted. Choosing option (ii), if the egg is OK, then you will unnecessarily dirty a plate, and so on. By analyzing the consequences of each alternative, it is therefore possible to estimate the best option.

As shown in the above example, each alternative can have several consequences, depending on the state of the egg. In decision theory's technical jargon, these uncertain factors (here the state of the egg) are called *events* and, as in probability theory, elementary events play a very special role and are called *states of nature*. For each state of nature (e.g. good egg or bad egg) the choice of any alternative (options (i), (ii) or (iii)) results in one and only one consequence. Thus, alternatives can be described as sets of pairs (state of nature, consequence). This is what is usually called an *act* in decision theory. More formally, let A be the set of all possible alternatives, let X be the set of all possible consequences and E be the set of the states of nature. Then, an act is a function $E \mapsto X$ which, to any state of nature $e \in E$, assigns a unique consequence in X. Thus, act f corresponding to the choice of option (i) is such that $f(\text{good egg}) = $ 'big omelette' and $f(\text{bad egg}) = $ 'five eggs wasted'.

Let us return to utility functions. We have already seen that such functions represent the decision maker's preferences. Since, from a cognitive point of view, alternatives can be described by acts, a preference relation over acts corresponds to the decision maker's preference relation over alternatives (see Savage [SAV 54] and von Neumann and Morgenstern [VON 44] for a deeper technical discussion on this matter). Hence, let $\mathcal{A}$ denote the set of acts and $\succsim_{\mathcal{A}}$ be the preference relation over the set of acts. A utility function representing $\succsim_{\mathcal{A}}$ is therefore some function $U : \mathcal{A} \mapsto \mathbb{R}$ such that $\text{act}_1 \succsim_{\mathcal{A}} \text{act}_2 \Leftrightarrow U(\text{act}_1) \geq U(\text{act}_2)$.

Of course, the decision maker's preferences over acts reveal both their preferences over consequences (they would probably prefer a big omelette rather than wasting five eggs) and their *belief* in the plausibility of occurrence of the events. Thus, if the decision maker is obsessed by use-by dates, then the pair (bad egg, five wasted eggs) will probably only be marginally taken into account in the evaluation of option (i), whereas it will be of greater importance if the decision maker is often inattentive. Utility function U must therefore not only take into account the decision maker's preferences on consequences, but also the plausibility of the possible events. This is possible only by taking into account the decision maker's knowledge about these events. Different decision models for U will correspond to different types of knowledge. The three most important ones are certainly:

1) *Decision making under certainty*: whatever the state of nature that is obtained, an act always results in the same consequence. This can be the case, for instance, when a decision maker chooses a given menu rather than another one in a restaurant: here, the consequences are entirely determined by the chosen menu.

Let $\succsim_{\mathcal{A}}$ denote the preference relation over acts and $\succsim$ be that over the consequences. Assume that $\succsim_{\mathcal{A}}$ and $\succsim$ are represented by utility functions $U : \mathcal{A} \mapsto \mathbb{R}$ and $u : X \mapsto \mathbb{R}$, respectively. We refer to x_{act} as the consequence of a given act. Then, choice under certainty amounts to asserting that: for all acts $\in \mathcal{A}$, $U(\text{act}) = u(x_{\text{act}})$.

2) *Decision making under risk*: here, the alternatives can have several consequences, depending on which event actually occurs. Moreover, it is assumed that there exists an 'objective' probability distribution over the events. This is the case, for instance, when a decision maker chooses whether or not to play games such as a

national lottery: the probabilities of winning as well as the resulting gain are known in advance.

The expected utility model described below is the standard tool for decision making under risk. It was axiomatized by von Neumann and Morgenstern [VON 44]. Since a probability and a consequence are assigned to each event, there exists an objective probability of obtaining a given consequence. Acts can therefore be represented as finite sets of pairs (probability of a consequence, consequence). These sets are called *lotteries*. Assume that an act corresponds to lottery $(x^1, p_1; \ldots; x^n, p_n)$, that is, this act has consequence x^1 with probability p_1, x^2 with probability p_2, and so on. Then von Neumann–Morgenstern axiomatics implies the existence of a function U such that $U(\text{act}) = \sum_{i=1}^{n} p_i u(x^i)$, where u is the restriction of U to the set of consequences.

3) *Decision making under uncertainty*: this is a situation quite similar to the preceding one. However, in this case, the existence of a probability distribution over the events is not assumed but rather is derived from a set of axioms defining the *rationality* of the decision maker [SAV 54]. This applies to situations, e.g. where you decide whether or not to bet on soccer games: the result of the games are not known at the time the decision is made. Moreover, the objectivist approach to probabilities cannot be applied since no infinite sequence of soccer games is available to estimate the probabilities of the possible events. Hence, in decision making under uncertainty, probabilities are subjective, i.e. they are estimated by the decision maker.

In this model, the decision maker assigns a (subjective) probability p_i of occurrence to each state of nature. The utility of a given act is, as in von Neumann–Morgenstern's model, $U(\text{act}) = \sum_{i=1}^{n} p_i u(x^i)$.

In the remainder of this chapter, we will consider various situations in which one or the other of these models can be applied. We will focus our attention on the utility functions over the consequences i.e. u.

15.2.3. *Multiattribute utility functions*

In practical situations, decision makers have multiple contradictory objectives in mind when making their decisions. This leads to describing the possible consequences using various *attributes*, that is, the set of consequences is a multidimensional space. Thus, a decision maker wishing to buy a new car may have as a choice set $X = \{\text{Opel Corsa, Renault Clio, Peugeot 206}\}$, but if the *choice criteria* (the attributes) are, among others, the engine size, the brand and the price of the car, then set X can also be described as $X = \{(1.2\text{L}; \text{Opel}; €11,400), (1.2\text{L}; \text{Renault}; €11,150), (1.1\text{L}; \text{Peugeot}; €11,600)\}$. Any utility function over this set therefore satisfies the equation:

$$\forall x = (x_1, x_2, x_3), y = (y_1, y_2, y_3) \in X, \ x \succsim y \Leftrightarrow u(x_1, x_2, x_3) \geq u(y_1, y_2, y_3).$$

This is precisely what is called a *multiattribute* utility function.

Of course, the meaning of the attributes of relation $\succsim$ heavily depends on the domain of application. For instance, Wakker [WAK 89, p. 28] and Bleichrodt [WAK 89] cite, among others, the following domains:

– In consumer theory, the attributes represent the amount of some commodity and, for any $x, y \in X$, $x \succsim y$ means that, from the decision maker's point of view, commodity bundle x is at least as good as y.

– In producer theory, $x \in X$ is a vector of inputs and $x \succsim y$ means that x provides at least as much output as y. The utility function is then called a 'production function'.

– In welfare theory, x is an allocation or a social situation. Each attribute represents the wealth of an agent or a player, and $x \succsim y$ means that the wealth of group x is greater than or equal to that of group y.

– In medical decision making, especially in QALYs (*Quality Adjusted Life Years*) theory, the first attribute represents the level of quality of life that can be expected after undergoing some medical treatment, and the second one corresponds to the expected number of years living at this level of quality of life.

Of course this list is not exhaustive and, to each new situation, there exists an appropriate set of attributes. Keeney and Raiffa [KEE 93] show how these attributes can be exhibited in practice (the so-called 'structuring of objectives').

15.2.4. *Decompositions of utility functions*

When the utility function over the consequences u is known, it is very easy to exploit it using a computer: it is sufficient to apply the formulas given by von Neumann–Morgenstern or Savage. Simple optimization software can then determine the best actions that the decision maker should take. However, in practice, the effective construction of function u raises numerous problems. Indeed, although the construction of single-attribute utility functions is generally quite easy, that of multiattribute utility functions is usually very hard to perform due to the cognitive limitations of decision makers. Hence, we have the usual requirement that u be decomposable as a simple combination of single-attribute (more easily constructed) utility functions.

Consider for instance the case of someone wishing to buy a desktop computer. The attributes of interest are the brand of the computer, its processor, the storage capacity of its hard drive, the size of its LCD display, its memory amount and, of course, its price. One can easily understand why the decision maker should not have too much trouble comparing tuples (Dell; core duo 2 GHz; 120GO; 17"; 2GO; €700) and (Apple; core duo 2 GHz; 120GO; 17"; 2GO; €700) as these computers differ only by their brand. On the contrary, from a cognitive point of view, it is much more difficult to compare (Dell; 3 GHz; 120GO; 24"; 1GO; €800) with (Apple; core duo 1.8 GHz; 200GO; 19"; 2GO; €600) as these computers have very different features.

This explains why it is usually not possible to directly construct a utility function representing the decision maker's preferences. Rather, it is more efficient to construct a special form of this function, the construction of which will be cognitively more 'feasible'.

Several such forms have been studied in the literature, the main ones being described below. In this list, X_i denotes the set of possible values for the ith attribute and it is assumed that $X \subseteq \prod_{i=1}^{n} X_i$. The axiomatizations guaranteeing the existence of these various forms differ depending on whether the decision problem is one of decision under certainty or decision under risk/uncertainty with an expected utility (EU) criterion $U(\cdot) = \sum_j p_j u(x^j)$ (as in von Neumann–Morgenstern's and Savage's models). Hence, for each item of the list, the context of application is explicitly mentioned:

1) The additive decomposition: there exist some functions $u_i : X_i \mapsto \mathbb{R}$ such that $u(x_1, \ldots, x_n) = \sum_{i=1}^{n} u_i(x_i)$. For decision making under certainty, see [DEB 60] [FIS 70, Chapters 4 and 5], [KEE 93, Chapter 3], [KRA 71, Chapter 6], [LUC 64] and [WAK 89, Chapter 3]. For the EU context, see [FIS 70, Chapter 11] and [KEE 93, Chapters 5 and 6].

2) The multiplicative decomposition: there exist some functions $u_i : X_i \mapsto \mathbb{R}$ such that $u(x_1, \ldots, x_n) = \prod_{i=1}^{n} u_i(x_i)$. This decomposition is closely related to the preceding one as it can be derived from it using a logarithmic transformation (assuming the u_i's are such that $u_i > 0$).

3) The multilinear decomposition (it is also called polynomial or multiplicative-additive): there exist functions $u_i : X_i \mapsto \mathbb{R}$ and, for every $j \in J$, where J is the set of subsets of $\{1, \ldots, n\}$, there exist some $\pi_j \in \mathbb{R}$ such that $u(x_1, \ldots, x_n) = \sum_{j \in J} \pi_j \prod_{k \in j} u_k(x_k)$. This decomposition is described in [BEL 87, FIS 75, FUH 91] and [KRA 71, Chapter 7] for decision making under certainty; and in [FAR 81] and [KEE 93, Chapters 5 and 6] for the EU situations.

4) The decomposable structure: there exist functions $u_i : X_i \mapsto \mathbb{R}$ and some function $F : \mathbb{R}^n \mapsto \mathbb{R}$ such that $u(x_1, \ldots, x_n) = F(u_1(x_1), \ldots, u_n(x_n))$. This representation under certainty is examined in [BOU 02] and [KRA 71, Chapter 7]. This structure is more general than the preceding ones but it has a major drawback: the uniqueness of both the u_i's and F cannot be guaranteed. As we shall see, this can raise some problems during the construction phase of the utility functions.

5) The additive non-transitive decomposition: there exist functions $v_i : X_i \times X_i \mapsto \mathbb{R}$ such that $x \succsim y \Leftrightarrow \sum_{i=1}^{n} v_i(x_i, y_i) \geq 0$. See [BOU 02, BOU 04, FIS 91] for decision making under certainty and [NAK 90] for cases in which a generalization of the EU criterion is applied. Among the additive non-transitive functions lies the special case of the additive difference model: there exist functions $u_i : X_i \mapsto \mathbb{R}$ and some functions $F_i : \mathbb{R} \mapsto \mathbb{R}$ such that $x \succsim y \Leftrightarrow \sum_{i=1}^{n} F_i(u_i(x_i) - u_i(y_i)) \geq 0$ See [BOU 02, FIS 92, TVE 69] for decision making under certainty.

In the remainder of this chapter, we will concentrate on models (1) (decomposition under certainty) and (3) (decomposition under risk/uncertainty). Let us now see the price to pay for guaranteeing that such decompositions actually represent the decision maker's preferences.

15.3. Decomposition under certainty

In this section, we consider situations in which every act has precisely one consequence, which is furthermore independent of the state of nature obtained. In addition, we assume that the set of consequences X is the Cartesian product of the attributes X_i's. In other words, $X = \prod_{i=1}^{n} X_i$. For instance, in the car example mentioned in the introduction, we would have $X_1 = \{1.1\text{L}; 1.2\text{L}\}$, $X_2 = \{\text{Opel}, \text{Renault}, \text{Peugeot}\}$, $X_3 = \{€11{,}400, €11{,}150, €11{,}600\}$ and $X = X_1 \times X_2 \times X_3$. Note that this implies that, from a cognitive point of view, we do not preclude the existence of cars such as (1.1L; Opel; €11,600), even if such cars do not actually exist. We will see later how to relax, at least partially, this restriction. Note however that it is not possible to cope with arbitrary subsets of Cartesian product $\prod_{i=1}^{n} X_i$: this is the price of having decomposable utility functions.

The rest of this section is devoted to the additive decomposability of function u. In the first subsection, such decomposability is studied in the case where $X = X_1 \times X_2$. Then, we consider the case where the set of consequences X is a Cartesian product of more than two attributes and, finally, special cases where $X \subsetneq \prod_{i=1}^{n} X_i$. For each case, our aim is to present some conditions that must be satisfied by the decision maker's preference relation $\succsim$ over the set of consequences in order to prove the existence of some functions $u_i : X_i \mapsto \mathbb{R}$ such that:

(a) $\forall\ x, y \in \prod_{i=1}^{n} X_i,\ x \succsim y \Leftrightarrow u(x) \geq u(y)$ and

(b) $\forall\ (x_1, \ldots, x_n) \in \prod_{i=1}^{n} X_i,\ u(x_1, \ldots, x_n) = \sum_{i=1}^{n} u_i(x_i).$

Of special interest, we will see that u_i functions are unique up to very particular transformations. This will prove useful for constructing the u_is (the so-called *elicitation* process).

15.3.1. *Additive decomposition in two-dimensional spaces*

In this section, we consider decision problems in which the possible consequences of every act can be described by two attributes, i.e. $X = X_1 \times X_2$. First, let us examine some necessary conditions for the existence of functions u_1 and u_2 such that:

$$\text{for all } x, y \in X_1 \times X_2, \ x \succsim y \Leftrightarrow u_1(x_1) + u_2(x_2) \geq u_1(y_1) + u_2(y_2). \quad (15.2)$$

The most obvious necessary condition for equation (15.2) to hold is that $\succsim$ can be represented by a utility function (not necessarily additive) $u : X_1 \times X_2 \mapsto \mathbb{R}$. Debreu [DEB 54] gave some necessary and sufficient conditions to ensure this. Among them is the completeness of $\succsim$, that is, for every pair of consequences x and y, either $x \succsim y$ or $y \succsim x$. Indeed, if $\succsim$ is representable by a utility function u, then $u(x)$ and $u(y)$ are real numbers and, consequently, either $u(x) \geq u(y)$ or $u(y) \geq u(x)$. By equation (15.1) this implies that either $x \succsim y$ or $y \succsim x$. Similarly, $\geq$ being a transitive relation, $\succsim$ must also be transitive, i.e. if $x \succsim y$ and $y \succsim z$ then $x \succsim z$. As a conclusion, in order to be representable by a utility function, $\succsim$ must be a weak order (this is of course a necessary condition, but it is not actually sufficient, see [DEB 54]).

Definition 15.1. *Weak ordering*
A weak order $\succsim$ is a binary relation that is transitive ($[x \succsim y$ and $y \succsim z] \Rightarrow x \succsim z$) and complete (for all $x, y \in X$, either $x \succsim y$ or $y \succsim x$).

Let us now see some properties specific to additive utilities. Assume there exists $u = u_1 + u_2$ representing $\succsim$. Then, for every $x_1, y_1 \in X_1$ and $x_2, y_2 \in X_2$,

$$\begin{aligned}(x_1, x_2) \succsim (y_1, x_2) &\Leftrightarrow u_1(x_1) + u_2(x_2) \geq u_1(y_1) + u_2(x_2) \\ &\Leftrightarrow u_1(x_1) \geq u_1(y_1) \\ &\Leftrightarrow u_1(x_1) + u_2(y_2) \geq u_1(y_1) + u_2(y_2) \\ &\Leftrightarrow (x_1, y_2) \succsim (y_1, y_2).\end{aligned}$$

This property expresses some independence among the attributes. In their preferences, the decision maker takes into account the attributes separately i.e. there is no synergy effect between them. This leads to the following axiom.

Axiom 15.1. *Independence*
For all $x_1, y_1 \in X_1$ and for all $x_2, y_2 \in X_2$,

$$(x_1, x_2) \succsim (y_1, x_2) \Leftrightarrow (x_1, y_2) \succsim (y_1, y_2),$$

$$(x_1, x_2) \succsim (x_1, y_2) \Leftrightarrow (y_1, x_2) \succsim (y_1, y_2).$$

Let us represent $\succsim$'s indifference curves in the outcome space $X_1 \times X_2$, that is, curves the points of which are all judged indifferent. If $X_1 = X_2 = \mathbb{R}$ then the independence axiom simply states that if a point (an outcome), say A, is preferred to

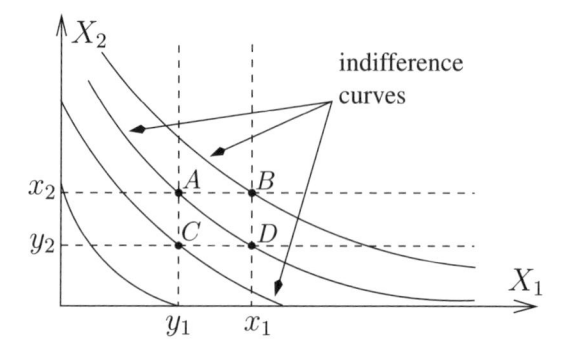

Figure 15.1. $\succsim$'s indifference curves and the independence axiom

another one on the same vertical line, say C, then for all pairs of points (B, D) such that $ABCD$ is a rectangle (see Figure 15.1), B must also be preferred to D. Similarly, if B is preferred to A, then for all pairs (C, D) such that $ABCD$ is a rectangle, D must be preferred to C.

The independence axiom is of utmost importance for the additive decomposability. To grab a strong understanding of this axiom, it may be worth working in a space slightly different from $X_1 \times X_2$: let $u(x_1, x_2) = u_1(x_1) + u_2(x_2)$ be an additive utility function representing $\succsim$. After assigning a given value x_2 to X_2, u only depends on X_1. Denoting this function from X_1 to $\mathbb{R}$ by $u_{[x_2]}$, we have $u_{[x_2]}(x_1) = u(x_1, x_2)$ for all $x_1 \in X_1$. We can now represent $u_{[x_2]}$ in the classical space $X_1 \times \mathbb{R}$ (see Figure 15.2). u's additive decomposition implies that:

for all $x_1 \in X_1$, for all $x_2, y_2 \in X_2$, $u(x_1, x_2) - u(x_1, y_2) = u_2(x_2) - u_2(y_2)$.

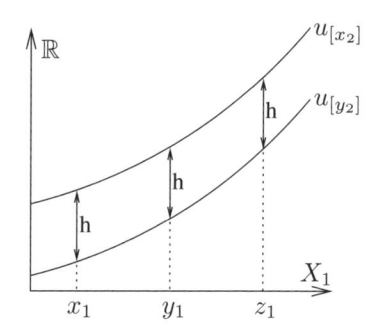

Figure 15.2. *Additive utilities in two-dimensional spaces*

Note that this value does not depend on x_1. This translates on Figure 15.2 as: the graph of any function $u_{[x_2]}, x_2 \in X_2$, can be deduced from that of any $u_{[y_2]}, y_2 \in X_2$, by a vertical translation. Conversely, if the graphs of functions $u_{[x_2]}, x_2 \in X_2$ can be deduced from one another by vertical translation, u is additively decomposable. Indeed, assume that the graph of $u_{[x_2]}$ is derived by a vertical translation from that of $u_{[x_2^0]}$, for a given value $x_2^0 \in X_2$. Then, for all $x_1 \in X_1$, $u(x_1, x_2) = u(x_1, x_2^0) +$ constant $h(x_2)$. However, as x_2^0 is fixed, $u(x_1, x_2^0)$ only depends on x_1. $u(x_1, x_2)$ is therefore the sum of a function of x_1, i.e. $u(x_1, x_2^0)$, and a function of x_2, i.e. $h(x_2)$. The following proposition summarizes the above discussion.

Proposition 15.1. *Additive decomposability*
Let $\succsim$ be a preference relation on $X_1 \times X_2$ representable by a utility function u. Then u is additive if and only if, for all $x_2, y_2 \in X_2$, the graph of function $u_{[x_2]}$ in space $X_1 \times \mathbb{R}$ can be deduced from that of $u_{[y_2]}$ by a vertical translation.

Now, let us return to the independence axiom: $(x_1, x_2) \succsim (x_1, y_2) \Leftrightarrow (y_1, x_2) \succsim (y_1, y_2)$ can be translated in terms of utility functions as $u_{[x_2]}(x_1) \geq u_{[y_2]}(x_1) \Leftrightarrow u_{[x_2]}(y_1) \geq u_{[y_2]}(y_1)$. This simply means that if the graph of $u_{[x_2]}$ is 'above' that of $u_{[y_2]}$ for a given point $x_1 \in X_1$, then the same holds for all the other points of X_1. However, if the graphs of the $u_{[\cdot]}$ are sufficiently close to each other, any slight variation of height between two graphs (which would rule out u's additive decomposition) would inevitably result in the intersection of at least two graphs, which would violate the independence axiom.

Under some structural conditions, it can be shown that when the outcome set X has at least three attributes, the $u_{[x_2]}$ graphs are always sufficiently close to each other such that the independence axiom is almost sufficient by itself to induce the additive decomposability of u. Unfortunately, this is not the case when $X = X_1 \times X_2$ and other necessary conditions such as the Thomsen condition are needed: assume again that u is additive. Then, for all $x_1, y_1, z_1 \in X_1$ and for all $x_2, y_2, z_2 \in X_2$,

$$(x_1, z_2) \sim (z_1, y_2) \Leftrightarrow u_1(x_1) + u_2(z_2) = u_1(z_1) + u_2(y_2)$$
$$(z_1, x_2) \sim (y_1, z_2) \Leftrightarrow u_1(z_1) + u_2(x_2) = u_1(y_1) + u_2(z_2)$$

Summing both equalities on the right hand side of $\Leftrightarrow$, we obtain:

$$u_1(x_1) + u_2(z_2) + u_1(z_1) + u_2(x_2) = u_1(z_1) + u_2(y_2) + u_1(y_1) + u_2(z_2).$$

Canceling out the terms belonging to both sides of the equality, we obtain $u_1(x_1) + u_2(x_2) = u_1(y_1) + u_2(y_2)$ and, consequently, $(x_1, x_2) \sim (y_1, y_2)$ since u is a utility function. We therefore have the following necessary condition for the additive decomposability.

Axiom 15.2. *Thomsen condition*
For all $x_1, y_1, z_1 \in X_1$, *for all* $x_2, y_2, z_2 \in X_2$,

$$[(x_1, z_2) \sim (z_1, y_2) \text{ and } (z_1, x_2) \sim (y_1, z_2)] \Rightarrow (x_1, x_2) \sim (y_1, y_2).$$

When we can exhibit sufficiently many indifferent ($\sim$) elements in X, the combination of independence and the Thomsen condition (Figure 15.3) is sufficiently strong to imply that the vertical distances between any two $u_{[\cdot]}$ graphs are constant, hence that u is additive. The Thomsen condition can be illustrated graphically using indifference curves: it simply states that if $A \sim B$ and $C \sim D$ then $E \sim F$.

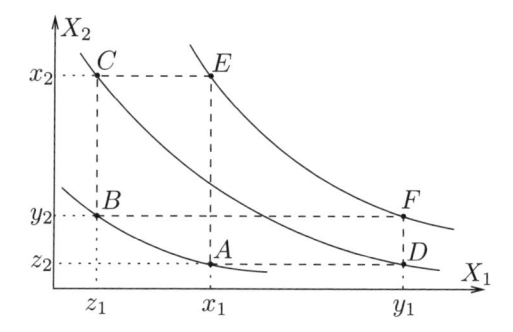

Figure 15.3. *Thomsen condition*

There still remains one important problem to fix in order to guarantee the additive decomposability: $\succsim$ must not have many more indifference curves than there are real numbers, or else it cannot be represented by a utility function. Indeed, by definition, all the points lying on the same indifference curve are indifferent among each other and, consequently, they have the same utility, i.e. the same real number is assigned to all of them. But if there exist much more indifference curves than there exist real numbers, how can we assign a different real number to each indifference curve? The following Archimedean axiom will prevent this kind of situation from occuring. Assume that $\succsim$ is representable by an additive utility function u. Let (x_1^0, x_2^0) and (x_1^0, x_2^1) be two arbitrary elements of X such that:

$$(x_1^0, x_2^0) \prec (x_1^0, x_2^1).$$

If there exists $x_1^1 \in X_1$ such that $(x_1^1, x_2^0) \sim (x_1^0, x_2^1)$ then, in terms of utility functions, this indifference is equivalent to:

$$u_1(x_1^1) = u_1(x_1^0) + (u_2(x_2^1) - u_2(x_2^0)).$$

Let $\alpha = u_2(x_2^1) - u_2(x_2^0)$. Since u represents $\succsim$, we must have $\alpha > 0$. Moreover, as by hypothesis u is additive, we know that the independence axiom holds. Hence, as X is a Cartesian product, (x_1^1, x_2^1) belongs to X and satisfies:

$$(x_1^1, x_2^0) \prec (x_1^1, x_2^1).$$

We can then iterate this process: if there exists $x_1^2 \in X_1$ such that $(x_1^2, x_2^0) \sim (x_1^1, x_2^1)$ then:

$$u_1(x_1^2) = u_1(x_1^1) + \alpha = u_1(x_1^0) + 2\alpha.$$

By induction, this creates a sequence $\{x_1^0, x_1^1, \ldots, x_1^k\}$ called a *standard sequence* such that $u_1(x_1^k) = u_1(x_1^0) + k\alpha$. So, as $\alpha > 0$, when k tends toward $+\infty$, $u_1(x_1^k)$ must also tend toward $+\infty$. Hence, if there existed $z \in X$ such that, for any k, $(x_1^k, x_2^0) \prec z$, the utility of z would be equal to $+\infty$, which is of course impossible. As a consequence, the following axiom is necessary for the additive decomposability.

Definition 15.2. Standard sequence with respect to the first attribute
For any set N of consecutive integers (no restriction is imposed on N; it may be finite or infinite and its integers may be positive or negative), a set $\{x_1^k \in X_1, k \in N\}$ is a standard sequence with respect to the the first attribute if and only if $\text{Not}(x_1^0, x_2^0) \sim (x_1^0, x_2^1)$ and $(x_1^k, x_2^1) \sim (x_1^{k+1}, x_2^0)$ for all $k, k+1 \in N$. $\{x_2^0; x_2^1\}$ is called the mesh of the sequence. A similar definition holds for standard sequences with respect to the other attributes.

Axiom 15.3. *Archimedean*
Any bounded standard sequence is finite: if (x_1^k) is a standard sequence of mesh $\{x_2^0; x_2^1\}$ such that there exist $y, z \in X$ such that $z \precsim (x_1^k, x_2^0) \precsim y$ for all $k \in N$, then sequence (x_1^k) is finite.

Figure 15.4 shows the graphical interpretation of this property: the construction of the standard sequence starts at the point on the lower left corner of the figure. Moving vertically from that point, when we reach the horizontal dotted line we have increased the utility by $\alpha > 0$. Moving down along the indifference curves (represented by solid curves on the figure) does not change the value of the utility. Consequently, the sequence of actions (vertical move, move along indifference curves) defines a sequence of points (x_1^k), the utility of which always increases by α. This is a standard sequence.

Of course, the Archimedean axiom is useful only if standard sequences can be constructed. One consequence is that there must exist some points such that $x_2^1 \succ x_2^0$ and $x_1^1 \succ x_1^0$. Hence the following axiom must be used in conjunction with the Archimedean axiom.

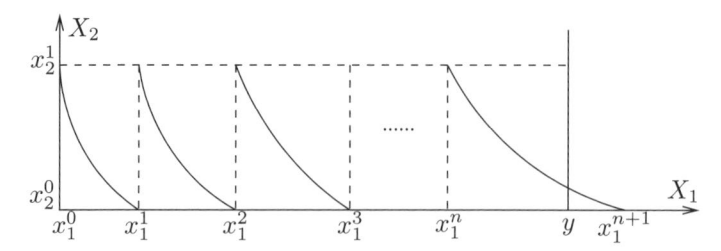

Figure 15.4. *The Archimedean condition*

Axiom 15.4. *Essentiality*
X_1 is essential if and only if there exist $a_1, b_1 \in X_1$ and $x_2 \in X_2$ such that $(a_1, x_2) \succ (b_1, x_2)$. A similar axiom holds for the other attributes.

The Archimedean axiom and the Thomsen condition are very powerful for structuring the consequence space. However, they have a major drawback: to be useful, they require indifferences between many points of X. When such indifferences do not exist, these axioms become useless and the additive decomposability cannot be proven to hold. For instance, when $X = \mathbb{R} \times \{0, 2, 4, 6\}$ and $\succsim$ is representable on X by the utility function:

$$u(x_1, x_2) = \begin{cases} x_1 + x_2 & \text{if } x_2 \leq 4 \\ 0,5(x_1 \bmod 2)^2 + \lfloor x_1/2 \rfloor + 6,5 & \text{if } x_2 = 6, \end{cases}$$

there are not enough indifferences in X. Although the independence axiom holds, it can be shown that the Thomsen condition does not. Similarly, if $X = [0, 2] \times \mathbb{N}$ and if $\succsim$ satisfies the properties:

$\succsim$ is representable by $u(x_1, x_2) = x_1 + 2^{x_2}$ on $[0, 2] \times \mathbb{N}^*$,
$\succsim$ is representable by $u(x_1, x_2) = x_1$ on $[0, 1] \times \{0\}$,
$(x_1, 0) \succ (y_1, y_2)$ for all $x_1, y_1 \in [0, 2]$ and for all $y_2 \neq 0$,

then the Archimedean axiom is utterly useless as it is impossible to construct standard sequences with more than two elements. In this very example, it can be shown that there exists no additive utility representing $\succsim$. To enable the Archimedean axiom and the Thomsen condition to strongly structure the outcome space, the following additional axiom is therefore traditionally required in the literature. It will induce the existence of a huge amount of indifferences within set X.

Axiom 15.5. *(Restricted) solvability with respect to the first attribute*
For all $y_1^0, y_1^1 \in X_1$, for all $y_2 \in X_2$ and for all $x \in X$, if $(y_1^0, y_2) \precsim x \precsim (y_1^1, y_2)$, then there exists $z_1 \in X_1$ such that $x \sim (z_1, y_2)$. A similar axiom holds for the other attributes.

In two-dimensional spaces $X_1 \times X_2$, the graphical interpretation of restricted solvability is quite simple, as shown on Figure 15.5. If points (y_1^0, y_2) and (y_1^1, y_2) lie on each side of the indifference containing point x, then the horizontal line passing through (y_1^0, y_2) and (y_1^1, y_2) intersects the indifference curve (of course this intersection belongs to X).

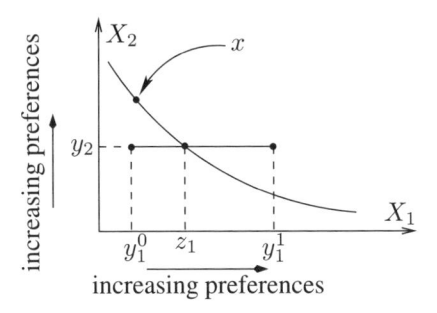

Figure 15.5. *Restricted solvability*

The combination of all the axioms presented so far is sufficient to ensure the additive representability of relation $\succsim$, as is shown by the following proposition [KRA 71, Chapter 6].

Proposition 15.2. *Existence and unicity of additive utilities*
Let $X = X_1 \times X_2$ be an outcome set, and let $\succsim$ be a binary relation on $X \times X$ satisfying restricted solvability and essentiality with respect to X_1 and X_2. Then, the following statements are equivalent:

1) $\succsim$ *is a weak order satisfying the Thomsen condition and, for each attribute, the independence axiom and the Archimedean axiom.*

2) There exists an additive utility $u = u_1 + u_2$ *representing* $\succsim$*. Moreover, this utility is unique up to scale and location. In other words, if there exists another additive utility* $v = v_1 + v_2$ *representing* $\succsim$*, then there exist* $\alpha > 0$ *and* $\beta_1, \beta_2 \in \mathbb{R}$ *such that* $v_1(\cdot) = \alpha u_1(\cdot) + \beta_1$ *and* $v_2(\cdot) = \alpha u_2(\cdot) + \beta_2$.

Assertion (2) implying assertion (1) has been shown previously. As for (1) ⇒ (2), the intuition of the proposition can explained using Figure 15.6. Start from an arbitrary point $x^0 = (x_1^0, x_2^0) \in X$. Assign utility value 0 to this point. By essentiality, there exists $x_2^1 \succ x_2^0$. Without loss of generality, assign utility value 1 to (x_1^0, x_2^1). Using restricted solvability and the Archimedean axiom, construct standard sequence (x_1^k) and assign $u_1(x_1^k) = k$. Similarly, construct a vertical standard sequence of mesh $\{x_1^0; x_1^1\}$, say (x_2^r), and assign $u_2(x_2^r) = r$.

The Thomsen condition guarantees that what has just been constructed is actually coherent since, if the decision maker is indifferent between A and B and between C

594   Decision-making Process

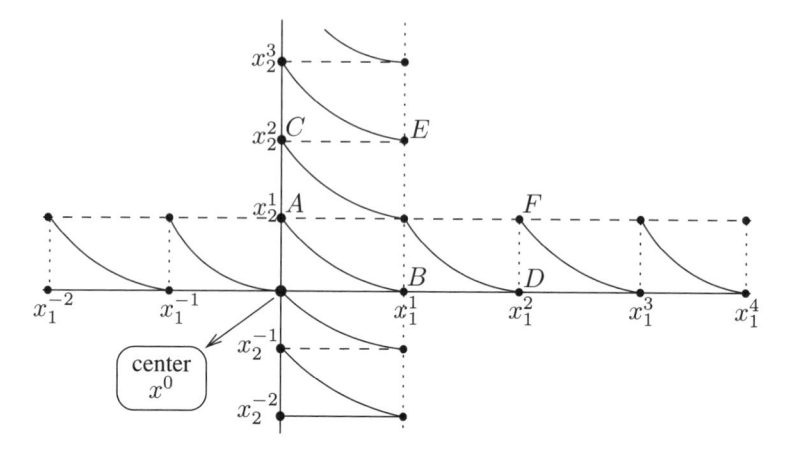

Figure 15.6. *Intuitions behind proposition 15.2*

and D, then they must also be indifferent between E and F. Fortunately, the utility assignment process used so far guarantees that the same values have been assigned to both E and F. More generally, the construction process ensures that the values assigned to all the points on the grid $\{(x_1^k, x_2^r)\}$ actually form a utility function representing $\succsim$. Either this grid corresponds to the whole set X and we just constructed an additive utility function on X, or there exist points in X that do not belong to this grid.

In the latter case, the model can be refined by doubling the set of points on the grid. Generally, the idea is to find a point $(x_1^{1/2}, x_2^{1/2})$ such that, in standard sequences of mesh $\{x_2^0; x_2^{1/2}\}$ and $\{x_1^0; x_1^{1/2}\}$, every other element corresponds to an element of (x_1^k) and (x_2^r) defined above. It is then obvious that $u_1(x_1^{1/2}) = u_2(x_2^{1/2}) = 1/2$. The process is iterated until a utility function is defined on the whole space X. This technique is used in particular in [WAK 89].

15.3.2. *Extension to more general outcome sets*

In this section, we will briefly examine two extensions of the additive decomposability results presented so far. First, we will consider outcome sets that are still Cartesian products but are described by more than two attributes. Then, we will briefly address the case of subsets of Cartesian products.

Additive decomposability for n-dimensional Cartesian products, $n \geq 3$, is not fundamentally different from that of 2D spaces. The main difference lies in the fact that the graphs of functions $u_{[\cdot]}$, which were not necessarily very close to each other in 2D, are now very close due to the combined effects of independence and restricted solvability in n-dimensional spaces. As a consequence the Thomsen condition, which was primarily used to ensure that the vertical distances between pairs of $u_{[\cdot]}$ graphs could not vary significantly, is no longer needed. The other axioms seen so far are still used and just require slight modifications to be adapted to the higher dimension of X. Only the independence axiom can be extended in several ways.

Axiom 15.6. *Independence (also know as coordinate independence)*
For all i, for all $z_i, t_i \in X_i$ and for all $x_j, y_j \in X_j$, $j \neq i$,

$$(x_1, \ldots, x_{i-1}, z_i, x_{i+1}, \ldots, x_n) \succsim (y_1, \ldots, y_{i-1}, z_i, y_{i+1}, \ldots, y_n)$$
$$\Leftrightarrow (x_1, \ldots, x_{i-1}, t_i, x_{i+1}, \ldots, x_n) \succsim (y_1, \ldots, y_{i-1}, t_i, y_{i+1}, \ldots, y_n).$$

Axiom 15.7. *Weak separability*
For all i, for all $z_i, t_i \in X_i$ and for all $x_j, y_j \in X_j$, $j \neq i$,

$$(x_1, \ldots, x_{i-1}, z_i, x_{i+1}, \ldots, x_n) \succsim (x_1, \ldots, x_{i-1}, t_i, x_{i+1}, \ldots, x_n)$$
$$\Leftrightarrow (y_1, \ldots, y_{i-1}, z_i, y_{i+1}, \ldots, y_n) \succsim (y_1, \ldots, y_{i-1}, t_i, y_{i+1}, \ldots, y_n).$$

Axiom 15.6 obviously implies axiom 15.7. On the other hand, the converse is false and axiom 15.7 is too weak to induce by itself the existence of additive utilities. Hence, we should rather extend the independence axiom of the preceding subsection by axiom 15.6. As we shall see later, weak separability can nevertheless also be used in some representation theorems.

In the context of n-dimensional spaces, we shall introduce new notation to simplify the formulae we need to manipulate. Let X_J denote the set of attributes with indices which belong to $J \subset N = \{1, \ldots, n\}$. Let $x_J y$ denote the consequence in X with attributes' values x_j for $j \in J$ and y_k for $k \in N - J$. Abusing notation, when $J = \{j\}$ we will write $x_j y$ instead of $x_J y$. Coordinate independence can therefore be stated as in axiom 15.8.

Axiom 15.8. *Independence*

For all i, for all $z_i, t_i \in X_i$ and for all $x, y \in X$, $z_i x \succsim z_i y \Leftrightarrow t_i x \succsim t_i y$.

Proposition 15.2 of the preceding section can now be extended to n-dimensional spaces by the following proposition.

Proposition 15.3. *Existence and unicity of additive utilities*
Let $X = \prod_{i=1}^n X_i$, $n \geq 3$, be an outcome set and let $\succsim$ be a binary relation on $X \times X$ satisfying essentiality and restricted solvability with respect to every attribute. Then the following statements are equivalent:

1) $\succsim$ *is a weak order satisfying, for every attribute, independence (axiom 15.8) and the Archimedean axiom.*

2) There exists an additive utility function $u = \sum_{i=1}^{n} u_i$ *representing* $\succsim$ *on* X. *Moreover, this utility is unique up to scale and location. In other words, if there exists another additive utility* $v = \sum_{i=1}^{n} v_i$ *representing* $\succsim$, *then there exist* $\alpha > 0$ *and* $\beta_i \in \mathbb{R}$, $i \in \{1, \ldots, n\}$, *such that* $v_i(\cdot) = \alpha u_i(\cdot) + \beta_i$ *for all* $i \in \{1, \ldots, n\}$.

This proposition, the proof of which can be found in [KRA 71, Chapter 6], is restrictive in two respects. First, the assumption that restricted solvability holds with respect to every attribute may be questionable in some practical situations. This is the case, for instance, when some attributes are naturally defined over continuums (e.g. money or time) while others are defined only over discrete sets (e.g. the number of rooms in a flat or some qualitative attributes like the job of a human being). For such cases, there exist some extensions of the above proposition requiring restricted solvability only with respect to a small number of attributes [GON 00, GON 03] or even substituting restricted solvability by 'lighter' axioms requiring some density properties [NAK 02]. Note, however, that these extensions are more difficult to use in practice than the above proposition. This is the price to pay to have theorems not requiring much structural conditions.

The second restriction imposed by proposition 15.3 is the fact that X must necessarily be the Cartesian product of the X_is. When X is only a subset of this Cartesian product, the axioms used so far can be significantly less powerful and can therefore be unable to ensure the additive representability. For instance, without solvability, we already saw that the Archimedean axiom can become utterly useless if X does not contain sufficiently many pairs of indifferent elements to ensure that lengthy standard sequences can be constructed. When X is only a subset of a Cartesian product, it can have an 'exotic' shape that prevents the existence of any long standard sequences, even when restricted solvability holds. Such a case is mentioned in [WAK 93] where X has the shape of an Eiffel tower lying at a 45° angle. Hence, when X is a subset of a Cartesian product, additive decomposability requires additional structural conditions on $(X, \succsim)$.

There are very few articles on this matter. This is first because we can often think of X as a Cartesian product even if, in reality, this is not precisely the case. Indeed, X corresponds to the very set of outcomes that the decision maker can imagine, not to the set of outcomes that are actually possible. The decision maker can also cognitively imagine outcomes that may be far from possible in the real world. Secondly, the additive decomposability on subsets of Cartesian products requires axioms that are much harder to use and to test than those presented so far. In addition, these axioms often have no real meaning in terms of preferences but rather are technical axioms only needed to complete mathematical proofs. See for instance proposition 15.4, due to Chateauneuf and Wakker [CHA 93]. Before providing it, however, we need a final additional notion. By the independence axiom (axiom 15.8), or even by weak separability (axiom 15.7), for every i,

$$(x_1, \ldots, x_{i-1}, x_i, x_{i+1}, \ldots, x_n) \succsim (x_1, \ldots, x_{i-1}, y_i, x_{i+1}, \ldots, x_n)$$
$$\Leftrightarrow (y_1, \ldots, y_{i-1}, x_i, y_{i+1}, \ldots, y_n) \succsim (y_1, \ldots, y_{i-1}, y_i, y_{i+1}, \ldots, y_n).$$

Since this preference should be satisfied for whatever $x_j, y_j \in X_j, j \neq i$, this means that, when the decision maker compares two outcomes, they only use the attributes that differ between outcomes. Hence, we can define for every i a new preference relation $\succsim_i$ such that $x_i \succsim_i y_i$ is equivalent to the above preference.

Proposition 15.4. *Additive representability on open spaces*
Let $X \subset \prod_{i=1}^{n} X_i$. Let $\succsim$ be a weak order on X. Assume that the X_is are endowed with the order topology with respect to $\succsim_i$. Assume that X is endowed with the product topology and that it is open. Moreover, assume that $\succsim$ is continuous over X and that the following sets are connected:

1) int(X), the interior of X;

2) all the sets of the form $\{x \in int(X) : x_i = s_i\}$ for all i, s_i; and

3) all the equivalence classes of int(X) with respect to $\sim$.

Then, if $\succsim$ is representable by an additive utility function on any Cartesian product included in X, then $\succsim$ is also representable by an additive utility on X.

As we can see, the interpretation in terms of preferences of the hypotheses of this proposition is not easy. The key idea behind this proposition is to construct an additive utility on a 'small' Cartesian product, to extend this construction on another Cartesian product in the neighborhood of the first one and to iterate this process. int(X) connexity hypothesis ensures for instance that this iterative construction process will result in an additive utility function defined over the whole of X.

Chateauneuf *et al.* and Segal [CHA 93, SEG 94] propose other representation theorems on even more general subsets. Here again, the axioms used in these theorems are rather technical and are not prone to a simple interpretation in terms of preferences. Nevertheless, there exist some subsets of Cartesian products in which the existence of additive utilities can be simply derived from that on full Cartesian products. This is the case, for instance, of rank dependent ordered sets, i.e. sets in which tuples $(x_1, \ldots, x_n)$ have the following property: all their attributes belong to the same set X_1 and there exists a weak order $\succsim'$ over X_1 such that $x_1 \succsim' x_2 \succsim' \ldots \succsim' x_n$ [WAK 91].

15.4. Decompositions under uncertainty

The preceding section concerned situations where each act had a unique consequence, known with certainty. In this section, we address uncertain situations where each act has $m > 1$ possible consequences depending on the state of nature that obtains. Thus, the act having consequence x^i when event E_i occurs is now denoted by $(x^1, E_1; \ldots; x^m, E_m)$, where $\{E_1, \ldots, E_m\}$ is a partition of the set of states of nature considered by the decision maker. Recall that the expected utility criterion for decision under risk (see von Neumann and Morgenstern [VON 44]) assumes that the probabilities of the events are known (objectively) whereas Savage's subjective expected utility criterion [SAV 54] allows a subjective probability that reflects the decision maker's beliefs to be assigned to each event. When the set of the states of nature is endowed with a probability measure, act $(x^1, E_1; \ldots; x^m, E_m)$ induces a lottery $(x^1, p_1; \ldots; x^m, p_m)$, where p_i denotes the probability of event E_i. Note that in Savage's axiomatics, acts can also have infinite support. Finally, in both of these expected utility axiomatics, consequences can be qualitative but also quantitative and unidimensional but also multidimensional.

In the remainder of this section, we will consider that the set of consequences X is equal to the Cartesian product $\prod_{i=1}^{n} X_i$, as in section 15.2. The set of lotteries $(x^1, p_1; \ldots; x^m, p_m)$ over X is now denoted by $\mathbb{P}$ and is assumed to be endowed with the usual preference relation $\succsim$. Indifference relation $\sim$ and the strict preference relation $\succ$ are defined as before. The expected utility criterion requires the existence of a utility function $u : X \to \mathbb{R}$, defined up to scale and location, such that:

$$\text{for all } P, Q \in \mathbb{P}, \ P \succsim Q \iff E(u, P) \geq E(u, Q)$$

where $E(u, P)$ and $E(u, Q)$ denote the mathematical expectations of the utilities of lotteries P and Q, respectively.

Similarly to the certain case, in practice, the construction of multiattribute utility function u raises numerous problems. For instance, consider the case of a decision maker having to make a decision involving h possible consequences $x^1, \ldots, x^h$. In theory, using the expected utility criterion, each consequence may be assigned a utility value as follows: assume that x^0 and x^* represent the least and most preferred consequences, respectively. As u is defined up to scale and location we can, without loss of generality, set $u(x^0) = 0$ and $u(x^*) = 1$. Now, for each consequence x^i putting a simple question to the decision maker, it is possible to determine probability p_i such that they are indifferent between receiving (1) a gain of x^i with certainty and (2) obtaining the lottery ticket providing consequence x^* with probability p_i and consequence x^0 with probability $1 - p_i$. According to the expected utility criterion, this indifference implies that $u(x^i) = p_i$ for every $i = 1, \ldots, h$.

Due to the cognitive limitations of decision makers, it is clearly impossible to use this kind of elicitation method when the number of attributes is high. Moreover, even when the latter stays relatively small, the combinatorial nature of X can induce a large set of consequences which, again, renders the above elicitation method unusable. Hence, in practice, analysts need to be able to decompose u in single-attribute utility functions, which are much easier and more intuitive to elicit [e.g. KEE 68, KEE 93, POL 67, VON 93]. Of course, as in the certain case, under uncertainty, utility function u being additively decomposable requires that additional constraints on the decision maker's preferences be satisfied. In this direction, Miyamoto and Wakker have proposed a decomposition approach based on models generalizing the classical expected utility model [MIY 96].

15.4.1. *Decomposition in two-dimensional spaces*

The additivity of von Neumann–Morgenstern utility function requires a more general independence condition than in the certain case. Indeed, assuming preferences can be modeled using the expected utility criterion, if $u = u_1 + u_2$, with $u_i : X_i \mapsto \mathbb{R}$ for $i = 1, 2$, then, for any $x_1, x'_1, y_1, y'_1 \in X_1, x_2, z_2 \in X_2$,

$$((x_1, x_2), \tfrac{1}{2}; (x'_1, x_2), \tfrac{1}{2}) \succsim ((y_1, x_2), \tfrac{1}{2}; (y'_1, x_2), \tfrac{1}{2})$$

$$\Updownarrow$$

$$\tfrac{1}{2} u(x_1, x_2) + \tfrac{1}{2} u(x'_1, x_2) \geq \tfrac{1}{2} u(y_1, x_2) + \tfrac{1}{2} u(y'_1, x_2)$$

$$\Updownarrow$$

$$\tfrac{1}{2} u(x_1, z_2) + \tfrac{1}{2} u(x'_1, z_2) \geq \tfrac{1}{2} u(y_1, z_2) + \tfrac{1}{2} u(y'_1, z_2)$$

$$\Updownarrow$$

$$((x_1, z_2), \tfrac{1}{2}; (x'_1, z_2), \tfrac{1}{2}) \succsim ((y_1, z_2), \tfrac{1}{2}; (y'_1, z_2), \tfrac{1}{2}).$$

The above equivalences show that preferences over lotteries differing only on attribute X_1 do not depend on their common level on attribute X_2. In such a case, attribute X_1 is said to be *utility independent* from attribute X_2. A similar reasoning implies that, for every $x_1, z_1 \in X_1, x_2, x'_2, y_2, y'_2 \in X_2$,

$$((x_1, x_2), \tfrac{1}{2}; (x_1, x'_2), \tfrac{1}{2}) \succsim ((x_1, y_2), \tfrac{1}{2}; (x_1, y'_2), \tfrac{1}{2})$$

$$\Updownarrow$$

$$((z_1, x_2), \tfrac{1}{2}; (z_1, x'_2), \tfrac{1}{2}) \succsim ((z_1, y_2), \tfrac{1}{2}; (z_1, y'_2), \tfrac{1}{2}).$$

In this case, attribute X_2 is said to be utility independent from attribute X_1. When X_1 is in addition utility independent from X_2, both attributes are said to satisfy *mutual utility independence*. Note that the independence axiom under certainty (axiom 15.1) is a special case of mutual utility independence in which probability 1/2 is substituted by probability 1.

Under expected utility, utility independence of attribute X_1 from attribute X_2 implies that, for any two $x_2, x_2' \in X_2$, utility functions $u(., x_2)$ and $u(., x_2')$ represent the same preferences over X_1. They are therefore identical up to scale and location. In other words, $u(., x_2) = \alpha u(., x_2') + \beta$, where $\alpha > 0$ and $\beta \in \mathbb{R}$ depend only on the given consequences x_2 and x_2'. Assuming that x_2 varies and that x_2' is fixed at a given level x_2^0, we can state more specifically:

$$\text{for all } (x_1, x_2) \in X_1 \times X_2, \ u(x_1, x_2) = \alpha(x_2) u(x_1, x_2^0) + \beta(x_2) \quad (15.3)$$

where $\alpha(.) > 0$ and $\beta(.) \in \mathbb{R}$ depend implicitly on consequence level x_2^0. Similarly, if attribute X_2 is utility independent from attribute X_1 then, for any consequence level x_1^0, we have that:

$$\text{for all } (x_1, x_2) \in X_1 \times X_2, \ u(x_1, x_2) = \gamma(x_1) u(x_1^0, x_2) + \delta(x_1) \quad (15.4)$$

where $\gamma(.) > 0$ and $\delta(.) \in \mathbb{R}$ depend implicitly on consequence level x_1^0.

Assume now that $u(x_1^0, x_2^0) = 0$. By equations (15.3) and (15.4), $\beta(x_2) = u(x_1^0, x_2)$, $\delta(x_1) = u(x_1, x_2^0)$ and

$$u(x_1, x_2^0)[\alpha(x_2) - 1] = u(x_1^0, x_2)[\gamma(x_1) - 1].$$

This equation obviously holds when $x_1 = x_1^0$ or when $x_2 = x_2^0$. Otherwise, i.e. when both $x_1 \neq x_1^0$ and $x_2 \neq x_2^0$, we obtain the equality:

$$\frac{\alpha(x_2) - 1}{u(x_1^0, x_2)} = \frac{\gamma(x_1) - 1}{u(x_1, x_2^0)} = k$$

where k is a constant which is independent of variables x_1 and x_2. Hence, it can be deduced that $\alpha(x_2) = ku(x_1^0, x_2) + 1$. Substituting into equation (15.3), we obtain:

$$\forall (x_1, x_2) \in X_1 \times X_2, \ u(x_1, x_2) = u(x_1, x_2^0) + u(x_1^0, x_2) + ku(x_1, x_2^0) u(x_1^0, x_2)$$
$$(15.5)$$

where $u(\cdot, x_2^0)$ and $u(x_1^0, \cdot)$ are single-attribute utility functions. Constant k represents a factor of interaction between attributes X_1 and X_2. The sign of this constant identifies explicitly the nature of this interaction [KEE 93, p. 240]. Thus, when $u(\cdot, x_2^0)$ and $u(x_1^0, \cdot)$ are increasing in x_1 and x_2 respectively, a positive (respectively, negative) k means that attributes X_1 and X_2 are complementary (respectively, substitutable).

The following proposition introduces the above multilinear decomposition in a slightly different manner substituting $u(x_1, x_2^0)$ and $u(x_1^0, x_2)$ by $k_1 u_1(x_1)$ and $k_2 u_2(x_2)$, respectively. k_1 and k_2 are *scaling constants* depending implicitly on the consequences used for normalizing functions $u_i(.)$, $i = 1, 2$ [FIS 65, KEE 93].

Proposition 15.5. *Assume that X_1 and X_2 are mutually utility independent. Utility function u can then be decomposed using the following multilinear form:*

$$\forall (x_1, x_2) \in X_1 \times X_2, \ u(x_1, x_2) = k_1 u_1(x_1) + k_2 u_2(x_2) + k k_1 k_2 u_1(x_1) u_2(x_2)$$

where

- *$u_i(.)$ is a single-attribute utility function normalized by $u_i(x_i^0) = 0$ and $u_i(x_i^*) = 1$, $i = 1, 2$, for x_1^* and x_2^* such that $(x_1^*, x_2^0) \succ (x_1^0, x_2^0)$ and $(x_1^0, x_2^*) \succ (x_1^0, x_2^0)$; and*
- *$k_1 = u(x_1^*, x_2^0) > 0$, $k_2 = u(x_1^0, x_2^*) > 0$ and $k_1 + k_2 + k k_1 k_2 = 1$.*

As shown above, mutual utility independence is not sufficient to induce the additive decomposition of u. The latter actually requires in addition that constant k be equal to 0. Let us now see a sufficient condition which, when combined with mutual utility independence, results in the additive decomposability of u. Assume that there *exist* some consequences $x_1, x_1' \in X_1$ and $x_2, x_2' \in X_2$ such that:

$$\left((x_1, x_2), \frac{1}{2}; (x_1', x_2'), \frac{1}{2} \right) \sim \left((x_1, x_2'), \frac{1}{2}; (x_1', x_2), \frac{1}{2} \right). \quad (15.6)$$

Translating this indifference in terms of expected utilities, and canceling out the terms appearing on both sides of the resulting equality, we obtain:

$$k[u(x_1, x_2^0) - u(x_1', x_2^0)][u(x_1^0, x_2) - u(x_1^0, x_2')] = 0.$$

If $\text{Not}[(x_1, x_2^0) \sim (x_1', x_2^0)]$ and $\text{Not}[(x_1^0, x_2) \sim (x_1^0, x_2')]$, then k should be constrained to be equal to 0. When $k \neq 0$, the multilinear decomposition equation (15.5) can be rewritten as:

$$v(x_1, x_2) = v(x_1, x_2^0) v(x_1^0, x_2)$$

where $v(x_1, x_2) = 1 + k u(x_1, x_2)$. This shows that mutual utility independence actually induces a *multiplicative* decomposition of utility function u.

Using scaling constants k_i as in proposition 15.5, this model can also be written as:

$$1 + k u(x_1, x_2) = \prod_{i=1}^{2} [1 + k k_i u_i(x_i)].$$

Now, since scaling constants k_1 and k_2 belong to the unit interval and since $1 + k_1 = \prod_{i=1}^{2}[1 + k k_i]$, constant $k = [1 - (k_1 + k_2)]/k_1 k_2$ lies necessarily between -1 and 0 for $k_1 + k_2 > 1$ and is greater than 0 for $k_1 + k_2 < 1$.

An extension of the cases in which indifference equation (15.6) holds induces a new condition called *additive independence*. This new condition is sufficient to guarantee the additive decomposition of utility function u.

Definition 15.3. Attributes X_1 and X_2 are said to be additively independent if indifference equation (15.6) holds for any consequences $x_1, x'_1 \in X_1$ and $x_2, x'_2 \in X_2$.

Substituting consequence (x'_1, x'_2) by the reference level consequence (x_1^0, x_2^0) in indifference equation (15.6), we obtain the following indifference:

$$\left((x_1, x_2), \frac{1}{2}; (x_1^0, x_2^0), \frac{1}{2}\right) \sim \left((x_1, x_2^0), \frac{1}{2}; (x_1^0, x_2), \frac{1}{2}\right).$$

Set $u(x_1^0, x_2^0) = 0$. The translation of the above indifference in terms of expected utilities then results in the equality:

$$\text{for all } (x_1, x_2) \in X_1 \times X_2, \ u(x_1, x_2) = u(x_1, x_2^0) + u(x_1^0, x_2) \quad (15.7)$$

The following proposition simply rewrites equation (15.7) in a more additive manner by introducing scaling constants.

Proposition 15.6. *Assume that attributes X_1 and X_2 are additively independent. Then utility function u can be written as:*

$$\text{for all } (x_1, x_2) \in X_1 \times X_2, \ u(x_1, x_2) = k_1 u_1(x_1) + k_2 u_2(x_2),$$

where:

- $u_i(.)$ *is a single-attribute utility function normalized by* $u_i(x_i^0) = 0$ *and* $u_i(x_i^*) = 1$, $i = 1, 2$, *for x_1^* and x_2^* such that* $(x_1^*, x_2^0) \succ (x_1^0, x_2^0)$ *and* $(x_1^0, x_2^*) \succ (x_1^0, x_2^0)$.
- $k_1 = u(x_1^*, x_2^0) > 0$, $k_2 = u(x_1^0, x_2^*) > 0$ *and* $k_1 + k_2 = 1$.

As can be seen above, the very fact that in a decision problem the consequences are described by several attributes raises the problem of choosing the appropriate decomposition of the utility function. Most often, the analyst must check with the decision maker whether mutual utility independence holds among the attributes. For this purpose, a simple approach consists of verifying whether the certainty equivalent, with respect to a given attribute X_i of a lottery with two equiprobable consequences having the same value of X_i, depends on the common level assigned to attribute X_i. More precisely, assume that $X_i = [x_i^0, x_i^*]$ for $i = 1, 2$. In order to check whether attribute X_1 is utility independent from attribute X_2, it is sufficient to choose three equidistant levels $\overline{x}_2, \overline{x}'_2, \overline{x}''_2$ in $[x_2^0, x_2^*]$ and to determine the certainty equivalents of lotteries $((x_1^*, a), \frac{1}{2}; (x_1^1, a), \frac{1}{2})$, $a = \overline{x}_2, \overline{x}'_2, \overline{x}''_2$. Identical certainty equivalents (within reasonable error) lead to the assumption that attribute X_1 is actually utility independent from attribute X_2. Utility independence of X_2 with respect to X_1 can be tested using a similar approach in which the roles of both attributes are exchanged.

In situations where it is reasonable to assume that the appropriate model is additively decomposable, it is possible to directly check additive independence. To do so, it is sufficient to fix three or four equidistant consequences in each of the intervals $X_i = [x_i^0, x_i^*]$, $i = 1, 2$, and to check condition (15.6) for the elements of the resulting Cartesian product.

15.4.2. *Extension of the two-dimensional decomposition*

The decompositions of the von Neumann–Morgenstern utility functions with more than two attributes result from quite simple extensions of the concepts and tools developed for the 2D case. We simply need to introduce some convenient notation to address the n-dimensional case.

Let us first recall that, if $J \subset N = \{1, \ldots, n\}$, $x_J y$ represents the consequence in X having coordinates x_j for $j \in J$ and coordinates y_j for $j \in N - J$. Moreover, when $J = \{j\}$, to simplify the notation, we write $x_j y$ instead of $x_J y$. In addition, $x_i x_j y$ means that the ith and jth coordinates of y have been substituted by x_i and x_j, respectively. Finally, x_J denotes the (sub) consequence constituted only by coordinates x_j, with $j \in J$.

Definition 15.4. *The set of attributes X_J, $J \subset N$, is said to be* utility independent *if for all $x, x', y, y', t, z \in X$*

$$(x_J t, \tfrac{1}{2}; y_J t, \tfrac{1}{2}) \succsim (x'_J t, \tfrac{1}{2}; y'_J t, \tfrac{1}{2}) \Leftrightarrow (x_J z, \tfrac{1}{2}; y_J z, \tfrac{1}{2}) \succsim (x'_J z, \tfrac{1}{2}; y'_J z, \tfrac{1}{2}). \quad (15.8)$$

There is mutual utility independence in the attributes of X if X_J is utility independent for every $J \subset N$.

Under certainty, the independence axiom (axiom 15.8) is a particular case of utility independence in which equivalence (15.8) above becomes $x_J t \succsim x'_J t \Leftrightarrow x_J z \succsim x'_J z$. Note that it is easy to show that, when u is additively decomposable, equivalence (15.8) holds for every $J \subset N$.

Under expected utility, for a given J, utility independence of X_J implies that, for any two distinct consequences t and z of X, utility functions $u(., t_{-J})$ and $u(., z_{-J})$ represent the same preferences. As in the two-attribute case, it can be deduced that these utilities are identical up to scale and location. Assuming that t_{-J} varies and that z_{-J} is set to a given reference level x^0_{-J}, we can write:

$$\text{for all } x \in X, \ u(x) = \alpha_J(x_{-J}) u(x_J x^0) + \beta_J(x_{-J})$$

where $\alpha_J(.) > 0$ and $\beta_J(.) \in \mathbb{R}$ depend implicitly on the reference level consequence x^0_{-J}.

In cases where mutual utility independence holds, a similar reasoning to that of the two-attribute case leads to the decomposition:

for all $x \in X$, $u(x) = u(x_1 x^0) + \sum_{j=2}^{n} \prod_{i=1}^{j-1} [ku(x_i x^0) + 1] u(x_j x^0)$ (15.9)

where k is a constant playing a role similar to that in equation (15.5). When this constant is equal to 0, the above equation results in an additive decomposition:

for all $x \in X$, $u(x) = \sum_{j=1}^{n} u(x_j x^0)$.

As in the two-attribute case, when $k \neq 0$ ($\sum_i k_i \neq 1$), equation (15.9) can be rewritten:

$$v(x) = \prod_{j=1}^{n} v(x_j x^0)$$

where $v(x_j y) = 1 + ku(x_j y)$ for every $x_j \in X_j$, $j = 1, \ldots, n$, and $y \in X$. Scaling constants $k_1, \ldots, k_n$ can also be emphasized by substituting $u(x_j x^0)$ by $k_j u_j(x_j)$ for every $j = 1, \ldots, n$. Hence the (equivalent) multiplicative decomposition:

$$ku(x) + 1 = \prod_{j=1}^{n} [kk_j u_j(x_j) + 1] \qquad (15.10)$$

where $u_j(x_j^0) = 0$ and $u_j(x_j^*) = 1$, $j = 1, \ldots, n$.

As an illustration, in the three-attribute case X_1, X_2, X_3, the decomposition of the utility function implied by equation (15.10) reduces to the equality:

$$u(x_1, x_2, x_3) = k_1 u_1(x_1) + k_2 u_2(x_2) + k_3 u_3(x_3) + kk_1 k_2 u_1(x_1) u_2(x_2)$$
$$+ kk_1 k_3 u_1(x_1) u_3(x_3) + kk_2 k_3 u_2(x_2) u_3(x_3)$$
$$+ k^2 k_1 k_2 k_3 u_1(x_1) u_2(x_2) u_3(x_3)$$

where, as in the two-attribute case, u_1, u_2 and u_3 are single-attribute utility functions and $k_1 + k_2 + k_3 + kk_1 k_2 k_3 + k^2 k_1 k_2 k_3 = 1$. When mutual independence is substituted by utility independence of X_J, for $J = \{1\}, \{2\}, \{3\}$, the resulting decomposition of the utility function is much richer. It can actually be shown that coefficient k, which represents the interaction between the attributes, is substituted by some specific interaction coefficients k_{12}, k_{13}, k_{23} and k_{123}:

$$u(x_1, x_2, x_3) = k_1 u_1(x_1) + k_2 u_2(x_2) + k_3 u_3(x_3) + k_{12} k_1 k_2 u_1(x_1) u_2(x_2)$$
$$+ k_{13} k_1 k_3 u_1(x_1) u_3(x_3) + k_{23} k_2 k_3 u_2(x_2) u_3(x_3)$$
$$+ k_{123} k_1 k_2 k_3 u_1(x_1) u_2(x_2) u_3(x_3).$$

The relative complexity of the above decomposition justifies why Keeney and Raiffa [KEE 93, p. 298] and other authors suggest limiting the set of admissible decompositions to the multiplicative and additive forms when $n \geq 4$. The following proposition generalizes proposition 15.5 [FIS 65].

Proposition 15.7. *Assume mutual utility independence. Utility function u can then be decomposed as in equation (15.9).*

When mutual utility independence holds, determining an additive utility function for $m > 2$ attributes requires checking a condition similar to that given by indifference equation (15.6). Indeed, it can be shown that if there exist some consequences $y \in X$, $x_i, x'_i \in X_i$ and $x_j, x'_j \in X_j$ with $i \neq j$ such that:

$$(x_i x_j y, \tfrac{1}{2}; x'_i x'_j y, \tfrac{1}{2}) \sim (x_i x'_j y, \tfrac{1}{2}; x'_i x_j y, \tfrac{1}{2}),$$

utility function u must therefore be additively decomposable [KEE 93].

Without mutual utility independence, the additive decomposability of function u requires a generalization of the additive independence condition introduced for the two-attribute case. Attributes $X_1, \ldots, X_n$ are said to be additively independent if, for any consequences $x, x', y, y' \in X$ and any $J \subset N$,

$$(x_J y, \tfrac{1}{2}; x'_J y', \tfrac{1}{2}) \sim (x_J y', \tfrac{1}{2}; x'_J y, \tfrac{1}{2}).$$

Pollak [POL 67] proposes a slightly different condition which is both necessary and sufficient for the additive decomposability.

As in the case of two-attribute decision problems, choosing between the multiplicative and the additive models for more than two attributes requires checking whether the corresponding conditions are approximately satisfied by the decision maker's preferences. This task is however slightly more complicated as it requests from the decision maker a deeper cognitive effort. Finally, note that Keeney and Raiffa in [KEE 93, p. 292] provide another set of conditions that enable utility independence to be checked while being more economical than those resulting directly from the definition given in this subsection.

15.5. Elicitation of utility functions

The aim of elicitation of multiattribute utility functions is to assign scores or utilities to the possible actions that can be chosen by the decision maker. These scores can then be used to rank the actions from the least desirable to the most desirable, and conversely. However, the very fact that such scores can be constructed from single-attribute utility functions requires some specific independence conditions to hold. In this section, we will only address the problem of eliciting utility functions in the two-attribute case. Similar methods can be used in situations where there are more than two attributes.

15.5.1. *Elicitation under certainty*

Assume that the decision maker faces a decision problem involving two attributes, and that their preferences can be represented by the additive model given by:

$$\text{for all } x, y \in X_1 \times X_2, \ x \succsim y \iff u_1(x_1) + u_2(x_2) \geq u_1(y_1) + u_2(y_2).$$

It is now well known that if there exist some additional functions v_1 and v_2 satisfying the above equivalence in place of u_1 and u_2, respectively, then there exist $\alpha > 0$ and $\beta_1, \beta_2 \in \mathbb{R}$ such that $v_i(.) = \alpha u_i(.) + \beta_i$ for $i = 1, 2$. As a consequence, the origins of u_1 and u_2 (which can be distinct) can be set as we wish, as well as a common unit for the scales of both u_1 and u_2. Assume that x_i^0 denotes the smallest consequence of set X_i, for $i = 1, 2$.

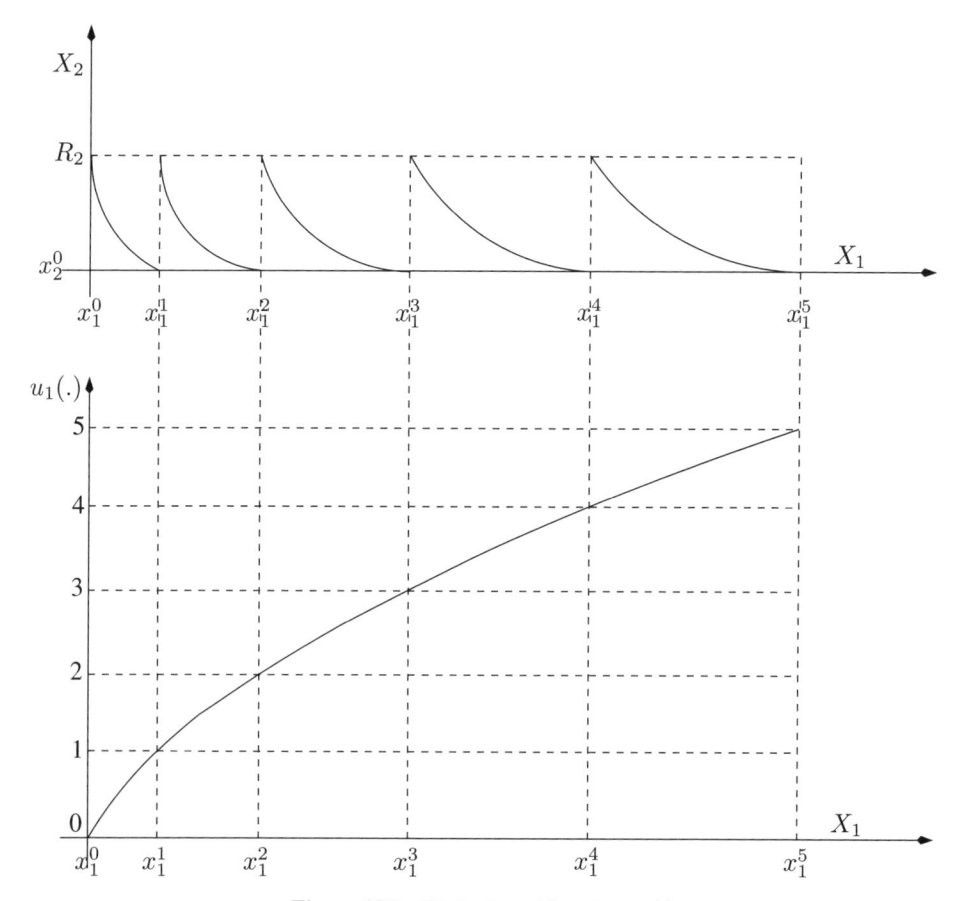

Figure 15.7. *Elicitation of function $u_1(.)$*

The first step in the elicitations of u_1 and u_2 consists of setting the origins of their utility scales as follows:

$$u(x_1^0, x_2^0) = u_1(x_1^0) = u_2(x_2^0) = 0. \tag{15.11}$$

Eliciting single-attribute utility function u_1 now requires a new consequence R_2 to be chosen such that $R_2 \succ x_2^0$ and determining consequence x_1^1 such that:

$$(x_1^1, x_2^0) \sim (x_1^0, R_2). \tag{15.12}$$

Intuitively, the closer to x_2^0 (in terms of preferences) the consequence R_2, the closer to x_1^0 the consequence x_1^1. The next step in the elicitation of u_1 consists of determining a new consequence x_1^2 such that:

$$(x_1^2, x_2^0) \sim (x_1^1, R_2). \tag{15.13}$$

Translating indifference equations (15.12) and (15.13) into the additive utilities model and subtracting the resulting equations leads to the equality:

$$u_1(x_1^1) - u_1(x_1^0) = u_1(x_1^2) - u_1(x_1^1). \tag{15.14}$$

To summarize, the elicitation of u_1 amounts to constructing a standard sequence of consequences $x_1^0, x_1^1, \ldots, x_1^{s_1}$ which 'covers' X_1 using indifferences:

$$(x_1^i, x_2^0) \sim (x_1^{i-1}, R_2), \; i = 1, \ldots, s^1.$$

Finally, setting $u_1(x_1^1) = 1$, we obtain $u_1(x_1^i) = i$, $i = 2, \ldots, s^1$. Figure 15.7 illustrates the elicitation process described.

Similarly, eliciting function u_2 begins by choosing a consequence R_1 such that $R_1 \succ x_1^0$ and determining consequence x_2^1 such that:

$$(x_1^0, x_2^1) \sim (R_1, x_2^0). \tag{15.15}$$

After the construction of the initial indifference equation (15.15), the elicitation process continues with the construction of a standard sequence of consequences $x_2^0, x_2^1, \ldots, x_2^{s_2}$ 'covering' X_2 and determined using the indifferences:

$$(x_1^0, x_2^i) \sim (R_1, x_2^{i-1}), \; i = 1, \ldots, s^2.$$

Figure 15.8 graphically illustrates the process.

By indifference equations (15.12) and (15.15), choosing $R_1 = x_1^1$ leads necessarily to $R_2 = x_2^1$. This choice therefore results in $u_2(x_2^i) = i$, $i = 1, \ldots, s^2$.

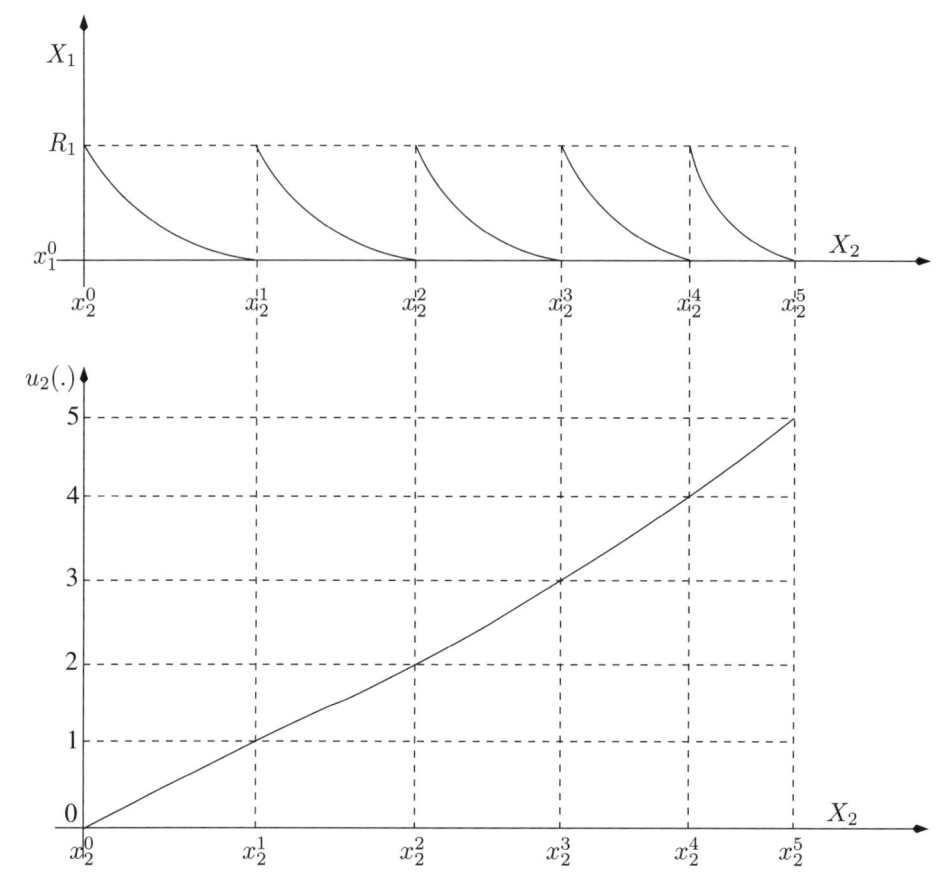

Figure 15.8. *Elicitation of function* $u_2(.)$

The value chosen for R_1 can also be different from x_1^1. This results inevitably in $x_2^1 \neq R_2$. In this case, the additive model:

$$\text{for all } x \in X_1 \times X_2, \ u(x_1, x_2) = k_1 u_1(x_1) + k_2 u_2(x_2) \tag{15.16}$$

is to be used, where $k_1 > 0$ and $k_2 > 0$ are *scaling constants* such that $k_1 + k_2 = 1$. These constants introduce an additional degree of freedom that allows us to assign to u_2 a utility unit independent from that resulting from $u_1(x_1^1) = 1$ and, therefore, to set $u_2(x_2^1) = 1$. Determining the scaling constants requires the use of (or construction of) an additional indifference. Thus, translating indifference equation (15.15) in terms of the model described in equation (15.16) results in the equality:

$$\frac{k_2}{k_1} = \frac{u_1(R_1) - u_1(x_1^0)}{u_2(x_2^1) - u_2(x_2^0)} = u_1(R_1).$$

Knowing $u_1(R_1)$ and $k_1 + k_2 = 1$, scaling constants can therefore be determined. These allow the utility scales of both u_1 and u_2 to be linked appropriately.

15.5.2. *Elicitation under uncertainty*

The essential hypothesis underlying the expected utility-based decision model is that the decision maker's preferences are sufficiently stable that they can be observed through very simple risky choices. These preferences are revealed through their utility function by the analyst. The latter can then use them to infer the decision maker's preferences over the set of all the possibles actions. Being able to perform this inference is essential: if we are unable to elicit the appropriate utility function, it may happen that we propose to the decision maker some ranking of the possible actions that is utterly unrelated to their own preferences.

In the rest of this section, we assume that $X_i = [x_i^0, x_i^*]$ for $i = 1, \ldots, n$. In addition, all the utility functions are considered to be normalized as follows: $u_i(x_i^0) = 0$ and $u_i(x_i^*) = 1$, $i = 1, \ldots, n$. Of course, these normalizations require some scaling constants, as in the certain case.

The most popular method for eliciting single-attribute utility functions is called the *fractile method*. The key idea is to choose a probability p, called a reference probability, and to ask the decision maker to state for which consequence x_i^1 in the interval $[x_i^0, x_i^*]$ they are indifferent. The choice is between x_i^1 with certainty (hence a degenerated lottery) and lottery $(x_i^*, p; x_i^0, 1-p)$, denoted from this point on by $(x_i^*, p; x_i^0)$.

Using the expected utility criterion, we immediately obtain $u_i(x_i^1) = p$. Applying a similar process to intervals $[x_i^0, x_i^1]$ and $[x_i^1, x_i^*]$, two other points of the utility function can be obtained: indifference $x_i^2 \sim (x_i^1, p; x_i^0)$ implies that $u_i(x_i^2) = p^2$ and indifference $x_i'^2 \sim (x_i^*, p; x_i^1)$ implies that $u_i(x_i'^2) = 2p-p^2$. Iterating this process, we obtain as many points $(x_i^j, u_i(x_i^j))$ as needed for determining utility function u_i over interval $[x_i^0, x_i^*]$. Figure 15.9 represents one such iterative utility construction process with reference probability $p = 1/2$ ($E_1 = px_i^* + (1-p)x_i^0$, $E_2' = px_i^* + (1-p)x_i^1$, $E_2 = px_i^1 + (1-p)x_i^0$).

The increasing number of experimental results against expected utility has attracted the attention of many researchers interested in applications of this theory in decision aid. MacCord and de Neufville [MCC 83] demonstrated that there was a direct connection between violations of expected utility and the systematic inconsistencies observed during the elicitation process of the single-attribute utility functions as early as the 1980s. Among these inconsistencies, it was observed that there exists a systematic dependence between the utility functions and the reference

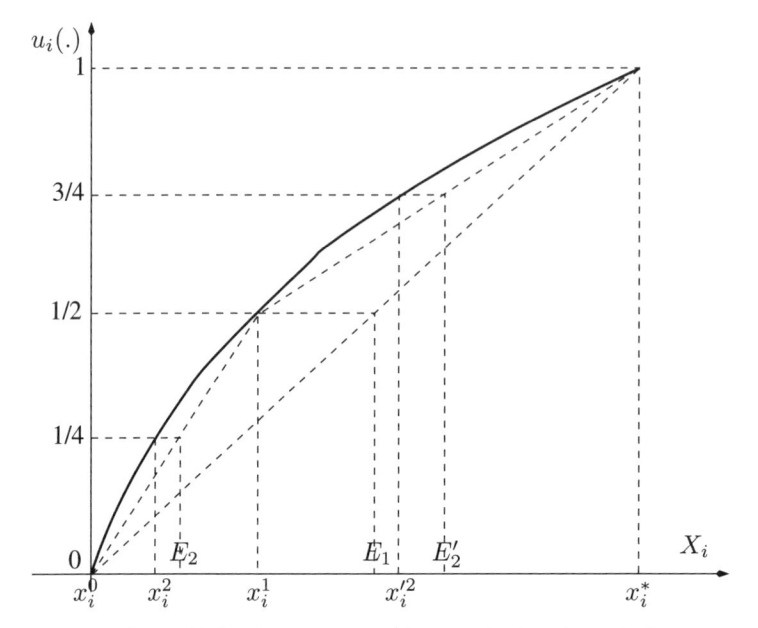

Figure 15.9. *Elicitation of $u_i(.)$ using the fractile method*

probabilities used for their elicitation. The higher this probability, the more concave the utility function elicited.

Numerous experimental results, dating back to the end of the 1940s [PRE 48], show a systematic trend from the decision makers facing simple risky choices to subjectively transform probabilities. Nowadays, this phenomenon is taken into account in many models of decision making under risk using a probability transformation function (*weighting*) in addition to the utility function (which actually can be thought of as a consequence transformation function). In both rank dependent utility models [QUI 82, TVE 92] and in Gul's model [GUL 91], lottery $P = (x, p; y)$ with $x \succ y$ is therefore evaluated by the utility defined:

$$V(P) = w(p)u(x) + (1 - w(p))u(y) \tag{15.17}$$

where probability weighting function w is an increasing function from $[0, 1]$ into $[0, 1]$, with $w(0) = 0$ and $w(1) = 1$. When $w(p) = p$ for every $p \in [0, 1]$, we obtain $V(P) = E(u, P)$. As compared with the expected utility model, in this new model probabilities p and $1 - p$ are substituted by *decision weights* $w(p)$ and $(1 - w(p))$, respectively. Knowing that $x \succ y$, it can easily be seen that the weight assigned to a given consequence actually depends on its rank.

Note however that rank dependent utility model (15.17) cannot be used to elicit function u using the fractile method or a similar method without prior knowledge of transformation function w. Only the tradeoff (TO) method, initially proposed by Wakker and Deneffe [WAK 96], can avoid this problem.

Eliciting a utility function by the tradeoff method TO essentially consists of constructing a standard sequence of consequences. A standard sequence of positive monetary consequences (gains) is usually constructed as follows. The process starts by the determination of consequence x_1 for which the decision maker is indifferent between lotteries $(x_0, p; R)$ and $(x_1, p; r)$, with $0 \leq r < R < x_0 < x_1$ and $p \in]0, 1[$, r, R, x_0 being fixed beforehand. As shown in Figure 15.10, the gain induced by substituting x_0 by x_1 on the p axis outweights the loss induced by substituting consequence R by r on the $(1-p)$ axis.

Next, consequence x_i^2 is determined such that the decision maker is indifferent between $(x_i^1, p; R)$ and $(x_i^2, p; r)$. Using general model (15.17), both indifferences constructed induce the equations:

$$w(p)u_i(x_i^0) + (1-w(p))u_i(R) = w(p)u_i(x_i^1) + (1-w(p))u_i(r) \qquad (15.18)$$

$$w(p)u_i(x_i^1) + (1-w(p))u_i(R) = w(p)u_i(x_i^2) + (1-w(p))u_i(r). \qquad (15.19)$$

Combining these equations and canceling out terms appearing on both sides of the equalities, we obtain the equality:

$$u_i(x_i^1) - u_i(x_i^0) = u_i(x_i^2) - u_i(x_i^1). \qquad (15.20)$$

It results from equation (15.20) that consequence x_i^1 is exactly halfway in terms of utilities between consequences x_i^0 and x_i^2. Consequences x_i^0, x_i^1, x_i^2 therefore build up a standard sequence. This conclusion clearly also holds under the expected utility hypothesis. Constructing a standard sequence of consequences $x_i^0, \ldots, x_i^q$ therefore requires the construction of q indifferences $(x_i^{j-1}, p; R) \sim (x_i^j, p; r)$, $j = 1, \ldots, q$. Setting $u_i(x_i^0) = 0$ and $u_i(x_i^q) = 1$, we obtain $u_i(x_i^j) = j/q$, $j = 1, \ldots, q$.

Miyamoto and Wakker [MIY 96] show that the propositions that enable the decomposition of the von Neumann–Morgenstern utilities still hold even when probabilities are subjectively transformed. This justifies the combination of the new TO utility elicitation method with some classical techniques used for eliciting scaling constants.

Determining scaling constants can be performed in two different ways, often used in combination by the analysts. These two methods can be easily illustrated in the 2D multiattribute case ($n = 2$). Assume that mutual utility independence holds. According to the preceding discussion, we then obtain:

$$U(x_1, x_2) = k_1 u_1(x_1) + k_2 u_2(x_2) + k k_1 k_2 u_1(x_1) u_2(x_2)$$

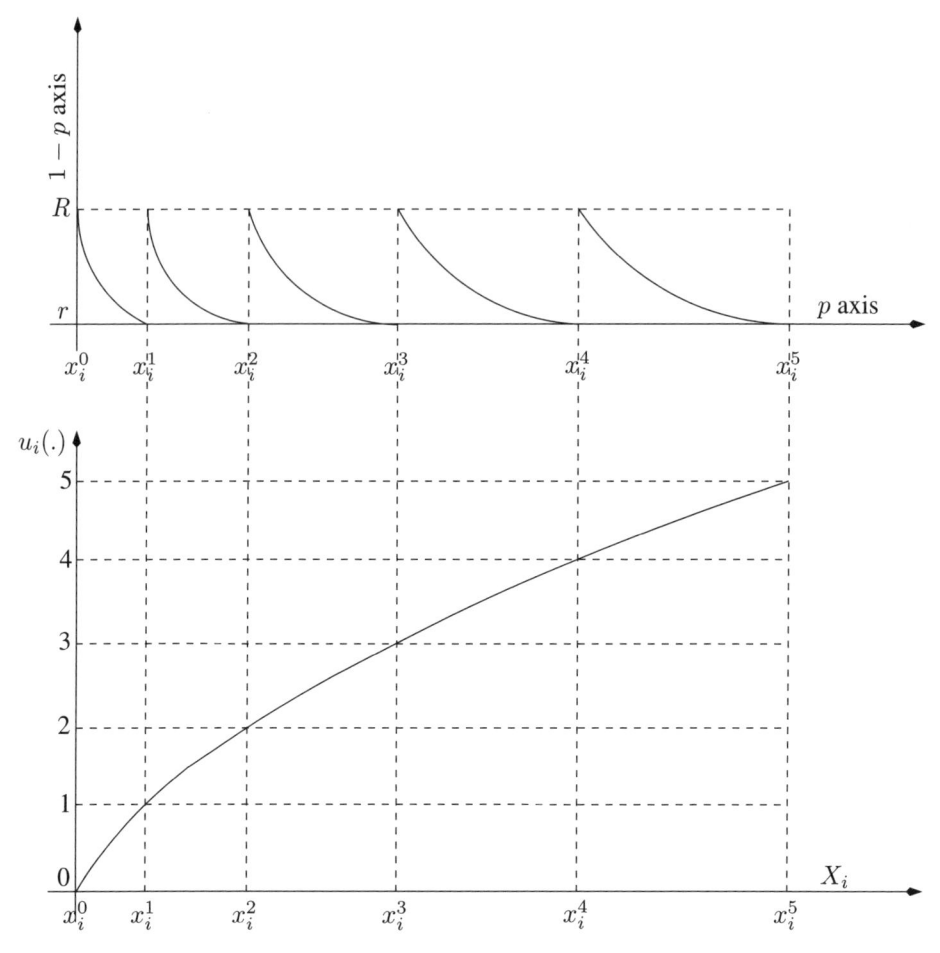

Figure 15.10. *Elicitation of function $u_i(.)$*

with $X_i = [x_i^0, x_i^*]$, $u_i(x_i^0) = 0$, $u_i(x_i^*) = 1$ for $i = 1, 2$ and $k_1 + k_2 + k k_1 k_2 = 1$. Constant k can be interpreted as an interaction factor among attributes X_1 and X_2.

Indeed, three scaling constants require three equations to be unambiguously determined. As we already know that $k_1 + k_2 + k k_1 k_2 = 1$, we just need two additional independent equations and therefore two additional indifferences under certainty and/or uncertainty.

Assume that $(x_1^0, x_2^*) \succ (x_1^*, x_2^0)$, i.e. that $k_2 > k_1$. By monotonicity, $(x_1^0, x_2^0) \prec (x_1^*, x_2^0)$. It is therefore possible to find a consequence $x_2^\downarrow (< x_2^*)$ such that $(x_1^0, x_2^\downarrow) \sim$

(x_1^*, x_2^0). Translating into the above multilinear form, we obtain:

$$k_2 u_2(x_2^\downarrow) = k_1. \qquad (15.21)$$

A second equation, independent from the first, can be obtained by substituting x_2^0 (in $(x_1^0, x_2^*) \succ (x_1^*, x_2^0)$) by $x_2^\uparrow$ ($> x_2^0$) such that $(x_1^0, x_2^*) \sim (x_1^*, x_2^\uparrow)$. In general, this results in the equation:

$$k_2 = k_1 + k_2 u_2(x_2^\uparrow) + k k_1 k_2 u_2(x_2^\uparrow). \qquad (15.22)$$

Combined with equality $k_1 + k_2 + k k_1 k_2 = 1$, the last two equations enable the determination of the scaling constants.

In the uncertain case, k_1 and k_2 can also be determined by finding probabilities p_1 and p_2 such that:

$$(x_1^*, x_2^0) \sim ((x_1^*, x_2^*), p_1; (x_1^0, x_2^0), 1 - p_1),$$
$$(x_1^0, x_2^*) \sim ((x_1^*, x_2^*), p_2; (x_1^0, x_2^0), 1 - p_2).$$

Translating these indifferences in terms of expected utilities, we obtain:

$$k_i = p_i, i = 1, 2. \qquad (15.23)$$

When probabilities are subjectively transformed, we obtain $k_i = w(p_i)$, which requires the additional elicitation of function w [ABD 00].

When there are more than two attributes in the decision problem, the necessity of having independent and compatible equations for evaluating the scaling constants makes their determination all the more complicated. Keeney and Raiffa [KEE 93, p. 301] describe for the additive and multiplicative models several procedures avoiding both redundancy and incompatibilities (of these equations).

15.6. Conclusion

The overview of multiattribute utility theory presented in this chapter is an introduction to a literature with a profusion of results covering a wide domain. We have attempted to present it in the most homogenous way possible. We suggest that readers interested in applications of the various techniques described in the chapter read [KEE 93, Chapters 7 and 8] and [CLE 96, Chapters 15 and 16]. [VON 93, Chapter 12] also contains some valuable material.

15.7. Bibliography

[ABD 00] ABDELLAOUI M., "Parameter-free elicitation of utilities and probability weighting functions", *Management Science*, vol. 46, p. 1497–1512, 2000.

[AND 86] ANDERSEN S. K., ANDREASSEN S., WOLDBYE M., "Knowledge representation for diagnosis and test planning in the domain of electromyography", *Proceedings of the 7th European Conference on Artificial Intelligence*, Brighton, p. 357–368, 1986.

[BEL 87] BELL D. E., "Multilinear representations for ordinal utility functions", *Journal of Mathematical Psychology*, vol. 31, p. 44–59, 1987.

[BOU 02] BOUYSSOU D., PIRLOT M., "Non-transitive decomposable conjoint measurement", *Journal of Mathematical Psychology*, vol. 46, p. 677–703, 2002.

[BOU 04] BOUYSSOU D., PIRLOT M., "'Additive difference' models without additivity or subtractivity", *Journal of Mathematical Psychology*, vol. 48, num. 4, p. 263–291, 2004.

[CHA 93] CHATEAUNEUF A., WAKKER P. P., "From local to global additive representation", *Journal of Mathematical Economics*, vol. 22, p. 523–545, 1993.

[CLE 96] CLEMEN R. T., *Making Hard Decisions: An Introduction to Decision Analysis*, Duxbury, Belmont, CA, 2nd edition, 1996.

[DEB 54] DEBREU G., "Representation of a preference ordering by a numerical function", THRALL R., COOMBS C. H., DAVIES R., Eds., *Decision Processes*, New York, Wiley, p. 159–175, 1954.

[DEB 60] DEBREU G., "Topological methods in cardinal utility theory", ARROW K. J., KARLIN S., SUPPES P., Eds., *Mathematical Methods in the Social Sciences*, p. 16–26, Stanford University Press, 1960.

[EDW 71] EDWARDS W., "Social utilities", *Engeenering Economist, Summer Symposium Series*, vol. 6, p. 119–129, 1971.

[FAR 81] FARQUHAR P. H., "Multivalent preference structures", *Mathematical Social Sciences*, vol. 1, p. 397–408, 1981.

[FIS 65] FISHBURN P. C., "Independence in utility theory with whole product sets", *Operations Research*, vol. 13, p. 28–45, 1965.

[FIS 70] FISHBURN P. C., *Utility Theory for Decision Making*, Wiley, New York, 1970.

[FIS 75] FISHBURN P. C., "Non-decomposable Conjoint Measurement for Bisymmetric Structures", *Journal of Mathematical Psychology*, vol. 12, p. 75–89, 1975.

[FIS 91] FISHBURN P. C., "Non-transitive additive conjoint measurement", *Journal of Mathematical Psychology*, vol. 35, num. 1, p. 1–40, 1991.

[FIS 92] FISHBURN P. C., "Additive differences and simple preference comparisons", *Journal of Mathematical Psychology*, vol. 36, p. 21–31, 1992.

[FUH 91] FUHRKEN G., RICHTER M. K., "Additive utility", *Economic Theory*, vol. 1, p. 83–105, 1991.

[GON 00] GONZALES C., "Two factor additive conjoint measurement with one solvable component", *Journal of Mathematical Psychology*, vol. 44, num. 2, p. 285–309, 2000.

[GON 03] GONZALES C., "Additive utility without restricted solvability on every component", *Journal of Mathematical Psychology*, vol. 47, num. 1, p. 47–65, 2003.

[GUL 91] GUL F., "A theory of disappointment aversion", *Econometrica*, vol. 59, num. 3, p. 667–686, 1991.

[KEE 68] KEENEY R. L., "Quasi-separable utility functions", *Naval Research Logistics Quarterly*, vol. 15, p. 551–565, 1968.

[KEE 93] KEENEY R. L., RAIFFA H., *Decisions with Multiple Objectives: Preferences and Value Tradeoffs*, Cambridge University Press, Cambridge, UK, 1993.

[KRA 71] KRANTZ D. H., LUCE R. D., SUPPES P., TVERSKY A., *Foundations of Measurement (Additive and Polynomial Representations)*, vol. 1, Academic Press, New York, 1971.

[LUC 64] LUCE R. D., TUKEY J. W., "Simultaneous conjoint measurement: A new type of fundamental measurement", *Journal of Mathematical Psychology*, vol. 1, p. 1–27, 1964.

[MCC 83] MCCORD M. R., DE NEUFVILLE R., "Fundamental deficiency of expected utility decision analysis", FRENCH S., HARTLEY R., THOMAS L C WHITE D. J., Eds., *Multi-Objective Decision Making*, p. 279–305, Academic Press, New York, 1983.

[MIY 96] MIYAMOTO J., WAKKER P. P., "Multiattribute utility theory without expected utility foundations", *Operations Research*, vol. 44, num. 2, p. 313–326, 1996.

[NAK 90] NAKAMURA Y., "Bilinear utility and a threshold structure for nontransitive preferences", *Mathematical Social Sciences*, vol. 19, p. 1–21, 1990.

[NAK 02] NAKAMURA Y., "Additive utilities on densely ordered sets", *Journal of Mathematical Psychology*, vol. 46, num. 5, p. 515–530, 2002.

[POL 67] POLLAK R. A., "Additive von Neumann-Morgenstern utility functions", *Econometrica*, vol. 35, p. 485–494, 1967.

[PRE 48] PRESTON M. G., BARATTA P., "An experimental study of the auction value of an uncertain outcome", *American Journal of Psychology*, vol. 61, p. 183–193, 1948.

[QUI 82] QUIGGIN J., "A theory of anticipated utility", *Journal of Economic Behavior and Organization*, vol. 3, p. 332–343, 1982.

[RAI 69] RAIFFA H., Preferences for Multi-attributed Alternatives, Report num. RM-58-68-DOT/RC, The Rand Corporation, Santa Monica, California, 1969.

[SAV 54] SAVAGE L. J., *The Foundations of Statistics*, Dover, New York, 1954.

[SEG 94] SEGAL U., "A Sufficient Condition for Additively Separable Functions", *Journal of Mathematical Economics*, vol. 23, p. 295–303, 1994.

[TVE 69] TVERSKY A., "Intransitivity of preferences", *Psychological Review*, vol. 76, p. 31–48, 1969.

[TVE 92] TVERSKY A., KAHNEMAN D., "Advances in prospect theory: Cumulative representation of uncertainty", *Journal of Risk and Uncertainty*, vol. 5, p. 297–323, 1992.

[VON 44] VON NEUMANN J., MORGENSTERN O., *Theory of Games and Economic Behaviour*, Princetown University Press, Princetown, New Jersey, 1944.

[VON 93] VON WINTERFELDT D., EDWARDS W., *Decision Analysis and Behavioral Research*, Cambridge University Press, Cambridge, UK, 1993.

[WAK 89] WAKKER P. P., *Additive Representations of Preferences: A New Foundation of Decision Analysis*, Kluwer Academic Publishers, Dordrecht, 1989.

[WAK 91] WAKKER P. P., "Additive representations on rank-ordered sets. I. The Algebraic Approach", *Journal of Mathematical Psychology*, vol. 35, p. 501–531, 1991.

[WAK 93] WAKKER P. P., "Additive representations on rank-ordered sets. II. The Topological Approach", *Journal of Mathematical Economics*, vol. 22, p. 1–26, 1993.

[WAK 96] WAKKER P. P., DENEFFE D., "Eliciting von Neumann-Morgenstern utilities when probabilities are distorted or unknown", *Management Science*, vol. 42, p. 1131–1150, 1996.

Chapter 16

Conjoint Measurement Models for Preference Relations

16.1. Introduction

Conjoint measurement [KRA 71, WAK 89] is concerned with the study of binary relations defined on Cartesian products of sets. Such relations are central in many disciplines, for example:

– multicriteria or multiattribute decision making, in which the preference of the decision maker is a relation that encodes, for each pair of alternatives, the preferred option taking into account all criteria [BEL 01, KEE 76, WIN 86];

– decision under uncertainty, where the preference relation compares alternatives evaluated on several states of nature [FIS 88, GUL 92, SHA 79, WAK 84, WAK 89];

– consumer theory, dealing with preference relations that compare bundles of goods [DEB 59];

– inter-temporal decision making, that uses preference relations for comparing alternatives evaluated at various instants in time [KOO 60, KOO 72, KEE 76]; and

– inequality measurement, that compares distributions of wealth across individuals [ATK 70, BEN 94, BEN 97].

Let $\succsim$ denote a binary relation on a product set $X = X_1 \times X_2 \times \cdots \times X_n$. Conjoint measurement searches for conditions that allow numerical representations of $\succsim$ to be built and possibly guarantee the uniqueness of such representations. The interest of numerical representations is obvious. They not only facilitate the manipulation

---

Chapter written by Denis BOUYSSOU and Marc PIRLOT.

of preference relations but also, in many cases, the proofs that such representations exist are constructive (or at least provide useful indications on how to build them). Very often, the conditions for the existence of a representation can be empirically tested [KRA 71]. All these reasons justify the interest for this theory in many research domains.

16.1.1. *Brief overview of conjoint measurement models*

In most classical models of conjoint measurement, the relation is assumed to be *complete* and *transitive*. The central model is the *additive utility* model in which we have:

$$x \succsim y \Leftrightarrow \sum_{i=1}^{n} u_i(x_i) \geq \sum_{i=1}^{n} u_i(y_i), \qquad (16.1)$$

where u_i denotes a real-valued function defined on the set X_i, for all $i = 1, \ldots, n$. x and y denote n-dimensional elements of the product set X i.e. $x = (x_1, \ldots, x_n)$ and $y = (y_1, \ldots, y_n)$.

The axiomatic analysis of this model is now well established and additive utility (also called additive value function) is at the root of many techniques used in decision analysis [FRE 93, KEE 76, WIN 86, WAK 89, POM 00].

This model has two main difficulties, however. The axiomatic analysis of equation (16.1) raises technical questions that are rather subtle yet important. Many systems of axioms have been proposed in order to guarantee the existence of a representation as described by equation (16.1) [KRA 71, WAK 89]. Two cases can be distinguished:

– If X is finite and no upper bound is fixed *a priori* on the number of its elements, Scott and Suppes [SCO 64] have shown that the system of axioms needed consists of an infinite (countable) set of *cancellation* conditions, which guarantee (via the use of the theorem of the alternative) that a system of (finitely many) linear equations possesses at least one solution (see also [KRA 71, Chapter 9] and, for more recent contributions, [FIS 96, FIS 97]). These conditions are hardly interpretable or testable.

– The case in which X is infinite is quite different but raises other problems. Non-necessary conditions are usually imposed on X in order to guarantee that the structure of X is 'close' to that of the real numbers and that $\succsim$ behaves consistently with this structure. In one approach, an archimedean axiom is imposed together with solvability conditions [KRA 71, Chapter 6]. In another approach, it is assumed that X is a topological space and that $\succsim$ is continuous [DEB 60, WAK 89]. Using such 'structural' assumptions, it is possible to characterize model equation (16.1) by means of a finite number of cancellation conditions (for recent contributions see [GON 96, GON 00, KAR 98]; for an alternative approach extending the technique used in the finite case to the infinite case, see [JAF 74]). In these axiomatic systems, the necessary properties interact with structural, unnecessary assumptions imposed on X [KRA 71, Chapter 6], which obscures the understanding of the model and does not allow for completely satisfactory empirical tests [KRA 71, Chapter 9]. In addition, the analysis of the two-dimensional case ($n = 2$) differs totally from that of the cases where n is greater than or equal to 3.

As we shall see, it is possible to avoid imposing unnecessary hypotheses (structural assumptions) provided the requirement of an additive representation is abandoned; this is the idea followed by the authors of [KRA 71, Chapter 7] when introducing the following *decomposable* model:

$$x \succsim y \Leftrightarrow U(u_1(x_1), u_2(x_2), \ldots, u_n(x_n)) \geq U(u_1(y_1), u_2(y_2), \ldots, u_n(y_n)) \quad (16.2)$$

where U is an increasing function of all its arguments.

There is another type of difficulty with the additive model (16.1) of a more fundamental nature: this model excludes all preference relations that fail to be transitive or complete from consideration. Several authors have now forcefully argued in favor of models tolerating intransitive or incomplete preferences [MAY 54, TVE 69] and there are multiple criteria decision analysis methods that do not exclude such relations [ROY 85, ROY 93].

The *additive difference* model proposed in [TVE 69] is among the first that does not assume transitive preferences; the preference $\succsim$ is supposed to satisfy:

$$x \succsim y \Leftrightarrow \sum_{i=1}^{n} \Phi_i(u_i(x_i) - u_i(y_i)) \geq 0 \quad (16.3)$$

where Φ_i are increasing and odd functions (which implies that the preference $\succsim$ is complete). An axiomatic characterization of this model has been proposed by Fishburn [FIS 92]. Due to the additive form of the representation, Fishburn could not avoid imposing unnecessary structural conditions in his characterization of model (16.3).

More recently, more general additive non-transitive models have been proposed (allowing in particular for incomplete preferences) [BOU 86, FIS 90a, FIS 90b, FIS 91, FIS 92, VIN 91]. They are of the type:

$$x \succsim y \Leftrightarrow \sum_{i=1}^{n} p_i(x_i, y_i) \geq 0 \quad (16.4)$$

where p_i are real-valued functions defined on X_i^2; they may enjoy additional properties (e.g. $p_i(x_i, x_i) = 0 \; \forall i \in \{1, 2, \ldots, n\}$ and for all $x_i \in X_i$).

In the spirit of decomposable model (16.2) that avoids the difficulties of the axiomatization of the additive models, Goldstein [GOL 91] has proposed a generalization of model (16.4) in which the sum has been substituted by a function G, increasing in its arguments. The underlying model is therefore:

$$x \succsim y \Leftrightarrow G(p_1(x_1, y_1), p_2(x_2, y_2), \ldots, p_n(x_n, y_n)) \geq 0. \quad (16.5)$$

In decision analysis, methods that may lead to intransitive and/or incomplete preference relations have been used for a long time [ROY 68, ROY 73]. They are known as *outranking* methods [ROY 91, ROY 93], and are inspired by social choice procedures, especially the Condorcet voting rule. In a basic version of the ELECTRE method [ROY 68, ROY 73], the outranking relation is obtained as follows:

$$x \succsim y \Leftrightarrow \sum_{\{i : x_i S_i y_i\}} w_i \geq \lambda \quad (16.6)$$

where w_i are weights associated with the criteria, x_i and y_i represent the performance of alternatives x and y on criterion i, S_i is a binary relation that orders the levels on the scale of criterion i and λ is a majority threshold (called *concordance threshold*), generally assigned a value larger than 50% of the sum of the weights. Clearly, binary relations obtained in this way may fail to be transitive or complete. Consider for instance the case where $n = 3$, $p_1 = p_2 = p_3 = \frac{1}{3}$, $x = (3, 2, 1)$, $y = (2, 1, 3)$, $z = (1, 3, 2)$, S_i is the usual order $\geq$ on the set of the real numbers and $\lambda = 60\%$. Denoting by $\succ$ the asymmetric part of $\succsim$ ($a \succ b$ if $a \succsim b$ and not $b \succsim a$) and applying rule (16.6) yields $x \succ y$, $y \succ z$, but not $x \succ z$: i.e. relation $\succ$ is not transitive. Moreover, since $z \succ x$, it has cycles. This is a version of the Condorcet paradox, appearing in a multiple criteria decision making context. In the same perspective, considering $n = 2$, $p_1 = p_2 = \frac{1}{2}$, $x = (2, 1)$, $y = (1, 2)$ and $\lambda = 60\%$, we have that neither $x \succsim y$ nor $y \succsim x$: the relation $\succsim$ is not complete.

As is easily verified, note that outranking relations obtained through equation (16.6) are representable in the additive non-transitive model (16.4), letting:

$$p_i(x_i, y_i) = \begin{cases} w_i - \frac{\lambda}{n} & \text{if } x_i S_i y_i \\ -\frac{\lambda}{n} & \text{otherwise.} \end{cases} \quad (16.7)$$

16.1.2. *Chapter contents*

Our goal is to propose a general framework as well as quite general analytical tools that allow the study of binary relations defined on a Cartesian product in a conjoint measurement perspective. Our framework encompasses most methods that have been proposed in multiple criteria decision analysis to construct a global preference relation.

We consider two main families of models of relations on a product set. To support the reader's intuition, consider the various manners of comparing objects characterized by their description on a set of n attributes. Let $x = (x_1, x_2, \ldots, x_n)$ and $y = (y_1, y_2, \ldots, y_n)$ be two alternatives described by n-dimensional vectors. In a first approach, in view of deciding whether 'x is at least as good as y', we may try to assess the 'value' of either alternative on each attribute and then combine these values in appropriate fashion. It is important to emphasize what we mean by 'value'; the 'value' of alternative x on criterion i is not simply the label describing this alternative on attribute i (which is denoted by x_i) but an assessment that reflects the way this label is perceived by a decision maker in a given decisional context, taking into account their objectives and preferences. Abandoning for the moment classical requirements such as transitivity or completeness, we may consider a model in which:

$$x \succsim y \Leftrightarrow F(u_1(x_1), u_2(x_2), \ldots, u_n(x_n), u_1(y_1), u_2(y_2), \ldots, u_n(y_n)) \geq 0, \quad (16.8)$$

where u_i are real-valued functions on X_i and F is a real-valued function on the product set $\prod_{i=1}^{n} u_i(X_i)^2$.

Another strategy relies on the idea of 'measuring' *differences of preference* between x and y on each attribute separately and then combining these differences in order to determine whether the balance of these is in favor of x or y. This suggests a model in which:

$$x \succsim y \Leftrightarrow G(p_1(x_1, y_1), p_2(x_2, y_2), \ldots, p_n(x_n, y_n)) \geq 0 \quad (16.9)$$

where p_i are real-valued functions on X_i^2 and G is a real-valued function on $\prod_{i=1}^{n} p_i(X_i^2)$.

Of course, the strategies just outlined are not incompatible. It can reasonably be expected that the differences of preference on each criterion can be expressed in terms of values assigned to the alternatives on each criterion. In the model that this suggests, we have:

$$x \succsim y \Leftrightarrow H(\varphi_1(u_1(x_1), u_1(y_1)), \varphi_2(u_2(x_2), u_2(y_2)), \ldots, \varphi_n(u_n(x_n), u_n(y_n))) \geq 0$$
$$(16.10)$$

where u_i are real-valued functions on X_i, φ_i are real-valued functions on $u_i(X_i)^2$ and H is a real-valued function on $\prod_{i=1}^{n} \varphi_i(u_i(X_i)^2)$.

As long as no additional property is imposed to the various functions that intervene in the above three models, these models are exceedingly general in the sense that any relation on X (provided that X is finite or denumerable) can be represented in all three models. If X is not denumerable, the generality of the models is only restricted by technical conditions (that are necessary and sufficient).

Consequently, to make these models interesting, we shall impose additional properties on the involved functions. For instance:

– in model (16.8), we shall lay down that F is non-decreasing in its first n arguments and non-increasing in its last n arguments;

– in model (16.9), we shall require that G is an odd function or that it is non-decreasing in its n arguments or that p_i is antisymmetric;

– in model (16.10), we shall consider the cases in which H is an odd function or is non-decreasing in its n arguments or the cases in which φ_i are odd functions or functions that are non-decreasing in their first argument and non-increasing in their second argument.

By adding such requirements, a large variety of models can be defined. A selection of them will be studied in the sequel. In particular, certain variants are rather close to classical models alluded to in section 16.1.1. Note, however, that our goal is not to characterize exactly classical models but instead to establish general frameworks in which such a characterization could be elaborated. The advantage of general frameworks is to allow for a better understanding of what is common to classical models and what distinguishes them.

Note that the frameworks (16.8), (16.9) and (16.10) rely on fundamental objects that possess nice interpretations in terms of preference and permit the analysis of preference relations on a product set. For understanding of the classical additive value function model, *marginal preference* is the crucial notion. This relation, defined on each factor X_i of the product set X as a projection (in a certain sense) of the global preference $\succsim$ on each attribute, is the relation that is numerically represented by the u_i functions in model (16.1). The process of 'elicitation' of an additive value function model, relies in an essential manner on marginal preferences.

In models (16.8) and (16.9), the central role is no longer played by marginal preferences since these relations do not enjoy, in these models, the properties that facilitate their interpretation in the additive value function model (16.1). In general, they are not transitive or complete. They are 'too rough' to allow for a sufficiently detailed analysis of the global preference, as we shall see in the following.

In our three frameworks (16.8), (16.9) and (16.10), the main tool for analyzing the preference relation is the *trace*, a notion that admits different variants. In model (16.8), we shall use the *marginal trace* of the preference on each component X_i; this relation provides an ordering of the labels of the scale X_i of each attribute i. In model (16.9), we shall be concerned with traces on each Cartesian product X_i^2 of each attribute scale with itself; here the trace rank-orders the differences of preference between two alternatives on attribute i. Finally, in model (16.10), both types of traces appear and interact.

The contents of this chapter are the following. In section 16.2, we introduce the main tools for analyzing preference relations: marginal traces on levels and marginal traces on differences. We discuss the position of the more classical marginal preferences w.r.t. these traces. We then show how any preference relation can be represented in any of the three general models introduced above.

We briefly describe various specializations of model (16.8) and their axiomatic characterizations. We shall see in section 16.2 that some of these axioms indeed express a fundamental requirement of aggregation procedures, namely that the relation obtained through aggregation should contain the dominance relation. The rest of the section shows how the marginal traces on levels tend to become increasingly similar to marginal preference relations while additional requirements are imposed on the model, driving it closer to the additive value function model.

Section 16.4 studies model (16.9). Much as in the previous section, we characterize several variants of the model. We show that the numerical representations of type (16.9) are well-suited to understand outranking methods.

In section 16.5, we consider the relations that can be described within model (16.10). We characterize some of their variants and analyze the position of some well-known models such as the model of additive differences (16.3) and some outranking methods in this framework.

A brief conclusion summarizes the main advantages of the new concepts for analyzing relations on a product set. Various applications are discussed.

All our results have elementary proofs. We present some which we feel useful for understanding the new concepts. The reader interested in more details is invited to refer to a series of articles in which all proofs are given: [BOU 02b, BOU 04b, BOU 05a, BOU 05b, BOU 09]. These articles contain a complete study of the general, non-denumerable case as well as the proof that our axioms are independent. We shall pay little attention to the latter aspects in this chapter.

16.2. Fundamental relations and trivial models

16.2.1. *Binary relations on a product set*

As far as binary relations are concerned, we adopt the terminology and definitions used in Chapter 2. Hence, we shall use notions such as reflexive, irreflexive, complete, symmetric, asymmetric, transitive, Ferrers and semi-transitive relation with the same meaning. We also assume that the definitions of (complete) weak order, interval order and semiorder are familiar to the reader (see also Chapter 2 for these definitions).

We generally work with binary relations on a product set $X = X_1 \times X_2 \times \ldots \times X_n$. The sets X_i, $i = 1, 2, \ldots, n$, may be sets of arbitrary cardinality and n is assumed to be at least equal to 2. The elements of X are n-dimensional vectors: $x \in X$ with $x = (x_1, x_2, \ldots, x_n)$. We interpret them as alternatives described by their values on n attributes.

A binary relation on the set X will usually be denoted by $\succsim$, its asymmetric part by $\succ$ and its symmetric part by $\sim$. A similar convention holds for the asymmetric and symmetric parts of a relation when the symbol $\succsim$ is subscripted or superscripted. Relation $\succsim$ is interpreted as a preference relation and $a \succsim b$ reads: 'a is at least as good as b'.

For any subset I of the set of attributes $\{1, 2, \ldots, n\}$, we denote by X_I (respectively, X_{-I}) the product set $\prod_{i \in I} X_i$ (respectively, $\prod_{i \notin I} X_i$). We denote by (x_I, a_{-I}) the vector $w \in X$ such that $w_i = x_i$ if $i \in I$ and $w_i = a_i$ otherwise. If I is a singleton $\{i\}$, we simply write X_{-i} and (x_i, a_{-i}), abusing notation.

16.2.2. *Independence and marginal preferences*

A preference relation $\succsim$ on a product set X induces relations called *marginal preferences* on the subspaces X_I, for any subset of attributes I. The marginal preference $\succsim_I$ induced by $\succsim$ on X_I is defined for all x_I, y_I by:

$$x_I \succsim_I y_I \Leftrightarrow (x_I, z_{-I}) \succsim (y_I, z_{-I}), \text{ for all } z_{-I} \in X_{-I}. \tag{16.11}$$

We do not assume in general that preferences have special properties such as completeness or transitivity. Even if $\succsim$ is complete, this property is not necessarily inherited by its marginal preferences $\succsim_I$. Let us define two properties that confer some regularity to marginal preferences.

Definition 16.1. Let $\succsim$ be a preference relation on a product set X and let I be a subset of attributes:

– We say that $\succsim$ is *independent for I* if, for all $x_I, y_I \in X_I$,

$$[(x_I, z_{-I}) \succsim (y_I, z_{-I}), \text{ for some } z_{-I} \in X_{-I}]$$
$$\Rightarrow [(x_I, w_{-I}) \succsim (y_I, w_{-I}), \text{ for all } w_{-I} \in X_{-I}].$$

– We say that $\succsim$ is *separable for I* if, for all $x_I, y_I \in X_I$,

$$[(x_I, z_{-I}) \succ (y_I, z_{-I}), \text{ for some } z_{-I} \in X_{-I}]$$
$$\Rightarrow Not[(y_I, w_{-I}) \succ (x_I, w_{-I})], \text{ for all } w_{-I} \in X_{-I}.$$

– If $\succsim$ is independent (respectively, separable) for all subset of attributes I, we say that $\succsim$ is independent (respectively, separable). If $\succsim$ is independent (respectively, separable) for all subsets consisting of a single attribute, we say that $\succsim$ is weakly independent (respectively, weakly separable).

Independence is a classical notion in measurement theory. Intuitively, it means that common values on a subset of attributes do not influence preference. It is well known that independence implies weak independence, but not the converse [WAK 89]. Similarly, independence implies separability but the converse is false. Separability is a weakening of the independence property. It is an interesting property since aggregation models based on the max or min operator yield preferences that are separable but not independent. Separability prohibits strict reversal of the preferences while letting common values on some attributes vary. Separability entails weak separability but the converse is not true.

Independence and separability are of course related to completeness of marginal preferences. The following results are either well known or obvious.

Proposition 16.1. *Let $\succsim$ be a binary relation on X:*

– if $\succsim$ is complete and independent for attribute i, $\succsim_i$ is complete;

– $\succsim_i$ is complete if and only if $\succsim$ is weakly separable and satisfies the following condition: for all $x_i, y_i \in X_i$ and for all $a_{-i} \in X_{-i}$,

$$(x_i, a_{-i}) \succsim (y_i, a_{-i}) \text{ or } (y_i, a_{-i}) \succsim (x_i, a_{-i}). \qquad (16.12)$$

Marginal preferences on each attribute i express the results of the pairwise comparison of levels x_i and y_i when these levels are adjoined common levels on all other attributes (*ceteris paribus* reasoning). We shall see in the next section that marginal preferences $\succsim_i$ do not exploit all the information contained in $\succsim$ relatively to attribute i, contrary to marginal traces on levels.

16.2.3. *Marginal traces on levels*

Various kinds of marginal traces ($\succsim_i^+, \succsim_i^-$ and $\succsim_i^\pm$) on X_i are defined as follows.

Definition 16.2. *For all $x_i, y_i \in X_i$, for all $a_{-i} \in X_{-i}$, for all $z \in X$,*

$$x_i \succsim_i^+ y_i \Leftrightarrow [(y_i, a_{-i}) \succsim z \Rightarrow (x_i, a_{-i}) \succsim z],$$
$$x_i \succsim_i^- y_i \Leftrightarrow [z \succsim (x_i, a_{-i}) \Rightarrow z \succsim (y_i, a_{-i})],$$
$$x_i \succsim_i^\pm y_i \Leftrightarrow \begin{cases} (y_i, a_{-i}) \succsim z \Rightarrow (x_i, a_{-i}) \succsim z, \\ \text{and} \\ z \succsim (x_i, a_{-i}) \Rightarrow z \succsim (y_i, a_{-i}). \end{cases}$$

These definitions clarify the difference between marginal preferences and marginal traces. Marginal traces use all the information available in $\succsim$ in order to compare x_i with y_i. These two levels in X_i are adjoined the same evaluations on X_{-i} and one observes how such alternatives compare with all other alternatives. In contrast, marginal preference results from the comparison of alternatives, evaluated by level x_i on attribute i, with alternatives that are evaluated by level y_i. Both alternatives are adjoined the same evaluations on X_{-i} (*ceteris paribus* comparison). The latter mode of comparison does not take into account the behavior of such alternatives with respect to others. Under a very weak hypothesis, namely reflexivity of $\succsim$, we have indeed that $x_i \succsim_i^+ y_i$ (or $x_i \succsim_i^- y_i$) entails $x_i \succsim_i y_i$. This is readily verified starting e.g. from $(y_i, a_{-i}) \succsim (y_i, a_{-i})$. Applying the definition of $\succsim_i^+$, we obtain $(x_i, a_{-i}) \succsim (y_i, a_{-i})$. Similarly, starting from $(x_i, a_{-i}) \succsim (x_i, a_{-i})$ and using the definition of $\succsim_i^-$, we obtain the other entailment.

Using their definitions, it is not difficult to see that $\succsim_i^+, \succsim_i^-$ and $\succsim_i^\pm$ are reflexive and transitive relations.

According to our conventions, we denote the asymmetric (respectively, symmetric) part of $\succsim_i^+$ by $\succ_i^+$ (respectively, $\sim_i^+$) and similarly for $\succsim_i^-$ and $\succsim_i^\pm$. In the following lemma we note a few links between marginal traces and the preference relation $\succsim$. These properties, which will be used in the sequel, describe the 'responsiveness' of the preference with respect to the traces. The proof of this lemma is left to the reader.

Lemma 16.1. *For all $i \in \{1, \ldots, n\}$ and $x, y, z, w \in X$:*

1) $[x \succsim y, z_i \succsim_i^+ x_i] \Rightarrow (z_i, x_{-i}) \succsim y$,

2) $[x \succsim y, y_i \succsim_i^- w_i] \Rightarrow x \succsim (w_i, y_{-i})$,

3) $[z_i \succsim_i^\pm x_i, y_i \succsim_i^\pm w_i] \Rightarrow \begin{cases} x \succsim y \Rightarrow (z_i, x_{-i}) \succsim (w_i, y_{-i}), \\ \text{and} \\ x \succ y \Rightarrow (z_i, x_{-i}) \succ (w_i, y_{-i}), \end{cases}$

4) $[z_i \sim_i^\pm x_i, y_i \sim_i^\pm w_i, \forall i \in \{1, \ldots, n\}] \Rightarrow \begin{cases} x \succsim y \Leftrightarrow z \succsim w, \\ \text{and} \\ x \succ y \Leftrightarrow z \succ w. \end{cases}$

Marginal traces are not necessarily complete relations. When this is the case, this has important consequences, as we shall see in section 16.3.

16.2.4. *Marginal traces on differences*

Wakker [WAK 88, WAK 89] has demonstrated the importance of traces on differences for understanding conjoint measurement models. We introduce two relations on preference differences $\succsim_i^*$ and $\succsim_i^{**}$ for each attribute i. These relations compare pairs of levels; they are subsets of $X_i^2 \times X_i^2$.

Definition 16.3. For all $x_i, y_i, z_i, w_i \in X_i$,

$$(x_i, y_i) \succsim_i^* (z_i, w_i) \quad \text{if and only if}$$
$$\forall a_{-i}, b_{-i} \in X_{-i}, (z_i, a_{-i}) \succsim (w_i, b_{-i}) \Rightarrow (x_i, a_{-i}) \succsim (y_i, b_{-i});$$

$(x_i, y_i) \succsim_i^{**} (z_i, w_i)$ if and only if $[(x_i, y_i) \succsim_i^* (z_i, w_i)$ and $(w_i, z_i) \succsim_i^* (y_i, x_i)]$.

Intuitively, we interpret $(x_i, y_i) \succsim_i^* (z_i, w_i)$ as stating that the difference of preference between levels x_i and y_i is at least as large as that between z_i and w_i. By definition, $\succsim_i^*$ is reflexive and transitive while, in contrast, there is no necessary link between (x_i, y_i) and the 'opposite' difference (y_i, x_i); that is why we introduce relation $\succsim_i^{**}$.

As for marginal traces on levels, the preference relation $\succsim$ is monotone with respect to marginal traces on differences. Moreover, traces on levels and traces on differences are not unrelated. The following lemmas describe the former and the latter links; their elementary proof is left to the reader.

Lemma 16.2. For all $x, y \in X$ and all $z_i, w_i \in X_i$,

1) $\succsim$ is independent if and only if $(x_i, x_i) \sim_i^* (y_i, y_i)$, $\forall i \in \{1, \ldots, n\}$,
2) $[x \succsim y$ and $(z_i, w_i) \succsim_i^* (x_i, y_i)] \Rightarrow (z_i, x_{-i}) \succsim (w_i, y_{-i})$,
3) $[(z_i, w_i) \sim_i^* (x_i, y_i), \forall i \in \{1, \ldots, n\}] \Rightarrow [x \succsim y \Leftrightarrow z \succsim w]$,
4) $[x \succ y$ and $(z_i, w_i) \succsim_i^{**} (x_i, y_i)] \Rightarrow (z_i, x_{-i}) \succ (w_i, y_{-i})$,
5) $[(z_i, w_i) \sim_i^{**} (x_i, y_i), \forall i \in \{1, \ldots, n\}] \Rightarrow \begin{cases} [x \succsim y \Leftrightarrow z \succsim w] \\ \text{and} \\ [x \succ y \Leftrightarrow z \succ w], \end{cases}$

Lemma 16.3. For all $i \in \{1, \ldots, n\}$ and all $x_i, y_i \in X_i$,

1) $x_i \succsim_i^+ y_i \Leftrightarrow [(x_i, w_i) \succsim_i^* (y_i, w_i), \forall w_i \in X_i]$,
2) $x_i \succsim_i^- y_i \Leftrightarrow [(w_i, y_i) \succsim_i^* (w_i, x_i), \forall w_i \in X_i]$,
3) $x_i \succsim_i^\pm y_i \Leftrightarrow [(x_i, w_i) \succsim_i^{**} (y_i, w_i), \forall w_i \in X_i]$,
4) $[\ell_i \succsim_i^+ x_i$ and $(x_i, y_i) \succsim_i^* (z_i, w_i)] \Rightarrow (\ell_i, y_i) \succsim_i^* (z_i, w_i)$,
5) $[y_i \succsim_i^- \ell_i$ and $(x_i, y_i) \succsim_i^* (z_i, w_i)] \Rightarrow (x_i, \ell_i) \succsim_i^* (z_i, w_i)$,
6) $[z_i \succsim_i^+ \ell_i$ and $(x_i, y_i) \succsim_i^* (z_i, w_i)] \Rightarrow (x_i, y_i) \succsim_i^* (\ell_i, w_i)$,
7) $[\ell_i \succsim_i^- w_i$ and $(x_i, y_i) \succsim_i^* (z_i, w_i)] \Rightarrow (x_i, y_i) \succsim_i^* (z_i, \ell_i)$,
8) $[x_i \sim_i^+ z_i$ and $y_i \sim_i^- w_i] \Rightarrow (x_i, y_i) \sim_i^* (z_i, w_i)$,
9) $[x_i \sim_i^\pm z_i$ and $y_i \sim_i^\pm w_i] \Rightarrow (x_i, y_i) \sim_i^{**} (z_i, w_i)$.

Marginal traces on differences are not generally complete. When they are, this has interesting consequences that will be studied in section 16.4.

16.2.5. *Three models for general relations on a Cartesian product*

Provided the cardinal of X is not larger than that of the set of real numbers, every binary relation on X can be represented in the three models described by equations (16.8)–(16.10). As we shall see in the proof of the following proposition, marginal traces on levels play a fundamental role for representation (16.8). Marginal traces on differences play a similar role in representation (16.9) and both types of traces are important for model (16.10). The importance of this role will be strengthened when we impose the completeness of the traces in the following three sections.

We use the notation $[u_i(x_i)]$ to denote the n-components vector $(u_1(x_1), \ldots, u_n(x_n))$.

Proposition 16.2. *Trivial representations on product sets*
Let $\succsim$ be a binary relation on the set $X = \prod_{i=1}^{n} X_i$, the cardinal of which is at most that of $\mathbb{R}$.

1) There are real-valued functions u_i on X_i and a real-valued function F defined on $[\prod_{i=1}^{n} u_i(X_i)]^2$ such that, for all $x, y \in X$,

$$x \succsim y \Leftrightarrow F([u_i(x_i)]; [u_i(y_i)]) \geq 0. \tag{L0}$$

2) There are real-valued functions p_i on X_i^2 and a real-valued function G defined on $\prod_{i=1}^{n} p_i(X_i^2)$ such that, for all $x, y \in X$,

$$x \succsim y \Leftrightarrow G([p_i(x_i, y_i)]) \geq 0. \tag{D0}$$

3) There exist real-valued functions u_i on X_i, real-valued functions φ_i on $u_i(X_i)^2$ and a real-valued function H defined on $\prod_{i=1}^{n} \varphi_i(u_i(X_i)^2)$ such that, for all $x, y \in X$,

$$x \succsim y \Leftrightarrow H([\varphi_i(u_i(x_i), u_i(y_i))]) \geq 0. \tag{L0D0}$$

Proof. Part (1). Let $i \in \{1, \ldots, n\}$. By construction, $\sim_i^{\pm}$ is an equivalence relation since it is reflexive, symmetric and transitive. Since X_i has at most the cardinality of $\mathbb{R}$, there exists a function u_i from X_i to $\mathbb{R}$ such that for all $x_i, y_i \in X_i$:

$$x_i \sim_i^{\pm} y_i \Leftrightarrow u_i(x_i) = u_i(y_i). \tag{16.13}$$

For all $i \in \{1, \ldots, n\}$, let u_i be a function that satisfies equation (16.13). We define F from $[\prod_{i=1}^{n} u_i(X_i)]^2$ to $\mathbb{R}$ by:

$$F([u_i(x_i)]; [u_i(y_i)]) = \begin{cases} +1 & \text{if } x \succsim y, \\ -1 & \text{otherwise.} \end{cases} \tag{16.14}$$

Lemma 16.1(4) guarantees that F is well defined.

Part (2). Since $\sim_i^{**}$ is an equivalence relation and in view of the cardinality of X_i, for all i there is a function p_i from X_i^2 to $\mathbb{R}$ that separates the equivalence classes of $\sim_i^{**}$, i.e. that is such that for all $x_i, y_i, z_i, w_i \in X_i$:

$$(x_i, y_i) \sim_i^{**} (z_i, w_i) \Leftrightarrow p_i(x_i, y_i) = p_i(z_i, w_i). \tag{16.15}$$

Using lemma 16.2(5), the following function G is well defined:

$$G([p_i(x_i, y_i)]) = \begin{cases} +1 & \text{if } x \succsim y, \\ -1 & \text{otherwise.} \end{cases} \tag{16.16}$$

Part (3). Let us consider, for all i, a function u_i that satisfies equation (16.13) and a function p_i that satisfies equation 16.15. We define φ_i on $u_i(X_i)^2$ by:

$$\varphi_i(u_i(x_i), u_i(y_i)) = p_i(x_i, y_i) \tag{16.17}$$

for all $x_i, y_i \in X_i$. Let us show that φ_i is welldefined i.e. that $u_i(x_i) = u_i(z_i)$ and $u_i(y_i) = u_i(w_i)$ imply $p_i(x_i, y_i) = p_i(z_i, w_i)$. By construction, we have $x_i \sim_i^{\pm} z_i$ and $y_i \sim_i^{\pm} w_i$; lemma 16.3(9) yields $(x_i, y_i) \sim_i^{**} (z_i, w_i)$, hence $p_i(x_i, y_i) = p_i(z_i, w_i)$.

Finally, we define H on $\prod_{i=1}^n \varphi_i(u_i(X_i), u_i(X_i))$ by:

$$H([\varphi_i(u_i(x_i), u_i(y_i))]) = \begin{cases} +1 & \text{if } x \succsim y, \\ -1 & \text{otherwise.} \end{cases} \tag{16.18}$$

Using lemma 16.2(3), we see that H is well defined.◇

Remark 16.1. The limitation on the cardinality of X imposed in proposition 16.2 is not a necessary condition. This condition can be weakened in the following way. For model ($L0$), it is sufficient that the number of equivalence classes of the relations $\sim_i^{\pm}$ is not larger than the cardinal of $\mathbb{R}$; in the same way, for model ($D0$), it is necessary and sufficient to impose the same restriction on the number of equivalence classes of relations $\sim_i^{**}$. For model ($L0D0$), the two previous restrictions are required.

16.3. Models using marginal traces on levels

16.3.1. *Definition of the models*

In model ($L0$), the role of u_i consists only of associating a numerical 'label' with each equivalence class of relation $\succsim_i^{\pm}$. The role of F is only to determine whether the profiles $[(u_i(x_i))], [(u_i(y_i))]$ correspond to a preference (see definition of F in equation (16.14)) or not. Things become more interesting when additional properties are imposed on F. We consider the following models:

– model (L1), obtained by imposing $F([u_i(x_i)]; [u_i(x_i)]) \geq 0$ on model (L0); and
– model (L2), obtained by imposing $F([u_i(x_i)]; [u_i(y_i)]) = -F([u_i(y_i)]; [u_i(x_i)])$ on model (L1).

Moreover, in each of the models (L0), (L1) and (L2), we consider the consequences of imposing that F is non-decreasing (respectively, increasing) in its first n arguments and non-increasing (respectively, decreasing) in its last n arguments. The resulting eight new models are defined in Table 16.1.

(L0) $x \succsim y \Leftrightarrow F([u_i(x_i)]; [u_i(y_i)]) \geq 0$
(L1) (L0) with $F([u_i(x_i)]; [u_i(x_i)]) \geq 0$
(L2) (L0) with $F([u_i(x_i)]; [u_i(y_i)]) = -F([u_i(y_i)]; [u_i(x_i)])$
....
(L3) (L0) with F non-decreasing, non-increasing,
(L4) (L0) with F increasing, decreasing,
....
(L5) (L1) with F non-decreasing, non-increasing,
(L6) (L1) with F increasing, decreasing,
....
(L7) (L2) with F non-decreasing, non-increasing,
(L8) (L2) with F increasing, decreasing,

Table 16.1. *Models using traces on levels*

A number of implications between these models result immediately from their definitions. We do not detail them here. We note in the following proposition a number of consequences of the properties of F introduced to define models (L1) and (L2).

Proposition 16.3. *A binary relation $\succsim$ on a product set $X = \prod_{i=1}^{n} X_i$, the cardinal of which is bounded by that of $\mathbb{R}$, can be represented in:*

1) model (L1) if and only if $\succsim$ is reflexive;
2) model (L2) if and only if $\succsim$ is complete.

Proof. Reflexivity and completeness of $\succsim$ are clear consequences of models (L1) and (L2), respectively. Reflexivity of $\succsim$ is evidently sufficient for model (L1). It remains to be shown that completeness is a sufficient condition for model (L2). This is readily done by reconsidering the construction of the representation of $\succsim$ in the proof of proposition 16.2; we simply change the definition of F, equation (16.14), to:

$$F([u_i(x_i)]; [u_i(y_i)]) = \begin{cases} +1 & \text{if } x \succ y, \\ 0 & \text{if } x \sim y, \\ -1 & \text{otherwise.} \end{cases} \quad (16.19)$$

Using the completeness of $\succsim$, we readily verify that F is still well defined and satisfies

$$F([u_i(x_i)];[u_i(y_i)]) = -F([u_i(y_i)];[u_i(x_i)]).$$

◇

In the next section, we introduce properties that are intimately connected to the monotonicity of F. Interestingly, the same properties ensure the completeness of marginal traces.

16.3.2. *Completeness of marginal traces and monotonicity of F*

We introduce the following three axioms for each dimension i.

Definition 16.4. Conditions $AC1$, $AC2$ and $AC3$
Let $\succsim$ be a binary relation on $X = \prod_{i=1}^{n} X_i$. For $i \in \{1,\ldots,n\}$, we say that relation $\succsim$ satisfies: $AC1_i$ if

$$\left.\begin{array}{c} x \succsim y \\ \text{and} \\ z \succsim w \end{array}\right\} \Rightarrow \left\{\begin{array}{c} (z_i, x_{-i}) \succsim y \\ \text{or} \\ (x_i, z_{-i}) \succsim w, \end{array}\right.$$

$AC2_i$ if

$$\left.\begin{array}{c} x \succsim y \\ \text{and} \\ z \succsim w \end{array}\right\} \Rightarrow \left\{\begin{array}{c} x \succsim (w_i, y_{-i}) \\ \text{or} \\ z \succsim (y_i, w_{-i}), \end{array}\right.$$

and $AC3_i$ if

$$\left.\begin{array}{c} z \succsim (x_i, a_{-i}) \\ \text{and} \\ (x_i, b_{-i}) \succsim y \end{array}\right\} \Rightarrow \left\{\begin{array}{c} z \succsim (w_i, a_{-i}) \\ \text{or} \\ (w_i, b_{-i}) \succsim y, \end{array}\right.$$

for all $x, y, z, w \in X$, for all $a_{-i}, b_{-i} \in X_{-i}$ and for all $x_i, w_i \in X_i$.

We say also that $\succsim$ satisfies $AC1$ (respectively, $AC2$, $AC3$) if it satisfies $AC1_i$ (respectively, $AC2_i$, $AC3_i$) for all $i \in \{1,\ldots,n\}$. We use $AC123$ as short-hand for the conjunction of properties $AC1$, $AC2$ and $AC3$.

These three conditions are called *cancellation conditions*, which is classical terminology in conjoint measurement theory. The denomination of the axioms comes from the fact that these axioms express 'intrA-Criterion' cancellation conditions (in contrast to axioms RC – 'inteR-Criterion' cancellation conditions; see section 16.4).

Conditions $AC1$, $AC2$ and $AC3$ were initially introduced in [BOU 99, BOU 97] and then used in [GRE 02].

Condition $AC1_i$ suggests that the elements of X_i can be ordered taking into account 'upward dominance': 'x_i upward dominates z_i' means that if $(z_i, c_{-i}) \succsim w$, then $(x_i, c_{-i}) \succsim w$. Condition $AC2_i$ has a similar interpretation taking into account 'downward dominance': 'y_i downward dominates w_i' if $x \succsim (y_i, c_{-i})$ entails $x \succsim (w_i, c_{-i})$. Condition $AC3_i$ ensures that it is possible to rank-order the elements of X_i taking into account both upward and downward dominance; these are not incompatible. It can be shown [BOU 04b, Appendix A] that $AC1$, $AC2$ and $AC3$ are logically independent axioms.

Conditions $AC1$, $AC2$, $AC3$ have consequences on marginal traces. We describe them in the following proposition.

Lemma 16.4. *Completeness of marginal traces*
Let $\succsim$ be a binary relation on X. We have:

1) $\succsim_i^+$ is complete if and only if $\succsim$ verifies $AC1_i$;
2) $\succsim_i^-$ is complete if and only if $\succsim$ verifies $AC2_i$;
3) $[\,Not\; x_i \succsim_i^+ y_i \Rightarrow y_i \succsim_i^- x_i]$ if and only if $\succsim$ verifies $AC3_i$;
4) $\succsim_i^\pm$ is complete if and only if $\succsim$ verifies $AC1_i, AC2_i$ and $AC3_i$.

Proof. To prove part (1), it is sufficient to observe that the negation of $AC1_i$ is equivalent to the negation of the completeness of $\succsim_i^+$. Part (2) is proven in a similar way.

Part (3). Assume that Not $x_i \succsim_i^+ y_i$; then there exist $z \in X$ and $a_{-i} \in X_{-i}$ such that $(y_i, a_{-i}) \succsim z$ and Not $(x_i, a_{-i}) \succsim z$. If $w \succsim (y_i, b_{-i})$, then $AC3_i$ entails $(x_i, a_{-i}) \succsim z$ or $w \succsim (x_i, b_{-i})$. Since by hypothesis, Not $(x_i, a_{-i}) \succsim z$, we must have $w \succsim (x_i, b_{-i})$ hence $\succsim_i^- x_i$. The converse implication results from the fact that the negation of $AC3_i$ is equivalent to the existence of $x_i, y_i \in X_i$ such that Not $y_i \succsim_i^+ x_i$ and Not $x_i \succsim_i^- y_i$.

Part (4) is a direct consequence of the first three parts. ◇

Conditions $AC1$, $AC2$ and $AC3$ together imply that the marginal traces $\succsim_i^\pm$ induced by $\succsim$ are (complete) weak orders. We can expect that these axioms have consequences on marginal preferences $\succsim_i$. Note, however, that marginal preferences and marginal traces on levels do not generally coincide, even under conditions $AC123$. The following results are given without proofs (these can be found in [BOU 04b, proposition 3]).

Proposition 16.4. *Properties of marginal preferences*
We have:

1) If $\succsim$ is reflexive and verifies $AC1_i$ or $AC2_i$ for all $i \in \{1, \ldots, n\}$, then $\succsim$ is weakly separable and satisfies condition (16.12).

2) If $\succsim$ is reflexive and verifies $AC1_i$ or $AC2_i$ then $\succsim_i$ is an interval order.

3) If, in addition, $\succsim$ satisfies $AC3_i$, then $\succsim_i$ is a semiorder.

From part (1), using proposition 16.1, we infer that $\succsim_i$ is complete as soon as $\succsim$ is reflexive and verifies $AC1_i$ or $AC2_i$.

We know that if $\succsim$ is reflexive and satisfies $AC123$, the marginal traces $\succsim_i^{\pm}$ are weak orders (lemma 16.4(4)). Under the same conditions, part (3) of the previous proposition tells us that marginal preferences $\succsim_i$ are semiorders. This suggests that marginal traces and preferences are distinct relations, which is confirmed by examples in [BOU 04b]; we shall see conditions ensuring that these relations are identical below. If they are distinct, we have seen that $x_i \succsim_i^{\pm} y_i$ entails $x_i \succsim_i y_i$ as soon as $\succsim$ is reflexive. Since under $AC123$, $\succsim_i^{\pm}$ and $\succsim_i$ are complete, this means that under these conditions $\succsim_i^{\pm}$ is more discriminant than $\succsim_i$ (in the sense that $\sim_i^{\pm} \subseteq \sim_i$: more pairs are indifferent with respect to marginal preference than to marginal trace).

Axioms $AC123$ are not only related to the completeness of marginal traces but also to the monotonicity properties of the function F that appears in models of type (16.8). In the next proposition, we establish a characterization of models (L5) and (L6). We prove the result only for the case where X is a countable set.

Proposition 16.5. *Characterization of (L5) and (L6)*
Let $\succsim$ be a binary relation on the countable set $X = \prod_{i=1}^{n} X_i$. We find that $\succsim$ verifies model (L6) if and only if $\succsim$ is reflexive and satisfies $AC1$, $AC2$ and $AC3$. Models (L5) and (L6) are equivalent.

Proof. Model (L5) is a particular case of model (L1); hence in that model the preference relation $\succsim$ is reflexive (proposition 16.3(1)). It is easily checked that any relation representable in model (L5) verifies $AC123$. Conversely, if $\succsim$ is reflexive and verifies $AC123$, we can construct a numerical representation that follows model (L6). As function u_i, we select a numerical representation of the weak order $\succsim_i^{\pm}$, i.e. $\forall x_i, y_i \in X_i$, we have:

$$x_i \succsim_i^{\pm} y_i \Leftrightarrow u_i(x_i) \geq u_i(y_i). \qquad (16.20)$$

Such a representation does exist since we have assumed that X is a countable set. We then define F on $[\prod_{i=1}^{n} u_i(X_i)]^2$ by setting:

$$F([u_i(x_i)]; [u_i(y_i)]) = \begin{cases} +\exp(\sum_{i=1}^{n}(u_i(x_i) - u_i(y_i))) & \text{if } x \succsim y, \\ -\exp(\sum_{i=1}^{n}(u_i(y_i) - u_i(x_i))) & \text{otherwise.} \end{cases} \qquad (16.21)$$

That F is well defined results from lemma 16.1(4). The fact that F is increasing in its first n arguments and decreasing in its last n arguments is a consequence of the definition of F and of lemma 16.1(3). ◇

The case in which X is not denumerable does not raise serious difficulties. A necessary and sufficient condition for its representability is that the marginal traces of $\succsim$ are representable on the real numbers, which is equivalent to imposing an 'order-density' condition. We say that $\succsim_i^\pm$ satisfies the 'order-density' condition $OD_i^\pm$ if there is a denumerable subset $Y_i \subseteq X_i$ such that $\forall x_i, z_i \in X_i$,

$$x_i \succ_i^\pm z_i \Rightarrow \exists y_i \in Y_i \text{ such that } x_i \succsim_i^\pm y_i \succsim_i^\pm z_i. \tag{16.22}$$

Conditional to this additional condition imposed on $\succsim$ for all $i \in \{1, \ldots, n\}$ is that the characterization of the above models remains valid.

Note also that the slightly more general case of models $(L3)$ and $(L4)$ is dealt with very similarly. These models are equivalent and the preferences that can be represented in these models are those that verify $AC1$, $AC2$ and $AC3$ (they need not be reflexive).

16.3.3. Model (L8) and strict monotonicity w.r.t. traces

In order to obtain a characterization of the more constrained model in Table 16.1, we introduce two new axioms that are effective only when the preference relation is complete. These axioms follow the scheme of the classical 'triple cancellation' axioms that are used in the characterization of additive value function models. That is the reason why we denote them by the acronym TAC (Triple intrA-Criteria annulation).

Definition 16.5. Conditions $TAC1$, $TAC2$
We say that $\succsim$ satisfies

$TAC1_i$ if
$$\left.\begin{array}{c}(x_i, a_{-i}) \succsim y \\ \text{and} \\ y \succsim (z_i, a_{-i}) \\ \text{and} \\ (z_i, b_{-i}) \succsim w\end{array}\right\} \Rightarrow (x_i, b_{-i}) \succsim w,$$

and $TAC2_i$ if
$$\left.\begin{array}{c}(x_i, a_{-i}) \succsim y \\ \text{and} \\ y \succsim (z_{-i}, a_{-i}) \\ \text{and} \\ w \succsim (x_i, b_{-i})\end{array}\right\} \Rightarrow w \succsim (z_i, b_{-i}),$$

for all $x_i, z_i \in X_i$, for all $a_{-i}, b_{-i} \in X_{-i}$ and for all $y, w \in X$.

We say that $\succsim$ satisfies $TAC1$ (respectively, $TAC2$) if it satisfies $TAC1_i$ (respectively, $TAC2_i$) for all $i \in \{1, \ldots, n\}$. We use also $TAC12$ as short-hand for $TAC1$ and $TAC2$.

The first two conditions in the premise of $TAC1_i$ and $TAC2_i$ suggest that level x_i is not lower than level z_i. $TAC1_i$ (respectively, $TAC2_i$) entail that x_i should then upward (respectively, downward) dominate z_i.

We give without proof a few consequences of $TAC1$ and $TAC2$. These axioms will only be imposed to complete relations; without this hypothesis, they have rather limited power.

Lemma 16.5. *Strictly positive responsiveness to the traces on levels*
If $\succsim$ is a complete binary relation on $X = \prod_{i=1}^n X_i$ then:
1) $TAC1_i \Rightarrow [AC1_i$ and $AC3_i]$
2) $TAC2_i \Rightarrow [AC2_i$ and $AC3_i]$
3) $TAC1_i$ is equivalent to the completeness of relation $\succsim_i^{\pm}$ together with the condition:

$$[x \succsim y \text{ and } z_i \succ_i^+ x_i] \Rightarrow (z_i, x_{-i}) \succ y. \quad (16.23)$$

4) $TAC2_i$ is equivalent to the completeness of relation $\succsim_i^{\pm}$ together with the condition:

$$[x \succsim y \text{ and } y_i \succ_i^- w_i] \Rightarrow x \succ (w_i, y_{-i}). \quad (16.24)$$

5) If $TAC1_i$ or $TAC2_i$, then $\succsim$ is independent for $\{i\}$ and $\succsim_i$ is a weak order. Moreover, if we have $TAC12$ then $\succsim_i = \succsim_i^{\pm}$.

As we can see, as soon as $\succsim$ is complete, the conjunction of $TAC1_i$ and $TAC2_i$ guarantees that $\succsim$ responds in a strictly increasing manner to the marginal trace $\succ_i^{\pm}$. These properties also imply that $\succsim$ is weakly independent on criterion $\{i\}$ and that the marginal preference $\succsim_i$ is a weak order and identical to the marginal trace $\succsim_i^{\pm}$. We do not examine in detail here the relationship between $TAC1_i$, $TAC2_i$ on the one hand and $AC1_i$, $AC2_i$, $AC3_i$ on the other. We shall return to this in section 16.3.6. It can be shown [BOU 04b, Appendix A] that for a complete relation, $TAC1$ and $TAC2$ are logically independent properties.

Note that the above system of axioms does not imply that the preference $\succsim$ has strong properties such as transitivity or even semi-transitivity or the Ferrers property. In these models (even in the more constrained i.e. model ($L8$)), the preference cannot even be supposed to be an interval order. The previous results lead directly to the characterization of model ($L8$).

Proposition 16.6. *Characterization of (L8)*
Let $\succsim$ be a binary relation on the denumerable set $X = \prod_{i=1}^{n} X_i$. The relation $\succsim$ verifies model (L8) if and only if $\succsim$ is complete and satisfies $TAC1$ and $TAC2$.

Proof. The proof follows exactly the same scheme as that of proposition 16.5. The only difference lies in the definition of function F which has to be altered in order to take into account the completeness of $\succsim$. We define F on $[\prod_{i=1}^{n} u_i(X_i)]^2$, substituting equation (16.21) by:

$$F([u_i(x_i)]; [u_i(y_i)]) = \begin{cases} +\exp(\sum_{i=1}^{n}(u_i(x_i) - u_i(y_i))) & \text{if } x \succsim y, \\ 0 & \text{if } x \sim y, \\ -\exp(\sum_{i=1}^{n}(u_i(y_i) - u_i(x_i))) & \text{otherwise.} \end{cases} \quad (16.25)$$

Parts (3) and (4) of lemma 16.5 entail that F is strictly increasing (respectively, decreasing) in its first (respectively, last) n arguments since, in this construction, the u_i have been chosen to be numerical representations of the weak orders $\succsim_i^{\pm}$. ◊

16.3.4. *Complete characterization of the models on levels*

To be complete, we give without proof [see BOU 04b] a characterization of all the models on levels described in Table 16.1. We limit ourselves to the case in which the set X is denumerable. The non-denumerable case can be dealt with without major difficulty by imposing order density conditions on the traces, starting from model (L4).

Theorem 16.1. *Models based on traces on levels*
Let $\succsim$ be a binary relation on the denumerable set $X = \prod_{i=1}^{n} X_i$. This relation can be represented in

  1) *model (L1) if and only if $\succsim$ is reflexive;*

  2) *model (L2) if and only if $\succsim$ is complete;*

  3) *model (L4) if and only if $\succsim$ verifies AC1, AC2 and AC3; models (L3) and (L4) are equivalent;*

  4) *model (L6) if and only if $\succsim$ is reflexive and verifies AC1, AC2 and AC3; models (L5) and (L6) are equivalent;*

  5) *model (L7) if and only if $\succsim$ is complete and verifies AC1, AC2 and AC3;*

  6) *model (L8) if and only if $\succsim$ is complete and verifies TAC1 and TAC2.*

Let us observe that increasing or non-decreasing (respectively, decreasing or non-increasing) do not make a difference in our models unless function F is also supposed to be antisymmetric (i.e. $F([u_i(x_i)]; [u_i(y_i)]) = -F([u_i(y_i)]; [u_i(x_i)])$). In this case, the value '0' plays a special role, which is to represent indifference. This is what led us to differentiate the increasing case from the non-decreasing one.

16.3.4.1. *Uniqueness and regular representations*

All these models have obviously rather poor properties regarding uniqueness of numerical representation. A large variety of functions can of course be used for F as well as for the u_i. Nevertheless, it is not difficult to determine necessary and sufficient conditions that these functions must fulfill. Let us consider, for instance, model ($L6$). Our proof of proposition 16.5 shows that it is always possible to use functions u_i that verify:

$$x_i \succsim_i^{\pm} y_i \Leftrightarrow u_i(x_i) \geq u_i(y_i). \tag{16.26}$$

Let us refer to a representation in which the functions u_i verify equation (16.26) as *regular*. According to our proof, any strictly increasing transformation of a function u_i verifying this condition can also be used and yields another valid representation. Other choices can be made, however. It is easy to see that any function u_i that satisfies

$$x_i \succ_i^{\pm} y_i \Rightarrow u_i(x_i) > u_i(y_i) \tag{16.27}$$

can be used in a representation of $\succsim$ in model ($L6$).

Regarding function F, we can substitute the exponential of the sum of the differences of the $2n$ arguments, that appears in equation (16.21), by any real-valued positive function defined on $\mathbb{R}^{2n}$ (or at least on the subset $[\prod_{i=1}^{n} u_i(X_i)]^2$) that is increasing in its first n arguments and decreasing in its last n ones. It is also clear that only such functions can be used.

The representations described above are the only possible ones for model ($L6$). It is easy to adapt the reasoning that we have just used to cover all the models considered here [BOU 04b].

16.3.5. *Relations compatible with dominance*

Why should we be particularly interested in models ($L5$), ($L6$) and ($L8$)? The major reason is related to the application of conjoint measurement models to multiple criteria decision analysis. In this field of application the preference is usually constructed; it is not known *a priori*. The process of constructing the preference relies upon data (that are the evaluations of the alternatives on the various attributes recognized as relevant for the decision) and their interpretation in terms of preference on each criterion.

We emphasize that we have not assumed any *a priori* structure on the sets X_i. We did not suppose that they are sets of numbers; they may be ordered sets or even nominal scales. The interpretation of the evaluations of the alternatives in terms of preference requires at least the definition of an ordering of the elements of X_i, an order that would correspond to the direction of increasing preference of the decision maker on the viewpoint attached to that attribute. The set X_i endowed with this interpretation is what we call a *criterion* [ROY 93].

We expect of course the existence of certain logical connections between the criteria and global preference. *Respect of dominance* is such a natural connection [ROY 85, ROY 93] and [VIN 89]. (This notion of dominance must not be confused with that introduced just after definition 16.4. The latter only deals with the relative positions of the levels on the scale of a single attribute. We called it 'upward dominance' and 'downward dominance' due to the lack of a more appropriate term.) In conjoint measurement theory, no order is *a priori* postulated on the sets X_i. Would it exist, such an order should be compatible with global preference. We can therefore formulate the principle of the respect of dominance in a conjoint measurement context as follows.

Definition 16.6. A reflexive binary relation $\succsim$ on a set $X = \prod_{i=1}^{n} X_i$ is *compatible with a dominance relation* if for all $i \in \{1, \ldots, n\}$, there is a weak order S_i on X_i such that for all $x, y \in X$ and all $z_i, w_i \in X_i$,

$$[x \succsim y, z_i S_i x_i \text{ and } y_i S_i w_i \text{ for all } i \in \{1, \ldots, n\}] \Rightarrow z \succsim w. \tag{16.28}$$

We say that this compatibility is *strict* if the conclusion of condition (16.28) is modified in $z \succ w$ as soon as, for some $j \in \{1, \ldots, n\}$, $z_j P_j x_j$ or $y_j P_j w_j$ (where P_j denotes the asymmetric part of S_j).

This definition requires a comment. It could be thought that a reasonable definition of the compatibility with a dominance relation would require the fulfillment of the following condition instead of condition (16.28):

$$[x_i S_i y_i \text{ for all } i \in \{1, \ldots, n\}] \Rightarrow x \succsim y. \tag{16.29}$$

The reader will easily be convinced that defining compatibility in this way would make this notion too weak in case the preference relation cannot be supposed transitive. Indeed, if $\succsim$ has cycles in its asymmetric part, it is possible that this relation verifies condition (16.28) while there exist alternatives $x, y, z \in X$ such that $x \Delta y$, $y \succ z$ and $z \succ x$ (where the dominance relation $x \Delta y$ is defined by $[x_i S_i y_i$ for all $i \in \{1, \ldots, n\}]$). In such a case, the non-dominated alternatives (w.r.t. relation Δ) need not always be considered as good choices in a multiple criteria choice decision problem since x could be non-dominated while there would exist an alternative z such that $z \succ x$.

Definition 16.6 avoids this drawback since, using condition (16.28), $x \Delta y$ and $y \succ z$ imply $x \succsim z$, which contradicts $z \succ x$.

In view of the results in section 16.3.2, establishing a link between relations $\succsim_i^\pm$ and the monotonicity of F, we can expect that when a preference $\succsim$ is compatible with a dominance relation, the relations S_i in definition 16.6 are related to the marginal traces $\succsim_i^\pm$. It is indeed the case as shown in the next proposition (in which we limit ourselves to reflexive preference relations; the case of asymmetric relations could be treated similarly).

Proposition 16.7. *Compatibility with dominance*
A reflexive binary relation $\succsim$ on a set $X = \prod_{i=1}^n X_i$ is compatible with a dominance relation if and only if it satisfies AC1, AC2 and AC3. In such a case, S_i is compatible with $\succsim_i^\pm$ in the following sense:

$$x_i \succ_i^\pm y_i \Rightarrow \text{Not } y_i S_i x_i. \tag{16.30}$$

Proof. The necessity of $AC1$, $AC2$ and $AC3$ is almost immediate. Consider the case of $AC1$, the cases of the other axioms being similar. Assume that $(x_i, a_{-i}) \succsim y$ and $(z_i, b_{-i}) \succsim w$. Relation S_i being complete, we have either $x_i S_i z_i$ or $z_i S_i x_i$. If we have $z_i S_i x_i$ then, using the definition of compatibility with dominance, $(x_i, a_{-i}) \succsim y$ entails $(z_i, a_{-i}) \succsim y$. If we have $x_i S_i z_i$, then $(z_i, b_{-i}) \succsim w$ entails $(x_i, b_{-i}) \succsim w$. As a consequence, $AC1$ is verified.

The fact that $AC1$, $AC2$ and $AC3$ are sufficient conditions is clear. We can indeed take $S_i = \succsim_i^\pm$ for all $i \in \{1, \ldots, n\}$. Under $AC123$, the relations $\succsim_i^\pm$ are complete weak orders (lemma 16.4(4)) and, using lemma 16.1(3), we obtain equation (16.28).

To show equation (16.30), let us suppose on the contrary that there exist $x_i, y_i \in X_i$ with $x_i \succ_i^\pm y_i$ and $y_i S_i x_i$. From the former relation we deduce that there exist either $a_{-i} \in X_{-i}$ and $z \in X$ such that $(x_i, a_{-i}) \succsim z$ and Not $(y_i, a_{-i}) \succsim z$, or $b_{-i} \in X_{-i}$ and $w \in X$ such that $w \succsim (y_i, b_{-i})$ and Not $w \succsim (x_i, b_{-i})$. In both cases, using $y_i S_i x_i$ and applying equation (16.28) leads to a contradiction. ◇

From this result we deduce, when the preference $\succsim$ is compatible with a dominance relation, that $\succsim_i^\pm$ cannot be finer than S_i. In other words, $S_i \subseteq \succsim_i^\pm$. From a practical point of view, if we consider that a global preference $\succsim$ compatible with a dominance relation is the result of the aggregation of relations S_i defining the criteria, we understand that $\succsim$ cannot induce a trace on X_i that would contradict S_i; $\succsim$ cannot even create a preference where S_i only sees indifference. Even though, for a reflexive preference satisfying $AC123$, we cannot guarantee the uniqueness of the relations S_i, we see that such relations are strongly constrained: S_i can only be a weak order included in $\succsim_i^\pm$.

With the previous proposition, model $(L6)$ (or the equivalent model $(L5)$) can be seen as a natural framework for describing preferences compatible with a dominance relation. This prompts the question of a similar framework for preferences that are *strictly* compatible with a dominance relation. Surprisingly, the natural framework for such preferences is not model ($L8$). This model imposes complete preferences which is not, as we shall see, a necessary condition for strict dominance.

16.3.6. *Strict compatibility with dominance*

Strict compatibility with dominance requires, of course, stronger axioms than AC_1, AC_2, AC_3. We refer to the following strengthening of $AC3$ as $AC4$.

Definition 16.7. Condition $AC4$
We say that $\succsim$ satisfies $AC4_i$ if $\succsim$ verifies $AC3_i$ and if, whenever one of the consequences in $AC3_i$ is false, then the other consequence is strictly satisfied, i.e. with $\succ$ instead of $\succsim$. We say that $\succsim$ satisfies $AC4$ if it satisfies $AC4_i$ for all $i \in \{1,\ldots,n\}$.

The following lemma that we state without proof [BOU 04b] collects a few consequences of $AC4$.

Lemma 16.6. *Consequences of $AC4$*
If $\succsim$ is a relation on X, we have:

1) If $\succsim$ is reflexive, $AC4_i$ is equivalent to the completeness of $\succsim_i^{\pm}$ and the conjunction of the following two conditions:

$$[x \succsim y \text{ and } z_i \succ_i^{\pm} x_i] \Rightarrow (z_i, x_{-i}) \succ y, \tag{16.31}$$

$$[x \succsim y \text{ and } y_i \succ_i^{\pm} w_i] \Rightarrow x \succ (w_i, y_{-i}). \tag{16.32}$$

2) If $\succsim$ is reflexive and satisfies $AC4_i$ then
  - $\succsim$ is independent for $\{i\}$,
  - $\succsim_i$ is a weak order and
  - $\succsim_i = \succsim_i^{\pm}$.

3) If $\succsim$ is complete, $[TAC1_i \text{ and } TAC2_i] \Leftrightarrow AC4_i$.

As soon as $\succsim$ is reflexive, condition $AC4$ (which, by definition, is stronger than $AC3$) also entails $AC1$ and $AC2$ since it implies the completeness of relations $\succsim_i^{\pm}$ (lemmas 16.6(1) and 16.4(4)). If $\succsim$ is complete, $AC4$ is equivalent to $TAC1$ and $TAC2$, which also provides (see proposition 16.6) an alternative characterization of model ($L8$): $\succsim$ satisfies ($L8$) if and only if $\succsim$ is complete and verifies $AC4$.

$AC4$ has the advantage over $TAC1$ and $TAC2$ that it implies a strictly positive response to marginal traces even when $\succsim$ is incomplete. It is the condition that we look for in view of obtaining a characterization of strict compatibility with dominance.

Proposition 16.8. *Strict compatibility with dominance*
A reflexive binary relation $\succsim$ on a set $X = \prod_{i=1}^{n} X_i$ is strictly compatible with a dominance relation if and only if it satisfies AC4. In such a case, the relations S_i are uniquely determined and $S_i = \succsim_i^{\pm}$, for all i.

The proof of this proposition is similar to that of proposition 16.7; see [BOU 04b].

Let us observe that the conditions ensuring strict compatibility with a dominance relation do not, however, guarantee that $\succsim$ possesses 'nice' properties such as completeness or transitivity. It is straightforward, using examples inspired by Condorcet's paradox, e.g. [SEN 86], to build a binary relation $\succsim$ that is strictly compatible with a dominance relation and has circuits in its asymmetric part (building for example $\succsim$ via the majority rule applied to relations S_i).

16.3.7. *The case of weak orders*

Visiting more classical models of preferences, i.e. models in which the preference is a weak order, we examine how this hypothesis combines with our axioms. When $\succsim$ is a weak order, the marginal trace $\succsim_i^{\pm}$ is identical to the marginal preference $\succsim_i$. We give the following results without proof; see [BOU 04b].

Lemma 16.7. *Case of a weak order*
If $\succsim$ is a weak order on the set $X = \prod_{i=1}^{n} X_i$, we have:

1) [$\succsim$ is weakly separable] $\Leftrightarrow$ [$\succsim$ satisfies AC1] $\Leftrightarrow$ [$\succsim$ satisfies AC2] $\Leftrightarrow$ [$\succsim$ satisfies AC3]; and

2) [$\succsim$ is weakly independent] $\Leftrightarrow$ [$\succsim$ satisfies AC4] $\Leftrightarrow$ [$\succsim$ satisfies TAC1 and TAC2].

In the case of weakly independent weak orders, we can neglect considering marginal traces; we do not need tools more refined than marginal preferences for analyzing preferences when these are weakly independent weak orders. Note that the case of weak orders is highly specific: see [BOU 04b, Appendix A] for examples of weakly separable (even weakly independent) semiorders which violate $AC1$, $AC2$ and $AC3$. In this slightly less constrained case, weak separability is not equivalent to $AC1$, $AC2$ or $AC3$.

Using these observations, it is easy to prove the following proposition.

Proposition 16.9. *Let $\succsim$ be a weak order on a denumerable set $X = \prod_{i=1}^{n} X_i$. There exist real-valued functions u_i defined on X_i and a real-valued function U on $\prod_{i=1}^{n} u_i(X_i)$ such that for all $x, y \in X$,*

$$x \succsim y \Leftrightarrow U(u_1(x_1), \ldots, u_n(x_n)) \geq U(u_1(y_1), \ldots, u_n(y_n)) \geq 0. \quad (16.33)$$

Function U in equation (16.33) can be chosen to be:

1) non-decreasing *in all its arguments if and only if* $\succsim$ *is weakly separable; and*

2) increasing *in all its arguments if and only if* $\succsim$ *is weakly independent.*

Proof. We start with applying Cantor's classical result [CAN 95]: any weak order $\succsim$ on a denumerable set X admits a numerical representation, i.e. there exists a function $f : X \to \mathbb{R}$ such that $x \succsim y \Leftrightarrow f(x) \geq f(y)$. In the general case, a factorization of f as $U(u_1(x_1), \ldots, u_n(x_n))$ obtains, as in the proof of proposition 16.2(1), the following. We choose functions u_i that separate the equivalence classes of $\succsim_i^{\pm}$ (see condition (16.13): $x_i \sim_i^{\pm} y_i \Leftrightarrow u(x_i) = u_i(y_i)$) and we define U setting $f(x) = U(u_1(x_1), \ldots, u_n(x_n))$. In the weakly separable and weakly independent cases, u_i will be a numerical representation of the marginal preference, the weak order $\succsim_i$ or the marginal trace $\succsim_i^{\pm}$ which is equivalent here. We define U as before. Combining the results of lemmas 16.4, 16.6 and 16.7 we show that U is non-decreasing (respectively, increasing) in each of its arguments. ◇

The non-denumerable case requires the adjunction of the usual hypothesis limiting the cardinality of X and guaranteeing the existence of numerical representations for the weak orders $\succsim$ and $\succsim_i$ (order-density condition).

While the case of a representation with an increasing function U is well known in the literature [KRA 71, theorem 7.1], the result in the case of non-decreasing U generalizes a theorem obtained by [BLA 78] under the hypothesis that $X \subseteq \mathbb{R}^n$.

16.3.8. *Examples*

Models (16.1), (16.3) and (16.6) enter into the framework of our models using traces on levels. Among them, the additive value function model (16.1) is the only one in which the preference is a weak order. However, all three models have marginal traces $\succsim_i^{\pm}$ that are weak orders.

In contrast, in the additive non-transitive model (16.4), the marginal traces of the preference relation are not necessarily complete. Postulating the latter condition in this model drives us closer to Tversky's additive differences model (16.3).

Let us briefly review the three models cited above, for the aim of illustration.

The additive value function model (16.1) belongs to model ($L8$), the more constrained of our models based on levels. In addition, the preferences representable by an additive value function are weak orders. In view of lemma 16.6, marginal traces and marginal preferences are identical and are weak orders. The functions u_i that appear in model (16.1) are numerical representations of the marginal preferences (or traces). The preference reacts in a strictly positive way to any progress of an alternative on any marginal trace.

Tversky's additive differences model (16.3) tolerates intransitive preferences. Like the additive value function it belongs to the more constrained class of models ($L8$). Lemma 16.6 also applies to this model, in which marginal traces and preferences are identical; the functions u_i that appear in (16.3) are numerical representations of these marginal preferences (or traces). We shall turn again to this model in section 16.5.2 since it is also based on the traces of differences (represented by the functions Φ_i).

Although the models based on levels are not the most adequate for describing relations obtained by outranking methods (a basic version of which is described by condition (16.6)), such relations nevertheless possess marginal traces that are weak orders. The preference relations representable in model (16.6) belong to class ($L5$) or ($L6$). The asymmetric part of their marginal preferences $\succ_i$ is usually empty. Indeed, the marginal preference on dimension j does not discriminate at all between levels unless the weight p_j of criterion j is 'dominant', i.e. if $\sum_{i=1}^{n} w_i \geq \lambda$, while $\sum_{i; i \neq j} w_i < \lambda$.

At this stage, it may come as a surprise to see that the additive value function model and the additive differences model belong to the same class ($L8$) of models on the levels. In particular, for those models, there is no distinction between marginal preferences and traces. Does this mean that the only interesting class of models on the levels is ($L8$), if we except the models inspired by the majoritarian methods in Social Choice (such as the ELECTRE methods)? If the answer were positive, the more refined analysis made here (which consists of carefully distinguishing marginal traces from marginal preferences) would lose a great deal of its interest. As well as the fact that our approach allows us to understand important issues such as the respect of a dominance relation (section 16.3.5), there exist models that are both genuinely interesting and cannot be described satisfactorily in terms of marginal preferences. Let us consider for instance a preference $\succsim$ which is representable in an additive value function model with a threshold:

$$\begin{aligned} x \succ y &\Leftrightarrow \sum_{i=1}^{n} u_i(x_i) \geq \sum_{i=1}^{n} u_i(y_i) + \varepsilon \\ x \sim y &\Leftrightarrow \left| \sum_{i=1}^{n} u_i(x_i) - \sum_{i=1}^{n} u_i(y_i) \right| \leq \varepsilon, \end{aligned} \quad (16.34)$$

where ε is a positive number representing a threshold above which a difference of preference becomes noticeable; differences that do not reach this threshold escape perception and lead to an indifference judgement ($\sim$). The preferences $\succsim$ that can be described by such a model are not weak orders but semiorders. The asymmetric part $\succ$ of the preference is transitive, while indifference $\sim$ is not [LUC 56, PIR 97]. Such a model can be used e.g. for describing a statistical test for the comparison of means (taking into account that, in this context, relation $\succsim$ should not be interpreted as a preference but rather as a comparative judgement on two quantities). It is impossible to analyze such a relation in terms of marginal preferences. Indeed, the latter can be represented by

$$x_i \succsim_i y_i \Leftrightarrow u_i(x_i) \geq u_i(y_i) - \varepsilon,$$

which implies that each marginal preference relation $\succsim_i$ is a semiorder. Generally, marginal traces are more discriminant. They are weak orders; if the set of alternatives is sufficiently rich (it is the case, for instance, when the image sets $u_i(X_i)$ are intervals of the real line), they can be represented by the functions u_i (i.e. $x_i \succsim_i^{\pm} y_i \Leftrightarrow u_i(x_i) \geq u_i(y_i)$). In this model, preference $\succsim$ is complete and its marginal traces are complete; hence it belongs to model ($L7$). It is likely that the reason why such models have received little attention is related to the fact that the dominant additive value function model does not require tools more refined than marginal preferences for its analysis. In the next section, we are interested in another fundamental tool for analyzing preferences: traces on differences.

Before closing this section, there is a final issue to be discussed. In the last part of this section, devoted to preferences that are weak orders (section 16.3.7), we distinguished weakly separable and weakly independent weak orders. The reader may wonder if there are interesting preference relations that are weak orders, weakly separable but not weakly independent. The answer is definitely positive. Consider for instance the additive value function model (16.1) and substitute the sum by a 'minimum' or a 'maximum' operator. We then obtain a weak order that is weakly separable but not independent. Indeed, let $(X_i) = [0, 10]$ and $u_i(x_i) = x_i$ for $i = 1, 2$. Preference $\succsim$ compares the alternatives only taking into consideration their 'weak point', that is $x \succsim y$ if and only if $\min x_i \geq \min y_i$. Clearly, marginal traces and marginal preferences are identical and correspond to the usual order of the real numbers of the interval $[0, 10]$. Let $x = (3, 5)$ and $y = (7, 3)$; we have $x \sim y$, but preference $\succsim$ does not strictly react if e.g. we raise the level of x on the second dimension. Even if we set x_2 to 10, we still have $(3, 10)$ indifferent to $(7, 3)$.

Other decision rules of practical importance, such as 'LexiMin' or 'LexiMax', the Choquet integral or the Sugeno integral (see section 17.5) lead in general to weak orders that are weakly separable but not weakly independent.

16.4. Models using marginal traces on differences

In this section we study preference models obtained in a similar manner to those in the previous section; we simply substitute marginal traces on levels by marginal traces on differences.

16.4.1. *Models definition*

We start from the trivial model ($D0$) based on marginal traces and introduced in section 16.2.5, in which:

$$x \succsim y \Leftrightarrow G([p_i(x_i, y_i)]) \geq 0.$$

We define the following variants:

– model ($D1$), by imposing that $p_i(x_i, x_i) = 0$ on ($D0$);
– model ($D2$), by imposing that each p_i is antisymmetric, i.e. $p_i(x_i, y_i) = -p_i(y_i, x_i)$, on ($D1$); and
– model ($D3$), by imposing that G is odd, i.e. $G(\mathbf{x}) = -G(-\mathbf{x})$, on ($D2$).

In the same way as in section 16.3, we also consider the models obtained by assuming in each variant ($D0$), ($D1$), ($D2$) and ($D3$), that G is non-decreasing or increasing in each of its n arguments which yields twelve models as defined in Table 16.2.

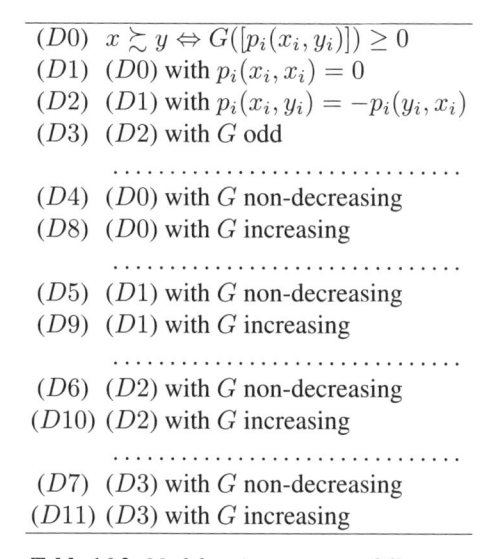

($D0$)	$x \succsim y \Leftrightarrow G([p_i(x_i, y_i)]) \geq 0$
($D1$)	($D0$) with $p_i(x_i, x_i) = 0$
($D2$)	($D1$) with $p_i(x_i, y_i) = -p_i(y_i, x_i)$
($D3$)	($D2$) with G odd
....	....
($D4$)	($D0$) with G non-decreasing
($D8$)	($D0$) with G increasing
....	....
($D5$)	($D1$) with G non-decreasing
($D9$)	($D1$) with G increasing
....	....
($D6$)	($D2$) with G non-decreasing
($D10$)	($D2$) with G increasing
....	....
($D7$)	($D3$) with G non-decreasing
($D11$)	($D3$) with G increasing

Table 16.2. *Models using traces on differences*

There are obvious implications linking these models; we do not detail them. As well as these implications, the properties of G in models ($D1$), ($D2$) and ($D3$) entail simple properties of the relations representable in these models. We shall lean on these properties to characterize the models.

Proposition 16.10. *Characterization of ($D1$), ($D2$) and ($D3$)*
A binary relation $\succsim$ on a product set $X = \prod_{i=1}^{n} X_i$ having at most the cardinality of $\mathbb{R}$ can be represented in

1) model ($D1$) or model ($D2$) if and only if $\succsim$ is independent; and
2) model ($D3$) if and only if $\succsim$ is independent and complete.

Proof. Part (1). We have $p_i(x_i, x_i) = 0$ in model (D1), which implies that $(x_i, a_{-i}) \succsim (x_i, b_{-i}) \Leftrightarrow G(0, (p_j(a_j, b_j))_{j \neq i}) \geq 0 \Leftrightarrow (y_i, a_{-i}) \succsim (y_i, b_{-i})$. As a consequence, $\succsim$ is independent as soon as $\succsim$ is representable in model (D1).

Assume conversely that $\succsim$ is independent and let us construct a representation of $\succsim$ in model (D2). We reconsider the construction of a representation described in the proof of part (2) of proposition 16.2, and slightly modify it. The alteration is related to the specification of functions p_i. These functions separate the equivalence classes of $\sim_i^{**}$: $(x_i, y_i) \sim_i^{**} (z_i, w_i) \Leftrightarrow p_i(x_i, y_i) = p_i(z_i, w_i)$. Nothing prevents us from imposing on p_i the verification of $p_i(x_i, x_i) = 0$ for a certain $x_i \in X_i$. Since $\succsim$ is independent, $(x_i, x_i) \sim_i^{**} (y_i, y_i)$ for all $y_i \in X_i$ and hence $p_i(y_i, y_i) = 0$ for all $y_i \in X_i$. We can also impose on p_i the verification of $p_i(x_i, y_i) = -p_i(y_i, x_i)$. Finally, G can be defined by equation (16.16) in the same way as for the trivial model, i.e.

$$G([p_i(x_i, y_i)]) = \begin{cases} +1 & \text{if } x \succsim y, \\ -1 & \text{otherwise.} \end{cases}$$

Clearly, G is well-defined and yields a representation of $\succsim$ in model (D2).

Part (2). The completeness of $\succsim$ is a direct consequence of the definition of model (D3); since model (D3) implies model (D1), $\succsim$ is independent. Reciprocally, let us assume that $\succsim$ is independent and complete. If this is the case, we use the same functions p_i as in part (1), but we change the definition of G as follows:

$$G([p_i(x_i, y_i)]) = \begin{cases} +1 & \text{if } x \succ y, \\ 0 & \text{if } x \sim y, \\ -1 & \text{otherwise.} \end{cases} \qquad (16.35)$$

We show, using independence of $\succsim$ that G is well defined. Since $\succsim$ is complete, function G is odd. ◇

The monotonicity properties of G are linked with specific axioms, rather similar to those defined in section 16.3.2. We introduce them in the next section.

16.4.2. *Completeness of marginal traces on differences and monotonicity of* G

There are two axioms for each attribute i. As with $AC1$, $AC2$ and $AC3$, these axioms appear as cancellation conditions. Their denomination, $RC1$, $RC2$ recalls the fact that they are 'inteR-Criteria' cancellation conditions.

Definition 16.8. Conditions $RC1$ and $RC2$
Let $\succsim$ be a binary relation on the set $X = \prod_{i=1}^n X_i$. We say that this relation satisfies

axiom: $RC1_i$ if

$$\left.\begin{array}{r}(x_i, a_{-i}) \succsim (y_i, b_{-i}) \\ \text{and} \\ (z_i, c_{-i}) \succsim (w_i, d_{-i})\end{array}\right\} \Rightarrow \left\{\begin{array}{l}(x_i, c_{-i}) \succsim (y_i, d_{-i}) \\ \text{or} \\ (z_i, a_{-i}) \succsim (w_i, b_{-i}),\end{array}\right.$$

and $RC2_i$ if

$$\left.\begin{array}{r}(x_i, a_{-i}) \succsim (y_i, b_{-i}) \\ \text{and} \\ (y_i, c_{-i}) \succsim (x_i, d_{-i})\end{array}\right\} \Rightarrow \left\{\begin{array}{l}(z_i, a_{-i}) \succsim (w_i, b_{-i}) \\ \text{or} \\ (w_i, c_{-i}) \succsim (z_i, d_{-i}),\end{array}\right.$$

for all $x_i, y_i, z_i, w_i \in X_i$ and for all $a_{-i}, b_{-i}, c_{-i}, d_{-i} \in X_{-i}$. We say that $\succsim$ satisfies $RC1$ (respectively, $RC2$) if it satisfies $RC1_i$ (respectively, $RC2_i$) for all $i \in \{1, \ldots, n\}$. We shall sometimes use $RC12$ for the conjunction of conditions $RC1$ and $RC2$.

Condition $RC1_i$ suggests that (x_i, y_i) corresponds to a difference of preference at least as large as (z_i, w_i) or vice versa. It is easily seen that assuming both Not $(x_i, y_i) \succsim_i^* (z_i, w_i)$ and Not $(z_i, w_i) \succsim_i^* (x_i, y_i)$ leads to a violation of $RC1_i$. From this we can see that $RC1_i$ is equivalent to the completeness of $\succsim_i^*$. The second axiom, $RC2_i$, suggests that the 'opposite' differences (x_i, y_i) and (y_i, x_i) are linked. In terms of the marginal trace on differences $\succsim_i^*$, this axiom tells us if the preference difference between x_i and y_i is not at least as large as that between z_i and w_i, then the difference between y_i and x_i is at least as large as that between w_i and z_i.

These observations are collected in the next lemma whose proof immediately results from the definitions and is omitted.

Lemma 16.8. *Completeness of the traces on differences*
We have:

1) $[\succsim_i^*$ is complete$]$ if and only if $RC1_i$;

2) $RC2_i$ if and only if $[$for all $x_i, y_i, z_i, w_i \in X_i$, Not $(x_i, y_i) \succsim_i^* (z_i, w_i) \Rightarrow (y_i, x_i) \succsim_i^* (w_i, z_i)]$; and

3) $[\succsim_i^{**}$ is complete$]$ if and only if $[RC1_i$ and $RC2_i]$.

Condition $RC1$ has been introduced in [BOU 86] under the name *weak cancellation*. The extension of condition $RC1$ to subsets of attributes (instead of singletons) is of fundamental importance in [VIN 91] where this condition receives the name of *independence*. Condition $RC2$ was first proposed in [BOU 99, BOU 97, BOU 09].

We note below two easy yet important consequences of $RC1$ and $RC2$ [BOU 05b].

Lemma 16.9. *Consequences of $RC1$ and $RC2$*
We have the following:
  1) if $\succsim$ satisfies $RC1_i$ then $\succsim$ is weakly separable for i; and
  2) if $\succsim$ satisfies $RC2$ then $\succsim$ is independent and either reflexive or irreflexive.

Axioms $RC1$ and $RC2$ allow us to analyze all the remaining models with the exception of the more constrained model ($D11$). We observe that the properties of non-decreasingness and increasingness with respect to the traces on differences do not lead to different models except in the more constrained case (models ($D7$) and ($D11$)).

Proposition 16.11. *Characterization of models ($D4$) to ($D10$)*
A binary relation $\succsim$ on a denumerable set $X = \prod_{i=1}^n X_i$ can be represented in
  1) model ($D4$) or model ($D8$) if and only if $\succsim$ satisfies $RC1$;
  2) model ($D5$) or model ($D9$) if and only if $\succsim$ is independent and satisfies $RC1$;
  3) model ($D6$) or model ($D10$) if and only if $\succsim$ satisfies $RC1$ and $RC2$;
  4) model ($D7$) if and only if $\succsim$ is complete and satisfies $RC1$ and $RC2$.

Proof. Part (1). Model ($D4$) verifies $RC1$. Assume that $(x_i, a_{-i}) \succsim (y_i, b_{-i})$ and $(z_i, c_{-i}) \succsim (w_i, d_{-i})$. Using model ($D4$) we have:

$$G(p_i(x_i, y_i), (p_j(a_j, b_j))_{j \neq i}) \geq 0 \text{ and}$$
$$G(p_i(z_i, w_i), (p_j(c_j, d_j))_{j \neq i}) \geq 0.$$

If $p_i(x_i, y_i) \geq p_i(z_i, w_i)$ then, using the non-decreasingness of G, we obtain $G(p_i(x_i, y_i), (p_j(c_j, d_j))_{j \neq i}) \geq 0$, hence $(x_i, c_{-i}) \succsim (y_i, d_{-i})$. If $p_i(z_i, w_i) > p_i(x_i, y_i)$, we have $G(p_i(z_i, w_i), (p_j(a_j, b_j))_{j \neq i}) \geq 0$, hence $(z_i, a_{-i}) \succsim (w_i, b_{-i})$. Consequently, $RC1$ is verified.

The second part of the proof constructs a representation in model ($D8$) of a relation $\succsim$ provided it verifies $RC1$. Using $RC1$, we know that $\succsim_i^*$ is a weak order. As function p_i, we choose a numerical representation of $\succsim_i^*$ (which exists since X_i has been supposed to be denumerable): $(x_i, y_i) \succsim_i^* (z_i, w_i) \Leftrightarrow p_i(x_i, y_i) \geq p_i(z_i, w_i)$. We then define G on $p_i(X_i^2)$ as follows:

$$G([p_i(x_i, y_i)]) = \begin{cases} + \exp(\sum_{i=1}^n p_i(x_i, y_i)) & \text{if } x \succsim y, \\ - \exp(-\sum_{i=1}^n p_i(x_i, y_i)) & \text{otherwise.} \end{cases} \quad (16.36)$$

We see that G is well defined using lemma 16.2(3) and the definition of the p_i. To show that G is increasing, let us assume that $p_i(z_i, w_i) > p_i(x,_i, y_i)$, i.e. that

$(z_i, w_i) \succ_i^* (x_i, y_i)$. If $x \succsim y$, lemma 16.2(2) implies that $(z_i, x_{-i}) \succsim (w_i, y_{-i})$ and the conclusion follows from the definition of G. If Not $x \succsim y$, we have either Not $(z_i, x_{-i}) \succsim (w_i, y_{-i})$ or $(z_i, x_{-i}) \succsim (w_i, y_{-i})$. In both cases the conclusion follows from the definition of G.

Part (2). Since model (D5) implies models (D1) and (D4), the necessity of the independence condition and of $RC1$ is straightforward. Under these hypotheses, we can build a representation of $\succsim$ in model (D9), as in part (1), with the exception that we require that p_i verifies $p_i(x_i, x_i) = 0$ (which is made possible as a consequence of the independence property; see lemma 16.2(1)).

Part (3). We readily check that if $\succsim$ is representable in model (D6), it satisfies $RC1$ and $RC2$. For $RC1$, it is a consequence of the fact that model (D6) implies model (D4). For $RC2$, we can proceed as for part (1) for $RC1$. The necessity of conditions $RC1$ and $RC2$ is thus proven.

Under the hypothesis that $\succsim$ satisfies $RC1$ and $RC2$, we can construct a representation of $\succsim$ in model (D10) as follows. By lemma 16.8(3), we know that relations $\succsim_i^*$ and $\succsim_i^{**}$ are weak orders. Since sets X_i are supposed to be denumerable, there exist functions $q_i : X_i \to \mathbb{R}$ that represent $\succsim_i^*$; we choose one such function for each i and we define p_i through $p_i(x_i, y_i) = q_i(x_i, y_i) - q_i(y_i, x_i)$. It is clear that these functions p_i are antisymmetric and provide numerical representations of relations $\succsim_i^{**}$. Using these functions p_i, we define G through equation (16.36). Lemma 16.2(5) shows that this definition makes sense. To show that G is increasing, let us assume that $p_i(z_i, w_i) > p_i(x_i, y_i)$, i.e. that $(z_i, w_i) \succ_i^{**} (x_i, y_i)$. This construction implies that $(z_i, w_i) \succsim_i^* (x_i, y_i)$. The increasingness of G can then be proven as in part (1).

Part (4). The necessity of the completeness of $\succsim$ results from proposition 16.10(2) and from the fact that model (D7) implies model (D3). The necessity of $RC1$ and $RC2$ is a consequence of the fact that model (D7) implies model (D6) and of part (3). Making these hypotheses on $\succsim$, a representation of $\succsim$ in model (D7) is obtained as for model (D10). The only difference lies in the definition of function G. We define G as follows:

$$G([p_i(x_i, y_i)]) = \begin{cases} +\exp(\sum_{i=1}^{n} p_i(x_i, y_i)) & \text{if } x \succ y, \\ 0 & \text{if } x \sim y, \\ -\exp(-\sum_{i=1}^{n} p_i(x_i, y_i)) & \text{otherwise.} \end{cases} \quad (16.37)$$

Since $\succsim$ is complete, G is odd; G is well defined as a consequence of the definition of the p_i and of lemma 16.2(5). It is non-decreasing due to lemma 16.2, parts (2) and (4). ◇

16.4.3. *Characterization of model* (D11)

Distinguishing between models (D7) and (D11) requires the introduction of a new axiom. It is similar to axioms $TAC1$ and $TAC2$, introduced in section 16.3.2, for studying the models based on traces on levels. Here, axiom TC will only deliver its full power for complete preferences. It is useful for characterizing the model in which increasingness with respect to marginal traces on differences is distinguished from non-decreasingness.

Definition 16.9. Condition TC
Let $\succsim$ be a binary relation on the set $X = \prod_{i=1}^{n} X_i$. We say that this relation satisfies axiom:
TC_i if
$$\left.\begin{array}{c}(x_i, a_{-i}) \succsim (y_i, b_{-i}) \\ \text{and} \\ (z_i, b_{-i}) \succsim (w_i, a_{-i}) \\ \text{and} \\ (w_i, c_{-i}) \succsim (z_i, d_{-i})\end{array}\right\} \Rightarrow (x_i, c_{-i}) \succsim (y_i, d_{-i}),$$

for all $x_i, y_i, z_i, w_i \in X_i$ and for all $a_{-i}, b_{-i}, c_{-i}, d_{-i} \in X_{-i}$. We say that $\succsim$ satisfies TC if it satisfies TC_i for all $i \in \{1, \ldots, n\}$.

Condition TC_i (*Triple Cancelation*) is a classical cancellation condition that has often been used [KRA 71, WAK 89] in the analysis of the additive value function model (16.1) or the additive utility model. In the next lemma, we state without proof two properties involving TC. See [WAK 88, WAK 89] for a detailed analysis of this axiom, including its interpretation in terms of differences of preference.

Lemma 16.10. *Strict monotonicity with respect to traces on differences*

1) If $\succsim$ is complete, TC_i implies $RC1_i$ and $RC2_i$.
2) If $\succsim$ is complete and verifies TC_i, we have: $[x \succsim y$ and $(z_i, w_i) \succ_i^{**} (x_i, y_i)] \Rightarrow (z_i, x_{-i}) \succ (w_i, y_{-i})$.

The second of the above properties clearly underlines that TC is related to the strict monotonicity of $\succsim$ with respect to its traces $\succsim_i^{**}$ (as soon as $\succsim$ is complete). It shows that TC is the missing link that will allow us to characterize model (D11).

Proposition 16.12. *Characterization of model* (D11)
A binary relation $\succsim$ on a denumerable product set $X = \prod_{i=1}^{n} X_i$ is representable in model (D11) *if and only if $\succsim$ is complete and satisfies TC.*

Proof. The necessity of these conditions is straightforward. Assuming that $\succsim$ is complete and verifies TC, we obtain by lemma 16.10(1) that $\succsim$ verifies $RC1$ and $RC2$. We thus define p_i and G as in the proof of part (4) of proposition 16.11. The increasingness of G is a consequence of lemma 16.10(2). ◇

For the reader's convenience, we summarize the characterization of all the models based on marginal traces on differences in Table 16.3.

Model	Definition	Conditions
(D0)	$x \succsim y \Leftrightarrow G([p_i(x_i, y_i)]) \geq 0$	∅
(D1) ⇕ (D2)	(D0) with $p_i(x_i, x_i) = 0$ (D0) with p_i antisymmetric	independent
(D3)	(D0) with p_i antisymmetric and G odd	complete, independent
(D8) ⇔ (D4)	(D0) with $G(\nearrow\nearrow)$	$RC1$
(D9) ⇔ (D5)	(D1) with $G(\nearrow\nearrow)$	$RC1$, independent
(D10) ⇔ (D6)	(D2) with $G(\nearrow\nearrow)$	$RC12$
(D7)	(D3) with $G(\nearrow)$	complete, $RC12$
(D11)	(D3) with $G(\nearrow\nearrow)$	complete, TC

Table 16.3. *Characterization of the models using traces on differences* ($\nearrow$: *non-decreasing,* $\nearrow\nearrow$: *increasing*)

16.4.4. *Remarks*

16.4.4.1. *Goldstein's model*

Models (D8) and (D4) were introduced by Goldstein [GOL 91] as particular cases of his 'decomposable model with thresholds'; the equivalence of models (D8) and (D4) had been noticed.

16.4.4.2. *Marginal preferences*

Which role is played by marginal preferences $\succsim_i$ in the models based on traces on differences? They certainly do not play a central role but some monotonicity properties linking them to the global preference $\succsim$ can nevertheless be established. We present some of them, without proof, in the next proposition.

Proposition 16.13. *Properties of models using differences*

1) If $\succsim$ is representable in model (D5) then: $[x_i \succ_i y_i \text{ for all } i] \Rightarrow \text{Not } y \succsim x$.
2) If $\succsim$ is representable in model (D6) then:
   - $\succsim_i$ is complete; and
   - $[x_i \succ_i y_i \text{ for all } i] \Rightarrow [x \succsim y]$.
3) If $\succsim$ is representable in model (D11) then:
   - $[x_i \succsim_i y_i \text{ for all } i] \Rightarrow [x \succsim y]$; and
   - $[x_i \succsim_i y_i \text{ for all } i \text{ and there exists } j \in \{1,\ldots,n\} \text{ such that } x_j \succ_j y_j] \Rightarrow [x \succ y]$.

The reader might feel somewhat disappointed while looking at the monotonicity properties of our models, except for model (D11). We must however keep in mind that we address preferences that are not necessarily transitive or complete. In such a framework, properties that could be seen as natural requirements for preferences could simply be undesirable. For example, when the marginal indifference relations $\sim_i$ are not transitive, it may be inadequate to require a property such as:

$$[x_i \sim_i y_i \text{ for all } i] \Rightarrow [x \sim y].$$

Were such a property verified, it would forbid that tiny but actual differences on several criteria, none of which yield a preference when taken separately, could interact or 'cooperate' and yield global preference. Let us consider, for example, comparing triplets $x = (x_1, x_2, x_3)$ of numbers x_i belonging to the $[0, 1]$ interval. We decide to compare these triplets using the following majoritarian method: $x \succsim y$ if and only if $x_i \geq y_i$ for at least 2 values of index i out of 3. We clearly have, on each dimension i, that $\succsim_i = \sim_i$ i.e. that there is no strict marginal preference, all pairs of levels being indifferent. Indeed, $(x_i, z_{-i}) \sim (y_i, z_{-i})$ for all x_i, y_i and z_{-i}. However, the global preference relation $\succsim$ is not reduced to indifference between all pairs of triplets (for example, $1 \succsim_i 0$ for all $i = 1, 2, 3$, but $(1, 1, 1) \succ (0, 0, 0)$).

For broader views on this topic, see [GIL 95] or [PIR 97]. As emphasized in section 16.3, marginal preferences are not a sufficiently refined tool to analyze preferences that are not necessarily transitive or complete; we have to use the marginal traces $\succsim_i^{\pm}$ instead. In the example introduced above, the traces $\succsim_i^{\pm}$ are, on each dimension i, the natural order on the $[0, 1]$ interval. The monotonicity properties of the preference with respect to marginal traces have been described in lemmas 16.1 and 16.5(4).

16.4.4.3. *Uniqueness of the representation*

Regarding the models on levels, the uniqueness properties of the representations described in propositions 16.11 and 16.12 are quite weak. In model (D8), for instance, we may always take any numerical representation of the weak order $\succsim_i^*$ (at least, in the finite or countable case) for $p_i(x_i, y_i)$. Regarding the models on levels, we shall call a representation in which p_i is a numerical representation of $\succsim_i^*$, for all i, *regular*. Other choices can be made, but it is necessary (and sufficient) that p_i satisfies the condition:

$$(x_i, y_i) \succ_i^* (z_i, w_i) \Rightarrow p_i(x_i, y_i) > p_i(z_i, w_i). \tag{16.38}$$

In other terms, the chosen numerical representation must be at least as discriminant as relation $\succ_i^*$. In more constrained models such as $(D7)$ or $(D10)$, a similar condition, involving $\succ_i^{**}$ instead of $\succ_i^*$, is needed. For more details, see [BOU 05b, lemma 5.5].

16.4.5. *Examples*

Among all the models described in the introduction, the only one that does not use traces on differences is the decomposable model (16.2), since this model aggregates the levels of each alternative independently of other alternatives. We briefly review the other models.

Let us start with the additive non-transitive preference model (16.4), which we recall here:

$$x \succsim y \Leftrightarrow \sum_{i=1}^{n} p_i(x_i, y_i) \geq 0.$$

If we do not assume any property of functions p_i, the appropriate model is $(D8)$ (equivalent to $(D4)$); the p_i functions represent the traces $\succsim_i^*$ that are weak orders; and function G, which reduces to addition of its n components, is strictly increasing. Assuming additional properties of functions p_i, such as $p_i(x_i, x_i) = 0$ or antisymmetry, leads us to models $(D9)$ (equivalent to $(D5)$) and $(D11)$, respectively. In the latter model, p_i represents the weak order $\succsim_i^{**}$ instead of representing $\succsim_i^*$ (function G is odd).

Tversky's model of additive differences (16.3) is a particular case of the latter model. Functions p_i reduce to algebraic differences $u_i(x_i) - u_i(y_i)$ of marginal value functions that representant the traces on levels. This is therefore a model which is based both on traces on differences and on traces on levels. Such models will be investigated in the next section.

Rewriting the additive value function model (16.1) as

$$x \succsim y \Leftrightarrow \sum_{i=1}^{n} (u_i(x_i) - u_i(y_i)) \geq 0,$$

we observe that it is a particular case of the additive differences model, in which functions Φ_i reduce to identity. The differences of marginal value functions $(u_i(x_i) - u_i(y_i))$ represent the traces $\succsim_i^{**}$.

The additive value function model sharply differentiates differences of preference since each value of the difference $(u_i(x_i) - u_i(y_i))$ corresponds to a specific equivalence class of relation $\succsim_i^{**}$. In contrast, outranking methods obtained by means of condition (16.6) distinguish differences of preference in a very rough manner. In the case of the majoritarian model (16.6), p_i represents $\succsim_i^*$ and distinguishes only two classes of differences of preference, as shown by equation (16.7). Either difference (x_i, y_i) is 'positive', in which case the whole weight of criterion i is assigned to this difference (diminished by a fraction of the majority threshold), or else this difference is 'negative' in which case it counts for nothing. Notice that equation (16.7) provides a representation of the preference obtained by the majoritarian method in model $(D8)$ while the properties of such a preference would allow it to be represented in model $(D10)$. Relations $\succsim_i^{**}$ have three equivalence classes and can be represented by function:

$$p_i(x_i, y_i) = \begin{cases} w_i & \text{if } x_i > y_i \\ 0 & \text{if } x_i = y_i \\ -w_i & \text{if } x_i < y_i. \end{cases} \quad (16.39)$$

We then define G as:

$$G(p_1, \ldots, p_n) = 1 - \sum_{i: p_i < 0} p_i - \lambda. \quad (16.40)$$

Using this representation, we obtain the same relation as that defined by condition (16.6). Indeed, assuming normalized weights ($\sum w_i = 1$), we see that G computes (in a somewhat bizarre way) the sum of the weights of the criteria in which difference (x_i, y_i) is 'positive', diminished by threshold λ.

These elementary observations open the way to a characterization of majoritarian methods within the framework of model $(D10)$. These methods are characterized by traces on differences $\succsim_i^{**}$ that distinguish no more than three classes of differences of preference [BOU 01, BOU 05a, BOU 07].

The ELECTRE methods, as they appear in [ROY 68, ROY 73, ROY 91, ROY 93], involve an additional element with respect to pure majoritarian methods. In order to decide whether x is preferred to y (x 'outranks' y), we 'weigh' the arguments in favor of x which corresponds to majoritarian model (16.6). If this weight is large enough, we then verify that no 'strong argument' opposes the statement that x is preferred to y. By 'strong argument', we mean a difference (x_i, y_i) on some criterion i that is 'very negative', in disfavor of x. If x_i and y_i represent numerical assessments of alternatives on criterion i, a 'very negative difference' may for instance result from trespassing a threshold ν_i, called *veto threshold*; we cannot state that x is preferred to y if, on at least one criterion i, we have:

$$x_i < y_i - \nu_i.$$

We observe that the idea of a 'very negative difference' introduced a third class of preference differences in $\succsim_i^*$, corresponding to a 'veto'. Relations $\succsim_i^*$ can therefore be represented by

$$p_i(x_i, y_i) = \begin{cases} w_i & \text{if } x_i \geq y_i \\ 0 & \text{if } y_i - \nu_i \leq x_i < y_i \\ -M & \text{if } x_i < y_i - \nu_i, \end{cases} \qquad (16.41)$$

where M is a large positive number. We define G as:

$$G(p_1, \ldots, p_n) = \sum_i p_i - \lambda. \qquad (16.42)$$

We easily verify that $x \succsim y$ if and only if the sum of the weights of the criteria on which x is at least as good as y passes λ and there is no criterion on which the level of x goes beyond that of y by more than the veto threshold (the value assigned to $-M$ is such that it prevents the λ threshold being reached as soon as it appears in any of the terms p_i).

A relation $\succsim$ obtained through the above-defined *majoritarian rule with veto* can be represented in model $(D10)$. Relations $\succsim_i^*$ distinguish at most three classes of preference differences; relations $\succsim_i^{**}$ at most five. Such preference relations can be fully characterized within model $(D10)$ [BOU 08, GRE 01a].

These examples show that models using traces on differences are well suited for describing and understanding outranking methods. We shall return to these models at the end of the following section where we shall show how relations obtained by comparing differences can generally be related to the description of the alternatives by levels on attributes (we have assumed above that the X_i are sets of real numbers endowed with their natural order which was supposed to be compatible with the decision maker's preferences).

16.5. Models using both marginal traces on levels and on differences

After studying models based on marginal traces on levels and those based on marginal traces on differences in the previous sections, it is quite natural to discuss models based on both types of traces. This is done by expressing the differences of preference in terms of the traces on the levels.

We recall the definition of the general model $(L0D0)$ presented in section 16.1.1; in this model, the preference relation $\succsim$ is defined as follows:

$$x \succsim y \Leftrightarrow H([\varphi_i(u_i(x_i), u_i(y_i))]) \geq 0. \tag{$L0D0$}$$

This model can be seen as a particular case of model $(D0)$, in which functions $p_i(x_i, y_i)$ have been substituted by functions $\varphi_i(u_i(x_i), u_i(y_i))$. It is also possible to view it as a generalization of the additive differences model (16.3) in which the simple addition and subtraction operations have been substituted by general, appropriately monotonic, functions.

A model in which $p_i(x_i, y_i)$ is substituted by $\varphi_i(u_i(x_i), u_i(y_i))$ corresponds to each of the 12 models $(D0)$ to $(D11)$ studied in section 16.3, without imposing any additional property.

This allows us to define models $(L0D0)$ to $(L0D11)$. These 'new' models have in fact very little interest since they are equivalent (if the cardinality of the set of alternatives X is not larger than that of the real numbers) to the corresponding models based on traces on differences $(D0)$ to $(D11)$. They simply provide another representation of the same models. Indeed, starting with a given function $p_i(x_i, y_i)$ defined on $X_i \times X_i$, it is always possible to factorize it by means of a real-valued function u_i defined on X_i. The only condition that u_i must fulfill is to separate the elements of X_i that belong to different equivalence classes of the marginal trace $\succsim_i^{\pm}$. Notice that we do not assume the completeness of the traces on levels $\succsim_i^{\pm}$ (at the moment). More formally, the functions u_i must verify the following condition:

$$u_i(x_i) = u_i(y_i) \Rightarrow x_i \sim_i^{\pm} y_i.$$

For any function u_i satisfying this basic requirement and for any given function p_i, we define unambiguously the function φ_i on subset $u_i(X_i) \times u_i(X_i)$ of $\mathbb{R}^2$ by setting:

$$p_i(x_i, y_i) = \varphi_i(u_i(x_i), u_i(y_i)).$$

Consequently, starting from any representation $G([p_i(x_i, y_i)])$ of a relation $\succsim$ in one of the models based on traces on differences, we automatically obtain a representation of this relation in the corresponding model based on traces on differences and levels. This is done by substituting $p_i(x_i, y_i)$ by the function $\varphi_i(u_i(x_i), u_i(y_i))$ we have just defined. Let us note that function H is identical to G. Notice also that this substitution can be done without problem only when the cardinality of X does not exceed that of $\mathbb{R}$, and if no additional requirement is imposed on φ_i. At this stage, we do not even assume that φ_i is monotonic in its two arguments.

To make φ_i more similar to subtraction, we consider two variants of each of the twelve models $(L0D0)$ to $(L0D11)$. In the first variant we impose that φ_i is non-decreasing in its first argument and non-increasing in its second argument. This leads to models $(L1D0)$ to $(L1D11)$. In the other variant, we impose that functions φ_i must be increasing in their first argument and decreasing in their second argument. This yields models $(L2D0)$ to $(L2D11)$.

In summary, we have now defined $3 \times 12 = 36$ new models (see Table 16.4) using both marginal traces on levels and marginal traces on differences. Skipping the first twelve models that are not interesting as already mentioned, we study the others in the rest of this section after discussing the relationships between traces on differences and traces on levels.

$(L0D0)$	$x \succsim y \Leftrightarrow H([\varphi_i(u_i(x_i), u_i(y_i))]) \geq 0$
$(L0D1)$	$(L0D0)$ with $\varphi_i(u(x_i), u_i(x_i)) = 0$
$(L0D2)$	$(L0D1)$ with φ_i antisymmetric
$(L0D3)$	$(L0D2)$ with H odd
	....
$(L0D4)$	$(L0D0)$ with H non-decreasing
$(L0D5)$	$(L0D0)$ with H increasing
	....
$(L0D6)$	$(L0D1)$ with H non-decreasing
$(L0D7)$	$(L0D1)$ with H increasing
	....
$(L0D8)$	$(L0D2)$ with H non-decreasing
$(L0D9)$	$(L0D2)$ with H increasing
	....
$(L0D10)$	$(L0D3)$ with H non-decreasing
$(L0D11)$	$(L0D3)$ with H increasing

Table 16.4. *Models based both on traces on levels and on differences. Models $(L1Dx)$ correspond to models $(N0Dx)$ where $\varphi_i(\nearrow, \searrow)$; models $(L2Dx)$ correspond to models $(L0Dx)$ where $\varphi_i(\nearrow\nearrow, \searrow\searrow)$*

16.5.1. *Relationships between traces on differences and on levels*

The traces on differences $\succsim_i^*$ and $\succsim_i^{**}$ are binary relations on the product set $X_i \times X_i$. We may define their own traces on levels in the usual way. For $\succsim_i^*$, we denote

– the left (respectively, right, left-right) trace on the first dimension by $(\succsim_i^*)_1^+$ (respectively, $(\succsim_i^*)_1^-$, $(\succsim_i^*)_1^\pm$);

– the left (respectively, right, left-right) trace on the second dimension by $(\succsim_i^*)_2^+$ (respectively, $(\succsim_i^*)_2^-$, $(\succsim_i^*)_2^\pm$).

Their definition is a straightforward transposition of definition 16.3 applied to $\succsim_i^*$ instead of $\succsim$ as follows.

Definition 16.10. *Left and right traces of the traces on differences*
Let $\succsim$ be a preference relation on the product set X and $\succsim_i^*$ its trace on differences relative to the ith dimension. The traces of $\succsim_i^*$ are defined as follows. For all $x_i, y_i \in X_i$,

1) $x_i \, (\succsim_i^*)_1^+ \, y_i$ if $\forall s_i, t_i, z_i \in X_i, (y_i, s_i) \succsim_i^* (z_i, t_i) \Rightarrow (x_i, s_i) \succsim_i^* (z_i, t_i)$;
2) $x_i \, (\succsim_i^*)_1^- \, y_i$ if $\forall s_i, t_i, z_i \in X_i, (z_i, t_i) \succsim_i^* (x_i, s_i) \Rightarrow (z_i, t_i) \succsim_i^* (y_i, s_i)$;
3) $x_i \, (\succsim_i^*)_2^+ \, y_i$ if $\forall s_i, t_i, z_i \in X_i, (s_i, y_i) \succsim_i^* (t_i, z_i) \Rightarrow (s_i, x_i) \succsim_i^* (t_i, z_i)$;
4) $x_i \, (\succsim_i^*)_2^- \, y_i$ if $\forall s_i, t_i, z_i \in X_i, (t_i, z_i) \succsim_i^* (s_i, x_i) \Rightarrow (t_i, z_i) \succsim_i^* (s_i, y_i)$.

The traces of $\succsim_i^{**}$ are defined similarly.

Are there relationships between these traces and the traces on levels of $\succsim$? The answer is positive as suggested by lemma 16.3. Referring to definitions 16.2 and 16.3 of $\succsim_i^+, \succsim_i^-$ and $\succsim_i^*$, it is easy to see that the traces on levels $\succsim_i^+$ and $\succsim_i^-$ can be defined in terms of $\succsim_i^*$ as follows:

$$\begin{array}{ll} x_i \succsim_i^+ y_i & \text{if and only if} \quad \forall z_i \in X_i, (x_i, z_i) \succsim_i^* (y_i, z_i) \\ x_i \succsim_i^- y_i & \text{if and only if} \quad \forall w_i \in X_i, (w_i, y_i) \succsim_i^* (w_i, x_i). \end{array} \quad (16.43)$$

This means that $\succsim_i^+$ and the inverse of relation $\succsim_i^-$, $(\succsim_i^-)^{-1}$, can be interpreted as the marginal relations of relation $\succsim_i^*$ defined on $X_i \times X_i$: they play the same role with respect to $\succsim_i^*$ as that played by the marginal preferences $\succsim_i$ with respect to $\succsim$.

The following result can easily be proven using lemma 16.3(5–8).

Proposition 16.14. *For all $i \in N$, for all $x_i, y_i \in X_i$ we have:*

1) $x_i \succsim_i^+ y_i$ if and only if $x_i \, (\succsim_i^*)_1^+ \, y_i$ if and only if $x_i \, (\succsim_i^*)_1^- \, y_i$ if and only if $x_i \, (\succsim_i^*)_1^\pm \, y_i$; and

2) $x_i \succsim_i^- y_i$ if and only if $y_i \, (\succsim_i^*)_2^+ \, x_i$ if and only if $y_i \, (\succsim_i^*)_2^- \, x_i$ if and only if $y_i \, (\succsim_i^*)_2^\pm \, x_i$.

As a consequence, $\succsim_i^\pm = \succsim_i^+ \cap \succsim_i^-$ is the intersection of the (left-right trace) of $\succsim_i^*$ on the first dimension, $(\succsim_i^*)_1^\pm$, and the inverse of the (left-right) trace of $\succsim_i^*$ on the second dimension $(\succsim_i^*)_2^\pm$:

$$x_i \succsim_i^\pm y_i \text{ if and only if } x_i \, (\succsim_i^*)_1^\pm \, y_i \text{ and } y_i \, (\succsim_i^*)_2^\pm \, x_i. \quad (16.44)$$

Regarding $\succsim_i^{**}$, it is not difficult to see that its left-right trace on the first dimension is identical to $\succsim_i^\pm$, while its left-right trace on the second dimension is the inverse of $\succsim_i^\pm$, $(\succsim_i^\pm)^{-1}$.

We emphasize that these observations are true without making any hypothesis on traces; in particular, they are true even if traces are incomplete. In the case where $\succsim_i^*$ is a weak order (hence, when $\succsim$ satisfies axiom $RC1_i$), we may apply proposition 16.9 to $\succsim_i^*$. This relation therefore admits a numerical representation of the type

$$(x_i, y_i) \succsim_i^* (z_i, w_i) \text{ if and only if } \varphi_i(u_i(x_i), u_i(y_i)) \geq \varphi_i(u_i(z_i), u_i(w_i)),$$

where u_i is a function that separates the equivalence classes of the traces of $\succsim_i^*$. In view of equation (16.44) we can take a function that separates the equivalence classes of $\succsim_i^\pm$ for u_i. The fact that $\succsim_i^*$ is a weak order on the product set $X_i \times X_i$, i.e. a product of a set by itself, allows us to use the same function u_i on both dimensions.

Assume that $\succsim_i^*$ is weakly separable (since the product set on which $\succsim_i^*$ is defined has only two dimensions, 'weakly separable' is equivalent to 'separable' and 'weakly independent' is equivalent to 'independent'). Using the rest of proposition 16.9, we can build a numerical representation of $\succsim_i^*$ by a function $\psi_i(v_{i1}(x_i), v_{i2}(y_i))$, where v_{i1} is a numerical representation of the trace $(\succsim_i^*)_1^\pm$, v_{i2} is a numerical representation of the trace $(\succsim_i^*)_2^\pm$ and ψ_i is a function of two variables that is non-decreasing in both variables.

Since $\succsim_i^+ = (\succsim_i^*)_1^\pm$ and $\succsim_i^- = ((\succsim_i^*)_2^\pm)^{-1}$, we can alternatively represent $\succsim_i^*$ by $\phi_i(u_{i1}(x_i), u_{i2}(y_i))$, where u_{i1} is a numerical representation of $\succsim_i^+$, u_{i2} is a numerical representation of $\succsim_i^-$ and ϕ_i is a function of two variables that is non-decreasing in its first variable and non-increasing in the second. (We can take, for instance, $u_{i1} = v_{i1}$, $u_{i2} = -v_{i2}$ and $\phi_i = \psi_i$.) The latter opens the door to a representation of $\succsim_i^*$ by a function $\varphi_i(u_i(x_i), u_i(y_i))$, with the same function u_i on both dimensions. Indeed, as soon as $\succsim_i^+$ and $\succsim_i^-$ are not incompatible, i.e. as soon as $\succsim_i^\pm$ is a weak order, we can use for u_i a numerical representation of the weak order $\succsim_i^\pm$.

The case of $\succsim_i^{**}$ is simpler. As above, its trace on the first dimension is $\succsim_i^\pm$ and on the second dimension is $(\succsim_i^\pm)^{-1}$. Hence, as soon as $\succsim_i^{**}$ is a weakly separable weak order and $\succsim_i^+$ a weak order, we can build a representation of $\succsim_i^{**}$ of the type $\varphi_i(u_i(x_i), u_i(y_i))$, where u_i is a numerical representation of the weak order $\succsim_i^\pm$ and φ_i is non-decreasing in its first argument and non-increasing in its second argument.

In the framework of our models, it is on $\succsim$ that we have to determine conditions which guarantee the separability or the independence of $\succsim_i^*$ or $\succsim_i^{**}$. Separability conditions for $\succsim_i^*$ and $\succsim_i^{**}$ are stated in the following proposition. In contrast (and this may sound strange initially) the independence of $\succsim_i^{**}$ is a consequence of none of our models, even the more constrained model ($L2D11$). We shall discuss this issue after we prove proposition 16.15 below.

Proposition 16.15. *If X_i is denumerable and $\succsim$ verifies $AC123_i$ and $RC1_i$, then $\succsim_i^*$ is a separable weak order on X_i^2 and any numerical representation $p_i(x_i, y_i)$ of $\succsim_i^*$*

factorizes into

$$p_i(x_i, y_i) = \varphi_i(u_i(x_i), u_i(y_i)), \tag{16.45}$$

where u_i is a numerical representation of weak order $\succsim_i^{\pm}$ and φ_i is a function defined on $u_i((X_i)^2)$, non-decreasing in its first argument and non-increasing in its second argument.

If, in addition, $\succsim$ satisfies $RC2_i$, the same can be said of relation $\succsim_i^{**}$ and of its numerical representations.

Proof. We know that $\succsim$ verifies $RC1_i$ if and only if $\succsim_i^*$ is a complete weak order on X_i^2. This weak order is separable if, for all x_i, y_i, z_i, w_i in X_i, neither of the following conjunctions occurs:

1) $(x_i, z_i) \succ_i^* (y_i, z_i)$ and $(y_i, w_i) \succ_i^* (x_i, w_i)$;
2) $(z_i, x_i) \succ_i^* (z_i, y_i)$ and $(w_i, y_i) \succ_i^* (w_i, x_i)$.

Since $\succsim_i^*$ is a complete relation, forbidding conjunction (1) is equivalent to ensuring that:

$$\left.\begin{array}{c}(x_i, z_i) \succsim_i^* (y_i, z_i) \\ \text{and} \\ (y_i, w_i) \succsim_i^* (x_i, w_i)\end{array}\right\} \Rightarrow \left\{\begin{array}{c}(y_i, z_i) \succsim_i^* (x_i, z_i) \\ \text{or} \\ (x_i, w_i) \succsim_i^* (y_i, w_i).\end{array}\right.$$

We know that $\succsim_i^{\pm}$ is the intersection of the first trace $(\succsim_i^*)_1^{\pm}$ of $\succsim_i^*$ and of the inverse of its second trace $(\succsim_i^*)_2^{\pm}$. Since $\succsim$ verifies $AC123_i$, $\succsim_i^{\pm}$ is a weak order. As a consequence, either $x_i \succsim_i^{\pm} y_i$ or $y_i \succsim_i^{\pm} x_i$. In the former case, starting from $(y_i, w_i) \succsim_i^* (y_i, w_i)$ and using definition (16.43), we obtain $(x_i, w_i) \succsim_i^* (y_i, w_i)$. In the latter case, starting from $(x_i, z_i) \succsim_i^* (x_i, z_i)$, we obtain $(y_i, w_i) \succsim_i^* (x_i, w_i)$.

We can show that conjunction (2) is also false in a similar way.

Let $p_i(x_i, y_i)$ and $u_i(x_i)$ be any numerical representation of the weak orders $\succsim_i^*$ and $\succsim_i^{\pm}$, respectively. Using the above conclusions, we verify directly that setting

$$\varphi_i(u_i(x_i), u_i(y_i)) = p_i(x_i, y_i)$$

defines unambiguously a function φ_i on $u_i(X_i)^2$ and that this function is non-decreasing in its first argument and non-increasing in its second argument.

Regarding $\succsim_i^{**}$, the same considerations apply as soon as $\succsim_i^{**}$ is a weak order, which is ensured by $RC2_i$. ◇

Let us now consider model ($L2D11$). It is straightforward that any preference $\succsim$ representable in this model is complete and satisfies $TAC12$ and TC. Hence, using lemmas 16.5(3), 16.5(4) and 16.10(2), we know that such a preference reacts in a strictly positive manner both to the traces on levels and to the traces on differences, i.e. if $(y_i, a_{-i}) \succsim (z_i, b_{-i})$, then

$$x_i \succ_i^+ y_i \Rightarrow (x_i, a_{-i}) \succ (z_i, b_{-i}),$$
$$z_i \succ_i^- w_i \Rightarrow (y_i, a_{-i}) \succ (w_i, b_{-i})$$
$$\text{and} \quad (x_i, z_i) \succ_i^* (y_i, z_i) \Rightarrow (x_i, a_{-i}) \succ (z_i, b_{-i}).$$

We cannot deduce from this, however, that $x_i \succ_i^+ y_i \Rightarrow (x_i, s_i) \succ_i^* (y_i, s_i)$ for all levels s_i or that $z_i \succ_i^- w_i \Rightarrow (t_i, w_i) \succ_i^* (t_i, z_i)$ for all levels t_i. In the former case (the other case being similar), for some levels s_i, it may indeed occur that comparing the difference (x_i, s_i) to the difference (y_i, s_i) does not reveal that x_i is at a higher level than y_i. One situation in which the higher level of x_i is certainly revealed is the following. If there exist $a_{-i}, b_{-i} \in X_{-i}$, such that $(y_i, a_{-i}) \sim (s_i, b_{-i})$ then, using the strict monotonicity of $\succsim$ with respect to $\succsim_i^+$, we have $(x_i, a_{-i}) \succ (s_i, b_{-i})$ hence $(x_i, s_i) \succ_i^* (y_i, s_i)$. If such a situation never occurs, it may happen that for all $a_{-i}, b_{-i} \in X_{-i}$ we always have either $(y_i, a_{-i}) \succ (s_i, b_{-i})$ and $(x_i, a_{-i}) \succ (s_i, b_{-i})$ or Not$[(y_i, a_{-i}) \succsim (s_i, b_{-i})]$ and Not$[(x_i, a_{-i}) \succsim (s_i, b_{-i})]$. In such a case, $(x_i, s_i) \sim_i^* (y_i, s_i)$ while this is not in contradiction with $x_i \succ_i^+ y_i$ [BOU 04a, example 17].

Condition $x_i \succ_i^\pm y_i \Rightarrow (x_i, w_i) \succ_i^* (y_i, w_i)$ is, however, necessary for the independence of $\succsim_i^{**}$. Indeed, $\succsim_i^{**}$ is independent if and only if for all x_i, y_i, z_i, w_i in X_i, $(x_i, z_i) \succsim_i^{**} (y_i, z_i) \Leftrightarrow (x_i, w_i) \succsim_i^{**} (y_i, w_i)$ and $(z_i, x_i) \succsim_i^{**} (z_i, y_i) \Leftrightarrow (w_i, x_i) \succsim_i^{**} (w_i, y_i)$. But $x_i \succ_i^\pm y_i$ implies $x_i \succ_i^+ y_i$ or $x_i \succ_i^- y_i$ (or both). In the former case, there exist levels a_{-i} and an alternative w such that $(x_i, a_{-i}) \succsim w$ and Not $(y_i, a_{-i}) \succsim w$. Hence, we have $(x_i, w_i) \succ_i^* (y_i, w_i)$. The latter case entails a similar conclusion. Hence, the independence of $\succsim_i^{**}$ implies that for all z_i, $(x_i, z_i) \succ_i^* (y_i, z_i)$.

Although we are unable to characterize the independence of $\succsim_i^{**}$ in terms of relation $\succsim$ and the previously introduced axioms (or the independence of $\succsim_i^*$), this will have no influence on the characterization of our models as we shall see. The only consequence is that we cannot guarantee the existence of *regular* representations for model $(L2D11)$ (i.e. of representations in which u_i represents $\succsim_i^\pm$ and $\varphi_i(u_i(x_i), u_i(y_i))$ represents $\succsim_i^{**}$).

16.5.2. *Study of models* $(L1D0)$ *to* $(L1D11)$ *and* $(L2D0)$ *to* $(L2D11)$

In this section, we assume that X is at most denumerable. The difficulties of the general case are mainly technical; they are fully dealt with in [BOU 04a]. Let us start with the study of the models where H is not supposed to be monotonic, i.e. models

Models E		Models $L0Dx$, $L1Dx$ and $L2Dx$	Conditions
$(D0)$	$\Leftrightarrow$	$(L0D0) \Leftrightarrow (L1D0) \Leftrightarrow (L2D0)$	$\varnothing$
$(D1)$	$\Leftrightarrow$	$(L0D1) \Leftrightarrow (L1D1) \Leftrightarrow (L2D1)$	
$\Updownarrow$		$\Updownarrow$	independent
$(D2)$	$\Leftrightarrow$	$(L0D2) \Leftrightarrow (L1D2) \Leftrightarrow (L2D2)$	
$(D3)$	$\Leftrightarrow$	$(L0D3) \Leftrightarrow (L1D3) \Leftrightarrow (L2D3)$	complete, independent

Table 16.5. *Models equivalent to (D0), (D1), (D2) and (D3)*

$(L1D0)$ to $(L1D3)$ and $(L2D0)$ to $(L2D3)$. It is easily understood that these models contribute nothing new with respect to the corresponding models on differences, that is models $(D0)$, $(D1)$ (which is equivalent to $(D2)$) and $(D3)$. Indeed, the monotonicity of functions φ_i does not impose any additional constraint, since we do not require that function H reacts monotonically to the variations of functions φ_i. We can easily build the new representations on the basis of those of the models on differences by substituting $\varphi_i(u_i(x_i), u_i(y_i))$ to $p_i(x_i, y_i)$. The models equivalences are noted in Table 16.5; the equivalences with models $(L0D0)$, $(L0D1)$, $(L0D2)$ and $(L0D3)$ are also noted as well as the models characterizations.

As soon as we assume that H is non-decreasing, variations of φ_i are transmitted and additional constraints appear and impact on the characterization of the preference relations. Model $(L1D4)$ is the first interesting one; it is equivalent to models $(L1D8)$, $(L2D4)$ and $(L2D8)$. We verify immediately that a preference representable in model $(L1D4)$ satisfies $AC123$ and these conditions, together with $RC1$, are necessary and sufficient for this model. To obtain a representation of a relation satisfying $RC1$ and $AC123$ in model $(L1D8)$, let us start with the representation in model $(D8)$ obtained through equation (16.36), i.e.

$$G([p_i(x_i, y_i)]) = \begin{cases} + \exp(\sum_{i=1}^n p_i(x_i, y_i)) & \text{if } x \succsim y, \\ - \exp(-\sum_{i=1}^n p_i(x_i, y_i)) & \text{otherwise} \end{cases}$$

where p_i is a numerical representation of $\succsim_i^*$ for all i.

Using proposition 16.15, we can decompose $p_i(x_i, y_i)$, which is any numerical representation of $\succsim_i^*$, into $\varphi_i(u_i(x_i), u_i(y_i))$ in which u_i represents weak order $\succsim_i^{\pm}$ and φ_i is non-decreasing in its first argument and non-increasing in its second argument. This shows that model $(L1D8)$ is not more constrained than model $(L1D4)$. We can show, starting from the just constructed representation, that it is possible to change functions φ_i into functions that are increasing in their first argument and decreasing in their second argument. This is possible without making any additional hypothesis on relation $\succsim$ [BOU 04a]. Note that this modified function will no longer, in general, be a numerical representation of $\succsim_i^*$. This proves that model $(L2D8)$ is not more constrained than model $(L1D4)$ and thus establishes the announced equivalence of the four models as well as their characterization.

Passing to model $(L1D5)$ and the equivalent models $(L1D9)$, $(L2D5)$ and $(L2D9)$, we first observe that independence of $\succsim$ is a necessary condition, in addition to $RC1$ and $AC123$. Assuming that these conditions are fulfilled, we then construct a representation of $\succsim$ in model $(L1D9)$ as in the previous paragraph. The only difference is that $p_i(x_i, y_i)$ is no longer any numerical representation of $\succsim_i^*$: the chosen representation satisfies an additional property, that is $p_i(x_i, x_i) = 0$. Using proposition 16.15, we decompose *this* numerical representation of $\succsim_i^*$ into $\varphi_i(u_i(x_i), u_i(y_i))$ where u_i represents weak order $\succsim_i^\pm$ and φ_i is non-decreasing in its first argument and non-increasing in its second argument. We find in addition that $\varphi_i(u_i(x_i), u_i(x_i)) = 0$. As before, $\varphi_i(u_i(x_i), u_i(y_i))$ can be modified into a function that is increasing in its first argument and decreasing in its second argument, while preserving the additional property $\phi_i(u_i(x_i), u_i(x_i)) = 0$. A representation of $\succsim$ in model $(L2D9)$ is therefore obtained.

Model $(L1D6)$ implies $RC12$ and $AC123$. The independence of $\succsim$ is a consequence of $RC12$ (as in model $(D6)$ of which it is a specialization). The procedure used with the previous models also applies here to characterize models $(L1D6)$, $(L1D10)$, $(L2D6)$ and $(L2D10)$ and show that they are equivalent. Let us start with equation (16.37). Here, function p_i is a representation of $\succsim_i^{**}$; it is antisymmetric. The antisymmetry of p_i is transferred to $\varphi_i(u_i(x_i), u_i(y_i))$ (as a consequence of proposition 16.15).

The last four models are not all equivalent. We distinguish three classes among them: $(L1D7)$ and $(L2D7)$ are equivalent; the last two are distinct models. Notice first that all these models correspond to complete relations. Models $(L1D7)$ and $(L2D7)$ correspond exactly to the complete relations $\succsim$ that fulfill conditions $RC12$ and $AC123$. A numerical representation can be constructed as before, starting from a representation in model $(D7)$.

For a preference $\succsim$ representable in model $(L1D11)$, it is clear that TC and $AC123$ are necessary since $(L1D11)$ is a special case of models $(L1D10)$ and $(D11)$. Under these hypotheses, the construction process used for model $(L1D7)$ leads to a representation in model $(L1D11)$.

Finally, for model $(L2D11)$, TC and $TAC12$ are necessary conditions. The construction of a representation starts as for model $(L1D7)$; we then transform function φ_i into a function non-decreasing in its first argument and non-increasing in its second argument, which no longer is, in general, a numerical representation of $\succsim_i^{**}$.

Models $L1Dx$	Models $L2Dx$	Conditions
$(L1D4) \Leftrightarrow (L1D8)$	$\Leftrightarrow (L2D4) \Leftrightarrow (L2D8)$	$RC1, AC123$
$(L1D5) \Leftrightarrow (L1D9)$	$\Leftrightarrow (L2D5) \Leftrightarrow (L2D9)$	independent, $RC1, AC123$
$(L1D6) \Leftrightarrow (L1D10)$	$\Leftrightarrow (L2D6) \Leftrightarrow (L2D10)$	$RC12, AC123$
$(L1D7)$	$\Leftrightarrow (L2D7)$	complete, $RC12, AC123$
$(L1D11)$		complete, $TC, AC123$
	$(L2D11)$	complete, $TC, TAC12$

Table 16.6. *Equivalences and characterization of models $(L1D4)$ to $(L1D11)$ and $(L2D4)$ to $(L2D11)$*

Table 16.6 summarizes all characterization and equivalence results relative to models $(L1D4)$ to $(L1D11)$ and $(L2D4)$ to $(L2D11)$.

16.5.3. *Examples*

Tversky's additive differences model (16.3) and the additive value function model (16.1) both use marginal traces on levels and on differences. They both verify, as we have seen in sections 16.3.8 and 16.4.5, the hypotheses of the more constrained models $(L8)$ and $(D11)$. As a result they belong to category $(L1D11)$ in the models using both traces on levels and on differences.

The additive differences model can be viewed as a particular case of model (16.4); functions $p_i(x_i, y_i)$ that occur in the latter factorize into algebraic differences: $p_i(x_i, y_i) = \Phi_i(u_i(x_i) - u_i(y_i))$ where functions u_i represent the marginal traces $\succsim_i^{\pm}$ that are identical (in this case) to marginal preferences $\succsim_i$.

In the versions of outranking methods described in literature, differences of preference are generally expressed in terms of the levels. In the simple versions that we have presented, the majoritarian method without veto (condition (16.6)) or with veto (equations (16.41) and (16.42)), we have assumed that preference differences can be expressed directly in terms of the alternative description on the relevant attributes, i.e. as a difference between corresponding coordinates of vectors x and y. In other words, it has been assumed implicitly that $u_i(x_i) = x_i$. It is easy of course to adapt the descriptions of the outranking methods in order to show explicitly a coding of the descriptions (i.e. of the elements of X_i) by functions u_i. These transform the possibly unstructured sets X_i into subsets of the real numbers $u_i(X_i)$. To do this, we simply substitute x_i and y_i by $u_i(x_i)$ and $u_i(y_i)$, respectively, in expressions (16.6), (16.41) and (16.42). Through this, we obtain models on the levels and on the differences of type ($L1D10$) or, equivalently, of type ($L2D10$). Note that the representations in models as constrained as possible are not always the most natural or the most useful ones, as already observed with models on differences (compare equations (16.39) and (16.40) with (16.6)).

16.6. Conclusion

In this chapter, we have presented a general approach for describing binary relations on a product set. This approach is based on conjoint measurement models that do not exclude intransitive or incomplete preferences. The main tools for analyzing such preferences are simple: we use two types of marginal traces induced on each dimension by the global preference. These tools are powerful: they permit a complete analysis of a rather large variety of models as we have shown, limiting ourselves to the case where X is denumerable.

Our project was to discover how far it is possible to go, in terms of numerical representations of relations, by using only a small number of cancellation conditions and without imposing transitivity conditions to the relations or unnecessary structural properties on the set of objects X. Surprisingly, we can go rather far while remaining in the relatively poor setting that we have chosen. In addition, the cancellation conditions that we are using ($RC1$, $RC2$, independence, TC, $AC1$, $AC2$, $AC3$, $TAC1$, $TAC2$, $AC4$) are reasonably simple and remain close to the conditions used in traditional conjoint measurement models.

The framework that has been developed and the results obtained are promising in terms of applications and further developments. Some of them have been evoked above; let us emphasize the following in particular:

– The characterization of all relations compatible with a dominance relation: such a characterization has been obtained using the models based on the marginal traces on levels (see sections 16.3.5 and 16.3.6; see also [BOU 04b]).

– The characterization of preference relations that can be obtained by means of an 'ordinal aggregation model' using marginal traces on differences: such models can be used for analyzing majoritarian methods and outranking relations such as those obtained by methods of the ELECTRE type. We illustrate how this suggestion can be put into practice in section 16.4.5 (see also [BOU 01, BOU 05a, BOU 08]). This offers an alternative to the approach developed in [DUB 01, DUB 02a, DUB 03b, FAR 01].

– The characterization of 'ordinal' models for decision in the uncertain (Chapter 11). The models described in this chapter adapt to the decision in the uncertain; it is sufficient to suppose that all components X_i of the product set X are copies of a single set. The n components of the vector describing an alternative correspond to the evaluations of this alternative in the various 'states of Nature' [BOU 03a, BOU 03b, BOU 04c]. As for ordinal aggregation, models of the type studied in this chapter offer an alternative to the approach developed in [DUB 97, FAR 99, DUB 02b, DUB 03a].

– The characterization of some particular functional forms for F, G or H [BOU 02a]: for instance, the cases where F, G or H are sums, the min operator, etc.

It is of course impossible to develop all these points here. The reader who will have followed us up to this point will not have any difficulty in imagining the spirit of these results.

Let us summarize in a few words the main message of this chapter:

– Faced with a non-transitive or incomplete relation, it is advisable to work with its marginal traces on levels and/or on differences.

– Conjoint measurement techniques can also be used to study non-transitive and incomplete relations.

– Setting aside the efficiency of elicitation procedures, we observe that substituting the additivity hypothesis by simple decomposability requirements often permits the fundamental features of a model to be captured in a simple way.

– Substituting additivity by a mere decomposability hypothesis amounts to using models that are intimately linked to rule-based modeling of preferences [GRE 99, GRE 01b, GRE 02]. In this way, one can consider the construction of elicitation procedures, using a machinery of rules induction issued from artificial intelligence.

The general framework and the results presented also contribute to a general theory of conjoint measurement. They allow us to outline a broad panorama of conjoint measurement models (Figure 16.1). The models are grouped according to whether:

– they use the traces on differences, in which case their functional form can be written in order to be non-decreasing in the functions $p_i(x_i, y_i)$;

– they use the traces on levels, in which case their functional form can be written in order to be non-decreasing in the functions $u_i(x_i)$ and non-increasing in the functions $u_i(y_i)$; or else

– they are transitive.

In Figure 16.1, **T** denotes a transitive model, **L** a model that has complete marginal traces on levels and **D** a model that has complete marginal traces on differences.

In the family **L**, all relations are weakly separable but it may happen that they are not weakly independent (and, *a fortiori*, not independent either). In contrast, family **D** contains only independent relations as soon as axiom $RC2$ is imposed. Marginal preference relations of preferences in family **L** tend to enjoy nice properties: they are

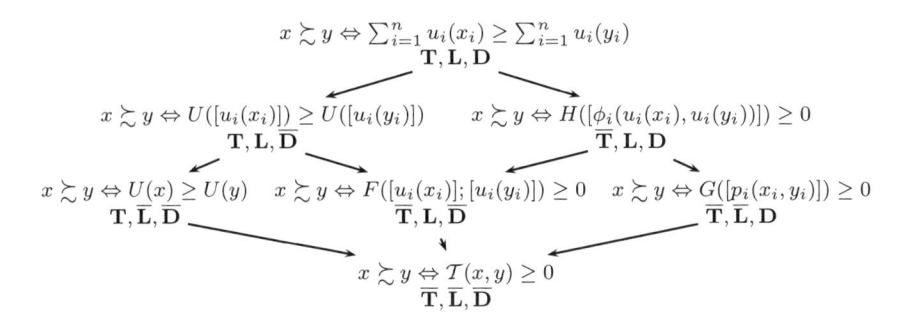

$$x \succsim y \Leftrightarrow \sum_{i=1}^{n} u_i(x_i) \geq \sum_{i=1}^{n} u_i(y_i)$$
$$\mathbf{T, L, D}$$

$$x \succsim y \Leftrightarrow U([u_i(x_i)]) \geq U([u_i(y_i)]) \qquad x \succsim y \Leftrightarrow H([\phi_i(u_i(x_i), u_i(y_i))]) \geq 0$$
$$\mathbf{T, L, \overline{D}} \qquad \mathbf{\overline{T}, L, D}$$

$$x \succsim y \Leftrightarrow U(x) \geq U(y) \quad x \succsim y \Leftrightarrow F([u_i(x_i)];[u_i(y_i)]) \geq 0 \quad x \succsim y \Leftrightarrow G([p_i(x_i, y_i)]) \geq 0$$
$$\mathbf{T, \overline{L}, D} \qquad \mathbf{\overline{T}, L, \overline{D}} \qquad \mathbf{\overline{T}, \overline{L}, D}$$

$$x \succsim y \Leftrightarrow \mathcal{T}(x, y) \geq 0$$
$$\mathbf{\overline{T}, \overline{L}, \overline{D}}$$

Figure 16.1. *Summary of preference models:* **T** *means 'transitive';* **L** *means 'uses marginal traces on levels';* **D** *means 'uses marginal traces on differences'; and for a property* **P**, **$\overline{\mathbf{P}}$** *means 'Not* **P***'*

complete and often semi-orders (as soon as axioms $AC3$ and either $AC1$ or $AC2$ are in force). The situation is quite different in family **D**.

Note that all combinations of **T**, **L** and **D** have been studied in literature except for the combination **T**, $\overline{\mathbf{L}}$, **D**. This is not surprising since, when **D** is in force, most models also use $RC2$; hence they are independent. When these properties are joined to transitivity and completeness of $\succsim$, $\succsim_i$ is a weak order, identical to $\succsim_i^{\pm}$. As a consequence, such models necessarily have complete marginal traces on levels.

16.7. Bibliography

[ATK 70] ATKINSON A. B., "On the measurement of inequality", *Journal of Economic Theory*, vol. 2, 244–263, 1970.

[BEL 01] BELTON V., STEWART T., *Multiple Criteria Decision Analysis: An Integrated Approach*, Kluwer, Dordrecht, 2001.

[BEN 94] BEN-PORATH E., GILBOA I., "Linear measures, the Gini index and the income-equality tradeoff", *Journal of Economic Theory*, vol. 64, p. 443–467, 1994.

[BEN 97] BEN-PORATH E., GILBOA I., SCHMEIDLER D., "On the measurement of inequality under uncertainty", *Journal of Economic Theory*, vol. 75, p. 194–204, 1997.

[BLA 78] BLACKORBY C., PRIMONT D., RUSSELL R., *Duality, Separability, and Functional Structure: Theory and Economic Applications*, North-Holland, New York, 1978.

[BOU 86] BOUYSSOU D., "Some remarks on the notion of compensation in MCDM", *European Journal of Operational Research*, vol. 26, p. 150–160, 1986.

[BOU 97] BOUYSSOU D., PIRLOT M., VINCKE PH., "A general model of preference aggregation", in KARWAN M. H., SPRONK J., WALLENIUS J., Eds., *Essays in Decision Making*, Berlin, Springer Verlag, p. 120–134, 1997.

[BOU 99] BOUYSSOU D., PIRLOT M., "Conjoint measurement without additivity and transitivity", in MESKENS N., ROUBENS M., Eds., *Advances in Decision Analysis*, Dordrecht, Kluwer, p. 13–29, 1999.

[BOU 01] BOUYSSOU D., PIRLOT M., "A characterisation of strict concordance relations", in BOUYSSOU D., JACQUET-LAGRÈZE É., PERNY P., SLOWIŃSKI R., VANDERPOOTEN D., VINCKE PH.. Eds., *Aiding Decisions with Multiple Criteria: Essays in Honour of Bernard Roy*, Dordrecht, Kluwer, p. 121–145, 2001.

[BOU 02a] BOUYSSOU D., GRECO S., MATARAZZO B., PIRLOT M., SLOWIŃSKI R., "Characterization of 'max', 'min' and 'order statistics' multicriteria aggregation functions", Presentation at *IFORS'2002*, 8 – 12 July, 2002, Edinburgh, UK, July 2002.

[BOU 02b] BOUYSSOU D., PIRLOT M., Ordinal aggregation and strict preferences for multiattributed alternatives, Working Paper, LAMSADE, University of Paris-Dauphine, 2002.

[BOU 03a] BOUYSSOU D., PIRLOT M., "A note on Wakker's cardinal coordinate independence", *Mathematical Social Sciences*, vol. 48, p. 11–22, 2003.

[BOU 03b] BOUYSSOU D., PIRLOT M., On some ordinal models for decision making under uncertainty, Working Paper, LAMSADE, University of Paris-Dauphine, 2003.

[BOU 04a] BOUYSSOU D., PIRLOT M., "'Additive difference' models without additivity and subtractivity", *Journal of Mathematical Psychology*, vol. 48, p. 263–291, 2004.

[BOU 04b] BOUYSSOU D., PIRLOT M., "Preferences for multiattributed alternatives: Traces, dominance and numerical representations", *Journal of Mathematical Psychology*, vol. 48, num. 3, p. 167–185, 2004.

[BOU 04c] BOUYSSOU D. , PIRLOT M., "A note on Wakker's cardinal coordinate independence", *Mathematical Social Sciences*, vol. 48(1), 11–22, 2004.

[BOU 05a] BOUYSSOU D., PIRLOT M., "A characterization of concordance relations", *European Journal of Operational Research*, 167(2), 427–443, 2005.

[BOU 05b] BOUYSSOU D., PIRLOT M., "Following the traces: An introduction to conjoint measurement without transitivity and additivity", *European Journal of Operational Research*, vol. 163, num. 2, p. 287–337, 2005.

[BOU 07] BOUYSSOU D., PIRLOT M., "Further results on concordance relations", *European Journal of Operational Research*, vol. 181, p. 505–514, 2007.

[BOU 08] BOUYSSOU D., PIRLOT M., An axiomatic analysis of concordance-discordance relations, Working Paper, LAMSADE, University of Paris-Dauphine, 2008.

[BOU 09] BOUYSSOU D., MARCHANT, T., PIRLOT M., "A conjoint measurement approach to the discrete Sugeno integral", in BRAMS, S., GEHRLEIN, W.V. and ROBERTS, F.S. (eds). *The Mathematics of Preference, Choice and Order. Essays in Honor of Peter C. Fishburn*, Springer, Berlin, 85–109, 2009 and *Journal of Mathematical Psychology*, vol. 46, p. 677–703, 2002.

[CAN 95] CANTOR G., "Beiträge zur Begründung der transfiniten Mengenlehre I", *Mathematische Annalen*, vol. 46, p. 481–512, 1895.

[DEB 59] DEBREU G., *Theory of Value: An Axiomatic Analysis of Economic Equilibrium*, Wiley, New York, 1959.

[DEB 60] DEBREU G., "Topological methods in cardinal utility theory", in ARROW K. J., KARLIN S., SUPPES P., Eds., *Mathematical Methods in the Social Sciences*, p. 16–26, Stanford University Press, Stanford, 1960.

[DUB 97] DUBOIS D., FARGIER H., PRADE H., "Decision-making under ordinal preferences and uncertainty", in GEIGER D., SHENOY P. P., Eds., *Proceedings of the 13th Conference on Uncertainty in Artificial Intelligence*, Morgan Kaufmann, Los Altos, p. 157–164, 1997.

[DUB 01] DUBOIS D., FARGIER H., PERNY P., PRADE H., "Towards a qualitative multicriteria decision theory", in *Proceedings of the EUROFUSE Workshop on Preference Modelling and Applications*, Granada, Spain, April 25–27, 2001, p. 121–129, 2001.

[DUB 02a] DUBOIS D., FARGIER H., PERNY P., "On the limitation of ordinal approaches to decision making", in FENSEL D., GUINCHIGLIA F., WILLIAMS M.-A., MCGUINNESS D., Eds., *Knowledge Representation 2002 — Proceedings of the 8th International Conference (KR'02)*, San Francisco, CA, Morgan Kaufmann, p. 133–144, 2002.

[DUB 02b] DUBOIS D., FARGIER H., PRADE H., PERNY P., "Qualitative decision theory: From Savage's axioms to nonmonotonic reasoning", *Journal of the ACM*, vol. 49, num. 4, p. 455–495, 2002.

[DUB 03a] DUBOIS D., FARGIER H., PERNY P., "Qualitative decision theory with preference relations and comparative uncertainty: An axiomatic approach", *Artificial Intelligence*, vol. 148, p. 219–260, 2003.

[DUB 03b] DUBOIS D., FARGIER H., PERNY P., PRADE H., "A characterization of generalized concordance rules in multicriteria decision-making", *International Journal of Intelligent Systems*, vol. 18, num. 7, p. 751–774, 2003.

[FAR 99] FARGIER H., PERNY P., "Qualitative decision models under uncertainty without the commensurability assumption", in LASKEY K. B., PRADE H., Eds., *Proceedings of Uncertainty in Artificial Intelligence*, Morgan Kaufmann Publishers, p. 188–195, 1999.

[FAR 01] FARGIER H., PERNY P., "Modélisation des préférences par une règle de concordance généralisée", in COLORNI A., PARUCCINI M., ROY B., Eds., *A-MCD-A, Aide Multicritère à la Décision/Multiple Criteria Decision Aid*, p. 99–115, European Commission, Joint Research Centre, 2001.

[FIS 88] FISHBURN P. C., *Nonlinear Preference and Utility Theory*, Johns Hopkins University Press, Baltimore, 1988.

[FIS 90a] FISHBURN P. C., "Additive non-transitive preferences", *Economic Letters*, vol. 34, p. 317–321, 1990.

[FIS 90b] FISHBURN P. C., "Continuous non-transitive additive conjoint measurement", *Mathematical Social Sciences*, vol. 20, p. 165–193, 1990.

[FIS 91] FISHBURN P. C., "Non-transitive additive conjoint measurement", *Journal of Mathematical Psychology*, vol. 35, p. 1–40, 1991.

[FIS 92] FISHBURN P. C., "On non-standard nontransitive additive utility", *Journal of Economic Theory*, vol. 56, p. 426–433, 1992.

[FIS 96] FISHBURN P. C., "Finite linear qualitative probability", *Journal of Mathematical Psychology*, vol. 40, p. 21–31, 1996.

[FIS 97] FISHBURN P. C., "Cancellation conditions for multiattribute preferences on finite sets", in KARWAN M. H., SPRONK J., WALLENIUS J., Eds., *Essays in Decision Making*, Berlin, Springer Verlag, p. 157–167, 1997.

[FRE 93] FRENCH S., *Decision Theory – An Introduction to the Mathematics of Rationality*, Ellis Horwood, London, 1993.

[GIL 95] GILBOA I., LAPSON R., "Aggregation of semiorders: Intransitive indifference makes a difference", *Economic Theory*, vol. 5, p. 109–126, 1995.

[GOL 91] GOLDSTEIN W. M., "Decomposable threshold models", *Journal of Mathematical Psychology*, vol. 35, p. 64–79, 1991.

[GON 96] GONZALES CH., "Additive utilities when some components are solvable and others not", *Journal of Mathematical Psychology*, vol. 40, p. 141–151, 1996.

[GON 00] GONZALES CH., "Two factor additive conjoint measurement with one solvable component", *Journal of Mathematical Psychology*, vol. 44, p. 285–309, 2000.

[GRE 99] GRECO S., MATARAZZO B., SLOWIŃSKI R., "The use of rough sets and fuzzy sets in MCDM", in GAL T., HANNE T., STEWART T., Eds., *Multicriteria Decision Making, Advances in MCDM Models, Algorithms, Theory and Applications*, Kluwer, p. 14.1–14.59, 1999.

[GRE 01a] GRECO S., MATARAZZO B., SLOWIŃSKI R., Axiomatic basis of noncompensatory preferences, Communication to *FUR X*, 30 May–2 June, Torino, Italy, 2001.

[GRE 01b] GRECO S., MATARAZZO B., SLOWIŃSKI R., "Rough sets theory for multicriteria decision analysis", *European Journal of Operational Research*, vol. 129, num. 1, p. 1–47, 2001.

[GRE 02] GRECO S., MATARAZZO B., SLOWIŃSKI R., "Preference representation by means of conjoint measurement and decision rule model", in BOUYSSOU D., JACQUET-LAGRÈZE É., PERNY P., VANDERPOOTEN D., VINCKE PH., Eds., *Aiding Decisions with Multiple Criteria: Essays in Honour of Bernard Roy*, p. 263–313, Kluwer, Dordrecht, 2002.

[GUL 92] GUL F., "Savage's theorem with a finite number of states", *Journal of Economic Theory*, vol. 57, p. 99–110, 1992.

[JAF 74] JAFFRAY J.-Y., "On the extension of additive utilities to infinite sets", *Journal of Mathematical Psychology*, vol. 11, p. 431–452, 1974.

[KAR 98] KARNI E., SAFRA Z., "The hexagon condition and additive representation for two dimensions: An algebraic approach", *Journal of Mathematical Psychology*, vol. 42, p. 393–399, 1998.

[KEE 76] KEENEY R. L., RAIFFA H., *Decisions with Multiple Objectives: Preferences and Value Tradeoffs*, Wiley, New York, 1976.

[KOO 60] KOOPMANS T. C., "Stationary ordinal utility and impatience", *Econometrica*, vol. 28, p. 287–309, 1960.

[KOO 72] KOOPMANS T. C., "Representation of preference orderings over time", in MCGUIRE C. B., RADNER R., Eds., *Decision and Organization*, p. 57–100, North-Holland, Amsterdam, 1972.

[KRA 71] KRANTZ D. H., LUCE R. D., SUPPES P., TVERSKY A., *Foundations of Measurement*, vol. 1: *Additive and Polynomial Representations*, Academic Press, New York, 1971.

[LUC 56] LUCE R. D., "Semi-orders and a theory of utility discrimination", *Econometrica*, vol. 24, p. 178–191, 1956.

[MAY 54] MAY K. O., "Intransitivity, utility and the aggregation of preference patterns", *Econometrica*, vol. 22, p. 1–13, 1954.

[PIR 97] PIRLOT M., VINCKE PH., *Semiorders: Properties, Representations, Applications*, Kluwer, Dordrecht, 1997.

[POM 00] POMEROL J.-C., BARBA-ROMERO S., *Multicriterion Decision in Management, Principles and Practice*, Kluwer, Dordrecht, 2000.

[ROY 68] ROY B., "Classement et choix en présence de points de vue multiples (la méthode ELECTRE)", *Revue francaise d'informatique et de recherche opérationnelle*, vol. 8, p. 57-75, 1968.

[ROY 73] ROY B., BERTIER P., "La méthode ELECTRE II: une application au media-planning", in ROSS M., Ed., *OR'72*, p. 291–302, North Holland, Amsterdam, 1973.

[ROY 85] ROY B., *Méthodologie multicritère d'aide à la décision*, Economica, Paris, 1985.

[ROY 91] ROY B., "The outranking approach and the foundations of ELECTRE methods", *Theory and Decision*, vol. 31, p. 49–73, 1991.

[ROY 93] ROY B., BOUYSSOU D., *Aide multicritère à la décision: méthodes et cas*, Economica, Paris, 1993.

[SCO 64] SCOTT D., "Measurement structures and linear inequalities", *Journal of Mathematical Psychology*, vol. 1, p. 233–247, 1964.

[SEN 86] SEN A. K., "Social choice theory", in ARROW K. J., INTRILIGATOR M. D., Eds., *Handbook of Mathematical Economics*, vol. 3, p. 1073–1181, North-Holland, Amsterdam, 1986.

[SHA 79] SHAPIRO L., "Conditions for expected uility maximization", *Annals of Statistics*, vol. 7, p. 1288–1302, 1979.

[TVE 69] TVERSKY A., "Intransitivity of preferences", *Psychological Review*, vol. 76, p. 31–48, 1969.

[VIN 89] VINCKE PH., *L'aide multicritère à la décision*, éditions de l'Université de Bruxelles-éditions Ellipses, Bruxelles, 1989, English Version *Multicriteria Decision Aid*, Wiley, New York, 1992.

[VIN 91] VIND K., "Independent preferences", *Journal of Mathematical Economics*, vol. 20, p. 119–135, 1991.

[WAK 84] WAKKER P. P., "Cardinal coordinate independence for expected utility", *Journal of Mathematical Psychology*, vol. 28, num. 1, p. 110–117, 1984.

[WAK 88] WAKKER P. P., "Derived strength of preference relations on coordinates", *Economic Letters*, vol. 28, p. 301–306, 1988.

[WAK 89] WAKKER P. P., *Additive Representations of Preferences: A New Foundation of Decision Analysis*, Kluwer, Dordrecht, 1989.

[WIN 86] VON WINTERFELDT D., EDWARDS W., *Decision Analysis and Behavioral Research*, Cambridge University Press, Cambridge, 1986.

Chapter 17

Aggregation Functions for Decision Making

17.1. Introduction

Aggregation functions are generally defined and used to combine several numerical values into a single one, so that the final result of the aggregation takes into account all the individual values in a given manner. Such functions are widely used in many well-known disciplines such as statistics, economics, finance and computer science. For a general background, see Grabisch *et al.* [GRA 09].

For instance, suppose that several individuals form quantifiable judgements either about a measure of an object (weight, length, area, height, volume, importance or other attributes) or about a ratio of two such measures (how much heavier, longer, larger, taller, more important, preferable, more meritorious etc. one object is than another). In order to reach a consensus on these judgements, classical aggregation functions have been proposed: arithmetic mean, geometric mean, median and many others.

In multicriteria decision making, values to be aggregated are typically *preference* or *satisfaction* degrees. A preference degree reveals to what extent an alternative a is preferred to an alternative b, and thus is a relative appraisal. By contrast, a satisfaction degree expresses to what extent a given alternative is satisfactory with respect to a given criterion. It is an absolute appraisal.

We assume that the values to be aggregated belong to numerical scales, which can be of ordinal or cardinal type. On an ordinal scale, numbers have no meaning other than defining an order relation on the scale; distances or differences between values

---

Chapter written by Jean-Luc MARICHAL.

cannot be interpreted. On a cardinal scale, distances between values are not quite arbitrary. There are actually several kinds of cardinal scales. On an interval scale, where the position of the zero is a matter of convention, values are defined up to a positive linear transformation i.e. $\phi(x) = rx + s$, with $r > 0$ and $s \in \mathbb{R}$ (e.g. temperatures expressed on the Celsius scale). On a ratio scale, where a true zero exists, values are defined up to a similarity transformation i.e. $\phi(x) = rx$, with $r > 0$ (e.g. lengths expressed in inches). We will come back on these measurement aspects in section 17.2.2.

Once values are defined we can aggregate them and obtain a new value. This can be done in many different ways according to what is expected from the aggregation function, the nature of the values to be aggregated and which scale types have been used. Thus, for a given problem, any aggregation function should not be used. In other terms, the use of a given aggregation function should always be justified.

To help the practitioner choose an appropriate aggregation function in a given problem, it is useful and even convenient to adopt an axiomatic approach. Such an approach consists of classifying and choosing aggregation functions according to the properties they fulfill. Thus, a catalog of 'desirable' properties is proposed and, whenever possible, a description of the family of aggregation functions satisfying a given set of properties is provided. This is the very principle of axiomatization.

Proposing an interesting axiomatic characterization of an aggregation function (or a family of aggregation functions) is not an easy task. Mostly, aggregation functions can be characterized by different sets of conditions. Nevertheless, the various possible characterizations are not equally important. Some of them involve purely technical conditions with no clear interpretation and the result becomes useless. Others involve conditions that contain the result explicitly and the characterization becomes trivial. On the contrary, there are characterizations involving only natural conditions which are easily interpretable. In fact, this is the only case where the result should be seen as a significant contribution. It improves our understanding of the function considered and provides strong arguments to justify (or reject) its use in a given context.

The main aim of this chapter is to present, on an axiomatic basis, the most used families of aggregation functions in decision making. We shall confine ourselves to aggregation functions that assign a numerical value to every profile of n values, which represent objects or alternatives. We will not deal with utility functions which, in a more general way, make it possible to rank alternatives without assigning precise values to them. For instance, procedures such as 'leximin' or 'discrimin' are ranking procedures, rather than aggregation functions.

The organization of this chapter is as follows. In section 17.2 we yield the list of the main properties that we shall use. This list is divided into three classes: (1) elementary properties (continuity, symmetry, etc.); (2) properties related to the scale types used to represent the data; and (3) certain algebraic properties such as associativity. In section 17.3 we present the concept of mean and its various definitions. Perhaps the most common definition of means is that of quasi-arithmetic means with a very natural axiomatization due to Kolmogoroff [KOL 30] and Nagumo [NAG 30].

In section 17.4 we present associative functions, which are at the root of the theory of semigroups. These functions were at the root of the concept of fuzzy connectives such as t-norms, t-conorms, and uninorms. In section 17.5 we present an important branch of the aggregation function theory, namely Choquet and Sugeno non-additive integrals. These integrals enable us to generalize the classical aggregation modes, such as the weighted arithmetic mean and the median, to functions that take into account the possible interactions among the considered attributes. Finally, in sections 17.6 and 17.7 we present particular functions designed for aggregating interval scales, ratio scales and ordinal scales.

We close this introduction by setting the notation that we will use in this chapter.

In a general manner, we shall denote an aggregation function with n variables by $A : E^n \to \mathbb{R}$ where E is a real interval, bounded or not. E° will denote the interior of E. We shall sometimes consider sequences of functions $(A^{(n)} : E^n \to \mathbb{R})_{n \geq 1}$, the superscript $^{(n)}$ being used only to specify the number of arguments of the function $A^{(n)}$.

We shall use N to denote the index set $\{1, \ldots, n\}$ and 2^N to denote the set of its subsets. Π_N will be used to denote the set of permutations on N. Finally, for any $S \subseteq N$, the characteristic vector of S in $\{0, 1\}^n$ will be denoted $\mathbf{1}_S$.

A standard notation for certain aggregation functions exists:
– The *arithmetic mean* is defined as

$$\mathrm{AM}(x) = \frac{1}{n} \sum_{i=1}^{n} x_i.$$

– For any weight vector $\omega = (\omega_1, \ldots, \omega_n) \in [0, 1]^n$ such that $\sum_i \omega_i = 1$, the *weighted arithmetic mean* and the *ordered weighted averaging function* are defined as

$$\mathrm{WAM}_\omega(x) = \sum_{i=1}^{n} \omega_i x_i,$$

$$\mathrm{OWA}_\omega(x) = \sum_{i=1}^{n} \omega_i x_{(i)},$$

respectively, where $(\cdot)$ represents a permutation on N such that $x_{(1)} \leq \ldots \leq x_{(n)}$.

- For any $k \in N$, the *projection* and the *order statistic* associated with the kth argument are defined as
$$P_k(x) = x_k,$$
$$OS_k(x) = x_{(k)},$$
respectively.
- For any $S \subseteq N$, $S \neq \emptyset$, the *partial minimum* and *partial maximum* functions associated with S are defined as
$$\min{}_S(x) = \min_{i \in S} x_i,$$
$$\max{}_S(x) = \max_{i \in S} x_i,$$

respectively.

In this chapter the min and max operations will often be denoted $\wedge$ and $\vee$, respectively.

17.2. Aggregation properties

As mentioned in the introduction, in order to choose a reasonable or satisfactory aggregation mode, it is useful to adopt an axiomatic approach and impose that the aggregation functions fulfill some selected properties. Such properties can be dictated by the nature of the values to be aggregated. For example, in some multicriteria evaluation methods, the aim is to assess a global absolute score to an alternative given a set of partial scores with respect to different criteria. Clearly, it would be unnatural to give as a global score a value which is lower than the lowest partial score, or greater than the highest score, so that only internal aggregation functions (means) are allowed. Another example concerns the aggregation of opinions in voting procedures. If, as usual, the voters are anonymous, the aggregation function must be symmetric.

In this section we present some properties that could be desirable or not depending upon the considered problem. Of course, all these properties are not required with the same strength, and do not pertain to the same purpose. Some of them are imperative conditions whose violation leads to obviously counterintuitive aggregation modes. Others are technical conditions that simply facilitate the representation or the calculation of the aggregation function. There are also facultative conditions that naturally apply in special circumstances but are not to be universally accepted.

17.2.1. Elementary mathematical properties

Definition 17.1. $A : E^n \to \mathbb{R}$ is *symmetric* if, for any $\pi \in \Pi_N$, we have

$$A(x_1, \ldots, x_n) = A(x_{\pi(1)}, \ldots, x_{\pi(n)}) \qquad (x \in E^n).$$

The symmetry property essentially implies that the indexing (ordering) of the arguments does not matter. This is required when combining criteria of equal importance or the opinions of anonymous experts.

Definition 17.2. $A : E^n \to \mathbb{R}$ is *continuous* if it is continuous in the usual sense.

One of the advantages of a continuous aggregation function is that it does not present any chaotic reaction to a small change of the arguments.

Definition 17.3. $A : E^n \to \mathbb{R}$ is

- *non-decreasing* if, for any $x, x' \in E^n$, we have

$$x \leq x' \Rightarrow A(x) \leq A(x'),$$

- *strictly increasing* if it is non-decreasing and if, for any $x, x' \in E^n$, we have

$$x \leq x' \text{ and } x \neq x' \Rightarrow A(x) < A(x'),$$

- *unanimously increasing* if it is non-decreasing and if, for any $x, x' \in E^n$, we have

$$x < x' \Rightarrow A(x) < A(x').$$

An increasing aggregation function presents a non-negative response to any increase of the arguments. In other terms, increasing a partial value cannot decrease the result. This function is strictly increasing if, moreover, it presents a positive reaction to any increase of at least one argument. Finally, a unanimously increasing function is increasing and presents a positive response whenever all the arguments strictly increase. For instance we observe that on $[0,1]^n$, the maximum function $A(x) = \max x_i$ is unanimously increasing whereas the bounded sum $A(x) = \min(\sum_{i=1}^n x_i, 1)$ is not.

Definition 17.4. $A : E^n \to \mathbb{R}$ is *idempotent* if $A(x, \ldots, x) = x$ for all $x \in E$.

Definition 17.5. $A : [a,b]^n \to \mathbb{R}$ is *weakly idempotent* if $A(a, \ldots, a) = a$ and $A(b, \ldots, b) = b$.

In a variety of applications, it is desirable that the aggregation functions satisfy the idempotency property, i.e. if all x_i are identical, $A(x_1, \ldots, x_n)$ restitutes the common value.

Definition 17.6. $A : E^n \to \mathbb{R}$ is
- *conjunctive* if $A(x) \leq \min x_i$ for all $x \in E^n$,
- *disjunctive* if $\max x_i \leq A(x)$ for all $x \in E^n$,
- *internal* if $\min x_i \leq A(x) \leq \max x_i$ for all $x \in E^n$.

Conjunctive functions combine values as if they were related by a logical **AND** operator. That is, the result of aggregation can be high only if all the values are high. t-norms are suitable functions for doing conjunctive aggregation (see section 17.4.5). At the opposite end, disjunctive functions combine values as an **OR** operator so that the result of aggregation is high if at least one value is high. The best known disjunctive functions are t-conorms.

Between these two extreme situations are the internal functions, located between the minimum and the maximum of the arguments. In this kind of functions, a bad (respectively, good) score on one criterion can be compensated for by a good (respectively, bad) one on another criterion, so that the result of aggregation will be medium. By definition, means are internal functions (see section 17.3).

17.2.2. Stability properties related to scale types

Depending on the kind of scale which is used, allowed operations on values are restricted. For example, aggregation on ordinal scales should be limited to operations involving comparisons only, such as medians and order statistics.

A *scale of measurement* is a mapping which assigns real numbers to objects being measured. The *type* of a scale, as defined by Stevens [STE 51, STE 59], is defined by a class of *admissible transformations*, transformations that lead from one acceptable scale to another.

For instance, we call a scale a *ratio scale* if the class of admissible transformations consists of the similarities $\phi(x) = rx$, with $r > 0$. In this case, the scale value is determined by the choice of a unit. Mass is an example of a ratio scale. The transformation from kilograms to pounds, for example, involves the admissible transformation $\phi(x) = 2.2x$. Length (inches, centimeters) and time intervals (years, seconds) are two other examples of ratio scales.

We call a scale an *interval scale* if the class of admissible transformations consists of the positive linear transformations $\phi(x) = rx + s$, with $r > 0$ and $s \in \mathbb{R}$. The scale value is then determined by choices of unit and zero point. Temperature (except where there is an absolute zero) defines an interval scale. Thus, transformation from Centigrade into Fahrenheit involves the admissible transformation $\phi(x) = 9x/5 + 32$.

We call a scale an *ordinal scale* if the class of admissible transformations consists of the strictly increasing bijections $\phi(x)$. Here the scale value is determined only by order. For example, the scale of air quality being used in a number of cities is an ordinal scale. It assigns a number 1 to unhealthy air, 2 to unsatisfactory air, 3 to acceptable air, 4 to good air and 5 to excellent air. We could just as well use the numbers 1, 7, 8, 15, 23 or the numbers 1.2, 6.5, 8.7, 205.6, 750 or any numbers that preserve the order. Definitions of other scale types can be found in the book by Roberts [ROB 79] on measurement theory; see also Roberts [ROB 90, ROB 94]. The reader will find further details on measurement in Chapter 18.

A statement using scales of measurement is said to be *meaningful* if the truth or falsity of the statement is invariant when every scale is replaced by another acceptable version of it [ROB 79, p. 59]. For example, a ranking method is meaningful if the ranking of alternatives induced by the aggregation does not depend on scale transformation.

In 1959, Luce [LUC 59] observed that the general form of a functional relationship between variables is greatly restricted if we know the scale type of the variables. These restrictions are discovered by formulating a functional equation from knowledge of the admissible transformations. Luce's method is based on the principle of theory construction, which states that an admissible transformation of the independent variables may lead to an admissible transformation of the dependent variable. For example, suppose that $f(a) = A(f_1(a), \ldots, f_n(a))$, where f and $f_1, \ldots, f_n$ are all ratio scales, with the units chosen independently. Then, by the principle of theory construction, we obtain the functional equation

$$A(r_1 x_1, \ldots, r_n x_r) = R(r_1, \ldots, r_n) A(x_1, \ldots, x_n),$$
$$r_i > 0, \quad R(r_1, \ldots, r_n) > 0.$$

Aczél *et al.* [ACZ 86] showed that the solutions of this equation are given by

$$A(x) = a \prod_{i=1}^{n} g_i(x_i), \quad \text{with } a > 0, g_i > 0,$$

and

$$g_i(x_i y_i) = g_i(x_i) g_i(y_i).$$

In this section we present some functional equations related to certain scale types. The interested reader can find more details in Aczél *et al.* [ACZ 89b, ACZ 86] and a good survey in Roberts [ROB 94].

Definition 17.7. $A : \mathbb{R}^n \to \mathbb{R}$ is

– *meaningful for the same input-output ratio scales* if, for any $r > 0$, we have
$$A(rx_1, \ldots, rx_n) = rA(x_1, \ldots, x_n) \qquad (x \in \mathbb{R}^n),$$

– *meaningful for the same input ratio scales* if, for any $r > 0$, there exists $R_r > 0$ such that
$$A(rx_1, \ldots, rx_n) = R_r A(x_1, \ldots, x_n) \qquad (x \in \mathbb{R}^n),$$

– *meaningful for the same input-output interval scales* if, for any $r > 0$ and $s \in \mathbb{R}$, we have
$$A(rx_1 + s, \ldots, rx_n + s) = rA(x_1, \ldots, x_n) + s \qquad (x \in \mathbb{R}^n),$$

– *meaningful for the same input interval scales* if, for any $r > 0$ and $s \in \mathbb{R}$, there exist $R_{r,s} > 0$ and $S_{r,s} \in \mathbb{R}$ such that
$$A(rx_1 + s, \ldots, rx_n + s) = R_{r,s} A(x_1, \ldots, x_n) + S_{r,s} \qquad (x \in \mathbb{R}^n),$$

– *meaningful for the same input-output ordinal scales* if, for any strictly increasing bijection $\phi : \mathbb{R} \to \mathbb{R}$, we have
$$A(\phi(x_1), \ldots, \phi(x_n)) = \phi(A(x_1, \ldots, x_n)) \qquad (x \in \mathbb{R}^n),$$

– *meaningful for the same input ordinal scales* if, for any strictly increasing bijection $\phi : \mathbb{R} \to \mathbb{R}$, there exists a strictly increasing function $\psi_\phi : \mathbb{R} \to \mathbb{R}$ such that
$$A(\phi(x_1), \ldots, \phi(x_n)) = \psi_\phi(A(x_1, \ldots, x_n)) \qquad (x \in \mathbb{R}^n).$$

17.2.3. Algebraic properties

The following properties concern the aggregation procedures that can be decomposed into partial aggregations, that is, procedures for which it is possible to partition the set of attributes into disjoint subgroups, build the partial aggregation for each subgroup, and then combine these partial results to get the global value. This condition may take several forms. Maybe one of the strongest is associativity. Other weaker formulations will also be presented: decomposability and bisymmetry.

We first present associativity for two variable functions.

Definition 17.8. $A : E^2 \to E$ is *associative* if, for any $x \in E^3$, we have
$$A(A(x_1, x_2), x_3) = A(x_1, A(x_2, x_3)).$$

A large number of papers deal with the associativity functional equation. For a list of references see Aczél [ACZ 66, section 6.2].

This property can be extended to sequences of functions as follows.

Definition 17.9. The sequence $(A^{(n)} : \mathbb{R}^n \to \mathbb{R})_{n \geq 1}$ is *associative* if $A^{(1)}(x) = x$ for all $x \in E$ and

$$A^{(n)}(x_1, \ldots, x_k, x_{k+1}, \ldots, x_n) = A^{(n)}(A^{(k)}(x_1, \ldots, x_k), A^{(n-k)}(x_{k+1}, \ldots, x_n))$$

for all $x \in E^n$ and all $k, n \in \mathbb{N}$ such that $1 \leq k \leq n$.

Implicit in the assumption of associativity is a consistent way of going unambiguously from the aggregation of n elements to $n + 1$ elements, i.e. if M is associative

$$A^{(n+1)}(x_1, \ldots, x_{n+1}) = A^{(2)}(A^{(n)}(x_1, \ldots, x_n), x_{n+1}),$$

for all $n \in \mathbb{N} \setminus \{0\}$.

Let us turn to the decomposability property. For this purpose, we introduce the following notation. For any $k \in \mathbb{N} \setminus \{0\}$ and any $x \in \mathbb{R}$, we set $k \cdot x = x, \ldots, x$ (k times). For example,

$$A(3 \cdot x, 2 \cdot y) = A(x, x, x, y, y).$$

Definition 17.10. The sequence $(A^{(n)} : \mathbb{R}^n \to \mathbb{R})_{n \geq 1}$ is *decomposable* if $A^{(1)}(x) = x$ for all $x \in E$ and

$$A^{(n)}(x_1, \ldots, x_k, x_{k+1}, \ldots, x_n)$$
$$= A^{(n)}(k \cdot A^{(k)}(x_1, \ldots, x_k), (n-k) \cdot A^{(n-k)}(x_{k+1}, \ldots, x_n))$$

for all $x \in E^n$ and all $k, n \in \mathbb{N}$ such that $1 \leq k \leq n$.

Here the definition is the same as for associativity, except that the partial aggregations are duplicated by the number of aggregated values.

Introduced first in Bemporad [BEM 26, p. 87] in a characterization of the arithmetic mean, decomposability has been used by Kolmogoroff [KOL 30] and Nagumo [NAG 30] to characterize the quasi-arithmetic means. More recently, Marichal and Roubens [MAR 93] proposed calling this property 'decomposability' in order to avoid confusion with classical associativity.

The *bisymmetry* property, which extends associativity and symmetry simultaneously, is defined for n-variables functions as follows.

Definition 17.11. $A : E^n \to E$ is *bisymmetric* if

$$A(A(x_{11},\ldots,x_{1n}),\ldots,A(x_{n1},\ldots,x_{nn}))$$
$$= A(A(x_{11},\ldots,x_{n1}),\ldots,A(x_{1n},\ldots,x_{nn}))$$

for all square matrices $(x_{ij}) \in E^{n \times n}$.

For two-variable functions, this property has been investigated from the algebraic point of view by using it mostly in structures without the property of associativity; see Aczél [ACZ 66, section 6.4] and Aczél and Dhombres [ACZ 89a, Chapter 17].

For a sequence of functions, this property becomes as described in the following definition.

Definition 17.12. The sequence $(A^{(n)} : \mathbb{R}^n \to \mathbb{R})_{n \geq 1}$ is *bisymmetric* if $A^{(1)}(x) = x$ for all $x \in E$ and

$$A^{(p)}(A^{(n)}(x_{11},\ldots,x_{1n}),\ldots,A^{(n)}(x_{n1},\ldots,x_{pn}))$$
$$= A^{(n)}(A^{(p)}(x_{11},\ldots,x_{p1}),\ldots,A^{(p)}(x_{1n},\ldots,x_{pn}))$$

for all $n, p \in \mathbb{N} \setminus \{0\}$ and all matrices $(x_{ij}) \in E^{p \times n}$.

17.3. Means

It would be very unnatural to propose a chapter on aggregation functions without dealing somehow with *means*. Already discovered and studied by the ancient Greeks [e.g. ANT 98, Chapter 3] the concept of mean has given rise today to a very wide field of investigation with a huge variety of applications. Actually, a tremendous amount of literature on the properties of several means (such as the arithmetic mean, the geometric mean, etc.) has already been produced, especially since the 19th century, and is still developing today. For a good overview, see the expository paper by Frosini [FRO 87] and the remarkable monograph by Bullen *et al.* [BUL 88].

The first modern definition of mean was probably due to Cauchy [CAU 21] who considered in 1821 a mean as an internal (definition 17.6) function.

The concept of mean as a *numerical equalizer* is usually ascribed to Chisini [CHI 29, p. 108], who provided the following definition.

Let $y = g(x_1, \ldots, x_n)$ be a function of n independent variables $x_1, \ldots, x_n$ representing homogenous quantities. A mean of $x_1, \ldots, x_n$ with respect to the function g is a number M such that, if each of $x_1, \ldots, x_n$ is replaced with M, the function value is unchanged, that is,

$$g(M, \ldots, M) = g(x_1, \ldots, x_n).$$

When g is considered as the sum, the product, the sum of squares, the sum of inverses or the sum of exponentials, the solution of Chisini's equation corresponds to the arithmetic mean, the geometric mean, the quadratic mean, the harmonic mean and the exponential mean, respectively.

Unfortunately, as noted by de Finetti [FIN 31, p. 378], Chisini's definition is so general that it does not even imply that the 'mean' (provided there exists a real and unique solution to Chisini's equation) fulfills Cauchy's internality property.

The following quote from Ricci [RIC 15, p. 39] could be considered as another possible criticism to Chisini's view.

> ...when all values become equal, the mean equals any of them too. The inverse proposition is not true. If a function of several variables takes their common value when all variables coincide, this is not sufficient evidence for calling it a mean. For example, the function
>
> $$g(x_1, x_2, \ldots, x_n) = x_n + (x_n - x_1) + (x_n - x_2) + \cdots + (x_n - x_{n-1})$$
>
> equals x_n when $x_1 = \cdots = x_n$, but it is even greater than x_n as long as x_n is greater than every other variable.

In 1930, Kolmogoroff [KOL 30] and Nagumo [NAG 30] considered that the mean should be more than just a Cauchy mean or a numerical equalizer. They defined a *mean value* to be a decomposable sequence of continuous, symmetric, strictly increasing (in each variable) and idempotent real functions

$$M^{(1)}(x_1) = x_1, M^{(2)}(x_1, x_2), \ldots, M^{(n)}(x_1, \ldots, x_n), \ldots.$$

They proved, independently of each other, that these conditions are necessary and sufficient for the quasi-arithmeticity of the mean, that is, for the existence of a continuous strictly monotonic function f such that $M^{(n)}$ may be written in the form

$$M^{(n)}(x_1, \ldots, x_n) = f^{-1}\left[\frac{1}{n}\sum_{i=1}^{n} f(x_i)\right] \qquad (17.1)$$

for all $n \in \mathbb{N} \setminus \{0\}$.

$f(x)$	$M^{(n)}(x_1,\ldots,x_n)$	Name
x	$\frac{1}{n}\sum_{i=1}^{n} x_i$	arithmetic
x^2	$\left(\frac{1}{n}\sum_{i=1}^{n} x_i^2\right)^{1/2}$	quadratic
$\log x$	$\left(\prod_{i=1}^{n} x_i\right)^{1/n}$	geometric
x^{-1}	$\dfrac{1}{\frac{1}{n}\sum_{i=1}^{n} \frac{1}{x_i}}$	harmonic
x^α ($\alpha \in \mathbb{R}\setminus\{0\}$)	$\left(\frac{1}{n}\sum_{i=1}^{n} x_i^\alpha\right)^{1/\alpha}$	root-mean-power
$e^{\alpha x}$ ($\alpha \in \mathbb{R}\setminus\{0\}$)	$\frac{1}{\alpha}\ln\left(\frac{1}{n}\sum_{i=1}^{n} e^{\alpha x_i}\right)$	exponential

Table 17.1. *Examples of quasi-arithmetic means*

Quasi-arithmetic means (17.1) comprise most of the algebraic means of common use (see Table 17.1). However, some means, such as the median, do not belong to this family.

The above properties defining a mean value seem to be natural enough. For instance, one can readily see that, for increasing means, the idempotency property is equivalent to Cauchy's internality; both are accepted by all statisticians as requisites for means.

The decomposability property of means is rather natural. Under idempotency, this condition becomes equivalent to

$$M^{(k)}(x_1,\ldots,x_k) = M^{(k)}(x'_1,\ldots,x'_k)$$
$$\Downarrow$$
$$M^{(n)}(x_1,\ldots,x_k,x_{k+1},\ldots,x_n) = M^{(n)}(x'_1,\ldots,x'_k,x_{k+1},\ldots,x_n)$$

which states that the mean does not change when altering some values without modifying their partial mean.

The purpose of this section is not to present a state of the art of all the known results in this vast realm of means. Instead, we just skim the surface of the subject by pointing out characterization results for the most-often used and best-known families of means.

The medians and, more generally, the order statistics (which are particular means designed to aggregate ordinal values), will be briefly presented in section 17.7.

17.3.1. *Quasi-arithmetic means*

As mentioned above, quasi-arithmetic means were introduced from a very natural axiomatization. In this section, we investigate those means both as n-variable functions and as sequences of functions. Results on this class of means can also be found in Bullen *et al.* [BUL 88, Chapter 4].

It was proven by Aczél [ACZ 48a] (see also [ACZ 66, section 6.4] and [ACZ 89a, Chapter 17]) that the quasi-arithmetic means are the only symmetric, continuous, strictly increasing, idempotent, real functions $M : E^n \to E$ which satisfy the bisymmetry condition. The statement of this result is formulated as follows.

Theorem 17.1. *$M : E^n \to E$ is a symmetric, continuous, strictly increasing, idempotent, and bisymmetric function if and only if there exists a continuous and strictly monotonic function $f : E \to \mathbb{R}$ such that*

$$M(x) = f^{-1}\left[\frac{1}{n}\sum_{i=1}^{n} f(x_i)\right] \qquad (x \in E^n). \tag{17.2}$$

Quasi-arithmetic means (17.2) are internal aggregation functions and cover a wide spectrum of means including arithmetic, quadratic, geometric and harmonic; see Table 17.1.

The function f occurring in equation (17.2) is called a *generator* of M. It was also proven that f is determined up to a linear transformation. With $f(x)$, every function

$$g(x) = rf(x) + s \qquad (r, s \in \mathbb{R}, r \neq 0)$$

belongs to the same M, but no other function.

In addition to Aczél's result, we also recall the Kolmogoroff–Nagumo results.

Theorem 17.2. *The sequence $(M^{(n)} : E^n \to E)_{n \geq 1}$ is a decomposable sequence of symmetric, continuous, strictly increasing and idempotent functions if and only if there is a continuous and strictly monotonic function $f : E \to \mathbb{R}$ such that*

$$M^{(n)}(x) = f^{-1}\left[\frac{1}{n}\sum_{i=1}^{n} f(x_i)\right] \qquad (x \in E^n).$$

Nagumo [NAG 30] investigated some subfamilies of the class of quasi-arithmetic means. He proved the following result (see also [ACZ 87, section 4] and [ACZ 89a, Chapter 15]).

Proposition 17.1. *Assume* $E =]0, \infty[$ *or a subinterval:*

1) $M : E^n \to E$ *is a quasi-arithmetic mean that is meaningful for the same input-output ratio scales if and only if*
 - either M is the geometric mean:

$$M(x) = \left(\prod_{i=1}^{n} x_i\right)^{\frac{1}{n}} \quad (x \in E^n),$$

 - or M is a root-mean-power: there exists $\alpha \in \mathbb{R} \setminus \{0\}$ *such that*

$$M(x) = \left(\frac{1}{n}\sum_{i=1}^{n} x_i^{\alpha}\right)^{\frac{1}{\alpha}} \quad (x \in E^n). \tag{17.3}$$

2) $M : E^n \to E$ *is a quasi-arithmetic mean that is meaningful for the same input-output interval scales if and only if M is the arithmetic mean.*

Let us denote the root-mean-power equation (17.3) generated by $\alpha \in \mathbb{R} \setminus \{0\}$ by $M_{(\alpha)}$. It is well known [BEC 65] that if $\alpha_1 < \alpha_2$ then $M_{(\alpha_1)}(x) \leq M_{(\alpha_2)}(x)$ for all $x \in]0, +\infty[^n$ (equality if and only if all x_i are equal).

The family of root-mean-powers was studied by Dujmović [DUJ 74, DUJ 75] and then by Dyckhoff and Pedrycz [DYC 84]. It encompasses most of traditionally known means: the arithmetic mean $M_{(1)}$, the harmonic mean $M_{(-1)}$, the quadratic mean $M_{(2)}$ and three limiting cases: the geometric mean $M_{(0)}$, the minimum $M_{(-\infty)}$ and the maximum $M_{(+\infty)}$ e.g. Abramowitz and Stegun [ABR 64].

Let us return to theorem 17.1. Note that Aczél [ACZ 48a] also investigated the case where symmetry and idempotency are dropped (see also [ACZ 66, section 6.4] and [ACZ 89a, Chapter 17]). He obtained the following result.

Theorem 17.3. *1)* $M : E^n \to E$ *is a continuous, strictly increasing, idempotent, and bisymmetric function if and only if there exists a continuous and strictly monotonic function* $f : E \to \mathbb{R}$ *and real numbers* $\omega_1, \ldots, \omega_n > 0$ *fulfilling* $\sum_i \omega_i = 1$ *such that*

$$M(x) = f^{-1}\left[\sum_{i=1}^{n} \omega_i f(x_i)\right] \quad (x \in E^n). \tag{17.4}$$

2) $M : E^n \to E$ is a continuous, strictly increasing, and bisymmetric function if and only if there exists a continuous and strictly monotonic function $f : E \to \mathbb{R}$ and real numbers $p_1, \ldots, p_n > 0$ and $q \in \mathbb{R}$ such that

$$M(x) = f^{-1}\left[\sum_{i=1}^{n} p_i\, f(x_i) + q\right] \quad (x \in E^n). \tag{17.5}$$

Quasi-linear means (17.4) and *quasi-linear functions* (17.5) are weighted aggregation functions. The question of uniqueness with respect to f is dealt with in detail in [ACZ 66, section 6.4]. Table 17.2 provides some special cases of quasi-linear means.

$f(x)$	$M(x)$	Name of weighted mean
x	$\sum_{i=1}^{n} \omega_i\, x_i$	arithmetic
x^2	$\left(\sum_{i=1}^{n} \omega_i\, x_i^2\right)^{1/2}$	quadratic
$\log x$	$\prod_{i=1}^{n} x_i^{\omega_i}$	geometric
$x^\alpha \ (\alpha \in \mathbb{R} \setminus \{0\})$	$\left(\sum_{i=1}^{n} \omega_i\, x_i^\alpha\right)^{1/\alpha}$	root-mean-power

Table 17.2. *Examples of quasi-linear means*

17.3.2. Lagrangian and Cauchy means

Let us consider the intermediate point M in the classical mean value formula

$$F(y) - F(x) = F'(M)(y - x) \quad (x, y \in E) \tag{17.6}$$

as a function of the variables x, y with the convention $M(x, x) = x$. $F : E \to \mathbb{R}$ is a given continuously differentiable and strictly convex or strictly concave function. Reformulating this definition in terms of integrals instead of derivatives, we can rewrite equation (17.6) as

$$M(x, y) = \begin{cases} f^{-1}\left(\frac{1}{y-x} \int_x^y f(\xi)\, d\xi\right), & \text{if } x \neq y, \\ x, & \text{if } x = y, \end{cases} \tag{17.7}$$

for $x, y \in I$, where $f : E \to \mathbb{R}$ is a continuous strictly monotonic function. This function $M(x, y)$ is called the *Lagrangian mean* associated with f. See for example Berrone and Moro [BER 98] and Bullen et al. [BUL 88, p. 343]. The uniqueness of the generator is the same as for quasi-arithmetic means, that is, defined up to a linear transformation; see Berrone and Moro [BER 98, corollary 7] and Matkowski [MAT 99, theorem 1].

Many classical means are Lagrangian. The arithmetic mean and the geometric means correspond to taking $f(x) = x$ and $f(x) = 1/x^2$, respectively, in equation (17.7). The harmonic mean, however, is not Lagrangian.

In general, some of the most common means are both quasi-arithmetic and Lagrangian. However, there are quasi-arithmetic means, such as the harmonic one, which are not Lagrangian. Conversely, the logarithmic mean

$$M(x,y) = \begin{cases} \frac{x-y}{\log x - \log y}, & \text{for } x, y > 0, x \neq y, \\ x, & \text{for } x = y > 0, \end{cases}$$

is an example of a Lagrangian mean ($f(x) = 1/x$) that is not quasi-arithmetic.

Let us now consider the Cauchy mean value theorem which asserts that, for any functions F and g continuous on an interval $[x, y]$ and differentiable on $]x, y[$, there exists $M \in \,]a, b[$ such that

$$\frac{F(y) - F(x)}{g(y) - g(x)} = \frac{F'(M)}{g'(M)}.$$

If the functions g and $f := F'/g'$ are strictly monotonic on $]x, y[$, the mean value $M(x, y)$ is unique and can be written as

$$M(x,y) = \begin{cases} f^{-1}\left(\frac{1}{g(y)-g(x)} \int_x^y f(\xi) dg(\xi)\right), & \text{if } x \neq y, \\ x, & \text{if } x = y, \end{cases}$$

for $x, y \in E$. It is then said to be the *Cauchy mean associated with the pair* (f, g); see Berrone and Moro [BER 00]. Such a mean is continuous, idempotent, symmetric and strictly increasing.

When $g = f$ (respectively, g is the identity function), we retrieve the quasi-arithmetic (respectively, the Lagrangian) mean generated by f. The *anti-Lagrangian mean* [BER 00] is obtained when f is the identity function. For example, the harmonic mean is an anti-Lagrangian mean generated by the function $g = 1/x^2$. The generators of the same anti-Lagrangian mean are defined up to the same non-zero affine transformation.

17.4. Associative aggregation functions

Before dealing with associative functions and their axiomatizations, we introduce some useful concepts. A *semigroup* (E, A) is a set E with an associative operation

$A : E^2 \to E$ defined on it. As usual, we assume that E is a real interval, bounded or not.

An element $e \in E$ is (a) an *identity* for A if $A(e, x) = A(x, e) = x$ for all $x \in E$, (b) a *zero* (or *annihilator*) for A if $A(e, x) = A(x, e) = e$ for all $x \in E$; or (c) an *idempotent* for A if $A(e, e) = e$. For any semigroup (E, A), it is clear that there is at most one identity and at most one zero for A in E, and both are idempotents.

We also need to introduce the concept of *ordinal sum*, well known in the theory of semigroups e.g. Climescu [CLI 46] and Ling [LIN 65].

Definition 17.13. Let K be a totally ordered set and $\{(E_k, A_k) \mid k \in K\}$ be a collection of disjoint semigroups indexed by K. Then the *ordinal sum* of $\{(E_k, A_k) \mid k \in K\}$ is the set-theoretic union $\cup_{k \in K} E_k$ under the following binary operation:

$$A(x, y) = \begin{cases} A_k(x, y), & \text{if } \exists k \in K \text{ such that } x, y \in E_k \\ \min(x, y), & \text{if } \exists k_1, k_2 \in K, k_1 \neq k_2 \text{ such that } x \in E_{k_1} \text{ and } y \in E_{k_2}. \end{cases}$$

The ordinal sum is a semigroup under the above-defined operation.

17.4.1. Strictly increasing functions

Aczél [ACZ 48b] investigated the general continuous, strictly increasing, real solutions on E^2 of the associativity functional equation (17.8). He proved the following result (see also [ACZ 66, section 6.2]).

Theorem 17.4. *Let E be a real interval, bounded or not, which is open on one side. $A : E^2 \to E$ is continuous, strictly increasing and associative if and only if there exists a continuous and strictly monotonic function $f : E \to \mathbb{R}$ such that*

$$A(x, y) = f^{-1}[f(x) + f(y)] \quad ((x, y) \in E^2). \tag{17.8}$$

It was also proved that the function f occurring in equation (17.8) is determined up to a multiplicative constant, that is, $f(x)$ and all functions $g(x) = r f(x)$ ($r \in \mathbb{R} \setminus \{0\}$) belong to the same A, and only these. Moreover, the function f is such that if $e \in E$ then

$$A(e, e) = e \Leftrightarrow f(e) = 0. \tag{17.9}$$

By equation (17.9) and because of strict monotonicity of f, there is at most one idempotent for A (which is, actually, the identity) and hence A cannot be idempotent. Therefore, there is no continuous, strictly increasing, idempotent and associative function. However, we can note that every continuous, strictly increasing and associative function is necessarily symmetric. The sum ($f(x) = x$) and the product ($f(x) = \log x$) are well-known examples of continuous, strictly increasing and associative functions.

According to Ling [LIN 65], any semigroup (E, M) satisfying the hypotheses of theorem 17.4 is called *Aczélian*.

Recall that each associative sequence $(A^{(n)} : E^n \to E)_{n \geq 1}$ of functions is uniquely determined by its 2-variable function. We therefore have the following result.

Corollary 17.1. *Let E be a real interval, bounded or not, which is open on one side. $(A^{(n)} : E^n \to E)_{n \geq 1}$ is an associative sequence of continuous and strictly increasing functions if and only if there exists a continuous and strictly monotonic function $f : E \to \mathbb{R}$ such that, for all $n \in \mathbb{N} \setminus \{0\}$,*

$$A^{(n)}(x) = f^{-1}\left[\sum_{i=1}^{n} f(x_i)\right] \qquad (x \in E^n).$$

17.4.2. Archimedean semigroups

Some authors attempted to generalize theorem 17.4 by relaxing the strict increasing monotonicity into non-decreasing monotonicity. However, it seems that the class of continuous, non-decreasing and associative functions has not yet been described. However, under some additional conditions, results have been obtained.

First, we state a representation theorem attributed very often to Ling [LIN 65]. In fact, her main theorem can be deduced from previously known results on topological semigroups; see Faucett [FAU 55] and Mostert and Shields [MOS 57]. Nevertheless, the advantage of Ling's approach is twofold: it treats two different cases in a unified manner and establishes elementary proofs.

Theorem 17.5. *Let $E = [a, b]$. $A : E^2 \to E$ is continuous, non-decreasing, associative and*

$$A(b, x) = x \qquad (x \in E) \tag{17.10}$$
$$A(x, x) < x \qquad (x \in E°) \tag{17.11}$$

if and only if there exists a continuous strictly decreasing function $f : E \to [0, +\infty]$, with $f(b) = 0$, such that

$$A(x, y) = f^{-1}[\min(f(x) + f(y), f(a))] \qquad (x, y \in E). \tag{17.12}$$

The requirement that E be closed is not really a restriction. If E is any real interval, finite or infinite with right endpoint b (b can be $+\infty$), we can replace condition (17.10) with

$$\lim_{t \to b^-} A(t,t) = b, \quad \lim_{t \to b^-} A(t,x) = x \quad (x \in E).$$

Any function f solving equation (17.12) is called an *additive generator* (or simply *generator*) of A. Moreover, we can easily see that any function A of the form equation (17.12) is symmetric and conjunctive.

Condition (17.10) expresses that b is a *left identity* for A. It turns out, from equation (17.12), that b acts as an identity and a as a zero. Condition (17.11) simply expresses that there are no idempotents for A in $]a,b[$. Indeed, by non-decreasing monotonicity and equation (17.10), we always have $A(x,x) \leq A(b,x) = x$ for all $x \in [a,b]$.

Depending on whether $f(a)$ is finite or infinite (recall that $f(a) \in [0, +\infty]$), A takes a well-defined form (Fodor and Roubens [FOD 94, section 1.3] and Schweizer and Sklar [SCH 83]):

– $f(a) < +\infty$ if and only if A has *zero divisors* (i.e. $\exists x, y \in]a,b[$ such that $A(x,y) = a$). In this case, there exists a continuous strictly increasing function $g : [a,b] \to [0,1]$, with $g(a) = 0$ and $g(b) = 1$, such that

$$A(x,y) = g^{-1}[\max(g(x) + g(y) - 1, 0)] \quad (x, y \in [a,b]). \tag{17.13}$$

To see this, it is sufficient to set $g(x) := 1 - f(x)/f(a)$.
For associative sequences $(A^{(n)} : [a,b]^n \to [a,b])_{n \geq 1}$, equation (17.13) becomes

$$A^{(n)}(x) = g^{-1}\left[\max\left(\sum_{i=1}^n g(x_i) - n + 1, 0\right)\right] \quad (x \in [a,b]^n, \, n \in \mathbb{N} \setminus \{0\}).$$

– $\lim_{t \to a^+} f(x) = +\infty$ if and only if A is strictly increasing on $]a,b[$. In this case, there exists a continuous strictly increasing function $g : [a,b] \to [0,1]$, with $g(a) = 0$ and $g(b) = 1$, such that

$$A(x,y) = g^{-1}[g(x)\,g(y)] \quad (x, y \in [a,b]). \tag{17.14}$$

To see this, it is sufficient to set $g(x) := \exp(-f(x))$.
For associative sequences $(A^{(n)} : [a,b]^n \to [a,b])_{n \geq 1}$, equation (17.14) becomes

$$A^{(n)}(x) = g^{-1}\left[\prod_{i=1}^n g(x_i)\right] \quad (x \in [a,b]^n, \, n \in \mathbb{N} \setminus \{0\}).$$

Of course, theorem 17.5 can also be written in a dual form as follows.

Theorem 17.6. *Let* $E = [a,b]$. $A : E^2 \to E$ *is continuous, non-decreasing, associative and*

$$A(a, x) = x \quad (x \in E)$$
$$A(x, x) > x \quad (x \in E°)$$

if and only if there exists a continuous strictly increasing function $f : E \to [0, +\infty]$, *with* $f(a) = 0$, *such that*

$$A(x, y) = f^{-1}[\min(f(x) + f(y), f(b))] \quad (x, y \in E). \tag{17.15}$$

Again, E can be any real interval, even infinite. Functions A of the form equation (17.15) are symmetric and disjunctive. There are no interior idempotents. The left endpoint a acts as an identity and the right endpoint b acts as a zero.

Once more, two mutually exclusive cases can be examined:

– $f(b) < +\infty$ if and only if A has zero divisors (i.e. $\exists x, y \in\,]a, b[$ such that $A(x, y) = b$). In this case, there exists a continuous strictly increasing function $g : [a, b] \to [0, 1]$, with $g(a) = 0$ and $g(b) = 1$, such that

$$A(x, y) = g^{-1}[\min(g(x) + g(y), 1)] \quad (x, y \in [a, b]). \tag{17.16}$$

To see this, it is sufficient to set $g(x) := f(x)/f(b)$.
For associative sequences $(A^{(n)} : [a, b]^n \to [a, b])_{n \geq 1}$, equation (17.16) becomes

$$A^{(n)}(x) = g^{-1}\left[\min\left(\sum_{i=1}^{n} g(x_i), 1\right)\right] \quad (x \in [a, b]^n,\ n \in \mathbb{N} \setminus \{0\}).$$

– $\lim_{t \to b^-} f(x) = +\infty$ if and only if A is strictly increasing on $]a, b[$. In this case, there exists a continuous strictly increasing function $g : [a, b] \to [0, 1]$, with $g(a) = 0$ and $g(b) = 1$, such that

$$A(x, y) = g^{-1}[1 - (1 - g(x))(1 - g(y))] \quad (x, y \in [a, b]), \tag{17.17}$$

To see this, it is sufficient to set $g(x) := 1 - \exp(-f(x))$.
For associative sequences $(A^{(n)} : [a, b]^n \to [a, b])_{n \geq 1}$, equation (17.17) becomes

$$A^{(n)}(x) = g^{-1}\left[1 - \prod_{i=1}^{n}(1 - g(x_i))\right] \quad (x \in [a, b]^n,\ n \in \mathbb{N} \setminus \{0\}).$$

Any semigroup fulfilling the assumptions of theorem 17.5 or 17.6 is called *Archimedean*; see Ling [LIN 65]. In other words, any semigroup (E, A) is said to be *Archimedean* if A is continuous, non-decreasing, associative, one endpoint of E is an identity for A and there are no idempotents for A in $E°$. We can make a distinction between conjunctive and disjunctive Archimedean semigroups depending on whether the identity is the right or left endpoint of E, respectively. An Archimedean semigroup is called *properly Archimedean* or *Aczélian* if every additive generator f is unbounded; otherwise it is *improperly Archimedean*.

Ling [LIN 65, section 6] proved that every Archimedean semigroup is obtainable as a limit of Aczélian semigroups.

17.4.3. *A class of non-decreasing and associative functions*

We now give a description of the class of functions $A : [a, b]^2 \to [0, 1]$ that are continuous, non-decreasing, weakly idempotent and associative. For all $\theta \in [a, b]$, we define $\mathcal{A}_{a,b,\theta}$ as the set of continuous, non-decreasing, weakly idempotent and associative functions $A : [a, b]^2 \to [0, 1]$ such that $A(a, b) = A(b, a) = \theta$. The extreme cases $\mathcal{A}_{a,b,a}$ and $\mathcal{A}_{a,b,b}$ will play an important role in the sequel [MAR 00c].

Theorem 17.7. $A : [a, b]^2 \to [0, 1]$ *is continuous, non-decreasing, weakly idempotent and associative if and only if there exist* $\alpha, \beta \in [a, b]$ *and two functions* $A_{a,\alpha \wedge \beta,\alpha \wedge \beta} \in \mathcal{A}_{a,\alpha \wedge \beta,\alpha \wedge \beta}$ *and* $A_{\alpha \vee \beta,b,\alpha \vee \beta} \in \mathcal{A}_{\alpha \vee \beta,b,\alpha \vee \beta}$ *such that, for all* $x, y \in [a, b]$,

$$A(x, y) = \begin{cases} A_{a,\alpha \wedge \beta,\alpha \wedge \beta}(x, y), & \text{if } x, y \in [a, \alpha \wedge \beta] \\ A_{\alpha \vee \beta,b,\alpha \vee \beta}(x, y), & \text{if } x, y \in [\alpha \vee \beta, b] \\ (\alpha \wedge x) \vee (\beta \wedge y) \vee (x \wedge y), & \text{otherwise.} \end{cases}$$

Now, let us turn to the description of $\mathcal{A}_{a,b,a}$. Mostert and Shields [MOS 57, p. 130] proved the following.

Theorem 17.8. $A : [a, b]^2 \to [a, b]$ *is continuous, associative and is such that a acts as a zero and b as an identity if and only if either*

– $A(x, y) = \min(x, y) \quad (x, y \in [a, b])$,

– *there exists a continuous strictly decreasing function* $f : [a, b] \to [0, +\infty]$, *with* $f(b) = 0$, *such that*

$$A(x, y) = f^{-1}[\min(f(x) + f(y), f(a))] \quad (x, y \in [a, b])$$

(conjunctive Archimedean semigroup) or

– there exist a countable index set $K \subseteq \mathbb{N}$, a family of disjoint open subintervals $\{]a_k, b_k[\mid k \in K\}$ of $[a,b]$ and a family $\{f_k \mid k \in K\}$ of continuous strictly decreasing function $f_k : [a_k, b_k] \to [0, +\infty]$, with $f_k(b_k) = 0$, such that, for all $x, y \in [a, b]$,

$$A(x,y) = \begin{cases} f_k^{-1}[\min(f_k(x) + f_k(y), f_k(a_k))], & \text{if } \exists k \in K \text{ s.t. } x, y \in [a_k, b_k] \\ \min(x,y), & \text{otherwise.} \end{cases}$$

(ordinal sum of conjunctive Archimedean semigroups and one-point semigroups).

We can show that $\mathcal{A}_{a,b,a}$ is the family of continuous, non-decreasing and associative functions $A : [a,b]^2 \to [a,b]$ such that a acts as a zero and b as an identity. Consequently, the description of the family $\mathcal{A}_{a,b,a}$ is also given by theorem 17.8. Moreover, it turns out that all functions fulfilling the assumptions of this result are symmetric, non-decreasing and conjunctive.

Theorem 17.8 can also be written in a dual form as follows.

Theorem 17.9. $A : [a,b]^2 \to [a,b]$ *is continuous, associative and is such that a acts as an identity and b as a zero if and only if either*

– $A(x,y) = \max(x,y) \quad (x, y \in [a,b])$,

– *there exists a continuous strictly increasing function $f : [a,b] \to [0, +\infty]$, with $f(a) = 0$, such that*

$$A(x,y) = f^{-1}[\min(f(x) + f(y), f(b))] \quad (x, y \in [a,b]).$$

(disjunctive Archimedean semigroup) or

– *there exist a countable index set $K \subseteq \mathbb{N}$, a family of disjoint open subintervals $\{]a_k, b_k[\mid k \in K\}$ of $[a,b]$ and a family $\{f_k \mid k \in K\}$ of continuous strictly increasing function $f_k : [a_k, b_k] \to [0, +\infty]$, with $f_k(a_k) = 0$, such that for all $x, y \in [a, b]$,*

$$A(x,y) = \begin{cases} f_k^{-1}[\min(f_k(x) + f_k(y), f_k(b_k))], & \text{if } \exists k \in K \text{ s.t. } x, y \in [a_k, b_k] \\ \max(x,y), & \text{otherwise.} \end{cases}$$

(ordinal sum of disjunctive Archimedean semigroups and one-point semigroups).

As above, we can see that $\mathcal{A}_{a,b,b}$ is the family of continuous, non-decreasing and associative functions $A : [a,b]^2 \to [a,b]$ such that a acts as an identity and b as a zero. The description of the family $\mathcal{A}_{a,b,b}$ is therefore given by theorem 17.9. Moreover, all functions fulfilling the assumptions of this result are symmetric, non-decreasing and disjunctive.

Theorems 17.7, 17.8, and 17.9, taken together, give a complete description of the family of continuous, non-decreasing, weakly idempotent and associative functions $A : [a,b]^2 \to [a,b]$. Imposing some additional conditions leads to the following immediate corollaries.

Corollary 17.2. $A : [a,b]^2 \to [a,b]$ *is continuous, strictly increasing, weakly idempotent and associative if and only if there exists a continuous strictly increasing function $g : [a,b] \to [0,1]$, with $g(a) = 0$ and $g(b) = 1$, such that either*

$$A(x,y) = g^{-1}[g(x)\,g(y)] \qquad (x,y \in [a,b]),$$

– *or*

$$A(x,y) = g^{-1}[g(x) + g(y) - g(x)\,g(y)] \qquad (x,y \in [a,b]).$$

Corollary 17.3. $A : [a,b]^2 \to [a,b]$ *is symmetric, continuous, non-decreasing, weakly idempotent and associative if and only if there exist $\alpha \in [a,b]$ and two functions $A_{a,\alpha,\alpha} \in \mathcal{A}_{a,\alpha,\alpha}$ and $A_{\alpha,b,\alpha} \in \mathcal{A}_{\alpha,b,\alpha}$ such that for all $x,y \in [a,b]$,*

$$A(x,y) = \begin{cases} A_{a,\alpha,\alpha}(x,y), & \text{if } x,y \in [a,\alpha] \\ A_{\alpha,b,\alpha}(x,y), & \text{if } x,y \in [\alpha,b] \\ \alpha, & \text{otherwise.} \end{cases}$$

Corollary 17.4. $A : [a,b]^2 \to [a,b]$ *is continuous, non-decreasing, weakly idempotent, associative and has exactly one identity element in $[a,b]$ if and only if $A \in \mathcal{A}_{a,b,a} \cup \mathcal{A}_{a,b,b}$.*

17.4.4. Internal associative functions

We now investigate the case of internal associative functions, that is, associative means. As these functions are idempotent, we actually investigate idempotent and associative functions. Although we have already observed that there are no continuous, strictly increasing, idempotent and associative functions, the class of continuous, non-decreasing, idempotent and associative functions is non-empty and its description can be deduced from theorem 17.7. However, Fodor [FOD 96] had already obtained this description in a more general framework, as follows.

Theorem 17.10. *Let E be a real interval, finite or infinite. $A : E^2 \to E$ is continuous, non-decreasing, idempotent and associative if and only if there exist $\alpha, \beta \in E$ such that*

$$A(x,y) = (\alpha \wedge x) \vee (\beta \wedge y) \vee (x \wedge y) \qquad ((x,y) \in E^2).$$

Notice that, by distributivity of $\wedge$ and $\vee$, A can also be written in the equivalent form:

$$A(x,y) = (\beta \vee x) \wedge (\alpha \vee y) \wedge (x \vee y) \qquad ((x,y) \in E^2).$$

For sequences of associative functions, the statement can be formulated as follows.

Theorem 17.11. *Let E be a real interval, finite or infinite. $(A^{(n)} : E^n \to E)_{n \geq 1}$ is an associative sequence of continuous, non-decreasing and idempotent functions if and only if there exist $\alpha, \beta \in E$ such that*

$$A^{(n)}(x) = (\alpha \wedge x_1) \vee \left(\bigvee_{i=2}^{n-1} (\alpha \wedge \beta \wedge x_i) \right) \vee (\beta \wedge x_n) \vee \left(\bigwedge_{i=1}^{n} x_i \right) \quad (x \in E^n,\ n \in \mathbb{N} \setminus \{0\}).$$

Before Fodor [FOD 96], the description of symmetric functions was obtained by Fung and Fu [FUN 75] and revisited by Dubois and Prade [DUB 84]. The result can now be formulated as follows.

Theorem 17.12. *Let E be a real interval, finite or infinite:*

1) $A : E^2 \to E$ is symmetric, continuous, non-decreasing, idempotent and associative if and only if there exists $\alpha \in E$ such that

$$A(x, y) = \mathrm{median}(x, y, \alpha) \quad (x, y \in E).$$

2) $(A^{(n)} : E^n \to E)_{n \geq 1}$ is an associative sequence of symmetric, continuous, non-decreasing and associative functions if and only if there exists $\alpha \in E$ such that

$$A^{(n)}(x) = \mathrm{median}\left(\bigwedge_{i=1}^{n} x_i, \bigvee_{i=1}^{n} x_i, \alpha \right) \quad (x \in E^n,\ n \in \mathbb{N} \setminus \{0\}). \quad (17.18)$$

The previous three theorems show that the idempotency property is seldom consistent with associativity. For instance, the associative mean (17.18) is not very decisive since it leads to the predefined value α as soon as there exist $x_i \leq \alpha$ and $x_j \geq \alpha$.

Czogala and Drewniak [CZO 84] have examined the case when A has an identity element $e \in E$, as follows.

Theorem 17.13. *Let E be a real interval, finite or infinite:*

1) If $A : E^2 \to E$ is non-decreasing, idempotent, associative and has an identity element $e \in E$, then there exists a decreasing function $g : E \to E$ with $g(e) = e$, such that for all $x, y \in E$,

$$A(x, y) = \begin{cases} x \wedge y, & \text{if } y < g(x), \\ x \vee y, & \text{if } y > g(x), \\ x \wedge y \text{ or } x \vee y, & \text{if } y = g(x). \end{cases}$$

2) If $A : E^2 \to E$ is continuous, non-decreasing, idempotent, associative and has an identity element $e \in E$, then $A = \min$ or $\max$.

17.4.5. *t-norms, t-conorms, and uninorms*

In fuzzy set theory, one of the main topics consists of defining fuzzy logical connectives which are appropriate extensions of logical connectives **AND**, **OR** and **NOT** in the case when the valuation set is the unit interval $[0, 1]$ rather than $\{0, 1\}$.

Fuzzy connectives modeling **AND** and **OR** are called *triangular norms* (t-norms for short) and *triangular conorms* (t-conorms) respectively; see Alsina *et al.* [ALS 83] and Schweizer and Sklar [SCH 83].

Definition 17.14. 1) A t-norm is a symmetric, non-decreasing and associative function $T : [0, 1]^2 \to [0, 1]$ having 1 as identity.

2) A t-conorm is a symmetric, non-decreasing and associative function $S : [0, 1]^2 \to [0, 1]$ having 0 as identity.

The investigation of these functions has been made by Schweizer and Sklar [SCH 61, SCH 63] and Ling [LIN 65]. There is now an abundant literature on this topic; see the book by Klement *et al.* [KLE 00].

Of course, the family of continuous t-norms is nothing other than the class $\mathcal{A}_{0,1,0}$, and the family of continuous t-conorms is the class $\mathcal{A}_{0,1,1}$. Both families have been fully described in this section. Moreover, corollary 17.4 gives a characterization of their union.

Corollary 17.5. *A* $: [0, 1]^2 \to [0, 1]$ *is continuous, non-decreasing, weakly idempotent, associative and has exactly one identity in $[0, 1]$ if and only if A is a continuous t-norm or a continuous t-conorm.*

It is well known that t-norms and t-conorms are extensively used in fuzzy set theory, especially in modeling fuzzy connectives and implications [WEB 83]. Applications to practical problems require the use of, in a sense, the most appropriate t-norms or t-conorms. On this issue, Fodor [FOD 91a] presented a method to construct new t-norms from t-norms.

It is worth noting that some properties of t-norms, such as associativity, do not play any essential role in preference modeling and choice theory. Recently, some authors [ALS 93, DYC 84, ZIM 80] have investigated non-associative binary operation on $[0, 1]$ in different contexts. These operators can be viewed as a generalization of t-norms and t-conorms in the sense that both are contained in this kind of operations. Moreover, Fodor [FOD 91b] defined and investigated the concept of weak t-norms. His results were usefully applied to the framework of fuzzy strict preference relations.

Further associative functions were recently introduced, i.e. *t-operators* [MAS 99] and *uninorms* [YAG 96] (see also [MAS 01, MAS 02]), which proved to be useful in expert systems, neural networks and fuzzy quantifiers theory.

Definition 17.15.   1) A *t-operator* is a symmetric, non-decreasing, associative function $F : [0,1]^2 \to [0,1]$, with 0 and 1 as idempotent elements, such that the sections $x \mapsto F(x,0)$ and $x \mapsto F(x,1)$ are continuous on $[0,1]$.

2) A *uninorm* is a symmetric, non-decreasing and associative function $U : [0,1]^2 \to [0,1]$ having an identity.

It is clear that a uninorm becomes a t-norm (respectively, a t-conorm) when the identity is 1 (respectively, 0).

We will not linger on this topic of t-norms, t-conorms, and uninorms. The interested reader can consult the book by Klement *et al.* [KLE 00]. For more recent results, we also recommend an article on associative functions by Sander [SAN 02].

17.5. Non-additive integrals

Many aggregation functions can be seen as non-additive discrete integrals with respect to non-additive measures. In this section we introduce Choquet and Sugeno integrals. The reader can find more details on this topic in Chapter 18.

17.5.1. *Motivations*

A significant aspect of aggregation in multicriteria decision making is the difference in the importance of criteria or attributes, usually modeled by using different weights. Since these weights must be taken into account during the aggregation phase it is necessary to use weighted functions, therefore giving up the symmetry property. Until recently, the most often used weighted aggregation functions were averaging functions, such as quasi-linear means (17.4).

However, the weighted arithmetic means and, more generally, the quasi-linear means present some drawbacks. None of these functions are able to model in an understandable way an interaction among attributes. Indeed, it is well known in multiattribute utility theory (MAUT) that these functions lead to *mutual preferential independence* among the attributes [e.g. FIS 95], which expresses in some sense the independence of the attributes. Since these functions are not appropriate when interactive attributes are considered, people usually tend to construct independent attributes or attributes that are assumed to be so, causing some bias effect in evaluation.

In order to have a flexible representation of complex interaction phenomena among attributes or criteria (e.g. positive or negative synergy among some criteria), it is useful to substitute the weight vector for a non-additive set function, allowing the definition of a weight not only on each criterion but also on each subset of criteria.

For this purpose, the use of fuzzy measures was proposed by Sugeno in 1974 [SUG 74] to generalize additive measures. It seems widely accepted that additivity is not suitable as a required property of set functions in many real situations, due to the lack of additivity in many facets of human reasoning. To be able to express human subjectivity, Sugeno proposed replacing the additivity property with a weaker one: monotonicity. These non-additive monotonic measures are referred to as fuzzy measures.

We consider a discrete set of n elements $N = \{1, \ldots, n\}$. Depending on the application, these elements could be players of a cooperative game, criteria in a multicriteria decision problem, attributes, experts or voters in an opinion pooling problem, etc. To emphasize that N has n elements, we will often write N_n.

Definition 17.16. A (discrete) *fuzzy measure* on N is a set function $\mu : 2^N \to [0, 1]$ that is monotonic, that is $\mu(S) \leq \mu(T)$ whenever $S \subseteq T$, and fulfills the boundary conditions $\mu(\varnothing) = 0$ and $\mu(N) = 1$.

For any $S \subseteq N$, the coefficient $\mu(S)$ can be viewed as the weight, importance or strength of the combination S for the particular decision problem under consideration. Thus, in addition to the usual weights on criteria taken separately, weights on any combination of criteria are also defined. Monotonicity then means that adding a new element to a combination cannot decrease its importance. We denote the set of fuzzy measures on N as $\mathcal{F}_N$.

When a fuzzy measure is available on N, it is interesting to have tools capable of summarizing all the values of a function to a single point, in terms of the underlying fuzzy measure. These tools are the *fuzzy integrals*, a concept proposed by Sugeno [SUG 74, SUG 77].

Fuzzy integrals are integrals of a real function with respect to a fuzzy measure, by analogy with Lebesgue integral which is defined with respect to an ordinary (i.e. additive) measure. As the integral of a function in a sense represents its average value, a fuzzy integral can be viewed as a particular case of averaging aggregation function.

Contrary to the weighted arithmetic means, fuzzy integrals are able to represent a certain kind of interaction among criteria, ranging from redundancy (negative interaction) to synergy (positive interaction). For this reason they have been thoroughly studied in the context of multicriteria decision problems [GRA 95a, GRA 96, GRA 98, GRA 00].

There are several classes of fuzzy integrals, among which the most representative are the Choquet and Sugeno integrals. In this section we discuss these two integrals as aggregation functions. In particular, we present axiomatic characterizations for these integrals. The main difference between them is that the former is suitable for the aggregation on interval scales, while the latter is designed for aggregating values on ordinal scales.

17.5.2. *The Choquet integral*

The concept of the Choquet integral was proposed in capacity theory [CHO 54]. Since then, it was used in various contexts such as non-additive utility theory [GIL 87, SAR 92, SCH 86, WAK 89], theory of fuzzy measures and integrals [CAM 91, HÖH 82, MUR 89, MUR 91] (see also the excellent edited book [GRA 00]) and also finance [DOW 92] and game theory [DOW 94].

Since this integral is viewed here as an n-variable aggregation function, we will adopt a function-like notation instead of the usual integral form, and the integrand will be a set of n real values denoted $x = (x_1, \ldots, x_n) \in \mathbb{R}^n$.

Definition 17.17. Let $\mu \in \mathcal{F}_N$. The (discrete) *Choquet integral* of $x \in \mathbb{R}^n$ with respect to μ is defined by

$$\mathcal{C}_\mu(x) := \sum_{i=1}^n x_{(i)} \left[\mu(A_{(i)}) - \mu(A_{(i+1)}) \right],$$

where $(\cdot)$ is a permutation on N such that $x_{(1)} \leq \ldots \leq x_{(n)}$. Also, $A_{(i)} = \{(i), \ldots, (n)\}$ and $A_{(n+1)} = \emptyset$.

For instance, if $x_3 \leq x_1 \leq x_2$, we have

$$\mathcal{C}_\mu(x_1, x_2, x_3) = x_3 \left[\mu(\{3,1,2\}) - \mu(\{1,2\})\right] + x_1 \left[\mu(\{1,2\}) - \mu(\{2\})\right] + x_2 \mu(\{2\}).$$

The Choquet integral is therefore a linear expression, up to a reordering of the arguments. It is closely related to the Lebesgue integral, since both coincide when the measure is additive:

$$\mathcal{C}_\mu(x) = \sum_{i=1}^n \mu(i) x_i \qquad (x \in \mathbb{R}^n).$$

In this sense, the Choquet integral is a generalization of the Lebesgue integral.

Let us now turn to axiomatizations of the Choquet integral. First of all, as we can see, this aggregation function fulfills a number of natural properties. It is continuous, non-decreasing, unanimously increasing, idempotent, internal and meaningful for the same input-output interval scales; see for instance Grabisch [GRA 96]. It also fulfills the *comonotonic additivity* property [DEL 71, SCH 86], that is,

$$f(x_1 + x'_1, \ldots, x_n + x'_n) = f(x_1, \ldots, x_n) + f(x'_1, \ldots, x'_n)$$

for all *comonotonic* vectors $x, x' \in \mathbb{R}^n$. Two vectors $x, x' \in \mathbb{R}^n$ are comonotonic if there exists a permutation σ on N such that

$$x_{\sigma(1)} \leq \cdots \leq x_{\sigma(n)} \quad \text{and} \quad x'_{\sigma(1)} \leq \cdots \leq x'_{\sigma(n)}.$$

An interpretation of this property in multicriteria decision making can be found in Modave *et al.* [MOD 97, MOD 98].

The following result [MAR 99, proposition 4.1] gives a characterization of the 2-variable Choquet integral in a very natural way.

Proposition 17.2. $f : \mathbb{R}^2 \to \mathbb{R}$ *is non-decreasing and meaningful for the same input-output interval scales if and only if there exists* $\mu \in \mathcal{F}_2$ *such that* $f = \mathcal{C}_\mu$.

The class of n-variable Choquet integrals was first characterized by Schmeidler [SCH 86] by using monotonic additivity; see also [CAM 91, CAM 92, GRA 93, GRA 95c]. Note that this result was stated and proved in the continuous case (infinite) instead of the discrete case.

Theorem 17.14. $f : \mathbb{R}^n \to \mathbb{R}$ *is non-decreasing, comonotonic additive and fulfills* $f(\mathbf{1}_N) = 1$ *if and only if there exists* $\mu \in \mathcal{F}_N$ *such that* $f = \mathcal{C}_\mu$.

Since the Choquet integral is defined from a fuzzy measure, it is sometimes useful to consider, for a given set N, the family of Choquet integrals on N as a set of functions

$$\{f_\mu : \mathbb{R}^n \to \mathbb{R} \mid \mu \in \mathcal{F}_N\}$$

or, equivalently, as a function $f : \mathbb{R}^n \times \mathcal{F}_N \to \mathbb{R}$.

Let us mention a first characterization of the family of Choquet integrals on N; see Groes *et al.* [GRO 98]. For any $S \subseteq N$, $S \neq \emptyset$, denote by μ_S the fuzzy measure on N defined by $\mu_S(T) = 1$ if $T \supseteq S$ and 0 otherwise.

Theorem 17.15. *The class of functions* $\{f_\mu : \mathbb{R}^n \to \mathbb{R} \mid \mu \in \mathcal{F}_N\}$ *fulfills the following properties:*

– *for any* $\mu, \nu \in \mathcal{F}_N$ *and any* $\lambda \in \mathbb{R}$ *such that* $\lambda\mu + (1-\lambda)\nu \in \mathcal{F}_N$, *we have*

$$f_{\lambda\mu + (1-\lambda)\nu} = \lambda f_\mu + (1-\lambda) f_\nu,$$

– for any $S \subseteq N$, we have $f_{\mu_S} = \min_S$,

if and only if $f_\mu = \mathcal{C}_\mu$ for all $\mu \in \mathcal{F}_N$.

A second characterization obtained by the author [MAR 98, MAR 00a] can be stated as follows.

Theorem 17.16. *The class of functions $\{f_\mu : \mathbb{R}^n \to \mathbb{R} \mid \mu \in \mathcal{F}_N\}$ fulfills the following properties:*

– *any function f_μ is a linear expression of μ, that is there exist 2^n functions $g_T : \mathbb{R}^n \to \mathbb{R}$ $(T \subseteq N)$ such that $f_\mu = \sum_{T \subseteq N} g_T \, \mu(T)$ for all $\mu \in \mathcal{F}_N$,*
– *for any $\mu \in \mathcal{F}_N$ and any $S \subseteq N$, we have $f_\mu(\mathbf{1}_S) = \mu(S)$,*
– *for any $\mu \in \mathcal{F}_N$, the function f_μ is non-decreasing and meaningful for the same input-output interval scales,*

if and only if $f_\mu = \mathcal{C}_\mu$ for all $\mu \in \mathcal{F}_N$.

These two characterizations are natural and similar to each other. The linearity condition proposed in the second characterization is useful if we want to keep the aggregation model as simple as possible. Technically, this condition is equivalent to the superposition condition, that is,

$$f_{\lambda_1 \mu + \lambda_2 \nu} = \lambda_1 f_\mu + \lambda_2 f_\nu$$

for all $\mu, \nu \in \mathcal{F}_N$ and all $\lambda_1, \lambda_2 \in \mathbb{R}$ such that $\lambda_1 \mu + \lambda_2 \nu \in \mathcal{F}_N$. Of course, linearity implies the first condition of the first characterization. Moreover, under this linearity condition, the other conditions are equivalent. In fact, in the proof of the second characterization [MAR 98, MAR 00a], the author replaced the condition $f_{\mu_S} = \min_S$ with the three conditions: $f_\mu(\mathbf{1}_S) = \mu(S)$, non-decreasing monotonicity and meaningfulness for the same input-output interval scales of f_μ.

We also have the following three results [MAR 98, section 4.2.3].

Proposition 17.3. *The Choquet integral $\mathcal{C}_\mu : \mathbb{R}^n \to \mathbb{R}$ is bisymmetric if and only if*

$$\mathcal{C}_\mu \in \{\min_S, \max_S \mid S \subseteq N\} \cup \{\mathrm{WAM}_\omega \mid \omega \in [0,1]^n\}.$$

Proposition 17.4. *The sequence of Choquet integrals $\mathcal{C} := (\mathcal{C}^{(n)}_{\mu^{(n)}} : \mathbb{R}^n \to \mathbb{R})_{n \geq 1}$ is bisymmetric if and only if either:*

– *for any $n \in \mathbb{N} \setminus \{0\}$, there exists $S \subseteq N_n$ such that $\mathcal{C}^{(n)}_{\mu^{(n)}} = \min_S$,*

– *for any $n \in \mathbb{N} \setminus \{0\}$, there exists $S \subseteq N_n$ such that $C_{\mu^{(n)}}^{(n)} = \max_S$, or*
– *for any $n \in \mathbb{N} \setminus \{0\}$, there exists $\omega \in [0,1]^n$ such that $C_{\mu^{(n)}}^{(n)} = \mathrm{WAM}_\omega$.*

Proposition 17.5. *The sequence of Choquet integrals $\mathcal{C} := (C_{\mu^{(n)}}^{(n)} : \mathbb{R}^n \to \mathbb{R})_{n \geq 1}$ is decomposable if and only if either*
– $\mathcal{C} = (\min^{(n)})_{n \geq 1}$,
– $\mathcal{C} = (\max^{(n)})_{n \geq 1}$, *or*
– *there exists $\theta \in [0,1]$ such that, for any $n \in \mathbb{N} \setminus \{0\}$, we have $C_{\mu^{(n)}}^{(n)} = \mathrm{WAM}_\omega$, with*

$$\omega_i = \frac{(1-\theta)^{n-i}\theta^{i-1}}{\sum_{j=1}^n (1-\theta)^{n-j}\theta^{j-1}} \qquad (i \in N_n).$$

Proposition 17.6. *The sequence of Choquet integrals $\mathcal{C} := (C_{\mu^{(n)}}^{(n)} : \mathbb{R}^n \to \mathbb{R})_{n \geq 1}$ is associative if and only if*

$$\mathcal{C} = (\min^{(n)})_{n \geq 1} \text{ or } (\max^{(n)})_{n \geq 1} \text{ or } (P_1^{(n)})_{n \geq 1} \text{ or } (P_n^{(n)})_{n \geq 1}.$$

Let us now consider certain special cases of the Choquet integral, namely the weighted arithmetic means (WAM) and the ordered weighted averaging functions (OWA).

The *weighted arithmetic mean* WAM_ω is a Choquet integral defined from an additive measure. It fulfills the classical *additivity* property, i.e.

$$f(x_1 + x_1', \ldots, x_n + x_n') = f(x_1, \ldots, x_n) + f(x_1', \ldots, x_n')$$

for all vectors $x, x' \in \mathbb{R}^n$. More precisely, we have the following results (see Marichal [MAR 98, section 4.2.4] and Murofushi and Sugeno [MUR 93]).

Proposition 17.7. *The Choquet integral $C_\mu : \mathbb{R}^n \to \mathbb{R}$ is additive if and only if there exists $\omega \in [0,1]^n$ such that $C_\mu = \mathrm{WAM}_\omega$.*

Proposition 17.8. *$A : \mathbb{R}^n \to \mathbb{R}$ is non-decreasing, meaningful for the same input-output interval scales and additive if and only if there exists $\omega \in [0,1]^n$ such that $A = \mathrm{WAM}_\omega$.*

The *ordered weighted averaging functions* OWA_ω were proposed by Yager [YAG 88]. Since their introduction, these aggregation functions have been applied to many fields as neural networks, database systems, fuzzy logic controllers and group decision making. An overview on these functions can be found in the book edited by Yager and Kacprzyk [YAG 97]; see also Grabisch *et al.* [GRA 00].

The following result, ascribed to Grabisch [GRA 95b] (see [MAR 02a] for a concise proof), shows that the OWA function is nothing but a Choquet integral with respect to a *cardinality-based* fuzzy measure i.e. a fuzzy measure depending only on the cardinalities of the subsets.

Proposition 17.9. *Let $\mu \in \mathcal{F}_N$. The following assertions are equivalent:*
1) For any $S, S' \subseteq N$ such that $|S| = |S'|$, we have $\mu(S) = \mu(S')$.
2) There exists a weight vector w such that $\mathcal{C}_\mu = \text{OWA}_w$.
3) $\mathcal{C}_\mu$ is a symmetric function.

The fuzzy measure μ associated with an OWA_w is given by

$$\mu(S) = \sum_{i=n-s+1}^{n} w_i \quad (S \subseteq N, \ S \neq \emptyset).$$

Conversely, the weights associated with OWA_w are given by

$$w_{n-s} = \mu(S \cup i) - \mu(S) \quad (i \in N, \ S \subseteq N \setminus i).$$

The class of OWA functions includes an important subfamily, namely the order statistics

$$\text{OS}_k(x) = x_{(k)},$$

when $w_k = 1$ for some $k \in N$. In this case, we have for any $S \subseteq N$

$$\mu(S) = \begin{cases} 1, & \text{if } s \geq n - k + 1, \\ 0, & \text{otherwise.} \end{cases}$$

This subfamily itself contains the minimum, the maximum and the median. Axiomatizations of the class of OWA functions can be immediately derived from those of the Choquet integral and from proposition 17.9.

17.5.3. *The Sugeno integral*

The Sugeno integral [SUG 74, SUG 77] was introduced as a fuzzy integral, that is, an integral defined from a fuzzy measure. This integral has then been thoroughly investigated and used in many domains (an overview can be found in Dubois *et al.* [DUB 01] and the volume edited by Grabisch *et al.* [GRA 00]).

As for the Choquet integral, we give here the definition of the Sugeno integral in its discrete (finite) version, which is nothing other than an aggregation function from $[0, 1]^n$ to $[0, 1]$.

Definition 17.18. Let $\mu \in \mathcal{F}_N$. The (discrete) *Sugeno integral* of $x \in [0,1]^n$ with respect to μ is defined by

$$\mathcal{S}_\mu(x) := \bigvee_{i=1}^{n} [x_{(i)} \wedge \mu(A_{(i)})],$$

where $(\cdot)$ is a permutation on N such that $x_{(1)} \leq \ldots \leq x_{(n)}$. Also, $A_{(i)} = \{(i), \ldots, (n)\}$ and $A_{(n+1)} = \varnothing$.

Exactly as in the definition of the Choquet integral, the 'coefficient' associated with each variable x_i is fixed uniquely by the permutation $(\cdot)$. For instance, if $x_3 \leq x_1 \leq x_2$, then we have

$$\mathcal{S}_\mu(x_1, x_2, x_3) = [x_3 \wedge \mu(\{3,1,2\})] \vee [x_1 \wedge \mu(\{1,2\})] \vee [x_2 \wedge \mu(\{2\})].$$

From the definition, we can immediately deduce that

$$\mathcal{S}_\mu(x) \in \{x_1, \ldots, x_n\} \cup \{\mu(S) \mid S \subseteq N\} \qquad (x \in [0,1]^n).$$

Moreover, similarly to the Choquet integral, we have

$$\mathcal{S}_\mu(\mathbf{1}_S) = \mu(S) \qquad (S \subseteq N),$$

which shows that the Sugeno integral is completely determined by its values at the vertices of the hypercube $[0,1]^n$.

It was proven [GRE 87, MAR 00b, SUG 74] that the Sugeno integral can also be set in the following form, which does not require the reordering of the variables:

$$\mathcal{S}_\mu(x) = \bigvee_{T \subseteq N} \left[\mu(T) \wedge \left(\bigwedge_{i \in T} x_i \right) \right] \qquad (x \in [0,1]^n).$$

It was also proven [KAN 78] that the Sugeno integral is a kind of weighted median:

$$\mathcal{S}_\mu(x) = \text{median}[x_1, \ldots, x_n, \mu(A_{(2)}), \mu(A_{(3)}), \ldots, \mu(A_{(n)})] \qquad (x \in [0,1]^n).$$

For instance, if $x_3 \leq x_1 \leq x_2$, then

$$\mathcal{S}_\mu(x_1, x_2, x_3) = \text{median}[x_1, x_2, x_3, \mu(1,2), \mu(2)].$$

The following result [MAR 01] shows that the Sugeno integral is a rather natural concept and, contrary to the Choquet integral, it is suitable for an aggregation in an ordinal context.

Proposition 17.10. *Any weakly idempotent function* $A : [0,1]^n \to [0,1]$, *whose (well-formed) expression is made up of variables* $x_1, \ldots, x_n$, *constants* $r_1, \ldots, r_m \in [0,1]$, *lattice operations* $\wedge = \min$ *and* $\vee = \max$ *and parentheses is a Sugeno integral (and conversely).*

Let us now turn to axiomatizations of the Sugeno integral. We can easily see that the Sugeno integral is a continuous, non-decreasing, unanimously increasing, idempotent and internal function. It also fulfills the *comonotonic minitivity* and *comonotonic maxitivity* properties [CAM 91], that is

$$f(x_1 \wedge x'_1, \ldots, x_n \wedge x'_n) = f(x_1, \ldots, x_n) \wedge f(x'_1, \ldots, x'_n)$$
$$f(x_1 \vee x'_1, \ldots, x_n \vee x'_n) = f(x_1, \ldots, x_n) \vee f(x'_1, \ldots, x'_n)$$

for all comonotonic vectors $x, x' \in [0,1]^n$. More specifically, it is *weakly minitive* and *weakly maxitive*, that is, it fulfills

$$f(x_1 \wedge r, \ldots, x_n \wedge r) = f(x_1, \ldots, x_n) \wedge r$$
$$f(x_1 \vee r, \ldots, x_n \vee r) = f(x_1, \ldots, x_n) \vee r$$

for all vectors $x \in [0,1]^n$ and all $r \in [0,1]$. Even more specifically, by replacing x with the Boolean vector $\mathbf{1}_S$ in the two equations above, we see that it is also *non-compensative*, that is it fulfills

$$f(r\mathbf{1}_S) \in \{f(\mathbf{1}_S), r\} \text{ and } f(\mathbf{1}_S + r\mathbf{1}_{N\setminus S}) \in \{f(\mathbf{1}_S), r\}$$

for all $S \subseteq N$ and all $r \in [0,1]$.

Comonotonic minitivity and maxitivity have been interpreted in the context of aggregation of fuzzy subsets by Ralescu and Ralescu [RAL 97]. Non-compensation has been interpreted in decision making under uncertainty in Dubois *et al.* [DUB 01].

The main axiomatizations of the Sugeno integral as an aggregation function are summarized in the following result; see Marichal [MAR 98, MAR 00b].

Theorem 17.17. *Let* $A : [0,1]^n \to [0,1]$. *The following assertions are equivalent:*
- *A is non-decreasing, idempotent and non-compensative;*
- *A is non-decreasing, weakly minitive and weakly maxitive;*
- *A is non-decreasing, idempotent, comonotonic minitive and maxitive; and*
- *there exists* $\mu \in \mathcal{F}_N$ *such that* $A = \mathcal{S}_\mu$.

The 2-variable Sugeno integral can be characterized in a very natural way by means of the associativity property. Indeed, theorem 17.10 can be rewritten as follows.

Proposition 17.11. $A : [0,1]^2 \to [0,1]$ *is continuous, non-decreasing, idempotent and associative if and only if there exists $\mu \in \mathcal{F}_2$ such that $A = \mathcal{S}_\mu$.*

Considering associative or decomposable sequences, we have the following result; see Marichal [MAR 98, p. 113].

Proposition 17.12. *Let $A := (A^{(n)} : [0,1]^n \to [0.1])_{n \geq 1}$ be a sequence of functions. Then the following assertions are equivalent:*

– *A is an associative sequence of Sugeno integrals;*

– *A is a decomposable sequence of Sugeno integrals;*

– *A is an associative sequence of continuous, non-decreasing and idempotent functions; and*

– *there exist $\alpha, \beta \in [0,1]$ such that*

$$A^{(n)}(x) = (\alpha \wedge x_1) \vee \left(\bigvee_{i=2}^{n-1} (\alpha \wedge \beta \wedge x_i) \right) \vee (\beta \wedge x_n) \vee \left(\bigwedge_{i=1}^{n} x_i \right) \quad (x \in [0,1]^n, n \in \mathbb{N} \setminus \{0\}).$$

Just as the Choquet integral includes two main subclasses, namely the weighted arithmetic means and the ordered weighted averaging functions, the Sugeno integral includes the weighted minimum and maximum and the ordered weighted minimum and maximum. These functions have been introduced and investigated in Dubois and Prade [DUB 86] and Dubois et al. [DUB 88], respectively.

For any vector $\omega = (\omega_1, \ldots, \omega_n) \in [0,1]^n$ such that $\bigvee_{i=1}^{n} \omega_i = 1$, the *weighted maximum* associated with ω is defined by

$$\text{pmax}_\omega(x) = \bigvee_{i=1}^{n} (\omega_i \wedge x_i) \quad (x \in [0,1]^n).$$

For any vector $\omega = (\omega_1, \ldots, \omega_n) \in [0,1]^n$ such that $\bigwedge_{i=1}^{n} \omega_i = 0$, the *weighted minimum* associated with ω is defined by

$$\text{pmin}_\omega(x) = \bigwedge_{i=1}^{n} (\omega_i \vee x_i) \quad (x \in [0,1]^n).$$

The functions pmax_ω and pmin_ω can be characterized as follows [DUB 86, MAR 98, RAL 96].

Proposition 17.13. *Let $\mu \in \mathcal{F}_N$. The following assertions are equivalent:*

- *μ is a possibility measure such that*

$$\mu(S \cup T) = \mu(S) \vee \mu(T) \quad (S, T \subseteq N);$$

- *there exists $w \in [0,1]^n$ such that $S_\mu = \mathrm{pmax}_w$; and*
- *$S_\mu(x_1 \vee x'_1, \ldots, x_n \vee x'_n) = S_\mu(x_1, \ldots, x_n) \vee S_\mu(x'_1, \ldots, x'_n)$* $(x, x' \in [0,1]^n)$.

Proposition 17.14. *Let $\mu \in \mathcal{F}_N$. The following assertions are equivalent:*

- *μ is a necessity measure, such that*

$$\mu(S \cap T) = \mu(S) \wedge \mu(T) \quad (S, T \subseteq N);$$

- *there exists $w \in [0,1]^n$ such that $S_\mu = \mathrm{pmin}_w$; and*
- *$S_\mu(x_1 \wedge x'_1, \ldots, x_n \wedge x'_n) = S_\mu(x_1, \ldots, x_n) \wedge S_\mu(x'_1, \ldots, x'_n)$* $(x, x' \in [0,1]^n)$.

For any vector $w = (w_1, \ldots, w_n) \in [0,1]^n$ such that $\bigvee_{i=1}^n w_i = 1$, the *ordered weighted maximum* associated with w is defined by

$$\mathrm{opmax}_w(x) = \bigvee_{i=1}^n (w_i \wedge x_{(i)}) \quad (x \in [0,1]^n).$$

For any vector $w = (w_1, \ldots, w_n) \in [0,1]^n$ such that $\bigwedge_{i=1}^n w_i = 0$, the *ordered weighted minimum* associated with w is defined by

$$\mathrm{opmin}_w(x) = \bigwedge_{i=1}^n (w_i \vee x_{(i)}) \quad (x \in [0,1]^n).$$

Surprisingly enough, the class of ordered weighted minima coincides with that of ordered weighted maxima and identifies with the symmetric Sugeno integrals. The result can be stated as follows [GRA 95b, MAR 98].

Proposition 17.15. *Let $\mu \in \mathcal{F}_N$. The following assertions are equivalent:*

- *μ depends only on the cardinalities of the subsets;*
- *there exists $w \in [0,1]^n$ such that $S_\mu = \mathrm{opmax}_w$;*
- *there exists $w \in [0,1]^n$ such that $S_\mu = \mathrm{opmin}_w$; and*
- *S_μ is a symmetric function.*

Using the fact that the Sugeno integral is also a weighted median, we can write

$$\operatorname{opmax}_\omega(x) = \operatorname{median}(x_1, \ldots, x_n, \omega_2, \ldots, \omega_n),$$
$$\operatorname{opmin}_\omega(x) = \operatorname{median}(x_1, \ldots, x_n, \omega_1, \ldots, \omega_{n-1}).$$

Another interesting subclass is that of lattice polynomials, which are nothing other than Sugeno integrals defined from fuzzy measures taking their values in $\{0, 1\}$. We will characterize these functions in the final section.

17.6. Aggregation on ratio and interval scales

In this section, we present the families of aggregation functions that are meaningful for ratio and interval scales (see definition 17.7). First of all, we have the following two results concerning ratio scales (see [ACZ 86, case #2], [ACZ 89a, Chapter 20], [ACZ 94, p. 439]).

Theorem 17.18. $A :]0, \infty[^n \to]0, \infty[$ is meaningful for the same input-output ratio scales if and only if

$$A(x) = x_1 F\left(\frac{x_2}{x_1}, \ldots, \frac{x_n}{x_1}\right) \quad (x \in]0, \infty[^n),$$

with $F :]0, \infty[^{n-1} \to]0, \infty[$ arbitrary ($F = $ constant if $n = 1$).

Theorem 17.19. $A :]0, \infty[^n \to]0, \infty[$ is meaningful for the same input ratio scales if and only if

$$A(x) = g(x_1) F\left(\frac{x_2}{x_1}, \ldots, \frac{x_n}{x_1}\right) \quad (x \in]0, \infty[^n),$$

with $F :]0, \infty[^{n-1} \to]0, \infty[$ arbitrary ($F = $ constant if $n = 1$) and $g :]0, \infty[\to]0, \infty[$ such that $g(xy) = g(x)g(y)$ for all $x, y \in]0, \infty[$. $g(x) = x^c$ if A is continuous (c arbitrary).

We have the following results regarding interval scales (see [ACZ 86, case #5] and [MAR 98, section 3.4.1]).

Theorem 17.20. $A : \mathbb{R}^n \to \mathbb{R}$ is meaningful for the same input-output interval scales if and only if

$$A(x) = \begin{cases} S(x) F\left(\frac{x_1 - \operatorname{AM}(x)}{S(x)}, \ldots, \frac{x_n - \operatorname{AM}(x)}{S(x)}\right) + \operatorname{AM}(x), & \text{if } S(x) \neq 0, \\ x_1, & \text{if } S(x) = 0 \end{cases}$$

where $S(x) = \sqrt{\sum_{i=1}^n (x_i - \operatorname{AM}(x))^2}$ and $F : \mathbb{R}^n \to \mathbb{R}$ arbitrary ($A(x) = x$ if $n = 1$).

Theorem 17.21. $A : \mathbb{R}^n \to \mathbb{R}$ *is meaningful for the same input interval scales if and only if*

$$A(x) = \begin{cases} S(x) \, F\left(\frac{x_1 - \text{AM}(x)}{S(x)}, \ldots, \frac{x_n - \text{AM}(x)}{S(x)}\right) + a \, \text{AM}(x) + b, & \text{if } S(x) \neq 0, \\ a \, x_1 + b, & \text{if } S(x) = 0, \end{cases}$$

or

$$A(x) = \begin{cases} g(S(x)) \, F\left(\frac{x_1 - \text{AM}(x)}{S(x)}, \ldots, \frac{x_n - \text{AM}(x)}{S(x)}\right) + b, & \text{if } S(x) \neq 0, \\ b, & \text{if } S(x) = 0 \end{cases}$$

where $a, b \in \mathbb{R}$, $S(x) = \sqrt{\sum_{i=1}^n (x_i - \text{AM}(x))^2}$, $F : \mathbb{R}^n \to \mathbb{R}$ *is arbitrary* ($A(x) = ax + b$ *if* $n = 1$) *and* $g : \mathbb{R} \to]0, \infty[$ *is such that* $g(xy) = g(x)g(y)$ *for all* $x, y \in \mathbb{R}$.

The restriction of these families to non-decreasing functions and strictly increasing functions is discussed in Aczél et al. [ACZ 94].

In the rest of this section, we present axiomatizations of some subfamilies of functions that are meaningful for the same input-output interval scales [MAR 99]. For instance, we observed in section 17.5.2 that the discrete Choquet integral fulfills this property. More generally, it is clear that any aggregation function obtained by composition of an arbitrary number of discrete Choquet integrals is again meaningful for the same input-output interval scales. These functions, called *composed Choquet integrals*, have been investigated in e.g. Narukawa and Murofushi [NAR 02].

If we confine ourselves to bisymmetric functions, we have the following results.

Proposition 17.16. $A : \mathbb{R}^n \to \mathbb{R}$ *is non-decreasing, meaningful for the same input-output interval scales and bisymmetric if and only if*

$$A \in \{\min_S, \max_S \mid S \subseteq N\} \cup \{\text{WAM}_\omega \mid \omega \in [0,1]^n\}.$$

Corollary 17.6. $A : \mathbb{R}^n \to \mathbb{R}$ *is symmetric, non-decreasing, meaningful for the same input-output interval scales and bisymmetric if and only if*

$$A \in \{\min, \max, \text{AM}\}.$$

Proposition 17.17. $(A^{(n)} : \mathbb{R}^n \to \mathbb{R})_{n \geq 1}$ *is a bisymmetric sequence of non-decreasing and meaningful functions for the same input-output interval scales if and only if either*

- *for any* $n \in \mathbb{N} \setminus \{0\}$, *there exists* $S \subseteq N_n$ *such that* $M^{(n)} = \min_S$;
- *for any* $n \in \mathbb{N} \setminus \{0\}$, *there exists* $S \subseteq N_n$ *such that* $M^{(n)} = \max_S$, *or*
- *for any* $n \in \mathbb{N} \setminus \{0\}$, *there exists* $\omega \in [0,1]^n$ *such that* $M^{(n)} = \text{WAM}_\omega$.

Corollary 17.7. $A := (A^{(n)} : \mathbb{R}^n \to \mathbb{R})_{n \geq 1}$ is a bisymmetric sequence of symmetric, non-decreasing and meaningful functions for the same input-output interval scales if and only if

$$A = (\min{}^{(n)})_{n \geq 1} \text{ or } (\max{}^{(n)})_{n \geq 1} \text{ or } (\text{AM}^{(n)})_{n \geq 1}.$$

Let us now consider the decomposable and associative sequences of aggregation functions. We have the following results.

Proposition 17.18. $A := (A^{(n)} : \mathbb{R}^n \to \mathbb{R})_{n \geq 1}$ is a decomposable sequence of non-decreasing and meaningful functions for the same input-output interval scales if and only if either

– $A = (\min{}^{(n)})_{n \geq 1}$;
– $A = (\max{}^{(n)})_{n \geq 1}$; or
– there exists $\theta \in [0,1]$ such that, for any $n \in \mathbb{N} \setminus \{0\}$ we have $A^{(n)} = \text{WAM}_\omega$ with

$$\omega_i = \frac{(1-\theta)^{n-i}\theta^{i-1}}{\sum_{j=1}^n (1-\theta)^{n-j}\theta^{j-1}} \qquad (i \in N_n).$$

Corollary 17.8. $A := (A^{(n)} : \mathbb{R}^n \to \mathbb{R})_{n \geq 1}$ is a decomposable sequence of symmetric, non-decreasing and meaningful functions for the same input-output interval scales if and only if

$$A = (\min{}^{(n)})_{n \geq 1} \text{ or } (\max{}^{(n)})_{n \geq 1} \text{ or } (\text{AM}^{(n)})_{n \geq 1}.$$

Proposition 17.19. $A := (A^{(n)} : \mathbb{R}^n \to \mathbb{R})_{n \geq 1}$ is an associative sequence of non-decreasing and meaningful functions for the same input-output interval scales if and only if

$$A = (\min{}^{(n)})_{n \geq 1} \text{ or } (\max{}^{(n)})_{n \geq 1} \text{ or } (\text{P}_1^{(n)})_{n \geq 1} \text{ or } (\text{P}_n^{(n)})_{n \geq 1}.$$

Corollary 17.9. $A := (A^{(n)} : \mathbb{R}^n \to \mathbb{R})_{n \geq 1}$ is an associative sequence of symmetric, non-decreasing and meaningful functions for the same input-output interval scales if and only if

$$A = (\min{}^{(n)})_{n \geq 1} \text{ or } (\max{}^{(n)})_{n \geq 1}.$$

17.7. Aggregation on ordinal scales

In this final section, we consider aggregation functions that are meaningful for the same input-output ordinal scales. Their description is not immediate and requires the concept of invariant sets. Denote the set of strictly increasing bijections of $\mathbb{R}$ by Φ.

Definition 17.19. A nonempty subset $I \subseteq \mathbb{R}^n$ is said to be *invariant* if
$$x \in I \to \phi(x) \in I \quad (\phi \in \Phi).$$
Such a set is said to be *minimal* if it does not contain any proper invariant subset.

The family $\mathcal{I}$ of all invariant subsets of $\mathbb{R}^n$ provides a partition of $\mathbb{R}^n$ into equivalence classes, where $x, y \in \mathbb{R}^n$ are equivalent if there exists $\phi \in \Phi$ such that $y = \phi(x)$. In fact, one can show that any invariant subset is of the form
$$I = \{x \in \mathbb{R}^n \mid x_{\pi(1)} \triangleleft_1 \cdots \triangleleft_{n-1} x_{\pi(n)}\},$$
where $\pi \in \Pi_N$ and $\triangleleft_i \in \{<, \leq\}$ for $i = 1, \ldots, n-1$.

The meaningful functions for the same input-output ordinal scales have been investigated by many authors [MAR 02b, MAR 93, MES 04, OVC 98]. They can be described as follows [OVC 98].

Theorem 17.22. $A : \mathbb{R}^n \to \mathbb{R}$ *is meaningful for the same input-output ordinal scales if and only if, for any* $I \in \mathcal{I}$, *there exists* $i \in N$ *such that* $A|_I = P_i|_I$ *is the ith projection.*

The meaningful functions for the same input ordinal scales have also been widely studied [MAR 02b, MAR 05, ORL 81, OVC 96, YAN 89]. They have been described as follows [MAR 05].

Theorem 17.23. $A : \mathbb{R}^n \to \mathbb{R}$ *is meaningful for the same input ordinal scales if and only if, for any* $I \in \mathcal{I}$, *there exists* $i_I \in N$ *and a constant or strictly monotone function* $g_I : P_{i_I}(I) \to \mathbb{R}$ *such that*
$$A|_I = g_I \circ P_{i_I}|_I,$$
where, for any $I, J \in \mathcal{I}$, *either* $g_I = g_J$, *or* $\operatorname{ran}(g_I) = \operatorname{ran}(g_J)$ *is a singleton, or* $\operatorname{ran}(g_I) < \operatorname{ran}(g_J)$, *or* $\operatorname{ran}(g_I) > \operatorname{ran}(g_J)$.

We therefore see that the meaningful functions for the same input-output ordinal scales reduce to projections on each invariant subset. In addition, the meaningful functions for the same input ordinal scales reduce to constants or transformed projections on these invariant subsets.

The restriction of these functions to non-decreasing and/or continuous functions has also been studied. To describe these subfamilies, we need the concept of lattice polynomials.

Definition 17.20. A *lattice polynomial* of n variables is a well-formed expression involving n variables $x_1, \ldots, x_n$ linked by the lattice operations $\wedge = \min$ and $\vee = \max$ in an arbitrary combination of parentheses.

For instance, $L(x) = (x_1 \vee x_2) \wedge x_3$ is a 3-variable lattice polynomial.

We can show [BIR 67, Chapter 2] that any n-variable lattice polynomial can be written in disjunctive form as

$$L_\gamma(x) = \bigvee_{\substack{S \subseteq N \\ \gamma(S)=1}} \bigwedge_{i \in S} x_i \quad (x \in \mathbb{R}^n),$$

where $\gamma : 2^N \to \{0,1\}$ is a binary fuzzy measure (i.e. with values in $\{0,1\}$). We denote the family of these fuzzy measures on N by Γ_N.

It was also proven [MAR 01] that the class of lattice polynomials restricted to the domain $[0,1]^n$ identifies with the intersection between the family of Choquet integrals on $[0,1]^n$ and the family of Sugeno integrals.

Regarding non-decreasing functions, we have the descriptions [MAR 02b, MAR 05] as follows.

Proposition 17.20. $A : \mathbb{R}^n \to \mathbb{R}$ *is non-decreasing and meaningful for the same input-output ordinal scales if and only if there exists $\gamma \in \Gamma_N$ such that $A = L_\gamma$.*

Proposition 17.21. $A : \mathbb{R}^n \to \mathbb{R}$ *is non-decreasing and meaningful for the same input ordinal scales if and only if there exists $\gamma \in \Gamma_N$ and a constant or strictly monotone function $g : \mathbb{R} \to \mathbb{R}$ such that $A = g \circ L_\gamma$.*

The functions in the above two theorems are continuous, up to discontinuities of function g. Regarding continuous functions, we have the following results [MAR 02b].

Corollary 17.10. $A : \mathbb{R}^n \to \mathbb{R}$ *is continuous and meaningful for the same input-output ordinal scales if and only if there exists $\gamma \in \Gamma_N$ such that $A = L_\gamma$.*

Corollary 17.11. $A : \mathbb{R}^n \to \mathbb{R}$ *is continuous and meaningful for the same input ordinal scales if and only if there exists $\gamma \in \Gamma_N$ and a constant or continuous and strictly monotone function $g : \mathbb{R} \to \mathbb{R}$ such that $A = g \circ L_\gamma$.*

Lattice polynomials are idempotent, but not necessarily symmetric. Actually, symmetric lattice polynomials are exactly the order statistics, which include the classical median. By adding symmetry and/or idempotency to the previous results, we obtain the following corollaries.

Corollary 17.12. $A : \mathbb{R}^n \to \mathbb{R}$ *is symmetric, non-decreasing (or continuous) and meaningful for the same input-output ordinal scales if and only if there exists* $k \in N$ *such that* $A = \mathrm{OS}_k$.

Corollary 17.13. $A : \mathbb{R}^n \to \mathbb{R}$ *is idempotent, non-decreasing (or continuous) and meaningful for the same input ordinal scales if and only if there exists* $\gamma \in \Gamma_N$ *such that* $A = L_\gamma$.

Corollary 17.14. $A : \mathbb{R}^n \to \mathbb{R}$ *is symmetric, non-decreasing and meaningful for the same input ordinal scales if and only if there exist* $k \in N$ *and a constant or strictly increasing function* $g : \mathbb{R} \to \mathbb{R}$ *such that* $A = g \circ \mathrm{OS}_k$.

Corollary 17.15. $A : \mathbb{R}^n \to \mathbb{R}$ *is symmetric, continuous and meaningful for the same input ordinal scales if and only if there exists* $k \in N$ *and a constant or continuous and strictly monotonic function* $g : \mathbb{R} \to \mathbb{R}$ *such that* $A = g \circ \mathrm{OS}_k$.

17.8. Conclusion

In this chapter we have discussed the most classical aggregation functions that are used in decision making. An appropriate classification of these functions into a catalog can be better done through an axiomatic approach, which consists of listing a series of reasonable properties and classifying or, better, characterizing the aggregation functions according to these properties.

With knowledge of the increasing need to define suitable aggregation functions fulfilling very precise conditions in various situations, it is not surprising that such a catalog of aggregation functions, which is already huge, is constantly growing and remains an important topic of research. We have only skimmed the surface of a still-growing domain here.

17.9. Bibliography

[ABR 64] ABRAMOWITZ M., STEGUN I. A., *Handbook of Mathematical Functions with Formulas, Graphs, and Mathematical Tables*, vol. 55 of *National Bureau of Standards Applied Mathematics Series*, For sale by the Superintendent of Documents, U.S. Government Printing Office, Washington, D.C., 1964.

[ACZ 48a] ACZÉL J., "On mean values", *Bulletin of American Mathematical Society*, vol. 54, p. 392–400, 1948.

[ACZ 48b] ACZÉL J., "Sur les opérations définies pour nombres réels", *Bulletin de la Société Mathématique de France*, vol. 76, p. 59–64, 1948.

[ACZ 66] ACZÉL J., *Lectures on Functional Equations and their Applications*, Academic Press, New York, 1966.

[ACZ 86] ACZÉL J., ROBERTS F. S., ROSENBAUM Z., "On scientific laws without dimensional constants", *Journal of Mathematical Analysis and Applications*, vol. 119, num. 1–2, p. 389–416, 1986.

[ACZ 87] ACZÉL J., ALSINA C., "Synthesizing judgements: a functional equations approach", *Mathematical Modelling*, vol. 9, num. 3–5, p. 311–320, 1987, The analytic hierarchy process.

[ACZ 89a] ACZÉL J., DHOMBRES J., *Functional Equations in Several Variables*, Cambridge University Press, Cambridge, 1989.

[ACZ 89b] ACZÉL J., ROBERTS F. S., "On the possible merging functions", *Mathematical Social Sciences*, vol. 17, num. 3, p. 205–243, 1989.

[ACZ 94] ACZÉL J., GRONAU D., SCHWAIGER J., "Increasing solutions of the homogeneity equation and of similar equations", *Journal of Mathematical Analysis and Applications*, vol. 182, num. 2, p. 436–464, 1994.

[ALS 83] ALSINA C., TRILLAS E., VALVERDE L., "On some logical connectives for fuzzy sets theory", *Journal of Mathematical Analysis and Applications*, vol. 93, num. 1, p. 15–26, 1983.

[ALS 93] ALSINA C., MAYOR G., TOMÁS M. S., TORRENS J., "A characterization of a class of aggregation functions", *Fuzzy Sets and Systems*, vol. 53, num. 1, p. 33–38, 1993.

[ANT 98] ANTOINE C., *Les moyennes*, vol. 3383 of *Que Sais-Je? [What Do I Know?]*, Presses Universitaires de France, Paris, 1998.

[BEC 65] BECKENBACH E. F., BELLMAN R., *Inequalities*, Second revised printing. Ergebnisse der Mathematik und ihrer Grenzgebiete. Neue Folge, Band 30, Springer-Verlag, New York, Inc., 1965.

[BEM 26] BEMPORAD G., "Sul principio della media aritmetica. (Italian)", *Atti Accad. Naz. Lincei*, vol. 3, num. 6, p. 87–91, 1926.

[BER 98] BERRONE L. R., MORO J., "Lagrangian means", *Aequationes Mathematicae*, vol. 55, num. 3, p. 217–226, 1998.

[BER 00] BERRONE L. R., MORO J., "On means generated through the Cauchy mean value theorem", *Aequationes Mathematicae*, vol. 60, num. 1–2, p. 1–14, 2000.

[BIR 67] BIRKHOFF G., *Lattice Theory*, Third edition. American Mathematical Society Colloquium Publications, Vol. XXV, American Mathematical Society, Providence, R.I., 1967.

[BUL 88] BULLEN P. S., MITRINOVIĆ D. S., VASIĆ P. M., *Means and their Inequalities*, vol. 31 of *Mathematics and its Applications (East European Series)*, D. Reidel Publishing Co., Dordrecht, 1988, Translated and revised from Serbo-Croatian.

[CAM 91] DE CAMPOS L. M., LAMATA M. T., MORAL S., "A unified approach to define fuzzy integrals", *Fuzzy Sets and Systems*, vol. 39, num. 1, p. 75–90, 1991.

[CAM 92] DE CAMPOS L. M., JORGE M., "Characterization and comparison of Sugeno and Choquet integrals", *Fuzzy Sets and Systems*, vol. 52, num. 1, p. 61–67, 1992.

[CAU 21] CAUCHY A. L., *Cours d'analyse de l'Ecole Royale Polytechnique, Vol. I. Analyse algébrique*, Debure, Paris, 1821.

[CHI 29] CHISINI O., "Sul concetto di media. (Italian)", *Periodico di matematiche*, vol. 9, num. 4, p. 106–116, 1929.

[CHO 54] CHOQUET G., "Theory of capacities", *Annals of Institute Fourier, Grenoble*, vol. 5, p. 131–295 (1955), 1953–1954.

[CLI 46] CLIMESCU A. C., "Sur l'équation fonctionnelle de l'associativité", *Bulletin of École Polytech. Jassy*, vol. 1, p. 211–224, 1946.

[CZO 84] CZOGALA E., DREWNIAK J., "Associative monotonic operations in fuzzy set theory", *Fuzzy Sets and Systems*, vol. 12, num. 3, p. 249–269, 1984.

[DEL 71] DELLACHERIE C., "Quelques commentaires sur les prolongements de capacités", *Séminaire de Probabilités, V (Univ. Strasbourg, année universitaire 1969-1970)*, p. 77–81. Lecture Notes in Mathematics, Vol. 191, Springer, Berlin, 1971.

[DOW 92] DOW J., WERLANG S. R. D. C., "Uncertainty aversion, risk aversion, and the optimal choice of portfolio", *Econometrica*, vol. 60, num. 1, p. 197–204, 1992.

[DOW 94] DOW J., WERLANG S. R. D. C., "Nash equilibrium under Knightian uncertainty: breaking down backward induction", *Journal of Economonic Theory*, vol. 64, num. 2, p. 305–324, 1994.

[DUB 84] DUBOIS D., PRADE H., "Criteria aggregation and ranking of alternatives in the framework of fuzzy set theory", *Fuzzy Sets and Decision Analysis*, vol. 20 of *Studies in Management Science*, p. 209–240, North-Holland, Amsterdam, 1984.

[DUB 86] DUBOIS D., PRADE H., "Weighted minimum and maximum operations in fuzzy set theory", *Information Sciences*, vol. 39, num. 2, p. 205–210, 1986.

[DUB 88] DUBOIS D., PRADE H., TESTEMALE C., "Weighted fuzzy pattern matching", *Fuzzy Sets and Systems*, vol. 28, num. 3, p. 313–331, 1988.

[DUB 01] DUBOIS D., MARICHAL J. L., PRADE H., ROUBENS M., SABBADIN R., "The use of the discrete Sugeno integral in decision-making: a survey", *International Journal of Uncertainty, Fuzziness and Knowledge-Based Systems*, vol. 9, num. 5, p. 539–561, 2001.

[DUJ 74] DUJMOVIĆ J. J., "Weighted conjunctive and disjunctive means and their application in system evaluation", *Univ. Beograd. Publ. Elektrotehn. Fak. Ser. Mat. Fiz.*, p. 147–158, 1974.

[DUJ 75] DUJMOVIĆ J. J., "Extended continuous logic and the theory of complex criteria", *Univ. Beograd. Publ. Elektrotehn. Fak. Ser. Mat. Fiz.*, p. 197–216, 1975.

[DYC 84] DYCKHOFF H., PEDRYCZ W., "Generalized means as model of compensative connectives", *Fuzzy Sets and Systems*, vol. 14, num. 2, p. 143–154, 1984.

[FAU 55] FAUCETT W. M., "Compact semigroups irreducibly connected between two idempotents", *Proceedings of American Mathematical Society*, vol. 6, p. 741–747, 1955.

[FIN 31] DE FINETTI B., "Sul concetto di media. (Italian)", *Giorn. Ist. Ital. Attuari*, vol. 2, num. 3, p. 369–396, 1931.

[FIS 95] FISHBURN P., WAKKER P., "The invention of the independence condition for preferences", *Management Sciences*, vol. 41, num. 7, p. 1130–1144, 1995.

[FOD 91a] FODOR J. C., "A remark on constructing t-norms", *Fuzzy Sets and Systems*, vol. 41, num. 2, p. 195–199, 1991.

[FOD 91b] FODOR J. C., "Strict preference relations based on weak t-norms", *Fuzzy Sets and Systems*, vol. 43, num. 3, p. 327–336, 1991.

[FOD 94] FODOR J. C., ROUBENS M., *Fuzzy Preference Modelling and Multicriteria Decision Support*, Kluwer, Dordrecht, 1994.

[FOD 96] FODOR J. C., "An extension of Fung-Fu's theorem", *International Journal of Uncertainty, Fuzziness and Knowledge-Based Systems*, vol. 4, num. 3, p. 235–243, 1996.

[FRO 87] FROSINI V., "Averages", *Italian Contributions to the Methodology of Statistics*, p. 1–17, Cleup, Padova, 1987.

[FUN 75] FUNG L. W., FU K. S., "An axiomatic approach to rational decision making in a fuzzy environment", *Fuzzy Sets and their Applications to Cognitive and Decision Processes*, p. 227–256, Proceedings US–Japan Seminar, Univ. Calif., Berkeley, Calif., Academic Press, New York, 1975.

[GIL 87] GILBOA I., "Expected utility with purely subjective nonadditive probabilities", *Journal of Mathematical Economics*, vol. 16, num. 1, p. 65–88, 1987.

[GRA 93] GRABISCH M., "On the use of fuzzy integral as a fuzzy connective", *Proceedings of the Second IEEE International Conference on Fuzzy Systems*, San Francisco, p. 213–218, 1993.

[GRA 95a] GRABISCH M., "Fuzzy integral in multicriteria decision making", *Fuzzy Sets and Systems*, vol. 69, num. 3, p. 279–298, 1995.

[GRA 95b] GRABISCH M., "On equivalence classes of fuzzy connectives: the case of fuzzy integrals", *IEEE Transactions on Fuzzy Systems*, vol. 3, num. 1, p. 96–109, 1995.

[GRA 95c] GRABISCH M., NGUYEN H. T., WALKER E. A., *Fundamentals of Uncertainty Calculi with Applications to Fuzzy Inference*, vol. 30 of *Theory and Decision Library. Series B: Mathematical and Statistical Methods*, Kluwer Academic Publishers, Dordrecht, 1995.

[GRA 96] GRABISCH M., "The application of fuzzy integrals in multicriteria decision making", *European Journal of Operational Research*, vol. 89, num. 3, p. 445–456, 1996.

[GRA 98] GRABISCH M., "Fuzzy integral as a flexible and interpretable tool of aggregation", *Aggregation and Fusion of Imperfect Information*, vol. 12 of *Studies in Fuzziness and Soft Computing*, p. 51–72, Physica, Heidelberg, 1998.

[GRA 00] GRABISCH M., MUROFUSHI T., SUGENO M., Eds., *Fuzzy Measures and Integrals, Theory and Applications*, vol. 40 of *Studies in Fuzziness and Soft Computing*, Physica-Verlag, Heidelberg, 2000.

[GRA 09] GRABISCH M., MARICHAL J.-L., MESIAR R., PAP E., *Encyclopedia of Mathematics and its Applications*, Cambridge University Press, Cambridge, UK, 2009.

[GRE 87] GRECO G. H., "On L-fuzzy integrals of measurable functions", *Journal of Mathematical Analysis and Applications*, vol. 128, num. 2, p. 581–585, 1987.

[GRO 98] GROES E., JACOBSEN J., SLOTH B., TRANÆS T., "Axiomatic characterizations of the Choquet integral", *Economic Theory*, vol. 12, num. 2, p. 441–448, 1998.

[HÖH 82] HÖHLE U., "Integration with respect to fuzzy measures", *Proceedings of IFAC Symposium on Theory and Applications of Digital Control*, New Delhi, p. 35–37, January 1982.

[KAN 78] KANDEL A., BYATT W. J., "Fuzzy sets, fuzzy algebra, and fuzzy statistics", *Proceedings of IEEE*, vol. 66, num. 12, p. 1619–1639, December 1978.

[KLE 00] KLEMENT E. P., MESIAR R., PAP E., *Triangular norms*, vol. 8 of *Trends in Logic—Studia Logica Library*, Kluwer Academic Publishers, Dordrecht, 2000.

[KOL 30] KOLMOGOROFF A. N., "Sur la notion de la moyenne (French)", *Atti Accad. Naz. Lincei*, vol. 12, num. 6, p. 388–391, 1930.

[LIN 65] LING C.-H., "Representation of associative functions", *Publicationes Mathematicae Debrecen*, vol. 12, p. 189–212, 1965.

[LUC 59] LUCE R. D., "On the possible psychophysical laws", *Psychological Review*, vol. 66, p. 81–95, 1959.

[MAR 93] MARICHAL J.-L., ROUBENS M., "Characterization of some stable aggregation functions", *Proceedings of 1st International Conference on Industrial Engineering and Production Management (IEPM'93)*, Mons, Belgium, p. 187–196, June 1993.

[MAR 98] MARICHAL J.-L., Aggregation operators for multicriteria decision aid, PhD thesis, Institute of Mathematics, University of Liège, Liège, Belgium, December 1998.

[MAR 99] MARICHAL J.-L., MATHONET P., TOUSSET E., "Characterization of some aggregation functions stable for positive linear transformations", *Fuzzy Sets and Systems*, vol. 102, num. 2, p. 293–314, 1999.

[MAR 00a] MARICHAL J.-L., "An axiomatic approach of the discrete Choquet integral as a tool to aggregate interacting criteria", *IEEE Transactions on Fuzzy Systems*, vol. 8, num. 6, p. 800–807, 2000.

[MAR 00b] MARICHAL J.-L., "On Sugeno integral as an aggregation function", *Fuzzy Sets and Systems*, vol. 114, num. 3, p. 347–365, 2000.

[MAR 00c] MARICHAL J.-L., "On the associativity functional equation", *Fuzzy Sets and Systems*, vol. 114, num. 3, p. 381–389, 2000.

[MAR 01] MARICHAL J.-L., "An axiomatic approach of the discrete Sugeno integral as a tool to aggregate interacting criteria in a qualitative framework", *IEEE Transactions on Fuzzy Systems*, vol. 9, num. 1, p. 164–172, 2001.

[MAR 02a] MARICHAL J.-L., "Aggregation of interacting criteria by means of the discrete Choquet integral", *Aggregation Operators: New Trends and Applications*, p. 224–244, Physica, Heidelberg, 2002.

[MAR 02b] MARICHAL J.-L., "On order invariant synthesizing functions", *Journal of Mathematical Psychology*, vol. 46, num. 6, p. 661–676, 2002.

[MAR 05] MARICHAL J.-L., MESIAR R., RÜCKSCHLOSSOVÁ T., "A complete description of comparison meaningful functions", *Aequationes Mathematicae*, vol. 69, num. 3, p. 309–320, 2005.

[MAS 99] MAS M., MAYOR G., TORRENS J., "t-operators", *International Journal of Uncertainty, Fuzziness and Knowledge-Based Systems*, vol. 7, num. 1, p. 31–50, 1999.

[MAS 01] MAS M., MONSERRAT M., TORRENS J., "On left and right uninorms", *International Journal of Uncertainty, Fuzziness and Knowledge-Based Systems*, vol. 9, num. 4, p. 491–507, 2001.

[MAS 02] MAS M., MAYOR G., TORRENS J., "The modularity condition for uninorms and t-operators", *Fuzzy Sets and Systems*, vol. 126, num. 2, p. 207–218, 2002.

[MAT 99] MATKOWSKI J., "Invariant and complementary quasi-arithmetic means", *Aequationes Mathematicae*, vol. 57, num. 1, p. 87–107, 1999.

[MES 04] MESIAR R., RÜCKSCHLOSSOVÁ T., "Characterization of invariant aggregation operators", *Fuzzy Sets and Systems*, vol. 142, num. 1, p. 63–73, 2004.

[MOD 97] MODAVE F., DUBOIS D., GRABISCH M., PRADE H., "A Choquet integral representation in multicriteria decision making", *AAAI Fall Symposium on Frontiers in Soft Computing and Decisions Systems*, Boston, MA, p. 30–39, November 7–9 1997.

[MOD 98] MODAVE F., GRABISCH M., "Preference representation by the Choquet integral: the commensurability hypothesis", *Proceedings of the 7th International Conference on Information Processing and Management of Uncertainty in Knowledge-Based Systems (IPMU'98)*, Paris, p. 164–171, 1998.

[MOS 57] MOSTERT P. S., SHIELDS A. L., "On the structure of semigroups on a compact manifold with boundary", *Annals of Mathematics (2)*, vol. 65, p. 117–143, 1957.

[MUR 89] MUROFUSHI T., SUGENO M., "An interpretation of fuzzy measures and the Choquet integral as an integral with respect to a fuzzy measure", *Fuzzy Sets and Systems*, vol. 29, num. 2, p. 201–227, 1989.

[MUR 91] MUROFUSHI T., SUGENO M., "A theory of fuzzy measures: representations, the Choquet integral, and null sets", *Journal of Mathematical Analysis and Applications*, vol. 159, num. 2, p. 532–549, 1991.

[MUR 93] MUROFUSHI T., SUGENO M., "Some quantities represented by the Choquet integral", *Fuzzy Sets and Systems*, vol. 56, num. 2, p. 229–235, 1993.

[NAG 30] NAGUMO M., "Über eine klasse der mittelwerte. (German)", *Japanese Journal of Mathematics*, vol. 7, p. 71–79, 1930.

[NAR 02] NARUKAWA Y., MUROFUSHI T., "The n-step Choquet integral on finite spaces", *9th International Conference on Information Processing and Management of Uncertainty in Knowledge-Based Systems (IPMU 2002)*, Annecy, France, p. 539–543, July 1-5 2002.

[ORL 81] ORLOV A. I., "The connection between mean values and the admissible transformations of scale", *Mathematical Notes*, vol. 30, p. 774–778, 1981.

[OVC 96] OVCHINNIKOV S., "Means on ordered sets", *Mathematical Social Sciences*, vol. 32, num. 1, p. 39–56, 1996.

[OVC 98] OVCHINNIKOV S., "Invariant functions on simple orders", *Order*, vol. 14, num. 4, p. 365–371, 1997/98.

[RAL 96] RALESCU D. A., SUGENO M., "Fuzzy integral representation", *Fuzzy Sets and Systems*, vol. 84, num. 2, p. 127–133, 1996.

[RAL 97] RALESCU A. L., RALESCU D. A., "Extensions of fuzzy aggregation", *Fuzzy Sets and Systems*, vol. 86, num. 3, p. 321–330, 1997.

[RIC 15] RICCI U., "Confronti tra medie. (Italian)", *Giorn. Economisti e Rivista di Statistica*, vol. 26, p. 38–66, 1915.

[ROB 79] ROBERTS F. S., *Measurement Theory*, vol. 7 of *Encyclopedia of Mathematics and its Applications*, Addison-Wesley Publishing Co., Reading, Mass., 1979.

[ROB 90] ROBERTS F. S., "Merging relative scores", *Journal of Mathematical Analysis and Applications*, vol. 147, num. 1, p. 30–52, 1990.

[ROB 94] ROBERTS F. S., "Limitations on conclusions using scales of measurement", *Operation Research and the Public Sector*, p. 621–671, Elsevier, Amsterdam, 1994.

[SAN 02] SANDER W., "Associative aggregation operators", *Aggregation operators*, vol. 97 of *Studies in Fuzziness and Soft Computing*, p. 124–158, Physica, Heidelberg, 2002.

[SAR 92] SARIN R., WAKKER P., "A simple axiomatization of nonadditive expected utility", *Econometrica*, vol. 60, num. 6, p. 1255–1272, 1992.

[SCH 61] SCHWEIZER B., SKLAR A., "Associative functions and statistical triangle inequalities", *Publicationes Mathematicae Debrecen*, vol. 8, p. 169–186, 1961.

[SCH 63] SCHWEIZER B., SKLAR A., "Associative functions and abstract semigroups", *Publicationes Mathematicae Debrecen*, vol. 10, p. 69–81, 1963.

[SCH 83] SCHWEIZER B., SKLAR A., *Probabilistic Metric Spaces*, North-Holland Series in Probability and Applied Mathematics, North-Holland Publishing Co., New York, 1983.

[SCH 86] SCHMEIDLER D., "Integral representation without additivity", *Proceedings of American Mathematical Society*, vol. 97, num. 2, p. 255–261, 1986.

[STE 51] STEVENS S. S., "Mathematics, measurement, and psychophysics", *Handbook of Experimental Psychology*, p. 1–49, Wiley, New York, 1951.

[STE 59] STEVENS S. S., "Measurement, psychophysics, and utility", *Measurement: Definitions and Theories*, p. 18–63, Wiley, New York, 1959.

[SUG 74] SUGENO M., Theory of fuzzy integrals and its applications, PhD thesis, Tokyo Institute of Technology, Tokyo, 1974.

[SUG 77] SUGENO M., "Fuzzy measures and fuzzy integrals: a survey", *Fuzzy Automata and Decision Processes*, p. 89–102, North-Holland, New York, 1977.

[WAK 89] WAKKER P., "Continuous subjective expected utility with nonadditive probabilities", *Journal of Mathematical Economics*, vol. 18, num. 1, p. 1–27, 1989.

[WEB 83] WEBER S., "A general concept of fuzzy connectives, negations and implications based on t-norms and t-conorms", *Fuzzy Sets and Systems*, vol. 11, num. 2, p. 115–134, 1983.

[YAG 88] YAGER R. R., "On ordered weighted averaging aggregation operators in multicriteria decisionmaking", *IEEE Transactions on Systems, Man, and Cybernetics*, vol. 18, num. 1, p. 183–190, 1988.

[YAG 96] YAGER R. R., RYBALOV A., "Uninorm aggregation operators", *Fuzzy Sets and Systems*, vol. 80, num. 1, p. 111–120, 1996.

[YAG 97] YAGER R., KACPRZYK J., Eds., *The Ordered Weighted Averaging Operators*, Kluwer Academic Publishers, USA, 1997, Theory and Applications.

[YAN 89] YANOVSKAYA E. B., "Group choice rules in problems with interpersonal preference comparisons", *Automation and Remote Control*, vol. 50, num. 6, p. 822–830, 1989.

[ZIM 80] ZIMMERMANN H.-J., ZYSNO P., "Latent connectives in human decision making", *Fuzzy Sets and Systems*, vol. 4, p. 37–51, 1980.

Chapter 18

Subjective Evaluation

18.1. Introduction

In the area of decision, an important topic is *evaluation*. When a director of human resources examines the profiles of candidates for a position, when a manager from the European Commission must choose which projects to fund among those submitted and when a marketing director evaluates the various models of a new car to be launched, all these people perform an evaluation process. Closer to everyday life, in an unconscious way, we constantly evaluate goods we have bought e.g. when saying that chocolate XXX is better than chocolate YYY, that the seat of this car is really very comfortable or that the keyboard of this computer is too soft.

In the above examples, the reader has certainly noticed the *subjective* character of evaluation: it seems impossible to give an objective measurement of the intellectual, managerial or commercial abilities of a candidate, of the social and economical consequences of the next five years of a given project, of the aesthetic of a car, of the comfort of a seat or of the bitterness, sweetness or salty degree of some edible good. Numerous attempts have nevertheless been made in order to reach objectivity in the measurement of many of the above cited examples. This can be seen in the various testing procedures to measure the abilities of people in a specific domain; e.g. the food industry uses trained and regularly tested experts (who could be called *human sensors*) to measure fundamental aspects of taste.

Even if we could achieve a precise measurement of these notions, the above examples in evaluation would remain nevertheless subjective in nature. A given

---

Chapter written by Michel GRABISCH.

candidate can be judged very differently by two different directors and, as the popular dicton states, nobody should discuss a matter of taste. The subjective character lies therefore more in the global perception we have of the object, rather than in the difficulty of measuring its characterstics. The global perception is proper to the individual and reflects its subjectivity, while the sensorial perception remains more or less invariant, up to physiological fluctuations.

Hence, among the above-mentioned *descriptors* or *attributes* (how the various characteristics or dimensions describing the object are referred to), we can distinguish two categories. There are those which are clearly objective descriptors, since they are measurable by sensors (physical or human) or by well-defined and repeatable procedures. These are e.g. the abilities (intellectual, managerial, etc.) of a given kind, the performance of a car, the volume of its trunk, the degrees of sweetness and bitterness.

The second category includes descriptors for which it seems nearly impossible to conceive a measurement procedure, mainly because these notions are very difficult to define. These are e.g. aesthetic, the design of a car or the comfort of a seat. Although everybody has a clear intuitive understanding of these descriptors, they are difficult to grasp because they are multidimensional in nature, each dimension being a new descriptor which is possibly itself multidimensional. Even if we could imagine an infinite power of analysis which would enable the extraction of the set of all objective descriptors forming such a descriptor, we must admit the fact that two different people having the same stimulus (for example, the photograph of a car in a magazine) would certainly have different global perceptions. Hence, these are subjective descriptors.

The aim of evaluation is to try to mathematically model this global perception, belonging to a given individual or a given population, in terms of objective descriptors measurable by human or physical sensors, or by clearly defined procedures.

This informal introduction should have made clear the fact that the problem taken as a whole is a complex one, and that it is connected to many disciplines. Let us mention at this stage that this topic is of great interest in Japan, where the word *kansei* (feeling) is used (even in English publications due to the difficulty of translating it). There exist some annual workshops on this topic (called 'Heart and Mind'), as well as a whole book devoted to the *kansei* data analysis [NAK 00].

The aim of this chapter is both more modest and more focused. In section 18.2, we set the borders of the problem we want to address and mention related domains. After a section giving the foundations of our approach, which is based on multicriteria decision making and measurement theory, we methodically build our approach in sections 18.4–18.8. Section 18.9 is devoted to applications. After a general presentation of potential applications, we detail the main applications using the methodology described in this chapter.

18.2. What is subjective evaluation?

The aim of this section is to formalize the problem of subjective evaluation and to define some general notation.

18.2.1. *General definition and related domains*

We simply call the parameter to be evaluated the *object*. The object can be a concrete object in the usual sense (a piece of chocolate, a car), an abstract one (a piece of music), or an unanimated being (candidate, cat, etc.). The evaluation of an object or of a collection of objects of the same type is done with respect to a *quality* which the object is supposed to have (the good taste of chocolate, the comfort of a car, the beauty of a piece of music, the cleverness of a candidate, etc.). This evaluation is carried out by an *evaluator* or a *subject*.

Subjective evaluation is restricted to the case where the quality cannot be directly evaluated by some sensor, either human or physical, or by some well-defined and repeatable procedure. By a *human sensor*, we mean an expert, tested and well trained for measuring a given quality, whose characteristics are known as for a physical sensor. We make the assumption that this quality has a multidimensional character, each dimension being called a *descriptor* or *attribute*. A descriptor is also a quality of an object which ideally is measurable, but it may be the case that some descriptors are themselves subjective qualities (not directly measurable), and therefore also multidimensional. Performing this process until the end, we obtain a tree of descriptors [ZIM 83] whose leaves are all directly measurable descriptors (*objective* descriptors).

Such a construction is only possible in ideal situations. In real situations, only an approximation of it can be reached with a limited number of descriptors. Given the recursive character of this representation, it is sufficient to consider here one quality defined by a set of descriptors as being all objective. We denote by X the quality of interest, and by $X_1, \ldots, X_n$ the n objective descriptors which describe it. X_i represents the set of all possible values (numerical, qualitative, etc.) taken by the corresponding descriptor.

The process of subjective evaluation relies on or is closely linked to a certain number of disciplines, which we briefly list below:

1) Multicriteria decision making, which is the study of choice procedures with respect to several criteria or points of view, is a central tool in subjective evaluation. It offers a solid theoretical background for the multidimensional aspect of choice, which underlies every problem of subjective evaluation. The approach we propose here lies within this perspective.

2) Data analysis is undoubtedly another fundamental and compulsory tool in this domain, which permits correlations between dimensions, principal components or

factors to be examined. It allows the most synthetic representation of the quality of the object of interest to be found.

This approach needs an important amount of data (measurements of descriptors, evaluation of the quality of several objects by several subjects). If data are quantitative, Principal Component Analysis (PCA) can be used; on the other hand, in case of qualitative data, the Multiple Correspondence Analysis (MCA) is used [SAP 90]. Lastly, data of the frequency type can be processed by the Factorial Analysis of Correspondences (FAC). There exists a method able to treat these different cases conjointly, called the Multiple Factorial Analysis (MFA) [ESC 88].

3) Measurement theory is concerned with the mathematical foundations of the act of measuring objects. It permits a numerical representation of relations between objects to be determined, as for the preference relation. In section 18.3.2, we will describe this theory.

4) Sensorial analysis allows a quantitative approach of descriptors based on the five senses of human perception (taste, smell, touch, sight, sounds), and leads to the concept of 'human sensor'. Measurement is made by a panel of calibrated judges, i.e. able to measure a descriptor in a repeatable way with an acceptable standard deviation.

5) Sensorial physiology studies how senses function. It informs us of all factors which may modify our perception. Lastly, some research in psychology has highlighted several phenomena which may influence, sometimes heavily, our perception.

The above list is deliberately ordered. Multicriteria decision making and data analysis apply to the values of descriptors; the different possibilities of how to use these values is controlled by measurement theory, which takes into account the way these values have been obtained. In turn, the way of obtaining measurements relies on sensorial analysis, which is itself based on sensorial physiology and psychology.

18.2.2. *Definition of our scope*

The previous section has demonstrated how large the topic is; it could easily fill an entire book. In this chapter we will restrict ourselves to an approach based on multicriteria decision making, leaving some room for measurement theory for the following reasons. First of all, we have neglected sensorial analysis, sensorial physiology and psychology, which are very large topics that cannot fit into this book devoted to decision theory. Nevertheless, we will devote a section to psychology since it is somehow related to the scales and measurement notions which we will introduce. In a similar way, data analysis is a well-known domain for which numerous textbooks already exist. On the other hand, multicriteria decision making, which clearly has an important place in this book, offers an original approach to the problem of subjective evaluation. This approach is, however, not applicable to every situation, a point which we detail below.

Let us consider the example of evaluating the comfort of car seats, which will be detailed in section 18.9. The aim is to analyze the sensations of discomfort felt by the driver of a car after a certain duration. There are basically two ways to proceed. A first method consists of questioning the subject about local discomfort sensations (back, legs, arms, etc.) and overall discomfort sensation. A second method consists of performing electromyographical measurements on the subject, in order to determine the overall sensation of discomfort.

In the first case, descriptors $X_1, \ldots, X_n$ will be expressed e.g. on a scale from 0 (no discomfort) to 10 (unbearable discomfort). Doing so, these descriptors are 'homogenous' and represent a degree of discomfort, as well as quality X represents the overall discomfort. We understand that an augmentation of X_i among the local sensations cannot lead to a reduction of the overall discomfort X.

In the second case, measurements can be of a very different nature. It is therefore not possible to know in advance if augmenting the value of X_i for a given i will cause an augmentation or a diminution of the overall sensation of discomfort.

Our approach is limited to the first case, where it is always possible to put the descriptors on homogenous scales (or more precisely, on *commensurate* scales), which can be thought of as satisfaction degrees or (in the present case) dissatisfaction degrees. This amounts to defining functions $u_i : X_i \longrightarrow \mathbb{R}$, which transform the values of descriptors into degrees of satisfaction or attractiveness. The degree of overall satisfaction is then a function $u : X = X_1 \times \ldots \times X_n \longrightarrow \mathbb{R}$ which is written

$$u(x) = F(u_1(x_1), \ldots, u_n(x_n)) \tag{18.1}$$

where $F : \mathbb{R}^n \longrightarrow \mathbb{R}$ is a non-decreasing function of each argument. Note that this formula is also used in fuzzy set theory: the $u_i(x_i)$ are then membership degrees. In the above example of discomfort, functions u_i are all the identity function.

The second case cannot be handled by this method since there is no way to build functions u_i; it is more related to data analysis.

Section 18.3 details the multicriteria approach.

18.3. A multicriteria approach to subjective evaluation

We consider descriptors $X_1, \ldots, X_n$, all assumed to be measurable, describing a quality X of an object. For each $i = 1, \ldots, n$, X_i denotes the descriptor itself, as well as the set of all possible values of the descriptor (denoted by x_i). We stress the fact that these values are not always numbers. We make the assumption that the set of descriptors is exhaustive, hence a n-tuple $(x_1, \ldots, x_n)$ defines without ambiguity an instance of the quality X. This can be seen as the quality of an object, possibly fictitious. We can therefore assimilate X to the Cartesian product $X_1 \times \ldots \times X_n$ and, considering that in a given problem we are interested only in a single quality, we can assimilate $x \in X$ to the object of quality x if it is unique or to one of the members of its equivalence class.

We make the assumption that we are able to associate a satisfaction or attractiveness degree $u_i(x_i)$ to each $x_i \in X_i$, i.e. to define a function $u_i : X_i \longrightarrow \mathbb{R}$ sometimes referred to as the *utility function*. The existence of this utility function, translating the values of the descriptor in satisfaction, allows us to speak of *criterion*. Strictly speaking, criterion i is the pair (X_i, u_i) and, with some abuse of notation, we will sometimes label X_i itself the criterion i. We then look for a function $F : \mathbb{R}^n \longrightarrow \mathbb{R}$ (called the *aggregation function*) which enables a numerical model of subjective evaluation of an object x by equation (18.1) to be built.

There are two problems underlying this representation:

1) Under which conditions does such a model exist? More precisely, when can we ensure the existence of utility functions u_i or of the aggregation function F?

2) Assuming that functions u_i do exist, they are not in general unique but instead defined by some transformation. Among all possible functions u_i, $i = 1, \ldots, n$, which one should we choose?

The answer to these questions is based on measurement theory. The MACBETH (Measuring Attractiveness by a Categorical Based Evaluation TecHnique) methodology offers a less general but more operational answer to these two questions. The following sections provide its essential elements. First, however, we recall some useful results obtained in psychology, which will help our construction.

18.3.1. *The importance of affect in evaluation*

Research in psychology, generally conducted by Slovic [SLO 02], has shown that our way of judging, evaluating and making decision is guided by *affect*. Quoting Slovic, this word can be defined as "specific quality of 'goodness' and 'badness', as it is felt consciously or not by the decision maker, and demarcating a positive or negative quality of stimulus". We limit ourselves to the main points of interest for our purpose:

– Evaluability: in multi-attribute evaluation, attributes whose perception is imprecise or without reference level have few impacts on the final decision. Hsee [HSE 96] has performed the following experiment. A population are asked how much they would pay for second-hand music dictionaries, one (a) having 10,000 entries and looking almost new, the other (b) having 20,000 entries and the cover being torn. The amount for B is far above the amount given for A, because of the number of entries. However, if the experiment is done with a second population who are asked to evaluate only A or B, the price for A is greater than that given for B. The reason is that most people are unable to tell whether 10,000 or 20,000 entries can be considered as sufficient for a music dictionary (absence of a reference level). The evaluation is therefore only made on the second attribute i.e. the condition of the book, which can be directly appreciated.

– Dominance of proportion: expressing an attribute with a proportion or percentage has more impact than if it is expressed in an absolute way. The reason is again the absence of reference level when the attribute is expressed in an absolute manner. As noticed by Slovic, people are more inclined to support policies in airports which save 95% of 150 human lives than to save 150 human lives, because this last figure does not give any reference level. Similarly, people prefer a small but overflowing cup of ice-cream, rather than a big cup which is half-filled even if the latter may contain more ice-cream than the former.

– Bipolarity: the *bipolar* character of affect, i.e. built on two opposite poles (good/bad, positive/negative), is central in evaluation, and it is important to represent it in the correct way. The representation based on a bipolar scale, i.e. one single axis for coding affect from negative to positive, has been until recently the dominant practice (see the works of Osgood *et al.* [OSG 57]). Recently, Cacioppo *et al.* have proposed the use of two unipolar separate scales, one for the positive part of affect and the other for the negative part [CAC 97]. The motivation for such an approach is that we may feel both a positive feeling *and* a negative feeling for the same object, while it is not possible to fuse them in a single *resulting* feeling (for example, eating some chocolate gives a gustative pleasure, but one can also feel guilty). A recent study of Peters and Slovic [PET 03] with the aim of comparing the two paradigms was not able to reach a clear conclusion. In our construction, we will adopt the bipolar version but we will indicate some research carried out on the 'doubly unipolar' side.

– Sign theory: recently proposed by Lin and Slovic [LIN 03], this makes the assumption that the evaluation of an object with respect to an attribute is done on three values coded by -1 (negative), 0 (neutral) and 1 (positive). Values 'positive' and 'negative' of course refer to positive and negative affects, value 'neutral' is used when the stimulus does not bear a clear affective value (which can be the case when there is no reference level; see above). For the overall judgment of an object, one counts the positive and negative signs.

18.3.2. *Measurement theory, notion of scale*

The reader is refered to [KRA 71, ROB 79] for more details.

Consider a set of objects A, on which we define a relation (most often binary) $\succsim$ such as 'greater than', 'warmer than', 'preferred to', etc. and a binary operation $*$. The prototype of a binary operation is concatenation, which amounts e.g. to laying end to end two objects when the relation of interest $\succsim$ is 'bigger than'. We call $\mathcal{A} := (A, \succsim, *)$ a *relational system*. In the following, we essentially consider relational systems $(A, \succsim)$ without concatenation law.

It is convenient to introduce the *symmetric* part $\sim$ and *asymmetric* part $\succ$ of the relation $\succsim$, defined by $a \sim b$ if and only if $a \succsim b$ and $b \succsim a$, and $a \succ b$ if and only if $a \succsim b$ and $\neg(b \succsim a)$. We will often use the quotient set $A/\sim$ (set of equivalence classes of $\sim$).

The fundamental problem of measurement is to find homomorphisms between relational systems $\mathcal{A}$ and $\mathcal{B} := (B, \succsim', *')$, the most common case being when $\mathcal{B} = (\mathbb{R}, \geq, +)$. This amounts to finding a function $f : A \longrightarrow B$ such that:

$$a \succsim b \Leftrightarrow f(a) \succsim' f(b)$$

and

$$f(a * b) = f(a) *' f(b).$$

We call *scale* a triple $(\mathcal{A}, \mathcal{B}, f)$, where f is an homomorphism from A to B. With some abuse of notation, we will sometimes say that f itself is the scale. The scale is said to be *numerical* if $B = \mathbb{R}$. Finally, we say that f is a *representation* of $\mathcal{A}$, numerical if $B = \mathbb{R}$.

In general f is not unique. Every function $\phi : B \longrightarrow B$ such that $\phi \circ f$ is still a homomorphism are *admissible transformations*. If we take the example of temperature measurement ($\succsim$='warmer than'), Celsius and Kelvin degrees are examples of scales.

We distinguish between several types of scales, according to the class of admissible transformations. The main examples of scale are:
– Absolute scales: the only admissible transformation is identity e.g. counting.
– Ratio scales: admissible transformations are $\phi(x) = \alpha x$, $\alpha > 0$ e.g. mass, temperature in Kelvin degrees.
– Interval scales: admissible transformations are $\phi(x) = \alpha x + \beta$, $\alpha > 0$ e.g. temperature in Celsius degrees, years of the calendar.
– Ordinal scales: every function ϕ which is increasing is admissible e.g. scale of hardness, scale of Richter.

A proposition on $\mathcal{A}/\sim$ (e.g. a is 2 times longer, or warmer or heavier than b) is *meaningful* if its truth remains unchanged for all admissible transformation. Hence, for the scale of Kelvin degrees, it is meaningful to say that a is twice as warm as b; this has no meaning for the scales of Celsius degrees, however.

Let us examine the simplest case of relational system $\mathcal{A} = (A, \succsim)$, where $\succsim$ is a binary relation. We want to find a homomorphism f from $\mathcal{A}$ to $\mathcal{B} = (\mathbb{R}, \geq)$ (this is called the *ordinal measurement* problem). In the case of a finite set A, it is easy to show that such a homomorphism exists if and only if $\succsim$ is a complete preorder. We can take as solution $f(x) := |\{y \mid x \succsim y\}|$. The result can be extended to the case where A is countable (in fact, it is sufficient that the quotient set $A/\sim$ is countable).

In the general case, it is not always possible to find a homomorphism. The counterexample of the lexicographic order, due to Debreu, is famous. Let us take $A = \mathbb{R}^2$, and define the lexicographic order (asymmetric part) by:

$$(a,b) \succ_{\text{lex}} (c,d) \Leftrightarrow \Big[a > c \text{ or } (a = c \text{ and } b > d)\Big].$$

Let us suppose that a homomorphism f exists; we should then have $f(a,1) > f(a,0)$. A rational number $g(a)$ therefore exists such that $f(a,1) > g(a) > f(a,0)$. Since this is valid for all $a \in \mathbb{R}$, we have defined a function $g : \mathbb{R} \longrightarrow \mathbb{Q}$. Let us remark that this function is injective. Indeed, if $a \neq b$, we necessarily have $a > b$ or $b > a$. In the case $a > b$, this implies that $g(a) > f(a,0) > f(b,1) > g(b)$. However, there exists no injective function from the reals to the rationals.

Roughly speaking, a numerical representation cannot exist if A has a cardinality greater than that of the real numbers. This is expressed by the result of Birkhoff-Milgram, based on the notion of *order-density*. Let $(A, \succsim)$ be a complete order (i.e. antisymmetric: $A/\sim = A$). We say that a part B of A is *order-dense* in $(A, \succsim)$ if $\forall a, b \in A \setminus B$ such that $a \succ b$, then $\exists c \in B$ such that $a \succsim c \succsim b$. We then have the following result.

Theorem 18.1. *Consider $(A, \succsim)$, with $\succsim$ a binary relation. There exists $f : A \longrightarrow \mathbb{R}$ such that $a \succsim b \Leftrightarrow f(a) \geq f(b)$ if and only if $\succsim$ is a complete preorder, and the quotient set $A/\sim$ has a order-dense subset at most countable. Moroever, if such an f exists, then $(\mathcal{A}, \mathcal{B}, f)$ is an ordinal scale.*

This result answers our first question in the case $n = 1$. The utility function u_i plays the role of a homomorphism, and $\succsim$ represents the preference of the subject. Moreover, since function u_i is defined up to an increasing transformation, we obtain an ordinal scale.

An ordinal scale is poor, and cannot allow numerical values to be handled. Is it possible to go farther, and to specify an interval scale? This question is related to difference measurements, of which we give a brief description. We consider a quaternary relation $\succsim$ on A. The meaning given to $ab \succsim st$ for $a, b, s, t \in A$ is the following: the intensity difference between a and b is greater than the difference of intensity between s and t, the intensity being expressed by a real-valued function f defined on A. We therefore have the following equivalence:

$$ab \succsim st \Leftrightarrow f(a) - f(b) \geq f(s) - f(t).$$

The question is to know which are the required conditions on $\succsim$ so that such a function f exists, and if this function is unique. Krantz et al. [KRA 71] have shown that the following five conditions are necessary and sufficient for the existence of f:

1) The binary relation R on A^2 defined by $(a,b)R(s,t) := ab \succsim st$ is a complete preorder.

2) $ab \succsim st \Rightarrow ts \succsim ba$.

3) $ab \succsim a'b'$ and $bc \succsim b'c'$ imply $ac \succsim a'c'$.

4) $ab \succsim st$ and $st \succsim xx$ imply the existence of $u, v \in A$ such that $au \sim st$ and $vb \sim st$ (solvability).

5) Every strictly bounded standard sequence is finite (Archimedian axiom). We say that $a_1, \ldots, a_n$ is a *standard sequence* if $a_{i+1}a_i \sim a_2a_1$, $i = 1, \ldots, n-1$ and $\neg(a_2a_1 \sim a_1a_1)$ (regular spacing). The standard sequence is strictly bounded if there exists $s, t \in A$ such that $st \succ a_i a_1 \succ ts$, $i = 1, \ldots, n$.

Moreover, if such an f exists, it is unique up to a positive affine transformation and it therefore defines an interval scale.

There exists a result due to Scott in the case where A is finite, which uses an infinite scheme of axioms.

There exists a third type of measurement called *extensive measurement*, where we look for a homomorphism between $(A, \succsim, *)$ and $(\mathbb{R}, \geq, +)$. A representation exists if and only if $(A, \succsim, *)$ is an Archimedean ordered group (Hölder's theorem). In this case, we obtain a ratio scale.

We have now studied the mono-dimensional case $n = 1$. What happens in the multidimensional case? According to our notation, we denote the set of objects by $X = X_1 \times \ldots \times X_n$. We are looking for a function $u : X \longrightarrow \mathbb{R}$ such that $x \succsim y$ if and only if $u(x) \geq u(y)$. The existence of this function is given by the theorem of Birkhoff-Milgram: it is necessary and sufficient that $(X/\sim, \succsim)$ has a countable order-dense subset and that $\succsim$ is a complete preorder. In order to make the dimensions X_i explicit, we are looking for functions which are called *decomposable*, i.e. of the form

$$u(x_1, \ldots, x_n) = F(u_1(x_1), \ldots, u_n(x_n)), \qquad (18.2)$$

with F increasing. A necessary condition for the existence of this form is *weak separability* or *independence* of $(X, \succsim)$. (Note that if there is no condition on F, we replace $\succsim$ by $\sim$ in equation (18.3). This condition is called *substitutability*. On the other hand, the independence condition can be found in expected utility theory within the sure-thing principle [SAV 72].)

$$(x_i, z_{i^c}) \succsim (y_i, z_{i^c}) \Leftrightarrow (x_i, z'_{i^c}) \succsim (y_i, z'_{i^c}), \quad \forall x, y, z, z' \in X. \qquad (18.3)$$

Notation $z = (x_A, y_{A^c})$ means that the object z is such that $z_i = x_i$ if $i \in A$, and $z_i = y_i$ otherwise. This property entails the existence of relations $\succsim_i$ on each X_i, and therefore of homomorphisms $u_i : X_i \longrightarrow \mathbb{R}$. To summarize, the result is as follows.

Theorem 18.2. *$(X, \succsim)$ is representable by a decomposable function u with $F : \mathbb{R}^n \longrightarrow \mathbb{R}$ being increasing if and only if $\succsim$ is a complete preorder, $(X/ \sim, \succsim^*)$ has a countable order-dense subset, and $(X, \succsim)$ is weakly separable.*

u defines an ordinal scale since it is unique up to an increasing transformation.

This result answers our two questions raised at the begining, since equations (18.1) and (18.2) are identical: F is then the aggregation function we were looking for, and the utility functions u_i are unique. However, it is nothing other than an existence theorem, with conditions which are difficult to check in practice. On the other hand, it would be interesting to obtain at least a difference scale. The MACBETH methodology, which we present below, permits a difference scale (non-unique) to be obtained, with an experimental protocol at the expense of some additional assumptions. We first introduce the fundamental notion of unipolar and bipolar scales.

18.3.3. *Unipolar and bipolar scales*

Let us examine the notion of scale from a different viewpoint, in the light of work done in psychology around the notion of affect (section 18.3.1). This work has shown the bipolar nature (good/bad, positive/negative) of evaluation, and the existence of a neutral level (theory of sign). We will attempt to formalize these notions, relying on measurement theory.

The distinction between unipolar and bipolar scales lies in the presence of a particular value of the scale, called *neutral value*, whose exact meaning is related to the nature of the relation $\succsim$. In many cases, however, and in particular for all relations $\succsim$ of physical nature, this distinction has no meaning at all. It seems however useful for all relations of a more subjective nature where affect is present, such as preference.

Let $(A, \succsim)$ be a relational system and f a scale which we will suppose to be numerical (it is however possible to work on any totally ordered set). There exists a particular value e in A, called the *neutral value*, which has the property that if $a \succ e$ then a is felt as 'good' while if $e \succ a$, then a is felt as 'bad'. It is convenient (but not compulsory) to assign the value $f(e) = 0$ to e. Doing so, positive numbers correspond to good values of the descriptor and negatives numbers to bad values. A neutral value exists whenever the relation $\succsim$ corresponds to two opposite notions of the language. This is the case for the relations 'more attractive than', 'better than', 'like more than', whose corresponding pairs of opposite notions are attractiveness/repulsion, good/bad and like/dislike, respectively. On the contrary, relations such as 'higher priority than', 'more permitted than' or 'belongs more to category C than' clearly do not correspond to pairs of opposite concepts (absence of affect), and therefore have no neutral value.

A *bipolar scale* has a neutral value, while a *unipolar scale* does not. Typically, for a bipolar scale the range of f will be $\mathbb{R}$ (bipolar *unbounded*) or a closed interval of $\mathbb{R}$, symmetric around 0 (bipolar *bounded*), considered as neutral value. For a unipolar scale, we generally consider that it has a least element, that is, there exists $a \in A/\sim$ such that $b \succsim a$ for all $b \in A$ (it is always the case if A is finite and $\succsim$ is a total preorder). It is convenient but not compulsory to assign the value $f(a) = 0$ to a. In this case, the range of f is $\mathbb{R}_+$ (unipolar unbounded) or a closed interval $[0, \alpha]$ (unipolar bounded). If we take again the examples of unipolar scales given above, the relations 'more permitted' and 'belongs more to category C than' have a least element, which we can express by 'forbidden' (in the strict sense) and 'outside category C', respectively. On the contrary, there is no least element for 'higher priority than' since one can always find something of less priority.

It is convenient to denote by **0** the neutral value of a bipolar scale, or the least element of a unipolar scale.

A scale has a greatest element if there exists a value $a_1 \in A$ such that $a_1 \succsim a$ for all elements a of A. We say that a unipolar scale is *bounded* if it has a greatest element. A bipolar scale is bounded if it has a least and a greatest element (because of the symmetry of this type of scale, the existence of a greatest element entails that of a least element). In the above examples, relations 'more attractive than', 'better than' and 'of higher priority than' are not bounded in general, while 'more permitted than' and 'belongs more to category C than' are clearly bounded. The greatest elements are 'fully permitted' and 'totally belongs to category C', respectively. We denote the greatest element by **1** and the least element of the bipolar scale by $-\mathbf{1}$, when they exist.

The absence of a greatest element can create a problem when several scales are used at the same time (commensurability). In this case, we must build another particular level which we call the *satisfactory level*, also denoted by **1**. This level is considered as *good and quite satisfactory* if the decision maker could obtain it, even if more attractive elements could exist in A, by the unboundedness assumption. As we will see in the next section, the existence of such a level is a basic assumption in the MACBETH approach. The existence of a 'satisfactory' level which would satisfy the decision maker, and would be such that they would not feel the need to find better elements, is one of the fundamental thesis of the economist Herbert Simon in his theory of *satisficing bounded rationality* [RAD 75, SIM 56, SIM 01]. The main idea is that in a real situation, hence naturally complex (e.g. chess game) and often under incomplete information (e.g. an animal looking for food), the decision maker or agent does not try to *optimize* but to *satisfy*: they will choose any solution which will be satisfactory for them.

In addition, the necessity to have a reference point on the scale has been well demonstrated in psychology: this is precisely the notion of *evaluability* (see section 18.3.1). When the scale is bounded, we can see in addition the phenomenon of *dominance of proportion* (section 18.3.1): to express a value in percentage or in proportion is indeed to make reference to a greatest element, to which all values are compared.

What is the relation between bipolar/unipolar and the different types of scales (ordinal, interval, ratio, etc.) explained above? There is no *a priori* relation; we can have for example a scale which is both ordinal and bipolar or unipolar. Nevertheless, the neutral value of a bipolar scale is linked to the 0 of a ratio scale, which is a fixed point of any admissible transformation. For a unipolar scale without a least element, the absence of any reference point would imply that it has an interval scale. If a least element exists, according to the meaning of the relation $\succsim$, we can have a ratio or interval scale.

18.3.4. *The MACBETH approach*

The MACBETH methodology is due to Bana e Costa and Vansnick [BAN 94, BAN 97, BAN 99].

Let us begin as above with the mono-dimensional case. We consider a finite set of objects $A = \{a, b, c, \ldots\}$. The subject is asked two types of questions for every pair $(a, b) \in A^2$:

– Is a more attractive (or preferred, etc.) than b? (yes/no) If the answer is 'yes', we write aPb.

– If aPb, is the difference of attractivity (or preference, etc.):
  - very weak ($aC_1 b$)
  - weak ($aC_2 b$)
  - moderate ($aC_3 b$)
  - strong ($aC_4 b$)
  - very strong ($aC_5 b$)
  - extreme ($aC_6 b$).

(only one answer is possible)

If neither aPb nor bPa holds, we say that a and b are indifferent which we denote by $aC_0 b$. We have $P = C_1 \cup C_2 \cup \ldots \cup C_6$, and we define $P_k := C_k \cup C_{k+1} \cup \ldots \cup C_6$, $k = 1, \ldots, 6$.

Referring to measurement theory, the answer to the first question brings an ordinal information. We are looking for a numerical representation $f : A \longrightarrow \mathbb{R}$ such that $f(a) > f(b)$ if and only if aPb. We know (section 18.3.2) that in this case there always exists one if P is a strict complete preorder, and that this defines an ordinal scale.

The second question is related to difference measurement. The quaternary relation $\succsim$ is implicitly defined by the ordered character of categories $C_1, \ldots, C_6$. We have seen that a representation by a difference scale does not always exists (result of Scott for the finite case and of Krantz et al. for the general case). In the present case, this amounts to looking for a function $f : A \longrightarrow \mathbb{R}$ such that aC_kb and $cC_{k'}d$, with $k > k'$ being equivalent to the condition $f(a) - f(b) > f(c) - f(d)$. Bana e Costa and Vansnick have found conditions of existence of such a function f [BAN 94] which are simpler that those of Scott. First, the existence of such a function f is equivalent to the existence of real numbers $0 =: t_1 < \ldots < t_6$ and of a function $f : A \longrightarrow \mathbb{R}$ such that

$$aP_kb \Leftrightarrow f(a) > f(b) + t_k, \quad k = 1, \ldots, 6. \tag{18.4}$$

This condition is in turn equivalent to a condition on the graph of the relation P. It can also be verified more simply by solving a linear program.

Let us suppose that the two ordinal and cardinal conditions are verified. By a linear program, we then look for the smallest function f imposing $t_k := k$. This function f defines an interval scale, since it is unique up to a positive affine transformation.

We consider now the multidimensional case. We denote as above the set of potential objects by X, of the form $X_1 \times \ldots \times X_n$. For every descriptor X_i, we suppose that it is either finite or that there exists a finite subset $\tilde{X}_i$ containing the remarkable values of X_i. This assumption is necessary, since MACBETH can only work on a finite set of low cardinality. In practice, this is not restrictive since we should not forget that the set of objects of interest (in the experiment) is necessarily finite: $x^1, x^2, \ldots, x^p$. It is sufficient to take $\tilde{X}_i := \{x_i^1, x_i^2, \ldots, x_i^p\}$ for all i such that X_i is infinite.

The MACBETH methodology belongs to the category of the methods which build a decomposable function u (equation (18.2)), with F being of the form $\sum_{i=1}^{n} w_i x_i$, $w_i \geq 0$ (weighted sum; for necessary and sufficient conditions on $\succsim$ for preference representation by a weighted sum see [KRA 71, ROB 79]). We know from section 18.3.2 that a decomposable representation needs an assumption of weak separability for $\succsim$. MACBETH implicitly makes this assumption, and builds the utility functions u_i on each X_i upon it. We proceed as follows. Suppose that we want to build function u_i on X_i. We consider the set of objects (most often fictitious)

$$A_i := \{(\mathbf{0}_1, \ldots, \mathbf{0}_{i-1}, x_i^j, \mathbf{0}_{i+1}, \ldots, \mathbf{0}_n)\}_{x_i^j \in \tilde{X}_i} \tag{18.5}$$

where $\mathbf{0}_j$ is a particular value of X_j. Under the assumption of weak separability, the application of the above described MACBETH methodology on the set of objects A_i determines, without ambiguity, an interval scale u_i i.e. defined up to a positive affine transformation $\alpha_i u_i + \beta_i$, $\alpha_i > 0$. As presented in [GRA 04b], it is possible to avoid the weak separability assumption. We can state that the function F satisfies the following property (which could be called *weak homogenity*) for $i = 1, \ldots, n$: there exists a non-negative real number α_i such that $F(a_i, 0_{i^c}) = \alpha_i a_i$ for all $a_i \in \mathbb{R}_+$. If we set $u_i(\mathbf{0}_i) = 0$, then equation (18.5) permits u_i to be determined without ambiguity. The weighted sum, as well as the Choquet integral, satisfy the weak homogenity property.

At first sight, any value of X_j can be chosen for $\mathbf{0}_j$. For commensurability reasons which will be clear, it is important that the values $\mathbf{0}_j$ could have an absolute meaning. Depending on whether the scale is unipolar or bipolar (section 18.3.3), we define $\mathbf{0}_j$ as the value of X_j felt by the subject as being completely inacceptable (case of unipolar scales: $\mathbf{0}_i$ is then the least element), or neutral (case of bipolar scales: $\mathbf{0}_i$ is the neutral value of the scale).

MACBETH makes the assumption that such a value having an absolute meaning exists on each descriptor, and that it can be expressed by the subject. The absolute meaning of these values means that for all $j = 1, \ldots, n$, the satisfaction induced by the value $\mathbf{0}_j$ for the subject is the same. Hence, We must have $u_i(\mathbf{0}_i) = u_j(\mathbf{0}_j)$, for each i, j. It seems natural to take as common value $u_i(\mathbf{0}_i) = 0$.

In order to fix the two constants α_i, β_i, it is necessary to fix a second particular point having an absolute meaning on each X_i, which will be denoted by $\mathbf{1}_i$. If the scale is bounded, then $\mathbf{1}_i$ corresponds to the greatest element of $A_i/\sim$ (the most satisfactory value). Otherwise, the value $\mathbf{1}_i$ is the *satisfactory* value of section 18.3.3. As above, the absolute meaning of these values implies that $u_i(\mathbf{1}_i) = u_j(\mathbf{1}_j)$ for all i, j. By convention, we set $u_i(\mathbf{1}_i) := 1$, $i = 1, \ldots, n$.

This being done, functions u_i are determined in a unique way. They are *commensurable* in the sense where an equality of the values implies an equality of the satisfaction for the subject.

The last step consists of determining the weights w_i of each descriptor in the weighted sum F. For this, we build the following set of (fictive) objects

$$B := \{\mathbf{0}_1, \ldots, \mathbf{0}_{i-1}, \mathbf{1}_i, \mathbf{0}_{i+1}, \ldots, \mathbf{0}_n\}_{i=1,\ldots,n} \qquad (18.6)$$

and apply the MACBETH methodology on B to find an interval scale w. Denoting the element of B having the value $\mathbf{1}_i$ at the ith coordinate by b_i, we obtain $w_i = w(b_i)$, $i = 1, \ldots, n$. By this method, the weights of a descriptor correspond to the value assigned to an object being satisfactory on this descriptor and neutral (or unacceptable) elsewhere.

18.3.5. *Construction of the model of subjective evaluation*

The application of the MACBETH methodology yields a constructive answer to the two questions asked at the beginning of this section, restricted to the case where F is the weighted sum. The weighted sum is a simple aggregation function, but of limited power. On the other hand, we know that there exist many other aggregation functions (see Chapter 4). We propose here a more general approach.

Consider the following example in order to show the limitations of the weighted sum and to motivate our approach.

Example 18.1. Let us take $X = X_1 \times X_2$, and suppose that we have built the two utility functions u_1, u_2. Consider three objects a, b, c, with the following utility values:

$$u_1(a_1) = 0.4 \quad u_1(b_1) = 0 \quad u_1(c_1) = 1$$
$$u_2(a_2) = 0.4 \quad u_2(b_2) = 1 \quad u_2(c_2) = 0,$$

assuming that $u_i : X_i \longrightarrow [0,1]$, $i = 1, 2$. The subject has as preference $a \succ b \sim c$. Let us find w_1, w_2 such that this choice is represented by the weighted sum. We obtain:

$$b \sim c \Leftrightarrow w_1 = w_2$$
$$a \succ b \Leftrightarrow 0.4(w_1 + w_2) > w_2$$

equivalent to $0.8w_2 > w_2$, which is impossible. This is because in the model, the subject specifies only the satisfaction on fictive objects which are satisfactory on the first criterion and unacceptable for the second, and vice versa. Obviously, the subject is sensitive to objects having an unacceptable criterion, and the two criteria must be equally satisfied.

This example suggests that to construct F we must determine the subject's preference on fictive objects with an arbitrary combination of $\mathbf{1}_i$ and $\mathbf{0}_i$, (we call such an object *binary*). Hence, the set B of fictive objects to consider is not that defined by equation (18.6), but the set of binary objects:

$$B := \{(\mathbf{1}_A, \mathbf{0}_{A^c}) \mid A \subset N\} \tag{18.7}$$

where $N := \{1, \ldots, n\}$ and the fictive object $z = (\mathbf{1}_A, \mathbf{0}_{A^c})$ is defined by $z_i = \mathbf{1}_i$ if $i \in A$ and $z_i = \mathbf{0}_i$ otherwise. Applying MACBETH to this set, we build an interval scale $\mu : \mathcal{P}(N) \longrightarrow \mathbb{R}$. Noting that $A = \emptyset, N$ leads to objects $(\mathbf{0}_1, \mathbf{0}_2, \ldots, \mathbf{0}_n)$ and $(\mathbf{1}_1, \mathbf{1}_2, \ldots, \mathbf{1}_n)$, it seems natural to set $\mu(\emptyset) = 0$ and $\mu(N) = 1$.

When $A \subset B$, we remark that the fictive object $(\mathbf{1}_B, \mathbf{0}_{B^c})$ *dominates* object $(\mathbf{1}_A, \mathbf{0}_{A^c})$, which means that the former is at least as good as the latter on each descriptor. It then seems reasonable to impose that $\mu(A) \leq \mu(B)$, a property which is called monotonicity or *isotonicity*.

The value $\mu(A)$ is the value assigned by the model to the fictive object $(\mathbf{1}_A, \mathbf{0}_{A^c})$. Since $u_i(\mathbf{1}_i) = 1$, $u_i(\mathbf{0}_i) = 0$, $\forall i \in N$, we have:

$$F(\mathbf{1}_A, \mathbf{0}_{A^c}) = \mu(A), \quad \forall A \subset N. \tag{18.8}$$

Otherwise, μ determines F on the vertices of the hypercube $[0,1]^n$. It remains to determine F on the whole hypercube $[0,1]^n$ or on $\mathbb{R}_+^n$ or $\mathbb{R}^n$ depending on the type of scale (unipolar, bipolar, bounded, etc.). This is the topic of section 18.4.

To summarize, the model of evaluation is built in the following way:

(0) Data: descriptors $X_1, \ldots, X_n$, and if necessary, finite subsets of these descriptors $\tilde{X}_1, \ldots, \tilde{X}_n$.

Fundamental assumptions:

(H1) The relation $\succsim$ on $X = X_1 \times \ldots \times X_n$ is a complete preorder weakly separable (this assumption cannot be verified since $\succsim$ cannot be known on X entirely).

(H2) On each descriptor, it is possible to identify two particular values $\mathbf{0}_i$ and $\mathbf{1}_i$, possessing an absolute meaning.

(1) Construction of utility functions u_i: we consider for $i \in N$ the set A_i given by equation (18.5). The application of the MACBETH methodology gives a function u_i up to a positive affine transformation. We determine functions u_i in a unique way, imposing $u_i(\mathbf{0}_i) = 0$, $u_i(\mathbf{1}_i) = 1$, $\forall i \in N$.

This construction supposes that:

(O_i) Relations $\succsim_i$ on A_i are complete preoders (implicitly satisfied if the fundamental assumption (H1) is satisfied).

(D_i) The conditions of difference measurement are satisfied (equation (18.4)).

(2) Construction of the weighting μ: we consider the set of fictive objects B defined by equation (18.7). We apply the MACBETH methodology to determine the function $\mu : \mathcal{P}(N) \longrightarrow \mathbb{R}$, defined up to a positive affine transformation. We choose the unique function such that $\mu(\varnothing) = 0$ and $\mu(N) = 1$. Doing so, the aggregation function F is defined on the vertices of the hypercube $[0,1]^n$ (equation (18.8)).

This construction supposes that:

(O) The relation $\succsim$ restricted to B is a complete preorder (implicitly satisfied if the fundamental assumption (H1) is satisfied).

(D) the conditions of difference measurement are satisfied (equation (18.4)).

We add the additional following assumption:

(I) $\succsim$ restricted to B satisfies dominance (or equivalently, under the condition that $\succsim$ restricted to B is a complete preorder, μ is isotone).

The construction which we have presented for the scale μ remains theoretical. It is given in order to define precisely all our working assumptions, and to lead in a natural way to our model. We will examine practical methods for identifying μ in section 18.6.

18.4. Construction of the aggregation function

Let us turn to the construction of the function F. We have shown above that this function is known on the vertices of the hypercube $[0,1]^n$ by equation (18.8), since it coincides with the function $\mu : \mathcal{P}(N) \longrightarrow [0,1]$. Recall that $N = \{1,\ldots,n\}$ is the set of indices of descriptors. Hence, F can be viewed as an extension of μ on the whole hypercube (even $\mathbb{R}^n$).

We have fixed the values of $\mu(\varnothing)$ and $\mu(N)$, and have imposed that μ is monotone (isotone) (assumption (I)).

Definition 18.1. A function $\mu : \mathcal{P}(N) \longrightarrow [0,1]$ such that $\mu(\varnothing) = 0$, $\mu(N) = 1$, and $A \subset B \Rightarrow \mu(A) \leq \mu(B)$ is called *fuzzy measure* [SUG 74] or *capacity* [CHO 53].

The notion of fuzzy measure extends that of (additive) measure theory [HAL 50] (not to be confused with measurement theory), and has given rise to a theory of non-additive measures [DEN 94]. Recall that μ is *additive* if $\mu(A \cup B) = \mu(A) + \mu(B)$, $A \cap B = \varnothing$. On the other hand, we say that μ is *symmetric* if, for all $A \subset N$, $\mu(A)$ depends only on $|A|$.

18.4.1. *Case of cardinal unipolar scales*

Consider the case of a unipolar bounded scale, typically $[0,1]$. Our aim is then to build F on $[0,1]^n$. There are of course infinitely many ways of extending F from μ, however, we look for a simple method. An easy way is to use interpolation: for any $x \in [0,1]^n$, $F(x)$ would be given by a formula involving values $F(1_A, 0_{A^c})$, for A in a set of vertices $\mathcal{A}(x)$, in order that the convex hull $\overline{\mathcal{A}(x)}$ of vertices of $\mathcal{A}(x)$ contains point x: this is the very meaning of the notion of interpolation. On the other hand, in order to avoid any ambiguity, a given point x must belong to a unique region. Consequently, the hypercube $[0,1]^n$ is partitioned into polyhedra defined by their sets of vertices $\mathcal{A}_1, \ldots, \mathcal{A}_q$ which are all vertices of $[0,1]^n$. These polyhedra contain the points whose interpolation is obtained from their vertices.

The simplest interpolation would be a linear interpolation:

$$F(x) = \sum_{A \in \mathcal{A}(x)} \left[\sum_{i=1}^{n} \alpha_i(A) x_i \right] F(1_A, 0_{A^c}),$$

where $\alpha_i(A) \in \mathbb{R}$, $i = 1, \ldots, n$, $\forall A \in \mathcal{A}(x)$, with polyhedra containing as few as possible vertices.

Let us examine in detail the case $n = 2$ (Figure 18.1). To interpolate F in x, it is necessary (except for particular cases of x) to have at least three vertices; otherwise, their convex hull could not contain x. There are only two possible cuttings (a) and (b). Let us examine the first, which divides $[0, 1]^2$ into two regions $\{(x_1, x_2) \mid x_1 \leq x_2\}$ and $\{(x_1, x_2) | x_2 \leq x_1\}$. Suppose that $x_1 \leq x_2$. The formula becomes (note that $F(0, 0) = 0$ and $F(1, 1) = 1$):

$$F(x_1, x_2) = (\alpha_1 x_1 + \alpha_2 x_2) F(0, 1) + (\beta_1 x_1 + \beta_2 x_2).$$

Taking $(x_1, x_2) = (0, 1)$ and $(1, 1)$, we obtain the equations:

$$\alpha_2 = 1, \qquad \beta_2 = 0$$
$$\alpha_1 + \alpha_2 = 0, \qquad \beta_1 + \beta_2 = 1,$$

from which we obtain the unique solution in the form:

$$F(x_1, x_2) = (x_2 - x_1)\mu(\{2\}) + x_1. \tag{18.9}$$

Proceeding similarly with the case $x_2 \leq x_1$, we obtain:

$$F(x_1, x_2) = (x_1 - x_2)\mu(\{1\}) + x_2. \tag{18.10}$$

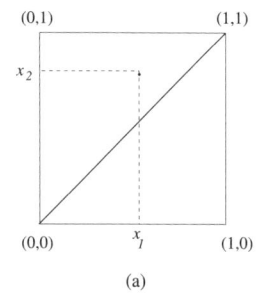

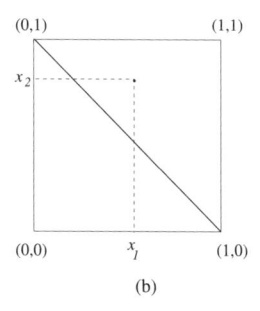

Figure 18.1. *Linear interpolation: two possible cuttings*

Let us examine now if the other cutting leads to a solution. Let us choose $x \in \{x_1 + x_2 \geq 1\}$; the interpolation equation then becomes:

$$F(x_1, x_2) = (\alpha_1 x_1 + \alpha_2 x_2)F(0, 1) + (\beta_1 x_1 + \beta_2 x_2)F(1, 0) + (\gamma_1 x_1 + \gamma_2 x_2)F(1, 1).$$

Setting $x = (1, 0)$ and $x = (0, 1)$, we necessarily have $\gamma_1 = \gamma_2 = 0$, which implies that the point $(1, 1)$ will never be recovered by the interpolation formula. We understand that, in order for the cutting to work, subsets corresponding to vertices chosen for the interpolation must form a chain $A_1 \subset A_2 \subset \ldots \subset A_n$, as is the case for cutting (a).

Generalizing this reasoning for any n, we can show that the unique solution with polyhedra containing the fewest number of vertices is given by:

- $q = n!$;
- each polyhedron is defined by a permutation σ on N:

$$\overline{\mathcal{A}_\sigma} = \{x \in [0,1]^n \mid x_{\sigma(1)} \leq x_{\sigma(2)} \leq \ldots \leq x_{\sigma(n)}\};$$

- each $\mathcal{A}_\sigma$ contains n vertices, plus the origin $(0,0,\ldots,0)$;
- for $x \in \mathcal{A}_\sigma$, the interpolation formula is

$$F(x) = \sum_{i=1}^{n} [x_{\sigma(i)} - x_{\sigma(i-1)}] \mu(\{\sigma(i), \ldots, \sigma(n)\}). \tag{18.11}$$

This result can also be found in Lovász [LOV 83] and in Marichal [MAR 02]. Equation (18.11) is in fact *the Choquet integral* of x (considered as a function of N to $[0,1]$).

Definition 18.2. *Let μ be a capacity on N, and a function $f : N \longrightarrow \mathbb{R}^+$. The Choquet integral of f w.r.t. μ is defined by:*

$$\mathcal{C}_\mu(f) := \sum_{i=1}^{n} [f(\sigma(i)) - f(\sigma(i-1))] \mu(\{\sigma(i), \ldots, \sigma(n)\}),$$

with σ a permutation on N such that $f(\sigma(1)) \leq \ldots \leq f(\sigma(n))$.

We have shown that the Choquet integral corresponds to the simplest linear interpolation to solve our problem in the case of unipolar bounded scales. However, there is no limitation for x to belong to $\mathbb{R}_+^n$, hence the unipolar unbounded case can be treated in the same way.

It is easy to verify that if μ is additive, then the Coquet integral reduces to the weighted sum $\sum_{i=1}^{n} \mu(\{i\}) x_i$. On the other hand, we have for all $x \in \mathbb{R}_+^n$ and all capacity μ, $\min_i x_i \leq \mathcal{C}_\mu(x) \leq \max_i x_i$, bounds being attained by capacities $\mu_{\min}, \mu_{\max}$, defined by $\mu_{\min}(A) := 0, \forall A \neq N$ and $\mu_{\max}(A) := 1, \forall A \neq \emptyset$.

The Choquet integral is the basis of numerous works in decision making theory. In decision under uncertainty or risk, it has given rise to models of Choquet expected utility [SCH 89, WAK 90] and to rank dependent utility [QUI 93] (see a survey of these models in [CHA 00]). In multicriteria decision making, the Choquet integral is used as a general aggregation function, permitting the interaction between criteria to be represented [GRA 96, GRA 03e, GRA 04b] (section 18.7).

The first result of characterization of the Choquet integral has been given by Schmeidler [SCH 86]; it has been followed by many others, in particular those of Marichal. for a general study of the properties of the Choquet integral, see [DEN 00, MAR 00a, MUR 00].

18.4.2. *Case of cardinal bipolar scales*

Consider now the case of bipolar scales; it will be enough to consider the interval $[-1, 1]$. Recall that a bipolar scale contains three remarkable points: the neutral value 0 and the values 1 and -1 (here 0, 1 and –1, respectively). It seems necessary that these values appear in the set of fictive objects to consider for constructing the model (see equation (18.7)).

The simplest solution is to suppose some symmetry between positive and negative parts, in which case the set B of binary objects defined by equation (18.7) suffices. For example, we could say that the evaluation of the object $(-1_A, 0_{A^c})$ is equal to the opposite to that of object $(1_A, 0_{A^c})$ (*symmetric* model) or of object $(1_{A^c}, 0_A)$ (*asymmetric* model). For an object having both positive and negative scores, the simplest is to compute overall scores for the positive and negative parts separately, then to add them. In the case $n = 2$, this procedure is illustrated in Figure 18.2(a).

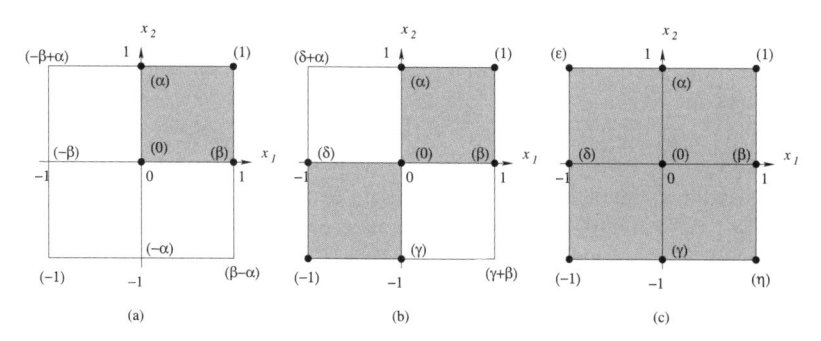

Figure 18.2. *Case of a bipolar scale: (a) symmetric model; (b) CPT; and (c) general bipolar. Black circles indicate fictive objects determining the model and values in parentheses indicate overall evaluations. Scores not in gray parts are computed from scores in gray parts*

If we take the Choquet integral C_μ to compute overall scores on the positive part of the scale, these two models, for $x \in \mathbb{R}^n$, are respectively:

$$\check{C}_\mu(x) := C_\mu(x^+) - C_\mu(x^-) \text{ (symmetric)} \tag{18.12}$$

$$C_\mu(x) := C_\mu(x^+) - C_{\bar{\mu}}(x^-) \text{ (asymmetric)} \tag{18.13}$$

with $x_i^+ := x_i \vee 0$ and $x_i^- = (-x_i)^+$, $i = 1, \ldots, n$. On the other hand, $\bar{\mu}$ is the conjugate capacity defined by $\bar{\mu}(A) := 1 - \mu(A^c)$, $A \subset N$. These expressions in fact define what is called the symmetric Choquet integral (or Šipoš integral [ŠIP 79]) and the asymmetric Choquet integral [DEN 94].

If there is no reason to suppose any symmetry between positive and negative parts, we can add the set of *negative binary objects* NB to the set of binary objects B:

$$NB := \{(-\mathbf{1}_A, \mathbf{0}_{A^c}) \mid A \subset N\}.$$

In this way we construct two capacities μ^+, μ^-, hence two unipolar models whose overall scores will be added:

$$C_{\mu^+,\mu^-}(x) := C_{\mu^+}(x^+) - C_{\mu^-}(x^-), \quad \forall x \in \mathbb{R}^n. \tag{18.14}$$

In decision under risk, this model corresponds to the model of cumulative prospects (cumulative prospect theory, CPT) of Tversky and Kahnemann [TVE 92]. For $n = 2$, the CPT model is illustrated in Figure 18.2(b).

Finally, if we do not want to make any independence assumption between positive and negative parts of the scale, we must consider as additional fictive objects those which have both satisfactory levels $\mathbf{1}$ and non-satisfactory levels $-\mathbf{1}$. We are then led to consider the set of *fictive ternary objects*:

$$T := \{(\mathbf{1}_A, -\mathbf{1}_B, \mathbf{0}_{(A \cup B)^c}) \mid A, B \subset N, \quad A \cap B = \varnothing\}. \tag{18.15}$$

This is illustrated in Figure 18.2(c) in the case $n = 2$. When applying the MACBETH methodology on T, we construct an interval scale $v : \mathcal{Q}(N) \longrightarrow \mathbb{R}$ denoted by $\mathcal{Q}(N) := \{(A, B) \in \mathcal{P}(N) \times \mathcal{P}(N) \mid A \cap B = \varnothing\}$. As before, we set $v(N, \varnothing) = 1$ and $v(\varnothing, \varnothing) = 0$, since these are the overall scores of objects being satisfactory everywhere and neutral everywhere, respectively. Similarly, one can set by convention $v(\varnothing, N) = -1$. Lastly, the notion of dominance applies as in section 18.3.5, which leads a property of isotonicity of v to be opposed in the following sense: $A \subset B$ implies $v(A, \cdot) \leq v(B, \cdot)$ and $v(\cdot, A) \geq v(\cdot, B)$. By analogy with the notion of capacity, we call such a function a *bicapacity* [GRA 02c, GRA 02d].

Definition 18.3. A *bicapacity* on N is a function $v : \mathcal{Q}(N) \longrightarrow \mathbb{R}$ satisfying:

1) $A \subset B \Rightarrow v(A, \cdot) \leq v(B, \cdot)$ and $v(\cdot, A) \geq v(\cdot, B)$; and

2) $v(N, \emptyset) = 1$, $v(\emptyset, \emptyset) = 0$, $v(\emptyset, N) = -1$.

A bicapacity is said to be of the *CPT type* if it can be written as the difference of two capacities μ^+, μ^-:
$$v(A, B) = \mu^+(A) - \mu^-(B), \quad \forall (A, B) \in \mathcal{Q}(N).$$
The bicapacity is said to be *symmetric* if, in addition, $\mu^+ = \mu^-$.

Thus, v assigns to each ternary object an overall score by $v(A, B) = F(1_A, -1_B)$, where $(1_A, -1_B)$ denotes the vector whose coordinate is 1 for $i \in A$, -1 for $i \in B$ and 0 elsewhere. This is in accordance with the bipolar view of the affect, as it has been initiated by Osgood et al. [OSG 57] (section 18.3.1). Greco et al. [GRE 02] have proposed a notion of *bipolar capacity* $\zeta : \mathcal{Q}(N) \longrightarrow [0, 1] \times [0, 1]$, where we assign two scores $\zeta^+(A, B)$ and $\zeta^-(A, B)$ to each element (A, B) of $\mathcal{Q}(N)$, one concerning the positive part of the score and the other the negative part of the score. The scores satisfy the properties:

– if $A \subset A'$ and $B \supset B'$, then $\zeta^+(A, B) \leq \zeta^+(A', B')$ and $\zeta^-(A, B) \geq \zeta^-(A', B')$;
– $\zeta^-(A, \emptyset) = 0$, $\zeta^+(\emptyset, A) = 0$, $\forall A \subset N$; and
– $\zeta(N, \emptyset) = (1, 0)$ and $\zeta(\emptyset, N) = (0, 1)$.

This notion corresponds to the *double unipolar* view of the affect [CAC 97], where we have the coexistence of positive and negative feelings.

Consider the first bicapacities to be given. Let us try to construct the aggregation function F, viewed as an extension of v on $[-1, 1]^n$, then on $\mathbb{R}^n$. Regarding the case of unipolar scales, we look for a solution which is the simplest linear interpolation. Points to be considered for the interpolation are no longer the vertices of the hypercube $[-1, 1]^n$, however, but all points corresponding to ternary objects i.e. points x such that $x_i = -1, 0$ or 1, $i = 1\ldots, n$.

Let us examine first the case $n = 2$ (Figure 18.3). Let us take a point x such that $x_1 \geq 0$, $x_2 \leq 0$ and $|x_1| \leq |x_2|$. For the point $|x|$ located in the positive quadrant, we already know the best linear interpolation by applying the result of section 18.4.1: it is the Choquet integral. It is now sufficient, by an adequate symmetry, to set the suitable vertices for interpolation:
$$F(x_1, x_2) := |x_1|F(1, -1) + (|x_2| - |x_1|)F(0, -1).$$
This expression is a Choquet integral with respect to a set function ν_1 defined by:
$$\nu_1(\{1, 2\}) = F(1, -1)$$
$$\nu_1(\{2\}) = F(0, -1).$$

Now consider the general case. Let us define $N^+ = \{i \in N \mid x_i \geq 0\}$, $N^- = N \setminus N^+$. With similar considerations of symmetry, we obtain:

$$F(x) = |x_{\sigma(1)}| F(1_{N^+}, -1_{N^-}) +$$

$$\sum_{i=2}^{n} (|x_{\sigma(i)}| - |x_{\sigma(i-1)}|) F(1_{\{\sigma(i),\ldots,\sigma(n)\} \cap N^+}, -1_{\{\sigma(i),\ldots,\sigma(n)\} \cap N^-})$$

where σ is a permutation on N such that $|x_{\sigma(1)}| \leq \ldots \leq |x_{\sigma(n)}|$. This expression is the Choquet integral of $|x|$ with respect to the set function ν_{N^+} defined by:

$$\nu_{N^+}(A) := F(1_{A \cap N^+}, -1_{A \cap N^-}).$$

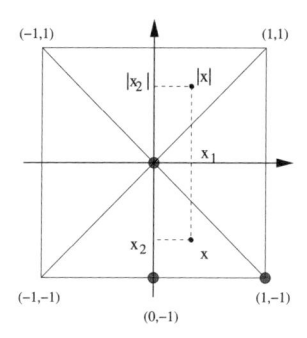

Figure 18.3. *Linear interpolation in the bipolar case ($n = 2$)*

Recalling that $F(1_A, -1_B) =: v(A, B)$, we obtain the following definition.

Definition 18.4. Let v be a bicapacity on N, and $x \in \mathbb{R}^n$. The *Choquet integral* of x with respect to v is defined by:

$$\mathcal{C}_v(x) := \mathcal{C}_{\nu_{N^+}}(|x|), \tag{18.16}$$

where $N^+ := \{i \in N \mid a_i \geq 0\}$, $N^- := N \setminus N^+$ and $\nu_{N^+}(A) := v(A \cap N^+, A \cap N^-)$.

It should be noted that ν_{N^+} is not in general a capacity, since it could be non-monotonic or take negative values.

If v is of the CPT type with $v(A, B) = \mu^+(A) - \mu^-(B)$, then we recover the CPT model $\mathcal{C}_{\mu^+,\mu^-}$ (and consequently we recover the symmetric Choquet integral when v is symmetric). This leads to two remarks:

– The Choquet integral for bicapacities is indeed a generalization of symmetric and CPT models.

– The symmetric and CPT models are particular cases of linear interpolation between the 'ternary' points x (with $x_i = -1, 0, 1$).

Let us return to the double unipolar model of Greco et al. [GRE 02]. The Choquet integral with respect to a bipolar capacity is defined as follows. For $x \in \mathbb{R}^n$, let us denote a permutation on N by σ such that $|x_{\sigma(1)}| \leq \ldots \leq |x_{\sigma(n)}|$, and define:

$$A_i^+ := \{\sigma(j), \quad j \in \{i, \ldots, n\} \mid x_{\sigma(j)} \geq 0\}$$
$$A_i^- := \{\sigma(j), \quad j \in \{i, \ldots, n\} \mid x_{\sigma(j)} \leq 0\}$$

and

$$\mathcal{C}_\zeta^+(x) := \sum_{i \in N} \left(x_{\sigma(i)}^+ - x_{\sigma(i-1)}^+\right) \zeta^+(A_i^+, A_i^-)$$

$$\mathcal{C}_\zeta^-(x) := \sum_{i \in N} \left(x_{\sigma(i)}^- - x_{\sigma(i-1)}^-\right) \zeta^-(A_i^+, A_i^-)$$

with the same notation as before. The Choquet integral with respect to ζ is then defined by

$$\mathcal{C}_\zeta(x) := \mathcal{C}_\zeta^+(x) - \mathcal{C}_\zeta^-(x), \quad \forall x \in \mathbb{R}^n. \tag{18.17}$$

There are two important remarks to make at this point. The first one is that if we want to keep the original spirit of the double unipolar model of Cacioppo, it is better to consider the couple $(\mathcal{C}_\zeta^+(x), \mathcal{C}_\zeta^-(x))$ as the Choquet integral without taking the difference. The second one is that, under the assumption that we take the difference equation (18.17), we can show that if the expression does not depend on the chosen permutation σ (if several are candidates), then the bipolar capacity ζ necessarily reduces to the bicapacity $v(A, B) := \zeta^+(A, B) - \zeta^-(\emptyset, B)$. The expression of $\mathcal{C}_\zeta$ then coincides with $\mathcal{C}_v$ given by equation (18.16) [GRA 04b].

18.5. The case of ordinal scales

18.5.1. *Introduction*

Until now we have assumed that the quantities and the scales we handle are numerical, either of interval or of ratio type (*cardinal scales*). However, in practice, it is often not possible to directly obtain cardinal information. The aim of the MACBETH methodology is indeed to obtain by a well-founded approach cardinal information from an ordinal information, at the price of some additional assumptions (measurement of difference, determination of neutral and satisfactory levels, etc.). In some situations, it may not be possible to get this information from the decision maker, the decision maker may be inconsistent or the basic assumptions may not be satisfied. In this case, we are obliged to use the ordinal information as such (despite the poor algebraic structure it induces) and avoid making arbitrary assumptions to return to the cardinal world.

Dealing with ordinal information in fact creates many difficulties. First, our construction of utility functions and of weighting explained in section 18.3.5 is no longer possible. Second, the above approach based on interpolation cannot be transposed, and the same happens with the multicriteria approaches of the Choquet integral proposed in [GRA 03e, LAB 03b]. In this section, we provide the existing tools to tackle this type of problem.

In this section, we consider finite ordinal scales (often denoted by L), with a least element $\mathbb{O}$ and greatest element $\mathbb{1}$. We have shown in section 18.3.2 that, for ordinal scales, the usual arithmetical operations are no longer meaningful. We are therefore restricted to the minimum ($\wedge$) and maximum ($\vee$) operators, and their combinations. We refer to any expression $P(x_1, \ldots, x_n)$ formed of n variables $x_1, \ldots, x_n$ taking values in L, of constants in L, and linked by $\vee, \wedge$ in an arbitrary combination of parentheses as a *Boolean polynomial*. An example is: $((\alpha \wedge x_1) \vee (x_2 \wedge (\beta \vee x_3))) \wedge x_4$. An important result of Marichal states that the *Sugeno integral* (defined later) coincides with the class of Boolean polynomials such that $P(\mathbb{O}, \mathbb{O}, \ldots, \mathbb{O}) = \mathbb{O}$, $P(\mathbb{1}, \mathbb{1}, \ldots, \mathbb{1}) = \mathbb{1}$ and P is non-decreasing with respect to each variable [MAR 01a]. Since these conditions are those on which we have based our study up to this point, we understand that the Sugeno integral is an unavoidable concept in the ordinal framework.

Let us emphasize the fact that other methods could exist. For example, Roubens has proposed a method based on the Choquet integral, where scores are related to the number of times that the concerned object is better or worse than the others on the same criterion [ROU 01] (section 18.6.2).

First, it seems important to emphasize the difficulties of the ordinal nature of the information:

1) Finiteness of scales: if we define the aggregation function F as a function from L^n to L, it is clear that it is impossible to have an increasing function. Moreover, there will be large indifference domains where the function will have the same value, which makes the construction not very interesting. This is why studies on t-norms and t-conorms on finite scales give a very poor class of functions [FOD 00]. It is better to have a larger scale for the image of F, built step by step. This approach has been chosen in [GRA 01b] for the Sugeno integral (see also a general study of this topic in [GRA 01a]).

On the other hand, in the finite case, there are very few results in measurement theory since most of the models suppose a condition of solvability or an Archimedian axiom. This cannot exist in a finite framework.

2) Ordinal nature of the scale: even if we consider a continuous scale such as $[0, 1]$, the Sugeno integral cannot be increasing. On the other hand, as shown by Marichal [MAR 01a], the Sugeno integral induces a preference relation which satisfies weak separability if and only if there is a criterion which is a dictator. In fact, the Sugeno integral induces a weaker property which is *weak directional separability*, defined by:

$$(x_i, z_{-i}) \succ (y_i, z_{-i}) \Rightarrow (x_i, z'_{-i}) \succeq (y_i, z'_{-i}), \quad \forall x, y, z, z' \in X.$$

This condition prevents a preference reversal occuring.

3) Construction of utility functions: contrary to the cardinal case, it is not possible to determine the utility functions without knowing the weighting. We will see later that the overall evaluation of an object $(x_i, \mathbf{0}_{i^c})$ by the Sugeno integral reads $u_i(x_i) \wedge \mu(\{i\})$. Therefore, it is not always possible to recover $u_i(x_i)$ since the value of $\mu(\{i\})$, either known or unknown, acts like a threshold. This explains why in most applications, and although this assumption is questionable, we suppose that all attributes are defined on a common scale L which serves for all scores of attributes. Grabisch *et al.* [GRA 01b] propose a method to construct the utility functions after having constructed the weighting μ.

18.5.2. *The Sugeno integral*

(See also Chapters 11 and 17.) Let μ be a capacity on N taking values in L, with $\mu(\emptyset) = \mathbb{0}$ and $\mu(N) = \mathbb{1}$. Let $a := (a_1, \ldots, a_n)$ be a vector of scores in L^n. The *Sugeno integral* of a with respect to μ is defined by [SUG 74]:

$$\mathcal{S}_\mu(a) := \bigvee_{i=1}^{n} [a_{\sigma(i)} \wedge \mu(A_{\sigma(i)})], \quad (18.18)$$

where σ is a permutation on N such that $a_{\sigma(1)} \leq a_{\sigma(2)} \leq \ldots \leq a_{\sigma(n)}$, and $A_{\sigma(i)} := \{\sigma(i), \ldots, \sigma(n)\}$ (note the similarity to the Choquet integral, see definition 18.2). If we take $L = [0, 1]$, the Choquet and Sugeno integrals coincide when either the capacity or the integrand is valued in $\{0, 1\}$. More precisely:

$$\mathcal{S}_\mu(1_A, 0_{A^c}) = \mu(A) = \mathcal{C}_\mu(1_A, 0_{A^c}), \quad \forall A \subset N$$
$$\mathcal{S}_\mu(a) = \mathcal{C}_\mu(a) \quad \forall a \in [0, 1]^n \Leftrightarrow \mu(A) \in \{0, 1\}, \quad \forall A \subset N.$$

The reader can refer to [DUB 01a, MUR 00] for survey papers and to [MAR 00b, MAR 01a] for detailed studies of properties of the Sugeno integral. We also mention an axiomatization of the Sugeno integral in a framework of decision under uncertainty, similar to that of Savage for expected utility [DUB 00, DUB 01b].

As described in the introduction, the ordinal framework leads to difficulties as well as some surprising results. For example, it may be that for $a, a' \in \mathbb{R}^n$ such that $a_i > a'_i$, $i = 1, \ldots, n$, we have $\mathcal{S}_\mu(a) = \mathcal{S}_\mu(a')$ (*drowning effect*). These unwanted effects are summarized in the following proposition [MAR 00b, MUR 01]. Let $\succeq$ be a complete preorder on $[0,1]^n$ and, for $a, b \in [0,1]^n$, we write $a \geq b$ if $a_i \geq b_i$ for all $i \in N$, $a > b$ if $a \geq b$ and $a_i > b_i$ for at least one $i \in N$ and $a \gg b$ if $a_i > b_i$ for all $i \in N$. We say that $\succeq$ satisfies *monotonicity* if $a \geq b$ implies $a \succeq b$, *strong Pareto dominance* if $a > b$ implies $a \succ b$ and *weak Pareto dominance* if $a \gg b$ implies $a \succ b$. The following proposition holds.

Proposition 18.1. *Let μ be a capacity on N and $\succeq_\mu$ the complete preorder induced by the Sugeno integral $\mathcal{S}_\mu$:*

1) $\succeq_\mu$ *always satisfies monotonicity;*
2) $\succeq_\mu$ *satisfies weak Pareto dominance if and only if μ is valued in $\{0,1\}$;*
3) $\succeq_\mu$ *never satisfies strong Pareto dominance.*

It is to be noted that the Choquet integral always satisfies weak Pareto dominance and strong Pareto dominance if and only if μ is strictly monotone.

18.5.3. *The symmetric Sugeno integral and bipolar models*

The above section presented the ordinal counterpart of the Choquet integral. This model does not suppose any particular point on the scale, except boundaries $\mathbb{O}$ and $\mathbb{1}$, so it can be considered as *unipolar*. The question is now to define a bipolar ordinal model, similar to that proposed in the cardinal framework. This section is based on work by [GRA 02a, GRA 03b, GRA 04a].

Let us begin by constructing a bipolar ordinal scale i.e. with a central point denoted by $\mathbb{O}$. The scale demarcates the limit between the domain of 'good' scores with a greatest element denoted by $\mathbb{1}$ and the domain of 'bad' scores with a least element denoted by $-\mathbb{1}$. It is sufficient to make a reversed copy of the ordinal scale L^+ with greatest and least elements $\mathbb{O}$ and $\mathbb{1}$ denoted by L^-, and to join them. In other words, $L^- := \{-a \mid a \in L^+\}$ with $(-a) \leq (-b)$ if and only if $b \leq a$. The bipolar scale is $L := L^+ \cup L^-$, making $\mathbb{O}$ and $-\mathbb{O}$ coincide.

The second step consists of endowing this bipolar scale with suitable operations which enable computations to be made taking into account the ordinal character and also the symmetry of the scale. As $\vee$ and $\wedge$ are the two basic operations in an ordinal framework, we want to construct operations denoted by $\varovee, \varowedge$ satisfying the following conditions in particular:

(C1) $\varovee, \varowedge$ coincide with $\vee, \wedge$ on L^+;

(C2) $-a$ is the opposite of a, in the sense that $a \varovee (-a) = \mathbb{O}$;
(C3) $a \varowedge b$ follows the rule of signs for the multiplication of real numbers: $-(a \varowedge b) = (-a) \varowedge b$, $\forall a, b \in L$.

The first condition states that the operations we are looking for are extensions of min and max. The second one states that $\varovee$ behaves like an addition of real numbers, and the third that $\varowedge$ is the counterpart of multiplication. These analogies are inspired by the comparison with expressions of the Choquet integral (definition 18.2) and of Sugeno (equation (18.18)). The conditions of symmetry (C2) and (C3) should enable models similar to CPT and to the general bipolar model to be defined.

A difficulty however becomes apparent. The conditions (C1) and (C2) imply that $\varovee$ cannot be associative in general. Indeed, let us take $\mathbb{O} < a < b$, and consider the expression $(-b) \varovee b \varovee a$. According to the location of parentheses, the results differ since we have $((-b) \varovee b) \varovee a = \mathbb{O} \varovee a = a$, but $(-b) \varovee (b \varovee a) = (-b) \varovee b = \mathbb{O}$. We can show that the best solution (that is, associative on the largest domain) is given by:

$$a \varovee b := \begin{cases} -(|a| \vee |b|) & \text{if } b \neq -a \text{ and } |a| \vee |b| = -a \text{ or } = -b \\ \mathbb{O} & \text{if } b = -a \\ |a| \vee |b| & \text{otherwise.} \end{cases} \quad (18.19)$$

Except for the case $b = -a$, $a \varovee b$ is equal to the one between a and b which has the greatest absolute value.

The non-associativity of $\varovee$ implies that we cannot write expressions such as $\varovee_{i=1}^n a_i$ if some computation rule is not specified. Several are possible, and in the following we will use the following rule, which simply consists of aggregating the positive and negative quantities separately:

$$\langle \varovee_{i=1}^n a_i \rangle := (\varovee_{i=1}^n a_i^+) \varovee (- \varovee_{i=1}^n a_i^-).$$

The definition of $\varowedge$ following the conditions (C1) and (C3) does not create a problem, and the operation is associative:

$$a \varowedge b := \begin{cases} -(|a| \wedge |b|) & \text{if sign } a \neq \text{sign } b \\ |a| \wedge |b| & \text{otherwise.} \end{cases} \quad (18.20)$$

We are now in the position to define the symmetric Sugeno integral and the ordinal counterpart of the CPT model. It reads:

$$\mathcal{S}_{\mu^+,\mu^-}(a) := \mathcal{S}_{\mu^+}(a^+) \varovee (-\mathcal{S}_{\mu^-}(a^-)).$$

When $\mu^+ = \mu^-$, we obtain the *symmetric Sugeno integral*, denoted $\check{\mathcal{S}}_\mu$.

From this point, we can define the Sugeno integral with respect to a bicapacity v. We proceed as in definition 18.4 i.e. setting $\mathcal{S}_v(a) := \mathcal{S}_{\nu_{N^+}}(|a|)$, with notation as above, and replacing $\vee, \wedge$ by $\oslash, \oslash$. It can be shown that the Sugeno integral can be written as follows [GRA 03c]:

$$\mathcal{S}_v(a) = \left\langle \oslash_{i=1}^n \left[|a_{\sigma(i)}| \oslash v(A_{\sigma(i)} \cap N^+, A_{\sigma(i)} \cap N^-) \right] \right\rangle, \quad (18.21)$$

where σ is a permutation on N such that $|a_{\sigma(1)}| \leq \ldots \leq |a_{\sigma(n)}|$, and $N^+ := \{i \in N \mid a_i \geq 0\}$, $N^- := N \setminus N^+$. A similar expression for the bipolar capacities has been proposed by Greco et al. [GRE 02].

We can show that if v is of the CPT type, the ordinal CPT model is recovered. Finally, we mention Denneberg and Grabisch [DEN 04] who have proposed a general formulation of the Sugeno integral on bipolar scales with an arbitrary structure (finite or infinite, with or without holes).

18.6. Identification of the parameters of the aggregation function

Suppose that we want to determine a model of subjective evaluation, using models described in this chapter, from experimental data and measurements. We have explained the general construction of the model based on MACBETH in section 18.3.5. If this methodology can be used for the determination of utility functions by contrast, the way to determine the aggregation function (which in our case amounts to determining the weighting μ (capacity) or v in the bipolar case (bicapacity)) is usually not possible in a framework of subjective evaluation. Indeed, the binary objects $(1_A, 0_{A^c})$ (ternary in the bipolar case) which are necessary for the determination of μ or of v are fictive objects with which it is not possible to make real experiments. We are then forced to use *physical* objects at disposal, often in limited number. Let us call the set of available objects $\mathcal{O} \subset X$, which we assimilate as before to their vectors of descriptors.

The general principle is to use optimization methods, after defining some suitable validity criterion. We can distinguish two main types of criteria:

– Minimization of an error or of a distance d between the output of the model $F(u_1(x_1), \ldots, u_n(x_n))$ (the computed overall score) and the 'desired' output $y(x)$, $x \in \mathcal{O}$. This implies that we must necessarily have a measurement of the overall score $y(x)$ for each object of $\mathcal{O}$, which is not always the case in practice.

– The criteria aiming at representing the preferences on $\mathcal{O}$. If for $x, x' \in \mathcal{O}$ the experiment reveals that x is 'at least as good as' x' (denoted by $x \succeq x'$) then, under the assumption that $\succeq$ is complete and transitive on $\mathcal{O}$, the model must represent the preference: $F(u_1(x_1), \ldots, u_n(x_n)) \geq F(u_1(x'_1), \ldots, u_n(x'_n))$.

In fact, a faithful representation of preferences induces constraints on μ or v, and does not define (strictly speaking) a validity criterion. Since the set of solutions is in general empty or infinite, it is necessary to define a validity criterion in order to choose one of the solutions (for example the one which produces the most distant overall scores).

The two approaches have their own advantages and drawbacks, and can be complementary. Note that when applying the MACBETH methodology on $\mathcal{O}$, it is possible to obtain overall scores on a difference scale. The advantage of the distance criterion is that we always find a solution, but there is no guarantee that this solution represents the preference induced by the overall scores.

We can have both $y(x) > y(x')$ and $F(u(x)) < F(u(x'))$, denoted $F(u(x)) := F(u_1(x_1), \ldots, u_n(x_n))$. In order to avoid this, we can incorporate constraints induced by preferences in the optimization problem, at the risk of finding no solution. The main drawback of the second approach is that there is not always a solution. In this case, it is not that easy to know how to modify the preference in order to get a solution.

We now describe these approaches in more detail, according to the type of scales (cardinal or ordinal).

18.6.1. Cardinal case

The most common error criterion is the sum of squared errors. When F is the Choquet integral with respect to a capacity, the optimization problem reads:

$$\text{minimize} \sum_{x \in \mathcal{O}} \left[\mathcal{C}_\mu(u_1(x_1), \ldots, u_n(x_n)) - y(x) \right]^2$$

under $\mu(A) \leq \mu(B), \quad \forall A, B \subset N, A \subset B,$

fixing $\mu(\emptyset) = 0, \mu(N) = 1$. We can show that this leads to a quadratic problem under linear constraints [GRA 95b, GRA 96] with $2^n - 2$ variables (the values taken on by μ, except for $\emptyset$ and N) and $n(2^{n-1} - 1)$ constraints.

There is always a solution to this problem, but not always unique. The set of solutions forms a convex set. A study of uniqueness of the solution is not easy, and can be found in [MIR 98]. Suppose that there are l data $x^1, \ldots, x^l$ in $\mathcal{O}$, and denote the vector of their overall scores by $\mathbf{y} := [y^1, \ldots, y^l]^T$. We can write under a vector form $[\mathbf{d}^k]^T \mathbf{u}$ the Choquet integral of $x^k \in \mathcal{O}$, where $\mathbf{u}$ is the vector of size $2^n - 2$ containing the values of μ, and $\mathbf{d}^k$ is a vector of size $2^n - 2$ containing the scores of x^k arranged in a suitable way. Defining the matrix $\mathbf{D}^T := [\mathbf{d}^1, \ldots, \mathbf{d}^l]$, the minimization of the criterion amounts to finding $\mathbf{u}^*$ such that:

$$d(\mathbf{D}\mathbf{u}^*, \mathbf{y}) = \min_{\mathbf{u} \in \mathcal{F}(N)} d(\mathbf{D}\mathbf{u}, \mathbf{y})$$

where $\mathcal{F}(N)$ is the set of capacities on N and d is the Euclidian distance. Since $\mathcal{F}(N)$ is convex, the set of products $\mathcal{Y} := \{\mathbf{Du} \mid \mathbf{u} \in \mathcal{F}(N)\}$ is also convex so that there exists a unique $y^* \in \mathcal{Y}$ which satisfies:

$$d(y^*, \mathbf{y}) = \min_{\mathbf{u} \in \mathcal{F}(N)} d(\mathbf{Du}, \mathbf{y}).$$

The linear system $\mathbf{Du}^* = y^*$ remains to be solved, whose uniqueness of the solution depends on the rank of the matrix $\mathbf{D}$. However, $\mathbf{u}^*$ must be a member of $\mathcal{F}(N)$, which makes the study of uniqueness complex. We can have a rank much smaller than $2^n - 2$ but a unique solution.

From the experimental point of view, the quadratic method, although optimal, has some drawbacks:

– If the amount of data is low, the set of possible solutions can be large and the solution returned by the software of quadratic programming is often 'extremal' (in the sense that it contains a lot of values set to 0 and 1). The capacity obtained in that way induces behaviors which are close to the minimum and maximum for the Choquet integral.

– The size of the matrices of the quadratic program increases exponentially with n. Computation time, memory size, as well as problems with ill-conditioned matrices also increase. Hence, $n = 8$ is a large value; it would be unreasonable to go beyond $n = 10$.

Suboptimal heuristic algorithms exist, e.g. that of Ishii and Sugeno [ISH 85] and Mori and Murofushi [MOR 89]. The author has proposed an optimization algorithm [GRA 95a] based on the latter. Although suboptimal, the algorithm performs better than that of previous methods. The criterion used here is again the quadratic error criterion, to which the gradient is applied. The basic idea of this algorithm is that, if no information is present, the less arbitrary way to aggregate scores is the arithmetic mean, i.e. the Choquet integral with respect to the equidistributed additive capacity. Any new information tends to depart from this initial point. Consequently, if there are few learning data, the values of μ which are not concerned with the computations are kept as close as possible to the initial point, while ensuring monotonicity of the capacity.

Experiments with classification problems have demonstrated the good performance of this algorithm, sometimes better than the optimal quadratic algorithm when n becomes large. In particular, the required memory size and computation time are far less than that required by the quadratic algorithm, and it is then possible to go beyond $n = 10$ ($n = 16$ in [MET 95]).

More recently, many authors have applied genetic algorithms for the identification of μ [COM 03, GRA 03a, KWO 00, WAN 99].

Let us examine now the approach of the second type. The overall scores of objects of $\mathcal{O}$ are replaced by an order relation $\succeq$, which we will suppose to be reflexive and transitive but not necessarily complete. We want to find a capacity μ such that

$$x \succ x' \Leftrightarrow \mathcal{C}_\mu(u_1(x_1), \ldots, u_n(x_n)) > \mathcal{C}_\mu(u_1(x'_1), \ldots, u_n(x'_n))$$

for all $x, x' \in \mathcal{O}$. The set of solutions, when non-empty, is a convex polyhedron. We must reduce its size as much as possible, and eventually choose a particular solution inside. In order to reduce its size, we can add constraints expressing desire for a given type of capacity (e.g. a k-additive capacity, see section 18.7), or some particular behavior of the aggregation function (importance of criteria, interaction: see section 18.7). To choose a solution, Marichal and Roubens [MAR 98b] propose maximizing the discrepancy between the overall scores computed by the model for all the objects in $\mathcal{O}$. Indeed, if the expert thinks that $x \succ x'$, it means that x is *significantly* better than x'; their overall scores must reflect this difference. This can be expressed by the following linear program:

maximize ϵ

subject to

$$\begin{aligned} \epsilon &\geq 0 \\ \mathcal{C}_\mu(u_1(x_1), \ldots, u_n(x_n)) &\geq \mathcal{C}_\mu(u_1(x'_1), \ldots, u_n(x'_n)) + \epsilon, \quad \forall x, x', x \succ x' \\ \mu(A) &\leq \mu(B), \quad \forall A, B \subset N, A \subset B, \end{aligned}$$

fixing $\mu(\emptyset) = 0, \mu(N) = 1$. See [GRA 00b] for a description of this method, an example treated by this approach and a comparison with the error criterion.

Everything described above concerns the Choquet integral with respect to a capacity. We can directly generalize these methods to bipolar models (bicapacities).

18.6.2. *Ordinal case*

We first remark that the specificities of the ordinal case make the approachs based on the error criterion irrelevant, since the notion of difference and therefore also of error or of distance do not make sense on an ordinal scale.

Even if we set $L = [0,1]$, which makes the definition of a mean quadratic error possible, the problem of minimizing the quadratic error when the model is the Sugeno integral is difficult to solv. This is because it involves the operations $\vee, \wedge, \oslash, \oslash$ which are nonlinear and non-differentiable. In this case, only the so-called meta-heuristic methods (genetic algorithms, simulated annealing, etc.) can resolve the problem. There has been some research in this direction, although most applied to the Choquet integral [GRA 03a, VER 03, WAN 99].

756   Decision-making Process

By contrast, the ordinal framework is quite compatible with the approach based on preference representation. A detailed study of this approach has been carried by Rico et al. [RIC 05] in the case where the model is the Sugeno integral with respect to a capacity. We briefly explain the results.

Suppose that the utility functions are known and take values on a unipolar scale L. We can therefore consider that the preference $\succeq$ of the expert is directly expressed on L^n. Let us call the set corresponding to $\mathcal{O}$ $\mathcal{A} \subset L^n$. Let us distinguish two levels of representation:

– strong representation, where the capacity μ must be such that $\mathcal{S}_\mu(a) \geq \mathcal{S}_\mu(b)$ if and only if $a \succeq b$; and

– weak representation, where only inversion is forbidden: $a \succ b$ implies $\mathcal{S}_\mu(a) \geq \mathcal{S}_\mu(b)$.

It appears initially that the weak representation is better suited to the Sugeno integral because of its properties (weak separability).

Suppose that the objects in $\mathcal{A}$ can be partitioned in p indifference classes $[a^1], \ldots, [a^p]$ by $\sim$, the symmetric part of $\succeq$, numbering them so that $a^1 \prec \ldots \prec a^p$. The problem of strong representation amounts to finding p values $\alpha_1 < \alpha_2 < \ldots < \alpha_p$ in L, such that there exists a capacity μ satisfying $\mathcal{S}_\mu(a) = \alpha_i$ for all $a \in [a^i]$, $i = 1, \ldots, p$. For the weak representation problem, it is sufficient to find $p-1$ numbers $0 =: \alpha_0 \leq \alpha_1 \leq \alpha_2 \leq \ldots \leq \alpha_p := 1$ in L such that there exists a capacity μ satisfying $\alpha_{i-1} \leq \mathcal{S}_\mu(a) \leq \alpha_i$ for all $a \in [a^i]$, $i = 1, \ldots, p$.

Denoting a permutation on N which rearranges scores by increasing order by σ as above, the set of capacities such that $\mathcal{S}_\mu(a) = \alpha$ is non-empty if $a_{\sigma(n)} < \alpha$ or $a_{\sigma(1)} > \alpha$, and is the interval $[\check{\mu}^{a,\alpha}, \hat{\mu}^{a,\alpha}]$ where for all $A \neq \varnothing, N$

$$\hat{\mu}^{a,\alpha}(A) := \begin{cases} \alpha & \text{if } A \subset A_{(i_{a,\alpha}^\geq)} \\ \mathbb{1} & \text{otherwise,} \end{cases}$$

$$\check{\mu}^{a,\alpha}(A) := \begin{cases} \alpha & \text{if } A_{(i_{a,\alpha}^\geq)} \subset A \\ \mathbb{0} & \text{otherwise,} \end{cases}$$

with $i_{a,\alpha}^\geq \in N$ such that $a_{(i_{a,\alpha}^\geq - 1)} < \alpha \leq a_{(i_{a,\alpha}^\geq)}$ and $i_{a,\alpha}^\geq \in N$ such that $a_{(i_{a,\alpha}^\geq - 1)} \leq \alpha < a_{(i_{a,\alpha}^\geq)}$. The set of solutions for the strong representation is then the intersection of all these intervals, for all α_i.

Since the set of capacities which are solutions of the problem of the weak representation is empty if and only if there exists i such that $a_{(1)} > \alpha_i$ for some $a \in [a^i]$ or if there exists i such that $b_{(n)} < \alpha_i$ for some $b \in [a^{i+1}]$. Otherwise, there exists an interval $[\check{\mu}, \hat{\mu}]$, with

$$\check{\mu}(A) = \bigvee_{i=1}^{p-1} \bigvee_{a \in [a^{i+1}]} \check{\mu}^{a,\alpha_i}(A), \quad \hat{\mu}(A) = \bigwedge_{i=1}^{p-1} \bigwedge_{a \in [a^i]} \hat{\mu}^{a,\alpha_i}(A).$$

Another approach has been proposed by Roubens [MAR 01b, ROU 01], based on the Choquet integral. We suppose that on each attribute X_i, the subject is able to compare the objects (relation $\succeq_i$). For objects x, y, we set $R_i(x,y) = 1$ if $x_i \succeq_i y_i$, and 0 otherwise. On the other hand, the subject is able to sort the different objects of $\mathcal{O}$ in ordered categories $C_1, \ldots, C_m$, thus defining a partition of $\mathcal{O}$ in $O_1, \ldots, O_m$. For $i < j$, the subject thinks that $x \in O_i$ is at least as good as (in the strict sense) $y \in O_j$. We defines the *net marginal score* of $x \in \mathcal{O}$ on the attribute i by:

$$S_i(x) := \sum_{y \in \mathcal{O}} [R_i(x,y) - R_i(y,x)].$$

We can easily show that S_i is a representation (ordinal measurement) of $\succeq_i$ in the sense that $x_i \succeq_i y_i \Leftrightarrow S_i(x) \geq S_i(y)$. The functions $S_1, \ldots, S_n$ are commensurable, since they all share a common meaning (number of times when x is better, minus the number of times where it is worse). On the other hand we can consider them as ratio scales, since a multiplication by a positive constant does not change the meaning. It is then possible to use $S_1^N, \ldots, S_n^N$, which are the normalized versions between 0 and 1. Marichal and Roubens proposed using these normalized scores in a Choquet integral to compute an overall score for each object, thus $\mathcal{C}_\mu(S_1^N(x), \ldots, S_n^N(x))$.

By doing so, the drawbacks of the Sugeno integral are avoided while respecting the ordinal character of the data. However, the net scores of an object $x \in \mathcal{O}$ strongly depend on all other objects in $\mathcal{O}$, although a score should reflect the intrinsic quality of an object according to a criterion.

Nevertheless, the capacity μ remains to be determined. If we wants the model to correctly separate classes $C_1, \ldots, C_m$, it is sufficient that

$$\mathcal{C}_\mu(S_1^N(x), \ldots, S_n^N(x)) - \mathcal{C}_\mu(S_1^N(x'), \ldots, S_n^N(x')) \geq \epsilon,$$

for all pairs $(x, x') \in O_j \times O_{j-1}, j = 2, \ldots, m$ and $\epsilon > 0$. We can reduce the number of constraints by introducing for each class the sets of dominated and dominating objects:

$$Nd_j := \{x \in O_j \mid \nexists x' \in O_j \setminus \{x\}, x \geq x'\}$$
$$ND_j := \{x \in O_j \mid \nexists x' \in O_j \setminus \{x\}, x' \geq x\}$$

with the relation of dominance defined by $x \geq y$ if and only if $x_i \succeq_i y_i, i = 1, \ldots, n$. It is then sufficient to consider the above constraints for the pairs $(x, x') \in Nd_j \times ND_{j-1}, j = 2, \ldots, m$. These constraints, added to those of monotonicity for μ, form a linear program where the objective function is simply $\max \epsilon$.

The model being entirely determined, we must now be able to evaluate any object x which does not belong to the learning set $\mathcal{O}$ i.e. to classify it in one of the categories $C_1, \ldots, C_m$. The rule is as follows:

$$x \in C_j \text{ if } z_j \leq \mathcal{C}_\mu(S_1^N(x), \ldots, S_n^N(x)) \leq Z_j$$

$$x \in C_j \cup C_{j-1} \text{ if } Z_{j-1} \leq \mathcal{C}_\mu(S_1^N(x), \ldots, S_n^N(x)) \leq z_j$$

where

$$z_j := \min_{x \in Nd_j} \mathcal{C}_\mu(S_1^N(x), \ldots, S_n^N(x))$$

and

$$Z_j := \max_{x \in ND_j} \mathcal{C}_\mu(S_1^N(x), \ldots, S_n^N(x)).$$

Intervals $[z_j, Z_j]$ form an interval order, but not necessarily a quasi-order. For a detailed exploitation of the ranking we refer the reader to [MEY 05].

18.7. Interpretation of the aggregation function

Suppose that the model has been obtained by one of the above identification methods i.e. we know the utility functions and the aggregation function F. The utility functions translate the attributes of the object in quantitative or qualitative scores; they have a clear interpretation for this reason. On the other hand, in the general case where F is a Choquet or a Sugeno integral, it is not easy to have an intuitive understanding of the way F aggregates scores. However, for some applications (section 18.9), this can be of primary importance.

There are numerous ways of interpreting F. The most significant include the following:

– The degrees with which F is close to min ($\wedge$) and to max ($\vee$): these degrees indicate if F aggregates scores in a rather conjunctive way (related by 'and') or disjonctive way (related by 'or'). These degrees were introduced by Dujmović [DUJ 74] for any aggregation function then by Yager [YAG 88] (degrees of *'orness'* and *'andness'*) for the weighted ordered average (OWA). These are Choquet integrals where the capacity is symmetric ($\mu(A)$ depends only on $|A|$).

– The presence of vetoes and of favors [GRA 97a]: we say that criterion i is a veto if for all vectors of scores $(a_1, \ldots, a_n)$, we have $F(a_1, \ldots, a_n) \leq a_i$. If the inequality is reversed, we say that i is a favor criterion. The situations where i is a veto or a favor being rather seldom, Marichal has defined a *degree of veto* (or favor) for the Choquet integral [MAR 03].

– The degree of importance of a criterion: this degree indicates the average weight of a criterion in the model. When F is the weighted sum, this degree of importance is simply the weighting of the concerned criterion. In the case of the Choquet integral, we will show that this degree can be defined as the Shapley value.

– The degree of interaction between criteria: if we take again the example of section 18.3.5 with the 3 objects a, b, c, we have an example of interaction between criteria. The satisfaction of one of them acts on the necessity that the other criterion are also satisfied in order to have a satisfactory overall score. (In this example, it is necessary that the other is satisfied: we then have a *conjunctive* aggregation.) This shows in an intuitive way that the weighted sum cannot represent interaction phenomena between criteria, and that the degrees of 'orness' and 'andness' are linked to interaction as well as the phenomena of veto and favor.

– The degree of improvement power of a criterion: this permits the following question to be answered. For a given object, if we want to significantly improve its overall score, on which criterion should we act first? Alternatively, on average, which criterion should we satisfy to have a high overall score? Although similar to the degree of importance, we will see that this notion is in fact different.

Before going into the details of these various degrees (which we will refer to as *indices*), we stress the fact that often, when the capacity (or any other parameter of a given model F) has been obtained by a learning procedure, it is an optimal solution among a convex set of other optimal solutions. Consequently, the pertinence of the interpretation of the capacity is becoming smaller if this set is large.

18.7.1. *Index of importance of a criterion*

Consider first the case of a unipolar cardinal scale. It seems natural to say that a criterion i is important if for any coalition of criteria A, the overall score of the object $(\mathbf{1}_{A \cup i}, \mathbf{0}_{-(A \cup i)})$ is significantly larger than that of $(\mathbf{1}_A, \mathbf{0}_{-A})$. Consequently, the index of importance is defined as an average value Δ_i of the quantity $\mu(A \cup i) - \mu(A)$, for all $A \subset N \setminus i$. On the other hand, we want the sum of indices on all the criteria to be constant so that comparisons can be made and that the numbering of criteria has no influence on the result. If, moreover, we calculate the average value Δ_i as a weighted sum, then Shapley [SHA 53] has shown that the expression of the index of importance is unique:

$$\phi^\mu(i) := \sum_{K \subset N \setminus i} \frac{(n-k-1)!k!}{n!} [\mu(K \cup i) - \mu(K)] \qquad (18.22)$$

where $k := |K|$ (we omit the superindex μ if there is no ambiguity). We have $\sum_{i=1}^n \phi(i) = \mu(N) = 1$ and, if μ is additive, then $\phi(i) = \mu(\{i\})$.

We can adapt this notion to the case of a bipolar scale. We say that a criterion i is important if each time we add it to a coalition of satisfied criteria or remove it from a coalition of unsatisfied criteria, we get a significant improvement of the overall score. In terms of bicapacities, this means that the index of importance should be an average of the quantities $v(A \cup i, B) - v(A, B)$ and $v(A, B) - v(A, B \cup i)$ on each $(A, B) \in \mathcal{Q}(N \setminus i)$. Summing these two expressions, we obtain $v(A \cup i, B) - v(A, B \cup i)$, where the term in which i has a neutral value has disappeared. In [GRA 02c, LAB 03a], it is this last expression which is chosen, making the assumption that the index of importance must not depend on situations where i is neutral. Felsenthal and Machover [FEL 97] take the other route and keep the two expressions in the average separated; see a detailed discussion of this point in [LAB 03c].

Regarding the capacities, under an assumption of linearity it is sufficient to impose symmetry conditions (no influence of the numbering of criteria) and normalization (the sum of indices on all the criteria is constant) to obtain a unique expression of the importance index, also called the Shapley importance index:

$$\phi^v(i) = \sum_{K \subset N \setminus \{i\}} \frac{(n-k-1)!k!}{n!} [v(K \cup \{i\}, N \setminus (K \cup \{i\})) - v(K, N \setminus K)].$$

(18.23)

This expression is very similar to the original i.e. equation (18.22). The property of normalization is written $\sum_{i=1}^{n} \phi(i) = v(N, \emptyset) - v(\emptyset, N) = 2$. If v is of the CPT type with $v(A, B) := \mu^+(A) - \mu^-(B)$, then $\phi^v(i) = \phi^{\mu^+}(i) + \phi^{\mu^-}(i)$.

If we work in an ordinal framework, then μ and v take their values on an ordinal scale and the above definitions no longer have any meaning. Definitions similar to that used for capacities, adapted to the ordinal case, have been proposed by the author [GRA 97c]. However, although they maintain similar properties, their interpretation in practice remains questionable.

18.7.2. *Index of interaction*

Let us give a precise definition of interaction. Consider first the case $n = 2$ and the four following objects (see Figure 18.4):
- $x = (\mathbf{0}_1, \mathbf{0}_2)$;
- $y = (\mathbf{1}_1, \mathbf{0}_2)$;
- $z = (\mathbf{0}_1, \mathbf{1}_2)$; and
- $t = (\mathbf{1}_1, \mathbf{1}_2)$

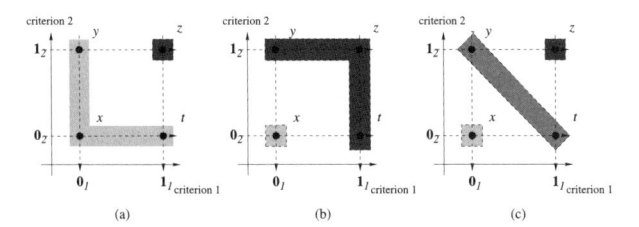

Figure 18.4. *Different cases of interaction*

It is clear that t is better than x, but the preference of the other pairs depends on the subject. Because of the condition of dominance, we have the following two extreme situations:

1) We set $\mu(\{1\}) = \mu(\{2\}) = 0$, which amounts to the preference $x \sim y \sim z$ (Figure 18.4(a)). This means that for the subject, the two criteria must be satisfied to have a satisfactory object, and the satisfaction of only one of the two is not enough. We say that the criteria are *complementary*.

2) We set $\mu(\{1\}) = \mu(\{2\}) = 1$, which amounts to the preference $y \sim z \sim t$ (Figure 18.4(b)). In this case, the subject thinks that the satisfaction of one of the two criteria is sufficient to have a satisfactory object, and satisfying both criteria is not rewarding. We say that the criteria are *substitutive*.

The criteria are not independent in these two situations, in the sense that the satisfaction of one of them influences the usefulness of the other to have a satisfactory object (necessary in the first case, useless in the second). We say that there is *interaction* between the criteria.

A situation without interaction is such that the satisfaction of each criterion brings its own contribution to the overall satisfaction, which can be expressed:

$$\mu(\{1,2\}) = \mu(\{1\}) + \mu(\{2\}) \tag{18.24}$$

(additivity) (see Figure 18.4(c)). In situation (1), we have $\mu(\{1,2\}) > \mu(\{1\}) + \mu(\{2\})$ with the reverse inequality for situation (2). This suggests that the interaction I_{12} between criteria (1) and (2) should be defined by:

$$I_{12}^{\mu} := \mu(\{1,2\}) - \mu(\{1\}) - \mu(\{2\}) + \mu(\emptyset). \tag{18.25}$$

We remark that this expression is nothing other tha the difference between the sum of overall scores of objects on the diagonal (where there is strict dominance), and the sum of scores on the antidiagonal (where there is no relation of dominance). The interaction is positive when the criteria are complementary, and negative when they are substitutive.

In the case of more than two criteria, the definition of the interaction is similar to that of the Shapley index, i.e. all coalitions of N must be taken into account. The following definition has been proposed by Murofushi and Soneda [MUR 93] for a pair of criteria i, j:

$$I_{ij}^{\mu} := \sum_{K \subset N \setminus \{i,j\}} \frac{(n-k-2)!k!}{(n-1)!} [\mu(K \cup \{i,j\}) - \mu(K \cup \{i\}) - \mu(K \cup \{j\}) + \mu(K)]. \quad (18.26)$$

We have $I_{ij} > 0$ (respectively, $< 0, = 0$) for complementary criteria (respectively, substitutive, independent). The definition of this index was extended by the author to any coalition of criteria $\varnothing \neq A \subset N$ [GRA 97b]:

$$I^{\mu}(A) := \sum_{K \subset N \setminus A} \frac{(n-k-|A|)!k!}{(n-|A|+1)!} \sum_{L \subset A} (-1)^{|A|-|L|} \mu(K \cup L), \forall A \subset N, A \neq \varnothing. \quad (18.27)$$

We note that we have $I_{ij} = I(\{i,j\})$ and also $I(\{i\}) = \phi(i)$, the Shapley importance index. For this reason, we call function I the *Shapley interaction index*. It is easy to see that, when the capacity is additive, we have $I(A) = 0$ for all A such that $|A| > 1$. Lastly, let us note that I has been axiomatized by Grabisch and Roubens [GRA 99] in a way similar to the Shapley importance index. Another axiomatization has been proposed by Fujimoto [FUJ 03].

We have seen that the interaction index contains as a particular case the Shapley importance index. In fact, it is possible to obtain the interaction index in a recursive way from the Shapley importance index, considering subproblems with less criteria [GRA 99]. For I_{ij}^{μ}, this relation reads:

$$I_{ij}^{\mu} = \phi^{\mu^{[ij]}}([ij]) - \phi^{\mu_{N \setminus i}}(j) - \phi^{\mu_{N \setminus j}}(i), \quad (18.28)$$

where $[ij]$ is a fictive criterion (i and j taken together), $\mu^{[ij]} : \mathcal{P}((N \setminus \{i,j\}) \cup \{[ij]\}) \longrightarrow [0,1]$, where $\mu^{[ij]}(A) := \mu((A \setminus [ij]) \cup \{i,j\})$ if $A \ni [ij]$ and $\mu(A)$ otherwise and $\mu_{N \setminus i}$ is the restriction of μ to $N \setminus i$.

Let us examine now how this concept can be generalized to the case of bicapacities. A first way would be to proceed recursively from the Shapley importance index (equation (18.23)) using a formula similar to equation (18.28) [GRA 02d]. However, because of bipolarity, it seems more natural to distinguish the satisfied criteria from the unsatisfied ones. Denoting the coalitions of satisfied and unsatisfied criteria by A, B, we are led to an interaction index with two arguments $I_{A,B}$ (called *bi-interaction* in [GRA 02d]). Let us detail this in the case $n = 2$, following the same argument as for capacities. Because of bipolarity, we now have nine ternary objects (see Figure 18.5).

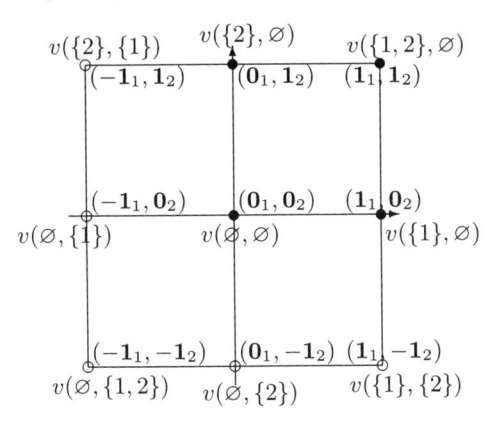

Figure 18.5. *Ternary objects for $n = 2$*

In each subsquare of $[-1, 1]^2$, it is sufficient to apply the definition of the classical interaction index given by equation (18.24). We obtain:

$$I_{\{1,2\},\varnothing} := v(\{1,2\},\varnothing) - v(\{1\},\varnothing) - v(\{2\},\varnothing) + v(\varnothing,\varnothing) \qquad (18.29)$$
$$I_{\varnothing,\{1,2\}} := v(\varnothing,\varnothing) - v(\varnothing,\{1\}) - v(\varnothing,\{2\}) + v(\varnothing,\{1,2\})$$
$$I_{1,2} := v(\{1\},\varnothing) - v(\varnothing,\varnothing) - v(\{1\},\{2\}) + v(\varnothing,\{2\})$$
$$I_{2,1} := v(\{2\},\varnothing) - v(\{2\},\{1\}) - v(\varnothing,\varnothing) + v(\varnothing,\{1\}).$$

Based on this principle, we can show that the general formula is:

$$I^v(A,B) = \sum_{K \subset N \setminus (A \cup B)} \frac{(n-a-b-k)!k!}{(n-a-b+1)!} \Delta_{A,B} v(K, N \setminus (A \cup K)),$$

with $\Delta_{A,B} v(S,T) := \sum_{K \subset A, L \subset B} (-1)^{(a-k)+(b-l)} v(S \cup K, T \setminus (K \cup L))$. We can check that the Shapley importance index for bicapacities reads:

$$\phi(i) = I_{i,\varnothing} + I_{\varnothing,i}.$$

In fact, we recover with $I_{i,\varnothing}$ and $I_{\varnothing,i}$ the averages of quantities $v(A \cup i, B) - v(A, B)$ and $v(A, B) - v(A, B \cup i)$ introduced in section 18.7.1, and which represent an index for the satisfied criteria and an index for the unsatisfied criteria, respectively.

If v is of the CPT type with $v(S,T) := \mu^+(S) - \mu^-(T)$, the interaction can be expressed in the following form:

1) $I^v_{S,T} = 0$ except if $S = \varnothing$ or $T = \varnothing$.

2) Denoting by I^{μ_i} the interaction index of the capacity μ_i, we have:

$$I^v_{S,\varnothing} = I^{\mu^+}(S), \quad \forall \varnothing \neq S \subseteq N$$

$$I^v_{\varnothing,T} = \overline{I^{\mu^-}}(T), \quad \forall T \subseteq N.$$

Property (1) clearly expresses the fact that for a CPT model, there is no interaction between the positive and negative parts. Property (2) shows the relation between the interaction for bicapacities and for capacities. For capacities there also exists an ordinal counterpart of the interaction [GRA 97c] which has the same drawbacks as the ordinal importance index.

18.7.3. *Maximum improving index*

The aim of this index is to quantify the interest we have in improving scores on a coalition A of criteria, in order to obtain a maximal effect on the overall score taken in average on all fictive objects (in fact, all vectors of scores). An axiomatic construction of this index has been proposed by Labreuche and Grabisch [GRA 01c], of which we give a brief description. For $A \subset N$, let us denote this index by $W_A(F)$, viewed as a functional assigning a real number to an aggregation function F.

We suppose first that W_A is continuous and linear. Consider a family of *threshold* aggregation functions, denoted by $\mathbf{1}_\alpha : [0,1]^n \longrightarrow \{0,1\}$, $\alpha \in [0,1]^n$ and defined for all $x \in [0,1]^n$ by:

$$\mathbf{1}_\alpha(x) = \begin{cases} 1, & \text{if } x_i \geq \alpha_i, \quad i=1,\ldots,n \\ 0, & \text{otherwise.} \end{cases}$$

Intuitively, $W_A(\mathbf{1}_\alpha)$ should be proportional to the number of vectors in $[0,1]^n$ whose overall score goes from 0 to 1 if only scores of criteria in A are improved. More precisely, let us define S_α as the set of situations $(x,y) \in [0,1]^n \times [0,1]^n$ such that $y \geq x$, x and y are identical on $N \setminus A$. Their scores are $\mathbf{1}_\alpha(x) = 0$ and $\mathbf{1}_\alpha(y) = 1$, respectively. Then $W_A(\mathbf{1}_\alpha)$ is proportional to the Lebesgue measure of S_α.

A normalization axiom remains to be added, saying that when F is the weighted sum $\sum_{i=1}^n \lambda_i x_i$, $W_A(F) = \sum_{i \in A} \lambda_i$. These four axioms determine the index in a unique way, which reads:

$$W_A(F) = 3 \cdot 2^{|A|} \int_{x \in [0,1]^n} \int_{y_A \in [x_A, 1]} \left[F(y_A, x_{A^c}) - F(x) \right] dx\, dy_A$$

with the usual notation. $y_A \in [x_A, 1]$ means that $y_i \in [x_i, 1]$ for all $i \in A$. When F is the Choquet integral, we get for $A = \{i\}$:

$$W_i(\mathcal{C}_\mu) = 6 \sum_{K \subset N \setminus i} \frac{(n-k)!(k+1)!}{(n+2)!}[\mu(K \cup i) - \mu(K)],$$

which is very similar to the Shapley index. We can show that, in general, $W_i(\mathcal{C}_\mu) \leq 3\phi^\mu(i)$. For $A = \{i, j\}$ we get:

$$W_{ij}(F) = W_i(F) + W_j(F),$$

but this additivity property is no longer true as soon as $|A| > 2$.

It is possible to construct an index which is proper to a particular object in a similar way, and not an average over all possible objects [LAB 04].

18.7.4. *Conjunction and disjunction indices*

Adapting a definition of Dujmović [DUJ 74], Marichal [MAR 98a, MAR 03] proposed the following general definition for the conjunction and disjunction indices of the Choquet integral with respect to a capacity μ:

$$\text{conj}_\mu := \frac{E(\max) - E(\mathcal{C}_\mu)}{E(\max) - E(\min)}$$

$$\text{disj}_\mu := \frac{E(\mathcal{C}_\mu) - E(\min)}{E(\max) - E(\min)}$$

where $E(F)$ is the average value of an aggregation function F on the unit hypercube:

$$E(F) := \int_{[0,1]^n} F(x)dx.$$

Recall that the minimum and the maximum are the limit cases of the Choquet integral. These indices therefore express a normalized distance to these bounds. Their definitions can be easily extended to other aggregation functions.

We can show that these indices generalize those introduced by Yager for ordered weighted averages [YAG 88].

18.7.5. *Veto and index of veto*

We have seen that i is a veto criterion (respectively, favor criterion) if $F(a_1, \ldots, a_n) \leq a_i$ (respectively, $\geq a_i$) for all vectors of scores. When F is the Choquet integral with respect to a capacity μ, it is easy to show that i is a veto if and only if μ is such that $\mu(A) = 0$ when $A \not\ni i$. It can also be shown that i is a veto implies that interaction I_{ij} is positive $\forall j \neq i$ [GRA 97a]. Similarly, i is a favor criterion is equivalent to $\mu(A) = 1$ when $i \in A$, which also implies that $I_{ij} \leq 0 \ \forall j \neq i$.

As it is very uncommon to find vetoes and favors in the above sense, Marichal has proposed veto and favor indices valued on $[0, 1]$ defined as follows [MAR 98a, MAR 03]:

$$\text{veto}_\mu(i) := 1 - \frac{1}{n-1} \sum_{T \subset N \setminus i} \frac{(n-t-1)!t!}{(n-1)!} \mu(T)$$

$$\text{favor}(i) := \frac{1}{n-1} \sum_{T \subset N \setminus i} \frac{(n-t-1)!t!}{(n-1)!} \mu(T \cup i) - \frac{1}{n-1}.$$

These definitions, which may look arbitrary, are in fact uniquely determined by four axioms. Regarding the Shapley index, we impose that these indices are linear in terms of μ and symmetric in the sense that they are insensitive to a renumbering of the criteria. We impose on the other hand that the veto index of the minimum operator is equal to 1, similarly for the favor index of the maximum. Lastly, a normalization condition says that if all criteria have the same veto index (respectively, favor index), then this value should coincide with the conjunction index (respectively, disjunction index).

We have the following properties:

$$\frac{1}{n} \sum_{i=1}^{n} \text{veto}_\mu(i) = \text{conj}_\mu$$

$$\frac{1}{n} \sum_{i=1}^{n} \text{favor}_\mu(i) = \text{disj}_\mu.$$

18.8. Particular families of capacities and bicapacities

We have seen in the preceding sections that capacities and bicapacities are powerful and very general means of constructing multicriteria models of evaluation. However, this richness has a cost which is non-negligible since the complexity of these models is exponential (of the order of 2^n for capacities and 3^n for bicapacities). The question then arises if it would be possible to have models based on capacities defined by less than 2^n coefficients, but keeping as far as possible the performances and richness of capacities. A first family of capacities of this type is that of *decomposable measures* [DUB 82, WEB 84] which include λ-measures of Sugeno [SUG 74], which are very often used in practice. These capacities are defined by a function on N

analogous to a density, and which need only $n-1$ coefficients. However, such models based on decomposable capacities have a limited power of modeling, since the interaction index I_{ij} always has the same sign for all i, j.

It is possible to generalize this concept to bicapacities [GRA 02c]. A more suitable family is that of k-additive capacities.

Definition 18.5. [GRA 97b] Let $k \in \{1, \ldots, n-1\}$. A capacity μ is said to be k-*additive* if $I(A) = 0$ when $|A| > k$, and there exists $A \subset N$ with exactly k elements such that $I(A) \neq 0$.

From the properties of the interaction index, a 1-additive capacity is in fact an additive capacity. Generally, k-additive capacity needs $1 + n + \binom{n}{2} + \ldots + \binom{n}{k} - 2$ coefficients to be defined.

A good compromise between richness and complexity is offered by 2-additive capacities, which need only $\frac{n(n+1)}{2} - 1$ coefficients since they permit the representation of interaction between two criteria (usually sufficient in practice). Experimentally, it is observed that the difference in precision between a 2-additive model and a general model is small [GRA 02b].

When the measure is 2-additive, it is possible to express the Choquet integral with I instead of μ [GRA 97a]:

$$\mathcal{C}_\mu(a_1, \ldots, a_n) = \sum_{I_{ij}>0} (a_i \wedge a_j) I_{ij} + \sum_{I_{ij}<0} (a_i \vee a_j) |I_{ij}|$$

$$+ \sum_{i=1}^{n} a_i \left(\phi_i - \frac{1}{2} \sum_{j \neq i} |I_{ij}| \right), \quad \forall a \in [0,1]^n, \quad (18.30)$$

for all $(a_1, \ldots, a_n) \in \mathbb{R}^n_+$. Moreover, we have $\phi_i - \frac{1}{2} \sum_{j \neq i} |I_{ij}| \geq 0$ for all i. This shows that the Choquet integral for 2-additive measures is a sum of a conjunctive part (corresponding to positive interactions), a disjunctive part (negative interactions) and a linear part (Shapley importance index). All this corresponds to the interpretation of the interaction that we have given. This sum is convex since $\sum_{i=1}^{n} \phi_i = 1$. The Choquet integral is therefore the convex closure of all the conjunctions and disjunctions of pairs of criteria and of all the dictators.

The concept of k-additive bicapacity can be defined in an analogous way; see [GRA 02c].

Definition 18.6. A bicapacity is said to be k-*additive* for k in $\{1, \ldots, n-1\}$ if its interaction index is such that $I_{A,B} = 0$ when $|B| < n-k$ and there exists (A, B) with $|B| = n-k$ such that $I_{A,B} \neq 0$.

A bicapacity needs $1 + 2\binom{n}{n-1} + 2^2\binom{n}{n-2} + \ldots + 2^k\binom{n}{n-k} - 3$ coefficients to be defined. For a 2-additive bicapacity, the number of coefficients is $2n^2 - 3$. The expression of the Choquet integral for a 2-additive bicapacity is however not easy [GRA 03d] and therefore not useful.

We also mention a third family of capacities introduced by Miranda and Grabisch [MIR 02] called *p-symmetric capacities*. The idea is to generalize the notion of symmetric measure (section 18.4), considering a partition $\{A_1, \ldots, A_p\}$ of N into *subsets of indifference*. These are sets such that $\mu(A)$ does not depend on $|A|$, for all $A \subset A_i$. A symmetric capacity is therefore a 1-symmetric capacity, where the partition is N. The number of coefficients for defining a p-symmetric capacity is $\prod_{i=1}^{p}(|A_i| + 1) - 2$.

This concept can be generalized to bicapacities [MIR 03].

18.9. Applications

Before briefly presenting some applications, it is worthwhile indicating several general facts about them. The question is the following: why construct a mathematical model of subjective evaluation? If we want to know how a new product is received by the consumer, why not evaluate it or test it on an individual or a population of individuals? If we want to know if a project or a candidate is good, why it is not sufficient to evaluate it by an expert?

Among the possible answers, let us give the most significant:

– The mathematical model allows an automatic or semi-automatic treatment in case of numerous data. Moreover, in this case, it can ensure a stability in time that a human expert would be unable to maintain.

– The mathematical model can predict the result of a test of a new product, without performing costly tests on a panel of consumers.

– The mathematical model allows the analysis of the process of evaluation. For an industry launching a new product on the market, it is more important to know *why* the product has had (will have) success, rather than to know whether it will have success. We provided tools for such an analysis in section 18.7: importance of criteria, interaction, conjunctive or disjunctive behavior, vetoes, etc.

– Lastly, the mathematical model allows an axiomatic approach. These axioms can be chosen and considered as being rational according to the situations. They determine a model or a family of models which will suit the problem.

We now cite several applications based on the presented methodology. The first examples using the Choquet or the Sugeno integral, although very empirical in nature, come from Japan. We refer the reader to [GRA 95b] for a presentation of them.

Several more recent examples can be found in [GRA 00a], among which an application on the evaluation of motorcycles by Kwon and Sugeno (see also [SUG 95]). Again in Japan, Nakamori has performed a certain number of studies on the evaluation of the environnement [NAK 95] and on the impression of space in a living room [NAK 00].

Mauris *et al.* have realized applications in project management aiding [MON 02], and evaluation of a web site [BÜY 03]. In the domain of environnement, Verkeyn *et al.* have applied the Sugeno integral to the evaluation of noise annoyance [VER 03].

Lastly, the author has also realized several applications, in particular for the evaluation of cosmetics [GRA 97d], of mental workload and of comfort in sitting position [GRA 02b]. We end this section by detailing this last application, in order to show how the analysis of the model can be used.

The problem is to measure the sensation of discomfort felt on a car seat, after having remained still for a long time. The human body is divided in 38 zones, and we consider 5 types of discomfort called: vibratory, overheating, pins and needles, hard point and contraction. The intensity of discomfort goes from 0 (no discomfort) to 10 (unbearable). The aim is to explain the overall sensation of discomfort felt, with local discomforts (zones and type of discomfort). Eleven subjects, two seats and two modes (with or without vibration of the road) have been used. In order to maintain the number of descriptors to a reasonable level because of the low number of data, two types of models have been constructed:

1) The descriptors are the 5 types of discomfort and we take an average of all zones of the body.

2) The descriptors are 5 macro-zones of the body (arm, legs, upper back, lower back, chest) and we take an average of the types of discomfort.

We have obtained the following two models (Choquet integral with respect to a 2-additive capacity):

1) Model by type of discomfort (variables are the levels of discomfort on the attributes: vibratory, overheating, pins and needles, hard point and contraction; e is the overall level of discomfort, with precision 10^{-3}).

$$e = 0.022(a_2 \wedge a_3) + 0.337(a_2 \vee a_4) + 0.256(a_2 \vee a_5)$$
$$+ 0.163(a_3 \vee a_5) + 0.142(a_4 \vee a_5) + 0.003(a_1 \vee a_3) + 0.028a_3.$$

2) Model by macro-zones (variables are the levels of discomfort on macro-zones legs, arms, lower back, upper back and chest; e is the overall level of discomfort, with

precision 10^{-3}).

$$e = 0.517(a_2 \vee a_4) + 0.134(a_4 \vee a_5) + 0.122(a_2 \vee a_3)$$
$$+ 0.095(a_1 \vee a_3) + 0.051(a_3 \vee a_4) + 0.039(a_1 \vee a_5) + 0.043a_5.$$

We can see that the linear part of these models is very small. The Shapley importance indices and the interaction indices are as listed in Tables 18.1 and 18.2.

Shapley index($\times 5$)		Interaction $I(i,j)$		
Vibratory	0.004897	$I(1,2)$ -0.000	$I(2,4)$	-0.337
Overheating	1.538209	$I(1,3)$ -0.002	$I(2,5)$	-0.256
Pins and needles	0.732960	$I(1,4)$ -0.000	$I(3,4)$	-0.050
Hard point	1.321827	$I(1,5)$ -0.000	$I(3,5)$	-0.163
Contraction	1.402106	$I(2,3)$ 0.022	$I(4,5)$	-0.142

Table 18.1. *Model by type of discomfort*

Shapley index ($\times 5$)		Interaction $I(i,j)$		
Legs	0.333036	$I(1,2)$ -0.000	$I(2,4)$	-0.517
Arms	1.599255	$I(1,3)$ -0.095	$I(2,5)$	-0.000
Lower back	0.669032	$I(1,4)$ -0.000	$I(3,4)$	-0.051
Opper back	1.755150	$I(1,5)$ -0.039	$I(3,5)$	-0.000
Chest	0.643526	$I(2,3)$ -0.122	$I(4,5)$	-0.134

Table 18.2. *Model by macro-zones*

These results can be interpreted as follows:

– Model by type of discomfort: the most important criteria are overheating, contraction and hard point. Criterion vibratory does not play any role in the overall discomfort. On the whole, the model is of the disjunctive type. We can summarize: 'It is sufficient that one discomfort of the type overheating, contraction or hard point is present for an overall discomfort to be felt. No sensation of discomfort can alleviate another sensation of discomfort.'

– Model by macro-zones: the most important macro-zones are the upper back and the arms, and then the lower back. Legs have little influence in the model, which is mainly expressed by a disjunction between discomforts in the upper back and the arms, the other pairs of criteria being more or less independent. This can be summarized: 'It is sufficient that one discomfort is felt in the arms or the upper back for an overall discomfort to be felt. Discomfort sensations appearing in other macro-zones (especially the lower back) will reinforce the overall sensation of discomfort.'

These results can be further analyzed and exploited for the design of car seats.

18.10. Conclusion

We have attempted to give a constructive and overall view of methods dealing with subjective evaluation based on a multicriteria approach. As we have emphasized, these approachs are a complement of the tools of data analysis, and can only be used if scores or degrees of satisfaction can be defined on the attributes. The reader has perhaps seen some similarity with Principal Component Analysis (PCA) which determines the most important axes, and the importance index of Shapley or the interaction. These indices effectively aim to detect the most important attributes in the model and to understand how they interact. Our indices are more useful in practice, however, as (in the case of ACP) axes which are found are in fact linear combinations of attributes, making their interpretation difficult. In contrast, the methods that we propose use the attributes without changing them.

18.11. Bibliography

[BAN 94] BANA E COSTA C., VANSNICK J., "A theoretical framework for Measuring Attractiveness by a Categorical Based Evaluation TecHnique (MACBETH)", *Proceedings of XIth International Conference on MultiCriteria Decision Making*, Coimbra, Portugal, p. 15–24, August 1994.

[BAN 97] BANA E COSTA C., VANSNICK J., "Applications of the MACBETH approach in the framework of an additive aggregation model", *Journal of Multicriteria Decision Analysis*, vol. 6, p. 107–114, 1997.

[BAN 99] BANA E COSTA C., VANSNICK J., "The MACBETH approach: basic ideas, software and an application", MESKENS N., ROUBENS M., Eds., *Advances in Decision Analysis*, p. 131–157, Kluwer Academic Publishers, 1999.

[BÜY 03] BÜYÜKÖZKAN G., MAURIS G., FEYZIOĞLU O., BERRAH L., "Providing elucidations of web site evaluation based on a multi–criteria aggregation with the Choquet integral", *International Fuzzy Systems Association World Congress (IFSA 2003)*, Istanbul, Turkey, p. 131–134, June 2003.

[CAC 97] CACIOPPO J., GARDNER W., BERNTSON G., "Beyond bipolar conceptualizations and measures: the case of attitudes and evaluative space", *Personality and Social Psychology Review*, vol. 1, num. 1, p. 3–25, 1997.

[CHA 00] CHATEAUNEUF A., COHEN M., "Choquet expected utility model: a new approach to individual behavior under uncertainty and to social welfare", GRABISCH M., MUROFUSHI T., SUGENO M., Eds., *Fuzzy Measures and Integrals – Theory and Applications*, p. 289–313, Physica Verlag, 2000.

[CHO 53] CHOQUET G., "Theory of capacities", *Annales de l'Institut Fourier*, vol. 5, p. 131–295, 1953.

[COM 03] COMBARRO E., MIRANDA P., "A genetic algorithm for the identification of fuzzy measures from sample data", *International Fuzzy Systems Association World Congress (IFSA 2003)*, Istanbul, Turkey, p. 163–166, June 2003.

[DEN 94] DENNEBERG D., *Non-Additive Measure and Integral*, Kluwer Academic, Heidelberg, 1994.

[DEN 00] DENNEBERG D., "Non-additive measure and integral, basic concepts and their role for applications", GRABISCH M., MUROFUSHI T., SUGENO M., Eds., *Fuzzy Measures and Integrals – Theory and Applications*, p. 42–69, Physica Verlag, Heidelberg, 2000.

[DEN 04] DENNEBERG D., GRABISCH M., "Measure and integral with purely ordinal scales", *Journal of Mathematical Psychology*, vol. 48, p. 15–27, 2004.

[DUB 82] DUBOIS D., PRADE H., "A class of fuzzy measures based on triangular norms", *International Journal of General Systems*, vol. 8, p. 43–61, 1982.

[DUB 00] DUBOIS D., PRADE H., SABBADIN R., "Qualitative decision theory with Sugeno integrals", GRABISCH M., MUROFUSHI T., SUGENO M., Eds., *Fuzzy Measures and Integrals – Theory and Applications*, p. 314–332, Physica Verlag, Heidelberg, 2000.

[DUB 01a] DUBOIS D., MARICHAL J.-L., PRADE H., ROUBENS M., SABBADIN R., "The use of the discrete Sugeno integral in decision making: a survey", *International Journal of Uncertainty, Fuzziness and Knowledge-Based Systems*, vol. 9, num. 5, p. 539–561, 2001.

[DUB 01b] DUBOIS D., PRADE H., SABBADIN R., "Decision-theoretic foundations of qualitative possibility theory", *European Journal of Operational Research*, vol. 128, p. 459–478, 2001.

[DUJ 74] DUJMOVIĆ J., "Weighted conjunctive and disjunctive means and their application in system evaluation", *Univ. Beograd. Publ. Elektrotechn. Fak.*, p. 147–158, 1974.

[ESC 88] ESCOFIER B., PAGES J., *Analyses factorielles simples et multiples*, Dunod, Paris, 1988.

[FEL 97] FELSENTHAL D., MACHOVER M., "Ternary voting games", *International Journal of Game Theory*, vol. 26, p. 335–351, 1997.

[FOD 00] FODOR J., "Smooth associative operations on finite ordinal scales", *IEEE Transactions on Fuzzy Systems*, vol. 8, num. 6, p. 791–795, 2000.

[FUJ 03] FUJIMOTO K., "An axiomatic approach to the Stieltjes integral representations of cardinal-probabilistic interaction indices", *Proceedings of the 10th IFSA (International Fuzzy Systems Association) World Congress*, Istanbul, Turkey, p. 147–150, June 2003.

[GRA 95a] GRABISCH M., "A new algorithm for identifying fuzzy measures and its application to pattern recognition", *International Joint Conference of the 4th IEEE International Conference on Fuzzy Systems and the 2nd International Fuzzy Engineering Symposium*, Yokohama, Japan, p. 145–150, March 1995.

[GRA 95b] GRABISCH M., NGUYEN H., WALKER E., *Fundamentals of Uncertainty Calculi, with Applications to Fuzzy Inference*, Kluwer Academic, Dordrecht, 1995.

[GRA 96] GRABISCH M., "The application of fuzzy integrals in multicriteria decision making", *European Journal of Operational Research*, vol. 89, p. 445–456, 1996.

[GRA 97a] GRABISCH M., "Alternative representations of discrete fuzzy measures for decision making", *International Journal of Uncertainty, Fuzziness, and Knowledge Based Systems*, vol. 5, p. 587–607, 1997.

[GRA 97b] GRABISCH M., "k-order additive discrete fuzzy measures and their representation", *Fuzzy Sets and Systems*, vol. 92, p. 167–189, 1997.

[GRA 97c] GRABISCH M., "On the representation of k-decomposable measures", *7th IFSA World Congress*, Prague, Czech Republic, p. 478–483, June 1997.

[GRA 97d] GRABISCH M., BARET J., LARNICOL M., "Analysis of interaction between criteria by fuzzy measure and its application to cosmetics", *International Conference on Methods and Applications of Multicriteria Decision Making*, Mons, Belgium, p. 22–25, May 1997.

[GRA 99] GRABISCH M., ROUBENS M., "An Axiomatic Approach to the Concept of Interaction among Players in Cooperative Games", *International Journal of Game Theory*, vol. 28, p. 547–565, 1999.

[GRA 00a] GRABISCH M., MUROFUSHI T., SUGENO M., *Fuzzy Measures and Integrals. Theory and Applications (edited volume)*, Studies in Fuzziness, Physica Verlag, 2000.

[GRA 00b] GRABISCH M., ROUBENS M., "Application of the Choquet integral in multicriteria decision making", GRABISCH M., MUROFUSHI T., SUGENO M., Eds., *Fuzzy Measures and Integrals – Theory and Applications*, p. 348–374, Physica Verlag, Heidelberg, 2000.

[GRA 01a] GRABISCH M., "On preference representation on an ordinal scale", BENFERHAT S., BESNARD P., Eds., *6th European Conference on Symbolic and Quantitative Approaches to Reasoning with Uncertainty (ECSQUARU'2001)*, Lecture Notes in Computer Science, Toulouse, France, Springer Verlag, p. 18–28, September 2001.

[GRA 01b] GRABISCH M., DIA S., LABREUCHE C., "A multicriteria decision making framework in ordinal context based on Sugeno integral", *Joint 9th IFSA World Congress and 20th NAFIPS International Conference*, Vancouver, Canada, July 2001.

[GRA 01c] GRABISCH M., LABREUCHE C., "How to improve acts: an alternative representation of the importance of criteria in MCDM", *International Journal of Uncertainty, Fuzziness, and Knowledge-Based Systems*, vol. 9, num. 2, p. 145–157, 2001.

[GRA 02a] GRABISCH M., "The Möbius function on symmetric ordered structures and its application to capacities and integrals", *9th International Conference on Information Proceedings of and Management of Uncertainty in Knowledge-Based systems (IPMU'2002)*, Annecy, France, p. 755–762, July 2002.

[GRA 02b] GRABISCH M., DUCHÊNE J., LINO F., PERNY P., "Subjective evaluation of discomfort in sitting position", *Fuzzy Optimization and Decision Making*, vol. 1, num. 3, p. 287–312, 2002.

[GRA 02c] GRABISCH M., LABREUCHE C., "Bi-capacities", *Joint International Conference on Soft Computing and Intelligent Systems and 3rd International Symp. on Advanced Intelligent Systems*, Tsukuba, Japan, October 2002.

[GRA 02d] GRABISCH M., LABREUCHE C., "Bi-capacities for decision making on bipolar scales", *EUROFUSE Workshop on Informations Systems*, Varenna, Italy, p. 185–190, September 2002.

[GRA 03a] GRABISCH M., "Modelling data by the Choquet integral", TORRA V., Ed., *Information fusion in data mining*, p. 135–148, Physica Verlag, Berlin, Heidelberg, 2003.

[GRA 03b] GRABISCH M., "The symmetric Sugeno integral", *Fuzzy Sets and Systems*, vol. 139, p. 473–490, 2003.

[GRA 03c] GRABISCH M., LABREUCHE C., Bi-capacities, Report num. 2003/002, LIP6, UPMC, http://www.lip6.fr/reports/lip6.2003.002.html, 2003.

[GRA 03d] GRABISCH M., LABREUCHE C., "The Choquet integral for 2-additive bi-capacities", *3rd International Conference of the European Society for Fuzzy Logic and Technology (EUSFLAT 2003)*, Zittau, Germany, p. 300–303, September 2003.

[GRA 03e] GRABISCH M., LABREUCHE C., VANSNICK J., "On the extension of pseudo-Boolean functions for the aggregation of interacting bipolar criteria", *European Journal of Operational Research*, vol. 148, p. 28–47, 2003.

[GRA 04a] GRABISCH M., "The Möbius function on symmetric ordered structures and its application to capacities on finite sets", *Discrete Mathematics*, vol. 287, num. 1–3, p. 17–34, 2004.

[GRA 04b] GRABISCH M., LABREUCHE C., "Fuzzy measures and integrals in MCDA", FIGUEIRA J., GRECO S., EHRGOTT M., Eds., *Multiple Criteria Decision Analysis*, p. 563–608, Kluwer Academic Publishers, New York, 2004.

[GRE 02] GRECO S., MATARAZZO B., SLOWINSKI R., "Bipolar Sugeno and Choquet integrals", *EUROFUSE Workshop on Informations Systems*, Varenna, Italy, p. 191–196, September 2002.

[HAL 50] HALMOS P., *Measure Theory*, Springer Verlag, New York, 1950.

[HSE 96] HSEE C., "The evaluability hypothesis: An explanation for preference reversals between joint and separate evaluations of alternatives", *Organizational Behavior and Human Decision Processes*, vol. 67, p. 242–257, 1996.

[ISH 85] ISHII K., SUGENO M., "A Model of Human Evaluation Process Using Fuzzy Measure", *International Journal of Man–Machine Studies*, vol. 22, p. 19–38, 1985.

[KRA 71] KRANTZ D., LUCE R., SUPPES P., TVERSKY A., *Foundations of Measurement*, vol. 1: Additive and Polynomial Representations, Academic Press, San Diego, 1971.

[KWO 00] KWON S., SUGENO M., "A hierarchical subjective evaluation model using non–monotonic fuzzy measures and the Choquet integral", GRABISCH M., MUROFUSHI T., SUGENO M., Eds., *Fuzzy Measures and Integrals – Theory and Applications*, p. 375–391, Physica Verlag, 2000.

[LAB 03a] LABREUCHE C., GRABISCH M., "Bi-cooperative games and their importance and interaction indices", *14th Mini–EURO Conference on Human Centered Processes (HCP'2003)*, Luxembourg, p. 287–291, May 2003.

[LAB 03b] LABREUCHE C., GRABISCH M., "The Choquet integral for the aggregation of interval scales in multicriteria decision making", *Fuzzy Sets and Systems*, vol. 137, p. 11–26, 2003.

[LAB 03c] LABREUCHE C., GRABISCH M., The Shapley value and the interaction indices for bi-cooperative games, Report num. 2003/001, LIP6, UPMC, http://www.lip6.fr/reports/lip6.2003.001.html, 2003.

[LAB 04] LABREUCHE C., "Determination of the criteria to be improved first in order to improve as much as possible the overall evaluation", *10th International Conference on Information Processing and Management of Uncertainty in Knowledge-Based Systems (IPMU 2004)*, Perugia, Italy, p. 609–616, July 2004.

[LIN 03] LIN S., SLOVIC P., "Sign theory: a non–extensional theory of preference", 2003, Working paper.

[LOV 83] LOVÁSZ L., "Submodular function and convexity", BACHEM A., GRÖTSCHEL M., KORTE B., Eds., *Mathematical Programming. The State of the Art*, p. 235–257, Springer Verlag, Berlin, 1983.

[MAR 98a] MARICHAL J., Aggregation operators for multicriteria decision aid, PhD thesis, University of Liège, 1998.

[MAR 98b] MARICHAL J., ROUBENS M., "Dependence between criteria and multiple criteria decision aid", *2nd International Workshop on Preferences and Decisions*, Trento, Italy, p. 69–75, 1998.

[MAR 00a] MARICHAL J., "An axiomatic approach of the discrete Choquet integral as a tool to aggregate interacting criteria", *IEEE Transactions on Fuzzy Systems*, vol. 8, num. 6, p. 800–807, 2000.

[MAR 00b] MARICHAL J., "On Sugeno integral as an aggregation function", *Fuzzy Sets and Systems*, vol. 114, p. 347–365, 2000.

[MAR 01a] MARICHAL J., "An axiomatic approach of the discrete Sugeno integral as a tool to aggregate interacting criteria in a qualitative framework", *IEEE Transactions on Fuzzy Systems*, vol. 9, num. 1, p. 164–172, 2001.

[MAR 01b] MARICHAL J., ROUBENS M., "On a sorting procedure in the presence of qualitative points of view", CHOJEAN J., LESKI J., Eds., *Fuzzy Sets and Their Applications*, Gliwice, Poland, Silesian University Press, p. 217–230, 2001.

[MAR 02] MARICHAL J., "Aggregation of interacting criteria by means of the discrete Choquet integral", CALVO T., MAYOR G., MESIAR R., Eds., *Aggregation Operators: New Trends and Applications*, vol. 97 of *Studies in Fuzziness and Soft Computing*, p. 224–244, Physica Verlag, Heidelberg, 2002.

[MAR 03] MARICHAL J., "On tolerant or intolerant character of interacting criteria in aggregation by the Choquet integral", BISDORFF R., Ed., *Proceedings of HCP'2003 (Human Centered Processes)*, Luxembourg, p. 267–271, May 2003.

[MET 95] METELLUS O., GRABISCH M., "Une approche de la classification par filtrage flou – Méthodologie et performances sur un problème de segmentation clientèle", *Proceedings of Rencontres Francophones sur la Logique Floue et ses Applications (LFA)*, Paris, France, p. 215–220, November 1995.

[MEY 05] MEYER P., ROUBENS M., "Choice, ranking and sorting in fuzzy multiple criteria decision aid", FIGUEIRA J., GRECO S., EHRGOTT M., Eds., *Multiple Criteria Decision Analysis*, p. 471–506, Kluwer Academic Publishers, New York, 2005.

[MIR 98] MIRANDA P., GRABISCH M., "Optimization issues for fuzzy measures", *7th International Conference on Information Processing and Management of Uncertainty in Knowledge-Based Systems (IPMU'98)*, Paris, France, p. 1204–1211, July 1998.

[MIR 02] MIRANDA P., GRABISCH M., GIL P., "p-symmetric fuzzy measures", *International Journal of Uncertainty, Fuzziness, and Knowledge-Based Systems*, vol. 10 (Suppl.), p. 105–123, 2002.

[MIR 03] MIRANDA P., GRABISCH M., "$p$symmetric bi-capacities", *International Summer School on Aggregation Operators and their Applications*, Alcala, Spain, p. 123–129, July 2003.

[MON 02] MONTMAIN J., AKHARRAZ A., MAURIS G., "Knowledge management as a support for collective decision-making and argumentation processes", *9th International Conference on Information Proceedings of and Management of Uncertainty in Knowledge-Based systems (IPMU'2002)*, Annecy, France, p. 91–98, July 2002.

[MOR 89] MORI T., MUROFUSHI T., "An analysis of evaluation model using fuzzy measure and the Choquet integral", *5th Fuzzy System Symposium*, Kobe, Japan, p. 207–212, 1989, in Japanese.

[MUR 93] MUROFUSHI T., SONEDA S., "Techniques for reading fuzzy measures (III): interaction index", *9th Fuzzy System Symposium*, Sapporo, Japan, p. 693–696, May 1993, in Japanese.

[MUR 00] MUROFUSHI T., SUGENO M., "Fuzzy measures and fuzzy integrals", GRABISCH M., MUROFUSHI T., SUGENO M., Eds., *Fuzzy Measures and Integrals – Theory and Applications*, p. 3–41, Physica Verlag, Heidelberg, 2000.

[MUR 01] MUROFUSHI T., "Lexicographic use of Sugeno integrals and monotonicity conditions", *IEEE Transactions on Fuzzy Systems*, vol. 9, num. 6, p. 783–794, 2001.

[NAK 95] NAKAMORI Y., IWAMOTO N., "Analysis of environmental evaluation structure by the Choquet integral model", *International Joint Conference of the 4th IEEE International Conference on Fuzzy Systems and the 2nd International Fuzzy Engineering Symp.*, Yokohama, Japan, p. 695–700, March 1995.

[NAK 00] NAKAMORI Y., *Kansei data kaiseki*, Morikita Publ. Company, Tokyo, 2000, in Japanese.

[OSG 57] OSGOOD C., SUCI G., TANNENBAUM P., *The Measurement of Meaning*, University of Illinois Press, Urbana, IL, 1957.

[PET 03] PETERS E., SLOVIC P., "Affective asynchrony and the measurement of the affective attitude component", 2003, Working paper.

[QUI 93] QUIGGIN J., *Generalized Expected Utility Theory: The Rank-dependent Model*, Kluwer Academic, Norwell, MA, 1993.

[RAD 75] RADNER R., "Satisficing", *Journal of Mathematical Economics*, vol. 2, p. 253–262, 1975.

[RIC 05] RICO A., GRABISCH M., LABREUCHE C., CHATEAUNEUF A., "Preference modelling on totally ordered sets by the Sugeno integral", *Discrete Applied Maths.*, vol. 147, p. 113–124, 2005.

[ROB 79] ROBERTS F., *Measurement Theory*, Addison-Wesley, Reading, MA, 1979.

[ROU 01] ROUBENS M., "Ordinal multiattribute sorting and ordering in the presence of interacting points of view", BOUYSSOU D., JACQUET-LAGRÈZE E., PERNY P., SLOWINSKY R., VANDERPOOTEN D., VINCKE P., Eds., *Aiding Decisions with Multiple Criteria: Essays in Honor of Bernard Roy*, p. 229–246, Kluwer Academic Publishers, 2001.

[SAP 90] SAPORTA G., *Probabilités, Analyse des données et Statistique*, Ed. Technip, Paris, 1990.

[SAV 72] SAVAGE L. J., *The Foundations of Statistics*, Dover, 2nd edition, 1972.

[SCH 86] SCHMEIDLER D., "Integral representation without additivity", *Proceedings of the American Mathematical Society*, vol. 97, num. 2, p. 255–261, 1986.

[SCH 89] SCHMEIDLER D., "Subjective probability and expected utility without additivity", *Econometrica*, vol. 57, num. 3, p. 571–587, 1989.

[SHA 53] SHAPLEY L., "A value for $n$person games", KUHN H., TUCKER A., Eds., *Contributions to the Theory of Games, Vol. II*, Annals of Mathematics Studies, p. 307–317, Princeton University Press, 1953.

[SIM 56] SIMON H., "Rational choice and the structure of the environment", *Psychological Review*, vol. 63, num. 2, p. 129–138, 1956.

[SIM 01] SIMON H., "Theories of bounded rationality", EARL P., Ed., *The Legacy of Herbert Simon in Economic Analysis*, vol. 1, Edward Elgar Publishing Ltd, 2001.

[ŠIP 79] ŠIPOŠ J., "Integral with respect to a pre–measure", *Math. Slovaca*, vol. 29, p. 141–155, 1979.

[SLO 02] SLOVIC P., FINUCANE M., PETERS E., MACGREGOR D., "The affect heuristic", GILOVITCH T., GRIFFIN D., KAHNEMAN D., Eds., *Heuristics and Biases: The Psychology of Intuitive Judgment*, p. 397–420, Cambridge University Press, 2002.

[SUG 74] SUGENO M., Theory of fuzzy integrals and its applications, PhD thesis, Tokyo Institute of Technology, 1974.

[SUG 95] SUGENO M., KWON S., "A clusterwise regression–type model for subjective evaluation", *Journal of Japan Society for Fuzzy Theory and Systems*, vol. 7, num. 2, p. 291–310, 1995.

[TVE 92] TVERSKY A., KAHNEMAN D., "Advances in prospect theory: cumulative representation of uncertainty", *Journal of Risk and Uncertainty*, vol. 5, p. 297–323, 1992.

[VER 03] VERKEYN A., BOTTELDOOREN D., BAETS B. D., TRÉ G. D., "Sugeno integrals for the modelling of noise annoyance aggregation", BILGIC T., BAETS B. D., KAYNAK O., Eds., *Fuzzy Sets and Systems – IFSA 2003*, p. 277–284, Springer Verlag, 2003.

[WAK 90] WAKKER P., "A behavioral foundation for fuzzy measures", *Fuzzy Sets & Systems*, vol. 37, p. 327–350, 1990.

[WAN 99] WANG Z., LEUNG K., WANG J., "A genetic algorithm for determining nonadditive set functions in information fusion", *Fuzzy Sets and Systems*, vol. 102, p. 462–469, 1999.

[WEB 84] WEBER S., "$\perp$-decomposable measures and integrals for Archimedean t–conorms $\perp$", *Journal of Mathematical Analysis and Applications*, vol. 101, p. 114–138, 1984.

[YAG 88] YAGER R., "On ordered weighted averaging aggregation operators in multicriteria decision making", *IEEE Transactions Systems, Man & Cybernetics*, vol. 18, p. 183–190, 1988.

[ZIM 83] ZIMMERMANN H.-J., ZYSNO P., "Decisions and evaluations by hierarchical aggregation of information", *Fuzzy Sets & Systems*, vol. 10, p. 243–260, 1983.

Chapter 19

Social Choice Theory and Multicriteria Decision Aiding

19.1. Introduction

Many organizations face such complex and important management problems that they sometimes want their decisions to be somehow supported by a 'scientific approach', sometimes called a *decision analysis*. The analyst in charge of this preparation faces many diverse tasks: stakeholder identification, problem statement, elaboration of a list of possible actions, definition of one or several criteria for evaluating these actions, information gathering, sensitivity analysis, elaboration of a recommendation (for instance a ranking of the actions or a subset of 'good' actions), etc. The desire or necessity to take multiple conflicting viewpoints into account for evaluating the actions often makes this task even more difficult. In that case, we speak of *multicriteria decision aiding* [POM 93, ROY 85, VIN 89]. The expert must then try to synthesize the partial preferences (modeled by each criterion) into a global preference on which a recommendation can be based. This is called *preference aggregation*.

A very similar aggregation problem has been studied for a long time in the framework of *voting theory*. It consists of searching a 'reasonable' mechanism (we call it voting system or aggregation method in the sequel) aggregating the opinions expressed by several voters on the candidates in an election, in order to determine a winner or to rank all candidates in order of preference. This problem is of course

---

Chapter written by Denis BOUYSSOU, Thierry MARCHANT and Patrice PERNY.

very old but its modern analysis dates back to the end of the eighteenth century [BOR 81, CON 85].

The diversity of voting systems actually used in the world shows that this problem is still important. In the 1950s, the works of [ARR 63, BLA 58, MAY 52] initiated a huge literature [KEL 91] forming what is today called *social choice theory*. It analyzes the links that exist (or should exist) between the *individual preferences* of the members of a society and the decisions made by this group when these decisions are supposed to reflect the *collective preference* of the group.

The many results obtained in social choice theory are valuable for multicriteria decision aiding. There are indeed links between these two domains: it is easy to go from one to the other by replacing the words 'action', 'criterion', 'partial preference' and 'overall preference' by 'candidate', 'voter', 'individual preference' and 'collective preference' [ARR 86].

The aim of this chapter is to present some important results in social choice theory in a simple way and to discuss their relevance for multicriteria decision aiding. Using some classical examples of voting problems (section 19.2), we will show some fundamental difficulties arising when aggregating preferences. We will then present some theoretical results that can help us better understand the nature of these difficulties (section 19.3). We will then try to analyze the consequences of these results for multicriteria decision aiding (section 19.4). A long list of references will help the interested reader to deepen their understanding of these questions.

19.2. Introductory examples

Choices made by a society often impact the individuals making up this society. It therefore seems reasonable to ground these choices on the preferences of the individuals. The choice of a candidate (law, project, social state, etc.) then depends on the outcome of an election in which the individuals (*voters*) express their preferences. A voting system (or aggregation method) uses the information provided by the voters in order to determine the elected candidate or, more generally, the decision made by the group.

In such conditions, how should we conceive a 'good' voting system? Common sense tells us that such a system must be democratic, i.e. it must yield collective preferences reflecting the individual preferences as much as possible. In many countries (groups, companies, committees), this is operationalized by the *majority rule* (or some variant of it): candidate a wins against b if the majority of the voters prefer a to b. This simple rule is very intuitive. As we will later see, when there are only two candidates this rule raises almost no problem [MAY 52].

This rule can be adapted in many ways to face situations with more than two candidates. These adaptations can lead to surprising outcomes, which will be illustrated by a few examples in this section. We will begin with *uninominal* voting systems, where each voter expresses their opinion through a ballot that only contains the name of one candidate (section 19.2.1), before moving to other systems where the voters can express their preferences in more complex ways (section 19.2.2).

In all examples, we will assume that each voter is able to rank (possibly with ties) all candidates in order of preference, i.e. can express preferences by means of a weak order. If a voter prefers a to b and b to c (thereby preferring a to c), we write '$a \succ b \succ c$'. Except if otherwise stated, we will suppose that the voters are sincere, i.e. they express their 'true' preferences. Finally, notice that most examples presented here are classic. Many more examples and the analysis of many voting systems can be found in [DUM 84, FIS 77, MOU 80, MOU 88, NUR 87].

19.2.1. *Uninominal systems*

Example 19.1. Dictatorship of majority
Let $\{a, b, c, \ldots, z\}$ be the set of 26 candidates for an election with 100 voters whose preferences are:

$$51 \text{ voters have preferences } a \succ b \succ c \succ \ldots \succ y \succ z,$$
$$49 \text{ voters have preferences } z \succ b \succ c \succ \ldots \succ y \succ a.$$

It is clear that 51 voters will vote for a while 49 vote for z. Thus a has an absolute majority and, in all uninominal systems we are aware of, a wins. But is a really a good candidate? Almost half of the voters perceive a as the worst one and candidate b seems to be a good candidate for everyone. Candidate b could be a good compromise. As shown by this example, a uninominal election combined with the majority rule allows a 'dictatorship of majority' and doesn't favor a compromise. A possible way to avoid this problem might be to ask the voters to provide their whole ranking instead of their preferred candidate. We will see some examples in section 19.2.2.

The possibility of a dictatorship of the majority was already acknowledged by classic greek philosophers. The following examples show that many other strange phenomena can occur with uninominal voting systems.

Example 19.2. Respect of majority in the British system
The voting system in the United Kingdom is *plurality voting*, i.e. the election is uninominal and the aggregation method is a simple majority. Let $\{a, b, c\}$ be the set of candidates for a 21 voters election (or 21×10^6 voters if one wishes a more realistic example). Suppose that

10 voters have preferences $a \succ b \succ c$,
6 voters have preferences $b \succ c \succ a$,
5 voters have preferences $c \succ b \succ a$.

Then a (respectively, b and c) obtains 10 votes (respectively, 6 and 5) so that a is chosen. Nevertheless, this might be different from what a majority of voters wanted. Indeed, an absolute majority of voters prefers any other candidate to a (11 out of 21 voters prefer b and c to a).

Let us see, using the same example, if such a problem could be avoided by the two-stage French system (also called plurality with runoff). After the first stage, as no candidate has an absolute majority, a second stage is run between candidates a and b. We suppose that the voters keep the same preferences on $\{a, b, c\}$. So

10 voters have preferences $a \succ b$,
11 voters have preferences $b \succ a$.

Thus a obtains 10 votes and b 11 votes so that candidate b is elected. This time, none of the beaten candidates (a and c) are preferred to b by a majority of voters. Nonetheless we cannot conclude that the two-stage French system is superior to the British system from this point of view, as shown by the following example.

Example 19.3. Respect of majority in the two-stage French system
Let $\{a, b, c, d\}$ be the set of candidates for a 21 voter election. Suppose that

10 voters have preferences $b \succ a \succ c \succ d$,
6 voters have preferences $c \succ a \succ d \succ b$,
5 voters have preferences $a \succ d \succ b \succ c$.

After the first stage, as no candidate has absolute majority, a second stage is run between candidates b and c. Candidate b easily wins with 15 out of 21 votes although an absolute majority (11/21) of voters prefer a and d to b.

Because it is not necessary to be a mathematician to figure out such problems, some voters might be tempted not to sincerely report their preferences as shown in the next example.

Example 19.4. Manipulation in the two-stage French system

Let us continue with the example above. Suppose that the six voters having preferences $c \succ a \succ d \succ b$ decide not to be sincere and vote for a instead of c. Then candidate a wins after the first stage because there is an absolute majority for him (11/21). If they had been sincere (as in the previous example), b would have been elected. Thus, casting an insincere vote is useful for those 6 voters as they prefer a to b. Such a system, that may encourage voters to falsely report their preferences, is called manipulable.

This is not the only weakness of the French system, as attested by the following three examples.

Example 19.5. Monotonicity in the two-stage French system

Let $\{a, b, c\}$ be the set of candidates for a 17 voters election. A few days before the election, the results of a survey are as follows:

> 6 voters have preferences $a \succ b \succ c$,
> 5 voters have preferences $c \succ a \succ b$,
> 4 voters have preferences $b \succ c \succ a$,
> 2 voters have preferences $b \succ a \succ c$.

In the French system, a second stage would be run between a and b and a would be chosen obtaining 11 out of 17 votes. Suppose that candidate a, in order to increase his lead over b and to lessen the likelihood of a defeat, decides to strengthen his electoral campaign against b. Suppose that the survey exactly revealed the preferences of the voters and that the campaign has the correct effect on the last two voters. Thus we observe the following preferences:

> 8 voters have preferences $a \succ b \succ c$,
> 5 voters have preferences $c \succ a \succ b$,
> 4 voters have preferences $b \succ c \succ a$.

After the first stage, b is eliminated, due to the campaign of a. The second stage opposes a to c and c wins, obtaining 9 votes. Candidate a thought that his campaign would be beneficial. He was wrong. Such a method is called non-monotonic because an improvement of a candidate's position in some of the voter's preferences can lead to a deterioration of his position after the aggregation.

It is clear with such a system that it is not always interesting or efficient to sincerely report our preferences. We will note in the next example that some manipulations can be very simple.

Example 19.6. Participation in the two-stage French system
Let $\{a, b, c\}$ be the set of candidates for a 11 voters election. Suppose that

> 4 voters have preferences $a \succ b \succ c$,
> 4 voters have preferences $c \succ b \succ a$,
> 3 voters have preferences $b \succ c \succ a$.

In the French system, a second stage should oppose a to c and c should win the election obtaining 7 out of 11 votes. Suppose that 2 of the first 4 voters (with preferences $a \succ b \succ c$) decide not to vote because c, the worst candidate according to them, is going to win anyway. What will happen? There will only be 9 voters:

> 2 voters have preferences $a \succ b \succ c$,
> 4 voters have preferences $c \succ b \succ a$,
> 3 voters have preferences $b \succ c \succ a$.

Contrary to all expectations, candidate c will loose while b will win, obtaining 5 out of 9 votes. Our two lazy voters can be proud of their abstention since they prefer b to c. Clearly such a method does not encourage participation.

Example 19.7. Separability in the two-stage French system
Let $\{a, b, c\}$ be the set of candidates for a 26 voters election. The voters are located in two different areas: countryside and town. Suppose that the 13 voters located in the town have the following preferences:

> 4 voters have preferences $a \succ b \succ c$,
> 3 voters have preferences $b \succ a \succ c$,
> 3 voters have preferences $c \succ a \succ b$,
> 3 voters have preferences $c \succ b \succ a$.

Suppose that the 13 voters located in the countryside have the following preferences:

> 4 voters have preferences $a \succ b \succ c$,
> 3 voters have preferences $c \succ a \succ b$,
> 3 voters have preferences $b \succ c \succ a$,
> 3 voters have preferences $b \succ a \succ c$.

Suppose now that an election is organized in the town, with 13 voters. Candidates a and c will go to the second stage and a will be chosen, obtaining 7 votes. If an election is organized in the countryside, a will defeat b in the second stage, obtaining 7 votes. Thus, a is the winner in both areas. Naturally we expect a to be the winner in a global election, but it is easy to observe that in the global election (26 voters) a is defeated during the first stage. Such a method is called non-separable.

The previous examples showed that, when there are more than 2 candidates, it is not an easy task to imagine a system that would behave as expected. Note that, in the presence of 2 candidates, the British system (uninominal and one-stage) is equivalent to all other systems and it suffers none of the above-mentioned problems [MAY 52]. We might therefore be tempted by a generalization of the British system (restricted to 2 candidates). If there are 2 candidates, we use the British system; if there are more than 2 candidates, we arbitrarily choose 2 of them and we use the British system to select the winner. The winner is opposed (using the British system) to a new arbitrarily chosen candidate, and so on until no more candidates remain. This would require $n-1$ votes between 2 candidates. Unfortunately, this method suffers severe drawbacks.

Example 19.8. Influence of the agenda in sequential voting
Let $\{a, b, c\}$ be the set of candidates for a 3 voters election. Suppose that

> 1 voter has preferences $a \succ b \succ c$,
> 1 voter has preferences $b \succ c \succ a$,
> 1 voter has preferences $c \succ a \succ b$.

The 3 candidates will be considered two by two in the following order or agenda: a and b first, then c. During the first vote, a is opposed to b and a wins with absolute majority (2 votes against 1). Then a is opposed to c and c defeats a with absolute majority. c is therefore elected.

If the agenda is a and c first, it is easy to see that c defeats a and is then opposed to b. Hence, b wins against c and is elected.

If the agenda is b and c first, it is easy to see that a is finally elected. Consequently, in this example, any candidate can be elected and the outcome depends completely on the agenda, i.e. on an arbitrary decision. Let us note that sequential voting is very common in different parliaments. The different amendments to a bill are considered one by one in a predefined sequence. The first one is opposed to the original bill using the British system; the second one is opposed to the winner and so on. Finally, the result is opposed to the status quo. Clearly, such a method lacks neutrality. It doesn't treat all candidates in a symmetric way. Candidates (or amendments) appearing at the end of the agenda are more likely to be elected than those at the beginning. We say that such a method is not *neutral*. Notice that the British and French systems are neutral because they do not favor any candidate.

Example 19.9. Violation of unanimity in sequential voting
Let $\{a, b, c, d\}$ be the set of candidates for a 3 voters election. Suppose that

1 voter has preferences $b \succ a \succ d \succ c$,
1 voter has preferences $c \succ b \succ a \succ d$,
1 voter has preferences $a \succ d \succ c \succ b$.

Consider the following agenda: a and b first, then c and finally d. Candidate a is defeated by b during the first vote. Candidate c wins the second vote and d is finally elected although all voters unanimously prefer a to d. Let us note that this cannot happen with the French and British systems.

Example 19.10. Tie-breaking chairperson
Suppose we use the two-stage French system and, at the second stage, the two candidates have the same number of votes. This is very unlikely in a national election but can often occur in small-scale elections (board of trustees, court jury, PhD jury, etc.). It is then usual to use the chairperson's vote to break the tie. In this case, the opinions of all voters are not treated in the same way. We then say that the voting system is not *anonymous*, unlike all systems we have seen so far. Note that using the chairperson's vote is not the only possibility: we could break the tie by choosing, for instance, the oldest of the two candidates (this would not respect neutrality).

Up until now, we have assumed that the voters are able to rank all candidates from best to worst without ties but the only information that we collected was the best candidate. We could try to palliate the many encountered problems by asking voters to explicitly rank the candidates in order of preference (some systems, like approval voting, use another kind of information; see [BRA 82]). This idea, although interesting, will lead us to many other pitfalls as discussed in the following section.

19.2.2. *Systems based on rankings*

In this kind of election, each voter provides a ranking without ties of the candidates. Hence the task of the aggregation method is to extract from all these rankings the best candidate or a ranking of the candidates reflecting the preferences of the voters as much as possible. Comparing all candidates pairwise in the following way has been suggested [CON 85].

Condorcet method (or majority method) Candidate a is preferred to b if and only if the number of voters ranking a before b is larger than the number of voters ranking b before a. In case of tie, candidates a and b are indifferent.

Condorcet states the following principle.

Condorcet principle If a candidate is preferred to each other candidate using the majority rule, then he should be chosen. The candidate, the *Condorcet winner*, is necessarily unique.

Note that neither the British nor the French system respect this principle. Indeed, in example 19.2, the British system leads to the election of a while b is the Condorcet winner and, in example 19.3, the French system elects b while a is the Condorcet winner.

The Condorcet principle seems very sensible and close to the intuitive notion of democracy (yet it can be criticized, as suggested in example 19.1 where candidate a is a Condorcet winner). It is not always operational: in some situations, there is no Condorcet winner; this is the so-called *Condorcet paradox*. Indeed, in example 19.8, a is preferred to b, b is preferred to c and c is preferred to a. No candidate is preferred to all others. In such a case, the Condorcet method fails to elect a candidate. One might think that example 19.8 is very bizarre and unlikely to happen. Unfortunately it isn't. If you consider an election with 25 voters and 11 candidates, the probability of such a paradox is significantly high: approximately $1/2$ [GEH 83]. The more candidates or voters, the higher the probability of such a paradox. Note that, in order to obtain this result, all rankings are supposed to have the same probability. Such an hypothesis is clearly questionable [GEH 83].

We must find how to proceed when there is no Condorcet winner. We may, for example, choose a candidate such that no other candidate defeats him according to the majority rule (weak Condorcet principle), but such a candidate does also not always exist (as in example 19.8). Many methods have been proposed for exploiting the relation constructed using the majority method [FIS 77, LAS 97, NUR 87].

An alternative approach has been proposed by [BOR 81]. He suggests associating a global score to each candidate. This score is the sum of his ranks in the rankings of the voters.

Borda method Candidate a is preferred to b if the sum of the ranks of a in the rankings of the voters is strictly smaller than the corresponding sum for b (we now assume that the rankings are without tie and we assign rank 1 to the best candidate in the ranking, rank 2 to the second best candidate, and so on; as we will see, the method can be easily generalized for handling ties).

Example 19.11. Borda and Condorcet methods
Let $\{a, b, c, d\}$ be the set of candidates for a 3 voters election. Suppose that

2 voters have preferences $b \succ a \succ c \succ d$,
1 voters have preferences $a \succ c \succ d \succ b$.

The Borda score of a is $5 = 2 \times 2 + 1 \times 1$. For b, it is $6 = 2 \times 1 + 1 \times 4$. Candidates c and d receive 8 and 11. Thus, a is the winner and the collective ranking is $a \succ b \succ c \succ d$. Using the Condorcet method, the conclusion is different: b is the Condorcet winner. Furthermore, the collective preference obtained by the Condorcet method is transitive and yields the ranking $b \succ a \succ c \succ d$. The two methods diverge; the Borda method does not verify the Condorcet principle. Nevertheless, it can be shown that the Borda method never chooses a Condorcet loser, i.e. a candidate that is beaten by all other candidates by an absolute majority (contrary to the British system, see example 19.2).

The Borda method has an important advantage with respect to the Condorcet method. In any situation, it selects one or several winners (those with the lowest sum of ranks). Furthermore, it always yields a ranking of the candidates from best to worse. The Condorcet method, on the contrary, sometimes yields non-transitive preferences and it is then impossible to rank the candidates or even to choose a subset of 'good' candidates (see example 19.8). It is easy to verify that the Borda method is neutral, anonymous, separable, monotonic and encourages participation.

The Borda method nevertheless sometimes behaves in a strange way. Indeed, consider example 19.11 and suppose that candidates c and d decide on the eve of the election not to compete because they are almost sure to lose. With the Borda method, the new winner is b. Thus b now defeats a just because c and d dropped out. The fact that a defeats or is defeated by b therefore depends not only on the relative positions of a and b in the rankings of the voters but is also contingent upon the presence of other candidates and on their position with respect to all other candidates. This can be a problem as the set of candidates is not always fixed. It is even more of a problem in decision aiding because the set of actions is seldom given and is, to a large extent, the outcome of a modeling process.

After all these examples, we would like to propose a democratic method with the advantages of the Borda method (transitivity of the collective preferences) and those of the Condorcet method (Condorcet principle and absence of contingency problems). We will see in section 19.3 that it is mainly hopeless.

Let us mention that we limited this discussion to voting systems aimed at choosing a candidate and not a subset of candidates. The reader might then be tempted to conclude that those systems are inferior to systems aimed at choosing a representative body with some 'proportional' method. However, this is too simple, for at least two reasons. First, the definition of what constitutes a fair or democratic proportional representation is complex and most proportional systems lead to paradoxical situations [BAL 82]. Second, representative bodies must make decisions and, to this end, they need voting systems aimed at choosing a single action.

19.3. Some theoretical results

Based on the preceding examples, we now have the intuition that conceiving 'good' preference aggregation methods raises serious problems. This is confirmed by some celebrated results in social choice theory.

19.3.1. *Arrow's theorem*

Arrow's theorem is central in social choice theory. It is about voting systems aimed at aggregating n ($n \geq 3$) weak orders (rankings possibly with ties) in a collective weak order. Just as in section 19.2.2, each voter ranks all the candidates, possibly with ties.

Formalization 19.1. *A binary relation R on a set A is a subset of $A \times A$. We often write aRb instead of $(a, b) \in R$. A weak order on A is a complete (for all $a, b \in A$ we have aRb and/or bRa) and transitive (for all $a, b, c \in A$, aRb and bRc imply aRc) binary relation on A. Let $\mathcal{WO}(A)$ denote the set of all weak orders on the set A. The asymmetric part of R is the binary relation P defined by $aPb \Leftrightarrow [aRb$ and Not $bRa]$. The symmetric part of R is the binary relation I defined by $aIb \Leftrightarrow [aRb$ and $bRa]$.*

Let $N = \{1, 2, \ldots n\}$ represent the set of voters and A the set of candidates. We assume that voter $i \in N$ expresses their preference by means of a weak order $R_i \in \mathcal{WO}(A)$ on the set A. We write P_i (respectively, I_i) for the asymmetric (respectively, symmetric) part of R_i.

Arrow was interested in the aggregation methods satisfying the following conditions.

Universality Every configuration of rankings is admissible.

Formalization 19.2. *We want to find an aggregation function F yielding a result (a collective weak order) for every element $(R_1, R_2, \ldots, R_n)$ of $\mathcal{WO}(A)^n$.*

This condition excludes any constraint on the set of admissible rankings. The examples of the previous section have shown that some problems are caused by some specific rankings or configurations of rankings. A possible way out would then consist of proposing a method that works only with 'simple' configurations. Imposing restrictions on the admissible configurations is sometimes reasonable. For instance, one may sometimes assume that all voters and candidates are located on a right-left axis and that each voter ranks the candidates in order of increasing distance between themself and the candidates. The preferences of the voters are then *single-peaked*; [BLA 58] showed that a Condorcet winner then necessarily exists. However, such restrictions imply e.g. the absence of atypical voters. This cannot be excluded *a priori*. With a non-universal aggregation method, some ballots would be impossible to analyze.

Transitivity The outcome of the aggregation method must always be a complete ranking, possibly with ties.

Formalization 19.3. *The aggregation function takes its values in $\mathcal{WO}(A)$. When there is no ambiguity, we write $R = F(R_1, R_2, \ldots, R_n)$ and P (respectively, I) the asymmetric part (respectively, symmetric) of R.*

This condition lays down that the outcome is transitive irrespective of the preference of the voters. Whenever the society prefers a to b and b to c, it must therefore prefer a to c. We have seen that the Condorcet method does not satisfy this condition. It is sufficient (but not necessary) to ensure that the method will, in all cases, designate one or several best candidates (those with the best positions in the ranking). We will later see that weakening this condition does not improve the situation formalized by Arrow's theorem.

Unanimity The outcome of the aggregation method may not contradict the voters when they vote unanimously.

Formalization 19.4. *The aggregation function F must be such that, for all $a, b \in A$, if aP_ib for all $i \in N$, then aPb.*

If a is ranked before b in each ranking, then it must be before b in the collective ranking. This condition is very sensible; Example 19.9 nevertheless shows that some methods violate it.

Independence The relative position of two candidates in the collective ranking only depends on their relative position in the individual rankings.

Formalization 19.5. *For all $(R_1, R_2, \ldots, R_n), (R'_1, R'_2, \ldots, R'_n) \in \mathcal{WO}(A)^n$ and all $a, b \in A$, if $aR_ib \Leftrightarrow aR'_ib$ and $bR_ia \Leftrightarrow bR'_ia$, then $aRb \Leftrightarrow aR'b$.*

This condition is more complex than the previous conditions. When comparing a and b, it forbids:

– taking preference intensities into account: the only thing that matters is that a is ranked by the voters before or after b; and

– taking other candidates into account.

Let us illustrate this condition with an example.

Example 19.12. The Borda method and independence
Let $\{a, b, c, d\}$ be the set of candidates. Suppose there are three voters with the following preferences:

> 2 voters have preferences $c \succ a \succ b \succ d$,
> 1 voters has preferences $a \succ b \succ d \succ c$.

The Borda method yields the ranking: a, c, b, d with the respective scores 5, 6, 8 and 11.

Suppose now that :

> 2 voters have preferences $c \succ a \succ b \succ d$,
> 1 voters has preferences $a \succ c \succ b \succ d$.

The Borda method yields the ranking: c, a, b, d with the respective scores 4, 5, 9 and 12.

Note that, in each individual ranking, the relative position of a and c did not vary across ballots: one voter prefers a to c while two voters prefer c to a. Independence then imposes that the position of a and c in the collective ranking be identical. This is not the case with the Borda method. Indeed, this method uses the fact that the 'distance' between a and c seems larger in the ranking $a \succ b \succ d \succ c$ than in the ranking $a \succ c \succ b \succ d$, because b and d lie between a and c in the first case.

The dependence of the relative position of a and c with respect to b and d is ruled out by the Independence condition. It also excludes any method using, in addition to the rankings, some information regarding preference intensities.

The last condition used by Arrow states that no voter can impose, in all circumstances, their preferences to the society. This condition is extremely sensible for anyone willing to use a democratic method.

Non-dictatorship There is no dictator.

Formalization 19.6. *For all $i \in N$ and all $a, b \in A$, there is a profile $(R_1, R_2, \ldots, R_n)$ $\in \mathcal{WO}(A)^n$ such that aP_ib and bRa.*

We are now ready to state the following celebrated theorem.

Theorem 19.1. *[ARR 63] If the number of voters is finite and there is at least three candidates, no aggregation method can simultaneously satisfy universality, transitivity, unanimity, independence and non-dictatorship.*

Proof. The proof of Arrow's theorem uses the following definitions. A subset $I \subseteq N$ of voters is *almost decisive* for the pair of candidates $(a, b) \in A^2$ if, for all $(R_1, R_2, \ldots, R_n) \in \mathcal{WO}(A)^n$, $[aP_ib, \forall i \in I \text{ and } bP_ja, \forall j \notin I] \Rightarrow aPb$. Similarly, the subset $I \subseteq N$ of voters is *decisive* for the pair of candidates $(a, b) \in A^2$ if, for all $(R_1, R_2, \ldots, R_n) \in \mathcal{WO}(A)^n$, $[aP_ib, \forall i \in I] \Rightarrow aPb$.

We first show that, if I is almost decisive for the pair (a, b), then I is decisive for all pairs of candidates.

Let c be a candidate distinct from a and b (such a candidate always exists because we assumed $n \geq 3$). Let $(R_1, R_2, \ldots, R_n) \in \mathcal{WO}(A)^n$ be a profile such that aP_ic, $\forall i \in I$. Let $(R'_1, R'_2, \ldots, R'_n) \in \mathcal{WO}(A)^n$ be a profile such that

- $aP'_ibP'_ic, \forall i \in I$,
- bP'_ja and $bP'_jc, \forall j \notin I$.

Since I is almost decisive for the pair (a, b), we have $aP'b$. Unanimity imposes $bP'c$. Transitivity then implies $aP'c$. Since the relation between a and c for the voters outside I in the profile $(R'_1, R'_2, \ldots, R'_n)$ has not been specified, Independence implies aPc. We have therefore proved that whenever I is almost decisive for the pair (a, b), then I is decisive for any pair of candidates (a, c) such that $c \neq a, b$. This reasoning is easily generalized to the case where c is not distinct from a or b.

We now show that there is always a voter $i \in N$ almost decisive for some pair of candidates. As shown above, this voter will be decisive for all pairs of candidates and will therefore be a dictator.

By unanimity, N is almost decisive for all pairs of candidates. Since N is finite, there is at least one subset $J \subseteq N$ almost decisive for the pair (a, b) with a minimal cardinality. Suppose $|J| > 1$ and consider a profile $(R_1, R_2, \ldots, R_n) \in \mathcal{WO}(A)^n$ such that:

- aP_ibP_ic, for $i \in J$,
- $cP_jaP_jb \,\forall j \in J \setminus \{i\}$,
- $bP_kcP_ka \,\forall k \notin J$.

Since J is almost decisive for the pair (a, b) we have aPb. It is impossible that cPb. Indeed, by independence, this would imply $J \setminus \{i\}$ is almost decisive for the pair (c, b) and, hence, decisive for all pairs, contrary to our hypothesis. We therefore have bRc and transitivity implies aPc. This implies that $\{i\}$ is almost decisive for the pair (a, c).
◊

This negative result applies only when there are at least three candidates. It is easy to verify that the majority method satisfies the five conditions of Arrow's theorem with two candidates. Arrow's theorem explains to a large extent the problems we met in section 19.2 when we were trying to find a 'satisfying' aggregation procedure. Observe, for instance, that the Borda method verifies universality, transitivity, unanimity and non-dictatorship. Hence, it cannot verify independence, as shown in example 19.12. The Condorcet method respects universality, unanimity, independence and non-dictatorship. It cannot therefore be transitive, as shown in example 19.8.

Notice that Arrow's theorem uses only five conditions. In addition to these, we might wish to impose also neutrality, anonymity, monotonicity, non-manipulability, separability or Condorcet's principle. What makes Arrow's theorem so strong is precisely that it uses only five conditions, all seemingly reasonable. This is enough to prove an impossibility.

Arrow's theorem initiated a huge literature, a good overview of which can be found in [CAM 02, FIS 87, KEL 78, SEN 86]. Let us mention that weakening transitivity does not solve the problem revealed by Arrow's theorem. For instance, if we impose quasi-transitivity (i.e. transitivity of the asymmetric part) instead of transitivity, then we can always determine one or several winners. However, it is possible to prove that replacing transitivity by quasi-transitivity in Arrow's theorem leads to an oligarchy instead of a dictatorship. An oligarchy is a subset of voters that can impose their preferences when they are unanimous and such that each of them can veto any strict preference i.e. if a member of the oligarchy strictly prefers a to b, then b cannot be strictly better than a in the collective preference [GIB 69, MAS 72].

Example 19.13. Let us consider six voters numbered from $i = 1$ to 6 and an aggregation method yielding the relation $R = F(R_1, R_2, \ldots, R_6)$ by means of:

$$xPy \Leftrightarrow \sum_{\{i: xP_iy\}} w_i > \lambda,$$
$$xIy \quad \text{otherwise,}$$

with $w_1 = w_2 = 0.4$, $w_3 = w_3 = w_5 = w_6 = 0.05$ and $\lambda = 0.7$. This method is oligarchic. Indeed, consider the set O containing voters 1 and 2. It is easy to verify that, for any profile of preferences,

$$[xP_1y \text{ and } xP_2y] \Rightarrow xPy,$$
$$[xP_1y \text{ or } xP_2y] \Rightarrow \text{Not } yPx.$$

The existence of an oligarchy is as problematic as the existence of a dictator. Indeed, if the oligarchy contains all voters (this is the only possibility if we want a democratic method) then, because of the veto right of each voter, the collective preference will not be very decisive since it will not discriminate much between candidates. On the contrary, an oligarchy containing only one voter is a dictatorship. Between these two extreme cases, no solution is satisfactory.

We can weaken transitivity even more and impose that there is no circuit in the asymmetric part of the collective preference relation. This condition is necessary and sufficient to guarantee the existence of maximal elements in any finite set of candidates [SEN 70]. However, it is then possible to prove the existence of a voter with an absolute veto [MAS 72] so this does not really help much.

19.3.1.1. *Arrow's theorem and fuzzy preferences*

Why is it impossible to aggregate voters' preferences in a satisfactory way (i.e. while respecting Arrow's conditions)? There are mainly two reasons:

– The information contained in the weak orders describing the voters' preferences is too poor; it is ordinal. If we use richer structures, we can hope to escape Arrow's theorem. In particular, if we represent the voters' preferences by means of fuzzy relations, we can not only speak of the preference of a over b but also of the intensity of this preference.

– The global preference must be a weak order and this is a strong constraint. If we weaken this condition, we may consider aggregation methods yielding relations with more flexibility, such as fuzzy relations.

Some authors [e.g. BAR 86, BAR 92, LEC 84, PER 92a] have analyzed the consequences of imposing that the outcome of the aggregation is a fuzzy relation, that is a mapping R from A^2 to $[0, 1]$. Their findings are unfortunately largely negative: if we impose that the fuzzy relation has some properties permitting the easy designation of a winner or construction of a ranking, then we find that the only possible aggregation methods give very different powers to the various voters (as in oligarchies or dictatorships). In particular, it is the case if we impose that the collective preference relation verifies min-transitivity, i.e. for all $a, b, c \in A$:

$$R(a, c) \geq \min(R(a, b), R(b, c)).$$

This condition guarantees that the relation R_λ defined by

$$a R_\lambda b \Leftrightarrow R(a, b) \geq \lambda,$$

is transitive for any value of λ. Hence, starting from a min-transitive relation, it is not difficult to designate a winner or to rank the candidates.

However, there are some positive results in the literature which use weaker transitivity conditions [e.g. OVC 91]. It is then tempting to believe that Arrow's theorem does not hold with fuzzy relations. But these apparently positive results are misleading: the transitivity condition they use is so weak that is not incompatible with Condorcet cycles, as shown in the following example.

Example 19.14. The transitivity condition used by [OVC 91] can be expressed as follows. For all $a, b, c \in A$:

$$R(a, c) \geq R(a, b) + R(b, c) - 1. \tag{19.1}$$

Suppose we want to aggregate the preferences of n voters. We can define the collective fuzzy preference relation by

$$R(a,b) = \frac{1}{n}\#\{i \in A : aR_ib\}.$$

It is easy to show that it satisfies equation (19.1). Let us now consider $3k$ voters with the following preferences:

k voters have preferences $a \succ b \succ c$,
k voters have preferences $b \succ c \succ a$,
k voters have preferences $c \succ a \succ b$.

We obtain $R(a,b) = 2/3$, $R(b,c) = 2/3$ and $R(c,a) = 2/3$; this is indeed compatible with equation (19.1). However, note that this relation is in some sense cyclic and does not permit us to designate a winner or to rank the candidates. Therefore, this does not solve the problem raised by Arrow's theorem.

In summary, unless we consider a very weak transitivity relation (without any practical interest), aggregation methods yielding fuzzy relations do not escape Arrow's theorem.

19.3.2. *Some other results*

Arrow's theorem and its many extensions represent only a part of the numerous results in social choice theory. For a comprehensive overview of this field, see [CAM 02, SEN 86]. In this paper, we will roughly group the results into three categories as follows:

1) Impossibility results, as for Arrow's theorem, show that some conditions are incompatible. These results help us to understand better why it is difficult to find a 'good' aggregation method.

2) Characterization results present a set of conditions that a given aggregation method and only this one simultaneously respects. Such results help us understand better the essential characteristics of a method. It is then easier to compare it with other methods.

3) 'Analysis' results: given a set of desirable conditions, these results compare different methods in order to see which satisfies the most axioms. This can help to find a satisfactory method (within the limits revealed by impossibility results).

This distinction is of course to some extent arbitrary, and the three kinds of results are not contradictory. They often use the same conditions.

We will now informally mention some results that we find important or interesting for understanding some phenomena presented in the examples of section 19.2.

19.3.2.1. Impossibility results

Among the impossibility results in social choice theory, two are particularly important:

1) Gibbard-Satterthwaite's theorem [GIB 73, SAT 75]. This result shows that there is no aggregation method (for choosing a single candidate) verifying universality, non-dictatorship and non-manipulability when there are at least three candidates. The French electoral system is clearly non-dictatorial and satisfies universality. If we neglect the ties than can occur during the second stage, Gibbard-Satterthwaite's theorem tells us that there is at least one situation where a voter would benefit from voting not sincerely. We have seen such a situation in example 19.4. Note that this result initiated a huge literature analyzing voting problems in terms of non-cooperative games [DUM 84, MOU 80, MOU 88, PEL 84].

2) Sen's theorem of the 'Paretian liberal' [SEN 70]. Suppose a society must vote to choose one of several social states. These are defined in such a way that they concern the private sphere of an individual. Clearly, there are conflicts between the majority principle, possibly yielding to a dictatorship of majority (see example 19.1), and the respect of this individual for his private sphere, in which he should decide alone. The theorem of the Paretian liberal tells us much more than this: it proves that the respect of a private sphere is incompatible with universality and unanimity. This result initiated a large literature, a good overview of which can be found in [SEN 83, SEN 92].

19.3.2.2. Characterizations

Among the many characterization results (many such results are presented in [SEN 86]), those about the Borda method (section 19.2.2) are particularly interesting. Indeed, this method satisfies most conditions encountered so far and it is very easy to implement.

19.3.2.2.1. A characterization of the Borda method

In this section, we present a characterization of the Borda method proved by [YOU 74]. This method is considered as a choice procedure, i.e. a procedure mapping each profile of weak orders on A to a non-empty subset of A. In this context, the Borda method works as follows: for each candidate a, we calculate a score (Borda score) $B(a)$ equal to the sum of the ranks of candidate a in the weak orders of the voters. In case of a tie, we use the mean rank. The choice set then contains the candidate(s) with the smallest score. Example 19.11 illustrates how the scores are computed. Note that, in this example, the Borda method is used to rank and not to choose.

Formalization 19.7. *A choice procedure is a function* $f : \mathcal{WO}(A)^n \to 2^A \setminus \varnothing$. *To each n-uple of weak orders, f associates a non-empty subset of A, interpreted as the set of the best candidates. The Borda method is defined by:*

$$f(R_1, R_2, \ldots, R_n) = \{a \in A : B(a) \leq B(b), \forall b \in A\},$$

where $B(a)$ is the Borda score of candidate a and is defined by:

$$B(a) = \sum_{i=1}^{n} \left[\#\{b \in A : bR_i a\} - \#\{b \in A : aR_i b\} \right]. \tag{19.2}$$

This formalization is not exactly the sum of the ranks, but the reader will easily check that $B(a)$, defined by equation (19.2), is an affine transformation of the sum of the ranks and therefore, using equation (19.2) or the sum of the ranks always yields the same result. We will use equation (19.2) because it is more convenient than the sum of the ranks.

In order to characterize the Borda method, [YOU 74] uses four conditions.

Neutrality The choice set depends only on the position of the candidates in the preferences of the voters and not, for instance, on the name of the candidates or on their age.

Formalization 19.8. *Let $\mathcal{P}$ be the set of all permutations on A, π an element of $\mathcal{P}$ and R a binary relation on A. We write $\pi(T)$ for the binary relation such that $\pi(a) \, \pi(T) \, \pi(b) \Leftrightarrow aRb$. A choice method is neutral if and only if $f(R_1, \ldots, R_n) = \pi(f(\pi(R_1), \ldots, \pi(R_n)))$ for any permutation π in $\mathcal{P}$.*

This condition imposes that all candidates be treated in the same way. It excludes, for instance, methods where the older candidate wins in case of tie. Similarly, sequential voting (example 19.8) is ruled out.

Faithfulness If there is only one voter, then the choice set must contain the best candidates according to this unique voter.

Formalization 19.9. $f(R_1) = \{a \in A : aR_1 b, \, \forall b \in A\}$.

This condition is extremely intuitive. Indeed, if there is only one voter, why not respect their preferences?

Consistency Suppose, as in example 19.7, that the voters are divided into two groups. We use the same choice method in both groups. If some candidates belong to both choice sets, then these candidates and only these should belong to the choice set which results from applying the same choice method to the whole set of voters.

Formalization 19.10.

$$f(R_1, \ldots, R_m) \cap f(R_{m+1}, \ldots, R_n) \neq \emptyset \Rightarrow$$
$$f(R_1, \ldots, R_n) = f(R_1, \ldots, R_m) \cap f(R_{m+1}, \ldots, R_n).$$

Consistency is quite sensible. If two groups agree that some candidate, say a, is one of the best, then it is difficult to understand why a would not be a winner when both groups vote together.

Many such conditions, involving two groups of voters, have been used in the literature. They are often called separability. Consistency is one of these conditions.

Cancellation Let us consider two candidates a and b and suppose the number of voters preferring a to b is equal to the number of voters preferring b to a. This is not very particular. Suppose now this is true not only for a and b but for all pairs of candidates, simultaneously. We then face a very particular situation. In such a situation, cancellation requires that the choice set contains all candidates.

Formalization 19.11.

$$\forall a, b \in A, \ \#\{i \in N : aR_i b\} = \#\{i \in N : bR_i a\} \Rightarrow f(R_1, \ldots, R_n) = A.$$

Among the four conditions used by Young, cancellation is probably the most questionable one. In some sense, it is reasonable: when, for each pair a, b of candidates, there are as many voters in favor of a as in favor of b, we can indeed prudently consider that no candidate is better than the other. But there are other situations when prudence recommends considering all candidates tied. For instance, when the majority relation is cyclic (see above, Condorcet paradox). Choosing cancellation rather than another condition imposing a complete tie in case of a cyclic majority relation or in another case is rather arbitrary.

The reader will easily verify that the Borda method verifies neutrality, faithfulness, consistency and cancellation. The following theorem, proved by Young, tells us much more.

Theorem 19.2. *[YOU 74] One and only one choice method verifies neutrality, faithfulness, consistency and cancellation: the Borda method.*

Since the proof of this theorem is quite long, we do not present it in this chapter. Notice that a similar characterization exists for the borda method used to rank [NIT 81]. Moreover, different generalizations of this result have been proved for the Borda method used to aggregate many different kinds of binary relations and even fuzzy binary relations [DEB 87, MAR 96, MAR 98, MAR 00, OUL 00].

19.3.2.3. *Generalizations of the Borda method*

The Borda method is a particular case of a general family of aggregation methods called *scoring rules*. These rules associate a number (a score) to each position in a binary relation. In order to aggregate n preference relations, we compute, for each candidate, the sum of its scores in the preference relations of the n voters. The winner is the candidate with the smallest total score. The Borda method is a particular scoring rule where the numbers associated with each rank are equally spaced. The British system is also a scoring rule where the best candidate in a preference relation receives 1 point and all the others receive the same score, say 2.

It has been shown that scoring rules are essentially characterized by neutrality, anonymity and separability [SMI 73, YOU 74, YOU 75]. (If we then add cancellation, we obtain a characterization of the Borda method.) For an overview of many results about scoring rules, see [SAA 94]. The French system is not a scoring rule because of the second stage. However, it is neutal and anonymous. It is therefore not separable, as shown in example 13.7. We have noticed in section 13.2 that the British system and the Borda method do not satisfy the Condorcet principle (see examples 19.2 and 19.10). This is not a surprise: indeed, it is possible to prove that no scoring rule can satisfy the Condorcet principle [MOU 88].

The French system can be considered as a scoring rule with iteration: at the first stage, it uses the British system for selecting two candidates. The same system is then used at the second stage. Note that there are many ways to iterate a scoring rule (one could for example use more than two stages). A result by [SMI 73] shows that no iterated scoring rule is monotonic. The violation of monotonicity by the French system (example 19.5) is simply a consequence of this.

19.3.2.4. *A characterization of simple majority*

In this section, we present the characterization of simple majority of [MAY 52] for two candidates. In this case, the distinction between choosing and ranking is no longer meaningful but, in order not to use a new formalism, we adopt here the choice formalism. May considers a choice procedure, i.e. a method designating one or several winners, based on the preferences of the voters. A formal definition of a choice method was presented above, in relation to the Borda method.

A candidate belongs to the choice set with a simple majority if the number of voters supporting them is not smaller than the number of voters supporting their contender.

Formalization 19.12. *The simple majority choice method is defined by:* $a \in f(R_1, \ldots, R_n)$ *if and only if*

$$\#\{i \in N : aR_ib\} \geq \#\{i \in N : bR_ia\}.$$

Note that voters that are indifferent between a and b have no effect on the outcome of the election. Their votes are counted on both sides of the inequality. The outcome would be the same if they did not exist. In order to characterize simple majority, [MAY 52] used three conditions.

Anonymity The choice set depends only on the preferences of the voters and not, for instance, on their name or age.

Formalization 19.13. *Let S be the set of all permutations on $N = \{1, \ldots, n\}$. A choice method is anonymous if and only if $f(R_1, \ldots, R_n) = f(R_{\sigma(1)}, \ldots, R_{\sigma(n)})$ for any permutation σ in S.*

This condition rules out, for example, the methods where some voters weigh more than others and methods where a voter (usually the chairperson of the committee) has the power to decide in case of a tie.

Neutrality See above.

Strict monotonicity Given the preferences of the voters, if the candidates a and b are chosen and if one of the voters changes his preferences in favor of a (the other voters do not change anything), then only a is chosen. If, only a was chosen at the beginning, then a stays alone in the choice set.

Formalization 19.14. *Consider two weak orders R_i and R'_i identical apart from the fact there is a pair of candidates (a, b) such that:*
- *Not aR_ib and aR'_ib or*
- *bR_ia and Not bR'_ia.*

Strict monotonicity then imposes:

$$f(R_1, \ldots, R_i, \ldots, R_n) = \{a\} \Rightarrow f(R_1, \ldots, R'_i, \ldots, R_n) = \{a\},$$

and

$$f(R_1, \ldots, R_i, \ldots, R_n) = \{a, b\} \Rightarrow f(R_1, \ldots, R'_i, \ldots, R_n) = \{a\}.$$

A consequence of this condition is that, in case of a tie, a single voter changing their mind is enough to break the tie. Simple majority clearly verifies the three above-mentioned conditions. Moreover, no other method satisfies them all.

Theorem 19.3. *[MAY 52] When there are exactly two candidates, the only choice method satisfying neutrality, anonymity and strict monotonicity is simple majority.*

To understand why this theorem only applies to the case of two candidates, note that many different choice methods coincide when there are only two candidates. In particular, the Borda method and many scoring methods always yield the same result as simple majority with two candidates. You may then question the interest of this characterization. Actually, Arrow's theorem has shown us that simple majority cannot be extended to more than two candidates (without deeply modifying it). The characterization with two candidates is therefore essential.

19.3.2.5. *Analysis*

The few aggregation methods presented so far are just a small sample of all the methods proposed in the literature. In particular, we did not mention the methods using the majority relation (constructed by the Condorcet method) to arrive at a choice set or a ranking. Similarly, the properties (such as neutrality or monotonicity) presented so far are also a very small subset of all those studied in the literature. For an overview of methods and properties, see [ARR 63, DED 00, FEL 92, FIS 77, LEV 95, NUR 87, RIC 75, RIC 78a, RIC 78b, RIC 81].

19.4. Multicriteria decision aiding and social choice theory

19.4.1. *Relevance and limits of social choice results*

We have seen in section 19.1 that aggregation problems in multicriteria decision aiding and social choice are formally very close to each other. The examples of section 19.2 and the results of section 19.3 taught us that conceiving a satisfactory aggregation method is a challenging task. Some authors [e.g. GAR 82] have then concluded that muticriteria decision aiding is doomed to failure. For a detailed answer to this objection, see [ROY 93]. We nonetheless mention the following points:

1) Such a conclusion flows from a biased and too radical interpretation of the available results in social choice theory. There are some impossibility results but this does not mean that resorting to an aggregation method to try to find a collective decision is a futile exercise. It is a demanding task requiring compromises to be made between several exigencies that are in general not compatible.

These results, when combined with characterization and analysis results, provide a good support to motivate the choice of a method. There is no ideal method but some are perhaps more satisfactory than others. See [SAA 94] for a convincing plea in favor of the Borda method or [BRA 82] for approval voting.

2) The formal proximity between both problems does not imply that both problems are identical. In particular:
   - The goal of a multicriteria decision aiding process is not always to choose one and only one action. There are many other kinds of outcomes, unlike in social choice theory [ROY 85].

– Some conditions look intuitive in social choice theory but are questionable in multicriteria decision aiding, and conversely. Let us mention, for example, that anonymity is not relevant in multicriteria decision aiding as soon as we wish to take criteria of different importance into account. Conversely, the set of potential actions to be evaluated is seldom given in multicriteria decision aiding (contrary to the set of candidates in social choice theory); it can evolve. The conditions telling us how an aggregation method should behave when this set changes (some actions are added or removed) are therefore more important in multicriteria decision aiding than in social choice theory.

– The preferences to be aggregated in multicriteria decision aiding are the outcome of a long modeling phase along each criterion [BOU 90]. This modeling phase can sometimes lead to incomplete preferences, fuzzy preferences or preferences such that indifference is not transitive [FOD 94, PER 92c, PER 98, ROU 85]. In some circumstances, it is possible to finely model preference intensities or even to compare preference differences on different criteria [KEE 76, VON 86]. Let us mention that handling uncertainty, imprecision or indeterminacy is often necessary to arrive at a recommendation in multicriteria decision aiding [BOU 89], contrary to social choice theory.

– In multicriteria decision aiding, contrary to social choice, it is not always necessary to completely construct the global preference. Indeed, it can occur that the decision maker can express their global preference with respect to some pairs of alternatives. For example, they are able to state that they prefer x to z and y to z but they hesitate between x and y. If they then use an aggregation method, it is in order to construct the preference only between x and y and not on the whole set of alternatives. Of course, these preferences that we construct on some pairs of alternatives must be based on the single-criterion preferences of the decision maker but also on the global preferences stated.

In multicriteria decision aiding, we therefore have a new element at our disposal: the global preferences. These do not exist in social choice theory. They are of course (very) incomplete but they can nevertheless help construct the global preference relation. In practice, these global preferences are often used by analysts in order to set the value of some parameters of the aggregation method they use. For instance, with the methods based on multi-attribute value theory (MAVT), the decision maker must compare (sometimes fictitious) alternatives in order to assess the value functions. The existence of these global preferences, totally non-existing in social choice theory, breaks the symmetry between multicriteria decision aiding and social choice theory. Few theoretical results have so far taken the global preferences of the decision maker into account. More research is needed [MAR 03].

Even if both domains are formally close to each other and if some conditions used in social choice theory can also be found in multicriteria decision aiding, we must beware of crude transpositions due to the many specificities of multicriteria aggregation.

Conversely, we must not conclude that both domains are unrelated and that the examples and results of sections 19.2 and 19.3 are of no consequence for multicriteria anlysis. It has clearly been shown [VAN 86a] that it is possible and useful to consider multicriteria aggregation methods in the light of social choice theory. Let us mention that, for example, the difference between the Condorcet and the Borda method can be found in multicriteria anlysis between the ordinal methods [ROY 91, ROY 93] and the cardinal ones where the idea of preference difference is central [KEE 76, VON 86]. In the light of Arrow's theorem, it is not surprising that ordinal methods often lead to global preference relations from which a recommendation is not always easy to derive [VAN 90].

Many results of social choice theory still need to be adapted and/or extended to make them relevant to multicriteria analysis. Among the works in this direction, let us mention:

– impossibility results [ARR 86, BOU 92a, PER 92b];

– characterization results [BOU 92b, BOU 86, BOU 92c, MAR 96, PIR 95, PIR 97]; and

– analysis results [BOU 97, LAN 96, LAN 97, PÉR 94, PÉR 95, PIR 97, VIN 92].

However, there is still much to do [BOU 93].

19.4.2. *Some results in close relation with multicriteria analysis*

So far, we have tried to sketch a global overview of social choice theory and to show the links with multicriteria decision aiding and the limits of this analogy. In this last section, we mention some results of social choice theory that are directly relevant for the analysis of some popular aggregation methods in multicriteria decision aiding.

19.4.2.1. *TACTIC [VAN 86b]*

The first relevant result is the characterization of a simple majority with two alternatives by [MAY 52], presented higher. This aggregation method can be seen as a particular case of TACTIC, with a concordance threshold equal to 1, without weights and without discordance. For the case of two alternatives, a result by [FIS 73] characterizes simple majority with weights.

Another article worth mentioning here is by [MAR 03]. It presents two characterizations of weighted simple majority with any number of alternatives. It is therefore slightly more general than the results of May and Fishburn. It corresponds to a particular case of TACTIC with a concordance threshold equal to 1 and no discordance.

19.4.2.2. *Multi-attribute value theory (MAVT) [KEE 76, VON 86]*

The methods of this family are usually analyzed in the framework of measurement theory [KRA 71, WAK 89]. There are however some relevant results in social choice theory and, in particular, in cardinal social choice theory. In this part of social choice theory, the information to be aggregated is not ordinal (not a binary relation) but cardinal: it consists of utilities, that is, numbers representing preferences [ROB 80]. As far as we know, none of these results have been transposed in multicriteria decision aiding.

19.4.2.3. *Weighted sum*

The weighted sum is a particular case of MAVT methods. The previous section is therefore relevant for the weighted sum. Let us highlight a particular result: [ROB 80, theorem 2] characterizes the weighted sum. See also [BLA 54, D'A 77].

19.4.2.4. *ELECTRE and PROMETHEE [ROY 91, ROY 93, VIN 89]*

With ELECTRE and PROMETHEE, each alternative is represented by a vector of $\mathbb{R}^n$, $x = (x_1, \ldots, x_n)$ where x_i represents the performance of x on criterion i (we suppose that all criteria are to be maximized).

The first step in PROMETHEE consists of choosing, for each criterion, a preference function f_i [MAR 88]. This is used to compute, for each pair of alternatives x, y, a number between 0 and 1 representing a preference degree denoted by $P_i(x, y)$ and defined by $P_i(x, y) = f_i(x_i, y_i)$. At the end of the first step, we therefore have a fuzzy preference relation for each criterion, P_i being the fuzzy relation associated with criterion i and $P_i(x, y)$ the value of this relation for the pair x, y.

In the next step, these fuzzy relations are aggregated by means of a generalization of the Borda method. This generalization has been characterized by [MAR 96]. Some variants of this characterization are presented in [MAR 98, MAR 00, OUL 00].

The ELECTRE methods use a somehow similar construction but with veto effects [ROY 91, ROY 93]. The preference relation constructed at the end of the aggregation phase uses some functions f_i and g_i with values in $[0; 1]$ in order to define (1) concordance indices $C_i(x, y) = f_i(x_i, y_i)$ representing to what extent x_i is at least as good as y_i and (2) discordance indices $D_i(x, y) = g_i(x_i, y_i)$ expressing to what extent the difference $y_i - x_i$ is compatible with a global preference of x over y. When $y_i - x_i$ exceeds a certain threshold (*veto threshold*), $D_i(x, y)$ equals 1 and the aggregation method then forbids a preference of x over y [PER 92c].

The ELECTRE and PROMETHEE methods therefore use aggregation procedures based on the construction and aggregation of fuzzy relations. They therefore do not escape the impossibility results mentioned in section 19.3.1.1 or about the aggregation of fuzzy relations [PER 92b]. This is why a last phase (exploitation) is necessary in order to reach a recommendation [ROY 93, VAN 90] This last phase is often difficult and the problems it raises can also be analyzed in the light of axiomatic results on ordinal aggregation of preferences. For instance, some non-monotonicity phenomena arising with exploitation procedures based on an iterated choice function [FOD 98, PER 92a] can be explained by Smith's theorem presented in section 19.3.2.3 or by more recent axiomatic analyses in the same direction [BOU 04, JUR 03].

Let us finally mention that [BOU 96] has extended the classic results of [MCG 53] regarding simple majority to ELECTRE and PROMETHEE.

19.5. Bibliography

[ARR 63] ARROW K. J., *Social Choice and Individual Values*, Wiley, New York, 2nd edition, 1963.

[ARR 86] ARROW K. J., RAYNAUD H., *Social Choice and Multicriterion Decision-making*, MIT Press, Cambridge, 1986.

[BAL 82] BALINSKI M. L., YOUNG H. P., *Fair Representation*, Yale University Press, New Haven, 1982.

[BAR 86] BARRETT C. R., PATTANAIK P. K., SALLES M., "On the structure of fuzzy social welfare functions", *Fuzzy Sets and Systems*, vol. 19, p. 1–10, 1986.

[BAR 92] BARRETT C. R., PATTANAIK P. K., SALLES M., "Rationality and aggregation of preferences in an ordinally fuzzy framework", *Fuzzy Sets and Systems*, vol. 49, p. 9–13, 1992.

[BLA 54] BLACKWELL D., GIRSHIK M. A., *Theory of Games and Statistal Decisions*, Wiley, New York, 1954.

[BLA 58] BLACK D., *The Theory of Committees and Elections*, Cambridge University Press, London, 1958.

[BOR 81] BORDA J.-CH. DE., *Mémoire sur les élections au scrutin*, Comptes Rendus de l'Académie des Sciences, 1781, Translation into English by Alfred de Grazia "Mathematical derivation of an election system", *Isis*, Vol. 44, 1953, pp. 42–51.

[BOU 86] BOUYSSOU D., VANSNICK J.-C., "Non-compensatory and generalized noncompensatory preference structures", *Theory and Decision*, vol. 21, p. 251–266, 1986.

[BOU 89] BOUYSSOU D., "Modelling inaccurate determination, uncertainty, imprecision using multiple criteria", LOCKETT A. G., ISLEI G., Eds., *Improving Decision Making in Organisations*, p. 78–87, Springer-Verlag, Heidelberg, 1989.

[BOU 90] BOUYSSOU D., "Building criteria: A prerequisite for MCDA", BANA E COSTA C. A., Ed., *Readings in Multiple Criteria Decision Aid*, p. 58–80, Springer-Verlag, Berlin, 1990.

[BOU 92a] BOUYSSOU D., "On some properties of outranking relations based on a concordance-discordance principle", DUCKSTEIN L., GOICOECHEA A., ZIONTS S., Eds., *Multiple Criteria Decision Making*, p. 93–106, Springer-Verlag, Berlin, 1992.

[BOU 92b] BOUYSSOU D., "Ranking methods based on valued preference relations: A characterization of the net flow method", *European Journal of Operational Research*, vol. 60, p. 61–67, 1992.

[BOU 92c] BOUYSSOU D., PERNY P., "Ranking methods for valued preference relations: A characterization of a method based on entering and leaving flows", *European Journal of Operational Research*, vol. 61, p. 186–194, 1992.

[BOU 93] BOUYSSOU D., PERNY P., PIRLOT M., TSOUKIÀS A., VINCKE PH., "The manifesto of the new MCDA era", *Journal of Multi-Criteria Decision Analysis*, vol. 2, p. 125–127, 1993.

[BOU 96] BOUYSSOU D., "Outranking relations: do they have special properties?", *Journal of Multiple Criteria Decision Analysis*, vol. 5, p. 99–111, 1996.

[BOU 97] BOUYSSOU D., VINCKE PH., "Ranking alternatives on the basis of preference relations: a progress report with special emphasis on outranking relations", *Journal of Multi-Criteria Decision Analysis*, vol. 6, p. 77–85, 1997.

[BOU 04] BOUYSSOU D., "Monotonicity of 'ranking by choosing' procedures: A progress report", *Social Choice and Welfare*, vol. 23, num. 2, p. 249–273, 2004.

[BRA 82] BRAMS S. J., FISHBURN P. C., *Approval Voting*, Birkhäuser, Basel, 1982.

[CAM 02] CAMPBELL D. E., KELLY J. S., "Impossibility theorems in the Arrovian framework", ARROW K. J., SEN A. K., SUZUMURA K., Eds., *Handbook of Social Choice and Welfare*, vol. 1, p. 35–94, North-Holland, Amsterdam, 2002.

[CON 85] CONDORCET J. A. N. CARITAT, MARQUIS DE., *Essai sur l'application de l'analyse à la probabilité des décisions rendues à la pluralité des voix*, Imprimerie Royale, Paris, 1785.

[D'A 77] D'ASPREMONT C., GEVERS L., "Equity and the informational basis of collective choice", *Review of Economic Studies*, vol. 44, p. 199–209, 1977.

[DEB 87] DEBORD B., Axiomatisation de procédures d'agrégation de préférences, PhD Thesis, Université Scientifique, Technique et Médicale de Grenoble, 1987.

[DED 00] DE DONDER PH., LE BRETON M., TRUCHON M., "Choosing from a weighted tournament", *Mathematical Social Sciences*, vol. 40, p. 85–109, 2000.

[DUM 84] DUMMET M., *Voting Procedures*, Oxford University Press, Oxford, 1984.

[FEL 92] FELSENTHAL D. S., MOAZ Z., "Normative properties of four single-stage multi-winner electoral procedures", *Behavioral Science*, vol. 37, p. 109–127, 1992.

[FIS 73] FISHBURN P. C., *The Theory of Social Choice*, Princeton University Press, Princeton, New Jersey, 1973.

[FIS 77] FISHBURN P. C., "Condorcet social choice functions", *SIAM Journal on Applied Mathematics*, vol. 33, p. 469–489, 1977.

[FIS 87] FISHBURN P. C., *Interprofile Conditions and Impossibility*, Harwood Academic Publishers, Chur, 1987.

[FOD 94] FODOR J., ROUBENS M., *Fuzzy Preference Modelling and Multiple Criteria Decision Support*, Kluwer, Dordrecht, 1994.

[FOD 98] FODOR J., ORLOVSKI S., PERNY P., ROUBENS M., "The use of fuzzy preference models in multiple criteria choice, ranking and sorting", SLOWIŃSKI R., Ed., *Fuzzy sets in decision analysis, operations research and statistics*, p. 69–101, Kluwer, Dordrecht, 1998.

[GAR 82] GARGAILLO L., "Réponse à l'article 'Le plan d'extension du métro en banlieue parisienne, un cas type de l'analyse multicritère'", *Les Cahiers Scientifiques de la Revue Transports*, vol. 7, p. 52–57, 1982.

[GEH 83] GEHRLEIN W. V., "Condorcet's paradox", *Theory and Decision*, vol. 15, p. 161–197, 1983.

[GIB 69] GIBBARD A., Intransitive Social Indifference and the Arrow Dilemma, Mimeographed, 1969.

[GIB 73] GIBBARD A., "Manipulation of voting schemes: A general result", *Econometrica*, vol. 41, p. 587–601, 1973.

[JUR 03] JURET X., "Conditions suffisantes de monotonie des procédures de rangement itératives", *Mathématiques et Sciences Humaines*, vol. 161, p. 59–76, 2003.

[KEE 76] KEENEY R. L., RAIFFA H., *Decisions with Multiple Objectives: Preferences and Value Tradeoffs*, Wiley, New York, 1976.

[KEL 78] KELLY J. S., *Arrow Impossibility Theorems*, Academic Press, New York, 1978.

[KEL 91] KELLY J. S., "Social choice bibliography", *Social Choice and Welfare*, vol. 8, p. 97–169, 1991.

[KRA 71] KRANTZ D. H., LUCE R. D., SUPPES P., TVERSKY A., *Foundations of Measurement*, vol. 1: *Additive and Polynomial Representations*, Academic Press, New York, 1971.

[LAN 96] LANSDOWNE Z. L., "Ordinal ranking methods for multicriterion decision making", *Naval Research Logistics Quarterly*, vol. 43, p. 613–627, 1996.

[LAN 97] LANSDOWNE Z. L., "Outranking methods for multicriterion decision making: Arrow's and Raynaud's conjecture", *Social Choice and Welfare*, vol. 14, p. 125–128, 1997.

[LAS 97] LASLIER J.-F., *Tournament Solutions and Majority Voting*, Springer-Verlag, Berlin, 1997.

[LEC 84] LECLERC B., "Efficient and binary consensus functions on transitively valued relations", *Mathematical Social Sciences*, vol. 8, p. 45–61, 1984.

[LEV 95] LEVIN J., NALEBUFF B., "An introduction to vote-counting schemes", *Journal of Economic Perspectives*, vol. 9, p. 3–26, 1995.

[MAR 88] MARESCHAL B., BRANS J.-P., "Geometrical representations for MCDA", *European Journal of Operational Research*, vol. 34, p. 69–77, 1988.

[MAR 96] MARCHANT TH., "Valued relations aggregation with the Borda method", *Journal of Multi-Criteria Analysis*, vol. 5, p. 127–132, 1996.

[MAR 98] MARCHANT TH., "Cardinality and the Borda score", *European Journal of Operational Research*, vol. 108, p. 464–472, 1998.

[MAR 00] MARCHANT TH., "Does the Borda rule provide more than a ranking?", *Social Choice and Welfare*, vol. 17, p. 381–391, 2000.

[MAR 03] MARCHANT TH., "Towards a theory of MCDM; Stepping away from social choice theory", *Mathematical Social Sciences*, vol. 45, p. 343–363, 2003.

[MAS 72] MAS-COLELL A., SONNENSCHEIN H. F., "General possibility theorems for group decisions", *Review of Economic Studies*, vol. 39, p. 185–192, 1972.

[MAY 52] MAY K. O., "A set of independent necessary and sufficient conditions for simple majority decisions", *Econometrica*, vol. 20, p. 680–684, 1952.

[MCG 53] MCGARVEY D. C., "A theorem on the construction of voting paradoxes", *Econometrica*, vol. 21, p. 608–610, 1953.

[MOU 80] MOULIN H., *La stratégie du vote*, Monographie du séminaire d'économétrie nR14, Éditions du CNRS, Paris, 1980.

[MOU 88] MOULIN H., *Axioms of Cooperative Decision Making*, Cambridge University Press, Cambridge, 1988.

[NIT 81] NITZAN S., RUBINSTEIN A., "A further characterization of Borda ranking method", *Public Choice*, vol. 36, num. 1, p. 153–158, 1981.

[NUR 87] NURMI H., *Comparing Voting Systems*, D. Reidel, Dordrecht, 1987.

[OUL 00] OULD-ALI S., Variations autour de la méthode de Borda: une approche axiomatisée, PhD Thesis, Joseph Fourier University, Grenoble, 2000.

[OVC 91] OVCHINNIKOV S., "Social Choice and Łukasiewicz Logic", *Fuzzy Sets and Systems*, vol. 43, p. 275–289, 1991.

[PEL 84] PELEG B., *Game Theoretic Analysis of Voting in Committees*, Cambridge University Press, Cambridge, 1984.

[PER 92a] PERNY P., Modélisation, agrégation et exploitation de préférences floues dans une problématique de rangement, PhD Thesis, Paris Dauphine University, 1992.

[PER 92b] PERNY P., "Sur le non-respect de l'axiome d'indépendance dans les méthodes de type ELECTRE", *Cahiers du CERO*, vol. 34, p. 211–232, 1992.

[PER 92c] PERNY P., ROY B., "The use of fuzzy outranking relations in preference modelling", *Fuzzy Sets and Systems*, vol. 49, p. 33–53, 1992.

[PÉR 94] PÉREZ J., "Theoretical elements of comparison among ordinal discrete multicriteria methods", *Journal of Multi-Criteria Decision Analysis*, vol. 3, p. 157–176, 1994.

[PÉR 95] PÉREZ J., BARBA-ROMERO S., "Three practical criteria of comparison among ordinal preference aggregating rules", *European Journal of Operational Research*, vol. 85, p. 473–487, 1995.

[PER 98] PERNY P., ROUBENS M., "Fuzzy preference modelling", SLOWIŃSKI R., Ed., *Fuzzy Sets in Decision Analysis, Operations Research and Statistics*, p. 3–30, Kluwer, Dordrecht, 1998.

[PIR 95] PIRLOT M., "A characterization of 'min' as a procedure for exploiting valued preference relations and related results", *Journal of Multi-Criteria Decision Analysis*, vol. 4, p. 37–56, 1995.

[PIR 97] PIRLOT M., "A common framework for describing some outranking procedures", *Journal of Multi-Criteria Decision Analysis*, vol. 6, p. 86–93, 1997.

[POM 93] POMEROL J.-CH., BARBA-ROMERO S., *Choix multicritère dans l'entreprise*, Hermès, 1993, English translation: *Multicriterion Decision in Management, Principles and Practic*, Kluwer, Dordrecht, 2000.

[RIC 75] RICHELSON J. T., "A comparative analysis of social choice functions", *Behavioral Science*, vol. 20, p. 331–337, 1975.

[RIC 78a] RICHELSON J. T., "A comparative analysis of social choice functions II", *Behavioral Science*, vol. 23, p. 38–44, 1978.

[RIC 78b] RICHELSON J. T., "A comparative analysis of social choice functions III", *Behavioral Science*, vol. 23, p. 169–176, 1978.

[RIC 81] RICHELSON J. T., "A comparative analysis of social choice functions IV", *Behavioral Science*, vol. 35, p. 346–353, 1981.

[ROB 80] ROBERTS K. W. S., "Interpersonal comparability and Social Choice theory", *Review of Economic Studies*, vol. 47, p. 421–439, 1980.

[ROU 85] ROUBENS M., VINCKE PH., *Preference Modelling*, Springer-Verlag, Berlin, 1985.

[ROY 85] ROY B., *Méthodologie multicritère d'aide à la décision*, Economica, Paris, 1985, English translation: *Multicriteria Methodology for Decision Aiding*, Kluwer, Dordrecht, 1996.

[ROY 91] ROY B., "The outranking approach and the foundations of ELECTRE methods", *Theory and Decision*, vol. 31, p. 49–73, 1991.

[ROY 93] ROY B., BOUYSSOU D., *Aide multicritère à la décision: Méthodes et cas*, Economica, Paris, 1993.

[SAA 94] SAARI D. G., *Geometry of Voting*, Springer-Verlag, Heidelberg, 1994.

[SAT 75] SATTERTHWAITE M. A., "Strategyproofness and Arrow's conditions: existence and correspondence theorems for voting procedures and social welfare functions", *Journal of Economic Theory*, vol. 10, p. 187–217, 1975.

[SEN 70] SEN A. K., "The impossibility of a paretian liberal", *Journal of Political Economy*, vol. 72, p. 152–157, 1970.

[SEN 83] SEN A. K., "Liberty and social choice", *Journal of Philosophy*, vol. 80, p. 5–28, 1983.

[SEN 86] SEN A. K., "Social choice theory", ARROW K. J., INTRILIGATOR M. D., Eds., *Handbook of Mathematical Economics*, vol. 3, p. 1073–1181, North-Holland, Amsterdam, 1986.

[SEN 92] SEN A. K., "Minimal Liberty", *Economica*, vol. 59, p. 139–159, 1992.

[SMI 73] SMITH J. H., "Aggregation of preferences with a variable electorate", *Econometrica*, vol. 41, p. 1027–1041, 1973.

[VAN 86a] VANSNICK J.-C., "De Borda et Condorcet à l'agrégation Multicritère", *Ricerca Operativa*, vol. 40, p. 7–44, 1986.

[VAN 86b] VANSNICK J.-C., "On the problem of weights in multiple criteria decision making: the noncompensatory approach", *European Journal of Operational Research*, vol. 24, p. 288–294, 1986.

[VAN 90] VANDERPOOTEN D., "The construction of prescriptions in outranking methods", BANA E COSTA C. A., Ed., *Readings in Multiple Criteria Decision Aid*, Springer-Verlag, p. 184–215, 1990.

[VIN 89] VINCKE PH., *L'aide multicritère à la décision*, Éditions de l'Université de Bruxelles: Éditions Ellipses, Brussels-Paris, 1989, English translation: *Multi-criteria Decision Aid*, Wiley, New York, 1992.

[VIN 92] VINCKE PH., "Exploitation of a crisp relation in a ranking problem", *Theory and Decision*, vol. 32, p. 221–240, 1992.

[VON 86] VON WINTERFELDT D., EDWARDS W., *Decision Analysis and Behavorial Research*, Cambridge University Press, Cambridge, 1986.

[WAK 89] WAKKER P. P., *Additive Representations of Preferences: A New Foundation of Decision Analysis*, Kluwer, Dordrecht, 1989.

[YOU 74] YOUNG H. P., "An axiomatization of Borda's rule", *Journal of Economic Theory*, vol. 9, p. 43–52, 1974.

[YOU 75] YOUNG H. P., "Social choice scoring functions", *SIAM Journal on Applied Mathematics*, vol. 28, p. 824–838, 1975.

Chapter 20

Metric and Latticial Medians

20.1. Introduction

Previous chapters of this book dealt with some aggregation problems arising in the field of collective choice or multicriteria decision. This chapter studies a family of aggregation methods often encountered in literature and which may be qualified as *median procedure*. In this introduction, we first consider the concept of median in general, then the medians of binary relations and finally latticial medians.

20.1.1. *Medians in general*

The concept of median comes first from geometry. Every one of us dealt in school with special lines in triangles. An angle bisector cuts an angle into two equal angles and comes to an end on the opposite side. An altitude is a straight line through a vertex and perpendicular to the opposite side. A median is a straight line through a vertex and the midpoint of the opposite side, which is divided into two equal parts. More generally, medians are based on equal shares. The median of a sorted statistical series divides it into two equal parts. In their famous *Dictionary of Statistical Terms*, Kendall and Buckland [KEN 57] distinguish between 'median' and 'median center' by writing that 'according to the Italian tradition', the median center is a point such that the sum of the distances to the points of a given set is a minimum. In fact, these two notions coincide as already pointed out by Laplace [LAP 74].

Chapter written by Olivier HUDRY, Bruno LECLERC, Bernard MONJARDET and Jean-Pierre BARTHÉLEMY.

Medians therefore relate two kinds of structures: an ordinal structure (here a linear order; more generally, a lattice or a semilattice) and a metric structure (we will speak about metric median in this case). It is interesting to observe that if the median is of metric nature, it is not of geometric nature. The intersection of the three medians of a triangle is its center of gravity and not the (metric) median of its three vertices. Moreover, the median of aligned points depends only on the succession of these points and not on the lengths of the intervals between them.

20.1.2. *Medians of binary relations*

The problem of the aggregation of binary relations (here, finite complete preorders) was formally raised by Arrow [ARR 51]. The notion of median occurred quickly in the prolongation of this work and according to the above-mentioned dimensions: ordinal and metric. With respect to the first, Guilbaud [GUI 52] dated back the Arrowian questions to the voting theories developed at the end of the 18th century by Borda [BOR 84], Condorcet [CAR 85] and others (e.g. [BLA 58]). In particular, Guilbaud insisted on the fact that the majority rule is not generally applicable, and wrote: 'The analytic study of Condorcet's paradox will lead us to perceive how we can build a *median* in various partially ordered structures.'

Indeed, Condorcet (and some others after him) noticed that the usual voting procedures made possible the election of a candidate defeated by another by a majority of voters. Condorcet then proposed to split the vote into duels (i.e. to compare the candidates pairwise) and to consider the candidate defeating all the others by a majority as the winner. Unfortunately, Condorcet realized that this voting procedure raised a major difficulty, referred to as *Condorcet's effect* by Guilbaud ('voting paradox' in the English literature): it can happen that each candidate is defeated majoritarily by another one (an example in section 20.2.4).

At the end of the 1950s, Kemeny [KEM 59] introduced the notion of metric median of linear orders in order to palliate Arrow's impossibility result. This notion of median is based on the symmetric difference distance, a distance given by the number of 'disagreements' between two binary relations. Kemeny's justification to use this distance was based on its axiomatic characterization. Since these pioneering works, the amount of research on the median of binary relations has considerably increased. We can find in [BART 81] a review of the already abundant literature devoted to this subject before the 1980s. From an algorithmic point of view, observe that except some rather obvious cases, the search for a median (in Kemeny's sense and for various types of binary relations) generally leads to NP-hard problems [HUD 08].

20.1.3. *Medians in lattices*

As is usual in mathematics, the understanding of a strong relation between two approaches is reached with the help of an abstract scheme in which both approaches are embedded. Here, the abstract model of lattices (and semilattices) will join ordinal (Guilbaud) and metric (Kemeny) approaches. In two seminal papers, Barbut [BAR 61, BAR 67] showed that Laplace's result on the equivalence of ordinal and metric medians (of a series of numbers) generalizes to distributive lattices. Moreover, he explicitly related these medians both with Condorcet's majority rule and with ordinal statistics as developed by Kendall [KEN 38] (the celebrated Kendall coefficient τ is nothing but a normalization between -1 and $+1$ of the symmetric difference distance, which was later extensively considered by Kemeny). Barbut's results were then systematized by Monjardet who introduced the notion of median interval [MON 80]. Significant extensions were then developed in two directions:

– to larger types of ordinal structures, especially modular lattices (and semilattices); and

– to the study of medians in trees (a topic undoubtedly initiated by Camille Jordan [JOR 69]).

Finally, any statement simultaneously valid in trees and in distributive lattices may be expected to remain valid in the more general abstract structure of median semilattices (previously considered by Sholander [SHO 54] and Avann [AVA 61]). For instance, Barbut's results on distributive lattices, together with those of Zelinka [ZEL 68] and Slater [SLA 78] on trees, were extended to median semilattices by Bandelt and Barthélemy [BAN 84].

The topic considered in this chapter is very prolific. Barthélemy and Monjardet's paper [BART 81] written almost 30 years ago contained about 200 references. This number has surely at least tripled (in particular, cluster analysis is becoming a big consumer of medians). We have therefore been forced to make drastic choices.

On the relational side, we essentially restrict the field to the cases of arbitrary binary relations, tournaments and linear orders (although other relations occur in the final section as an application of the latticial median).

On the metric side, we insist on the symmetric difference distance and its extension to semilattices. We do not deal with the 'geodesic' aspects (for example, in the permutohedron lattice) which also refer to graph theory and ordered set theory.

On the latticial side, we insist on the structure where medians have a natural algebraic expression, namely the median semilattices. This is not a reason to forget that similar or more general results (in semimodular and even arbitrary semilattices) have been obtained e.g. [LEC 93, LEC 94].

This chapter is divided into five sections, including this introduction. Section 20.2 gives the general frame, with the main definitions that will be useful later. It includes a study of the medians in the simple cases of general binary relations and tournaments. Section 20.3 deals with median (linear) orders, and considers the problem of their effective computation. It includes developments about several questions relevant from a combinatorial optimization point of view.

Medians in (semi)lattices are considered in section 20.4. It is first observed that several sets of binary relations, conveniently ordered, are lattices or semilattices. The attention then moves from binary relations to lattices. First, the extension of the symmetric difference metric to lattices involves a definition of medians in such structures. We focus on median semilattices, previously described as a favored frame for the unification of almost all the positive results of the literature. This section also returns to the uses, pointing out how the lattice approach may provide results about several types of binary relations but also about other models of preferences (e.g. some types of choice functions).

Finally, in the conclusion of the chapter, we recapitulate the different notions of medians encountered, their relationships and the situations where the median procedure turns out to be an easy method.

20.2. Median relations

20.2.1. *The model*

We consider in this chapter:

– a finite set $V = \{1, 2, \ldots, v\}$ of v elements referred to as *voters*, but which could also be agents, criteria, etc.

– a finite set $X = \{x, y, z, \ldots\}$ of n elements referred to as *candidates*, but which could also be decisions, objects, etc.

Each voter is assumed to compare the candidates pairwise. Their preferences between the candidates are therefore expressed by a binary relation R defined on X. We assume that R belongs to a given set $\mathcal{D}$ of binary relations defined on X. So if $\mathcal{R} = P(X^2)$ is the set of all the subsets of X^2 i.e. the set of all binary relations defined on X, we have $\mathcal{D} \subseteq \mathcal{R}$. When the preference relation R_i of each voter i is given, we obtain the so-called *profile* of the individual preferences of the voters. We denote such a profile by $\Pi = (R_1, R_2, \ldots, R_v)$. The set of all possible preference profiles is therefore $\mathcal{D}^v$.

The collective preference must often belong to the same set of relations as the individual preferences i.e. it must belong to $\mathcal{D}$. We can also allow the collective relation to belong to a set $\mathcal{M}$ (for 'models') of relations, generally with $\mathcal{D} \subseteq \mathcal{M} \subseteq \mathcal{R}$. Then, an *aggregation procedure* is a map from $\mathcal{D}^v$ to $\mathcal{M}$. Later, we will extend this definition by considering that the aggregation procedure can lead to several collective preference relations for the same profile of individual preferences. Then, an *aggregation procedure* becomes a map from $\mathcal{D}^v$ to $P^*(\mathcal{M})$, where $P^*(\mathcal{M})$ denotes the set of non-empty subsets of $\mathcal{M}$.

The applied aggregation procedure is required to satisfy 'good properties'. For instance, if all the voters prefer a certain candidate to another, this unanimous preference must be kept in the collective preference. To find 'good' aggregation procedures is not an easy task. Indeed, we face strong obstacles such as the Condorcet effect (section 20.3) or Arrow's theorem [ARR 51] (see Chapter 19 and the articles in issue number 163 of *Mathématiques et Sciences Humaines* [MSH 03]). We cannot then be too ambitious on the qualities of the considered aggregation procedures.

The aggregation procedures that we are going to study in this chapter belong to the large class of the so-called *metric aggregation procedures*. They are based on a very natural idea found in various contexts, for example in data analysis. We look for the collective preference that is the closest – in a sense to specify – to the profile of individual preferences. In order to specify this closeness, we begin by defining a distance d on the set $\mathcal{M}$ of possible collective preference relations, which therefore becomes a metric space $(\mathcal{M}, d)$. Afterwards in this metric space we define a remoteness [BART 81] between a profile of individual preferences and an arbitrary relation of $\mathcal{M}$. The collective preference relations associated with this profile are the relations of $\mathcal{M}$ minimizing this remoteness.

20.2.2. *The median procedure*

Let $(\mathcal{M}, d)$ be the metric space where $\mathcal{M}$ is the set of all possible collective preference relations and d a distance on $\mathcal{M}$. The median procedure is the metric aggregation procedure where the remoteness $E(\Pi, R)$ between a profile $\Pi = (R_1, R_2, \ldots, R_v)$ of individual preferences and a relation R of $\mathcal{M}$ is obtained as the sum of the distances of the relations R_i of this profile to the relation R:

$$E(\Pi, R) = \sum_{i=1}^{v} d(R_i, R).$$

Definition 20.1. Let $\Pi \in \mathcal{D}^v$ be a profile of individual preferences and $\mathcal{M} \subseteq \mathcal{R}$. An $\mathcal{M}$-median of Π is a relation of $\mathcal{M}$ that is a solution of the following optimization problem:

$$\text{minimize } \{E(\Pi, M) : M \in \mathcal{M}\}.$$

As $\mathcal{M}$ is a finite set, there always exists at least one $\mathcal{M}$-median of a profile and there can exist several $\mathcal{M}$-medians. We denote by $Med_{\mathcal{M}}(\Pi)$ the set of $\mathcal{M}$-medians of a profile Π. Obviously, the $\mathcal{M}$-medians of a profile depend on the chosen distance d on $\mathcal{M}$. Hereafter, we will only consider the most natural and used distance between binary relations, namely the symmetric difference distance δ. Recall the definition of this distance. Let R and R' be two binary relations defined on a set X and $|R \Delta R'|$ be their symmetric difference. Then,

$$\delta(R, R') = |R \Delta R'| = |R \cup R'| - |R \cap R'| = |R \backslash R'| + |R' \backslash R|$$

which can also be written:

$$\delta(R, R') = |\{(x,y) : [(x,y) \in R \text{ and } (x,y) \notin R'] \text{ or } [(x,y) \notin R \text{ and } (x,y) \in R']\}|.$$

In other words, the symmetric difference distance between R and R' is the number of ordered pairs of X belonging to one of these relations and not to the other. It counts the number of *disagreements* between these two relations.

Then, for the chosen distance δ, the remoteness of a profile $\Pi = (R_1, R_2, \ldots, R_v)$ to a relation R is:

$$E(\Pi, R) = \sum_{i=1}^{v} \delta(R_i, R).$$

20.2.3. *The $\mathcal{R}$-medians of a profile of relations*

We begin by considering the case where the individual preferences of the voters on the candidates can be arbitrary binary relations i.e. $\mathcal{D} = \mathcal{R}$. This case, unrealistic in a voting context, can be achieved for other aggregation contexts. Moreover, the results obtained for this case remain valid for particular relations. We need to define parameters associated with a profile $\Pi = (R_1, R_2, \ldots, R_v)$. We set:

$$
\begin{aligned}
V_\Pi(x,y) &= \{i \in V : xR_iy\}, \\
V_\Pi^c(x,y) &= \{i \in V : (x,y) \notin R_i\}, \\
v_\Pi(x,y) &= |V_\Pi(x,y)| = |\{i \in V : xR_iy\}|, \\
v_\Pi^c(x,y) &= |V_\Pi^c(x,y)| = |\{i \in V : (x,y) \notin R_i\}|, \\
w_\Pi(x,y) &= v_\Pi(x,y) - v_\Pi^c(x,y).
\end{aligned}
$$

$V_\Pi(x,y)$ is therefore the set of voters preferring candidate x to candidate y, $v_\Pi(x,y)$ is the number of these voters and $v_\Pi^c(x,y)$ is the number of voters that do not prefer x to y (which generally does not mean that they prefer y to x). We obviously have $v_\Pi(x,y) + v_\Pi^c(x,y) = v$ and $w_\Pi(x,y) = 2v_\Pi(x,y) - v$. When there is no risk of ambiguity i.e. almost always, we drop the index Π in the above notation (e.g. $V_\Pi(x,y)$ becomes $V(x,y)$).

A first result states the remoteness of a profile to an arbitrary relation R by means of the previous parameters, and the changes in this remoteness when an ordered pair is removed from or added to R.

Lemma 20.1. *For* $\Pi = (R_1, R_2, \ldots, R_v) \in \mathcal{R}^v$ *and* $R \in \mathcal{R}$, *we have:*
1) $E(\Pi, R) = \sum_{(x,y) \in R} v^c(x,y) + \sum_{(x,y) \notin R} v(x,y)$;
2) $E(\Pi, R) = \sum_{i=1}^{v} |R_i| - \sum_{(x,y) \in R} w(x,y)$;
3) *if* $(x,y) \in R$, $E(\Pi, R \setminus \{(x,y)\}) = E(\Pi, R) + w(x,y)$;
4) *if* $(x,y) \notin R$, $E(\Pi, R \cup \{(x,y)\}) = E(\Pi, R) - w(x,y)$.

Proof. Let us first prove (1). By definition of $E(\Pi, R)$, we have:

$$E(\Pi, R) = \sum_{i=1}^{v} \delta(R_i, R) = \sum_{i=1}^{v} |R_i \Delta R|.$$

Let us introduce the characteristic function δ_i of $R_i \Delta R$ defined by:

$$\forall (x,y) \in X^2, \delta_i(x,y) = \begin{cases} 1 & \text{if } (x,y) \in R_i \Delta R, \\ 0 & \text{otherwise.} \end{cases}$$

Then

$$E(\Pi, R) = \sum_{i=1}^{v} \sum_{(x,y) \in X^2} \delta_i(x,y).$$

By partitioning X^2 into R and its complement $X^2 \setminus R$, we obtain:

$$\begin{aligned} E(\Pi, R) &= \sum_{(x,y) \in R} \sum_{i=1}^{v} \delta_i(x,y) + \sum_{(x,y) \notin R} \sum_{i=1}^{v} \delta_i(x,y) \\ &= \sum_{(x,y) \in R} v^c(x,y) + \sum_{(x,y) \notin R} v^c(x,y) \end{aligned}$$

which proves the first relation. Adding and subtracting $\sum_{(x,y)\in R} v(x,y)$, we obtain (2):

$$\begin{aligned} E(\Pi, R) &= \sum_{(x,y)\in R} v(x,y) + \sum_{(x,y)\notin R} v(x,y) - \left[\sum_{(x,y)\in R} v(x,y) - \sum_{(x,y)\in R} v^c(x,y) \right] \\ &= \sum_{(x,y)\in X^2} v(x,y) - \sum_{(x,y)\in R} w(x,y) \\ &= \sum_{i=1}^{v} |R_i| - \sum_{(x,y)\in R} w(x,y). \end{aligned}$$

Formulae (3) and (4) are immediate consequences of (2). ◇

In the simple cases, the median relations of a profile are linked to the 'majority' relations associated with this profile. We now define these relations after introducing some notation: for $\Pi \in \mathcal{R}^v$ and for an integer σ, we set:

$$R(\Pi, \sigma) = \{(x,y) \in X^2 : v(x,y) \geq \sigma\}.$$

We also denote this relation by $R(\sigma)$. It contains all the pairwise preferences supported by at least σ voters. On the other hand, if r is a real number, the notation $\lceil r \rceil$ (respectively $\lfloor r \rfloor$) denotes the integer part by excess (respectively by defect) of r. Finally, we set $\alpha = \lceil (v+1)/2 \rceil$ and $\beta = \lfloor (v+1)/2 \rfloor$ (thus, if $v = 2p+1$, $\alpha = \beta = p+1$; if $v = 2p$, $\alpha = p+1$ and $\beta = p$).

Definition 20.2. For $\Pi \in \mathcal{R}^v$, the strict majority relation associated with Π is the relation

$$R(\alpha) = \{(x,y) \in X^2 : v(x,y) \geq \alpha = \lceil (v+1)/2 \rceil\}$$

and the majority relation associated with Π is the relation

$$R(\beta) = \{(x,y) \in X^2 : v(x,y) \geq \beta = \lfloor (v+1)/2 \rfloor\}.$$

A candidate x is therefore preferred to a candidate y in the strict majority relation (respectively, in the majority relation) if the number of voters preferring x to y in profile Π is strictly greater than (respectively, greater than or equal to) half the voters. Obviously, these two relations are the same if the number of voters is odd. We also have the equalities:

$$R(\alpha) = \{(x,y) \in X^2 : v(x,y) > v^c(x,y)\} = \{(x,y) \in X^2 : w(x,y) > 0\}$$

and

$$R(\beta) = \{(x,y) \in X^2 : v(x,y) \geq v^c(x,y)\} = \{(x,y) \in X^2 : w(x,y) \geq 0\}.$$

The set $R(\beta)\backslash R(\alpha) = \{(x,y) \in X^2 : w(x,y) = 0\}$ is the set of the ordered pairs (x,y) of candidates for which there are as many voters preferring x to y as voters not preferring x to y. In the case where, for all the voters, x is not preferred to y if and only if y is preferred to x, $R(\beta)\backslash R(\alpha)$ is the set of the ordered pairs of candidates which are *ex æquo*, i.e. of candidates for which the numbers of voters preferring one of the candidates to the other are equal.

Recalling the notion of *interval* in a lattice (see section 6.4.1), we can state the first result on the (arbitrary) medians of a profile of (arbitrary) relations. In the Boolean lattice $(\mathcal{R}, \subseteq)$ of all the binary relations defined on X, the interval $[S,T]$ associated with two relations S and T satisfying $S \subseteq T$ is the set $\{R \in \mathcal{R} : S \subseteq R \subseteq T\}$.

Proposition 20.1. *Let* $\Pi \in \mathcal{R}^v$ *be a profile of binary relations on* X. *We have:*

$$Med_{\mathcal{R}}(\Pi) = [R(\alpha), R(\beta)].$$

The number of $\mathcal{R}$-medians of Π is $2^{|R(\beta)\backslash R(\alpha)|}$. If $R(\beta)\backslash R(\alpha) = \emptyset$ (in particular if the number of voters is odd), then Π has a unique median.

Proof. Let R be an $\mathcal{R}$-median of Π. If $R(\alpha) \subseteq R$ is not satisfied, there exists $(x,y) \in X^2$ with $w(x,y) > 0$ and $(x,y) \notin R$. By lemma 20.1(4), we have:

$$E(\Pi, R \cup \{(x,y)\}) = E(\Pi, R) - w(x,y) < E(\Pi, R),$$

which is impossible, since R is a median of Π. Likewise, if $R \subseteq R(\beta)$ is not satisfied, there exists $(x,y) \in X^2$ with $(x,y) \in R$ and $w(x,y) < 0$. By lemma 20.1(3), we have:

$$E(\Pi, R\backslash\{(x,y)\}) = E(\Pi, R) + w(x,y),$$

which is still a contradiction.

The $\mathcal{R}$-medians of Π are therefore in the interval $[R(\alpha), R(\beta)]$ and, since all the relations R of this interval have the same remoteness to the profile i.e.

$$E(\Pi, R) = E(\Pi, R(\alpha)) = \sum_{i-1}^{v} |R_i| - \sum_{w(x,y)>0} w(x,y),$$

this interval provides all the $\mathcal{R}$-medians of Π.

Since we may or may not add any element of $R(\beta)\backslash R(\alpha)$ to form an $\mathcal{R}$-median of Π, we immediately obtain the number of these $\mathcal{R}$-medians. ◇

The $\mathcal{R}$-medians of Π are therefore all the relations between the two majority relations of Π. They form the interval $[R(\alpha), R(\beta)]$ (the *median interval*) of the Boolean lattice $(\mathcal{R}, \subseteq)$ of all the binary relations. The last section of this chapter will return to the links between medians and lattices, but we can already observe that the majority relations are obtained by means of the operations of this lattice i.e. by means of the union and of the intersection of relations. Indeed, we have

$$R(\alpha) = \bigcup_{W \subseteq V \text{ and } |W| \geq \alpha} \left(\bigcap_{i \in W} R_i \right) \text{ and } R(\beta) = \bigcup_{W \subseteq V \text{ and } |W| \geq \beta} \left(\bigcap_{i \in W} R_i \right).$$

20.2.4. *The $\mathcal{M}$-medians of a profile of relations*

We now consider the case where the collective preference relations associated with a profile Π are not arbitrary relations but must belong to a given set $\mathcal{M}$ of binary relations i.e. must be the $\mathcal{M}$-medians of Π. We can always consider the $\mathcal{R}$-medians of Π i.e. the median interval $[R(\alpha), R(\beta)]$, but this interval may contain no relation belonging to $\mathcal{M}$. For example, if $\mathcal{D}$ and $\mathcal{M}$ are both the set of the linear orders on three candidates x, y and z, it is easy to see that the $\mathcal{R}$-medians of the profile formed by the three linear orders $x > y > z$, $y > z > x$ and $z > x > y$ is the reflexive relation R defined by xRy, yRz and zRx; this relation is not a linear order (it is a 3-cycle). In fact, we have the following obvious but not uninteresting result.

Proposition 20.2. *Let $\Pi \in \mathcal{R}^v$ and $\mathcal{M} \subseteq \mathcal{R}$. If $\mathcal{M} \cap Med_\mathcal{R}(\Pi) \neq \emptyset$, then $Med_\mathcal{M}(\Pi) = \mathcal{M} \cap Med_R(\Pi)$.*

Proof. Indeed, if a relation of $\mathcal{M}$ belongs to the median interval of a profile Π, then this relation (as well as all the other relations of $\mathcal{M}$ belonging to this interval) minimizes the remoteness of the profile to any relation of $\mathcal{M}$, since it minimizes this remoteness on the set of all binary relations. ◇

20.2.5. *The $\mathcal{T}$-medians of a profile of tournaments*

We now restrict the relations modeling the individual and collective preferences of the voters by assuming that they are tournaments. A *tournament* T on X is a *complete* (i.e. xTy not satisfied implies yTx) and *antisymmetric* (i.e. xTy and yTx imply $x = y$) relation. A tournament that is also transitive (i.e. xTy and yTz imply xTz) is a *linear order* (the classical and simplest model of transitive preference). However, preference relations which are non-transitive tournaments often appear, e.g. when a voter is asked what their preferred candidate is in each pair of candidates (the so-called paired-comparison method). We denote by $\mathcal{T}$ (respectively, $\mathcal{L}$) the set of tournaments (respectively, linear orders) defined on X. It immediately follows from the properties of tournaments that, for a profile $\Pi = (T_1, T_2, \ldots, T_v) \in \mathcal{T}^v$ (and in particular for $\Pi \in \mathcal{L}^v$), we have for all x and y:

$$v_\Pi^c(x, y) = v_\Pi(y, x) \text{ if } x \neq y; v_\Pi^c(x, x) = 0,$$
$$w_\Pi(x, y) = 2v_\Pi(x, y) - v; w_\Pi(x, x) = v,$$
$$v_\Pi(x, y) + v_\Pi(y, x) = \begin{cases} v & \text{if } x \neq y; \\ 2v & \text{if } x = y. \end{cases}$$

As above, when there is no risk of ambiguity i.e. almost always, we omit the index Π in the notation. The remoteness of a tournament T to a profile of tournaments $\Pi = (T_1, T_2, \ldots, T_v)$ is then given by:

$$E(\Pi, T) = \sum_{(x,y) \in T} v(y, x) + \sum_{(x,y) \notin T} v(y, x)$$
$$= \frac{v.n(n+1)}{2} - \sum_{(x,y) \in T} w(x, y).$$

With this formula and proposition 20.2, we easily find all the *median tournaments* of a profile of tournaments i.e. all the tournaments T minimizing $E(\Pi, T)$ in the set $\mathcal{T}$ of all the tournaments defined on X.

Proposition 20.3. *Let $\Pi \in \mathcal{T}^v$ be a profile of tournaments. Then $Med_\mathcal{T}(\Pi) = \mathcal{T} \cap [R(\alpha), R(\beta)]$. Moreover, the number of median tournaments of Π is $2^{|R(\beta) \setminus R(\alpha)|/2}$. The remoteness of a median tournament T to the profile Π is:*

$$E(\Pi, T) = \frac{v.n(n+1)}{2} - \sum_{w(x,y) > 0} w(x, y).$$

Proof. By proposition 20.2, we have only to show that there always exists a tournament in the median interval $[R(\alpha), R(\beta)]$ of Π. However, we obtain such a tournament by adding to the antisymmetric relation $R(\alpha)$ one and only one of the two ordered pairs (x, y) and (y, x) whenever x and y are *ex æquo*, i.e. when $v(x, y) = v(y, x)$. ◇

20.3. The median linear orders ($\mathcal{L}$-medians) of a profile of linear orders

Let us consider now the case for which the voters' preferences are linear orders. Since linear orders are particular tournaments, we can apply the previous results to find the median tournaments of a profile Π of linear orders. These are the tournaments belonging to the median interval of Π which always contains some tournaments according to proposition 20.3 stated above.

Everything may change if we now search for the *median linear orders* of Π i.e. the linear orders L minimizing $E(\Pi, L)$ among the set $\mathcal{L}$ of linear orders defined on X. Indeed, as shown in the example given in section 20.2.4, the median interval of a profile of linear orders may contain no linear order (in this example, the median interval is reduced to the majority relation and this single tournament is a circuit i.e. a directed cycle).

We must then distinguish between two cases. In the first case, there exists a linear order in the median interval of Π or, equivalently, the strict majority relation $R(\alpha)$ of Π has no circuit. In this case (according to proposition 20.3), the median orders of Π are all the linear orders belonging to the median interval, i.e. all the linear orders that contain the relation $R(\alpha)$ (it is well known that a relation is contained in a linear order if and only if the relation has no circuit).

The second case is that where the median interval of the profile contains no linear order or, equivalently, the case where the strict majority relation contains a circuit. In this case, we say that a *Condorcet effect* occurs. (The possible existence of circuits in the majority relation was indeed shown by Condorcet [CAR 85]. A sharp analysis [YOU 88] of Condorcet's propositions – not always very clear – in order to overcome the existence of such circuits has also led to him being credited with the paternity of the process providing the median orders of a profile of linear orders. This process may actually be defined in many ways [MON 90a], which explains the fact that it has been proposed by several authors, the first of whom was Kemeny [KEM 59].) The possible existence of a Condorcet effect has the following consequence. Whereas obtaining median relations or median tournaments of a profile was easy, the problem of searching for a median linear order becomes hard (actually NP-hard, see section 20.3.4) and requires the study of the properties of such orders and the use of combinatorial optimization methods to provide exact or approximate solutions. This issue will be the subject of section 20.3; in section 20.4, we will return to the easy case which can be dealt with in the framework of 'median semilattice'.

20.3.1. *Binary linear programming formulation*

Consider a profile of linear orders $\Pi = (L_1, L_2, \ldots, L_v) \in \mathcal{L}^v$ and a linear order L. We have seen in section 20.2.3 (lemma 20.1) that the remoteness $E(\Pi, L)$ can be

stated as:
$$E(\Pi, L) = \sum_{i=1}^{v} |L_i| - \sum_{(x,y) \in L} w(x, y).$$

In order to formulate the remoteness with 0-1 variables, let us introduce the *characteristic function* $\rho = (\rho_{xy})_{(x,y) \in X^2}$ of L. It is defined from X^2 to $\{0, 1\}$ by $\rho_{xy} = 1$ if xLy, and $\rho_{xy} = 0$ otherwise. Since for any $L_i (1 \leq i \leq v)$ we have the relation

$$|L_i| = \frac{n(n+1)}{2},$$

we obtain for the remoteness:

$$E(\Pi, L) = \frac{v.n(n+1)}{2} - \sum_{(x,y) \in X^2} w(x, y).\rho_{xy}.$$

Since the variables are the terms ρ_{xy} for $(x, y) \in X^2$, this formulation allows us to consider $E(\Pi, L)$ as the objective function of a linear programming problem with binary variables ρ_{xy}. Since minimizing a function is the same as maximizing its opposite (with opposite signs for the optima), minimizing $E(\Pi, L)$ is the same as maximizing

$$\sum_{(x,y) \in X^2} w(x, y).\rho_{xy}$$

up to an additive constant, which will be omitted in the following.

It simply remains to state the characteristic properties of a linear order as linear constraints. The reader will easily convince themself that these properties can be expressed as the following constraints:

- reflexivity: $\forall x \in X, \rho_{xx} = 1$;
- antisymmetry: $\forall (x, y) \in X^2$ with $x \neq y$, $\rho_{xy} + \rho_{yx} \leq 1$;
- completeness: $\forall (x, y) \in X^2$ with $x \neq y$, $\rho_{xy} + \rho_{yx} \geq 1$;
- transitivity: $\forall (x, y, z) \in X^3$, $\rho_{xy} + \rho_{yz} - \rho_{xz} \leq 1$.

The determination of a median order is therefore the same as the resolution of the following binary linear programming problem:

$$\text{Maximize} \sum_{(x,y) \in X^2} w(x, y).\rho_{xy}$$

under the constraints

$$\begin{cases} \forall x \in X, \rho_{xx} = 1 \\ \forall (x, y) \in X^2 \text{ with } x \neq y, \rho_{xy} + \rho_{yx} \leq 1 \\ \forall (x, y, z) \in X^3, \rho_{xy} + \rho_{yz} - \rho_{xz} \leq 1 \\ \forall (x, y) \in X^2, \rho_{xy} \in \{0, 1\}. \end{cases}$$

20.3.2. *Formulation using weighted directed graphs*

Since a binary relation can be associated with a graph and vice versa, we can formulate the problem with the help of graphs. The previous considerations show that the voters' preferences can be summarized by the data contained in the terms $w(x,y)$ for any element x and any element y of X (with $w(y,x) = -w(x,y)$ for $x \neq y$ since we consider individual preferences that are linear orders; in the general case, the preferences can be summarized by the terms $v(x,y)$). Previous considerations show that minimizing the remoteness is the same as maximizing the sum $\sum_{(x,y) \in X^2} w(x,y) \cdot \rho_{xy}$.

We can therefore summarize a profile $\Pi = (L_1, L_2, \ldots, L_v)$ defined on X by a directed graph $G = (X, X^2)$ (in other words, G contains all the possible arcs i.e. directed edges) in which each arc (x,y) is weighted by $w(x,y)$; we will say that the weighted graph G *represents* the profile Π. Note that the weights of the arcs (x,y) and (y,x), for $x \neq y$, are opposite. Moreover, since $w(x,y)$ is equal to $2v(x,y) - v$, all the weights have the same parity as v and are between $-v$ (no voter prefers x to y) and v (all the voters prefer x to y, which is the case in particular if $x = y$). We may wonder which graphs represent profiles of linear orders. The works of Debord [DEB 87], extending those of McGarvey [MCG 53], give such a characterization when the number of linear orders is large enough.

Theorem 20.1. *Let $G = (X, X^2)$ be a graph containing all the possible arcs, which are weighted by a function w. Then G represents a profile of v ($v > 0$) linear orders if the following properties are satisfied:*
1) $\forall (x,y) \in X^2$, $w(x,y)$ has the same parity as v;
2) $\forall x \in X$, $w(x,x) = v$;
3) $\forall (x,y) \in X^2$ with $x \neq y$, $w(x,y) = -w(y,x)$;
4) $v \geq 1/2(\sum_{x \neq y} |w(x,y)|)$ if this sum is not equal to 0 and $v \geq 2$ otherwise.

In the following, we will say that a weight-function w satisfies the property (P) if it verifies the following conditions:
1) all the values taken by w have the same parity;
2) the quantities $w(x,x)$ are the same for all $x \in X$; and
3) $\forall (x,y) \in X^2$ with $x \neq y$, $w(y,x) = -w(x,y)$.

We will say that w satisfies the property (P') if its values are non-negative and if it verifies conditions (1) and (2) stated above.

Debord's proof of theorem 20.1 consists of building a profile of linear orders from the graph G. The minimum number v of linear orders involved in this construction is about $1/2(\sum_{x \neq y} |w(x,y)|)$. The exact value depends on the parity of the weights $w(x,y)$; this quantity is not necessarily the minimum number of required linear orders. (There exist graphs G representing profiles of linear orders but which do not satisfy condition (4) of theorem 20.1. Except for some simple cases, we do not know how to characterize these graphs, or even how to recognize them in polynomial time.)

Let us also note that the construction performed by Debord to build the profile is polynomial if the quantities $w(x,y)$ are upper-bounded by a polynomial in n or if the profile is represented in a slightly different manner than before: instead of describing the profile Π by enumerating the v orders of Π, we enumerate only the orders which are pairwise distinct and which appear in Π along with the number of occurrences for each such order [HUD 89].

This graph theoretic representation of the profiles of linear orders is used to study the problem complexity in particular, since its polynomiality allows the representative graphs to be dealt with rather than the profiles without changing qualitatively the obtained results. On the other hand, theorem 20.1 also provides the characterization of a profile of v tournaments with a slight adaptation: it is sufficient to replace condition (4) by the inequality $v \geq \max_{(x,y)} |w(x,y)|$. This inequality, with the parity of v and the fact that v is non-negative, then gives all the possible values for v. A particular case is the one for which v is equal to 1 (the profile is reduced to one tournament e.g. the majority tournament of a profile of linear orders). We obtain the problem stated by Slater [SLA 61] to fit a tournament to a linear order; in this case, all the weights w are equal to 1 or -1.

Similarly, we may associate a graph with the searched median order L. For this, it is sufficient to consider the graph of which the adjacency matrix admits the ρ_{xy} as its entries, where $(\rho_{xy})_{(x,y) \in X^2}$ denotes the characteristic function of L. From a graph theoretic point of view, determining a linear order maximizing $\sum_{(x,y) \in X^2} w(x,y) \rho_{xy}$ is then the same as selecting some arcs of G constituting a linear order such that the sum of the weights of the selected arcs is maximum. These arcs (x,y) will be those defined by the equality $\rho_{xy} = 1$.

Beyond this formulation, the properties of linear orders (constituting the profile as well as that searched for the median relation) permit the search of a median order to be expressed in several equivalent ways, the subject of the following section.

20.3.3. *Equivalent formulations for the search of a median order of a profile of linear orders*

We note that, because of the relation $w(y,x) = -w(x,y)$ for $x \neq y$, the weights of the arcs of the graph G (representing the profile Π) are partially redundant. We may therefore only keep the arcs with positive weights or, for the pairs of arcs (x,y)

and (y, x) weighted by zero, one of the two arcs chosen arbitrarily. We then obtain a non-negatively weighted tournament, which also represents the profile Π. This model can often be found in the literature, leading to new formulations for the problem of the search for a median linear order of a profile of linear orders. We give some examples below without proving their equivalences; see [CHARO 96, CHARO 07]. These formulations are often known under different names. Some of them have been mentioned above, such as *problem of the median order* or *Kemeny rule*, but there is also *linear order problem* or *linear ordering problem*, etc. We specify some of these names in the following.

We start by recalling the three statements previously mentioned. The first is the original one, the second is the one permitting the expression of the problem as a 0-1 linear programming problem and the third is that obtained by considering the graph representing the profile. The solutions of problems 20.1–20.3 below are therefore the same, but are considered according to several points of view: as a binary relation for problem 20.1, as a set of binary variables (defining the characteristic function of the solution of problem 20.1) for problem 20.2, or even as a graph (of which the adjacency matrix is given by the solution of problem 20.2) for problem 20.3.

Problem 20.1. Given a profile Π of v linear orders defined on X, determine a median linear order of Π.

Problem 20.2. Given the integers $w(x, y)$ satisfying the property (P), determine an optimal solution of the problem:

$$\text{Maximize} \sum_{(x,y) \in X^2} w(x, y) \rho_{xy}$$

under the four constraints listed at the end of section 20.3.1.

In order to state some of the following problems, we introduce some new notation. Let $G = (X, A)$ be a graph whose arcs a are weighted by $w(a)$. For any subset B of A, the quantity $w(B) = \sum_{b \in B} w(b)$ will be called the *weight of B*.

Problem 20.3. Given a graph $G = (X, X^2)$ containing all the possible arcs and such that each arc (x, y) is weighted by $w(x, y)$, these weights satisfying property (P), determine $L \subset X^2$ with a maximum weight $w(L)$ and such that (X, L) is the graph of a linear order defined on X.

For the following formulation, let us recall that a linear order is a transitive tournament and conversely. If we only keep from G the positively weighted arcs and some arcs with weights equal to zero in order to obtain a tournament T as specified above (see section 20.3.3), selecting in G an arc (x, y) with a non-positive weight (such an arc does not appear in T, but the reversed arc (y, x) does) is the same as reversing in T the arc (x, y) in order to recover (y, x). We therefore obtain the formulation of problem 20.4 (known as the *minimum reversing set problem* if all the weights are equal to 1; see [BART 95a,CHARO 07]). Note that an optimal solution of problem 20.4 (a transitive tournament) still defines an optimal solution of problem 20.1, i.e. a median order.

Problem 20.4. Given a tournament $T = (X, A)$ whose arcs (x, y) are weighted by weights $w(x, y)$ which satisfy property P', determine a subset A' of A with a minimum weight and such that reversing the elements of A' in T transforms T into a transitive tournament.

A tournament T is transitive (i.e. represents a linear order) if and only if T contains no circuit of length greater than or equal to 3 (in terms of number of arcs). (In other words, there must be no circuit except the loops (x, x), for $x \in X$, which are characteristic of the reflexivity. Remember that, by definition of a tournament, there is no circuit of length 2.) This remark could permit the equivalence between the statement of problem 20.4 and that of problem 20.5 to be proved. More precisely, the optimal solutions of problem 20.4 (subsets of arcs) are not necessarily the same as those of problem 20.5. However, it is easy to show that the weights of the optimal solutions of problems 20.4 and 20.5 are equal: the optimal subsets of arcs of these problems can differ only by some arcs with a weight equal to zero.

Problem 20.5. Given a tournament $T = (X, A)$ whose arcs (x, y) are weighted by weights $w(x, y)$ that satisfy property P', determine a subset A' of A with a minimum weight such that the graph obtained from T by deleting the arcs of A' contains no circuit of length greater than or equal to 3.

The following formulation is a consequence of problem 20.5. Its only interest is to relate two problems that are sometimes studied separately. Example 20.5 is a weighted formulation of the *minimum feedback arc set problem*, and problem 20.6 is a weighted formulation of the *maximum arc consistent set problem*, also called the *acyclic subdigraph problem*. We will see in the following that problems 20.5 and 20.6 do not behave similarly with respect to approximation algorithms.

Problem 20.6. Given a tournament $T = (X, A)$ whose arcs (x, y) are weighted by weights $w(x, y)$ that satisfy property P', determine a subset A' of A with a maximum weight such that the graph (X, A') contains no circuit of length greater than or equal to 3.

Example 20.7 states problems 20.4 and 20.5 in terms of a matrix (Slater [SLA 61] adopts this formulation to define the problem of fitting a tournament in which all the weights are equal to 1 into a linear order; see also [YOUN 63]). For this, given a tournament $T = (X, A)$ whose arcs (x, y) are weighted by weights $w(x, y)$ that satisfy property P', we define the matrix $M = (m_{xy})_{(x,y) \in X^2}$ of the weights of T by:

$$m_{xy} = \begin{cases} w(x, y) & \text{if } (x, y) \in A \\ 0 & \text{otherwise.} \end{cases}$$

Problem 20.7. Given the matrix M of the weights of a tournament weighted by w that satisfies property P', determine a same ordering on the lines and the rows of M such that the sum of the terms located below the diagonal is minimum. (A variant, linked to problem 20.6, would consist of maximizing the sum of the terms located above the diagonal. It is then a particular case of the problem met in economics under the name of 'triangulation' of a square table of coefficients that reflect industrial exchanges [GRÖ 84, REI 85].)

For the final formulation, we need some more sophisticated tools: *hypergraphs*, or *systems of sets*, are a generalization of undirected graphs. More precisely, a hypergraph $H = (Y, F)$ is a pair of sets constituted by a set Y, whose elements are called *vertices*, and by a subset F of the set of non-empty parts of Y covering all the elements of Y. If all the elements of F have cardinality equal to 2, we recover the usual notion of undirected graph without isolated vertex. Given a tournament $T = (X, A)$, we consider here the hypergraph $H(T)$ of the circuits of T. The vertices of $H(T)$ are the arcs of T which are not loops and which the circuits of T go through. The elements of F are the subsets of X defining the circuits of T. A *vertex cover* of a hypergraph $H = (Y, F)$ is a subset Y' of Y such that any element of F (a non-empty subset of Y) contains at least one element of Y'. For a tournament T whose arcs are weighted, each vertex of $H(T)$ has a weight which is the weight of the arc of T associated with the considered vertex of $H(T)$. We can therefore define the weight of a vertex cover as the sum of the weights of its vertices. We then obtain the last formulation considered here (already given in [BER 72] for Slater's problem).

Problem 20.8. Given a tournament $T = (X, A)$ whose arcs (x, y) are weighted by weights $w(x, y)$ that satisfy property P', determine a vertex cover with a minimum weight of the hypergraph $H(T)$ of the circuits of T.

Any vertex cover of $H(T)$ selects a subset of arcs of T which is a solution of problem 20.5: removing these arcs in T leaves a graph without any circuit. In particular, a minimum vertex cover will provide an optimal solution of problem 20.5, and hence an optimal solution of problem 20.4, i.e. will define a median linear order by reversing these arcs.

20.3.4. *Complexity of the search of a median order of a profile of linear orders*

The complexity theory [BART 96, GAR 79] studies the efficiency of algorithms and the intrinsic difficulty of a problem. Broadly speaking, an algorithm is said to be a polynomial if the number of elementary operations (such as arithmetic operations or comparisons, etc.) performed to solve any given instance can be upper-bounded by a polynomial of the size of the considered instance. A problem is said to be *polynomial* if there exists an algorithm of polynomial complexity to solve it. There exist many problems for which we do not know any polynomial algorithm to solve them (which does not mean that such an algorithm does not exist). It is the case in particular for the NP-complete and the NP-hard problems.

Note that a *NP-complete* problem is a decision problem (i.e. a problem in which a question is set whose answer is 'yes' or 'no') which belongs to the NP class (the class of non-deterministic polynomial decision problems; for any instance admitting the answer 'yes' it is possible to check, in polynomial time with respect to the size of the instance, that the answer is really 'yes' with the help of an estimate) and which is at least as difficult as any other problem of NP. Indeed, NP-complete problems constitute the most difficult problems inside the NP class. The existence of a polynomial algorithm solving such a problem would involve the existence of polynomial algorithms for all the problems of NP. A *NP-hard problem*, which may be a decision problem or not, is a problem at least as difficult as a NP-complete problem. A decision problem can be associated canonically with an optimization problem. If this decision problem is NP-complete, then the optimization problem is itself NP-hard.

From a practical point of view, the consequence of the NP-hardness of a problem is that the algorithms designed to solve this problem have large complexities, typically exponential. The computation time required to solve such a problem exactly may become prohibitive quickly when the size of the data increases. In order to illustrate the increasing complexity of a non-polynomial algorithm, let us consider the method consisting of enumerating the $n!$ linear orders and keeping the best one. If we run a computer that can deal with one thousand million linear orders per second, it would take around 4 msec for $n = 10$, 77 years for $n = 20$, 8.4×10^{13} centuries for $n = 30$, 2.6×10^{29} centuries for $n = 40$ and almost 10^{46} centuries for $n = 50$. It is therefore important, when dealing with the resolution of a problem from a practical point of view, to know its complexity. Theorem 20.2 gives the complexity of the aggregation of a profile of linear orders into a linear order; see [BART 89, DWO 01, HUD 89].

Theorem 20.2. *The problem of the determination of a median linear order of a profile of linear orders is NP-hard.*

Other complexity results (as well as references) can be found in [HUD 08, WAK 86] and [WAK 98] about the computation of median relations (including the proof of theorem 20.2; for the complexity of other voting procedures see [HUD 09a]). Except for some trivial cases, the problems of preferences aggregation are generally NP-hard or of unknown complexity. For instance, the aggregation of a profile of linear orders into a complete preorder is also NP-hard; similarly, Slater's problem (i.e. fitting a tournament into a linear order, which corresponds to a profile reduced to one tournament) is also NP-hard [ALO 06, CHAR 07, CHARO 07, CONI 06, HUD 09b]. On the other hand, if there is no Condorcet effect (the majority tournament representing the profile has no circuit), the median linear orders are exactly the majority linear orders and therefore can be computed in polynomial time.

Let us mention a polynomial case which is not trivial: the aggregation of a profile of *unimodal linear orders* [BLA 48]. In order to define the structure of a unimodal order, we assume that the candidates are ordered following a criterion independent of the voters, and defining a linear order $\prec$ on the candidates (e.g. a political election, the usual scale going from extreme-left to extreme-right, if we can always identify (not an easy task in practice) the political membership of a candidate and distinguish any two candidates according to this criterion).

Let $x_1 \prec x_2 \prec \ldots \prec x_n$ be the order of the candidates with respect to $\prec$, for an appropriate numbering of the candidates. We assume moreover that each voter attributes a numerical value to each candidate. With respect to the numbering induced by $\prec$, let γ_k^i be the value attributed by voter i (for $1 \leq i \leq v$) to candidate x_k (for $1 \leq k \leq n$), all these values being distinct for any given i. We will say that the preference order L_i of voter i is unimodal with respect to $\prec$ if there exists an index $k(i)$, with $1 \leq k(i) \leq n$, such that the series $(\gamma_k^i)_{1 \leq k \leq k(i)}$ is increasing and the series $(\gamma_k^i)_{k(i) \leq k \leq 1}$ is decreasing.

In the example given previously of a political election, it means that voter i has a favorite candidate $x_{k(i)}$. The further we move away from this candidate, towards the left or the right, the less appreciated is the candidate. However, nothing is said about the respective values of two candidates located on both sides of $x_{k(i)}$. This order is therefore defined by $x_k L_i x_{k'}$ if and only if we have $\gamma_k^i > \gamma_{k'}^i$.

A profile of linear orders is said to be a *profile of unimodal linear orders* if there exists an order $\prec$ defined on X such that all the orders of the profile are unimodal with respect to the order $\prec$. In this case, as stated above, the computation of a median linear order can be completed in polynomial time. More precisely, the majority relation of unimodal linear orders is a unimodal linear order.

20.3.5. *Exact and approximate methods*

From the algorithmic point of view, a consequence of theorem 20.2 is that we do not know, in general, any polynomial algorithm computing a median order exactly (and such an algorithm does not exist if P is different from NP). We will simply present the main algorithmic directions to compute median orders, the problem being often stated through a weighted tournament (the interested reader will find some bibliographical references in [BART 81, CHARO 07, HUD 97] in addition to those given below).

Because of the NP-hardness of the problem, exact methods have large complexities and therefore do not allow large problems to be solved. These methods are mainly based on branch and bound methods, with several more or less sophisticated components. Note in particular, for the design of an evaluation function, the application of the continuous relaxation to the formulation of problem 20.2 stated above (the constraints $\rho_{xy} \in \{0,1\}$ are replaced by $\rho_{xy} \in [0,1]$), the Lagrangian relaxation of the transitivity constraints [ARD 84, CHARO 06] and the application of polyhedral theory using cutting planes. These methods are called *branch and cut*; see for instance [JÜN 85, MIT 96, MIT 00, REI 85].

Other attempts are based on combinatorial properties [CHARO 97, CHARO 06] or on appropriate structures in order to store extra information. For instance, the use of a heap speeds up the search of the leaf of the search-tree to be developed in a 'Best-First' strategy [WOI 97], and the use of a beginning-sections-tree permits the search-tree to be pruned in another way than the usual application of the evaluation function [GUÉ 95].

The performance of these algorithms depends on the considered instances. It is possible to solve some real instances with sizes up to a hundred candidates in a 'reasonable' time. For example, the software available at http://www.enst.fr/~charon/-tournament/median.html can deal with instances simulating real data with 100 candidates in about 1 sec. Random instances seem more difficult to solve; the same software requires about 1000 sec to solve random instances of Slater's problem with 36 candidates [CHARO 06].

Another possibility is to look for approximate solutions, with the hope of computing 'good' solutions in a 'reasonable' time. Some of these heuristics are specific to the considered problem. Several dealt initially with Slater's problem, but they can often be generalized to the case of a weighted tournament; see [BART 89, BEC 67, CHA 96, COO 88, GOD 83, KAY 95, MEN 00, SMI 74].

Other methods come from *metaheuristics* (general approximate methods) such as simulated annealing, tabu search, noising methods, genetic algorithms or even some hybridization between these different methods e.g. [CAM 99, CAM 01, CHARO 98, CHARO 06, CON 00, HUD 89, LAG 99, SCH 03]. If the quality of some specific heuristics can decrease quite fast with the size of the considered instance, metaheuristics seem to provide good results in a limited amount of computation time. For instance, in the experiments reported in [CHARO 06] dealing with 5790 tournaments with up to 100 vertices, the noising methods [CHARO 02] could provide an exact solution in a negligible time for 5784 tournaments (the other six tournaments were solved exactly by a second application of the method).

We can also mention another type of method to solve difficult problems: the probabilistic methods. These methods have been applied to tournaments in which all the weights are equal to 1 in [POL 86, POL 88]. In [POL 86], a recursive algorithm is designed to deal with several optimization problems, including the search for a partial graph without circuit in a given directed graph. Suppose we have a graph $G = (X, A)$ weighted by a function c with non-negative values. The algorithm provides, for some values of a real parameter λ belonging to $[0, 1]$, a partial graph $H = (X, B)$ with

$$\sum_{b \in B} c(b) \geq \lambda \sum_{a \in A} c(a) + \frac{1-\lambda}{2} \zeta(G),$$

where $\zeta(G)$ denotes the weight of a minimum (with respect to c) spanning tree of G.

For the search of a maximum partial graph without circuit of a directed antisymmetric graph weighted by c which is the constant function equal to 1, the value $\lambda = 0.5$ gives some interesting results. Indeed, we obtain an algorithm that selects in a tournament at least

$$\frac{n(n+3)}{4} + \frac{n-1}{4}$$

arcs without circuit of length (in number of arcs) greater than or equal to 3. This therefore reverses at most

$$\frac{(n-1)^2}{4}$$

arcs to obtain a linear order. This result is improved in [POL 88], due to a probabilistic method with a complexity of $O(n^3 \log n)$ that computes (at least for n large enough) a partial graph without circuit of length (in number of arcs) greater than or equal to 3 in a tournament in which all weights are equal to 1, with at least

$$\frac{n(n+3)}{4} + \frac{n\sqrt{n}}{8\sqrt{\pi}}$$

arcs of the tournament, and therefore a linear order is obtained by reversing at most

$$\frac{n(n-1)}{4} - \frac{n\sqrt{n}}{8\sqrt{\pi}}$$

arcs.

The final possibility considered here is relative to approximation algorithms with performance guarantees [VAZ 03]. Indeed, we can design a deterministic algorithm for problem 20.6 stated above (search for a partial subgraph without circuit and of maximum weight) which perhaps does not provide an optimal solution systematically but permits a solution not too far from an optimal solution to be obtained. For this, it is sufficient to put the vertices of the tournament on a horizontal line, according to any numbering of the vertices e.g. $x_1, x_2, \ldots, x_n$.

With respect to this alignment, some arcs (that are not loops) are directed from the left to the right and the others from the right to the left. The selection of the loops and of the arcs directed from the left to the right provides a partial graph without circuit of length greater than or equal to 3. Let w_1 be the sum of the weights of these arcs. If w_{max} denotes the weight of an optimal solution of problem 20.6 for the considered tournament, we obtain then $w_{max} \geq w_1$. By doing the same with the loops and the arcs directed from the right to the left, we obtain another solution of weight w_2 which also verifies the inequality $w_{max} \geq w_2$.

Let W be the sum of all the weights of the tournament:

$$W = \sum_{a \in A} w(a).$$

The loops (of weight v) are counted twice in the sum $w_1 + w_2$. We obtain the relations: $w_1 + w_2 = W + n.v$ and $w_{max} \leq W$. We may assume without loss of generality that w_2 is at least as great as w_1 (otherwise we reverse the vertices numbering). We then obtain the relations

$$\frac{w_{max}}{2} < w_2 \leq w_{max},$$

or equivalently

$$\frac{w_{max} - w_2}{w_{max}} < \frac{1}{2}.$$

The relative error if we choose the solution associated with w_2 instead of an optimal solution cannot be greater than 50%, for any considered tournament. We can therefore make a mistake but, to some extent, not too large. (Note that, for the existence of algorithms with performance guarantees, the eight problems given in section 20.3.3 are not necessarily equivalent. Indeed, the process described above cannot be applied to problem 20.5 due to the lack of a lower bound for the minimum value of this problem, proportional to W but not equal to zero.)

20.3.6. *Properties of median orders*

In this section, we mention some properties of the median linear orders of profiles of linear orders. The first property can be established from a reasoning close to that which ends the previous section. We assume here that the considered profile of linear orders is described by its representative tournament (section 20.3.3) and we focus on problem 20.4 (inversion of a set of arcs of minimum weight in order to transform the tournament associated with the profile into a linear order).

Proposition 20.4. *Let $T = (X, A)$ be the tournament associated with a profile Π of linear orders and let w be its weight function. Let $L = x_1 > x_2 > \ldots > x_n$ be a median order of Π. We then have, for any i between 1 and $n-1$:*

$$\sum_{(x_j, x_k) \in A, 1 \leq j \leq i < k \leq n} w(x_j, x_k) \geq \sum_{(x_k, x_j) \in A, 1 \leq j \leq i < k \leq n} w(x_k, x_j).$$

Proof. Assume that there exists an index i for which the previous inequality is not satisfied. Set the vertices of T on a horizontal line, the indices increasing from the left to the right. If we split the vertices with indices between 1 and i from the others by a vertical line, the arcs which cross the vertical line from the right to the left have a total weight strictly greater than the total weight of the arcs crossing the line from the left to the right. Let us consider then the linear order L' obtained by swapping the left part of the vertical line and the right part, i.e. the linear order $L' = x_{i+1} > \ldots > x_n > x_1 > \ldots > x_i$. Since L' requires the inversion of the same arcs as L except for the arcs which cross the vertical line (i.e. the arcs involved in one of the two sums in the statement of the proposition), it is easy to see that L' would be necessarily better than L, a contradiction with the optimality of L, hence the result. ⋄

As shown by the following proposition [JAC 69, YOUN 63], any interval of a median linear order is a median order of the subtournament induced by this interval.

Proposition 20.5. *Let $T = (X, A)$ be the weighted tournament associated with a profile Π of linear orders and let $L = x_1 > x_2 > \ldots > x_n$ be a median order of Π. Then, for any i and any j with $1 \leq i < j \leq n$, $x_i > x_{i+1} > \ldots > x_j$ is a median order of the subtournament of T induced by $x_i, x_{i+1}, \ldots, x_j$.*

Proof. Assume that there exist two indices i and j for which proposition 20.5 is false. Let L' be the linear order obtained by replacing $x_i > \ldots > x_j$ in L by a median order of the subtournament of T induced by $x_i, \ldots, x_j$. It is easy to see that L' would be better than L, a contradiction with the optimality of L. ⋄

We can deduce the following corollary.

Corollary 20.1. *Let $T = (X, A)$ be the weighted tournament associated with a profile Π of linear orders and let w be its weight function. Let $L = x_1 > x_2 > \ldots > x_n$ be a median order of Π. We assume that, for $a \in A$, no weight $w(a)$ is equal to 0. Then, for any i between 1 and $n-1$, the arc between x_i and x_{i+1} is directed from x_i to x_{i+1}.*

Proof. It is sufficient to apply proposition 20.5 with $j = i + 1$. ⋄

In particular, if we apply corollary 20.1 to a tournament T whose weights are equal to 1 (Slater's problem), we obtain a well-known result [REM 66], specifying that the arcs between two consecutive vertices in any Slater order of T define a Hamiltonian path of T. (Recall that a Hamiltonian path of T is a path going through each vertex of T exactly once.) The link between median orders and Hamiltonian paths is also involved in the proof of theorem 20.3.

Theorem 20.3. *Let Π be a profile of v linear orders defined on a same set X of n elements. Then, if v is even, the number of median orders of Π is between 1 and $n!$, and the bounds may be reached. If v is odd and large enough, the number of median orders of Π is between 1 and*

$$\frac{\mu n \sqrt{n} n!}{2^n},$$

where μ is a constant.

Proof. In both cases, the lower bound is trivial: it suffices for instance to consider the case of a profile consisting of the same linear order repeated v times.

If v is even, let us consider two opposite linear orders $L_1 = x_1 > \ldots > x_n$ and $L_2 = x_n > \ldots > x_1$. The profile consisting of L_1 repeated $v/2$ times and in L_2 also repeated $v/2$ times is represented by a tournament in which all the weights are equal to 0 (for each candidate x and each candidate y, there exist as many voters preferring x to y as y to x). In this case, it is easy to see that all the linear orders defined on X are optimal solutions; hence the result, since on the other hand $n!$ is a trivial upper-bound of the number of median linear orders.

If v is odd, the weights of the arcs of the tournament T that represents Π are all odd, and so are not equal to 0. Therefore, according to the previous results, we can upper-bound the number of median orders of Π by the number of Hamiltonian paths in T. Alon [ALO 90] showed that this number is upper-bounded by

$$\frac{\mu n \sqrt{n} n!}{2^n},$$

for some constant μ and for n large enough. ◇

The maximum number of median orders of a profile of v linear orders is not known exactly when v is odd. Some results (combinatorial or experimental) for some profiles seem to indicate that the maximum number of median orders admitted by a profile consisting of an odd number of linear orders is significantly lower than the number of Hamiltonian paths in the tournament representing this profile. The number of median orders can nevertheless be exponential for some profiles. More precisely, it has been shown [WOI 97] that for a tournament whose weights are equal to 1 (Slater's problem), the number of optimal solutions can reach

$$\exp\left[\frac{\ln 3}{4}(3n - 2\log_3 n - 3)\right]$$

when n is a power of 3. Since such a tournament can via theorem 20.1 be associated with a profile of linear orders, we deduce that this exponential number is a lower bound for the maximum number of median orders of a profile of linear orders.

Another property satisfied by the median linear orders is the *unanimity rule* (or *Pareto principle*). For a profile $\Pi = (L_1, L_2, \ldots, L_v)$ of v linear orders, let $U(\Pi) = \cap_{1 \leq i \leq v} L_i$ be the unanimous part of Π. The following theorem [BART 76, FEL 73, MON 73] shows that, if all the voters prefer a candidate x to a candidate y, then x must also be preferred to y in every median order of Π.

Theorem 20.4. *Let Π be a profile of v linear orders and L be a median order of Π. We then have: $U(\Pi) \subseteq L$.*

Finally, let us mention a last property: the *consistency*. If two profiles Π and Π' of linear orders defined on X admit some common median orders, then the set of median orders of the concatenation of Π and Π' is the set of median orders that are common to Π and Π'.

Theorem 20.5. *Let $\Pi = (L_1, L_2, \ldots, L_v)$ and $\Pi' = (L'_1, L'_2, \ldots, L'_v)$ be two profiles of linear orders v and v', respectively. Let $\Pi\Pi'$ be the profile obtained by the concatenation of Π and Π' i.e. $\Pi\Pi' = (L_1, L_2, \ldots, L_v, L'_1, L'_2, \ldots, L'_v)$. We then have:*

$$Med_{\mathcal{L}}(\Pi) \cap Med_{\mathcal{L}}(\Pi') \neq \emptyset \Rightarrow Med_{\mathcal{L}}(\Pi\Pi') = Med_{\mathcal{L}}(\Pi) \cap Med_{\mathcal{L}}(\Pi').$$

This property of consistency is the most important in an outstanding axiomatic characterization of the median procedure due to Young and Levenglick [YOU 78], as well as in the characterization of the median procedure in median semilattices. Moreover, it remains true for all the metric medians [BART 91]. Other properties of median orders are described in [BART 81, CHARO 96, CHARO 97, CHARO 07] or, for the tournaments whose weights are equal to 1, in [LAS 97].

20.4. Medians in lattices and semilattices

Until now, we tackled the consensus problem by searching for medians of profiles of binary relations. We established that such research, easy in some cases (arbitrary relations or tournaments), may become quite hard in other instances (median orders). The purpose of this section is to show that these results generalize to a large extent. Indeed, one may define and search medians in any ordered set where a direct generalization of the symmetric difference distance exists, especially in every (finite) semilattice. The search of median consensus then follows similar lines in any set of objects (to aggregate) endowed with such an order, while the ease of this search depends on the structural properties of the obtained ordered set. The 'good' case corresponds to median semilattices, as presented in section 20.4.3.

Previously, we give the required basic notions on ordered sets in section 20.4.1, with the examples of sets of binary relations ordered by inclusion. In particular, we survey the ordered set structure of the sets of those relations which are useful in preference modeling. In section 20.4.2, we give a standard generalization of the symmetric difference distance in semilattices, with the associated formulae for the remoteness between a v-tuple and a single element. Section 20.4.4 gives a brief description of the arising difficulties when the semilattice is no longer a median one. Finally, some situations showing evidence of the efficiency of such latticial generalizations are presented in section 20.4.5.

20.4.1. *Ordered structures*

We frequently consider a set $\mathcal{D}$ of relations which is (partially) ordered. That is, $\mathcal{D}$ is endowed with an *order relation* $\leq$ satisfying three properties: for any R, R', R'' belonging to $\mathcal{D}$, $R \leq R$ (reflexivity), $R \leq R'$ and $R' \leq R$ imply $R = R'$ (antisymmetry), $R \leq R'$ and $R' \leq R''$ imply $R \leq R''$ (transitivity). In most cases, this order is just the restriction to D of the inclusion order on the set $P(X^2)$ of all binary relations on X. Without other hypotheses, we consider this situation and write $R \subseteq R'$ instead of $R \leq R'$, and $R \subset R'$ if, moreover, $R \neq R'$. The considered orders are generally 'partial' orders in the sense of Chapter 2, but linear orders are allowed.

Given a subset $\mathcal{A}$ of $\mathcal{D}$, a *lower bound* of $\mathcal{A}$ is a relation R in $\mathcal{D}$ such that $R \subseteq A$, for any $A \in \mathcal{A}$. The subset $\mathcal{A}$ is *lower bounded* if it admits at least one lower bound. Similarly, an *upper bound* of $\mathcal{A}$ is a relation R in $\mathcal{D}$ such that $A \subseteq R$ for any $A \in \mathcal{A}$, and $\mathcal{A}$ is *upper bounded* if it admits at least one upper bound. If there is a greatest lower bound g of $\mathcal{A}$, then g is the *meet* of $\mathcal{A}$, denoted $\wedge \mathcal{A}$ (the meet of two elements R and R' is denoted $R \wedge R'$). When the intersection $\cap \mathcal{A}$ of all the relations in $\mathcal{A}$ is again an element of $\mathcal{D}$, we have $\wedge \mathcal{A} = \cap \mathcal{A}$. Similarly, if there is a least upper bound ℓ of $\mathcal{A}$, then ℓ is the *join* of $\mathcal{A}$, denoted $\vee \mathcal{A}$ or $\cup \mathcal{A}$ if it corresponds to set union (the join of R and R' is denoted $R \vee R'$). We note that, if it exists, the minimum (respectively, the maximum) of $\mathcal{A}$ is its meet (respectively, its join).

The ordered set $\mathcal{D}$ is:
– a *meet semilattice* if any pair $\{R, R'\}$ of its elements has a meet $R \wedge R'$;
– a *join semilattice* if any pair $\{R, R'\}$ of its elements has a join $R \wedge R'$;
– a *lattice* if any pair has a meet and a join i.e. it is simultaneously a meet and a join semilattice.

When $\mathcal{D}$ is linearly ordered, it is therefore a lattice with the minimum as meet and the maximum as join, respectively. The set $P(X^2)$ is a lattice with set intersection and set union as meet and join, respectively. Table 20.1 gives the ordinal structures for the inclusion order of often considered sets of reflexive and transitive binary relations on X.

Set $\mathcal{D}$	Properties	Meet	Join	Ordinal structure
$\mathcal{Q}$, (partial) preorders		Set intersection ∩	Transitive closure of set union	Lattice
$\mathcal{E}$, equivalences	Symmetry	Set intersection ∩	Transitive closure of set union	Lattice
$\mathcal{O}$, (partial) orders	Antisymmetry	Set intersection ∩	—	Meet semilattice
$\mathcal{W}$, complete pre-orders	Completeness	—	Transitive closure of set union	Join semilattice
$\mathcal{L}$, linear orders	Antisymmetry and completeness	—	—	—

Table 20.1. *Ordered structures of sets of reflexive and transitive binary relations*

Set inclusion on the set $\mathcal{L}$ of linear orders and, more generally, on the set $\mathcal{T}$ of tournaments, corresponds to an *antichain* structure where, for $T, T' \in \mathcal{T}, T \subseteq T'$ implies $T = T'$. Nevertheless, the set $\mathcal{T}$ may be endowed with a lattice order as follows: start with a given arbitrary tournament T_0. It is often convenient to choose T_0 as follows: set $X = \{1, 2, \ldots, n\}$ and take $T_0 = \{(i, j) \in X^2 : i \leq j\}$.

Let $T_0^d = \{(i, j) \in X^2 : j < i\}$ be the *(irreflexive) dual tournament* of T_0; with any tournament T, we associate the relation $I(T)$ of all *inverse* pairs in T (with respect to T_0) i.e. $I(T) = \{(i, j) \in T : j < i\} = T \cap T_0^d$. The correspondence $T \leftrightarrow I(T)$ is one-to-one between, on the one hand, the set $\mathcal{T}$ of all the tournaments on X and, on the other, the set $P(T_0^d)$ of the sets of inverse pairs. The (lattice) inclusion order on $P(T_0^d)$ induces on $\mathcal{T}$ the order defined by: $T \leq T'$ if and only if $I(T) \subseteq I(T')$. The minimum for this order is T_0 (with $I(T_0) = \emptyset$) and the maximum is T_0^d (with $I(T_0^d) = T_0^d$). The restriction to $\mathcal{L}$ of this order on $\mathcal{T}$ is still a lattice (*permutohedron lattice*), although this property is less immediate [GUI 63].

We have just observed that, either directly with set inclusion or with some change on this order, the considered sets of binary relations are all endowed with lattice structures (they are lattices or semilattices; see [DAV 90] for ordered sets and lattices). This observation is strengthened by the fact that such structures are again found in other models of preferences or choices: valued (or fuzzy) relations [LEC 95] or choice functions [MON 04]. The study of the consensus problem at the more abstract level of lattice structures themselves has led to results particular to various situations e.g. [BART 91, DAY 03, LEC 93, LEC 95. MON 90b]. We therefore now consider the general case of a meet semilattice (possibly a lattice) D whose elements are denoted s, t, etc. For the case $\mathcal{M} = \mathcal{D}$, we aim to aggregate a profile $\Pi = (t_1, t_2, \ldots t_v)$ belonging to D^v into a unique element $t \in D$.

In the case of binary relations on X, each ordered pair of elements of X may be considered as an elementary relation, a given relation R being decomposable into such elementary ones. Such a decomposition still exists in any semilattice D by taking into account its *irreducible* elements. An element t of D is said to be *join-irreducible* if it cannot be obtained as the join of a subset of D not containing t. Similarly, t is *meet-irreducible* if it is not the meet of a subset of other elements. Here, we only investigate the role of join-irreducibles, and just mention that the same considerations apply to meet-irreducibles (although more rarely in practice). Let $t \in D$. We denote:

- S or $S(D)$ the set of all the join-irreducibles of D;
- S_t the set of all the join-irreducibles s of D satisfying $s \leq t$.

We then have a representation of the elements of D by subsets of S, with two essential properties which are recalled in the following theorem.

Theorem 20.6. *Let D be an ordered set. For any $t \in D$, the equality $t = \vee S_t$ holds; for all $t, t' \in D$ such that $t \wedge t'$ exists, the equality $S_{t \wedge t'} = S_t \cap S_{t'}$ holds.*

So, the mapping $t \mapsto S_t$ from D to $P(S)$ is a *meet-morphism* in the sense that it preserves meets, and an *order encoding* since it may be verified that, for any $t, t' \in D$, we have $t \leq t' \Leftrightarrow S_t \subseteq S_{t'}$. In the lattices and semilattices of Table 20.1: $S(\mathcal{Q}) = S(\mathcal{O})$ is the set of the orders on X with a unique ordered pair (x, y) of distinct elements; $S(\mathcal{E})$ is the set of the equivalences on X with a unique double ordered pair $(x, y), (y, x)$ with distinct x and y; $S(\mathcal{W})$ is the set of the linear orders on X (it is known that a complete preorder is the union and the join of the linear orders that it contains).

Each join-irreducible element of the lattice $\mathcal{T}$ of tournaments corresponds to an ordered pair of T_0^d, with $S(\mathcal{T}) = \{T \in \mathcal{T} : |I(T)| = 1\}$. The join-irreducibles of the permutohedron lattice $\mathcal{L}$ are still associated with the ordered pairs of T_0^d, but in a more complex way: the join-irreducible associated with the ordered pair $(x, y) \in T_0^d$ is the lowest linear order containing this ordered pair.

An important remark for the following is that, if $t \vee t'$ exists, then we have $S_t \cup S_{t'} \subseteq S_{t \vee t'}$, but equality is not true in general. For instance, consider the lattice $\mathcal{Q}$ of preorders on X, three elements x, y, z of X and two preorders Q and Q' such that $(x, y) \in Q$ and $(y, z) \in Q'$. Then, by transitivity, we have $(x, z) \in Q \vee Q'$, although this pair does not necessarily belong to $Q \cup Q'$.

20.4.2. *Symmetric difference distance in semilattices and remoteness*

The symmetric difference distance was previously defined in section 20.2.2. It easily generalizes to any semilattice D with the use of the join-irreducible representation described just above. We now set, for any $t, t' \in D$,

$$\begin{aligned}\delta(t,t') &= |S_t \Delta S_{t'}| = |S_t \cup S_{t'}| - |S_t \cap S_{t'}| = |S_t \setminus S_{t'}| + |S_{t'} \setminus S_t| \\ &= |\{s \in S : [s \in S_t \text{ and } s \notin S_{t'}] \text{ or } [s \notin S_t \text{ and } s \in S_{t'}]\}|.\end{aligned}$$

In lattices or semilattices $P(X^2)$ (binary relations), $\mathcal{Q}$ (preorders), $\mathcal{E}$ (equivalences), $\mathcal{O}$ (orders) and $\mathcal{T}$ (tournaments), we recover the number of ordered pairs by which the two relations R and R' differ, that is the symmetric difference distance as defined above. The situation of the permutohedron lattice $\mathcal{L}$ is the same. It differs in the join-semilattice $\mathcal{W}$ (complete preorders) where the count of differences is made on the linear orders which are or are not included in R and R'.

We now consider a profile $\Pi = (t_1, \ldots, t_i, \ldots, t_v) \in D^v$. The following parameters are associated with Π and with any join-irreducible $s \in S(D)$:

$$\begin{aligned}v_\Pi(s) &= |\{i \in V : s \leq t_i\}|; \\ v_\Pi^c(s) &= |\{i \in V : s \not\leq t_i\}|; \\ w_\Pi(s) &= v_\Pi(s) - v_\Pi^c(s).\end{aligned}$$

As above, the subscript Π is omitted in the notation when no ambiguity could arise (i.e. always in practice). The equalities $v(s) + v^c(s) = v$ and $w(s) = 2v(s) - v$ are satisfied. We say that a join-irreducible s is a *majority* one if $2v(s) > v$ (then s belongs to the representations of a strict majority of elements of the profile) and *balanced* if $2v(s) = v$.

In order to tackle the aggregation of a profile Π of D^v into a unique element t of D, we first give an expression of the remoteness $E(\Pi, t) = \sum_{i=1}^{v} \delta(t, t_i)$ between Π and an arbitrary element t of D in terms of the previous parameters.

Lemma 20.2. *For* $\Pi = (t_1, \ldots, t_i, \ldots, t_v) \in D^v$ *and* $t \in D$, *we have:*

$$E(\Pi, t) = \sum_{i=1}^{v} |S_{t_i}| - \sum_{s \in S_t} w(s).$$

This is merely a lattice version of the equality (2) of lemma 20.1 (section 20.2.3). Indeed, it is obtained in a similar way. The quantity $-w(s)$ then appears as the contribution of the join-irreducible s of S_t to the remoteness of t. As described previously, this contribution is negative if s is a majority join-irreducible, equal to zero if it is balanced and positive otherwise. To obtain a remoteness as low as possible (i.e. corresponding to a median), the best would be to find an element t of D of which the representation S_t would contain all the majority join-irreducibles (and possibly some balanced ones), but no others. The aim of the next section is the recognition of those semilattices where such an element always exists.

20.4.3. *Medians in median semilattices*

We now assume that D is a meet semilattice, possibly a lattice, and we go further in the transposition to this case of some notions presented in section 20.2.3. With S still being the set of the join-irreducibles of D, we set for $\Pi \in D^v$ and for any integer σ:

$$S(\Pi, \sigma) = \{s \in S : v(s) \geq \sigma\}.$$

In general, this set will simply be denoted as $S(\sigma)$. In particular, with the numbers α and β of section 20.2.3, $S(\alpha)$ is the set of the majority join-irreducibles and $S(\beta)\backslash S(\alpha)$ is the set of the balanced join-irreducibles (empty for odd v).

Proposition 20.6. *For any $s, s' \in S$, $s \in S(\sigma)$ and $s' \leq s$, $s' \in S(\sigma)$.*

Proof. If $s \in S(\sigma)$, then there exists a subset $W \subseteq V$ such that $|W| \geq \sigma$ and $s \leq t_i$ for any $i \in W$. Then, $s' \leq s$ implies $s' \leq t_i$ for all $i \in W$. Therefore, $s' \in S(\sigma)$. ◇

Provided that such elements exist, we set

$$t(\sigma) = \vee S(\sigma)$$

and

$$t'(\sigma) = \vee\{\wedge\{t_i : i \in W\} : W \subseteq V, |W| \geq \sigma\}.$$

The latter expression has the form of a 'lattice polynomial'.

Recall a general property of meet semilattices: any upper bounded subset admits a join, precisely the meet of its upper bounds. As a consequence, for any $t \in D$, the ordered subset $\{t' \in D : t' \leq t\}$ is a lattice.

Proposition 20.7. *If one of the elements $t(\sigma)$ and $t'(\sigma)$ exists, then the other also exists and $t(\sigma) = t'(\sigma)$.*

Proof. Assume that $t'(\sigma)$ exists, and let $s \in S(\sigma)$. There is therefore a subset $W \subseteq V$ such that $|W| \geq \sigma$ and $s \leq t_i$ for all $i \in W$. Then $s \leq \wedge\{t_i : i \in W\} \leq t'(\sigma)$ and $t'(\sigma)$ is an upper bound of $S(\sigma)$. Thus, $t(\sigma) = \vee S(\sigma)$ exists, with $t(\sigma) \leq t'(\sigma)$.

On the other hand, according to theorem 20.6, the join-irreducible representation is a meet-morphism. Thus, for $|W| \geq \sigma$, $S_{\wedge\{t_i : i \in W\}} = \cap_{i \in W} S_{t_i}$ is a subset of $S(\sigma)$. Then, the element $t(\sigma) = \vee S(\sigma)$ exists, according to the first part of this proof, and is an upper bound of $\wedge_{i \in W} t_i = \vee S_{\wedge\{t_i : i \in W\}}$. Since $t'(\sigma)$ is the join of elements which all admit $t(\sigma)$ as an upper bound, we have $t(\sigma) \geq t'(\sigma)$.

Conversely, assume that $t(\sigma)$ exists. It is then an upper bound of each meet $\wedge\{t_i : i \in W\}$ with $|W| \geq \sigma$, which implies that $t'(\sigma)$ exists, and one may apply the previous results. ◇

Following this proposition, we have a polynomial expression for $t(\alpha)$:

$$t(\alpha) = \vee\{\wedge\{t_i : i \in W\} : W \subseteq V, |W| \geq \alpha\}.$$

This lattice formalization of the majority rule generalizes the expression given at the end of section 20.2.3.

The element $t(\alpha)$ is also given by its representation $S_{t(\alpha)}$:

$$t(\alpha) = \vee S_{t(\alpha)} = \vee\{s \in S : s \leq t(\alpha)\}.$$

The representation $S_{t(\alpha)}$ contains all the majority join-irreducibles but also, in general, other join-irreducibles which are neither majority nor balanced ones.

We now describe a particular type of meet semilattices, where the join-irreducible representation is not only a meet-morphism but also a join-morphism. First, a lattice D is said to be *distributive* if it satisfies one of the following equivalent conditions:

1) for any $t, t', t'' \in D$, $t \wedge (t' \vee t'') = (t \wedge t') \vee (t \wedge t'')$;
2) for any $t, t', t'' \in D$, $t \vee (t' \wedge t'') = (t \vee t') \wedge (t \vee t'')$;
3) $s \in S, D' \subseteq D$ and $s \leq \vee D'$ imply $s \leq t$ for at least one element $t \in D$;
4) for any $t, t' \in D$, the equality $S_t \cup S_{t'} = S_{t \vee t'}$ holds.

We do not give a complete proof of these classical equivalences. Observe, for instance, that when (1) is satisfied, the inequality $s \leq \vee D'$ implies $s = s \wedge (\vee D') = \vee\{s \wedge t : t \in D'\}$. Since s is join-irreducible, $s = s \wedge t'$ follows, that is $s \leq t'$, for at least one element t' of D'. Similarly, assume that (3) is satisfied and consider $t, t' \in D$ and $s \in S_{t \vee t'}$. Then, $s \leq t$ or $s \leq t'$. Thus, $S_{t \vee t'} \subseteq S_t \cup S_{t'}$, which implies (4) since the converse inclusion is always true.

The class of distributive lattices is particularly important since it includes linear orders (with the maximum and minimum operations as join and meet), products of linear orders and also lattices of subsets endowed with set union and set intersection (that is, Boolean lattices). For instance, in the previous examples, the lattices $P(X^2)$ and $\mathcal{T}$ are distributive.

By extension, a meet semilattice D is said to be distributive if, for any $t \in D$, the lattice $\{t' \in D : t' \leq t\}$ is distributive. A *median semilattice* [AVA 61] is a distributive meet semilattice D in which, for all $t_1, t_2, t_3 \in D, t_1 \vee t_2 \vee t_3$ exists as soon as the three elements $t_1 \vee t_2, t_1 \vee t_3$ and $t_2 \vee t_3$ all exist. In such a semilattice, the element $(t \wedge t') \vee (t' \wedge t'') \vee (t'' \wedge t)$ exists for any $t, t', t'' \in D$. By straightforward algebraic calculations on its lattice polynomial form, the existence of $t(\alpha)$ follows (but not that of $t(\beta)$). We obtain the following characterization of medians for the distance δ in such semilattices [BAN 84]. It generalizes a series of results on medians in distributive lattices originated in [BAR 61].

Theorem 20.7. *Let D be a median semilattice and $\Pi \in D^v$ be a profile of D. If v is odd, then $t(\alpha)$ is the unique median of Π; if v is even, then the set of all the medians of Π is $Med_D(\Pi) = \{\vee S' : S(\alpha) \subseteq S' \subseteq S(\beta) \text{ and } \vee S' \text{ exists}\}$.*

Proof. It was observed just after lemma 20.2 that, when it exists, an element t satisfying $S(\alpha) \subseteq S_t \subseteq S(\beta)$ minimizes $E(\Pi, t)$. From the previous considerations and proposition 20.7, $t(\alpha) = \vee S(\alpha)$ exists for any profile of a median semilattice. Let $s \in S$ such that $s \leq t(\alpha)$. From property (3) of distributive lattices, there exists $s' \in S(\alpha)$ such that $s \leq s'$. Then, from proposition 20.6, $s \in S(\alpha)$. So, $S_{t(\alpha)} = S(\alpha)$, which implies that $t(\alpha)$ is a median. We show in the same way that $s \leq \vee S'$ with $S' \subseteq S(\beta)$ implies $s \in S(\beta)$. Thus, the elements that have the same remoteness as $S(\alpha)$ are those with the form $\vee S'$, where $S(\alpha) \subseteq S' \subseteq S(\beta)$. If v is odd, then $S(\alpha) = S(\beta)$ and $t(\alpha)$ is the unique median. ◇

In particular, if D is a (distributive) lattice, we have the simple expression $Med_D(\Pi) = \{t \in D : t(\alpha) \leq t \leq t(\beta)\}$, which generalizes the result given by proposition 20.1 on the medians of a profile of binary relations. We shall emphasize in section 20.4.5 the interest of generalizing to median semilattices.

It is implicit, particularly when considering theorem 20.5, that the median procedure constitutes an aggregation multiprocedure which associates a non-empty subset $c(\Pi) \subseteq D$ to any profile of finite length $\Pi \in D^* = \bigcup_{v \in \mathbb{N}} D^v$. In median semilattices, this procedure has been axiomatically characterized [MCM 00]. Recall that an element s of a meet semilattice D is a join irreducible if and only if there exists a unique element s^- of D such that $s^- \leq s, s^- \neq s$, and $s^- \leq s' \leq s$ imply $s' = s^-$ or $s' = s$. For any two profiles $\Pi = (t_1, t_2, \ldots, t_v)$ and $\Pi' = (t'_1, t'_2, \ldots, t'_{v'})$ belonging to D^*, recall that the concatenation of Π and Π' is the profile $\Pi\Pi' =$

$(t_1, \ldots, t_v, t'_1, \ldots, t'_{v'})$. We then obtain the following theorem. Although considered structures and statements differ, we observe that the consistency property below is a direct generalization of that appearing in the characterization of the median procedure applied to profiles of linear orders mentioned at the end of section 20.3.6.

Theorem 20.8. *Let D be a median semilattice and let $c : D^* \to (P(D)\backslash\{\varnothing\})$ be an aggregation multiprocedure. Then, c is the median procedure if and only if it satisfies the following three properties:*

1) Condorcet: $\Pi \in D^v$ *with even* $v, s \in S(D), 2v(s) = v, t \in D$ *and* $t \vee s$ *exists imply* $[t \vee s^- \in c(\Pi) \Leftrightarrow t \vee s \in c(\Pi)]$.

2) Consistency: $\Pi, \Pi' \in D^*$ *and* $c(\Pi) \cap c(\Pi') \neq \varnothing$ *imply* $c(\Pi\Pi') = c(\Pi) \cap c(\Pi')$.

3) Faithfulness: $\Pi \in D^1$ *and* $\Pi = (t)$ *imply* $c(\Pi) = \{t\}$.

As it is most frequently done in the literature, we have developed in this section the case of meet semilattices and therefore considered median (meet) semilattices. Of course, the above considerations may be done about join semilattices, with the exchange of joins and meets (meet irreducibles then replacing join irreducibles). We shall see in section 20.4.5 that the join semilattice $\mathcal{W}$ of complete preorders is precisely a 'median join semilattice'.

20.4.4. *Other semilattices*

As observed above, median semilattices constitute a type of structure where medians are simply characterized. Moreover, the median $t(\alpha)$ is easy to determine as soon as the join operation and, for any $t \in S$, the computation of the set S_t is easy. Otherwise, the search for medians for the symmetric difference distance in a lattice or semilattice of another type is generally difficult [LEC 94].

In a distributive meet semilattice which is not a median one, the conclusions of theorem 20.7 apply to every profile such that $t(\alpha)$ exists. Otherwise, the problem is to find the elements t of D of the type $t = (\vee S_1) \vee (\vee S_2)$, where S_1 is a set of majority join-irreducibles such that $\vee S_1$ exists and maximizes $\sum_{s \in S_1} w(s)$ under this condition, and such that S_2 is a set of balanced join-irreducibles such that t exists. Such a problem may become difficult.

When D is a meet semilattice which is not distributive, even the property that $t(\alpha)$ is a median is no longer guaranteed, since the representation $S_{t(\alpha)}$ may include join-irreducibles s belonging to $S\backslash S(\beta)$, for which the quantity $w(s)$ is negative. Nevertheless, some relations between medians and majority rule remain. They apply, for example, to the lattices of equivalences (or partitions) [BART 95b] and of preorders, or to the semilattice of orders [LEC 03] as follows.

Theorem 20.9. *Let D be a meet semilattice. For any profile Π of D such that $t(\beta)$ exists and for any median t of Π, the inequality $t \leq t(\beta)$ holds; for any profile Π such that $t(\alpha)$ exists and for any median t of Π, there exists a median t' such that $t' \leq t \wedge t(\alpha)$ and every element t'' satisfying $t' \leq t'' \leq t$ is a median.*

20.4.5. *Applications*

Theorem 20.7, which characterizes medians in structures including distributive lattices, applies to the lattice of the subsets of any set and therefore to the lattice $P(X^2)$ of binary relations and to the lattice $\mathcal{T}$ of tournaments described above. A class of distributive lattices generalizing lattices of subsets is provided by direct products of linear orders. Such lattices naturally appear in many problems and modelizations. For instance, consider a multicriteria evaluation with k criteria, each of them taking its values in a finite linearly ordered set D_i. An element t of D is then equivalent to a k-tuple $(t^1, t^2, \ldots, t^k) \in D = D_1 \times D_2 \times \ldots \times D_k$. It is not difficult to see that the medians of a v-tuple of such objects are obtained by taking one median value for each criterion.

Another example is given by the choice functions satisfying some properties. A *choice function* on X is a mapping $ch : P^*(X) \to P^*(X)$ (as in section 20.2.1, $P^*(X)$ is the set of non-empty subsets of X) satisfying $ch(Y) \subseteq Y$ for any $Y \subseteq X$. Such a function is assumed to represent the selection made by an agent among the elements of any non-empty subset Y of X. It is then natural to consider the collective choice of a group of agents as a consensus of choice functions. Among many axioms defining interesting classes of choice functions [ALE 07, MON 04] we have the following *heritage* property (H):

(H) For any $Y, Z \subseteq X$, $Y \subseteq Z$ implies $Y \cap ch(Z) \subseteq ch(Y)$.

The set $\mathcal{X}$ of all the choice functions on X is naturally ordered by the pointwise order: for $ch, ch' \in \mathcal{X}$, $ch \leq ch'$ if $ch(Y) \subseteq ch'(Y)$ for any $Y \subseteq X$. It is then shown that the ordered subset $\mathcal{X}_H$ of those choice functions which satisfy the heritage property is a distributive lattice.

The previous examples deal with distributive lattices. Nevertheless, the extension to median semilattices in theorem 20.7 is justified by the observation that such semilattices, which are not lattices, are frequently encountered. Consider a finite set E endowed with a symmetric binary relation C modeling a 'compatibility' of some type. We are concerned with the set $\mathcal{F}$ of subsets F of E whose elements are pairwise compatible. In other terms, the subgraph induced by C on F is a *clique* (i.e. it is a complete subgraph). Then, ordered by inclusion, $\mathcal{F}$ is a median semilattice. For instance, if E is an ordered set and C its comparability relation, the cliques of C correspond to the linearly ordered subsets of E (also called the *chains* of E) and they constitute a median semilattice.

We provide an example of median semilattices of chains. Let us associate with any complete preorder W on X the (linearly ordered by inclusion) family $N(W)$ of subsets of X defined by $N(W) = \{\{y \in X : yWx\}, x \in X\}$. We may check that there is a one-to-one correspondence between the set $\mathcal{W}$ of all the complete preorders on X and the set $\mathcal{N}$ of all the chains of $P(X)$ including X. Moreover, we have $W \subseteq W' \Leftrightarrow N(W') \subseteq N(W)$. From the above considerations, $\mathcal{N}$ is a median semilattice. Since the inclusion order on $\mathcal{N}$ is (order) dual to the semilattice $\mathcal{W}$ described in Table 20.1, the latter is a so-called median join semilattice. The join irreducible elements of $\mathcal{N}$ correspond to the meet irreducibles of $\mathcal{W}$, and the symmetric difference distance δ on $\mathcal{N}$ counts the subsets of X present in exactly one of the chains $N(W)$ and $N(W')$. In fact, with this metric, we often obtain median chains with few subsets of X, corresponding to poorly discriminant complete preorders.

The choice functions satisfying the following *Arrow condition* (A) correspond to a similar case:

(A) For any $Y, Z \subseteq X, Y \subseteq Z$ and $Y \cap ch(Z) \neq \emptyset$ imply $Y \cap ch(Z) = ch(Y)$.

This condition (A) implies the heritage (H) and characterizes those choice functions which are *rationalizable by a complete preorder* i.e. if ch satisfies (A), there exists a complete preorder W on X such that $ch(Y)$ is the set of the maximal (for W) elements of Y. The set $\mathcal{X}_A$ of the choice functions satisfying Condition (A) is a median semilattice, isomorphic to $\mathcal{N}$ and dual to $\mathcal{W}$.

20.5. Conclusion

We return to the various notions of medians seen in this chapter, in particular to give some historical information [MON 91, MON 08]. We begin with the notions found in all books on statistics. Consider a population totally preordered according to the values of a linearly ordered variable, e.g. the age for a population of individuals. The *median age* of this population is that for which there are as many individuals with an age lower than the median age as individuals with a greater age. When there are $v = 2p$ individuals ranked by increasing age, each age (strictly) included between the ages of the pth and the $(p+1)$th individual satisfies this property and is therefore a median.

We have a 'median interval' (in this case, statisticians often choose as median age the mean between the two ages that are the bounds of the median interval). Two observations can be made on the median(s) of a distribution:

1) A median is a solution of an optimization problem: it minimizes the sum of its distances to the different values taken by the variable on the population (these values being weighted by their number of occurrences). This is a consequence of a more general result, due to Laplace, on the median of a probability distribution [LAP 74].

2) At least when the median is unique, it can be obtained by an algebraic expression using the operations Max and Min. For instance, in the simplest case where the values of the variable for three individuals are a, b, c with $a < b < c$, the median b is given by the formula $b = \min[\max(a, b), \max(b, c), \max(c, a)]$. (When there is a median interval, its two bounds are given by algebraic formulas.)

The first observation leads to the notion of metric median. In a metric space (E, d), a median of a v-tuple $(t_1, t_2, \ldots, t_v)$ is an element t of E minimizing the sum $\sum_{i=1}^{v} d(t, t_i)$ of the distances of t to the elements of the v-tuple. This is in fact an old notion since it appears in a famous challenge proposed by Fermat in his *Essai sur les maximas et les minimas* [FER 29]: "Let he who does not approve of my method attempt the solution of the following problem: given three points of the plane, find a fourth point such that the sum of its distances to the three given points is a minimum". Here, the distance between two points P and Q is the length of the segment PQ. We must therefore find the median point of three points of the plane for the usual Euclidean metric.

(Contrary to a frequent error, this median point is not the intersection point of the three medians of the triangle formed by the three points. This last point, the *gravity center* of the three points, minimizes the sum of the squared distances.)

Fermat's problem and its numerous various generalizations will be a recurrent topic in pure or applied mathematics literature. In particular, one of these generalizations appears in Alfred Weber's book *Über den Standort der Industrien* [WEB 09] where the problem consists of finding the median of v weighted points of the plane (in the theory of optimal location, we speak of Fermat–Weber's problem). On the other hand, at the beginning of the 20th century the Italian statistician Gini considered the problem of finding the central value of a multidimensional statistical series [GIN 14]. He proposed adopting the (multidimensional) value nearest (according to the sum of the Euclidean distances) the observed values as central value, and he called it the *median* of the statistical series.

One of Gini's motivations was to palliate Quételet's *mean man* paradox. Recall that Quételet considered a population of men described by several measurable characteristics and he defined the mean man as the man obtained by taking the means (in the usual sense) of the values of the attributes in the population. The problem (quickly pointed out by Cournot) is that this mean man will generally be an impossible man. With the same motivation to palliate Quételet's defective definition, the mathematician Fréchet (creator of the notion of metric space in 1904) proposed [FRÉ 49] introducing a distance in the space of the observations (which can be elements of any nature) and to take as a 'typical value' of a v-tuple of observations their (metric) median.

Note that this median (just as the mean in an Euclidean space) has no reason to be one of the observed values. Thus, this notion of metric median has been for a long time a possible solution of the problem to find the central value of data of a various nature. In order to use this median, it is sufficient to be able to define a distance in the set of possible data. An example of this approach is described in section 20.2 when data are binary relations. There, the distance between two relations is the symmetric difference distance. The studied relations are first arbitrary (20.2.3), afterwards tournaments (20.2.5) and then linear orders (20.3). However, in this last case which is e.g. the one where we want to aggregate voters' preferences assumed to be linear orders into a 'consensus' linear order, computing the median (linear orders) can be a very difficult combinatorial optimization problem (since it is NP-hard; section 20.3.4). This is why section 20.3 develops different formulations of the problem consisting of searching for the median (linear) orders (especially as a 0-1 linear programming problem) and gives several properties of these median orders useful for this research.

Of the opposite nature, when in sections 20.2.3 and 20.2.5 we search for the medians of a profile of arbitrary relations or the median tournaments of a profile of tournaments, the answer is easily obtained from the two (strict and not strict) majority relations associated with the profile. We recover the notion of metric median: indeed, as shown by formulae just before section 20.2.4, these two majority relations are expressed by algebraic formulae in the Boolean lattice of the subsets of a set with the two binary operations of this lattice, namely the intersection and the union. Moreover, the definition of these relations as the union of majority ordered pairs (definition 20.2) makes them a generalization of the definition of medians in a linearly ordered set as the element(s) dividing the population into two halves. If, for example, we consider the case of a $(2p+1)$-tuple of distinct elements of a linearly ordered set, the median is the maximum of the *majority elements* in the sense of section 20.4.2 (i.e. the maximum of these elements less than a majority of elements of this tuple).

Finally, the interesting question both for practical and theoretical reasons is therefore to be able to recognize the 'good' discrete (since here we only consider finite structures) metric spaces. These are those metric spaces where finding medians is possible since they are given by algebraic expressions generally easily computable. These metric spaces are the so-called *median semilattices*. (For the sake of brevity *median graphs*, which are the undirected graphs that, suitably oriented, are the covering graphs of the median semilattices, are not covered here. These graphs, which in particular contain chains and trees, have many characterizations [BAN 84] and various generalizations [MUL 80].)

Median semilattices are endowed with a distance which generalizes the symmetric difference distance between sets (and relations). The median semilattices that are lattices are exactly the distributive lattices. Two special cases of distributive lattices seen above are the linearly ordered sets and the Boolean lattices (for instance, the Boolean lattices of all the binary relations defined on a set). In sections 20.4.1 and

20.4.2 we first consider the natural distance, which can be defined on any (finite) semilattice. Afterwards, section 20.4.3 is devoted to median semilattices. In such semilattices the so-called *join-irreducible* elements generalize either the elements of a linearly ordered set or the ordered pairs of binary relations. The formulae of theorem 20.7 show that in a median semilattice the medians of a v-tuple of elements are obtained by the join operation on the (strict or not strict) *majority join-irreducible* elements of this v-tuple. When the median semilattice is a distributive lattice, we obtain the formulae using the meet and the join operations which generalize the formulae given just before section 20.2.4. Finally, section 20.4.4 returns to the case of some other semilattices for which we can give indications on the location of medians.

To conclude, we see that various motivations and research on 'pure' and 'applied' mathematics have met for the elaboration of a theory of the median procedure. As for any central value, the median procedure has good properties but it also has drawbacks. The main drawback is probably the possible non-uniqueness of the median. This procedure is useful in the many domains where discrete data must be aggregated. However, we must take care not to confuse different levels. On the one hand, the theory shows that the median procedure is conveniently usable when the data can be considered as elements of a particular ordered structure: namely a median semilattice (and, as a very particular case, a linearly ordered set) since then the computation of medians is generally easy. On the other hand, we can apply the median procedure to data that are themselves orders. This is precisely the case when we search to aggregate profiles of linear orders into a median (linear) order. However, since the set of all linear orders is not a median semilattice, it is difficult to obtain these median orders. The final section of this chapter gives some other examples of 'good' cases, e.g. the cases of some sets of choice functions. The final slogan therefore could be: if you have to aggregate non-numerical discrete data, first look for an underlying median semilattice.

20.6. Acknowledgements

Olivier Hudry would like to thank Lucile Denœud-Belgacem for her help in the translation of his part of this chapter.

20.7. Bibliography

[ALE 07] ALESKEROV F., BOUYSSOU D., MONJARDET B., *Utility Maximization, Choice and Preference*, Springer-Verlag, Berlin, 2007.

[ALO 90] ALON N., "The maximum number of Hamiltonian paths in tournaments", *Combinatorica* 10, pp. 319–324, 1990.

[ALO 06] ALON N., "Ranking tournaments", *SIAM Journal on Discrete Mathematics* 20(1), pp. 137–142, 2006.

[ARD 84] ARDITTI D., "Un nouvel algorithme de recherche d'un ordre induit par des comparaisons par paires", in *Data Analysis and Informatics III*, E. Diday, M. Jambu, L. Lebart, J. Pagès, R. Tomassone (eds), North-Holland, Amsterdam, pp. 323–343, 1984.

[ARR 51] ARROW K.J., *Social Choice and Individual Values*, Wiley, New York, 1951.

[AVA 61] AVANN S.P., "Metric ternary distributive semi-lattices", *Proceedings of American Mathematical Society*, 12, pp. 407–414, 1961.

[BAN 84] BANDELT H.J., BARTHÉLEMY J.-P., "Medians in median graphs", *Discrete Applied Mathematics*, 8, pp. 131–142, 1984.

[BAR 61] BARBUT M., "Médiane, distributivité, éloignements", *Publications du Centre de mathématiques sociales*, Paris, 1961 and *Mathématiques et Sciences Humaines*, 70, pp. 5–31.

[BAR 67] BARBUT M., "Médiane, Condorcet et Kendall", *Note SEMA*, Paris, 1967, and *Mathématiques et Sciences Humaines*, 69, pp. 5–13, 1980.

[BART 76] BARTHÉLEMY J.-P., "Sur les éloignements symétriques et le principe de Pareto", *Mathématiques et Sciences Humaines*, 56, pp. 97–125, 1976.

[BART 81] BARTHÉLEMY J.-P., MONJARDET B., "The median procedure in cluster analysis and social choice theory", *Mathematical Social Sciences*, 1, pp. 235–267, 1981.

[BART 89] BARTHÉLEMY J.-P., GUÉNOCHE A., HUDRY O., "Median linear orders: heuristics and a branch and bound algorithm", *European Journal of Operational Research*, 41, pp. 313–325, 1989.

[BART 91] BARTHÉLEMY J.-P., JANOWITZ M.F., "A formal theory of consensus", *SIAM Journal on Discrete Mathematics*, 4, pp. 305–322, 1991.

[BART 95a] BARTHÉLEMY J.-P., HUDRY O., ISAAK G., ROBERTS F.S., TESMAN B., "The reversing number of a digraph", *Discrete Applied Mathematics*, 60, pp. 39–76, 1995.

[BART 95b] BARTHÉLEMY J.-P., LECLERC B., "The median procedure for partitions", in *Partitioning data sets*, I.J. Cox, P. Hansen and B. Julesz (eds), *DIMACS Series in Discrete Mathematics and Theoretical Computer Science* 19, American Mathematical Society, Providence, RI, pp. 3–34, 1995.

[BART 96] BARTHÉLEMY J.-P., COHEN G., LOBSTEIN A., *Algorithmic Complexity and Communication Problems*, UCL Press, London, 1996.

[BEC 67] BECKER O., "Das Helmstädtersche Reihenfolgeproblem: die Effizienz verschiedener Näherungsverfahren", in *Computers Uses in the Social Sciences*, Berichteiner Working Conference, Vienna, 1967.

[BER 72] BERMOND J.-C., "Ordres à distance minimum d'un tournoi et graphes partiels sans circuits maximaux", *Mathématiques et Sciences Humaines*, 37, pp. 5–25, 1972.

[BLA 48] BLACK D., "On the rationale of group decision-making", *Journal of Political Economy*, 56, pp. 23–34, 1948.

[BLA 58] BLACK D., *The Theory of Committees and Elections*, Cambridge University Press, London, 1958.

[BOR 84] BORDA J.-C., *Mémoire sur les élections au scrutin, Histoire de l'Académie royale des sciences pour 1781*, Paris, 1784.

[CAM 99] CAMPOS V., LAGUNA M., MARTÍ R., "Scatter search for the linear ordering problem", in *New Ideas in Optimization*, D. Corne, M. Dorigo, F. Glover (eds), McGraw-Hill, New York, pp. 331–339, 1999.

[CAM 01] CAMPOS V., GLOVER F., LAGUNA M., MARTÍ R., "An experimental evaluation of a scatter search for the linear ordering problem", *Journal of Global Optimization*, 21 (4), pp. 397–414, 2001.

[CAR 85] CARITAT M.J.A.N., marquis de CONDORCET, *Essai sur l'application de l'analyse à la probabilité des décisions rendues à la pluralité des voix*, Imprimerie Royale, Paris, 1785.

[CHA 96] CHANAS S., KOBYLANSKI P., "A new heuristic algorithm solving the linear ordering problem", *Computational Optimization and Applications* 6, pp. 191–205, 1996.

[CHAR 07] CHARBIT P., THOMASSE S., YEO A., "The minimum feedback arc set problem is NP-hard for tournaments", *Combinatorics, Probability and Computing*, 16(1), pp. 1–4, 2007.

[CHARO 96] CHARON I., HUDRY O., WOIRGARD F., "Ordres médians et ordres de Slater des tournois", *Mathématiques, Informatique et Sciences Humaines*, 133, pp. 23–56, 1996.

[CHARO 97] CHARON I., GUÉNOCHE A., HUDRY O., WOIRGARD F., "New results on the computation of median orders", *Discrete Mathematics*, 165–166, pp. 139–154, 1997.

[CHARO 98] CHARON I., HUDRY O., "Lamarckian genetic algorithms applied to the aggregation of preferences", *Annals of Operations Research*, 80, pp. 281–297, 1998.

[CHARO 02] CHARON I., HUDRY O., "The noising methods: a survey", in *Essays and Surveys in Metaheuristics*, P. Hansen, C.C. Ribeiro (eds), Kluwer Academic Publishers, Amsterdam, pp. 245–261, 2002.

[CHARO 06] CHARON I., HUDRY O., "A branch and bound algorithm to solve the linear ordering problem for weighted tournaments", *Discrete Applied Mathematics*, 154, pp. 2097–2116, 2006.

[CHARO 07] CHARON I., HUDRY O., "A survey on the linear ordering problem for weighted or unweighted tournaments", *4OR*, 5(1), pp. 5–60, 2007.

[CON 00] CONGRAM R. K., Polynomially searchable exponential neighbourhoods for sequencing problems in combinatorial optimisation, PhD thesis, University of Southampton, Great Britain, 2000.

[CONI 06] CONITZER V., "Computing Slater rankings using similarities among candidates", in *Proceedings of the 21st National Conference on Artificial Intelligence (AAAI-06)*, Boston, MA, USA, pp. 613–619, 2006.

[COO 88] COOK W.D., GOLAN I., KRESS M., "Heuristics for ranking players in a round robin tournament", *Computers and Operations Research*, 15(2), pp. 135–144, 1988.

[DAV 90] DAVEY B.A., PRIESTLEY H.A., *Introduction to Lattices and Order*, Cambridge University Press, Cambridge, 1990.

[DAY 03] DAY W.H.E., MCMORRIS F.R., *Axiomatic Consensus Theory in Group Choice and Biomathematics. Frontiers in applied mathematics* 29, SIAM, Philadelphia, 2003.

[DEB 87] DEBORD B., "Caractérisation des matrices de préférences nettes et méthodes d'agrégation associées", *Mathématiques et Sciences Humaines*, 97, pp. 5–17, 1987.

[DWO 01] DWORK C., KUMAR R., NAOR M., SIVAKUMAR D., "Rank aggregation methods for the Web", in *Proceedings of the 10th International Conference on World Wide Web (WWW10)*, Hong Kong, pp.613–622, 2001.

[FEL 73] FELDMAN J., "Pôles, intermédiaires et centres dans un groupe d'opinions", *Mathématiques et Sciences Humaines*, 43, pp. 39–54, 1973.

[FER 29] FERMAT P., "Essai sur les maximas et les minimas", *1629 and Œuvres de Fermat*, P. Tannery, C.Henry (eds), Gauthier-Villars, Paris, 1891–1912.

[FRÉ 49] FRÉCHET M., "Réhabilitation de la notion statistique de l'homme moyen", Les Conférences du Palais de la Découverte, Paris, 1949.

[GAR 79] GAREY M.R., JOHNSON D.S., *Computers and Intractability, a Guide to the Theory of NP-completeness*, Freeman, New York, 1979.

[GIN 14] GINI C., "L'uomo medio", *Giornali degli economiste e revista de statistica*, 48, pp. 1–24, 1914.

[GOD 83] GODDARD S.T., "Tournament rankings", *Management Science*, 29 (12), pp. 1385–1392, 1983.

[GRÖ 84] GRÖTSCHEL, M., JÜNGER M., REINELT G., "Optimal triangulation of large real-world input-output-matrices", *Statistische Hefte*, 25, pp. 261–295, 1984.

[GUÉ 95] GUÉNOCHE A., "How to choose according to partial evaluations", in *Advances in Intelligent Computing*, B. Bouchon-Meunier, R.R. Yager, L.A. Zadeh (eds), IPMU'94, *Lecture Notes in Computer Sciences*, num. 945, Springer-Verlag, Berlin-Heidelberg, pp. 611–618, 1995.

[GUI 52] GUILBAUD G. Th., "Les théories de l'intérêt général et le problème logique de l'agrégation", *Économie appliquée*, 5, pp. 501–584, 1952, and *Éléments de la théorie des jeux*, Dunod, Paris, 1968. English translation "Theories of the general interest and the logical problem of aggregation" in *Electronic Journal for History of Probability and Statistics*, 4(1), 2008.

[GUI 63] GUILBAUD G. Th., ROSENSTIEHL P., "Analyse algébrique d'un scrutin", *Mathématiques et Sciences Humaines*, 4, pp. 9–33, 1963.

[HUD 89] HUDRY O., *Recherche d'ordres médians: complexité, algorithmique et problèmes combinatoires*, PhD thesis, ENST, Paris, 1989.

[HUD 97] HUDRY O., "Algorithms for the aggregation of ordinal preferences: a review", in *Proceedings of the First Conference on Operations and Quantitative Management* (ICOQM), pp. 169–176, 1997.

[HUD 08] HUDRY O., "NP-hardness results on the aggregation of linear orders into median orders", *Annals of Operations Research*, 163(1), pp. 63–88, 2008.

[HUD 09a] HUDRY O., "Complexity of voting procedures", in the *Encyclopedia of Complexity and Systems Science*, R. Meyers (ed.), Springer, forthcoming.

[HUD 09b] HUDRY O., "NP-hardness of Slater's problems and of Kemeny's problems", submitted for publication.

[JAC 69] JACQUET-LAGRÈZE É., "L'agrégation des opinions individuelles", *Informatique et Sciences Humaines*, 4, pp. 1–21, 1969.

[JOR 69] JORDAN C., "Sur les assemblages de lignes", *Journal für die reine und andgewandte Mathematik*, 70, pp. 185–190, 1869.

[JÜN 85] JÜNGER M., *Polyhedral Combinatorics and the Acyclic Subdigraph Problem*, Heldermann Verlag, Berlin, 1985.

[KAY 95] KAYKOBAD M., AHMED Q.N.U., SHAFIQUL KHALID A.T.M., BAKHTIAR R.-A., "A new algorithm for ranking players of a round-robin tournament", *Computers and Operations Research*, 22(2), pp. 221–226, 1995.

[KEM 59] KEMENY J.G., "Mathematics without numbers", *Daedalus*, 88, pp. 577–591, 1959.

[KEN 38] KENDALL M.G., *Rank Correlation Methods*, Hafner, New York, 1938.

[KEN 57] KENDALL M.G., BUCKLAND W.R., *A Dictionary of Statistical Terms*, Oliver and Boyd, Edinburgh, 1957.

[LAG 99] LAGUNA M., MARTÍ R., CAMPOS V., "Intensification and diversification with elite tabu search solutions for the linear ordering problem", *Computers and Operations Research*, 26(12), pp. 1217–1230, 1999.

[LAP 74] LAPLACE P.-S., *Mémoire sur la probabilité des causes par les événements*, Œuvres complètes, tome VIII, pp. 141–153, 1774 and *Théorie analytique*, 2(4), 1812.

[LAS 97] LASLIER J.-F., *Tournament Solutions and Majority Voting*, Springer, Berlin, Heidelberg, New York, 1997.

[LEC 93] LECLERC B., "Lattice valuations, medians and majorities", *Discrete Mathematics*, 111, pp. 345–356, 1993.

[LEC 94] LECLERC B., "Medians for weight metrics in the covering graphs of semilattices", *Discrete Applied Mathematics*, 49, pp. 281–297, 1994.

[LEC 95] LECLERC B., MONJARDET B., "Latticial Theory of Consensus", in *Social Choice, Welfare, and Ethics*, W. Barnett, H. Moulin, M. Salles, N. Schofield (eds), Cambridge University Press, Cambridge, pp. 145–160, 1995.

[LEC 03] LECLERC B., "The median procedure in the semilattice of orders", *Discrete Applied Mathematics*, 127, pp. 241–269, 2003.

[MCG 53] MCGARVEY D., "A theorem on the construction of voting paradoxes", *Econometrica*, 21, pp. 608–610, 1953.

[MCM 00] MCMORRIS F.R., MULDER H.M., POWERS R.C., "The median function on median graphs and semilattices", *Discrete Applied Mathematics*, 101, pp. 221–230, 2000.

[MEN 00] MENDONCA D., RAGHAVACHARI M., "Comparing the efficacy of ranking methods for multiple round-robin tournaments", *European Journal of Operational Research*, 123, pp. 593–605, 2000.

[MIT 96] MITCHELL J.E., BORCHERS B., "Solving real world linear ordering problems using a primal-dual interior point cutting plane method", *Annals of Operations Research*, 62, pp. 253–276, 1996.

[MIT 00] MITCHELL J.E., BORCHERS B., "Solving linear ordering problems with a combined interior point/simplex cutting plane algorithm", in *High Performance Optimization*, H.L. Frenk, K. Roos, T. Terlaky, S. Zhang (eds), Kluwer Academic Publishers, Dordrecht, The Netherlands, pp. 349–366, 2000.

[MON 73] MONJARDET B., "Tournois et ordres médians pour une opinion", *Mathématiques et Sciences Humaines*, 43, pp. 55–73, 1973.

[MON 80] MONJARDET B., "Théorie et applications de la médiane dans les treillis distributifs", *Annals of Discrete Mathematics*, pp. 87–91, 1980.

[MON 90a] MONJARDET B., "Sur diverses formes de la règle de Condorcet d'agrégation des préférences", *Mathématiques Informatique et Sciences Humaines*, 111, pp. 61–71, 1990.

[MON 90b] MONJARDET B., "Arrowian characterizations of latticial federation consensus functions", *Mathematical Social Sciences*, 20, pp. 51–71, 1990.

[MON 91] MONJARDET B., "Éléments pour une histoire de la médiane métrique", in *Moyenne, milieu et centre: histoires et usages*, collection Histoire des sciences et techniques, num. 5, éditions de l'École des hautes études en sciences sociales, pp. 45–62, 1991.

[MON 04] MONJARDET B., RADERANIRINA V., "Lattices of choice functions and consensus problems", *Social Choice and Welfare*, 23, 2004, 349–382.

[MON 08] MONJARDET B., "'Mathématique Sociale' and Mathematics. A case study: Condorcet's effect and medians" *Electronic Journal for History of Probability and Statistics*, 40(1), 2008.

[MSH 03] MONJARDET B., HUDRY O. (eds), Théorie du choix social: cinquantenaires, *Mathématiques et Sciences Humaines*, 163, 2003.

[MUL 80] MULDER H.M., *The Interval Function of a Graph*, Mathematical Centre Tracts 132, Mathematisch Centrum, Amsterdam, 1980.

[POL 86] POLJAK S., TURZÍK D., "A polynomial time heuristic for certain subgraph optimization problems with guaranteed lower bound", *Discrete Mathematics*, 58, pp. 99–104, 1986.

[POL 88] POLJAK S., RÖDL V., SPENCER J., "Tournament ranking with expected profit in polynomial time", *SIAM Journal Discrete Mathematics*, 1(3), pp. 372–376, 1988.

[REI 85] REINELT G., *The Linear Ordering Problem: Algorithms and Applications*, Research and Exposition in Mathematics 8, Heldermann Verlag, Berlin, 1985.

[REM 66] REMAGE R., THOMPSON W.A., "Maximum likelihood paired comparison rankings", *Biometrika*, 53, pp. 143–149, 1966.

[SCH 03] SCHIAVINOTTO T., STÜTZLE T., "Search space analysis of the linear ordering problem", in *Applications of Evolutionary Computing*, G.R. Raidl et al. (eds), Lecture Notes in Computer Science 2611, Springer Verlag, Berlin, pp. 322–333, 2003.

[SHO 54] SHOLANDER M., "Medians, lattices and trees", *Proceedings of American Mathematical Society*, 5, pp. 808–812, 1954.

[SLA 61] SLATER P., "Inconsistencies in a schedule of paired comparisons", *Biometrika*, 48, pp. 303–312, 1961.

[SLA 78] SLATER P.J., "Centers to centroids in graphs", *Journal of Graph Theory*, 2, pp. 209–222, 1978.

[SMI 74] SMITH A.F.M., PAYNE C.D., "An algorithm for determining Slater's i and all nearest adjoining orders", *British Journal of Mathematical and Statistical Psychology*, 27, pp. 49–52, 1974.

[VAZ 03] VAZIRANI V.V., *Approximation Algorithms*, Springer, Berlin, 2003.

[WAK 86] WAKABAYASHI Y., Aggregation of Binary Relations: Algorithmic and Polyhedral Investigations, PhD thesis, University of Augsbourg, 1986.

[WAK 98] WAKABAYASHI Y., "The Complexity of Computing Medians of Relations", *Resenhas*, 3(3), pp. 323–349, 1998.

[WEB 09] Weber A., *Über den Standort der Industrien*, Teil I: *Reine Theorie des Standorts*, Mohr, Tübingen, 1909. English translation *Alfred Weber's Theory of the Location of Industries*, University of Chicago Press, Chicago, 1929.

[WOI 97] WOIRGARD F., *Recherche et dénombrement des ordres médians des tournois*, PhD thesis, ENST, Paris, 1997.

[YOU 78] YOUNG H.P., LEVENGLICK A., "A consistent extension of Condorcet's election principle", *SIAM Journal on Applied Mathematics*, 35, pp. 285–300, 1978.

[YOU 88] YOUNG H.P., "Condorcet theory of voting", *American Political Science Review*, 82, pp. 1231–1244, 1988.

[YOUN 63] YOUNGER D.H., "Minimum feedback arc sets for a directed graph", *IEEE Transactions of the Professional Technical Group in Circuit Theory*, 10(2), pp. 238–245, 1963.

[ZEL 68] ZELINKA B.L., "Median and peripherian of trees", *Archivum Mathematicum (Brno)*, pp. 87–95, 1968.

List of Authors

Mohammed ABDELLAOUI
GRID
Cachan
France

Jean-Pierre BARTHÉLEMY
ENST-Bretagne
Brest
France

Denis BOUYSSOU
LAMSADE-CNRS
Paris-Dauphine University
France

Alain CHATEAUNEUF
Cermsem
Paris 1 University
France

Michèle COHEN
EUREQua
Paris 1 University
France

Didier DUBOIS
IRIT-CNRS
Paul Sabatier University
Toulouse
France

Hélène FARGIER
IRIT-CNRS
Paul Sabatier University
Toulouse
France

Christophe GONZALES
LIP6
Paris 6 University
France

Michel GRABISCH
LIP6
Paris 6 University
France

Denis J. HILTON
Psychology department
Toulouse 2 University
France

Olivier HUDRY
ENST Paris
France

Jean-Yves JAFFRAY
LIP6
Paris 6 University
France

Jérôme LANG
IRIT-CNRS
Paul Sabatier University
Toulouse
France

Bruno LECLERC
CAMS
EHESS
Paris
France

Thierry MARCHANT
University of Gand
Belgium

Jean-Luc MARICHAL
Luxembourg University
Luxembourg

Bernard MONJARDET
CAMS
EHESS
Paris
France

Patrice PERNY
LIP6
Paris 6 University
France

Marc PIRLOT
Math RO
Faculté Polytechnique de Mons
Belgium

Jean-Charles POMEROL
LIP6
Paris 6 University
France

Henri PRADE
IRIT-CNRS
Paul Sabatier University
Toulouse
France

Eric RAUFASTE
Psychology department
Toulouse 2 University
France

Régis SABBADIN
INRA
Toulouse
France

Thomas SCHIEX
INRA-MIA
Toulouse
France

Jean-Marc TALLON
EUREQua
Paris 1 University
France

Jacques TEGHEM
Math RO
Faculté Polytechnique de Mons
Belgium

Alexis TSOUKIÀS
LAMSADE-CNRS
Paris-Dauphine University
France

Gérard VERFAILLIE
ONERA-DCSD
Toulouse
France

Philippe VINCKE
SMG
Université libre de Bruxelles
Belgium

Index

act, 366, 386, 402
    constant, 386
    simple step, 386
acyclic, 72, 76
additive
    generator, 691
    value functions, 64
affect, 495
aggregation, 829, 840, 843
    binary relation, 812
    conjunctive, 759
    fuzzy preference, 794, 838
    method, 63
    ordinal, 665
    preference, 673, 779, 811, 830
    satisfaction degree, 673
aggregation function, 673
    algebraic property, 675
    associative, 675, 688
    associative and internal, 676
    bisymmetric, 682
    conjunctive, 678
    continuous, 677
    decomposable, 681
    definition, 676
    disjunctive, 678
    idempotence, 677
    increasing, 677
    interval scale, 686
    Lagrangian mean, 687
    mean, 682
    non-additive integral, 675

    ordinal scale, 689
    OWA, 675, 703, 704
    quasi-arithmetic mean, 675, 681, 685
    quasi-linear mean, 687
    ratio scale, 686
    symmetry, 674, 676
    t-conorm, 697
    t-norm, 697
    t-operator, 698
    uninorm, 697
    WAM, 675, 702
    weighted mean, 675
algorithm
    genetic, 755
    linear programming, 755, 826
alternative, 326
analysis
    data, 725, 815
    multiple correspondence, 726
    principal component, 726
    sensorial, 726
anchor point, 183
andness, 758
anonymity, 800
Anscombe and Aumann theory, 396
antisymmetric, 52
approval voting, 786, 801
Arrow's theorem, 5, 14, 63, 73, 76, 789, 792–795, 801, 815
artificial intelligence, 6, 49
asymmetric, 52
attentional focusing, 487

axiom
    $AC1$, 631
    $AC2$, 631
    $AC3$, 631
    additive independence, 602
    anonymity, 799
    Archimedean, 591
    Arrow independence, 790
    cancellation, 798
    conjunctive dominance, 454
    consistency, 797
    continuity, 373
    disjunctive dominance, 454
    faithfulness, 797
    independence, 374, 587, 595, 624
    mutual utility independence, 601, 603
    neutrality, 800
    non-compensation, 455
    ordinal invariance, 450
    $RC1$, 646
    $RC2$, 646
    separability, 625
    solvability, 592
    $TAC1$, 634
    $TAC2$, 634
    TC, 650
    Thomsen, 590
    unanimity, 790
    utility independence, 599, 603
    weak directional separability, 749
    weak separability, 595, 732, 736, 739, 749
axiomatization, 674
Bayesian network, 506, 511
    construction, 528
belief function, 112
bicapacity, 744
    Choquet integral, 742
    decomposable, 766
    symmetric, 744
binary relation, 49, 811
    aggregation, 811
    linear order, 812
    matrix representation, 53
    outranking, 620, 655, 665
bipolarity, 329, 729, 762
Borda, 812

    method, 787, 788, 790, 798
Bowman theorem, 208
calibration, 476
capacity
    2-additive, 767
    decomposable, 767
    k-additive, 767
causal graphs, 531
causality, 530
certainty, 108
    equivalent, 371
ceteris paribus comparison, 339, 340
choice
    of computer, 584
    of problem, 62
choosing, 62
classical preference structures, 57
cognitive
    capacity, 168
    psychology, 7
collective preference, 73
commensurability, 734
comonotonic sure-thing principle, 412
comonotony, 403
complete, 52
    ignorance, 366
complexity, 271, 829
    decision problem, 829
    NP-complete, 829
    NP-hard, 829
    theory, 272
concordance, 620
conditioning, 130
    by intervention, 531
    qualitative, 132
Condorcet
    method, 786, 788
    paradox, 63, 77
    principle, 787
    winner, 787
confidence interval, 87, 127, 476, 477
congnitive bias, 178
conjunctive dominance axiom, 456
consistency, 269
    arc-consistency, 275
    graph, 268
    local, 275

path-consistency, 278
constraint
    continuous domain, 298
    distributed decision, 310
    graph, 267
    interactive decision, 310
    preference, 301
    propagation, 282, 293
    satisfaction, 13
    satisfaction problem, 265
    uncertainty, 308
CP-net, 343
CSP, 265
    additive, 301
    conditional, 300
    dynamic, 300
    possibilistic, 302
    probabilistic, 302
    valued, 302
cumulative prospect theory, 744
cut-cycle, 522
d-separation, 513
decision
    analysis, 579
    case-based, 173
    inter-temporal, 617
    medical, 584
    multiattribute, 617
    process, 1
    satisfactory, 171
    theory, 1
    under certainty, 582, 585
    under multiple criteria, 63
    under risk, 63, 77, 598
        rank dependent, 611
    under uncertainty, 63, 582, 585, 597, 599, 612, 617, 666
decision-aiding
    constructive, 7
    constructive approach, 19, 23
    descriptive approach, 18, 19, 50, 480–482, 490
    ELECTRE, 804
    importance of criteria, 802
    interactive system DSS, 175
    MAVT, 804
    methodology, 1, 3, 16
    multicriteria, 725, 780, 811, 845
    normative approach, 17–19, 23, 50, 186, 380, 480, 482, 490, 497
    preference modeling, 802
    process, 3, 11, 16, 20
    PROMETHEE, 804
    social choice theory, 801
    TACTIC, 803
    weighted sum, 804
descriptor, 725
desire, 182
    conditional, 347
diagnosis, 172
difference
    symmetric, 812
disjunctive dominance axiom, 457
distance, 811
    between binary relations, 812
    semilattice, 839
    Tchebytchev, 207
dominance, 637, 641, 665
    relation, 203
    rule, 483
Dutch book, 65, 77
ecological rationality, 489
economics, 49
ELECTRE, 620, 643, 654
epistemic possibility, 108
equivalence, 52
evaluation
    affect, 728
    cosmetic, 769
    discomfort, 769
    model, 23
    subjective, 723
        structure, 725
evaluator, 725
exhaustive, 56
expected utility, 65, 438, 460
    model, 372
    subjective, 65, 386
expertise, 723
expressivity, 353
Fermat–Weber problem, 847
Ferrers, 52, 66
first-order stochastic dominance, 368
framing effect, 477

864 Decision-making Process

French system
    manipulation, 783
    monotonicity, 783
    participation, 784
    separability, 784
function
    scalarizing, 207
fusion information, 87
fuzzy
    number, 253
    relations, 55
    set, 7, 14, 94, 727
GAI-net, 331
genetic algorithm, 243, 831
Geoffrion theorem, 208
goal, 326
    ideal, 350
    negative, 329
    positive, 329
    programming, 9, 211
granularity, 87, 96
heuristic
    anchoring-adjustment, 493
    availability, 492
    evaluation, 489
    representativeness, 491
hierarchical optimization, 211
human sensor, 723
impossibility results, 796
incomparability, 73, 76
increasing risk, 369
independence, 508
    axiom, 162
    conditional, 510
    generalized additive, 331
    preferential, 343
index
    conjunction, 765
    disjunction, 765
    Gini, 847
    importance of a criterion, 759
    interaction, 760
    maximum improving, 764
    Shapley, 760, 762, 763
    veto, 765
indifference
    relation, 443

threshold, 67
influence diagram, 507, 532, 535, 565
information
    gradual, 96
    granularity, 96
    imprecise, 118, 138
    propagation, 518
    uncertain, 131, 138
integral
    Choquet, 467, 700, 742
    Sugeno, 644, 699, 704, 748
    Sugeno bicapacity, 751
    Sugeno symmetric, 751
intensity of preference, 55
interactive phase, 230, 249
interval
    order, 76
    scale, 65
    weak order, 70
irreflexive, 52
isotonicity, 739
join-irreducible, 839
junction tree, 523
language
    graphical, 331
    preference representation, 327
    with priorities, 332
lattice polynomial, 713
level of expectancy, 182
Likely Dominance rule, 442
logical interpretation, 324
lottery, 420, 438, 454, 457, 458, 488, 498
MACBETH, 728, 733, 735
macrostructure, 267
majority
    British system, 781
    dictatorship, 781
    French system, 782
Markov equivalence class, 529
matrix representation, 54, 68
maximin
    criterion, 438
maximum, 686
    partial, 676
    weighted, 707
maxitivity, 93, 126, 706
mean, 673, 682

Index   865

arithmetic, 673, 675
Cauchy, 682, 687
geometric, 673
harmonic, 683
Lagrangian, 687
quadratic, 686
quasi-arithmetic, 686
mean man paradox, 847
meaningful, 61
meaningfulness, 78
measure
fuzzy, 699, 740
measurement
conjoint, 579, 617
extensive, 732
inequality, 617
scale, 673
standard sequence, 591
theory, 726
median, 704, 713, 811
algebraic, 813, 847
application, 845
binary linear proramming, 822
binary relation, 812
in lattices, 836
in semilattices, 836
L-medians, 822
lattical, 811
median center, 811
methods, 830
metric, 811
order, 825
ordinal, 813
probability distribution, 846
procedure, 811
R-medians, 816
relation, 814
statistics, 846
T-medians, 820
tournament, 820
tree, 813
weighted, 705
weighted graph, 824
meet-irreducible, 839
method
Borda, 787
characterizations, 796

Condorcet, 786
elicitation, 605
fractile, 609
tradeoff, 611
Geoffrion et al., 223
Gonzales et al., 228
interactive, 170, 200, 214, 215, 222, 228
junction tree, 523, 537
Kiziltan and Yucaoglu, 227
Klein and Hannan, 226
MOMIX, 229
Pearl, 517
STEM, 215, 230, 248
Steuer and Choo, 219
STRANGE, 217, 246, 247, 252
Sylva and Crema, 226
Zionts and Wallenius, 222
metric space, 815, 847
microstructure, 268, 304
min-transitivity, 794
minimum
partial, 676
weighted, 707
minitivity, 93, 706
model
additive differences, 619, 654, 664
additive non-transitive, 585, 619
additive utility, 436, 618
difference, 644, 655
expected utility, 65
Gilboa and Schmeidler, 416
level, 629, 633, 635, 644
level and difference, 655, 665
non-transitive non-additive, 620
Olympian, 167
Quiggin, 420
Schmeidler, 415
von Neumann and Morgenstern, 408
Yaari, 420
multicriteria
analysis, 9
decision aid, 199
paradigm, 200
multiple objective combinatorial
optimization, 231, 232
direct method, 235

exact method, 233
metaheuristics, 241
two phases method, 237
mutually exclusive, 56
necessity, 119
   measure, 440
negatively transitive, 52
non-classical logics, 55
non-discordance, 620
normality, 345, 350
numerical representation, 59, 65, 71
oligarchy, 793
omelette, 581
operational research, 4, 49
order
   interval, 66, 69, 624, 758
   interval (numerical representation), 71
   partial, 73, 129, 345, 837
   statistic, 676
   total, 57, 74, 171, 303
   total (numerical representation), 59
   weak, 60
   weak (numerical representation), 61
ordinal scale, 69
orness, 758
outranking
   concordance, 620
   method, 15
overconfidence, 476
paradox
   Allais, 419, 422
   Ellsberg, 405, 409, 415
Paretian liberal, 796
partial order, 76
   dimension, 74
payoff matrix, 205, 248
plausibility function, 114
point
   anti-ideal, 206
   ideal, 205, 248
   nadir, 205, 206, 230
   reference, 206
political sciences, 49
possibilistic qualitive criterion, 439
possibility, 90, 119
   distribution, 439
   measure, 440

theory, 14
potential surprise, 439
preference, 580
   a posteriori, 213
   a priori, 210
   ceteris paribus, 323, 338
   aggregation, 63
   collective, 780, 814
   completeness, 621
   conditional, 344
   constraint, 301
   contradictory, 352
   data, 78
   defeasible, 345
   fuzzy, 794
   incomplete, 352
   independence, 64
   individual, 780, 814
   marginal, 624
   modeling, 49, 617
   parameter, 206
   product set, 623
   progressive, 213
   relation, 7, 326
   representational logic, 327
   reversal, 477
   structure, 54
   transitivity, 76, 621
   voting, 780
principle
   sure-thing, 387, 446
priority, 332
probability, 98
   a priori, 163
   Bayesian, 104
   comparative, 128
   conditional, 101, 130, 509
   imprecise, 108
   joint, 507
   marginal, 507
   pignistic, 116
   qualitative, 391
   subjective, 104
problem
   assignment, 233
   constraint satisfaction, 265
   deterministic, 247

Fermat–Weber, 847
formulation, 11
knapsack, 235, 236
optimization, 294
SAT, 272
programming
   dynamic, 534
   linear, 4
   multi-objective, 201
      fuzzy linear, 253
      integer, 224
      integer linear, 224
      linear, 202
      stochastic linear, 245
   with constraints, 297
project management, 769
prospect theory, 478
pseudo-distance, 335
psychology, 49, 735
quasi-order, 74, 76
quasi-transitivity, 793
query, 269
rank-dependent expected utility, 420
rankings, 786
rationality, 20, 168
   bounded, 5, 170
   procedural, 168
   substantive, 166
recognition, 173
recommendation, 24
reflexive, 52
reinforcement learning, 558
relation
   binary, 50
   dominance, 203
   equivalence, 53
   outranking, 620, 654, 665
   tournament, 77
remoteness, 815
representation function, 340
reservation level, 206
risk, 366
   aversion, 370, 372, 377, 378, 380, 420
   premium, 372
robustness, 178
rough set, 97
sagittal representation, 54

SAT problem, 272
satisfaction degrees, 727
satisficing, 734
Savage's theory, 387
scalarizing function, 206
scale
   absolute, 730
   bipolar, 729
   interval, 730, 731
   ordinal, 730, 733
   ratio, 730, 732
   unipolar, 729
scenario, 176
scoring rules, 799
search
   greedy, 291
   local, 292
   Tabu, 243
   tree, 283
second-order stochastic dominance, 369
semi-order, 66, 76
   numerical representation, 68
   partial, 76
   weak order, 67
semi-transitive, 52, 66
semigraphoïd, 511
semigroup
   Aczélian, 690
   Archimedean, 690
   improperly Archimedean, 693
   ordered, 689
   properly Archimedean, 693
semilattice, 813, 840, 844
   distributive, 844
   median, 822, 836
sequential voting, 785
simple majority, 800
simulated annealing, 241
social choice, 4, 77, 335, 442, 779
   theory, 5, 780
Soland theorem, 209
solution
   compromise, 200, 201
   efficient, 203
   Pareto optimal, 203
   supported efficient, 224
   weakly efficient, 203

space
    decision, 201, 202
    objective, 202
state of nature, 582
subjective expected utility, 386
substitution rate, 206, 223
sure-thing principle, 387, 446
    comonotonic, 412
symmetric, 52
t-norm, 697
Tabu search, 243
Tchebytchev distance, 207
theorem
    Anscombe and Aumann, 396
    Gibbard-Satterthwaite, 796
    May, 799
    Sen, 796
    Young, 798
threshold, 72
tie-break, 786
total order, 76
trace, 67, 623
    difference, 621, 626
    left, 70
    level, 621, 625, 629
    level and difference, 621
    right, 70
tradeoffs, 579
transitivity, 52, 789
    of indifference, 73
triangular conorm, 697
unanimity, 786
uncertainty, 14
universality, 789
utility function, 5, 15, 95, 160, 174, 210, 222, 326, 366, 579
    additive, 618
    additive under certainty, 586
    decomposable, 585
    decomposition, 585
    multilinear decomposition, 585
    multiplicative decomposition, 585
    subset of the Cartesian product, 596
    von Neumann and Morgenstern, 598
V-structure, 515
value
    iteration, 545

value function, 62
    additive, 619
    decomposable, 619
variable elimination, 288
veto, 655, 758, 765
    right, 793
voters, 780
voting
    plurality, 781
    sincerity, 783
    theory, 779
voting procedure
    abstention, 784
    analysis, 795
    anonymity, 786
    Borda method, 796, 799
    cancellation, 798
    characterization, 795
    Condorcet, 786
    consistency, 797
    dictator, 791
    faithfulness, 797
    fuzzy preference, 794
    impossibility results, 795
    independence, 790
    majority, 780
    majority in two stages, 782
    manipulation, 783
    monotonicity, 783
    neutrality, 797
    oligarchy, 793
    scoring method, 799
    separability, 785
    simple majority, 799
    strict monotonicty, 800
    transitivity, 793
    veto, 793
voting system, 780
    uninominal, 781
weak
    order, 76
    separability, 756
weakly complete, 52
weighted Leximax/Leximin criteria, 463
weights, 206
    associated with a criterion, 249
zero divisor, 691